Resort to War

RESORT TO WAR

A DATA GUIDE TO INTER-STATE, EXTRA-STATE,
INTRA-STATE, AND NON-STATE WARS, 1816–2007

Meredith Reid Sarkees
and
Frank Whelon Wayman

CQ PRESS

A Division of SAGE
Washington, D.C.

CQ Press
2300 N Street, NW, Suite 800
Washington, DC 20037
Phone: 202-729-1900; toll-free, 1-866-4CQ-PRESS (1-866-427-7737)

Web: www.cqpress.com

Cover design: Paula Goldstein, Blue Bungalow Design
Cover photo: London, 1940–1941, showing damage inflicted by German air raids
    during World War II. ullstein bild/The Granger Collection
Composition: C&M Digitals (P) Ltd.

⊚ The paper used in this publication exceeds the requirements of the American
National Standard for Information Sciences—Permanence of Paper for Printed Library
Materials, ANSI Z39.48-1992.

Printed and bound in the United States of America

14   13   12   11   3   4   5

Library of Congress Cataloging-in-Publication Data

Sarkees, Meredith Reid, 1950-
  Resort to war : a data guide to inter-state, extra-state, intra-state, and non-state wars,
1816-2007 / Meredith Reid Sarkees and Frank Whelon Wayman.
      p. cm.
  Includes bibliographical references and index.
  ISBN 978-0-87289-434-1 (alk. paper)
1. War—Causes. 2. War—Prevention. 3. War—Statistical methods. I. Wayman, Frank
Whelon. II. Title.

  JZ6385.S27 2010
  355.02—dc22

                                                                    2009049728

This book is dedicated to all
those who study war in the
hopes of preventing it.

Especially to J. David Singer, whose passing
we mourn and whose life we celebrate.

Contents

Tables and Figures

Acknowledgments

This book would not have been possible without the tremendous teamwork of the entire Correlates of War (COW) community. Extraordinary recognition is owed to J. David Singer, the founder of the COW Project, and Melvin Small, the project historian, who were the authors of the two preceding COW war handbooks. They created a groundbreaking quantitative study of war and established a wide-ranging research project that has been a model throughout the world politics community. Their dedication as scholars and their political commitments as individuals have inspired a countless number of colleagues. They have encouraged and sustained this war update, and their professional and personal support has been invaluable. The entire COW Project is also indebted to Phil Schafer, who has done a lifetime of archival work that forms the bases of many of the COW datasets. His research and insights are behind many of the war narratives, and his dataset on States, Nations, and Entities has informed the discussions of the typologies of wars and of the war participants. Jeffrey Dixon, COW intra-state data co-host, has devoted tremendous effort in studying the intra-state wars and has contributed significantly to the further development and increasing specificity of the COW coding rules. Many COW colleagues have furnished helpful commentary and insights, especially Scott Bennett, Zeev Maoz, and Paul Diehl, the current COW director. The University of Michigan, the Pennsylvania State University, and the University of Illinois, which have hosted the COW Project over the years, merit special recognition. The staff of CQ Press have been wonderful to work with. Andrea Pedolsky, Editorial Director, Reference Information Group, and Doug Goldenberg-Hart, Senior Acquisitions Editor, have been most encouraging, understanding, and supportive. David Arthur, Anastazia Skolnitsky, Janine Stanley-Dunham, and Anne Stewart were instrumental in ensuring the professionalism of this work.

In addition to our heartfelt joint expression of gratitude, each of us as co-authors need to acknowledge special work that was done for us separately. Frank Wayman would like to thank those who contributed on his end. Peter Brecke, a professor at Georgia Tech, kindly provided his own, unpublished war data to Frank Wayman and Atsushi Tago in 2003, permitting us to start with a cross-check on other published figures. At the University of Michigan-Dearborn, Courtney Dean, Kenn Dunn, Salam Elia, Dr. Mark Hoeprich, Nura Lutfi, Meaghan Ograyensek, Kim Ostrenga, Beth Rivard, Bianca Rus, Michael Taggert, Sarah Wright, and Sarah Yousif provided research support, often with special language skills. Thanks also to Dr. Robert Donia and Prof. Ronald R. Stockton. Especially helpful advice came from three skilled political scientists and treasured friends: Drs. Bruce Bueno de Mesquita, Michael Levy, and Paul R. Williamson. Bram Wayman, a Yale University computer coordinator, and Eric Wayman, a web developer in Ann Arbor, supplied computer assistance to "dad" along the way. Professor Ellen C. Schwartz, Frank's wife and also a scholar of Byzantine studies, deserves special praise. She was a constant source of much inspiration and support, as well as such sage advice as only a published author and skillful writer can provide.

As for the special support team for Meredith Reid Sarkees, we are also grateful for the dedicated research assistance of Amy Frame, Carol Reid, Christine Sarkees, and John R. Sarkees. Further thanks go to Karen O'Connor of the Women & Politics Institute at American University for providing Meredith with a research home. Meredith is particularly indebted to J. David Singer for his willingness to read and comment upon the manuscript. She is also profoundly appreciative of the advice and the constant support and encouragement so generously proffered by David Singer and Diane Macauley. Most important, enduring gratitude goes to John R. Sarkees, who truly understands the magnitude of effort that this book has entailed. He has borne the many costs of this work with grace and an optimism that it would one day be completed.

Finally, we are grateful to the COW "invisible college" of associates at universities across the globe who work together selflessly in support of the COW Project and in pursuit of a greater understanding of all types of armed conflict.

Foreword

As I watch the coauthors of this volume, and the research assistants who have done so much to move the enterprise along, my emotions are mixed. Certainly there is pride that I initiated this ambitious Correlates of War Project in 1963 and recruited an impressive team of students and colleagues, who have done much of the creative work and heavy lifting for more than four decades here at the University of Michigan as well as other places far and wide. It has been said that this project has been a driving force behind a major paradigm shift in the study of world politics. One result is that we have played a central role in moving the study of world politics in general, and armed conflict in particular, from a largely anecdotal field of study to one that is today considerably more rigorous, systematic, and scientific. Many questions that had been mere matters of opinion for decades or even centuries are now getting answers that, while not always conclusive, evoke considerably more confidence and consensus, and can be realistically affirmed or challenged.

When I had initially described my ideas to Michigan colleagues and confessed my aspirations, Anatol Rapoport warned me not to hope for too much; we were not likely to come up with an integrated explanatory theory of war, he said, but at the least we would lay to rest many of the foolish and self-serving platitudes that had characterized the field and led all too many nations into the brutal abyss of war. To date, his prediction has been correct—an interesting mix of success and failure. To be sure, we know quite a bit more about the origins and etiology of war, but at the same time we are not yet close to an adequate theory. Wars are all too different; nor are the roads to war that visible.

While the number of scholars and their students who follow the scientific style has gone from a few intrepid souls to hundreds in the United States, we have yet to see our ideas penetrate the national security circles around the world. This is certainly true here in the United States, where the policy community remains skeptical of quantitative analysis, despite its acceptance in the academic community. Given the motivation that propelled me into this project, I can hardly express great satisfaction in terms of its broader impact. Thus, as the COW team and its allies continue to chalk up valuable gains in research design, theoretical models, and empirical discoveries, we need to develop intellectual and educational strategies that will make our research more relevant to the political process and make the members of the policy communities more competent and more responsive to our growing bodies of knowledge. This new war data handbook—*Resort to War*—will play a crucial role in fulfilling that dream.

J. David Singer, founder of the Correlates of War Project and emeritus professor of political science at the University of Michigan

Preface

I was skeptical when I hired on in 1964 as the "historian" on a project filling up with political scientists eager to quantify virtually any activity having to do with international diplomatic and military interactions. I did have some interest in social science, since my dissertation involved public opinion and foreign policy, but when it came to numbers, I was, as Dave Singer would accurately contend, "preoperational." Needless to say, I learned a lot about the folks across the interdisciplinary wall, while I think I was of assistance to some of them who could not find Tuscany on a map or whose historical references went back only as far as the Korean War. They, of course, helped me to see how history could be more than a series of unrelated anecdotes. Along the way, they were amused by those same anecdotes at the legendary weekly seminars.

The main problem I encountered working on the project at the start was one of data-quality control. COW was omnivorous, eager for whatever data I could provide and not always as interested as I was in their provenance. More important, I found myself often playing the role of historical grand poobah, pointing out that certain kinds of data were simply unavailable, or especially, that even when we had accurate data-sets, some fanciful indicators that could easily be developed did not have face validity.

On the other hand, I think I was of some assistance in constructing surrogate variables for complicated historical processes that did not do violence to history and that could be aggregated and analyzed with our then primitive tools in a meaningful way. Speaking of primitive tools, it would have been so much easier to begin COW in the present time, with the vast resources of the Internet available in multiple languages. We had to do it the old way in libraries, with dusty tomes such as our perennial favorite, the *Almanach de Gotha*, which is so little used now that one has to file special requests to retrieve it from storage.

At the least, most of those tomes were more reliable than some of the seemingly authoritative information we might pluck from the Internet today. Indeed, I frequently have to tell students engaged in historical research with me that they should go the library to perform most of their work. When informed, some ask, "Where is the library?" Many of the political science students working as assistants on the project learned their way around the stacks, especially in the "D," or Eurocentric area.

I enjoyed working on the COW team. Almost all historians do their work alone. When I was an undergraduate, I looked forward to the time when I would be in a history department, talking with colleagues about our mutual research. Alas, although we share our ideas with one another at seminars and brown bags, most of us are too busy with our own work to take a serious interest in our counterparts' work and generally do not have the expertise in narrow subdisciplines to offer more than theoretical and stylistic commentary.

Of course, working on an ever-growing team meant the need for larger grants. I was concerned about the amount of time COW people spent discussing, planning, and writing grant proposals every two years or so.

One role that I played with some gusto was as the official respondent to Karl Deutsch. Deutsch, a brilliant polymath who knew a good deal about history, came into town periodically as COW's most distinguished consultant. On occasion, it was my task to gently challenge his memory of facts when he confidently lectured to COW political scientists about an obscure nineteenth-century Middle European war. It was difficult competing with him, since his charming Middle-European accent lent authenticity to his account.

Despite some interest in quantification among economic and social historians in the 1960s and 1970s, most were not impressed with the work I did with COW. Leading two lives, I generally was careful to leave numbers out of my writing in modern American history. Once, when I included two figures depicting the opinion-policy relationship during the Vietnam War era, a colleague in an otherwise friendly review wondered why I needed to use them.

More interesting, perhaps, my work with COW social scientists has taught me to begin my articles and books with lengthy methodological introductions and to insist that my students do likewise. And for this I am most grateful to my more scientifically oriented colleagues. Although explicit concern about "coding rules" may seem elementary to most other scholars, many accomplished historians still pay little attention to how they go about their business. Even though political science is the softest of the "sciences" and history is the hardest of the humanities, the twain still do not meet.

Over the years I have been gratified to see how many students who worked on COW have achieved prominence in their discipline. It is also rewarding to witness the vast number of scholars outside of the project who have used and continue to use some of the data that I had a hand in developing. This important new volume will surely add to the utility of COW for the next generation of social scientists interested in trying to understand the problem of war in modern society.

Melvin Small, Correlates of War Project historian and
professor of history at Wayne State University

Introduction

In the midst of World War II, Quincy Wright, a leader in the quantitative study of war, noted that people view war from contrasting perspectives:

> To some it is a plague to be eliminated; to others, a crime which ought to be punished; to still others, it is an anachronism which no longer serves any purpose. On the other hand, there are some who take a more receptive attitude toward war, and regard it as an adventure which may be interesting, an instrument which may be legitimate and appropriate, or a condition of existence for which one must be prepared.[1]

Despite the millions of people who died in that most deadly war, and despite widespread avowals for peace, war remains as a mechanism of conflict resolution. As Sven Chojnacki and Gregor Reisch recently observed: "[V]iolence at the highest level of armed conflict is still a way of enforcing decisions and allocating values."[2]

Given the prevalence of war, the importance of war, and the enormous costs it entails, one would assume that substantial efforts would have been made to comprehensively study war. However, the systematic study of war is a relatively recent phenomenon. Generally, wars have been studied as historically unique events, which are generally utilized only as analogies or examples of failed or successful policies. There has been resistance to conceptualizing wars as events that can be studied in the aggregate in ways that might reveal patterns in war or its causes. For instance, in the United States there is no governmental department of peace with funding to scientifically study ways to prevent war, unlike the millions of dollars that the government allocates to the scientific study of disease prevention. This reluctance has even been common within the peace community, where it is more common to deplore war than to systematically figure out what to do to prevent it. Consequently, many government officials and citizens have supported decisions to go to war without having done their due diligence in studying war, without fully understanding its causes and consequences.

The Correlates of War (COW) Project was founded by J. David Singer in the hopes that the world would be more likely to avoid war if we understood it more completely. Over the years, the COW Project has produced a number of interesting observations about wars. For instance, an important early finding concerned the process of starting wars. A country's goal in going to war is usually to win. Conventional wisdom was that the probability of success could be increased by striking first. However, a study found that the rate of victory for initiators of inter-state wars (or wars between two countries) was declining: "Until 1910 about 80 percent of all interstate wars were won by the states that had initiated them.... In the wars from 1911 through 1965, however, only about 40 percent of the war initiators won."[3] A recent update of this analysis found that "pre-1900, war initiators won 73% of wars. Since 1945 the win rate is 33%."[4] In civil war the probability of success for the initiators is even lower. Most rebel groups, which are generally the initiators in these wars, lose. The government wins 57 percent of the civil wars that last less than a year and 78 percent of the civil wars lasting one to five years.[5]

1

So, it would seem that those initiating civil and inter-state wars were not able to consistently anticipate victory. Instead, the decision to go to war frequently appears less than rational. Leaders have brought on great carnage with no guarantee of success, frequently with no clear goals, and often with no real appreciation of the war's ultimate costs. This conclusion is not new. Studying the outbreak of the first carefully documented war, which occurred some 2,500 years ago in Greece, historian Donald Kagan concluded: "The Peloponnesian War was not caused by impersonal forces, unless anger, fear, undue optimism, stubbornness, jealousy, bad judgment and lack of foresight are impersonal forces. It was caused by men who made bad decisions in difficult circumstances."[6] Of course, wars may also serve leaders' individual goals, such as gaining or retaining power. Nonetheless, the very government officials who start a war are sometimes not even sure how or why a war started. During the Cuban missile crisis, President John F. Kennedy was concerned with developing a more rational foreign policy decision-making process. Kennedy had recently read Barbara Tuchman's *Guns of August,* which detailed the miscalculations that led to World War I. He encouraged his advisers to read Tuchman's book and warned his crisis managers: "If this planet is ever ravaged by nuclear war—if the survivors of that devastation can then endure the fire, poison, chaos, and catastrophe—I do not want one of the survivors to ask the other, 'How did it all happen?' and to receive the incredible reply, 'Ah, if only we knew.'"[7] Santayana once said that if we do not remember the past, we will be condemned to relive it.[8] In our age of nuclear weapons, the stakes of war are higher: If we do not understand the past and its wars, we may not survive to relive it —as individuals, perhaps even as a species.

The Debate: Is War Evolving?

Quincy Wright's observation about war is as applicable today as it was during World War II. War is seen differently by various groups of people, both within the general public and within the community of researchers who study war. Some see war as an unfortunate but still pervasive element of human experience. Others see war as a phenomenon that is undergoing fundamental changes in its origins and in the ways in which it is conducted. Others see war as an atavistic savagery left over from humankind's cruel past. This latter perspective has recently found support among both policymakers and scholars. Generally, they see history as a story of human progress, entailing not only advances in our standard of living but also movement toward a more peaceful, less warlike future. When the Cold War ended as the Berlin Wall was torn down, on November 9, 1989, euphoria was widespread. Francis Fukuyama, who was working at the Policy Planning Staff of the U.S. State Department, described the end of the Cold War as "The End of History."[9] In his view there was a growing convergence of states into a liberal democratic model. Wars, which in the past predominantly had had ideological components (liberals vs. communists, liberals vs. monarchists, liberals vs. fascists, communists vs. monarchists, communists vs. fascists, and so forth), would mostly disappear. In the same vein, President George H. W. Bush, for whom Fukuyama worked, announced a "New World Order," which for many people meant that war was now obsolete. Similarly, President George W. Bush argued in his 2005 State of the Union address, "It should be clear that the advance of democracy leads to peace, because governments that respect the rights of their people also respect the rights of their neighbors."[10]

This same optimism was prevalent within the scholarly community as well. Following in the philosophical tradition of the early liberals, a plethora of scholars argued that the spread of democracy was going to bring about a "democratic peace." Though there had been a wide diversity of opinion among the early liberals (including John Locke, Jeremy Bentham, and Adam Smith), common elements of liberalism included a generally positive view of human nature, a focus on individual rights, a pacific view of the state of nature, and a positive view of the role of citizens in government as a mediating force against unwise governmental actions, including war.[11] Probably one of the most well-known statements of this perspective was put forward by Immanuel Kant, who, in arguing that democracies would be less warlike than their predecessors, claimed that a republic was "by nature inclined to seek perpetual peace."[12]

The reasoning as to why democracies would be peaceful has generally relied on either a monadic or a dyadic analysis. The monadic view (which emphasizes the attributes of a single country) argues that democracies are always more peaceful than nondemocracies because of their nonviolent norms or the restraint of the citizenry. The more constrained dyadic view (which looks at the relationships between a pair of countries) argues that democracies are less likely to go to war only with other democracies.[13] Both variations of this democratic peace perspective have become increasingly popular among international relations scholars, and support for the democratic peace in a variety of statistical studies has led many to claim that the democratic peace is "as close as anything we have to an empirical law in world politics."[14]

A corollary of the democratic peace argument is the conclusion that since the number of democracies is growing worldwide, then the number of wars must be declining as well. This conclusion has recently been presented in the *Human Security Report 2005*. The report relies on the data generated by the Uppsala University's Conflict Data Program and the International Peace Research Institute, Oslo (PRIO), and it looks at wars from 1946 to 2003 to conclude that there has been a dramatic decline in armed conflicts around the world since the end of World War II. Thus it claims that those who believe that violence has increased are wrong.[15]

Other scholars have rejected this optimistic view, on both theoretical and data-analysis grounds. John Mearsheimer declared, "[W]e will soon miss the Cold War," and anticipated a bloodier set of conflicts.[16] Others see the "democratic peace" as a statistical artifact that correlates, mistakenly, a decline in war with ideology, when it could more aptly be understood by political similarities, economic systems, trade, polarity, or alliances. For instance, was the low level of war in post–World War II Europe due to the spread of democracy or was it due to the fact that many of the pairs of democracies were in the North Atlantic Trade Organization (NATO) alliance against the Soviet Union and, so, less likely (as allies) to fight each other? Errol A. Henderson replicated one of the major democratic peace studies, that done by Oneal and Russett,[17] and concluded that his finding should disabuse scholars of the notion that democracies are more peaceful.[18] He found that democracies are not particularly more peaceful in relation with other democracies and that democracies are in fact more likely to initiate inter-state wars than are nondemocracies.[19] Recent events have even led one of the primary proponents of the democratic peace, Bruce Russett, to claim that their point of view had been undercut and in particular that U.S. policy was "Bushwhacking the Democratic Peace."[20]

In addition to these competing perspectives, there have been a number of scholars who have claimed that wars are evolving or experiencing fundamental change. A common observation within international relations' scholarship is that the end of the twentieth century was marked by the relative decline in inter-state war and a corresponding increase in intra-state war. Many have seen these developments as harbingers of a complete alteration in the practices and incidence of war, in which new types of war are emerging.[21] Consequently, there have been calls for the development of an innovative war typology to describe these "new" wars, including ethnic wars, peoples' wars, postmodern wars, and "wars of the third kind." For instance, Donald Snow has argued that contemporary internal wars are more like international wars than traditional civil wars, leading him to call them "uncivil wars."[22]

In a related vein, Kal Holsti has argued: "War today is not the same phenomenon it was in the eighteenth century, or even in the 1930s. It has different sources and takes on significantly different characteristics."[23] He concludes that the wars we are currently facing are wars of a third kind, which he contrasts to institutionalized war and total war.[24] The objective of "wars of the third kind" is to create a state, and Holsti argues that this process is fundamentally different from state formation in Europe.[25] The characteristics of these "wars of the third kind" include: no fronts, no campaigns, no set strategies, the use of terror, the high number of casualties—especially civilian casualties—and little distinction between the armed forces and the civilian population.[26] Similarly, Mary Kaldor highlighted new types of wars based on economic conflict and the activities of paramilitary actors.[27]

Perhaps the most common of the claims for a new type of war is the argument that ethnicity is one of the most powerful forces in contemporary international relations, and that the contemporary international system is characterized by a proliferation of ethnic wars and ethnic conflicts, which are unlike conflicts in the past. This perspective was popularized by Samuel Huntington, who argued that the ideological conflict of the Cold War would be replaced by ethnic conflict along historical cleavage lines, or a "clash of civilizations."[28] Along these lines, it has become common to argue, as do Rajat Ganguly and Raymond Taras, that nationalism, ethnicity, and religion are the fault lines of contemporary international relations in the post-bipolar world.[29] Michael Brown summarized this point of view: "Many policymakers and journalists believe that the causes of internal conflict are simple and straightforward. The driving forces behind these violent conflicts, it is said, are the 'ancient hatreds' that many ethnic and religious groups have for each other."[30] Similarly, David Lake and Donald Rothchild argued that the early 1990s can be characterized as a "new world disorder" characterized by "ethnic conflict." They further note:

> Since the end of the Cold War, a wave of ethnic conflict has swept across parts of Eastern Europe, the former Soviet Union, and Africa. Localities, states, and sometimes whole regions have been engulfed in convulsive fits of ethnic insecurity, violence, and genocide. Early optimism that the end of the Cold War might usher in a new world order has been quickly shattered. Before the threat of nuclear Armageddon could fully fade, new threats of state melt down and ethnic cleansing have rippled across the international community.[31]

The focus on ethnic wars also parallels research that conceptualizes the contemporary world as dominated by the North-South divide. In this view, wars, particularly inter-state wars, are being fought almost exclusively in the South, while wars in the North are less likely.[32] While some theorists relate this divide to the importance of ethnicity in the South, others see the dividing line as being more one of development and technology.[33] For instance, David Singer argued that the geocultural divide was being breached by the divide between the nuclear haves and have-nots.[34] He concluded: "All of which reminds us that any reference to a clear dichotomous division on the basis of race or geographic position will lead to a gross oversimplification."[35]

Many of the theories that posit major changes in war are derived from examinations of only one type of war, generally inter-state or intra-state, and from examinations of war during relatively short time periods, frequently the post–Cold War era or the post–World War II period. A differing perspective arises when one examines the data on all types of war throughout a long historical period in order to gain an adequate understanding of war in all its manifestations. Here the evidence seemed more mixed, revealing a relative consistency in the overall experience of war, though there were fluctuations within the various categories of war. For instance, extra-state wars (or wars between a state and a non-state entity outside its borders, such as colonial wars) had stopped in the 1970s. Yet, intra-state, or civil, wars were becoming more common and more bloody. In the late 1980s, inter-state wars had been occurring at their usual expected frequency, rather than declining, and were still at higher levels than in earlier periods of our history.[36] If these post–Cold War patterns continued until the new millennium, we predicted that the 1990s, which were supposed to be the first decade of the "New World Order," would witness more wars than any decade since 1816. When we updated this analysis after the twentieth century had ended, our warning against premature optimism was confirmed. Inter-state wars in the 1990s (as in the 1980s) were still at higher levels than average.[37] Intra state wars were at a record high in the 1990s. Even extra-state war, which had seemed to cease in the 1970s and 1980s, reappeared in the 1995–2004 period. Consequently, the 1990s ended up being the decade with the most war onsets since Napoleon. Some of the patterns revealed in these earlier data would be consistent with a thesis positing that types of war may be substituted for each other and that reducing one type may just displace war into another form.

The new data presented throughout this book constitute both an update of the war list and an attempt to increase its comprehensiveness by the inclusion of non-state wars. The implications of these data for the discussion of the evolution of war will be addressed in the concluding chapter, Chapter 7.

The Need for Systematic Studies of War

To both understand the nature of war and determine whether it has been increasing or decreasing, one needs to study it scientifically, to categorize it, and to measure it carefully and consistently over a long span of time. Though a discrete analysis of a particular war can provide a wealth of detail, context, and specific information, it can also be misleading if people attempt to utilize one case as an analogy for all wars. When trying to understand war, people have felt a need for such detailed and comprehensive information, and, sadly, they are often let down and misled. When writing *The Wages of War, 1816–1965* in 1972, J. David Singer and Melvin Small discussed one particularly egregious example of a lack of scientific information, "a series of reports whose appearance can only be explained by a complete disregard for the most elementary rules of scholarship."[38] As revealed in *The Great Statistics of War Hoax*,[39] several impressive-sounding sources, such as the United States Naval Institute Proceedings ("The Art of War," 1960), the *New York Times Magazine* (1963), and *Military Review* ("The Art of War," 1960, 1962), had all published almost identical reports on the frequency and magnitude of war. They reported that there had been only 292 years of peace since 3600 B.C., and that 3,640,000,000 people had been killed in a total of 14,531 wars during that period."[40] Each of these studies and a subsequent article in *Time* magazine (1965) cited a Norwegian source, but David Singer, during a year in Norway, was unsuccessful in locating this purported study. Brownlee Haydon, then at the Rand Corporation, finally discovered an article by Norman Cousins in the *St. Louis Post-Dispatch*, December 13, 1953, saying that it was too bad that we did not have good data on wars, but if we had, scholars might find that since 3600 B.C., 3,640,000,000 people had been killed in war, and so on.[41] Soon, these made-up "facts," which Cousins had labeled "fanciful," were being treated as real. One might have hoped that Singer and Small's report, amplifying Haydon's detective work, would have put this hoax to rest. But a decade later, in *World Politics: Trend and Transformation* (1981), Charles Kegley and Eugene Wittkopf wrote, "It has been hypothesized by Norman Cousins [cited in Beer 1974: 7] that since 3600 B.C. there have been over 14,500 major and minor wars which have taken the lives of over 3.5 billion people."[42] These two authors provide no words of warning to the reader concerning the misleading implications of what they had said in their widely used textbook.

To appreciate the value of a scientific understanding of war, it may be helpful to view war as a disease, for which a cure might be sought. Such a cure requires some scientific knowledge of what cases have broken out, what course the affliction has taken, and what forces seem to be most strongly associated with a worsening or an improvement in the condition. To do this properly, it seems best to begin with distinguishing the cases into useful categories. Physicians, for example, have learned that it is useful to distinguish between two types of stroke, those originating from clots, which improve with the administration of blood thinners, and those originating from hemorrhaging, which are made fatally worse by the administration of blood thinners. Once these different categories are defined, cases of each type of disease can be identified and records can be kept of what is associated with the onset or cure of their condition. For instance, a great accomplishment in the twentieth century was the discovery that tobacco smoking is a major cause and risk factor in the onset of lung cancer.

In this vein of discovery, J. David Singer created the Correlates of War Project in an attempt to apply the methods and procedures of the scientific method to the study of war—beginning with categorizing the participants in war, the various types of war, and the incidences of war, and identifying the elements related to the onset of war. Singer and Melvin Small hoped to provide sound data that would make possible the understanding of war and would facilitate steps toward peace. They hoped to ensure that people would be able to rely on factual rather than fanciful information.

Brief History of the Correlates of War Project

The rise of scientific and quantitative analyses of war began in the 1930s with the work of Quincy Wright and Lewis Fry Richardson, who developed comprehensive lists of wars.[43] In 1963 J. David Singer launched the Correlates of War (COW) Project as a continuation of this endeavor to systematically describe and understand war, and the social and political conditions associated with war onset, with the ultimate goal of hopefully controlling or eliminating it.[44] This book tells of the story of that COW Project, which continues as perhaps the longest-running research program in the study of international relations.

The initial problems facing the project were daunting. Singer and his collaborator, Melvin Small, decided to develop a typology of wars that was based on differentiating between or among the different types of war participants. Wars were initially defined as armed conflicts that resulted in a minimum of 1,000 battle deaths. Their three basic types of war were: (1) inter-state, wars that were between or among states or members of the interstate system; (2) extra-state (initially referred to as extrasystemic), wars that were between a state and a non-state entity outside the state's borders; and (3) civil, wars that involved a conflict between the government and another group within a state. Singer and Small wanted to begin their study of wars by examining international wars, which encompassed inter-state and extra-state wars; however, before they could identify the wars, they had to first identify the potential war participants, or the members of the interstate system. Thus their project began with an attempt to identify the population of states, the results of which were published in 1966 as "The Composition and Status Ordering of the International System 1815–1940."[45] Subsequently, Singer, Small, and Bruce Russett expanded this list to include other entities that either had not qualified for system membership or were part of the broader international system in the twentieth century.[46] With the potential war participants now identified, Singer and Small were able to focus on the primary project of identifying all of the international wars (entailing a minimum of 1,000 battle-related fatalities for inter-state wars and 1,000 battle-related fatalities per year for the system member in extra-state wars) that occurred after 1816. They also developed a dataset concerning the alliance behavior between/among system members. In 1968 David Singer edited a volume, *Quantitative International Politics,* which included both discussions of the quantitative method and some of the early statistical findings.[47]

The first COW war handbook, *The Wages of War, 1816–1965: A Statistical Handbook,* was published in 1972, and it included lists of all of the inter-state and extra-state wars. The data on each war included variables for battle deaths, start and end dates, initiators, and the victors in each. From these data, it was possible to compute such fundamental information as the percentage of war initiators who won, magnitudes of wars (measured by nation-months or the total of the number of states multiplied by the length in months of their war participations), duration, severity (battle-connected deaths), and intensity (fatalities per nation-month, per capita, and so forth). The second handbook for the project was published in 1982 as *Resort to Arms: International and Civil Wars, 1816–1980.*[48] Here Small and Singer not only updated the data on international war but also included new data on civil wars.

In addition to the specific data on wars, the Correlates of War Project was also interested in the correlates of war, that is to say, the other elements that might be associated with war. Thus additional datasets were developed that tapped into the correlates of war, beginning with the national material capabilities of states. For each year, the military expenditures, military personnel, energy consumption, iron and steel production, total population, and urban population were determined for each state in the system. From these data, each state's share of the overall system capabilities (or power) was computed. This allowed, further, an analysis of the structure and polarity of the international system. Subsequent datasets focused on alliance patterns between states, diplomatic representation, memberships in intergovernmental organizations, territorial contiguity, cultural groups, and trade. All these elements have been utilized by scholars in a multitude of studies that have enhanced our understanding of various aspects of war onsets. In 1985 Melvin Small and J. David Singer published an edited volume, *International War, An Anthology and Study Guide,* which included articles about the various ways in which war had been studied.[49] This book not only included Small and Singer's discussion of international warfare, but it also presented an article by Charles S. Gochman and Zeev Moas (Maoz) that described a major advance in the project, the development of the Militarized Interstate Dispute (MID) dataset.[50] MIDs are conflicts between states that entail fewer than 1,000 fatalities.[51] In general, each MID, such as the Cuban missile crisis, represents a sequence of interstate interactions, including at least one threat, display, or use of force. Over 2,000 MIDs have been recorded by COW in the period since 1816, so there are over ten MIDs per decade. In most instances, inter-state wars are preceded by interstate disputes, and the MID dataset allows a study of the process leading to war. Additional data-gathering projects were established to examine conditions relating to the formation of MIDs. For instance, the Behavioral Correlates of War (BCOW) Project has examined in greater detail the sequences of military and diplomatic moves of these dangerous confrontations.

Overall, the COW Project and its growing number of datasets have begun identifying many attributes of the international system and the issues leading to war. Some of the findings were collected in a 1990 volume edited by J. David Singer and Paul F. Diehl, *Measuring the Correlates of War.*[52] The Project has also prompted the accumulation of a vast array of related data. A comparison of COW to other datasets was prepared by Claudio Cioffi-Revilla and published as *The Scientific Measurement of International Conflict.*[53] Similarly, a comprehensive list of a vast array of empirical studies using COW data was presented by Brian Gibbs and J. David Singer.[54] A former student of Professor Singer, Bruce Bueno de Mesquita, has written a book also available through CQ Press, *Principles of International*

Politics, which is a sophisticated introductory textbook to international politics that presents students with a summary of many studies using COW data and allows them to learn how to test hypotheses using the data.[55]

Work on the data is continuing throughout the COW Project, and it is anticipated that much of it will be published in the new Correlates of War series offered by CQ Press. Most recently, a two-volume work concerning alliances was written by Douglas Gibler as *International Military Alliances 1648–2008,* which is the first book in the COW series.[56] This current book is the second work in this series, and it will be followed by a book on intra-state war by Jeffrey Dixon and Meredith Reid Sarkees and an examination of international rivalries by William Thompson. The reader may also wish to examine the COW datasets, which are available at the COW Web site, www.correlatesofwar.org. The current director of the Correlates of War Project is Paul F. Diehl of the University of Illinois. Previous directors have been J. David Singer of the University of Michigan and Stuart Bremer of the Pennsylvania State University.

Purpose of This Work

This book is the third war data handbook of the Correlates of War Project, following in the tradition of *The Wages of War* and *Resort to Arms.* The goal of all these books is to serve as a primary resource on wars that will be accessible on a number of levels to both students and senior scholars. The fundamental purpose of this volume is to gather together the COW data on wars—retaining the information from the previous handbooks yet giving particular emphasis to the developments of the past twenty-seven years since *Resort to Arms* was published. Not only does this volume update the data on all wars through 2007, but it also presents information on a number of newly identified historical wars, which were included as more original source material has become available. To a significant degree this work is also a chronicle of COW's theoretical evolution. It presents the coding decisions and rules that drove the data-gathering process and also describes the ways in which these guidelines changed and gathered specificity as the scope of the project grew and new types of wars were added.

In this vein this handbook provides information on a new COW type of war, "non-state" wars, and describes the relationship of these wars to our other war categories. In fact, the discussion of non-state wars represents a major innovation in the Project, since for the first time COW has gathered data on conflicts that do not involve the governments of countries (or system members). The combatants in such wars could be entities such as nongovernmental organizations, private militaries, political entities that have not yet developed the requisite characteristics of system membership, or ethnic groups. From a historical perspective this category includes wars such as that between the Boers and the Zulus. This category is significant, since it constitutes about 10 percent of all wars and is a classification that has been omitted in other war studies. It is hoped that this expanded examination will provide a more comprehensive understanding of not only the trends in war but also the interplay among the types of war.

Overall, this handbook is structured around four primary tasks: (1) to address the theoretical basis of the COW Project, which is the understanding of the international system that emerged after the Napoleonic Wars, upon which depend the COW definitions of system membership and the war categories; (2) to present the data of all categories of war—these data will include updates of the existing war types but also introduce a new category of war; (3) to provide brief descriptions of each war; and (4) to offer some analyses of war patterns, focusing on trends in the separate classes of war over time and their spatial distribution in regions. These patterns should reveal ways in which wars are evolving and which particular types of war are becoming more or less common over time. In addition to the separate analyses of each individual class of war, a composite list of all wars has been prepared and presented in the Appendix. A discussion of trends in evidence in this comprehensive dataset will return to the theme of war evolution that began this introduction. It will also facilitate consideration of the question as to whether there are connections among all the different types of war.

Those of us associated with the COW Project are exceedingly fortunate to have been involved in discussions concerning the most important problems of peace and security in the modern world. The coherent framework of the project and the careful data gathering by a multitude of people have laid the foundations for this handbook. It is hoped that this work will be of assistance to the next generation of scholars who appreciate the value of quantitative analyses for addressing issues of war and peace.

NOTES

1. Quincy Wright, *A Study of War*, 2 vols. (Chicago: University of Chicago Press, 1942): I:3.
2. Sven Chojnacki and Gregor Reisch, "Perspectives on War: Collecting, Comparing and Disaggregating Data on Violent Conflicts," *Beiträge aus Sicherheitspolitik und Friedensforschung* 26 (April 2008): 244.
3. Karl W. Deutsch, "An Interim Summary and Evaluation," in *The Correlates of War II: Testing Some Realpolitik Models*, ed. J. David Singer (New York: Free Press, 1980), 292.
4. Dan Lindley, "Is War Rational? The Extent of Miscalculation and Misperception as Causes of War" (paper presented at the annual meeting of the Midwest Political Science Association, Chicago, April 2006), 23.
5. T. David Mason, Joseph Winegarten, and Patrick Fett, "Win, Lose, or Draw: Predicting the Outcome of Civil Wars," *Political Research Quarterly* 52, no. 2 (1999): 239–268.
6. Donald Kagan, *The Origins of the Peloponnesian War* (Ithaca, N.Y.: Cornell University Press, 1969), 356.
7. Theodore Sorenson, *Kennedy* (New York: Bantam Books, 1966), 577–578.
8. Santayana, quoted in William L. Shirer, *The Rise and Fall of the Third Reich* (New York: Simon and Schuster, 1960), vii.
9. Francis Fukuyama, "The End of History?" *The National Interest* 16 (Summer 1989): 3–5, 8–15, 18.
10. Quoted in T. Purdon, "For Bush, No Boasts, but a Taste of Vindication," *New York Times*, March 9, 2005.
11. See the discussion by Michael W. Doyle in *Ways of War and Peace* (New York: W.W. Norton , 1997), 205–311.
12. From "Perpetual Peace," cited in Doyle, *Ways of War and Peace*, 251.
13. For a complete discussion and testing of these two democratic peace propositions, see Errol A. Henderson, *Democracy and War: The End of an Illusion?* (Boulder, Colo.: Lynne Rienner, 2002).
14. Jack Levy, "Domestic Politics and War," in *The Origin and Prevention of Major Wars*, ed. Robert Rotberg and Theodore Rabb (Cambridge: Cambridge University Press, 1989), 88.
15. Human Security Centre, *Human Security Report 2005: War and Peace in the 21st Century* (Oxford: Oxford University Press, 2005), 15, 17.
16. John Mearsheimer, "Back to the Future: Instability in Europe after the Cold War," *International Security* 15 (1990): 5–56.
17. John R. Oneal and Bruce Russett, "The Classical Liberals Were Right: Democracy, Interdependence, and Conflict, 1950–1985," *International Studies Quarterly* 41 (June 1997): 267–293.
18. Henderson, *Democracy and War*, 156.
19. Henderson, *Democracy and War*, 146.
20. Bruce Russett, "Bushwhacking the Democratic Peace," *International Studies Perspectives* 6, no. 4 (2005): 395–408.
21. For a more complete discussion, see Meredith Reid Sarkees, "Trends in Intra-state (not Ethnic) Wars" (paper presented at the international, joint meeting of the International Studies Association, Hong Kong, July 26–28, 2001), 2.
22. Donald M. Snow, *Uncivil Wars* (Boulder, Colo.: Lynne Rienner, 1996), 1–2.
23. Kalevi J. Holsti. *The State, War, and the State of War* (Cambridge: Cambridge University Press, 1996), xi.
24. Holsti. *The State, War, and the State of War*, 28.
25. Holsti. *The State, War, and the State of War*, 38, 61.
26. Holsti. *The State, War, and the State of War*, 37.
27. Mary Kaldor, *New and Old Wars: Organized Violence in a Global Era* (Stanford: Stanford University Press, 1999).
28. Samuel Huntington, "The Clash of Civilizations," *Foreign Affairs* 72 (1993): 56–73.

29. Rajat Ganguly and Raymond C. Taras. *Understanding Ethnic Conflict* (New York: Longman, 1998), xi.

30. Michael Brown, "The Causes of Internal Conflict," in *Nationalism and Ethnic Conflict*, ed. Michael E. Brown, Owen R. Coté Jr., Sean M. Lynn-Jones and Steven E. Miller (Cambridge, Mass.: MIT Press, 1997), 3.

31. David A. Lake and Donald Rothchild, eds. *The International Spread of Ethnic Conflict* (Princeton: Princeton University Press, 1998), 97.

32. Rafael X. Reuveny and William R. Thompson. "The North-South Divide and International Studies: A Symposium," *International Studies Review* 9, no. 4 (Winter 2007): 558.

33. J. David Singer. "Nuclear Proliferation and the Geocultural Divide: The March of Folly," *International Studies Review* 9, no. 4 (Winter 2007): 664.

34. Singer. "Nuclear Proliferation and the Geocultural Divide," 665.

35. Singer. "Nuclear Proliferation and the Geocultural Divide," 671.

36. Meredith Reid Sarkees and J. David Singer, "Old Wars, New Wars and an Expanded War Typology" (paper presented at the joint meeting of the International Studies Association and the Japan Association of International Relations, Tokyo, September 20–23, 1996) and Meredith Reid Sarkees, J. David Singer, and Frank Wayman, "System Structure and Inter-State, Extra-Systemic, and Intra-State Wars" (paper presented at the annual meeting of the International Studies Association, San Diego, April 1996).

37. Meredith Reid Sarkees, Frank W. Wayman, and J. David Singer, "Inter-State, Intra-State and Extra-State Wars: A Comprehensive Look at Their Distribution over Time, 1816–1997," *International Studies Quarterly* 47, no. 1 (March 2003): 49–79.

38. J. David Singer and Melvin Small, *The Wages of War, 1816–1965: A Statistical Handbook* (New York: Wiley, 1972), 10.

39. Brownlee Haydon, *The Great Statistics of War Hoax* (Santa Monica, Calif.: Rand, 1962).

40. Singer and Small, *The Wages of War*, 11.

41. Norman Cousins in the *St. Louis Post-Dispatch*, December 13, 1953.

42. Charles Kegley and Eugene Wittkopf, *World Politics: Trend and Transformation* (New York: St. Martin's Press, 1981), 352.

43. Wright, *A Study of War*, and Lewis F. Richardson, *Statistics and Deadly Quarrels* (Pittsburgh: Boxwood, 1960).

44. Singer and Small, *The Wages of War*, 4.

45. J. David Singer and Melvin Small, "The Composition and Status Ordering of the International System 1815–1940," *World Politics* 18 no. 2 (January 1966): 236–282.

46. Bruce Russett, J. David Singer, and Melvin Small, "National Political Units in the Twentieth Century: A Standardized List," *American Political Science Review* 67 (1968): 932–951.

47. J. David Singer, ed., *Quantitative International Politics, Insights and Evidence.* (New York: Free Press, 1968).

48. Melvin Small and J. David Singer, *Resort to Arms: International and Civil Wars, 1816–1980* (Beverly Hills, Calif.: Sage, 1982).

49. Melvin Small and J. David Singer, eds., *International War, An Anthology and Study Guide* (Homewood, Ill.: Dorsey Press, 1985).

50. Charles S. Gochman and Zeev Moas, "Militarized Interstate Disputes, 1816–1976," in *International War, An Anthology and Study Guide*, ed. Melvin Small and J. David Singer (Homewood, Ill.: Dorsey Press, 1985), 27–36.

51. Daniel Jones, Stuart Bremer, and J. David Singer, "Militarized Interstate Disputes, 1816–1992: Rationale, Coding Rules, and Empirical Patterns," *Conflict Management and Peace Science* 15, no. 2 (Summer 1996): 163–215; Faten Ghosn, Glenn Palmer, and Stuart Bremer, "The MID3 Data Set, 1993–2001: Procedures, Coding Rules, and Description," *Conflict Management and Peace Science* 21, no. 2 (Summer 2004): 133–154.

52. J. David Singer and Paul F. Diehl, eds., *Measuring the Correlates of War* (Ann Arbor: University of Michigan Press, 1990).

53. Claudio Cioffi-Revilla, *The Scientific Measurement of International Conflict* (Boulder, Colo.: Lynne Rienner, 1990).

54. Brian H. Gibbs and J. David Singer, *Empirical Knowledge on World Politics: A Summary of Quantitative Research, 1970-1991* (Westport, Conn.: Greenwood Press, 1993).

55. Bruce Bueno de Mesquita, *Principles of International Politics: People's Power, Preferences, and Perceptions,* 3rd ed. (Washington, D.C.: CQ Press, 2006).

56. Douglas M. Gibler, *International Military Alliances 1648–2008* (Washington, D.C.: CQ Press, 2009).

CHAPTER ONE

The Interstate and International Systems

Theoretical Foundations: State Actors in the International System

The study of world politics is beset by terminological confusion. This is especially problematic when the lack of clarity surrounds the primary actors in international relations, alternatively referred to as countries, nations, nation-states, or states. Even though these terms are related, they do in fact refer to different entities. However, most people tend to use the terms *state, nation,* and *country* as synonyms and use them interchangeably. For instance, during the past century, when the sovereign states of the world have assembled themselves globally, they have come together as the League of *Nations* and the United *Nations.* Similarly, the Olympic Games were organized by an Inter*national* Olympic Committee" (the IOC for short) [emphasis added throughout this paragraph], and the IOC Charter is filled with the terms *nation* and *country,* used synonymously at some points yet with an awareness of the differences at others. A typical passage reads: "The mission of the NOCs [*National Olympic Committees*] is to develop, promote and protect the Olympic Movement in their respective *countries.*"[1] Yet, at the Olympics, Puerto Rico, a Commonwealth dependency of the United States (not a country), marches under its own flag in the opening parade and fields its own team. In all, as of the start of 2007, the Olympic Movement Web site announced that there were 203 NOCs, which was 11 more than the number of UN members at that time. Using *National* in a way inconsistent with *nations,* the Movement blithely announces, "Although most NOCs are from nations, the IOC also recognizes independent territories, commonwealths, protectorates and geographical areas."[2] This is largely because areas that are not politically independent but that have a degree of autonomy and what is seen as a sufficiently distinctive culture or way of life (such as Hong Kong and Puerto Rico) are treated as countries for purposes of the Olympics. Yet, Puerto Rico and Hong Kong are not considered to be eligible for membership in the UN, nor for inclusion in the Correlates of War (COW) state membership list.

Social scientists tend to use the terms *nation* and *state* more widely than *country,* yet even they are not immune to the linguistic slippage among these words. In their earlier war handbooks, David Singer and Melvin Small developed a list of what they considered to be the primary actors in world politics, and they referred to their list as the "*nation* members of the inter*state* system."[3] One of the most influential associates of the COW Project, Karl Deutsch, tried to bring clarity to the distinction between *nations* and *states* in his formative book *Nationalism and Social Communication,*[4] though his terminology was not entirely successful. Subsequently, he described a *people* as a group of human beings with complementary habits of communication; they usually speak the same language.[5] People were then contrasted with the state:

> A *state* is an organization for the enforcement of decisions or commands, made practicable by the existing habits of compliance among the population.... If a significant proportion of the

members of a people are trying to get control of some substantial part of the machinery of enforcement and government ... we call them a *nationality*. If they succeed in getting hold of significant capabilities of enforcement over a large area—that is, usually, if they get control over a state—we call them a *nation*, and ordinarily they will so call themselves. A nation, then, is a people in control of a state.[6]

This understanding of *nation* shifts the focus to a group of people, though many use the term *nation* regardless of the degree of national unity or control that they possess. Part of this terminological confusion derives from one of the significant developments of the modern era: the drive to create nation-states. Under this paradigm, a *nation* is a group of people with a common history, culture, and language, while the *state* is a territorial entity organized under the government. Nationalism is then the drive to provide a nation (people) with its own territory, or to create a nation-state, like the drive to create a specific homeland for the Jewish people (a nation).[7] Despite the trend toward the creation of nation-states, which was particularly evident in the aftermath of World War I, most countries are in fact multinational. In a number of cases, the multiethnic character of modern countries was a result of colonialism, under which the colonial powers drew borders with little regard for the peoples living in the regions. In other cases, a multiethnic population resulted from previous conquests of one nation by another. The lack of a cohesive national identity in such countries contrasts with a more unified entity such as present-day Japan, which is more representative of the conception of a nation-state. Most countries fall quite short of being such a culturally unified nation-state, even if such unity is the aspiration of some of their leaders or dominant groups.

In order to sidestep the complex discussion of how much national cohesion is necessary for an entity to be considered a nation-state, the COW project has focused instead on territorial entities that are classified as being the members of the interstate system and that are referred to as *states* (which will be discussed in greater detail below). As Singer and Small noted, this list includes both "national and *quasi*-national political entities [emphasis added]."[8] COW states (or interstate system members) are in essence a subset of what people commonly refer to as countries, in that an additional key requirement is that the states must interact with one another within the broader international system. Unfortunately, the term *state* has a multitude of meanings as well. Although *state* is frequently used for regional subunits that are part of the United States, such as California and Alaska, in the study of international relations the term *states* refers to the countries, or the sovereign political units that conduct foreign policy with other sovereign states. In fact, the widely used term *international relations* highlights the idea that the *relationships* that these sovereign political units have with each other are the primary focus of the study of world politics. The set of those relationships between and among states is called the interstate system. Even so, the terminology used to define or describe a state is also not consistent within the scholarly community. In particular, the COW definition of a state differs from the commonly used Weberian conception of the state.

The Weberian concept of a state was developed within the subfield of comparative politics by political scientists including Max Weber. Comparative politics is, as the name suggests, the field of study that compares the political systems of the world, generally looking at such internal characteristics as their government form (for example, monarchies vs. republics); degree of centralism (unitary vs. federal); political party system (one-party, two-party, multi-party, non-party); degree of democracy (frequently on a continuum from authoritarian to democratic), and so on. This tradition focuses on state sovereignty in an internal way, looking at whether the central government does or does not have control over its territory, a tax base, bureaucrats and loyal soldiers. In a famous lecture in 1919, Max Weber provided a brief definition of a state:

> A state is a human community that (successfully) claims the monopoly of the legitimate use
> of physical force within a given territory.... Specifically, at the present time, the right to use
> physical force is ascribed to other institutions or to individuals only to the extent to which the
> state permits it. The state is considered the sole source of the "right" to use violence.[9]

This definition thus highlights the criteria of territory, population (or "community," in Weber's word), and the legitimate use of force. Though these elements are important for the COW definition of a state, the COW Project also includes statehood criteria that focus on external, or international, actions as well. These external relations are deemphasized and indeed basically ignored in the Weberian approach, which is appropriate for comparative politics, which deals with isolated geopolitical units. However, when studying war and peace, external interactions are too central a feature to ignore. These external relations can be both peaceful and conflictual. In terms of peaceful interactions, one criterion for COW statehood is diplomatic recognition of each system member by other states. Conversely, there is a specific link between statehood and conflict. In an oft-cited aphorism, it has been said that "war made the state, and the state made war."[10] War has increased, or even created, the need for a state, yet states, in turn, became frequent sources of war. For instance, a group of people who were under attack by outsiders often felt a need for an organized state to protect themselves. Conversely, during the process of decolonization, a colony's desire for a state of its own frequently led to a war between the colony and the colonial power. Then, once established as new states, these former colonies sometimes became embroiled in inter-state wars themselves, as the case of Vietnam demonstrates. Inter-state war is an example of a conflictual *interaction* between *independent* political units. It is the focus on interactions between and among entities that forms the basis of the COW understanding of states and the system in which they operate. It was perhaps put best by Stuart Bremer, during the period when he was director of the COW project: "We must remind ourselves that Singer and Small were not just defining states but rather a state system. A system implies some degree of interaction and interdependence between and among its constituent units; without this we have a set of states but not a system of states."[11]

Another difference between the COW and the Weberian approach concerns Weber's famous assertion that the state claims (successfully) a monopoly on the legitimate use of force within its borders. Such a requirement, with its moralistic focus on the "right" to use force, becomes problematic particularly when studying civil wars, where the rebels similarly claim the "right" or necessity of utilizing force to promote their cause. During civil wars, in which the rebels are fighting against the government for a sustained period, the government does not have a monopoly on the use of force within its territory—the rebels are deadly evidence to the contrary, regardless of which party has the moral "right" to do so. As COW colleague Zeev Maoz recently commented, "The essence of civil war outbreak is the collapse of the government's authority; the government no longer possesses a monopoly over the use of organized force."[12] To adopt Weber's definition of a state, COW would have to remove states from the list of system members when they entered a period of civil war (or else define a state in such a way that rebels holding territory would have a state of their own for the duration of their rebellion).

A useful analogy that reflects the ramifications of a similar disagreement over classification of system members is the recent debate over the size of our solar system.[13] In the year 1846 this system encompassed all eight of the known planets. Then, in 1930, the object Pluto was found circling our sun, and thereafter, Pluto was called the ninth planet. This view persisted despite Pluto's odd orbit, small size, and unusual composition. However, recently astronomers reconsidered the problem of what constitutes a planet and decided that Pluto does not fit the criteria. This decision was based on criteria that addressed not only the internal planetary qualities but solar system relational qualities as well. Likewise in politics, there are difficult cases involving the exact dividing lines between states and other entities. To resolve these difficulties, a standard definition must be adopted based insofar as possible on the observable characteristics of the entity and its relation with other actors. This relational system approach has also enabled the COW Project to examine historical transformations within the international system.

One such transformation that was particularly significant for world politics since the nineteenth century was the expansion of the interstate system, from one that was predominately a European system to a worldwide system, as the states (or members of the interstate system) solidified and expanded their control over territory. Thus two major features of this modern interstate system are the spread throughout the globe of those interactions that had characterized the European system and the increasing extent to which independent states controlled territory. Though some areas of the earth's surface, such as Antarctica and the pelagic areas of midocean, are not the domain of any sovereign state, states now control most of the world's inhabited landmass—as well as those waters adjacent to such land. Melvin Small, the COW project historian, believed with J. David Singer that this globalization accelerated in the early nineteenth century and that the COW Project should consequently focus on the global phase of the international system, starting in 1816. Hans Morgenthau, perhaps the leading political scientist studying international politics in the period up to 1965, dated this transformation to a very similar moment, the issuing of the Monroe Doctrine in 1823:

> From the beginning of the modern state system at the turn of the fifteenth century to the end of the Napoleonic Wars in 1815, European nations were the active elements in the balance of power. Turkey was the one notable exception…. The century from 1815 to the outbreak of the First World War saw the gradual extension of the European balance of power into a worldwide system. One might say that this epoch started with President Monroe's message to Congress in 1823, stating what is known as the Monroe Doctrine. By declaring the mutual political independence of Europe and the Western Hemisphere and thus dividing the world, as it were, into two political systems, President Monroe laid the groundwork for the subsequent transformation of the European system into a world-wide balance-of-power system.[14]

Furthermore, today's sovereign states mostly control just the territory of their own "country." In contrast, as recently as 1945, much of the world's landmass was made up of the colonies or dependencies of some of the great imperial powers, such as Britain, France, and Portugal. Some geopolitical entities, such as Algeria, have at times been colonies or otherwise dependencies of a sovereign state, whereas other geopolitical units, such as the United States, have remained independent throughout the entire period since 1816.

These independent states, or members of the interstate system, have been the focus of the COW Project, since they are not only the ones that most often wage war but also the ones that have initiated the bloodiest wars of the modern era. Yet, states are merely one type of actor in world politics. Extra-state wars and civil wars both involve states fighting against non-state entities. Thus it is also important to situate states within the broader array of global actors.

Five Nested Systems

In developing a comprehensive view of world politics, Singer and Small conceived of a nested hierarchy of five major levels of analysis or systems, beginning with the global system and then subsequent systems that were based on ever smaller aggregations of units and lower levels of analysis. At the highest, or most comprehensive, level is the global system, which is composed of all humankind and all the worldwide groupings that people have formed. These groupings can take any form, from informal to regimented, and need not have an international or political focus. The global system thus includes a virtually infinite number of actors, and it encompasses all of the subsequent systems.

At the next lower, and more restricted, level is the international system, made up of all the geopolitical units (defined below) and a plethora of existing subnational and extranational groupings, including nonterritorial entities. This is followed by the interstate system, which is composed of territorial entities that satisfied the criteria of system membership or statehood (as defined by Singer and Small). Within the interstate system are two systems of a more restricted nature—the central system and the major power system. The central system embraces all those states that are particularly interdependent and that play especially vigorous parts in interstate politics: essentially identical to what was known as the European state system plus a few other states. Finally, at the lowest level of analysis is the major power system.

Since we are concerned particularly with international political behavior, the discussion here will focus on the international, interstate, central, and major power systems and the entities that participate in each. Singer and Small briefly described the international system as including the national political units (later termed geopolitical units), as well as the existing subnational and extranational groupings that are of interest to the researcher.[15] Subsequently, Bob Bennett referred to the international system as the universe of entities that have "some minimum structural potential for autonomous political action."[16] To be a bit more specific, the international system will be defined as consisting of entities that have an international political goal (including, among other things, state creation or survival), engage in international political behavior (including inter-state or extra-state conflict, alliances, trade, or international organizations), or engage in political behavior that has international consequences (such as civil wars). The international system thus includes both geopolitical, or territorial, entities, as well as nonterritorial entities. This would therefore exclude uninhabited areas, areas that are completely isolated, and the multitude of entities without an international political focus that would be part of the larger global system.

The international system includes all of the elements of the lower levels of analysis; or in other words, it includes the members of the major power system, the central system, and the interstate system. In developing a typology to classify these various actors in the international system, five primary elements will be utilized: territory, population, sovereignty, independence, and diplomatic recognition. Though it might logically make sense to start describing the members of the larger international system and then work down to the smaller subsystems, Singer and Small saw the interstate system as the key system. In a sense, all the other members of the international system are defined or classified in terms of their relationships to the system members, or the characteristics that define the members of the interstate system. Thus we shall first describe the interstate system before returning to a broader discussion of the other members of the international system.

The Correlates of War Interstate System

The interstate system was seen by Singer and Small as a particular phenomenon that was defined both in temporal fashion and by the characteristics of its members.[17] In particular, the interstate system was seen as a distinctive set of relations that emerged among relevant actors after the end of the

Congress of Vienna. After November 20, 1815, with the signing of the Treaty of Paris agreements the so-called concert system, or Singer and Small's interstate system, was launched. The distinguishing characteristic of this system was the recurring international interactions between and among the interstate system members. Thus membership in this interstate system was not meant to encompass all global actors, nor all sovereign entities, but only those that actively participated in the interstate system.[18] In determining which actors participated in the system, or were eligible to be considered system members (whenever the word *system* was used without a modifier, Singer and Small were referring to the interstate system), the initial criterion was whether the entity was "large enough in population or other resources to play a moderately active role in world politics, to be a player more than a pawn, and to generate more signal than noise in the system."[19] Second, "was the entity sufficiently unencumbered by legal, military, economic, or political constraints to exercise a fair degree of sovereignty and independence?"[20] In making the first determination, Singer and Small included only entities that controlled territory with its associated resources, including population. In determining whether a state was "large enough," they considered several possible criteria or measures, including population, size of territory, unity, self-sufficiency, and armed forces. However, they decided on a minimum population figure because (1) population is always a basic requirement of national survival; (2) it frequently correlates highly with a number of other criteria of national power; and (3) it is one of the variables for which adequate data have existed over a long period of time. Thus their first criterion for treating an entity as an active member of the interstate system was a population minimum of 500,000. That particular number was chosen because setting the population threshold at 1,000,000 would have excluded a number of important international actors, such as Greece from 1830 to 1845, while setting it below 500,000 would have brought in a large number of city-states and small principalities in Germany and Italy that lacked the population to be substantial players in the nineteenth-century interstate system.[21]

The second determination was whether the entity was sufficiently "unencumbered" to be sovereign (having a supreme political authority) and independent (free from the influence or control of others). Initially, Singer and Small decided to utilize diplomatic recognition as their measure here. Diplomatic recognition served to "differentiate between independent actors on the one hand, and colonies, protectorates, or more ambiguously independent entities on the other."[22] They argued that in the pre–World War I period, there was a consistency of diplomatic practice such that almost all national governments tended to agree on the status of another national entity:

> That agreement was manifested in a most operational fashion via the granting or withholding of diplomatic recognition, and it will be remembered that this was rarely used as a political weapon until after World War I. Such decisions were not based on one government's approval or disapproval of another, but strictly on the judgment as to whether it could and would effectively assume its international obligations.[23]

For the period through World War I (1816 to 1919), diplomatic recognition was determined by the "legitimizers." In this period England and France served as legitimizers, and an entity was considered to have diplomatic recognition as soon as both legitimizers had dispatched a permanent mission headed by an officer at or above the chargé d'affaires level to the capital city of an entity with the requisite half-million population. They utilized the establishment of the mission rather than the granting of recognition as the determinant, since there were occasions on which one government might "recognize" another but delay sending its representative for long periods. For example, during the 1820s many of the newly independent Latin American states were "recognized" by European powers, but few permanent missions were dispatched for several decades.[24] A historian of this era speaks of the vast distances and difficulty of communication in those times and places, which would have tended toward excluding areas from meaningful participation in the system. In our age of air travel, we think of Chile and Argentina as neighbors, but 200 years ago the land journey from Buenos Aires to Santiago, Chile, took two months and a sea journey from Buenos Aires to Acapulco in Mexico took four months.[25]

A contemporary example of the importance of diplomatic recognition is the case of Palestine. At the turn of the twenty-first century, the Palestinian Authority in Gaza and the West Bank had a bureaucracy and military; it garnered taxes and other revenues but was not generally granted diplomatic recognition. Thus it is not considered to be a state or member of the interstate system. Much of the Israeli-Palestinian diplomacy of the 1990s, in fact, was aimed at trying to develop a framework in which Israel would be secure in a "two-state solution" (a diplomatic settlement in which Israel and the Palestinian Authority would each be recognized as sovereign states). The Palestinian example is somewhat unusual in recent times, and the matter of diplomatic recognition was more commonly problematic in the early nineteenth century, when, partly because of transportation and communication limitations, the world was less integrated. In that era a number of independent entities, in Asia and Latin America, lacked the diplomatic recognition to be in the system.

After World War I, power in the system became somewhat more diffused and the capacity to extend or withhold legitimacy became increasingly a perquisite of other states, directly (by other major powers) as well as through international organizations. Thus for the period since 1920, Singer and Small developed a number of means by which an entity could attain system membership status, partially in order to deal with eight ambiguous cases. The League of Nations and later the United Nations took on the role of legitimizer, and a state was dated as becoming a system member when it became a member of either organization or when it was recognized by the method of permanent diplomatic missions. In this later period, therefore, an entity was classified as a system member if it either was a member of the League of Nations or the United Nations at any time during its existence, or met the half-million-population minimum and received diplomatic missions from *any two* (rather than the *specific* two) *major* powers.[26] The minimum population requirement was thus effectively omitted because membership in the League or the UN reflected active involvement in the interstate system. An entity could also become a system member when it attained the requisite population or was released from de facto dependence. These criteria were summarized succinctly by Stuart Bremer:

> The Correlates of War definition of what constitutes a modern state (and by implication the membership of the interstate system) has been widely accepted and adopted for over thirty years.

The defining criteria are:

a) Between 1816 and 1919 a geopolitical entity is a state if its population is at least 500,000 and it receives accredited diplomatic missions (at the chargé d'affaires level or higher) from Britain and France.

b) After 1919 a geopolitical entity is a state if it is a member of the League of Nations or the United Nations or its population is at least 500,000 and it receives accredited diplomatic missions (at the chargé d'affaires level or higher) from two major powers.[27]

Though Singer and Small emphasized these two major criteria for interstate system membership, as they dealt with a number of complex cases both in terms of system membership and wars, they utilized two additional criteria for system membership more specifically, independence and sovereignty. For instance, loss of membership in the system was strictly a function of loss of sovereignty and independence, through a member being occupied, conquered, annexed, or federated with others.[28] If the entity suffered only a partial occupation and it retained effective control over a viable sector of its population and territory, it was not classed as occupied and it retained its system membership. They also treated a state as continuing in existence if an effective fighting force of 100,000 or more troops persisted in its struggle against the enemy elsewhere along the front, even if the home territory were completely overrun. On the other hand, if an entity was not under the control of a foreign power but its legitimate government went into exile or was replaced by a puppet regime, the entity was treated as experiencing the occupied status and thus was no longer a system member. However, any change in an entity's status that did not last for one month or more was not included.

Similarly, certain members of the two international organizations (the League of Nations and the United Nations) could still be excluded from system membership if they were not considered to be independent according to historical consensus. The independence criterion required that an entity be in full control of its foreign policy. Thus members of the League or United Nations (or those that had diplomatic recognition) that did not control their own foreign policy (such as India, Slovakia, and Manchukuo in the 1920s and 1930s and Ukraine and Byelorussia after 1945) were not considered to be members of the interstate system. Singer and Small also utilized this criterion of independence when discussing the participants in extra-state wars. Extra-state wars are those that are fought by a system member against a nonsystem member, and, in particular, wars in the subcategory of imperial wars are fought against "an independent political entity that did not qualify for membership because of serious limitations on its independence, a population insufficiency, or a failure of other states to recognize it as a legitimate member."[29]

The importance of sovereignty also appeared in the discussions of civil wars. According to the COW definition of civil wars, one of the primary actors must be the national government in power at the time hostilities begin.[30] Yet, even determining who the government is can be complicated, as in cases of rival claims. In such cases Small and Singer defined "the government" in terms of sovereignty, as those forces in de facto control of the nation's institutions, regardless of the legality or illegality of their claim. The control of the nation's institutions need not necessarily include control of the armed forces.[31] Initially, they considered the only circumstance by which a system member could lose its membership status was through loss of sovereignty and independence, by being occupied, conquered, annexed, or federated with others. There are other ways besides occupation, however, through which states can lose sovereignty. In particular, the contemporary "failed states" discussion focuses on states that no longer have sovereign control over their territory or population through internal collapse. Consequently, the COW Project is considering criteria by which system members that suffer internal collapse might be removed from system membership.

Thus, in differing contexts, Singer and Small mentioned five general criteria that are critical for membership in the interstate system: territory, population, sovereignty, independence, and diplomatic recognition (or involvement in the interstate system).[32] The entities that met these criteria for system membership became the central focus of the COW project. Each state was assigned a state number, and the dates of its entry into and exit from the system were recorded. These were the participants in inter-state wars, the parties that created alliances and intergovernmental organizations, and the entities whose capabilities (or power) COW measured. Table 1.1 illustrates the classification

TABLE 1.1 **DETERMINANTS OF MEMBERSHIP IN THE COW INTERSTATE SYSTEM**

Entity		Criteria for membership				
	Territory	Population more than 500,000	Diplomatic recognition	Sovereign control	Independence	Classification: as COW state
United Kingdom	Yes	Yes	Yes	Yes	Yes	Yes
Vatican	Yes	No	Yes	Yes	Yes	No
China pre-1860	Yes	Yes	No	Yes	Yes	No
Vichy France (11/12/ 1942–8/24/1944)	Yes	Yes	Yes	No	No	No
Ukraine 1945–1991	Yes	Yes	Yes	Yes	No	No

criteria for statehood: *1) territory; 2) population; 3) diplomatic recognition; 4) sovereignty;* and *5) independence,* with some salient examples.

What this table illustrates is that one really does need to look at all five criteria to accurately determine each entity's full statehood status. Places such as the Vatican fall short on the population standard and so do not count as COW states. Pre-1860 China fell short on diplomatic recognition. The Ukraine during the Cold War met these two criteria (including being in the United Nations) but was not independent of the Soviet Union. Another prominent example is India in the 1920s and 1930s, which, like the Ukraine later, met the population and recognition standards but not the independence threshold.

There are a number of specific benefits to the way in which Singer and Small constructed their interstate system and its membership criteria; however, one of the most important is that the state numbers were assigned in a way that was as consistent and noncapricious as possible. The state numbers represent the geopolitical unit, not the regime, so that they can be utilized as a marker of continuity for those states that evolved through history. On the other hand, changes in system membership (or state numbers) are also signifiers of major transformations in the states themselves. For example, system membership is coded as ending when a state is occupied or ceases to exist. Alternatively, the creation of a new state number highlights the fact that a fundamentally different geopolitical unit has emerged. For example, Germany (#255) exited the system at the end of World War II and does not appear as a member of the system during its period of occupation. In 1954 and 1955 two new states emerge, the German Democratic Republic (#265) and the German Federal Republic (#260). These two states leave the system in 1990 with the return of the reunited Germany (#255). Other data projects present information on Germany from 1950 to the present, without noting in any way the change in its composition or size. Consequently, comparing gross national product (GNP) figures between Germany and France during this period could be quite misleading.

Table 1.2 consists of the list of the members of the interstate system. The states are organized by the major regions of: the Western Hemisphere, Europe, Africa, the Middle East, Asia, and Oceania. These regions will also be utilized later to describe the locations of wars. The five criteria of system membership will also be utilized as the basis of our classification of the other actors in the broader international system.

TABLE 1.2 **MEMBERS OF THE INTERSTATE SYSTEM** (1816–2007)

State num	State name	State abb	Start date	End date
	WESTERN HEMISPHERE			
2	United States of America	USA	January 1, 1816	December 31, 2007
20	Canada	CAN	January 10, 1920	December 31, 2007
31	Bahamas	BHM	July 10, 1973	December 31, 2007
40	Cuba	CUB	May 20, 1902	September 26, 1906
40	Cuba	CUB	January 23, 1909	December 31, 2007
41	Haiti	HAI	January 1, 1859	July 28, 1915
41	Haiti	HAI	August 15, 1934	December 31, 2007
42	Dominican Republic	DOM	January 1, 1894	November 29, 1916
42	Dominican Republic	DOM	September 29, 1924	December 31, 2007
51	Jamaica	JAM	August 6, 1962	December 31, 2007
52	Trinidad and Tobago	TRI	August 31, 1962	December 31, 2007
53	Barbados	BAR	November 30, 1966	December 31, 2007
54	Dominica	DMA	November 3, 1978	December 31, 2007
55	Grenada	GRN	February 7, 1974	December 31, 2007
56	St. Lucia	SLU	February 22, 1979	December 31, 2007
57	St. Vincent and the Grenadines	SVG	October 27, 1979	December 31, 2007
58	Antigua & Barbuda	AAB	November 1, 1981	December 31, 2007
60	St. Kitts and Nevis	SKN	September 19, 1983	December 31, 2007
70	Mexico	MEX	January 1, 1831	December 31, 2007
80	Belize	BLZ	September 21, 1981	December 31, 2007
90	Guatemala	GUA	January 1, 1868	December 31, 2007
91	Honduras	HON	January 1, 1899	December 31, 2007
92	El Salvador	SAL	January 1, 1875	December 31, 2007
93	Nicaragua	NIC	January 1, 1900	December 31, 2007
94	Costa Rica	COS	January 1, 1920	December 31, 2007
95	Panama	PAN	January 1, 1920	December 31, 2007
100	Colombia	COL	January 1, 1831	December 31, 2007
101	Venezuela	VEN	January 1, 1841	December 31, 2007
110	Guyana	GUY	May 26, 1966	December 31, 2007
115	Suriname	SUR	November 25, 1975	December 31, 2007
130	Ecuador	ECU	January 1, 1854	December 31, 2007
135	Peru	PER	January 1, 1839	December 31, 2007
140	Brazil	BRA	January 1, 1826	December 31, 2007
145	Bolivia	BOL	January 1, 1848	December 31, 2007
150	Paraguay	PAR	January 1, 1846	June 20, 1870
150	Paraguay	PAR	June 22, 1876	December 31, 2007
155	Chile	CHL	January 1, 1839	December 31, 2007
160	Argentina	ARG	January 1, 1841	December 31, 2007
165	Uruguay	URU	January 1, 1882	December 31, 2007

(Continued)

TABLE 1.2 **MEMBERS OF THE INTERSTATE SYSTEM** (1816–2007)

State num	State name	State abb	Start date	End date
	EUROPE			
200	United Kingdom	UKG	January 1, 1816	December 31, 2007
205	Ireland	IRE	December 6, 1922	December 31, 2007
210	Netherlands	NTH	January 1, 1816	July 14, 1940
210	Netherlands	NTH	June 26, 1945	December 31, 2007
211	Belgium	BEL	December 20, 1830	May 28, 1940
211	Belgium	BEL	June 26, 1945	December 31, 2007
212	Luxembourg	LUX	November 15, 1920	May 10, 1940
212	Luxembourg	LUX	September 10, 1944	December 31, 2007
220	France	FRN	January 1, 1816	November 11, 1942
220	France	FRN	August 25, 1944	December 31, 2007
221	Monaco	MNC	May 28, 1993	December 31, 2007
223	Liechtenstein	LIE	September 18, 1990	December 31, 2007
225	Switzerland	SWZ	January 1, 1816	December 31, 2007
230	Spain	SPN	January 1, 1816	December 31, 2007
232	Andorra	AND	July 28, 1993	December 31, 2007
235	Portugal	POR	January 1, 1816	December 31, 2007
240	Hanover	HAN	January 1, 1838	July 26, 1866
245	Bavaria	BAV	January 1, 1816	January 18, 1871
255	Germany	GMY	January 1, 1816	May 8, 1945
255	Germany	GMY	October 3, 1990	December 31, 2007
260	German Federal Republic	GFR	May 5, 1955	October 2, 1990
265	German Democratic Republic	GDR	March 25, 1954	October 2, 1990
267	Baden	BAD	January 1, 1816	January 18, 1871
269	Saxony	SAX	January 1, 1816	April 17, 1867
271	Württemberg	WRT	January 1, 1816	January 18, 1871
273	Hesse Electoral	HSE	January 1, 1816	July 26, 1866
275	Hesse Grand Ducal	HSG	January 1, 1816	April 17, 1867
280	Mecklenburg Schwerin	MEC	January 1, 1843	April 17, 1867
290	Poland	POL	November 3, 1918	September 27, 1939
290	Poland	POL	June 28, 1945	December 31, 2007
300	Austria-Hungary	AUH	January 1, 1816	November 12, 1918
305	Austria	AUS	September 10, 1919	March 13, 1938
305	Austria	AUS	July 27, 1955	December 31, 2007
310	Hungary	HUN	November 16, 1918	December 31, 2007
315	Czechoslovakia	CZE	October 28, 1918	March 15, 1939
315	Czechoslovakia	CZE	May 10, 1945	December 31, 1992
316	Czech Republic	CZR	January 1, 1993	December 31, 2007
317	Slovakia	SLO	January 1, 1993	December 31, 2007
325	Italy	ITA	January 1, 1816	December 31, 2007
327	Papal States	PAP	January 1, 1816	November 5, 1860

(Continued)

TABLE 1.2 **MEMBERS OF THE INTERSTATE SYSTEM** (1816–2007) (Continued)

State num	State name	State abb	Start date	End date
329	Two Sicilies	SIC	January 1, 1816	February 13, 1861
331	San Marino	SNM	March 2, 1992	December 31, 2007
332	Modena	MOD	January 1, 1842	March 15, 1860
335	Parma	PMA	January 1, 1851	March 15, 1860
337	Tuscany	TUS	January 1, 1816	March 15, 1860
338	Malta	MLT	September 21, 1964	December 31, 2007
339	Albania	ALB	January 1, 1914	April 7, 1939
339	Albania	ALB	November 17, 1944	December 31, 2007
341	Montenegro	MNG	June 12, 2006	December 31, 2007
343	Macedonia	MAC	April 8, 1993	December 31, 2007
344	Croatia	CRO	January 15, 1992	December 31, 2007
345	Yugoslavia	YUG	July 13, 1878	April 20, 1941
345	Yugoslavia	YUG	October 20, 1944	December 31, 2007
346	Bosnia and Herzegovina	BOS	April 7, 1992	December 31, 2007
349	Slovenia	SLV	January 15, 1992	December 31, 2007
350	Greece	GRC	January 1, 1828	April 23, 1941
350	Greece	GRC	October 13, 1944	December 31, 2007
352	Cyprus	CYP	August 16, 1960	December 31, 2007
355	Bulgaria	BUL	October 5, 1908	December 31, 2007
359	Moldova	MLD	December 26, 1991	December 31, 2007
360	Romania	ROM	July 13, 1878	December 31, 2007
365	Russia	RUS	January 1, 1816	December 31, 2007
366	Estonia	EST	February 24, 1918	June 16, 1940
366	Estonia	EST	September 6, 1991	December 31, 2007
367	Latvia	LAT	November 18, 1918	June 16, 1940
367	Latvia	LAT	September 6, 1991	December 31, 2007
368	Lithuania	LIT	February 16, 1918	June 15, 1940
368	Lithuania	LIT	September 6, 1991	December 31, 2007
369	Ukraine	UKR	December 26, 1991	December 31, 2007
370	Belarus	BLR	December 26, 1991	December 31, 2007
371	Armenia	ARM	December 26, 1991	December 31, 2007
372	Georgia	GRG	December 26, 1991	December 31, 2007
373	Azerbaijan	AZE	December 26, 1991	December 31, 2007
375	Finland	FIN	December 6, 1917	December 31, 2007
380	Sweden	SWD	January 1, 1816	December 31, 2007
385	Norway	NOR	June 7, 1905	April 30, 1940
385	Norway	NOR	May 7, 1945	December 31, 2007
390	Denmark	DEN	January 1, 1816	April 9, 1940
390	Denmark	DEN	May 7, 1945	December 31, 2007
395	Iceland	ICE	May 17, 1944	December 31, 2007

(Continued)

TABLE 1.2 MEMBERS OF THE INTERSTATE SYSTEM (1816–2007)

State num	State name	State abb	Start date	End date
	AFRICA			
402	Cape Verde	CAP	July 5, 1975	December 31, 2007
403	São Tomé and Principe	STP	July 12, 1975	December 31, 2007
404	Guinea-Bissau	GNB	September 10, 1974	December 31, 2007
411	Equatorial Guinea	EQG	October 12, 1968	December 31, 2007
420	Gambia	GAM	February 18, 1965	December 31, 2007
432	Mali	MLI	June 20, 1960	December 31, 2007
433	Senegal	SEN	August 20, 1960	December 31, 2007
434	Benin	BEN	August 1, 1960	December 31, 2007
435	Mauritania	MAA	November 28, 1960	December 31, 2007
436	Niger	NIR	October 3, 1960	December 31, 2007
437	Ivory Coast	CDI	August 7, 1960	December 31, 2007
438	Guinea	GUI	October 2, 1958	December 31, 2007
439	Burkina Faso	BFO	August 5, 1960	December 31, 2007
450	Liberia	LBR	June 30, 1920	December 31, 2007
451	Sierra Leone	SIE	April 27, 1961	December 31, 2007
452	Ghana	GHA	March 6, 1957	December 31, 2007
461	Togo	TOG	April 27, 1960	December 31, 2007
471	Cameroon	CAO	January 1, 1960	December 31, 2007
475	Nigeria	NIG	October 1, 1960	December 31, 2007
481	Gabon	GAB	August 17, 1960	December 31, 2007
482	Central African Republic	CEN	August 13, 1960	December 31, 2007
483	Chad	CHA	August 11, 1960	December 31, 2007
484	Congo	CON	August 15, 1960	December 31, 2007
490	Democratic Republic of the Congo	DRC	June 30, 1960	December 31, 2007
500	Uganda	UGA	October 9, 1962	December 31, 2007
501	Kenya	KEN	December 12, 1963	December 31, 2007
510	Tanzania	TAZ	December 9, 1961	December 31, 2007
511	Zanzibar	ZAN	December 19, 1963	April 26, 1964
516	Burundi	BUI	July 1, 1962	December 31, 2007
517	Rwanda	RWA	July 1, 1962	December 31, 2007
520	Somalia	SOM	July 1, 1960	December 31, 2007
522	Djibouti	DJI	June 27, 1977	December 31, 2007
530	Ethiopia	ETH	January 1, 1898	May 5, 1936
530	Ethiopia	ETH	May 5, 1941	December 31, 2007
531	Eritrea	ERI	May 24, 1993	December 31, 2007
540	Angola	ANG	November 11, 1975	December 31, 2007
541	Mozambique	MZM	June 25, 1975	December 31, 2007
551	Zambia	ZAM	October 24, 1964	December 31, 2007
552	Zimbabwe	ZIM	November 11, 1965	December 31, 2007
553	Malawi	MAW	July 6, 1964	December 31, 2007

(Continued)

TABLE 1.2 **Members of the Interstate System** (1816–2007) (Continued)

State num	State name	State abb	Start date	End date
560	South Africa	SAF	January 10, 1920	December 31, 2007
565	Namibia	NAM	March 21, 1990	December 31, 2007
570	Lesotho	LES	October 4, 1966	December 31, 2007
571	Botswana	BOT	September 30, 1966	December 31, 2007
572	Swaziland	SWA	September 6, 1968	December 31, 2007
580	Madagascar	MAG	June 26, 1960	December 31, 2007
581	Comoros	COM	December 31, 1975	December 31, 2007
590	Mauritius	MAS	March 12, 1968	December 31, 2007
591	Seychelles	SEY	June 29, 1976	December 31, 2007
	MIDDLE EAST			
600	Morocco	MOR	January 1, 1847	March 30, 1912
600	Morocco	MOR	March 2, 1956	December 31, 2007
615	Algeria	ALG	July 5, 1962	December 31, 2007
616	Tunisia	TUN	January 1, 1825	May 12, 1881
616	Tunisia	TUN	March 20, 1956	December 31, 2007
620	Libya	LIB	December 24, 1951	December 31, 2007
625	Sudan	SUD	January 1, 1956	December 31, 2007
630	Iran	IRN	January 1, 1855	December 31, 2007
640	Turkey	TUR	January 1, 1816	December 31, 2007
645	Iraq	IRQ	October 3, 1932	December 31, 2007
651	Egypt	EGY	January 1, 1855	September 15, 1882
651	Egypt	EGY	May 26, 1937	December 31, 2007
652	Syria	SYR	April 17, 1946	February 1, 1958
652	Syria	SYR	September 29, 1961	December 31, 2007
660	Lebanon	LEB	March 10, 1946	December 31, 2007
663	Jordan	JOR	March 22, 1946	December 31, 2007
666	Israel	ISR	May 14, 1948	December 31, 2007
670	Saudi Arabia	SAU	May 22, 1927	December 31, 2007
678	Yemen Arab Republic	YAR	September 2, 1926	May 21, 1990
679	Yemen	YEM	May 22, 1990	December 31, 2007
680	Yemen People's Republic	YPR	November 30, 1967	May 21, 1990
690	Kuwait	KUW	June 19, 1961	December 31, 2007
692	Bahrain	BAH	August 15, 1971	December 31, 2007
694	Qatar	QAT	September 3, 1971	December 31, 2007
696	United Arab Emirates	UAE	December 2, 1971	December 31, 2007
698	Oman	OMA	October 7, 1971	December 31, 2007
	ASIA			
700	Afghanistan	AFG	January 1, 1920	December 31, 2007
701	Turkmenistan	TKM	December 26, 1991	December 31, 2007
702	Tajikistan	TAJ	December 26, 1991	December 31, 2007
703	Kyrgyzstan	KYR	December 26, 1991	December 31, 2007
704	Uzbekistan	UZB	December 26, 1991	December 31, 2007

(Continued)

TABLE 1.2 **MEMBERS OF THE INTERSTATE SYSTEM** (1816–2007)

State num	State name	State abb	Start date	End date
705	Kazakhstan	KZK	December 26, 1991	December 31, 2007
710	China	CHN	October 25, 1860	December 31, 2007
712	Mongolia	MON	January 1, 1921	December 31, 2007
713	Taiwan	TAW	December 8, 1949	December 31, 2007
730	Korea	KOR	January 1, 1887	November 17, 1905
731	North Korea	PRK	September 9, 1948	December 31, 2007
732	South Korea	ROK	June 29, 1949	December 31, 2007
740	Japan	JPN	January 1, 1860	August 14, 1945
740	Japan	JPN	April 28, 1952	December 31, 2007
750	India	IND	August 15, 1947	December 31, 2007
760	Bhutan	BHU	September 21, 1971	December 31, 2007
770	Pakistan	PAK	August 14, 1947	December 31, 2007
771	Bangladesh	BNG	January 1, 1972	December 31, 2007
775	Myanmar	MYA	January 4, 1948	December 31, 2007
780	Sri Lanka	SRI	February 4, 1948	December 31, 2007
781	Maldives	MAD	July 26, 1965	December 31, 2007
790	Nepal	NEP	January 1, 1920	December 31, 2007
800	Thailand	THI	January 1, 1887	December 31, 2007
811	Cambodia	CAM	November 9, 1953	December 31, 2007
812	Laos	LAO	October 23, 1953	December 31, 2007
816	Vietnam	DRV	July 21, 1954	December 31, 2007
817	South Vietnam	RVN	June 4, 1954	April 30, 1975
820	Malaysia	MAL	August 31, 1957	December 31, 2007
830	Singapore	SIN	August 9, 1965	December 31, 2007
835	Brunei	BRU	January 1, 1984	December 31, 2007
840	Philippines	PHI	July 4, 1946	December 31, 2007
850	Indonesia	INS	December 27, 1949	December 31, 2007
860	East Timor	ETM	September 27, 2002	December 31, 2007
	OCEANIA			
900	Australia	AUL	January 10, 1920	December 31, 2007
910	Papua New Guinea	PNG	September 16, 1975	December 31, 2007
920	New Zealand	NEW	January 10, 1920	December 31, 2007
935	Vanuatu	VAN	September 15, 1981	December 31, 2007
940	Solomon Islands	SOL	July 7, 1978	December 31, 2007
946	Kiribati	KIR	September 14, 1999	December 31, 2007
947	Tuvalu	TUV	September 5, 2000	December 31, 2007
950	Fiji	FIJ	October 10, 1970	December 31, 2007
955	Tonga	TON	September 14, 1999	December 31, 2007
970	Nauru	NAU	September 14, 1999	December 31, 2007
983	Marshall Islands	MSI	September 17, 1991	December 31, 2007
986	Palau	PAL	December 15, 1994	December 31, 2007
987	Federated States of Micronesia	FSM	September 17, 1991	December 31, 2007
990	Samoa	WSM	December 15, 1976	December 31, 2007

Note: num = number; abb = abbreviation

CHARACTERISTICS OF MEMBERS OF THE INTERSTATE SYSTEM: OTHER DATASETS

The Correlates of War Project has amassed a wealth of data concerning the members of the interstate system, in terms of both their internal characteristics and their external behaviors.[33] The most commonly used datasets are those that relate to the external behaviors of system members: wars, militarized disputes, alliances, intergovernmental relations, diplomatic missions, and bilateral trade. The data on wars (inter-state, extra-state, intra-state, and non-state) that by definition involve a minimum of 1,000 battle-deaths per year will be discussed in this book. Armed confrontations between system members that involve fewer than 1,000 battle deaths per year are included in the Militarized Interstate Dispute dataset. The COW Formal Alliances dataset records each state's alliance commitments in defense pacts, ententes, and neutrality or nonaggression pacts. A Dyadic Alliance dataset is also available, which breaks down bilateral and multilateral alliances into dyadic alliance commitments (the relational commitments between two parties). The Intergovernmental Organization (IGO) dataset records the various IGOs and their state members. The Diplomatic Exchange dataset codes not only the number of diplomatic missions received but also the levels of diplomatic representation, such as chargé d'affaires, minister, and ambassador. The Bilateral Trade dataset begins with trade data from 1870 for most of the system members.

In terms of the internal characteristics of system members, probably the most frequently utilized of the datasets is that relating to material capabilities. In matters of war and peace, the strength of nations is often at issue. One side may initiate a war because it believes it is stronger and therefore can win a war. For such reasons, COW has developed and maintained the National Material Capabilities dataset, designed to measure the elements that might contribute to superior strength. These capability elements try to capture three general aspects of power: demographic, economic, and military. Each of these three aspects is measured by two specific indicators. Demographic capability includes the total population of the state and its urban population. Levels of economic development are measured by assessing a state's energy consumption and its iron and steel production. Finally, two dimensions of a state's military capability are the number of military personnel and the amount of its military expenditures. All six of these material capabilities are then summed up into a capabilities index, called a Composite Index of National Capability (CINC) score, which represents a composite of each state's share of the total worldwide capability for each of the six dimensions. These CINC scores give a rough indication of the relative overall material capability of states in any given year. Other datasets that examine the characteristics of the state system members are those that deal with cultural and territorial attributes. The Cultural dataset records for each decade the linguistic, religious, and ethnic composition of the state. The Territorial Change dataset has recently been expanded into three separate datasets. Territorial Change records peaceful and violent changes in territory, while the Direct Contiguity registers the land and sea borders of all system members and the Colonial/Dependency Contiguity dataset examines the contiguity relationship between the colonies and other dependencies. Finally, COW also developed a National Political Units dataset (later known as the Geopolitical Units dataset) that includes other types of international territorial actors (besides interstate system members), and it will be discussed in detail below.

The International System

Having identified the membership of the interstate system, we shall now return to addressing the components of the broader international system. As mentioned above, the international system will be defined as consisting of entities that have an international political goal (including, among other things, state creation or survival), engage in international political behavior (including inter-state or extra-state conflict, alliances, trade, or international organizations), or engage in political behavior that has international consequences (such as civil wars). The system thus includes both geopolitical units (GPUs) and nonterritorial entities (NTEs), such as international organizations or terrorist groups. The goal here is to create a comprehensive typology of international actors that can be utilized in categorizing the participants in wars. Though the members of the interstate system constitute a significant group of the actors within the international system, there are clearly a multitude of other actors. In developing a comprehensive typology to describe and classify these various actors in the international system, we shall utilize the five primary elements that Singer and Small identified in discussing members of the interstate system: (1) territory; (2) population; (3) sovereignty; (4) independence; and (5) diplomatic recognition (involvement in interstate interactions). This classification has also been structured in a way to facilitate the incorporation of existing COW datasets. Before proceeding, it should be noted that Stuart Bremer and Faten Ghosn proposed a similar, but more complex, system for categorizing international actors (and specifically geopolitical units) within the COW project that included these same elements within their two indices—one an internal measure of size, autonomy, and cohesion and the other an external measure of interaction, interdependence, and recognition. Examining "stateness" along these two dimensions was meant to highlight the fact that no single attribute of a GPU automatically qualified it for statehood.[34]

Within our typology of international system members, territoriality is considered to be the primary distinguishing characteristic. The international system includes both political actors that are territorially based and those that are not. Thus international actors will initially be classified as territorially based geopolitical units or nonterritorial political entities.

GEOPOLITICAL UNITS

GPUs have control of territory with its accompanying resources as their raison d'être and do in fact control a defined territory at the time of their classification. Within the category of GPUs, we rely on the elements of population, sovereignty, independence, and diplomatic recognition to differentiate the classifications of entities. The discussion here follows the work that was done by Bruce Russett, J. David Singer, and Melvin Small for the National Political Units dataset. This dataset was subsequently updated and expanded as the Bennett/Zitomersky/Wallace Autonomous Political Units dataset, and later as the States, Nations and Entities dataset (by Phil Schafer and Dan Jones). It is currently referred to as the Geopolitical Units dataset. Following the coding rules developed in the later updates, the concept of sovereignty is utilized to divide GPUs into two classifications: autonomous entities and nonsovereign entities. The "autonomous entity" category consists of all areas that were judged to have sovereignty or effective control over domestic affairs, whether or not they were in control of foreign policy.[35] Thus autonomous entities in essence include two major groups: those with sovereignty and independence as well as those with sovereignty but not independence (though the datasets did not initially subdivide them in this fashion). In the Autonomous Political Units version of these data, Bob Bennett had specified the criteria for determining whether an entity was autonomous: that an entity's government maintain an autonomous military organization (that is, independence) and that the government is recognized as legitimate or maintains control over some portion, however small, of the territory that it claims (that is, sovereignty).[36] In combining these considerations with the discussion of sovereignty that appeared in terms of interstate system members, we are defining an entity as sovereign if it maintains control over some portion, however small, of the territory it claims and if it maintains control over the national institutions. An entity would be independent if it had control over its foreign policy and was able to maintain an autonomous military organization.

The first class of autonomous entities, those that are sovereign and independent (or control both domestic and foreign policy), encompasses four subgroups. The first is the members of the interstate system. The second subgroup consists of independent territorial entities that did not meet the system-membership population requirement. The data on these two aforementioned groups were initially developed for the National Political Units dataset by Russett, Singer, and Small.[37] GPUs with a minimum population of 10,000 were referred to as National Political Units, and Russett, Singer, and Small considered them to be "the territorially based political units which are, have been since 1900, or are likely to become national political entities."[38] Thus their dataset included members of the interstate system (with a 500,000 population requirement) and territorial actors that failed system membership due to low population (or thus had populations between 10,000 and 500,000). We refer to the latter group as ministates. A third subgroup would be territorial entities with populations of fewer than 10,000 (some of which were included in the Schafer and Jones data). These are referred to as microstates. The final subgroup in this category includes entities that were sovereign and independent but did not meet the diplomatic recognition requirement for interstate system membership (herein referred to as protostates).

The second major category of autonomous entities consists of those entities that are sovereign but not independent, or that control domestic affairs but not foreign policy. These are what Adam Hochschild referred to as pseudostates.[39] These entities may claim independence, but their independence is not recognized and can in fact be constrained by others. Within this category, Schafer and Jones included entities such as Texas (1836–1845) and Hawaii (1816–1898) before they became dependencies of the United States. This category also included rebel-controlled areas in civil wars if the rebels were considered to have effective control over the domestic affairs in their territory, such as the Confederate States of America (1861–1865).

The category of geographical entities that do not have a sovereign government includes two major types of areas. The first group does not have a sovereign government, but the area has independence in the sense that it is not controlled by another entity. Such areas include both territories in historical pre-state-formation phases in which there are no national institutions, and territories in which there is no one group that has control over the national institutions (as in failed states).

The second group lacks independence, and entities in this group can be termed dependencies. In the National Political Units dataset, Russett, Singer, and Small described dependencies as belonging to one of three relatively general categories: (1) colonies and dependencies; (2) mandate and trust territories; and (3) occupied territories.[40]

1. Colonies and dependencies were characterized by a fairly durable status in which the entity exercised almost no control over its foreign affairs, armed forces, immigration, or trade.

2. Mandate and trust territories were entities whose dependent status was intended by the major powers to be fairly temporary, and whose gradual transition to independence was the moral and legal responsibility of the states to which they were assigned by the League of Nations, the United Nations, or international responsibility.

3. Occupied territories referred to those entities that had enjoyed independence until being overrun and occupied by foreign military forces.

In their subsequent updating of these data, Schafer and Jones added a substantial amount of information concerning entities that were parts of system members, and, relatedly, they differentiated ten codes for type of dependency control:

0 = associated state, protected state, or feudal relationship

1 = part of a larger or another entity

2 = colony

3 = protectorate

4 = claimed by this entity

5 = mandated to this entity

6 = occupation

7 = possession

8 = neutral zone or demilitarized zone

9 = leased to this entity

Finally, any change in an entity's status that did not last for one month or more was not included. Their data also included a couple of international intergovernmental organizations, such as the United Nations, which will be addressed below in the nonterritorial entity category.

In coding dependencies, one of the complicated coding decisions is determining which entities remain as colonies, mandates, protectorates, and occupied territories, and which become incorporated into a member of the interstate system. As Singer and Small noted, "Many states find it advantageous to blur this distinction through legal shams in order to demonstrate that its dependencies are integral parts of its territory...."[41] However, they ultimately decided to make a distinction among territories on the basis of whether their subjects had a direct role in the functioning of the central authority. Consequently, dependencies that were mandates, occupied territories, or non-contiguous (not adjacent by land nor within 150 uninterrupted miles by sea) were not generally incorporated into the system member.[42] A noncontiguous territory would be considered to be incorporated into a system member only when de facto control was established and the territory's incorporation was recognized by the members of the interstate system. Furthermore, territories were regarded as integrated only if there were no constitutional or statutory provisions that limited the rights of the subjects of the territory in question, nor any institutionalized discriminatory practices that would limit the subjects' rights.[43] For example, Pennsylvania is coded as a colony of the United Kingdom from 1681 to 1783 and then a part of the United States thereafter. Hawaii is coded as an autonomous entity from 1775 to 1898, a U.S. colony from 1898 to 1960, and a part of the United States thereafter. There are 191 distinct entities in the Western Hemisphere during the 500 years from 1492 to 1992. In the same period, there are 381 in Europe. For instance, in Europe the Papal States is in the COW interstate system for the period 1816–1860 but also is an autonomous entity from 1492 to 1796. From 1796 to 1814, it is occupied by France, and from 1860 to 1993 it is coded as part of Italy.

NONTERRITORIAL ENTITIES

In our typology of international actors (or members of the international system), the largest category of entities to be added to the preexisting datasets is that of the nonterritorially based entities or actors (NTEs). As nonstate actors develop greater capabilities, they have greater potential to engage in significant international behavior, including war. Thus we need a schema to describe their activities in relation to other more traditional actors. Categorization of NTEs will be based on four of the same general elements as GPUs, though they will be defined in slightly different terms. Needless to say, since we are describing nonterritorial entities, possession of territory will not be a prerequisite, though entities will be described as operating within states or across state borders. Population will be a requirement for nonstate unarmed groups, though there will be only two classifications: entities with large memberships and entities with limited memberships. The categories of sovereignty and independence will be similar to the conceptions for territorial actors, though they will be measured in slightly more constrained terms. Following the work of Ted Gurr and Phil Schrodt, sovereignty will be defined as having a persistent political organization that governs or commands some of the loyalties of a significant national group. Independence will refer to the ability to conduct policies in pursuit of its goals. The possession of an organized military will not be seen as an element of independence, but it will be utilized as a characteristic for differentiating among NTEs. Recognition will not be tied to specific diplomatic representation but will refer to acceptance of the NTE as a legitimate international actor by members of the international system.

These considerations will be utilized to categorize nonterritorial entities along two general dimensions of military capability and level of organization. Initially, NTEs will be categorized by their possession of, or lack of, armed forces. A common practice in discussing civil wars is to refer to the opponents in civil wars as merely insurgents or armed groups. In this vein, the term *nonstate armed groups* (NSAs) has been used to describe conflict participants including rebel movements, progovernment militias, community-based vigilante groups, some religious movements, and foreign mercenaries.[44] The nonstate armed groups will be contrasted with entities that do not have armed forces, called nonstate unarmed groups (NSUs). Secondly, NTEs will be distinguished by their relationships to the members of the interstate system, contrasting entities that are composed of representatives of the members of the interstate system, such as international intergovernmental organizations (IGOs), with entities that do not represent system members (or nongovernmental organizations [NGOs]). Third, entities will be subdivided on the basis of level of organization into those with little or no overarching political organization (nations) and quasi states that have an enduring political organization. This distinction derives from Gurr and Schrodt, who created a brief list of "groups" or "transnational actors." This listing included both groups of people (nations), such as the Kurds, and specific organizations. These groups and organizations could operate both within system members and across system member borders. They were not necessarily territorially based organizations, but Gurr and Schrodt referred to them as "quasi-state" actors because they had "persisting political organizations and aspirations either to the creation of a new state or revolutionary seizure of power in an existing state. Each governs or commands some of the loyalties of a significant national group, and has demonstrated substantial military and/or diplomatic capabilities to pursue that end."[45] For the NSAs, the next distinction is based on the size of the armed forces (greater or less than 100 armed personnel). The NSUs will be grouped based on population, differentiating those actors with large memberships from those with limited memberships.

In conclusion, there are two relatively simple ways to summarize the arguments being made here and to represent the typology of actors in the international system, both of which are included below. The first (Tables 1.3 and 1.4) focuses on the five major attributes of statehood and the extent

TABLE 1.3 GEOPOLITICAL UNITS (GPUs): TERRITORIAL MEMBERS OF THE INTERNATIONAL SYSTEM

Classification	Characteristics	Actor	Territory	Population	Sovereignty	Independence	Diplomatic recognition
Autonomous entities	All five	Interstate system member	X	>500,000	X	X	X
	Population disqualification	Ministates	X	>10,000 <500,000	X	X	X
		Microstates	X	<10,000	X	X	X
	Recognition disqualification	Protostates	X	>500,000	X	X	
	Independence limitations	Pseudostates	X	>500,000	X	Partial	
	Sovereignty disqualification	Detached governments	X	>500,000		X	X
		Occupied states (puppet government)	X	>500,000	Partial		X
		Failed states	X	>500,000		Perhaps	Perhaps
Dependencies	Independence disqualification	Rebel territories	X	X	X		
		Dependencies and subunits—types 0 to 9	X	X	Perhaps		

to which these attributes are possessed by various international actors. The first table examines the territorially based geopolitical units, and the second summarizes the types of nonterritorial entities. The second schema (Table 1.5) is merely an outline that shows the overall relationships among the actors in the international system and the location of some of the data concerning these actors. It is hoped that this typology will be useful in framing our discussions about international politics and its evolving nature. Though consensus or a common understanding on such a typology is not always desired or desirable, it can be instrumental in promoting collaborative research. This schema shows both where there are existing data on the actors in the international system and where such data are lacking. Despite the fact that significant data-gathering projects are under way, there is much work yet to be done.

TABLE 1.4 **NONTERRITORIAL ENTITIES (NTEs): NONTERRITORIALLY BASED MEMBERS OF THE INTERNATIONAL SYSTEM**

Classification	Actor	Territory: relations to states	Size of population/ armed forces	Sovereignty	Independence	Diplomatic recognition
Nonstate armed groups (NSAs)	Intergovernmental organizations (IGOs)	Members are territorial entities	Large armed forces >100; small armed forces <100		X	X
	Foreign NGOs: Foreign armed organizations	Operate across state borders or in nonstate areas	Large armed forces >100; small armed forces <100	X	X	
	Domestic NGOs: Indigenous armed organizations	Operate within states	Large armed forces >100; small armed forces <100	X	X	
	Foreign nations: Foreign armed aggregated groups	Operate across state borders or in nonstate areas	Large armed forces >100; small armed forces <100		Perhaps	
	Domestic nations: Indigenous aggregated groups	Operate within states	Large armed forces >100; small armed forces <100		Perhaps	
Nonstate unarmed groups (NSUs)	IGOs	Members are territorial entities	Large >50 members; small <50 members		X	X
	Foreign NGOs: Foreign organizations	Operate across state borders or in nonstate areas	Large >10,000 members; small <10,000 members	X	X	X
	Domestic NGOs: Indigenous organizations	Operate within states	Large >10,000 members; small <10,000 members	X	X	X
	Foreign nations: Foreign aggregated groups	Operate across state borders or in nonstate areas	Large > 50,000 members; small <50,000		Perhaps	Perhaps
	Domestic nations: Indigenous aggregated groups	Operate within states	Large > 50,000 members; small <50,000		Perhaps	Perhaps

TABLE 1.5 **THE INTERNATIONAL SYSTEM**

I. Geopolitical units (GPUs)
  A. Autonomous entities—States, Nations and Entities dataset
    1. Those with sovereignty and independence
      a. Members of the interstate system (states)—Interstate System Membership dataset, National Political Units dataset
      b. Ministates, population between 10,000 and 500,000—National Political Units dataset
      c. Protostates—lacking the diplomatic recognition requirement for interstate system membership (or not active in the interstate system)
      d. Microstates, population below 10,000
    2. Those with sovereignty but not independence
      a. Pseudostates
      b. Rebel-held territories
    3. Sovereignty limitations: former interstate system members that no longer have sovereignty
      a. Detached governments—governments in exile or governments that continue to function internationally, that is, by fielding a military force
      b. Failed states—former interstate system members whose governments no longer have sovereignty
      c. Occupied states with puppet regimes
  B. Dependencies or nonindependent entities—though there may be restrictions on sovereignty as well—States, Nations and Entities dataset
    1. Dependencies—colonies, mandates, and occupied territories (at all three population levels)—National Political Units dataset
    2. Rebel territories
II. Nonterritorial entities (NTEs)
  A. Nonstate armed groups (NSAs)
    1. Representing interstate system members—international intergovernmental organizations (IGOs) and alliances—IGO dataset, Alliance dataset
    2. Nongovernmental organizations (NGOs): quasi-states (groups with persistent political institutions), entities with limited memberships (armed gangs), small NSAs, private military companies (PMCs)
      a. Foreign
      b. Domestic
    3. Armed nations—armed unorganized hordes
      a. Foreign
      b. Domestic
  B. Nonstate unarmed groups (NSUs)
    1. Intergovernmental Organizations (IGOs)—representing interstate system members:—international intergovernmental organizations (IGOs) and alliances are in the IGO dataset, Alliance dataset
    2. Nongovernmental organizations (NGOs): quasi-states (groups with persistent political institutions), entities with limited memberships (armed gangs), small NSAs, PMCs
      a. Foreign
      b. Domestic
    3. Unarmed nations (groups with common bonds, but no overarching persisting political organization and having no substantial military capability) are in the Cultural dataset
      a. Foreign
      b. Domestic

The Central System and the Major Power System

In his political fable *Animal Farm*, George Orwell once said, "All animals are equal, but some animals are more equal than others."[46] Likewise, while all UN members are treated as equally deserving of one vote in the General Assembly, the role played by the Security Council (in particular, its permanent members) demonstrates that not all these territorial political entities are equal in political power. In the COW Project there is a similar rank order of importance of international actors, based on which states have the most ability to exercise power or influence.[47] Consequently, there are two particular subsets of the interstate system that Singer and Small considered to be especially important: the central system and the major power system. Membership in these systems is indicated in Table 1.6. The central system was defined by Singer and Small as "the most powerful, industrialized, and diplomatically active members of the interstate system, generally coinciding with the 'European state system.'"[48] The states of the central system did much to define the rules of the entire interstate system; therefore, they were singled out by Singer and Small for particular attention. It is the central European system that dominated much of the military and economic aspects of the world, for instance, through colonization and war. Only the larger states of Europe are included in this subsystem; thus it excludes the smaller city-states and regional states of Germany and Italy from the central system. The central subsystem was deemed relevant in the period 1816–1919 and was phased out at the end of World War I.

Within the interstate system, the states with the most power are considered to be the major powers. The major powers are states with especially high levels of material capabilities, so that their military reach is global; they are also those that are informally treated as great powers by the other members of the great power club.[49] Singer and Small initially noted that major power membership could be ascertained by the "high degree of scholarly consensus" concerning the "composition of this oligarchy," though they did note that there was less consensus on the list of the major powers in the post–World War II period than in the earlier period.[50] A decade later they add an important qualification:

> Since we completed the first version of this study, we have become even less confident of our major power classifications, especially for the period since 1965. In economic terms, West Germany and Japan have indeed become major powers, but we are reluctant to include them as major military actors because of the several constitutional provisions that preclude them—through the 1970s—from exercising a global military presence.[51]

With that qualification, they stuck with the scholarly consensus of who were the majors, although they admitted that this decision represented only the best of a number of imperfect solutions.

Over the past two centuries, the majors are the states with the greatest capabilities at any particular time, those that in fact have sufficient capability to launch military campaigns anywhere in the globe. It is generally true that these major powers form a "club," in the sense that they each, as well as we in the "scholarly consensus," realize which states are in their exclusive circle. Thus in 1816 the major powers were the United Kingdom (of Great Britain and Northern Ireland), France, Russia, Prussia, and Austria-Hungary. Austria-Hungary dropped off the list in 1918, when it broke up at the end of World War I. During the Cold War, it was generally recognized that the first five nations to acquire nuclear weapons (which are now also the five permanent members of the UN Security Council) were the major powers. One disagreement over the list of members occurred in the wake of the Chinese civil war of 1927–1949, when each of the two surviving Chinese governments claimed that it was entitled to China's Security Council seat. The confusion about the place of rival Chinese governments clarified gradually as the government controlling Beijing got the upper hand. Especially after Communist China's nuclear bomb test, it gained the Chinese Security Council seat from Taiwan.

TABLE 1.6 **MEMBERS OF THE CENTRAL AND MAJOR POWER SYSTEMS** (1816–2007)

Code	Abb	State name	Central system	Major power system
2	USA	United States	1899–1919	1899–2007
200	UKG	United Kingdom	1816–1919	1816–2007
210	NTH	Netherlands	1816–1919	
211	BEL	Belgium	1831–1919	
220	FRN	France	1816–1919	1816–1940; 1945–2007
225	SWZ	Switzerland	1816–1919	
230	SPN	Spain	1816–1919	
235	POR	Portugal	1816–1919	
255	GMY	Germany/Prussia	1816–1919	1816–1918; 1925–1945; 1990–2007
290	POL	Poland	1919–1919	
300	AUH	Austria-Hungary	1816–1918	1816–1918
305	AUS	Austria	1919–1919	
310	HUN	Hungary	1919–1919	
325	ITA	Italy/Sardinia	1816–1919	1860–1943
339	ALB	Albania	1914–1919	
345	YUG	Yugoslavia/Serbia	1878–1919	
350	GRC	Greece	1828–1919	
355	BUL	Bulgaria	1908–1919	
360	ROM	Romania	1878–1919	
365	RUS	Russia (USSR)	1816–1919	1816–1917; 1922–2007
366	EST	Estonia	1918–1919	
367	LAT	Latvia	1918–1919	
368	LIT	Lithuania	1918–1919	
380	SWD	Sweden	1816–1919	
385	NOR	Norway	1905–1919	
390	DEN	Denmark	1816–1919	
640	TUR	Turkey/Ottoman Empire	1816–1919	
710	CHN	China	1895–1919	1950–2007
740	JPN	Japan	1895–1919	1895–1945; 1990–2007

Examining the major power subsystem has been a relatively popular subject for researchers. For instance, Jack Levy has conducted a well-known study entitled *War in the Modern Great Power System, 1495–1975*. Though Levy's modern system begins 321 years before COW's interstate system, for all intents and purposes his description of the "great powers" is synonymous with the COW understanding of the "major powers." One difference, however, is that Singer and Small were trying to avoid the use of the word *great* lest it convey an unseemly approval of the often-reprehensible major power behavior. Levy, after a useful review of definitions of great powers, settled on the definition that a great power is "a state that plays a major role in international politics with respect to security-related issues."[52] Since security can be treated as a synonym for strategic or military objectives, and since states that play a major role on security issues are almost all of high capability and recognized as members of the informal great power club, the Levy and COW definitions overlap to the point of being almost indistinguishable in practice during their common time frame. Levy positions his argument for the importance of studying the members of the great power system within the overarching realist paradigm by explaining that within the anarchic international system, there is a hierarchy of actors based on differing levels of power.[53] It is the great powers that drive the international system through their ability to project military power. Since the level of interactions among the great powers is higher that those of other states, the great powers constitute an independent system of their own. As Levy noted, a relatively high proportion of great power alliance commitments and war behavior is with one another.[54] Other studies focusing on the major powers have also demonstrated the usefulness of examining this small system of states, since the major powers tend to be a particularly war-prone group. Thus the full list of the members of the COW central and major power systems appears in Table 1.6. The behavior of the major powers also serves as a bridge to the discussion in our next chapter, which focuses on the definition and classification of war.

NOTES

1. International Olympic Committee, "National Olympic Committees," *Olympic Charter*, September 1, 2004, http://multimedia.olympic.org/pdf/en_report_122.pdf.
2. The Olympic Movement, "National Olympic Committees," www.olympic.org/uk/index_uk.asp.
3. J. David Singer and Melvin Small, *The Wages of War, 1816–1965: A Statistical Handbook* (New York: Wiley, 1972), 24; Melvin Small and J. David Singer, *Resort to Arms: International and Civil Wars, 1816–1980* (Beverly Hills, Calif.: Sage, 1982), 47.
4. Karl Wolfgang Deutsch, *Nationalism and Social Communication* (New York: Wiley, 1953).
5. Karl W. Deutsch, *The Analysis of International Relations*, 2nd ed. (Englewood Cliffs, N.J.: Prentice-Hall, 1978), 81.
6. Deutsch, *The Analysis of International Relations*, 79.
7. See the discussion in Joshua S. Goldstein, *International Relations* (New York: HarperCollins, 1994), 28–30.
8. Singer and Small, *The Wages of War*, 19.
9. Max Weber, "Politics as a Vocation," in *From Max Weber: Essays in Sociology*, ed. H.H. Gerth and C. Wright Mills (New York: Oxford University Press, 1958), 78.
10. C. Tilly, "Reflections on the History of European State Making," in *The Formation of National States in Western Europe*, ed. C. Tilly (Princeton, N.J.: Princeton University Press, 1975), 3–83.
11. Stuart A. Bremer with Faten Ghosn, "Defining States: Reconsiderations and Recommendations," *Conflict Management and Peace Science* 20, no. 1 (2003): 24.
12. Zeev Maoz, e-mail message to authors, December 2006.
13. See Bremer, "Defining States," for another discussion of this analogy.
14. Hans Morgenthau, *Politics among Nations: The Struggle for Power and Peace*, 5th ed. (New York: Knopf, 1973), 190.
15. Singer and Small, *The Wages of War*, 16.
16. Robert Bennett, "Redefining the Interstate System" (draft manuscript, University of Michigan, March 25, 1975), 18.
17. See J. David Singer and Melvin Small, "The Composition and Status Ordering of the International System 1815–1940," *World Politics* 18, no. 2 (January 1966), 236–282; Bruce M. Russett, J. David Singer, and Melvin Small, "National Political Units in the Twentieth Century: A Standardized List," *American Political Science Review* 62, no. 3 (September 1968), 932–951; Singer and Small, *The Wages of War*.
18. As some critics have rightly pointed out, many scholars have utilized the system membership list without much thought about what it was designed to capture.
19. Singer and Small, *The Wages of War*, 20.
20. Ibid.
21. Small and Singer, *Resort to Arms*, 40.
22. Singer and Small, "The Composition and Status Ordering of the International System," 246. In Singer and Small, *The Wages of War*, diplomatic recognition is also more specifically described as a means to identify those entities that play a more significant role in the interstate system.

23. Singer and Small, *The Wages of War*, 20.
24. Small and Singer, *Resort to Arms*, 41.
25. John Lynch, *The Spanish-American Revolutions, 1808–1826* (New York: W. W. Norton, 1973), 25–26, cited in Benedict Anderson, *Imagined Communities: Reflections on the Origin and Spread of Nationalism*, rev. and ext. ed. (London: Verso, 1991), 52.
26. Singer and Small, *The Wages of War*, 21.
27. Bremer, "Defining States," 23.
28. Singer and Small, "The Composition and Status Ordering of the International System," 247–249.
29. Small and Singer, *Resort to Arms*, 51.
30. Other scholars utilize a definition of civil war that does not require participation by the national government. For instance, see Stathis N. Kalyvas, *The Logic of Violence in Civil War* (New York: Cambridge University Press, 2006), 17.
31. Small and Singer, *Resort to Arms*, 214.
32. For a detailed description of the evolution of these criteria, see Meredith Reid Sarkees, "A Typology of International Political Actors and War Participants" (draft manuscript, 2007).
33. Most of these datasets can be obtained from the COW Web site: www.correlatesofwar.org.
34. Bremer, "Defining States," 32.
35. Phil Schafer and Daniel M. Jones, "States, Nations and Entities, 1816–1993" (introduction to the dataset, University of Michigan, 1994), 2.
36. Bennett, "Redefining the Interstate System," 19.
37. Bruce M. Russett, J. David Singer, and Melvin Small, "National Political Units in the Twentieth Century: A Standardized List," *American Political Science Review* 62, no. 3 (September 1968), 932–951. In this article, the interstate-international system distinction was not made as clearly as it might have been. As Singer and Small admitted in *The Wages of War* (p. 19), their application of the label of "international system" to what is really the more restricted interstate system had the effect of treating as outside of the international system the many national entities (colonies, mandates, annexed or occupied regions, and so forth) that, while clearly not in the sovereign state category, definitely are constituent units of that larger *international* system. This subsequently became one of the reasons for the change in terminology from intra-systemic war to inter-state war and extra-systemic war to extra-state war.
38. Russett, Singer, and Small, "National Political Units in the Twentieth Century," 933.
39. Adam Hochschild, "A Pseudostate Is Born," *Global Policy Forum*, June 27, 2004, www.globalpolicy.org/nations/future/2004/0627pseudostate.htm.
40. Russett, Singer and Small, "National Political Units in the Twentieth Century," 934.
41. Small and Singer, *Resort to Arms*, 211.
42. Robert Bennett (internal COW memo, University of Michigan , October 1973), 12.
43. Small and Singer, *Resort to Arms*, 211.
44. Malian Ministry of Foreign Affairs and International Cooperation, "Mapping of Non-state Armed Groups in the ECOWAS Region" (draft presented at the 6th Ministerial Meeting of the Human Security Network, Bamako, Mali, May 27–29, 2004), 26.
45. T. R. Gurr and Phil Schrodt, "Updating and Expanding the Singer and Small Codes" (internal COW memo, September 30, 1988), 1–2.
46. George Orwell, "Politics and the English Language," (Garden City, N.Y.: Doubleday Anchor Books, 1954) 162–176.
47. J. David Singer, "Inter-Nation Influence: A Formal Model," *American Political Science Review* 57, no. 2 (June 1963): 420–430; Frank Wayman, J. David Singer, and Gary Goertz, "Capabilities, Allocations and Success in Militarized Disputes and Wars, 1816–1976," *International Studies Quarterly* 27 (December 1983), 497–516.
48. Singer and Small, *The Wages of War*, 381.
49. Frank Wayman, Meredith Reid Sarkees, and J. David Singer, "Inter-State, Intra-State, Extra-State, and Non-State Wars, 1816–2004" (paper presented at the annual meeting of the International Studies Association, Honolulu, Hawaii, March 5, 2005), 5.
50. Singer and Small, *The Wages of War*, 23.
51. Small and Singer, *Resort to Arms*, 45.
52. Jack S. Levy, *War in the Modern Great Power System, 1495–1975* (Lexington: University Press of Kentucky, 1983), 16.
53. Levy, *War in the Modern Great Power System*, 8.
54. Levy, *War in the Modern Great Power System*, 9.

CHAPTER TWO

Defining and Categorizing Wars

By Meredith Reid Sarkees

Defining War and a Typology of War

"Our goal is to be as operational as possible while doing as little harm as possible to history."

—Mel Small and David Singer

War is a word infused with epic drama, attracting a host of politicians, headline writers, and story-tellers to employ it for their own rhetorical purposes. The United States has seen the War on Poverty, the war on drugs, and the war on crime, as well as the Cold War, the deficit reduction war, and, more recently, the war on terror. Within the political science community, the term *war* has also been utilized in a variety of contexts.[1] There is Carl von Clausewitz's famous description of war as "a continuation of political activity by other means."[2] Thomas Hobbes described the state of nature as a "condition which is called war, and such a war is of every man against every man."[3] Marx and Engels defined history in terms of class struggles and argued for the need for a "war ... where the violent overthrow of the bourgeoisie lays the foundation for the sway of the proletariat."[4] In its more classical understanding, war has been studied from a variety of perspectives, and it has been both praised and condemned. Machiavelli argued that for the Prince, war not only would help to secure the state but also would satisfy the princely drive for glory.[5] In the last century, Leon Trotsky also argued for the necessity of war, particularly the "permanent revolution,"[6] and Rosa Luxemburg claimed that "the Russian Revolution is the mightiest event of the World War."[7] In contradiction, Jane Addams argued that "war is not a natural activity for mankind."[8] Woodrow Wilson apparently saw both the positive and negative aspects of war when he described World War I as the war to "bring peace and safety to all nations."[9] Jean Bethke Elshtain, among many others, has discussed whether there could be a "just war."[10] Joshua Goldstein investigated the links between war and gender.[11]

In contrast to these myriad expansive conceptions of war, COW wanted to develop a more limited definition of war, lest any situation involving tension, contention, and conflict be deemed as war. Quite a significant number of international relations scholars have attempted to do the same thing, yet the disagreements in the definition and categorization of wars have led to competing data-gathering projects that have produced conflicting understandings of war. A useful review of the various scholarly definitions of war as they are used in international relations can be found in *The War Puzzle* by John Vasquez.[12] He described conceptions of war that include contending by force, legal contests, social inventions, biological imperatives, and political instruments. Ultimately, Vasquez adopted a definition of war that was a modification of a classic definition provided by Hedley Bull. Bull's definition was: "War is organized violence carried on by political units against each other."[13] To this, Vasquez adds only the qualification that the organized violence must aim to "kill members of another group, not simply to do them harm."[14] These words of Bull, as refined by Vasquez, are very close to the definition of war adopted by Mel Small and David Singer. Small and Singer began *Resort to Arms* with a quote from Quincy Wright's groundbreaking *A Study of War*, which summarized the differing perspectives on war:

> To some it is a plague which ought to be eliminated; to others, a crime which ought to be punished; to still others, it is an anachronism which no longer serves any purpose. On the other hand, there are some who take a more receptive attitude toward war, and regard it an adventure which may be interesting, an instrument which may be legitimate and appropriate, or a condition of existence for which one must be prepared.[15]

This contrast in normative valuations of war entered into Wright's classification of war, whereby he distinguished four types of war: balance-of-power wars; civil wars; defensive wars that "defend modern civilization against alien culture"; and imperial wars that seek "to expand modern civilization at the expense of alien culture."[16] Wright's distinctions led to the exclusion of certain conflicts, so Small and Singer developed what they referred to as a coding mechanism for wars that was in their estimation "somewhat more discriminating—as well as more complex."[17] Their definition of war hinged on two primary criteria: the threshold of battle-related fatalities or troops in combat, and the status of the war participants. Small and Singer began with the definition that war is sustained combat involving substantial fatalities: "We must define war in terms of violence. Not only is war impossible without violence (except of course in the metaphorical sense), but we consider the taking of human life the primary and dominant characteristic of war."[18] Yet, not all taking of human life is war. A murder of an individual or a slaughter or massacre of civilians would not be considered as fatalities resulting from sustained combat. Small and Singer ultimately decided on a threshold of 1,000 battle-related deaths as the level of hostilities that differentiates war from other types of conflict. This threshold has proven to be empirically significant in describing wars, and variations of it have been adopted by an assortment of other war data–gathering projects. For instance, the Uppsala Conflict Data Project (UCDP) utilizes the 1,000 death requirement for a war, but the deaths must occur within a calendar year. Their fatalities also include the deaths of civilians that were the result of hostilities, while such fatalities are not included in the Correlates of War (COW) wars. For example, the approximately 3,000 people killed at the World Trade Center in 2001 were considered as combat-related hostilities by the UCDP, but they are not seen as the result of sustained combat, and therefore the attack was not counted as a war by COW.

The second major criterion in describing war is the status of the war participants. Wars had to have participants on both sides that had organizations able to conduct combat (armed forces). Thus their overarching definition of war was sustained combat, involving organized armed forces, resulting in a minimum of 1,000 battle-related fatalities. Singer and Small's primary interest, however, was in developing a typology that differentiated the various types of war. As described in the previous chapter, Singer and Small focused their attention on the members of the interstate system, or states, which by definition had to have the means of exerting their independence and playing a role in international relations. Just as the distinction between states and nonstate entities was the basis of their understanding of the international system, it was also the basis of their understanding of war. Singer and Small developed a typology of war, or categories of war, determined by the political status of the participants (unlike other data-gathering projects that focus on the issues over which there is conflict or the types of weapons used). Inter-state wars were those that were conducted between or among members of the interstate system. Extra-systemic wars were those that were conducted between a system member and a nonstate entity (not a system member). Civil wars were conducted between a state and a group within its borders. The remainder of this chapter will be devoted to describing in more detail Singer and Small's initial classification of wars and the changes and additions that have been made to their war typology. The variables that are used in describing or measuring wars will be discussed, including the temporal domain; battle-related deaths, or battle-deaths; the "bulk of the fighting"; the war's duration; the initiator; the outcome; and the location of the war. It is possible for conflicts to change classifications, and the conditions under which such transformations take place will be enumerated. Most importantly, the discussion will focus upon the characteristics of each of the classes of wars and examine the ways in which the specific variables are delineated in each of the categories.

Focusing on wars, and setting the death threshold at 1,000 deaths, does not imply that conflict at lower levels is unimportant but merely that conflict involving 1,000 fatalities per year is different from conflict that results in fewer deaths. In fact, the COW Project has developed other datasets that contain information on either instances of conflict between states that involved less than 1,000 battle-deaths or instances of fatalities from other causes. The Militarized Interstate Dispute (MID) dataset focuses on conflict between or among interstate system members with hostility levels that ranged from merely a show of force up through conflicts with fewer than 1,000 battle-related deaths. A second COW data-gathering project has been developed by Phil Schafer, who initially collected a list of all instances, from 1816 to the present, in which at least 20 people were killed in violence. He has recently updated this list to include deaths by natural disasters as well. The basic differentiating factor separating the wars from the mass political killings is the requirement for "sustained combat," which is not in evidence in the latter case.

The Initial Classification

The classification of wars by J. David Singer and Mel Small originally appeared in 1972 in *The Wages of War 1816–1965: A Statistical Handbook,* which described the two types of international wars, inter-state and extra-systemic. Small and Singer updated the data on these wars in 1982 in *Resort to Arms: International and Civil War, 1816–1980,* which also included data on civil wars. Since this latter work not only represented an updating and expansion of the data but also included further clarification of some of the coding rules, it will be the primary source for the following discussion of the initial COW categorization of wars.

International War

As noted above, war has been defined by the COW Project as sustained combat between or among military organizations involving substantial casualties of 1,000 deaths. Wars were classified into two major groupings: international wars and civil wars. International wars were further subdivided into two major types, inter-state and extra-systemic wars. Inter-state wars were defined as those in which a territorial state that qualifies as a member of the interstate system is engaged in a war with another system member. An inter-state war must have sustained combat involving regular armed forces on both sides and 1,000 battle-related fatalities among all of the system members involved. Any individual member state qualified as a war participant through either of two alternative criteria:

a minimum of 100 fatalities or a minimum of 1,000 armed personnel engaged in active combat.[19] The Inter-state War dataset that was developed described the experience of each interstate system member involved in each war, utilizing 44 variables, including the entry and exit dates; the prewar population; the number of persons serving in the armed forces (exclusive of police forces, unorganized militias, border guards, and gendarmerie); the geographical location of the war; the severity of the war as determined by the number of battle-related deaths; and the magnitude as reflected in duration (nation-months, or the sum of the number of months each participating nation is involved in a war).

Extra-systemic wars were those in which the interstate system member engaged in a war with a political entity that was not a system member. Extra-systemic wars were initially defined as those in which the system member's forces were engaged in sustained combat with forces (however irregular and disorganized) of a political entity that failed the requirements for system membership. Since Small and Singer were concerned with the war experience of system members, sustained combat required a minimum of 1,000 battle-related fatalities for the system member alone during each year of the war. Extra-systemic wars were further divided into two major subtypes, depending once more on the political status of the adversary. The first subtype, the "imperial war," involved an adversary that was an independent political entity, that was seeking to maintain that independence, and that did not qualify as a member of the interstate system (because of limitations on its independence, insufficient population to meet the interstate system membership criteria, or a failure of other states to recognize it as a legitimate member). The war was classified as "colonial" if, on the other hand, the adversary was already a colony, a dependency, or a protectorate composed of ethnically different people and located at some geographical distance from the given system member, or at least peripheral to its center of government. Small and Singer indicated that internationalized civil wars should be considered international wars as well. In internationalized civil wars, a system member intervenes in a civil war that is ongoing within another state. A state's involvement in a war outside its borders thus represents international warfare, though such wars were included in the Civil War dataset.

It should be noted that extra-systemic wars derived their identity from the involvement of a system member's active participation in a war beyond its own "metropolitan" territory and against the forces of a political entity that was not a recognized member of the system.[20] This distinction of classifying wars on the basis of being peripheral to the center of government (or the "metropole") is the key to understanding the initial differences between extra-systemic and civil wars. For millennia, the main form of legitimacy of a state was to claim that its monarch ruled by the will of heaven, or God. As such, a state was the personal property of the monarch, and it had an extent co-terminus with the reach of his or her army. Depending upon the efficacy of the army, the state could develop an extensive imperial range. Within the empire, a distinction was sometimes made between a part of the core, called the metropole, and the peripheral area of the empire, often called the colonies. The word *metropole* derives from the Greek words for "mother" (*métér*) and "city" (*polis*) and involves the notion that in antiquity the mother countries, or "metropoles" such as Corinth, were the ones that established colonies, such as Corcyra (the island known today as Corfu). The same distinction between metropoles and colonies was used to describe the European colonial empires. Thus, speaking of the independence wars of the United States and Latin America from 1776 to 1826, Benedict Anderson wrote: "Whether we think of Brazil, the USA, or the former colonies of Spain, language was not an element that differentiated them from their respective imperial *metropoles* [emphasis added]."[21] Hence, wars that took place between colonies and the mother country (or extra-systemic wars) were described as wars between the periphery and the metropole. Small and Singer utilized the metropole distinction not only in terms of describing extra-systemic wars but also in their definition of civil wars. It is critical to understand the initial emphasis on the metropole/periphery distinction because the elimination of this distinction was the one major change in the COW war typology that is reflected in the new expanded typology (which will be described below).

CIVIL WAR

The classification of civil war was built on three dimensions: internality, types of participants, and the degree of effective resistance. In general, a civil war was defined as any armed conflict that involved (1) military action internal to the metropole of the state system member; (2) the active participation of the national government; (3) effective resistance by both sides; and (4) a total of at least 1,000 battle-deaths during each year of the war.

One distinction made here (and conversely in the definition of extra-systemic wars above) was that significant military action had to occur between political entities within the boundaries of the metropole. However, unlike the distinction in extra-state wars, the metropole is not contrasted with distant colonies; here the metropole is the core of the system member itself. When examining civil wars (and adding them to the database), Small and Singer concluded that there were wars that took place within states having characteristics that resembled extra-state conflicts between a metropole and a periphery, particularly when there were areas within the state boundaries that were not well integrated into the central government, or had characteristics that were different from those of the metropole or the capital of the state. In such cases, wars between these distant areas (often seeking autonomy) were more like extra-systemic wars than they were like civil wars that frequently were urban conflicts for control of the capital city. Consequently, Small and Singer classified wars that took place between the metropole and a periphery within a state as extra-systemic wars as well. Civil wars were then specifically defined as involving military action internal to the metropole of the system member. Given this criterion, it was necessary to construct rules for distinguishing the metropole of a state from its non-integrated areas, and this distinction between the metropole (or core) of a state and the periphery was reflective of the degree of the internal cohesion of a state. A territory was regarded as integrated (or part of the metropole) if all the following conditions were true: (1) there were no constitutional provisions denying the subjects the right to participate in the government; (2) there were no restrictive provisions based on ethnicity, race, or religion; and (3) districts included in the national capital or federal district were considered to be integrated, regardless of the manner in which they were administered.[22] To reiterate, in terms of wars that took place within the boundaries of a system member, wars that were fought by the central government against actors or territories not integrated into the metropole were considered extra-systemic wars, and wars within the metropole were civil wars. The extent to which this classification seemed to be in conflict with the COW Project's emphasis on the territorial state as the basis of many of its datasets became one of the motivations for the endeavor to expand upon and revise the initial COW war typology.

The second criterion for civil wars was that the national government had to be an active participant. This requirement has made the COW discussion of civil wars more specific and limited than those in other research projects. In surveying the civil war research in 1982, Small and Singer concluded:

> Conceptually the field (studies of civil war, insurgency, rebellion, coups, and revolution) is a morass. There is neither a unified approach to the task of defining a typology of internal violence (violence with a COW state or similar geo-political entity) nor even a single agreed-upon concept of what civil war is or is not.… At worst they (the authors and their terminology) are confusing and internally inconsistent.[23]

As Small and Singer pointed out, the terminologies used to describe internal wars were inconsistent, and even though the term *war* might have been used, there was not even necessarily a requirement for violence as a means of bringing about change.[24] The term *civil war* had its roots primarily in English and American history, not political science. A basic dictionary definition of civil war is "a war between factions or regions of one country."[25] In political science, terms such as *revolution* (Crane Brinton, Theda Skocpol)[26], *internal war* (Harry Eckstein)[27], *insurgency,* and even *rebellion* (Ted Gurr)[28] were more common. Frequently, such conflicts were described in terms of the motivations of the participants along ideological or political lines or in terms of the tactics used (guerrilla war). Small and Singer saw the basic definition of civil war and the descriptions of revolution, internal war, and rebellion as too broad, including conflicts of disparate types. Since they were primarily concerned with war as it was experienced by the members of the interstate system, they included the requirement that civil wars must involve the "national government in power at the time hostilities begin."[29] However, in their overall typology of war, they did create space for the other types of internal war that involved other types of actors. Their category of internal war included three subcategories: civil wars (involving the national government); regional internal war (involving a subnational government); and communal violence (not involving government at any level).[30] Small and Singer did not gather data on the latter two types of war, though this has been part of the recent progress within the COW Project.

Unfortunately, the lack of definitional clarity about what constitutes a civil war still remains, and in this context Small and Singer's requirement of the involvement of the national government is controversial.[31] Even a member of the COW community, Zeev Maoz, has argued against the restrictive nature of requiring national government involvement:

> Allow me to dissent from the general consensus about civil wars. The characteristics of war in general—and they apply to civil wars as well—are threefold: (1) Organized violence: Acts of violence are deliberate and conducted under the guidance of recognizable—overt or secret—organizations on at least two sides. (2) Sustained violence: Actions of violence occur fairly regularly over time, rather than in a sporadic and disparate manner. (3) Severe violence: the 1,000 deaths per year criterion is essential. The way I view it, the presence or absence of a government is immaterial in civil war. The essence of civil war outbreak is the collapse of the government's authority; the government no longer possesses a monopoly over the use of organized force. Hence, the extent of the collapse of such authority—whether the government functions at all in terms of management of force—is not an element of the definition. The notion of "failed state" is nice but it has to do with government control over the principal functions of governance. It is conceivable that a state would fail in this sense without a resort to mass violence. Moreover, the government-insurgent notion is overly narrow as it does not include cases of multiple organized groups fighting each other in a fairly intense way, e.g., Angola, 1977–1990; Rhodesia/Zimbabwe (about the same period); Lebanon (1974–91), and others.[32]

Currently, the debate about what constitutes a civil war has become important in the discussion of how to describe the conflict in Iraq. The United States' administration has resisted calling the situation in Iraq a civil war in an effort to downplay the level of violence occurring there. COW is in the uncomfortable position of agreeing that it is not a civil war, but for a different reason. For the conflict to be a COW civil war, the government of Iraq would have to be the major participant. Since the bulk of the fighting is being conducted by the United States against the Iraqi insurgency, the war is classified as an extra-state war, not a civil war.

An Expanded Typology of War

On the whole, the classification of wars and the coding rules established by Singer and Small have proven to be so effective that they have remained unchanged over the past forty years. In 1994, however, the COW Project began a process of slightly modifying and updating its war typology and coding rules. The motivating factors for these changes included the desires to expand the war typology to include additional types of armed conflict; modify a coding rule (the metropole distinction) that had previously allowed similar types of war to be assigned to different classifications; change the coding of certain variables in order to make them more comparable across all the war types; and change some of the terminology and coding practices that had been perceived as Eurocentric. Descriptions of the initial stages of this process were presented by Meredith Reid Sarkees and J. David Singer at conferences in 1996 and 2001,[33] and were published by Meredith Reid Sarkees in 2000 as "Correlates of War Warsets: An Update."[34]

To some members of the COW Project, it seemed that there was a need for an expanded classification of wars, in that since World War II there appeared to be a growing number of armed conflicts and/or important combatants that did not fit comfortably within the existing COW categories. In particular, trends have signaled the importance in international interactions of other subnational (or intranational) and extranational entities alongside the territorial state. Globalization can be seen as a historical trend marked by the proliferation of transnational movements of information, goods, money, and, to a lesser extent, people. Some of these movements have become institutionalized in nongovernmental international organizations that exercise significant influence. Thus, as noted in Chapter 1, the dominance of the territorial state as the primary actor in international relations is being challenged by the rise in efficacy of intergovernmental organizations (IGOs) and nongovernmental organizations (NGOs), including the multinational corporations (MNCs). States are also being threatened from within. For instance, there are states that are no longer as institutionalized as in the past, such as "failed states" or "quasi-legitimate" states. In addition, multinational states are being threatened by the reappearance of the support for the creation of "nation-states." At the end of World War I, U.S. president Woodrow Wilson included in his peace plan the notion that each national, linguistic, religious, or ethnic identity group was entitled to its own sovereign and independent state. Few at the time appreciated the volatile nature of national self-determination. To put it bluntly, there is no cultural identity group that cannot be further subdivided by political and religious elites who are capable of mobilizing one or another subpopulation by claims of historical or contemporary insults, humiliations, defeats, victories, or entitlements that warrant separation and perhaps war in pursuit of their own state.

In the absence of effective institutions (domestic and/or international), many problems have led to the emergence of new actors and new types of conflict. For instance, the flourishing of nonstate actors has been related to, among other things, the increase in worldwide arms trade and the development of private armies; the growth of international drug trafficking; the expanding power of multinational corporations; the fact that boundaries are increasingly permeable by people, weapons, drugs; and the formation of diverse coalitions that acquire weapons and form armies. Separately, and in combination, these forces have contributed to the increasing number of nonstate actors that have the motivation and capacity to engage in warfare both within traditional states and across state borders. The variety of groups involved in contemporary "civil wars" and the activities of international "terrorist groups" are forerunners of a potential plethora of actors that may soon be willing and able to inflict and sustain casualties severe enough to qualify as wars.[35] Other

TABLE 2.1 **THE COW PROJECT'S TWO TYPOLOGIES OF WAR**

Traditional typology	Expanded typology
I. International wars	
A. Inter-state wars	I. Inter-state wars (war type 1)
B. Extra-systemic wars	II. Extra-state wars
(1) Colonial	A. Colonial—conflict with colony (war type 2)
(2) Imperial	B. Imperial—state vs. nonstate (war type 3)
	III. Intra-state wars
	A. Civil wars
II. Civil wars	1. for central control (war type 4)
	2. over local issues (war type 5)
	B. Regional internal (war type 6)
	C. Inter-communal (war type 7)
	IV. Non-state wars
	A. In nonstate territory (war type 8)
	B. Across state borders (war type 9)

scholars have noted these trends as well. For instance, Kal Holsti (1996) has argued that we are seeing the emergence of new "wars of the third kind," [36] and many others, including Lake and Rothchild [37] and Carment and James, [38] have decried the proliferation of "ethnic wars." Donald Snow has argued that contemporary internal wars diverge from their predecessors owing to their more violent nature. Such wars are more like international wars than what were traditionally referred to as civil wars, leading him to call them "uncivil wars." [39] We shall examine our evidence in assessing these claims in Chapter 7. Similarly, Dennis Sandole argued that there are such significant similarities among violent conflicts occurring at various levels of aggregation, that there is a need for a *generic theory* for "Capturing the Complexity of Conflict." [40] The COW Project began such an endeavor by looking at the ways in which these new international actors may lead to different types and patterns of warfare, and the project has consequently reformulated and expanded its war classifications, or typology of wars.

The expanded typology, presented in Table 2.1, incorporates several additions and changes to the initial COW war typology. In terms of the additions, the primary one is the addition of wars conducted by nonstate actors. These can be found in four places on the chart. Subsection IV, Non-state Wars, includes those wars conducted by nonsystem member actors that take place beyond the confines of one state. Category IV-A contains those wars that take place in a nonstate territory, or generally the territory of autonomous entities, or territory in pre-state-formation areas (war type 8). Category IV-B includes wars by nonstate entities that take place within two or more states (war type 9). Wars between or among nonstate actors also appear within the category of Intra-state Wars as Regional Internal Wars (war type 6) and Inter-communal Wars (war type 7). Regional Internal Wars and Inter-communal Wars were categories mentioned by Small and Singer as elements of internal wars but were never included in their databases. Both categories take place within the territory of a state. Inter-communal wars involve at least two parties, none of which is a government, while regional internal wars have a local or regional government (not the national government) as one of the parties to the war.

As hinted at above, the expanded typology does contain one major change in the coding rules promulgated by Small and Singer. A consequence of the metropole distinction, which was utilized in both the extra-systemic and civil war categories, was that disparate conflicts were being grouped together, and, conversely, similar conflicts were placed in different classifications. In particular, some wars that took place within the territory of the system member (as identified by the datasets on entities, on territorial change, and on material capabilities) and which were often commonly referred to as civil wars, were categorized as extra-systemic wars because the area of the conflict was considered part of the periphery, which was not incorporated into the state's metropole. The classification of these wars as extra-systemic wars and thus international wars appeared inconsistent with COW's state-centric perspective in which emphasis is placed on territory as a defining characteristic of system members. Though we are sympathetic to the argument that highlights the ways in which intra-state metropole-periphery wars are similar to extra-systemic metropole-periphery wars, it was decided that the metropole distinction would be eliminated in an attempt to maintain the consistency of the territorial focus of the growing number of COW datasets. Thus both the extra-systemic and civil war categories have been redefined (see below). Finally, in an attempt to rectify what some critics saw as the Eurocentric bias within the data, some of the terminology and variable descriptions have been changed. In particular, the variable of battle-related deaths has been redefined, and extra-systemic wars are now referred to as extra-state wars.

Consequently, an expanded and redefined war typology has been adopted that clarifies the relationship between and among the various types of war and provides more latitude for the inclusion of different types of conflict. Utilizing the focus on the members of the state system, an elemental four-pronged grouping of wars emerged: wars between or among states, wars between a state and nonstate forces outside of the state, wars within states, and wars between or among nonstate actors taking place outside of states. This change involved the deemphasizing of the initial international–civil war distinction, and focusing instead on a quadripartite typology of: inter state wars (definition remains the same); extra-state wars (redefined); intra-state wars (also redefined); and non-state wars (a new category). The new master typology, or expanded typology, of war (shown in Table 2.1) allows for an examination of the totality of modern war, including—to the limits of our ability to detect them—all the cases of sustained combat with substantial fatalities over the past 192 years.

The primary definitional change in the new typology was removing the distinction between the metropole and the periphery within both categories of extra-systemic (now extra-state) war and civil war. This change ensured that all wars that take place within the recognized territory of a state would fall under the intra-state war category and, conversely, that only wars between a state and a nonstate entity outside its borders would be included in the extra-state war category. This redefinition of terminology has resulted in the reclassification of thirty wars that were included as extra-systemic wars in the 1992 version of the data, so that they are now coded as intra-state wars. Of these thirty (see Table 2.2), fourteen had been included as extra-systemic in *Resort to Arms*[41] and sixteen had been included in subsequent data updates. Those familiar with the extra-systemic list in *Resort to Arms* may also note that two other wars have been removed. On the basis of additional information, war #427, First Kashmir, has been reclassified as an inter-state war and war #409, and Russian Nationalities, has been subdivided into three inter-state wars.

We shall now turn to a more detailed discussion of the war categories under the expanded typology and to a description of some of the variables utilized in coding the wars.

TABLE 2.2 **EXTRA-SYSTEMIC WARS RECLASSIFIED AS INTRA-STATE WARS**

1992 Extra-systemic war number	1992 Extra-systemic war name	Current intra-state war number	Start year
304	Greek	506	1821
312	Albanian	512	1830
315	Belgian Independence	515	1830
316	First Polish	517	1831
319	First Syrian	518	1831
322	Texan	527	1835
323	First Bosnian	528	1836
328	Second Syrian	533	1839
333	Second Bosnian	540	1841
340	Hungarian	554	1848
346	First Turco-Montenegran	556	1852
352	Second Turco-Montenegran	562	1858
354	Second Buenos Aires	573	1861
355	Second Polish	580	1863
360	First Cretan	583	1866
366	Mitre Rebellion	600	1874
367	Balkan	601	1875
395	Third Cretan	631	1896
396	Druze-Turkish	630	1895
406	Ilinden	640	1903
408	Yunnan	675	1916
416	Chinese Muslim	703	1928
417	Soviet-Turkistani	711	1931
436	Tibetan	741	1956
437	First Kurdish	752	1961
439	Philippine-MNLF	786	1972
442	Ethiopian-Eritrean	798	1975
443	Kurdish Autonomy	797	1974
451	Ogaden	805	1976
454	Tigrean	808	1978

The Coding of Wars

In coding wars, or in determining the specific classification of war into which a conflict might fall, there are several criteria that relate to all the categories of war. Each of these criteria will be described in a general fashion, followed by a discussion of how these elements are applied within each of the four categories of war.

THE TEMPORAL DOMAIN

As described in the preceding chapter, Singer and Small believed that the international system that emerged after the Napoleonic Wars was distinctive. Thus when gathering information about wars, they utilized the same temporal domain of 1816 to the present. Especially when examining wars, there were a number of reasons they considered this long historical approach to be particularly important. In their judgment, "no social phenomena are comprehensible except in the context of the historical flow in which they are embedded. Prior events and conditions, along with the direction and rate of change in them, must be taken into account if we hope to explain the present or predict the future."[42] Indeed, Singer once expressed the following aphorism on forecasting: "One should not predict further into the future than one's data extend into the past." Consequently, Small and Singer were particularly critical of the war projects that were only concerned with wars in the post–World War II era. Such projects frequently defended their shorter time span with the argument that the contemporary system is radically different from previous eras. While Small and Singer agreed that "as conditions change, the relationships among variables will change, and regularities that hold in the early nineteenth century will often not hold in the late twentieth, or perhaps even the mid-nineteenth century,"[43] they argued that an important reason for not restricting one's research to a brief (and usually quite contemporary) time span is that one cannot understand exactly how things are different unless one includes other historical eras with which to make comparisons. Consequently, this study examines war that occurred after January 1, 1816.

SUSTAINED COMBAT—BATTLE-RELATED DEATHS

As described above, Singer and Small began with a definition of war as sustained combat, involving organized armed forces, resulting in a minimum of 1,000 battle-related fatalities. For most wars, the concept of sustained combat was left relatively undefined by Singer and Small, who argued that there was no temporal definition of sustained combat and that such combat could be lengthy or brief.[44] It is only within the category of civil wars that the requirement of sustained combat is more specifically described (see below). However, the criterion of sustained combat has two fundamental purposes. Initially the requirement of sustained combat (or mutual military action) is instrumental in contrasting war with one-sided violence, such as massacres. Thus incidents in which there were large-scale massacres of disarmed combatants (or prisoners) outside of combat operations would not be considered wars. Second, the requirement for sustained combat serves to eliminate from consideration as wars any hide-and-seek operations that involve no combat over an extended period but nevertheless kill many troops through disease. For example, the Ottoman Empire frequently had trouble simply moving troops within its own borders without losing hundreds or thousands to cholera and dysentery.[45]

The related issue is how Singer and Small then defined what constituted battle-related deaths. They began their consideration of battle-deaths by examining Lewis Richardson's *Statistics of Deadly Quarrels*:

> In computing his figures, he first listed *all possible* war-connected death categories, which we rearrange and paraphrase as follows: (a) belligerent military personnel killed in fighting or drowned in action at sea, or who died from wounds or from poison or from starvation in a siege or from other malicious acts of their enemies; (b) belligerent military personnel who died from disease or exposure; (c) civilians belonging to the belligerent nations who died from malicious acts of their enemies; (d) members of neutral populations (civilian or military) accidentally killed in the war; (e) neutral or belligerent civilians who died from exposure and disease; and (f) the additional number of babies that would presumably have been born if war had not occurred. In Richardson's estimates, the military and civilian deaths resulting from enemy action were included "because they were intentionally inflicted," and military deaths

due to disease and exposure were included "because they were accepted as a risk contingent to planned operations" (1960a: 9). In sum, he included military *and* civilian deaths that could be attributed to the hostile actions of the participants (a, b, and c), but excluded those that could not reasonably be so explained (d, e, and f).[46]

Despite their general agreement with Richardson, Singer and Small ultimately decided to include only elements a and b in their definition of battle-related deaths.

> Given this range of considerations, then, we settled on *battle-related fatalities among military personnel only* as our measure of war's severity. This was defined to include not only those personnel killed in combat but those who subsequently died from combat wounds or from diseases contracted in the war theater. It should also be noted that these figures include not only personnel of the system member but native troops from the colonies, protectorates, and dominions who fought alongside them.[47]

The deaths of civilians were not included in their definition of battle-related deaths owing to questions about the validity of civilian death numbers and because of concerns about their comparability over time. In the nineteenth century, wars rarely involved large numbers of civilian fatalities. However, one of the trends that Singer and Small noted in the twentieth century was the increasing incentive and technological capability to include targeting civilians as an integral component of war strategy. Thus in order to make nineteenth- and twentieth-century fatality figures more comparable, civilian fatalities were excluded from data on international wars.

Though Singer and Small decided on a threshold of 1,000 battle-related fatalities to differentiate wars from lower levels of violence, this requirement was framed in slightly different terms for each of the three categories of war in *Resort to Arms.* In terms of inter-state wars, the requirement was for a total of 1,000 fatalities between or among all the state war participants. Since Small and Singer were primarily interested in examining the war experience of the members of the interstate system, when they examined extra-systemic wars, they gathered information only on the fatalities suffered by the system members (not the nonstate participants). The criterion for an extra-systemic war was that the system member involved in the war had to suffer at least 1,000 battle-related fatalities per year. The requirement was also phrased so that if the war lasted more than a year, the system member's battle-deaths had to reach an annual average of 1,000, a threshold that was established to eliminate colonial or imperial struggles that dragged on for long periods of time, but which suffered variable levels of fatalities.[48] The fatality figures for the nonstate participants were not included because "while such deaths did not go unmourned, they often went uncounted or unrecorded."[49] Thus the lack of reliable information contributed to the decision not to include nonstate deaths in the war threshold. The result was, however, that the battle-death threshold was significantly higher for extra-systemic wars than for inter-state wars.

The same decision was not made by Small and Singer in regard to the definition of battle-deaths in civil wars. Since terrorizing the populace and civilian fatalities are fundamental parts of guerrilla wars, Small and Singer included civilian combat-connected fatalities in their total civil war deaths. This distinction also made practical sense in that in civil wars it is much more difficult to distinguish the combatants from the civilian population. Thus historical accounts of civil wars frequently provide only total fatality figures, combining combatants and civilians. However, since including civilian deaths put the civil war data at odds with the other war categories, the battle-related death definition for civil wars has been changed.

In order to provide consistency among the COW war datasets, the decision was made to standardize the definition of battle-related deaths. The current requirement for all categories of wars is for 1,000 battle-related deaths per year (twelve-month period beginning with the start date of the war) among all the qualified war participants. Battle-deaths include not only those armed personnel killed in combat but also those who subsequently died from combat wounds or from diseases contracted in the war theater.[50] In determining if the war battle-related death threshold has been reached, civilian fatalities are excluded regardless of which type of war is under consideration. There are a couple of reasons for including deaths by wounds and disease. Deaths due to disease in the combat zone are an integral repercussion of a state's war participation, and they can be significantly higher than the deaths caused directly by the enemy. Furthermore, it may not be recorded whether a combatant died during actual battle or later from a bullet wound, or the virus that swept through the army hospital, for instance. Most fatality records do not report separately on deaths by disease; thus it would be easier and more consistent to include them in the battle-related fatalities rather than to try to disaggregate them. Civilian fatalities, however, are excluded. Currently, the requirement for 1,000 battle-related deaths per year could only be considered to be an average of 1,000 battle-deaths per year in circumstances in which there was evidence of significant sustained combat within all years of the war yet insufficient evidence to establish concretely the exact fatalities per year. The impact of this change in definition was felt most within the extra-state war category, where we have now gathered data on the deaths among the nonstate war participants. Including the non-state-participant deaths in the total to meet the war threshold has significantly increased the number of extra-state wars.

Gathering fatality figures is a complex endeavor. Many historical accounts of war contain only vague generalizations about battles that resulted in severe (or light) casualties. Authors frequently utilize the terms *deaths* and *casualties* interchangeably, for instance, noting in two different sentences that a specific war resulted in 1,000 casualties or 1,000 deaths, though generally the term *casualties* refers to the combination of the number of those who died and the number of wounded. Many sources report only total death figures, combining deaths of civilians and combatants.

There are also wide differences even within the death figures provided for a specific war. The death numbers from a variety of sources, each of which claims to be accurate, can vary widely, with one source reporting deaths that are two or three times as high as those reported in other sources. Probably more significant, however, is the reality that war fatalities represent valuable and contestable political information. States often have an incentive to minimize their own losses in battle to protect themselves from criticism for failure or an incentive to inflate their deaths in order to garner international sympathy and support. Conversely, states may also downplay the fatalities they caused their opponent so that they do not appear to be excessively bloodthirsty, or they may inflate the opponent's fatalities as a way of proving the efficacy of their own military campaign. Small and Singer noted related problems during the initial stages of the COW Project:

> It is worth bearing in mind the possible sources of erroneous data. First, not all armed forces have been consistent in differentiating among dead, captured, missing, wounded, and deserting. As Dumas (*Losses of Life Caused by War*, 1923: 21) reminds us, the field commander "attaches no importance to the cause of the absences . . . for him it is all the same." Second, there is the simple matter of accurate estimates, compounded by the fact that the size of a force may not be known with any accuracy even by its commanders.[51]

Although gathering fatality estimates was difficult in the past, especially in extra-state wars that were sometimes fought in remote areas, the process has not necessarily become easier in the present.

Even though today there is an impressive array of nongovernmental agencies with resources devoted to gathering statistics on the costs of war (though many are primarily concerned with civilian deaths), governments have also displayed their ability to utilize technology as a means of concealing war fatality figures. For instance, in its 2003 war against Iraq, the United States made a specific policy decision not to count the numbers of Iraqis killed in order to avoid the "body count" problems common in the Vietnam War. The United States has also proven to be adept at controlling media coverage of the war in order to limit the information about American fatalities and the impact it would have on the American public in general.

All war data–gathering projects have responded to these perennial challenges in different ways. In an attempt to reduce the effects of the low reliability of death statistics, Lewis Richardson utilized a logarithmic (to the base 10) scale for reporting fatality statistics.[52] The Uppsala/PRIO Project provides the low estimate, the high estimate, and their best guess for fatality figures (though they include the deaths of civilians killed during combat and exclude military deaths due to disease).[53] Our procedure for finding the best death statistics generally begins with consulting existing war compilations, such as those by Richardson, Wright, Kohn, Clodfelter, and Phillips and Axelrod.[54] We then refer to general histories, specific war monographs, and articles, or we calculate overall deaths by adding up the fatality numbers presented for specific battles in monographs or sources such as the battle lists by Harbottle and Bruce and Jaques.[55] Our final procedure is the same as that utilized by Small and Singer:

> Once all the available estimates were in for a given war and adjustments were made of the varying classificatory criteria, the semi-operational estimating began. Among the considerations affecting our final figure were army size, weapons and medical technology available, number of major battles, others' estimates of the wounded-to-killed ratio (Bodart, 1916, seems to have discovered a constant of about 3.5 to 1), and historians' appraisals of the war's intensity.[56]

In many cases, battle-death figures are not available, and sources provide only casualty numbers, which include deaths and those wounded. In dealing with casualty numbers, scholars have developed techniques for estimating battle-deaths when given casualty figures. Bodart found that in nineteenth-century wars there were about 10 killed for every 35 wounded in battle, but 10 to 15 percent of those classified as "wounded" later died of wounds, producing a final ratio of killed to wounded very close to 1:3.[57] Livermore (1957) found a "usual ratio of killed to wounded of 1 to 2.5" in the American Civil War.[58] Similarly, Clodfelter found a general 3:1 ratio of wounded to killed.[59] Jeffrey Dixon summarized the findings of Trevor Dupuy in this regard:

> Dupuy, examining studies of wounded to killed in ancient battles to the modern era, terms the ratio of wounded to killed "one of the most consistent relationships in battle statistics" (1990, 48–9). The number of wounded per combat death is listed for a number of wars: 2.1–2.2 (ancient battles), 1–2.6 (Germans in Franco-Prussian War), about 4.4 (several wars from 1704–1871), 2.18 (US in Mexican War), 2.38 (Union in American Civil War), and ratios of 2.41 to 4.16 in later American wars. Dupuy concludes that, on average, the historical relationship appears to be about 3 wounded for every 1 killed in combat.[60]

Consequently, given the widespread agreement on this standard, we utilize a 3:1 ratio of wounded to killed in order to calculate the number of battle-related deaths when only casualty estimates are available. However much we have attempted to discern accurate battle-death statistics, we reiterate Small and Singer's caution: "Despite these multiple cross-checks and a large dose of skepticism at every turn, we must reemphasize the fact that our battle death figures are only estimates."[61] The figures can best be seen as general guides concerning the relative magnitude of the costs of war participation.

Who Is Fighting Whom? Organized Armed Forces

In developing the COW project, David Singer and Melvin Small wanted to create a comprehensive study of war. After examining existing compendia of war and considering a number of alternative ways of describing or categorizing war, Singer and Small decided to base their typology of war on the characteristics of the war participants. The key determination in the classification of wars was based on the judgment of who was fighting whom. To begin, they thus needed a list of those entities that might be involved in international politics (including war). Consequently, they developed a list of what they referred to as the interstate system members (described in Chapter 1). Membership in the interstate system was based on criteria of population, territory, independence, sovereignty, and diplomatic recognition. Since states generally possess organized armed forces (a requirement in the definition of war), the members of the interstate system were considered to be the predominant actors in war. Any individual member state qualified as a war participant through either of two alternative criteria: a minimum of 100 fatalities or a minimum of 1,000 armed personnel engaged in active combat. Singer and Small also decided to prioritize their data-gathering efforts, beginning with the type of war that they saw as the most important (international war), and data on such wars were published in *The Wages of War*. International war included two major types of war, based on who was fighting whom. Inter-state wars (originally also called intra-systemic wars) involved system members fighting one another, while extra-systemic (now extra-state) wars involved system members fighting against another entity outside its borders. The goal of identifying these other entities led to the creation of the States, Nations, and Entities dataset, which not only included the members of the interstate system but also identified other autonomous entities and dependencies, which might be participants in extra-state wars.[62]

In *Resort to Arms*, Small and Singer expanded the "who" to include nongovernmental entities within states that were sufficiently organized to engage in combat. Wars involving states and such entities within their borders were civil wars, and the data on these wars were a major addition to the COW data presented in *Resort to Arms*. The discussion of civil wars also raised the issue of the status of territorial entities. Whether a territory is an integral part of a state or is instead one of its dependencies would determine the type of a war in which it is involved. If a war took place within an integral part of a state, it would be a civil war; however, if it took place within territory that was not part of the state, then the war would be an extra-state war. The States, Nations, and Entities dataset (updated to the Geopolitical Units dataset) was also instrumental in defining the status of specific territories by indicating ten different types of dependencies, including whether a territory was an integral part of a state (dependency code 1) or whether it was a colony or protectorate (codes 2 and 3). For example, the rebellion of the Paris Commune took place within the territory of France and was thus coded as a civil war. The revolt by the Vietminh against French rule in Indochina took place in a French colony and was thus coded as an extra-state war. Though most of the territorial status determinations seem relatively straightforward, probably the most complex involved determining the status of the various parts of the Ottoman Empire and the question of Algeria, which France claimed to be integrating into French territory.

The Bulk of the Fighting

Once the participants in the war have been identified, the question of "who is fighting whom?" devolves into the issue of describing the war in a way that identifies the primary combatants. This is done by determining which of the parties involved in the war were doing the "bulk of the fighting." Singer and Small do not specifically mention this criterion when describing their initial war classifications, though they did utilize it as the basis for war transformations (which will be described below). However, they did require that inter-state wars must include system members as sufficiently active participants on each side of the war. They also clearly utilized a related judgment when delineating wars that had both inter-state and intra-state components, such as the Franco-Spanish War of 1823, which was divided into two separate wars—a civil war and an inter-state war. As wars have become more complex, involving not only multiple state actors but a plethora of nonstate entities as well, the task of ensuring that wars are placed within the appropriate categories has become more complicated. Thus we have decided to make the "bulk of the fighting" criterion a bit more explicit.

We considered a number of measures that could be used to try to capture the essence of which of several participants on one side of a war are doing the bulk of the fighting. Probably the easiest measure (favored by historian Mel Small) is merely the judgment of historians about who the major war participants were. A slightly more operational measure would be to ascertain which party had the greater number of troops in the theater of war; however, a party's being there does not necessarily mean that it was fighting. Alternatively, one could argue that the party that suffered the largest number of fatalities did the bulk of the fighting. As COW colleague Jeffrey Dixon remarked: "There is no surer proof of engaging in fighting than getting shot."[63] In that same vein, instead of focusing on fatalities, one could count casualties (which include those wounded) or compute ratios of deaths or casualties per troops committed. Yet all these indicators seem to measure who suffered the most in the war and to downplay the role of participants who were able to perhaps utilize technology to fight on a less personal level and thus reduce their fatalities. Consequently, we have instead decided to utilize the determination of which party was causing the greatest number of battle-deaths as the measure of which combatant was doing the bulk of the fighting. Though the information needed to make this determination may be slightly more difficult to discern than the number of fatalities suffered, this definition ensures that we are identifying the participants engaged in the violence that is at the core of war. It also allows us, for instance, to classify states that use bombs or missiles to cause significant fatalities (while suffering few themselves) as the major war participants.

WAR DURATION

The coding rules governing the duration of wars have remained unchanged from *Resort to Arms* and rely on the war's start date, end date, and breaks in the hostilities.

> Each war's *opening date* is that of the formal declaration, but only if it is followed immediately by sustained military combat. If hostilities precede the formal declaration and continue in a sustained fashion up to and beyond that latter date, the first day of combat is used. Even in the absence of a declaration, the sustained continuation of military incidents or battle, producing the requisite number of battle deaths, is treated as a war, with the first day of combat again used for computing duration.[64]

The war then continues until its termination, or as long as there is sustained military combat resulting in 1,000 battle-related deaths per year. The end date may be the date of an armistice or cease-fire agreement, as long as conflict does not resume thereafter. If there is a delay between the cessation of military action and the armistice, or if the armistice fails to halt the hostilities, then the end date is the day that most clearly demarcates the close of sustained military conflict. The date of the final peace treaty would not be used unless it coincided with the end of combat.[65]

In the descriptions of the wars presented in the subsequent chapters, the overall dates for the wars indicated in fact represent the maximum duration of the war (or the minimum start date and the maximum end date). Within the datasets themselves, each individual war participant is described in terms of the dates that it entered and left the war. Frequently participants join an ongoing war at a later date, while in other multiparticipant wars one party may be defeated or just withdraw from the war before the others. In such cases, the entity's active participation period (start date to end date) delineates the period of its own forces' involvement in sustained military combat. Relatedly, for wars that require participants to be members of the interstate system, a state may be included as a war participant only for the period during which it is a system member. For example, Baden, Bavaria, and Württemberg entered the Franco-Prussian War of 1870–1871 on the first day (July 19, 1870). Even though they had troops in active combat during the entire war (until 1871), their war participation is coded as ending in November 1870, when they became integrated into the new German empire and thus ceased to be independent system members.

Coding the end date of a war or a combatant's participation in a war is not always clear-cut and can be related to the difficulties in ascertaining fatality figures. Wars (especially civil wars) may not necessarily end through a cease-fire or an agreement of any sort but may instead peter out as the rebels just cease fighting or retreat to fight another day. In such cases a judgment has been made about the date at which the last sustained combat took place that contributed to 1,000 battle-related deaths within a year. In essence, a war ends if: (1) there is a truce or other agreement that ends combat for a year or more; (2) if the apparent defeat of one side (absent a formal surrender or truce) ends combat for one year or more; or (3) if a twelve-month period passes without 1,000 battle-deaths. In the last case, the termination date for the war is the last day in which in can be said that 1,000 battle-deaths were suffered during the previous twelve months.[66] There must be clear evidence that fighting has shrunk to this level. If we have only an overall total fatality figure for multiple years, and we cannot find how many died within a particular twelve-month period, unless we have specific evidence of a lull, we continue to classify the conflict as a war as long as there are on average 1,000 battle-deaths per year.

A war's duration is generally calculated by subtracting the start date from the end date, and resulting in a measurement of the war's duration in months or days. One exception to this procedure concerns wars in which there is a break in the fighting. Small and Singer raised the concern about a cessation of hostilities arising out of a truce, a temporary cease-fire, or an armistice agreement. In general, if the fighting stopped for thirty days or less, no break in the war was coded; however, if there was a cessation of hostilities that endured for more than thirty days, this break was marked by essentially ending participation (end date 1) and then resuming the war on a second start date. This break then led to a reduction in the war's overall duration measure equal to the length of the interruption.

> To illustrate, the three-week truce (December 19, 1933 to January 8, 1934) arranged by the League of Nations during the Chaco War is not counted as a break, and the war is treated as if it had run continuously for the three years from June 15, 1932 through June 12, 1935, for a duration of 35.9 months. On the other hand, because a formal truce lasted for two of the total six months between the onset and termination of the Second Schleswig-Holstein War (February 1, through August 20, 1864), that war is treated as having a duration of only 3.6 months.[67]

Yet Small and Singer did not specify how long such breaks could last or what to do about lulls in hostilities that resulted from other causes than specific agreements. In wars there are periods when the level of violence drops for a time and then rises again. For instance, fighting may be informally halted during a rainy season, only to resume when weather conditions improve. In a sense, these breaks in fighting are not the same. Truces, cease-fires, and armistice agreements represent a commitment to end hostilities, at least on some level, whereas temporary lulls in the fighting do not. Thus we shall continue the practice of treating them in slightly different fashion. Temporary lulls in the fighting will not be recorded as breaks in the fighting; however, should such a lull last for more than a year and there are not 1,000 battle-related fatalities within that year, the war will be coded as having ended. Should the hostilities resume after that point, a new war will have begun. A break in the fighting that is the result of a specific agreement such as a truce, cease-fire, or armistice agreement, however, will continue to be coded as a break in the war (with secondary start dates and end dates) as long as it lasts over thirty days. Such a break can last up to a year in length. If hostilities resume after more than a year, a new war will be coded.

These restrictions on the length of a break do not apply to individual participants who withdraw from a multiparty war that remains ongoing with other participants. In such instances, one combatant can withdraw from a war and reenter it at any time. For instance, in World War II, France is coded as fighting on the side of the allies from September 3, 1939, until June 22, 1940. There is then a break in France's war participation from then until the country reenters the war, on October 23, 1944. It is important to note that should a combatant cease its war participation and then reenter the war on the other side, that is not coded as a break in the entity's participation. Instead the combatant is given a second participant record with the new start and end dates. Again, France's experience in World War II is an example here. In addition to its record as a participant on the allied side of the war as indicated above, France has a second participant record that represents Vichy France's war participation on the side of the Axis from July 7, 1940, to July 14, 1941.

WAR TRANSFORMATIONS

Wars themselves are often not as clearly delineated as our typologies and can often contain elements of different types of wars, and a war can, over its life span, metamorphose from one type to another. For instance, wars can be partially civil wars between the government and a rebel group yet can also include interventions by other states. COW has attempted to deal with such complexity by relying on the two major determinants: the principle of the mutual exclusivity of wars and the classification of wars based upon the decision concerning which parties are doing the bulk of the fighting. Since wars are classified by the status of the participants, *mutual exclusivity* merely means that wars involving the same participants should not simultaneously appear in more than one war classification. This principle is utilized to prevent confusion or the multiple recording of fatalities that can result from having a war appear with two different names and in two different categories. It is possible for a state to be involved in two different wars at the same time, assuming that they involve different participants. A state could be involved in a civil war and an inter-state war at the same time, or even two civil wars (as discussed below). Yet a single war is never entered simultaneously at two points in the database. For instance, we would not enter the Vietnam War of the late 1960s as simultaneously an inter-state war and an intra-state war. It is assigned to one or the other category during a specific period based on its predominant characteristics.

Wars can also be complex, involving more actors than the standard two-party conflict. COW has attempted to capture this complexity through the concepts of internationalized wars and war transformations. Since the classification of any war is based on the types of participants involved, a war must thus change if the nature of the participants should fundamentally alter. For example, the nature of an inter-state war between two system members does not significantly change when one (or more) additional states join in the conflict, since the war remains one among system members. Extra-state and civil wars, on the other hand, are wars between a state and a nonstate entity either outside or within its borders. Such wars are classified as internationalized when other states intervene. The state intervener must qualify as a war participant either by committing over 1,000 troops to the conflict or by suffering 100 battle-deaths. The intervener may join the conflict on either the side of the government or the nonstate participant. This type of change may be a relatively minor one within the COW classification system. Within the datasets, a variable is included indicating whether the war is internationalized or not, and individual records are included for each system member involved that code the side of the war on which they are participating (for instance, on the side of the government or the side of the rebels in a civil war). This procedure holds as long as the initial combatants continue doing the bulk of the fighting. If, on the other hand, there is a change in the parties that are conducting the conflict that is sufficiently significant to alter the character of the war or the nature of the actors, then the primary classification of the war also must change. If the party that is doing the bulk of the fighting changes, the classification of the war must change as well. Since COW has provided a mutually exclusive typology of wars, when the character of a war changes, the war in one category ends and a new war in another category begins. Probably the most well-known example that demonstrates these levels of change would be the Vietnam War. The war started out as a civil war in 1960 between the government of South Vietnam and the National Liberation Front (also known as the Viet Cong), and it was transformed into an internationalized civil war with the involvement of the United States in 1961. In 1965, however, the United States fundamentally altered the type of conflict when it started bombing North Vietnam, making this into a conflict between two system members, or between the United States and its ally South Vietnam on one side and North Vietnam on the other. At that point, the civil war ceased and an inter-state war had begun.

There are two general circumstances under which COW has decided that there is sufficient significant change to cause a shift in war classification. The first is when the outside intervener takes an action that fundamentally alters the nature of the conflict, for instance, in the Vietnam case, discussed above. The second and more common form of shift takes place when a state intervener takes over the bulk of the fighting from one of the original war participants. It thus replaces one of the parties as the major combatant, and the classification of the war must change to reflect the reality of who is fighting whom. As described above, the *bulk of the fighting* is defined in terms of which combatant is causing the greatest number of deaths among the opposition. Transformations in this regard are frequently marked by an increase in the armed forces committed to the war by the intervener, which then takes over the dominant combat role. Frequently, such transformations take place within civil wars, or wars between the central government and a rebel group. If the outside state intervener is fighting on the side of the rebels and then takes over the bulk of the fighting, the conflict becomes an inter-state war between the intervener and the central government (such as when the United States took over the bulk of the fighting from the Northern Alliance against the Taliban government of Afghanistan in 2001). If the outside state is intervening against the rebels on the side of the government and takes up the bulk of the fighting, the war becomes an extra-state war between a state and a nonstate actor outside the intervener's territory.

This process of wars changing categories can work the other way as well. If a major combatant decides to withdraw from a conflict and the conflict continues with other parties, that specific war may end and the conflict may be classified as a different type of war based on the categorization of the war participants. For instance, the USSR had been involved in an extra-state war in Afghanistan against the mujahideen. When the Soviet troops withdrew, the extra-state war ended, though the conflict continued as a civil war when the Afghan government then took over the bulk of the fighting in its conflict with the mujahideen. Similarly, the United States and the "Coalition of the Willing" were involved in an inter-state war against Saddam Hussein's government in Iraq. When Iraq was defeated and withdrew from the war, the inter-state war ended and the conflict continued as an extra-state war between the Coalition and the Iraqi resistance.

Though transformations most commonly take place in the context of civil wars, they can take place within virtually any type of war: civil or intra-state to extra-state; intra-state to inter-state; intra-state regional to intra-state civil; extra-state to intra-state; extra-state to inter-state; extra-state to non-state; inter-state to intra-state; inter-state to extra-state; non-state to inter-state; and non-state to extra-state. The most complex set of transformations has taken place in Afghanistan, which over the past thirty years has experienced a series of wars, beginning with intra-state war #810, the Saur Revolution in 1978. This war was followed by intra-state war #812, the First Afghan Mujahideen Uprising in 1978–1980, which was transformed by the USSR taking over the bulk of the fighting into extra-state war #476, the Soviet Quagmire in 1980–1989. The extra-state war was transformed by the withdrawal of the USSR into intra-state war #851, the Second Afghan Mujahideen Uprising in 1989–2001. The civil war was transformed again by the intervention of the United States and its allies into inter-state war #225, the Invasion of Afghanistan in 2001, which then became extra-state war #481, Afghan Resistance, 2001–present after the defeat of the Taliban government. Table 2.3 lists the major transformations that have taken place.

INITIATOR AND OUTCOME

The final variables that apply generally to all wars are those of the war initiator and the war outcome. In both of these cases, the general procedures utilized by Small and Singer have been maintained. In determining which combatant was the war initiator, Small and Singer were merely determining which party started the war. Specifically, they relied on the consensus of historians to classify the initiator as the actor whose battalions made the first attack in strength on their opponent's armies or territories.[68] They emphasized that this was not in any way a moral judgment: "As our language should make very clear, we are not labeling any government the 'aggressor' in these wars, or trying to reach a firm, data-based conclusion as to which participant 'caused' the war, whether by action, threat, or other provocation."[69] As Small and Singer made clear, the initiator was not necessarily the party that provoked the war, and this distinction is particularly important for those seeking to examine the stages in conflict escalation. Though in most cases the initiator was one party, it could be several combatants that acted in concert in the initial attack, as in the Boxer Rebellion, in which Japan, the United Kingdom, Russia, France, and the United States are coded as the initiators. Where determining the initiator can be tricky is if one side enters the other's territory, without having to fight, and the other side is the first to engage in combat. Is the initiating side the side that seizes undefended territory or the side that tries to drive them off? Small and Singer[70] seemed ambivalent on this point, giving different interpretations with regard to the Mexican-American and Sino-Indian inter-state wars. This ambivalence is especially problematic when considering extra-state wars of imperialism, in which a European power would often invade an autonomous entity with a poorly defended border. If only a little disputed territory is occupied and then there is a massive attack by the other side, there is a better case that the attacker, rather than the occupier, was the initiator. On the other hand, if the occupying army is marching through core territory and even attempting to take the capital city of its target, and the invaded side then launches a massive offensive against the dug-in troops of the occupier, then it seems clear that the invader was the initiator. The Small and Singer definition of the war initiator is different from that used in the Militarized Interstate Dispute (MID) dataset, where all the states that are on the side of the initiator are listed as the initiating side. Furthermore, the initiator of the war need not necessarily be the same as the initiator of the MID, since a MID can be started by a show of force, whereas the initiator of a war begins the actual combat.

TABLE 2.3 **WAR TRANSFORMATIONS**

War Transformed From			War Transformed Into		
War number	War name	Dates	War number	War name	Dates
Inter-state war into extra-state war					
189	Vietnamese-Cambodian	9/24/1977–1/8/1979	475	Khmer Insurgency	1/9/1979–9/25/1989
225	Invasion of Afghanistan	10/7/2001–12/22/2001	481	Afghan Resistance	12/23/2001–present
227	Invasion of Iraq	3/19/2003–5/2/2003	482	Iraqi Resistance	5/3/2003–present
Inter-state war into intra-state war					
40	Franco-Mexican	4/16/1862–2/5/1867	587	Queretaro	2/6/1867–5/14/1867
176	Communist Coalition	3/23/1970–7/2/1971	785	Khmer Rouge	7/3/1971–7/17/1975
186	War over Angola	10/23/1975–2/12/1976	804	Angolan Control	2/13/1976–5/15/1991
187	Second Ogaden phase 2	7/23/1977–3/9/1978	808	Second Ogaden phase 3	3/10/1978–12/3/1980
215	Bosnian Independence	4/7/1992–6/5/1992	877	Bosnian–Serb Rebellion	6/6/1992–12/14/1995
Extra-state war into inter-state war					
327	Uruguay War	2/16/1843–7/18/1851	19	La Plata	7/19/1851–2/3/1852
352	Garibaldi Expedition	5/11/1860–10/14/1860	37	Neapolitan	10/15/1860–2/13/1861
373	Serbian-Turkish	6/30/1876–4/23/1877	61	Second Russo-Turkish	4/24/1877–1/31/1878
385	Third Franco-Vietnamese	4/25/1882–6/14/1884	67	Sino-French	6/15/1884–6/19/1885
404	Second Spanish-Cuban	2/24/1895–4/21/1898	79	Spanish-American	4/22/1898–8/12/1898
410	Spanish-Philippine	8/30/1896–5/1/1898	79	Spanish-American	4/22/1898–8/12/1898
Extra-state war into intra-state war					
472	East Timorese phase 2	10/16/1975–7/17/1976	806	East Timorese phase 3	7/18/1976–5/26/1979
475	Khmer Insurgency	1/9/1979–9/25/1989	857	First Cambodian Civil	9/26/1989–10/23/1991
476	Soviet Quagmire	2/22/1980–2/15/1989	851	Second Afghan Mujahideen	2/16/1989–10/6/2001
Extra-state war into non-state war					
469	Angolan-Portuguese	2/3/1961–10/14/1974	1581	Angola Guerrilla	10/15/1974–10/22/1975
Intra-state war into inter-state war					
503	Spanish Royalists	12/1/1821–4/6/1823	1	Franco-Spanish	4/7/1823–11/13/1823
506	Greek Independence	3/25/1821–4/25/1828	4	First Russo-Turkish	4/26/1828–9/14/1829
551	Milan Five-Day Revolt	3/18/1848–3/23/1848	10	Austro-Sardinian	3/24/1848–3/30/1849
631	Second Cretan	3/10/1896–2/14/1897	76	Greco-Turkish	2/15/1897–5/19/1897
650	Second Albanian Revolt	3/?/1910–10/16/1912	100	First Balkan	10/17/1912–4/19/1913
681	Western Ukrainian	11/1/1918–2/13/1919	109	Russo-Polish	2/14/1919–10/18/1920
748	Vietnam phase 1	1/1/1960–2/6/1965	163	Vietnam phase 2	2/7/1965–4/30/1975
756	Second Laotian phase 1	3/19/1963–1/12/1968	170	Second Laotian phase 2	1/13/1968–4/17/1973
782	Pakistan-Bengal	3/25/1971–12/2/1971	163	Vietnam phase 2	2/7/1965–4/30/1975

(Continued)

TABLE 2.3 **WAR TRANSFORMATIONS** (Continued)

	War Transformed From			War Transformed Into	
War number	War name	Dates	War number	War name	Dates
805	Second Ogaden phase 1	7/1/1976–7/22/1977	170	Second Laotian phase 2	1/13/1968–4/17/1973
851	Second Afghan Mujahideen	2/16/1989–10/6/2001	178	Bangladesh	12/3/1971–12/17/1971
872	Nagorno-Karabakh	12/26/1991–2/5/1993	187	Second Ogaden phase 2	7/23/1977–3/9/1978
900	Kosovo Independence	2/28/1998–3/23/1999	225	Invasion of Afghanistan	10/7/2001–12/22/2001
			216	Azeri-Armenian	2/6/1993–5/12/1994
			221	War for Kosovo	3/24/1999–6/10/1999
Intra-state war into extra-state war					
601	Bosnia and Bulgaria Revolt	6/30/1875–6/29/1876	373	Serbian-Turkish	6/30/1876–4/23/1877
812	First Afghan Mujahideen	9/1/1978–2/21/1980	476	Soviet Quagmire	2/22/1980–2/15/1989
Intra-state regional war into intra-state civil war					
545	Mayan Caste phase 1	1/15/1847–8/16/1848	553	Mayan Caste phase 2	8/17/1848–3/4/1855
772	Cultural Revolution phase 1	1/9/1967–9/4/1967	776	Cultural Revolution phase 2	9/5/1967–9/1/1968
Non-state war into inter-state war					
1572	Palestine	11/29/1947–5/14/1948	148	Arab-Israeli	5/15/1948–1/7/1949
1581	Angola Guerrilla	10/15/1974–10/22/1975	186	War over Angola	10/23/1975–2/12/1976
Non-state war into extra-state war					
1571	Hyderabad War	8/15/1947–9/12/1948	461	Indo-Hyderabad	9/13/1948–9/17/1948
1582	East Timorese phase 1	8/11/1975–10/15/1975	472	East Timorese phase 2	10/16/1975–7/17/1976
Non-state war into intra-state war					
1527	Anti-Rosas	2/24/1839–12/31/1840	538	First Argentina phase 2	1/1/1841–12/6/1842
1534	Taiping Rebellion phase 1	12/?/1850–10/24/1860	567	Taiping Rebellion phase 2	10/25/1860–2/9/1866
1537	Han-Miao	3/24/1854–10/24/1860	570	Miao Revolt phase 2	10/25/1860–5/1/1872
1541	Han-Panthay	5/19/1856–10/24/1860	571	Panthay Rebellion phase 2	10/25/1860–12/26/1872

Similarly, Small and Singer had no operational indicators for determining the outcome of a war or the side that was victorious in the war. Instead of developing complex schemas for weighing the relative benefits attained in a war, they admitted to merely following the consensus among the acknowledged specialists in deciding which side "won" each war.[71] They noted that determining the consensus on the winner was difficult in only a few cases and that among the inter-state wars, only two wars in the 1982 list were coded as ties: the Korean War of 1950–1953 and the Israeli-Egyptian War of Attrition in

1969–1970. In terms of coding the individual combatants as winners or losers, they treated "every nation that qualified as an active participant on the victorious side as a 'victor,' regardless of its contribution to that victory or the costs it sustained; the same holds for all those that fought on the vanquished side in these inter-state wars."[72] In several instances, a combatant could be coded as an ultimate winner despite its complete defeat in an earlier stage of the war:

> On occasion, some of the nations we labeled victors suffered far more than the vanquished. Pyrrhic victors like Poland and Belgium in World War II were defeated on the field of battle and returned only at war's end as political victors. Despite their total absorption by the "vanquished," we consider them to have been part of the winning coalition that shared in the spoils in 1945.[73]

This coding is also somewhat complex in those cases in which a combatant switches sides during the war. In such cases, the combatant will have two separate participant records and two separate outcome determinations, both as a winner and a loser. For instance, for most of World War II, Italy was on the side of the Axis powers and has one participant record for the period from 1940 to 1943 on this side. Here Italy is coded as having lost (or being on the losing side). After that point, however, Italy then participates in the war on the side of the Allies and thus has a second participant record for the 1943–1945 period, for which Italy is then coded as a winner, or being on the victorious side.

As the Project began to gather more information on intra-state wars in particular, it became clear that there were more outcomes than merely winning, losing, or having a tie. Thus several new outcome codes have been developed. Though this variable may continue to evolve, at this point the following outcome codes are being used: 1 = Side A wins; 2 = Side B wins; 3 = compromise (a solution is reached in which both sides gain something); 4 = war is transformed into another category; 5 = war ongoing; 6 = stalemate (fighting ceases without a satisfactory agreement); 7 = conflict continues but at below war-level fatalities.

We shall now turn to a brief description of each of the four categories of war and a discussion of any differences in the ways in which these general variables apply within each category.

Describing Inter-state War

Inter-state war is the most straightforward of the categories of war, in that Singer and Small initially developed their war typology and its related variables as a means of describing wars between system members. It is also the war classification that remained virtually unchanged in the switch from the initial typology to the revised expanded war typology. The general definition of war developed above is that war is sustained combat between or among military organizations involving substantial casualties of 1,000 deaths per year (or twelve-month period). To reiterate, inter-state war is war in which at least one sufficiently active participant on each side of the war is a member of the interstate system. Thus inter-state war is war in which the regular armed forces of a state that qualifies as a member of the interstate system engage in sustained combat with the forces of one or more other members of the interstate system resulting in 1,000 battle-related deaths (among all the state participants) per year (or twelve-month period from the start date of the war). Any individual interstate system member qualifies as a war participant through either of two alternative criteria: a minimum of 100 fatalities or a minimum of 1,000 armed personnel engaged in active combat.

In looking at the determination of "who is fighting whom" in terms of inter-state wars, on each side of the conflict, the combatant that is conducting the "bulk of the fighting" must be a member of the interstate system, and each state that is considered to be a war participant must either suffer 100 battle-related deaths or commit 1,000 armed personnel to active combat. Small and Singer claimed that the criterion that was most often used in judging which states were war participants was the requirement that the state sustain a minimum of 100 fatalities, however, there were a few cases in which a member not only declared war but also sent combat units into the war theater without sustaining even this low number of casualties. In such cases, they wanted to be able to distinguish between (and include) a state that was an active war participant but fortunately sustained few casualties and (still exclude) one that sent only a very few troops and suffered very few losses. Thus an alternative route to qualified participation was necessary: a minimum of 1,000 armed personnel engaged in active combat. Without having the two alternative paths for a state to qualify as a participant would have meant that a state that dispatched 2,000 troops but used them so skillfully or cautiously as to lose only 50 would not qualify, whereas one that sent 200 and lost half would be included.[74] This second route was used in only a few instances (such as including France and England in the Sinai War of 1956), yet it may be utilized more frequently in the future as the technology of warfare increasingly enables states to engage in warfare while sustaining few battle-related deaths. Conversely, the participant requirements can also be used to exclude marginal participants. For example, New Zealand committed troops to the Korean War yet neither sustained the necessary 100 battle deaths nor committed 1,000 troops to active combat, and thus it is not listed as a participant in that war.

The requirement that in inter-state wars a member of the interstate system must assume the bulk of the fighting on each side of the war does not mean that there are not other entities involved in the war as well. States have frequently been assisted in war not only by other state participants but also by partisans, rebel groups, nonstate autonomous entities, and their colonies or possessions. Within interstate wars, however, only system members are coded as war participants. Small and Singer did not gather information on the nonstate war participants, though some research is currently progressing along these lines. When calculating the battle-related deaths for the war, the deaths among the nonstate war participants are not included (although state deaths caused by such combatants would be included within a state's fatality figure). The only exception to this generalization relates to a state's colonies. Battle-related deaths for a system member include not only the deaths among its own uniformed military personnel but also the "native troops from the colonies, protectorates, and dominions who fought alongside them."[75]

The change in the battle-related death requirement for wars impacted the category of inter-state wars only slightly. Under the Small and Singer initial typology, an inter-state war had to include sustained combat resulting in a total of 1,000 battle-related deaths among all the state participants. The revised requirement is for 1,000 battle-related deaths among all the system-member participants per year (twelve-month period). This more stringent requirement was already being met by the inter-state wars in the dataset, so its application did not lead to the removal of any inter-state wars.

As indicated above, when describing the initiator of a war, Small and Singer were merely determining which party started the war. In terms of inter-state wars, this generally means identifying which state's forces crossed the border into its opponent's territory first. Identifying the initiator might be particularly useful for those seeking to examine the stages in conflict escalation. Examining conflict escalation was also one of the motivations for the development of the COW MID dataset. Most interstate wars are preceded by MIDs, which can involve uses of military force that range from mere displays of force to combat resulting in fewer than 1,000 battle-deaths. For each MID, an initiator is also coded, and it is important to note here that the initiator of the inter-state war and the initiator of the

MID are not necessarily the same state. The initiator in an inter-state war is not the party that caused the war, by action, threat, or other provocation, yet it is such actions and provocations that are integral components of MIDs.

In terms of war transformations, inter-state wars can be the originators of, or the results of, war transformations. System members are increasingly intervening in civil wars, creating international- ized civil wars; however, should the intervener take over the bulk of the fighting on behalf of the rebels, the war becomes inter-state, whereas if it takes over the bulk of the fighting from the initial government, the war becomes extra-state. Conversely, inter-state wars can be transformed into extra- state wars or intra-state wars if a state participant withdraws from the conflict.

Describing Extra-state War

As indicated above, under the expanded COW typology, the definition and description of extra-state war changed to a significant degree with the elimination of the metropole distinction. Extra-state wars are those in which a member of the interstate system is engaged in sustained combat outside its borders against the forces (however irregular and disorganized) of a political entity that is not a member of the state system.[76] In addition, there must be at least 1,000 battle-deaths for every year for all participants. The subcategories of extra-state wars have not changed from the original two basic types:

1. Colonial war (or State vs. Dependent Nonstate Actor): The member of the interstate system engages in sustained combat against the forces of a political entity that is geographically outside the internationally accepted boundaries of the state and that is a dependency, colony, protectorate, mandate, or otherwise under its suzerainty or control and not merely within a claimed sphere of influence. The French-Indochina War, for independence from French control, fought from 1946 to 1954, is a colonial war.

2. Imperial war (State vs. Independent Nonstate Actor): A member of the system is engaged in sustained combat outside its borders with the forces of an independent nonstate entity. The adversary might be an independent political entity that does not qualify for system membership because of serious limitations on its independence, a population insufficiency, or a failure of other states to recognize it as a legitimate member. Such entities might be included as autonomous entities within the Geopolitical Units dataset. However, one by-product of this imperial-colonial terminology is that it obscures the fact that extra-state wars can be fought against nonterritorially identified entities as well. The adversary might be a nonterritorially based entity, such as pirates, an international terrorist organization, or the private army of a multinational corporation. The 1879 British war against the Zulus, when the British were trying to establish colonies "from Cape Town to Cairo" in Africa, is a classic example of an imperial extra-state war; yet, the current war by the United States and its allies against nonstate, nonterritorial entities such as al-Qaida in Afghanistan would be an imperial war as well.

In addition to the changes in extra-state wars brought about by the elimination of the metropole distinction, the understanding of extra-state wars has also been affected by changes in the definition of battle-related deaths. Initially, Small and Singer defined extra-state wars as those in which the sys- tem member itself sustained a minimum of 1,000 battle-related fatalities per year. They did not mea- sure or record the battle-deaths suffered by the nonstate participants. It was even more difficult than usual to determine the severity of these extra-state (imperial and colonial) wars because the Europeans who generally kept the records did not do as thorough a job of ascertaining (or curtailing) the number of non-European dead. However, the new classification of extra-state wars changes the requirements so that an extra-state war must involve 1,000 battle-related fatalities over a twelve-month period, and battle-deaths include those deaths suffered by both the state and nonstate war participants.

The category of other participants in extra-state wars is a broad one, including potentially any political entity that was not a system member, whether it was organized or not. Owing to its focus on the members of the interstate system, the COW Project did not specifically gather data on the other participants in extra-state wars. Though some of the extra-state war participants were listed in the Geopolitical Political Units (GPU) data, there was no particular effort to code or categorize the nonstate participants beyond the dichotomous classification of extra-state wars as *imperial* or *colonial*. As noted above, one by-product of this imperial-colonial classification is that it obscures the fact that according to the definition of extra-state wars, such wars can be fought against nonterritorially based entities as well. Efforts are under way to categorize and gather more information on the nonstate entities. Such entities would need to have some sort of identifiable organizational structure. From the GPU data, these would include both the dependencies (such as colonies, protectorates, possessions, and occupied territories) and the "near-state" entities within the autonomous entities category that fail system membership because of limitations on population (range 20,000–500,000), independence, sovereignty, or lack of diplomatic recognition. In addition, the nonstate entities would include political actors that are not territorially identified but have an organized armed force capable of engaging in sustained combat. Such entities are frequently referred to as nonstate armed groups (NSAs). To be considered a war participant, such nonstate entities would need to commit a minimum of 100 armed troops to sustained combat or suffer a minimum of twenty-five battle-related deaths.[77]

The definitional changes in the expanded typology have had a significant impact on the category of extra-state war. In *Resort to Arms*, Small and Singer identified 51 extra-systemic wars. Of these, 14 were reclassified as intra-state civil wars and 3 others shifted. However, an additional 129 wars have been added to this category, many because of the change in the definition of battle-deaths to now include deaths suffered by the nonstate participant.

Describing Intra-State War

An intra-state war is sustained combat between or among organized armed forces taking place within the territorial boundaries of a state system member and leading to 1,000 battle-related deaths per year. As described above, the expanded typology of wars includes three subcategories of intra-state war: civil wars, regional internal wars, and inter-communal wars. Since the description of civil wars was included in *Resort to Arms,* they will be discussed first and used as the basis for distinguishing the other two classes of intra-state war.

Civil War

Small and Singer's categorizing of civil wars was based on three dimensions: internality, types of participants, and the degree of effective resistance. As described above, the elimination of the metropole distinction for civil wars means that internality merely refers to the requirement of military action within the borders of the system member. In terms of participants, civil wars had to involve the active participation of the national government. There also had to be effective resistance by both sides.[78] In addressing the issue of "who is fighting whom," Small and Singer noted that there had to be organized armed forces on both sides of the war, and they argued that the "bulk of the fighting" on one side had to be conducted by the national government of an interstate system member. In other words, civil war is sustained military conflict "pitting the central government against an insurgent force capable of effective resistance."[79] Thus their discussion of civil war participants is interesting, both in terms of the need to define the "government" and in its description of the other war participants.

Determining who the government is can be complicated, for instance, in cases of rival entities claiming the right to govern all or part of a state. In such cases, Small and Singer defined "the government" as those forces that were at the start of the war in de facto control of the nation's institutions, regardless of the legality or illegality of their claim.[80] They did not, however, specifically define what was meant by the "nation's institutions." Within the general discussion of the members of the interstate system (see Chapter 1), Singer and Small had argued that a state could continue to be a war participant even if its territory were occupied, as long as it could field an army of 100,000 troops. Yet in terms of civil wars, they noted that the control of the nation's institutions need not necessarily include control of the armed forces, since the armed forces might be the combatants in a war against the government. The COW MID dataset operationalizes "the government" somewhat differently:

> In cases of militarized interstate disputes within the context of a civil war, the side that controls the pre-war capital is said to be in control of the government. When effective control of the capital, and hence the central government, is lost by one side and gained by another faction, a change in government is said to have occurred.[81]

As Jeffrey Dixon has pointed out, however, even this criterion has several difficulties, such as when the capital city is occupied by a foreign power (though a government in exile exists elsewhere); when the location of the capital city is in dispute; and when control of the capital city is divided between or among factions. Consequently, he suggests returning to the Small and Singer reference to national institutions, though making it somewhat more specific by referring to the institutions of governance: whichever party begins the war in possession of the institutions of government (parliament, the palace, and so forth) may be termed the government. When each side controls an institution (for example, Chile's Congressist rebellion, which pitted the president against Congress), then the executive or monarch's faction ought to be termed the government.[82] This further refinement of the definition is maintained here.

As noted above, control of the nation's institutions need not necessarily include control of the armed forces. Although a government can generally expect its armed forces to defend it, in a civil war the armed forces may actually be fighting against the government. In such cases, the government must rely on civilian combatants or other branches of the civilian or military infrastructure that remain loyal.[83] Consequently, within the category of civil war, Small and Singer also included in the general category of "the government," or the side of the national government, all those—from national military forces to local police and citizens—who enter the conflict in the name of that government.[84] This decision makes sense because it then includes as civil wars some of the ambiguous cases, such as when the national army declines to fight and the war is fought by private militias affiliated with the government—for instance, Lebanon's military remained neutral for a period during its civil wars—or when the government seems to switch its support between two rival contenders.[85] This criterion would become particularly difficult to apply only in cases where two or more groups claim to be fighting in support of the national government.

Consequently, here we seem to have a slightly different conception of sovereignty than that which appeared in the discussion of system membership. There, a system member continued to exist (or was not considered to be occupied) if it could field an army of 100,000 (despite loss of its territory), whereas here the focus is on a more classical understanding of sovereignty where the government has to control the nation's institutions in order to be considered to exist. It should also be mentioned that determining which party is the government is not dependent on diplomatic recognition. Although diplomatic recognition (or membership in the United Nations) is a requirement for an entity to be a member of the interstate system, that is not a de jure recognition (or approval) of a specific government. Thus it is possible for one party to be considered by COW as the government of a state because of its control of the national institutions while another party may be diplomatically recognized by other states, or even retain the United Nations seat (as was the case when the Northern Alliance retained the UN seat for Afghanistan, despite the fact that the Taliban government was in control in Afghanistan).

In defining civil wars, Small and Singer also began to describe the other participant(s) in the civil war. Unlike the description of extra-state wars in which the characteristics of the nonstate entity involved are relatively undefined, the requisite condition of a civil war is that the government is fighting against an internal insurgent force capable of "effective resistance." Small and Singer developed a two-part definition of effective resistance: "[A] violent episode of sustained military combat shall be considered a civil war if (a) both sides are initially organized for violent conflict and prepared to resist the attacks of their antagonists, or (b) the weaker side, although initially unprepared, is able to inflict upon the stronger opponents at least five percent of the number of fatalities it sustains."[86] The effective resistance criterion was specifically utilized to differentiate civil wars from massacres. The application of these two alternative criteria is similar to the two alternative means by which a state can be considered a war participant (suffering 100 fatalities, or committing 1,000 armed troops to combat). The primary requirement is that each participant must have an organized armed force capable of engaging in sustained combat; however, application of this criterion alone would eliminate as civil wars such cases in which the nonstate actor is perhaps not initially well organized but relatively soon develops an armed organization. For example, the 1923 Agrarian Rising in Bulgaria initially was not considered to be a COW civil war, because of organizational concerns, but it was later added to the civil war list (through the application of criterion b) when it became clear that the peasants became nominally organized and armed.[87] Dixon has suggested a complementary way through which to conceptualize these two criteria, what he calls the "rebuttable presumption" standard:

> [G]iven that a candidate conflict meets the other standards for inclusion, one should code effective resistance as present unless one has affirmative evidence that a conflict was really a massacre. In other words, if military action within a state occurs between that state's government and a non-state actor and 1000 battle-related fatalities result, coders should assume for purposes of war inclusion/exclusion that both sides were capable of effective resistance unless there is evidence that indeed one side suffered more than 20 battle-deaths for every one suffered by its opponent. This "rebuttable presumption" standard acknowledges the paucity of historical data on casualties while still preserving transparency and being applicable to all wars.[88]

Small and Singer also consider a number of alternative ways in which to categorize the "other side" in civil wars. Two possibilities would be to categorize the rebels by differing degrees of organization: by indicating a range of organizational abilities, from the disciplined military to the untrained rebellious masses; alternatively one could categorize participants in terms of the types of weapons they used. Such distinctions have often been used to differentiate civil wars (seen as wars against organized forces that have their own governmental institutions and effective territorial control) from insurrections and riots. Small and Singer ultimately rejected such a classification as unreliable.[89] Ted Gurr and Phil Schrodt did continue the discussion of COW civil war participants by creating a brief list of "groups" or "transnational actors." This listing included both groups of people (nations), such as the Kurds, as well as specific organizations. These groups could operate both within system members and across system member borders. These groups were not necessarily territorially based organizations, but Gurr and Schrodt referred to them as "quasi-state" actors because they had "persisting political organizations and aspirations either to creation of a new state or revolutionary seizure of power in an existing state. Each governs or commands some of the loyalties of a significant national group, and has demonstrated substantial military and/or diplomatic capabilities to pursue that end."[90] A more common practice is to refer to the opponents in civil wars as merely insurgents or armed groups. In this vein, the term *nonstate armed groups* (NSAs) has been used to describe conflict participants, including rebel movements, progovernment militias, community-based vigilante groups, some religious movements, and foreign mercenaries.[91] Such considerations move our specificity beyond a reliance on vague historical judgments of the existence of an organized armed force. Hence, as we move forward in gathering data on the nonstate participants in extra-state and intra-state wars, we shall be utilizing the criteria that an NSA can be considered a war participant if it either commits 100 armed personnel to combat or suffers 25 battle-related deaths. These requirements are appropriately less than the requirements for state war participation (either committing 1,000 troops or suffering 100 battle-deaths), since rebel groups or nonstate participants would not generally have the same size population as would states. Civil wars may involve the central government in conflict with a number of smaller rebel groups, which individually might not be able to hit the 1,000 personnel threshold though together could still be engaged in sustained combat causing significant fatalities. The lower troop and fatality figures are also appropriate at this stage, since the lower threshold has the advantage of flexibility—it is far easier for a researcher using the data to drop consideration of certain participants than to add in participants that have been excluded by a higher threshold.

Just as they rejected classifying civil wars by the types of weapons or tactics used (overt vs. covert, or conventional military vs. guerrilla), Small and Singer also initially rejected categorizing civil wars by the purposes and goals of the rebels. Requests from scholars, however, led COW to reconsider the issue. Despite the difficulty of ascertaining the objectives of political protagonists or most other entities, COW nonetheless concluded that motives and goals are the most relevant criteria for differentiating the various forms that civil war might take. COW adopted a minimalist categorization of the objectives of the nonstate participants, and in later versions of the data, civil wars were grouped into two categories based on the apparent motives of the nonstate actors: (1) conflicts for control of the central government and (2) conflicts over regional interests. In category 1, for central control, the insurgent forces seek to overthrow the existing national regime and replace it with one that is more receptive to their material, cultural, or psychic interests. But at the more restricted local, provincial, or regional level, in category 2 the insurgents fight in order to modify the national regime's treatment of this particular region or group of people, to replace the local regime with a friendlier one, or to secede from the larger statewide political system in order to set up their own regime. In trying to make this distinction between local as distinct from central government/statewide objectives, not only do we recognize the ambiguities and uncertainties involved in the behavior of the different elements that make up the insurgency, but we must also recognize that their objectives are far from constant. These will change as the insurgent coalition changes in its composition and in the relative power of its constituent groups, but also as the fortunes of war fluctuate. It is this changeable nature of objectives that has dissuaded the project from trying to subdivide this category further. It must also be noted, however, that in both of these categories, the NSA is fighting against the forces of the national government. Should the NSA be fighting against a regional or local government merely over local issues, the war would be categorized as an intra-state regional war (see below).

When conceptualizing battle-related deaths for civil wars, Singer and Small included civilian combat-connected fatalities in their total civil war deaths. This decision made practical sense because in civil wars it is much more difficult to distinguish the combatants from the civilian population, and consequently historical accounts frequently provide only total fatality figures, combining combatants and civilians. However, as described above, in the new expanded typology of wars the same battle-related death definition of 1,000 fatalities among the combatants per year applies to all wars, including civil wars. We have thus undertaken a major initiative to exclude civilian fatalities and to develop relatively accurate estimates of the deaths suffered both by the state and nonstate war participants, while admitting the frequent lack of adequate information in this regard.

In terms of examining civil war duration, the general rules concerning start dates, end dates, and breaks in the fighting apply here as well. These definitions become somewhat more significant here than in discussions of inter-state war because civil wars frequently encompass periods when combat waxes and wanes. In particular, COW codes the end of a civil war when there is a period of more than a year in which combat does not lead to 1,000 battle-related deaths. This coding procedure has not necessarily been accepted by other projects that examine civil wars. Many such projects consolidate multiple COW wars or recode start and end dates so that conflicts encompass long periods of time. For instance, the Uppsala/PRIO Armed Conflict dataset codes one conflict between the Philippines and the Moro National Liberation Front (MNLF) from 1970 through 2002, though they do indicate multiple periods in which the intensity level of the combat varies.[92]

The category of civil wars is also the category in which wars are frequently internationalized and/or transformed into wars of a different type. Civil wars can become internationalized when a system member intervenes either on the side of the regime of another state member fighting against insurgents within its territory or on the side of the insurgents. However, should the intervener subsequently take over the bulk of the fighting on behalf of the regime, the war is transformed into an extra-state war between the intervener and a nonstate armed group outside its borders. If the intervener takes over the bulk of the fighting on behalf of the nonstate actor, the war becomes an inter-state war between the intervener and the state involved in the original civil war. In both these instances, the civil war is coded as ending and a new inter-state or extra-state war is coded as beginning.

The final coding decision that especially affects civil wars is the issue of multiple simultaneous wars. In general, COW categorizes wars as mutually exclusive, utilizing the processes of war internationalization and war transformation to recode wars rather than having simultaneous wars of different types, but there are instances when states can conduct two or more separate wars against separate opponents (for example, the current American and British involvements in extra-state wars in Iraq and Afghanistan). However, it becomes more difficult to distinguish separate wars when they take place within the confines of a state. The COW Militarized Interstate Dispute (MID) dataset confronted a similar issue in determining whether a militarized interstate dispute could coexist within an ongoing war. The rule that was finally adopted held that a militarized interstate dispute or war can concurrently exist within the context of a larger internationalized civil war or extra-state war as long as the two (or more) states fight one another to the exclusion of all other combat activity in the immediate region. To date, COW has not had explicit rules for making such decisions regarding civil wars. In particular, COW has not had criteria for distinguishing between a single civil war involving many nonstate armed groups opposed to the central government and several simultaneous civil wars, each characterized by the same government fighting a different NSA or rebel group.

Consequently, there have been cases in which it was not clear why certain wars seemed to be consolidated (the Russian civil war) while other conflicts were coded as separate conflicts (Ethiopian civil war).[93] The primary determinant in our differentiation will be the degree of coordination between or among the various NSAs. If a state is facing combat with a variety of NSAs that are coordinating their opposition, it will be coded as one single civil war. If, on the other hand, the state is facing combat against multiple NSAs that are operating in geographically distinct regions and are not coordinating their operations, then the conflict will be coded as multiple wars (assuming that all the other criteria for a war are met). The key difficulties with this categorization are, of course, identifying all of the NSAs involved in the war and then determining how much coordination existed between or among them. Wars frequently involve multiple groups, some more organized and larger than others, thus just identifying all the combatants can be complicated. For instance, Jeffrey Dixon has now identified at least sixty participants in the fighting in Russia from 1917 to 1922. Some have clear "Red" or "White" loyalties, but most have their own agenda, from "Green" peasant groups to nationalities seeking independence. While it is relatively easy to recognize evidence of coordination, such as common command structures, frequent meetings or communication among NSA leaders, or joint offensives, it is much more difficult to measure the absence of such coordination. Consequently, we are in essence utilizing negative coordination criteria. In instances in which a state is engaged in combat with multiple NSAs, each of which is operating in a distinct geographic area, multiple wars will be considered to exist unless there is specific evidence of coordination and cooperation between or among the NSAs. It should also be apparent that distinct civil wars will be coded if they occur within different states (against different state governments) even though the NSA may be identical in both cases.

REGIONAL WAR

Regional wars are intra-state wars in that they occur within the boundaries of an interstate system member; however, they are similar to the category of non-state wars in that neither of the major war participants (who are conducting the bulk of the fighting on each side) is a system member. In virtually all respects, regional intra-state wars function like civil wars, but what gives them their distinct identity is that the major combatant on one side of the war is a local or regional government (not the national government). The armed forces on this side of the war would be regional (similar to the New York State National Guard); however, as with civil wars, the side of the local or regional government would include all those who enter the conflict in the name of that government, from regional military forces to local police and citizens.

The key difficulty in identifying these wars, and in differentiating them from civil wars, is in determining the purpose for which the regional government is fighting. If the regional government is fighting against an NSA for local issues, including the perpetuation of the regional government itself, then the war would be a regional intra-state war. On the other hand, a regional or local government could also be merely a participant in a civil war involving the national government. A regional government could fight alongside or in the name of the national government in a civil war opposing an NSA seeking local autonomy or independence. Conversely, the regional government could be a participant in a civil war against the national government if the regional government itself is seeking autonomy or independence.

Inter-communal War

The third category of intra-state war is inter-communal war. Inter-communal wars are intra-state wars in that they occur within the boundaries of a member of the interstate system. In many respects they are similar to civil wars; however, they are also similar to our category of non-state wars in that neither of the major war participants (who are conducting the bulk of the fighting on each side) is a system member or a regional or local government. This type of warfare, between nongovernmental forces within a state, is obviously not new, and many scholars have become interested in what they call "ethnic conflict." We consider this terminology and many of the purported explanations of ethnic conflict to be misguided, so that term will not be used here.[94] However, inter-communal wars are becoming more common as advanced weapons technology boosts the probability that conflicts between or among NSAs will reach the requisite battle-death threshold for war. Conceivably, inter-communal wars could also take place within a "failed state," or a system member that no longer has a central government or an NSA that controls the capital city's institutions of executive power.

Describing Non-state War

The final category of war in our expanded schema is that of non-state war. These are wars between two (or among possibly more) combatants, none of which is a member of the COW interstate system. What distinguishes this category from the previously discussed two types of nonstate intra-state wars (regional and inter-communal) is that here the wars do not take place within the boundaries of a particular system member. We have identified two subcategories of non-state wars based on the location of the war. In the first class, "In nonstate territory," combat takes place in territory that is not part of the territory of a member of the interstate system. Such territory could involve a dependency, or a nonstate autonomous entity, that does not meet the criteria of system membership. Such conflicts were also common in pre-state-formation periods (for instance, in South America in the early nineteenth century or in China prior to it becoming a system member). The second category, "Across state borders," involves wars that take place across the borders of existing states but do not involve the state or regional governments in the conflict.

Adding these categories of war is part of an overarching project to expand our examination to entities that are not members of the interstate system. As we discussed in Chapter 1, the broader international system encompasses a variety of actors beyond the state members of the more narrow interstate system, including other geopolitical units (GPUs), such as other autonomous entities and dependencies, as well as nonterritorial entities (NTEs), including nonstate armed groups (NSAs). The war experiences of such entities had previously been included in the COW datasets when they served as objects of system members' activities (as the targets for extra-state or civil wars). But through the expansion of the intra-state war category and the addition of the non-state war category, we are trying to examine the war experiences of these nonstate entities between and among themselves. We hope that these incremental improvements in the Correlates of War Project war data files will permit the most comprehensive examination to date of longitudinal variations in all of the classifications of modern war from the end of the Napoleonic Wars to the present day.

Notes

1. For a detailed comparison see Michael Doyle, *Ways of War and Peace* (New York: W. W. Norton, 1977), 93–110.
2. Carl von Clausewitz, *On War*, ed. and trans. Michael Howard and Peter Paret (Princeton, N.J.: Princeton University Press, 1976), 87.

3. Thomas Hobbes, *Leviathan Parts I and II* (Indianapolis: Bobbs-Merrill, 1958), 106.

4. Karl Marx and Friedrich Engels, "The Communist Manifesto," in *Dogmas and Dreams,* ed. Nancy S. Love (Chatham, N.J.: Chatham House, 1991), 229.

5. Niccolo Machiavelli, *The Prince and the Discourses* (New York: Modern Library, 1950), 53.

6. Leon Trotsky, *The Permanent Revolution and Results and Prospects* (New York: Pathfinder Press, 1969).

7. Rosa Luxemburg, "Fundamental Significance of the Russian Revolution," in *Rosa Luxemburg Speaks,* ed. Mary Alice Waters (New York: Pathfinder Press, 1970), 367.

8. Jane Addams, "War Is Not a Natural Activity," in *Women on War,* ed. Daniela Gioseffi (New York: Simon and Schuster, 1988), 182.

9. Woodrow Wilson, *Declaration of War,* S. Doc. 5, 55th Cong., April 2, 1917.

10. Jean Bethke Elshtain, *Just War against Terror* (New York: Basic Books, 2004).

11. Joshua S. Goldstein, *War and Gender* (Cambridge: Cambridge University Press, 2001).

12. John Vasquez, *The War Puzzle* (Cambridge: Cambridge University Press, 1993).

13. Hedley Bull, *The Anarchical Society* (New York: Columbia University Press, 1977), 184.

14. Vasquez, *The War Puzzle, 23.*

15. Melvin Small and J. David Singer, *Resort to Arms: International and Civil Wars, 1816–1980* (Beverly Hills, Calif.: Sage, 1982), 14.

16. Quincy Wright, *A Study of War,* 2nd ed., 2 vols. (Chicago: University of Chicago Press, 1965), 641.

17. Small and Singer, *Resort to Arms,* 38 (hereafter cited as *Resort*).

18. Small and Singer, *Resort,* 205–206.

19. Small and Singer, *Resort,* 56.

20. Small and Singer, *Resort,* 52.

21. Benedict Anderson, *Imagined Communities: Reflections on the Origin and Spread of Nationalism* (London: Verso, 1991), 47.

22. Small and Singer, *Resort,* 211–212.

23. Small and Singer, *Resort,* 210.

24. Small and Singer, *Resort,* 205.

25. *American Heritage Dictionary,* 2nd college ed. (Boston: Houghton Mifflin, 1985), 277.

26. Crane Brinton, *The Anatomy of Revolution* (New York: Prentice-Hall, 1938); Theda Skocpol, *States and Social Revolutions: A Comparative Analysis of France, Russia, and China* (Cambridge: Cambridge University Press, 1979).

27. Harry Eckstein, ed. *Internal War* (Glencoe, Ill.: Free Press, 1964).

28. Ted R. Gurr, *Why Men Rebel* (Princeton, N.J.: Princeton University Press, 1970).

29. Small and Singer, *Resort,* 213.

30. Small and Singer, *Resort,* 217.

31. Other scholars utilize a definition of civil war that does not require participation by the national government. For instance, see Stathis N. Kalyvas, *The Logic of Violence in Civil War* (New York: Cambridge University Press, 2006), 17.

32. Zeev Maoz, e-mail memo to Correlates of War Community, 2007.

33. Meredith Reid Sarkees and J. David Singer, "Old Wars, New Wars, and an Expanded War Typology" (paper presented at the joint meeting of the International Studies Association and the Japan Association of International Relations, Tokyo, September 20–23, 1996); Meredith Reid Sarkees and J. D. Singer, "Armed Conflict Past and Future: A Master Typology?" (paper presented at the European Union Conference on Armed Conflict Data Collection, Uppsala, Sweden, June, 2001).

34. Meredith Reid Sarkees, "Correlates of War Warsets: An Update," *Conflict Management and Peace Science* 18 (2000): 123–144.

35. Sarkees and Singer, "Old Wars, New Wars, and an Expanded War Typology," 2.

36. Kal Holsti, *The State, War, and the State of War* (Cambridge: Cambridge University Press, 1996).

37. David A. Lake and Donald Rothchild, eds. *The International Spread of Ethnic Conflict* (Princeton, N.J.: Princeton University Press, 1998).

38. David Carment and Patrick James, *Wars in the Midst of Peace: The International Politics of Ethnic Conflict* (Pittsburgh: University of Pittsburgh Press, 1997).

39. Donald Snow, *Uncivil Wars* (Boulder, Colo.: Lynne Rienner, 1996), 1–2.

40. Dennis Sandole, *Capturing the Complexity of Conflict: Dealing with Violent Ethnic Conflicts of the Post–Cold War Era* (London: Pinter, 1999), 1.

41. Small and Singer, *Resort*, 96–99.
42. J. David Singer and Melvin Small, *The Wages of War, 1816–1965: A Statistical Handbook* (New York: Wiley, 1972), 15 (hereafter cited as *Wages*).
43. Small and Singer, *Resort*, 33.
44. Singer and Small, *Wages*, 45.
45. Jeffrey Dixon and Meredith Reid Sarkees, "Intervention, Recognition, and War Transformation: A Consistent Standard for Distinguishing Inter-state, Extra-state, and Intra-state Wars" (paper presented at the annual meeting of the International Studies Association, Honolulu, Hawaii, March 1–5, 2005), 5.
46. Singer and Small, *Wages*, 47–48.
47. Singer and Small, *Wages*, 48–49.
48. Small and Singer, *Resort*, 56.
49. Ibid.
50. It should be mentioned that the COW definition of battle-related deaths differs substantially from that utilized by the Uppsala/PRIO Project. They include civilian deaths that resulted from combat (which COW does not), yet they exclude deaths of military personnel in the theater of combat due to disease (which COW includes). Uppsala/PRIO also requires 1,000 battle-deaths per calendar year; thus, for instance, a conflict with 1,000 deaths split between two calendar years would not be considered a war.
51. Small and Singer, *Resort*, 73.
52. Lewis Richardson, *Statistics of Deadly Quarrels* (Pittsburgh: Boxwood, 1960).
53. Bethany Lacina and Nils Petter Gleditsch, "Monitoring Trends in Global Combat: A New Dataset of Battle Deaths," *European Journal of Population* 21, 2–3 (2005): 135–166.
54. Richardson, *Statistics of Deadly Quarrels*; Quincy Wright, *A Study of War*; George Childs Kohn, *Dictionary of Wars* (New York: Checkmark Books, 1999); Michael Clodfelter, *Warfare and Armed Conflicts: A Statistical Reference to Casualty and Other Figures, 1500–2000*, 2nd ed. (Jefferson, N.C.: McFarland, 2002); Charles Phillips and Alan Axelrod, *Encyclopedia of Wars*, vols. I–III (New York: Facts on File, 2005).
55. Thomas Benfield Harbottle and George Bruce, *Dictionary of Battles* (New York: Stein and Day, 1971); Tony Jaques, *Battles and Sieges: A Guide to 8,500 Battles from Antiquity through the Twenty-first Century*, vols. I–III (Westport, Conn.: Greenwood Press, 2007).
56. Small and Singer, *Resort*, 73.
57. Gaston Bodart, *Losses of Life in Modern War* (Oxford: Clarendon, 1916).
58. Thomas L. Livermore, *Numbers and Losses in the Civil War in America: 1861–65* (Bloomington: Indiana University Press, 1957). Cited in Jeffrey Dixon, "Suggested Changes to the COW Civil War Dataset 3.0" (paper presented at the annual meeting of the International Studies Association, Portland, Ore., February 25–March 1, 2003), 15.
59. Michael Clodfelter, *Warfare and Armed Conflicts: A Statistical Reference to Casualty and Other Figures, 1618–1991* (Jefferson, N.C.: McFarland, 1992), 1086.
60. Dixon, "Suggested Changes to the COW Civil War Dataset 3.0," 15; Trevor N. Dupuy, *Attrition: Forecasting Battle Casualties and Equipment Losses in Modern War* (Fairfax, Va.: Hero Books, 1990), 48–49.
61. Small and Singer, *Resort*, 73.
62. Phil Schafer, "States, Nations, and Entities from 1492 to 1992," Ann Arbor: University of Michigan Terminal System, for the Correlates of War Project, 1995.
63. Jeff Dixon, "Coding Rules Memo," e-mail communication to Sarkees, May 6, 2006: 1.
64. Small and Singer, *Resort*, 66.
65. Ibid.
66. Wording from Dixon, "Suggested Changes to the COW Civil War Dataset 3.0," 9 (hereafter cited as "Suggested Changes").
67. Small and Singer, *Resort*, 66.
68. Small and Singer, *Resort*, 194.
69. Ibid.
70. Small and Singer, *Resort*, 194–195.
71. Small and Singer, *Resort*, 182.
72. Ibid.
73. Ibid.
74. Small and Singer, *Resort*, 185.
75. Small and Singer, *Resort*, 71.

76. Small and Singer, *Resort*, 52.
77. Meredith Reid Sarkees, "A Typology of International Political Actors and War Participants" (draft manuscript, December 2006).
78. Small and Singer, *Resort*, 210.
79. Small and Singer, *Resort*, 216.
80. Small and Singer, *Resort*, 213.
81. MID 3.0 dispute code book.
82. Dixon, "Suggested Changes," 4.
83. Small and Singer, *Resort*, 214.
84. Small and Singer, *Resort*, 213.
85. Dixon, "Suggested Changes," 5.
86. Small and Singer, *Resort*, 215.
87. Dixon, "Suggested Changes," 10.
88. Dixon, "Suggested Changes," 11.
89. Small and Singer, *Resort*, 216.
90. T. R. Gurr and Phil Schrodt, "Updating and Expanding the Singer and Small Codes" (internal COW memo, September 30, 1988), 1–2.
91. Malian Ministry of Foreign Affairs and International Cooperation, "Mapping of Non-state Armed Groups in the ECOWAS Region" (paper presented at the 6th Ministerial Meeting of the Human Security Network, Bamako, Mali, May 27–29, 2004), 26.
92. Bethany Lacina, "The Battle Deaths Dataset, 1946–2005, Version 2.0, Documentation of Coding Decisions for Use with Uppsala/PRIO Armed Conflict dataset, 1946–2005, Version 4—2006," Oslo: Centre for the Study of Civil War (CSCW), International Peace Research Institute, September 2006, 261–262.
93. Jeffrey Dixon and Meredith Reid Sarkees, "Intervention, Recognition, and War Transformation: A Consistent Standard for Distinguishing Inter-state, Extra-state, and Intra-state Wars," 13–14.
94. For a detailed discussion, see Meredith Reid Sarkees, "Trends in Intra-state (Not Ethnic) Wars" (paper presented at the joint convention titled Globalization and Its Challenges in the 21st Century, sponsored by the International Studies Association, the University of Hong Kong, and eleven international studies associations, Hong Kong, July 26–28, 2001).

CHAPTER THREE

The Inter-state Wars

When people think about or discuss wars, they generally reference inter-state wars, or wars between states or members of the interstate system. These are the wars that are often seen as the epic struggles: World War I and World War II; the wars that shape the fates of countries, marking the expansion of Japanese influence, or the destruction of the Ottoman Empire; wars that are fought to spread ideologies; or wars that are fought for national glory, interest, security, or resources. Similarly, most scholars of war have focused on inter-state wars, studying them to understand their characteristics, their causes, and their roles in the history of humankind. When discussing the "long peace," the democratic peace, or zones of peace, researchers are generally referring to the supposed absence of inter-state wars. Given this priority placed on examining inter-state wars, we shall begin our more detailed assessment of war with a description of the inter-state wars that have occurred over the past 192 years, from 1816 to 2007.

As discussed in the previous chapter, inter-state wars are those that involve armed forces of two or more members of the interstate system (states) in sustained combat. Each party must commit a minimum of 1,000 troops to the war (or suffer over 100 battle-deaths) to be considered a war participant. Hostilities must also involve a minimum of 1,000 fatalities between or among the armed forces per year (or twelve-month period), beginning with the start date of the war. Table 3.1 consists of a list of the ninety-five wars included in the Correlates of War (COW) dataset on inter-state wars. Following the list, each of these wars will then be described individually, indicating the participants, the initiator of the war, the outcome (or winner), and the battle-related deaths. All of these variables are defined in Chapter 2. The dates given for each war indicate the earliest start date and the latest end date for war participation, though individual combatants may have entered or left the war at various points within the period provided. The war narratives will also attempt to provide a general description of the war, including its context or historical background. The comments within the brief sections on coding rules will attempt to explain instances in which classifying the war was unusually complicated. This section may also provide information about the relationship between the war and data in the Militarized Interstate Dispute (MID) dataset. Finally, a comparison may be made here concerning the ways in which the war is categorized by COW in contrast to other war compendiums, in particular Michael Clodfelter's *Warfare and Armed Conflicts: A Statistical Reference to Casualty and Other Figures, 1500–2000;* George Kohn's *Dictionary of War;* and Charles Phillips and Alan Axelrod's *Encyclopedia of Wars.*[1]

TABLE 3.1 **LIST OF INTER-STATE WARS IN CHRONOLOGICAL ORDER**

Inter-state war number	War name	Page no	Inter-state war number	War name	Page no
1	Franco-Spanish War of 1823	78	67	Sino-French War of 1884–1885	104
4	First Russo-Turkish War of 1828–1829	78	70	Second Central American War of 1885	105
7	Mexican-American War of 1846–1848	79	73	First Sino-Japanese War of 1894–1895	106
10	Austro-Sardinian War of 1848–1849	80	76	Greco-Turkish War of 1897	107
13	First Schleswig-Holstein War of 1848-1849	81	79	Spanish-American War of 1898	109
			82	Boxer Rebellion of 1900	110
			83	Sino-Russian War of 1900	112
16	War of the Roman Republic of 1849	82	85	Russo-Japanese War of 1904–1905	113
19	La Plata War of 1851–1852	83	88	Third Central American War of 1906	115
22	Crimean War of 1853–1856	84			
25	Anglo-Persian War of 1856–1857	85	91	Fourth Central American War of 1907	116
28	War of Italian Unification of 1859	86	94	Second Spanish-Moroccan War of 1909–1910	117
31	First Spanish-Moroccan War of 1859–1860	87	97	Italian-Turkish War of 1911–1912	118
34	Italian-Roman War of 1860	87	100	First Balkan War of 1912–1913	119
37	Neapolitan War of 1860–1861	89	103	Second Balkan War of 1913	120
40	Franco-Mexican War of 1862–1867	89	106	World War I of 1914–1918	121
43	Ecuadorian-Colombian War of 1863	91	107	Estonian War of Liberation of 1918–1920	124
46	Second Schleswig-Holstein War of 1864	91	108	Latvian War of Liberation of 1918–1920	125
49	Lopez War of 1864–1870	92	109	Russo-Polish War of 1919–1920	126
52	Naval War of 1865–1866	94			
55	Seven Weeks War of 1866	95	112	Hungarian Adversaries War of 1919	128
58	Franco-Prussian War of 1870–1871	96	115	Second Greco-Turkish War of 1919–1922	129
60	First Central American War of 1876	98	116	Franco-Turkish War of 1919–1921	130
61	Second Russo-Turkish War of 1877–1878	99	117	Lithuanian-Polish War of 1920	131
			118	Manchurian War of 1929	132
64	War of the Pacific of 1879–1883	101	121	Second Sino-Japanese War of 1931–1933	133
65	Conquest of Egypt of 1882	102	124	Chaco War of 1932–1935	135

(Continued)

TABLE 3.1 **LIST OF INTER-STATE WARS IN CHRONOLOGICAL ORDER**

Inter-state war number	War name	Page no	Inter-state war number	War name	Page no
125	Saudi-Yemeni War of 1934	136	178	War for Bangladesh of 1971	162
127	Conquest of Ethiopia of 1935–1936	137	181	Yom Kippur War of 1973	163
130	Third Sino-Japanese War of 1937–1941	138	184	Turco-Cypriot War of 1974	164
133	Changkufeng War of 1938	139	186	War over Angola of 1975–1976	166
136	Nomonhan War of 1939	140	187	Second Ogaden War Phase 2 of 1977–1978	167
139	World War II of 1939–1945	140	189	Vietnamese-Cambodian Border War of 1977–1979	168
142	Russo-Finnish War of 1939–1940	143	190	Ugandan-Tanzanian War of 1978–1979	170
145	Franco-Thai War of 1940–1941	144	193	Sino-Vietnamese Punitive War of 1979	171
147	First Kashmir War of 1947–1949	145	199	Iran-Iraq War of 1980–1988	171
148	Arab-Israeli War of 1948–1949	146	202	Falklands War of 1982	173
151	Korean War of 1950–1953	147	205	War over Lebanon of 1982	173
153	Off-shore Islands War of 1954–1955	148	207	War over the Aouzou Strip of 1986–1987	174
155	Sinai War of 1956	149	208	Sino-Vietnamese Border War of 1987	175
156	Soviet Invasion of Hungary of 1956	150	211	Gulf War of 1990–1991	176
158	Ifni War of 1957–1958	152	215	War of Bosnian Independence of 1992	177
159	Taiwan Straits War of 1958	153	216	Azeri-Armenian War of 1993–1994	178
160	War in Assam of 1962	154	217	Cenepa Valley War of 1995	180
163	Vietnam War Phase 2 of 1965–1975	155	219	Badme Border War of 1998–2000	181
166	Second Kashmir War of 1965	156	221	War for Kosovo of 1999	181
169	Six-Day War of 1967	157	223	Kargil War of 1999	184
170	Second Laotian War Phase 2 of 1968–1973	158	225	Invasion of Afghanistan of 2001	184
172	War of Attrition of 1969–1970	159	227	Invasion of Iraq of 2003	186
175	Football War of 1969	160			
176	War of the Communist Coalition of 1970–1971	161			

Individual Descriptions of Inter-state Wars

INTER-STATE WAR #1:
The Franco-Spanish War of 1823

Participants: France vs. Spain
Dates: April 7, 1823, to November 13, 1823
Battle-Related Deaths: Spain—600;
  France—400
Where Fought: Europe
Initiator: France
Outcome: France wins

Narrative: The origins of this war were tied to the international struggles between monarchical and revolutionary forces. In this case the conflict dated from 1808, when Napoleon placed his own brother on the throne of Spain, replacing the Spanish king Ferdinand VII, whom Napoleon had imprisoned in France. Ferdinand VII was returned to power in Spain after Napoleon's defeat. His absolutist rule and penchant for military adventures in the Americas led to an army revolt in 1820, whereby the king was encouraged to support the liberal constitution of 1812. Enduring conflict between the liberal and royalists forces led to a civil war (intra-state war #503). The royalist forces were unable to defeat the army of Spain and appealed to France (which had been aiding the royalist forces with money and arms) to directly intervene. Meanwhile, at the October 1822 Congress of Verona, the Holy Alliance of Russia, Prussia, and Austria decided on the need to act to support the Spanish monarchy. The post-Napoleonic monarchy of France desired to restore its royalist reputation, and, despite British opposition, France agreed to act as the mandatory of the powers by intervening in the Spanish war to oust the liberal constitutional government and restore the complete authority of the monarchy. The civil war ended on April 6 and the inter-state war began on April 7, 1823, when the French forces crossed the border and took over the "bulk of the fighting" from the Royalists. The French army, with a peak strength of 100,000 men, marched into Spain and reached Madrid by May 23, 1823. Ferdinand VII, in the custody of the liberal government (Cortes), was evacuated to Seville and then moved to the isle of Leon. By August 31 the Trocadero was in the hands of the invaders, and by October 1 Cadiz had fallen and Ferdinand was freed. Ferdinand VII returned to Madrid on November 13, 1823, which marks the end of the war.

Coding: Clodfelter (2002) describes the entire period of 1820–1823 as the "Riego Rebellion." Phillips and Axelrod are in accord with us in treating this as the "Franco-Spanish War" of 1823.

Sources: Artz (1934); Bodart (1916); Carr (1982); Clarke (1906); Clodfelter (2002); Geoffrey de Grandmaison (1928); Hume (1900); Phillips (1914); Phillips and Axelrod (2005); Richardson (1960a); Smith (1965).

INTER-STATE WAR #4:
The First Russo-Turkish War of 1828–1829

Participants: Russia vs. Ottoman Empire
  (Turkey)
Dates: April 26, 1828, to September 14, 1829
Battle-Related Deaths: Ottoman
  Empire—80,000; Russia—50,000
Where Fought: Europe, Middle East
Initiator: Russia
Outcome: Russia wins

Narrative: This war is part of the struggle of Greece for independence from the Ottoman

Empire. Ottoman control of the European Balkans dated from the fourteenth century; however, in a series of wars in the 1700s, Russia had begun to encroach on the territories held by the Ottoman Turks. In the late 1700s, under Catherine the Great, this expansion allowed Russia to reach the Black Sea, bringing it into conflict with the Ottoman Empire. Growing Russian influence continued into the nineteenth century (eroding Ottoman control over the Balkans) as Russia supported Eastern Orthodox Christian nations such as Greece and Serbia. The Greeks conducted a war of independence against the Ottoman Empire from 1821 to 1828 (intra-state war #506). Greek independence garnered international support, and on April 4, 1826, an Anglo-Russian protocol was signed that established a common policy toward promoting Greek independence. Nevertheless, a joint TurkishOttoman-Egyptian force overcame the Greeks, and by June 5, 1827, almost all of Greece was under Ottoman control. On October 20, 1827, Great Britain, France, and Russia intervened, sending a joint fleet to confront the Turkish-Egyptian ships at Navarino Bay. The allied fleet destroyed the Turkish fleet, which ensured Greek independence. An armistice was enforced by France in southern Greece, though conflict did continue between the Greek rebels and the Turks in northern Greece. The Ottoman sultan demanded compensation from the allies for the destruction at Navarino Bay. The Russians proposed further joint military action against the Turks, but Britain and France demurred. The Ottoman sultan closed the Dardanelles to Russian ships. Russia had been involved in another war (extra-state war #316) against Persia. When that war ended on February 28, 1828, Russia felt free to act against Turkey and declared war on April 26, 1828. This marks the transformation of the Greek Civil War into this First Russo-Turkish War. The war began with early Russian military advances. The Russians met stiff resistance in the Danube region but were more successful in the Caucasus, storming the fortress of Kars on June 23, 1828. By the end of August the troops had advanced within a few miles of Constantinople. The European powers, fearing Russian occupation of Constantinople, pressed the sultan for concessions, and on September 14, 1829, the Treaty of Adrianople was signed on Russian terms. The sultan was forced to grant Russia territorial gains around the Black Sea.

Coding: Greece gains its independence and becomes a system member on January 1, 1828. This war is preceded by bilateral militarized interstate dispute (MID) #189, initiated by Russia in November 1827.

Sources: Allen and Muratoff (1953); Crawley (1930); Dumas and Vedel-Petersen (1923); Florinsky (1953); Palmer (1992); Russell (1877); von Sax (1913); von Sternegg (1891–1895); Wolff (1978); Woodhouse (1952).

INTER-STATE WAR #7:

The Mexican-American War of 1846–1848

Participants: United States vs. Mexico
Dates: April 25, 1846, to September 14, 1847
Battle-Related Deaths: United States—13,283; Mexico—6,000
Where Fought: W. Hemisphere
Initiator: United States
Outcome: United States wins

Narrative: This war was a part of the trend of U.S. expansionism toward the Pacific. The proximate cause was the U.S. annexation of the formerly Mexican territory of Texas. Texas had gained independence from Mexico in the 1835–1836 intra-state war #527 and was annexed to the United States, becoming a state on December 29, 1845. The Texas border with Mexico was still in dispute, with the United States claiming the Rio Grande as the border, whereas Mexico claimed to the Nueces River. American president Polk was interested both in settling the border dispute and in further westward expansion, so he sent the Slidell mission to Mexico in November 1845 to negotiate and to offer to purchase California and New Mexico. The Mexican rejection of this mission led Polk to send troops into the disputed territory between the Nueces and the Rio Grande. On April 25, 1846, Mexican troops crossed the Rio Grande and attacked U.S. troops. Though fatalities were limited, this prompted the United States to send additional troops into the region. There were subsequent battles at Palo Alto and Resaca de la Palma, and in response, Polk sent a war message to Congress; on May 13, Congress declared war on Mexico. The U.S. Army planned a three-pronged attack: one going west toward Monterrey, Mexico; one going south toward Chihuahua, Mexico; and a third that was to head toward Santa Fe and then on toward San Diego. Former Mexican president Santa Anna (who was in exile in Cuba) offered to mediate the conflict; however, after the United States facilitated his return to Mexico, he began to raise an army to confront the U.S. Army. Even though the United States had initially planned a relatively shallow expedition into Mexico, successful military advances ultimately led them to Mexico City. The war ended with the battle of Chapultepec and the fall of Mexico City on September 14, 1847. This ended the fighting and thus the war. The treaty of Guadalupe Hidalgo was not signed until February 2, 1848. In the treaty, Mexico renounced claims to Texas above the Rio Grande and transferred New Mexico and Alta California to the United States in exchange for $15,000,000.

Coding: While never a member of the interstate system, Texas was a COW autonomous entity from 1836 to 1845. The war was preceded by a bilateral MID #1552, beginning August 23, 1843, in which the United States is coded as both the initiator and the revisionist side. In the war only slightly over 1,700 men were killed in direct combat. The remaining fatalities, which numbered above 11,500, were caused by disease.

Sources: Axelrod (2007); Bailey (1964); Bemis (1936); Clodfelter (1992); LaFeber (1989); Peterson (1957); Scheina (2003a); Singletary (1960); Smith (1919); Wilcox (1892).

INTER-STATE WAR #10:
The Austro-Sardinian War of 1848–1849

Participants: Austria vs. Tuscany, Sardinia, Modena
Dates: March 24, 1848, to March 30, 1849
Battle-Related Deaths: Austria—3,927; Sardinia—3,400; Modena—100; Tuscany—100
Where Fought: Europe
Initiator: Sardinia
Outcome: Austria wins

Narrative: After the fall of the Roman Empire, Italy was no longer united and quarrels among the Italian states led to foreign interventions, particularly by France, Spain, and Austria. Napoleon was unsuccessful in uniting Italy, and the Congress of Vienna restored the pre-Napoleonic status quo with Lombardy and Venetia (northeastern Italy) being given to Austria. Thereafter, Austria was the major opponent of the Italian unification movement. The leading proponent of Italian unification was the Kingdom of Sardinia/Piedmont. This kingdom included not only the island of Sardinia but also Savoy and the Piedmont area, around the city of Turin. In 1848 revolutionary war broke out across much of Europe, pitting republican rebels against entrenched monarchies. Austria was faced with an early revolt, an uprising in Vienna (intra-state war #550) in March 1848. In the context of this continental-scale revolution, subsequent revolts in Venice and Milan (intra-state war #551, Milan Five-Day Revolt) broke Austrian control. Furthermore, King Charles Albert of Sardinia/Piedmont proposed a risorgimento, a movement to both liberate Italy from Austrian domination and unify the Italian states under a single government. Responding to appeals for support from the Milanese, King Charles Albert declared war on Austria on March 23, 1848, in an attempt to make the rebellious Austrian provinces of Lombardy and

Venetia part of Sardinia (the civil war thus ends at this point and the inter-state war begins as Sardinia takes over the bulk of the fighting). King Charles Albert was able to field a large allied Italian army, with Tuscany and Modena joining as war participants. The Papal States also sent a small contingent (but not a large enough number to be considered a war participant). Though Sardinia saw an early victory, the Austrian forces (under the command of Austria's famed Field Marshal Joseph Radetzky) were able to regroup and defeat the Italians at Custoza on July 24, 1848. Milan was then reconquered, and Sardinia/Piedmont was forced to accept an armistice on August 9, 1848. King Charles Albert renounced the armistice on March 12, 1849, and fighting resumed between Sardinia and Austria. Modena and Tuscany did not take part in the war at this stage. The Austrian forces were able to defeat the less-well-trained Sardinians, and fighting ended with the Sardinian defeat at a battle at Brescia (March 30, 1849). Consequently, Charles Albert abdicated in favor of his son, Victor Emmanuel II, who later became the king of a united Italy. Victor Emmanuel II concluded a treaty with Austria under disadvantageous terms on August 9, 1849.

Coding: In 1848, COW codes the following Italian states as system members: Sardinia/Piedmont (#325); Papal States (#327); Two Sicilies (#329); Modena (#332); and Tuscany (#337). Sardinia/Piedmont (#325) was the only Italian member of the COW central system. The Austro-Sardinian War is preceded by MID #19, commencing January 15, 1848, and pitting Austria as the initiator against Sardinia, Modena, and Tuscany. Sardinia is the revisionist side in this MID. During the war, the period of August 9, 1848, to March 12, 1849, is coded as a break in the war.

Sources: Albrecht-Carrié (1958); Berkeley (1940); Bodart (1916); Clodfelter (2002); Friedjung (1912); Kohn (1999); Palmer and Colton (1964); Phillips and Axelrod (2005); Smith (1971); Smyth (1950); Sorokin (1937); Urlanis (1960).

INTER-STATE WAR #13:

The First Schleswig-Holstein War of 1848–1849

Participants: Prussia vs. Denmark
Dates: April 10, 1848, to July 10, 1849
Battle-Related Deaths: Denmark—3,500; Prussia—2,500.
Where Fought: Europe
Initiator: Prussia
Outcome: Prussia wins

Narrative: This war begins two weeks after the start of the Austro-Sardinian War, an appropriate parallel in that they both can be seen as the first inter-state wars in a sequence of wars leading, respectively, to Italian and German national unification. German-speaking Schleswig and Holstein were part of a hereditary fief to the king of Denmark, though they were held by a personal union only. Thus any attempts to tie them more closely to Denmark (such as the Danish king Christian VIII's attempt to apply Danish succession rules to Schleswig in 1846) aroused opposition. Nevertheless, Christian's successor, Frederick VII, declared the complete union of Schleswig to Denmark in 1848. As part of the revolutions of 1848 that were sweeping across the continent, the German-speaking majority in both duchies, Schleswig and Holstein, rebelled against Denmark, and a provisional government was created at Kiel. The rebels were unable to prevent the occupation of Schleswig by Danish troops in early April 1848 and appealed to the German Confederation for assistance. The German Confederation came to the aid of the rebels, commissioning Prussia to conduct the war. Prussian troops soon occupied both duchies. While this is an inter-state war between Prussia and Denmark, forces from the two duchies fought on the Prussian side, while Sweden assisted Denmark (though not at war-participant levels). The Prussians were militarily successful in driving the Danes from the two duchies. Denmark then blockaded Prussian ports, leading the Prussians to invade Jutland (in Denmark proper) on May 2. This escalation of the conflict aroused the concern of Russia, Sweden, France, and Britain. British intervention led to an armistice that began on August 26, 1848, and lasted for seven months (coded as a break in the war). Denmark launched a new offensive when the armistice expired on March 25, 1949. A second armistice was reached on July 10, 1849, and the final peace settlement was signed on July 2, 1850, by which both sides preserved their rights. The issue remained unresolved, leading to a second Schleswig-Holstein War in 1864 (inter-state war #46) and contributing to the Seven Weeks War in 1866 (inter-state war #55).

Coding: Schleswig was a COW autonomous entity from 1492 to 1863. Holstein was autonomous from 1492 to 1865. Both are under Danish control from 1816 to 1848. The First Schleswig-Holstein War is preceded by MID #375, initiated on April 1, 1848, by Prussia against Denmark. Prussia is later joined in this MID by the German states of Hanover, Saxony, and Bavaria, while Sweden, the United Kingdom, and Russia sided with Denmark.

Sources: Bodart (1916); Clodfelter (2002); Jennings (1971); Orr (1978); Phillips and Axelrod (2005); Pinson (1966); Sorokin (1937); Urlanis (1960); von Sternegg (1892–1898).

INTER-STATE WAR #16:
The War of the Roman Republic of 1849

Participants: Two Sicilies, France, Austria vs. Papal States
Dates: April 30, 1849, to July 2, 1849
Battle-Related Deaths: Papal States—1,400; France—1,000; Austria—100; Two Sicilies - 100
Where Fought: Europe
Initiator: France
Outcome: Two Sicilies, France, Austria win

Narrative: In 1848 both France and Austria held territories in what is now Italy. The republican revolutionary movement of 1848 (which swept the capitals of Europe), coupled with the Sardinia-sponsored risorgimento to unite Italy, contributed to a series of wars in Italy, including the civil war in the Two Sicilies (intra-state war #547), the Milan Five-Day Revolt (intra-state war #551), and the Austro-Sardinian War (inter-state war #10). The risorgimento actually encompassed three major groups: the radicals led by Giuseppe Mazzini, who sought to create a republic; the moderate liberals, who regarded the house of Savoy (which ruled the Kingdom of Sardinia/Piedmont) as the means for unification; and the conservative Catholics, who favored an Italian confederation under the Pope. Though there were several attempts to establish a republic, such as the one described here in Rome, Italian unification was ultimately achieved by Sardinia/Piedmont, and in particular King Victor Emmanuel II, with the assistance of his premier (Count Camillo Benso Cavour) and military leader Giuseppe Garibaldi.

As the revolutionary movement reached Rome, or the Papal States, Pope Pius IX declared that the old order of foreign domination could not continue. Thus he was popularly perceived as a leader in the national war of liberation from Austria. Yet, the people were to be disappointed. On April 29, 1848, the pope announced that he would not declare war on Austria. He did mobilize his forces during the Austro-Sardinian War but only to protect the Papal States, not to support liberation from Austria. As a result of the subsequent rioting, the pope fled from Rome. The Italian liberals were retreating south after being defeated by Austria in the Austro-Sardinian War. When they arrived in Rome, they established a Roman Republic on February 9, 1849, under the leadership of Giuseppe Mazzini. This new Roman Republic deprived the pope of his long-standing control of the Papal States (Rome and central Italy). When the pope was unsuccessful in his attempts to be reinstated, France sent an army under

Gen. Nicholas Oudinot to restore papal rule. An initial attack by the French on April 30, 1849, was repulsed by the Garibaldian Republican troops. Forces from Austria and the Two Sicilies (Naples) soon joined the French in a coalition supporting the pope against the fledgling republican government of the Papal States. The allies soon greatly outnumbered the republicans, and, after enduring a siege of Rome, the republic surrendered on July 2, 1849, and papal authority was restored. The dream of Italian unification remained, however, and it was instrumental in a series of wars that shook Italy ten years later.

Coding: In 1849, COW codes the following Italian states as system members: Sardinia/Piedmont (#325); Papal States (#327); Two Sicilies (#329); Modena (#332); and Tuscany (#337). Clodfelter (2002) bundles this event into the "Italian Revolutions" of 1848–49.

Sources: Berkeley (1932); Bodart (1916); Bruce (1981); Clodfelter (2002); Harbottle (1904); Johnston (1901); King (1899); Palmer and Colton (1964); Phillips and Axelrod (2005); Pieri (1962); Smith (1971); Sorokin (1937).

INTER-STATE WAR #19:
The La Plata War of 1851–1852

Participants: Brazil vs. Argentina
Dates: July 19, 1851, to February 3, 1852
Battle-Related Deaths: Argentina—800; Brazil—500
Where Fought: W. Hemisphere
Initiator: Brazil
Outcome: Brazil wins

Narrative: Buenos Aires lies on the Río de la Plata, an estuary between present-day Argentina and Uruguay. The name La Plata also refers to a viceroyalty formed by the Spanish in 1776, encompassing most of the area of contemporary Argentina, Uruguay, Bolivia, and Paraguay. The United Provinces of the Río de la Plata declared their independence on July 9, 1816; however, independence was followed by virtually continuous warfare. Most of these wars are classified as non-state wars because Argentina became a COW system member only in 1841, Paraguay in 1846, Bolivia in 1848, and Uruguay in 1882. For instance, there was a non-state war (#1503, Buenos Aires vs. several Provinces) in 1820; the war from 1826 to 1828 between Brazil and Argentina (extra-state war #315); the Argentine War for Unity (non-state war #1513; 1829–1831); a war between Argentina and the Ranqueles Indians of Patagonia (non-state war #1518 of 1833–1834); and a war between the Unitarios and the Federalists under Juan Manuel de Rosas (non-state war #1527). The La Plata War of 1851–1852 was the first inter-state war involving Argentina, yet it can be better understood in the context of the preceding five wars, plus a subsequent intrastate civil war and a following extra-state war.

The non-state war (#1527) between the Federalists and the Unitarios was transformed by Argentina gaining system membership in 1841 into an intra-state civil war (#538, The First Argentine War Phase 2) between Argentina and the Unitarios. Finally, between the end of the war in 1842 and 1851, Argentina enjoyed an almost-decade period without internal war. Yet, during this time it was able to shift the zone of armed conflict to combat over Uruguay. Argentina besieged Montevideo, the capital of Uruguay, for nine years on behalf of the conservative Blancos (under Manual Oribe) against the liberal Colorados. Uruguay was not at that time a member of the COW interstate system; thus this war, #327, the Uruguay War of 1843-1851, was classified as an extra-state war, which also involved Britain and France in support of Uruguay. While this conflict was winding down, civil unrest was increasing in Argentina, led by the governor of Entre Rios (Justo Jose de Urquiza) against the tyrant Juan Manuel de Rosas. On May 29, 1851, an alliance was signed in Montevideo among Entre Rios, Uruguay, and Brazil. Brazil wanted to maintain Uruguay's independence as a buffer for Argentina. Brazil entered the war on July 19, 1851. Since Brazil took over the bulk of the fighting, this ends the extra-state war and begins this inter-state war #19, The LaPlata War between Brazil, aided by Entre Rios and Uruguay (nonsystem members) against Argentina aided by the Uruguay Blancos. By October 7, 1851, the Blancos and Oribe had surrendered, and Argentina's Rosas was unable to stop the allied advance. In January 1852 a large united army invaded Argentina. The decisive battle of Monte Caseros was fought near Buenos Aires on February 3, 1852. Clodfelter (2002, 354) describes the climax as the largest single battle in South America since Incan times, with 46,000 troops engaged. This battle, in which Rosas suffered an overwhelming defeat, marked the end of the war. Under British protection, Rosas sought exile in Britain.

Coding: Clodfelter (2002) treats this war as the beginning of a civil war in Argentina, lasting from 1851 to 1876. Lemke (2006) identifies twenty entities in the Río de la Plata region from 1810 to 1862 and ten wars among them in this period. The 1851 war was preceded by bilateral MID #1528, beginning in April 1851. This MID was initiated by Brazil but with Argentina as the revisionist.

Sources: Best (1960, vol. 2); Cady (1929); Calogeras (1963); Clodfelter (2002); Dawson (1935); Lemke (2006); Levene (1937);

INTER-STATE WAR #22:
The Crimean War of 1853–1856

Participants: France, Ottoman Empire, Sardinia/Piedmont, United Kingdom vs. Russia
Dates: October 23, 1853, to March 1, 1856
Battle-Related Deaths: Russia—100,000; France—95,000; Ottoman Empire—45,000; United Kingdom—22,000; Sardinia/Piedmont—2,200
Where Fought: Europe
Initiator: Ottoman Empire

Outcome: France, Sardinia/Piedmont, Ottoman Empire, United Kingdom win

Narrative: This is the first major-power inter-state war (a war with at least one major power on each side) since the Napoleonic Wars. Since there were more fatalities in this war than in all the prior COW inter-state wars combined, the Crimean War is popularly associated with the deadly Charge of the Light Brigade and the nursing innovations of Florence Nightingale. The primary combatants were Ottoman Empire (Turkey), which was trying to defend its empire against Russian incursions (a theme that had been apparent in the First Russo-Turkish War of 1828–1829; inter-state war #4). The British and French, who had fought against the Ottoman Turks at Navarino Bay in 1827 (during the war of Greek Independence, intra-state war #506), switched to the Ottoman side in this war, fighting against the Russians. For Russia, the proximate issue was a demand for Eastern Orthodox control of Christian sites in the Holy Land, though in reality Russia was more concerned with gaining control of Constantinople and access to the Mediterranean. Russia had championed the concerns of the Christians in the Balkans, and in 1853 it secretly proposed to the British that they expel the Turks from Europe. The British demurred, not wanting to see the dismemberment of the Ottoman Empire. The British and French were concerned about the growth of Russian naval power beyond the Dardanelles, and gradually they formed a partnership to preserve the Ottoman Empire. Despite Russian entreaties, Austria initially remained neutral. On October 23, 1853, Russia began hostilities against the Ottoman Empire and initially enjoyed naval success. The Russian army, however, was less successful, becoming bogged down in an attack on Turkish Bulgaria. On March 31, 1854, France and Britain entered the fray and sent troops to defend the Turkish Balkans. In September the allied army launched the siege of the Crimean capital of Sevastopol. Initially, because of British global naval supremacy and the inferior Russian railroad network, the British were better equipped to bring men and supplies to the Russian Crimean than were the Russians; however, the troops endured a cholera epidemic and long periods of stationary fronts. Sardinia/Piedmont, which had remained neutral while waiting for Austria to assert its position, finally entered the war on January 10, 1855, partially as a means to promote Italian unity. The defenders of Sevastopol endured a siege for 349 days. Eventually the alliance of Britain, France, and Sardinia prevailed and the Russians were forced to abandon Sevastopol. Fighting also took place in the Caucasus, where the Russians won several battles against the Turks. The war exacted a terrible toll on the participants, and Russia finally agreed to make peace. Preliminary terms were ready by March 1, 1856, the war's end, though the final Treaty of Paris, which included the neutralization of the Black Sea, was not signed until March 30, 1856.

Coding: The war is preceded by MID #57, begun by Russia on May 31, 1853. Russia is also the revisionist side in that MID. MID participants are all the war participants, plus Austria one year after the start of the war.

Sources: Allen and Muratoff (1953); Bodart (1916); Clodfelter (2002); Dumas and Vedel-Peterson (1923); Finkel (2005); Phillips and Axelrod (2005); Russell (1877); Sorokin (1937); Thayer (1911); Urlanis (1960).

INTER-STATE WAR #25:
The Anglo-Persian War of 1856–1857

Participants: United Kingdom vs. Iran
Dates: October 25, 1856, to April 5, 1857
Battle-Related Deaths: Iran—1,500; United Kingdom—500
Where Fought: Middle East
Initiator: United Kingdom
Outcome: United Kingdom wins

Narrative: In 1821 Persia had gone to war with the Ottoman Empire (extra-state war #309), and in 1826 with Russia (extra-state war #316). By 1855, however, Persia had become a member of the interstate system, and thus this war with Britain is classified as an inter-state war. Britain saw Persia as a buffer zone for India and did not wish to see Persian (or Russian) advances in the area of present-day Afghanistan, then primarily the principality of Herat. However, the British at the time were not considering an expedition on the level of their campaign in the region in 1839–1842 (extra-state war #322). Yet, Persia had taken the side of Russia in the Crimean War (raising British suspicions), though Persia had resisted Russian blandishments to enter the war. The Persian shah switched his focus back to Herat. Dost Muhammad, the ruler of Kabul, aimed to unify Kandahar, Kabul, and Herat under his authority, whereas the Persian shah had similar designs on Herat. An unusual diplomatic struggle led to the closing of the British mission in Teheran in November 1855. Meanwhile, Dost Muhammad captured Kandahar in December 1855 and planned to proceed to Herat. The ruler of Herat appealed to Persia for assistance, and Persian troops entered the region, unfortunately with designs on Herat themselves. Faced with the Persian refusal to retreat, British troops in India began preparations for a military mission to the Persian Gulf. On September 26, orders were sent to launch the expedition. The force departed and on October 25, instructions declaring a state of war were received (marking the start of the war). The British attacked Persian soil on the shores of the Persian Gulf and near the Shatt-al-Arab (Tigris and Euphrates estuary). Military defeats there in early 1857 forced the Persian shah to sue for peace. The Treaty of Paris (March 4, 1857) required the shah to withdraw from Herat and Afghanistan. News of the treaty did not arrive in the Gulf till later that month, so fighting continued until April 5, 1857.

Coding: This war was a fight over what appears on today's maps as the country of Afghanistan (COW state #700) but was back then three distinct entities. For a few decades up until 1855, Kandahar and Kabul were separate and distinct COW autonomous entities, which in 1855 merged into the autonomous entity of Afghanistan. Herat, the third piece of today's Afghanistan, remained distinct as an autonomous entity in its own right until 1863. This war is preceded by MID #8, starting in July 1856, in which England is the initiator and revisionist state.

Sources: Clodfelter (2002); Fortescue (1930, vol. 13); Kelly (1968); Phillips and Axelrod (2005); Schafer (1995).

INTER-STATE WAR #28:

The War of Italian Unification of 1859

Participants: France, Sardinia/Piedmont vs. Austria
Dates: April 29, 1859, to July 12, 1859
Battle-Related Deaths: Austria—12,500; France—7,500; Sardinia/Piedmont—2,500
Where Fought: Europe
Initiator: Austria-Hungary
Outcome: France, Italy win

Narrative: Initial attempts to unite Italy and end its subjugation by foreigners had not gone well for the Italians, particularly in inter-state wars #10 (Austro-Sardinian) and #16 (Roman Republic). Both France and Austria-Hungary maintained possessions within Italy, and both had acted to defeat the Roman Republic in 1849. Ten years later, however, the situation had changed, and French emperor Napoleon III decided to aid the king of Sardinia/Piedmont, Victor Emanuel II, in driving out the Austrians. Though the French did not favor revolution, Napoleon saw the benefits of nationalism in unifying Italy and promoting peace in Europe. Sardinian policy was directed by premier Count Camillo Benso Cavour. In 1855 he had been instrumental in bringing Sardinia into the Crimean War (inter-state war #22) in assistance

to Great Britain and France. Emperor Napoleon III met Cavour and explained that France could not provoke a war with Austria but would support Sardinia if it were attacked. Thus they planned for a revolt against Austria by the people of Massacara. When Austria responded, Sardinia and France would come to the aid of the people. Sardinia was to get the Austrian territories in Lombardy and Venetia, and France would receive the French-speaking parts of Sardinia (Savoy and Nice) in compensation. Events leading up to the war developed as planned. On April 28, 1859, the Austrian emperor Franz Joseph I announced that he had ordered his troops to attack Sardinia to defeat the forces of revolution. The Austrian advance began the following day, and the French forces joined the conflict a few days later, on May 3, 1859. The French emperor arrived in Genoa on May 12 and took command of the "Army of Italy." A major battle on May 20 at Montebello was an allied victory, and subsequent advances led to the withdrawal of Austrian forces from Sardinia. The decisive battle of Magenta was won by France and Sardinia on June 4, 1859, crushing Austria's army in Italy. By July 12, 1859, Emperors Napoleon and Franz Joseph had arranged the general terms of peace. Lombardy was ceded to Napoleon, who could pass it over to Sardinia/Piedmont. Italy would be united in a confederation under the honorary presidency of the pope. Austria would retain Venetia, and a European congress would ratify the agreement. Sardinia did pass Nice and Savoy to the French. In 1860 Modena, Parma, and Tuscany were incorporated into Sardinia/Italy, and ceased to be members of the interstate system on March 16, 1860. Sardinia/Italy, however, was not entirely happy with its dependence on France in this war, nor the agreement reached between the two emperors. Future wars (see inter-state wars #34 and 37) reflected a break with the great powers and led to further Italian unification.

Coding: In 1859, COW codes the following Italian states as system members: Sardinia/Piedmont

(#325); Papal States (#327); Two Sicilies (#329); Modena (#332); Parma (#335); and Tuscany (#337). The war was preceded by MID #115, started January 29, 1859, with Austria and Prussia as the initiators against France and Sardinia but with Sardinia as the revisionist state. Clodfelter (2002) refers to this war as the "Franco-Austrian War: 1859" but also describes it as part of the "Italian Risorgimento" of 1859–1861. Phillips and Axelrod (2005) have an "Italian War of Independence" (1859–1861).

Sources: Bodart (1916); Case (1970); Clodfelter (2002); Dumas and Vedel-Peterson (1923); King (1899); Nolan (1865); Phillips and Axelrod (2005); Richardson (1960a); Sorokin (1937); Thayer (1911); Urlanis (1960).

INTER-STATE WAR #31:
The First Spanish-Moroccan War of 1859–1860

Participants: Spain vs. Morocco
Dates: October 22, 1859, to March 25, 1860
Battle-Related Deaths: Morocco—6,000; Spain—4,000
Where Fought: Middle East
Initiator: Spain
Outcome: Spain wins

Narrative: The European powers had begun to extend their influence in northern Africa, and Spain attempted to both ensure its security and promote national glory through expansion in northern Morocco. France had engaged in a war with Morocco in 1844 (extra-state war #330). However, Morocco, which had been an autonomous entity since 1492, became a member of the interstate system in 1847; thus this war between Spain and Morocco is coded as an inter-state war. This war represents the first big step in the Spanish conquest of portions of Morocco, completed in 1926. Moroccan sultan Abd el Rahman (Abderrahmane) died in 1858 and was succeeded by his son, Sidi Mohammed XVIII. The Spanish took advantage of the transition to press for concessions in Morocco,

including the granting of a neutral zone around Ceuta and Melilla. When Morocco finally resisted, Spain attacked. The Spaniards landed at Ceuta on October 25, 1859, and Tetuan was occupied on February 4, 1860. Spain had the upper hand in capabilities and had isolated Morocco from any allied help, and thus prevailed in the conflict. Fighting was concluded by March 25, 1860. One of the terms of the peace agreement was to be the continued occupation of Tetuan by the Spanish. Thus this conflict is sometimes referred to as the Tetuan War. In the aftermath Britain intervened in defense of the territorial integrity of Morocco and was able to negotiate the Spanish evacuation of Tetuan on May 2, 1862. Colonial expansionism would continue in Morocco, which would endure an additional six wars over a twenty-year period at the beginning of the twentieth century (extra-state war #431; intra-state war #646, inter-state war #94, extra-state war #434, extra-state war #436, and extra-state war #449). By 1912 most of Morocco would be reduced to the status of a French protectorate, while three relatively small Moroccan sectors would remain under Spanish control.

Coding: The war is preceded by bilateral MID #1580, in which Spain was the initiator and revisionist. This MID started only six days before the start of the war.

Sources: Clodfelter (2002); Dumas and Vedel-Peterson (1923); Harbottle (1904); Miege (1961); Phillips and Axelrod (2005); Richardson (1948); Richardson (1960a); Schafer (1995); Sorokin (1937); Spain, Servicio Historico Militar (1947); Urlanis (1960).

INTER-STATE WAR #34:
The Italian-Roman War of 1860

Participants: Sardinia/Piedmont vs. Papal States
Dates: September 11, 1860 to September 29, 1860
Battle-Related Deaths: Papal States—700; Sardinia/Piedmont—300
Where Fought: Europe

Initiator: Sardinia/Piedmont
Outcome: Sardinia/Piedmont wins

Narrative: This war continued the process of the unification of Italy that had played a prominent role in the Austro-Sardinian War of 1848-1849 (inter-state #10), the War of the Roman Republic in 1849 (inter-state #16), and the War of Italian Unification in 1859 (inter-state #28). In the War of Italian Unification (which was less than a year before this Italian-Roman War), Sardinia had captured (with French help) much of northern Italy from Austria. Giuseppe Garibaldi had participated in this war within the army of the king of Sardinia/Piedmont. Soon thereafter, Garibaldi and his "Thousand Red Shirts" launched a private expedition against Sicily and Naples (extra-state war #352, May 11, 1860 to October 14, 1860), whereby the Two Sicilies and Naples were liberated from the rule of the Bourbon king Francis I. As Garibaldi pushed the Neapolitan forces northward, the king of Sardinia decided to use the opportunity to confront the Papal States. Prior to the War of the Roman Republic of 1849 (inter-state war #16), a republic had been established in the Papal States, but armed intervention by Austria, France, and the Two Sicilies had destroyed the republic and restored Pope Pius IX to power. The pope maintained an army, ostensibly for self-defense; however, King Victor Emmanuel II feared that the Pope's army could be used in conjunction with the armies of Austria and the Two Sicilies (Naples) against Sardinia. Victor Emmanuel's premier, Camillo Paolo Filippo Giulio Benso, Count of Cavour, favored attacking the pope, who he felt had abandoned his once-more-liberal views. As a pretext for invasion, Cavour encouraged uprisings among the pope's subjects. Initial actions began on August 28, and a general insurrection was planned for the second week of September. Cavour then warned the commander of the papal forces, French general Lamoriciere, that if they attempted to suppress the National movement, the king's troops would attack. On September 11, 1860, the Sardinian army marched against the army of the Papal States. The Sardinian army greatly outnumbered the papal forces, and the war was brief—only eighteen days—but bloody. Lamoriciere retreated to Ancona, where he was attacked by both the Sardinian army and its fleet. Lamoriciere had hoped that either Austria or France would come to the pope's aid, but with no such assistance in sight, Lamoriciere surrendered, on September 29, 1860. As a result, Sardinia occupied most of the geographic expanse of the pope's temporal domains. In late 1860 two-thirds of the Papal States voted to join the Kingdom of Sardinia; the Papal States ceased to exist as a system member as of November 11, 1860. The city of Rome remained under the jurisdiction of the pope until 1870. The success of the Sardinian army against the Papal States freed Cavour to consider his remaining problem, the situation in Naples, which would be resolved by the upcoming Neapolitan War (inter-state war #37).

Coding: In September 1860 COW codes the following Italian states as system members: Sardinia/Piedmont (#325); Papal States (#327); and Two Sicilies/Naples (#329). Our coding of the wars in Italy in 1860–1861 is determined by the characteristics of the major combatants, causing the period to encompass three distinct wars: extra-state war #352, the Garibaldi Expedition between Garibaldi's Red Shirts and Two Sicilies; inter-state war #34, the Italian-Roman War between Sardinia/Piedmont and the Papal States; and inter-state war #37, the Neapolitan War between Sardinia/Piedmont and Two Sicilies. September 7, 1860, marks the first day of MID #112, which precedes the Italian-Roman War by only four days. Sardinia is the initiator and revisionist state in this MID, opposed by France and the Papal States. Clodfelter (2002) describes the entire period of 1859–1861 as one war, the "Italian Risorgimento." Phillips and Axelrod (2005) divide this period into two wars: "Garibaldi's invasion of Sicily," and "The Italian War of Independence."

Sources: Case (1970); Clodfelter (2002); Harbottle (1904); King (1899); Nolan (1865); Phillips and Axelrod (2005); Thayer (1911).

INTER-STATE WAR # 37:
The Neapolitan War of 1860–1861

Participants: Sardinia/Piedmont vs. Two Sicilies
Dates: October 15, 1860, to February 13, 1861
Battle-Related Deaths: Sardinia/Piedmont—600;
  Two Sicilies—400
Where Fought: Europe
Initiator: Sardinia/Piedmont
Outcome: Sardinia/Piedmont wins

Narrative: This is the third in a sequence of inter-state wars from 1859 to 1861 that were won by Sardinia, leading to Italian unification (see inter-state wars #28 and #34 above). After defeating the Papal States in the Italian-Roman War (#34), the troops of Sardinia/Piedmont marched south hoping to take over the fighting against the Kingdom of Two Sicilies from Garibaldi's Red Shirts. In extra-state war #352, Garibaldi and his Red Shirts had defeated the army of Francis II, the Bourbon king of Two Sicilies/Naples. After occupying Sicily, Garibaldi had landed on the mainland and followed the Bourbon troops toward Naples. Following Naples's surrender to Garibaldi on September 7, 1860, the royal troops retreated north. King Francis's offensive to retake Naples was halted by the Garibaldian troops on October 1, 1860. The army of Two Sicilies took refuge in Capua and Gaeta, whose fortifications could withstand a siege. Meanwhile, Premier Camillo Paolo Filippo Giulio Benso, Count of Cavour, whose Sardinian army had just defeated the Papal forces in the Italian-Roman War (#34), had concluded that Garibaldi was under the influence of the revolutionary radicals and thus had to be stopped. Cavour sent the Sardinian army south from Rome to take over the fighting against the king of Two Sicilies. The Sardinian army assumed the bulk of the fighting by October 15, 1860, thus ending the extra-state war and transforming it into this inter-state war #37, the Neapolitan War between Sardinia/Piedmont and Two Sicilies. The forces of the Kingdom of

Two Sicilies made a last stand at Gaeta, a port city between Rome and Naples, in a siege lasting from November 3, 1860, to February 13, 1861. The Sardinian army and naval forces, in conjunction with the Garibaldians, attacked the city and forced its surrender. The fall of Gaeta marked the end of the reign of Francis II, and of the Kingdom of Two Sicilies, which ceased to be a COW system member as of that date. Italian nationalist forces were now in control of virtually all of Italy. Plebiscites were held in most of the former city states, and people voted overwhelmingly to be annexed by Sardinia. The Kingdom of Sardinia became Italy on May 17, 1861, and Victor Emmanuel II became king of Italy. The region of Venetia was still controlled by Austria and was ceded to Italy in only 1866, after the Austro-Prussian (or Seven Weeks) War (inter-state war #55).

Coding: In October 1860 COW codes the following Italian states as system members: Sardinia/Piedmont (#325); Papal States (#327); and Two Sicilies/Naples (#329). The Neapolitan War is preceded by MID #113, beginning September 18, 1860, in which Sardinia is the initiator and revisionist and France and the Kingdom of Two Sicilies are on the other side. Clodfelter (2002) describes the entire period of 1859–1861 as one event, the "Italian Risorgimento."

Sources: Case (1970); Clodfelter (2002); Harbottle (1904); Jaques (2007); King (1899); Nolan (1865); Thayer (1911).

INTER-STATE WAR #40:
The Franco-Mexican War of 1862–1867

Participants: Mexico vs. France
Dates: April 16, 1862, to February 5, 1867
Battle-Related Deaths: Mexico—12,000;
  France—8,000
Where Fought: W. Hemisphere
Initiator: France
Outcome: France withdraws and fighting is transformed into intra-state war #587

Narrative: Mexico gained independence from Spain in 1821 and is coded as becoming a COW state system member in 1831. It subsequently suffered through a series of wars: the First Mexican War of 1832 (intra-state war #520); the Texan War of 1835–1836 (intra-state war #527); the Mexican-American War of 1846–1848 (inter-state war #7); the Mayan Caste War Phase 1 of 1847–1848 (intra-state war #545); the Mayan Caste War Phase 2 of 1848–1855 (intra-state war #553); and the Mexican Reform War of 1858–1861 (intra-state war #561. This series of wars created severe financial difficulties for Mexico, in particular, during the Mexican Reform War. In 1857 a liberal constitution had been drafted that reduced the powers of the church and the army. Conservative opposition led to the Mexican Reform War, in which acting president Benito Juarez finally led the liberals to victory. During the war, however, Juarez's government desperately needed money for its armies and consequently confiscated church property. These monetary difficulties continued after the war, and in an attempt to provide economic relief, Juarez instituted in 1861 a two-year moratorium on the payment of foreign debts.

Meanwhile, the U.S. Civil War created a temporary situation in which the United States was not able to enforce its Monroe Doctrine, which prohibited foreign powers from colonizing or attacking the Americas. Consequently, France tried to take advantage of this situation to expand its influence in Mexico. The pretext for French involvement was the issue of Mexican debts. However several Mexican conservatives (unhappy with the policies of the liberal government) had also been able to persuade France that there was popular support in Mexico for French intervention. Napoleon III was even persuaded that he could bring good government to Mexico. Initially, France was able to convince Britain and Spain to participate in a joint military campaign to recoup their financial losses. On December 17, 1861, British, French, and Spanish forces occupied Veracruz. The British and Spanish, however,

withdrew from the operation before hostilities began once they were persuaded that the Juarez government intended to ultimately pay its debts. France, on the other hand, was still desirous of expanding its empire. Thus on April 16, 1862, the French army began its advance toward Mexico City. On May 5, the French forces were defeated at Puebla by the smaller Mexican army. The following year, after having received reinforcements from France, the French army, aided by Mexican conservatives, again attacked the Mexican army at Puebla. This time the French prevailed. The French marched into Mexico City, while the Juarez government fled to the north. In 1864 the French proceeded to install Austrian archduke Maximilian as emperor of Mexico. Fighting between the Mexican and French armies continued, as Maximilian became increasingly unpopular. With the conclusion of the U.S. Civil War, the United States was able to pay more attention to the situation in Mexico and began to demand the removal of French forces. The French began a phased withdrawal in 1866, which was completed by February 5, 1867. With the French troops gone, the inter-state war ended and an intra-state civil war began. Maximilian refused to abdicate and remained, supported by the Mexican Imperialist (conservative) army and a number of Austrian and Belgian soldiers. Fighting continued between Maximilian's troops and those of the liberal government (see intra-state war #587, Queretaro War). Unable to regain support from France, Maximilian was finally captured and executed on June 19, 1867.

Coding: The war is preceded by MID #135, beginning October 31, 1861. This is a MID initiated by England, France, and Spain, which are the revisionist side, against Mexico. Spain and England withdrew from the MID on April 8, 1862, eight days before the outbreak of the war. Scheina (2003a) treats this as the "French Intervention in Mexico," 1861–1867, and Clodfelter (2002) describes this as the "War of the French Intervention: 1862–1867." In an interesting aside, Egypt sent 500 troops as part of the French expedition, though Egypt did not qualify as a war participant.

Sources: Bodart (1916); Bock (1966); Clodfelter (2002); Dawson (1935); Dumas and Vedel-Peterson (1923); Guérard (1959); Hanna and Hanna (1971); Harbottle (1904); Niox (1874); Phillips and Axelrod (2005); Ridley (1992); Scheina (2003a).

INTER-STATE WAR #43:
The Ecuadorian-Colombian War of 1863

Participants: Colombia vs. Ecuador
Dates: November 22, 1863, to December 6, 1863
Battle-Related Deaths: Ecuador—700;
    Colombia—300
Where Fought: W. Hemisphere
Initiator: Colombia
Outcome: Colombia wins

Narrative: Both Colombia and Ecuador had been under Spanish colonial rule. After gaining independence in 1819, Colombia existed as part of Greater Colombia, which also included Panama, Venezuela, and Ecuador (after 1822). Greater Colombia soon began to disintegrate, with Ecuador and Venezuela becoming independent. One vestige of Spanish rule was the lack of clear borders between the new countries, which would lead to a number of border conflicts. The former colonies also retained societal divisions, such as tensions and conflicts between more conservative and liberal groups. For instance, after 1831, Colombia suffered two intra-state wars, the first, 1840–1842 (intra-state war #536), and the second from May 15, 1860, to July 18, 1861 (intra-state war #565). As a consequence of the latter war, a relative liberal, Tomas Cipriano de Mosquera (who opposed the power of the church), became president. Similarly, in Ecuador tensions between the conservative landowners and the more liberal business community led to a virtual collapse of government (1845–1860). However, in this case, in 1861 a conservative, Gabriel Garcia Morena, became president, and he tried to unify the country by giving enhanced power to the Catholic Church. Predictably, conflict developed between Mosquera and Garcia Moreno. In addition to persistent border disputes, Mosquera provoked Garcia Moreno by wanting to re-create Greater Colombia under Colombian leadership. Mosquera also provided aid to rebellious Ecuadorian liberals in an effort to topple Garcia Moreno. Garcia Moreno responded to these perceived threats by sending a 6,000-man army to invade Colombia on November 22, 1863. The smaller Colombian army (of 4,000) resoundingly defeated the invaders at Cuaspad on December 6, 1863. Mosquera responded by sending troops into Ecuador, though they did not encounter any resistance. The parties agreed to an armistice, ending the war on December 6, 1863. The final Treaty of Pinsaqui was signed on December 30, 1863.

Coding: Colombia was an autonomous entity since 1819 and a state system member since 1831, while Ecuador joined the interstate system in 1854. After Colombia's second intra-state civil war, when one might expect Colombia to be weakened by internal fighting, it instead initiated two bilateral MIDs against Ecuador, #1520 on June 19, 1862, then #1519 in August.

Sources: Berthe (1903); Harbottle (1904); Howe (1936); Le Gouhir y Rodas (1925); Pattee (1941); Richardson (1960a); Scheina (2003a); Spindler (1987).

INTER-STATE WAR #46:
The Second Schleswig-Holstein War of 1864

Participants: Prussia, Austria vs. Denmark
Dates: February 1, 1864, to July 20, 1864
Battle-Related Deaths: Denmark—2,933;
    Prussia—1,048; Austria—500;
Where Fought: Europe
Initiator: Prussia
Outcome: Prussia, Austria win

Narrative: This is the first of three swift wars by which the Prussian chancellor Otto von Bismarck was able to unite Germany under Prussian control (followed soon thereafter by the Seven Weeks War [inter-state war #55] and the Franco-Prussian War [inter-state war #58]). The earlier First Schleswig-Holstein War of 1848–1849 (#13) was precipitated by German-speaking residents of Schleswig and Holstein who opposed further integration into Denmark and appealed to the German Confederation for assistance. On behalf of the German Confederation, Prussia occupied the two duchies, driving out Danish forces. Great power intervention led to a peace settlement in 1850 that left the status of Schleswig and Holstein unresolved but preserved the general rights of both Denmark and Prussia. In 1863 the future of the Danish monarchy was challenged by the lack of a direct male heir. On November 15, 1863, on the death of King Frederick VII, the House of Oldenburg, which had ruled Denmark since 1448, was replaced by King Christian IX of the House of Schleswig-Holstein-Sonderburg-Glücksburg. As might be expected from the first half of this family name, the new dynasty wanted closer ties between Schleswig-Holstein and Denmark. The London Conference of 1852 had settled on King Christian in the contested succession to Schleswig and Holstein, and in 1863, Denmark's parliament annexed Schleswig (which had a significant Danish population) directly. In December 1863 the German Confederation proposed instead the complete separation of both duchies from Denmark, and a Confederation army began the occupation of Holstein. Furthermore, Prussia proposed that a German prince rule Schleswig and Holstein, and Bismarck was able to persuade Austria to join Prussia in war of the two Germanic major powers against Denmark. On February 1, 1864, German and Austrian forces began the invasion of Schleswig, driving out Danish troops. By February 18, Austria and Prussia began the invasion of Denmark itself. A major Danish garrison at Duppel was captured

on April 18. Denmark appealed for assistance, but the other signatories to the London Protocol offered merely to arbitrate the conflict. An armistice stopped the fighting for two months, April 25–June 25 (coded as a break in the war); however, when fighting resumed, the outcome of the war was a Prussian-Austrian victory. Denmark sued for peace, with the result that Prussia gained control of Schleswig and Austria gained control of Holstein. Friction over this joint management of Schleswig-Holstein would provide Bismarck with issues over which Prussia could launch the Seven Weeks War (inter-state war #55) in 1866, thereby crushing Austria and uniting Germany under Prussian control.

Coding: Schleswig was a COW autonomous entity from 1492 to 1863. Holstein was autonomous from 1492 to 1865. This war is preceded by MID #194, beginning April 17, 1863. In this MID, Denmark is alone against the United Kingdom and seven German-speaking states (two of them major powers). Although all eight of these states are coded as the initiators of the MID, Prussia is coded as the only revisionist state.

Sources: Bodart (1916); Clark (1934); Clodfelter (2002); Dumas and Vedel-Peterson (1923); Friedjung (1935); Mosse (1963); Pinson (1966); Schafer (1995); Steefel (1932); Urlanis (1960); Warming (1902); Ziegler (1997).

INTER-STATE WAR #49:
The Lopez War of 1864–1870

Participants: Brazil, Argentina vs. Paraguay
Dates: November 12, 1864, to March 1, 1870
Battle-Related Deaths: Paraguay—200,000; Brazil—100,000; Argentina—10,000
Where Fought: W. Hemisphere
Initiator: Paraguay
Outcome: Brazil, Argentina win

Narrative: In terms of battle deaths, this is the biggest war among the states of South America. Events in Uruguay, in particular, the conflict between the conservative Blancos and the more liberal Colorados, had involved a number of states in wars over the years. Uruguay did not become a member of the interstate system until 1882, thus Argentina's involvement in a conflict against Uruguay beginning in 1843 was coded as extra-state war #327, the Uruguay War. The war also involved the United Kingdom and France. After their withdrawal and the entrance of Brazil, the war was transformed into inter-state war #19 between Argentina and Brazil. This war, the La Plata War of 1851–1852, ended with the overwhelming defeat of Argentina and the Uruguayan Blancos by Brazil and the Colorados. Conflict between the Blancos and the Colorados continued, and the Lopez War was the result of Paraguayan and Brazilian intervention into that conflict, prompted by Francisco Solano Lopez, Paraguay's leader. At the time the war broke out, Paraguay and Brazil were supporting opposite sides within Uruguay. Lopez, who was desirous of incorporating Uruguay and a portion of Brazil into Paraguay, sided with the Uruguayan Blancos (who were in power at that time), while Brazil (and later Argentina) sided with the Colorados. Brazil and the Colorados signed a secret agreement of cooperation on October 20, 1864. Though the population of Paraguay was dwarfed in numbers by those of Argentina and Brazil, Paraguay had arguably the best army in South America. Lopez decided to utilize this army to begin his war of conquest against Brazil, and the war began on November 12, 1864, when a Paraguayan gunboat seized a Brazilian ship.

Paraguay was initially successful in the military excursion that followed, occupying most of the Brazilian province of Mato Grosso. Brazil began by focusing its efforts on crushing the Blancos in Uruguay and was able to capture Montevideo in February 1865. Owing to the support of Brazil, the Colorados leader Venancio Flores became the head of the Uruguayan government at that time. Meanwhile, Lopez set his sights on the Brazilian province of Rio Grande do Sul; however, the easiest way there led through Argentinean territory. Argentina's refusal to allow the Paraguayans passage led to an attack by Paraguayan forces, and Argentina thus entered the war on March 5, 1865. Paraguay was successful in seizing the Argentine port of Corrientes. Subsequently, on May 1, 1865, Brazil, Uruguay, and Argentina signed the Triple Alliance, committing themselves to the defeat of Lopez (though Uruguay is not a member of the COW interstate system at that time and thus is not a recognized war participant). The allies, Brazil and Argentina, launched a counteroffensive, retaking Corrientes on May 25. Undeterred, Lopez decided on a second offensive against Brazil and Brazilian forces in Uruguay in June 1865. Though the Paraguayans made early advances, the allies' superiority in numbers of troops soon began to take its toll. The Paraguayans suffered a major defeat at Tuyuty on May 24, 1866, having 5,000 soldiers killed in just this engagement. From then on, Paraguay conducted a defensive war. After six years of fighting against three countries, Paraguay had lost most of its adult soldiers, most of its male population, and half of its total population. The allies occupied Asuncion on January 5, 1869. Though he had fewer than 2,000 troops remaining, Lopez refused to capitulate. He was captured and killed in March 1, 1870, which finally ended the war. As a result of the war, Paraguay ceased to be an independent state, was occupied by Brazil from 1870 to 1876, and thus lost its system membership. Paraguay rejoined the interstate system in 1876 as a smaller country, having lost much of its land permanently to Brazil and Argentina. Brazil's victory came at significant costs as well and can be tied to the overthrow of the regime in 1889 and a series of intra-state civil wars (#620, #621, and #632) in the 1890s.

Coding: As of 1865, Brazil, Argentina, and Paraguay are all members of the interstate system (Brazil joining in 1826, Argentina in 1841, and Paraguay in 1846). Uruguay, however, is not a system member and does not join until 1882. The war is preceded by MID #1590, beginning in

August 1863. In this MID, Paraguay is the initiator, but Brazil and Argentina are listed as the revisionist side. Our name for this war is the name of the Paraguayan dictator who started the war and whose death ended it. Cockcroft, Raine, Warren, and Scheina call it the "War of the Triple Alliance." Clodfelter (2002), Box (1927), Levene (1937), and Calogeras (1963) call it the "Paraguayan War." Fatality figures for this war are unreliable and vary widely. Frequently, fatalities have been determined by comparing population data from before and after the war. Fatalities include not only combat deaths but also a significant number of deaths of military personnel from epidemics. Clodfelter (2002) notes that Uruguay also suffered heavy casualties, though Uruguay is a nonstate participant under COW coding.

Sources: *Almanach de Gotha* (1865); Best (1960, vol. 2); Box (1927); Calogeras (1963); Clodfelter (2002); Cockcroft (1989); Kolinski (1965); Levene (1937); Phillips and Axelrod (2005); Raine (1956); Scheina (2003a); Warren (1949).

INTER-STATE WAR #52:
The Naval War of 1865–1866

Participants: Peru, Chile vs. Spain
Dates: September 25, 1865, to May 9, 1866
Battle-Related Deaths: Peru—600; Spain—300; Chile—100
Where Fought: W. Hemisphere
Initiator: Spain
Outcome: Peru, Chile win

Narrative: In 1864 Spain and Peru had a conflictual relationship. In 1824 Simón Bolívar had assured Peru's independence by defeating Spain; however, Spain had not recognized the independence of Peru and saw its cessation of hostilities against Peru as merely a truce. Thus Spain tended to see Peru as colony over which it needed to reassert control. Since becoming independent, Peru had experienced some civil unrest, including two civil wars (intra-state war #557 in 1853–1855 and #560 in 1856–1858). Consequently, Peru did not have extensive monetary reserves and thus had not paid Spain some of the moneys due from the colonial period. Spain had built up one of the world's top navies and was intent on reestablishing some of its global preeminence. Thus in 1863 it sent part of its fleet to the western coast of South America, ostensibly to conduct scientific observations. In the company of the fleet was a "commissary" sent to discuss financial matters with Peru. Since a commissary was seen as a colonial official, Peru refused to meet with him because he lacked the appropriate diplomatic rank to negotiate with a sovereign state. The commissary moved the Spanish fleet to the guano-rich islands of Chincha and seized them on April 14, 1864, in the name of Spain. Peru's president did try to negotiate with the admiral of the fleet, but his willingness to do so angered the populace, who then overthrew him in order to install a leader willing to confront Spain. Meanwhile, popular opinion in Chile was concerned about Spanish imperialist intentions. When the Spanish fleet arrived in Valparaiso on September 24, the admiral issued an ultimatum and ultimately announced a blockade of Chilean ports. The Chileans responded on September 25, 1865, with a declaration of war, and in November, Chile captured a Spanish ship. In December Chile entered into an alliance with Peru, and on January 14, 1866, Peru declared war on Spain. A similar treaty was signed by Chile and Ecuador on January 30, and on February 27, Ecuador declared war on Spain as well. In March an alliance was made joining Bolivia to the three allies (forming the Quadruple Alliance). Though neither Ecuador nor Bolivia provided military assistance to the allies, they did close their ports to the Spanish fleet. A naval battle took place among ships from Spain, Chile, and Peru, causing significant Spanish casualties on February 7. On March 31, 1866, the Spanish fleet bombed Valparaiso, Chile; and Callao, Peru, on April 27, 1866. On May 9, 1866, the Spanish fleet ceased hostilities, thus ending the war as a victory for Chile and Peru. In 1879, however, the Pacific littoral powers of South America would resume the fight among themselves in the War of the Pacific (inter-state war #64, 1879–1883).

Coding: Peru is coded as joining the interstate system in 1839. The war is preceded by MID #1482, of all the coastal regional states (Ecuador, Peru, Bolivia, and Chile) against Spain, with Spain as the initiator and revisionist. The nomenclature on this war is varied. Scheina, perhaps enjoying the oxymoron, calls it the "Pacific War," 1865–1866. Clodfelter (2002) calls it "Naval War with Spain: 1865–66." Phillips and Axelrod (2005) call it the "Spanish-Peruvian War" of 1866. www.onwar.com calls it the "Spain Peru Chincha War" of 1864–1866. Clodfelter (2002) cites both Bolivia and Ecuador as war participants, and they were part of the MID; however, they did not engage Spanish forces sufficiently to be considered war participants.

Sources: Clodfelter (2002); Cockcroft (1971); Davis (1950); Dellepiane (1943); Encina (1950); Galdames (1941); Galvez (1919); Markham (1892); Phillips and Axelrod (2005); Richardson (1960a); Scheina (2003a).

INTER-STATE WAR #55:
The Seven Weeks War of 1866

Participants: Mecklenburg-Schwerin, Italy, Prussia vs. Baden, Austria, Hesse Grand Ducal, Hesse Electoral, Saxony, Bavaria, Hanover, Württemberg
Dates: June 15, 1866, to July 26, 1866
Battle-Related Deaths: Austria—28,000; Prussia—10,000; Italy—4,000; Saxony—600; Hanover—500; Bavaria—500; Baden—100; Württemburg—100; Hesse Electoral—100; Hesse Grand Ducal—100; Mecklenburg-Schwerin—100
Where Fought: Europe
Initiator: Prussia
Outcome: Mecklenburg-Schwerin, Italy, Prussia win

Narrative: The Seven Weeks War is the second in a series of three short, victorious wars by which Prussian chancellor Otto von Bismarck unified Germany under Prussian domination (also including the Second Schleswig-Holstein War, inter-state war #46, and the Franco-Prussian War, inter-state war #58). Austria had traditionally been considered the leader of the Germanic states of Europe through the Holy Roman Empire. At the beginning of the nineteenth century, the Holy Roman Empire ceased to exist but was in essence replaced by the German Confederation, a loose mutual defense union of 39 Germanic states, also under Austrian leadership. As Prussia became increasingly powerful, however, Prussian chancellor Otto von Bismarck envisioned a smaller German confederation, one that excluded Austria and would be under Prussian leadership instead. The stage for the Seven Weeks War was set at the conclusion of the Second Schleswig-Holstein War of 1864 (inter-state war #46). The results of the war were ambiguous in that Prussia and Austria were to jointly administer the territories taken from Denmark, with Prussia dominant in Schleswig and Austria controlling Holstein. Ultimately, Bismarck was determined that Prussia should gain control of both duchies as a prelude to German unification under Prussian leadership. Thus he developed a plan for a confrontation with Austria.

One of Bismarck's strengths was in diplomatic maneuvering, and he wanted to ensure both that Prussia would have an ally in the upcoming war and that the other major powers (particularly France) would not intervene. In discussions with Napoleon in October 1865, Bismarck was assured that French-Austrian cooperation was unlikely. Napoleon also facilitated an alliance between Italy and Prussia. The alliance (the cost of which was a guarantee of Venetia for Italy) would mean that Austria would have to fight a two-front war (from the north and the south). Austria became convinced that war was inevitable and began to mobilize its forces. Bismarck then precipitated the conflict by proposing an alteration in the structure of the German Confederation. Most of the smaller German states sided with Austria (Hanover, Bavaria, Baden, Saxony, Württemberg, Hesse

Electoral, and Hesse Grand Ducal were war participants on Austria's side), while Mecklenburg-Schwerin fought alongside Prussia and Italy. Prussia sent troops into Holstein on June 14 and declared war against Hanover, Saxony, and Hesse on June 15, which marks the start of the war. Austria declared war on June 17, followed by Prussia (against Austria) on the 18th and Italy on the 20th. Austria's allies Hanover, Hesse, Bavaria, and Saxony were overrun, and Prussia advanced into the Hapsburg province of Bohemia. The Prussians encircled Austria's North Army, while Italy attempted the same with the Austrian South Army in Venetia. The Italians did suffer a defeat at Custoza; however, Austria was caught between two pincers. The major Prussian forces advanced on Koniggratz (or Sadowa), where the Prussians defeated the Austrian army on July 3. Clodfelter (2002) describes Sadowa as the biggest battle on earth from Waterloo until the twentieth century in terms of fatalities and the troops engaged. Though the overall war was short, it involved over a million men in combat. Austria surrendered, and the preliminary peace agreement was signed on July 26 (marking the end of the war). The final treaty, the Treaty of Prague, was signed on August 23, 1866. Two important outcomes of the Seven Weeks War were that Austria was to withdraw from German affairs and was forced to cede Venetia to Italy. Austria renounced all rights to Schleswig and Holstein and agreed to the dissolution of the German Confederation, which was replaced in 1867 by the new North German Confederation under Prussian leadership. As a result, a number of the German states ceased to be system members at that point: Saxony, Hesse Grand Ducal, and Mecklenburg-Schwerin on April 17, 1867, and Hesse Electoral on July 26, 1866. The Seven Weeks War was followed by the Franco-Prussian War (inter-state war #58), which completed German unification. Though the people of Holstein were overwhelmingly German, Schleswig had significant Danish and German populations. After World War I, plebiscites were conducted in Schleswig, which resulted in localities being able to rejoin Denmark.

Coding: The Seven Weeks War is preceded by MID #261, starting March 19, 1866, and involving eleven states. Prussia is listed as the only revisionist state. Saxony is the initiator of the MID, with Bavaria joining it first, then Austria, then Hanover, then the two Hesses, Württemberg, and Baden. The target side in the MID consists of Prussia, Mecklenburg, and Italy. The Seven Weeks War is also known as the Austro-Prussian War, the German Civil War, the Deutscher Krieg (the German War), or the Bruderkrieg (War of the Brothers) because it pitted the two major German powers, Prussia and Austria, against each other. It is also referred to as the Unification War because it leads to the creation of Germany through combining the smaller German states under Prussian leadership.

Sources: Albrecht-Carrié (1958); Bodart (1916); Clark (1934); Clodfelter (2002); Dumas and Vedel-Peterson (1923); Friedjung (1935); Gade and Jones (1997); Hozier (1867); Malet (1870); Phillips and Axelrod (2005); Pinson (1966); Urlanis (1960).

INTER-STATE WAR #58:

The Franco-Prussian War of 1870–1871

Participants: Prussia, Baden, Württemberg, Bavaria vs. France
Dates: July 19, 1870, to February 26, 1871
Battle-Related Deaths: France—152,000; Prussia—44,781; Bavaria—5,600; Württemburg—976; Baden—956
Where Fought: Europe
Initiator: France
Outcome: Prussia, Baden, Württemberg, Bavaria win

Narrative: The Franco-Prussian War was the war that completed Prussian chancellor Otto von Bismarck's unification of Germany. However, the underlying reason for the war was the

French desire to expand its influence and territory in response to the increase in Prussia's power that resulted from the Seven Weeks War of 1866 (inter-state war #55). French policy was in the hands of Emperor Napoleon III. Napoleon's plan was to balance the power of Prussia and Austria in Central Europe by encouraging a bloc among the South German states, over which France might exert influence. After Austria's defeat in the Seven Weeks War and the dissolution of the German Confederation, a new North German Confederation was created in 1867 under the leadership of Prussia. Prussian chancellor Otto von Bismarck had plans for the South German states as well, hoping to utilize their anti-French sentiments to encourage them to join Germany. Napoleon began his plans for expansion by attempting to purchase the duchy of Luxembourg, which was ruled by Holland. Napoleon's plan did not succeed, though he ultimately accepted the withdrawal of a Prussian garrison there and the neutralization of Luxembourg by the great powers. The next clash between French and Prussian goals concerned Spain. There had been a revolution in Spain in 1868 (intra-state war #591), whereby Queen Isabella had been deposed. Since Spain wanted to retain the monarchy, it began to search for a suitable royal replacement. Spain offered the crown to Prussian prince Leopold of Hohenzollern-Sigmaringen, an option Otto von Bismarck supported. The French were, however, diametrically opposed, and the proposal was withdrawn. Some have claimed that the Spanish incident was created by Bismarck as a planned trigger for the war with France that he desired. Lord Acton of Britain wrote at the time (Pinson 1966, 144) that he had it on good authority that "Bismarck arranged the Hohenzollern affair in order to bring on war."

It was actually France, however, that, in response to the inflammatory Ems telegram released by Bismarck (which supposedly was insulting), declared war on Prussia on July 19, 1870. The South German states (Bavaria, Baden, and Württemberg), in fulfillment of their secret treaties with Prussia, then joined Prussia's King Wilhelm (later Kaiser Wilhelm of the united Germany) in common front against France. The French army was outnumbered by that of Prussia, and France was not able to match the military organization and leadership of the Prussian count Helmuth von Moltke. The forces of Prussia and its allies were organized into three large armies, while the French loosely structured their initial eight armies into two, the Army of Alsace (the southernmost) and the Army of Lorraine (in the north). The Army of Alsace attacked eastward, meeting the Prussians near Saarbrücken on August 2, 1870. After fierce battles, the French were driven back westward to Metz. The French army in the north also faced Prussian attacks and retreated toward Chalons-sur-Marne. When the army tried to relieve the forces at Metz, it was trapped by the Prussians at Sedan on August 31. There, on September 2, Napoleon III surrendered himself and half of the French army. As a result, Napoleon was deposed and the Third French Republic was proclaimed. Negotiations between the new French government and the Prussians broke down over Prussian demands for Alsace and Lorraine, and the French continued to fight. The siege of Metz lasted for fifty-four days before the French surrendered. Meanwhile, the Prussians advanced to Paris. There the Prussian siege caused severe deprivation and destruction, which contributed several months later to the conflagration of the Paris Commune (intra-state war #596). The French army was also besieged at the fortress of Belfort, near the border with Switzerland, but it held on, even after Paris surrendered on January 28, 1871. Meawhile, adding insult to injury, on January 18, 1871, in the Hall of Mirrors at Versailles, the Prussian king was proclaimed the German emperor (kaiser). By the Treaty of Frankfurt, signed on May 10, 1871, France had ceded all of Alsace and part of Lorraine to Germany and was forced to pay huge reparations (terms of which became the source of future conflict). The Franco-Prussian War was one of the most significant wars in Europe: it marked the end of French domination of central Europe, and it led to the creation of a united Germany. The war also decisively ended the long peace in which there had been very few inter-state wars in Europe since the Congress of Vienna in 1816. Paradoxically, it is also followed by over forty years of peace between France and Germany, a peace that ended cataclysmically with the First World War in 1914.

Coding: Bavaria, Baden, and Württemberg began the war as independent states; however, they became part of the emerging German Empire by late 1870 and consequently ceased being independent belligerents as of November 15, 1870, November 22, 1870, and November 25, 1870, respectively. Clodfelter (2002) includes Hesse and Saxony as war participants. However, after the Seven Weeks War (inter-state war #55), Bavaria, Baden, and Württemberg entered the North German Confederation, and thus ceased to be COW independent system members. The fatalities suffered by their troops are included with those of Prussia. The bloody fighting concerning the Paris Commune was not included here because of its civil war nature (it is included as intra-state war #596). The Franco-Prussian War is preceded by MID #88, in which Prussia is the sole revisionist state. The MID, however, was initiated by France, which was joined by Baden, Bavaria, and Württemberg. Although the MID and war were initiated by Napoleon III of France, who was hardly an innocent party, it is also clear that Bismarck was working tirelessly to create a diplomatic and political situation in which France would initiate a war he could win.

Sources: Albrecht-Carrie (1958); Bodart (1916); Clodfelter (2002); Dumas and Vedel-Peterson (1923); Echard (1985); France, Ministry of Foreign Affairs (1915); Howard (1962); Keller (1934); Kohn (1999); Lord (1966); Phillips and Axelrod (2005); Pinson (1966); Sorokin (1937); Urlanis (1960); von Moltke (1992).

INTER-STATE WAR #60:

The First Central American War of 1876

Participants: Guatemala vs. El Salvador
Dates: March 27, 1876, to April 25, 1876
Battle-Related Deaths: Guatemala—2,000; El Salvador—2,000
Where Fought: W. Hemisphere
Initiator: Guatemala
Outcome: Guatemala wins

Narrative: This war is one of twenty "Mini-Wars among Caudillos of Central America, 1844–1907" identified by Scheina. These conflicts tended to be class-based ideological conflicts between liberals and conservatives; however, political developments were complicated by the fact that the ideological interests were often trumped by power grabs by one of the caudillos on behalf of his own more narrow patron-client group. The ideological conflicts could also cross state boundaries, leading to inter-state wars, as in this case. After having been part of the Spanish Empire and then the Mexican Empire, the Central American Confederation (or the Union of Central America) was created in 1823, consisting of Guatemala, El Salvador, Honduras, Nicaragua, and Costa Rica. Though the Central American liberals had hoped that the Confederation would evolve into a stable democracy, this goal was opposed by the conservatives, who were frequently wealthy landowners allied with the Catholic Church. The federation was finally torn apart by internal strife in 1839–1840 (non-state war #1528). Attempts to revive the confederation were made in 1842 and 1852 though they were short-lived. The former members then evolved as independent states and ultimately became members of the COW interstate system.

One of the leaders of the revolt against the federation was Rafael Carrera, a conservative who dominated Guatemalan politics until 1865. Guatemala's "Liberal Revolution" came in 1871, led by Justo Rufino Barrios. However, the success of the liberal project in Guatemala was affected by events in El Salvador and Honduras. The Liberal party had also come to power in El Salvador in 1871. Both Guatemala and El Salvador faced conservative and clerical opposition, which was assisted by the conservative regime in Honduras. Thus in 1872, Guatemala and El Salvador declared war on Gen. Jose Maria Medina, the president of Honduras. Though the conflict was short-lived and did not reach war-level fatalities, it was successful in putting a liberal regime in power in Honduras. The three governments then entered into an alliance to maintain the liberal regimes. The ideological conflict again assumed prominence in 1876, when General Medina returned to Honduras and was attempting to overthrow the liberal government. El Salvador proposed a conference with Guatemala at Chingo, where, on February 15, 1876, they agreed to aid the liberals in Honduras. However, following change in the government in El Salvador, instead of fulfilling the Chingo agreement, El Salvador appeared to be preparing for war with Guatemala, its erstwhile ally. On March 20, 1876, diplomatic relations between the two countries were broken, and on March 27, Guatemala declared war on El Salvador. Barrios and his forces crossed into El Salvador on April 1. The Guatemalan troops prevailed against the Salvadorans, and on April 25, El Salvador sued for peace, thus ending the war. Barrios then established a supportive government in El Salvador, and the two governments signed a treaty of friendship.

Coding: Guatemala joins the interstate system in 1868 and El Salvador in 1875. Though Honduras is also a party to this conflict, since it does not become a system member until 1899, it is not coded as a state war participant. This particular war of 1876 is preceded by MID #1533, a bilateral MID between Guatemala and El Salvador, with Guatemala the initiator and revisionist, beginning in February 1876. Clodfelter (2002) calls this the "Central American War" of 1876. Scheina (2003a) has two miniwars during 1876, designated as

"Liberal Guatemalans Defeat Conservative Hondurans, 1876" followed by "Liberal Guatemalans and Honduras Defeat Liberal Salvadorians, 1876."

Sources: Burgess (1926); Clodfelter (2002); Flemion (1972); Scheina (2003a).

INTER-STATE WAR #61:
The Second Russo-Turkish War of 1877–1878

Participants: Russia vs. Ottoman Empire
Dates: April 24, 1877, to January 31, 1878
Battle-Related Deaths: Ottoman Empire—165,000; Russia—120,000
Where Fought: Europe, Middle East
Initiator: Russia
Outcome: Russia wins

Narrative: This war is the last of three wars that confronted the Ottoman Empire in the Balkans between 1875 and 1878. The conflict began as an intra-state civil war (#601 the Bosnia and Bulgaria Revolt); however, it soon came to involve outside powers and was transformed into the Serbian-Turkish War of 1876-1877(extra-state war #373). The conflict was finally transformed into this inter-state war due to the intervention of Russia. Russia and the Ottoman Empire had long been rivals for influence in the Balkans, and this war reflected Russian support for the Balkan states in their struggles against the Ottomans. The overall conflict had begun with the revolt of Bosnia and Hercegovina against the Ottoman Empire, partially due to the persecution against Christians that occurred in the Ottoman Empire. The fundamental nature of the war changed in June 1876, when Serbia and then Montenegro declared war against the Ottomans. Serbia and Montenegro (unlike Bosnia and Hercegovina) were autonomous entities (not integrated into the Ottoman Empire). Thus when Serbia took over the bulk of the fighting from Bosnia and Hercegovina, the war became an extra-state war between a system member and a nonstate actor outside its borders (#373, the Serbian-Turkish War). Prior to the declaration of war, Serbia had sought Austrian and Russian assistance in the case of war, but assurances were not forthcoming; however, Russia did try to reach an understanding with Austria concerning protecting the Christian populations in the Balkans. The Austro-Russian negotiations continued until January 15, 1877, when two secret agreements were signed, one of which contained an Austrian promise of benevolent neutrality should Russia go to war with the Ottoman Empire. As a consequence, Russia would be permitted to occupy Bulgaria and Austria could occupy Bosnia and Hercegovina.

As of November 1876, Russia had already begun to mobilize its military, and in March, Romania did as well. On April 16, 1877, Russia and Romania signed a convention to allow the passage of Russian troops through Romanian territory on the way to Bulgaria. Russia declared war on April 24, 1877. Since Serbia had already been defeated, Russia immediately took over the bulk of the fighting in the war. This means that the war was no longer an extra-state war but had become an inter-state war between two members of the interstate system (though Russia is also aided by Romania, which is an autonomous, nonstate actor). The war was conducted on two fronts—in the Balkans, particularly along the Danube, and in the Transcaucasus, though the European front was more important. Although the Russian campaign in the Caucasus went smoothly, the campaign in the Balkans proved unexpectedly bloody and difficult. The Ottomans began their offensive by attacking Romanian cities along the Danube, and by April 26 the Romanian artillery had begun bombing the Ottoman garrison of Vidin on the Bulgarian shore of the Danube. On May 9, Bulgaria proclaimed independence, followed by Romania on May 21. For Russia the initial months of the war mostly involved military preparations to cross the Danube and invade Bulgaria. The first major

Russian assault began on July 20, though the Russian advance was halted at Plevna. The Russians made a second assault ten days later and a third attack on September 11. Even after the three assaults, the Russian troops had not succeeded in conquering the Plevna fortifications, so they decided to surround it in a lengthy siege. The delay at Plevna made the Russians more eager to accept the help of the smaller Balkan states, and Romania contributed to the capture of Plevna on November 30, 1877. By the end of the war, Russia occupied all of the Ottoman Balkans except the peninsula of Gallipoli and immediate vicinity of Constantinople. Overall, hostilities were terminated by the armistice of January 31, 1878, and the subsequent Treaty of San Stefano (February 19).

Phillips and Axelrod (2005) list seven Russo-Turkish Wars within a 200-year period (1678–1878). This litany of bilateral clashes does not count the multilateral wars, such as the Crimean War and World War I, in which the Russians fought the Turks as part of a larger war. Considering only the bilateral Russo-Turkish wars, Clodfelter (2002, 219) judged the 1877–1878 war to be the biggest. The Ottoman Empire was clearly in near-terminal decline, and immediately after the war its periphery was carved up. By the Treaty of Berlin in 1878, the eastern shores of the Black Sea, south of the Caucasus (regions then known as Kars and Batum), were transferred from the Ottoman Empire to Russia. In addition to the victorious Russians, many other states joined in the division of Ottoman domains. The Serbs and Romanians attained national independence. Bulgaria (although temporarily split into three parts) gained autonomy.

Coding: The coding of this war and its transformation from an intra-state war to an extra-state war and then an inter-state war was determined by changes in which parties were doing the bulk of the fighting and the status of these war participants. In 1875 Serbia, Bulgaria, Bosnia, Hercegovina, Romania, and Montenegro were not members of the interstate system;

however, their status differed. Bulgaria, Bosnia, and Hercegovina were integrated parts of the Ottoman Empire, thus conflict between any of these three against the Ottoman Empire was coded as a civil or intra-state war. Though Serbia and Montenegro had been parts of the Ottoman Empire, by 1817 they were independent autonomous entities, as was Romania after 1860. Thus the war of Serbia and Montenegro against the Ottoman Empire was coded as an extra-state war between a system member and a nonstate actor. After Serbia was defeated and Russia intervened in the war and took over the bulk of the fighting, the war then became an inter-state war between two system members. Hentea refers to the Romanian participation in this war as the "Romanian War of Independence." This war is preceded by MID #187 (beginning October 31, 1876), in which Russia is the initiator and revisionist state.

Sources: Allen and Muratoff (1953); Clodfelter (2002); Dumas and Vedel-Peterson (1923); Finkel (2005); Florinsky (1953); Hentea (2007); Hozier (1878); Palmer (1964); Phillips and Axelrod (2005); Richardson (1960a); Schafer (1995); Seton-Watson (1952); Sumner (1937); von Sax (1913); von Sternegg (1866–1899).

INTER-STATE WAR #64:
The War of the Pacific of 1879–1883

Participants: Chile vs. Peru, Bolivia
Dates: February 14, 1879, to December 11, 1883
Battle-Related Deaths: Peru—9,672; Chile—3,276; Bolivia—920
Where Fought: W. Hemisphere
Initiator: Chile
Outcome: Chile wins

Narrative: The area where Chile, Peru, and Bolivia come together is a sparsely populated, arid region, but it became economically important in the late nineteenth century with the enhanced commercial interest in mining nitrates, useful in fertilizer and other applications. Bolivia had won its independence from the Spanish

through the efforts of Simón Bolívar. Bolivia and Peru were later united in a Bolivia-Peru Confederation from 1836 to 1839, the dissolution of which led to the Peru-Bolivian War of 1841 (extra-state war #325). The two countries subsequently entered into a defensive alliance in 1873. Conflict between the two allies later surfaced regarding the mineral-rich Atacama region, a province of Bolivia, which Chile had started exploiting for its mineral wealth, sending settlers into the region. Bolivia had given a Chilean company the rights to extract the nitrate-rich deposits, but Chile then began to make territorial claims in an attempt to alter the territorial boundaries that had been established in 1810 and to annex the area. In response, Bolivia's president, Hilarion Daza, rescinded the Chilean contract in February 1879. Chile initiated war against Bolivia on February 14, 1879, by occupying Antofagasta. Peru offered to mediate the conflict, but Chile alleged grievances against Peru as well, accusing Peru of establishing interests in Peru's portion of the desert that harmed the Chilean company. Thus Chile declared war on Peru as well, on April 5, 1879.

The first real engagements of the war were naval battles, partially because Chile felt that the Peruvian navy stood no chance against Chile's new ironclad ships. Although the Peruvian navy was outgunned, it was able to delay the Chilean land invasion for six months. In a naval battle on May 21, 1879, Peru lost its ironclad ship the *Independencia*. During summer 1879 the Peruvian ship the *Huascar* protected the Peruvian coast and harassed the Chilean navy; however, on October 8, 1879, the refitted Chilean ironclads engaged the *Huascar* and forced it to surrender. Chile then controlled the seacoast, and preparations could be made for the land invasion. A joint Peruvian and Bolivian army stationed at Pisagua was defeated on November 2, 1879, and was driven inland toward Tarapaca, where it successfully stopped the Chilean advance. In 1880 the Chileans blockaded the ports of Arica and Callao (near Lima). In attacks around Tacna in May and June 1880, the Chileans were able to conquer the coveted nitrate region. The decisive battle of the war began at Callao and then led to a march against Lima. The Chilean forces landed on December 22, 1880, and reached the first line of defense around Lima on January 23, 1881. In fierce fighting, the Chileans captured Lima on January 17, 1881. The Peruvians established a new seat of government at Arequipa, where its congress met in March 1883. Meanwhile, the Chileans conducted raids throughout the country against small Peruvian forces, some of which were under the command of Col. Miguel Iglesias. Disregarding the congress at Arequipa, Iglesias agreed to surrender his forces and signed a Treaty of Ancon with the Chileans on October 23, 1883 (ending Peru's participation in the war). Iglesias then declared himself president and entered Lima on October 25. Fighting between Chile and Bolivia ceased on December 11, 1883, though an armistice was not signed until April 1884 in Valparaiso, and the final peace treaty was not signed until 1904. The war resulted in significant changes in the borders of all three parties. Before the war Bolivia had access to the sea, Peru had a longer coastline by 200 miles, and Chile was limited to the regions south of the tropics. By the end of the war Bolivia was landlocked and Peru had lost much of its southern extent (the provinces of Tacna and Arica) while Chile had gained a few hundred miles of coastline. The ultimate status of Tacna and Arica was supposed to have been resolved in a plebiscite, which never occurred. In 1929, however, mediation sponsored by the United States allowed Peru to regain Tacna province while Chile retained Arica.

Coding: The war is preceded by MID #1518, initiated by Chile against Bolivia on November 8, 1878. Chile initiated the war against Bolivia on February 14, 1879, and Peru joined the MID on the Bolivian side the following day. In an unusual coding, all three parties are coded as revisionists, indicating that all hoped to improve their position by resort to force. Clodfelter (2002) and Phillips and Axelrod (2005) generally agree with our treatment, but they end the war in 1884, when Chile and Bolivia concluded their treaty, ceding the Bolivian coast to Chile. (Our ending year marks the end of the fighting as well as the Chilean-Peruvian Treaty, since these events both date to 1883.)

Sources: Clodfelter (2002); *Columbia Encyclopedia* (1993); Dellepiane (1943); Dumas and Vedel-Peterson (1923); Galdames (1941); Markham (1892); Moriarity (2005); Palmer (1957); Phillips and Axelrod (2005); Richardson (1960a); Sater (1986); Scheina (2003a); U.S. Department of State (early 1900s); Welch (1978).

INTER-STATE WAR #65:

The Conquest of Egypt of 1882

Participants: United Kingdom vs. Egypt
Dates: July 11, 1882, to September 15, 1882
Battle-Related Deaths: Egypt—10,000; United Kingdom—79
Where Fought: Middle East
Initiator: United Kingdom
Outcome: United Kingdom wins

Narrative: This war marked the beginning of Egypt's tenure as a British colony. Throughout the modern era, Egypt had been only marginally independent, and more often colonized. Independent from 1492 to 1517, Egypt was made part of the Ottoman Empire in 1517. A brief period of French military occupation, 1798–1801, under Napoleon weakened the Ottoman grip but did not change Egypt's status. Egyptian forces fought on the side of the Ottomans in extra-state war #301 in the Hejaz in 1816 and in the First Russo-Turkish War of 1828–1829 (inter-state war #4). Egypt gradually began to assert its independence, engaging in regional intra-state wars (#516 in 1831, #521 in 1834, #532 in 1837, and #535 in 1840). Egypt also began to directly challenge Ottoman rule, fighting against the Turks in intra-state wars #518 in 1831, #533 in 1839, and #537 in 1840. By 1855, Egypt had become independent and thus a member of the interstate system. Even so, up to 1882, the Ottomans continued to claim that Egypt was still a part of the Ottoman Empire; however, the Ottomans had been crushed in the 1877–1878 Second Russo-Turkish War (inter-state war #61) and were in no position to defend their tenuous claim to Egypt.

In 1869 the French built the Suez Canal, considerably enhancing Egypt's strategic and economic importance. This was particularly true for Britain, since the canal served as a link between Britain and its largest colony, India. Many in Egypt, however, resented the foreign control of the canal and foreign influence in Egypt in general. As the crisis unfolded, Egyptian khedive Ismail was forced to abdicate by the Europeans, and his son, Tewfik, became khedive in 1879. The minister of war, Colonel Arabi, was instrumental in galvanizing Egyptian nationalists opposed to both European influence and Tewfik, whom they saw as a tool of the Europeans. The concern that supposedly prompted the British to act was the claim that Christians were being massacred on a regular basis in Egypt. For instance, Europeans in Alexandria, attacked by rioters, had to flee to sanctuary aboard French and English ships in the harbor. Critics have argued instead that it was the Europeans themselves who deliberately tried to create a situation of anarchy as a pretext for further intervention. In June 1882 batteries were being constructed in Alexandria that could be used to attack the British fleet stationed there. On July 9 the British admiral sent an ultimatum to Tewfik demanding that the forts be surrendered to him. Although the khedive offered to dismount several guns at the forts, this reply was insufficient for the British, who initiated the bombardment of the Alexandria forts on July 11, 1882, beginning the war. The Egyptian troops evacuated Alexandria, which was severely damaged by fire and looters. On July 13 the British started landing troops in Alexandria and took control of the city. Khedive Tewfik placed himself under the protection of the British, who then encouraged the khedive to brand Arabi a rebel. In response, Arabi claimed that the khedive had defected to the enemy and thus was no longer able to represent Egypt. Britain appealed to both the Ottoman Empire and Italy for assistance. Italy refused, though the Ottomans did agree to send 5,000 troops (which did not participate in the war). The British government also decided to send another 20,000 troops to the region. Arabi withdrew his army to the southeast, establishing a base at Kafr Dewar. In August the British sent an expeditionary force to the Suez Canal to attack Arabi's force from the rear. Once the British disembarked, the outcome of the conflict was determined because the Egyptians were badly outnumbered. In brief but bloody fighting on September 13, the Egyptian army was destroyed. Arabi fled to Cairo, where he considered making another stand. Instead he surrendered, and on September 15, 1882, the British took control of Egypt. Egypt ceased to be an interstate system member as of this date. Egypt remained a colony of the United Kingdom until 1914, after which COW classifies it a protectorate until 1922. Only then did it again become an autonomous entity. Egypt does not become a full member of interstate system again until May 26, 1937.

Coding: A series of events triggered this war, which is preceded by MID #3725, starting one week before the onset of the war. In this MID, France and Britain are the initiators and revisionists against Egypt; France, however, refused to join Britain in the war. Clodfelter (2002) calls this the "Egyptian Revolt of 1882." Phillips and Axelrod (2005) do not include it; they do include an "Egyptian Revolt," but it is against the Romans in ancient times.

Sources: Blunt (1967); Clodfelter (2002); Finkel (2005); Goldschmidt (1988); Lenczowski (1980); Mansfield (1971); Palmer (1964); Perry (2004); Phillips and Axelrod (2005); Schafer (1995); Vatikiotis (1980).

INTER-STATE WAR #67:
The Sino-French War of 1884–1885

Participants: France vs. China
Dates: June 15, 1884, to June 19, 1885
Battle-Related Deaths: China—10,000; France—2,100
Where Fought: Asia
Initiator: France
Outcome: France wins

Narrative: France had begun its conquest of Indochina in 1858 in southern Vietnam (see extra-state war #349, First Franco-Vietnamese). In 1873 France tried to spread its influence northward by attacking Tonkin in northern Vietnam (see extra-state war #369). Vietnam was technically independent, though it had strong ties to China. From 1882 to 1884 the French waged an imperial war against the Annamese (in central Vietnam) and the Chinese-supported Black Flag guerrillas of Tonkin (see extra-state war #385). Though the king of Annam had requested direct Chinese assistance, it did not arrive. After French victories at Hanoi in April 1883 and Hue in August 1883, the king sued for peace and signed the Treaty of Hue, by which the French protectorate was established. The agreement did not, however, end the fighting between the French and the Black Flag. China became concerned about the growing French influence along its southern border and began negotiations with the French. Meanwhile, China began to send its troops into Tonkin. On May 11 and June 9, 1884, China acknowledged the terms of the Hue Treaty; however, this temporary agreement between France and China broke down, leading to full-scale war. The conflict was thus transformed from an extra-state war into this inter-state war because China took over the bulk of the fighting.

The inter-state war began on June 15, 1884. In the first major battle, the French were defeated by Chinese forces at Bac Le on June 23, 1884. The fighting also spread to China itself. Adm.

Sébastien-Nicolas-Joachim Lespès utilized two ships to attack the port of Chilung (Keelung) on northern Taiwan and to establish a blockade. French admiral Anatole-Amédée-Prosper Courbet assembled a fleet and attacked the Chinese harbor of Foochow (Fuzhou), on the Chinese coast near Taiwan. There the French destroyed the Chinese fleet in the harbor and bombed the city, causing great destruction. The attack led to the official declaration of war by China on August 27, 1884. The French were having less success in fighting in Tonkin and along the Chinese border, where the French confronted both the Chinese and the Black Flag guerrillas. A large Chinese force laid siege to the French at Tuyen Quang from January 23 to March 3, 1885. The French captured Lang Son on February 13, 1885, but suffered a major defeat at Bang Bo on March 24, 1885, causing a French retreat. The French then sued for peace, and the war was concluded on June 9, 1885, with the Treaty of Tientsin, which restored the status quo ante. The French were victorious, however, in that China was obliged to accept a French protectorate over Tonkin.

Coding: The coding of this war, and its transformation from an extra-state into an inter-state war, depends on the status of the participants and the determination of who is doing the bulk of the fighting. In 1882 France and China were system members, while Vietnam was not. Thus COW coding considers the earlier conflicts as extra-state wars between a system member (France) and nonstate actors. The new inter-state war is coded as beginning when China becomes the major combatant. Prewar tensions between China and France are codified in COW MID #202, beginning on April 14, 1883. Clodfelter (2002) describes the entire period of 1883–1885 as one war, the "Tonkin War." Phillips and Axelrod (2005) refer to the entire period of 1882–1885 as the "French Indochina War," and they also include a listing for the "Sino-French War."

Sources: Bodart (1916); Buttinger (1958); Clodfelter (2002); Cordier (1902); Eastman (1967); Elleman (2001); Jaques (2007); Khoi

(1955); Kiernan (1939); Lancaster (1961); Li (1956); McAleavy (1968); Phillips and Axelrod (2005); Roberts (1963); Taboulet (1955).

INTER-STATE WAR #70:
The Second Central American War of 1885

Participants: El Salvador vs. Guatemala
Dates: March 28, 1885, to April 15, 1885
Battle-Related Deaths: Guatemala—800; El Salvador—200
Where Fought: W. Hemisphere
Initiator: Guatemala
Outcome: El Salvador wins

Narrative: From 1825 to 1838 the Central American Confederation (or Union of Central America) had united Costa Rica, Guatemala, Honduras, Nicaragua, and El Salvador (which had all been combined under the Spanish Empire). Conflicts between liberals and conservatives, however, led to the dissolution of the Federation in 1839–1840 (see non-state war #1528). Subsequently there were a number of attempts to reinstitute the confederation, though they frequently involved military force to put into power a more like-minded government. For instance, in 1876 Guatemalan president Justo Rufino Barrios, a proponent of integration, launched a war against El Salvador (inter-state war #60) in order to install a more supportive government there. General Barrios was still the leader of Guatemala in 1885. He had returned from a trip to Europe in 1884 impressed by the successes of Italy and Germany in moving toward unity. Thus Barrios encouraged discussions for unity among Guatemala, El Salvador, and Honduras, and the presidents of the three countries developed a provisional plan for union in discussions on September 15, 1884. On February 28, 1885, the decree declaring the Union of Central America was announced by Barrios, who also volunteered to serve as its president. President Luis Bográn Barahona of Honduras

was supportive and ensured that the decree was ratified by Honduras on March 7. Events took a different turn in El Salvador, where President Rafael Zaldivar responded slowly to the decree. Salvadoran public opinion opposed the decree, and it was defeated by the Salvadoran congress. President Zaldivar then issued a statement on March 14, 1885, in which he called on Salvadoran citizens to oppose Barrios. Zaldivar also contacted Nicaragua, Costa Rica, the United States, and Mexico, seeking support for his opposition to Guatemala. Nicaragua did contact Barrios, announcing the Nicaraguan congressional rejection of the unity decree and of Barrios's planned military dictatorship. Costa Rica replied in a similar fashion, and both governments prepared to send armies to invade Honduras. Mexico also sent messages of opposition to the planned union, and the United States reminded Guatemala that any attack on Nicaragua would be hostile to American interests. In response Barrios developed a military campaign in which Guatemala would attack El Salvador (and then Mexico, if necessary) while Honduras was to keep the armies of Nicaragua and Costa Rica at bay. Barrios headed toward the front on March 23, and on March 30, the Guatemalan troops began to fire at the Salvadorans across the river. The first battle led to a rout of the Salvadorans. On April 2, Barrios impulsively decided to lead a critical maneuver and was shot dead. Though the Guatemalan army continued to fight for several days, the troops were demoralized by Barrios's death. Honduran president Bogran was left alone to negotiate a peace agreement with El Salvador and Nicaragua. This abrupt end to the war prevented other states from becoming participants in what had been shaping up as a broad Central American conflict.

Coding: The war was preceded by MID #1535, beginning on February 28, 1885. In the MID, Guatemala was the initiator and revisionist against El Salvador, Mexico, and the United States. Mexico had mobilized its army, and the United States had engaged in a show of ships before the MID ended. Scheina (2003a, 256–257) labels this war the "Conservative Nicaraguans and Liberal Costa Ricans and Salvadorans Defeat Liberal Guatemalans and Hondurans, 1885." Phillips and Axelrod and Kohn term this the "Guatemalan War."

Sources: Burgess (1926); Karnes (1961); Kohn (1999); Meza (1935); Phillips and Axelrod (2005); Richardson (1960a); Scheina (2003a).

INTER-STATE WAR #73:
The First Sino-Japanese War of 1894–1895

Participants: Japan vs. China
Dates: July 25, 1894, to March 30, 1895
Battle-Related Deaths: China—10,000; Japan—5,000
Where Fought: Asia
Initiator: Japan
Outcome: Japan wins

Narrative: From the close of the sixteenth century, Korea was a target of both Manchu and Japanese aspirations. The Manchus ruled China, along with their native Manchuria, from 1644 on, and the ties between the Manchus and Korea steadily increased. The Manchus occupied Korea militarily in 1627, after which Korea, although autonomous, remained a tributary state to the Manchus until 1905. In essence Korea was a land closed to foreigners, a fact that lead to Korea being referred to as "the Hermit Kingdom." However, "for the Western powers, which were extending their juridical as well as their economic system to the rest of the world, the tributary system was too vague to be an acceptable basis of international relations. The tributary system could work only so long as China was strong" (Michael and Taylor 1964, 154). Chinese power was, however, declining. China had tried to restrict foreign trade in its country, but the First Opium War of 1839–1842 (extra-state war #323) forced China to open five ports for trade. The Second Opium War (extra-state war #343),

also known as the Arrow War of 1856–1860, forced the Chinese to open further ports for trade and persuaded the Chinese to allow the creation of foreign legations in Beijing. Similarly, the Western powers, particularly France and then the United States, began to push to open Korea to foreign trade. The Japanese also began to press the Korean government about such matters as its treatment of missionaries, converts, and surveyors. In 1875, in an attempt to maintain its isolation, Korea fired on a Japanese gunboat. The Japanese responded by sending a fleet that ultimately was successful in opening "the Hermit Kingdom" to foreign trade.

In 1876 Japan extracted a treaty from Korea in which Korea was declared independent, ending Chinese suzerainty—at least to the extent that this treaty held sway. China attempted to reassert its control, and the factions in the Korean court were divided over whether Korea was independent or a suzerainty of China. The Progressive party was pro-Japanese, while the Conservative party favored China. The conflict simmered for decades. In 1882 the conservatives attacked the Japanese legation in Seoul. The Japanese had planned to avenge the attack but were deterred by the presence of a Chinese fleet. In 1884 a revolution broke out in Seoul, with the Japanese assisting the Progressive party in seizing the palace. After the Japanese legation was again attacked by mobs supported by China, Japan was able to secure from China the Convention of Tientsin, which committed both parties not to send an armed force into Korea without notifying the other. During this period, a new religion, Tonghak, had developed in Korea, combining elements of Catholicism, Confucianism, Taoism, and Buddhism. The Tonghaks also developed a political agenda, and by 1894 they were openly defying the government. Korea appealed to China for assistance in restoring order, and China sent several ships and 2,000 soldiers. On the basis of the Tientsin convention, Japan also began sending troops into Korea. By June 1894 the Japanese had the superior force in

Korea; they occupied Seoul while the Chinese were stationed further south.

The war began on July 25, 1894, when the Japanese sank a ship carrying Chinese troops to Korea. The Chinese developed a battle plan to attack the Japanese from both the north and south; however, the Japanese attacked first, defeating the Chinese at Yashan. The Japanese then turned and attacked the Chinese in the north as well, with great success. With the Japanese victory at Pyengyand on September 15, the Chinese withdrew from Korea. The war then shifted to a naval battle, in which the Japanese were also victorious. After crippling the Chinese fleet, the Japanese began a two-front assault on China in October, one through Port Arthur and the other in Manchuria. Port Arthur fell on November 21, 1894. The Chinese sued for peace. Hostilities ceased by the end of March 1895, and the peace treaty was signed at Shimonoseki on April 17, 1895. During the war, China had sought foreign intervention to no avail; however, Russia, France, and Germany intervened in the peace negotiations to reduce Japanese territorial gains. Nonetheless, Japan wound up acquiring the island of Formosa (Taiwan), cash, and equal status with the Western powers in China (meaning most-favored-nation treatment and extra-territoriality). Referencing the original cause of the war, China agreed that Korea was an independent state. This set the stage for Japanese conquest of Korea during the Russo-Japanese War (inter-state war # 85) ten years later.

Coding: The war is preceded by MID #1490, which Japan initiated against Korea and China on June 5, 1894. Japan was also the revisionist state. Korea engaged Japan to the level of a clash and lost 26 to 100 troops but dropped out of the MID on July 23.

Sources: Bing (1914); Clodfelter (2002); Cordier (1902); Elleman (2001); Huth (1988); Kajima (1978); Li (1914); Michael and Taylor (1964); Morse (1918); Ono (1922); Phillips and Axelrod (2005); Richardson (1960a); Schafer (1995).

INTER-STATE WAR #76:
The Greco-Turkish War of 1897

Participants: Ottoman Empire vs. Greece
Dates: February 15, 1897, to May 19, 1897
Battle-Related Deaths: Ottoman Empire—1,400; Greece—600
Where Fought: Europe
Initiator: Greece
Outcome: Ottoman Empire wins

Narrative: This was a short war (often called the "Thirty Days' War") between Greece and the Ottoman Empire over the status of Crete. Crete had been part of the Ottoman Empire since 1669. Though the inhabitants had at first welcomed Ottoman rule, they ultimately became disenchanted. In particular, the Cretan Christians favored independence or union with Greece. Earlier in the nineteenth century, the Cretans had rebelled against Ottoman rule three times: in 1821–1828, during the Greek War of Independence (intra-state war #506); in 1866–1867, the First Cretan War (intra-state war #583); and in the Second Cretan War, 1896–1897 (intra-state war #631). The current Greco-Turkish War actually represents the transformation of the Second Cretan civil war into an inter-state war upon Greece's entry to the conflict. The intra-state war began as a rebellion against Ottoman rule by Crete, instigated by Greece. In 1894 the Christians in Crete formed a committee called Epitropi, which soon became a revolutionary organization. At the same time, another nationalist organization, the Ethnike Hetairia, was formed among Greek army officers, and it began agitation against the Ottomans in Macedonia. The Epitropi launched a war in March 1896, and even though the Epitropi were aided by Ethnike Hetairia, the Turks were generally successful in suppressing the rebellion.

Hostilities flared again in January 1897, and it was reported that the Christians were about to be massacred. The Greek government decided it had to act, and on February 10, 1897, the Greek navy sent several ships to intercept the Turkish transports that were attempting to reinforce the Turkish garrison on Crete. Three days later, Greece sent additional regular forces to Crete. When the Greek troops arrived in Crete, on February 15, 1897, a proclamation was issued indicating that the king of Greece, George I, had decided on the military occupation of Crete. Thus February 15 marks the start of the interstate war. The Greeks continued taking measures toward the annexation of Crete, claiming that Crete had ceased to be Ottoman territory. In an attempt to stop a war between Greece and the Ottomans, the major powers (Britain, France, Russia, Italy, and Austria-Hungary) sent a small contingent of 450 troops to oppose the Greek force. The Greek government ordered its troops to halt their advance and to avoid conflict with the foreign powers; however, on February 21, 1897, the Cretan rebels were attacked by the Turkish troops and those of the foreign powers. On March 2 the great powers presented a proposal to the Greek and Ottoman governments, suggesting autonomy for Crete and the removal of all Greek troops. When the Greeks failed to comply, the foreign powers began a blockade on March 21 to prevent Greece from sending additional troops to Crete. Within days the Ottomans granted autonomy to Crete.

Meanwhile, activities shifted from Crete to the mainland, where the Greek government ordered a full military mobilization on March 15. Simultaneously, Ethnike Hetairia increased its attacks against Turkish fortifications in Macedonia. The Ottomans also mobilized their army and sent additional troops to Turkey's borders with Greece. On March 29, 1897, the Greek crown prince, Constantine, arrived to take command of the Greek forces at Larisa (Greece). The Ottomans accused the Greek army of being involved in the Ethnike Hetairia raids, and in response to the deteriorating conditions, the Ottoman Empire declared war on Greece on April 17, 1897. The Ottoman forces crossed the border, though their advance was initially stopped at Nezeros. However, the conflict soon turned into a series of defeats of the Greeks by Turkish forces under Edhem Pasha. The Greeks made a final stand at Domokos, but the defeated Greeks were again forced to retreat. Hostilities were terminated on May 19, and the ceasefire was signed on May 20, 1897. Peace negotiations between the Ottoman Empire and the great powers representing Greece began on June 4. The final peace treaty was signed on December 4 in Istanbul. Although the Ottomans had occupied almost all of Thessaly during the war, the peace treaty generally restored the prewar borders (a preference of the great powers). Both Greek and Turkish troops evacuated Crete, which had been made an international protectorate. Crete was finally ceded to Greece in 1913 (see inter-state war #100).

Coding: The war was preceded by MID #1569, beginning in December 1896, a bilateral MID initiated by Greece with Greece as the revisionist. One of the coding decisions that affected this war was determining when the intra-state (civil) war ended and the inter-state war began. Clodfelter (2002) described this as the "Greek-Turkish War" of 1897; however, he also referred to it as the "Thirty Days War" that lasts from April 17 to May 20, 1897. Clodfelter thus starts the war with the declaration of war by the Ottoman Empire. Nevertheless, COW codes the beginning of the war with the start of armed clashes on February 15, 1897, when the Greeks attempted to occupy a foreign country. As Ekinci noted (2006, 25), "The dispatch of Greek troops in Crete internationalized the Cretan crisis, which had initially been a local problem within the Ottoman Empire."

Sources: Clodfelter (2002); Dumas and Vedel-Peterson (1923); Ekinci (2006); Finkel (2005); Harbottle (1904); Jaques (2007); Phillips and Axelrod (2005); Richardson (1960a); Sorokin (1937).

INTER-STATE WAR #79:

The Spanish-American War of 1898

Participants: United States vs. Spain
Dates: April 22, 1898, to August 12, 1898
Battle-Related Deaths: United States—2,910;
   Spain—775
Where Fought: W. Hemisphere, Asia
Initiator: United States
Outcome: United States wins

Narrative: Christopher Columbus visited Cuba in 1492, and the Spanish conquest of Cuba began in 1511. Even though the British had briefly occupied Havana, Cuba had been returned to the Spanish by the Treaty of Paris in 1763. It remained a Spanish possession while independence movements erupted throughout the Spanish Empire. In the nineteenth century, however, Cuban discontent and desires for independence grew, leading to the First Spanish-Cuban War in 1868 (extra-state war #363), or the Ten Years' War. The results of the war included Spanish promises of reform and greater autonomy for Cuba, promises that were never fully realized. A second revolutionary war began in 1895 (extra-state war #404) under the leadership of José Marti. The brutality of Spanish general Valeriano Weyler in attempting to defeat the rebels created greater sympathy for the Cubans in the United States. Public opinion, enflamed by the yellow journalism of William Randolph Hearst, prompted U.S. president Grover Cleveland to discuss the possibility of American intervention against Spain in his Presidential Message of December 1896. The sinking of the U.S. battleship *Maine* in Havana harbor on February 15, 1898 (for which the United States, fairly or not, blamed Spain), led U.S. president William McKinley to request that Congress authorize an invasion of Cuba. Congress went further and voted to recognize Cuban independence on April 19. The United States began a blockade of Cuba on April 22, and this date thus marked the end of the extra-state war and its transformation into an inter-state war as the United States took over the bulk of the fighting. In reaction Spain declared war on April 23, followed by a U.S. declaration two days later. Though the United States subsequently conducted a bipolar war, attacking Spanish forces in both Cuba and the Philippines, it was in the Philippines that the war really began. A Spanish fleet was stationed in Manila harbor. The headquarters of the American Asiatic fleet was in Hong Kong, where Adm. George Dewey had been preparing the fleet for war. On the night of April 30, the American fleet sailed into Manila harbor, and on the morning of May 1, the Americans destroyed the Spanish fleet. Dewey then instituted a blockade of Manila to force its surrender while he awaited the arrival of ground troops. The American troops finally landed on June 30, 1898, and captured Manila by August 14.

Meanwhile, back in the Caribbean, the U.S. Navy had begun a bombardment of Puerto Rico on May 12. An American army landed there on July 25, quickly defeating the Spanish troops. In Cuba the insurgents had been successful in spreading their influence and capturing a number of important towns. Spain sent a fleet toward Cuba, and it was able to arrive unobserved into the harbor at Santiago de Cuba. The United States began a bombardment of the Spanish there on June 6, 1898, with American troops landing at the end of June. On June 24 the American forces under Gen. Joseph Wheeler captured Las Guasimas and decided to then attack the Spanish on the San Juan Heights. The assault, which began on July 1, included the famous "Rough Riders" led by Theodore Roosevelt. Despite problems caused by the heat and disease, the American troops were successful in securing the surrender of the Spanish garrison at Santiago on July 17. The U.S. campaign was suspended on August 14, 1898, after the fall of Manila, when word arrived that an armistice had been signed on August 12. The United States and Spain signed a final peace treaty on December 10, 1898, in Paris. The United States gained the Philippines from Spain. Cuba was declared independent but provided the

United States with the naval base at Guantanamo and the right to intervene in Cuban affairs (through the Platt Amendment to the Cuban constitution). Prior to this war, the United States had largely limited its geopolitical interests to the Western Hemisphere. This war ushered America into the world stage, and the United States was considered a major power after 1898.

Coding: The war is preceded by MID #1557, initiated by the United States against Spain on January 3, 1898, in which the United States is the revisionist. More than 2,000 of the American battle-deaths in this war were attributed to disease.

Sources: Axelrod (2007); Clodfelter (2002); Phillips and Axelrod (2005); Scheina (2003a); Sorokin (1937); White (1909).

INTER-STATE WAR #82:
The Boxer Rebellion of 1900

Participants: United States, United Kingdom, France, Russia, Japan vs. China
Dates: June 17, 1900, to August 14, 1900
Battle-Related Deaths: China—2,000; Japan—622; Russia—302; United Kingdom—34; France—24; United States—21
Where Fought: Asia
Initiator: United States, United Kingdom, Russia, France, Japan,
Outcome: United States, United Kingdom, France, Russia, Japan win

Narrative: China's gradual opening to foreign trade led to competition among the foreign powers for influence in China. China had tried to restrict foreign trade within its borders, but the First Opium War of 1839–1842 (extra-state war #323) forced China to open five ports for trade. The Second Opium War (extra-state war #343), also known as the Arrow War, of 1856–1860 led to the opening of additional ports for trade and persuaded the Chinese to allow the creation of foreign legations in Beijing. The First Sino-Japanese War of 1894–1895 (fought over Korea, inter-state war #73), during which the Japanese had successfully invaded China,

had further weakened the Chinese government. The United States had supported the "Open Door" policy (of free trade for all), which was generally ignored by the other powers. Instead, China was divided up into spheres of influence under the control of the various foreign legations (there were eleven legations in Beijing, most of whom had been assigned to one sector of the city by the Manchu Court). This situation led to an increased hostility toward foreigners in China, which was the primary motivation for the Boxer Rebellion. The war is named for a group of Chinese martial artists, known in China as the society of "righteous, harmonious fists" and in the West as the "Boxers." The Boxers were a secret group from northern China that wanted to end the contamination of China by foreigners. They garnered attention when they began attacking Chinese converts to Christianity in 1898. By 1900, attacks against foreigners had become more common, and by the end of May 1900, a more general uprising had begun. The foreign legations in Beijing sent messages to Tientsin, where foreign troops were stationed, asking for military assistance. A contingent of 340 marines from the United States, Britain, France, Italy, Japan, and Russia arrived in Peking on May 30. The presence of these troops was insufficient to stop the threats against the foreign legations, so an appeal was sent for more foreign troops. A contingent of 2,000 troops from eight different countries, under the command of British vice-admiral Edward Seymour, left Tientsin by train for Beijing on June 11. The Seymour expedition made it about halfway to Beijing when it was stopped by the Boxers' destruction of the railroad. The Seymour expedition had to fight its way back to Tientsin and was probably saved by its seizure of weapons and ammunition from an imperial Chinese arsenal. The expedition did not make it back to Tientsin until June 26, 1900.

Meanwhile, as of June 17, Chinese troops had begun working with the Boxers, to resist the violation of their territory, and the government of China was in military combat with the international armies (thus marking the start of the inter-state war). Initially, a fleet of nine foreign ships attacked, and ultimately seized, the Chinese forts at Taku at the mouth of the Pei Ho (thirty-five miles downstream from Tientsin) on June 17. The same day, the Chinese attacked the foreign concessions at Tientsin and established a siege that lasted until July 14, when sufficient foreign reinforcements arrived from Taku to capture the city. Also in June the situation in Beijing had worsened; foreigners were being killed and foreign properties destroyed. Coincidentally, June 17 is also the date of the killing of German minister Baron von Ketteler, shot by Chinese government troops while trying to negotiate a settlement of the dispute. The legations had made preparations to defend themselves while they awaited the arrival of the Seymour expedition; however, after the foreign seizure of the Taku forts, the foreign ministers were ordered to leave Beijing within twenty-four hours. Many of the foreigners took shelter at the British Legation, and the legations were besieged from June 20 until August 14. Once Tientsin was back in foreign control, the foreign allies were able to launch an expedition to relieve the legations in Beijing. An army of 20,000 troops fought toward Beijing, defeating the Chinese forces in their path. As the foreign forces entered Beijing, the imperial court fled. After August 14, 1900, the bulk of the inter-state fighting stopped; however, the Russians were engaged in a separate war with China, the Sino-Russian War (inter-state war #83) in Manchuria. A preliminary peace agreement was signed on January 16, 1901, and the final settlement was approved on August 7, 1901. The foreign powers won a huge financial indemnity in the diplomatic settlement, termed the "Boxer Protocol." They also won the right to station troops between Beijing and the port of Tientsin. The latter provision enabled the Japanese to attack north China (see inter-state war #130, the Third Sino-Japanese War, and #139, World War II). The infamous

punitive expeditions that took place from fall 1900 through much of 1901 involved primarily German and Russian forces shooting at whatever Chinese they encountered, very few of whom were uniformed Chinese regulars.

Coding: In 1816 China was coded as a COW autonomous entity because it only gradually involved itself in international affairs. Great Britain was dissatisfied with its limited trade opportunities and provoked the First Opium War, 1839–1842 (extra-state war #323), which provided it with commercial concessions. The Taiping Rebellion of 1850 began as a non-state war (#1534) but shifted to an intra-state war (#567) when China became a member of the interstate system, on October 25, 1860. The Boxer Rebellion was preceded by MID #31, initiated on May 30 by the United Kingdom, Japan, Russia, Austria, the United States, France, Germany, and Italy, all of whom targeted China for expanded influence and export markets. In the MID, however, only the United Kingdom, Japan, and Russia were revisionists. This is because the other five intervening powers opposed the British, Japanese, and Russian efforts to colonize China or divide it into spheres of foreign influence. Of the MID initiators, Germany, Italy, and Austria were not considered war participants because they did not commit enough troops (sending fewer than 1,000 troops and suffering fewer than 100 battle-deaths). Nonetheless, even on this lesser level of engagement, the Germans lost somewhere between 26 and 100 battle-dead in the war (which is more than the French or the United States who were war participants), and even the Italians and Austrians lost up to 25 each.

The key coding question in classifying this as an inter-state war was whether the government of China was involved. The conflict had begun as one between the foreign states and the Boxers, who initially were not supported by the Chinese government. Had the conflict continued on these terms, it would have been classified as an extra-state war between five system members and a nonstate actor; however, two events on June 17, 1900, changed the nature of the conflict. In the first, foreign ships attacked Chinese forces at the forts at Taku. Second, the empress dowager summoned the imperial council to discuss the issue of the Boxers. After receiving a document that purported to be an ultimatum from the legations, the empress proclaimed that the foreigners were the aggressors and that the Chinese must send troops to fight in Beijing in aid of the Boxers (Fleming 1959, 97). Thus June 17, 1900, is seen as the start of the inter-state war. Phillips and Axelrod extend the war by setting the start date of the rebellion at 1899, when Boxer armed attacks commenced. Clodfelter (2002) and Phillips and Axelrod (2005) also extend the end date of the war to 1901 to include the punitive expeditions by the allied powers against Boxers in the Beijing region. Phillips and Axelrod (2005) and Kohn (1999) also include within the Boxer Rebellion the Russian offensives in Manchuria (which they only briefly mention), while COW codes these separately as the Sino-Russian War of 1900 (inter-state war #83).

Sources: Anthouard (1902); Bing (1914); Clements (1967); Clodfelter (2002); Columbia University (1915); *Deutschland in China* (1902); Elleman (2001); Fleming (1959); Frey (1904); Lensen (1967); Michael and Taylor (1964); Phillips and Axelrod (2005).

INTER-STATE WAR #83:

The Sino-Russian War of 1900

Participants: Russia vs. China
Dates: July 17, 1900, to October 10, 1900
Battle-Related Deaths: China—3,758;
  Russia—242
Where Fought: Asia
Initiator: Russia
Outcome: Russia wins

Narrative: This war had origins related to those of the Boxer Rebellion of 1900 (inter-state war #82). The Boxers were a secret group from northern China that wanted to end the contamination of China by foreigners. They led a revolt (later joined by the Chinese government) against the influence of foreigners, including the Russians, particularly in Beijing; however, Chinese opposition to Russian influence had a particular focus in Manchuria. China had been conquered by Manchuria in 1644, after which the Manchus became the ruling dynasty of China and Manchuria in the Ch'ing dynasty (1644–1911). As the power of the Chinese rulers declined, competition increased among the foreign powers for influence in China. China had tried to restrict foreign trade in China, but the First Opium War, 1839–1842 (extra-state war #323), forced China to open five ports for trade. The Second Opium War (extra-state war #343, also known as the Arrow War, 1856–1860) forced the Chinese to open further ports for trade and persuaded them to allow the creation of foreign legations in Beijing. The First Sino-Japanese War of 1894–1895 (inter-state war #73), during which the Japanese had successfully invaded China, also had led to the expansion of foreign interests.

Similarly, Manchuria increasingly became an object of Russian and Japanese expansionism. In 1858 China was forced to cede a portion of Manchuria north of the Amur River to Russia (except for an area known as the Sixty-Four Villages, east of the Heilongjiang River). In 1860 the Treaty of Beijing (see the Second Opium War, extra-state war #343) awarded another part of Manchuria (east of the Ussuri River) to Russia. During the Boxer Rebellion, which ended on August 14, 1900, the Boxers had also killed dozens of Russians in Manchuria. In July 1900 the Russians launched a separate invasion of Manchuria, the Sino-Russian War, with an army of 176,900 men. The Russians basically conducted three separate campaigns. The war began in western Manchuria, when the Russians crossed the Argun River on July 17, 1900, and began advancing eastward into Manchuria along the Chinese Eastern Railway. The army under General Orlov defeated a large Chinese force at Ongon on July 30 and captured the nearby city of Hailar before heading east toward Xing-an, where he forced the Chinese to withdraw on August 24. Meanwhile, Russian forces in the east along the Amur River, under the command of Gen. Deian Subotich, seized Aigun during fierce fighting on August 2–5, before marching south to Qiqihar, which fell after heavy fighting on August 28. A third Russian offensive began from the south, where the Russian general Fleisher drove north into Manchuria from Port Arthur. Fleisher's troops attacked Haicheng, which was held by 4,000 Chinese regulars and 1,000 Boxer militia, on August 11–12. Additional Russian victories occurred at Qiqihar (August 28), Jilin (September 23), and Shaho (September 27). The Chinese suffered a decisive defeat at Liaoyang on September 28, after which they abandoned Mukden. The war ended on October 10, 1900, with the occupation of Tienchwangtai. As a result of the war, China lost access to the Sea of Japan. Another consequence of this war was the subsequent Russo-Japanese War of 1904–1905 (inter-state war #85).

Coding: The war is preceded by bilateral MID #3250, starting on August 15, in which Russia is the initiator and the revisionist side and China of course is the target. Clodfelter (2002) agrees with COW in seeing the Russian offensive in Manchuria as a separate war, which he describes under the title of the "Russo-Chinese War" of 1900. Phillips and Axelrod (2005) and Kohn (1999) include the Russian offensives in Manchuria, which they only briefly mention, within the Boxer Rebellion.

Sources: Clodfelter (2002); Fairbank and Lice (1980); Jaques (2007); Langer (1948); Mackerras (1982); Michael and Taylor (1964); Morse (1918); Schafer (1995).

INTER-STATE WAR #85:
The Russo-Japanese War of 1904–1905

Participants: Japan vs. Russia
Dates: February 8, 1904, to September 15, 1905
Battle-Related Deaths: Japan—80,378; Russia— 71,453
Where Fought: Asia
Initiator: Japan
Outcome: Japan wins

Narrative: This war is the sixth in a series of wars that originate in attempts by foreign states to expand their influence in China. China had attempted to protect itself from foreign influence by restricting foreign trade; however, the First Opium War, 1839–1842 (extra-state war #323), forced China to open five ports for trade. The Second Opium War of 1856–1860 (extra-state war #343, also known as the Arrow War) led to additional ports being opened and persuaded the Chinese to allow the creation of foreign legations in Beijing. The First Sino-Japanese War of 1894–1895 (inter-state war #73) removed Korea from Chinese influence. The Boxer Rebellion of 1900 (inter-state war #82) led to expanded rights for foreign powers in China. The Sino-Russian War of 1900 (inter-state war #83) led to the increase of Russian influence in Manchuria and the loss of significant parts of Manchuria to Russia. Both Russia and Japan wanted to further the gains they had made in these wars. Essentially, Russia wanted to maintain its dominant position in Manchuria and hoped for gains in Korea that would require that Japan not be given a free hand there. Japan, on the other hand, wanted to protect its dominant interest in Korea and asserted its commitment to Chinese independence. In 1903 Japan issued a proposal to Russia for negotiations to resolve their competing interests. The Russian reply on October 3 basically reiterated its position that Russia should have a free hand in Manchuria, without granting the same to Japan in Korea. The French made an attempt to mediate the conflict on January 6, 1904, though neither side responded.

Japan then began to prepare for war. On February 5 Japan declared an end to negotiations and broke diplomatic relations with Russia. On February 8 Japan launched a surprise attack on the Russian warships at Port Arthur, marking the start of the war. The war would become known for the number of troops involved and for the level of fatalities. The subsequent war consisted of conflict in three distinct but interrelated arenas: the siege of Port Arthur, land operations in

Manchuria, and naval battles. The Japanese began on February 17 by landing troops in Korea. The army crossed the Yalu River, which marked the border between Korea and Manchuria and on May 1 scored its first victory over a small Russian force. The Japanese then proceeded into Manchuria. They had established a naval blockade of Port Arthur, and on May 5 they began landing troops on the Liaotung Peninsula (at the tip of which Port Arthur is located) in order to surround Port Arthur on land as well. The siege of Port Arthur, which included several failed Japanese assaults, lasted 148 days and has been considered "one of the greatest sieges of history" (Clodfelter 1992, 646). On January 2, 1905, the Russians surrendered Port Arthur. Meanwhile, after their defeat at the Yalu, the Russians moved deeper into Manchuria, retreating westward after engaging in fierce combat with the Japanese army. The Russians attacked a force that included three Japanese armies at Liaoyang on August 25, 1904, causing heavy casualties on both sides. Ultimately, the Russians retreated toward Mukden. The subsequent Battle of Mukden, which took place from February 21 to March 10, 1905, has been called one of the greatest in history due to the number of participants involved (Florinsky 1953, 1274). The Russians had 310,000 troops compared with the Japanese force of 300,000. The Japanese launched a pincer movement attack threatening to encircle the Russians. Fighting caused horrific losses on both sides before the Russians retreated. The final battle arena was a naval confrontation in Tsushima Strait, leading to the Sea of Japan. The Russians had called on its Baltic fleet, which arrived at the Tsushima Strait on May 27, 1905. There the Russian fleet was destroyed.

Thus through superior seamanship and willingness to take very high levels of fatalities, the Japanese prevailed decisively in a massive war on sea and land. At this point both Japan and Russia decided that they wanted to end the war.

Though both sides still retained significant military resources, the war was causing a severe economic strain on both countries. On May 31 the Japanese encouraged U.S. president Theodore Roosevelt to initiate peace negotiations. Roosevelt invited Japan and Russia to send representatives to Portsmouth, New Hampshire, where talks began on August 10. The treaty was signed on September 5, 1905, and it represented compromises by both parties. Among other things, the treaty provided that the lease on the Liaotung Peninsula (including Port Arthur) would be transferred from the Russians to the Japanese. Russian influence in Northern Manchuria would remain the same. The island of Sakhalin was divided between the two powers. Japanese rights in Korea were recognized: Korea was militarily occupied by Japan in 1905, becoming a Japanese protectorate in 1907 and an outright colony from 1910 to 1945. This war established Japan as an important revisionist military actor on the Asian mainland, a role it would maintain until 1945. In terms of its significance, the Russo-Japanese was the first inter-state war since the industrial revolution in which a non-European major power defeated a European major power.

Coding: With Russia having taken a diplomatic position that in retrospect was too unyielding, it initiated the militarized interstate dispute that led to this war. Russia was also coded as the revisionist in that dispute, MID #180, which erupted on June 29, 1903, and Japan was the initial target. Korea entered the MID on the Japanese side on October 1—as Russia was attempting to enhance its own influence in Korea at the expense of the Japanese. Korea dropped out of the dispute in January 1905, having gone no higher than a show of troops.

Sources: Akagi (1936); Clodfelter (1992); Dumas and Vedel-Peterson (1923); Florinsky (1953); Huth (1988); Martin (1967); Michael and Taylor (1964); Nish (1985); Ogawa (1923); Phillips and Axelrod (2005); Richardson (1960a); Schafer (1995); Seton-Watson (1952); Urlanis (1960).

INTER-STATE WAR #88:
The Third Central American War of 1906

Participants: Guatemala vs. El Salvador, Honduras
Dates: May 27, 1906, to July 20, 1906
Battle-Related Deaths: Guatemala—400; Honduras—300; El Salvador—300
Where Fought: W. Hemisphere
Initiator: Guatemala
Outcome: Guatemala wins

Narrative: The countries of Guatemala, El Salvador, Nicaragua, Honduras, and Costa Rica had once been part of the short-lived Central American Confederation (or Union of Central America). The Confederation had been created in 1823, but was torn apart by internal strife in 1839–1840 (see non-state war #1528). Attempts to revive the confederation were initially made in 1842. Subsequently, there were periodic attempts by a dictator (or "caudillo") in one country to resort to armed conflict to unite the countries (usually the four core countries of Guatemala, El Salvador, Nicaragua, and Honduras) under his leadership. In general, the Central American liberals hoped that the Federation would evolve into a stable democracy, an idea opposed by the conservatives, who were frequently wealthy landowners allied with the Catholic Church. Thus at times a conservative caudillo in one country would launch an armed attack against a liberal in another country (or vice versa), in order to force a change in government and thus a change in its position regarding confederation. For instance, the First Central American War of 1876 (inter-state war #60) was instigated by Guatemala's liberal leadership against El Salvador. Guatemala prevailed and then established a supportive government in El Salvador. The two governments then signed a treaty of friendship. The Second Central American War of 1885 (inter-state war #70) again involved Guatemala's liberal president Barrios trying to unify Guatemala, El Salvador, and Honduras under his leadership.

El Salvador's President Zaldivar opposed the proposal, and he prompted Nicaragua and Costa Rica to voice opposition as well. In response Guatemala attacked El Salvador in a war in which Barrios was killed, ending the unification movement for the time being. In 1906 and again in 1907, such wars again broke out: the Third Central American War (inter-state war #88) and the Fourth Central American War (inter-state war #91. Indeed, Scheina (2003a) calls the nineteenth century "the age of the caudillo." But in Central America, this age persisted until at least 1907. After that the next Central American inter-state war was not until 1969 (inter-state war #175, the Football War).

At the beginning of the twentieth century, two men fought for control of Central America: Manuel Estrada Cabrera and José Santos Zelaya. Estrada Cabrera ruled Guatemala from 1898 to 1920 as an absolute dictator. Zelaya was president of Nicaragua from 1894 to 1909, and although he was the leader of a liberal party, he also established a dictatorship. It was Zelaya who at this point in time was interested in re-creating the Central American Confederation, with himself at its head. Both this war and the Fourth Central American War (inter-state #91), which occurs the following year, originated in Zelaya's unification attempts. Zelaya's plan began by demanding that Honduras join with Nicaragua in attacking Guatemala. Honduras at the time was aligned with El Salvador and Costa Rica. Initially, nongovernmental forces from El Salvador infiltrated Guatemala to try to help overthrow the president, Estrada Cabrera. In response, on May 27, 1906, Guatemala began the war by invading El Salvador, which brought Honduras into the war as well. The United States, which at the time had significant investments in Honduras, wanted the war stopped before the whole region was in chaos. Thus U.S. president Theodore Roosevelt persuaded Mexico that the two countries should intervene. Roosevelt sent a ship into the region and was ultimately successful in persuading Guatemala, Honduras, and El Salvador to stop the fighting. Zelaya was unhappy both with American intervention and with the cessation of hostilities. Thus he would initiate a second war within seven months—the Fourth Central American War.

Coding: The Third Central American War is preceded by MID #1205, in which Guatemala is the initiator, in March 1906, against El Salvador. Guatemala and El Salvador are both revisionists. Nicaragua joins the MID on El Salvador's side on May 28, and Honduras joins with them on July 13. Nicaragua limits itself to a show of ships and pulls out in June, a month before the end of the war, and thus is not a war participant. Clodfelter (2002) describes this war as the "Central American War" of 1906. Phillips and Axelrod (2005) do not include it.

Sources: Bailey (1964); Castellanos (1925); Clodfelter (2002); Karnes (1961); LaFeber (1983); Scheina (2003a).

INTER-STATE WAR #91:
The Fourth Central American War of 1907

Participants: Nicaragua vs. El Salvador, Honduras
Dates: February 19, 1907, to April 23, 1907
Battle-Related Deaths: Nicaragua—400;
   Honduras—300; El Salvador—300
Where Fought: W. Hemisphere
Initiator: Nicaragua
Outcome: Nicaragua wins

Narrative: Attempts to unify the countries of Central America were a frequent source of conflict in the region. The Central American Confederation had united Guatemala, El Salvador, Honduras, Nicaragua, and Costa Rica from 1823 until it was torn apart by strife in 1839–1840 (non-state war #1528). The First Central American War (inter-state war #60), the Second Central American War (inter-state war #70), and the Third Central American War (inter-state war #88) were all related to attempts at regional integration in 1876, 1885, and 1906, respectively. In particular, the 1906 Third Central American War was the immediate cause of this fourth war.

Prior to the preceding war, President José Santos Zelaya of Nicaragua aimed to promote regional unity (under his leadership) by overthrowing his major regional opponent, President Manuel Estrada Cabrera of Guatemala. Zelaya was successful in persuading Honduras and El Salvador to become involved in the war with Guatemala (inter-state war #88).

Zelaya was particularly unhappy that the war ended without accomplishing its mission. He was further dismayed when peaceful moves toward confederation were being made by the other four Central American states. Thus Zelaya decided to change the regional dynamics by promoting regime change in Honduras. Honduras was ruled by conservative president Manuel Bonilla, who had come to power in 1903 by overthrowing a liberal government that had been supported by Zelaya. At first, Zelaya began to assist Honduran rebel groups that were trying to overthrow Bonilla; however, when Honduran troops crossed the Nicaraguan border in pursuit of the rebels, Zelaya demanded reparations. When Honduras refused, Zelaya started a war by attacking Honduras and then El Salvador. Nicaragua won the decisive Battle of Namasigue on March 18, 1907. Nicaragua occupied the capital of Honduras, and Bonilla fled to the United States. Mexico and the United States intervened diplomatically again (as they had done in the previous war) to stop the fighting and organize a settlement. The United States sponsored the Washington Conference of 1907, which attempted to link the Central American states together through a treaty of peace and a Central American court of justice. Although the Nicaraguan dictator Zelaya had been victorious in the war, he had been outspokenly anti-American. This was perceived as dangerous for the United States, in that Nicaragua was the main alternative to Panama for a canal from the Atlantic to the Pacific. In 1909 the U.S. Taft administration supported a revolution that ousted him from power. The U.S. military was then stationed in Nicaragua from 1912 to 1933, effectively ending the era of Central American wars but breeding new problems in their place.

Coding: Honduras and El Salvador behaved provocatively enough to be coded as the initiators of the MID that preceded the current war (#1202). This MID began on January 5, 1907, with Honduras the initial target and then the MID spreading to El Salvador. Clodfelter (2002) agrees with us in calling this the "Central American War" of 1907. Phillips and Axelrod (2005) call it the "Honduran-Nicaraguan War."

Sources: Bailey (1964); Castellanos (1925); Clodfelter (2002); Cockcroft (1989); Kohn (1999); LaFeber (1983); Phillips and Axelrod (2005); Scheina (2003a).

INTER-STATE WAR #94:
The Second Spanish-Moroccan War of 1909–1910

Participants: Spain vs. Morocco
Dates: July 7, 1909, to March 23, 1910
Battle-Related Deaths: Morocco—8,000; Spain—2,000
Where Fought: Middle East
Initiator: Spain
Outcome: Spain wins

Narrative: At the beginning of the twentieth century, the major European powers were trying to expand their colonial empires, and France, Spain, Britain, and Germany had shown particular interest in Morocco. France had been involved in wars in Morocco in 1844 (extra-state war #330) and in 1907 (extra-state war #431 and intra-state war #646), and Spain and Morocco had gone to war in 1859 (inter-state war #31). The 1859 First Spanish-Moroccan War represented Spain's first major step in its conquest of portions of Morocco. The war had started when Morocco resisted Spanish requests for the grant of a neutral zone around Ceuta and Melilla (in which Spain had long had interests). In 1904 Spain and France entered into an agreement to divide Morocco between themselves, and in

1905 the French had asked Morocco for a protectorate. Germany was concerned about such French advances, and at German insistence the Algeciras Conference was held in 1906 to discuss the Moroccan question. While the conference supposedly reaffirmed support for Moroccan integrity, it also allowed France and Spain to police the country. Morocco endured domestic instability as well. Morocco's Sultan Abd al-Aziz IV was overthrown by his brother in 1908 (in intra-state war #646). The new sultan could not maintain order and sought help from the Spanish and the French.

Spain was interested in expanding its control in Morocco, and did so by authorizing the military to protect the growing commercial activities. The Second Spanish-Moroccan War was then precipitated by the killing of four rail line workers by Rif tribesmen near the Spanish-controlled town of Melilla in July 1909. Spanish forces there then went on the offensive, leading to a widening war. The Spanish premier mobilized troops and dispatched reinforcements to Melilla. The mobilization and the sending of troops were unpopular with the Spanish people, and the recruits fought poorly, leading to Spanish defeats and heavy losses. These losses were sufficient to alter Spanish public opinion, which then supported a further Spanish military commitment to avenge its early defeats. A Spanish army of 40,000 troops was able to take the offensive, winning a battle at Tagdirt. The reinforcements were sufficient to win the war, and fighting ceased by March 23, 1910. A treaty was signed on November 16, 1910, between Spain and Morocco, adding territory to Spain's Moroccan possessions. Morocco also paid to cover the costs Spain had incurred in the war. Even though 10,000 soldiers died in this war, and the Spanish committed 40,000 troops to Morocco for the fighting, in the larger scheme of things this has been described as a minor campaign (Carr 1982, 483). During the next year, fighting in Morocco dragged on at a subwar level. In 1912 France would be involved in another war in Morocco (extra-state war #434), and by 1912 most of Morocco, which had been a state system member since 1847, was encompassed within a French protectorate, while three relatively small Moroccan sectors remained in Spanish control. In 1913 both France and Spain would fight against the Moroccan Berbers (extra-state war #436). Finally in 1921–1926, 70,000 troops would die in battle, as the Berber Rif rebels fought, successfully at first, against the Spanish and then the French (extra-state war #449). Only with the defeat of the Rif rebellion were the positions of the Spanish and French in Morocco stabilized. Morocco did not become independent again until 1956 (extra-state war #465).

Coding: Morocco was unusual in the region in terms of its relationship to the interstate system. While many of its neighbors did not become members of the system until they obtained independence from colonial powers (frequently in the 1950s and 1960s), Morocco joined the interstate system in 1847. Morocco lost its system membership during the period of the French protectorate, 1912 to 1956. Preceding this war, in the bilateral MID #1086 beginning May 9, 1909, Spain is the initiator and revisionist. Clodfelter (2002) concurs in describing this as the "Spanish-Moroccan War: 1909–1910." Kohn (1999) includes this war in an entry on the "Moroccan War" of 1907-1912.

Sources: Andrews (1911); Carr (1982); Clodfelter (2002); Kohn (1999); Smith (1965); Sorokin (1937); Usborne (1936).

INTER-STATE WAR #97:

The Italian-Turkish War of 1911–1912

Participants: Italy vs. Ottoman Empire
Dates: September 29, 1911, to October 18, 1912
Battle-Related Deaths: Ottoman
   Empire—14,000; Italy—6,000
Where Fought: Middle East
Initiator: Italy
Outcome: Italy wins

Narrative: In the late nineteenth and the early twentieth century, Italy, which had only recently attained the status of a unified state, desired to emulate the other European countries in developing a colonial empire, particularly in North Africa. The Italians had been able to briefly establish a protectorate over Ethiopia as the result of an 1887 war (extra-state war #392); however, an 1895 war (extra-state war #407) was won by the Ethiopians, thereby reducing the Italian holdings to Eritrea. Italy then shifted its focus to Tripoli (Libya). Tripoli (Libya), which had been an autonomous entity from 1711 to 1835, had been absorbed into the Ottoman Empire. Since 1880 Italy had sent merchants to the area. Tripoli was the last potentially unclaimed segment of North Africa (presuming the collapse of the Ottoman Empire), and Italy gradually obtained the agreement of most of the major powers to an official Italian presence there. In 1911, however, Italy began to be concerned about German interest in Tripoli. In early 1911 German objections to French activities in Morocco had led to the Agadir Crisis. Thus the Italians felt it was a propitious time to act. Claiming that Italians in Tripoli were being mistreated, Italy issued an ultimatum to the Ottomans on September 28, 1911, threatening to invade in twenty-four hours.

When Italy launched its attack, it caught the Turkish forces unprepared. After bombing Tripoli, the Italian forces seized control in October 1911 and faced a major offensive by Ottoman troops and pro-Turkish Senussi tribesmen wanting to recapture the capital. Fighting continued until October 1912. In addition to operations in Libya, the Italians began a naval campaign, bombing Beirut, seizing the Dodecanese Islands, and forcing the closure of the Dardanelles. The Treaty of Ouchy (near Lausanne, Switzerland) concluded the war with the Ottomans ceding control of Tripoli. The Italians continued fighting in Tripoli against Senussi tribesmen until the 1920s but at fatality levels below that necessary for a war classification. The immediate outcome of the war was that Italy gained control of Libya and the Dodecanese (including Rhodes) for thirty years. Libya was not yet an oil-producing area; earlier discovery of its oil could have substantially enhanced Axis prospects during World War II. Meanwhile, an immediate and real consequence of the Italian-Turkish War was that the poor Turkish performance persuaded the Balkan peoples to immediately launch the First Balkan War against the Ottoman Empire (inter-state war #100).

Coding: The war is preceded by bilateral MID #114, initiated by Italy on September 12, 1911. Clodfelter (2002) also calls this the "Italian-Turkish War" of 1911–1912. Albrecht-Carrié (1958) refers to this as the "Tripolitan War." Phillips and Axelrod (2005) and Kohn (1999) refer to it as the "Italo-Turkish War."

Sources: Albrecht-Carrié (1958); Askew (1942); Barber (1995); Beehler (1913); Clodfelter (2002); Kohn (1999); McClure (1913); Phillips and Axelrod (2005); Sorokin (1937); Urlanis (1960).

INTER-STATE WAR #100:
The First Balkan War of 1912–1913

Participants: Greece, Serbia, Bulgaria vs. Ottoman Empire
Dates: October 17, 1912, to April 19, 1913
Battle-Related Deaths: Bulgaria—32,000; Ottoman Empire—30,000; Serbia—15,000; Greece—5,000
Where Fought: Europe, Middle East
Initiator: Serbia
Outcome: Greece, Serbia, Bulgaria win

Narrative: The Ottoman Empire, the "Sick Man of Europe," was in a period of decline. Over the previous ninety years (1821–1911), the Ottoman Empire had been involved in thirty wars related in one way or another to the dissolution of the Ottoman Empire. This war started one day before the end of the immediately preceding inter-state conflict, the Italian-Turkish War of 1911–1912 (inter-state war #97). The Italian

victory in that war in particular had demonstrated the weaknesses of the Ottoman Empire. Especially for Greece and its Balkan neighbors, Italy's capture of the Dodecanese, where people spoke Greek, was especially relevant. The three initiators of the First Balkan War had gained independence from the Ottoman Empire in the nineteenth century: Greece in 1828 (the War of Greek Independence #506), Serbia in 1829 (The First Russo-Turkish War #4), and Bulgaria in 1878 (The Second Russo-Turkish War #61). All these achievements had occurred with Russian military help. By 1912 all three had become members of the interstate system—Greece in 1828, Serbia in 1878, and Bulgaria in 1908. These three predominantly Orthodox Christian Balkan states were still dissatisfied and were now ready to try to gain more from the Ottomans on their own.

At this stage, the Ottomans' European holdings were reduced to a band of territory that stretched between the Adriatic Sea on the west and the Black Sea on the east and was bounded by Serbia and Bulgaria on the north and Greece on the south. In order to liberate these territories from the Ottomans, Greece, Serbia, and Bulgaria decided to act together. On March 13, 1912, Serbia and Bulgaria concluded an alliance that provided for joint military action. The addition of a Greco-Bulgarian understanding in May 1912 led to the creation of the Balkan League. On October 8 Montenegro, which was an independent autonomous entity but not an interstate system member, declared war on the Ottoman Empire, followed on October 17 by a similar declaration by the Balkan League. The forces of the Balkan League invaded Turkish territory, and fighting led to Turkish defeats everywhere. The Bulgarian armies beat the Turks at Seliolu and Thrace October 22 to 24. Three Serbian armies crossed into Macedonia, winning a major victory at Kumanovo. The Greek forces crossed into southern Macedonia, defeating the Turks at Elasson on October 23. On December 3, 1912, an armistice was signed between Turkey and Serbia and Bulgaria. Thus the war participation of Serbia and Bulgaria is coded as ending that day; however, Greece continued to fight.

In the meantime, on December 16, two meetings were held in London to design the terms of peace. One conference was for the delegations from the Balkan states; the other was for the representatives of the great powers. Among the great powers, Austria wished to restrict Serbian gains from the war and thus proposed the creation of an independent Albania. Also according to the great powers, Bulgaria would not receive as much territory as it desired. Both Serbia and Bulgaria returned to fighting on February 3, 1913. The war finally ended on April 19, 1913, and a peace treaty was signed in London on May 30, 1913, in which the Ottoman Empire ceded its territory in Europe west of the Enos-Midia line (thereby allowing the Ottomans to keep some European territory near Istanbul). According to the great power plan, Albania was also granted independence, despite Serbia's hope of annexing it. The rest of the territorial divisions, however, turned on the resolution of the Second Balkan War, which started a month later; in the latter war the victors in the First Balkan War fought over the contested occupied land.

To gain a sense of the importance of the stakes to the participants, it may be helpful to consider that before the First Balkan War, Greece, though independent, was confined to the impoverished Peloponnesian peninsula and the area around Athens, which was then a village of a few thousand people. Greece doubled its size by its victory in the First Balkan War. This and many similar assets were the motivation for the conflict that cost so many thousands of lives.

Coding: The war is preceded by MID #1250, initiated by Bulgaria against the Ottomans on September 3, with Greece and Serbia joining on the Bulgarian side at the end of the month. Bulgaria, Greece, and Serbia were all revisionists. Since Montenegro was an independent autonomous entity but not a member of the interstate system, it is not included as a participant in this inter-state war. Thus the start date of this war is coded not as October 8 but as October 17 with the declaration by the Balkan League. A high percentage of the battle-related deaths were from disease.

Sources: Albrecht-Carrié (1958); Barber (1995); Clodfelter (2002); Dumas and Vedel-Peterson (1923); Fried (1914); Helmreich (1938); Phillips and Axelrod (2005); Report of International Commission (1914); Schafer (1995); Urlanis (1960); Wolff (1978); Young (1915).

INTER-STATE WAR #103:

The Second Balkan War of 1913

Participants: Greece, Romania, Serbia, Ottoman Empire vs. Bulgaria
Dates: June 30, 1913, to July 30, 1913
Battle-Related Deaths: Ottoman Empire—20,000; Serbia—18,500; Bulgaria—18,000; Greece—2,500; Romania—1,500
Where Fought: Europe
Initiator: Bulgaria
Outcome: Greece, Romania, Serbia, Ottoman Empire win

Narrative: The Balkan League had started the First Balkan War (inter-state war #100) with the intention of liberating the remainder of the Ottoman possessions in Europe. The war, which had begun on October 17, 1912, had led to Ottoman defeats on all fronts. During a temporary armistice, two meetings were held in London on December 16, to design the terms of peace, held separately for the Balkan and great power delegations. Austria promoted the creation of an independent Albania at the great powers' conference, in order to limit the expansion of Serbian territory after the war. The great powers also decided that Bulgaria would not receive as much territory as it desired. The war finally ended on April 19, 1913, as a complete defeat for the Ottoman Empire, and a peace treaty was signed in London on May 30, 1913, in which the Turks ceded Ottoman territory in Europe west of the Enos-Midia line (thereby allowing Turkey to keep some European territory near Istanbul). Plans were drawn for a new independent Albanian state (which in fact did become a member of the state system by 1914), despite Serbia's hope of annexing it. The Serbs, angry about their "loss" of Albania, asked Bulgaria to give them a bigger share of Macedonia, but the Bulgarians refused to renegotiate that part of the treaty. Meanwhile, the Romanians, who had not been participants in the First Balkan War, demanded that Bulgaria give them some of the territories the Bulgarians had won from the Ottomans. Finally, Bulgaria and Greece were unable to agree on who would get Thessaloniki, the most important city to be taken from the Ottomans in the First Balkan War. Greek forces had reached it just hours before the Bulgarian troops, so the Bulgarian government was determined to get it from Greece, even at the expense of a war.

Thus on June 30, 1913, Bulgaria attacked its former Greek and Serbian allies without warning. Bulgaria was no match for its opponents, especially since Romania and the Ottoman Empire decided to enter the war in opposition to Bulgaria on July 11 and July 15, respectively. The war, which lasted just one month before Bulgaria sued for peace, ended on July 30, 1913, and the terms of the peace were established by the Treaty of Bucharest on August 13, 1913. Since Bulgaria had been the instigator of the conflict, it had to bear its costs, and therefore the four opponents gained territory at Bulgaria's expense. Turkey recovered Adrianople (Edirne), site of one of the world's most beautiful mosques. The Romanians won the Dobrudja region near the mouth of the Danube at Bulgaria's expense, while Greece extracted a clear title to Thessaloniki. Bulgaria was evicted from Macedonia, which was divided between the Serbs and the Greeks. Albania's independence from Serbian designs was secured through the efforts of Germany and to the relief of Austria. Anticipating the First World War, German chancellor Otto von Bismarck had famously predicted that the next great war in Europe would break out because of "some damn fool thing in the Balkans." Indeed, within a year World War I would break out, triggered by similar struggles in the region.

Coding: The Second Balkan War was preceded by MID #1251, which had begun one day before the Second Balkan War ended. Bulgaria initiated this militarized dispute against Serbia. Ten days later, Greece entered the dispute. In a matter of weeks, Romania came in, too, just before the war. After the war had started, Turkey became the last state to enter the dispute.

Sources: Albrecht-Carrié (1958); Barber (1995); Clodfelter (2002); Dumas and Vedel-Peterson (1923); Fried (1914); Helmreich (1938); Hentea (2007); Luckett (1971); Mazower (2005); Phillips and Axelrod (2005); Report of International Commission (1914); Schafer (1995); Urlanis (1960); Wolff (1978); Young (1915).

INTER-STATE WAR #106:
World War I of 1914–1918

Participants: Russia, Greece, United States, United Kingdom, Belgium, France, Portugal, Serbia, Romania, Japan, Italy vs. Germany, Austria-Hungary, Bulgaria, Ottoman Empire
Dates: July 29, 1914, to November 11, 1918
Battle-Related Deaths: Germany—1,773,700; Russia—1,700,000; France—1,385,000; Austria-Hungary—1,200,000; United Kingdom—908,371; Italy—650,000; Romania—335,706; Ottoman Empire—325,000; United States—116,516; Bulgaria—87,500; Serbia—70,000; Belgium—13,716; Portugal—7,222; Greece—5,000; Japan—300
Where Fought: Europe, Africa, Middle East, Asia
Initiator: Austria-Hungary
Outcome: Russia, Greece, United States, United Kingdom, Belgium, France, Portugal, Serbia, Romania, Japan, Italy win

Narrative: For a number of years before World War I, Europe's major powers were polarized into two major camps: the Triple Alliance of Germany, Austria, and the Ottoman Empire against the Triple Entente of Great Britain, France, and Russia. Each of these alignments contained, in one form or another, commitments of assistance should an ally be attacked.

Once a conflict between states began, these ties served to bring an ever-widening circle of states into the war. As noted earlier, German chancellor Otto von Bismarck had famously predicted that the next great European war would be initiated by of "some damn fool thing in the Balkans." Desires for autonomy that had not been addressed in the previous Balkan Wars (interstate wars #100 and #103) did in fact provide the catalyst for World War I.

The progression of events is well known. The growing power of Serbia, as evidenced in the two Balkan Wars, made Serbia the foremost Slavic power in the Balkans and an inspiration to Slavs living under Austro-Hungarian rule. Austrian archduke Franz Ferdinand was assassinated in Sarajevo on June 28, 1914, by Gavrilo Princip, a politically motivated man of Serbian ethnicity. In response, Austria decided that Serbia should be eliminated as a power in the Balkans. Germany supported its ally Austria with the famous "blank check," promising support virtually no matter how much Austria escalated against the out-matched Serbia. On July 23 Austria issued an ultimatum to Serbia. Serbia's response was conciliatory though not the unqualified acceptance demanded by Austria. Russia had acted as a protector of Slavic interests in the past, and Russia let it be known that it would not allow Serbia to be destroyed. Nevertheless, Austria preemptively declared war on Serbia on July 28, and hostilities began the next day. Within a week most of the European powers were pulled into the war. To restrain Austria, Russia mobilized its army. In support of its Austrian ally, Germany responded with its own mobilization and declared war against Russia on August 1. In support of Russia, France ordered a mobilization as well. Germany, whose war plan depended on a victory against France before Russia mobilized, declared war against France on August 3 and then attacked France through Belgium on August 4. The United Kingdom, which had guaranteed the neutrality of Belgium, entered the war on the French side on August 5.

Other countries subsequently joined the war: Turkey and Japan later in 1914; Bulgaria and Italy in 1915; Portugal and Romania in 1916; and finally Greece and the United States in 1917.

The war lasted for over four years, until November 11, 1918, and virtually destroyed a generation of young men. During the war, combat took place in widely dispersed geographical locations that can be loosely grouped into the Western Front, the Eastern Front, the Balkans, and naval battles (though fighting also took place in the Middle East and Africa). In terms of the Western Front, the German Schlieffen Plan attempted to avoid the possibility of Germany having to fight a two-front war by quickly defeating France. The initial German invasion quickly routed the Belgians and rushed into France. The French forces fell back as the Germans headed toward Paris and the channel ports. The allied forces of France, Britain, and Belgium were finally able to halt the German advance, and by the end of 1914 both sides had established entrenched positions that would remain relatively stationary for the next three years. On the European Eastern Front, Russia initially went on the offensive, invading East Prussia and Austria; however, the tide changed in 1915, when the Austro-German armies launched a counteroffensive, driving the Russians back eastward. In the Balkans, Austria launched three invasions of Serbia, all of which were repulsed. In October 1915, in advance of Bulgaria entering the war on the side of the Central Powers, Britain and France sent troops to assist Serbia from the south, while an Austro-German force invaded from the north. By the end of 1915, the Central Powers had conquered Serbia. The general stalemate continued in 1916. On the Western Front, the Germans tried to break the Allied line with an attack on Verdun, while the Allies tried to break through the German line at the Somme. Both offensives caused severe loss of life but were unsuccessful. On the Eastern Front in 1916, the situation remained relatively stable as well. The Russians were able to launch several offensives westward against the Austrians, but reinforcements from Germany ultimately helped stop their advance.

During the intervening period, the United States under President Woodrow Wilson was still a neutral state, and Wilson tried unsuccessfully to bring about peace negotiations to end the war. The year 1917 marked a number of significant changes in the war. The United States had tried to maintain its neutrality and stay out of the war (except for trading with the participants); however, in January 1917 Germany announced that is was going to engage in unrestricted submarine warfare against all shipping to and from Great Britain. Attacks on American ships led to an American declaration of war against Germany on April 6, 1917, but American troops would not start to play a major role in the fighting until spring 1918. Germany had envisioned that its submarine attacks on British shipping would be sufficient to force Britain to withdraw from the war. Though the Germans were successful in destroying ships and supplies, it was not enough to force a British surrender.

Meanwhile on the Eastern Front, the most significant event in 1917 was the Russian withdrawal from the war. The costs of the war led to the Russian Revolution, and the Bolshevik party that came to power in November negotiated an armistice with the Germans on December 5, 1917. In the Treaty of Brest-Litovsk, signed in March 1918, the Germans imposed harsh penalties on Russia, including loss of territory. The year 1918 marked gains for the Allies in a number of regions. In the Balkans a united Allied force launched a large-scale attack against the Central Powers in Serbia. The successful offensive shortly forced Bulgaria out of the war. The Allied offensive in Italy was also successful against the Austrian army. On the Western Front, Germany launched a major offensive to occupy Paris before the American forces could enter the fighting in

significant numbers. The Allies were able to halt the German offensive and instead began to advance against German positions. By November 1918 the German line had been broken, and the Germans were in retreat along the entire Western Front. On November 11, 1918, an armistice was signed between Germany and the Allies. World War I is the second most severe war in our catalogue (trailing only World War II), with over 8.5 million military fatalities. The First World War and its settlement through the Treaty of Versailles had wide repercussions and set the stage for the rise of Hitler to power in Germany and the onset of the Second World War (inter-state war #139).

Coding: World War I is preceded by MID #257. Several states had entered this dispute before the onset of the war. Of these, only Austria is coded as a revisionist state. Austria was the first country on the initiating side of the dispute, which it began on July 23, 1914. Germany joined on the Austrian side on July 25. The first target to become party to the dispute is Serbia, which entered on July 23. Also on the target side, Russia and France entered on July 25 and England on July 26. Some historians and political scientists have argued that Germany would not have started the war had it known in time that England would join France, Russia, and Serbia in the war effort. Battle-death figures are most likely conservative, since fatality statistics are unreliable for Eastern Europe and Russia. Lacina and Gleditsch (2005) and the Uppsala/PRIO Data Project subdivide World War I into four separate wars based on geographical theaters. Clodfelter (2002) and Phillips and Axelrod (2005) describe the entire conflict as "World War I, 1914–1918." At the time the war was occurring, though, it was widely known as the "Great War."

Sources: Albertini (1952–1957); Albrecht-Carrié (1958); Clodfelter (2002); Dumas and Vedel-Peterson (1923); Esposito (1964a); Falls (1959); Fay (1928); Lacina and Gleditsch (2005); Moriarity (2005); Palmer and Colton (1964); Phillips and Axelrod (2005); Schmitt (1930); Sorokin (1937); Tuchman (1994); Urlanis (1960).

INTER-STATE WAR #107:
The Estonian War of Liberation of 1918–1920

Participants: Estonia, Finland vs. Russia
Dates: November 22, 1918, to January 3, 1920
Battle-Related Deaths: Russia—8,000;
    Estonia—3,600; Finland—150
Where Fought: Europe
Initiator: Russia
Outcome: Estonia, Finland win

Narrative: Estonia was part of the Russian Empire from 1710 to the end of the First World War (inter-state war #106). The Russians had implemented a policy of Russification in the 1890s, and a growth in Estonian nationalism developed in response. Initially there were calls for greater Estonian autonomy, but they later evolved into demands for independence. As the First World War gradually exhausted Russia, Czar Nicholas was overthrown in the February Revolution of 1917. A provisional Russian government then began to manage the war effort. Meanwhile, the Germans, thinking further revolution in Russia would be best for their war effort, moved Russian revolutionary Vladimir Ilyich Ulyanov (Lenin) from Switzerland to Russia through Finland. Lenin subsequently led the Bolsheviks to seize power in Russia during the October Revolution of 1917. Having pledged to remove Russia from the war, the new government signed an armistice with the Central Powers on December 5, 1917. The terms for peace were harsh, and at one point Leon Trotsky, who was negotiating for Russia, suspended the talks. This prompted the Germans to resume fighting, and German troops marched their way across Estonian territory toward Russia's czarist capital, Saint Petersburg. As the Russians fled before the advancing Germans, the Estonian capital of Tallinn was freed from occupation for one day, February 24, 1918. Seizing the opportunity, Estonian leaders declared independence, and

that day is still celebrated in Estonia as Independence Day. The next day the Germans installed Franz Adolf Freiherr von Seckendorff as the military governor in Estonia. Russia finally accepted the harsh terms of the Treaty of Brest-Litovsk on March 3, 1918, ending Russian participation in World War I. Russia renounced its sovereignty over each of the three Baltic States, Latvia, Lithuania, and Estonia, though it later tried to rescind that concession.

Several months later, when Germany signed the armistice ending World War I on November 11, 1918, Estonia reaffirmed its independence and an Estonian provisional government was established. In 1918 Estonian independence was finally recognized, though the Allies requested that German troops remain in Estonia to keep order. At the same time, the Soviets established an Estonian Bolshevik government in exile in Soviet Russia. The Bolsheviks invaded Estonia on November 22, 1918, in an attempt to reestablish control. The Soviets would also invade Latvia with the same goal (see inter-state war #108, Latvian Liberation). Initially, the Soviets advanced quickly toward Narva as the German army disintegrated, leaving the city in the hands of weak Estonian forces. On November 28 the Soviets occupied Narva and proclaimed an Estonian Workers' Commune. By the end of December, 1918, the Soviets, aided by the Estonian Communists, would control half of Estonia; however, the Estonian army grew stronger, invigorated by 2,750 White Russians placed under Estonian commend as well as Baltic Germans and volunteers from Latvia, Denmark, and Sweden. The British did provide weapons and naval support to the Estonians, and Finland agreed to send 2,000 troops (which qualifies it as a war participant). By early January 1919 the Soviets were approaching the Estonian capital of Tallinn; however, the Estonians were able to launch an offensive that drove most of the Soviet forces out of Estonia by early February. The Estonian army subsequently sent troops to aid Latvia in its conflict with Russia (see inter-state war #108). Soviet forces were still active in the east, so on May 13 the Estonians and White Russians launched a successful offensive that crossed the border into Russian territory. In June 1919 the White Russians were removed from the Estonian army and renamed the Russian Northwestern Army under the command of Gen. Nikolai Yudenich. Yudenich began a new offensive, heading toward Petrograd (which is not included in this war but as part of the Russian Civil War, intra-state war #677). By August, Estonia was looking for ways to withdraw from the war. Preliminary negotiations with the Soviets began in September. The Soviets attempted a brief offensive in December 1919, but they were repulsed. The two sides agreed to an armistice on January 3, 1920, and on February 2, 1920, the formal peace treaty, the Treaty of Tartu, was signed, by which the Soviet Union recognized Estonia's independence. Estonia remained independent until 1940, when it was conquered by the Soviet Union as part of Stalin's efforts to prepare Russia for a possible German invasion. Estonia regained its independence and rejoined the interstate system in 1991, during the disintegration of the Soviet Union.

Coding: In the corresponding MID (#2605), starting November 22, 1918, the Soviet Union is the initiator and revisionist, and the United Kingdom, which sent weapons to the Estonians, is on the Estonian side. At the time of the war, Estonia is a member of the COW interstate system. Consequently, this is an inter-state war, unlike most wars of independence, which are extra-state. Phillips and Axelrod (2005) describe this as the "Estonian War of Independence" and give slightly different dates, 1917–1920.

Sources: Brecher and Wilkenfeld (1997); Clemens (1991); Davies (1996); Lieven (1994); Palmer (2005); Phillips and Axelrod (2005); Stewart (1933); Urlanis (1960).

INTER-STATE WAR #108:
The Latvian War of Liberation of 1918–1920

Participants: Latvia, Estonia, Germany vs. Russia, Germany
Dates: December 2, 1918, to February 1, 1920
Battle-Related Deaths: Russia—8,000; Latvia—3,046; Germany—1,200; Estonia—1,000
Where Fought: Europe
Initiator: Russia
Outcome: Latvia, Estonia, win

Narrative: In 1629 Sweden conquered Latvia, which it lost to Russia in 1721. The Russians then ruled Latvia for almost 200 years, until the end of World War I (inter-state war #106). The war gradually exhausted Russia, and Czar Nicholas was overthrown in the February Revolution of 1917. A provisional Russian government then began to manage the war effort, but it soon fell as the Bolsheviks, led by Lenin, appropriated the reins of government in the October Revolution of 1917. The Bolsheviks had pledged to remove Russia from the war, and they signed an armistice with the Central Powers on December 5, 1917. The peace negotiations were difficult, but Russia accepted the stringent terms of the Treaty of Brest-Litovsk on March 3, 1918, ending its participation in World War I and its control over the three Baltic States: Latvia, Lithuania, and Estonia (though the Soviets later rescinded their agreement to independence). Latvia had actually declared its independence on November 18, 1917, and had sent representatives abroad to seek diplomatic recognition without success. Several months later, when Germany signed the armistice ending World War I (November 11, 1918), the Latvian Council met on November 19 and declared Latvian independence. Latvian independence was recognized, though the Allies requested that German troops remain in Latvia to keep order. At the time, the Latvians were divided between those who supported the

Communists and those who desired a noncommunist government. The Soviets installed a Latvian Bolshevik government and published its manifesto on December 17, 1918. Russia wished to utilize the Latvian Reds to reestablish its own control over Latvia. The Latvian Communists also were involved in helping the Russians plan the upcoming invasion of Latvia. In particular, they encouraged the incorporation of Latvian rifle units, so that the army would have some claim to being a Latvian army. The Latvian rifle regiments (sometimes referred to as the "Red Rifles") had been formed in 1915, and they had been instrumental in halting the German advance toward Riga up until 1917.

Germany, on the other hand, had very different plans for Latvia. The Germans had long felt that the Baltic States should become a province of Germany. As the Russian army disintegrated after the overthrow of the czar, the Germans were able to advance and capture Riga on September 3, 1917. The Germans remained in Latvia at the end of World War I (according to the armistice terms), supposedly in place only until a Latvian national army could be organized; however, Germany sent Gen. Rüdiger von der Goltz to assume command of all the German forces in the Baltics (including the Freikorps, the German paramilitary organization). Latvia thus became the setting for a Russo-German conflict when Russia invaded Latvia on December 2, 1918. By January 3, 1919, the Russian forces had entered Riga, and the Latvian government fled. The Latvian and German forces, under General von der Goltz, were able to regroup, and they were poised to recapture Riga. On April 16, 1919, the Germans engineered a coup d'etat against the Latvian government so that Germany could put a less independence-minded government in power. The Latvian government, under Prime Minister Karlis Ulmanis, was able to flee and gain protection on a British ship, and the Latvian army declared that it would remain loyal to Ulmanis. Thus as of April 16, the Germans went from being allied with the Latvians

to being at war with them. The Germans captured Riga on May 22, 1919. As early as January 1919, Latvia had obtained military assistance from Estonia in its conflict against the Russians. The Latvian Northern Army and the Estonians were able to drive the Soviets out of portions of northern Latvia. On June 1 this force reached Cesis. There the Germans under von der Goltz attacked the Latvian and Estonian forces leading to the defeat (on June 22) of the numerically superior Germans. This became the turning point in the war. The Germans retreated to Riga, where an armistice was signed on July 3, 1919. The war continued against the Russian forces, however, and on February 1, 1920, an armistice was signed between Russia and Latvia, with the final peace treaty being signed on August 11, 1920, securing Latvian independence After the conclusion of the fighting in Latvia, many of the Latvian Red Rifles were reorganized and sent to fight in the Russian civil war.

Coding: There are two MIDs that are related to this war. MID #2604 begins on January 3, 1919, and involves Russia against Latvia, which is later joined by Germany and the United Kingdom. The second MID (#1269) begins on March 15, 1919, and pits Germany against Latvia, which is later joined by Estonia, the United Kingdom, and Poland. These two MIDs reflect the fact that Germany changes sides in the war, going from being an ally of Latvia to being an opponent.

Sources: Laserson (1943); Luckett (1971); Mangulis (1983); Page (1948); Phillips and Axelrod (2005); Plakans (1995); Rabinavisius (1943); Urlanis (1960); White (1994).

INTER-STATE WAR #109:

The Russo-Polish War of 1919–1920

Participants: Poland vs. Russia
Dates: February 14, 1919, to October 18, 1920
Battle-Related Deaths: Russia—60,000; Poland—40,000
Where Fought: Europe

Initiator: Russia
Outcome: Poland wins

Narrative: This war is the third in a series of wars that broke out in northern Europe as a result of the confluence of turmoil caused by the end of World War I (inter-state war #106) and the beginning of the Russian Civil War (intra-state war #677). Like Estonia (inter-state war #107) and Latvia (inter-state war #108), Ukraine was interested in independence from the newly formed Soviet Union. The German army stayed in the region after the November 11, 1918, end of World War I, partially to support Ukrainian independence (as it had done in Latvia). The conflict between the Red Army of the Ukraine allied with forces from the USSR against the White Army in Ukraine is included as part of the Russian Civil War (intra-state war #677). Meanwhile, the Western Ukraine, which had a significant Polish population, had declared its independence from the Soviet Union. The Polish population responded by launching a rebellion of its own against the Ukrainians on November 1, 1918 (intra-state war #681). Poland wanted to both assist the Ukrainian Poles and take advantage of the turmoil in the Ukraine to further its own territorial goals. Poland had been given the "Polish Corridor," which provided access to the Baltic Sea, by the Treaty of Versailles. Yet this strip separated East Prussia from the main part of Germany, and was occupied by German forces. Poland, under the leadership of Gen. Jozef Pilsudski, also wanted to expand Poland's territory eastward, into the Ukraine, as part of his plan to organize a federation of countries along the Soviet border (which would also bring Poland into conflict with Lithuania in inter-state war #117). The Soviet Union was in turn interested in Polish territory as a bridge to inciting revolution in Germany. As German troops began withdrawing from the area, both Polish and Soviet troops advanced, and they clashed in Byelorussia on February 14, 1919, marking the start of the Russo-Polish War. The Polish troops then took over the bulk of the fighting and the war in the Western Ukraine (intra-state war #681) ends as the fighting is transformed or subsumed into this inter-state war.

Both parties fielded large armies, though early engagements resulted in Polish advances. The major Polish offensive took place after Pilsudski entered into an alliance with the Ukraine Directory in April 1920 and their joint forces attacked toward Kiev, capturing it on May 7, 1920. The Soviets launched a counteroffensive that drove the Polish troops back toward Warsaw. Both parties fielded armies of about 750,000 troops. The Battle of Warsaw began on August 16, and for a while the tide of battle swung back and forth, with at one point the Poles being willing to agree to a small Poland (bounded on the east by the so-called "Curzon line"), as proposed by neutrals. However, the Poles were finally able to break the Soviet line, pushing the Soviets back in fierce fighting. A ceasefire on October 18, 1920, ended the war. In the Treaty of Riga (March 18, 1921), the Soviets were forced to partition Byelorussia and the Ukraine with Poland. Poland remained independent until it was again divided between Nazi Germany and the Soviet Union in the attack beginning September 1, 1939, the starting date of World War II (inter-state war #139).

Coding: Poland, an independent entity from 1492 until 1795, first became a member of the COW interstate system on March 11, 1918. This date ended a century of partition, in which the pieces of Poland had been incorporated into Russia, Germany, and Austria-Hungary. By March 1918, World War I was well on its way to destroying all three of those monarchies. On January 1, 1919, Poland became engaged in a militarized interstate dispute with the Soviets. In this bilateral dispute (MID #1219), the Soviet Union was the initiator and revisionist.

Sources: Clodfelter (2002); Davies (1996); Davies (1972); Figes (1996); Lukowski and Zawadzki (2006); Phillips and Axelrod (2005); Reddaway (1941); Wandycz (1969).

INTER-STATE WAR #112:
The Hungarian Adversaries War of 1919

Participants: Czechoslovakia, Romania vs.
  Hungary
Dates: April 16, 1919, to August 14, 1919
Battle-Related Deaths: Hungary—6,000;
  Romania—3,000; Czechoslovakia—2,000
Where Fought: Europe
Initiator: Romania
Outcome: Czechoslovakia, Romania win

Narrative: Austrian control over Hungary had been established in 1711. During the wave of European revolutions in 1848, Hungary unsuccessfully revolted against Austrian rule (intrastate war #554). After Austria's defeat in the Seven Weeks War in 1866 (inter-state war #55), however, Austria was forced to recognize Hungarian national aspirations in the Ausgleich of 1867, which made Austria and Hungary virtual equals in the Austro-Hungarian Empire. The Dual Monarchy dissolved in the aftermath of its defeat in World War I (inter-state war #106). Toward the end of the war, King Charles I (or Charles IV of Hungary) appointed Count Mihaly Karolyi as prime minister. As the Dual Monarchy collapsed, Karolyi proclaimed Hungarian independence, and Hungary became a member of the interstate system on November 16, 1918, five days after the armistice ending World War I. A republican form of government was established, and Karolyi was elected president in January 1919. He faced harsh demands by the victorious Allies, as well as domestic opposition from both the conservatives and the Communists. Karolyi then resigned to protest the Allied demands, effectively surrendering the government to the Communists. Communist leader Béla Kun declared the creation of the Hungarian Soviet Republic in March 1919 and immediately created the Hungarian Red Army, which he utilized on the domestic front to enforce nationalization of Hungary's estates (see intra-state war #683).

Meanwhile, negotiations, which eventually led to the Treaty of Trianon in 1920, were still taking place among the participants of World War I. Romania, Czechoslovakia, and the new Yugoslavia all put forward demands for additional territory (much of which they already occupied) at Hungary's expense. Hungary recognized the Belgrade agreement, which had already resolved Yugoslavia's territorial goals, so Yugoslavia was hesitant about military action. With the support of France and Italy, however, Romania attacked northeast Hungary on April 16, 1919, starting the war. Though initially denying that it would join the Romanian attack, Czechoslovakian forces crossed the demarcation line on April 26. Having accomplished most of its goals, the Romanians heeded the request of the Allied powers to stop fighting; nevertheless, the Czechs continued their advance on Salgotarjan. On May 20, the Hungarians launched a counterattack, pushing the Czechs out of Hungarian territory and occupying eastern Slovakia. On June 16 the Slovak Soviet Republic was proclaimed. On June 13 the Allies established the demarcation lines between Hungary and Romania and urged the parties to cease hostilities. Though the Hungarians began to retreat, the Romanians and Czechs launched a new offensive that brought their troops into Budapest on August 14, marking the end of the war. The Treaty of Trianon was signed on June 4, 1920, formally concluding Hungary's participation in World War I. It was arguably the harshest of the post-WWI treaties, in that Hungary lost nearly three-fourths of its territory and two-thirds of its population, removing all non-Magyar populations. Hungary remained a dissatisfied and bitter state for the next twenty years, leading it to join the Axis side in World War II (inter-state war #139).

Coding: Militarized interstate dispute #1265 was initiated on March 20, 1919, by the Allies in World War I (Italy, the United Kingdom, France, Yugoslavia, and Czechoslovakia) against Hungary. These five initiators were also the revisionist side, since they were seeking territorial changes at Hungary's expense. On April 16, 1919, Romania and Czechoslovakia escalated the MID by initiating this war against Hungary. This is one of the few cases in which we code a state as fighting two separate wars at almost the same time. On March 25, 1919, Kun had launched an attack on the anticommunists, who were trying to overthrow him, which we code as intra-state war #683. Then on April 16, 1919, Czechoslovakia and Romania invaded, seeking territory, which we code as inter-state war #112. Though Czechoslovakia and Romania tried to claim that they were acting on the basis of anticommunism, Adám (1993, 37) argues that this was merely a pretext to more forcibly pursue their territorial goals in negotiations with the Allies. The wars were also territorially separate for most of the time, with the fighting for the inter-state war taking place mostly in north-eastern Hungary. Other authors have combined the two wars into one and named it according to whether they think the inter-state or civil war is dominant. For instance, Clodfelter (2002) describes this as the "Hungarian War: 1919," while Phillips and Axelrod (2005) call this "Kun's Red Terror," though they do cross-reference it as the "Hungarian-Czechoslovakian War."

Sources: Adám (1993); Clodfelter (2002); Hentea (2007); Hupchick and Cox (2001); Kiritzesco (1934); Phillips and Axelrod (2005).

INTER-STATE WAR #115:
The Second Greco-Turkish War of 1919–1922

Participants: Turkey vs. Greece
Dates: May 5, 1919, to October 11, 1922
Battle-Related Deaths: Greece—30,000; Turkey—20,000
Where Fought: Europe, Middle East
Initiator: Greece
Outcome: Turkey wins

Narrative: Ever since Greece attained independence from the Ottoman Empire in 1828, Greece and Turkey had a contentious relationship, fighting inter-state wars against each other in 1897

(Greco-Turkish War, inter-state war #76) and 1912 (First Balkan War, inter-state war #100). This particular war had its origins in the partitioning of the Ottoman Empire that took place at the end of World War I (inter-state war #106). World War I had partially been fought over issues of nationalism and representation. Thus the victorious powers were supposedly committed to utilizing the principle of self-determination in breaking up the defeated empires and drawing the postwar borders; however, it was particularly difficult to apply this principle in the Ottoman case, about which the Triple Entente (France, Russia, and Great Britain) had made contradictory commitments. Greece had been promised territorial gains at the expense of the Ottoman Empire if Greece entered World War I on the Allied side.

On November 13, 1918, only two days after the signing of the armistice ending World War I, troops of the Triple Entente plus Italy arrived to occupy the Ottoman capital of Istanbul. The Ottoman authorities were at the mercy of the occupying allied powers, and Turkish nationalists disliked what this meant for Turkey. The French took the imperial core of the city, the British the European side north of the Golden Horn, and the Italians the Asian side of the Bosphorus. Meanwhile, Greece pursued the "Megale Idea," or the desire to incorporate Greek populations into a Greek-controlled Aegean empire. On May 5, 1919, Greek forces began occupying areas around Smyrna that had historically been Greek and still had resident Greek populations. These areas also had large Turkish populations and had been under Ottoman government for centuries. This surge of Greek forces into Ottoman Turkish areas (and the Turkish resistance) is what began the inter-state war. In November 1919, by the Treaty of Neuilly, Greece was given the Aegean coast taken from Bulgaria. Also in November 1919, France attempted to occupy Cilicia (which led to the Franco-Turkish War, inter-state war #116). The Greek forces continued advancing in 1920, expanding their zone of control.

Then in August 1920 the Treaty of Sèvres ceded large portions of the Ottoman Empire to other countries, including Greece. Concurrently, by April 23, 1920, an Ottoman army officer, Kemal Ataturk, had established a nationalist Turkish movement with a rival government in Ankara—away from foreign armies. Turkish forces loyal to Kemal Ataturk fought against the Greeks and halted the Greek advance in early 1921 at Inonu. The arrival of Greek reinforcements enabled another Greek offensive, which resulted in thousands of fatalities. Beginning on August 26, 1922, the Turks launched their Great Offensive, leading to the decisive Battle of Dumlupinar, during which Greek forces were driven back to the Mediterranean. The retreating Greek army and the advancing Turks destroyed the cities in their paths, causing the deaths of thousands of civilians. The Armistice of Mudanya ended the war on October 11, 1922, and Greece was forced to evacuate. As a consequence of the war, in 1923 the Treaty of Lausanne produced Turkish boundaries very close to those of the present day; these were much smaller than the Ottoman Empire but much larger than those left to Turkey by the 1920 Treaty of Sèvres. Also in 1923, the allied armies of Italy, Britain, and France withdrew from Istanbul. The caliphate was abolished, the Ottoman dynasty ended, and the Turkish Republic was officially established.

Coding: The war emerges from a MID (#1270) in which Greece is the initiator and revisionist. Allied participation was limited in terms of both troops actively engaged and battle-deaths.

Sources: Clodfelter (2002); Finkel (2005); Hughes (1961); Phillips and Axelrod (2005); Urlanis (1960).

INTER-STATE WAR #116:
The Franco-Turkish War of 1919–1921

Participants: France vs. Turkey
Dates: November 1, 1919, to October 20, 1921

Battle-Related Deaths: Turkey—35,000; France—5,000
Where Fought: Middle East
Initiator: France
Outcome: Tie

Narrative: This war is similar to the previous war, the Second Greco-Turkish War, 1919–1922 (inter-state war #115), in that both are linked to the dismemberment of the Ottoman Empire after its loss in World War I (inter-state war #106). Though the Armistice of Mudros, signed on October 30, 1918, ended the Ottoman participation in World War I, it took a special body of the Paris Peace Conference to begin resolving the secret commitments the Entente powers had made concerning the dissolution of the Ottoman Empire. In the Sykes-Picot agreement of March 1916, Britain and France had agreed to a partition of the Levant, encompassing parts of present-day Jordan, Syria, Lebanon, Israel, and the Sinai in Egypt. In 1916 France had also signed the French-Armenian agreement that promised the creation of an Armenian state. For its part, Italy sought control over southern Anatolia under the agreement of St. Jean-de-Maurienne, and Greece sought the creation of a new Hellenic empire on the basis of promises made to Greece by the British. Thus on November 13, 1918, only two days after the signing of the armistice ending World War I, troops of the Triple Entente and Italy arrived to occupy not only the Ottoman capital of Istanbul but also other sectors of Turkey itself, as well as establish mandates in the Arab portion of the former Ottoman Empire. The French took the imperial core of Istanbul, the British the European side north of the Golden Horn, the Italians the Asian side of the Bosphorus; the Greeks began occupying areas around Smyrna (which precipitated the Greco-Turkish War). The sultan lacked the power to confront the foreign powers, so government officials in the Turkish Nationalist Movement began creating alternative government organizations outside of Istanbul, in Anatolia.

Meanwhile, Mustafa Kemal Pasha (later known as Kemal Ataturk) began to unify the Turkish armed forces under his command. Mustafa Kemal was concerned with the activities of both the Greeks and the French, though he assumed that if the Greeks were beaten, the French would fold. As per the Sykes-Picot agreement, France was to gain control over Syria; however, the French wanted to control southern Anatolia as well. Thus in November 1919 French forces landed near Adana. This region is also called Cilicia, and it once was the site of an Armenian kingdom. Thus it was apropos that the French forces were also aided by the French Armenian Legion, which had been created pursuant to the French-Armenian agreement, in order to give the Armenians an opportunity to contribute to the dismemberment of the Ottoman Empire. The French also at one time considered establishing Armenian sovereignty here. France faced Turkish resistance initially, though hostilities particularly increased in January 1920. Meanwhile, the French desire for control in the region also involved them in a war in Syria in 1920 (extra-state war #444). The Franco-Turkish War officially ended with the Accord of Ankara on October 20, 1921. French forces withdrew in early 1922, prior to the final agreement, known as the Armistice of Mudanya. As a consequence of the war, in 1923 the Treaty of Lausanne produced Turkish boundaries very close to those of the present day; these were much larger than those left to Turkey by the 1920 Treaty of Sèvres.

Coding: This war is linked to MID #3134, in which France is the initiator and revisionist. Both the war and the MID start on the same day. This war is sometimes referred to as the Cilicia War. Several scholars refer to this conflict as the Turkish War of Independence (which sometimes includes both this war and the war against Greece), while others tend to ignore or minimize it. Clodfelter (2002) does not treat this as a war but does devote a couple of sentences to it in his description of the Greco-Turkish War. Phillips and Axelrod (2005) do mention a "Turkish War of Independence" (1919–1923) but devote only one sentence to the French and Italians. This lack of attention is problematic, especially since in the Franco-Turkish War, Turkey had to fight a major power and suffered almost twice the number of battle-deaths it suffered against the Greeks.

Sources: Clodfelter (2002); Finkel (2005); Kaplan (2002); Lenczowski (1980); Phillips and Axelrod (2005).

INTER-STATE WAR #117:
The Lithuanian-Polish War of 1920

Participants: Poland vs. Lithuania
Dates: July 15, 1920, to December 1, 1920
Battle-Related Deaths: Poland—500; Lithuania—500
Where Fought: Europe
Initiator: Poland
Outcome: Poland wins

Narrative: Though Lithuania had been part of Poland, by the eighteenth century it had come under Russian control. In the nineteenth century a growing Lithuanian national movement led to frequent anti-Russian uprisings. During World War I (inter-state war #106), Lithuania was occupied by German troops. In February 1918 Lithuania was proclaimed an independent kingdom, under German protection. Russian troops immediately invaded, but they were driven out by the Germans. Germany then forced Soviet Russia to abandon all claims to Lithuania in the Treaty of Brest-Litovsk on March 3, 1918, and an independent Lithuanian republic was created in November 1918. After the conclusion of the war, however, the Soviets wanted to recover some of the lost former Russian territory and invaded Estonia (inter-state war #107) and Latvia (inter-state war #108), forcing German troops to retreat. The Soviets had similar plans for Lithuania, and a Lithuanian Soviet composed of exiles was created in Moscow in December 1918. After advancing into Estonia and Latvia, the Soviet Union entered into negotiations with the Germans for an evacuation of Lithuania. The Germans withdrew from Vilna (Vilnius). The Soviets arrived on January 5, 1919, and created the Lithuanian Provisional Government, planning to continue from there to unite with the Marxist revolution in Germany, which was anticipated according to communist theory. The revolution did not come to fruition, however, and suppression of the Spartacist uprising (intra-state war #682) convinced the Germans to halt their withdrawal from Lithuania. The Soviets then abandoned their plans for further advances.

Lithuania faced two additional problems: a dispute over Memel with the Allies and a dispute over Vilna with Poland stemming from competing land claims addressed in the Treaty of Versailles. Poland, under the leadership of Gen. Józef Klemens Pilsudski, wanted to regain from Russia territory that had belonged to the kingdom of Poland-Lithuania in the eighteenth century (including Vilna). Polish aims led to the Russo-Polish War (inter-state war #109) in February 1919, and within the context of that war, Polish forces captured Vilna in April 1919. At the Versailles Peace Conference, Polish nationalists had claimed all of Lithuania, and Polish patriot Ignacy Jan Paderewski proposed a union of Poland and Lithuania, an offer rejected by Lithuania. Versailles ultimately awarded Vilna to Lithuania. By early 1920 the Soviets decided to come to terms with the Baltic States and signed peace treaties with Estonia (February 2, 1920), Lithuania (July 12, 1920), and Latvia (August 11, 1920). In the bilateral peace treaty between Moscow and Lithuania, the Soviet Union recognized a large Lithuania, including the city of Vilna; however, in spring 1920 this city was still under Polish military occupation. In July 1920 fighting began between the Lithuanians and Poland over control of Vilna. As the Soviet troops were pushing Polish troops back during the Russo-Polish War, Lithuania reoccupied Vilna. A commission from the League of Nations intervened, and on October 7, 1920, the Armistice of Suwalki was signed according to which the Poles were to keep twenty-five miles south of Vilna. Nevertheless, on October 9 the Poles launched a new offensive and recaptured Vilna. The League attempted to encourage negotiations between the two countries without success. On November 23, 1920, however, Poland and Lithuania did accede to League demands to stop hostilities, though the two countries remained technically at war until 1927. In January 1922 Poland held a general election in Vilna, and the people voted to become part of Poland. Vilna was officially incorporated into Poland on March 22, 1923, and it remained under Polish control until World War II.

Coding: Lithuania became a member of the COW interstate system on February 16, 1918. Poland joined slightly later, on November 3, 1918. Hence this war occurred almost two years after they were both founded. Poland was the initiator and revisionist in the militarized interstate dispute (#1272) "leading" to the war (though this dispute started on the same day as the war). Latvia mobilized troops (a display of force) on the Lithuanian side but did not escalate to use of force. Kohn (1999) and Phillips and Axelrod (2005) refer to this as the "Lithuanian War of Independence" and include all the events from 1918 to 1920.

Sources: Clodfelter (2002); Davies (1972); Hupchick and Cox (2001); Kohn (1999); Langer (1931); Lieven (1994); Mowat (1927); Page (1948); Palmer (2005); Phillips and Axelrod (2005); Rabinavisius (1943); White (1994).

INTER-STATE WAR #118:

The Manchurian War of 1929

Participants: Union of Soviet Socialist Republics (USSR) vs. China
Dates: August 17, 1929, to December 3, 1929
Battle-Related Deaths: China—3,000; USSR—200
Where Fought: Asia

Initiator: Russia
Outcome: Russia wins

Narrative: This war primarily concerns the status of Manchuria. In the Sino-Russian War of 1900 (inter-state war #83), Russia had seized Manchuria from the Chinese Manchu dynasty. In the Russo-Japanese War of 1904–1905 (inter-state war #85), the Japanese, in turn, had taken southern Manchuria, though the Russians remained entrenched in the north. Despite the subsequent removals from power of the Manchu dynasty in China (see intra-state wars #657, and 671) and the czarist empire in Russia (see intra-state war #677), conditions in northern Manchuria had changed very little by 1929. The Soviet Union still held the former czarist Chinese Eastern Railway (which the Soviets used to connect Vladivostok with Moscow), and the Chinese Republic continued to press for Chinese control of the area. From 1926 to 1929 the Nationalist Nanking government continued to expand its control over opposition groups, such as the Muslims and the northern warlords (intra-state war #698) and was also able to capture Beijing despite Japanese intervention (intra-state war #700). The new leader of Manchuria, Chang Hsuehliang, soon embraced the Nationalist cause as well, and resentment of the Soviet influence there steadily grew. In May 1929 officials in the Manchurian city of Harbin disrupted what they said was a meeting of Russian Communists who were plotting the overthrow of the Chinese Nationalist government. Claiming that the Soviets had thereby violated the Beijing and Mukden agreements of 1924, Chinese officials in Manchuria in July began to seize the Chinese Eastern Railway and to close Soviet consulates and trade missions. The Soviets responded with an ultimatum, demanding the return of the pre-conflict status quo. Both sides began to mobilize troops along the Siberian-Manchurian border. The Chinese response suggesting negotiations was deemed unacceptable by the Soviets, who then broke diplomatic relations. Other states became concerned by the growing crisis, and France offered to mediate the dispute.

Meanwhile, Soviet forces began firing artillery shells across the border. The armed clashes began to assume the character of regular warfare when, on August 17, 1929, 10,000 Soviet troops crossed the border and attacked Chinese positions. At this point, the German government also offered to negotiate a settlement, an offer accepted by the Chinese but not the Soviets. Hostilities increased in October, and on November 18 the Soviets launched a major offensive along the western Manchurian border, seizing Manchuli and Chalainor. International pressure increased, and the United States urged the signatories of the Paris Peace Pact to urge both sides to negotiate. On December 3, 1929, an agreement was announced concerning Chinese and Soviet cooperation on the railroad. On December 22 a more comprehensive agreement restored the status quo ante in Manchuria, and Soviet troops were then withdrawn. Manchuria would soon be more effectively overrun by the Japanese (inter-state war #121).

Coding: The war is preceded by bilateral MID #41, starting May 27, 1929, in which China is the initiator. Neither side is coded as the revisionist in this MID, though China could be regarded as being revisionist in trying to reduce the Soviet presence in Manchuria. The forces combating the Soviets in Manchuria were clearly acting for the new central government. Clodfelter (2002) calls this the "Sino-Russian Border War" of 1929. Phillips and Axelrod (2005) do not include it.

Sources: Chow (1960); Clodfelter (2002); Ho (1935); Ulam (1968); Wei (1956).

INTER-STATE WAR #121:

The Second Sino-Japanese War of 1931–1933

Participants: Japan vs. China
Dates: December 19, 1931, to May 22, 1933

Battle-Related Deaths: China—50,000;
Japan—10,000
Where Fought: Asia
Initiator: Japan
Outcome: Japan wins

Narrative: Though this war is part of Japan's overall plan for expansion in Asia, it is similar to the preceding inter-state war (#118, the Manchurian War) in that it began over the status of Manchuria. In the Sino-Russian War of 1900 (inter-state war # 83), Russia had seized Manchuria from the Chinese Manchu dynasty. In the Russo-Japanese War of 1904–1905 (inter-state war #85), the Japanese, in turn, had taken southern Manchuria, though the Russians remained entrenched in the north. Following the period of the Chinese Warlord wars (intra-state wars #685, #692, and #698), the Nationalist Nanking government of China began to reassert its control in 1928 and 1929 by confronting opposition groups in intra-state wars #703 and #706. The Nationalists also repelled Japanese intervention in securing Beijing (intra-state war #700). Even though China was unable to counter the Soviet presence in Manchuria during the 1929 war (inter-state war #118), China still aimed to regain control over Manchuria and combat Japanese influence. In 1930, however, China became embroiled in new civil wars against the Chinese Communists (intra-state war #710) and the western Muslims (intra-state war #711). Japan saw this as an opportunity to act in contradiction to Chinese goals and to expand its own influence and control in Manchuria. Hostilities between China and Japan increased after the Mukden incident of September 18, 1931, when an explosion occurred on the tracks of the Japanese-owned South Manchuria Railway. Though damage was light, the Japanese troops in Mukden responded by beginning offensive operations against Chinese forces in the area, killing 320. Critics have claimed that the explosion was staged by the Japanese themselves as a pretext for seizing the Manchurian capital city of Mukden. The Japanese then began the seizure of other sectors of Manchuria. Initially, the Chinese government was too preoccupied elsewhere to offer much resistance, and the Japanese generally confronted only irregular forces; however, in December the Japanese significantly increased the size of their force in Manchuria, while the Chinese army finally decided to take a stand at the Great Wall. On December 19, 1931, the Japanese issued an ultimatum demanding a Chinese withdrawal. The Chinese refused, marking the start of the first phase of the war.

Despite protests by Britain, France, and the United States, Japan continued its advance, gaining complete control over South Manchuria. The Japanese then turned north, attacking the Chinese troops at Harbin. The Japanese took the city on January 5, 1932. The Japanese invited former Chinese emperor Pu-Yi to become head of state of the puppet state of Manchukuo (meaning Manchu Nation), which was proclaimed on February 18, 1932. The second phase of the conflict began with what is known as the "January 28 Incident." Japan was also interested in extending its influence in Shanghai, where it had concessions. On January 18 five Japanese monks were attacked in Shanghai, leading to further protests against the Japanese presence. On January 28 the Japanese attacked various targets, including the Chinese army stationed there. Fierce fighting took place involving attacks by both Japanese ships and airplanes. The Chinese forces withdrew on March 2, 1932. Delegates from the League of Nations soon arrived to stop the fighting. The Shanghai cease-fire was signed on May 5, 1932, making Shanghai into a demilitarized zone. Fighting continued, though in 1933 the locus of the war was the former Chinese province of Jehol (spelled Rehe in Pinyin). This province, just north of the Great Wall, west of Manchuria, and east of Mongolia, was also conquered by Japan and annexed to Manchukuo. The presence of Japanese troops so close to Beijing forced the Chinese to accept an armistice. On May 22 fighting generally ceased and a preliminary truce was arranged, ending the war. The final Armistice of T'ang-ku was signed on May 31, 1933. China appealed to the League of Nations for assistance, and the League's investigation, the Lytton Report, condemned the Japanese invasion. However, this just led to the Japanese withdrawal from the League. The Japanese would soon launch an invasion of China proper (inter-state war #130, the Third Sino-Japanese War of 1937–1941).

Coding: The preceding militarized interstate dispute (#129), which began on September 18, 1931, and ended on May 31, 1933, was initiated by Japan, and Japan is also the revisionist side. Clodfelter separates this conflict into two distinct wars: the "Manchurian and Jehol Campaigns" of 1931–1933 and the "Battle of Shanghai, 1932." Phillips and Axelrod and Kohn only briefly discuss this war in the context of the Chinese Civil War (1927–1937). Though the Japanese argued that Manchukuo was independent, it had minimal rights to autonomous government in reality. Thus this entity lacked sufficient independence to be considered a member of the COW interstate system. The conquest of Manchuria was also an integral part of the struggle for control of the domestic politics of Japan, over which the Japanese army was gradually gaining influence. The Imperial Way and Control Factions gradually cemented control of Japan in the period 1932–1936. A substantial part of their political leverage came from their demonstrating the effectiveness of military governance in Manchukuo and from the fact that the Army General Staff in Tokyo had planned the 1931 invasion of Manchuria without cabinet approval.

Sources: Brecher and Wilkenfeld (1997); Chow (1933); Clodfelter (2002); Elleman (2001); Lei (1932); Michael and Taylor (1964); Richardson (1960a); Schurmann and Schell (1967); Snow (1933).

INTER-STATE WAR #124:
The Chaco War of 1932–1935

Participants: Paraguay vs. Bolivia
Dates: June 15, 1932, to June 12, 1935

Battle-Related Deaths: Bolivia—56,661; Paraguay—36,000
Where Fought: W. Hemisphere
Initiator: Bolivia
Outcome: Paraguay wins

Narrative: Only seventy years after half its population died in the Lopez War (inter-state war #49), Paraguay, a tiny, landlocked country, entered a bloody war against Bolivia. This time, instead of initiating a war against Argentina and Brazil, Paraguay fought a defensive war against Bolivia, a country three times more populous than itself. In the War of the Pacific (inter-state war #64, 1879–1883), Bolivia had lost its access to the sea to Chile, which had gained a few hundred miles of coastline. For a long time, Bolivia had dreamed of regaining its lost territory, though that hope finally died; however, the disputed Chaco region was an area in which Bolivia might expand instead. Though the territory was an impoverished region about the size of Italy, there was hope that it might hold oil reserves, and it did offer access to the Atlantic via the Río Paraguay and Río de la Plata. Both Bolivia and Paraguay had claims to the Chaco dating back to the sixteenth and seventeenth centuries. Unfortunately, as a colonial power, Spain was not particularly diligent about defining the borders of its colonies, so the dispute had never been resolved, and it became a key element in the countries' domestic politics. Argentina had ceded its claim to the northern Chaco to Paraguay in the Hayes Award of 1878. Bolivia, however, still maintained its claim, and there were numerous attempts to negotiate the rival interpretations. Argentina offered to settle the dispute between the two states in 1924, but negotiations in 1927–1928 were inconclusive. There were brief skirmishes between the parties starting in 1927, and by 1931, they were mobilizing for war, purchasing vast amounts of weaponry from Europe. Bolivia, as the better armed and trained party, anticipated an easy victory, and began preparing a chain of posts (*fortines*) in the Chaco.

On June 15, 1932, Bolivia apparently attacked the Paraguayan military post at Pitiantuta, starting the war, though Bolivia accused Paraguay of firing the first shots. Paraguay was relatively unprepared for war and initially developed a defensive battle plan. Nevertheless, Paraguay was able to recapture its post in August and began capturing Bolivian posts in the fall. Bolivia became sufficiently concerned about the turn in the war that it recalled German general Hans Kundt (who had trained the Bolivian army) to assume command of its forces. Kundt's primary objective was the capture of Fort Nanawa, which blocked Bolivian access to the river. The first assault on Nanawa, made on January 9, 1933, failed, and the Bolivians kept up the assault for six months. Paraguay finally formally declared war on May 10, 1933, and the League of Nations tried to stop the war, to no avail. The fighting around Nanawa was so severe that journalists began to refer to it as the Verdun of South America (Warren 1949, 308). The battles were fought in the Chaco, where disease, lack of water, and difficulties in supplying the troops decimated the forces of both sides. Paraguay was able to mount an offensive attack and by December 1934 was advancing toward the Bolivian oil fields. Because its losses had been so horrific, Bolivia issued a general mobilization call, recruiting young boys and old men into the army. Attempts to end the war were complicated by the fact that Paraguay withdrew from the League of Nations on February 23, 1935. However, a mediation commission of Argentina, Chile, Uruguay, Brazil, and the United States was eventually able to mediate a truce between Paraguay and Bolivia, signed June 12, 1935. A final peace treaty was signed on July 21, 1938. The boundary was to be arbitrated, though it would leave Paraguay with most of its conquests.

Coding: Paraguay is coded as the initiator of the militarized interstate dispute (#1027) that precedes the war by a year. Both sides are coded as revisionist in the MID. There is disagreement about which state started the actual war, each side accusing the other. Warren (1949), Raine (1956), Scheina (2003b), Clodfelter (2002), and COW conclude that Bolivia initiated the hostilities, partially because Paraguay was much less prepared for war.

Sources: Clodfelter (2002); Garner (1966); Ireland (1938); La Foy (1946); Phillips and Axelrod (2005); Raine (1956); Richardson (1960a); Scheina (2003b); Warren (1949); Zook (1960).

INTER-STATE WAR #125:

The Saudi-Yemeni War of 1934

Participants: Saudi Arabia vs. Yemen
Dates: March 20, 1934, to May 13, 1934
Battle-Related Deaths: Yemen—2,000; Saudi Arabia—100
Where Fought: Middle East
Initiator: Saudi Arabia
Outcome: Saudi Arabia wins

Narrative: Yemen had been part of the Ottoman Empire. In general, the Ottomans exercised only minimal control over Imam Yahya Hamad al Din, who ruled Yemen from 1908 to 1948. Yemen became independent with the collapse of the Ottoman Empire at the end of World War I. Although small, poor, and lacking in oil, Yemen was known as Arabia Felix because of an abundant water supply that led to the development of agriculture, which was able to support a population of several million in the twentieth century. After the Ottoman withdrawal in 1918, Imam Yahya wanted to re-create the historical Greater Yemen by expanding Yemen's territory. Yemen's northern neighbor, Asir, had once been part of this Greater Yemen. Asir had also been part of the Ottoman Empire but had gained autonomy in 1914. With the fall of the Ottoman Empire, however, the British, who had a protectorate south of Yemen in Aden, temporarily occupied the port of Hodeida and returned it to Asiri control in 1921. Meanwhile, Yemen's eastern neighbor, Saudi Arabia, was consolidating its control over most of the Arabian Peninsula. In 1920 the Saudi king, Abdul

Aziz al Saud, conquered the Asir region along the Red Sea. After defeating a rival, the ruler of the Hejaz, in non-state wars #1567 and #1568, Abdul Aziz al Saud sought international recognition for Saudi Arabia in 1926 (and it became a system member in 1927). In 1925 Imam Yahya was able to gain control of the Asir port of Hodeida. In effect, this split Asir between Saudi and Yemeni control. The border between Asir and Saudi Arabia was not demarcated, and the dispute between Yemen and Saudi Arabia over Asir resulted in war in 1934. In January 1934 Yemen sent troops into the disputed territory. On March 15 Saudi Arabia issued a threat to Yemen, declaring war on March 20, 1934. The Saudis advanced quickly, capturing the Asir cities of Haraja on April 7 and Najran on April 21 and entering Yemen to seize Hodeida on April 28. The better-armed Saudis won the seven-week war decisively, ending the conflict on May 13, 1834. In the Treaty of Taif, signed June 23, 1934, Yemen was forced to renounce its claims to most of Asir.

Coding: Yemen has been a member of the interstate system since 1926, initially as state #678, the Yemen Arab Republic, 1926–1990, and subsequently as member #679, under the name Yemen after the unification with #680, the People's Democratic Republic of Yemen. Saudi Arabia has been a system member since 1927. Saudi Arabia was the initiator and revisionist in the militarized interstate dispute (MID #1129), begun on November 15, 1933, which is the MID preceding the war.

Sources: Burrowes (1987); Clodfelter (2002); Hiro (1996); Kostiner (1993); Lenczowski (1987); Schofield (1999); Wenner (1991); Wenner (1967).

INTER-STATE WAR #127:
The Conquest of Ethiopia of 1935–1936

Participants: Italy vs. Ethiopia
Dates: October 3, 1935, to May 9, 1936
Battle-Related Deaths: Ethiopia—16,000;
Italy—4,000

Where Fought: Africa
Initiator: Italy
Outcome: Italy wins

Narrative: After its relatively late unification, Italy had wanted to catch up to the other powers in developing a colonial empire; however, Italian plans had initially been frustrated by French activities in Tunisia in 1881 (extra-state war #383). The Italians were able to briefly establish a protectorate over Ethiopia as the result of a war in 1887 (extra-state war #392). Italy was also able to gain control over a portion of Somaliland in 1889. Italian colonial designs were destroyed, however, by Italy's loss to Ethiopia at Aduwa in 1896 during the Second Italian-Ethiopian War (extra-state war #407), where 80,000 Ethiopians had mauled and routed 20,000 Italians. Italy then shifted its focus to Tripoli (Libya) and gained control of Libya and the Dodecanese as a result of the Italian-Turkish War in 1911 (inter-state #97). The Italian defeat in 1896 had for a long time discouraged further attempts to colonize Ethiopia, but in 1935, under Mussolini's rule, Italy decided to try again. A clash at Wal Wal, along the border between Ethiopia and Italian Somaliland, on December 5, 1934, raised tensions. Ethiopia proposed arbitration, which Italy rejected, prompting Ethiopia to appeal to the League of Nations. This became a famous test case of the ability (or inability) of the League of Nations to prevent the aggressions that were leading up to World War II. The League Council initially declined to act. On October 3, 1935, Italy invaded Ethiopia in a two-front attack, from Eritrea in the northeast and from Italian Somaliland in the southeast. On October 7 the League Council did find Italy guilty of aggression, though Britain and France ruled out any meaningful sanctions. France had some sympathy for the Italians, and the United Kingdom feared that stronger actions, such as closing the Suez Canal to Italian shipping, might induce Italy to widen the war. Italy, boasting modern weaponry, quickly defeated Ethiopia, capturing the capital of Addis Ababa on May 5, 1936. On June 1, 1936, the king of Italy was also declared the emperor of Ethiopia. Subsequently, Ethiopia was combined with Eritrea and Italian Somaliland to form Italian East Africa. In 1941, during WWII, British and South African troops conquered Ethiopia and restored Emperor Haile Selassie to his throne.

Coding: Ethiopia was a member of the COW interstate system from 1898 through 1936, so the war between Italy and Ethiopia was an inter-state war. The war is preceded by MID #111, which was initiated by Ethiopia against Italy on November 22, 1934. Italy is, however, coded as the revisionist state. The United Kingdom entered the MID on the Ethiopian side on August 22, 1935, but its highest use of force was a show of ships, so it is not a war participant.

Sources: Albrecht-Carrié (1958); Badoglio (1937); Clodfelter (2002); Palmer and Colton (1964); Phillips and Axelrod (2005); Richardson (1960a); Sandford (1946).

INTER-STATE WAR #130:
The Third Sino-Japanese War of 1937–1941

Participants: Japan vs. China
Dates: July 7, 1937, to December 6, 1941
Battle-Related Deaths: China—750,000;
  Japan—250,000
Where Fought: Asia
Initiator: Japan
Outcome: Japan wins

Narrative: This war continued a long struggle between Japan and China that had included the First Sino-Japanese War of 1894–1895 (inter-state war #73), Japanese intervention in 1927 during the Chinese Northern Expedition (intra-state war #700), and the Second Sino-Japanese War of 1931–1933 (inter-state war #121). It also marked a shift in Japanese policies from one of more gradual encroachment into one in which Japan aimed at continental and regional domination. After conquering Manchuria, Japan began to spread its influence southward, hoping to persuade China to provide it with special concessions along the coast. Meanwhile, the Chinese Kuomintang (KMT) government was occupied with the Chinese Communist revolt, particularly in the Long March (see intra-state war #710). Consequently, as the Japanese advanced, the Chinese vacated northern China. The Chinese Communists had officially declared war against Japan in 1932; however, the KMT had hoped to be able to destroy the Communists before confronting Japan. The growing influence of Japan served to create a common threat, and the two Chinese forces finally developed a united front against Japan in 1936.

The specific precipitant of this war was referred to as the Marco Polo Bridge Incident. On July 7, 1937, Japanese and Chinese forces clashed near the Marco Polo Bridge, slightly south of Beijing (Peking), and the Japanese used this incident as the excuse for war. Japan launched two general offensives, one in the north heading toward Beijing and the other spreading out from Shanghai. Beijing was captured at the end of July. Japanese forces then pushed south across much of the rest of the urban areas and coastal provinces of China. During their advances, the Japanese brutalized the Chinese population, for instance in the "Rape of Nanking," which may have led to the deaths of over 600,000 civilians in 1937 alone. The Chinese government fled from Nanking to Hankow, and from 1938 the war was fought along the middle of China with significant casualties. Hankow fell in October 1938, and the Chinese government evacuated farther west to Chungking. The Japanese continued to advance southward along the coast as well, seizing Canton, also in October 1938. A Chinese offensive in 1939–1940 involved significant fatalities yet produced few tangible gains, and the fighting reached a general stalemate (though by this point Japan occupied extensive Chinese territory). U.S. opposition to this invasion of China led the United States to impose economic sanctions against Japan. These, in turn, led the

Japanese to attack Pearl Harbor on December 7, 1941. With this attack, this inter-state war #130 ends (as of the previous day) and the subsequent Sino-Japanese fighting is subsumed into World War II (inter-state war #139).

Coding: The Sino-Japanese War can be seen as an escalation of bilateral MID #157, in which Japan is the initiator and revisionist, but since the MID and the war started on the same day, this is another of the few wars that is not preceded temporarily by the MID. This war can be seen as the beginning phase of the Pacific portion of World War II; however, it is the period in which China was fighting against Japan alone. Japan is coded as winning the war because of the territorial gains it made against China. The Sino-Japanese War does not so much "end" in 1941 in the fullest sense but is, in the COW classification, subsumed after December 7, 1941, into the global conflict of the Second World War. Other scholars, including Clodfelter and Phillips and Axelrod, attempt to segregate this war from World War II, referring to "the Sino-Japanese War" of 1937–1945. They thus report fatalities for this war and the period of World War II together (1937–1945). Clodfelter (2002, 412–413) listed Chinese military deaths as 1,319,958 and Japanese deaths as 388,605 for the eight years. Fatality figures that include civilian deaths range from 3 million to over 6 million.

Sources: Clodfelter (2002); Elleman (2001); Esposito (1964b); Michael and Taylor (1964); Phillips and Axelrod (2005); Schurmann and Schell (1967); Snow (1961); Williamsen (1997).

INTER-STATE WAR #133:

The Changkufeng War of 1938

Participants: Japan vs. Union of Soviet Socialist Republics
Dates: July 29, 1938, to August 11, 1938
Battle-Related Deaths: USSR—1,200; Japan—526
Where Fought: Asia
Initiator: Japan
Outcome: USSR wins

Narrative: While Japan was involved in the war with China (inter-state war #130), Japanese expansionism also brought it increasingly into conflict with the Soviet Union. In particular, Japan's forces in Manchukuo began to confront Soviet forces. In 1937 Japan sank a Soviet gunboat in the Amur River, killing thirty-seven crewmen. This incident helped to persuade the Soviets of their need to resist Japanese pressure. The Changkufeng War was a battle for a hill in the area where the Soviet Union, Manchukuo, and Korea met, within 100 miles to the southwest of the key Russian port of Vladivostok. The Soviets apparently felt that Changkufeng hill had some strategic value, so they occupied it on July 11, 1938. Sustained combat began on July 29, 1938, when the Japanese, who occupied the surrounding territory, attacked. The Soviets responded with an overwhelming air and ground offensive. A cease-fire was agreed to on August 11, 1938, and Japan withdrew, ending the war. Neither side scored an overwhelming victory, and they continued to test each other in the Nomonhan War the next spring. This small war and the following, much larger Nomonhan War (inter-state war #136) were important in convincing Japan to divert its military expansion away from the Soviet Union and toward Southeast Asia. Thus these wars helped lead up to the Japanese attacks of December 1941 at Pearl Harbor and across the Asia-Pacific region.

Coding: This war is preceded by MID #184, a bilateral dispute that had been initiated three weeks earlier, on July 9, 1938, by the Soviet Union. Both the Soviet Union and Japan are coded as the revisionist in the dispute. Clodfelter (2002) combines both the Changkufeng and Nomonhan Wars into the "Russo-Japanese Border War: 1938–39." Phillips and Axelrod do not include either war in their war list.

Sources: Clodfelter (2002); Coox (1977); Jaques (2007); Kikuoka (1988).

INTER-STATE WAR #136:
The Nomonhan War of 1939

Participants: Union of Soviet Socialist Republics, Mongolia vs. Japan
Dates: May 11, 1939, to September 16, 1939
Battle-Related Deaths: Japan—20,000; USSR—5,000; Mongolia—3,000
Where Fought: Asia
Initiator: Japan
Outcome: USSR, Mongolia win

Narrative: Following a year after the Changkufeng War in 1938 (inter-state war #133), this war represents part of the continued border conflicts between Japan and the Soviet Union. This time, however, Mongolia also is involved. Outer Mongolia had broken away from Chinese rule to become a member of the interstate system in 1921. In 1924 the Communist-led Mongolian People's Republic was established, and in 1936 it signed a mutual aid pact with the Soviet Union. The Nomonhan (or Nomohan) Bridge, the location of the war, was at almost the extreme eastern point of Mongolia, where it penetrated the Japanese puppet regime of Manchukuo. The border here was ill defined, and Nomonhan had a hill of some strategic value. On May 11, 1939, Japanese troops attacked Mongolian and Soviet forces stationed along the Khalkan Gol River. Fighting in June also involved significant air battles. Initially, the Japanese had some success, advancing into Mongolian territory. In August, however, the Soviets sent reinforcements into the region. The Soviet troops, under the leadership of the yet-to-be-famous Gen. Georgy Zhukov, drove the Japanese back to the border. The Japanese sought a cease-fire, which ended the war on September 16, 1939. The Japanese defeat is widely seen as inducing them to subsequently expand militarily in the direction of Southeast Asia and the nearby Pacific, including the attacks on U.S. military bases in the Philippines and Hawaii in December 1941 (inter-state war #139).

Coding: Mongolia and the Soviet Union are coded as constituting the initiating side of MID #183, which is the MID associated with the war. Both sides are coded as revisionists. Clodfelter combines both the Changkufeng and Nomonhan Wars into the "Russo-Japanese Border War: 1938–39." Phillips and Axelrod do not include either war in their war list. Jaques describes this conflict as the "Battle of Khalkan Gol."

Sources: Clodfelter (2002); Coox (1985); Coox (1977); Coox (1973); Erickson (1962); Friters (1949); Ikuhiko (1976); Jaques (2007); Jones (1954); Keegan (1997); Kikuoka (1988); Phillips (1942); Rupen (1964).

INTER-STATE WAR #139:
World War II of 1939–1945

Participants: Brazil, Bulgaria, Greece, Yugoslavia, Italy, Poland, France, Belgium, United Kingdom, Canada, Ethiopia, United States, Romania, Netherlands, Norway, USSR, South Africa, China, Mongolia, Australia, New Zealand vs. Japan, (Vichy) France, Germany, Hungary, Italy, Bulgaria, Romania, Finland
Dates: September 1, 1939, to August 14, 1945
Battle-Related Deaths: USSR—7,500,000; Germany—3,500,000; Japan—1,740,000; China—1,350,000; United Kingdom—418,765; United States—405,400; Poland—320,000; Yugoslavia—305,000; Romania—300,000; Italy—226,900; France—213,324; Hungary—136,000; Finland—65,000; Canada—41,992; Australia—33,826; Greece—18,300; New Zealand—12,200; Bulgaria—10,000; Belgium—9,600; South Africa—8,700; Netherlands—7,900; Ethiopia—5,000; Norway—3,000; Mongolia—3,000; Brazil—1,000
Where Fought: Europe, Africa, Middle East, Asia, Oceania
Initiator: Germany
Outcome: Brazil, Bulgaria, Greece, Yugoslavia, Italy, Poland, France, Belgium, United Kingdom, Canada, Ethiopia, United States, Romania, Netherlands, Norway, USSR, South Africa, China, Mongolia, Australia, New Zealand win

Narrative: Through the Treaty of Versailles, at the end of World War I (inter-state war #106), Germany was forced to pay heavy reparations, especially in terms of lost territory. Consequently, Adolf Hitler came to power in Germany in 1933 representing German nationalism (and the Nazi party) and the desire to regain lost German prestige and territory. In violation of the Versailles agreements, Germany began to remilitarize the Rhineland in 1935. During 1936–1937, agreements among Germany, Italy, and Japan created the Rome-Berlin-Tokyo Axis (later known collectively as the Axis Powers). Germany then annexed Austria in 1938. That same year, Hitler's threat to annex Czechoslovakia's Sudetenland precipitated the Munich Conference, where the meeting of Germany, Italy, France, and Britain sealed Czechoslovakia's fate in exchange for what British prime minister Neville Chamberlain called "peace in our time." His misplaced optimism caused the name Munich to become the symbol for failed appeasement. The USSR, which had been ignored at Munich, entered into the Nazi-Soviet Pact in 1939, which guaranteed Soviet neutrality in a future war. Meanwhile, the cycle of increasing hostilities had begun. Italy, under Benito Mussolini, conquered Ethiopia (inter-state war #127) and Japan invaded Manchuria in 1931, leading to war with China in 1937 (inter-state war #130). The USSR also became involved in two wars with Japan: Changkufeng in 1938 (inter-state war #133) and Nomonhan in 1939 (inter-state war #136), which also involved Mongolia.

It was Hitler's blitzkrieg attack on Poland on September 1, 1939, however, that started World War II. Britain and France, which had had commitments to protect Poland, entered the war two days later. Ultimately, the war would grow to include twenty-five interstate system members. After the French and British declarations of war, the war entered a phase called the "phony war," because of the lack of combat between Germany and the French and British allies until May 1940. During the interim, Germany did attack Denmark and Norway in early 1940, while the USSR went to war with Finland (inter-state war #142). In May 1940 Hitler launched his major invasion westward, marching through Belgium, the Netherlands, and Luxembourg to attack France and break its famous Maginot Line. The German advance also forced the evacuation of British troops at Dunkirk. Germany then proceeded to occupy northern France, and the French surrendered on June 22, 1940. Marshal Henri Pétain established a collaborationist French government in Vichy, in southern France, and in early July, French naval warships in the Mediterranean were attacked by the British fleet. Also in July 1940, Germany launched the Battle of Britain, its attempt to bomb Britain from the air into surrendering.

The war expanded into other regions as well, particularly the Balkans and the Middle East. In the Balkans, Italy launched an invasion of Greece in 1940, and Germany sent troops to aid its Italian ally, forcing the surrender of Greece in 1941. In the Middle East, Britain invaded Iraq in an attempt to prevent the region from being occupied by the Axis powers. The Free French troops and the British were able to take Syria from the Vichy French in 1941, and they stayed there for the remainder of the war.

Having been successful in the western war, Hitler turned on his former ally and on June 22, 1941, invaded the Soviet Union, seeking "living room," or *Lebensraum,* in the east. With the Japanese attack on the United States forces in Pearl Harbor on December 7, 1941, and the German declaration of war on the United States the next day, the war spread to the Asia-Pacific theater and became unquestionably a world war. Prior to 1941 the United States had followed a policy of neutrality in the war, though it had begun supplying war materiel to the Allies. In December 1941 the United States and Great Britain met in Washington, D.C., where U.S. president Franklin D. Roosevelt and British prime minister Winston Churchill developed a strategy of defeating Germany first before fighting Japan, though it would be some time before U.S. troops could enter the war. Meanwhile, the German offensive against the USSR was initially successful, with the Germans driving toward Moscow. Joseph Stalin appealed to Great Britain and the United States to attack by opening a "second front" in the west to draw German troops away from the assault on the USSR. In summer 1942, however, the Germans attacked in the south and the eastern front, advancing in the Caucasus and toward Stalingrad, the site of the determined Soviet defense. In the Pacific the Japanese had been making significant gains as well. They had captured the Philippines and Thailand, and had advanced down the Malay Peninsula so that they soon controlled all of East Asia. Summer 1942 also marked advances for the Allies. American planes confronted the Japanese at the Battle of Midway in June, where the Japanese suffered heavy losses. American troops went on the offensive at Guadalcanal in August. The same month the British troops in North Africa stopped the advance of the Germans under Gen. Erwin Rommel at Al 'Alamein.

In 1943 the tide of war began to turn against the Axis powers. By January 1943 the Germans, having suffered their greatest defeat, had been forced to withdraw from Stalingrad. The Soviet offensive in summer 1943 had then forced widespread German retreats. On July 10, 1943, the Allies landed troops on Sicily for the beginning of the war against Italy. Italian premier Benito Mussolini was overthrown on July 24; however, Hitler sent German troops southward to ensure that the Allied march up through Italy would not be easy. June 6, 1944, was D-Day, the beginning of the Allied second front in Europe. Troops from the United States, the United Kingdom, Canada, Poland, and the Free French made an amphibious landing in Normandy that led to the liberation of Paris on August 25, 1944. Allied forces continued their advance north and east toward Germany. By early 1945 Germany was being encircled by Soviet armies in the east and American and British troops in the west. Hitler remained in Berlin, where he committed suicide on April 30, 1945. Germany signed an unconditional surrender on May 7, and May 8, 1945, was declared V-E (Victory in Europe) Day. Meanwhile, American forces had been capturing islands in the Pacific from the Japanese, landing on the Philippines in October 1944 and on Iwo Jima on February 19, 1945. As American forces advanced, they were able to begin bombing Japan in November 1944. In order to avoid what was expected to be a costly land invasion of Japan, the United States dropped atomic bombs on Hiroshima and Nagasaki, which led to the Japanese surrender on August 14, 1945, thus ending the war.

Coding: This is the most complex war we have seen in terms of numbers of participants and battle locations, and it is impossible to adequately describe it in the space we have available here. The war traces back to MID #258, between Poland and Germany, beginning March 25, 1939, with Poland the initiator yet Germany the revisionist. The dispute began over Memel, Lithuania's outlet to the sea, which had been German before World War I and which was annexed to Germany again (to East Prussia) in March 1939. The next logical expansion of East Prussia would be in the other direction, southwesterly toward Danzig and the Polish corridor between East Prussia and the rest of Germany. Poland resisted these pressures of Nazi revisionism and, in that resistance, became the initiator of the militarized dispute, which did not subside until Germany invaded Poland on September 1, 1939. As in World War I, battle-death figures are on the conservative side because of unreliable reports from Eastern Europe. When Germany established de facto control of the governments in such countries as France, Belgium, and Poland, these nations were dropped as Allied participants in the war, even though the Free French, Free Belgian, and other similar military contingents fought with the

Allies until the war's end. In the case of Holland, although a sizable Dutch force resisted the Japanese in Indonesia in early 1942, the contingent was, for all intents and purposes, an arm of the Anglo-American command in the Far East, supplied and, indeed, directed by the Allies. Consequently, Dutch participation is said to have ceased when it capitulated to Germany in 1940.

Partisan and underground fighting in France, Yugoslavia, and Greece is not included as state participation. Thailand and Mexico, which sent fewer than 1,000 troops into active combat, suffered few battle-deaths and were therefore excluded as war participants. The Soviet invasion of Poland in September 1939 was not included because it was relatively unopposed and resulted in few battle-deaths for both sides. Also excluded was the participation of Spain's "volunteer" Blue Legion on the Fascist side against the Soviet Union. The British–Vichy French combat in 1940–1941 in Syria was included. Italy, Bulgaria, and Romania all enter the war on the side of the Axis; however, as the Axis was being defeated, they switched sides and re-entered the war on the side of the Allied powers. Conversely, France began the war on the side of the Allies, but after being occupied by Germany, the Vichy government of France participated in the war on the side of the Axis powers. Thus Italy, Bulgaria, Romania, and France are coded as being on both sides of the war and are coded as both losers and winners. Several sources divide World War II into a number of individual wars, generally on the basis of the various geographical fronts. For instance, Blainey (1988) divides it into the "European War" and the "Pacific War." Most scholars tend to treat it as one war, though Kohn lists seven separate war fronts and Clodfelter divides it into the "European Theater" and the "Pacific Theater."

Sources: Arnold-Forster (1973); Aron (1958); Blainey (1988); Burt (1956); Chambers et al. (1950); Cline (1963); Clodfelter (2002); Esposito (1964b); *Geschichte des Zweiten Weltkrieges,* 1939–1945 (1960); Keegan (1997); Kohn (1999); Miller (1975); Moriarity (2005); Paxton (1972); Phillips and Axelrod (2005).

INTER-STATE WAR #142:
The Russo-Finnish War of 1939–1940

Participants: Union of Soviet Socialist Republics vs. Finland
Dates: November 30, 1939, to March 12, 1940
Battle-Related Deaths: USSR—126,875; Finland—24,923
Where Fought: Europe
Initiator: USSR
Outcome: USSR wins

Narrative: This war takes place in the context of the beginning of World War II. After being ignored at the Munich Conference in 1938, the Soviet Union was increasingly suspicious of the intentions of Britain and France and fearful of a German attack. To forestall the latter possibility, the Soviets entered into a nonaggression pact with Hitler's government (the Nazi-Soviet Pact) on August 23, 1939. A secret protocol to the pact included a division of spheres of influence, with the Baltic States (except Lithuania) going to the USSR and a division of Poland between the two. World War II (inter-state war #139) began with the German attack on Poland and the partitioning of the country by Germany and the USSR. The USSR still feared an eventual German invasion and thus began to secure "buffer states" between itself and Germany. One area in which the USSR could have been vulnerable to attack was along its border with Finland, especially in the vicinity of Leningrad. Initially, the Soviets sought an alliance with Finland, but when that was rejected, the Soviets launched an invasion of Finland on November 30, 1939. The Soviet offensive began with an air attack on Helsinki and a ground invasion along the Finnish Mannerheim Line between Lake Ladoga and the Gulf of Finland. Despite the fact that they were at a severe military disadvantage, the Finns were able to repulse the Soviet advances. The Finns fought effectively for a long time, even winning a victory at Suomussalmi following fighting from

December 11 to January 8, 1940; however, the Soviets' numerical strength finally broke the Finnish line on February 13, 1940. On March 12 the Finns accepted Soviet terms for peace, whereby the Soviet Union took about 10 percent of Finland (near Leningrad) but Finland was able to maintain its independence. In June 1940 the Soviet Union seized additional buffer territory in Latvia, Lithuania, and Estonia without organized resistance. These countries remained part of the Soviet Union until it was dissolved in 1991. Finland, on the other hand, remained unhappy with the terms of the 1940 agreement and entered World War II in June 1941 as part of the German invasion of the USSR.

Coding: The war is preceded by bilateral MID #179, starting October 8, 1939. In this MID, the Soviet Union is the initiator and revisionist. Clodfelter (2002) describes this as the "Russo-Finish War" of 1939–1940, including it as part of "World War II European Theater." Phillips and Axelrod (2005) refer to it as the "Russo-Finnish 'Winter War'" (1939–1940).

Sources: Albrecht-Carrié (1958); Brody et al. (1940); Coates (1941); Chew (1971); Clodfelter (2002); Phillips and Axelrod (2005); Plakans (1995).

INTER-STATE WAR #145:

The Franco-Thai War of 1940–1941

Participants: Thailand vs. France
Dates: December 1, 1940, to January 28, 1941
Battle-Related Deaths: France—700;
   Thailand—700
Where Fought: Asia
Initiator: Thailand
Outcome: Thailand wins

Narrative: Thailand (Siam) was unique among the countries of Southeast Asia in its ability to maintain its independence from European colonization. The French, however, saw Siam's growing influence as threatening to French colonial interests, and a dispute between Siam and France over the border between French Indochina and

Siam became a military confrontation, though not a war, in 1893. The treaty that ended the conflict gave France all of Laos east of the Mekong River. Additional territory west of the Mekong was obtained from Siam by France without a war in 1907. Resentment over territorial losses to France contributed to this Franco-Thai War in 1940. In December 1938 a nationalist government (with fascist sympathies) came to power in Siam. In 1939 the country's name was changed from Siam to Prathet Thai, or Thailand. Thailand then set out to regain territory that it had lost to France. In Europe the German invasion of France led to German occupation and the creation of the Vichy government. The French Vichy regime was isolated from Southeast Asia and ineffective in exerting military control over the French colonial empire in Indochina. The Japanese occupied much of French Indochina in September 1940, pushing back the weak French forces there. Thailand began amassing weapons, with Japan's assistance. The Thais then took advantage of French weakness to issue demands in October 1940 for the return of the former Thai provinces in Cambodia and Laos. By early November border skirmishes had broken out on the Cambodian border. By December 1940 sustained fighting was under way as the Thais attacked the remaining French forces in Indochina. An offensive launched on January 9, 1941, initially saw Thai success, but in fierce fighting on January 16 both sides withdrew. The last major encounter was a naval battle, which was a French victory. The Japanese offered to mediate, and the two sides agreed to a cease-fire on January 28, 1941 (ending the war). The final Tokyo agreement between Thailand and Vichy France, signed on March 11, 1941, gave the disputed provinces, with a population of about 1.5 million people, to Thailand. Thailand's status changed substantially later that year. Although much of the Japanese attack of December 1941 was against European colonies in Southeast Asia, it is also true (though less noted) that the

Japanese forces moved through Thailand on December 8, 1941. Thailand concluded a military alliance with Japan on December 12, 1941. Thailand retained its monarchy, but the autonomy of its government was compromised.

Coding: Thailand initiated the bilateral MID (MID #613) against France on November 23, 1940. Thailand was also the revisionist. Clodfelter (2002) describes this as the "Franco-Thai War" of 1941. Phillips and Axelrod (2005) do not index it, nor do they include it as an aspect of World War II. Thailand initiated and completed this war against France while Thailand was still free of Japanese control. Hence this Franco-Thai War is clearly a distinct war and not just a part of World War II.

Sources: Clodfelter (2002; Decoux (1949); Keegan (1997); Michael and Taylor (1964); *New York Times* (1941); Paloczi-Horvath (1995); Paxton (1972); Wyatt (1984).

INTER-STATE WAR #147:
The First Kashmir War of 1947–1949

Participants: India vs. Pakistan
Dates: October 26, 1947, to January 1, 1949
Battle-Related Deaths: India—2,500; Pakistan—1,000
Where Fought: Asia
Initiator: India
Outcome: Stalemate

Narrative: After the conclusion of World War II, Britain was no longer willing or able to maintain its colonial empire. Britain's initial preference was to create a single Indian state with a federal structure that would provide representation to Muslims and other minorities; however, when agreement along those lines was not possible, Britain accepted the demands of the Muslim League for partition into two states: India, which would be predominantly Hindu, and Pakistan for the Muslims. The agreement, which took effect on August 14, 1947, led to a period of mass migrations by 10 million individuals: Hindus into India and Muslims into Pakistan. Furthermore, although British rule in India ended without a colonial (extra-state) war against England, there nonetheless was a bloodbath. Most of this killing took the form of inter-communal violence (see the Partition Communal War of 1946–1947, non-state war #1570). Deaths of combatants and civilians may have reached as high as 1 million, so this was one of the most severe recorded instances of inter-communal violence in modern history.

A hotly contested area was Kashmir, an independent kingdom bordering West Pakistan. Kashmir's ruler, Maharaja Hari Singh (who was Hindu), favored either independence or joining India, even though about 66 percent to 75 percent of his population was Muslim. In August 1947 the Kashmiri Muslim peasants revolted against their Hindu landowners. In October Pakistani troops disguised as local tribesmen entered Kashmir in support of the Muslim peasants. On October 24, 1947, Hari Singh appealed to India for assistance. India agreed to send troops only if Kashmir agreed to join India. On October 26, 1947, Hari Singh assented, and India airlifted troops into Kashmir (which marks the start of the war). The Indians troops were ultimately able to halt the Pakistani advance. As violence in India continued, along with the escalating tensions between Pakistan and India, Mohandas Gandhi was assassinated, on January 30, 1948, which dampened conflict briefly. Major assaults were launched in February, March, and April. The final Indian major assault began on May 18 and involved fierce fighting. The battlefront soon stalemated, however, with one-third of Kashmir under Pakistani control (hence the war is coded as a stalemate). In August 1948 the United Nations called for an end to the hostilities, and a UN-ordered cease-fire was enacted on January 1, 1949 (thereby ending the war). The cease-fire line, which was referred to as the line of control (LOC), remains, even though India and Pakistan would fight two more wars over Kashmir, inter-state wars #166 and #223.

Coding: The war is preceded by bilateral MID #1238, initiated by India but with Pakistan the revisionist, running from September 26, 1947, to January 1, 1949. A cease-fire was arranged by the UN for December 1948 though it took effect on January 1, 1949. Initially in *The Wages of War,* Singer and Small tenuously classified this as an extra-state war between the Indian government and the people of Kashmir based on claims by Pakistan that Pakistan's army was not a major war participant. However, as the evidence became clearer that the Pakistani troops had done the bulk of the fighting, this war was transferred into the inter-state war category as a war between India and Pakistan.

Sources: Brecher and Wilkenfeld (1988); Ciment (2007); Clodfelter (2002); Ganguly (1996); Margolis (2002); Paul (2005); Phillips and Axelrod (2005); Rummel (1997).

INTER-STATE WAR #148:

The Arab-Israeli War of 1948–1949

Participants: Israel vs. Jordan, Iraq, Egypt,
  Lebanon, Syria
Dates: May 15, 1948, to January 7, 1949
Battle-Related Deaths: Israel—3,000;
  Egypt—2,000; Syria—1,000; Jordan—1,000;
  Lebanon—500; Iraq—500
Where Fought: Middle East
Initiator: Jordan
Outcome: Israel wins

Narrative: The origins of this war can, in many ways, be found in Europe. During World War I the Entente powers had begun planning for the dismemberment of the Ottoman Empire after the war, and the agreements into which they entered sometimes contained competing commitments. In 1915 the British entered into an agreement with Sherif Hussein of Mecca whereby the British would support Arab movements for independence in the area south of Turkey. The Sykes-Picot agreement between Britain and France in 1916 envisioned a division of the Levant between the two countries. In the Balfour Declaration of 1917, Britain committed itself to the establishment of a home for the Jews in Palestine. Following the Sykes-Picot agreement, Britain and France created a mandate system over the former Ottoman territory, and their control lasted through World War II, despite terrorist attacks by Zionist organizations determined to force Britain to agree to the creation of a Jewish state. World War II also significantly increased the flow of Jews into Palestine, despite Arab opposition. At the end of World War II, however, Britain decided to divest itself of many of its imperial commitments, including that over Palestine.

The British were unable to get the parties (Arabs and Jews) to reach an agreement on the future of Palestine and thus turned the issue over to the United Nations, which on November 27, 1947, proposed a plan for the partition of Palestine. The Arabs opposed any plan that would lead to the creation of a Jewish state in Arab territory. Arab volunteers were recruited for the defense of Palestine, and armed groups began attacking Jewish settlements (non-state war #1572). During the last months of British occupation (fall 1947 through May 1948), the British army lost several hundred troops in clashes with both Arab and Jewish forces, and many civilians were killed in the savage fighting. Britain terminated its mandate on May 14, 1948, and on the same day the Jewish state of Israel was proclaimed (and it was promptly recognized, making it a member of the interstate system as of that date). This ended the non-state war, and the fighting is transformed into this inter-state war. The war is coded as beginning the next day, as armies from the Arab states of Egypt, Iraq, Syria, Lebanon, and Jordan entered Palestine. Arab forces initially seized control over southern and eastern Palestine. The United Nations engineered two truces (resulting in a break in the war from July 18, 1948, to October 15, 1948). Iraq, Syria, Lebanon, and Jordan withdrew from the war on October 31, 1948, after which Israel concentrated its attacks against the Egyptian troops. Egypt finally ceased fighting on

January 7, 1949, thus ending the war. As a result of the war, Israel controlled almost 80 percent of the Palestine mandate. The West Bank came under the control of Jordan, while the Gaza Strip was administered by Egypt. One million Arabs were driven from their homes, creating a Palestinian refugee problem in neighboring states. The Palestinian problem would continue to bedevil the Middle East, leading to further inter-state wars in 1956 (#155), 1967 (#169), 1969 (#172), 1973 (#181), 1982 (#205); intra-state wars in 1958 (#743), 1970 (#780), 1975 (#801), 1978 (#807), 1983 (833), 1989 (#850); and an extra-state war in 2000 (#480).

Coding: Israel gained independence on May 14, 1948, and was instantly embroiled in MID #1793. The Arab-Israeli inter-state war broke out the next day. In the militarized interstate dispute, Egypt, Iraq, Jordan, Lebanon, and Syria initiated against Israel. Those five Arab states were also the revisionist side in the dispute. Arab-Israeli incidents between 1949 and 1956 and 1957 and 1967 do not reach our battle-death threshold. Clodfelter (2002) describes the entire period, including the phases before and after Israeli independence, as the "Israeli War of Independence: 1947–49." Phillips and Axelrod refer to the "Arab-Israeli War" of 1948–1949.

Sources: Abdel-Kader (1962); Albrecht-Carrié (1958); Clodfelter (2002); Glubb (1957); Israel Office of Information (1960); Kimche (1960); Lenczowski (1987); Lorch (1961); O'Ballance (1956); Phillips and Axelrod (2005).

INTER-STATE WAR #151:

The Korean War of 1950–1953

Participants: France, Netherlands, Thailand, South Korea, Turkey, Australia, Greece, Belgium, Philippines, Colombia, Canada, United States, Ethiopia, United Kingdom vs. North Korea, China

Dates: June 24, 1950, to July 27, 1953

Battle-Related Deaths: China—422,612; North Korea—316,579; South Korea—133,248; United States—54,487; Turkey—717; United Kingdom—710; Canada—309; Australia—291

France—288; Greece—169; Colombia—140; Ethiopia—120; Thailand—114; Netherlands—111; Belgium—97; Philippines—92

Where Fought: Asia

Initiator: North Korea

Outcome: Stalemate

Narrative: On their way to the "Big Three" meeting in Teheran in 1943, U.S. president Franklin Roosevelt and British prime minister Winston Churchill stopped in Cairo to meet with China's Generalissimo Chiang Kai-shek. The purpose of the meeting was to discuss the postwar arrangements in Asia, and the Cairo Declaration of December 1, 1943, committed the Allies to punishing Japan by removing from its control all of its prior conquests, including Korea (over which Japan had gained control in 1894 through inter-state war #73). In 1945, when preparing for the Japanese surrender, the USSR and the United States agreed to split Korea temporarily into two zones along the 38th parallel, so that each party could accept the surrender of Japanese troops in its zone (the USSR in the North and the United States in the South). Though it was not planned that the dividing line would be permanent, in February 1946 the Soviets announced the formation of an all-Korean (and Communist) government in North Korea. During 1947 the United States took the issue of Korea to the United Nations, which created a commission to oversee elections that were to lead to unification of Korea. The Soviet Union, however, refused to cooperate with the commission, and by 1948 it became clear that Korea would remain divided for the foreseeable future. North Korea became a member of the interstate system in September 1948 and South Korea in June 1949.

The United States began to reduce its commitments to South Korea, and in a famous speech on January 12, 1950, Secretary of State Dean Acheson did not include South Korea within Americas defense perimeter in Asia. North Korea, however, wanted to unify Korea under its leadership, and on June 25, 1950,

North Korean forces attacked South Korea. On June 27 the United Nations Security Council, in the absence of the USSR, which was boycotting the meeting, approved an American-sponsored resolution requesting UN members to commit troops to a UN army to be sent to Korea under United States' auspices (which marks the U.S. entry into the war). The Communists rapidly advanced, capturing the southern capital of Seoul on June 28 and driving the forces of South Korea and the United States back to the Pusan perimeter in the southeast corner of the Korean peninsula. On July 8 the UN appointed American general Douglas MacArthur the commander of the UN forces, which reinforced the Pusan perimeter and gradually pushed north. On August 29 Great Britain joined the UN contingent, which ultimately would include troops from fourteen UN members. On September 15 a dramatic UN amphibious landing at Inchon, far behind North Korean lines, routed the North Koreans and led to their rapid retreat to the extreme northern edge of Korea. At that point, the People's Republic of China entered the war on the side of North Korea and pushed the UN forces south, back across the 38th parallel, and recaptured Seoul. Fighting then bogged down along approximately the old border between North and South Korea. Shortly after the death of Stalin in the Soviet Union and the replacement of the Truman administration with the Eisenhower administration in the United States, long-stalled armistice talks were brought to a speedy conclusion, on July 27, 1953. Since the war ended at approximately the same boundaries at which it had started, the war is considered a stalemate.

Coding: North Korea and China are considered to be the initiating side of MID #51, the MID associated with the Korean War. In that MID (involving the sixteen war participants plus New Zealand), North Korea and South Korea are the two revisionist states. The MID is one of those rare ones that begins on the same day as the war it "leads to." In terms of nation-months (COW

"war magnitude") this is one of the largest inter-state wars, trailing World Wars I and II. Given the size of the contingent and the structure of the command, the Chinese "volunteers" have been considered official representatives of the Chinese government in this war.

Sources: Barclay (1954); Ciment (2007); Clodfelter (2002); Keesing's (1952); Leckie (1962); Rees (1964); Phillips and Axelrod (2005); United Nations Command (1953).

INTER-STATE WAR #153:

The Off-shore Islands War of 1954–1955

Participants: China vs. Taiwan
Dates: September 3, 1954, to April 23, 1955
Battle-Related Deaths: Taiwan—1,367;
China—1,003;
Where Fought: Asia
Initiator: China
Outcome: China wins

Narrative: As a result of the Chinese Civil War (intra-state wars #710 and #725), the Chinese Nationalists were driven out of mainland China in 1949 to a refuge on Taiwan. There, the Nationalists established a government (displacing the local peoples), which was referred to as the Republic of China (ROC), in contrast to the Communist People's Republic of China (PRC), which ruled on the mainland. Both the ROC and PRC claimed to be the legitimate government of all China (both Taiwan and the mainland), though ROC held China's UN Security Council seat in 1954. Also at stake were a number of offshore islands held by Taiwan, including Quemoy and Matsu in the harbors of Amoy and Fukien. These islands were strategically important as potential launching points for a Nationalist attempt to retake the mainland, were communist control of the mainland to falter. In 1949 the PRC forces unsuccessfully tried to capture Quemoy. After assisting North Korea in the Korean War (inter-state war #151), the PRC was able to return its attention to Taiwan. In early 1954 the PRC launched limited air and naval attacks on the Dachen (Tachen) Islands.

More important, on August 11, 1954, the PRC called for the liberation of Taiwan. Consequently, on September 3, 1954, the Communists began shelling Jinmen, or Quemoy (an attack that started the war and in which two Americans were also killed). The ROC garrison on Quemoy was heavily shelled on over seventy occasions from September to November 1954. On November 1 the conflict moved northward with PRC bombing raids on the Dachen Islands. Even the signing of the mutual defense treaty between the United States and the ROC in December 1954 did not dissuade the Communist government nor end the dispute. The PRC launched a major landing offensive on January 18, 1955, on Yijiangshan Island, which was seized by the PRC after all 720 Nationalist (Taiwanese) troops fought to the last soldier. Bombing raids continued against the Dachens, which were finally evacuated by the Nationalists with American naval assistance in February 1955. The PRC resumed naval battles and the shelling of Quemoy in March 1955. Consequently, in March 1955, U.S. secretary of state John Foster Dulles threatened to attack mainland China with U.S. nuclear weapons if it did not cease the attacks. Whether because of this threat of "massive retaliation" or because the engagement was becoming a draw, the Communists announced a willingness to negotiate on April 23, thus ending the war. Taiwan ultimately evacuated all the offshore islands except Quemoy and Matsu. The People's Republic has never released the battle-deaths its troops suffered in this war. The fatality figures cited above may be understated, since some estimates of PRC casualties (fatalities and wounded) are as high as 20,000. The status of Quemoy and Matsu would remain an issue of disagreement between the PRC and ROC and would flare into war again in 1958 (inter-state war #159). These struggles in the Taiwan Straits were important enough in the overall course of

the Cold War that Quemoy and Matsu became one of the major items of debate between Richard Nixon and John F. Kennedy in the first televised U.S. presidential election debate in 1960.

Coding: In the bilateral MID covering this period (MID #2987, starting on August 24, 1954), the initiator and revisionist is Taiwan. Some scholars do not include this as an inter-state war due to questions about the status of Taiwan and the controversy over whether there is one China or two Chinas, and which government is the legitimate government of China. The COW classification of Taiwan as a system member is not meant to take sides in the debate on one or two Chinas. Both Taiwan and the PRC simply meet the criteria for state system membership. If Taiwan were not a state system member, this war would be classified as intra-state.

Sources: Brecher and Wilkenfeld (1997); Clodfelter (2002); Keesing's (1955); Li (2003); Wortzel (1999).

INTER-STATE WAR # 155:
The Sinai War of 1956

Participants: France, Israel, United Kingdom vs. Egypt
Dates: October 29, 1956, to November 6, 1956
Battle-Related Deaths: Egypt—3,000; Israel—189; United Kingdom—22; France—10
Where Fought: Middle East
Initiator: Israel
Outcome: France, Israel, United Kingdom win

Narrative: The Suez Canal opened in 1867, and it paved the way for British control of Egypt. In 1875 Egypt's increasing debt led it to sell shares in the canal to the British, who were interested in it as a passage to India. Britain expanded its interests and its colonial control over Egypt subsequent to the Conquest of Egypt (inter-state war #65), and during World War I (inter-state war #106), Britain made Egypt a direct British protectorate. After the war the Egyptian nationalist Wafd party worked toward Egyptian independence. The British granted independence in

1922 though they maintained the protectorate till 1936. Egypt then became a recognized member of the interstate system in 1937. Egypt remained neutral in World War II, though Egyptian facilities were utilized by the British. After the war, Egypt was opposed to the creation of the state of Israel and sent troops that participated in the Arab-Israeli War of 1948–1049 (inter-state war #148). The defeat of the Arab states by the newly formed state of Israel led to the growing power of the Wafd party, with its opposition to the king and to the remnants of the British military presence. The Egyptian monarchy was abolished as the result of a coup, a republic was created, and Gamal Abdel Nasser was elected as president in 1954. Nasser tried to navigate the waters of the Cold War by following a "third way" between U.S. and Soviet interests. Initially, Britain and the United States offered to finance the building of the Aswan Dam; however, Nasser began pursuing anti-Western policies: entering into an arms deal with the Soviet Union, forming a military alliance with Syria, and extending diplomatic recognition to the People's Republic of China. The United States and Britain retaliated by rescinding the offer to finance the Dam.

One of Nasser's goals had been to force the withdrawal of all British troops from Egypt, and Britain finally completed the withdrawal of its military forces from the Suez Canal in June 1956. On July 27, 1956, Nasser nationalized the Suez Canal (which had been operated by Britain and France) in order to pay for the Aswan Dam and expelled British officials from Egypt. On October 13, 1956, the USSR vetoed attempts by the United Nations to place the Suez under international control. As a result Britain and France decided that they needed to punish Egypt, and Israel (whose shipping had been excluded from the Canal) wanted to utilize the crisis to enhance the security of its borders. The three states decided on a plan to invade Egypt. The war began on October 29, 1956, when Israeli troops spread out across the Sinai Peninsula, routing the Egyptian army, and Israeli paratroopers landed near the Suez Canal. On October 31, British bombers attacked Port Said in preparation for a British and French landing there on November 5. British and French planes destroyed the Egyptian air force, and the two powers seized the northern half of the Suez Canal. Both the United States and the Soviet Union applied pressure and/or threats to encourage the cessation of hostilities. On November 6 a UN cease-fire was put in place, supervised by a UN peacekeeping force. Britain and France were forced to give up their territorial gains, and by December 22 their forces had been evacuated. It was not until March 1957 that Israel finally yielded the Gaza Strip. Nasser emerged from the crisis with an enhanced reputation. In 1967 Egyptian pressure led to the withdrawal of the UN peacekeeping force by UN secretary-general U Thant. The subsequent closing of the Straits of Tiran to Israeli shipping initiated the Six Day War (inter-state war #169).

Coding: Egypt is the initiator of (and revisionist in) MID #200, begun on September 1, 1955—the MID that precedes the Sinai War. Other participants in the MID are the USSR, on the Egyptian side, and the United States, the United Kingdom, France, and Israel, on the target side. Clodfelter describes this as the "Suez War" of 1956. Phillips and Axelrod refer to it as the "Arab-Israeli War (Suez War, Sinai War)" (1956).

Sources: Bromberger and Bromberger (1957); Ciment (2007); Clodfelter (2002); Dupuy (1978); Henriques (1957); Lenczowski (1987); Marshall (1958); Phillips and Axelrod (2005); Thomas (1967).

INTER-STATE WAR #156:

The Soviet Invasion of Hungary of 1956

Participants: Union of Soviet Socialist Republics vs. Hungary
Dates: November 4, 1956, to November 14, 1956
Battle-Related Deaths: Hungary—926; USSR—720

Where Fought: Europe
Initiator: USSR
Outcome: USSR wins

Narrative: During World War II (inter-state war #139) Hungary had entered the war on the side of the Axis powers, declaring war on the United States and the Soviet Union in 1941; however, when Hungary tried to withdraw from the war, it was occupied by German forces. The Germans were finally driven out by the Soviets by April 1945. In 1949 the Hungarian Communist Party declared the creation of the People's Republic of Hungary. Communist leader Imre Nagy served as premier from 1953 until 1955. During radical purges, Nagy was removed from his position and expelled from the Communist Party in 1956. On October 23, 1956, a popular revolt led to three days of fighting between Hungarian citizens and the Soviet troops stationed in Hungary. Nagy was restored to power, and on October 28 he secured terms from the Soviets for the withdrawal of their tanks and seemingly embarked on a new course of liberalization for Hungary. Several features had made the growth of the popular movements possible in 1956. The death of Stalin in 1953 had ushered in an era of "de-Stalinization" across the communist world. For instance, in Poland in June 1956, riots against Soviet control led to a new government under communist leader Wladyslaw Gomulka, who was able both to be a symbol of resistance against Moscow and to reassure Khrushchev and the rest of the USSR leadership that Communists would remain in control. In Hungary, however, the Nagy government was clearly more reform minded and nationalist.

Hungarian Communist Party leader Janos Kadar appealed to the Soviet Union for assistance. Soviet domination of Eastern Europe after World War II was based on several factors, one of which was the threat of military invasion by Soviet troops. As Nagy realized that the Soviet withdrawal was a ruse and the threat of invasion appeared imminent, he appealed to the United

Nations for assistance on November 2. Furthermore, many Hungarians anticipated American support. However, the United Nations and the United States were preoccupied with the Suez crisis (inter-state war #155) and did not respond to Hungarian pleas. More than 200,000 Soviet troops invaded Hungary on November 4, 1956, and engaged Hungarian troops, marking the start of the inter-state war. The Soviets surrounded all the major Hungarian cities and attacked both the Hungarian military and the civilian Freedom Fighters. Some of the fiercest fighting took place on Csepel Island and at the Kilian barracks. In heavy fighting the forces of Hungarian reform were defeated. This demonstration of Soviet power dampened the forces for reform within the Soviet bloc, and the next such crisis did not occur until twelve years later, during the "Prague Spring" of 1968, when Soviet forces again intervened, this time against Czech Communists who were planning free elections. That invasion did not lead to war, however. Finally, in the 1980s, when similar unrest broke out during the Solidarity movement in Poland, Gorbachev renounced the Brezhnev Doctrine, and by 1989 the Soviet domination of Eastern Europe finally came to an end, a little over forty years after it had begun.

Coding: The bilateral MID preceding the war (MID #606) is initiated by the USSR on October 20, 1956, and the USSR is also the revisionist. A detailed military history of the Hungarian revolt remains to be written. Completely accurate figures for the size of the "Freedom Fighter" army, let alone its casualties, probably never will be ascertained. Fatality figures have ranged as high as 25,000 Hungarians and 7,500 Russians killed, though these figures probably include fatalities among the civilians (which COW does not include). Though COW initially used the fatality figures provided by Indian prime minister Nehru of 25,000 Hungarians and 7,500 Soviets killed, the fatality figures used here are from Clodfelter (2002, 599), for the month of November for the Hungarians. Unlike some other scholars, COW does not consider this war to be a civil war (or a war between the government and another domestic group). In a sense, the civil or "revolutionary" phase of the struggle might refer to the popular uprisings that led to Nagy being returned to power, though there were insufficient fatalities at that point for it to be coded as a war. The primary fighting took place as a clash between two states, the Soviet Union and Hungary. Similar to our perspective, Ciment refers to this conflict as "Hungary: Soviet Invasion," 1956. Clodfelter, however, describes this as the "Hungarian Revolution" of 1956, and Phillips and Axelrod refer to the "Hungarian Revolt" of 1956.

Sources: Ciment (2007); Clodfelter (2002); Ignotus (1972); Mackintosh (1963); Meray (1959); Phillips and Axelrod (2005); Tatu (1981); Vali (1961); Zinner (1962).

INTER-STATE WAR #158:
The Ifni War of 1957–1958

Participants: Spain, France vs. Morocco
Dates: November 21, 1957, to April 10, 1958
Battle-Related Deaths: Morocco—1,000; Spain—122; France—0
Where Fought: Middle East
Initiator: Morocco
Outcome: Spain, France win

Narrative: The Ifni War was part of the broad decolonization movement that was sweeping through Africa in the mid-twentieth century. It is also the last in a series of wars that were part of the Spanish colonial enterprise in Morocco. In inter-state wars #31 (1859–1860) and #94 (1909–1910), Spain began its colonial expansion in Morocco. In extra-state wars #431 and #434, France established colonial outposts, which ultimately led to a French protectorate in Morocco, while three relatively small Moroccan sectors remained under Spanish control. In extra-state wars #436 and #449, Spain and France attempted to expand their influence over Moroccan rebels. Finally in extra-state war #465, Morocco secured its independence from France. Consequently,

Morocco became a member of the interstate system on March 2, 1956. After attaining its independence, Morocco expressed an interest in regaining the remaining Spanish possessions as well. Ifni was one such possession, which had become a Spanish colonial outpost in 1860 (inter-state war #31).

In April 1956 public demonstrations demanding the reunion of Ifni with Morocco began, and France and Morocco announced an agreement to create a new Moroccan army. This development was particularly noteworthy owing to the relationship between the new Royal Moroccan Army and the "Liberation Army." The Liberation Army was a group of irregular insurgents, which in June 1956 had engaged in clashes with the French. Later that month the Liberation Army asked to be incorporated into the newly emerging Moroccan army, and by August about half of the 10,000 members of the Liberation Army were incorporated into the Royal Army. In early 1957 elements of the Liberation Army had engaged in clashes with French troops near the Spanish colony of Rio de Oro, and the Moroccan government had disclaimed responsibility for their actions. Then on November 21, 1957, large-scale coordinated attacks were launched against the Ifni enclave and Spanish outposts in the Spanish Sahara. The Moroccan government again disclaimed responsibility, indicating that the troops were parts of the Liberation Army irregulars, not official Moroccan forces; however, subsequent reports showed that the large Moroccan force included soldiers of the Moroccan Royal Army, members of the Liberation Army, and Saharan tribesmen (Saharauis). Initially, the Moroccan attacks were relatively successful, with the Spanish yielding some of their outposts and retreating to Ifni. The Spanish government responded by sending an additional 10,000 reinforcements to Ifni from Spain and the Canary Islands. In January 1958 Morocco increased its commitment to the anti-Spanish campaign, reorganizing its army units into the "Saharan Liberation Army," a division of which attacked the Spanish garrison at El Aaiun, where Spanish forces repelled the attack in fierce fighting. The war was expanded on February 10, 1958, when France joined it. Spain and France launched a coordinated offensive by troops supported by aircraft and were successful in driving back the Moroccan forces. Despite the Spanish-French victory, the war ended with an agreement on April 10, 1958, providing for the return of Spanish-held territory to Morocco. Ifni itself was not returned to Morocco until January 4, 1969.

Coding: The related bilateral MID is #1117. Clodfelter includes this war as the "Spanish-Moroccan Conflict: 1957–58," and Jaques refers to it as the 1957 "Ifni War." As mentioned above, the Moroccan government at first denied responsibility for the attacks on Ifni, claiming that they were the responsibility of the irregular "Liberation Army." If that were true, then this war would have been an extra-state war between Spain and a nonstate actor. However, the initial incorporation of parts of the Liberation Army into the Royal Army, the degree of coordination among the attacks, and the reports indicating that the large Moroccan force included soldiers of the Moroccan Royal Army, members of the Liberation Army and Saharan tribesmen (Saharauis) all indicate that the war was fought by and on behalf of the government of Morocco, thus making this an inter-state war.

Sources: Clodfelter (2002); Jaques (2007); Keesing's (1957); Mercer (1976).

INTER-STATE WAR #159:
Taiwan Straits War of 1958

Participants: People's Republic of China (PRC) vs. Republic of China (Taiwan)
Dates: August 23, 1958, to November 23, 1958
Battle-Related Deaths: Taiwan—1,500; China (PRC)—300
Where Fought: Asia
Initiator: China (PRC)
Outcome: Stalemate

Narrative: At the conclusion of inter-state war #153, the Off-shore Islands War of 1954-1955,

the status of the islands of Quemoy and Matsu was unresolved. The islands, off the coast of China, were controlled by the Republic of China (ROC), or Taiwan. The People's Republic of China (PRC) wanted to reunify the islands with the PRC and had tried to capture the islands in 1949 and in 1954 (inter-state war #153). As a result of the 1954 war, Taiwan had in fact withdrawn from the other offshore islands, except for Quemoy and Matsu. The basic elements of the 1954 crisis remained in 1958. The PRC had continued to subject the islands to intermittent shelling. The PRC rejected UN mediation in the dispute, claiming that the status of the islands was an internal Chinese matter. The United States had signed a mutual defense treaty with Taiwan in 1954 in an attempt to persuade Beijing of its commitment to the protection of its Nationalist/ROC ally.

In 1958, however, the situation was more dangerous because of the increased involvement of the American and Soviet superpowers. In particular, it was the decision by the United States in May 1957 to send missiles to Taiwan that served to precipitate the current war. Beijing responded by announcing a new attempt to liberate the islands. On August 23, 1958, the PRC began a sustained bombardment of Quemoy and Matsu. The war also involved air fights and a fierce sea battle on September 2. On September 4 the PRC extended its claim to territorial waters to twelve miles off its coast, thus blockading Quemoy and Matsu. The American fleet intervened to assist the Taiwanese navy and to supply the ROC garrisons. The PRC attacked the Taiwanese naval vessels, causing heavy damage, but were careful not to shell the American ships. The rhetoric for the conflict escalated when U.S. secretary of state John Foster Dulles pointed out America's commitment to the ROC and suggested that the United States might be willing to use nuclear weapons in its defense. On September 7, Soviet leader Nikita Khrushchev sent a letter to American president Dwight D. Eisenhower, warning that an attack on the PRC would be interpreted as an attack on the USSR as well. After a brief truce, the PRC resumed shelling the islands on October 20, but the Nationalist ROC garrisons held out. The war subsided after November 23, 1958. These struggles in the Taiwan Straits were important enough in the overall course of the Cold War that Quemoy and Matsu became one of the major items of debate between Richard Nixon and John F. Kennedy in the first televised U.S. presidential election debate in 1960.

Coding: The preceding MID #173 begins on July 22, 1958, involving Taiwan, China, and the United States. The Soviet Union joins the dispute on August 9, 1958.

Sources: Brecher and Wilkenfeld (1997); Clodfelter (2002); Keesing's (1958); Li (2003); *The Defense of Quemoy and the Free World* (1959); Wortzel (1999).

INTER-STATE WAR #160:
The War in Assam of 1962

Participants: People's Republic of China (PRC) vs. India
Dates: October 20, 1962, to November 22, 1962
Battle-Related Deaths: India—1,353; China—500
Where Fought: Asia
Initiator: China
Outcome: China wins

Narrative: While the world's attention was focused on the Cuban missile crisis of 1962, the People's Republic of China (PRC) attacked India in the Himalayas. India's troops were completely routed, and China gained prestige vis-à-vis India in their rivalry for leadership of the non-aligned movement. This war resulted from a dispute over the border between China and India, which had not been clearly demarcated by Britain during its colonial period. Britain had in fact continually tried to move India's border northward. There were two regions in dispute between the two countries, particularly after China's takeover of Tibet in 1950 (extra-state

war #462): Assam, or the Northeast Frontier territory of India (NEFA), and Ladakh (or Aksai Chin), in the northwest portion of India (north of Kashmir). Tensions between India and the PRC increased during the uprisings by Tibet against Chinese rule between 1956 and 1959 (intra-state war #741), when refugees fled into India. China was also irritated when India gave refuge to the Dalai Lama, after he fled across the border in 1959. Later that year, shots were exchanged by border guards in the Aksai Chin, an approach route from China to Tibet, which was particularly valuable to China. Assam (NEFA), high in the Himalayas, was equally vast but less strategic. China had volunteered to negotiate the dispute, giving India dominance in the east and China in the west, and India had refused. In late 1961 both India and China sent troops to establish outposts in the disputed regions, and by October 1962, Indian officers had advanced deep into Chinese territory. The Chinese responded on October 20 by attacking the Indian troops in both the eastern and western zones. The Chinese People's Liberation Army (PLA) had the advantage and advanced quickly against ill-prepared Indian troops. By the end of November, China had captured all the disputed territory in the west and most of the disputed territory in Assam. On November 22, China announced a cease-fire, ending the war. China kept control over Aksai Chin, while allowing India to reoccupy the northern portions of Assam. Though this war did not alter the de facto border, it is probable that India's poor showing in the war encouraged Pakistan to move against India in the Second Kashmir War in 1965 (inter-state war #166).

Coding: India is the initiator and revisionist in MID #199, beginning on November 2, 1961, which led to this war; however, China also is coded as revisionist, since both sides wanted to gain territory in Ladakh and the NEFA. Early in this war some Indian sources suggested that their forces had suffered 2,500 battle deaths. At war's end, however, this figure, according to Prime

Minister Jawaharlal Nehru, was around 200, excluding the "missing." Unofficial estimates range from 200 to 5,000 for India and a similar number for China.

Sources: *Britannica Book of the Year* (1963); Ciment (2007); Clodfelter (2002); *Communist China, 1962* (1963); Facts on File (1963); Feng and Wortzel (2003); Foreign Languages Press (1960); Kaul (1967); Maxwell (1970); *New York Times* (1962); Phillips and Axelrod (2005); Rouland (1967); *United Asia* (1962).

INTER-STATE WAR #163:
The Vietnam War Phase 2 of 1965–1975

Participants: North Vietnam vs. United States, South Vietnam, Philippines, Australia, South Korea, Cambodia, Thailand
Dates: February 7, 1965, to April 30, 1975
Battle-Related Deaths: North Vietnam—700,000; South Vietnam—254,257; United States—58,153; South Korea—4,687; Cambodia—2,500; Philippines—1,000; Australia—494; Thailand—351
Where Fought: Asia
Initiator: United States
Outcome: North Vietnam wins

Narrative: France had developed a colonial empire in Indochina through a series of colonial wars, starting with the First Franco-Vietnamese War concerning Cochin China in 1858 (extra-state war #349). This was followed by the Second Franco-Vietnamese War over Tonkin in 1873 (extra-state war #369) and the Third Franco-Vietnamese War in 1882 (extra-state war #385). Finally, the French-Indochina War (#457) of France against the Vietminh, ended French domination in 1954, when the Vietnamese Communists, who had been waging war since 1945 to gain control of Vietnam, defeated the French at the famous battle of Dienbienphu. The Geneva Accords that ended that war called for the division of Vietnam into two separate districts, divided at the 17th parallel. The pro-French forces would be relegated to the south, while the northern sector would be given to the Vietminh, a Nationalist/Communist front headed by Ho Chi Minh. This division was supposed to be temporary, until general elections could be held; however, the division solidified, and South Vietnam, or the Republic of Vietnam, became an interstate system member on June 4, 1954, and the North joined the interstate system on July 21, 1954. France decided to withdraw from Vietnam altogether on January 1, 1956, after turning power over to Ngo Dinh Diem.

South Vietnam's Communists, the Viet Cong, launched a civil war against the Republic of Vietnam on January 1, 1960 (intra-state war #748). The United States entered the war on the side of the South Vietnamese government on January 1, 1961. The war continued as an internationalized civil war until February 6, 1965. The next day, the United States began to bomb North Vietnam, and this action transformed the war from an intra-state civil war into the current inter-state war (Vietnam War Phase 2). After the Viet Cong launched an attack on the American military base at Pleiku, U.S. president Lyndon Johnson decided to respond forcefully by bombing North Vietnam, which had been supplying and training the Viet Cong from the south. The bombing campaign was expanded further into Operation Rolling Thunder on March 2, 1965. In order to support the bombing campaign, additional American troops were brought into Vietnam. Though they were initially deployed only to protect the planes, by June 1965 the American forces had become involved in direct combat missions alongside the Army of Vietnam (ARVN). As the ground war against the Viet Cong became a more complex guerrilla war, the United States committed an increasing number of soldiers to the war. Meanwhile, South Vietnam also received support from five other states that sent troops into the war (South Korea, Thailand, Cambodia, the Philippines, and Australia.) After three years of combat, the leadership of the Viet Cong and the

Vietminh decided to undertake a massive invasion of the South in January 1968. The Tet Offensive consisted of coordinated attacks on thirty-six South Vietnamese cities, including the South's capital, Saigon. Though the North was ultimately unable to retain many of its military gains, its ability to launch such a large-scale offensive stunned the Americans, and the Tet Offensive produced a major advantage for the North, as it served to fuel American disenchantment with the war. It also convinced President Johnson not to seek another presidential term. Richard Nixon was elected the next U.S. president, and he gradually began to withdraw American troops from Vietnam. At the same time, however, he also expanded the bombing campaigns into Laos and Cambodia. Nixon started secret negotiations to end the war. Under the terms of the agreement, the 17th parallel would remain the border between North and South Vietnam. The United States withdrew from Vietnam on January 27, 1973, though the war continued as a war between North and South Vietnam until the fall of Saigon on April 30, 1975. Ramifications of the wars in Vietnam spread throughout the region, contributing to wars in Laos (intra-state wars #751 and #756, and inter-state war #170); wars in Cambodia (inter-state war #176, intra-state war #785, extra-state war #475); a war between Vietnam and Cambodia (inter-state war #189); and two wars between Vietnam and China (inter-state wars #193 and #208).

Coding: From January 1960 through February 6, 1965, this was considered an intra-state civil war (#748) of the Republic of Vietnam against the Viet Cong, or National Liberation Front (NFL). The war was also coded as becoming an internationalized civil war on January 1, 1961, because of the participation of the United States, effective when a sufficient number of U.S. "advisors" assisted the Saigon government against the NLF for the United States to be considered a war participant (a minimum of 1,000). On February 7, 1965, after the NLF attack on Pleiku, the United States started to bomb North Vietnam

and thus transformed the war into this inter-state war. New Zealand, which participated on the U.S.-Saigon side, never sent more than 1,000 troops; nor did it suffer the requisite 100 battle-deaths to be coded as a war participant. Similarly, Clodfelter (2002) divides the Vietnam War chronologically into the "U.S. Advisory War: 1961–1964"; "Ground Operations in 1965 to 1972"; "The Cease-Fire War: 1973–1974"; and the "NVA Conquest of South Vietnam: 1975," as well as having separate warfare type subsections. While this war is a continuation of the intra-state war, the inter-state Vietnamese War Phase 2 of 1965–1975 is also an outgrowth of MID #611, begun on February 23, 1964, with the United States as the initiator and the Democratic Republic of Vietnam (North Vietnam) as the revisionist.

Sources: Buttinger (1967); Ciment (2007); Clodfelter (2002); Cooper (1970); Fall (1967); Gettleman (1970); Grant (1970); Herring (1979); Kahin and Lewis (1969); Karnow (1983); Phillips and Axelrod (2005); Pike (1966); U.S. Senate (1969).

INTER-STATE WAR #166:

The Second Kashmir War of 1965

Participants: Pakistan vs. India
Dates: August 5, 1965, to September 23, 1965
Battle-Related Deaths: Pakistan—3,800; India—3,261
Where Fought: Asia
Initiator: Pakistan
Outcome: Pakistan wins

Narrative: The First Kashmir War (inter-state war #147) occurred in 1947–1949 during the decolonization of the states of India and Pakistan following years of British rule. Both India and Pakistan had wanted to incorporate Kashmir. The war had ended in a stalemate in which one-third of Kashmir came under Pakistani control, with the remainder controlled by India. The United Nations arranged a cease-fire, enacted on January 1, 1949, establishing the line of control (LOC) between the two sectors. Pakistan desired to incorporate all of Kashmir because both shared overwhelmingly Muslim populations. Pakistan had expressed a willingness to have the issue settled by a plebiscite, to which India, content with the status quo, would not agree.

In 1965 skirmishes began along the LOC in April, when India unsuccessfully attacked Pakistani positions. Britain brokered another cease-fire in June, which held for only two months. On August 5, 1965, Pakistan sent its troops into the Indian-controlled section of Kashmir, marking the start of the war. Indian troops responded, attacking Pakistani positions. In September major escalations took place. Pakistani troops penetrated eighteen miles into Indian territory in Kashmir. India also expanded the war beyond Kashmir when it launched a major offensive against Pakistani areas near Lahore, which then became the focus of the war. Pakistan launched a counterattack on September 7, driving the Indians back into Indian territory. A major tank battle also took place around Sialkot, where India tried to cut communication and supply links between Pakistan and Pakistani troops in Kashmir. India also attacked farther south, into Sind, and the war was soon fought to a stalemate. From September 7 to September 15, UN secretary general U Thant tried to mediate the dispute, but Pakistan resisted because India had ignored previous UN resolutions that called for a plebiscite. However, the UN was able to broker another cease-fire, which took effect on September 23, at which time India controlled parts of Pakistan and Pakistan controlled parts of India. The cease-fire required that each state return to the positions it held before the war. The Indians did promise, at the Tashkent conference ending the war, to hold a plebiscite in Kashmir, and in this sense the war could be coded as a Pakistani victory. The plebiscite was not held, however, and India and Pakistan would fight another war over Kashmir in 1999, the Kargil War (inter-state war #223).

Coding: This war, although part of an ongoing Indo-Pakistani rivalry (inter-state wars in 1948–1949, 1965, 1971, and 1999), was immediately preceded by bilateral MID #1312, in which Pakistan is the initiator and revisionist. The MID began on March 5, 1965. The prewar phase of this MID included the fighting in the Rann of Kutch in April, considered by some to be substantial enough to be treated as part of the war, though fatalities at that time did not reach war levels. A cease-fire reestablished in June 1965 held until August. Clodfelter (2002) describes this war as the "India-Pakistan War: 1965 (Second Kashmir War)." Phillips and Axelrod (2006) refer to the "Indo-Pakistani War" of 1965.

Sources: Ciment (2007); Clodfelter (2002); Facts on File (1965); Lamb (1967); Paul (2005); Phillips and Axelrod (2005).

INTER-STATE WAR #169:
The Six Day War of 1967

Participants: Israel vs. Egypt, Jordan, Syria
Dates: June 5, 1967, to June 10, 1967
Battle-Related Deaths: Egypt—10,000; Jordan—6,100; Syria—2,500; Israel—1,000
Where Fought: Middle East
Initiator: Israel
Outcome: Israel wins

Narrative: As a consequence of the wars in 1948 (inter-state war #148) and 1956 (inter-state war #155), Israel sought to bolster its security by expanding its ties to the West, particularly with the United States. The Arab states sought to strengthen their positions by supporting the idea of Pan-Arabism, though they tended to be divided into more conservative and comparatively radical camps. Meanwhile, an unending series of low-level conflicts erupted along the demilitarized zone between Israel and its neighbors. The Palestine Liberation Organization (PLO) had been created in 1964 as a voice for the Palestinian people in opposition to the Israeli presence in Palestinian territory. An alternative perspective was offered by Fatah, whose primary goal was to liberate Palestine by armed struggle. Fatah launched its first military strikes against Israel in 1965. In August 1966 Israel responded by striking at targets in Syria, arguing that Syria was the primary supporter of Fatah. On November 13, 1966, Israel also launched a brief assault on Jordan. A majority of Jordan's population was Palestinian, and the Palestinians began agitating for action against Israel. Consequently, King Hussein of Jordan traveled to Cairo to sign a mutual defense pact with Egypt on May 30, 1967. The pact's being signed by the Arab states led to the perception in Israel that it was being surrounded by a tightening circle of opponents. In May Israeli chief of staff Yitzhak Rabin indicated that Israel was considering military action against Syria. The Soviet Union then informed its Syrian and Egyptian allies of evidence supposedly showing Israeli troop mobilizations. Egypt's president Gamal Abdel Nasser responded by ordering Egyptian troops into the Sinai and requesting the withdrawal of the UN peacekeeping force that had been stationed there after the 1956 war. Egypt also closed the Straits of Tiran to Israeli shipping. Support grew within Israel for a preemptive attack, which began on the morning of June 5, 1967. The Israelis launched an air strike on the Egyptian air force, destroying it on the ground on the first day of the war, and then took the Sinai Peninsula from Egypt. When the Jordanians attacked Israel, Israel counterattacked and seized the Old City of Jerusalem and the West Bank.

Finally, in the last days of the brief war, Israel drove Syrian forces from the Golan Heights. Both the United States and the Soviet Union were eager to contain the conflict and thus supported a UN resolution calling for a cease-fire. The war ended on June 10. By its conquests, Israel radically changed the map of the Middle East by gaining control over the Sinai, the Gaza Strip, and the Golan Heights; however, Israeli possession of these territories engendered additional hostility and became the basis of over forty years of crises and wars, including inter-state wars in 1969 (#172), 1973 (#181), and 1982 (#205); an extra-state war, #480; and intra-state civil wars in Jordan (#780) and Lebanon (#801,

#807, #833, #850). Small and Singer (1989, 30) identified the Six Day War, among 185 international wars, as the most intense, measured in terms of battle-deaths per day. Some Arab leaders had felt that the Arab advantage in population would be able to wear down Israel in a long war; the problem for them in 1967 was that the war had been so short and intense.

Coding: The war is preceded by MID #1035, beginning between Syria and Israel on December 16, 1966. In this MID, Syria, Egypt, Saudi Arabia, Kuwait, Jordan, and Iraq are the initiators against Israel. Of these, all continue in the MID until the end of the war, but only Syria, Egypt, and Jordan—the ones that proved willing to join the war—are coded as revisionist states. Focusing upon the territory that is in dispute, the Uppsala/PRIO dataset (Lacina and Gleditsch) divides this conflict into three separate wars: #104, Israel v. Egypt; #105, Israel v. Jordan; and #106, Israel v. Syria. The temporal domains of #104 and #106 are also expanded to include the 1969 and 1973 wars.

Sources: Cashman and Robinson (2007); Clodfelter (2002); Ginor and Remez (2007); Lacina and Gleditsch (2005); Phillips and Axelrod (2005); Safran (1969); Small and Singer (1989).

INTER-STATE WAR #170:

The Second Laotian War Phase 2 of 1968–1973

Participants: Vietnam vs. Laos, Thailand, United States
Dates: January 13, 1968, to April 17, 1973
Battle-Related Deaths: Laos—11,250; Vietnam—2,250; United States—375; Thailand—[ ]
Where Fought: Asia
Initiator: Vietnam
Outcome: Vietnam wins

Narrative: In the nineteenth century, France decided to create a colonial empire in Indochina, and in the 1880s and 1890s it expanded its control in the area around the Mekong River. Laos was one of the three nations that once constituted French Indochina. During World War II,

Japan allowed Vichy France to continue to rule the county. However, in 1945, even though Japan tried to declare the independence of Laos, postwar France sent its forces back into the region and asserted its control. The Vietminh in Vietnam conducted a nine-year-long extra-state war (#457) to gain their independence from France, in which the Vietminh had the support of the Pathet Lao (the nationalist rebel group formed in Laos). Laos finally gained its independence and became a member of the interstate system on October 23, 1953.

The Pathet Lao then began their opposition to the Laotian government and in 1960 launched the unsuccessful Laotian civil war, which lasted until 1962 (intra-state war #751). The Second Laotian War Phase 1 (#756) began on March 19, 1963, and the current inter-state war (or Phase 2 of that war) began on January 13, 1968. At that time the war fundamentally became one between North Vietnam (assisted by the Pathet Lao) and the government of Laos (aided by the United States and later Thailand). Beginning in 1968 there was a significant increase in the level of hostilities in Laos, which corresponded to the Tet Offensive in the war in Vietnam (see inter-state war #163). The North Vietnamese dominated the Communist activities, relegating the Pathet Lao to a subordinate role. The United States, which had stopped bombing North Vietnam at the time, shifted its targets and launched a sustained bombing campaign against the North Vietnamese troops in Laos instead. The bombing caused considerable destruction in northern Laos, particularly around the Plain of Jars. Nevertheless, the forces of the Laotian government were ineffective and could not take advantage of the situation. In 1971, at U.S. urging, Thailand sent a force that would eventually number 20,000 troops into Laos to assist the Laotian government. By this point, American enthusiasm for the war was dissipating. The United States withdrew from the Vietnam War on January 27, 1973, and American bombing in Laos ended on February 22, 1973. The fighting in Laos died out relatively soon after that, with the war ending in April 1973. On September 14, 1973, a coalition government was created in Laos, including all the factions; however, the Pathet Lao gradually took over the government.

Coding: The Second Laotian War Phase 1 (intra-state war #756) began on March 19, 1963, and it became an internationalized civil war with the interventions of North Vietnam on the side of the Pathet Lao and the United States on the side of the Laotian government. This intra-state civil war was transformed into the current inter-state war on January 13, 1968, when North Vietnam took over the bulk of the fighting from the Pathet Lao and the war fundamentally became one between North Vietnam (assisted by the Pathet Lao) and the government of Laos (aided by the United States and later Thailand).

Sources: Brown and Zasloff (1976); Brown and Zasloff (1974); Ciment (2007); Clodfelter (2002); Isaacs et al. (1987); Leary (1995); Zasloff (1973); Zasloff (1970); Zhang (2002).

INTER-STATE WAR #172:
The War of Attrition of 1969–1970

Participants: Israel vs. Egypt
Dates: March 6, 1969, to August 7, 1970
Battle-Related Deaths: Egypt—5,000; Israel—368
Where Fought: Middle East
Initiator: Egypt
Outcome: Stalemate

Narrative: In the previous Arab-Israeli inter-state war (#169, The Six Day War), Arab forces had been crushed by the Israeli preemptive strike in the most severe of all wars, based on battle-deaths per day (Small and Singer 1989, 30). Some Arab leaders felt that the Arab advantage in population would wear down Israel in a long war and that the problem in 1967 was that the war had been so short and intense. In contrast, this Israeli-Egyptian war, in 1969–1970, is one of the least intense wars, hence its name, "the War of Attrition." As a consequence of the Six Day War, Israel was in control of "the occupied territories" in the Sinai, Gaza Strip, and Golan Heights. On November 22, 1967, UN Security Council Resolution 242 called on Israel to withdraw from the occupied territories; however, efforts to implement the 242 recommendations were unsuccessful. One of the consequences of the lack of progress on the diplomatic front was the gradual deterioration of the cease-fire arrangements along the Suez Canal.

The war began on March 6, 1969, when Egyptian president Gamal Abdel Nasser declared the beginning of a war of attrition against Israel. The war generally consisted of heavy artillery barrages launched by Egypt and aircraft strikes and periodic land raids launched by Israel. The installation of Soviet SAM missile defenses began to inflict heavier damages on the Israeli air force. On January 22, 1970, however, Israeli troops were able to capture an island in the Gulf of Suez. Fatalities were much higher for Egypt than for Israel. The war ended in a stalemate when the Egyptians and Israelis realized that neither side was achieving its aims. A new cease-fire was arranged in August 1970 under the auspices of the United States. This war is followed within three years by the Yom Kippur War of 1973 (inter-state war #181), which is the last inter-state war to date between Israel and Egypt.

Coding: The MID leading up to the war is a bilateral MID (#1480), initiated by Israel but with Egypt being the revisionist state. This dispute begins on June 26, 1967, two weeks after the end of the Six Day War and almost two years before the outbreak of this 1969–1970 War of Attrition. The constant artillery and air duels along the cease-fire lines of the Six Day War satisfied our definition of an inter-state war. Clodfelter (2002) also lists this war but does so as a subheading under the overarching topic of "Terrorism in the Middle East since 1967." Phillips and Axelrod (2005) do not list it.

Sources: Bar-Siman-Tov (1980); Clodfelter (2002); Dupuy (1978); Heikal (1975); Lenczowski (1987); Small and Singer (1989); Whetten (1974).

INTER-STATE WAR #175:
The Football War of 1969

Participants: El Salvador vs. Honduras
Dates: July 14, 1969, to July 18, 1969
Battle-Related Deaths: Honduras—1,200; El Salvador—700
Where Fought: W. Hemisphere
Initiator: El Salvador
Outcome: El Salvador wins

Narrative: Most of El Salvador's border is shared with the much larger country of Honduras. There had been an attempt in 1895 to demarcate the border between the two neighbors, though the agreement was never ratified. In the four Central American inter-state wars of 1876–1907 (inter-state wars #60, #70, #88, and #91), El Salvador had never fought against Honduras. In fact, they had been allied with each other in the last two regional conflicts. In 1967, however, tensions between the two states increased as they accused each other of border violations. The Hondurans also began to blame their economic woes on the presence of Salvadorans in Honduras and began to send them back to El Salvador, where they in turn spread stories of mistreatment. The Salvadoran president, Julio Adalberto Rivera, came under increasing pressure to deal with Honduras.

In June 1969 the national football (soccer) teams from El Salvador and Honduras met in a qualifying match to decide which would advance to the 1970 World Cup. This World Cup is now remembered for the efforts of Pelé of Brazil, and many people consider it the finest World Cup ever. The Honduran team won the first of the three matches against El Salvador in Honduras. El Salvador won the second match, played on June 15, in San Salvador. Consequently, Honduran fans traveling home after the match were attacked and beaten. El Salvador won the final game played against Honduras in Mexico City on June 28, 1969. In Honduras, the Hondurans began attacking, beating, and killing Salvadorans who lived there. Over the next two weeks, the violence spread to the border area, causing thousands of Salvadorans to flee back to El Salvador. In response, El Salvador planned to overthrow the Honduran president. On July 14, El Salvador launched a preemptive attack in an attempt to offset Honduran air force superiority. The Salvadoran air force bombed Honduran cities, and troops crossed the border. The Hondurans responded by attacking Salvadoran aircraft and bombing its petroleum facilities. Relatively soon, both sides began to feel the costs of war. The Organization of American States (OAS) also tried to encourage the parties to cease hostilities. The cease-fire went into effect on July 18, so the war lasted only five days, though sporadic fighting did occur until the end of the month. The Hondurans had won the air war, while the Salvadorans had won on the ground. El Salvador is seen as the winner in the war because it occupied Honduran territory, which it subsequently relinquished in exchange for a pledge by Honduras to protect Salvadorans living in Honduras. Despite our title for the war, there is, of course, some dispute whether the war was really caused by the games.

Coding: Just days before the third and deciding soccer match, on June 24, 1969, a bilateral interstate dispute (MID #1206) was initiated by El Salvador against Honduras, with the latter, which was trying to limit Salvadoran migration to Honduras, deemed the revisionist. Both Ciment (2007) and Clodfelter (2002) refer to this as the "Soccer War."

Sources: Ciment (2007); Clodfelter (2002); Keesing's (1969); *New York Times* (1969); Phillips and Axelrod (2005); Scheina (2003b).

INTER-STATE WAR #176:
The War of the Communist Coalition of 1970–1971

Participants: North Vietnam vs. Cambodia, South Vietnam, United States
Dates: March 23, 1970, to July 2, 1971

Battle-Related Deaths: Cambodia—5,000; South Vietnam—1,000; North Vietnam—400; United States—125
Where Fought: Asia
Initiator: North Vietnam
Outcome: Transformed into intra-state war #785

Narrative: As France was establishing its colonial empire in Indochina, it responded to appeals for assistance from the king of Cambodia in 1854 and established a protectorate there in 1863. Cambodia formally became part of the Union of Indochina in 1887. After World War II, France granted Cambodia its independence, and Cambodia became a member of the interstate system in 1953. In the 1960s Cambodia's flamboyant leader, Norodom Sihanouk, dominated Cambodian politics. The only major opposition group was the Kampuchean Communist Party (later called the Khmer Rouge), which had strong ties to the Communist party in North Vietnam. By the late 1960s, the Vietnam War (inter-state war #163) spilled over into Cambodia, particularly since the supply lines from North Vietnam to the Viet Cong in the South (called the Ho Chi Minh Trail) ran along the Cambodian-Vietnamese border. Sihanouk tried to balance his policies between suppressing the Cambodian Communists while allowing the Vietnamese Communists to use bases in Cambodia.

Starting in 1968 the Khmer Rouge Communists launched a small guerrilla campaign against the government. As the Khmer attacks increased, the conservative elements within the Cambodian elite became increasingly disenchanted with Sihanouk's policies. In March 1970 a coup toppled Sihanouk from power while he was visiting the Soviet Union. Lon Nol became the leader of the new Cambodian government. Sihanouk fled to China, where he met with North Vietnam's premier, Pham Van Dong. On March 23, 1970, Sihanouk established the National United Front of Kampuchea (FUNK) as an umbrella organization for all groups opposed to the Lon Nol government. FUNK troops were to be trained and assisted by North Vietnam. Sihanouk's public appeal constituted a virtual declaration of war against the government of Cambodia, and thus March 23 marks the start of the war. Within days 40,000 North Vietnamese and Viet Cong troops launched strikes at Cambodian government positions. During April the North Vietnamese and Viet Cong forces easily pushed back the government forces. On May 1 U.S. president Richard Nixon announced that the United States and South Vietnam would also launch incursions into Cambodia, but they aimed at keeping Lon Nol's government afloat. By the end of 1970, the joint North Vietnamese, Viet Cong, and Khmer Rouge forces controlled one-half of Cambodia. During early 1971 tension between the Khmer Rouge and the North Vietnamese grew as the size of the Khmer army increased. On July 2, 1971, the North Vietnamese began withdrawing their troops from Cambodia, which ends the Communist Coalition and the inter-state phase of the war. The conflict continues as intra-state civil war #785.

Coding: Many scholars (including Ciment [2007], and Phillips and Axelrod [2005]) refer to the conflict in Cambodia in 1970–1971 as Cambodia's civil war; however, under COW coding rules, a civil war is defined as combat between the government and another armed group within the state borders. In this case the bulk of the fighting was not being done by the Khmer Rouge (which was still relatively small) but by the forces of North Vietnam against the government of Cambodia. Thus this is coded as an inter-state war. The United States and Cambodian officials even referred to the conflict as a "foreign invasion" aimed at conquering Cambodia (Isaacs et al. 1987, 94). The inter-state war ends on July 2, 1971, and the conflict is transformed into a civil war when the North Vietnamese decided to withdraw from Cambodia and the Khmer Rouge took over the bulk of the fighting at that point. Further evidence of the complexity involved in coding or describing this war is Clodfelter's descriptions of the same 1970–1971 battles both as the "Cambodian Campaign" (which is part of the Vietnam War) and as the "Cambodian Civil Wars: 1970–75, 1979–1998."

Sources: Ciment (2007); Girling (1972); Isaacs et al. (1987); Kirk (1974); Leifer (1975); Poole (1974); Short (2004); Simmonds (1973); Suhrke (1971).

INTER-STATE WAR #178:
The War for Bangladesh of 1971

Participants: India vs. Pakistan
Dates: December 3, 1971, to December 17, 1971
Battle-Related Deaths: Pakistan—7,982;
  India—3,241
Where Fought: Asia
Initiator: Pakistan
Outcome: India wins

Narrative: The partition of British India in 1947 created two distinct but interrelated problems. The configuration of India as a Hindu state and Pakistan as a Muslim state immediately led to tensions between the two and produced two wars between them over Kashmir (inter-state wars #147 and #166). The partition process also created Pakistan as a state consisting of two geographically separated parts, East and West Pakistan, with significantly different cultures. Bengali-speaking East Pakistan (known as East Bengal until 1955) was more populous, but the Urdu-speaking political elite in West Pakistan dominated the state. The confluence of these two issues in 1971 created a situation in which an intra-state civil war (#782) broke out between the two parts of Pakistan, and it was transformed into this inter-state war by the intervention of India.

In the late 1960s, the Pakistani government was becoming increasingly repressive, and demonstrations of popular discontent in East Pakistan were suppressed. Finally, in response to the growing violence, martial law was imposed. The East Pakistanis responded with increasing demands for either autonomy or independence. The Awami League was the political party that generally favored independence. Delayed elections and the collapsing political process in Pakistan contributed to growing civilian violence in

East Pakistan, and on March 25, 1971, the Pakistani military intervened in East Pakistan and began terrorizing the citizens. This date marks the beginning of the civil war (see intra-state war #782). India was interested in the conflict for a number of reasons: Indians have a number of cultural attributes in common with East Pakistan, particularly since Bengal had been divided between East Pakistan and India at the time of partition. India was also concerned about the number of refugees fleeing the war and entering India; and India saw the civil war as a way to reduce the power of West Pakistan, which was its rival in Kashmir. Thus Indian prime minister Indira Gandhi decided to enter the war on the side of East Pakistan. Beginning in November 1971, Indian troops began supporting the East Pakistani (Bengali) rebels. Full-scale inter-state war erupted on December 3, 1971, when Pakistan launched what it hoped would be a successful preemptive air strike against Indian installations in Kashmir and Punjab in the West and India's West Bengal in the East. At this point India immediately took over the bulk of the fighting from East Pakistan, making this an inter-state war between two system members. The war had two major fronts, the west (including Kashmir) and the east, and it involved not only an air war but ground and naval operations as well. Pakistan's forces in the west were somewhat inferior to those of India, but its forces in the east were insufficient to confront both the local insurgency and the Indian army. India quickly launched retaliatory air strikes and soon dominated the air war. In naval battles in both the western and eastern fronts, India was similarly successful, and Pakistan suffered heavy losses. In East Pakistan, Pakistan decided to disperse its relatively small forces across the entire front with India. India launched its offensive on December 4, and by December 14 it was shelling the Pakistani positions at the East Pakistani capital of Dacca. On December 16 the Pakistani forces there surrendered. The ground war in the west was more difficult. Pakistani forces

launched a series of attacks against Indian positions along the western front on December 3–6. India responded and in places advanced into Pakistani territory. On December 16 India won a large-scale tank battle and captured the Shakargarh salient. Even though the war in the west was less decisive than the Indian victory in the east, Pakistani president Yahya Kahn called for an end to the war on December 17, 1971. Pakistan was forced to agree to the independence of East Pakistan, now known as Bangladesh (meaning Bengal nation). The war eased the military pressures on India for future decades by reducing India's rival Pakistan to about half its former size.

Coding: There are a number of militarized disputes between India and Pakistan in the two years prior to the outbreak of this war: #2633 in March 1969; #2634 in August 1969; #2535 in December 1969; #2647 in July 1970; and finally #1447 which lasts from April 1971 until December 1971. Coding the initiator in this war is complicated. India did decide to intervene in the civil war and began assisting the Bengali forces; however, it was Pakistan that ultimately began the inter-state war with its preemptive strike. Clodfelter (2002) describes this as the "India-Pakistan War (Bangladesh War): 1971." Phillips and Axelrod (2005) refer to it as the "Indo-Pakistani War" (1971).

Sources: Clodfelter (2002); Keesing's (1971–1972); Paul (2005); Phillips and Axelrod (2005); Ziegler (1997).

INTER-STATE WAR #181:

The Yom Kippur War of 1973

Participants: Israel vs. Egypt, Iraq, Jordan, Saudi Arabia, Syria
Dates: October 6, 1973, to October 24, 1973
Battle-Related Deaths: Egypt—7,700; Syria—3,500; Israel—2,838; Iraq—278; Saudi Arabia—100; Jordan—23
Where Fought: Middle East
Initiator: Egypt, Syria
Outcome: Israel wins

Narrative: The Six Day War (inter-state war #169) had left Israel in control of the "occupied territories," land that it had captured from the Arab states, including the Gaza Strip and the Sinai Peninsula from Egypt, the Golan Heights from Syria, and the West Bank from Jordan. Consequently, Israel remained in a technical state of war with the Arab states. Egypt had unsuccessfully tried to persuade Israel to return some of the territory through the War of Attrition (inter-state war #172). The Arab states then began planning a war to try to retake the territory. In initiating the war on Yom Kippur, a Jewish holy day, the Arab states hoped to be able to take advantage of the celebrations to catch the Israelis unaware. On October 6, 1973, Syria and Egypt launched coordinated attacks: Egypt into the Sinai Peninsula and Syria (aided by Iraqi troops) into the Golan Heights. Jordan and Saudi Arabia entered the war four days later. Israel was caught by surprise, and the Arab states, which were the beneficiaries of Soviet weaponry, made initial advances. The Syrians attacked along the very well-fortified "purple line" in the Golan. The offensive in the northern Golan led to the capture of an Israeli post at Mount Hermon. In the southern Golan, Syria attacked with about 1,400 Soviet-provided tanks, at least half of which were destroyed, in some of the heaviest armored warfare in history, yielding some territorial gains. Though the Syrians made initial gains in the Golan Heights, they were gradually forced back behind their initial positions by Israeli counterattacks. Similar developments occurred in the Sinai front with Egypt. Initially, Egyptian forces succeeded in crossing the Suez Canal and pushing the Israeli forces back across much of the Sinai Peninsula, but an Israeli counterattack enveloped the remaining Egyptian forces on the east side of the Canal, while the Israelis took territory on the west side. On October 22 Syria agreed to a cease-fire called for by the United Nations, as did Israel on October 24, ending the war. A cease-fire led to a series of peace agreements between Egypt and Israel in the 1970s, culminating in the Camp David Accords and the Israeli-Egyptian Peace Treaty of 1979. In this treaty, Egypt made peace with Israel in return for Israel's return of the Sinai Peninsula to Egypt. The treaty further provided a framework for negotiation of an overall peace between Arabs and Israelis, but that overall peace proved more elusive.

Coding: On October 18, 1971, a militarized interstate dispute (#1046) broke out between Israel and Syria, leading to this war. In this dispute Syria was the initiator and revisionist. One month later, Egypt joined the Syrian side in the dispute and is also classified as revisionist. Later, Jordan, then Iraq, and finally Saudi Arabia join on the Arab side of this dispute, though none is classified as revisionist and Saudi Arabia does not come into even the militarized dispute until four days after the war had broken out. Although minor players, Jordan and Saudi Arabia did commit more than 1,000 troops each to the anti-Israeli effort and thus are coded as war participants.

Sources: Aker (1985); Clodfelter (2002); Lenczowski (1980); O'Ballance (1978); Phillips and Axelrod (2005).

INTER-STATE WAR #184:

The Turco-Cypriot War of 1974

Participants: Turkey vs. Cyprus
Dates: July 20, 1974, to August 16, 1974
Battle-Related Deaths: Turkey—1,000; Cyprus—500
Where Fought: Europe
Initiator: Turkey
Outcome: Turkey wins

Narrative: Cyprus had been controlled by a variety of political entities over its history, including Venice from 1492 to 1571, the Ottoman Turks from 1571 to 1878, and the British from 1878 to 1959. It also had two different communities within its borders, the Greek majority and the Turkish minority, that have had difficulty coexisting, partially due to the influence of Greece and Turkey (which had been involved in a number of wars against each other: inter-state wars #76 in 1897, #100 in 1912, #106 in 1914, and #115 in 1919). Though Britain had gained control of Cyprus from the Ottoman Empire in 1878, it was only after World War I that Britain formally made it into a British colony. During the nationalist fervor that spread after World War II, the Greek Cypriots demanded the end of British rule and a union with Greece. Britain, however, wanted to maintain control in Cyprus because it had become its main base in the region after the British had withdrawn their troops from Egypt and the Suez Canal. In 1955 conflict broke out between the Greek Cypriots and the Turkish Cypriots, many of whom preferred British rule to union with Greece. Ultimately, the 1959 London-Zurich agreements, among Britain, Greece, and Turkey, provided for independence for Cyprus and stipulated that the island could not be partitioned, though Britain, Greece, and Turkey were able to maintain military bases there.

Cypriot Greek and Turkish communities soon clashed over the distribution of power in the new joint government. In 1964 the UN dispatched a peacekeeping force in the hopes of creating peace between the two communities. By then the united government of Cyprus had collapsed into two separate governments and most of the international community recognized the Greek Cypriot government as Cyprus. Small units of Greek and Turkish troops were still stationed in Cyprus, and when Greek Cypriot president Archbishop Makarios requested their removal in 1974, the Greek forces staged a coup on July 15, 1974, removing him from power. It seemed likely that the military would turn Cyprus over to Greece, which itself was under military rule. Turkey, perceiving a threat to the Turkish Cypriot community, sent an additional 8,000 troops to augment its contingent of 750 already in Cyprus. Further reinforcement increased the Turkish troop level to 40,000, facing about 13,000 troops from the Greek Cypriot government and Greece.

Attempts by Greece to reinforce its forces in Cyprus were turned back by the Turks. On July 18 Turkey sent an ultimatum to Greece demanding the withdrawal of the Greek forces in Cyprus. The Greeks refused to accept the terms, and the Turks launched air attacks and a ground invasion of the island on July 20, 1974, marking the start of the war. The Turks advanced rapidly from their small enclave. Meanwhile, the Greek Cypriot troops exacted revenge on many of the Turkish Cypriot civilians.

On July 22 the UN issued a call for a cease-fire, and though the parties agreed, hostilities continued until the agreement was reached on July 30 under which hostilities were to cease and neither side was to expand its territory. A second round of negotiations, on August 8–14, collapsed. The second phase of the war began on August 14 with air strikes and troop offensives. The Turkish forces advanced and captured Morphou and much of the north. On August 16 Turkish premier Mustafa Bülent Ecevit agreed to the second cease-fire. By then, there was a de facto partitioning of the island. The Turks controlled about 40 percent of the island as a Turkish enclave for the 20 percent or so of the population that was Turkish. One of the enduring results of the war was the problem of refugees. Most of the Greek Cypriot population of the north moved across the "Attila Line" and into the south, while the Turkish Cypriots were moving to the north. UN troops were stationed as a barrier between the two sides. Meanwhile Greece returned President Makarios to power in Cyprus in December 1974. The overall situation has remained about the same to the present day.

Coding: Cyprus became an interstate system member as of August 16, 1960. The coding of this war includes a pause in the fighting as a result of the UN cease-fire that lasts from July 30 to August 13, 1974.

Sources: Ciment (2007); Clodfelter (2002); Markides (1977); Mirbagheri (1998); Oberling (1982); Phillips and Axelrod (2005); Scherer (1997); U.S. Congress (1975); Ziegler (1997).

INTER-STATE WAR #186:
The War over Angola of 1975–1976

Participants: Angola, Cuba vs. Democratic
  Republic of the Congo, South Africa
Dates: October 23, 1975, to February 12, 1976
Battle-Related Deaths: Cuba—1,500; Angola—
  1,000; Democratic Republic of the Congo—
  100; South Africa—100
Where Fought: Africa
Initiator: South Africa
Outcome: Transformed into intra-state
  war #804

Narrative: Angola had gained its independence
from Portugal through a thirteen-year war
(extra-state war #469). The war had ended when
the new government in Lisbon, which promised
independence to all its colonies, entered into
cease-fire agreements with the rebels. However,
fighting had continued among the various rebel
groups (non-state war #1581). Under the terms
of the Alvor agreement of January 1975, the
rebel groups were to establish a coalition government that would set the stage for elections to
be held prior to independence on November 11,
1975. The agreement soon broke down, and
while Portugal was still nominally in control of
Angola, fighting broke out between competing
Angolan rebel groups over which would become
the government at independence. The Popular
Movement for the Liberation of Angola (MPLA),
under the leadership of Agostinho Neto, was the
most radical of the groups. The National Union
for the Total Independence of Angola (UNITA),
led by Jonas Savimbi, was more moderate; and
the National Front for the Liberation of Angola
(FNLA), led by Holden Roberto, was the most
conservative. Since Angola was not a system
member at the time, the war at this stage is
coded as a non-state war (#1581) from 1974 to
1975. Each of the participants began receiving
assistance from outside powers that hoped to
further their own political interests. Soon this
outside intervention transformed the non-state
conflict into this inter-state proxy war.

The inter-state war began on October 23,
1975, when South Africa, in support of the then-
existing alliance of UNITA and FNLA, invaded
and occupied territory along the Namibian border. Opposing these troops were 18,000 Cuban
troops, with several Soviet advisers, who were
assisting the MPLA. This date marks the start of
the inter-state war, since the bulk of the fighting
was conducted by South Africa and Cuba. Initially the South African and UNITA forces made
advances in the south, matched by FNLA and
Zairian (or Democratic Republic of the Congo;
DRC) troop advances in the north. The MPLA
had gained control over the capital in July 1975,
though its control of the capital was threatened
just as independence was being achieved. When
Angola attained independence on November 11,
1975, it immediately became a member of the
interstate system and officially entered the war.
At that point, there were declarations of two
separate Angolan governments: the People's
Republic of Angola formed by the MPLA in
Luanda and the Social Democratic Republic of
Angola formed by the FNLA and UNITA in
Huambo. The MPLA was reinforced by an airlift
of additional Cuban troops and an increase in
Soviet arms, tipping the balance in favor of the
MPLA, which was then considered to be the
Angolan government.

The FNLA/DRC offensive soon collapsed,
and the UNITA/South African alliance was also
beginning to fracture. In December 1975 UNITA
launched an independent offensive, which was
initially successful but ultimately driven back by
the Angolan and Cuban attacks in January and
February 1976. By February 12, 1976, the Cuban/
Angolan forces had captured ten of the fourteen
provincial capitals and had driven most of the
UNITA/South African troops from Angola. This
marks the end of the inter-state war. Nevertheless, fighting continued, and on February 24 the
FNLA announced that it would now resort to
guerrilla warfare. By this time the MPLA Angolan government had become strong enough to
do the bulk of the fighting itself, so the next

phase of the conflict becomes an intra-state civil war between the Angolan government and UNITA/FNLA rebels, though it is internationalized by the involvement of South Africa and Cuba (intra-state war #804).

Coding: This war is coded as beginning on October 23, 1975, when South Africa launched its Task Force Zulu invasion. Though South Africa was supposedly acting in support of the UNITA and FNLA (which also had the support of 1,200 troops from the Democratic Republic of the Congo) and Cuba was supposedly acting in support of the MPLA, the initial stage of the war really was an external proxy war, with the bulk of the fighting done by the South African and Cuban troops, thus leading to the coding of this war as an inter-state war between Cuba and South Africa (aided by the DRC). Angola became a member of the interstate system with the Portuguese withdrawal on November 11, 1975. At that point the MPLA became the government of Angola and entered the war on that date, though the bulk of the fighting was still being done by Cuba and South Africa. After the Angolan government became sufficiently strong and was able to conduct most of the fighting itself, the war is transformed into a civil war between the Angolan government and the rebel groups (intra-state war #804). Clodfelter (2002) groups his discussion of the conflicts in Angola together as the "Angolan Civil Wars: 1975–1991, 1992–1994, 1998–."

Sources: Clodfelter (2002); Human Rights Watch (1994); Keesing's (1976); Malaquias (2007).

INTER-STATE WAR #187:
The Second Ogaden War Phase 2 of 1977–1978

Participants: Cuba, Ethiopia vs. Somalia
Dates: July 23, 1977, to March 9, 1978
Battle-Related Deaths: Somalia—8,000; Ethiopia—1,800; Cuba—700
Where Fought: Africa
Initiator: Somalia
Outcome: Somalia withdraws and fighting is transformed into intra-state war #808

Narrative: The Ogaden was a region east of Ethiopia (inhabited mostly by Somali nomadic tribes) that had been incorporated into Ethiopia in 1890 (a status confirmed in the Second Italian-Ethiopian War of 1895–1896 (extra-state war #407). As part of its desire for colonies, Italy had conquered what are now southern Somalia and Ethiopia (see inter-state war #127, the Conquest of Ethiopia of 1935–1936). Subsequently, in 1940 an Italian army conquered British Somaliland, and Italy combined it with Ethiopia, Eritrea, and Italian Somaliland to form Italian East Africa. In 1941, during WWII, British and South African troops conquered Ethiopia and restored Emperor Haile Selassie to his throne. Eritrea remained semi-independent until it was forced into a federal union with Ethiopia in 1952 and became a direct province in 1962. The British, however, kept control over Somalia, though Italy did temporarily regain control over Italian Somaliland. Somalia began to assert claims to the Ogaden, which Ethiopia opposed. In 1948 Haile Selassie took the issue of Ogaden to the United Nations, which ruled in Ethiopia's favor. Ultimately, Italy gave independence to Italian Somaliland, and the British did the same with British Somaliland. The two entities united into the Somali Republic on July 1, 1960 (and Somalia became a system member as of that date).

Not long after obtaining its independence, Somalia returned to its goal of annexing areas occupied by Somali people, including the Ogaden and French Somaliland (which became Djibouti). In this vein Somalia supported the Western Somali Liberation Front (WSLF) that formed in the Ogaden. From 1960 to 1977, the WSLF launched minor skirmishes against the Ethiopian forces. Meanwhile Gen. Mohammed Siad Barre, a communist, came to power through a coup in Somalia in 1969. Since Somalia and Ethiopia were of interest to the Cold War superpowers because of their strategic location, the Soviet Union began to provide assistance to Somalia (as did Cuba), while the United States aided Ethiopia. At that time Ethiopia was facing internal dissent on two fronts. Eritrea and the Eritrean Liberation Front (ELF) sought independence (intra-state war #798, 1975–1978). Ethiopia also faced a challenge from the military. Dissident military officers formed a committee, the Dergue, which overthrew Haile Selassie in 1974, replacing him with Dergue leader Maj. Mengistu Haile Mariam. Subsequently, the Dergue faced opposition as well from the Ethiopian People's Revolutionary Party (EPRP). The EPRP was a socialist party, and though the EPRP had initially cooperated with the Dergue, the EPRP wanted greater influence and revolted against Dergue leader Mariam. Somalia decided to take advantage of the chaos in Ethiopia to reassert its claims to the Ogaden. Somalia encouraged the WSLF to attack Ethiopian troops in the Ogaden, and Somali troops soon became involved in the conflict on a relatively small level (intra-state war #805).

The intra-state war was transformed into this inter-state phase of the war on July 23, 1977, when Somali troops invaded Ethiopia in support of the WSLF. Initially the well-armed Somali contingents scored some success, capturing 60 percent of the Ogaden; however, at that point a reversal in Cold War politics affected the war. The Soviet Union had aided Somalia while trying also to displace the United States as Ethiopia's patron. The Ogaden War forced the Soviets to choose sides, and they switched their support to Ethiopia, airlifting supplies and 17,000 Cuban troops into Ethiopia in November 1977. Thus when the Somali/WSLF forces tried to continue their advance in January 1978, they were repulsed. The Ethiopian/Cuban troops launched a counteroffensive in February. Their numerical superiority turned the tide, driving the Somali forces back into Somalia. On March 9, Somalia announced the end of the war. The WSLF continued attacks against Ethiopian troops, thus the war reverts back to an intra-state civil war, the Second Ogaden War Phase 3 (#808). One result of this inter-state Ogaden War was the realignment of superpower ties. After the Soviets switched their support to Ethiopia, the United States began supporting Somalia. Both Somalia and Ethiopia continued to face internal discord. Ethiopia faced the continuing Eritrean drive for independence, which was coupled with a revolt in Tigray province in intra-state war #826. The leaders of both Ethiopia and Somalia fell in 1991, leading to a period of warfare in Somalia (intra-state wars #870 and #938).

Coding: The overall conflict over the Ogaden is coded into three distinct phases and three distinct wars based on the application of the "bulk of the fighting" rule. The war began as the Second Ogaden War Phase 1, #805, a civil war between Ethiopia and the Ogaden WSLF rebels. The Somalis and Cubans do provide minimal aid and troops at this stage; however, the civil war is transformed into an inter-state war between Ethiopia and Somalia by the invasion of Somali troops in July 1977. At this point the Somalis take over the bulk of the fighting. Cuba also enters the war in November 1977. The war is transformed again from an inter-state war back into an intra-state war (#808) by the withdrawal of Somalia from the war in March 1978.

Sources: Ciment (2007); Clodfelter (1992); Fitzgibbon (1982); Kohn (2007); Lefebvre (1996); Rubinstein (1989).

INTER-STATE WAR #189:
The Vietnamese-Cambodian Border War of 1977–1979

Participants: Vietnam vs. Cambodia
Dates: September 24, 1977, to January 8, 1979
Battle-Related Deaths: Cambodia—5,000; Vietnam—3,000
Where Fought: Asia
Initiator: Cambodia
Outcome: The Cambodian government is overthrown and the fighting is transformed into extra-state war #475

Narrative: These two former allies (Cambodia and North Vietnam) began skirmishing almost immediately after the Khmer Rouge seized control of Phnom Penh. In inter-state war #176 (the War of the Communist Coalition), North Vietnam (assisted by the Khmer Rouge) had fought against the conservative government of Cambodia (aided by the United States and South Vietnam). After North Vietnam withdrew from the fighting in Cambodia, the war continued as a civil war between the Cambodian government and the Khmer Rouge (intra-state war #785). The Khmer Rouge won the civil war, coming to power in April 1975. At the same time, the war in Vietnam (inter-state war #163) had ended with the victory of North Vietnam over the South. Within days the two victorious parties, Vietnam and the new Khmer Rouge government, would be involved in conflict with one another.

The origins of this conflict date back to the borders drawn during the French colonial period, which left Vietnamese and Cambodians living outside the borders of their states. The Khmer government wanted to rectify the situation by changing its border with Vietnam, whereas Vietnam wanted to expand its control in the region. The conflict began as cross-border attacks, generally instigated by the Cambodians but frequently involving Vietnamese dissident groups as well. This low level conflict lasted for over two years. Meanwhile, the Cambodians launched similar incursions against Thailand and attacked the U.S. freighter *Mayaguez* in May 1976. Cambodia was experiencing domestic turmoil as well. On April 2, 1976, Prince Norodom Sihanouk resigned as head of state, and on April 14 Democratic Kampuchea was established with Pol Pot as its leader. Pol Pot initiated a purge against any vestige of Vietnamese influence within Kampuchea. On June 7, 1977, the Vietnamese government proposed negotiations to resolve the border conflict, but Pol Pot declined. Subsequently, Cambodia increased the intensity of its attacks. There was also a major power element to the growing conflict as well in that Cambodia was receiving assistance from China,

while the Soviet Union was aiding Vietnam. In September Vietnam began placing regular military units, instead of the local militias, along the border. A Cambodian attack on September 24, 1977, along the border of Tay Ninh province, led to the first major Vietnamese military counterattack, so this date marks the start of the war. On December 26, 1977, Vietnam responded with a large-scale invasion that penetrated fifteen miles into Cambodian territory. By January 1978 the Vietnamese offensive had stalled. Hostilities generally subsided but began increasing in intensity during the summer and resumed their ferocity in November and December 1978. On December 26, 1978, the Vietnamese launched another offensive, advancing on Phnom Penh. At the end of 1978, Cambodia also formally announced that diplomatic ties between Cambodia and Vietnam had been broken. This announcement served to reveal the extent of the war that the communist states had tried to hide. Though both sides accused each other of targeting civilians, the Khmer government was also engaged in "cleansing" its own citizenry. Phnom Penh was captured on January 7, 1979, and Pol Pot and the other Khmer leaders fled from Phnom Penh into the west. The Vietnamese installed Heng Samrin as the chairman of the new Kampuchean People's Revolutionary Council on January 8 (which marks the end of the inter-state war). This brought to an end the regime responsible for killing over 1,000,000 innocent people in one of the worst mass killings in recorded history. A war between the new Cambodian government and its Vietnamese allies against the Khmer Rouge continued in the jungles (see extra-state war #475). A month later, on February 17, 1979, Cambodia's ally China launched an attack against the northern Vietnamese border in the hope of reducing Vietnamese pressure on Cambodia (see inter-state war #193). The commitment to the Samrin regime created a long-lasting quagmire for Vietnam, which did not remove its troops from Cambodia until 1989.

Coding: Initially when this war was added to the COW dataset in *Resort to Arms,* the exact levels of fatalities for this war were not entirely known. Thus the war was coded as starting in 1975 with the cross-border attacks. It now appears, however, that the fatalities in the 1975–1977 period were mostly civilians (not the military battle-deaths required for a COW war classification). The start date of this war has thus been moved to September 24, 1977, which marks the beginning of sustained combat between Cambodia and Vietnam. The war ended with the installation of Vietnam's ally Heng Samrin as the chairman of the new Kampuchean People's Revolutionary Council, on January 8, 1979. At this point, the Heng Samrin regime took control of the major institutions of government and was considered the de facto government of Cambodia, despite the fact that diplomatic recognition was still being awarded to the Khmer regime. Fighting continued between the Khmer and its allies against the new Cambodian government, though since Vietnam conducted the bulk of the fighting on behalf of the Cambodian government, the war is classified as an extra-state war (#475, The Khmer Insurgency). Clodfelter (2002) describes the entire period of 1977–1989 as the "Vietnamese-Cambodian War," while Phillips and Axelrod (2005) treat it as part of the "Kampuchean Civil War" of 1978–1998.

Sources: Chanda (1988); Clodfelter (2002); Evans and Rowley (1990); Isaacs et al. (1987); Keesing's (1975–1980); Leighton (1978); *New York Times* (1975–1980); Phillips and Axelrod (2005).

INTER-STATE WAR #190:

The Ugandan-Tanzanian War of 1978–1979

Participants: Tanzania vs. Libya, Uganda
Dates: October 28, 1978, to April 11, 1979
Battle-Related Deaths: Uganda—1,500;
Tanzania—1,000; Libya—500
Where Fought: Africa
Initiator: Uganda
Outcome: Tanzania wins

Narrative: This is the war that led to the ouster of the infamous Ugandan dictator Idi Amin. Idi Amin came to power in Uganda in January 1971 through a coup that overthrew Milton Obote. Although he was initially popular, Amin soon began winning enemies, both outside Uganda and within. For instance, relations between Uganda and Tanzania were strained by Socialist Tanzanian president Julius Nyerere's opposition to President Amin. In 1972 members of former Ugandan president Obote's army invaded Uganda from Tanzania with the intention of overthrowing Amin, leading to the severing of diplomatic ties between the two countries. Subsequently, Idi Amin repeatedly accused Nyerere of planning to invade Uganda in order to reinstall Obote, whereas it was apparently Uganda that had designs on Tanzanian territory. Uganda invaded Tanzania on October 28, 1978, starting this war. Ugandan troops advanced 20 miles into Tanzania, capturing the Kagera Salient, and Uganda declared its intention of annexing the captured 710-square-mile territory in order to give Uganda access to the Indian Ocean. On November 11, Tanzania counterattacked, pushing the Ugandan forces out of Tanzania by November 14. In January 1979 the Tanzanian troops, with the encouragement of other East African governments, then pushed into Uganda, advancing about 30 miles into Ugandan territory. In February 1979 Tanzania sent additional forces into Uganda. Most of the Ugandan army vanished, though a force of 2,700 Libyan troops helped to defend Amin's government, marking Libya's entry as a war participant. After an April battle at Entebbe, most of the Libyans were airlifted out of the country. Tanzanian forces, aided by Ugandan rebels organized as the Uganda National Liberation Army, then captured the capital of Kampala on April 11 and forced Amin to flee to Jinja and then into exile in Libya. Obote returned to power through elections in December 1980. The contested legality of the elections led to a six-year conflict against the National Resistance Army (NRA) in which 300,000 civilians were killed (intra-state war #822). The NRA came to power in January 1986. Domestic conflict continued, with one of the more interesting challenges being raised by the Holy Spirit Movement (intra-state war #843 in 1986).

Coding: In addition to the military fatalities, this war cost over 2,000 civilian fatalities and thousands injured. It has been estimated that during the eight-year reign of Idi Amin, 500,000 Ugandans were killed (Ciment 2007, 312).

Sources: Avirgan and Honey (1982); Ciment (2007); Clodfelter (1992); Cutter (2007); Keesing's (1979); Meredith (2005); *New York Times* (1979); Phillips and Axelrod (2005).

INTER-STATE WAR #193:

The Sino-Vietnamese Punitive War of 1979

Participants: People's Republic of China (PRC) vs. Vietnam
Dates: February 17, 1979, to March 16, 1979
Battle-Related Deaths: China—13,000; Vietnam—8,000
Where Fought: Asia
Initiator: China
Outcome: China wins

Narrative: This case is one of the few inter-state wars between two well-established communist states. Following the Vietnam War that ended in 1975 (intra-state war #748 and inter-state war #163), North Vietnam began to consolidate its control over the former South Vietnam. It also began to extend its influence in the region, particularly through its war with Cambodia (inter-state war #189), in which China had supported Cambodia. Thus on some levels China wanted to "punish" Vietnam for this conflict. Meanwhile, Vietnam became more closely aligned with the Soviet Union (China's competitor at this stage). Vietnam's growing power also brought it into increasing conflict with China; for instance, both states claimed the Paracel and Spratley islands. Consequently, when China's Deng Xiaoping visited Washington, Vietnam suspected international collusion against it.

The particular precipitant of this war was the dispute over the location of the border between the two states. Each side accused the other of moving the border-marking stones to increase its territory, and Vietnam responded by expelling ethnic Chinese from Vietnam. In January 1979 China began massing troops along the border. On February 17, 1979, Chinese troops launched a major invasion of Vietnam at a number of points along the border. The Chinese forces advanced in six main thrusts toward the Vietnamese provincial capital cities and soon were about twenty miles into Vietnam. The Soviet Union issued a statement demanding the cessation of hostilities. Though the Chinese forces were numerically superior, they were hampered by the rugged terrain, and the Vietnamese border defense forces were able to stop the Chinese advance. Consequently, on March 5, China announced that it had punished Vietnam sufficiently, and the withdrawal of its troops was completed by March 16, 1979, ending the war. Though the war was short, it cost thousands of fatalities and ruined four Vietnamese provincial capitals.

Coding: In naming this war, we follow Chen (1987), who refers to this as "China's Punitive War."

Sources: Chen (1987); Ciment (2007); Clodfelter (2002); Clodfelter (1995); Keesing's (1979); Isaacs et al. (1987); Kohn (1999); *New York Times* (1979); Phillips and Axelrod (2005); Sagar (1991).

INTER-STATE WAR #199:

The Iran-Iraq War of 1980–1988

Participants: Iran vs. Iraq
Dates: September 22, 1980, to August 20, 1988
Battle-Related Deaths: Iran—750,000; Iraq—500,000
Where Fought: Middle East
Initiator: Iraq
Outcome: Stalemate

Narrative: Iran and Iraq previously had differences, including disputes over the Shatt-al-Arab waterway (the estuary of the Tigris and Euphrates rivers into the Persian Gulf). This river, Iraq's outlet to the sea, had at one time been totally under Iraqi control but was split down the mid-channel by an agreement between Iran and Iraq in 1975. Adjacent to that waterway to the east lay Iran's oil-rich province of Khuzistan. Iran had been destabilized by the Shiite revolution of Ayatollah Khomeini, which had resulted in the fall of the shah (intra-state war #813), disputes between institutions of the old monarchical order and the new theocratic regime (intra-state war #816), and the seizure of the hostages at the American embassy. Iraq's Saddam Hussein decided to take advantage of Iran's turmoil in order to resolve the border dispute and gain the entire waterway, remove the threat posed by Iran's Shiite government to the secular and Sunni regimes in the region, and gain access to Iranian oil and an Arab population that might welcome unification with predominantly Arab Iraq. Hussein apparently judged that military prospects were also favorable in that Iran was now estranged from its former ally and arms supplier, the United States. This would mean there would be no spare parts for the expensive and sophisticated U.S. military equipment in the arsenal of the Iranian military. Hussein also anticipated receiving assistance from other states threatened by the new Iranian regime, including the United States, Saudi Arabia, and Kuwait. A fundamental problem that Iraq faced was that Iran boasted twice the population of Iraq as well as a numerically superior military.

Iraq launched an aerial attack of Iran on September 22, 1980. The land invasion began the next day along a 300-mile front in the south, with Iraqi forces initially advancing steadily into Iran. At the end of November 1980, Iran launched a naval attack at the Iraqi port of Mina-al-Bakr, but the momentum seemed to remain with Iraqi forces, which opened a new front the following month. In December Iraq launched a fresh attack by way of Kurdistan in the north, where it was aided by the Iranian Kurds who had been periodically revolting against the Khomeini regime. Iran launched its first major counteroffensive on January 5, 1981, though it soon stalled. In 1982, however, Iran went on the offensive, and by the end of May the Iraqis had been driven out of Iranian territory. Nevertheless, Iran's attempt in summer 1982 to advance into Iraqi territory was unsuccessful. The war became a bloody stalemate between the Iranians (with lots of troops) and Iraq (with the edge in military technology). The year 1984 saw costly Iranian "human wave" assaults (or attacks by large numbers of poorly armed, frequently young combatants) against Iraq and the use of poison gas by Iraq to repel them. One of Iran's most significant victories occurred in late 1986 and early 1987 as it won a battle for the Iraqi city of Basra. The city finally fell on February 25, 1987, at a cost of 50,000 Iranian lives. As the land war dragged on, both sides launched attacks on the oil tankers in the Persian Gulf. This ultimately involved the United States in the war. Kuwait had requested American protection for its ships in the Gulf. On May 17, 1987, an Iraqi bomber attacked the American ship the *Stark* (supposedly in error), causing 37 American deaths. American ships were also damaged by Iranian mines on April 14, 1988, leading to an American retaliatory strike against Iranian ships and oil platforms. The conflict with Iran also led to the *Vincennes* incident, in which the American ship supposedly accidentally shot down an Iranian commercial airliner. In 1988 most of the Iranian territorial gains were reversed by Iraqi offensives. After eight years of unusually deadly warfare, this war ended in a stalemate. Both sides accepted a UN proposed cease-fire that went into effect on August 20, 1988.

Coding: The fatality estimates vary widely; many include significant civilian fatalities in the total war deaths of over a million.

Sources: Clodfelter (2002); Keesing's (1980–1981); Kohn (1999); *New York Times* (1980–1981); Phillips and Axelrod (2005).

INTER-STATE WAR #202:
The Falklands War of 1982

Participants: United Kingdom vs. Argentina
Dates: March 25, 1982, to June 15, 1982
Battle-Related Deaths: Argentina—746; United
    Kingdom—255
Where Fought: W. Hemisphere
Initiator: Argentina
Outcome: United Kingdom wins

Narrative: The Falkland Islands, or Islas Malvinas, have often been disputed territory. There are alternative historic claims, depending on whether one focuses on who first sighted, landed on, or permanently inhabited the islands. The early claimants were English and Spanish, so the islands have been known by their English and Spanish names; however, the islands have long been settled by English-speaking peoples, most of whom wished to remain part of the United Kingdom. A possession of Britain from 1766 to 1774, the islands reverted to Spain from 1774 to 1810. They were then part of Spain's successor state in the region, Argentina, from 1816 to 1833. Since 1833 the Falklands have been a colony of the United Kingdom of Great Britain and Northern Ireland. From the Argentine point of view, the islands were off the coast of Argentina, in Argentine waters, and thousands of miles from Britain.

    Thus in 1982 Argentina decided to reassert its claim to the islands and invaded the Falklands, easily defeating the small British force there. The war was heavily influenced by the character of the leaders of Argentina and Britain at the time. Argentine general Leopoldi Galtieri represented a military junta that had a limited understanding of Britain's worldview. To the junta, which was precariously clinging to power, it made sense to win popular support at home by throwing British imperialists off the islands. The junta also assumed that since Britain had not taken the trouble to defend the islands adequately, it was unlikely to take the much greater trouble involved in recapturing them. To British prime minister Margaret Thatcher, however, allowing Galtieri to keep the islands was akin to the appeasement of dictators that had shamed Britain ever since Neville Chamberlain had given in to Hitler at Munich. Britain also did not want to set a precedent that might encourage the Spanish to try to capture Gibraltar or the Chinese to try to take Hong Kong. Consequently, immediately after the fall of the Falklands, Thatcher organized a counterattack to retake the islands. The British sent a fleet of more than 100 ships toward the Falklands, while Argentina reinforced its garrison there. The British landed first on South Georgia Island on April 25, 1982, and forced the Argentine troops there to surrender. On May 2 a naval battle occurred that led to the sinking of the Argentine ship the *General Belgrano,* costing 368 Argentine lives. The British fleet continued its naval attacks. On May 21 the British began the landing of troops on the Falklands, and the troops advanced steadily. Meanwhile, an air and sea battle was being waged, leading to significant shipping losses on both sides. The British soon reached the outskirts of the Falklands city of Port Stanley, and on June 15 the Argentine forces there surrendered.

Coding: The war is preceded by MID #3630, which starts on March 1, 1982, and in which Argentina is coded as the revisionist state. There has been some disagreement about the number of fatalities in this war. Clodfelter (2002, 720–722) provides a detailed description of the military action, and his fatality figures, cited here, total 1,001, which is just sufficient for a war classification.

Sources: Clodfelter (1992); Keesing's (1982); Lebow (1985); Phillips and Axelrod (2005); Schafer (1995).

INTER-STATE WAR #205:
The War over Lebanon of 1982

Participants: Israel vs. Syria
Dates: April 21, 1982, to September 15, 1982

Battle-Related Deaths: Syria—1,200; Israel—455
Where Fought: Middle East
Initiator: Israel
Outcome: Stalemate

Narrative: Lebanon had long been troubled by constitutional rigidities that kept the growing Muslim population, which had become a majority, from exercising political power in accord with its demographic size. The ruling Christian factions refused to renegotiate the Lebanese constitutional covenant that had given them a dominant place in the government for decades. This tense situation was exacerbated by the arrival of large numbers of Palestinians (including members of the Palestine Liberation Organization [PLO]) who were expelled from Jordan in 1970 (Black September War, intra-state civil war #780). Consequently, an intra-state war broke out in Lebanon in 1975 in which Syria intervened (see intra-state war #801). Another intra-state war occurred in 1978 in which both Syria and Israel intervened (intra-state war #807), and in which both Syrian and Israeli forces occupied portions of Lebanon. The Israelis withdrew in 1978 but were not satisfied with developments in the following years, and starting in 1980, Israel launched attacks on the PLO positions in Lebanon. In 1981 these attacks led to a direct conflict with Syria.

In 1982 the Israelis launched air attacks against PLO targets in Beirut as the beginning phase of a major invasion of 60,000 troops. The Israeli "Operation Peace for Galilee" aimed to remove the PLO from Lebanon and to punish Lebanon for permitting the PLO attacks against Israel. Syria rushed reinforcements for their troops into Lebanon and were almost immediately engaged in an air battle against the Israelis. This battle is ranked among the most extensive supersonic fighter plane combat incidents in history, involving some 200 planes. In June the parties attempted to negotiate cease-fire agreements, with Syria and Israel meeting on June 11 and Israel and the PLO holding discussions on

June 12. The fighting continued, however, and the two-month-long siege of Beirut was particularly intense, causing heavy civilian casualties. Ultimately, the PLO agreed to evacuate Beirut on August 21, 1982, after which the Israelis helped install a Christian Phalangist government. On September 15 the new Lebanese president, Bashir Gemayel, was killed, prompting a reoccupation of Beirut by the Israeli forces. The Israelis did not prevent a Phalange attack against Palestinian refugees in the Sabra and Shatila refugee camps in Beirut on September 17–18. U.S. forces that tried to serve as peacekeepers were attacked by suicide bombers, killing 248 marines. The United States soon withdrew. Fighting between Israelis and Syrians eventually stopped, but both maintained troops in areas of Lebanon for many years. Additional intra-state wars in Lebanon occurred in 1983 (#833, in which the U.S. and France were involved) and in 1989 (#850 involving Syria).

Coding: Clodfelter (2002) describes this as the "Lebanon War: 1982." Phillips and Axelrod (2005) simply cover this as part of their "Lebanese Civil War (1975–1992)."

Sources: Clodfelter (2002); Dupuy and Martell (1986); Evron (1987); Gabriel (1984); Laffin (1985); Moriarity (2005); Phillips and Axelrod (2005); Schiff and Ya'ari (1984)

INTER-STATE WAR #207:
The War over the Aouzou Strip of 1986–1987

Participants: Chad vs. Libya
Dates: November 15, 1986, to September 11, 1987
Battle-Related Deaths: Libya—7,000; Chad—1,000
Where Fought: Middle East, Africa
Initiator: Chad
Outcome: Chad wins

Narrative: This war is the third in a series of wars that confronted Chad between 1966 and

1987. The first two were internationalized civil wars (intra-state wars #771 and #820). The first was a civil war between Chad and the forces of the National Liberation Front of Chad (FROLI-NAT) rebels in which France intervened; and the second, in 1980, was another civil war with the FROLINAT in which both France and Libya intervened. This latter war set the stage for this inter-state war in 1986–1987. Libya's leader, Muammar al-Gadhafi, had been expanding Libya's influence in Chad. In 1973 Libya had seized the Aouzou Strip, a disputed territory in northern Chad. In 1980 Libya intervened in the civil war in Chad on the side of President Goukouni Oueddei and Goukouni's Popular Armed Forces (FAP) against the Armed Forces of the North (FAN) of the minister of defense, Hissène Habré. Libya marked its military victory by proclaiming the unity of Chad and Libya in January 1981. As the Libyan forces withdrew from Chad in 1982, Habré's forces returned, driving Goukouni from office. Subsequently, the Libyans resumed an offensive on Goukouni's behalf, while the French entered the war on the side of Habré. In 1984 the war ended with Habré still in office and with both France and Libya agreeing to remove their forces; however, Libyan forces remained and began to expand their presence in the Aouzou Strip. At this stage the alliance within the rebel Transitional Government of National Unity (GUNT), which included Goukouni's FAP faction and the Democratic Revolutionary Council (CDR) led by Acheikh ibn Oumar, began to disintegrate. Many former GUNT troops shifted their support to Habré's FAN against their former ally Libya.

In November 1986 Habre's forces were able to down a Libyan plane and inflict heavy casualties (which marks the beginning of the inter-state war). In December Habré's forces began a more sustained offensive against the Libyan forces in the Aouzou Strip. During January and March 1987, Libyan bases rapidly fell to Habré's forces, aided by France. In August 1987 heavy fighting took place around the town of Aouzou,

during which the United States provided intelligence to Habré's forces. The Organization of African Unity (OAU) was able to broker the cease-fire that ended the war on September 11, 1987, though the status of the Aouzou Strip was not resolved. Chad appealed to the International Court of Justice, which backed Chad's claim to the Aouzou Strip. On May 31, 1994, Libya formally returned the Aouzou Strip to Chad.

Coding: This war is a war that evolved from a civil war (Habré Revolt #820) into an inter-state war (though there is a break between the two). During the Habré Revolt, Libya and France had intervened, making it an internationalized civil war. France withdrew from the conflict, though Libya remained involved. What changes the type of war is the disintegration of the rebel groups, the decision of some of their forces to unite with the government, and the government's decision to pursue a more sustained effort against the Libyans directly. Clodfelter (1992) refers to this as the "Chadian-Libyan Border War: 1987."

Sources: Clodfelter (1992); Cordesman (2004); Keesing's (1987); Meredith (2005); Nolutshungu (1996).

INTER-STATE WAR #208:

The Sino-Vietnamese Border War of 1987

Participants: People's Republic of China (PRC) vs. Vietnam
Dates: January 5, 1987, to February 6, 1987
Battle-Related Deaths: Vietnam—2,200; China—1,800
Where Fought: Asia
Initiator: China
Outcome: Tie

Narrative: Low-level armed struggle between the PRC and Vietnam had continued along their 800-mile shared border since their 1979 war (the Sino-Vietnamese Punitive War, inter-state war #193). At the time, China had about 400,000 troops stationed in the area; however, its strategy seems to have been one of maintaining a low level of fighting, often just below the war threshold, against Vietnam. Early in 1987 the fighting flared up briefly to the level of inter-state war. On January 5, 1987, the Chinese began the war with an artillery barrage, followed by a ground attack (though China blamed Vietnam for starting the conflict). Vietnamese forces also advanced across the border, and fighting continued in the rugged terrain for about a month. This 1987 war, with only one-fifth the battle-deaths of the 1979 war, has gone largely unreported, but the 4,000 battle-dead we record is hardly insignificant.

Coding: This war is preceded by bilateral MID #3628, beginning in October 1986, with China the initiator and revisionist. Neither Clodfelter (2002) nor Phillips and Axelrod (2005) list this war.

Sources: *New York Times* (1987); Sagar (1991).

INTER-STATE WAR #211:
The Gulf War of 1990–1991

Participants: Canada, Egypt, France, Italy, Kuwait, Morocco, Oman, Qatar, Saudi Arabia, Syria, United Arab Emirates, United Kingdom, United States vs. Iraq
Dates: August 2, 1990, to April 11, 1991
Battle-Related Deaths: Iraq—40,000; Kuwait—1,000; United States—376; Saudi Arabia—44; United Kingdom—24; Egypt—14; United Arab Emirates—6; France—2; Canada—0; Italy—0; Morocco—0; Oman—0; Qatar—0; Syria—0
Where Fought: Middle East
Initiator: Iraq
Outcome: Egypt, Oman, Saudi Arabia, Kuwait, Qatar, United Arab Emirates, Syria, Morocco, Italy, France, United Kingdom, Canada, United States win

Narrative: The origins of this war can be found in the Iran-Iraq War, 1980–1988 (inter-state war #199). During that war Kuwait and Saudi Arabia had provided assistance to Iraq. Though Iraq had apparently believed that the assistance was in the form of grants, the Kuwaitis began seeking repayment for its "loans." The Iraqi government, under Saddam Hussein, decided to pursue a different

policy to resolve the dispute, and in summer 1990 Iraq began threatening Kuwait and Saudi Arabia. Suddenly, on August 2, the Iraqi army attacked and overran Kuwait, encroaching slightly into Saudi Arabia. At the request of the Saudi government, the United States sent a large force to the region in fall 1990 (Operation Desert Shield) to discourage any potential Iraqi invasion of Saudi Arabia and to persuade the Iraqis to withdraw from Kuwait. By November 1990 U.S. president George H.W. Bush had decided on a military offensive to liberate Kuwait. A UN resolution authorized use of force by member states after January 15, 1991, if Iraq did not withdraw by that time. On the next morning a coalition of forces, led by the United States, began the war with an aerial attack on Iraq. The coalition would ultimately include twenty-eight states (though not all of them sent enough troops to be considered war participants). The Iraqis responded with an offensive against the Saudi border town of Khafji on January 29, 1991. The coalition's major ground offensive followed on February 24, and the invasion drove Iraqi forces out of Kuwait and moved swiftly into southern Iraq. The Iraqis mounted only minimal resistance, and a cease-fire was issued on February 28. President Bush's administration in Washington then ceased further attacks, allowing Saddam Hussein's government to remain in power in Bagdad. This war contributed to the 2003 war the Invasion of Iraq (inter-state war #227), in which U.S. forces under the younger President Bush captured Bagdad and overthrew the regime of Saddam Hussein. After the fall of the Iraqi government, fighting continued between the coalition and Iraqi resistance groups, including al-Qaida in Iraq (extra-state war #482).

Coding: Related MID is #2115. One of the main difficulties in analyzing this war was in determining battle fatalities. The United States and the other members of the coalition made a conscious decision not to count the number of Iraqis (military or civilian) killed in the war. Consequently, estimates of Iraqi fatalities vary widely, ranging from several thousand to over 150,000.

Sources: Clodfelter (1992); Cordesman and Wagner (1996); Heidenrich (1993); Phillips and Axelrod (2005).

INTER-STATE WAR #215:

The War of Bosnian Independence of 1992

Participants: Bosnia, Croatia vs. Yugoslavia
Dates: April 7, 1992, to June 5, 1992
Battle-Related Deaths: Bosnia—2,850; Yugoslavia—1,890; Croatia—500
Where Fought: Europe
Initiator: Yugoslavia
Outcome: Yugoslavia withdraws and the fighting is transformed into intra-state war #877

Narrative: Yugoslavia was a federation of six republics, Bosnia-Hercegovina, Croatia, Macedonia, Montenegro, Serbia, and Slovenia. Following the collapse of the Soviet Cold War–era domination of Eastern Europe, multiparty elections throughout 1990 in the Yugoslav republics led to the election of nationalist candidates who supported the autonomy of their respective republics. The disintegration of Yugoslavia began when Slovenia and Croatia declared independence in June 1991, Macedonia in November 1991, and Bosnia-Hercegovina in 1992. Fighting between Yugoslavia and Slovenia ended with relatively few fatalities and with Slovenian independence. Croatia gained its independence through the bloody Croatian War of Independence (intra-state war #864).

Bosnia-Hercegovina was a multiethnic society of Muslims, Serbians, and Croatians. In October 1991 the Croat and Muslim members of Bosnia's government voted to secede from Yugoslavia, and the Bosnian Serbs responded by proclaiming their own republic in January 1992. Each group had its own paramilitary organizations, and conflict began in early 1992 between the Yugoslav Army (the JNA) and the Bosnian

Serbs against the Bosnian Muslims, the Bosnian Croats, and the army of Croatia (though conflict did not reach a war level at this stage). International recognition of the independence of Bosnia-Hercegovina on April 7, 1992 (making Bosnia a COW system member on that date), led to an increase in hostilities between Yugoslavia and Bosnia, and the COW inter-state war began on that date. Intense conflict continued involving JNA troops within Bosnia, leading to international pressure on Yugoslavia to withdraw its troops and end the war. Yugoslavia agreed and claimed to have withdrawn its JNA forces by May 1992, though the evacuation of the Marshal Tito barracks in Sarajevo on June 5, 1992, marks the end of direct Yugoslav participation and the end of the inter-state phase of the war. However, 80,000 former JNA members did remain in Bosnia and continued fighting with the Bosnian Serb forces against the Bosnian government. Fighting continued until December 1995 as an intra-state civil war between the Bosnian regulars and the Bosnian Serb forces, though the involvement of the Croatian army and forces from North Atlantic Treaty Organization (NATO) members led to its classification as an internationalized civil war (see intra-state war #877). The Dayton Peace Accords, signed December 14, 1995, finally ended the war in Bosnia.

Coding: This war is not preceded by a MID. Though hostilities had begun in early 1992 between Yugoslavia and Bosnia, Bosnia was not a member of the interstate system at that time. The inter-state war is coded as beginning simultaneously with Bosnia's entry into the system, on April 7, 1992. This war was not initially coded as a war in the COW MID dataset version 3.0, due to the difficulties involved in separating out the inter-state and intra-state war phases and in counting battle-deaths. This is a rare instance in which there is a discrepancy between the war list in the existing COW MID dataset and the COW inter-state war data (though this may change in the future). The inter-state phase of the overall conflict is brief, lasting only for the period in which the regular armed forces of Yugoslavia/Serbia are involved in the fighting. When

Yugoslavia formally withdrew its troops from Bosnia, the war was transformed into an intra-state war between Bosnia and the Bosnian Serbs. However, since, as mentioned above, 80,000 Yugoslav troops did remain in Bosnia and continued fighting with the Bosnian Serbs against Bosnia, it has been argued that these troops were still really controlled by Yugoslavia and paid by Yugoslavia and that in reality the war remained an inter-state one for its duration.

All sources indicate the difficulty of establishing accurate fatality statistics for this conflict, both in terms of determining overall fatalities and in distinguishing combatants from civilians. Most of the human rights organizations were concerned primarily with civilian fatalities and reported figures that were only civilian deaths or aggregate numbers that may have combined civilian and combatant deaths. Fatality figures have also been either exaggerated or minimized, often to either promote or dissuade international intervention in the conflict. Most fatality figures are presented for the entire conflict, rarely by time periods or specific battles. Since we are dividing this conflict into two wars, our battle-death figures (1,000 of which are needed to code each phase as a war) were derived from calculations that divided the number of battle-dead over three years by the number of months, to arrive at an average number killed per month. Robert Donia (2007) examined our method and figures and reported that our estimate is probably low, because the months included in this inter-state war were particularly deadly months. His remarks reconfirm our conviction that this phase of the conflict was indeed severe enough to be an inter-state war. Similarly, the UN Commission of Experts described the beginning phase of the war as a conflict between Bosnia and the Yugoslav army. "At first, the Bosnian government and the JNA opposed each other. This lasted from April to June 1992" (Bassiouni 1992). This would seem to support classifying this period as an inter-state war. The entire conflict (inter-state and intra-state phases) lasts until the peace treaty is signed on December 14, 1995. During the total course of the conflict, there are three general parties involved in the conflict (the Bosnians, the Croats, and the Serbians)—including three system-member militaries and approximately

eighty-three paramilitary organizations. (For details see Bassiouni, 1992, the Final Report of the United Nations Commission of Experts.) The UN Commission of Experts divides its report into Annex III, which discusses what it calls the "regular military forces engaged in the conflict," and Annex IIIA, which describes the paramilitary and special forces units.

Sources: Bassiouni (1992); Bercovitch and Fetter (2004); Brogan (1998); Center for Balkan Development (1996); CIA (2002); Donia (2006); Donia and Fine (1994); Holbrooke (1999); Kaldor (1999); Keesing's (1992); Kenney (1995); Malcolm (1996); Nilsen (2004); Power (2002); Research and Document Center Sarajevo (2006); Rogel (1998); Sanz (1992); Sremac (1992); Sullivan (2003); Uppsala Universitet (1995).

INTER-STATE WAR #216:

The Azeri-Armenian War of 1993–1994

Participants: Armenia vs. Azerbaijan
Dates: February 6, 1993, to May 12, 1994
Battle-Related Deaths: Azerbaijan—8,500; Armenia—5,500
Where Fought: Europe
Initiator: Armenia
Outcome: Armenia wins

Narrative: The people of Nagorno-Karabakh are generally Christian and ethnically Armenian. In the early nineteenth century Russia had incorporated both Armenia and Azerbaijan into the Russian Empire. In 1813 Russia also acquired Nagorno-Karabakh from Turkey. Until 1920 Nagorno-Karabakh was considered a part of Armenia, but an agreement in 1921 between Russia and Turkey gave the region to Azerbaijan (which is overwhelmingly Turkic-speaking Muslims). This decision, needless to say, angered the Armenians. From the 1950s onward, the Armenians living in Nagorno-Karabakh petitioned Moscow to be annexed to Armenia. As the USSR began to liberalize (and ultimately disintegrate), the Armenians of Nagorno-Karabakh took the opportunity to push their cause. In February 1988 the regional council in Nagorno-Karabakh voted to be integrated into Armenia, leading to the imposition of direct rule by Moscow over the territory. In December 1989 Armenia declared that the region should be part of a unified Armenia, leading to conflicts with the USSR for two years (though the skirmishes did not reach a war level). Armenia ultimately declared that it was no longer interested in Nagorno-Karabakh, and the latter decided to seek independence for itself from Azerbaijan in 1990, a demand that led to sporadic conflict in 1991, killing 800 people.

In September 1991 Nagorno-Karabakh declared independence. After the fall of the USSR, Azerbaijan became a system member on December 26, 1991, and this date technically marks the beginning of an intra-state war between Azerbaijan and Nagorno-Karabakh (see war #872). In January 1992 Azerbaijani forces attacked the capital of Nagorno-Karabakh, and the forces of Nagorno-Karabakh responded, going on an offensive that captured an increasing amount of Azeri territory. Most important, on May 18 Nagorno-Karabakh captured Lachin, which created a land link, the "Lachin Corridor," between Nagorno-Karabakh and Armenia. In June 1992 the tide turned when Azerbaijani forces launched a major offensive, seizing northern Nagorno-Karabakh and attacking the Lachin Corridor, though they were finally repulsed after heavy fighting by Karabakh and Armenian forces, though at this stage Armenia continued to insist that it was not a formal party to the conflict. There were a number of attempts to mediate the conflict by Moscow, Iran, Kazakhstan, the Commission on Security and Cooperation in Europe (CSCE), the UN, and the Organization for Security and Co-operation in Europe (OSCE).

The year 1993 saw a significant increase in the level of conflict. A major offensive began on February 6, 1993, aimed at both attacking the Azeri forces in the north and relieving the Azeri pressure around Lachin by opening a new land link between Armenia and Karabakh. This offensive represents the point at which Armenia takes over the bulk of the fighting from the forces of Nagorno-Karabakh. It thus marks the end of the intra-state war and the transformation of the fighting into this inter-state war between Armenia and Azerbaijan. In fierce fighting in March and April 1993, Karabakh and Armenian forces attacked Azeri areas outside of Nagorno-Karabakh, leading to international protests and the mobilization of Turkish troops along the border with Armenia. Iran, claiming that its security was also being threatened, asked Armenia to withdraw its forces from Azerbaijan. Azerbaijan suffered through another coup, in which Russia may have played a role. Azerbaijan then joined the successor to the Soviet Union, the Commonwealth of Independent States (CIS), in September 1993. Meanwhile, the Armenian and Karabakh forces continued their advance in July and August 1993, consolidating Armenian control over most of southwestern Azerbaijan. After further Armenian gains in October 1993, the Azeris launched a counterattack in December, aided by volunteer Afghan mujahideen fighters and Russian advisers. The war became essentially a stalemate as each side depleted its resources. A CIS-brokered cease-fire was signed on May 12, 1994, with Armenia, Nagorno-Karabakh, and Azerbaijan attending the ceremony on July 27, 1994, in Yerevan. The cease-fire ended the war, and though it led to de facto autonomy for Nagorno-Karabakh, the ultimate status of Nagorno-Karabakh was unresolved. Minor clashes continued on the border between Armenia and Azerbaijan in 1997, 1998, 1999, and 2000.

Coding: The related MID is #3564, which lasts from 1992 to 1995. There were several interrelated problems in coding these wars (the intra-state and the inter-state). One problem was determining the number of battle-deaths. Most sources (see Mooradian and Druckman [1999]) give death totals that include civilian deaths; however, all sources agree that the fatality levels were highest during April 1993 to May 1994 (the period of the inter-state war). It was frequently difficult to separate out the actual war participants. Sources tended to refer to "Armenians" which included both the regular army forces from Armenia as well as the forces of the Armenian residents of Nagorno-Karabakh. Finally, in terms of differentiating the civil war phase from the inter-state war, it was necessary to determine when the Armenian army took over the bulk of the fighting from the Nagorno-Karabakh forces.

Sources: Chorbajian, Donabedian, and Mutafian (1994); Cornell (1999); Croissant (1998); de Waal (2003); Esposito (2001); Mooradian and Druckman (1999); United Nations Committee on Rights of the Child (1996); Uppsala Universitet (1997).

INTER-STATE WAR #217:

The Cenepa Valley War of 1995

Participants: Peru vs. Ecuador
Dates: January 9, 1995, to February 27, 1995
Battle-Related Deaths: Peru—950; Ecuador—550
Where Fought: W. Hemisphere
Initiator: Ecuador
Outcome: Compromise

Narrative: The roots of the conflict concerning the demarcation of the border between Ecuador and Peru derive from the period when the two countries declared their independence from Spain. Palmer (2001, 29) has referred to this as "the longest running boundary conflict without resolution in the Western Hemisphere." The two countries were involved in at least thirty-four bloody military confrontations since 1884. Major conflicts took place in 1829, 1859, 1941, and January 1981, though there were insufficient casualties for the conflicts to be considered wars. In 1941 Peru had invaded Ecuador and forced a settlement under the 1942 Rio Protocol. The governments of Brazil, Argentina, Chile, and the United States were to serve as the guarantors of the protocol. Under the protocol 95 percent of the border was demarcated in the plains region; however, the demarcation in the mountainous area was never completed due to 1946 aerial photography that revealed distinctive geographical characteristics of the watershed in the upper Cenepa Valley. Thus since 1960 Ecuador insisted that the Rio Protocol was not executable. In the early 1990s the Fujimori government of Peru tried to improve relations with Ecuador and proposed arbitration of the border, which Ecuador refused.

Peru had military superiority in numbers. Thus Ecuador adopted a strategy of secretly establishing military bases in the disputed territory. In December 1994 Peru discovered that Ecuador had established military bases at Tiwintza, Cueva de los Tallos, and Base Sur, in the disputed region. The war began with an exchange of fire on January 9 and 11, 1995, and lasted for six weeks. On January 26 fighting escalated to air attacks by Ecuador and Peru's responding air and ground attacks in the region. This led to large troop mobilizations by both sides. A battlefield stalemate developed in which Peru succeeded in driving the Ecuadorians from two bases, but Ecuador maintained control over Tiwintza, which was perceived as an Ecuadorian victory. A cease-fire was announced on February 15, 1995, yet hostilities continued until February 27. A peace agreement, the Declaration of Itamaraty, was signed on March 17, 1995, under the sponsorship of Brazil and the other three guarantors. The U.S. Military Observer Mission Ecuador/Peru (MOMEP) served as a peacekeeping force, though minor border incidents continued through September 1995. The remaining border issues were settled in the Brasilia Presidential Act on October 26, 1998. The accord reaffirmed Peru's claim about the border; however, it did give Ecuador a small area in Peru at Tiwintza to build a memorial to the war dead. It also gave Ecuador navigation rights on the Amazon within Peru.

Coding: Determining the fatality levels in this case has been difficult because, as Simmons (1999, note 29) noted, "Official figures are toward the low end, while 'reliable sources' place estimates toward the high end." Recent research by Palmer (2007–2008) and Mares (2007–2008) affirms Bonilla's (1995) earlier estimate of 1,500 total fatalities.

Sources: Bercovitch and Fretter (2004); Bonilla (1995); Dominguez (2003); Herz and Nogueira (2002); Mares (2007–2008); Mares (2001); Palmer (2007–2008); Palmer (2001); Palmer (1997); Scheina (2003b); Sethi (2002); Simmons (2007); Simmons (1999); Weidner (1996).

INTER-STATE WAR #219:
The Badme Border War of 1998–2000

Participants: Eritrea vs. Ethiopia
Dates: May 6, 1998, to December 12, 2000
Battle-Related Deaths: Ethiopia—70,000;
    Eritrea—50,000
Where Fought: Africa
Initiator: Eritrea
Outcome: Stalemate

Narrative: Eritrea had fought for its independence from Ethiopia between 1975 and 1991 (intra-state wars #798 and #826). Even though Eritrea was able to peacefully secede from Ethiopia in 1993, negative effects of the independence struggle remained. The border between them was never resolved, Ethiopia came out of the war with a huge debt, and it resented the loss of its ports on the Red Sea to Eritrea. Conflicts between the two states also concerned foreign policy and economic policy. The immediate cause of this inter-state war was the border dispute. In May 1998 Eritrean troops entered an area under Ethiopian control, and Ethiopian troops fired on them, marking the start of the war. Ground fighting escalated to air attacks in June 1998. In late 1998 U.S. president Bill Clinton appointed former national security adviser Anthony Lake as a

special envoy to help resolve the conflict. Lake worked with the Organization of African Unity (OAU) to produce a peace framework that was, among other things, supposed to prohibit the use of air strikes. Despite Eritrea's reservations, the agreement did reduce the level of violence for several months. In February 1999 however, fighting once again escalated, including the use of air attacks. In May and June 1999 thousands of combatants were killed in fierce fighting that involved both air strikes and trench warfare (reminiscent of World War I). In 1999 Eritrea and Somalia also assisted the Oromo Liberation Front in its war against Ethiopia (intra-state war #913). Heavy fighting continued in 2000 in which Ethiopia launched a major offensive and was able to regain some of the disputed territory in May. A new mediation effort was launched, and in June 2000 Eritrea accepted a new OAU plan that called on the parties to withdraw to May 1998 positions and for the UN to maintain a fifteen-mile buffer zone between the parties. Sporadic fighting continued. The peace agreement was finally signed in Algiers on December 12, 2000.

Coding: MID #4258 begins on May 6, 1998, the day the war begins.

Sources: Benson, Matuszak, and O'Meara (2001); Bercovitch and Fretter (2004); Clodfelter (1992); Peace Pledge Union (2001); Pendergast (2001); Project Ploughshares (2000); Salopek (2000); Uppsala Universitet (2005).

INTER-STATE WAR #221:
The War for Kosovo of 1999

Participants: France, Germany, Italy, Netherlands, Turkey, United Kingdom, United States vs. Yugoslavia
Dates: March 24, 1999, to June 10, 1999
Battle-Related Deaths: Yugoslavia—5,000; United States—2; France—0; Germany—0; Italy—0; Netherlands—0; Turkey—0; United Kingdom—0
Where Fought: Europe

Initiator: France, Germany, Italy, Netherlands, Turkey, United Kingdom, United States

Outcome: France, Germany, Italy, Netherlands, Turkey, United Kingdom, United States win

Narrative: Kosovo's desire for independence from Yugoslavia had led to war in 1998, intrastate war #900 (Kosovo Independence). International attempts to mediate the conflict between Kosovo and Yugoslavia failed. The North Atlantic Treaty Organization (NATO) had stationed 13,000 troops in Macedonia as a potential peacekeeping force had the mediation talks at Rambouillet succeeded. Though the Kosovars signed the Rambouillet Accord on March 18, the Yugoslav delegation refused to do so. Ambassador Richard Holbrooke flew to Belgrade in a final attempt to persuade Yugoslav president Slobodan Milošević to stop the attacks on Kosovo. Instead, on March 20, 1999, Yugoslavia launched Operation Horseshoe to expel the ethnic Albanians from Kosovo. In an attempt to stop the "ethnic cleansing," on March 24, 1999, NATO began a phased bombing campaign in an attempt to persuade Yugoslavia back to the bargaining table. This offensive marks the start of the interstate war. Of the nineteen NATO members, thirteen made their aircraft available for the operation: Belgium, Canada, Denmark, France, Germany, Italy, the Netherlands, Norway, Portugal, Spain, Turkey, the UK, and the United States. Eight of the NATO countries were involved in the bombing campaign on the first night (Canada, France, Germany, Italy, the Netherlands, Spain, the UK, and the United States) against targets throughout Yugoslavia. On March 25, 1999, Yugoslavia responded by declaring a state of war and broke off relations with France, Germany, the UK, and the United States.

The success of the NATO air strikes was limited by the necessity of keeping the planes above 15,000 feet owing to the Yugoslav air defense system. The air strikes were also initially ineffectual in stopping the atrocities occurring within Kosovo. Indeed, the Yugoslav military and paramilitary forces increased their attacks in Kosovo after NATO's bombing campaign had begun. As a result, over 90 percent of the Kosovars were displaced: over 863,000 civilians were forced out of Kosovo, and another 590,000 were internally displaced. Kosovars fled their homes at a rate that was ten times greater than in 1998. Many NATO governments had hoped that the air campaign would be a short one, yet Yugoslavia appeared to be unmoved by the air campaign's initial phase. Consequently, the number of attacks and the variety of targets grew during the war's second phase, which was implemented after a NATO summit in Washington, D.C., on April 23, 1999. That month NATO began planning for a ground invasion as well. Yet this expanded activity led to increasing collateral damage, including 3 killed in an attack on the Chinese embassy in Belgrade on May 8, 1999. Five NATO missiles landed in Bulgaria, and NATO strikes killed civilians in Kosovo and Yugoslavia (perhaps 527 Serb civilians). The ground war also expanded during this period, and the Kosovo Liberation Army (KLA) started to inflict Serb losses five to ten times higher than at the beginning of the conflict. NATO's collaboration with the KLA also grew, combining NATO's air power with KLA ground forces. For example, on June 7, during a significant battle between KLA and Yugoslav forces along the Albanian border, NATO sent two B-52s to bomb the Yugoslav positions.

In all, the NATO air campaign lasted seventy-eight days and involved aircraft flying 37,200 sorties and 9,500 strike sorties. The United States flew over 60 percent of all the sorties and 53 percent of the strike sorties. Ultimately, a final round of negotiations in June 1999 negated the need for the NATO ground invasion. The G8 had developed a plan for an internationally monitored Kosovo as an alternative to regulation by NATO. This plan was approved by the Yugoslav parliament on June 3. The Yugoslav army began withdrawing from Kosovo, and NATO suspended the bombing campaign on June 10, 1999, thus ending the war. The UN took over the administration of Kosovo. NATO's Kosovo Force (KFOR) peace-keeping troops began deploying in Kosovo on June 12. Kosovo was divided into five sectors under the command of the British, German, French, Italian, and U.S. contingents. Russia also deployed troops, though it did not have a territorial sector. At its peak, KFOR consisted of 50,000 personnel from thirty-four NATO and non-NATO states, yet that number declined to 38,000 by 2000. Violence continued between the Kosovars and Serbian civilians (though deaths did not reach war levels). The status of Kosovo remained unresolved for some time. Kosovo finally declared its independence on February 17, 2008. By the next day, Kosovo's independence had been recognized by seven countries, including the United Kingdom, France, Turkey, and the United States. Kosovo thus became a COW system member as of that date. Kosovo's independence was not universally accepted, however; it was rejected as illegal by Russia, and China also voiced its reservations. By May 21, 2008, only 41 of the 192 UN members had extended recognition.

Coding: This conflict posed coding issues in two general areas: in determining the type of conflict and in determining battle-deaths. In reference to the first issue, conflict began as an intra-state civil war that changed category due to the intervention of outside actors (system members). When an outside actor intervenes on the side of the insurgents and either takes some action that changes the nature of the conflict or assumes the bulk of the fighting (defined as causing the most fatalities), then the civil war takes on the characteristics of an inter-state war. The civil war is then coded as ending and an inter-state war is coded as beginning. In this case, when the members of NATO intervened in the ongoing civil war of the Kosovars against Yugoslavia and launched the bombing campaign against Yugoslavia, the war became an inter-state war of the NATO members aided by the KLA against Yugoslavia. COW discussed whether to code NATO as the primary actor in this conflict (which would then have resulted in a classification of an extra-state war between Yugoslavia and a nonstate entity, NATO). However, the decision was made

that it was more appropriate to code the individual NATO system members as the war participants because of the existence of parallel U.S. and NATO command structures, the overall dominance of actions by the United States, and independent (non-NATO) U.S. actions. Only those NATO members that met the war participation criterion of committing more than 1,000 troops were coded as participants. An inter-state war requires a minimum of 1,000 battle-related fatalities suffered by the system members per year during the period of the war. Since this is a war between NATO—aided by the KLA—and Yugoslavia, battle-deaths would include deaths suffered by NATO and those suffered by Yugoslavia (both those caused by NATO and those caused by the KLA). Estimates of fatality levels for the KLA and civilians are included here for informational (not coding) purposes only. All sources indicate the difficulty of establishing accurate fatality statistics for this conflict, in terms of both determining overall fatalities and distinguishing combatants (both Kosovars and Yugoslavs) from civilians. Most of the human rights organizations were concerned primarily with civilian fatalities and reported figures that were only civilian deaths or aggregate numbers that may have combined civilian and combatant deaths. Some fatality figures are presented for calendar years, not war durations. Fatality figures have also been either exaggerated or minimized, often to promote or dissuade international intervention in the conflict. Jones (2000) argues that early estimates of those killed (as opposed to missing) were low. As new evidence emerges, fatality levels are growing. He estimates between 10,000 and 20,000 total number of Kosovars killed in both wars. Others concluded that civilian casualties were smaller than anticipated in comparison with combatants.

Sources: BBC News (1999a, b, and c); CNN (1999); CNN (1998); Congressional Research Service (2000); Congressional Research Service (1998); Daalder and O'Hanlon (2000); Deployment Health Clinical Center (2006); Duke, Ehrhart, and Karadi (2000); FAS Intelligence Resource Program (2005); Global Security (2006); Haglund and Sens (2000); Human Rights Watch (2001); Human Rights Watch (2000); Independent International Commission on

Kosovo (2000); Jane's Defense (1999); Jones (2000); Judah (2000); Kostakos (2000); Lampe (2000); Loeb (1999); Mennecke (2004); Møller (2000); NATO (1999); Project Ploughshares (2005); Waller, Drezov, and Gökay (2001); Youngs, Oakes, and Bowers (1999).

INTER-STATE WAR #223:
The Kargil War of 1999

Participants: India vs. Pakistan
Dates: May 8, 1999, to July 17, 1999
Battle-Related Deaths: Pakistan—698;
   India—474
Where Fought: Asia
Initiator: Pakistan
Outcome: India wins

Narrative: Pakistan and India have rival claims to Kashmir dating from the 1947 partition of India by the British. Kashmir (a predominantly Muslim region) was given to India, rather than to Muslim Pakistan. India and Pakistan fought two previous wars over Kashmir (inter-state #147 in 1947–1949 and #166 in 1965). The first war left Kashmir divided, with Pakistan occupying about one-third of its territory, and the cease-fire line became the de facto border between India and Pakistan. Kashmir has a militant Kashmiri guerrilla movement seeking either independence or incorporation into Pakistan. In 1990 Kashmiri guerrillas seeking independence began a fifteen-year revolt that was suppressed by India (intra-state war #861). Tensions increased when both India and Pakistan conducted nuclear tests in 1998. Though the Lahore summit in February 1999 tried to de-escalate tensions, Pakistan wanted to revive international attention to the issue of Kashmir. On May 8, 1999, Pakistani heavy artillery fired into the Indian sector of Kashmir, and Pakistani troops and Islamic guerrillas (estimated at 1,200 to 1,500 troops) crossed the cease-fire line in order to secure the highlands near Kargil. This marks the start of the war. When the Pakistanis were

discovered, India retaliated in force on May 26, and heavy air and ground combat continued. The fighting in May was inconclusive; however, in June India increased its attempts to regain its mountain positions and successfully regained most of its territory. The fighting was the bloodiest confrontation in thirty years. Pakistan agreed to withdraw its troops on July 17, 1999 (ending the war), and India claimed victory. It is estimated that 80,000 people were displaced during the conflict. Meanwhile, the intra-state violence continued between Islamic militants (backed by Pakistan) and the Indian government (see intra-state war #861).

Coding: The militarized dispute that precedes this war (MID #4007) begins in September 1973.

Sources: Global Security (1999); Keesing's (1999); Peace Pledge Union (2001); Report of the Kargil Review Committee (2000).

INTER-STATE WAR #225:
The Invasion of Afghanistan of 2001

Participants: Australia, Canada, France, United
   Kingdom, United States vs. Afghanistan
Dates: October 7, 2001, to December 22, 2001
Battle-Related Deaths: Afghanistan—4,000;
   United States—2; Australia—0; Canada—0;
   France—0; United Kingdom—0
Where Fought: Asia
Initiator: United Kingdom, United States
Outcome: Transformed into extra-state war #481

Narrative: The stage for this war had been set by the preceding four wars in Afghanistan. The earlier civil wars (#810 and 812) had led to the Soviet Union's ten-year struggle for control of Afghanistan (the Soviet Quagmire, extra-state war #476). In 1989 the Soviets withdrew, leaving a communist government in power, which ultimately collapsed amid fighting with the Islamic mujahideen. A period of fighting among Afghan Islamic factions followed, with a new group, the Taliban, ultimately coming to power. Fighting between the Taliban and other mujahideen linked together as the Northern Alliance (intra-state war #851) continued until 2001, when the conflict was transformed into this inter-state war. The radical Islamic Taliban also provided a haven for al-Qaida, a terrorist group founded in 1989 by Saudi-born Osama bin Laden and directed against the perceived enemies of Islam. Bin Laden had moved to Afghanistan originally in 1979 to assist the mujahideen against the Soviets. He returned to Afghanistan in 1996, and al-Qaida was implicated in a number of terrorist incidents after that. Al-Qaida gained particular notoriety owing to its links to the attacks on the World Trade Center in New York City and the Pentagon on September 11, 2001. At this stage bin Laden was the personification of al-Qaida. He had forged an alliance with the Taliban and had integrated some al-Qaida fighters into the Taliban army.

The United States was determined to bring the perpetrators of the World Trade Center attack to justice, to destroy their organization through its "War on Terror," and to topple the Taliban government of Afghanistan in retaliation for its support of al-Qaida. With the concurrence of the UN Security Council, the U.S. demanded that Afghanistan turn over the leaders of al-Qaida in Afghanistan. When the Taliban refused, the United States began assembling an antiterrorism coalition with the assistance of the United Kingdom; however, their decision to target the Taliban government and to force regime change made it more difficult to assemble a coalition. The UN imposed sanctions and an arms embargo on September 16, 2001. Pakistan under the leadership of President Pervez Musharraf, which had been a supporter of the Taliban, changed its position and joined the coalition, despite the opposition of over 80 percent of the Pakistani population. On September 17 Pakistan urged the Taliban to surrender bin Laden. Meanwhile, the links between al-Qaida and the Taliban were becoming stronger. Their troops and bases melded together, and bin Laden was reportedly named commander in chief of the Taliban forces.

The United States and the United Kingdom began planning an attack on Afghanistan, titled Operation Enduring Freedom (British participation was named Operation Veritas). The allies also began supplying limited assistance to the anti-Taliban Northern Alliance, and U.S. and British Special Forces began entering Afghanistan. The war that began on October 7, 2001, ended the intra-state civil war and is coded as an inter-state war because the primary battle participants are interstate system members: the coalition states of the United States, United Kingdom, France, and Australia (aided by the Northern Alliance, a nonstate actor) against the Taliban government of Afghanistan (assisted by al-Qaida, a nonstate actor). The first battle plan (devised to limit allied casualties) involved aerial bombing raids (both land and sea based) around the major cities, conducted primarily by the United States and the United Kingdom, targeting both Taliban and al-Qaida positions. The United States and the United Kingdom are coded as initiating and participating in the war on the first day. Even though France had stationed a warship in the region and had special forces operating within Afghanistan, it is only after the UN Security Council resolution that French aircraft contributed to the air campaign, on October 21, 2001. Canada and Australia also committed more than the COW requisite 1,000 troops to the coalition and are thus considered to have joined the war on November 15, 2001, when their forces arrived. In conjunction with the air strikes, a ground war was conducted primarily (and ineffectively at this stage) by the Northern Alliance. By October 17, 2001, the U.S. and coalition forces had destroyed virtually all of the Taliban air defenses. The bombing campaign did, however, entail a number of costs, including civilian casualties, exacerbated refugee problems, alienation of world opinion, and disruption of humanitarian efforts.

The allies decided to shift their strategy to more directly support the Northern Alliance, and on October 20 U.S. and British ground troops launched a major ground offensive. Tensions rose within Pakistan as thousands of pro-Taliban fighters attempted to cross into Afghanistan. The United Nations sponsored negotiations to create a new government for Afghanistan, but divisions among the anti-Taliban opposition remained problematic. In early November, attacks against the Taliban increased and the Northern Alliance seized much of northern Afghanistan. On November 9, 2001, the battle for Mazari Sharif led to a major Taliban retreat and a massacre of Taliban supporters by the Northern Alliance. On November 13, 2001, the Afghan capital city of Kabul was occupied by Northern Alliance troops, and the Taliban withdrew to Kandahar, where U.S. ground forces were involved in the fighting. Meanwhile, al-Qaida forces concentrated their efforts in the Tora Bora area. The major anti-Taliban groups met in Bonn for UN-sponsored talks that led to an agreement on December 5 for the creation of an interim government. By early December, the United States had occupied the Kandahar airport. December 17, 2001, marked the last day of bombing (though the fighting continued). The allies were successful in driving the Taliban from power. After seventy-eight days of combat, a new Afghan interim government under Hamid Karzai was installed on December 22, 2001. Since the installation of a new government in Afghanistan meant that the coalition members were no longer fighting against the government of Afghanistan, this ends the inter-state phase of the conflict. Unfortunately, the conflict itself continued. The coalition continued to search for the remnants of the Taliban and al-Qaida forces, which had retreated to the mountains. Thus Operation Enduring Freedom then took on the characteristics of an extra-state war (see war #481) between system members and nonstate actors outside their borders.

Coding: Germany, Italy, and Turkey all sent forces but numbered less than 1,000 during this period, and so they are not coded as war participants. In their fatality figures, Uppsala/PRIO (2004) and Phillips and Axelrod (2005) include those killed in the attacks of September 11, 2001, but COW does not include these.

Sources: Al Jazeera Magazine (2003); Center for Defense Information (2001a); Center for Defense Information (2001b); Conetta (2002); Global Security (2005); Herold (2002); icasualties.org (2007); Keesing's (2001); Phillips and Axelrod (2005); Project Ploughshares (2005); U.S. Central Command (2007); Uppsala Universitet (2004).

INTER-STATE WAR #227:

The Invasion of Iraq of 2003

Participants: Australia, United Kingdom, United States vs. Iraq
Dates: March 19, 2003, to May 2, 2003
Battle-Related Deaths: Iraq—7,000; United States—140; United Kingdom—33; Australia—0
Where Fought: Middle East
Initiator: Australia, United Kingdom, United States
Outcome: Transformed into extra-state war #482

Narrative: Iraq was seen by some as a threat to peace in the Middle East. Under the leadership of Saddam Hussein, Iraq had engaged in an eight-year war with Iran (inter-state war #199) and had launched an invasion of Kuwait that had drawn another twelve countries into the subsequent Gulf War (inter-state war #211). Iraq was also seen as a supporter of, and a haven for, international terrorist organizations. Consequently, it was initially claimed that the purpose behind U.S. opposition to Iraq was the U.S. desire to reduce the threat posed by Iraq, which supposedly possessed "weapons of mass destruction" (WMDs). On November 8, 2002, the UN passed a resolution encouraging Iraq to divest itself of its WMDs; however, international opinion was divided about the issue of Iraq and what degree of threat it posed.

In March 2003 U.S. president George W. Bush issued an ultimatum to Saddam Hussein urging him to resign, and when he failed to do so, the United States began a series of air strikes against Iraq on March 19, 2003, which marks the start of the war. The United States assembled a "coalition of the willing" to aid it in this endeavor, and thirty states indicated that they would provide some level of support. Only five of them, however, provided troops (Albania, Australia, Poland, Romania, and the United Kingdom). Of these only two, Great Britain and Australia, contributed the over 1,000 troops necessary for them to be coded as war participants. The ground invasion began the following day, with U.S. and allied forces advancing from the south. The allied troops made rapid progress, reaching the capital, Baghdad, by early April, thereby forcing Saddam Hussein to go into hiding. The British were successful in occupying the southern city of Basra. On May 2, 2003, President Bush declared that major conflict had been concluded. The government of Iraq had been overthrown; thus this ended the inter-state war. Fighting continued, however, consisting of conflict between states and non-system members (al-Qaida in Iraq). The war was thus transformed into an extra-state war (#482). Saddam Hussein was finally captured by American forces on December 13, 2003, and he was later executed by the Iraqi government on December 30, 2006.

Coding: On May 2, 2003, President Bush declared that major conflict in Iraq had been concluded. The government of Iraq had been overthrown. Since the new government of Iraq was no longer in direct armed conflict against the United States and other states, this ended the inter-state war; however, fighting did continue at fatality levels sufficient for a war coding. There has been much debate about whether the subsequent conflict should be called a civil war. From the COW perspective, at this point the fighting is between the intervening states and nonsystem members (militias and al-Qaida in Iraq), and therefore the war was transformed into an extra-state war (#482). For it to be an intra-state civil war, the primary combatants would have to be the government of Iraq against nonstate armed groups within its borders.

Sources: Conetta (2004); Iraq Body Count (2005); Keesing's (2006); Kneisler (2005); Phillips and Axelrod (2005); Project Ploughshares (2005).

Analyzing Inter-state Wars

Inter-state wars are relatively rare, with only ninety-five inter-state wars over the past 192 years. As Figure 3.1 shows, most years have no inter-state war onsets at all. Sixty-four years have one war onset, and there were twelve years with two war onsets.

If we look at the distribution of war onsets over time, it becomes apparent that inter-state wars have not been evenly distributed. As Figure 3.2 shows, the most war-prone year in terms of war onsets was 1919, with four war onsets. The year 1939 had three war onsets. The nineteenth century was significantly less war prone than was the twentieth, with only twenty-nine war onsets. During the time span of our study, 1816–2007, there were only thirty-six inter-state war onsets in the first ninety-five years, compared with fifty-nine war onsets in the second half, with the least war-prone era being the period from 1816 to 1850.

The comparative peacefulness of the beginning of the nineteenth century is also visible if we collapse the dates into decades from 1817 to 2006 as seen in Figure 3.3 (the first and last years have been removed from the analysis to make the period evenly divisible into decades; however, there were no inter-state wars in either of those years). The earliest thirty years of the interstate system were its least war prone, with only one inter-state war breaking out per decade between 1817 and 1846. This finding is also related to the relatively small number of interstate system members at this time. However, the decade 1857–1866, which also had a relatively small number of system members, was the most war prone, with ten inter-state wars starting during that decade. If wars were evenly distributed by decade, there would be an average of five war onsets per decade. The decades of 1967–1976 and 1977–1986 are thus more war prone than average, while inter-state wars have been occurring with average frequency in the period of 1987 to 2006.

Inter-state wars are also not evenly distributed geographically. As Figure 3.4 shows, the plurality of inter-state wars have taken place in Asia, followed closely by Europe. Oceania experienced only one

FIGURE 3.1 **INTER-STATE WAR ONSETS BY NUMBER OF YEARS, 1816–2007 (NUMBER OF YEARS IN WHICH THE ONSET OF 0, 1, 2, 3, OR 4 INTER-STATE WARS OCCURRED)**

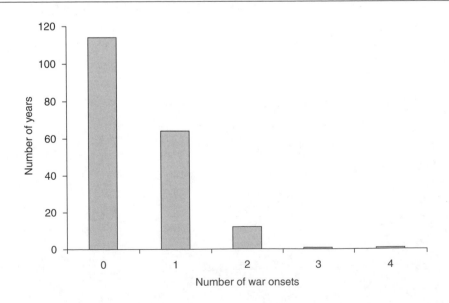

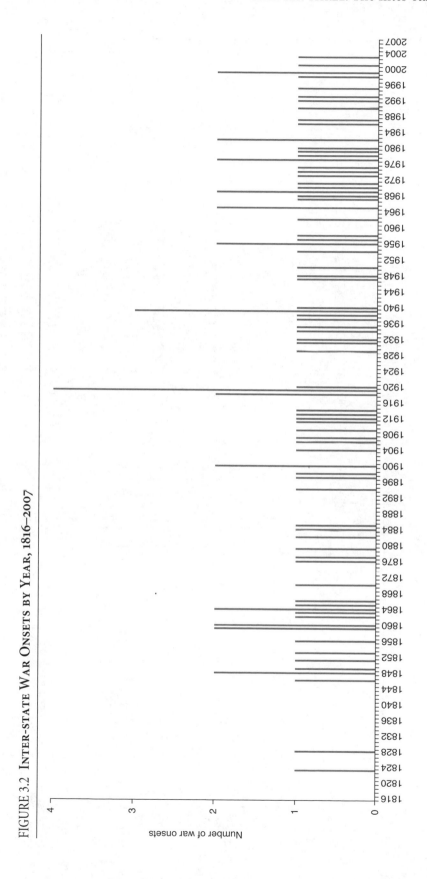

FIGURE 3.2 INTER-STATE WAR ONSETS BY YEAR, 1816–2007

FIGURE 3.3 **Inter-state War Onsets by Decade, 1817–2006**

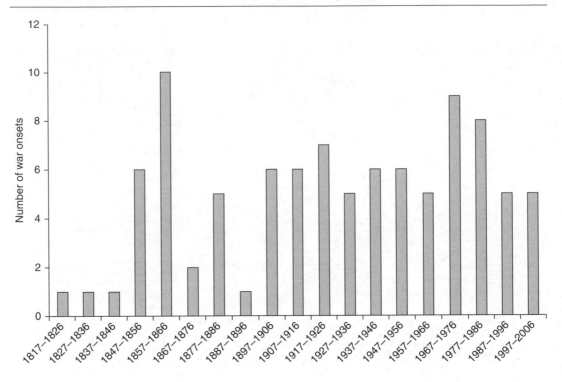

FIGURE 3.4 **Inter-state War Onsets by Region, 1816–2007**

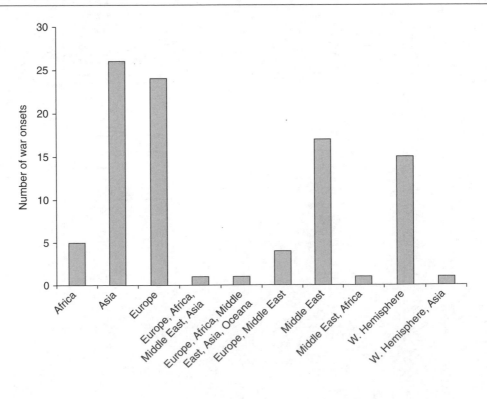

inter-state war, World War II, while Africa is the second-least common region for inter-state war. The regional distribution of inter-state wars is slightly different from that for other categories of war because of the presence of wars that take place in more than one region—most notably World Wars I and II, which take place in multiple regions, but also wars such as the Spanish-American War, which takes place both in the Western Hemisphere and in Asia. This regional dispersion does not occur in other types of war.

NOTES

1. Michael Clodfelter, *Warfare and Armed Conflicts: A Statistical Reference to Casualty and Other Figures, 1500–2000,* 2nd ed. (Jefferson, N.C.: McFarland, 2002); George Kohn, ed., *Dictionary of War,* 3rd ed. (New York: Checkmark Books, 2007); Charles Phillips and Alan Axelrod, *Encyclopedia of Wars,* 3 vols. (New York: Facts on File, 2005).

CHAPTER FOUR

The Extra-state Wars

Most of our readers will have already understood the basic idea of an inter-state war, as distinct from a civil war or an intra-state war. Extra-state wars are a bit more subtle. As detailed in Chapter 2, an extra-state war involves fighting by a state system member outside its borders against the armed forces of an entity that is not a member of the interstate system. For example, when France colonized much of West Africa, extra-state wars were frequently involved in that conquest. Similarly, at the other end of colonization, when African areas fought for independence from European colonialism, there were additional extra-state wars. Consequently, extra-state wars, as described by Melvin Small and J. David Singer in *Resort to Arms,* are of two general types: imperial and colonial. In imperial wars the system member fights an adversary that is "an independent political entity that did not qualify for system membership because of serious limitations on its independence, a population insufficiency, or a failure of other states to recognize it as a legitimate member."[1] In practice, most of our imperial wars involved an attempt to colonize a previously independent area, though extra-state wars can also be fought against nonterritorially based entities. The second type of extra-state war occurs if the adversary is a "colony, dependency, or protectorate."[2] In other words, these "colonial wars" tend to occur when a colony rebels and tries to become independent. In addition, in less extreme circumstances, the colonial people may resort to war to seek relief on a policy question (for example, the "Hut Tax War"), rather than seeking full-scale independence.

Finally, wars can be transformed into extra-state wars. This occurs most commonly within civil wars. If an outside state intervenes in another state's civil war (on the side of either the government or the rebels), the war becomes an "internationalized" civil war; however, if the intervening state assumes the "bulk of the fighting" from either of the parties, then the war is transformed into a different classification. If the intervener takes over the bulk of the fighting from the rebels, then the war becomes an inter-state war between two system members; however, if the intervener takes over the bulk of the fighting on behalf of the initially involved state, the war becomes an extra-state war between the intervener and a nonstate entity outside its borders (in this case the rebels within the other state). For instance, when the Soviet Union first intervened in 1979 in the ongoing civil war in Afghanistan, it did so on the side of the government of Afghanistan, making intra-state war #812, the Mujahideen Uprising, into an internationalized civil war (with both Afghanistan and the USSR coded as participants). However, in February 1980, when the USSR took over the bulk of the fighting from the Afghan government, the war became an extra-state war (#476, the Soviet Quagmire) between the Soviet Union and the Afghan insurgents.

Owing to their distinctive characteristics, extra-state wars have undergone phases that are unlike those that have affected inter-state and intra-state wars. Since extra-state wars are conducted by a state system member against a nonstate entity, they tend to be more prevalent when nonstate entities are numerous. For instance, within the Correlates of War (COW) time frame of 1816 to the present, most of the imperial wars occurred in the nineteenth century, as the European (and Japanese) colonial system expanded, generally taking over areas that had not yet attained all the requirements of system membership. Conversely, most of the colonial wars occurred in the mid-twentieth century, as colonies and dependencies helped bring the era of European colonialism to an end. As the former colonies gained independence and quickly joined the interstate system, they thereby reduced the number of nonstate entities in existence and thus lessened the possibilities for extra-state wars. In fact, there were no extra-state wars that began between 1964 and 1975, and we began to expect the demise of this war classification. However, one of the interesting trends within international relations currently is the growing number of nonstate entities that have the capability to wage war across state borders. Thus within the twenty-first century, we have seen a revival of extra-state wars.

As described in Chapter 2, the variables that the COW Project utilizes to classify and describe wars have had slightly different repercussions in the extra-state war category as compared with the inter-state wars. The requirements for a state to be a war participant are the same: a state must commit a minimum of 1,000 troops to the war, or suffer over 100 battle-deaths, to be considered a war participant. In terms of the nonstate war participants, Singer and Small initially required only that they have an organized armed force capable of engaging in sustained combat. As we continually gather more information about these nonstate participants, however, we have developed the additional requirements that nonstate entities need to commit a minimum of 100 armed troops, or suffer a minimum of 25 battle-related deaths. The requirement for sustained combat resulting in a minimum of 1,000 battle-related deaths per year among all parties is now the same for extra-state wars, though this is a shift from the initial practice of counting only the system-member deaths. In the new, expanded war typology and dataset, the elimination of the metropole distinction (described in Chapter 2) that was part of the original definition of extra-state wars had a significant impact on the number of wars in the extra-state category. In *Resort to Arms,* Small and Singer identified 51 extra-systemic wars. As a consequence of the definitional change, of these, 14 were reclassified as intra-state civil wars, (along with another 16 extra-state wars that had been added to the dataset since 1982; see Table 2.2 in Chapter 2 for a list). Two additional extra-systemic wars were reclassified or subdivided, and one was removed. However, an additional 129 wars have been added to the extra-state category, partially due to new historical information, partially because of the new wars that occurred since 1982, and especially due to the change in the definition of battle-deaths, which now includes the deaths suffered by the nonstate participant. Finally, the variables of the war's initiator and outcome are the same as for inter-state wars. In terms of extra-state wars, it is interesting to note that the party that initiated the war can be either the state or the nonstate entity, even in an imperial war. If an empire is spreading across an area and is suddenly attacked by the local people, the locals have initiated the war, even though it is an imperial war and may result in a defeat for the local people and a further expansion of the empire.

Table 4.1 is a list of the 163 wars included in the Correlates of War dataset on extra-state wars. Each of these wars will then be described individually, indicating the initiator of the war, the outcome (or winner), and the battle-related deaths, all of which are specifically defined in Chapter 2. The dates given for each war indicate the earliest start date and the latest end date for war participation, though individual combatants may have entered or left the war at various points within the period provided. The only additional variable added to the extra-state descriptions that was not included in the inter-state war histories is that of war type. As indicated in Chapter 2, Table 2.1 (and defined in Chapter 2), extra-state wars are of two types: Colonial (War Type 2) and Imperial (War Type 3).

TABLE 4.1 LIST OF EXTRA-STATE WARS IN CHRONOLOGICAL ORDER

(Continued)

TABLE 4.1 List of Extra-state Wars in Chronological Order (Continued)

Extra-state war number	War name	Page no	Extra-state war number	War name	Page no
360	British-Bhutanese War of 1865	239	386	First Franco-Madagascan War of 1883–1885	257
361	Russian-Bukharan War of 1866	239	387	Third British-Burmese War of 1885–1889	258
362	British-Ethiopian War of 1867–1868	240	389	French-Mandinka War of 1885–1886	259
363	First Spanish-Cuban War of 1868–1878	241	390	Russo-Afghan War of 1885	259
364	Attack on Bahr el-Ghazal of 1869–1870	242	391	Serbian-Bulgarian War of 1885	260
365	Ottoman Conquest of Arabia of 1870–1872	242	392	First Italian-Ethiopian War of 1887	261
366	Second Franco-Algerian War of 1871–1872	243	393	Zambezi Conquest of 1888	262
367	Second British-Ashanti War of 1873–1874	244	394	First Franco-Dahomeyan War of 1890	263
369	Second Franco-Vietnamese War of 1873–1874	244	395	Franco-Jolof War of 1890–1891	263
370	First Dutch-Achinese War of 1873–1878	245	396	Second Franco-Dahomeyan War of 1892–1893	264
371	Kokand Rebellion of 1875–1876	246	397	Belgian-Tib War of 1892–1894	264
372	Egypt-Ethiopian War of 1875–1876	247	398	Third British-Ashanti War of 1893–1894	265
373	Serbian-Turkish War of 1876–1877	248	399	Melilla War of 1893–1894	266
374	Third British-Xhosa War of 1877–1878	249	400	Mahdist-Italian War of 1893–1894	267
375	Egypt-Sudanese Slavers War of 1878–1879	249	401	Second Franco-Madagascan War of 1894–1895	267
376	Russo-Turkoman War of 1878–1881	250	402	Second Dutch-Bali War of 1894	268
377	Austrian-Bosnian War of 1878	251	403	Portuguese-Gaza Empire War of 1895	269
379	Second British-Afghan War of 1878–1880	251	404	Second Spanish-Cuban War of 1895–1898	269
380	Second British-Zulu War of 1879	252	405	Japan-Taiwanese War of 1895	271
381	Gun War of 1880–1881	253	406	Mazrui Rebellion of 1895–1896	271
382	First Boer War of 1880–1881	254	407	Second Italian-Ethiopian War of 1895–1896	272
383	Franco-Tunisian War of 1881–1882	255	409	Second British-Mahdi War of 1896–1899	274
384	First British-Mahdi War of 1881–1885	255	410	Spanish-Philippine War of 1896–1898	274
385	Third Franco-Vietnamese War of 1882–1884	257	411	British-South Nigerian War of 1897	276
			412	British-Pathan War of 1897–1898	276
			413	Hut Tax War of 1898	277
			414	American-Philippine War of 1899–1902	278

(Continued)

TABLE 4.1 LIST OF EXTRA-STATE WARS IN CHRONOLOGICAL ORDER

Extra-state war number	War name	Page no	Extra-state war number	War name	Page no
415	French Conquest of Chad of 1899–1900	279	451	Franco-Druze War of 1925–1927	305
416	Second Boer War of 1899–1902	280	452	Yen Bai Uprising of 1930–1931	306
417	Last Ashanti War of 1900	281	453	Saya San's Rebellion of 1930–1932	307
419	Somali Rebellion of 1901–1904	281	454	British-Palestinian War of 1936–1939	308
420	Bailundu Revolt of 1902–1903	283	455	Second British-Waziristan War of 1936–1938	310
421	Kuanhama Rebellion of 1902–1904	283	456	Indonesian War of 1945–1946	310
422	British Conquest of Kano and Sokoto of 1903	284	457	French-Indochina War of 1946–1954	311
423	South West African Revolt of 1904–1906	284	459	Third Franco-Madagascan War of 1947–1948	312
424	Second Dutch-Achinese War of 1904–1907	285	460	Malayan Rebellion of 1948–1957	313
425	Younghusband Expedition of 1904	286	461	Indo-Hyderabad War of 1948	314
426	Maji-Maji Revolt of 1905–1906	287	462	Third Sino-Tibetan War of 1950	314
427	Sokoto Uprising of 1906	288	463	Franco-Tunisian War of 1952–1954	315
429	Third British-Zulu War of 1906	288	464	British-Mau Mau War of 1952–1956	316
430	Dembos War of 1907–1910	289			
431	Anti-Foreign Revolt of 1907	289	465	Moroccan Independence War of 1953–1956	317
432	Japan-Korean Guerrillas War of 1907–1910	290	466	Third Franco-Algerian War of 1954–1962	318
433	French Conquest of Wadai of 1909–1911	291	467	French-Cameroon War of 1957–1958	319
434	French-Berber War of 1912	291	469	Angolan-Portuguese War of 1961–1974	320
435	First Sino-Tibetan War of 1912–1913	293	471	Mozambique-Portuguese War of 1964–1975	321
436	Moroccan-Berber War of 1913–1915	294	472	East Timorese War Phase 2 of 1975–1976	321
437	Moro Rebellion of 1913	295	473	Namibian War of 1975–1988	322
440	Second Sino-Tibetan War of 1918	296	474	Western Sahara War of 1975–1983	323
441	Caco Revolt of 1918–1920	297	475	Khmer Insurgency of 1979–1989	324
442	Third British-Afghan War of 1919	298	476	Soviet Quagmire of 1980–1989	325
443	First British-Waziristan War of 1919–1920	299	477	First PKK in Iraq of 1991–1992	327
444	Franco-Syrian War of 1920	300	479	Second PKK in Iraq of 1997	327
445	Iraqi-British War of 1920	301	480	Al Aqsa Intifada of 2000–2003	328
446	Conquest of Mongolia of 1920–1921	301	481	Afghan Resistance of 2001–present	329
447	Italian-Sanusi War of 1923–1931	302			
449	Rif Rebellion of 1921–1926	303	482	Iraqi Resistance of 2003–present	331
450	Moplah Rebellion of 1921–1922	305			

Individual Descriptions of Extra-state Wars

The Allied Bombardment of Algiers of 1816

Participants: Netherlands, United Kingdom vs. Algiers

Dates: August 26, 1816, to August 29, 1816

Battle-Related Deaths: Algeria—6,000; United Kingdom—129; Netherlands—13

Where Fought: Middle East

Initiator: Netherlands, United Kingdom

Outcome: Netherlands, United Kingdom win

War Type: Imperial

Narrative: Algiers is the capital of Algeria, which was a part of the Ottoman Empire from 1492 to 1705 and became an autonomous entity from 1705 to 1831. During this period, many countries paid tribute to the "Barbary pirates," yet Europeans continued to be kidnapped off ships and enslaved in Algiers and elsewhere along the North African coast. At the start of the nineteenth century the Americans took action against pirates further east, in Tripoli. These U.S. naval engagements from 1801 to 1805, remembered in the opening lines of the U.S. Marine Corps battle hymn ("From the halls of Montezuma to the shores of Tripoli"), were eventually followed by a U.S. Navy attack on Algiers in 1815. By 1816, with the Napoleonic Wars over, England had a larger fleet at its disposal to deal more decisively with the problems of Algerian piracy and the enslavement of European hostages. Along with Dutch allies, British ships pulled up off Algiers and leveled a good part of the city in a one-day bombardment. The battle pitted twenty-four British and five Dutch warships against 8,000 Algerian soldiers firing cannons from coastal forts. The allied flotilla won. On August 29 the Algerians accepted the British ultimatum, ending

the war. Immediately after, 1,600 Christian slaves were released. On September 24, 1816, the Algerians signed a treaty, settling matters, at least in the short run, to the satisfaction of the allies. Later, pirate raids resumed but were brought to an end by the French colonization of Algeria in 1830 (extra-state war #319).

Coding: Clodfelter (2002) describes the 1816 war as the "Bombardment of Algiers." Phillips and Axelrod cover the "Algerine War" of the United States versus the Algerian pirates in 1815, which resulted in fifty-seven battle-deaths but do not have an entry for this British-Dutch war.

Sources: Clodfelter (2002); Earle (2003); Leiner (2006); Lowenheim (2003); Nelson (1979).

The Ottoman-Wahhabi War of 1816–1818

Participants: Ottoman Empire vs. the Wahhabis

Dates: September [ ], 1816, to September 11, 1818

Battle-Related Deaths: Wahhabis—14,000; Ottoman Empire—13,500

Where Fought: Middle East

Initiator: Ottoman Empire

Outcome: Ottoman Empire wins

War Type: Imperial

Narrative: Egypt was a part of the Ottoman Empire, and in 1816 its ruler, Muhammad 'Ali, was one of the Ottoman sultan's more efficient vassals. Consequently, the Ottoman sultan Mahmud II asked the disciplined Egyptian army to deal with the problem of revolts by the Wahhabis in Arabia. Earlier revolts had ended in an 1815 negotiated agreement, which the Ottomans did not ratify. Thus in September 1816 a new army was sent consisting of Egyptian forces, local Ottoman recruits, and some

Moroccans, all under the command of the Egyptians. The combined force attacked the Wahhabis, who had taken over the Holy Places in the Arabian Peninsula. Despite bloody setbacks, the Egyptian-Ottoman forces eventually succeeded in returning control of Mecca and Medina to the Ottoman sultan. The sultan appointed the successful battlefield commander Ibrahim Pasha (son of the Egyptian leader) as the Ottoman governor of the Hejaz.

In World War I, Arab forces aligned with the British (famously including Lawrence of Arabia) to drive the Ottomans out of Arab lands. Consequently, almost exactly a century after this war, Mecca and Medina fell under the control of the Arab clan called the Hashemites. This family remains until now the ruling family in Jordan. In the 1920s, reversing their losses in 1816–1818, the Wahhabis of Nejd under the leadership of Abdul Aziz ibn Saud did retake the cities of Mecca and Medina from the Hashemites (see non-state wars #1567 and #1568).

Coding: Clodfelter (2002) describes this war as part of an 1811–1818 "Wahhabi War." Similarly, Phillips and Axelrod have an 1811–1818 "Wahhabi War." We find that the warfare stopped before 1815, so the resumption of the fighting in 1816 qualified this phase as a separate war.

Sources: Blaxland (1966); Clodfelter (2002); Finkel (2005); Marlowe (1965); Marsot (1984); McGregor (2006); Palmer (1992); Schafer (1995); Vassiliev (2000).

EXTRA-STATE WAR #302:
The Liberation of Chile of 1817–1818

Participants: Spain vs. Chilean independence army
Dates: January 9, 1817, to April 5, 1818
Battle-Related Deaths: Spain—1,700; Independence Army—1,140
Where Fought: W. Hemisphere
Initiator: Chilean independence army (San Martín's army, and others)

Outcome: Chile wins
War Type: Colonial

Narrative: This war is a segment of the general liberation of South America from Spain and Portugal, which covered the years 1810–1831. The geographic isolation of Chile (with the Andes to the east, desert to the north, and ocean elsewhere) rendered the fighting there a separate war. Chile, under the leadership of José Miguel Carrera and Bernard O'Higgins, had launched a struggle for independence from Spain in 1810. The Spanish royalist forces launched a successful counteroffensive. The Treaty of Lircay on May 3, 1814, halted the fighting by promising the Chileans autonomy within the Spanish Empire; however, the Spanish viceroy ultimately rejected the accord and sent another expedition against the revolutionaries. O'Higgins made a final stand at Rancagua, about fifty miles outside the capital, where the revolutionaries were defeated in October 1814. Spanish rule was thus restored, followed by a period of repression designed to destroy liberalism in Chile.

The Chilean independence movement continued to exist, though its hopes now shifted to Gen. José de San Martín, who had wanted to use an independent Chile as a base for launching attacks to secure the independence of Peru. O'Higgins, and some of his troops, joined San Martín's army, which crossed the Andes and launched a new attack on the Spanish royalists in Chile in January 1817. As the revolutionaries reached Santiago, O'Higgins was chosen as the director of the new state of Chile. The war against the royalists continued, however. In February 1818 O'Higgins proclaimed the independence of Chile despite the ongoing war. The royalists in fact defeated the revolutionaries near Talca on March 19, 1818. San Martín was able to rally the revolutionary forces, and they defeated the Spanish troops at Maipó (just outside Santiago) on April 5, 1818. The Spanish defeat ended the war and won Chilean independence. O'Higgins and San Martín then redirected their activities toward the liberation of Peru (extra-state war #312).

Coding: Scheina (2003a) includes this in the "Wars for Independence," in which South America becomes independent of Spain, France, and Portugal. Scheina divides the anti-Spanish wars on the basis of the various Spanish viceroyalties. In Scheina's scheme, this Chilean struggle becomes part of his wars in the Viceroyalty of Peru because Peru had a loose supervisory relationship over the Spanish Captaincy-General of Chile. Clodfelter (2002) treats this as just part of "South American Wars of Independence: 1810–1825," though he indicates that there was no substantial warfare in Chile in 1815 or 1816 and that the battles for Chilean independence were renewed during 1817 and 1818. Phillips and Axelrod have recorded the 1810–1818 "Chilean War of Independence."

Sources: Clodfelter (2002); Collier and Slater (2004); Loveman (1979); Phillips and Axelrod (2005); Scheina (2003a); Thomas (1956).

EXTRA-STATE WAR #303
First Bolívar Expedition of 1817–1819

Participants: Spain vs. New Granada revolutionaries
Dates: April 11, 1817, to August 10, 1819
Battle-Related Deaths: Spain—3,000; revolutionaries—2,000
Where Fought: W. Hemisphere
Initiator: Spain
Outcome: Revolutionaries win
War Type: Colonial

Narrative: The revolutionary wars to end Spanish rule in colonial Latin America went through several phases prior to the start date of this dataset on January 1, 1816. The dataset does not include periods in which fighting was light, and thus it starts the war when major periods of sustained combat resumed, in this case on April 11, 1817, in the Viceroyalty of New Granada. New Granada was the Spanish viceroyalty covering today's Venezuela, Colombia, and Ecuador. Spanish colonies in the Americas had always been dominated by a Spanish-born minority.

These *peninsulares* discriminated against "creoles," who were people of Spanish ancestry born in the Americas. The creoles, who vastly outnumbered the *peninsulares,* sustained the republican movement for the independence of South America from the Spanish crown. The timing of the creole revolution was strongly influenced by wars in Europe. The Peninsular War, waged by Napoleon against the Spanish and Portuguese in the Iberian Peninsula, occupied the Spanish military, but when that war ended, Spanish forces were available to respond to Simón Bolívar and the other rebels in the Americas.

Bolívar, leader of the revolutionaries in northern South America, had been driven from South America by royalist forces. However, Bolívar returned in spring 1816, gathered his forces, and was able to start renewed combat by the following spring. On April 11, 1817, revolutionary general Manuel Carlos Piar won a major victory at San Felix in what is now Venezuela. This began a major period of combat lasting until August 10, 1819. Subsequent battles ended in both Spanish and revolutionary victories. The revolutionaries succeeded in recruiting veterans of the Napoleonic Wars from Britain, and these battle-tested troops helped to turn the tide against the Spanish. In early 1819 Bolívar crossed the Andes from Venezuela into Colombia, where the Spanish forces were weaker. On April 2 the revolutionary forces won a victory at Queseras del Medio. On August 7 the revolutionary forces defeated the Spanish at the Battle of Boyacá near Bogotá. On August 10 Bolívar entered Bogotá, thus ending the war. Most of the major battles during this war involved forces numbering some three to five thousand soldiers on each side.

Bolívar then decided to shift his efforts back to Venezuela, where major combat began in April 1821 (extra-state war #308).

Coding: Clodfelter (2002) covers this within the "South American Wars of Independence, 1810–1825." Scheina (2003a) treats all armed conflict in the Viceroyalty of New Granada and the Captaincy-General of Venezuela, from 1810 to 1823, as one unit. Phillips and Axelrod (2005) have a separate "Colombian War of Independence, 1810–1818," and "Venezuelan War of Independence, 1811–1821."

Sources: Anderson (1991); Clodfelter (2002); Fisher, Kuethe, and McFarlane (1990); Herring (1966); Jaques (2007); Palmer (1957); Phillips and Axelrod (2005); Schafer (1995); Scheina (2003a); Thomas (1956).

EXTRA-STATE WAR #304:

The War of Mexican Independence of 1817–1818

Participants: Spain vs. Mina expedition
Dates: August 15, 1817, to January 1, 1818
Battle-Related Deaths: Spain—1,000; Mina
    expedition—1,000
Where Fought: W. Hemisphere
Initiator: Mina expedition
Outcome: Spain wins
War Type: Colonial

Narrative: Revolutionary movements had begun in Mexico (New Spain) in 1810, and though they had initially been successful, the end of the Peninsular War in Spain allowed the Spanish king Ferdinand to more effectively deal with colonial revolts. Spanish reinforcements contributed to the defeat of the rebels and the execution of revolutionary leader José María Morelos in 1815. This defeat deprived the independence movement of its organizational core, and subsequently there was a lack of coordination among the various revolutionary groups and leaders. This lack of cooperation was in evidence during the revolt that broke out in 1817–1818. The leader was Francisco Javier Mina, who had fought with Spain against France in the Peninsula War. In support of revolutionary movements, Mina recruited an international army. They landed in Mexico on August 15, 1817, and captured Soto la Marina. Mina then marched toward Guanajuato, hoping to join with Mexican revolutionaries.

The revolutionaries were able to defeat a royalist force in June; however, most of Mina's troops were defeated by royalist forces on October 24, 1817, at Guanajuato. Mina was captured and executed on November 11, 1817. The remainder of the revolutionaries continued the fight until they were defeated on January 1, 1818. Mina's expedition did not receive the support he had expected. In general, the revolutionaries capitulated and accepted pardons, so that by 1820 Mexico was virtually pacified.

Augustín Iturbide, the commander of the Spanish forces in northern Mexico, experienced a gradual conversion to the Mexican cause. When he and his army went over to the Mexican side in 1821, the Spanish yielded, and he entered Mexico City without having to actually wage further war. In this sense, the Mexican "War of Independence" eventually was successful.

Coding: Clodfelter (2002) has a "Mexican War of Independence" for the entire period from 1810 to 1821. Scheina (2003a) covers all the fighting in the Viceroyalty of New Spain in 1810–1829 as one conflict. Phillips and Axelrod (2005) are closer to our treatment. They include "Mexican Revolts (1810–1815)," with a hiatus followed by a "Mexican Revolution (1821)." We differ from Phillips and Axelrod in that we focus on battle-deaths; therefore, we use the dates 1817–1818, when the combat was most intense, rather than an end date of 1821, when political independence was finally attained.

Sources: Clodfelter (2002); Meyer and Beezley (2000); Meyer and Sherman (1983); Miller (1985); Palmer (1957); Phillips and Axelrod (2005); Scheina (2003a).

EXTRA-STATE WAR #305:

The British-Kandyan War of 1817–1818

Participants: United Kingdom vs. Kandyan rebels
Dates: October [ ], 1817, to November, 26, 1818
Battle-Related Deaths: Kandyans rebels—10,000;
    United Kingdom—1,000

Where Fought: Asia
Initiator: Kandyan rebels
Outcome: United Kingdom wins
War Type: Colonial

Narrative: Sri Lanka (also widely known as Ceylon) was a Portuguese colony from 1508 until 1658, after which it became a Dutch colony. The European colonizers had subjugated the coastal areas of the island mostly inhabited by the Tamil people, who had migrated centuries before from India. The Buddhist interior of Sri Lanka was the domain of the Kingdom of Kandy. The people there were, and remain, predominantly Sinhalese. Neither the Portuguese nor the Dutch were able to conquer Kandy. In 1795 the British took the island from the Dutch. During wars in 1803 and 1804, the British were able to occupy Kandy but not hold it, finally capturing Kandy in 1815, which consolidated their control over the entire island they now named Ceylon. In 1817 the Kandyans began a rebellion against British rule. There was a year of intense warfare, in which the Kandyans were defeated by the British, though many of the battle-related deaths were due to disease. Through this war and the almost-simultaneous British-Maratha War (extra-state war #306), the United Kingdom did much to establish all of South Asia as the jewel of the empire's crown. Ceylon gained its independence and became a member of interstate system in 1948, after which it adopted the name Sri Lanka.

Coding: Clodfelter (2002) dates this war 1815–1818. Phillips and Axelrod (2005) do not include it.

Sources: Burrows (1929); Clodfelter (2002); Powell (1973).

EXTRA-STATE WAR #306:
The British-Maratha War of 1817–1818

Participants: United Kingdom vs. Maratha clans
Dates: November 6, 1817, to June 3, 1818

Battle-Related Deaths: United Kingdom—2,800; Maratha—2,000
Where Fought: Asia
Initiator: Maratha
Outcome: United Kingdom wins
War Type: Colonial

Narrative: Maratha has given its name to the current Indian state of Maharashtra, the second most populous state in India. This state is probably best known by its most famous city, Mumbai, formerly Bombay. Maratha, which had been part of Moghul India from 1550 to 1653, became an autonomous entity from 1653 to 1802. It possessed a linguistic unity provided by its Indo-European language, Marathi. In the middle of the eighteenth century, the Maratha confederacy at least nominally controlled almost one-half of present-day India. In earlier wars (1775–1782 and 1803–1805), however, the British East India Company had gained control of territory from the Maratha confederacy.

The precipitant of this particular war was provided in raids executed by the Pindari bandits (supported by the Maratha confederacy) against Britain's ally, the nizam of the Decca and the British East India Company. In September 1817 the British governor-general received authorization to conduct a campaign against the Pindari. The British army of Bengal, under the command of the governor-general, and the army of the Deccan, under the command of Sir Thomas Hislop, marched to surround the Pindari. When British forces pursued the bandits into Maratha territory, three Maratha clans rose against the British in support of the bandits on November 6, 1817, marking the start of the war. A cholera epidemic attacked both the British and the Marathas, leading to significant fatalities and a halt in the fighting. However, when the British resumed their offensive later that month, they were successful in defeating the Maratha confederacy on several fronts. The rajah of Nagpur was defeated on November 26, 1817, and the Holkar on December 21. Finally the peshwa of the Marathas (Marattas) surrendered to the

British in June 1818. Thus the British were able to consolidate their control over the area.

Coding: In *Resort to Arms,* Singer and Small refer to this war as the "British-Maharattan War." Clodfelter (2002) calls this the "Third Maratha (Pindari) War" of 1817–1818, and Phillips and Axelrod (2005) refer to it as the "Third Maratha War." The fighting by troops of the British East India Company raises the question of whether this might be treated as a non-state war (depending on one's sense of the degree to which the Company should be seen as an agent ultimately subservient to the British state).

Sources: Clodfelter (2002); Fortescue (1923, vol. 11); Frazer (1897); Gordon (1993); Kohn (1986); Phillips and Axelrod (2005); Schafer (1995); Williams (1907).

EXTRA-STATE WAR #307:
The Ottoman Conquest of Sudan of 1820–1821

Participants: Ottoman Empire vs. Sudanese states
Dates: [ ]/[ ]/1820, to June [ ], 1821
Battle-Related Deaths: Ottomans—4,000;
 Sudanese—2,500
Where Fought: Middle East
Initiator: Ottoman Empire
Outcome: Ottoman Empire wins
War Type: Imperial

Narrative: In 1820 Egypt, which was still part of the Ottoman Empire, launched a campaign to conquer the Sudan at the request of the Ottoman sultan Mahmud II. The Ottomans were primarily interested in preventing European expansionism in the region. Egypt's ruler Muhammad Ali had a number of motivations for participating in this endeavor. The borders between Egypt and the Sudan were relatively undefined, and several Sudanese Muslim leaders had requested Egyptian protection to end conflicts in the region. Second, Muhammad Ali reportedly feared that the Mamluks, who had escaped to the Sudanese state of Dongola following the 1811 massacre in Cairo, were going to create their own state in the Sudanese Ethiopian border region with the assistance of Ethiopia. Finally, Muhammad Ali hoped to be able to secure gold and slaves from the region. This plethora of motivations has contributed to a historical dispute as to whether the 1820 campaign was beneficial for its imposition of order in Sudan or whether it was an unwarranted act of aggression against a Muslim state. Whatever the motivation, an Ottoman-Egyptian force of 4,000 troops was sent to the Sudan in 1820. The first expedition conquered the northern Sudanese provinces (Nubia, Sennar, Kordofan, and the Red Sea Province) with relative ease, though a significant number of fatalities were the result of disease. The northern states were also coerced into cooperating with the Ottoman army in massive slave raids. In 1821 a second expedition was sent against Darfur and Kordofan. The war ended at this point, though there were reports that the Egyptian forces massacred 30,000 people near Shindi the following year.

Coding: As a consequence of this war, the Sudanese provinces come under the control of Egypt, a period referred to as the Turkiyya. Egypt attempted to expand its control in the region in intra-state #507 and extra-state wars #364 and #375. Egyptian and British control would be overthrown by the Mahdist state in extra-state war #384.

Sources: Baddour (1960); Blaxland (1966); Brecke (1999); Collins and Tignor (1967); Johnson (2004); Marlowe (1965); McGregor (2006); Mowafi (1981); Oliver and Atmore (1994); Warburg (1991).

EXTRA-STATE WAR #308:
Second Bolívar Expedition of 1821–1822

Participants: Spain vs. New Granada
Dates: April 28, 1821, to May 24, 1822
Battle-Related Deaths: Spain—1,000;
 New Granada—500
Where Fought: W. Hemisphere

Initiator: New Granada
Outcome: New Granada wins
War Type: Colonial

Narrative: In the First Bolívar Expedition (extra-state war #303), only portions of the old Viceroyalty of New Granada were liberated from Spanish rule by Simón Bolívar and his generals. Parts of Venezuela and modern Ecuador were still under Spanish rule. On January 28, 1821, the city of Maracaibo began a revolt against the Spanish authorities. The Spanish announced that these events broke the terms of the earlier armistice, and they resumed military action on April 28, 1821, thus beginning this war. On June 24 the Spanish took a stand at the Battle of Carabobo in which the royalist troops faced an estimated 6,300 revolutionaries, and here the Spanish were defeated. The revolutionary forces were also successful in naval battles along the Venezuelan coast in summer 1821. In May Bolívar sent forces to assist revolutionaries in the province of Guayaquil (in contemporary Ecuador). Though initially successful, the revolutionaries under General Sucre suffered a defeat at Guachi (on their way to Quito) on September 12. In December 1821 Bolívar as well moved inland, also toward Quito. General Sucre was finally able to assemble an army of Argentines, Colombians, Ecuadorians, Peruvians, and Venezuelans to defeat the Spanish at Quito on May 24, 1822. The independence of Ecuador was thereby achieved, and the war ended.

Coding: As a result of five years of fairly continuous fighting, 1817–1822, the Spanish crown was driven permanently from what we now know as Venezuela, Colombia, and Ecuador. What emerged was a new country, called "Gran Colombia." Gran Colombia existed as an autonomous entity (though not a member of the interstate system) until 1830, when Bolívar resigned as president. At that juncture it broke apart (without a civil war) into present-day Ecuador, Venezuela, and Colombia. Of these pieces, Ecuador did not enter the COW interstate system until 1854; Colombia did almost

immediately, in 1831; and it was followed by Venezuela in 1841.

Sources: Anderson (1991); Clodfelter (2002); Fisher, Kuethe and McFarlane (1990); Herring (1966); Jaques (2007); Palmer (1957); Phillips and Axelrod (2005); Schafer (1995); Scheina (2003a); Thomas (1956).

EXTRA-STATE WAR #309:

The Turco-Persian War of 1821–1823

Participants: Ottoman Empire vs. Persia
Dates: August [ ], 1821, to May [ ], 1822
Battle-Related Deaths: Ottoman Empire—1,000; Persia—[ ]
Where Fought: Middle East
Initiator: Persia
Outcome: Stalemate
War Type: Imperial

Narrative: This is the ninth (and last) in the series of Turko-Persian wars listed by Phillips and Axelrod (2005) since 1500. The two traditional rivals generally fought for territory along their long common border. In this war the Ottoman Empire fought against Persia, which was not an interstate system member. At the start of this war, the Ottomans were aiding rebels in Azerbaijan who were revolting against Persian rule. In retaliation, Persian crown prince Abbas Mirza sent his army against the Ottomans directly. The recently modernized Persian army of 30,000 met and defeated the larger Ottoman force at Erzurum, before having to retreat during the winter. The following year the Persian army returned to Azerbaijan and again routed an Ottoman army at Khoi. The Persian army suffered significant fatalities due to cholera and decided to sue for peace in May 1822, which ended the war. The subsequent Treaty of Erzurum in 1823 did not change the border or the balance of power between the two parties.

Coding: Persia had sufficient internal characteristics of statehood but lacked the diplomatic recognition necessary to be considered a member of the interstate system. Thus this war is coded as an extra-state war. Iran does not become a state system member until 1855. Clodfelter does not include this war.

Sources: Farmanfarmaian (2007); Goodwin (1998); Jaques (2007); Kohn (1986); Phillips and Axelrod (2005); Schafer (1995).

EXTRA-STATE WAR #310:

The First British-Burmese War of 1823–1826

Participants: United Kingdom vs. Burma
Dates: September 24, 1823, to February 24, 1826
Battle-Related Deaths: United Kingdom—15,000; Burma—15,000
Where Fought: Asia
Initiator: Burma
Outcome: United Kingdom wins
War Type: Imperial

Narrative: Bengal had come under British control in 1757. As Britain expanded its influence in the region, it came into conflict with Burma (which was an autonomous entity but not an interstate system member), which also had been engaged in a project of expanding its territory. In 1823 Burma wished to annex Bengal and attacked British forces in an attempt to take Bengal from British India. Britain formally declared war against Burma on March 5, 1824, and attempted to force the invaders from Bengal. A British fleet also seized Rangoon on May 24, 1824. The British fortified Rangoon, which was subsequently attacked by the Burmese during the summer. In December a force of 60,000 Burmese launched another attack on Rangoon, though they were driven back after a week of severe fighting. Although fighting was intense, disease caused the greatest fatalities among both the Burmese and the British. In February 1825 Anglo-Indian troops advanced along the Irawadi River into the interior of Burma, where they were repulsed at Donabew (Danubyu). On

March 25 the British undertook the siege of Donabew, which fell after a week of bombardment. The British continued to advance, though their progress was halted by the monsoon season. Fighting resumed later that year, and the British nearly reached the Burmese capital of Ava in early 1826. At that point the Burmese king sued for peace. In the February 24 Treaty of Yandabo that ended the war, Burma was forced to cede territory (including Assam) to the British. Sixty years later, in 1885, Burma itself would be conquered and incorporated into British India, where it would remain for over fifty years (see extra-state war #387, the Third British-Burmese War of 1885-89).

Coding: Clodfelter (2002) calls this the "First Burma War of 1824–26." Phillips and Axelrod (2005) call it the "First Anglo-Burmese War." Clodfelter reports 15,000 deaths of the Anglo-Indian forces in the theatre, mostly from disease, but adds that fewer than 1,000 of these died from Burmese fire. Burma does not become a state system member (#775, currently called Myanmar) until 1948.

Sources: Bruce (1973); Cady (1958); Clodfelter (2002); Fortescue (1923, vol. 11); Harvey (1929); Williams (1907).

EXTRA-STATE WAR #311:

The First British-Ashanti War of 1824–1826

Participants: United Kingdom vs. Ashanti
Dates: January 20, 1824, to August 7, 1826
Battle-Related Deaths: Ashanti—5,000; United Kingdom—1,400
Where Fought: Africa
Initiator: Ashanti
Outcome: United Kingdom wins
War Type: Imperial

Narrative: The Ashanti had a well-organized kingdom based on gold mines and profiting from the slave trade. This kingdom was firmly established in the 1700s and early 1800s in

Asante, the Ashanti homeland (the central part of the current country of Ghana). The Ashanti confederation had as many as 100,000 warriors who could be mobilized at one time, and it dominated the tribes over which it held suzerainty. Meanwhile, the British controlled Ghana's coast (called the Gold Coast) along with the tribes there. These coastal tribes (primarily the Fante) were being harassed by the Ashanti and turned to the British for help. Charles MacCarthy, the British governor of the Gold Coast, agreed to intervene and in late 1823 gathered a force of British and native troops into four separate armies. One army encountered 10,000 Ashanti soldiers on January 20, 1824, near the Pra River, and virtually all the British troops were killed, including MacCarthy. Next, a force of 20,000 Ashanti stopped the advance of a combined force of 2,000 British with Fante allies. The British finally succeeded in bringing in outside troops that did not simply die of tropical diseases. Then, with a force of about 11,000 locals and 100 British officers and marines, the British finally prevailed, utilizing new Congreve rockets to defeat 10,000 Ashanti at Dodowah on August 7, 1826. With half the Ashanti force killed, captured, or taken out of action by wounds, the Ashanti realized that they could not survive in a series of such battles and agreed to leave the coastal tribes alone. The issue was soon to be contested afresh, however, and further rounds of fighting erupted in the latter part of the nineteenth century (extra-state wars #367 and 398) which led to the British annexation of the Asante region in 1896.

Coding: The COW Project codes the territorial entity of Asante an autonomous entity from 1701 to 1896. Clodfelter (2002) has a "First Ashanti War of 1824–1826," and Phillips and Axelrod (2005) have the same war listed as lasting from 1824–1831.

Sources: Clodfelter (2002); Edgerton (1995); Edgerton (2002); Kohn (1986); Oliver and Atmore (1994); Phillips and Axelrod (2005).

EXTRA-STATE WAR #312:

The Liberation of Peru of 1824–1825

Participants: Spain vs. Latin American revolutionaries
Dates: February 4, 1824, to April 2, 1825
Battle-Related Deaths: Spain—2,000; revolutionaries—400
Where Fought: W. Hemisphere
Initiator: Latin American revolutionaries
Outcome: Revolutionaries win
War Type: Colonial

Narrative: Peru had been the first focus of Spanish conquest of South America, with the quest for Incan gold. Peru remained a Spanish possession, with the emphasis remaining on extraction of precious metals, long after the liberation of the rest of the Spanish American mainland. Chile had been liberated by José de San Martín by the end of 1818. Early in the 1820s, Mexico and Gran Colombia had attained independence from Spain (see extra-state wars #304 and 308). Then, the revolutionaries' focus turned to Peru.

On July 21, 1821, San Martín boldly declared Peruvian independence from Spain. However, his move did not have the popular support he had anticipated, so he assumed the position of provisional governor himself. San Martín and his army controlled northern Peru and its coast, while the Spanish viceroy La Serna retained control of the central and southern regions. Discontent in Lima soon forced San Martín to resign, and subsequent president José de la Riva Agüero began a new military campaign against the Spanish (though this does not attain war level). After suffering defeats at the hand of the Spanish, the Peruvian congress asked for assistance from Simón Bolívar, who arrived in Peru on September 1, 1823, to take command of the four disparate revolutionary armies (from Peru, Chile, Colombia, and Río de la Plata). The war begins with attacks in February 1824. Facing an advancing royalist army, Bolívar ordered the evacuation of Lima. By March most of Peru was back under Spanish control; nevertheless, Bolívar was able to unite the revolutionary forces and launch a counteroffensive on July 15, 1824. Bolívar's army defeated Spanish royalist forces at Junín on August 8, 1824, and reoccupied Lima on October 1, 1824. Subsequently, a revolutionary contingent under General Sucre engaged a royalist army at the battle of Ayacucho on December 9, 1824. The revolutionaries overwhelmingly defeated the royalist forces, and their surrender led to the liberation of Peru; however, the royalist forces in Upper Peru refused to obey the surrender order. Thus the armies of Bolívar and Sucre advanced into Upper Peru, defeating royalist forces on December 24, 1824, and April 2, 1825 (which marks the end of the war). On August 6, 1825, Upper Peru declared its independence and named itself Bolivia in honor of Bolívar.

Coding: Clodfelter (2002) includes this war as part of an overall treatment of "South American Wars of Independence: 1810–1825." Scheina examines all armed conflict in the Viceroyalty of Peru from 1810 to 1831 as one unit. Phillips and Axelrod (2005) speak of an 1820–1825 "Peruvian War of Independence." Following this war, Peru joined the interstate system in 1839, and Bolivia joined in 1848.

Sources: Anna (1979); Clodfelter (2002); Collier and Slater (2004); Hunefeldt (2004); Klarén (2000); Phillips and Axelrod (2005); Scheina (2003a); Thomas (1956).

EXTRA-STATE WAR #313:

The Dutch-Javanese War of 1825–1830

Participants: Netherlands vs. Javanese rebels
Dates: July 23, 1825, to March 28, 1830
Battle-Related Deaths: Javanese rebels—200,000; Netherlands—15,000
Where Fought: Asia
Initiator: Javanese rebels
Outcome: Netherlands wins
War Type: Colonial

Narrative: From 1609 there had been a Dutch colony in Indonesia, with the exception of a brief interlude of British military occupation. In reality, the Dutch effectively controlled only the coast of the central island of Java, while the interior remained under the control of the kingdom of Mataram, which dissolved in 1755. By the Treaty of Giyanti of 1755, the United East India Company reached an understanding with the kingdom's successors, the city-states of Surakarta and Jogjakarta, under which they would both rule half of the interior. The Dutch withdrew to the coast, and a long period of peace ensued. Following a battle between the British and the Dutch in 1810, Java came under British control, though it was returned to the Dutch at the end of the Napoleonic Wars. The Dutch then began to meddle with economic institutions in the interior. Prince Dipo Negoro of Jogjakarta, motivated partly by these economic dislocations, partly by Islamic texts, and partly by older Javanese and Hindu traditions, withdrew into the mountains and prepared for war against the Dutch, which lasted five years. It was a guerrilla war, without major pitched battles. In the fighting the Dutch gradually prevailed, aided by a set of strategic hamlets connected by good roads. Two of Dipo Negoro's lieutenants defected when things began to go badly, and the Dutch eventually negotiated a peace with the prince, who surrendered on March 28, 1830 (marking the end of the war). He was banished to the Celebes and afterward to Madagascar, where he died.

Coding: This war was a major rebellion, involving 100,000 Dutch forces, yet most fatalities were caused by disease. Clodfelter (2002) calls this the "Java War: 1825–30" and estimates that 200,000 Javanese may have died (only 10 percent of those would have died in battle). After the end of this bloody guerrilla war, the Dutch had peace in Java until the Japanese invasion in World War II (inter-state war #139).

Sources: Clodfelter (2002); Hall (1981); Klerk (1938); Phillips and Axelrod (2005); Raffles (1985); Vlekke (1960).

EXTRA-STATE WAR #314:
The British-Bharatpuran War of 1825–1826

Participants: United Kingdom vs. Bharatpuran rebels
Dates: November 23, 1825, to January 18, 1826
Battle-Related Deaths: Bharatpuran rebels—4,500; United Kingdom—400
Where Fought: Asia
Initiator: Bharatpuran rebels
Outcome: United Kingdom wins
War Type: Colonial

Narrative: Rajasthan, a province of India, has a strategic location east of the Thar Desert and Pakistan and just west of Agra and Delhi. Close to the Indian capital, and at the eastern edge of the province, lies the city of Bharatpur (Bhurtpore). The city was heavily besieged in the British-Maratha War in 1804. The British were unsuccessful in capturing the city at that time, primarily because of a lack of siege cannon. Then in 1825, during the last year of its war with Burma (extra-state war #310), Britain found itself involved in another conflict in the subcontinent, again around the city of Bharatpur. Before his death in early 1825, the rajah of Bharatpur had named his son as his successor and had included him in an alliance with the (British) East India Company. After the rajah's death, a nephew raised a successful revolt to challenge the succession. The prince who had been deposed feared that the British would be unable to conduct the war in Burma and support him as well. Given Bharatpur's reputation as invincible, the British were at first reluctant to act on his behalf; however, on November 23, 1825, the British siege and bombardment of Bharatpur began. On January 18, 1826, the British exploded a mine that destroyed one of the fortress salients. Within hours the citadel had surrendered and the prince was restored. This war can be seen as just one step in the extended process of Britain's colonization of all of India. The Gwalior War of 1843 (extra-state war #329),

the next British extra-state war in India, has many similarities.

Coding: Clodfelter (2002) calls this the "Siege of Bhurtpore, 1825–26." Clodfelter says that as a city, Bhurtpore was second only to Lucknow (in the 1857 Indian Mutiny, war #347) in terms of casualties sustained by the British army in all their campaigns in India.

Sources: Clodfelter (2002); Jaques (2007); Luard (1929); Williams (1907).

EXTRA-STATE WAR #315:
The Brazil-Argentine War of 1826–1828

Participants: Brazil vs. Argentina
Dates: January 1, 1826, to October 27, 1828
Battle-Related Deaths: Brazil—4,000; Argentina—2,000
Where Fought: W. Hemisphere
Initiator: Argentina
Outcome: Argentina wins
War Type: Imperial

Narrative: Both the Spanish and the Portuguese established settlements in the area of what is now Uruguay. In 1724 the Spanish drove the Portuguese out, and Spain remained in control over the Banda Orientale (Uruguay) until it attained independence. Just as the Banda Orientale was a buffer zone between the Portuguese and Spanish colonies, it would later serve the same function between Argentina and Brazil. When the drive for independence from Spain began in Argentina in 1810, Banda Orientale accepted the revolutionary movement. In 1814, however, Banda Orientale broke with Argentina and began its own struggle for independence, which lasted until Brazil occupied Montevideo in 1817. In April 1825 a small group known as the Thirty Three Immortals declared Uruguay's independence from Brazil, though little conflict followed. On December 1, 1825, Argentina decided to support Banda Orientale against Brazil and took over the bulk of the fighting. Little military action occurred until after Brazil became a system member, on January 1, 1826; thus at that point the current extra-state war of Brazil versus Argentina and Banda Orientale (neither of which was an interstate system member) began.

In 1826 the initial fighting took place on both land and sea, with victories going to each side. The Argentine ships attacked Brazilian vessels along the coast and in the Uruguay River. On land Brazil had reinforced its troops in Banda Orientale, where it faced an offensive by the united Argentine and Uruguay troops. By 1827 the cost of the war was causing hardships in Argentina, and the government sent an envoy to Brazil to discuss an end to the war. The Argentine representative returned with terms that were unacceptable, and the war continued; however, a revolt in Rio de Janeiro on June 11, 1828, persuaded the Brazilians to accept British mediation efforts. The treaty signed on October 27, 1828, created the Oriental State of Uruguay, with Britain guaranteeing its sovereignty for five years. Uruguay continued to be a source of conflict in subsequent periods, as well, including the later extra-state war #327, the related inter-state war #19, and a civil war in 1904—intra-state war #641.

Coding: Uruguay becomes a member of the interstate system in 1882. Although we are following Brecke's estimate of total battle-dead, Clodfelter reports a higher number (8,000) just for Brazil but with no estimated deaths for Argentina.

Sources: Brecke (1999); Burns (1980); Clodfelter (2002); Lemke (2006); Palmer (1957); Phillips and Axelrod (2005); Schafer (1995); Scheina (2003a).

EXTRA-STATE WAR #316:
The Russo-Persian War of 1826–1828

Participants: Russia vs. Persia
Dates: September 28, 1826, to February 28, 1828
Battle-Related Deaths: Russia—5,000;
Persia—2,000

Where Fought: Middle East
Initiator: Persia
Outcome: Russia wins
War Type: Imperial

Narrative: Russia and Persia, which does not become a member of the interstate system until 1855, had gone to war in 1804 when Persia had assisted rebels in Georgia and Karabakh who were resisting their annexation by Russia. Persia's defeat in 1813 led to further territorial losses in the Caucasus to Russia under the Treaty of Gulistan. In 1826 Persia, led by an overconfident ruler, Fath Ali, tried to recover the lost territories by launching an attack in Georgia. There the Persians were defeated at the Battle of Ganja. The Russian forces then advanced, pushing the Persians back across their own border. In late 1827 the Russians were victorious in battles at Erivan and Tabriz, and ultimately occupied Teheran. The Persian defeat cost them additional holdings in Armenia as well as a cash indemnity. Both the defeat in this war and the stalemate in its war with the Ottoman Empire (extra-state war #309) marked the onset of a long period of decline of Persia's power.

Coding: Clodfelter (2002) and Phillips and Axelrod (2005) describe this as the "Russo-Persian War (1825–28)."

Sources: Atkin (1980); Baddeley (1908); Clodfelter (2002); Cohen (1996); Palmer (1957); Phillips and Axelrod (2005); Schiemann (1913); Sykes (1951); von Schlechta-Wssehrd (1866); Williams (1907).

EXTRA-STATE WAR #317:
The Spanish Reconquest of Mexico of 1829

Participants: Spain vs. Mexico
Dates: July 16, 1829, to September 11, 1829
Battle-Related Deaths: Spain—1,700;
Mexico—135
Where Fought: W. Hemisphere
Initiator: Spain

Outcome: Mexico wins
War Type: Imperial

Narrative: The Mexican movement for independence from Spain had been reflected in extra-state war #304. Though the rebels were defeated at that time, Augustín Iturbide, the commander of the Spanish forces, gradually came to favor Mexican independence. In February 1821 Iturbide presented a plan for Mexico to become an independent kingdom. When the Spanish viceroy rejected the plan, Iturbide marched his army toward the capital. A July 5, 1821, revolt in the capital forced the viceroy to resign. Though the advance of the revolutionary forces (united as the Army of the Three Guarantees) involved little sustained combat, it was sufficient to persuade the newly appointed Spanish Captaincy-General to come to terms. The Treaty of Córdoba of August 24 proposed Mexican independence. The Army of the Three Guarantees marched into Mexico City on September 27, 1821, and Iturbide became Emperor Augustín I. At this point, Mexico is no longer considered to be a colony of Spain but an autonomous entity, though not yet a member of the interstate system.

Spanish king Ferdinand VII hoped to regain his rebellious Viceroyalty of New Spain (Mexico), though the planning for this endeavor was incomplete. Disaffected Spaniards who had fled from Mexico to Cuba began to plot their return, and they were able to persuade the Cuban and Spanish authorities that the Spanish in Mexico would support a Spanish reconquest of Mexico. On July 6, 1829, Spain sent a fleet from Cuba to retake Mexico. After 3,500 Spanish troops landed near Tampico on July 16, 1829, Gen. Antonio López de Santa Anna, governor of Vera Cruz, gathered an army to confront them. They sailed north, landing near Tampico. On August 21, Santa Anna attacked the Spanish forces near Tampico. The Spanish then settled in at Tampico to await the anticipated general uprising in support of Spain. Meanwhile they suffered an outbreak of yellow fever. At the same time, another Mexican army was advancing from the north. The combined forces attacked the Spanish on September 10. The weakened Spanish, who had not received the popular support they had expected, surrendered the next day, and the surviving Spaniards were forced to sail back to Cuba. The fighting made General Santa Anna a Mexican hero, and he was thereafter a force in Mexican politics for a quarter-century.

Coding: Clodfelter (2002) also describes this as an 1828–1829 war. Scheina (2003a), however, treats all armed conflict in the Viceroyalty of New Spain from 1810 to 1829 as one unit. Phillips and Axelrod (2005) do not include it.

Sources: Anna (1998); Clodfelter (2002); Crawford (1967); Fowler (2000); Meyer and Sherman (1983); Miller (1985); Scheina (2003a).

EXTRA-STATE WAR #319:
The French Occupation of Algiers of 1830

Participants: France vs. Algeria
Dates: June 12, 1830, to July 5, 1830
Battle-Related Deaths: Algeria—3,000; France—600
Where Fought: Middle East
Initiator: France
Outcome: France wins
War Type: Imperial

Narrative: The kingdom of Algiers and its "Barbary pirates" had long bedeviled European and American shipping in the Mediterranean. Earlier attacks on Algiers (including extra-state war #300) had been unsuccessful in stopping the pirates. France in particular was interested in expanding its influence in North Africa. Thus a slight to the French consul delivered by the bey of Algiers on April 30, 1827, became the pretext for this war. On May 25, 1830, a large French naval force sailed for the Algerian coast.

It arrived on June 12 and anchored west of Algiers. The 34,000 troops disembarked and marched toward Algiers. On June 29 they reached the outskirts of Algiers and confronted 45,000 Algerian soldiers. The French began a bombardment of the fortifications, and the Algerians withdrew from the fort, leading to a panic in the city. The convention of Algerian surrender went into effect on July 5, 1830.

This war illustrates the interrelation among wars of all types. The French occupation of Algiers was not only an international incident, but it also reflected the tensions within France that produced a revolution and change of government a month later (intra-state war #513, France vs. the Liberals). As the Bourbons teetered on their last legs, in June 1830 they tried to distract attention from domestic problems in France with this "diversionary war." This, in turn, led to extra-state war #324, the conquest of the rest of Algeria, from 1839 to 1847. The French mistreatment of the civilians in Algiers after this war foreshadowed a pattern that damaged relations between the French and the Algerians for over a century.

Coding: Algeria had been part of the Ottoman Empire but is coded as an autonomous entity from 1816 until the French attack on Algiers in 1830. Clodfelter (2002) bundles almost two decades of fighting into "The French Conquest of Algeria: 1830–47." Phillips and Axelrod (2005) have an entry for "French Conquest of Algeria" but do not include the occupation of Algiers, referencing instead three subsequent "Wars of Abd El-Kader," only one of which reached our battle-death threshold (see extra-state war #324). Brecke (1999) estimates 10,000 total deaths in the 1830 fighting, but we assume that that figure includes civilian deaths.

Sources: Brecke (1999); Clodfelter (2002); Confer (1966); Entelis (1986); Evans and Phillips (2007); Great Britain (1942); Joestin (1964); Nelson (1979); Oliver and Atmore (1994); Phillips and Axelrod (2005); Ruedy (1992).

EXTRA-STATE WAR #320:
Ottoman-Bilmez-Asiri War of 1832–1837

Participants: Ottoman Empire vs. Bilmez army and Asiris
Dates: June [ ], 1832, to [ ]/[ ]/1837
Battle-Related Deaths: Bilmez army—800; Ottoman Empire—[ ]; Asiris—[ ]
Where Fought: Middle East
Initiator: Bilmez army
Outcome: Ottoman Empire wins
War Type: Imperial

Narrative: By 1520 Yemen had become part of the Ottoman Empire, though the Ottomans frequently exercised only nominal dominion. In 1636 Yemen's Imam Muhammad expelled the Ottomans from Yemen and extended Yemeni control from the Hawdramat in the south to Asir in the north. The subsequent imams were unable to control the entire area and faced challenges from the tribes in Asir, which is located in the north of Yemen along the Red Sea. The Ottomans, who wanted to reassert their control in this region, had intervened in the Arabian Peninsula in 1816 to counter the threat posed by Wahhabism, a puritanical sect of Islam. The Wahhabis drove out the traditional Yemeni Zaidi imams. Egypt's Ibrahim Pasha, acting in the name of the Ottoman sultan, was successful in defeating the Wahhabis in 1818 (see extra-state war #301). The Egyptians then remained in the region

Egypt's ruler, Muhammad Ali, had not initially planned on establishing military bases in Yemen; however, an uprising in the Hejaz, a region in the northwest Arabian Peninsula along the Red Sea, provided the opportunity to do so. The war began in June 1832 when a slave, Muhammad Agha, known as Turkçe Bilmez, led a revolt of his Albanian followers in Mecca against the Ottomans because they had not been paid in several months. Bilmez and 2,000 rebels marched from Mecca to Jeddah, where they seized the treasury. In December 1832 they commandeered ships and sailed south along the Red Sea coast, where they soon occupied the Yemeni cities of Mocha, Hodeida, and Aden. There the Hejaz rebels were soon joined by some of the region's discontented tribes, including some of the Asiri Wahhabis. On behalf of the Ottoman Empire, Muhammad Ali decided to send an expedition to restore order to the region. He was particularly interested in removing the rebels from Aden, where they might be able to prey on Egyptian shipping. In June 1833 Bilmez and his forces were being besieged at Mocha by the warriors of another of the Asiri chiefs, Ali ibn Mukhtar. Muhammad Ali's navy arrived and destroyed Bilmez's ships. The Egyptians also sent an army of 4,000 to assist in the siege at Mocha. Bilmez was able to escape from Mocha and flee to India, but the rebellion continued. Throughout 1834 the Egyptian army was unsuccessful in establishing order. The cities of Luhayya and Hodeida were heavily garrisoned by the rebels, and the Egyptians decided to delay military advances until the arrival of 4,000 reinforcements under Muhammad Ali's nephew. Even though the Asiris and their allies among the Yemeni tribes put up fierce resistance, the Egyptians were able to capture the capital city of Asir; however, the Egyptians were unable to capture the surrounding area and requested additional reinforcements from Egypt. The additional troops were somewhat more successful. Hodeida surrendered on January 19, 1835, and Mocha fell to the Egyptians five days later. Despite these successes along the coast, the Egyptians suffered heavy losses in confrontations inland. Additional reinforcements in 1837 finally enabled the Egyptians to restore order in the interior cities, as well. The Ottomans forced Egypt to withdraw its forces in 1840 and in 1849 compelled the Zaydi imam in Sanaa to become the Ottoman Empire's vassal. Yet opposition to the Ottomans did not end, and three more wars against them would occur in this region, extra-state wars #338, #342, and #365.

Coding: Both Asir and North Yemen are coded as autonomous entities from 1816 to 1871 and as being militarily occupied by the Ottoman Empire after that.

Sources: Baldry (1976); Cole and Momen (1986); Farah (2002); Farah (1984/1985); Ingrams and Ingrams (1993); Playfair (1978).

EXTRA-STATE WAR #321:
The First British-Zulu War of 1838

Participants: United Kingdom vs. Zulu
Dates: April 17, 1838, to April [ ], 1838
Battle-Related Deaths: United Kingdom—800; Zulu—[ ]
Where Fought: Africa
Initiator: United Kingdom
Outcome: Zulu win
War Type: Imperial

Narrative: The Zulu Empire existed along the eastern coast of what is now South Africa's Natal province. The Correlates of War Project recognizes the Zulu as an autonomous entity starting in 1818, when the Zulu came together under Shaka, who ruled till 1828. Shaka revolutionized Zulu society and made the Zulu into a powerful fighting force. Shaka was assassinated and replaced as king by his half-brother Dingaan. Soon thereafter, the Zulu, located near Natal, faced the expansionism of two groups, the British and the Boers. The Boers were the rural descendants of Dutch colonists who had come to the Cape starting in 1650. When the British took the Cape a century and a half later, the Boers began to move north, away from the coast. In what became known as the Great Trek of 1836, the Boers moved north in two columns, both of which came into contact with black South African tribes. One group headed toward the Transvaal and fought against the Matabele (non-state war #1521) in 1836–1837. The second Boer group, led by Peter Retief, headed toward Natal , which led to a war with the Zulu in 1838–1840 (non-state war #1525).

At the same time, the British were interested in expanding their Cape Colony. In the 1820s and 1830s the British acquired territory in Natal from the Zulu. While the Zulu were fighting against the Boers, the British sent an expeditionary force into Natal in April 1838. The Zulu were able to lure the British into a trap, and in brief but heavy fighting the Zulu killed all of the invaders. The Zulu then attacked and destroyed Durban. Ultimately, the Boers were able to establish a state in southern Natal for three years, and in 1843 the British annexed the Afrikaner Republic of Natal to the Cape Colony. The British would confront the Zulu again in 1879 (extra-state war #380).

Coding: Clodfelter (2002), Kohn (1999), and Phillips and Axelrod (2005) include this war as part of the "Boer-Zulu War."

Sources: Clodfelter (2002); Featherstone (1973); Knight (2003); Kohn (1999); Oliver and Atmore (1994); Phillips and Axelrod (2005).

EXTRA-STATE WAR #322:
The First British-Afghan War of 1839–1842

Participants: United Kingdom vs. Afghanistan
Dates: Feburary 14, 1839, to October 12, 1842
Battle-Related Deaths: United Kingdom—20,000; Afghan tribes—[ ]
Where Fought: Asia
Initiator: United Kingdom
Outcome: Afghanistan wins
War Type: Imperial

Narrative: On September 10, 1838, the British governor in India, Lord Auckland, announced his intention to send an expedition beyond the North-West Frontier. The ostensible purpose the British were stationed at Jalalabad and Kandahar was to return Shah Shuja to the throne of Kabul. Shah Shuja, an ally of the East India Company, had been driven from power by Dost Muhammed Khan. Though Dost Muhammed had initially sought British assistance against Persia, the British feared that he had become allied with Russia. Britain came to the conclusion that the best way to stop Russian ambition was to unseat Dost Muhammed and return Shah Shuja to the throne.

The British sent an army of 21,000 men into Afghanistan (including a small contingent under the orders of Shah Shuja). The army crossed the Indus River on February 14, 1839, which marks the start of the war. The British suffered losses to enemy fire as they moved through the Bolan Pass. By April 1839 the British forces had reached Kandahar, which was taken without a fight. The British then marched north toward Ghazni. On July 23 the fortress was captured, opening the way to Kabul. On August 7, 1839, the victorious British entered Kabul, where Shah Shuja was restored to his throne. British troops remained in Kabul. In November 1840 Dost Muhammed did launch a counterattack, but when that did not succeed, he went into exile in India. Anti-British agitation continued, however. On October 10 the British Bombay Division began its return march toward India and was attacked all along the way. An uprising against the remaining British began on November 2, 1841, partially in the name of Dost Muhammed's son. One Afghan force besieged the British in Kabul, while the other besieged Kandahar. The British soldiers in Kabul refused to take action and soon began to suffer from starvation. On December 26 the British surrendered. On January 6, 1842, the British began their withdrawal from Kabul toward Jalalabad. Thousands of retreating British soldiers and civilians were shot by the Ghilzais, one of the most fanatic tribes. As they continued their retreat, the native regiments were nearly annihilated by the cold and hunger as well as by the enemy. In attacks on January 12 and 13, virtually all the British and native forces perished, except for a few taken as prisoners of war. Jalalabad itself was then besieged. British reinforcement arrived to assist the troops at Jalalabad and Kandahar, and by September 15 the

British had advanced back to Kabul. On October 12, 1842, however, the British began their withdrawal from Afghanistan. Dost Muhammed was released, and he returned to power in Kabul in 1843.

Coding: Clodfelter (2002) and Phillips and Axelrod (2005) both cover what they call a "First Afghan War" of 1839–1842.

Sources: Clodfelter (2002); Featherstone (1973); Fletcher (1965); Macrory (1966); Majumdar (1948); Norris (1967); O'Balance (1993); Phillips and Axelrod (2005); Richards (1990); Sykes (1940); Thompson and Garrett (1934); Williams (1907).

EXTRA-STATE WAR #323:
The First Opium War of 1839–1842

Participants: United Kingdom vs. China
Dates: September 4, 1839, to August 29, 1842
Battle-Related Deaths: China—2,000; United Kingdom—450
Where Fought: Asia
Initiator: United Kingdom
Outcome: United Kingdom wins
War Type: Imperial

Narrative: The British wished to establish trade with China on a more equal footing. Many Chinese goods were in demand in Britain, but very few British goods were being bought in China, owing to various restrictions. Chinese officials were especially keen to put restrictions on the illicit opium imports to China. To stop the drug traffic, Chinese officials in Canton burned 6 million taels worth of opium. This was worth a considerable sum of money, enough to anger the British and to trigger the war. The British sent ships to protect the opium shipments and to attack Chinese ports. The ships were attacked on September 4, 1839. The war involved subsequent naval battles and British landings in Canton and along the coast. The island of Amoy was captured in August 1840. In difficult fighting, the city of Chusan was captured in October 1840, though more fatalities were due to disease than

battle. As the fighting gathered momentum, British military assaults became so successful that when the British reached Nanking in August 1842, the Chinese sought peace. In 1842 the Treaty of Nanking ended the war.

The treaty was the first of a series of agreements the Chinese called the "unequal treaties." The Treaty of Nanking did not deal with opium, which continued to be traded illicitly. Ironically, one of the main points of the treaty, from the British point of view, was the establishment of the principle that the British were equals of China diplomatically. Up to that time the Chinese throne had insisted that England was a tributary state. Indeed, John Quincy Adams wrote that the cause of the war had been "the arrogant and insupportable pretensions of China, that she will hold commercial intercourse with the rest of mankind, not upon equal reciprocity, but upon the insulting and degrading form of relation between lord and vassal." (Michael and Taylor 1964, 128–129)

Coding: This treaty was the beginning of the introduction of China into the modern state system. China becomes a state system member in 1860. But as late as the First Sino-Japanese War of 1894–1895 (inter-state war #73), the Chinese tribute system remained an issue, as the Japanese insisted that China stop treating Korea as a Chinese tributary state. Another important effect of the First Opium War is that the Treaty of Nanking gave Hong Kong to Britain and extended to the British the right to trade and reside in Shanghai and other cities.

Sources: Clodfelter (2002); Featherstone (1973); Kuo (1935); Michael and Taylor (1964); Phillips and Axelrod (2005).

EXTRA-STATE WAR #324:
The First Franco-Algerian War of 1839–1847

Participants: France vs. Algerian forces led by Abd el-Kader
Dates: November 1, 1839, to December 23, 1847

Battle-Related Deaths: Algerian forces—20,000; France—15,000
Where Fought: Middle East
Initiator: Algerian forces led by Abd el-Kader
Outcome: France wins
War Type: Imperial

Narrative: After the French occupation of Algiers in 1830 (extra-state war #319), fighting quieted down but for only a couple of years. In 1834 the French resumed their drive to occupy all of Algeria, and by 1837 they took Constantine, which was the last city to retain its independence. However, the Sufi spiritual leader Abd el-Kader (Abd al-Qadir), whose power was centered in the hinterland of Oran, held out against the French. In 1832 Abd el-Kader declared a jihad against the Christian invaders, though fighting in 1832–1834 and 1835–1837 did not reach COW war levels. The 1837 Treaty of Tafna enabled Abd el-Kader to develop a regime outside the French zones. Abd el-Kader engaged the French again in this war in 1839, with his forces mainly engaging in small skirmishes. The French, however, were determined to defeat him. By the end of the war, the French had 108,000 troops in Algeria, while Abd el-Kader's army was at most 50,000 men. Abd el-Kader did receive some assistance from Morocco until September 10, 1844, when the Moroccan assistance was brought to a halt after French naval bombardment of Tangiers, as well as a successful ground assault by 7,500 French troops on a combined Algerian and Moroccan force of 45,000 in Morocco. Abd el-Kader continued his resistance in Algeria, and the French modified their tactics so that they could better confront his mobile style of warfare. The French also developed tactics for attacks on civilians and destruction of the countryside that were intended to terrorize the Algerian population. Ultimately, Abd el-Kader realized that further opposition was futile, and he surrendered to the French in late 1847. Abd el-Kader was then taken to France, where he lived under close supervision until 1852, when he was given his freedom as long as he did not return to Algeria.

Coding: This war spreads laterally into the Franco-Moroccan War of 1844 (extra-state war #330). Clodfelter (2002) describes the events of the entire period of 1830–1847 (and thus our three extra-state wars #319, #324, and #330) as the "French Conquest of Algeria: 1830–1847." Kohn (1999) includes a listing for "Abd el-Kader" in which he differentiates three wars, with the last one named the "Third War of Abd-el-Kader (1840–47)." Making things even more complicated, Phillips and Axelrod (2005) have one listing for all these events under the title "French Conquest of North Africa (1830–1847)" and then have separate listings for three wars: "Abd el-Kader, First War (1832–1834)," "Abd el-Kader, Second War (1835–1837)," and "Abd el-Kader, Third War (1840–1847)."

Sources: Clodfelter (2002); Confer (1966); Entelis (1986); Evans (2007); Great Britain (1942); Joestin (1964); Kohn (1999); Martin (1963); Nelson (1979); Oliver and Atmore (1994); Phillips and Axelrod (2005); Vandervort (1998); Williams (1907).

EXTRA-STATE WAR #325:
The Peru-Bolivian War of 1841

Participants: Peru vs. Bolivia
Dates: October 19, 1841, to November 28, 1841
Battle-Related Deaths: Peru—600; Bolivia—400
Where Fought: W. Hemisphere
Initiator: Bolivia
Outcome: Bolivia wins
War Type: Imperial

Narrative: In colonial times Bolivia had been part of the Spanish Viceroyalty of Peru. Peru gained its independence in 1821 and Bolivia in 1825 (extra-state war #312). During the early 1830s, Peru and Bolivia engaged in several conflicts over the issue of reuniting these two entities. Finally the attempt to re-create that earlier unity took the form of the Bolivia-Peru Confederation (or the Confederation of the Andes) from 1836 to 1839. Opposition to the union by Chile and some Peruvian exiles led to a war for the "restoration of Peru" in 1837 (non-state war #1523). The Chilean victory meant the end of the Confederation. As a consequence, the situation in Bolivia deteriorated into chaos. By 1841 Peruvian president Augustin Gamarra decided to try to reunify the countries again and invaded Bolivia. The two armies met at Ingavi on November 18, where the Peruvians were soundly defeated and President Gamarra was killed. The Bolivians then crossed the border into Peru, capturing several cities, which marks the end of the war. The final peace treaty was signed on June 7, 1842. This defeat ended the series of armed attempts to unite Peru and Bolivia. Decades later, in the War of the Pacific (interstate war #64), Chile attacked Peru and Bolivia and defeated them, taking all of Bolivia's coastline and much of Peru's.

Coding: After the destruction of the Bolivia-Peru Confederation, Peru became a member of the interstate system in 1839. Bolivia became an autonomous entity in 1839 but did not become a system member until 1848. Thus the war in 1841 is coded as an extra-state war between a system member and a nonstate entity outside its borders. Clodfelter (2002) describes this as the "Bolivian-Peruvian War: 1841."

Sources: Arguedas (1923); Clodfelter (2002); Dellepiane (1943); Dobyns and Doughty (1976); Phillips and Axelrod (2005); Scheina (2003a); Vasquez-Machicado, Mesa, and Gisbert (1963).

EXTRA-STATE WAR #326:
The British-Sind War of 1843

Participants: United Kingdom vs. Sind
Dates: January 6, 1843, to June 14, 1843
Battle-Related Deaths: Sind Army—4,000; United Kingdom—200
Where Fought: Asia
Initiator: United Kingdom
Outcome: United Kingdom wins
War Type: Imperial

Narrative: The British were expanding their empire in India by moving into Sind, along the delta of the Indus River between India and Afghanistan in what is now Pakistan. They needed to be able to send troops through Sind in order to conduct the wars in Afghanistan, and Britain had signed several agreements with the amirs (or mirs, the Baluchi rulers of Sind) by which the amirs were forced to give assistance to British expeditions, though the amirs were not pleased with the arrangement. After the defeat of the British in Afghanistan (extra-state war #322), the amirs hoped that they might regain some of their independence. The British, however, wanted the amirs to sign a new treaty with additional concessions. Hearing that the amirs had assembled an army, the British decided to act first. On January 6, 1843, a British regiment advanced toward Emaun-Ghur, a fortress in the desert. By the time the British arrived, the fortress had been abandoned. So the British troops destroyed it before returning to Hyderabad. On February 13, Baluchis attacked and besieged the small British garrison at Hyderabad. A British relief column rescued the garrison by defeating the Baluchis at the Battle of Miani (near Hyderabad) on February 22. The British pursued the Baluchi forces, and on March 24, a British force of 5,000 overwhelmingly defeated an army of 20,000 Baluchis at Dubba. Further British assaults on the Baluchis were launched in June, and the Baluchi defeat on June 14 signaled the end of the war. Britain then annexed Sind and the Indus delta to its empire in India.

Coding: Sind is coded as an autonomous entity until 1843, when it is incorporated into India. Clodfelter (2002) describes this as the "Sind War" of 1843. Phillips and Axelrod (2005) do not include it.

Sources: Clodfelter (2002); Farwell (1972); Featherstone (1992b); Featherstone (1973); Williams (1907).

EXTRA-STATE WAR #327:
The Uruguay War of 1843–1851

Participants: Argentina vs. France, United Kingdom, Uruguay
Dates: February 16, 1843, to July 18, 1851

Battle-Related Deaths: Uruguay—3,500; Argentina—1,500; France—600; United Kingdom—400
Where Fought: W. Hemisphere
Initiator: Argentina
Outcome: Transformed into inter-state war #19
War Type: Imperial

Narrative: After 1842 conflict within Argentina subsided, yet Argentina shifted the zone of armed conflict to combat over Uruguay. In Uruguay there were two primary political factions, the liberal Colorados and the conservative Blancos. In 1835 a Blanco, Manuel Oribe, was elected president. The Colorados, led by Jose Fructuoso Rivera, revolted and overthrew Oribe in 1838. Oribe sought the assistance of Argentina, which had previously intervened in Uruguayan affairs (see the extra-state war #315 between Argentina and Brazil 1826–1828). Argentine dictator Juan Manuel de Rosas wished to conquer Uruguay and thus began a siege of the Uruguayan capital of Montevideo on February 16, 1843, which marks the start of the war. The war initially involved attempts by the Uruguayans to break out of Montevideo. However, Britain and France wanted to preserve Uruguay's independence as well as their commercial interests in the country, so they entered the war on the side of Uruguay. In 1845 French and British naval forces created a blockade of the Río de la Plata, which blocked Argentina's approaches to Montevideo, and engaged in several naval clashes with Argentine ships there.

Both Britain and France withdrew their forces in 1849. Even though the French did attempt to negotiate a withdrawal of Argentine forces from Uruguay, a treaty was signed on August 31, 1850, that allowed Argentine troops to remain in Montevideo. Despite appeals to the Monroe Doctrine, the United States made it clear it would not intervene. It appeared that Argentina would prevail. However, wanting to maintain the independence of Uruguay as a buffer between itself and Argentina, Brazil did not wish to see Argentina annex Uruguay. Therefore, Brazil broke relations with Argentina in October 1850; formed an alliance with Paraguay, a system member, in December 1850; and decided to enter the war. Meanwhile within Argentina, the governor of Entre Ríos declared war against Argentina in April 1851. An anti-Argentina league among Brazil, Uruguay, and Entre Ríos (later joined by Paraguay) was subsequently formed on May 29, 1851. This extra-state war ends on July 18, 1851. After that, Brazil took over the bulk of the fighting against Argentina, sending troops to relieve Montevideo and providing forces to support the revolt against Rosas within Argentina. Thus the conflict is transformed into an inter-state war, #19, the La Plata War, between Brazil and Argentina. Ultimately, Argentine forces were driven out of Uruguay, which then formed a long-standing alliance with Brazil.

Coding: Uruguay was not at that time a member of the COW interstate system; thus this war is classified as an extra-state war between a state, Argentina, and an autonomous entity, Uruguay. Kohn refers to this war as the "Siege of Montevideo (1843–1851)." Clodfelter refers to it as the "Uruguayan War: 1843–1851."

Sources: Best (1960, vol. 2); Cady (1929); Calogeras (1963); Clodfelter (2002); Dawson (1935); Kohn (1999); Lemke (2006); Levene (1937); Phillips and Axelrod (2005); Scheina (2003a).

EXTRA-STATE WAR #329:

The Gwalior War of 1843

Participants: United Kingdom vs. Gwalior
Dates: December 28, 1843, to December 29, 1843
Battle-Related Deaths: Gwalior—1,330; United Kingdom—106
Where Fought: Asia
Initiator: United Kingdom
Outcome: United Kingdom wins
War Type: Imperial

Narrative: Gwalior is a fortress town in north-central India, within about 100 miles of Agra and the Taj Mahal, in the current state of Madhya

Pradesh. Gwalior was one of the three members of the Maratha confederation (states ruled by the Maratha of the Mahratta people). In 1804 Gwalior was an autonomous entity, though it had been placed under the protection of the British. The British then subdued most of the Marathas in 1817 (extra-state war #306). When the rajah of Gwalior died in 1843, his successor was a minor, so a regent was appointed. The initial regent, who had British support, was expelled and replaced by Dada Khasji-wala, who attempted to reduce British influence. The British could not accept a hostile regime in Gwalior, in part owing to their fear of a combined opposition of the Marathas and the Sikhs. Britain thus sent troops against Gwalior. One British army advanced from the north and another from the south, and they converged at the Gwalior capital of Maharajpur. In brief but heavy fighting at Maharajpur and Punniar approximately 20,000 British overcame about 30,000 Maratha defenders. The usurping government submitted, and the fortress at Gwalior was occupied by the British. Under the terms of the treaty of January 13, 1844, Gwalior maintained its independence, but was to conduct its foreign affairs with the advice of the British resident.

Coding: Extra-state war #314, the British-Bharatpuran War of 1825–1826, was fought over the nearby city of Bharatpur. Clodfelter (2002) calls this current war the "Gwalior War: 1843–1844." Phillips and Axelrod (2005) do not include it.

Sources: Clodfelter (2002); Dodwell (1929); Farwell (1972); Featherstone (1992b); Featherstone (1973); Gordon (1898); Malleson (1875); Williams (1907).

EXTRA-STATE WAR #330:
The Franco-Moroccan War of 1844

Participants: France vs. Morocco (in support of Algerian resistance)
Dates: August 6, 1844, to September 10, 1844

Battle-Related Deaths: Morocco—800; France—200
Where Fought: Africa
Initiator: France
Outcome: France wins
War Type: Imperial

Narrative: Often wars between two countries occur when nearby events finally spill over a border. In this case, the French conquest of Algeria (extra-state war #324) had finally reached the stage where the Algerian leader Abd el-Kader was being driven out of Algeria and into Morocco. This induced the Moroccans to give him assistance, and that assistance in turn prompted a short war between the French and the Moroccans. In August 1844 the French fleet under Captain François-Ferdinand-Philippe-Louis-Marie d'Orléans, prince de Joinville, bombarded Tangier and Mogador. The French army, led by Marshal Robert Thomas Bugeaud, the governor-general of Algeria, confronted the Moroccans at Isly. In the Battle of Isly on August 15, the French, with 8,000 infantry, enveloping cavalry, and superior artillery, confronted a force of 40,000 Moroccans and soundly beat them. Hostilities were ended by the Treaty of Tangier on September 10, 1844. Two years later, in 1846, when Abd el-Kader again attempted to enter Morocco, the sultan denied him entry, and within a year the Algerian resistance to the French collapsed. This war marked the beginning in a series of wars through which France would gain a protectorate over Morocco in 1912.

Coding: Clodfelter (2002) includes this in the "French Conquest of Algeria: 1830–47." Phillips and Axelrod (2005) cover it as part of both the "French Conquest of North Africa (1830-1847) and "Abd el-Kader, The Third War of, (1840–1847)."

Sources: Churchill (1867); Clodfelter (2002); Oliver and Atmore (1994); Phillips and Axelrod (2005); Usborne (1936); Williams (1907).

EXTRA-STATE WAR #331:
The First British-Sikh War of 1845–1846

Participants: United Kingdom vs. Sikhs
Dates: December 13, 1845, to February 10, 1846
Battle-Related Deaths: Sikhs—7,000; United Kingdom—1,500
Where Fought: Asia
Initiator: Sikhs
Outcome: United Kingdom wins
War Type: Imperial

Narrative: The Sikhs inhabited the Punjab (northwest of India). During the early nineteenth century, they were ruled by Ranjit Singh, the "Old Lion," who had promoted the military prowess of the Sikhs. Consequently, the Punjab had been too strong militarily to be attacked by Britain, and was one of the last significant entities on the Indian subcontinent not absorbed into the British Empire. The Sikhs had a very disciplined and effective army of 20,000 infantry and 4,000 cavalry. During their period of unity, there was cohesion among not only the Sikhs but also neighboring Muslims. However, divisions among the Sikhs following the death of Ranjit Singh in 1839 led to confusion and misrule. The British needed free passage through the Punjab for their troops in Afghanistan and thus sent several regiments to the frontiers to protect the British possessions. The Sikhs, assuming that they were going to be attacked by the British, struck first, sending an army of 20,000 warriors toward the British force of 10,000 men at Mudki in December 1845. After heavy fighting, the Sikhs were repulsed, and they suffered a second defeat at Ferozesha three days later in what some have called "the most terrible battle in British-Indian History" (Featherstone 1992b, 49). Initially the Sikhs had attacked British India, but after they were repelled, the British then invaded Punjab, where they won further victories. The final battle at Sobraon on February 10, 1846, involved heavy casualties on both sides, resulting in the defeat of the Sikh army. The British then advanced into the capital of Lahore, where the final treaty was signed on March 10, 1846. The Sikhs yielded their portion of Kashmir, as well as other territory, to the British; however, fighting would resume two years later (see extra-state war #335).

Coding: This was treated as an imperial war because the Sikhs had never been a part of the British raj. Clodfelter (2002) and also Phillips and Axelrod (2005) call this the "First Sikh War" of 1845–1846.

Sources: Bond (1967); Burt (1956); Clodfelter (2002); Farwell (1972); Featherstone (1992b); Featherstone (1973); Fortescue (1927, vol. 12); Gough and Innes (1897); Majumdar (1948); Metcalf and Metcalf (2006); Phillips and Axelrod (2005); Singh (1966); Williams (1907).

EXTRA-STATE WAR #332:
The Cracow Revolt of 1846

Participants: Austria, Prussia, Russia vs. Cracow rebels
Dates: February 15, 1846, to March 3, 1846
Battle-Related Deaths: Austria—1,000; Cracow rebels—1,000; Prussia—[ ]; Russia—[ ]
Where Fought: Europe
Initiator: Austria
Outcome: Austria wins
War Type: Imperial

Narrative: As a result of the Congress of Vienna, Cracow was created as an independent republic from 1816 while the rest of traditional Poland was partitioned by Russia, Prussia, and Austria. A Polish revolt against Russian rule was suppressed in 1831 (see intra-state war #517). The Austrian region of Galicia included the Austrian-incorporated portion of Poland. Both the socialists and the nobles residing in Galicia were unhappy with Austrian rule, and the Polish nationalists living in Cracow tried to instigate their discontent in order to inspire a revolt that might reestablish Polish independence. An insurrection was planned to take place in Prussia, Russia, and Galacia for February 24, 1846. The Austrians became aware of the revolutionary plans and began rounding up the planners on February 15. The Austrians also enlisted the assistance of Austrian peasants, who went on a rampage, killing local noblemen. On February 18, Austrian forces entered Cracow. Even though an initial attack on the Austrians by the Polish insurgents was unsuccessful, the magnitude of the insurgent forces persuaded the Austrians to withdraw on February 22. The insurgents declared the formation of a national government and announced plans for abolishing the nobility. Meanwhile, insurgents in Galacia, following the original plan, attacked an Austrian post at Chocholow. The insurgency was sufficient to threaten all three of the partitioning powers, and armies from Austria, Prussia, and Russia all converged on Cracow, and the insurgents were defeated. Subsequently, the partitioning parties repealed the treaty of 1815, and Cracow was incorporated into Austria.

Coding: Clodfelter (2002) describes "Polish Rebellions" of 1830–1831 and 1846. Phillips and Axelrod (2005) call it the "Cracow Insurrection" of 1846. Bridge (1990) refers to this war as the "Galician Revolt of 1846."

Sources: Bridge (1990); Clodfelter (2002); Davies (1984); Lukowski and Zawadzki (2006); Phillips and Axelrod (2005); Williams (2007).

EXTRA-STATE WAR #333:
The First British-Xhosa War of 1846–1847

Participants: United Kingdom vs. Xhosa locals
Dates: April 16, 1846, to December 23, 1847
Battle-Related Deaths: Xhosa—2,000; United Kingdom—1,000
Where Fought: Africa
Initiator: United Kingdom
Outcome: United Kingdom wins
War Type: Imperial

Narrative: The Xhosa are a Bantu-speaking people who lived just to the east of the city of Port Elizabeth, in the watersheds of the Great Fish River and the Kei River as well as the land between. The Bantu were particularly united, since Bantu is a large language family, spoken across almost all of southern Africa. The Xhosa maintained a reasonably prosperous life by raising cattle and growing corn. As British and Dutch settlers from the Cape Colony sought more land, they came into conflict with the local tribes. As the Boers moved north from the Cape in the Great Trek of 1835–1836, they became involved in wars with the Matabele and the Zulu (non-state wars #1521 and #1525). The British had also engaged in a brief war with the Zulu (extra-state war #321) and then became involved in this conflict with the Xhosa. In the 1830s British patrols rampaged through Xhosa territory, stealing cattle and driving the Xhosa further north. An incident in which a Xhosa warrior stole an axe to free a comrade was enough to trigger this war (which is sometimes referred to as the Axe War).

The British initially had 2,600 troops against a force of 2,000 Xhosa warriors, though the British commander's troop strength eventually reached 14,000 (of whom 3,000 were British, with the rest Boers, Khoikhoi, and others), while it is estimated that the Xhosa had a maximum of 12,000 warriors. On April 16, 1846, the British attacked the Xhosa near Burn's Hill, and later the Xhosa attacked the British as they encamped there. The Xhosa also attacked a reinforcing column, and the British abandoned their supply wagons. Several British forts were attacked, and in just one battle near Fort Pierre in June 1846, five hundred Xhosa died in combat. Later in the war, however, the British commander could not lure the Xhosa into big pitched battles, and the British resorted to seizing the Xhosas' cattle, thus inflicting grievous economic harm. Finally the Xhosa chiefs tired of the war and made peace overtures to the British in September 1846; however, the Xhosa were unwilling to accept all of the British terms. Thus hostilities resumed, and the British won several decisive victories in 1847. The Xhosa, who were further weakened by starvation and disease, surrendered unconditionally to the British on December 23, 1847, ending the war.

Coding: In earlier versions of the COW dataset, this war was referred to as the First Kaffir War, after the locals who were called "Kaffirs" by the British but known to themselves and us as the Xhosa. *Kaffir* is the Arabic word for "infidel." Hence, the Afghan region appears as "Kafiristan" in the Rudyard Kipling story "The Man Who Would Be King." From these linguistic roots the word was generalized, during the Victorian days of the British empire building into widespread English usage meaning "native," and so *Kaffir* was generally a derogatory term. In South Africa it was used by the British to demean the Xhosa and to describe wars to subdue them. Likewise, Clodfelter (2002) describes this war as part of the "Kaffir Wars: 1811–78." Phillips and Axelrod (2005) call this war the "War of the Axe (1846–1847)," but the fighting is the seventh of a sequence of nine wars they call the "Kaffir Wars" of whites against the Xhosa, starting in 1779.

Sources: Clodfelter (2002); Featherstone (1992a); Mostert (1992); Peires (1982); Phillips and Axelrod (2005).

EXTRA-STATE WAR #334:

The First Dutch-Bali War of 1848–1849

Participants: Netherlands vs. Bali
Dates: April 12, 1848, to June 14, 1849
Battle-Related Deaths: Balinese—2,000; Netherlands—300
Where Fought: Asia
Initiator: Netherlands
Outcome: Stalemate
War Type: Imperial

Narrative: At the beginning of the nineteenth century, Bali was relatively isolated from international trade, unlike the nearby island of Java. Bali was also internally divided into eight kingdoms, ruled by eight rajas, the most important of whom was the raja of Klungkung. These kingdoms were frequently in conflict with one another. The Netherlands was desirous of spreading its colonial empire in the region and had fought a war with Java from 1825 to 1830 (extra-state war #313). By 1840 the Dutch had decided to bring Bali under their control in order to preclude the advances of other colonial powers. From 1841 to 1843 the Dutch entered into a series of agreements with the rajas, though some resisted Dutch claims of sovereignty. This led to a Dutch attack on the raja of Buleleng in 1846. Though the Dutch won a quick victory (fighting was at below war fatality levels), the raja ultimately refused to pay an indemnity, setting the stage for the second Dutch offensive.

The rajas then began to create a coalition against the Dutch. The Dutch then issued ultimatums to the rajas, and when evasive replies were received, the Dutch began bombarding coastal villages on April 12, 1848. On April 29 the Dutch on Java announced that a state of war existed between the Netherlands and the kingdoms of Buleleng, Karangasem, and Klungkung. A Dutch force of 4,000 men landed near Buleleng on June 7, 1848. The Dutch expected a quick victory and were surprised to be confronted by thousands of Balinese warriors. They made initial advances but were later forced to retreat from the major fortification at Jagaraga. The Dutch finally retreated to Java on June 21, and this stage of the war was seen as a major Dutch defeat. This loss made the Dutch only more determined to defeat the Balinese, and they immediately began planning the next offensive.

In January and February 1849 the Dutch assembled an army and navy of 13,000 men, who were also aided by 4,000 warriors sent by the raja of the nearby island of Lombok. The united rajas of Bali fielded an army of 33,000 warriors. On April 2, 1849, the Dutch fleet arrived at Buleleng. After heavy fighting, the Dutch captured the fortress at Jagaraga on April 16. The Dutch and Lombok forces then attacked Karangasem, which was defeated in May. The Dutch then advanced against the raja of Klungkung. In defense of Klungkung, the Balinese assembled a force of 33,000 warriors, who, though not well armed, vastly outnumbered the available Dutch troops. Both sides ultimately decided it was better to avoid a potential bloodbath (which would involve a mass "puputan," or battle to the death by the raja, his family, and his followers). Dutch forces began to withdraw on June 14, 1849, ending the war. The final treaty was signed on July 13, 1849. The war is coded as ending in a stalemate, because neither side won an outright victory. The Dutch were successful in the sense that the Balinese accepted Dutch sovereignty; however, the Dutch also promised that they would not attempt to station civilian or military troops in Bali. The next extra-state war that involves Bali is in 1894 (extra-state war #402).

Coding: The period of June 22, 1848, to April 1, 1849, is coded as a break in the war. The island of Bali was an independent entity from 1492 to 1856, after which it was incorporated into Dutch Indonesia for almost all of the following one hundred years. Fighting in peripheral areas of Bali continued, however, until the island was totally subdued in the fighting of 1906–1908. Clodfelter (2002) calls the Dutch imperial war against Bali the "Conquest of Bali: 1856–1908" and says the Dutch "left [the island] alone until 1849." Phillips and Axelrod (2005) include only the "Java Revolt" of 1849.

Sources: Agung (1991); Clodfelter (2002); De Klerk (1938); Phillips and Axelrod (2005); Ricklefs (2001); Robinson (1995); van der Kraan (1995); Zainu'ddin (1968).

EXTRA-STATE WAR #335:

The Second British-Sikh War of 1848–1849

Participants: United Kingdom vs. Sikhs
Dates: May 18, 1848, to March 10, 1849
Battle-Related Deaths: Sikhs—5,000; United Kingdom—1,500
Where Fought: Asia

Initiator: United Kingdom
Outcome: United Kingdom wins
War Type: Imperial

Narrative: This war completed the British conquest of the Punjab. The treaty that had ended the First British-Sikh War of 1845–1846 (extra-state war #331) had awarded some Punjab territory to the British, and in early 1848 two British officers had been sent to take control of the Sikh province of Moultan. They were murdered on April 19, 1848. The British, seeing this as a threat to their supremacy, dispatched a military expedition to Moultan. An attack there by the Sikhs on May 18 was repulsed. The expedition was joined by a second British army, and the united force defeated a large army of the Sikh viceroy of Moultan, Dewan Moolraj, on May 20. Moolraj's army (of 7,000–10,000 warriors) was defeated in several engagements in June before taking refuge in a fortress at Suddoosam. The British besieged the fortress (containing 12,000 Sikhs) with an army that soon reached 32,000 men; however, the British force contained a contingent of 5,000 "friendly" Sikhs. On September 14 the Sikhs deserted the British and aligned themselves with Moolraj. Meanwhile skirmishes took place elsewhere, resulting in several notable British defeats involving foolish charges against enemy positions. Moolraj finally surrendered on January 22, 1849. The decisive battle then took place at Gujrat, where a British force of 24,000 faced a Sikh army estimated at 60,000 men. On February 21 the Sikh army was completely defeated. The remaining Sikh forces surrendered at Rawalpindi on March 10, 1849. The outcome was that the Sikh territory, Punjab, was totally absorbed into British India. Queen Victoria also gained the great Koh-i-noor diamond.

Coding: Clodfelter (2002) as well as Phillips and Axelrod (2005) refer to this as the "Second Sikh War" of 1848–1849.

Sources: Bond (1967); Burt (1956); Clodfelter (2002); Farwell (1972); Featherstone (1992b); Featherstone (1973); Fortescue (1927, vol. 12);

Gough and Innes (1897); Jaques (2007); Majumdar (1948); Metcalf and Metcalf (2006); Phillips and Axelrod (2005); Singh (1966); Williams (1907).

EXTRA-STATE WAR #336:
Chinese Pirates War of 1849

Participants: United Kingdom vs. Chinese pirates
Dates: October 20, 1849, to October 22, 1849
Battle-Related Deaths: Chinese pirates—2,800; United Kingdom—0
Where Fought: Asia
Initiator: United Kingdom
Outcome: United Kingdom wins
War Type: Imperial

Narrative: A Chinese pirate fleet, led by Shap-ng-tsai, had been causing havoc in South China Sea shipping routes during the 1840s. Finally, in October 1849 the British government in Hong Kong sent a naval squadron to deal with the problem. The pirates were found near Haiphong in northern Vietnam. The pirate ships, or junks, were destroyed one by one, and only six escaped. The pirate leader soon surrendered. The British sailors were paid £20 for each pirate captured or killed.

Coding: Clodfelter (2002) calls this the "Expedition against the Chinese Pirates" of 1849.

Sources: Clodfelter (2002); Farwell (1972).

EXTRA-STATE WAR #337:
The Second British-Xhosa War of 1850–1852

Participants: United Kingdom vs. Xhosa
Dates: December 24, 1850, to April 8, 1852
Battle-Related Deaths: Xhosa—6,000; United Kingdom—1,400
Where Fought: Africa
Initiator: United Kingdom
Outcome: United Kingdom wins
War Type: Colonial

Narrative: This is part of a series of wars involving the growth of the British colony in South Africa in the nineteenth century. The conflict involved three groups that were already there: the Zulu, the Boers, and the Xhosa. The British fought two wars against the Zulus, two against the Boers, and three against the Xhosa. Of these, the wars against the Xhosa were called "Kaffir Wars" by the British. In chronological order, the British wars against these groups started with a war against the Zulu (extra-state war #321) in 1838. Then there were the wars against the Xhosa: extra-state war #333, in 1846–1847; extra-state war #337, in 1850–1852; and finally extra-state war #374, in 1877–1878. The British fought their second and last Zulu war in 1879 (extra-state #380). After having defeated the Xhosa and the Zulu, the British completed their consolidation of power in South Africa by fighting wars against the Boers in 1880–1881 (extra-state war #382) and 1899–1902 (extra-state war #416). In addition, there are several non-state wars (see Chapter 6) in which these ethnic groups fought against each other or factions within the same ethnic group fought against each other in an inter-communal war.

This 1850–1852 war was perhaps the biggest of the three Xhosa wars. Here the Xhosa began agitating against British rule over Xhosa territory that had been lost after the preceding war. Consequently, the British deposed and outlawed one of the Xhosa chiefs. The British then sent a small expedition to capture him, and the war started on December 24, 1850, when the Xhosa attacked this patrol. Xhosa forces swarmed across the border into British territory. Though the British force was initially small, ultimately about 10,000 soldiers on the British side fought against 20,000 Xhosa. During the first year, most of the fighting was relatively limited, with the Xhosa making forays from two strongholds; however, in late 1851 the British expedition began to drive the Xhosa from their bases, a task that was completed in March 1852. By April 8, 1852, the Xhosa, despite their numerical superiority in terms of soldiers, had been defeated by the British. The peace treaty was not signed until March 2, 1853. This time the British destroyed tens of thousands of head of cattle, the economic base of Xhosa power. Perhaps because of this decisive British victory, there was not another British-Xhosa war until a quarter-century later.

Coding: In earlier versions of the COW dataset, this war was referred to as the Second Kaffir War, after the locals who were called "Kaffirs" by the British. Since *Kaffir* is a derogatory term, it is not utilized here. Clodfelter (2002) describes nine "Kaffir Wars" of 1811–1878 and points out that this one, in 1850 to 1852, was the largest. Phillips and Axelrod (2005) also have nine "Kaffir Wars," though they call the seventh one the "War of the Axe" and this one the "Eighth Kaffir War." They date its end to a peace agreement of March 2, 1853.

Sources: Clodfelter (2002); Featherstone (1992a); Featherstone (1973); Mostert (1993); Oliver and Atmore (1994); Peires (1982); Phillips and Axelrod (2005); Thompson (2001).

EXTRA-STATE WAR #338:
The Ottoman-Yam War of 1851

Participants: Ottoman Empire vs. Yam tribe
Dates: April 21, 1851, to July 9, 1851
Battle-Related Deaths: Yam—1,600; Ottoman Empire—[ ]
Where Fought: Middle East
Initiator: Yam
Outcome: Ottoman Empire wins
War Type: Imperial

Narrative: The Ottoman Empire had reached its limit of power, territorial expansion, and influence in the sixteenth century. The seventeenth century was marked by imperial neglect, followed by the eighteenth century's period of decline. The nineteenth century then reflected a period of reform and reassertion of Ottoman power. During the period of Ottoman decline, some of the more remote parts of the Ottoman Empire, such as Yemen, had slipped into virtual independence due to Ottoman neglect. Meanwhile, the British took advantage of the opportunity to establish trading centers at Mocha, Lahij, and Aden. Consequently, Ottoman sultans, beginning with Mahmud II, began to try to regain control over the entire Arabian Peninsula, including Yemen (see also extra-state wars #301, #320, and #342), primarily by requesting the military intervention of Muhammad Ali of Egypt. In 1840, however, the Egyptians were encouraged to leave the area, and consequently Egypt ceded its territory along the coast to Husayn, sharif of Abu Arish, who proceeded to occupy the port city of Hodeida. In 1842 Husayn, as a result of a conflict with the British, was forced to acknowledge his allegiance to the Ottoman Empire. Then in 1849, when the Ottomans decided to establish more direct control by forcing the Zaydi imam in Sanaa to become an Ottoman vassal, Sharif Husayn was forced out of Hodeida, surrendering his territory to the Ottomans, though he remained sharif of Abu Arish and temporary governor of the coastal area. Opposition to Ottoman rule endured in the region, and during the 1850s the Ottomans attempted to extend their control over the local tribes and kingdoms.

The Yam was one of the five most powerful tribes in northern Yemen. They operated in the Tihamah, the coastal plain along the Red Sea coast of Yemen. In 1821 the Yam had plundered the port of Luhayyah and had seized the city of Zabid (located between Mocha and Hodeida). This brought the Yam into potential conflict with both the imam in Sanaa and the British in Mocha and precipitated a diplomatic crisis between Britain and the Ottoman Empire in 1822. This encouraged the British to shift their operations from Mocha to Aden in 1839. After 1849 the Ottomans organized Yemen into five administrative *sancaks,* or regions (Hodeida, Mocha, Luhayyah, Abu Arish, and Sanaa), each headed by a sharif, and they based their administration at Hodeida, rather than at Sanaa in the interior highlands.

In 1851 the coastal tribes were fighting among themselves. The local inhabitants invited the emir of Asir (north of Yemen) to intervene, and in January he was successful in removing Husayn as the sharif of Abu Arish and replacing him with his cousin, al-Hasan. The Asiri then withdrew to their mountain strongholds as the Ottomans headed toward Abu Arish. The Ottoman administrator removed al-Hasan as sharif and appointed Sharif Haydar in his place. Consequently, Sharif Hasan became determined to recover control over Abu Arish. Hasan, along with 7,000 Yam followers attacked and occupied the Ottoman fort at Luhayyah. Ottoman troops met the Yam at Zaydidah, where the Yam suffered a major defeat. Sharif Hasan continued plotting against the Ottomans until he was imprisoned at Jiddah in June 1852.

Coding: Resistance to Ottoman rule continued in Yemen and Asir in the 1860s, leading to the Ottoman conquest of Arabia in 1870–1872 (extra-state war #365). Yemen is coded as an autonomous entity from 1816 to 1871, when it is incorporated into the Ottoman Empire as a result of that war.

Sources: Baldry (1976); Baynard et al. (1986); Farah (2002); Lewis (1958); Palmer (1992).

EXTRA-STATE WAR #339:

The Second British-Burmese War of 1852

Participants: United Kingdom vs. Burma
Dates: April 5, 1852, to November 20, 1852
Battle-Related Deaths: Burma—800; United
    Kingdom—400
Where Fought: Asia
Initiator: United Kingdom
Outcome: United Kingdom wins
War Type: Imperial

Narrative: Burma was an autonomous entity dating back to 1555. This war of 1852 was a step on the way to the establishment of British colonial control of Burma. There had already been a British-Burmese war (extra-state war #310) in 1823–1826, over border territory, and there would be another war, in 1885–1886, in which all of Burma, upon its defeat, became a British colony. Almost halfway between those two wars, in 1852 the British attacked Burma supposedly as a result of the Burmese mistreatment of British citizens. On March 15, 1852, the British sent an ultimatum to the king of Burma. On March 28, 1852, a British fleet sailed toward the mouth of the Irawadi River. The fort of Martaban (which housed 5,000 Burmese troops) was seized on April 5. The expedition then sailed up the river to the capital, Rangoon. The garrison there was destroyed and the city surrendered. Then, on April 19, the British seized the fort at Bassein. Meanwhile, the troops that the British had left at Martaban were attacked by a large Burmese force, which was repulsed with a great loss of life. The offensive resumed in the fall, and the British took control of the province of Pegu (called Bago today). This takeover of the Pegu region required not only a victory in the initial attack on Burmese armed forces, but then a follow-up struggle in which the British were able to subdue local rebels in the captured province. The battle here on November 20, 1852, marks the end of the war. After that the British and Burmese ceased fighting. On December 10, 1852, the British East India Company announced the annexation of South Burma in the name of the United Kingdom. The Burmese, however, did not recognize the British colonial government in Pegu. Fighting continued, albeit at below war levels, for the next thirty years, until the Third British-Burmese War of 1885–1889 (extra-state war #387).

Coding: Clodfelter (2002) describes this as "the Second Burma War" of 1852–1853. Phillips and Axelrod (2005) call it the "Second Anglo-Burmese War", and restrict it to 1852.

Sources: Bruce (1973); Clodfelter (2002); Farwell (1972); Featherstone (1973); Jaques (2007); Phillips and Axelrod (2005); Williams (1907).

EXTRA-STATE WAR #340:
The French-Tukulor War of 1854–1857

Participants: France vs. Tukulor
Dates: [ ]/[ ]/1854, to July 15, 1857
Battle-Related Deaths: Tukulor—2000;
   France—100
Where Fought: Africa
Initiator: Tukulors
Outcome: Stalemate
War Type: Imperial

Narrative: The Tukulors inhabited an area called Tekrur in West Africa along the Senegal River (in what is now Guinea). In the eleventh century, they converted to Islam and extended their influence northward into Morocco. The Mali Empire conquered Tekrur in the fourteenth century and remained dominant until the mid-nineteenth century. In 1826 a Tukulor cleric named Umar went to Mecca and was initiated into an Islamic brotherhood (Tijaniyya). This gave him the honorific name al-Hajj Umar. He wanted to revive the importance of Tekrur by waging a jihad, and, in the 1850s, Umar began to attack and conquer a number of neighboring entities. This period is included as non-state war #1535, the First Tukulor War of 1852 to 1854. Umar's expansionist policies, however, brought him into conflict with the French.

The French had established a colony in Senegal in the seventeenth century, though they had lost it to Britain on several occasions. In the mid-nineteenth century, the French were limited to the coastal region; however, during the period of 1854 to 1865, Capt. Lewis Faidherbe was governor of Senegal, and he wanted to extend French influence eastward. As he did so, the French came into conflict with Umar's 1854 westward turn. The French and Tukulor forces engaged in skirmishes, in which the Tukolor sometimes achieved victory, and Umar attacked the French garrisons, in which the Tukolor were generally defeated. The French saw Umar's activities as threatening the security of all of western Senegal and thus wanted access to the strategic region of Futa Toro to block Umar's advance. Futa Toro is east of the French coastal outpost of Dakar and west of Umar's kingdom. There, in 1855, the French constructed a fort at Médine. In 1857 Umar launched an assault on Médine and besieged it from April to July. On July 15 Governor Faidherbe and 500 men dispersed the Tukulor and relieved the fort. The French captured Futa Toro and thus halted Umar's advances. At this point, the extra-state war ended, though a treaty of peace between Umar and Faidherbe was not signed until September 10, 1860. Umar's kingdom remained intact, and he returned to his jihad and attacking non-French areas for another six years from 1857 to 1863, seizing the kingdom of Segu in 1861. Umar was killed in 1864, one year after that war ended.

Coding: Both Kohn (1999) and Phillips and Axelrod (2005) include "Tukulor-French Wars (1853–1864)." This war is not included in Clodfelter (2002).

Sources: *Columbia Encyclopedia* (1993); Fage (1969); Kohn (1999); Oliver and Atmore (1994); Phillips and Axelrod (2005); Robinson (1988); Vandervort (1998).

EXTRA-STATE WAR #341:
The British-Santal War of 1855–1856

Participants: United Kingdom vs. Santal
Dates: [ ]/[ ]/1855, to [ ]/[ ]/1856
Battle-Related Deaths: Santal—15,000; United
   Kingdom—[ ]
Where Fought: Asia
Initiator: Santal
Outcome: United Kingdom wins
War Type: Colonial

Narrative: In the nineteenth century, the Santal were a tribal group in India, living mostly in Bihar, which is a province lying just south of Nepal, north of the Ganges Delta. The Santal felt exploited by both the British East India Company and some native Indian groups who had become integrated into the British economic system of capitalism. Thus the Santal revolt has sometimes been called one of the "forest peoples" (Metcalf and Metcalf 2006, 87) who rose up against the imposition of British rule in the nineteenth century. In this war the Santal forces marched on Calcutta, but the rebellion did not succeed. That city was defended by British forces, including not only troops from Britain but also local Indian allies. After driving the Santal column back, the British forces then carried the battle into Santal territory and inflicted serious damage.

Coding: Today the Santals remain an important tribal group in India. However, in earlier centuries, as a tribal group living in the hills south of the Himalayas, they did not form a state-like sovereign entity and so were never marked as an autonomous entity in our States, Nations, and Entities list (Schafer 1995). Clodfelter (2002) describes this as the "Santal Insurrection" of 1855–1856. Phillips and Axelrod (2005) do not cover it.

Sources: Clodfelter (2002); Metcalf and Metcalf (2006); Schafer (1995).

EXTRA-STATE WAR #342:
Hodeida Siege of 1856

Participants: Ottoman Empire vs. Beni Aseer tribe
Dates: January 22, 1856, to February 22, 1856
Battle-Related Deaths: Beni Aseer tribe—15,000; Ottoman Empire—1,700
Where Fought: Middle East
Initiator: Beni Aseer tribe
Outcome: Stalemate
War Type: Colonial

Narrative: In the earlier wars (extra-state war #301 and extra-state war #320), the Ottoman Empire had tried to reassert its control over the Red Sea coast of the Arabian Peninsula. In 1816

the Ottomans sent Egyptian troops to counter the threat posed by Wahhabism, a puritanical sect of Islam. In 1832 the Ottomans again commissioned the Egyptians to fight against a rebellion by the Asiri tribes. By 1837 the Egyptians controlled the entire eastern Red Sea coast. However, in 1840 pressure by Britain, Russia, Austria, Italy, and the Ottoman Empire persuaded Egypt's Muhammad Ali to withdraw from Yemen, and consequently Egypt ceded its territory along the coast to Husayn, sharif of Abu Arish. In 1842 Husayn, as a result of a conflict with the British, was forced to acknowledge his allegiance to the Ottoman Empire. Then in 1849, when the Ottomans decided to reassert their claim to all of Yemen, Sharif Husayn surrendered his territory to the Ottomans. The Ottomans were, however, unsuccessful in extending their control into the interior, most of which was controlled by the Yemeni imams in Sanaa. Ottoman expeditions in 1850 and 1852 were beaten back (though at below war levels).

In 1856 the Ottomans directly controlled the coastal area, including the port city of Hodeida; however, there was opposition to Ottoman control from the Sanaa imams, the sharifs of Asir, and a number of fiercely independent tribes. John Baldry (1976, 163) concluded that "In south-west Arabia, Turkey encountered more opposition to its rule than in any other part of the Arab World in the late nineteenth and early twentieth centuries...." In order to resist the Ottoman control along the Red Sea coast, the Beni Aseer tribe in 1856 decided to take advantage of the fact that the Ottomans were engaged in struggles elsewhere. The tribe's 60,000 warriors marched southward from Asir and besieged the Ottoman forces at Hodeida. Though the siege lasted only a month, a cholera epidemic struck the rebels, causing many fatalities. The rebels were then forced to withdraw, and the war ended in a stalemate. Opposition to the Ottomans did not end, however, and another war would occur in this region, extra-state war #365.

Coding: Both Asir and North Yemen are coded as autonomous entities from 1816 to 1871 and as being militarily occupied by the Ottoman Empire after that.

Sources: Baldry (1976); Cole and Momen (1986); Farah (1985/86); Ingrams and Ingrams (1993); Playfair (1978).

EXTRA-STATE WAR #343:

The Second Opium War of 1856–1860

Participants: France, United Kingdom vs. China
Dates: October 22, 1856, to October 24, 1860
Battle-Related Deaths: China—3,000; United
　　Kingdom—200; France—100
Where Fought: Asia
Initiator: France, United Kingdom
Outcome: France and United Kingdom win
War Type: Imperial

Narrative: Chinese opposition to the sale of opium to its subjects had led to the First Opium War against Britain beginning in 1839 (extra-state war #323). One result of that war had been the opening of even more Chinese cities to foreign trade. Similarly, this war centered on foreign powers wanting to secure expanded trade in China. The opium-smuggling ship the *Arrow,* flying the British flag, was seized by Chinese officials in 1856. The British objected, insisting that the Chinese were interfering with legitimate commerce. The British then began the war against the Chinese with the assistance of the French, who cited the killing of a French missionary as justification for their involvement. The European forces seized both Canton (now Guangzhou) on December 30, 1857, and Tientsin (now usually called Tianjin) on May 20, 1858. At this point negotiations took place among the warring parties, leading to the Treaties of Tientsin; however, the Chinese government renounced the treaties and fought on, despite the loss of these two major cities. The British and French won battles near Peking (now Beijing), looted the Summer Palace lying to the northwest of the city, and forced the Chinese emperor to flee from the capital itself. The Chinese government had also been weakened by the lengthy Taiping Rebellion (non-state war #1534 and intra-state war #567), which had begun in 1850. Consequently, the Chinese agreed to the terms of the Treaty of Peking, which ended the war with Britain and France. The Europeans were able to secure major concessions from the Chinese. The Chinese ceded to the British the southern tip of the Kowloon Peninsula, thus greatly expanding their colony of Hong Kong. New treaty ports were added, including Tientsin, the port of Peking. Foreigners gained both the right to travel freely in China and extraterritoriality (meaning that legal disputes involving them would be settled by Western law). China was forced to agree to a low tariff of 5 percent, and opium was included in the taxed goods, thus legalizing the opium trade.

Coding: Clodfelter (2002) describes this as the "Arrow War: 1856–1860," after the ship of that name that was seized by the Chinese—the event that triggered the war. Phillips and Axelrod (2005) call this the "Opium War, Second" of 1856–1860. As noted above, this war is loosely linked to the internal struggle within China called the Taiping Rebellion. This fact may merit special note because the Taiping Rebellion is relatively unknown, despite the fact that the rebellion is the only modern war that comes even close to the number of casualties suffered during the two world wars.

Sources: Clodfelter (2002); Featherstone (1973); Hurd (1967); Michael and Taylor (1964); Phillips and Axelrod (2005).

EXTRA-STATE WAR #345:

The French Conquest of Kabylia of 1856–1857

Participants: France vs. Kabylia
Dates: May 17, 1856, to December [ ], 1857
Battle-Related Deaths: France—1,000; Kabylia—[ ]

Where Fought: Middle East
Initiator: France
Outcome: France wins
War Type: Colonial

Narrative: Kabylia is the predominantly mountainous, Berber-inhabited region of Algeria, lying to the east of Algiers. From there came the people who took over Egypt in the famous Fatimid dynasty of the tenth to the twelfth century. More recently, in the mid-twentieth century, this Berber area was a key part of the Algerian independence war against France.

By 1856 it had almost been a decade since the end of extra-state war #324, in which the Berber forces under Abd el-Kader had been defeated and France secured all Algeria as a French colony. Since then, France had established further European settlements in Algeria and pursued an aggressive military policy against the Kabuli (Kabyle) tribes in the southwest mountain region. Tribal resistance to French rule, however, had been persistent in Kabylia, led by Bou Baghla (Bu Baghla), who had fought with Abd el-Kader in the earlier war. Bou Baghla had even been successful in defeating French forces at Tachekkirt in July 1854. Bou Baghla was killed later that year, and one of Baghla's compatriots, a female mystic named Lalla Fadhma (Fatma), was chosen to replace him as commander (along with her brothers). The French, who were impressed with her spirit referred to her as "Joan of Arc of the Djurdjura" (Naylor 2006, 230).

Meanwhile, France had been involved in the Crimean War (inter-state war #22), and once the war had ended, on March 1, 1856, France could deal with the unrest in Algeria. The French made much of the distinction between the Kabyle and the Arabs, who, led by Abd el-Kader, had waged a lengthy war against the French (extra-state war #324). In contrast, the French felt that Kabylia would remain peaceful if left alone. In the end the French decided to attack the Kabyle, not because they had attacked the French, but because a free Kabylia might encourage the Arab

tendency to revolt (Lorcin 1995, 33). French general Jacques Louis Randon was to lead the mission to pacify Kabylia. On May 17, 1856, France sent a force of 35,000 French soldiers, supported by 10,000 indigenous troops, against the Kabyle forces of about 30,000. The Kabyle were vastly outnumbered and were gradually defeated. The French employed their strategy of total warfare, destroying villages as well as olive and fig groves. In July 1856 Lalla Fadhma was captured. By the end of 1857 the French had established permanent military installations in the region to ensure its control. There were, however, subsequent uprisings in the region against the French in 1858 and 1860, though not at war levels.

Coding: The Kabyle were considered to be inhabitants of the French colony Algeria, so this is treated as a colonial war. Neither Clodfelter (2002) nor Phillips and Axelrod (2005) cover this war.

Sources: Guérard (1959); Lorcin (1995); Naylor (2006); Ruedy (1992); Williams (1907).

EXTRA-STATE WAR #347:

The Indian Mutiny of 1857–1859

Participants: United Kingdom vs. Indian sepoys
Dates: May 10, 1857, to April 7, 1859
Battle-Related Deaths: Indian sepoy rebels—11,500; United Kingdom—11,000
Where Fought: Asia
Initiator: Indian sepoy rebels
Outcome: United Kingdom wins
War Type: Colonial

Narrative: The sepoys were the Indian natives who served in the armies of the British East India Company, and they constituted a large portion of the British armed forces (of the total army of 300,000 men, only 43,000 were British). So it was important for the British to keep the sepoys relatively content; however, the sepoys were gradually becoming restless. The underlying issue may have been the recent British annexation of the kingdom of Oudh in 1856 and the overall denationalizing trend they saw within the British Empire. The sepoys' fear of a loss in their status or of forced religious conversions contributed to a widespread conspiracy within the army to rebel against British domination. Originally an army mutiny, this conflict reached such proportion as to qualify as an Indian war for liberation from the British. The immediate cause of the uprising was the introduction of new rifle cartridges, which had to be bitten apart, and which the sepoys claimed were greased with cow or pig fat, which was against their religion to consume. Dismay about the cartridges began to spread in February 1857, with troops refusing to use the new ammunition.

The war itself broke out in Bengal, where in 1857 there were 118,663 sepoys and only 22,698 regular British soldiers. Cavalry troops who refused to use the cartridges were arrested, and on May 10, 1857, the remaining troops mutinied and stormed the prison. As the British regiments advanced, the mutineers fled to Delhi, where British troops and civilians were slaughtered. All of India was soon beset by fighting. In June a British force advanced toward Delhi and besieged the city, which held a much larger Indian force. Delhi was recaptured by the British on July 20, 1857. The city of Lucknow, the capital city of Oudh, became well known owing to the fact that the British there endured a siege of 133 days, until they received reinforcements, on September 25, 1857, though they were not evacuated until November. Throughout the war the sepoys carried out numerous massacres, and the British responded in kind. Gradually the British began to regain control of India. Lucknow was retaken on March 22, 1858. The final rebel leader was captured on April 7 and executed on April 18, 1859, effectively ending the war, though peace was formally proclaimed on July 8, 1859. Thousands died on both sides, well beyond the combatant battle-death figures. In the end the British prevailed. The rule of India

by the East India Company was replaced by direct rule by the British crown.

Coding: Clodfelter (2002) describes this by the common term, "The Sepoy Mutiny: 1857–59." Phillips and Axelrod (2005) call it the "Indian Mutiny (1857–1858)." Clodfelter also includes, as a single entry, two earlier "Sepoy Mutinies" of 1806 and 1824.

Sources: Clodfelter (2002); Collier (1963); Edwardes (1963); Farwell (1972); Featherstone (1992b); Phillips and Axelrod (2005); Williams (1907).

EXTRA-STATE WAR #349:

The First Franco-Vietnamese War of 1858–1862

Participants: France vs. Vietnam
Dates: August 31, 1858, to June 5, 1862
Battle-Related Deaths: Vietnam—2,500; France—1,500
Where Fought: Asia
Initiator: France
Outcome: France wins
War Type: Imperial

Narrative: After coming to power in France in 1848, Louis-Napoleon (later to become Emperor Napoleon III of France) wanted to increase the power and prestige of France, which during this period could be aided by securing a colonial empire. Thus France had engaged in imperial wars in West Africa (extra-state war #340), North Africa (extra-state war #345), and now finally Asia.

From the seventeenth century onward, the French had attempted to expand their commercial ties in Indochina. In the eighteenth century the area that we now refer to as Vietnam consisted of three entities: Annam (in the center), Tonkin (in the north), and Cochin China (in the south). In 1802, with French support, the three united into the kingdom of Vietnam, and the French developed a supportive relationship with the Vietnamese emperor. After the emperor died, his son was less favorably inclined toward the French, and the French, as well as Europeans in general, began to be persecuted. In 1857 a Spanish bishop was arrested and killed in Tongking. As a result, France and Spain decided to unite to seek reparations for the violence done to their citizens. On August 31, 1858, a French army with Spanish assistance arrived in Indochina. The fleet attacked Da Nang, in the narrow central portion of Vietnam, where the army established a fort. It was besieged and held out for about a year and a half until terrible losses, many of which were due to disease, encouraged the French to abandon the fort in March 1860. Meanwhile, the French fleet had sailed south and attempted another, more successful, probe at Saigon, beginning in February 1859. The citadel there fell after heavy fighting but was then besieged. The French survived the efforts of the Annamites to drive them out, and by 1861 the three upper provinces of Cochin China (which is the southern tip of Annam) were in French possession. On February 25, 1861, in the most intense battle of the war, a French relief force defeated the Annamite forces at nearby Chi Hoa. The French victory was sufficiently decisive that emperor Tu Duc sued for peace and agreed to terms on June 5, 1862, ending the war. By the terms of the treaty, signed in 1863, the emperor recognized French control of three additional provinces, including Saigon. Nonetheless, the French remained harassed for the next eighteen years by persistent guerrilla fighting. In the French colonization of Vietnam, the next war is the Second Franco-Vietnamese War of 1873–1874 (extra-state war #369), as the French extended their colonial control from Cochin China into northern Vietnam.

Coding: Vietnam is coded as an autonomous entity from 1802 to 1887, when a long period of French colonial rule began. In 1887 Annam, Cochin China, Tonkin, and Cambodia were joined together into French Indochina, and Laos was

added in 1893. Clodfelter (2002) describes this as the "Franco-Vietnamese War: 1858–1862." Phillips and Axelrod (2005) refer to the "French Indochina War" of 1858–1863.

Sources: Cady (1954); Clodfelter (2002); Jaques (2007); Kohn (1999); O'Brien (1999); Osborne (1969); Phillips and Axelrod (2005); Schafer (1995); Thompson (1968); Williams (1907).

EXTRA-STATE WAR #350:
The Netherlands-Bone War of 1859–1860

Participants: Netherlands vs. Bone
Dates: February 20, 1859, to January 20, 1860
Battle-Related Deaths: Netherlands—500; Bone—500
Where Fought: Asia
Initiator: Netherlands
Outcome: Netherlands wins
War Type: Imperial

Narrative: Bone (or Boni) was an indigenous monarchy in the southwestern area of the island of Sulawesi (also known as Celebes). It remained autonomous from 1492 to 1905 but was eventually absorbed into the Dutch East Indies (present-day Indonesia).

The Netherlands had been attempting to expand its colonial empire throughout Southeast Asia. In that pursuit it had fought extrastate wars #313 against Java in 1825 and war #334 against Bali in 1848. The resultant Dutch shipping was a target for the Bone, who harassed Dutch ships for years, despite growing Dutch warnings. In 1824 the Dutch organized a military attack to punish the Bone, and the conflict ended in 1838, when the Bone reaffirmed the Treaty of Bungaya, which reflected acquiescence to the Dutch. When the Bone king died on February 16, 1859, he was succeeded by King Besse Kajura, who refused to accept Dutch domination. Thus the Netherlands decided to undertake a military expedition, partially to deter other states from joining the Bone. The Dutch forces stationed at Makassar, a city in South Sulawesi, were augmented by a Dutch fleet from Java. The Dutch were able to land troops at Bajoa despite heavy Bone resistance. The expedition advanced into the interior and seized the capital, though the queen had fled. The Dutch withdrew in April, and a garrison they left behind was soon decimated by disease. Consequently, they planned a second, larger expedition in November 1859. The Dutch landed on November 28, 1859, and advanced to the Boni capital of Watampone, though the queen had fled. The Bone representatives surrendered, ending the war on January 20, 1860. In the treaty signed on February 13, 1860, Bone was reduced to feudal status, with the Dutch appointing Aru Palaka as the new king. Conflict between the Bone and the Dutch flared up again in 1905–1906 (though at below war level).

Coding: Clodfelter (2002) and Phillips and Axelrod (2005) do not cover this war. Hall gives it one sentence.

Sources: Brecke (1999); De Klerk (1938); Hall (1981); ter Keurs (2007); O'Brien (1999); Richardson (1960a); Ricklefs (1993).

EXTRA-STATE WAR #351:
The Argentine-Buenos Aires War of 1859

Participants: Argentina vs. Buenos Aires
Dates: May 29, 1859, to October 23, 1859
Battle-Related Deaths: Argentina—500; Buenos Aires—500
Where Fought: W. Hemisphere
Initiator: Argentina
Outcome: Argentina wins
War Type: Imperial

Narrative: Argentina attained its independence from Spain in 1816 but did not become a state system member until January 1, 1841. While under Spanish rule, the province of Buenos Aires, or Río de la Plata, had its own administration, and it was subject to the Spanish viceroy in Peru until 1776, when it became the capital of the new Viceroyalty of Río de la Plata (which included much of Argentina, Uruguay, Paraguay, and Bolivia). The people of the city of Buenos Aires, however, were in many ways distinct from those in the periphery of the region, and during the early years these differences led to conflict. The province of Buenos Aires, stretching far to the south and west from the city, was often opposed to the port of Buenos Aires. The provincials did not want to be ruled by the *porteños* (people of the port of Buenos Aires), and the *porteños* did not want to be ruled by provincials. Owing to this conflict, the city of Buenos Aires became an autonomous entity in 1827–1831 and again in 1852, when the city refused to participate in a national congress and seceded from Argentina. Consequently, the 400,000 people of Buenos Aires were in an autonomous entity, separate from the rest of Argentina, which had about 1,000,000 people.

Fighting, at below war level, between Buenos Aires and the Argentine province of Buenos Aires began in 1852 as the city was besieged. The siege collapsed in 1855, and Buenos Aires and the United Provinces signed a peace treaty, which was not honored. On May 29, 1859, the Argentine officials authorized their military leader, Gen. Justo José de Urquíza, who had participated in extra-state war #327 and inter-state war #19, to recapture Buenos Aires by force. Buenos Aires established a blockade in an attempt to prevent the Argentine force from advancing up the Paraná River; nevertheless, Urquíza's 10,000 troops were able to fight past the fortifications and marched on Buenos Aires, defended by about 8,300 troops. In a battle at Cépeda on October 23, 1859, the Argentine forces prevailed, ending the war. The Buenos Aires governor resigned, and as a result of the war, Buenos Aires was reunited with the Argentine Confederation on November 11, 1859.

Coding: Clodfelter (2002) describes a period of "Argentine Civil Wars: 1851–76," without trying to separate out each war. Phillips and Axelrod (2005) have an "Argentine Civil War (1851–1861)."

Sources: Clodfelter (2002); *Columbia Encyclopedia* (1993); Herring (1966); Phillips and Axelrod (2005); Schafer (1995); Scheina (2003a).

EXTRA-STATE WAR #352:
The Garibaldi Expedition of 1860

Participants: Two Sicilies vs. Garibaldi's Redshirts
Dates: May 11, 1860, to October 14, 1860
Battle-Related Deaths: Two Sicilies—4,500; Redshirts—1,500
Where Fought: Europe
Initiator: Redshirts
Outcome: Transformed into inter-state war #37
War Type: Imperial

Narrative: This war continued the process of the unification of Italy that had played a prominent role in the Austro-Sardinian War of 1848–1849 (inter-state #10), the War of the Roman Republic of 1849 (inter-state #16), and the War of Italian Unification of 1859 (inter-state #28). In the latter war Sardinia/Piedmont, with French help, had captured much of northern Italy from Austria. Giuseppe Garibaldi had participated in this war within the army of the king of Sardinia. Soon thereafter, Garibaldi and his "Thousand Redshirts" launched what was to be one of his most well-known accomplishments, the conquest of the kingdom of Two Sicilies (including Naples). Though this expedition had the support of Sardinian king Victor Emmanuel II, it was really a private expedition by a nonstate actor against a system member, Two Sicilies (Sicily and Naples, system member #329). Thus this war is classified as an extra-state war.

Sicily had already begun a rebellion against its Bourbon king, Francis II. The rebels called for assistance in the name of Italian unity, and Garibaldi responded. On May 11, 1860,

Garibaldi landed in Sicily with his 1,000 irregulars and conquered the island in spectacular fashion. His forces were augmented by 3,000 to 10,000 Sicilians, including the *picciotti* (Sicilian guerrillas) and a band of 100 led by a monk. The Redshirts, however, conducted most of the fighting against numerically superior royal forces. By the beginning of June, Garibaldi had captured Palermo, and then Milazzo later that month. After liberating Sicily, Garibaldi crossed over to the mainland and began driving the royal forces north toward Naples. On September 5 King Francis II announced his decision to leave Naples and move northward to the coastal resort of Gaeta (between Naples and Rome). Naples surrendered to Garibaldi on September 7. Though the populace hailed Garibaldi as their liberator, Garibaldi remained loyal to King Victor Emmanuel II and ultimately handed Sicily over to the emerging Italy. The army of King Francis withdrew from Naples as well and headed northward, where it was able to regroup, later defeating the Garibaldians near the Volturno River on September 12. King Francis hoped to crush Garibaldi and return to Naples in triumph. Thus on October 1 the 31,000 Bourbon troops attacked the 21,000 Garibaldians. After a daylong battle, reserves arrived to bolster the Garibaldian forces, which were ultimately victorious. The royal army retreated to Capua. Meanwhile Prime Minister Camillo Paolo Filippo Giulio Benso, Count of Cavour, whose Sardinian army had defeated the papal forces in the Italian-Roman War of 1860 (inter-state war #34), had decided that Garibaldi was under the influence of the revolutionary radicals and thus had to be stopped. Therefore, he sent the Sardinian army south from Rome to take over the fighting against the king of Two Sicilies. The Sardinian army took over the bulk of the fighting, thus ending the extra-state war and transforming it into inter-state war #37, the Neapolitan War, which starts the next day.

Coding: As of May 1860, COW codes the following Italian states as system members: Sardinia/Piedmont (#325), Papal States (#327), and Two Sicilies (#329). Our coding of the wars in Italy in 1860– 1861 is determined by the characteristics of the major combatants, causing the period to encompass three distinct wars: extra-state war #352, the Garibaldi Expedition between Garibaldi's Redshirts and the Two Sicilies; inter-state war #34, the Italian-Roman War between Sardinia and the Papal States; and inter-state war #37, the Neapolitan War between Sardinia and the Two Sicilies. The date September 7, 1860, marks the first day of the MID #112, which precedes the Italian-Roman War by only four days. Sardinia is the initiator and revisionist state in this MID, opposed by France and the Papal States. Clodfelter (2002, 204–205) describes the entire period of 1859–1861 as one war, the "Italian Risorgimento." Phillips and Axelrod (2005) divide this period into two wars: "Garibaldi's Invasion of Sicily" and "The Italian War of Independence."

Sources: Case (1970); Harbottle (1904); King (1899); Nolan (1865); Phillips and Axelrod (2005); Thayer (1911).

EXTRA-STATE WAR #353:

The Spanish–Santo Dominican War of 1863–1865

Participants: Spain vs. Santo Domingo
Dates: April [ ], 1863, to May 3, 1865
Battle-Related Deaths: Spain and local militia—28,000; Santo Domingo—4,000
Where Fought: W. Hemisphere
Initiator: Spain
Outcome: Santo Domingo wins
War Type: Colonial

Narrative: This is a war between Spain and its colony of Santo Domingo, on the large Caribbean island of Hispañola. Today the island contains the Dominican Republic on the eastern side, while the western region is Haiti. Haiti, which had been a French colony, became a member of the interstate system in 1859, and the Dominican Republic, formerly a Spanish colony, joined the system in 1894.

Spain's activities on the island had begun with the explorations of Christopher Columbus (1492) and were followed by the founding of the city of Santo Domingo by Christopher's brother Bartholomew Columbus in 1496. The city became the seat of the Spanish Captaincy-General of Santo Domingo, which administered the Spanish Caribbean islands. In 1697 the Spanish, who were unable to control all of Hispañola, ceded the western one-third of it to France. In 1795 the Spanish gave up the whole island to the French, though Spanish control over the eastern portion was restored after a rebellion against the French in 1808–1809. The Spanish were ousted in 1821, and by 1822 the Haitians controlled the whole island. In 1844, however, the Haitians were expelled from the east and the Dominican Republic was proclaimed. The Dominican Republic was an autonomous entity from 1844 to 1861, when it fell back under Spanish colonial control during the American Civil War.

In March 1861 internal fighting within the Dominican Republic, plus a threat of invasion from Haiti, reached a point at which one of the Dominican leaders, Pedro Santana, invited the Spanish to return. The Spanish sent an army to recolonize the area, and the Spanish queen appointed Pedro Santana her governor of the colony. Santana reportedly told the Spanish queen, "I have made you an immensely valuable gift, for I have given you a people without journalists and devoid of lawyers" (Scheina 2003a, 347). There were, however, those who opposed Spanish rule on the island, similar to the independence movements throughout the Spanish colonial empire. In 1862, as Spanish rule became increasingly unpopular, Santana resigned, and his replacement was unsuccessful in stopping the growing guerrilla warfare.

By February 1863 the Spanish authorities considered Santo Domingo to be under siege because of the spreading guerrilla attacks. In April the Spaniards engaged, and defeated, a contingent of

Dominican revolutionaries at Cibao, which marks the start of the war. In September reinforcements arrived from Spain and Pedro Santana was recalled to lead the offensive against the rebels. Santana's offensive stalled at Monte Plata. Rebel forces continued to attack, and the Spanish authorities refused to send more troops. Santana died on June 14, 1864; however, the guerrilla warfare persisted, though yellow fever continued to take a heavy toll. A relief mission from Santiago de Cuba arrived and was able to capture Monte Cristi, which was the only major Spanish victory. The Spanish retreated to Santo Domingo, and on May 3, 1865, the Spanish queen authorized the abandonment of the colony, which marks the end of the war.

Since then, the Dominican Republic has remained an autonomous entity and entered the state system in 1894. In the twentieth century the Dominican Republic remained subject to occasional interventions, invasions, and occupations by the United States. The Dominican Republic was militarily occupied by the United States from 1916 to 1925. A one-family dictatorship, that of the Trujillos, took over, and unstable conditions at the end of their rule led to another U.S. invasion and occupation in 1965–1966.

Coding: Clodfelter (2002) and Scheina (2003a) describe this as the "War of the Restoration." Phillips and Axelrod (2005) and Kohn (1999) do not cover this war.

Sources: Clarke (1906); Clodfelter (2002); *Columbia Encyclopedia* (1993); Herring (1966); *New York Times* (1863–1865); Schafer (1995); Scheina (2003a).

EXTRA-STATE WAR #355:
The British-Maori War of 1863–1866

Participants: United Kingdom vs. New Zealand Maori
Dates: June 4, 1863, to January 14, 1866
Battle-Related Deaths: New Zealand Maori— 2,000; United Kingdom—700

Where Fought: Oceania
Initiator: United Kingdom
Outcome: United Kingdom wins
War Type: Colonial

Narrative: The Maori are the indigenous people of New Zealand. New Zealand was visited three times by British captain James Cook between 1769 and 1778, followed by a period of trading and European settlement. The Maori were organized as tribes, and a period of intertribal warfare between 1815 and 1840 led to tens of thousands of deaths (non-state war #1500). In 1840 the first British settlement was established at Wellington, and the same year the Treaty of Waitangi guaranteed Maori lands in exchange for their recognition of British sovereignty. As the number of European settlers increased, however, so did the Maori opposition, leading to antiforeign conflicts in 1843–1848 (at below war levels). As the British colonial government structure developed, the Maori were unhappy about the policies enabling the government acquisition of Maori lands. When a tribe resisted the confiscation of land, it was attacked by the British in March 1860. Overall, the conflict lasted for over twelve years (1860–1872) but consisted of only occasional periods of significant hostilities. During the first year there was stiff Maori resistance to British advances mostly in the Taranaki region of the North Island, but after a British victory at Te Arei on March 18, 1861, the Maori surrendered and a cease-fire was established. Since fatality levels did not meet the war threshold during this period, this phase is not included in the extra-state war. The war begins when hostilities resumed, in 1863.

On June 4, 1863, the British attacked a fortified *pa* (or temporary fort) near Katikara and were successful in defeating the Maori. The British were similarly successful in heavy fighting at Koheroa in July, and at Rangiriri in November 1863, where the local Maori surrendered. Conflict continued elsewhere in 1864 with a string of British victories, though the Maori

235

were successful in repulsing a British attack against Gate Pa on April 29, 1864. The next day 200 warriors from the religious Hauhau led an assault on the British at Sentry Hill. The Hauhau had assumed that they were immune to bullets, and consequently suffered significant casualties. The final battle at Otapawa also ended in a British victory, in January 1866. Hostilities then tapered off, though they resumed again from 1868 to 1872 (though at below war levels). Combatant battle-related deaths for this war are relatively low, yet it has been estimated that during the entire decade of hostilities, the Maori lost 54 percent of their population, or at least 27,000 people (Phillips and Axelrod 2005, 1122).

Coding: COW codes New Zealand as a British colony from 1840 till 1920 and as a state system member after that. We have no other entities on that archipelago, since no statelike organizations had formed there among the indigenous people (Schafer 1995). Clodfelter (2002) describes the "Maori Wars: 1843–46, 1860–1872." Phillips and Axelrod (2005) separate out three distinct wars: the "First Taranaki (1860–1861)," the "Second Taranaki (1863–1864)," and the "Third Taranaki (1864–1872)."

Sources: Belich (1986); Clodfelter (2002); Featherstone (1973); Jaques (2007); Kohn (1999); Langer (1952); Phillips and Axelrod (2005); Schafer (1995); Sinclair (1980); Turbull (1975).

EXTRA-STATE WAR #356:
The Shimonoseki War 1863–1864

Participants: Choshu Daimyo of Japan vs. France, Netherlands, United Kingdom, United States
Dates: June 25, 1863, to September 7, 1864
Battle-Related Deaths: Choshu—1,000; United Kingdom—13; France—6; United States—5; Netherlands—2
Where Fought: Asia
Initiator: Choshu Daimyo
Outcome: France, Netherlands, United Kingdom, and United States win
War Type: Imperial

Narrative: The shogun was the feudal military leader who administered Japan as the emperor's military deputy and was in essence the ruler of Japan. The shogunate was held by various Japanese families. The Tokugawa family was the last of the shoguns, ruling in Tokyo from 1603 until 1867. The daimyo were the feudal landowning families, who owed allegiance to the Tokugawa but were allowed great autonomy in their own domains. From 1858 to 1868 some of the more powerful daimyo were the western daimyo, including Choshu, whose territory stretched along the Shimonoseki Strait that separates the island of Kyushu from Honshu, the central island of Japan. The Choshu came into conflict with the shogun partly over disagreements on how to deal with foreign vessels. Adm. Matthew Perry had "opened" Japan in 1853, and the subsequent unequal treaties with Great Britain, France, and Russia had engendered hostility within Japan toward foreigners. The Choshu were part of a group that favored expelling foreigners from Japan.

In line with their antiforeign sentiments, the Choshu daimyo attacked an American ship in the Strait of Shimonoseki on June 25, 1863. Similar attacks took place against French, British, and Dutch ships as well. Initially, the Americans responded by sinking Choshu ships, and the French attacked a village; however, as the attacks by the Japanese continued, the Americans and French destroyed the fort at Shimonoseki in July, though it was quickly rebuilt. In 1864 the British were able to persuade France, the Netherlands, and the United States that a joint expedition would be necessary to halt the attacks. On September 5, 1864, an allied fleet began a three-day bombardment of the Choshu coast, leading to fatalities that were overwhelmingly one-sided. As a result, a treaty was negotiated ensuring free passage for shipping in the strait.

Another consequence of this war was that Choshu decided to modernize its military along Western lines. These Western-type forces would soon enable the daimyo to overthrow the shogun (in intra-state war #588), thus ushering in the modern imperial era, which would dominate Japan from 1868 to 1945.

Coding: This war is classified as extra-state because the Choshu were neither directed by nor acting on behalf of the Japanese government, with which they were, in fact, in conflict. Thus Choshu is considered to be a nonstate entity. Clodfelter (2002) treats the fighting in the Shimonoseki Strait as part of the 1863–1869 armed conflicts of the Meiji Restoration. Phillips and Axelrod (2005) join us in calling it the "Shimonoseki War" of 1863–1864.

Sources: Beasley (1955); Clodfelter (2002); Craig (1961); Dumas and Vedel-Peterson (1923); Fairbank et al. (1958, 1960); Featherstone (1973); Fox (1969); Frédéric (2002); Kohn (1999); Michael and Taylor (1964); Phillips and Axelrod (2005); Schafer (1995).

EXTRA-STATE WAR #357:
The British Umbeyla Campaign of 1863

Participants: United Kingdom vs. Pathan tribe
Dates: October 20, 1863, to December 21, 1863
Battle-Related Deaths: Pathan tribes—1,500;
 United Kingdom—900
Where Fought: Asia
Initiator: United Kingdom
Outcome: United Kingdom wins
War Type: Imperial

Narrative: This is a war that took place near the Buner Valley in what became in 1902 the North-West Frontier province of India. The area (also known as the Brunewals) was inhabited by the Pathan (Pashtun) tribe, and was annexed by Pakistan after its partition from India in 1947. More recently, it is an area made famous in the twenty-first century as a sanctuary for forces loyal to Osama bin Laden.

In the 1860s this region was a problem area for the British, since it bordered the frontier of the growing British colony of India. This war represented a British attempt to secure the borders of the British Empire against the Pathan, who had since 1849 launched raids into British territory. In 1863 the particular problem was a group of Pathan the British simply called the "Hindustani fanatics," because they were followers of Sayyid Ahmad. Sayyid Ahmad had used religious appeals to arouse his followers to pursue a jihad against the British unbelievers. In 1862 the sayyid's followers had begun an attack against the British, who, in response, had initiated a general blockade of the region. This action encouraged other tribes to join with sayyid's followers to oppose the British. The British then decided to undertake a military campaign against those who were raiding into British India. The mission was named the Umbeyla (Ambela) Campaign after the strategic pass where most of the fighting occurred.

In October 1863, 9,000 British and Indian troops began the expedition under the command of Neville Chamberlain. The British forces were divided into two groups, one of which would go through the Umbeyla Pass, while the other would wait in Topi. With great difficulty, the troops wended their way through the pass and established a base at two high spots, Crag Picket and Eagle's Nest, from which the British could fire down into the valley. The long trek had deprived the expedition of the element of surprise, and thousands of tribesmen were amassing against them. The British were surrounded and pinned down for over a month. Finally the 6,000 tribesmen advanced against the British, and Crag Picket was attacked four times and overrun three times, earning itself the name "Place of Slaughter." After six weeks the British received reinforcements and went on the offensive into the Chamla Valley. A smaller force advanced further and demolished the Pathan stronghold at Malka and thus suppressed the raiding for a while. The British refrained from attacking the Pathan again until the Bruner campaign of 1897 (extra-state war #412). In all, the British undertook fifty-four expeditions against the frontier tribes between 1849 and 1902 (Spain 1963, 174).

Coding: Clodfelter (2002) also calls this the "Umbeyla Campaign" of 1863. Phillips and Axelrod (2005) do not cover it.

Sources: Caroe (1958); Clodfelter (2002); Farwell (1972); Featherstone (1973); Sivard (1991); Spain (1963).

EXTRA-STATE WAR #359:
Russian-Kokand War of 1864–1865

Participants: Russia vs. Kokand
Dates: April 24, 1864, to June 17, 1865
Battle-Related Deaths: Kokand—1,500; Russia—120
Where Fought: Asia
Initiator: Russia
Outcome: Russia wins
War Type: Imperial

Narrative: Kokand was the capital city of an Uzbek-speaking, Sunni Muslim kingdom (the Khanate of Kokand) located in the mountainous region of Central Asia, along the upper reaches of the Syr-Daria River that flows to the Aral Sea. In the middle of the eighteenth century, Kokand became independent of Bukhara and was an autonomous entity from 1740 to 1867, when it was absorbed into Russia. The area remained Russian or Soviet until 1991, and today this area includes Kirgizia and Tajikistan.

In the nineteenth century Russia was interested in expanding its influence in Central Asia, including in Khiva, Kokand, and Bukhara, which were kingdoms with ill-defined borders and which were frequently at war with one another. Responding to a relative power vacuum in the region, and in order to forestall British expansionism, Russian expeditions had been undertaken in 1839 and 1847, though they were generally unsuccessful in expanding Russian control. During this period, Kokand was also involved in wars against China (non-state wars #1515 and #1533). The Russians began another

campaign against Kokand in April 1864 with a relatively small force of 4,000 men. Kokand had a regular army of 12,000 men plus another 28,000 irregulars. Thus the Russian advances were generally confronted by superior numbers, though the Kokand forces were generally neither well trained nor well armed. Even though the Russians were able to defeat the Kokand troops at Chimkent (near Tashkent) on July 19–22, 1864, they ultimately retreated when they realized that they had insufficient troops to storm the fortified city.

A reinforced Russian army returned to Chimkent in September 1864 and quickly captured the city on September 22. The Russians then advanced toward Tashkent, though they suffered a minor defeat in December at Ikan. Consequently, they developed an alternative strategy. Russia's official policy was of nonintervention in Kokand, as long as Kokand was peaceful; however, given the instability in the region, Russia developed a plan to gain a foothold in Central Asia by promoting the independence of the commercially important city of Tashkent from Kokand. The Russians would foment the independence movement in Tashkent and then send in Russian troops to guarantee the success of the rebellion. Tashkent could then be used as a base for Russian armed forces. Thus on April 24, 1865, Russian troops headed for Tashkent. When they arrived, the pro-Russian independence movement was unable to act, so on May 7 the Russians laid siege to the city. On May 19, 1865, near Tashkent, the Russian force of 1,300 men defeated the 6,000-man army of Alim Kul, the Kokand commander, who was killed in the battle. A reinforced Russian army launched a final attack in June 1865 against the Tashkent fortifications. Tashkent surrendered on June 17, thus ending the war. The Russians were then faced with the issue of what to do with Kokand. Their initial plan had not been to occupy it directly but instead to utilize it as a buffer zone against Bukhara. In fact, the Russian war against Bukhara would begin the next year (extra-state war

#361). The issue of Russian-Kokand relations would reemerge in extra-state war #371.

Coding: Clodfelter (2002) mentions this as part of the "Russian Conquests in Central Asia: 1839–85."

Sources: Abedin (1988); Becker (1968); Clodfelter (2002); Hopkirk (1992); Khalfin (1964); Palmer (1957); Seton-Watson (1967); Sorokin (1937); Wieczynski (1977).

EXTRA-STATE WAR #360:
The British-Bhutanese War of 1865

Participants: United Kingdom vs. Bhutan
Dates: January [ ], 1865, to November 11, 1865
Battle-Related Deaths: Bhutan—900; United Kingdom—100
Where Fought: Asia
Initiator: United Kingdom
Outcome: United Kingdom wins
War Type: Imperial

Narrative: Assam was an independent Buddhist entity that had sustained its own independence from 1492 until 1819. But then Burma, in an expansionist period, was able to capture Assam and make it part of Burma from 1819 to 1824. Burma then committed a major strategic error in attacking British India (see extra-state war #310). In the Treaty of Yandabo, which ended that war, Burma was forced to cede Assam to Britain, and Assam was incorporated into British India in 1826. Britain and Burma fought a second war in 1852 (extra-state war #339), by which southern Burma became a British colony.

After Assam was incorporated into British India, border disputes began with Assam's neighbor to the north, Bhutan, which had been an autonomous entity since 1700. Particularly in the early 1860s, Bhutan seized various mountain passes from Assam (British India) and ignored Assamese and British objections and demands for compensation. In 1863 the British sent a delegation to Bhutan to discuss the territory and the British subjects who had been seized in the

raids. The mission was a complete failure, and the British envoy was forced to sign an agreement surrendering the lands under dispute to Bhutan. In response to this outrage, the British viceroy of India, Sir John Lawrence, declared war on Bhutan in November 1864. The war began in January 1865, when the British invaded Bhutan with a small force. The British expedition was unsuccessful and included a rout of British forces on February 5, 1865, and the seizure of the British garrison at Dewangiri. A second punitive expedition by the much larger Bhutan Field Force engaged in fierce fighting in March 1865. The British were able to recapture Dewangiri and gradually suppressed the Bhutanese, who agreed to peace on November 11, 1865. Bhutan was thereby reduced to a British protectorate from 1865 to 1949, after which it was an Indian protectorate for twenty-two years, until 1971.

Coding: Clodfelter (2002) describes the entire period of 1864–1865 as the "Bhutan War." Phillips and Axelrod (2005) refer to the "Bhutan War (1865)"

Sources: Clodfelter (2002); Collister (1987); Dorji (1995); Featherstone (1973); Gupta (1974); Kohn (1999); Phillips and Axelrod (2005); Williams (1907).

EXTRA-STATE WAR #361:
Russian – Bukharan War of 1866

Participants: Russia vs. Bukhara
Dates: January 12, 1866, to October 18, 1866
Battle-Related Deaths: Bukhara—1,000; Russia—100
Where Fought: Asia
Initiator: Russia
Outcome: Russia wins
War Type: Imperial

Narrative: Bukhara, like the more famous Samarkand, is a city between the Amu-Daria and Syr-Daria rivers in Central Asia, to the southeast of the Aral Sea. It is one of the oldest units in the COW States, Nations and Entities dataset, being an autonomous entity from 1492 to 1867, when it was absorbed into the Russian czarist empire by conquest.

After completing its war against Kokand in 1865 (extra-state war #359), Russia turned its attention southwestward, toward Bukhara. Russian control of Kokand had proven to be more difficult than the Russians had expected, partially because of Bukharan raids into Kokand and their demand for the withdrawal of Russian troops. Initially, the Russians tried to negotiate with Bukhara's Emir Muzaffar ad-Din; however, talks broke down over the emir's demand for control of Kokand. The Russians were also concerned about the possibility of the emir organizing an anti-Russian coalition among Bukhara, Kokand, Khiva, Shahr-i Sabz, and Afghanistan. Russia's suspicions were heightened when the emir seized the Russian diplomatic mission in December 1865. In January 1866, in an attempt to intimidate the emir, the Russians launched a small expedition against Bukhara. When the emir refused to be intimidated, the Russians crossed the Syr-Daria River in force. The Russian efforts to take the fort at Dzhizak failed, and they were forced to withdraw back across the river. Skirmishes between the forces of Russia and Bukhara continued. In April 1866, when the emir evaded the question of releasing the Russian envoys, the Russians resumed military action. A major battle took place at Irdzhar on May 8, 1866, where the Bukharan forces were defeated. Negotiations between the Russians and the emir were resumed, but when the emir failed to accept the Russian terms, the Russians launched another invasion on September 23, quickly seizing Bukharan territory. The war ended in October 1866, and a short-lived peace agreement was signed in 1867.

The Bukharans were unhappy with the prospect of permanent Russian domination and tried to forge an alliance of the Central Asian states with the Ottoman Empire and Britain against Russia. A Bukharan Muslim cleric declared a holy war against Russia, leading to renewed conflict between Russia and Bukhara in May and June 1868, though at below war levels. Russia had disavowed any plans for territorial expansion, but by 1868 it had gained control over large portions of Central Asia.

Coding: Clodfelter only briefly mentions this war in his entry "Russian Conquests in Central Asia: 1839–1885."

Sources: Abedin (1988); Becker (1968); Clodfelter (2002); Hopkirk (1992); Khalfin (1964); Sivard (1991); Wieczynski (1977).

EXTRA-STATE WAR #362:
The British-Ethiopian War of 1867–1868

Participants: United Kingdom vs. Ethiopians
Dates: December [ ], 1867, to April 13, 1868
Battle-Related Deaths: Ethiopians—800; United Kingdom—400
Where Fought: Africa
Initiator: United Kingdom
Outcome: United Kingdom wins
War Type: Imperial

Narrative: Ethiopia was an autonomous entity from 1492 to 1700, after which it was disaggregated into separate areas (including, from north to south, Tigre, Gondar, Amhara, Gojjam, and Shoa). It remained disunited like this for almost two centuries, until 1885, when Ethiopia was united again as an autonomous entity. Even when disunited, Ethiopia had at its core a national Ethiopian Christian Church, which, along with the church-educated elite, kept alive a dream of national unity. As early as the 1850s, unification had begun under Emperor Tewodros II (Theodore the Second), who, starting from a base in Gondar, seized a number of dissident areas in the period from 1852 to 1855.

Things did not go as smoothly for Tewodros II on the international front. Tewodros asked Queen Victoria for British aid, and when the queen did not respond, Tewodros seized British officials, thereby triggering this war with Britain in 1867. The queen was not amused and sent an Anglo-Indian force of 13,000 troops to rescue the imprisoned consular officers. The British landed at Zula, on the coast, and worked their way 400 miles inland. In a battle at Arogi on April 10, 1868, the British decisively defeated the Ethiopian army. The column then stormed the emperor's fortress at nearby Magdala on April 13. Tewodros committed suicide, and the British rescued the captives, ending the war. The British withdrew, and the Ethiopian state endured and was later one of the indigenous sub-Saharan African states to survive and become a member of the League of Nations.

Coding: Clodfelter (2002) calls this the "British-Abyssinian War" of 1867–1868. Phillips and Axelrod (2005) call it the "British Expedition in Ethiopia (British-Abyssinian War)" of 1867–1868.

Sources: Clodfelter (2002); Farwell (1972); Featherstone (1973); Jaques (2007; Marcus (2001); Oliver and Atmore (1994); Phillips and Axelrod (2005); Sorokin (1937).

EXTRA-STATE WAR #363:
The First Spanish-Cuban War of 1868–1878

Participants: Spain vs. Cuba
Dates: October 10, 1868, to February 11, 1878
Battle-Related Deaths: Spain—100,000; Cuba—50,000
Where Fought: W. Hemisphere
Initiator: Cuba
Outcome: Spain wins
War Type: Colonial

Narrative: Although Christopher Columbus visited Cuba in 1492, the Spanish conquest of the island did not really begin until the establishment of several settlements in 1511. Cuba was at times a target for pirates or European powers, but it generally prospered under Spanish rule and thus remained a Spanish colony while other Spanish colonies sought their independence. In fact, as the independence movements succeeded in South America and Central America, many of the royalists from these newly independent countries fled to Cuba. The desire for independence, however, ultimately developed in Cuba, as well, as a result of Spanish taxation and slavery policies. The success of the Spanish Revolution (intra-state war #591) in September 1868 in overthrowing the autocratic Isabella II inspired the Cubans seeking independence.

On October 9, 1868, Carlos Manuel de Céspes, supported by thirty-eight Cuban planters, proclaimed a revolution at Yara in the southeast. The initial group of revolutionaries included refugees from Santo Domingo and a number of foreign adventurers. They had hoped for a widespread popular uprising, which did not materialize, and the war that began the next day settled into a long-term guerrilla conflict. On October 18 the small rebel force was able to seize the town of Bayamo (in southeast Oriente Province), where they established their base. The rebels faced a Spanish army of 7,000 troops, which ultimately became a force of 95,000 men. In 1869 a revolutionary republic was proclaimed, which abolished slavery and favored Cuban annexation to the United States. The Spanish began digging a ditch from the south to the north of the island in an attempt to barricade the rebels in the eastern region. Most of the war consisted of raids and reprisals, though there were occasional naval exchanges with Cuban ships running the Spanish blockade. One of the few large-scale battles began on February 19, 1874, when the revolutionaries attacked westward. Fighting continued until March 18, when the Spanish retreated after having suffered significant losses, though the revolutionaries ultimately returned to the eastern side of the island.

By 1876 the Third Carlist War in Spain (intra-state war #597) had ended and the Spanish were able to send additional troops to Cuba. Consequently, the rebels began to suffer significant losses. Spain also began to ameliorate its policies in Cuba, promising reforms and an end to slavery. The rebels had tired of fighting, and the Treaty of Zanjón ended the war on February 11, 1878. As a result of the Spanish victory, Cuban independence was delayed by twenty years. Cuban independence would require two more wars, namely, extra-state war #404, the Second Spanish-Cuban War of 1895–1898, and inter-state war #79, the Spanish-American War of 1898.

Coding: This war, also known as the Ten Years War, was the deadliest extra-state war in the nineteenth century, with many combatants dying from disease (which was common). Clodfelter (2002) and Phillips and Axelrod (2005) refer to this war as the "Ten Years War."

Sources: Barrios y Carrion (1888–1890); Beals (1933); Bethell (1993); Carr (1982); Clarke (1906); Clodfelter (2002); Guerra y Sanchez (1950); Payne (1967); Phillips and Axelrod (2005); Ponte Dominguez (1958); Scheina (2003a).

EXTRA-STATE WAR #364:
The Attack on Bahr el-Ghazal of 1869–1870

Participants: Egypt vs. Bahr el-Ghazal
Dates: [ ]/[ ]/1869, to [ ]/[ ]/1870
Battle-Related Deaths: Bahr el-Ghazal—1,500; Egypt—[ ]
Where Fought: Middle East
Initiator: Egypt
Outcome: Bahr el-Ghazal wins
War Type: Imperial

Narrative: In 1869 the khedive of Egypt sent Samuel Baker to lead an expeditionary force to try to expand Egyptian control in southern Sudan, especially the Bahr el-Ghazal region. The purported aim of the expedition was to try to suppress the slave trade, especially that controlled by Zubayr (Zobeir, Zubair) Pasha. For many years there had been a profitable slave trade between Egypt and Bahr el-Ghazal in southern Sudan (see extra-state war #307 and

intra-state war #507), and the slave trade had significantly depopulated the area. Now, under pressure from European public opinion, Egypt was trying to find alternative commerce for the region. Baker's expedition met with only limited success. Baker did advance along the upper Nile as far as Unyoro, and he did start the process to suppress the slave trade; however, in 1870 the Egyptian army suffered a defeat at the hand of Zubayr Pasha (ending the war). By 1874 Zubayr Pasha controlled much of Darfur. Egypt negotiated the incorporation of Bahr el-Ghazal into Egypt, with Zubayr as governor. He finally ended up as a counselor to the British regime in Sudan in 1899.

Coding: Charles Gordon would lead a similar expedition in 1878–1879 (extra-state war #375). These campaigns provoked the war by the Mahdi in 1881, who wanted to purify Islam and end Egyptian control in the Sudan.

Sources: Bouthoul and Carrere (1978–1979); Brecke (1999); Langer (1952); "Mohammedanism and Slave-Trade in Africa" (1888); Stearns (2001); Wickens (1970).

EXTRA-STATE WAR #365:
The Ottoman Conquest of Arabia of 1870–1872

Participants: Ottoman Empire vs. Yemen, Asir, Hasa
Dates: November 30, 1870, to December 30, 1872
Battle-Related Deaths: Ottoman Empire—4,000; Yemen, Asir, Hasa—1,500
Where Fought: Middle East
Initiator: Asir
Outcome: Ottoman Empire wins
War Type: Imperial

Narrative: Although much of the Arabian Peninsula had once been part of the Ottoman Empire, the decline in Ottoman power and its general neglect of the area in the seventeenth and eighteenth centuries had led to the situation in the nineteenth century where the Ottoman

Empire ruled little of the Arabian Peninsula except for the Hejaz, the location of the Muslim holy cities of Mecca and Medina. The Ottomans wanted to restore their position in the region and began a series of diplomatic negotiations and military expeditions to restore their control (see extra-state wars #301, #338, and #342). Through these wars the Ottomans established footholds along the Red Sea coast. In 1870 they decided to expand their control into central Arabia (Najd), in al-Hasa (on the eastern coast), and along the western Red Sea coast (to Asir and Yemen). This undertaking was partly prompted by an 1869 uprising of the Asir tribe that could have threatened the Ottoman foothold at the port of Hodeida (Hudaydah). It was also made easier by the recent opening of the Suez Canal, which facilitated the shipping of troops from Constantinople to Hodeida.

This war included two general expeditions by the Ottomans. On November 30, 1870, the Asir tribe again attacked Hodeida but was repulsed by the 2,000 Ottoman troops stationed there. The following month, reinforcement from Constantinople arrived, and the Ottoman force of 6,000 was able to drive the Asiris back into the mountains. After subduing the Asir tribe and consolidating Ottoman control over the coastal Tihama region, the Ottoman force advanced southward toward Yemen. The Yemeni imam was a titular vassal of the Ottoman Empire, but he was unable to rule the highland tribes. Several tribal forts fell to the Ottomans as they advanced toward the capital of San'a, which surrendered to the Ottomans quickly (April 1872), and the heaviest fighting of the war took place at the nearby fortress of Manakha. The Ottoman forces then fanned out to conquer a number of tribes in the region. Meanwhile the other expedition was advancing from the east, capturing several towns through 1871. In May 1871 the Ottomans attacked al-Hasa. After a siege of several months, hundreds of Ottoman troops were dead of starvation, fighting, and disease. Nevertheless, by November much of the al-Hasa territory had fallen to the Ottomans. San'a then became the capital of the new Ottoman government in Yemen. Attempting to control the tribes would, however, continue to be a challenge.

Coding: Asir, al-Hasa, and Yemen are coded as autonomous entities until 1871, after which they are incorporated into the Ottoman Empire.

Sources: Baldry (1976); Farah (2002); Gavin (1975); Kour (1981); Stearns (2001).

EXTRA-STATE WAR #366:
The Second Franco-Algerian War of 1871–1872

Participants: France vs. Algeria
Dates: March [ ], 1871, to January [ ], 1872
Battle-Related Deaths: Algeria—10,000; France—2,686
Where Fought: Middle East
Initiator: Algeria
Outcome: France wins
War Type: Colonial

Narrative: Kabylia is the predominantly mountainous, Berber-inhabited region of Algeria, lying to the east of Algiers. The area had already been engulfed in extra-state war #345, the French Conquest of Kabylia in 1856–1857. Fifteen years later another war occurred in the area, the war of 1871–1872. This extra-state war illustrates, as a number of other wars do, the interconnectedness of the war system. The French had just lost interstate war #58, the Franco-Prussian War, and the loss of Alsace-Lorraine to Prussia in that war aroused French resentment. A less well-known result of that war was that a large number of French-speaking people from Alsace-Lorraine were displaced by the German takeover of their homeland and that the French government resettled them in Algeria. This resettlement required taking land from the Algerians, which in turn triggered the Franco-Algerian War of 1871–1872.

Approximately 4,000 Alsatian refugee families were resettled in Algeria, and through the power of the French colonial government, land was made available to these settlers. Not surprisingly, the French government in turn displaced the native Algerians from their homeland and provoked them to fight back in resistance. Following 1871 the French government also established additional laws and policies to punish and control the Muslims. Consequently, the Kabyle (particularly tribal groups led by Muhammad Mukrani) attacked the French in pursuit of their independence and their land. Within ten months, the French had defeated them, deprived them of their autonomy, and taken even more of their land.

Coding: Neither Clodfelter (2002) nor Phillips and Axelrod (2005) nor Oliver and Atmore (1994) cover this war. Clodfelter does cover "the French Conquest of Algeria: 1830–47" and mentions subsequent revolts occurring in 1873 and 1881. However, from the point of view of sustained combat leading to substantial casualties, we find the 1871–1872 period, just before 1873, to be the one time that war resumes. Abun-Nasr (1975) lists 2,686 French dead from the war; Martin Stone (1997), the author of *Agony of Algeria*, says the Algerian losses were many times higher, so we use 10,000 as our estimate of those.

Sources: Abun-Nasr (1975); Confer (1966); Entelis (1986); Evans (2007); Great Britain, Naval Intelligence Division (1942); Nelson (1979); Stone (1997).

EXTRA-STATE WAR #367:

The Second British-Ashanti War of 1873–1874

Participants: United Kingdom vs. Ashanti
Dates: January [ ], 1873, to February 4, 1874
Battle-Related Deaths: Ashanti—1,400; United Kingdom—100
Where Fought: Africa
Initiator: Ashanti
Outcome: United Kingdom wins
War Type: Imperial

Narrative: As a result of the First British-Ashanti War of 1824–1826 (extra-state war #311), the Ashanti (or Asante, which is now Central Ghana) had given up their claims to the Gold Coast (of west Africa) to Britain, which organized the Gold Coast as a colony. The Ashanti, however, continued raiding British forts along the Gold Coast. In January 1873 this war began when an estimated 20,000 Ashanti troops invaded the coastal area and seized most of the British posts, and in October the Ashanti threatened the British port at Elimina. Gen. Garnet Wolseley, who had been appointed the new British governor and who would later become famous in the Sudan, took an auxiliary force and on October 13 defeated the Ashanti at Essaman, driving them away from the coast. With a reinforced army, the British went on the offensive and defeated the Ashanti at Abakrampa in November 1873 and Amoafo in January 1874. The British then captured the Ashanti capital of Kumasi on February 4, 1874, ending the war. Under the Treaty of Fomena, the Asante kingdom paid an indemnity of 50,000 ounces of gold to the United Kingdom. War between Britain and the Ashanti would flare up again in 1893 (extra-state war #398). The Ashanti would be defeated in 1896, and in 1901 Asante would be annexed to the Gold Coast.

Coding: Both Clodfelter (2002) and Phillips and Axelrod (2005) cover this as the "Second Ashanti War" of 1873–1874.

Sources: Brackenbury (1968); Clodfelter (2002); Edgerton (1995); Fage (1969); Farwell (1972); Featherstone (1992a); Featherstone (1973); Jaques (2007); Kohn (1986); Oliver and Atmore (1994); Phillips and Axelrod (2005).

EXTRA-STATE WAR #369:

The Second Franco-Vietnamese War of 1873–1874

Participants: France vs. Vietnam
Dates: November 20, 1873, to [ ]/[ ]/1874

Battle-Related Deaths: Vietnam—600;
France—400
Where Fought: Asia
Initiator: France
Outcome: Compromise
War Type: Imperial

Narrative: In the eighteenth century, the area that we now refer to as Vietnam consisted of three entities: Annam (in the center), Tonkin (in the north), and Cochin China (in the south). In 1802, with French support, the three united into the kingdom of Vietnam. For most of the nineteenth century (1802–1887), Vietnam was an autonomous entity; however, as a result of the First Franco-Vietnamese War (extra-state war #349), parts of Cochin China were ceded to France in 1862, and 1867 it became a direct French colony.

French explorers and traders continued their activities in other parts of Vietnam, as well. In 1873 a small French force was sent to Hanoi to settle a dispute involving a French trader. When the Vietnamese refused to accept the French decision in the settlement, the French captured Hanoi on November 20, 1873, initiating this war. The French continued their offensive, gaining control over most of the Vietnamese cities in the north. There the French were confronted by a Vietnamese-Chinese force called the Black Flag. After the Taiping Rebellion in China (non-state war #1534 and intra-state war #567), groups of the Chinese rebels fled into Tonkin (northern Vietnam) and were ravaging the population. The Vietnamese emperor Tu-Duc could not stop them, so he asked for assistance from the Chinese governor of Canton. The Cantonese armed forces simply joined in the pillaging of Vietnam and the raiding of French shipping. The Black Flag confronted the French in a battle on December 21, 1873, and the leader of the French expedition, Francis Gamier, was killed. Fighting continued in early 1874, with French ships captured and pro-French Christian towns destroyed. The French decided to withdraw from Hanoi

and the north (which ends the war), though Emperor Tu Duc was forced to grant the French free passage on the Red River and to promise not to persecute Christians.

War would break out again between France and Vietnam in 1882 (extra-state war #385) which is linked to the Sino-French War of 1884–1885 (inter-state war #67). By 1887 all of Vietnam was under French control, and the French united it with Cambodia to form the Union of Indochina.

Coding: Clodfelter (2002) has a "Tonkin War: 1883–1885." Phillips and Axelrod (2005) describe two distinct "French Indochina Wars," one in 1873–1874 and the other in 1883–1884.

Sources: Cady (1954); Clodfelter (2002); Kohn (1986); Osborne (1969); Phillips and Axelrod (2005); SarDesai (1998); Thompson (1968).

EXTRA-STATE WAR #370:

The First Dutch-Achinese War of 1873–1878

Participants: Netherlands vs. Aceh
Dates: March 26, 1873, to October 13, 1878
Battle-Related Deaths: Netherlands—12,000;
Achinese—11,000
Where Fought: Asia
Initiator: Achinese
Outcome: Dutch win
War Type: Imperial

Narrative: Aceh, located at the northern tip of Sumatra, had been an autonomous entity for centuries, and it held on to its independence more tenaciously than any other precolonial Indonesian quasi-state. Traders from both the United Kingdom and the Netherlands had long been operating in the area of Indonesia, and pirates operating from Aceh had attacked ships from both countries. The Netherlands, however, sought to expand its colonial empire throughout the island chain (see extra-state wars #313, #334, and #350). In an 1824 treaty, the British had ceded their control over Sumatra to the

245

Dutch East India Company. The Dutch had initially promised to respect Aceh's independence; however by 1873 they wished to expand their protectorate to include the Muslim sultanate of Aceh. The pretext of the Dutch expedition was to deal with the pirates; however, the Dutch also wished to preclude American activities in the region. In 1873 an Achinese emissary had discussed signing a treaty with the United States under the auspices of the American consul in Singapore.

In 1873 the Dutch launched two expeditions to Aceh. Their first assault, in March, was repulsed, and its leader, Maj. Gen. Johan Harmen Rudolf Köhler, was killed A second expedition landed a force of about 12,000 troops in December 1873, defeating the Achinese in several battles. By January 1874 the Dutch had surrounded the Achinese capital and the sultan fled from the palace and took refuge in the interior. The Dutch proclaimed annexation of the sultanate on January 24, 1874. Significant Achinese resistance lasted through September 1878, and on October 13, 1878, the colonial government announced that the war had ended.

Coding: Most of the Dutch battle-related deaths are due to disease. The Dutch did not completely subdue the Achinese until 1908, but the first major phase of the conflict ended in 1878. Fighting continued but at below war levels until 1904, when the level of hostilities rose again. Since there is more than a year between these two war episodes, they are coded as separate wars, and the second phase appears as the Second Dutch-Achinese War of 1904–1907 (extra-state #424). In 1949 Aceh became an autonomous province of Indonesia, and Achinese resistance to integration into Indonesia contributed to several civil wars starting in 1953 (see intra-state wars #738 and #742). Clodfelter (2002) has an "Atjeh (Aceh) War" of 1873–1914, while Phillips and Axelrod (2005) have an "Achinese War" of 1873 to 1907.

Sources: Clodfelter (2002); Kielstra (1883); Phillips and Axelrod (2005); Ricklefs (1993); Rose (1915); Vlekke (1960); Williams (1907).

EXTRA-STATE WAR #371:
The Kokand Rebellion of 1875–1876

Participants: Russia vs. Kokand
Dates: August 9, 1875, to February 28, 1876
Battle-Related Deaths: Kokand—4,800; Russia—100
Where Fought: Asia
Initiator: Kokand
Outcome: Russia wins
War Type: Imperial

Narrative: In extra-state wars #359 and #361, Russia had occupied parts of Kokand and Bukhara, expanding its influence in Central Asia. Although the Russians had initially disclaimed any intent on annexing these areas, on June 14, 1867, Tsar Alexander II created Turkestan, which included parts of the two khanates. The remainder of Kokand was considered to be a Russian protectorate, which often meant a period of gradually increasing Russian control. As Russian control increased, so did the taxes imposed on Kokand. As a result, in 1875 a Kokand rebellion broke out. A holy war was declared by Kokand's leaders against Russia, and on August 9, 1875, the Kokand troops surrounded the Russian-held city of Khojend. A Russian relief column of 3,000 troops arrived from Tashkent on August 18, and the rebel force retreated to the fortress at Makhram. The Russians advanced into Kokand, defeating the rebels there on August 22, 1875. The Russians continued their offensive, defeating the Kokand troops in several engagements, including a major confrontation at Namangan in October. The rebels fled back to their stronghold at Andizhan, where they were defeated again in January 1876. In the meantime, Tsar Alexander II had decided that Kokand should no longer remain autonomous, and on February 19, 1876, he signed a decree annexing Kokand to Russia. The war itself finally ended on February 28,

1876, when the Russians stormed the fortress at Uch-Kurgan, seizing several of the revolutionary leaders.

Coding: As a result of this war, Kokand ceases being a dependency of Russia and becomes part of the territory of Russia itself.

Sources: Becker (1968); Hopkirk (1992); Jaques (2007); Palmer (1957); Seton-Watson (1967); Wieczynski (1977); Zuljan (2003).

EXTRA-STATE WAR #372:
The Egypt-Ethiopian War of 1875–1876

Participants: Egypt vs. Ethiopia
Dates: September [ ], 1875, to March 9, 1876
Battle-Related Deaths: Ethiopia—4,550;
    Egypt—4,250
Where Fought: Africa
Initiator: Egypt
Outcome: Ethiopia wins
War Type: Imperial

Narrative: Egypt under Ismail Pasha embarked on programs for economic development and aggrandizement, both internally and externally. Earlier, Egypt had expanded its control into Sudan (extra-state war #364), and now Ismail Pasha wanted to extend his domain eastward from Sudan to the Red Sea. Ethiopia had been weakened by its war with the British (extra-state war #362) in 1867–1868. Thus in 1875 Egypt launched an attack on Eritrea, which was at that time (from 1855 to 1882), part of Ethiopia. Egypt's advance would have cut off Ethiopia from the Red Sea and rendered the country landlocked, motivating the resistance of Ethiopian king John IV (Yohannes IV). During the war, Egypt launched two separate invasions, one in 1875 and the other in 1876. In 1875 the Egyptians occupied several Ethiopian cities along the Red Sea. From one of them, Massawa, the Egyptians then march inland. The expedition was attacked by the much larger Ethiopian army (estimated at 70,000 men) at Gundet and almost completely destroyed on November 15–16, 1875. The second Egyptian expedition had over six times as many troops as the first, but it was similarly unsuccessful. In March 1876 the Egyptians again set out from Massawa. They encamped at a fort near Gura but then went out to attack the Ethiopian army on March 7, 1876. The Egyptians were again defeated, suffering significant casualties, after which they retreated to the fort. Two days later the Ethiopians attempted to attack the fort but suffered severe casualties and withdrew. The Egyptians then gave up their offensive and withdrew.

The costs for this war contributed to the financial difficulties that Egypt faced, ultimately prompting Egypt to sell shares in the Suez Canal to Great Britain. The Ethiopians soon thereafter gained the attention of the world by inflicting the same fate on the Italian imperialists in 1887 (extra-state war #392) and again in 1895–1896 (extra-state war #407). Eventually, Ethiopia did become an Italian colony (inter-state war #127).

Coding: Egypt, which had been part of the Ottoman Empire, had become increasingly autonomous in the nineteenth century and had become a state system member in 1855 (partly as a result of activities surrounding the Suez Canal). Ethiopia remained an autonomous entity, despite its defeat by Great Britain in 1868 in extra-state war #362; however, Ethiopia did not become a state system member until 1898, thus this is an extra-state war. Clodfelter (2002) covers this as the "Egyptian-Abyssinian War" of 1875–1879, while Phillips and Axelrod refer to it as the "Ethiopian-Egyptian War (1875–1877)."

Sources: Baddour (1960); Becker (1968); Clodfelter (2002); Darkwah (1975); Gillespie (2002); Goldstein (1992); Jaques (2007); Kohn (1986); Marcus (2001); McGregor (2006); Oliver and Atmore (1994); Phillips and Axelrod (2005); Schafer (1995); Williams (1907).

EXTRA-STATE WAR #373:
The Serbian-Turkish War of 1876–1877

Participants: Ottoman Empire vs. Serbia and
  Montenegro
Dates: June 30, 1876, to April 23, 1877
Battle-Related Deaths: Serbia—5,000;
  Montenegro—[ ]; Ottoman Empire—[ ]
Where Fought: Europe
Initiator: Serbia
Outcome: Transformed into inter-state war #61
War Type: Imperial

Narrative: This war is the second of three wars that confronted the Ottoman Empire in the Balkans between 1875 and 1878. The conflict began as a civil war of Bosnia and Bulgaria against the Ottoman Empire (intra-state war #601); however, when outside entities (Serbia and Montenegro) became involved, the war transformed into this extra-state war. Finally, when Russia intervened, the war evolved into the Second Russo-Turkish War of 1877–1878 (inter-state war #61). The Bosnian and Bulgarian civil war began on June 30, 1875, when peasants in Hercegovina revolted against the rule of the Ottoman Empire, followed soon thereafter by Bosnia and Bulgaria. Bosnia and Hercegovina appealed to Serbia for assistance, and on June 30, 1876, Serbia declared war on the Ottoman Empire, followed by Montenegro on July 1, 1876. Both Serbia and Montenegro were autonomous entities at this time, not integrated parts of the Ottoman Empire, and consequently had more resources available than Bosnia or Bulgaria. Thus Serbia, in particular, entered the war with a significantly greater number of troops than the rebels (124,500 compared with 25,000). Serbia thus assumed the bulk of the fighting as soon as it entered the war, on June 30, 1876. This marks the end of the intra-state war and its transformation into this extra-state war.

Particularly after the Crimean War (inter-state war #22), the Pan-Slavic movement spread throughout the Balkans, linking Russia to the Balkan desire for independence form the Ottoman Empire. Serbia's decision to declare war against the Ottoman Empire was influenced by its desire to secure its own independence, as well as that of Bosnia and Hercegovina. The Serbs were also aware of the Ottomans' brutal repression of the independence movement in Bulgaria earlier that year and were hopeful that they would receive the support of Russia should they declare war on the Ottomans. Prince Milan of Serbia had, in fact, requested Austrian and Russian support should Serbia declare war on Turkey. Instead the two powers tried to deter Serbia's entry into the war. Several thousand Russian volunteers did flock to the Serbian forces as a gesture of Slavic solidarity, but the lack of Russian support doomed the Serb offensive.

As the war began, the Montenegrins were initially victorious, defeating the Turks in Hercegovina, where they stayed for the duration of the war. The Serbian forces were less successful. The Ottomans launched an attack toward Belgrade in August 1876. Although their advance was initially stalled, a second offensive in October overwhelmed the defenders. Serbia was defeated, and only Russian intervention prevented Serbia's destruction. Russia issued an ultimatum to the Turks, demanding a cease-fire. The Ottomans acquiesced on October 18, 1876, and the subsequent peace agreement between the Ottomans and Serbia (February 28, 1877) established the status quo ante. The cease-fire did not, however, end the hostilities entirely, particularly in Bosnia and Hercegovina. Meanwhile, on March 31, 1877, Romania began to mobilize its forces. Also on March 31, the London Protocol signed by the major powers invited the Ottomans to demobilize and institute reforms in the Christian provinces. This proposal was rejected by the Turks on April 9. On April 16, 1877, Russia and Romania signed a convention to allow the passage of Russian troops through Romanian territory on the way to Bulgaria. Russia declared war on April 24, 1877. This marked the beginning of the inter-state war and the ending of the extra-state war (on the previous day).

Coding: The coding of this war and its transformation from an intra-state war into an extra-state war and then into an inter-state war were determined by changes in which parties were doing the bulk of the fighting and the status of these war participants. In 1875 Serbia, Bulgaria, Bosnia, Hercegovina, and Montenegro were not members of the interstate system; however, their status differed. Bulgaria, Bosnia, and Hercegovina were integrated parts of the Ottoman Empire; thus a war between any of these three against the Ottoman Empire was coded as a civil or intra-state war. Though Serbia and Montenegro had been part of the Ottoman Empire, by 1817 they were independent autonomous entities. Thus the war of Serbia and Montenegro against the Ottoman Empire was coded as an extra-state war between a system member and a nonstate actor. After the war the Congress of Berlin (1878) gave Serbia, Montenegro, and Romania their independence. Serbia and Romania became interstate system members on July 13, 1878.

Sources: Allen and Muratoff (1953); Clodfelter (2002); Dumas and Vedel-Peterson (1923); Finkel (2005); Florinsky (1953); Hentea (2007); Hozier (1878); Kohn (1986); *London Times* (1875–1876); MacKenzie (1967); Palmer (1992); Phillips and Axelrod (2005); Richardson (1960a); Schafer (1995); Seton-Watson (1952); von Sax (1913); von Sternegg (1866–1899).

EXTRA-STATE WAR #374:

The Third British-Xhosa War of 1877–1878

Participants: United Kingdom vs. South Africa Xhosa
Dates: August [ ], 1877, to June [ ], 1878
Battle-Related Deaths: South Africa Xhosa— 3,700; United Kingdom—200
Where Fought: Africa
Initiator: South Africa Xhosa
Outcome: United Kingdom wins
War Type: Colonial

Narrative: From its Cape Colony, Great Britain had fought two wars against the Xhosa (extra-state war #333 in 1846–1847 and #337 in 1850–1852). This was the last of this series of wars, though the Xhosa continued to play a very prominent role in South Africa. In this war the Xhosa again rose up in desperate rebellion against the British and white colonists and attempted to recover the lands lost in the earlier wars. This in turn produced a crushing retaliatory blow by British troops. In the attacks two important Xhosa chiefs, Sandile and Siyolo, were both killed, along with thousands of their troops. Britain suffered some casualties but succeeded in completely subjugating the Xhosa to British control and annexing all the Xhosa territory, ending the "Kaffir Wars."

Coding: In earlier versions of the COW dataset, wars with the Xhosa were referred to as the Kaffir Wars, after the locals who were called "Kaffirs" by the British but known to themselves as the Xhosa. *Kaffir* is the Arabic word for "infidel," and it was generalized in English usage as a derogatory term meaning "native" and was used in South Africa as a term to demean the Xhosa. Clodfelter (2002) covers this as one of a series of "Kaffir Wars." Phillips and Axelrod (2005) have this designated as the "Kaffir War, Ninth (1877–1878)."

Sources: Clodfelter (2002); Featherstone (1992a); Featherstone (1973); James (1985); Mostert (1992); Oliver and Atmore (1994); Peires (1982); Phillips and Axelrod (2005); Williams (1907).

EXTRA-STATE WAR #375:

Egypt-Sudanese Slavers War of 1878–1879

Participants: Egypt vs. Sudanese slavers
Dates: Feburary [ ], 1878, to July [ ], 1879
Battle-Related Deaths: Slavers—4,000; Egypt—[ ]
Where Fought: Middle East
Initiator: Egypt
Outcome: Egypt wins
War Type: Imperial

Narrative: Early in the nineteenth century, Egypt had been led by the effective Ottoman viceroy Muhammad Ali. Under his rule Egypt had conquered Sudan (extra-state war #307), and Egyptian rule there lasted over fifty years. Muhammad Ali was succeeded by a dynasty that persisted through three descendants, none of whom approached his level of power and influence. Ismail Pasha was the third of these successors. Ismail did much to modernize Egypt, but his idealism prompted him to spend beyond Egypt's available resources. His expenses included military expeditions to try to extend Egypt's influence and control of trade in areas within Sudan (extra-state war #364), and into Ethiopia to the east along the Red Sea (extra-state war #372). One of Pasha's purported motives was to try to stamp out the very persistent slave trade in Sudan.

In February 1877 Ismail appointed the famous British soldier Col. Charles George Gordon as the governor-general of Sudan with the mandate to suppress the slave trade and to extend Egyptian rule throughout the region. In response to the Egyptian expeditions, the Sudanese slavers, led by Zebehr (or Zubair) Pasha and his son Suleiman, went on the offensive in Bahr el-Ghazal in the southwest part of Sudan, massacring the government garrison at Dem Idris. Gordon delegated the subsequent military expedition to Romolo Gessi, who, with an Egyptian army of 7,656 troops, was sent to hunt down the slavers and free the slaves. The mission was accomplished in July 1879, when Suleiman surrendered. Meanwhile, the Egyptian government went bankrupt and Ismail Pasha was overthrown in June 1879, prompting Gordon to resign his position. Conflict in the region soon reappeared in one of the bloodiest wars in nineteenth-century colonialism: the Mahdi's war against the British and Egyptians in the Sudan (extra-state war #384).

Coding: Clodfelter (2002) covers this war; Phillips and Axelrod (2005) do not.

Sources: Baddour (1960); Clodfelter (2002); Collins and Tignor (1967); Holt and Daly (1979); Marlowe (1975); McGregor (2006); Mowafi (1981); Oliver and Atmore (1994); Pakenham (1991).

EXTRA-STATE WAR #376:
The Russo-Turkoman War of 1878–1881

Participants: Russia vs. Turkomans
Dates: May [ ], 1878, to January 24, 1881
Battle-Related Deaths: Turkomans—8,000; Russia—2,000
Where Fought: Asia
Initiator: Russia
Outcome: Russia wins
War Type: Imperial

Narrative: During the late nineteenth century, Russia engaged in three wars in an attempt to extend its control over Central Asia (extra-state wars #359, #361, and #371). The next target of Russian expansionism was the Turkoman people (of the present Republic of Turkmenistan). The Turkomans (or the Tekke tribe) had become subjects of the khan of Khiva in the early nineteenth century, and as the Russians attempted to establish their control over Khiva, they faced stiff resistance from the Turkomans. In 1867 Russia appointed its first governor-general to Turkestan, giving him the mandate to secure control over these regions for Russia. In 1873 Russia sent an expedition to map the region and begin to plan fortifications. The Russians occupied several Turkoman villages from which they subsequently launched a number of small forays into the region, destroying villages in an attempt to intimidate the tribes. After the conclusion of the Second Russo-Turkish War (inter-state war #61) in 1878, Russia again turned its focus to expanding its sphere of influence in Central Asia. In May 1878 the Russian governor-general mobilized a force of 20,000 men, and they advanced into Turkestan. The Russians launched an unsuccessful offensive against the Turkoman stronghold of Geok Tepe in August 1879, in which they suffered significant casualties. The defeat prompted the Russians to launch a second offensive, led by Gen. Mikhail Skobelev, who had distinguished himself in the Second Russo-Turkish War, against Geok Tepe in December 1880. The fortress withstood the initial bombardment, but a Russian assault on January 24, 1881, captured the town, ending the war. Afterward, the Russians massacred 8,000 to 16,000 civilians attempting to flee. In 1899 the region became part of the governate-general of Russian Turkistan.

Coding: Clodfelter (2002) covers this as a stage in "Russia's Conquest of Central Asia: 1839–85." Phillips and Axelrod (2005) do not cover this war.

Sources: Clodfelter (2002); Coates and Coates (1951); d'Encausse (1994); Jaques (2007); Latimer 1903); MacKenzie (1974); Schuyler (1876); Seton-Watson (1967).

EXTRA-STATE WAR #377:
The Austrian-Bosnian War of 1878

Participants: Austria-Hungary vs. Bosnia
Dates: July 29, 1878, to October 1, 1878
Battle-Related Deaths: Austria-Hungary—3,500; Bosnia—2,500
Where Fought: Europe
Initiator: Austria-Hungary
Outcome: Austria-Hungary wins
War Type: Imperial

Narrative: The desire for Bosnian independence from the Ottoman Empire was the precipitant leading to a civil war (intra-state war #601), an extra-state war (#373), and an inter-state war (#61), all between 1875 and 1878. After the defeat of the Ottoman Empire in the Second Russo-Turkish War (#61), the Congress of Berlin (June-July 1878) was called to reexamine the harsh terms imposed by Russia in the Treaty of San Stefano, which had ended that war. As a result of the congress, Serbia, Montenegro, and Romania attained their independence, while

Bosnia and Hercegovina were to be administered by Austria-Hungary, though still under nominal Ottoman sovereignty. Austria-Hungary would have preferred to annex the provinces outright, and to accomplish this goal, in July 1878 Austria-Hungary marched about 200,000 troops into Bosnia. Ottoman resistance was nil, but the locals, especially the Bosnian Muslims, fought back, and the war became quite deadly, though brief. At the war's conclusion, Austria-Hungary occupied Bosnia.

Coding: From 1878 to 1908, Bosnia was occupied by Austria-Hungary, and after that for a decade it was part of Austria-Hungary until the end of World War I. Only after World War I did Bosnia become part of Yugoslavia. Bosnia did not become an autonomous entity until 1991 and did not become a state system member until 1992. Clodfelter (2002) calls this the "Austrian Conquest of Bosnia." Phillips and Axelrod (2005) do not cover this war.

Sources: Clodfelter (2002); Donia (2006); Dumas and Vedel-Petersen (1923); Gerolymatos (2002).

EXTRA-STATE WAR #379:
The Second British-Afghan War of 1878–1880

Participants: United Kingdom vs. Afghanistan
Dates: November 21, 1878, to September 2, 1880
Battle-Related Deaths: Afghanistan—11,000; United Kingdom—10,000
Where Fought: Asia
Initiator: United Kingdom
Outcome: United Kingdom wins
War Type: Imperial

Narrative: Great Britain had been involved in a number of wars on the fringes of its colony in India. Britain was concerned with both tribal resistance and growing Russian expansionism in Central Asia. Consequently, Britain began to see Afghanistan as an emerging buffer state. After the earlier conflict with Afghanistan (extra-state war #322, 1839–1842), Britain had essentially ignored Afghanistan until it resumed relations and signed a treaty in 1855 that committed each party to respect each other's territorial integrity. The British also signed an accord with Russia by which Russia pledged to respect the borders of Afghanistan. British growing support of Afghanistan also applied to its borders with Persia. It was the Persian seizure of the Afghan city of Herat that had led to the Anglo-Persian War (inter-state war #25 in 1856–1857).

In 1878 both Russia and Britain sent diplomatic missions to Afghanistan. Afghanistan's emir, Sher Ali, initially tried to prevent the missions from entering Afghan territory, though the Russian mission was able to reach Kabul on July 22, 1878. However, as Britain's mission headed toward Kabul, it was turned back as it approached the Khyber Pass on September 21, 1878. The British government then sent the emir an ultimatum, demanding an apology, and when that was not forthcoming, Britain made plans to invade. The British invasion force of 35,300 men faced a potential 100,000 Afghans. On November 21, 1878, the British force attacked Afghanistan on three fronts. One prong quickly defeated the Afghans, reaching Kandahar on January 8, 1879. The other two prongs also were successful, though they faced stiffer resistance. Sher Ali fled (dying on February 21, 1879), and his son Yakub Khan concluded a treaty with the British on May 26, 1879. This treaty proved to be merely a temporary break in the war. On September 3, 1879, a force of 2,000 Afghans attacked the British in Kabul, killing the entire 80-man detachment. On October 6, 1879, a British relief column defeated the Afghans at Charasia (twelve miles south of Kabul). The British entered Kabul on October 12. Yakub Khan abdicated at that point, and the British proclaimed Abdur Rahman as the emir; however, thousands of Afghan troops then besieged Kabul. The British were able to break out of the city and defeat the Afghans; nevertheless, Yakub Khan's brother, who was also Abdur Rahman's cousin, Ayub Khan, claimed the throne and advanced on Kandahar. On July 27, 1880, at Maiwand, Ayub Khan defeated the British, who lost over 1,000 troops. Ayub Khan then besieged the British at Kandahar on August 6. A British relief force arrived on September 1 and routed Ayub Khan's army. This ended the war, and British troops withdrew from Afghanistan. The following year Ayub Khan led a rebellion against Abdur Rahman, which was suppressed.

Coding: At this time Afghanistan is considered an autonomous entity but not a member of the interstate system. The period between May 26, 1879, and September 3, 1879, is coded as a break in the war. Of the British battle-related deaths, 80 percent were the result of disease.

Sources: Clodfelter (2002); Featherstone (1973); Hanna (1910); Jaques (2007); O'Balance (1993); Phillips and Axelrod (2005); Richards (1990).

EXTRA-STATE WAR #380:
The Second British-Zulu War of 1879

Participants: United Kingdom vs. Zulu (Zululand)
Dates: January 11, 1879, to July 4, 1879
Battle-Related Deaths: Zulu—8,000; United Kingdom—2,500
Where Fought: Africa
Initiator: United Kingdom
Outcome: United Kingdom wins
War Type: Imperial

Narrative: Prior to this war, the British had had only one war with the Zulu, extra-state war #321, in 1838. In the first half of the nineteenth century, most of the British wars in southern Africa had been against the Xhosa (extra-state wars #333, #337, and #374). However, British conflict with the Zulu was revived in 1868, when huge diamond deposits were discovered near the confluence of the Vaal and Orange rivers, in Boer country. This ushered in a period of more than a century in which diamonds were a major part of the South African economy. Immediately, the British and others were drawn to the area of the diamond deposits, where the British again came into contact with the Zulu.

In 1843 Britain had annexed Natal, the site of the First British-Zulu war, to the Cape Colony. As a result, the Boers moved out of Natal toward the northwest and in 1857 founded the South African Republic (Transvaal). The Zulu, who were among the most formidable warriors in Africa, disputed the border between Transvaal and Zululand. After the British annexed the Transvaal in 1877, they decided to deal with the border challenges posed by the Zulu. The British demanded control of the disputed territory. They sent the Zulu king, Cetewayo, a list of humiliating demands, and when he refused to acquiesce and to pay homage to Queen Victoria, the British attacked. A force of 13,300 British regulars and native troops invaded in January 1879 and faced 50,000 native troops known as impis. While 30 percent of the British troops went on a scouting mission, the remainder, encamped at Isandhlwana, was attacked by the Zulu. There the British suffered one of their greatest colonial battle defeats. Of the 950 British troops, 895 died, along with 550 of their African allies. Despite 2,000 Zulu casualties that day, it was a great Zulu victory. The same day, the Zulu went on to attack a small British force at Rorke's Drift. Numerous Zulu assaults were repulsed at significant cost to both sides. Over the next several months, British forces faced additional losses to Zulu attacks; however, the British began to turn the tide with a victory at Gingindlovu on April 2, 1879. The British troops then advanced to relieve the British fort at Eahowe, which had been besieged by the Zulu for ten weeks (since January 23). The army then returned south into Natal and then invaded Zululand a second time in June 1879. On July 4 the British were attacked near the Zulu capital of Ulundi. There the Zulu were defeated. King Cetewayo was captured, ending the war. Although Zulu independence was not yet lost, their power was broken. Britain would annex Zululand in 1887.

Coding: Zululand is coded as an autonomous entity from 1818 to 1880.

Sources: Clodfelter (2002); Farwell (1972); Featherstone (1992a); Featherstone (1973); Jaques (2007); Knight (1992); Morris (1965); Oliver and Atmore (1994); Phillips and Axelrod (2005).

EXTRA-STATE WAR #381:
The Gun War of 1880–1881

Participants: United Kingdom vs. Basuto
Dates: September [ ], 1880, to April [ ], 1881
Battle-Related Deaths: Basuto—1,400; United Kingdom—[ ]
Where Fought: Africa
Initiator: United Kingdom
Outcome: United Kingdom wins
War Type: Colonial

Narrative: Located in southern Africa, Basutoland (the home of the Basuto people, also called the Sotho) was an autonomous entity from 1818 to 1868. In 1852 and 1857 the Basuto had turned back British expeditions (at below war levels), and in 1858 and 1865 the Basuto had fought wars against the Boers of the Orange Free State (non-state wars #1544 and #1552). As a consequence, in 1868 King Moshoeshoe put Basutoland under British protection, and the British incorporated it into the Cape Colony in 1871. By the late 1870s, however, cattle raiding by the Basuto (now ruled by Morosi) caused problems for the British. In 1880 the British authorities attempted to extend the 1878 Peace Preservation Act to Basutoland, which would have required a general disarmament of the Basuto, and the Basuto objected. The resulting war has thus been referred to as the Gun War. The Basuto began to arm themselves, and the British sent in troops to disarm them. Morosi led the Basuto onto a mountaintop position. A small British contingent stormed the mountain, annihilating the Basuto and killing Morosi. In one battle, on September 22, 1880, the Basuto forces under Letherodi attacked the British at

Mafeteng, causing heavy fatalities. The rebellion was not long-lived. Fairly quickly the two sides agreed to arbitration, and the Basuto accepted the conditions that they license their weapons and pay an indemnity. This agreement, however, was never carried out.

Coding: The Basuto today inhabit the independent state of Lesotho, which is surrounded by South Africa. Clodfelter has one brief entry for all the wars, the "Basuto Wars, 1852–1883." Phillips and Axelrod (2005) call this war the "Basuto Gun War."

Sources: Evans (2000); Featherstone (1992a); Halpern (1965); James (1985); Phillips and Axelrod (2005); Schafer (1995); Williams (1907); Wilson and Thompson (1971).

EXTRA-STATE WAR #382:
The First Boer War of 1880–1881

Participants: United Kingdom vs. Transvaal
Dates: December 16, 1880, to April 5, 1881
Battle-Related Deaths: United Kingdom—900; Transvaal—100
Where Fought: Africa
Initiator: Transvaal
Outcome: Transvaal wins
War Type: Colonial

Narrative: In 1836 the Dutch Boers (or Afrikaners), who objected to the expansion of the British Empire around Cape Town, began what came to be known as the Great Trek, in which the Boers moved northward. This migration brought them into contact with black South African tribes. One Boer group, led by Andries Potgier, headed toward the Transvaal where it fought the Matabele (non-state war #1521) in 1836–1837. The second Boer group, led by Peter Retief, headed toward Natal (along the Indian Ocean), where they fought the Zulu (non-state war #1525). Ultimately, the Boers moved into two general areas. The more southerly area was annexed by the British in 1848 as the Orange River Sovereignty. After the British were unable to establish control over the area, they gave it independence, as the Orange Free State, in 1854. The other group of Boers created the South African Republic (Transvaal) in 1857. Partially because of its financial difficulties, the Transvaal was annexed by the British in 1877. Many of the Boers were unhappy with this turn of events. In particular, when the British administrator, Colonel Lanyon, began to try to enforce a system of taxation, many of the Boers refused to pay.

In November 1880 the crisis was precipitated by the British seizure of a wagon because of its owner's nonpayment of taxes. The Boers utilized the occasion to appoint a provisional government for a South African Republic. Three commando groups were organized, and the first shots of the war occurred on December 16, 1880, at Potchefstroom, where the proclamation of independence was printed. In the first major engagement of the war, on December 20, 1882, the Boers ambushed and defeated a small British column at Bronkhorst Spruit. The Boers then attacked and besieged a small British garrison at Potchefstroom. On December 29 a small British contingent was attacked, and its 240 soldiers were killed, wounded, or taken prisoner. Some Boers from the Orange Free State also took the opportunity to go to Transvaal to fight against the British. On January 24, 1881, the Boers went on the offensive, occupying Laing's Nek in British Natal. The British in Pretoria sent a relief column, which made an unsuccessful attempt to dislodge the Boers at Laing's Nek. The British suffered further defeats at Ingogo. On February 27, 1881, the British, hoping to attack the flank of the Boers at Laing's Nek, took a position on top of Majuba Hill. The Boers stormed the hill, killing half of the British positioned there. Exhausted, the British signed an armistice with the Boers, giving them autonomy under British suzerainty on March 6, 1881. It was some time before the news of the agreement reached the combat zone, and it was often not believed. For instance, the Boer commander of the siege at Potchefstroom continued the siege for another ten days after he heard of the armistice. The relationship between Britain and the Boers would rise again in 1899, in the Second Boer War (extra-state war #416).

Coding: This war is sometimes referred to as the First South African War, the Transvaal War, or the First Freedom War. At the conclusion of this war, Transvaal is coded as becoming an autonomous entity, a status it maintains until the conclusion of the Second Boer War, in 1902, when it reverts to being a colony of Britain.

Sources: Bruce (1981); Clodfelter (2002); Farwell (1972); Featherstone (1992a); Featherstone (1973); Jaques (2007); Kohn (1999); Langer (1948); LeMay (1995); Pakenham (1994); Phillips and Axelrod (2005); Smith (1996); Sorokin (1937); Stearns (2001); Williams (1907).

EXTRA-STATE WAR #383:
The Franco-Tunisian War of 1881–1882

Participants: France vs. Tunisia
Dates: June [ ], 1881, to April 4, 1882
Battle-Related Deaths: France—3,500; Tunisia—[ ]
Where Fought: Middle East
Initiator: Tunisia
Outcome: France wins
War Type: Imperial

Narrative: Both France and Italy sought to gain influence and control in Tunisia. France's excuse for direct intervention was provided by a border dispute between Tunisia and the French colony of Algeria as a local Tunisian tribe launched a raid into Algeria in late March 1881. On April 25, 1881, the French sent an expedition from Algeria into Tunisia. Although there was some initial Tunisian resistance, for the most part the French advanced unhindered. The Tunisian leader (known as a bey), Muhammed es-Saduk (Sadok), appealed unsuccessfully for European assistance. On May 12, 1881, the French forced the bey to accept a French protectorate through the Treaty of Kasr as-Said; however, the rest of

Tunisia did not accept the French offer as quickly and a rebellion against the French broke out in southern Tunisia. The French began a siege of the city of Safaqis (Sfax) on July 1, 1881. In October and November 1881 the French conquered a number of Tunisian strongholds. By early 1882 the resistance had been subdued. The number of French troops that were killed in battle numbered only about 500, but another 3,000 succumbed to disease.

Coding: Tunisia had been an autonomous entity in 1492–1534 but afterward had been part of the Ottoman Empire until 1705. After that it was an autonomous entity and was a state system member from 1825 until just prior to this war (May 12, 1881), when it became a French protectorate. The subsequent war is thus an extra-state war in which France tries to extend its colonial control. Phillips and Axelrod (2005) do not cover this war.

Sources: Abun Nasr (1975); Bodart (1916); Clodfelter (2002); Pakenham (1991); Sorokin (1937); Williams (1907).

EXTRA-STATE WAR #384:
The First British-Mahdi War of 1881–1885

Participants: United Kingdom, Egypt vs. Mahdist Empire
Dates: August [ ], 1881, to March 22, 1885
Battle-Related Deaths: United Kingdom, Egypt—25,000; Mahdist Empire—17,000; Egypt (until 1882)—5,000
Where Fought: Middle East
Initiator: Mahdist Empire
Outcome: Mahdist Empire wins
War Type: Colonial

Narrative: In 1881 Egypt was still a member of the interstate system but was facing the growing influence of Britain in the region. Almost simultaneously, Egypt was threatened by problems in the Sudan, which would lead to one of the bloodiest wars in the nineteenth century. In earlier wars (extra-state wars #364 and #375), the Ottoman Empire and then Egypt had gained control over Sudan, though that relationship was not acceptable to many Sudanese. In particular, Muhammed Ahmed, who styled himself the Mahdi, or successor of the Prophet Muhammad, developed a substantial following in Sudan in the 1880s. The Mahdi wanted to remove the foreign influences from Sudan, and after amassing a large army, he declared war in August 1881 and began to attack cities, forces, and social groups associated with the British and Egyptian interests. The Egyptians and British sent a small force to capture the Mahdi, though they were annihilated at the Battle of Aba on August 12, 1881. The Mahdi and his force then moved westward and established a base in the Sudanese province of Kordofan. In December 1881 a British-Egyptian force attempting to attack the stronghold was similarly annihilated, losing 70 percent of the 2,000-man joint force. These victories emboldened the Mahdi forces (also referred to as the Dervishes by the British), which took advantage of Egypt's problems by attacking Egyptian outposts throughout Kordofan in 1882. In fall 1882 the Mahdi army attacked an Egyptian garrison at El Obeid (in central Sudan). There, the defenders were successful, repulsing the Mahdi army, which lost 10,000 of its 30,000 troops. The Mahdi forces then besieged the fort, a siege that would last seven months.

Also in 1882, Britain conquered Egypt in a brief war (inter-state war #65), ending on September 15, 1882. Thereafter, the British took the lead in the ongoing Egyptian effort to quell the Sudanese rebellion. An Anglo-Egyptian force was sent to relieve El Obeid; however, the troops were ambushed and defeated, leading to the surrender of El Obeid to the Mahdist Empire on January 17, 1883. The British launched a new offensive, sending 10,000 troops toward El Obeid in late 1883. The Anglo-Egyptian force was attacked and utterly defeated in a battle on November 3–5, 1883. Fighting was also taking place along the Red Sea, where the Anglo-Egyptian forces were also defeated in February 1884. After very bloody fighting, the Mahdists were briefly defeated at Tamai in March 1884. Concluding that it was going to be impossible to maintain control in Sudan, the British sent Gen. Charles Gordon to evacuate the British from Khartoum. Instead, Gordon decided to defend the city, where he withstood a Mahdi siege for almost a year. On January 26, 1885, the Mahdi army was able to breach the fortifications and slaughtered all of the defenders upon entry. A British relief column arrived two days later but immediately withdrew. While the Anglo-Egyptian forces retreated from central Sudan, some fighting continued along the Red Sea. A British expedition was defeated there on March 22, 1885, ending the war. The British forces remained along the coast for another month, but ultimately the British and Egyptians were driven out of Sudan.

After their losses, the British temporarily gave up hopes for the reconquest of Sudan. The Mahdi forces would later fight against Italy in 1893 (extra-state war #400). The British then resumed their campaign against the Mahdi from 1896 to 1899 (extra-state war #409).

Coding: This war starts with both the United Kingdom and Egypt coded as interstate system member participants; however, in 1882 Britain conquered Egypt in a brief war (inter-state war #65). Thus Egypt lost its status as a member of the interstate system, which it would not regain until 1937. During the phase of the war after September 1882, losses suffered by Egyptian forces under British command in the Sudan were considered British battle-related deaths. The Mahdist Empire is coded as part of Egypt until 1882, when the Mahdist Empire is considered to have sufficient unity and territory to be coded as an autonomous entity from 1882 to 1898. Clodfelter (2002) calls this the "First Mahdist War" of 1881–85. Phillips and Axelrod (2005) call this the "Sudanese War (First Mahdist War)" of 1881–1885.

Sources: Alford and Sword (1932); Baddour (1960); Churchill (1900); Clodfelter (2002); Featherstone (1973); Holt (1958); Jaques (2007);

Magnus (1958); McGregor (2006); Pakenham (1991); Phillips and Axelrod (2005); Schafer (1995); Shibeika (1952); Theobald (1951); Williams (1907).

EXTRA-STATE WAR #385:

The Third Franco-Vietnamese War of 1882–1884

Participants: France vs. China, the Black Flag, Vietnam,
Dates: April 25, 1882, to June 14, 1884
Battle-Related Deaths: France—4,500; Vietnam—2,000; China—1,000; Black Flag—[ ]
Where Fought: Asia
Initiator: France
Outcome: Transformed into inter-state war war #67
War Type: Imperial

Narrative: As a result of the First and Second Franco-Vietnamese wars of 1858–1862 and 1873–1874 (extra-state wars #349 and #369), France had gained control of Cochin China and access to the Red River from Vietnam. France wanted to expand its control into central Vietnam (Annam) and northern Vietnam (Tonkin) and hoped that the Red River would provide access to these regions. As with the earlier war, banditry by the Black Flag against French activities and persecution of Christians in the north remained problems. China became concerned at the growing French influence and in 1881 reasserted a historical claim to Annam as a Chinese vassal state.

Meanwhile, in France proponents of imperialism began to advance an aggressive colonial policy in Asia and elsewhere (Madagascar, Tunisia, and Niger). Commercial interests were one of the driving forces in this policy, and in this case France used alleged Vietnamese violations of the 1873 treaty as an excuse for military action. A small French force landed at Tonkin on April 25, 1882, which marks the start of the war. The French captured Hanoi and then advanced along the Red River. There the French were ambushed by the Black Flag on May 19, 1883. The French government sent reinforcements, which bombed the fortress at Hue on August 18, 1883. At this time the French and Vietnamese signed an agreement, on August 25, 1883, that gave the French protectorates over Tonkin and Annam. The Chinese rejected the agreement, and in the next major engagement the French attacked a joint Chinese–Black Flag fortress at Sontay on December 14–16, 1883, which marks the entry of China into the war. The fortress fell to the French, prompting China to start negotiations with France. Skirmishes continued throughout early 1884, and the talks broke down, though there was an agreement between the French and the Black Flag in May 1884. By this time the French had 17,000 troops deployed in Vietnam. At this point the participants in the war changed; thus the war is transformed into an inter-state war. As of June 15, 1884, the Chinese increased their involvement in the war, taking over the bulk of the fighting against the French from Vietnam and the Black Flag. Thus this extra-state war is ended on June 14 and is transformed into the Sino-French War (inter-state war #67), which starts on June 15.

Coding: The end date of this war is the day before the start date of inter-state war #67, as China took over the bulk of the fighting. Many of the French fatalities were from disease.

Sources: Bodart (1916); Buttinger (1958); Cady (1954); Clodfelter (2002); Cordier (1920); Jaques (2007); Khoi, (1955); Kiernan (1939); Lancaster (1961); Li (1956); Osborne (1969); Phillips and Axelrod (2005); Roberts (1963); SarDesai (1998); Thompson (1968); Williams (1907).

EXTRA-STATE WAR #386:

The First Franco-Madagascan War of 1883–1885

Participants: France vs. Madagascar
Dates: May [ ], 1883, to December 12, 1885
Battle-Related Deaths: Madagascar—700; France—300

Where Fought: Africa
Initiator: France
Outcome: France wins
War Type: Imperial

Narrative: In the seventeenth century, Madagascar, an island located off the southeast coast of Africa, was divided into several small kingdoms. The Portuguese had tried to establish missions there, though from 1642 onward they came into conflict with the French, who also established settlements. By the early nineteenth century, the Hova had been able to take control of almost all the island. The Hova, a group that had emigrated from Indonesia a millennium earlier, was the main highland group, and they created a unified Madagascar state with the help of the British. In 1861 there was a treaty among France, Great Britain, and Madagascar; however, disputes between the French and the Hova ensued. In 1880, when France was under the sway of the imperialists, the French began to assert greater control over Madagascar. In 1882 they attempted to assert a protectorate over northwest Madagascar. The Hova-dominated government refused to accept its loss of independence and sent appeals to the French and British governments. In response, the French began a military operation in 1883. In May the French fleet occupied Majunga and then sailed along the eastern coast. In June 23,000 French troops bombarded and then occupied the coastal town of Tamatave. Over the next two years low levels of sustained combat occurred. Finally, in 1885, the French were permitted to impose a protectorate in the northwest. A French "resident" was also allowed to be stationed in the capital, Tananarive. Conflict between Madagascar and France would resume in 1894 (extra-state war #401), at the conclusion of which France would establish direct colonial rule over Madagascar.

Coding: Madagascar is coded as a French protectorate until 1895, when it comes under direct French colonial rule. Phillips and

Axelrod (2005) cover this war, while Clodfelter (2002) mentions it only in the context of the 1894 war.

Sources: Brown (2001); Jaques (2007); Kent (1976); Phillips and Axelrod (2005); Schafer (1995); Stearns (2001); Williams (1907).

EXTRA-STATE WAR #387:
The Third British-Burmese War of 1885–1889

Participants: United Kingdom vs. Burma
Dates: November 10, 1885, to [ ]/[ ]/1889
Battle-Related Deaths: United Kingdom—3,000; Burma—3,000
Where Fought: Asia
Initiator: United Kingdom
Outcome: United Kingdom wins
War Type: Imperial

Narrative: Related to Britain's Empire in India, the British had fought wars against Burma (present-day Myanmar) in 1823–1826 (extra-state war #310) and in 1852 (extra-state war #339). As a result of these wars, Britain had gained control over southern Burma. This war would complete the British conquest of Burma.

Only upper Burma remained independent when its new king, Thibaw Min, came to power in 1878. Thibaw Min tried to reduce British influence in Burma by conducting negotiations with Britain's colonial rival France to build a railroad or enter into a treaty. Such an arrangement would have threatened British economic interests. Furthermore, the Burmese threatened to seize the assets of the British-owned Bombay-Burma Trading Company. The British objected and issued an ultimatum to the Burmese on October 22, 1885. When the Burmese king refused to address British concerns and rejected their terms on November 9, the British decided to take military action. On November 10, 1885, fifty-five ships of the Royal Navy transported almost 12,000 British troops up the Irawadi River toward the capital city at Ava (Mandalay).

The Burmese were taken completely by surprise. The British immediately began a bombardment of the fortifications. The British ground attack began on November 16, and initially the 15,000-man Burmese army put up only minimal resistance. There was a brief battle at nearby Minhla the following day in which the Burmese were defeated. Attacks were made against the other fortresses along the river, and the British quickly advanced toward the capital. When they arrived, they were presented with the king's surrender, on November 27; however, the pacification of the remainder of the country was more difficult. The British continued their advance and seized Bhamo on December 28, but this still did not end the conflict. British expeditions followed one upon another. It took 29,000 British troops over the next four years to subdue the resistance, primarily by establishing an extensive system of posts all over the country.

Coding: Most of the fatalities take place during the four-year period of pacification.

Sources: Bruce (1973); Clodfelter (2002); Featherstone (1973); Phillips and Axelrod (2005); Sorokin (1937); Williams (1907).

EXTRA-STATE WAR #389:

The French-Mandinka War of 1885–1886

Participants: France vs. Mandinka
Dates: [ ]/[ ]/1885, to [ ]/[ ]/1886
Battle-Related Deaths: France—1,000; Mandinka—[ ]
Where Fought: Africa
Initiator: France
Outcome: France wins
War Type: Imperial

Narrative: The Mandinka (Mandingo) are one of the largest ethnic groups in West Africa. They formed the great Empire of Mali, which dominated the area in the sixteenth century, stretching along the Gambia River from the Atlantic coast to the upper reaches of the Niger River. In the eighteenth century many of the Mandinka people converted to Islam. In the nineteenth century, a number of the Mandinka in the region of the Upper Milo (a Niger River tributary) were united by a religious chief named Samori Touré, known by the British and French as "the African Napoleon." Samori was interested in utilizing modern weapons to create an Islamic state. In 1878 he proclaimed himself the leader of his own Wassoulou Empire, with its capital at Bissandugu. The empire expanded into what is now northern Côte d'Ivoire, where the Mandinka came into contact with the equally expansionist French, who had established trading posts along the coast in the late seventeenth century. The two parties had their first skirmish in 1882, which prompted Samori to make overtures to the British in Sierra Leone. In 1885 a large French expedition attempted to seize the Burcé gold field, which was the main source of the Mandinka's wealth. Thus the Mandinka counterattacked and were successful in forcing the French to retreat. The next year, 2,000 French troops defeated 40,000 Mandinka, resulting in the annexation of much of the interior of Côte d'Ivoire. Samori then recognized the Niger River as his frontier.

Coding: The conflict between the Mandinka and the French continued as low-level guerrilla war, though there were increases in hostilities in 1894–1895 and in 1898.

Sources: Ajayi and Crowder (1987); Catchpole and Akinjogbin (1983); Clodfelter (2002); Edgerton (2002); Fage (1969); Fage and Oliver (1975–1980); Lewis (1987); Phillips and Axelrod (2005); Steel (2003).

EXTRA-STATE WAR #390:

The Russo-Afghan War of 1885

Participants: Russia vs. Afghanistan
Dates: March 30, 1885, to April [ ], 1885
Battle-Related Deaths: Russia—1,000; Afghanistan—[ ]

Where Fought: Asia
Initiator: Russia
Outcome: Compromise
War Type: Imperial

Narrative: This conflict was part of the "Great Game," through which the United Kingdom and Russia vied for influence in Central Asia for much of the nineteenth century. Russia had followed a policy of expanding its control in Central Asia, partially to subdue disorder there and partially to deter further British expansionism from India. Russia had gained control over Kokand (extra-state wars #359 and #371), Bukhara (extra-state war #361), and Turkoman (extra-state war #376). The next area of concern was Afghanistan. Great Britain had already been involved in two wars there, extra-state war #322 in 1839–1842 and extra-state war #379 in 1878–1880. Prior to the last war, Britain and Russia had signed an agreement to respect the territorial integrity of Afghanistan. Britain's involvement in Afghanistan was motivated to some degree by a desire to have an Afghan ruler who was not under Russian influence.

As the Russians advanced further southward, border clashes with Afghanistan became more common. Finally, in 1885, Russian troops attacked the Afghans and drove them out of the Penjdeh region. Local Russian troops, ignoring orders to hold their position, then attacked and defeated Afghan forces at Ak-Teppe on March 30, 1885. Britain, fearing a threat to its control of the city of Herat, considered a war with Russia. Instead, the British negotiated an agreement under which Russia obtained the Penjdeh district in exchange for Afghan sovereignty over the Zulfkan Pass.

Coding: Clodfelter (2002) has an entry on "Russian Conquests in Central Asia: 1839–1885." Phillips and Axelrod include the "Russo-Afghan War" of 1885.

Sources: Clodfelter (2002); Kohn (1999); Langer (1948); O'Balance (1993); Phillips and Axelrod (2005).

EXTRA-STATE WAR #391:

The Serbian- Bulgarian War of 1885

Participants: Serbia vs. Bulgaria
Dates: November 2, 1885, to December 7, 1885
Battle-Related Deaths: Bulgaria—3,000;
    Serbia—2,000
Where Fought: Europe
Initiator: Serbia
Outcome: Bulgaria wins
War Type: Imperial

Narrative: The Serbian-Bulgarian War of 1885 lies at the heart of the process that led to World War I. The events leading to the Serbian-Bulgarian War started with the financial bankruptcy of the Ottoman Empire in 1875, when the Turks were hopelessly swallowed by a vicious cycle of mounting interest payments to west European bankers. Meanwhile, the Balkan states had been agitating for independence from the Ottoman Empire, which led to the Serbian-Turkish war in 1876–1877 (extra-state war #373), followed by the Ottoman loss in the Second Russo-Turkish War of 1877–1878 (inter-state war #61). The Congress of Berlin, at which the major powers settled the outcomes of the later war, ended 500 years of Ottoman rule in the Balkans for the most part. Bulgaria was divided into three entities: Bulgaria would be autonomous, Eastern Roumelia was a new creation with intermediary status, and Macedonia remained under Ottoman rule. In one view, "The disposition of Macedonia, perhaps the one issue that more than any other doomed the region to future conflict, was not even taken up seriously at the Congress of Berlin" (Medlicott 1963, 38). Both Serbia and Bulgaria had interests in Macedonia, which had been part of the Bulgarian state, from 681 to 1018, and then later had been placed under the control of the Greek patriarch within the Ottoman Empire. But Skopje, the capital of Macedonia, had also been the capital of the Serbian tsar Stefan Dušan, who was crowned there in 1346 after he had captured Macedonia. The fate of Macedonia would be determined in the Serb-Bulgarian War of 1885.

On September 18, 1885, a conflict broke out in Eastern Roumelia, a thin strip south of Bulgaria that stretched from Plovdiv to the Black Sea. The next day Bulgaria proclaimed its union with Roumelia. Serbia, fearing that Bulgaria would aim to acquire Macedonia next, demanded compensation for this enlargement of Bulgaria. Although a new international conference was arranged to address the issue, King Milan of Serbia decided instead to invade Bulgaria with 28,000 troops in November 1885. The able military commander of the Bulgarians, Prince Alexander, met the Serbs with 15,000 Bulgar troops at Slivnitza and won a victory. Then, larger armies, on the order of 40,000 troops on each side, met at the battle of Pirot, and again the Bulgars won. Only the threat by Austria to intervene in defense of Serbia ended the war and prevented a complete Bulgarian occupation of Serbia. The treaty in 1886 reaffirmed the prewar Serb-Bulgarian border and recognized the union of Roumelia and Bulgaria. The next time Serbia and Bulgaria (by then a system member) would fight (inter-state war #103, in 1913), Serbia would need to round up two allies, Greece and Romania, in order to win.

Coding: In our dataset, the cast of characters is as follows: Serbia is a state system member as of 1878, but Bulgaria was an autonomous entity until 1908; so, with just one of the protagonists in the system, this is an extra-state war. Eastern Roumelia, which had been part of the Ottoman Empire since 1492, becomes an autonomous entity in 1878 and then a part of Bulgaria from 1885 on. Macedonia, always previously a part of some other entity, does not become an autonomous entity until 1991 and does not become a state system member until 1993. Phillips and Axelrod (2005) have this war with the same start date but extend it into 1886.

Sources: Albrecht-Carrié (1958); Clodfelter (2002); Dumas and Vedel-Peterson (1923); Gerolymatos (2002); Hupchick and Cox (2001);

MacDermott (1962); Mallat (1902); Medlicott (1963); Mijatovich (1917); Miller (2007); Phillips and Axelrod (2005).

EXTRA-STATE WAR #392:

The First Italian-Ethiopian War of 1887

Participants: Italy vs. Ethiopia
Dates: January 24, 1887, to March [ ], 1887
Battle-Related Deaths: Italy—1,000; Ethiopia—400
Where Fought: Africa
Initiator: Italy
Outcome: Compromise
War Type: Imperial

Narrative: After its relatively late unification, Italy had wanted to catch up to the other powers in developing a colonial empire. Its first attempt had been frustrated by French activities in Tunisia in 1881 (extra-state war #383). The Italians then turned to the other side of the African continent, focusing on the Red Sea coast, and Ethiopia in particular. The Ethiopian state had survived a military defeat at the hands of the British Empire in 1867–1868 (extra-state war #362). Next, the Ethiopians impressively beat off an Egyptian attempt to conquer the Ethiopian province of Eritrea (extra-state war #372), in 1875–1876. But Ethiopia had not been tested in an all-out European attempt to turn it into a colony. The Italians were about to give it a try— twice in the nineteenth century and then, the third time, under Mussolini in the 1930s.

In 1882 the Italians began their colonial enterprise with the purchase of Assab, a small city on the Eritrean coast. In 1885 Great Britain, which was involved in a war against the Mahdi (extra-state war #384), helped the Italians secure an outpost at Massawa on Ethiopia's Red Sea coast. From there, the Italians began their excursions into Ethiopia's interior. Italy's offensive was met with a skirmish at Saati on January 24, 1887. Two days later, an Italian reinforcement column was ambushed and annihilated by 15,000 Ethiopians at Dogali (ten miles west of Massawa). Italy then dispatched an army of 20,000 troops, stationing them in Eritrea. There they faced little fighting because Ethiopian emperor Yohannes IV withdrew into the interior. The Italians were decimated by disease, however, and withdrew, ending the war in March 1887. Meanwhile, Yohannes IV was killed in fighting a Mahdi invasion in the north (non-state war #1559). His successor, Menelik, an ally of Italy, assumed the throne and signed the Treaty of Uccialli with Italy on May 2, 1889. The conclusion of the war is coded as a compromise because Italy failed to defeat Ethiopia but was able to withdraw effectively while maintaining its colony in Eritrea. The conflict would be resumed in extra-state war #407, the Second Italian-Ethiopian War of 1895–1896.

Coding: Although most scholars see this war as beginning at approximately the same time, the end date of the war varies considerably. Kohn (1999) and Phillips and Axelrod (2005) call this the "Italo-Ethiopian War" and extend the end date to 1889 with the Treaty of Uccialli. Jaques describes the "1st Italo-Ethiopian War" as lasting from 1887 to 1896, encompassing what we refer to as the First and the Second Italian-Ethiopian Wars. Clodfelter (2002) calls this the "Italian-Abyssinian War," though he also limits it to 1887. Our coding is based on the lack of fighting between Italy and Ethiopia leading to 1,000 battle-related deaths per year in the 1887–1895 period.

Sources: Clodfelter (2002); Jaques (2007); Kohn (1999); Langer (1948); Marcus (1995); Pakenham (1991); Phillips and Axelrod (2005).

EXTRA-STATE WAR #393:
The Zambezi Conquest of 1888

Participants: Portugal vs. Prazero da Cruz
Dates: [ ]/[ ]/1888, to [ ]/[ ]/1888
Battle-Related Deaths: Prazero da Cruz—6,000; Portugal—[ ]
Where Fought: Africa
Initiator: Portugal
Outcome: Portugal wins
War Type: Imperial

Narrative: Portuguese colonial expansion along the coast of East Africa began with Vasco da Gama in 1498, and by the end of the sixteenth century, the Portuguese had developed trading outposts and forts within most of the Arab sultanates along the coast. As Portugal's fortunes declined, Portuguese influence was concentrated on the island of Mozambique and the southern coast. A colonial conference was held among the great powers in Berlin from November 1884 to February 1885, and the Act of Berlin preserved Portuguese rights in the region, though Portugal lost colonial territory on the west coast of Africa (in the Angola-Congo region). Portugal resisted surrendering its objective to spread its colonial control between Mozambique and Angola, particularly in the face of growing German aspirations in the region. Although Portugal was gradually able to extend its control inland, its power was restricted by the autonomy of individual settlers. Within the region, a *prazo* was a private estate granted to a private individual by the Portuguese government. Several of these were granted in the Zambezi Valley in the Portuguese colony of Mozambique. The da Cruz family had established their *prazo* in the Tete region in 1767. During the mid-nineteenth century the Pereira clan of the *prazo* (or *prazero*) of Macanga was attacked by the da Cruz clan of Massangano. The Portuguese authorities were unable to stop the fighting despite sending four small expeditions. Consequently, the da Cruz family continued to give the Portuguese authorities unending problems. The precipitant for this particular war was João Santana da Cruz (Bonga da Cruz), who refused to pay taxes in 1888. Portuguese governor-general Augusto da Castilho sent an expedition to force compliance and attacked the stockade at Massangano, defeating da Cruz.

Coding: Mozambique would remain a Portuguese colony until gaining its independence in 1975 (extra-state war #471).

Sources: Albrecht-Carrié (1958); Azevedo (1991); Clodfelter (2002); Duffy (1962).

CHAPTER FOUR: The Extra-state Wars

EXTRA-STATE WAR #394:
The First Franco-Dahomeyan War of 1890

Participants: France vs. Dahomey
Dates: March 1, 1890, to April 20, 1890
Battle-Related Deaths: Dahomey—800; France (and native auxiliaries)—200
Where Fought: Africa
Initiator: France
Outcome: France wins
War Type: Imperial

Narrative: In the late nineteenth century, France engaged in colonial expansions in Asia, the Middle East, and particularly Africa. The French gained footholds along the coast of West Africa, and as they began to expand their areas of control, they became involved in wars with the Tukulor (extra-state war #340) and the Mandinka (extra-state war #389). The French objective in this war was Dahomey (currently known as Benin). Both Great Britain and France wanted to control West Africa's Niger River region but agreed to divide control in 1889. France received the town of Cotonou, where it landed an expedition in 1890. King Behanzin of Dahomey sent his forces against the French on March 1, though this attack and a subsequent attack three days later were repulsed. After receiving reinforcements, the French went on the offensive in April, advancing to Atchoupa, where they were attacked by 9,000 Dahomeyan troops, including 2,000 Amazons led by King Behanzin himself. The French inflicted heavy casualties but were forced to withdraw when the native auxiliaries faltered. A truce was signed in which Cotonou and Porto Novo were ceded to the French. Hostilities between the two parties would begin again in 1892 (extra-state war #396).

Coding: Kohn (1999) and Phillips and Axelrod (2005) start the war in 1889, apparently with the British and French agreement.

Sources: Catchpole and Akinjogbin (1983); Clodfelter (2002); Dalzel (1967); Jaques (2007);

Phillips and Axelrod (2005); Ross (1971); Sivard (1991).

EXTRA-STATE WAR #395:
The Franco-Jolof War of 1890–1891

Participants: France vs. Jolof/Tukulor
Dates: April [ ], 1890, to Feburary 24, 1891
Battle-Related Deaths: Jolof/Tukulor—3,000; France—100
Where Fought: Africa
Initiator: France
Outcome: France wins
War Type: Imperial

Narrative: In 1854 the French had engaged in a war with the Tukulor people (extra-state war #340). The French had sought to expand their colonial control in Senegal eastward, while the Tukulor were trying to expand their empire westward. The war had ended in a stalemate, with each side turning its attention elsewhere; however, the conflict (or jihad) between the French and various local Islamic leaders continued throughout the years. War started in the region again in 1890, when the French launched a two-pronged attack. Senegal's Governor Clément-Thomas invaded two semiautonomous areas in the region: the Jolof Empire and Futa Toro. The French, breaking an 1889 treaty, attacked long-time leader Albury Njay. Although Albury Njay was a member of the traditional ruling elite in Jolof, he supported the marabout (strict Muslims) and was seen as continuing the work of Shaikh Amadu Ba, who had brought the emphasis on jihad to Jolof. As the French advanced, Albury withdrew into what is now Mali and then to present-day Mauritania. Meanwhile, Commandant Supérieur Louis Archinard attacked further east against Tukolar leader Ahmadu Seku, seizing the religious center of Ségu on April 6, 1890. The Tukulors were also defeated at Koniakary, Nioro, and Diena (on February 24, 1891). These combined offensives broke the ties between the eastern and western

Islamic movements and enabled the French to consolidate their control.

Coding: This entire region was incorporated into French West Africa, which remained a French colony until 1958. Senegal did not become a member of the interstate system until 1960.

Sources: Catchpole and Akinjogbin (1983); Charles (1975); Clark and Phillips (1994); Clodfelter (2002); Phillips and Axelrod (2005); Robinson (1988).

EXTRA-STATE WAR #396:
The Second Franco-Dahomeyan War of 1892–1893

Participants: France vs. Dahomey
Dates: September 19, 1892, to November 9, 1893
Battle-Related Deaths: Dahomey—1,800;
   France—80
Where Fought: Africa
Initiator: France
Outcome: France wins
War Type: Imperial

Narrative: French colonial expansion involved France in numerous conflicts in West Africa. Although many of the conflicts did not reach the level of wars (such as Senegal in 1857), the French did become involved in wars with the Tukolar (extra-state war #340) and the Mandinka (extra-state war #389), Dahomey (extra-state war #394), and Jolof (extra-state war #395).

In the First Franco-Dahomeyan War of 1890, France had fought against King Behanzin and had gained control over Cotonou and Porto Novo. To an extent, the French had rationalized their colonial expansion in the region as a means to end the slave trade. However, King Behanzin remained involved in the slave trade and continued to make raids into neighboring areas. In 1892 he attacked a French gunboat, which precipitated this war. A French force of 2,000 troops advanced inland toward Dogba, where the Dahomeyans attacked on September 19, 1892.

The French suffered heavy losses but were finally able to repulse the Dahomeyans. The French continued their advance, occupying the holy city of Kana before entering King Behanzin's capital at Abomey on November 17, 1892. Despite a truce, the Dahomeyans continued their resistance until a second French expedition defeated them at Acheribe on November 9, 1893. The French installed Behanzin's brother Gouchili as the new king. Behanzin surrendered in January 1894 and was exiled.

Coding: Owing to the existence of a truce and the fact that there appears to be only minor fighting between November 17, 1892, and November 9, 1893, this period is coded as a break in the war. Jaques (2007) refers to the 1893 expedition as a separate "3rd Franco-Dahomeyan War."

Sources: Catchpole and Akinjogbin (1983); Clodfelter (2002); Dalzel (1967); Jaques (2007); Phillips and Axelrod (2005); Ross (1971); Sivard (1991).

EXTRA-STATE WAR #397:
The Belgian-Tib War of 1892–1894

Participants: Belgium vs. Tippu Tib Empire
Dates: October [ ], 1892, to February [ ], 1894
Battle-Related Deaths: Tib Empire—13,000;
   Belgium/auxiliaries—7,000
Where Fought: Africa
Initiator: Belgium
Outcome: Belgium wins
War Type: Imperial

Narrative: The Congo Free State was the privately owned preserve of Belgium's King Leopold II. The Congo Free State existed from 1885 to 1908 and encompassed the area of what is now the Democratic Republic of the Congo (also known as Zaire). European awareness about the region was heightened in 1877 by the work of explorer Henry Morton Stanley. In 1885 King Leopold II was faced with two problems in the Congo: the Tippu Tib Empire and Cecil Rhodes, who was attempting to expand British territory northward from the Cape Colony into the Congo. The problem of British encroachment was solved in 1891 through a treaty with the Yeke Kingdom in Katanga. King Leopold II then turned to the issue of Hamed bin Muhammed el Murjebi, known as Tippu Tib.

Tippu Tib was an Arab chieftain who had gained prominence by assisting western explorers, such as Stanley, and by leading trading expeditions for the sultans of Zanzibar. He then was able to develop his own plantations and create an extensive empire, based on slave trading, in the eastern part of the Congo. In order to gain control over this region, King Leopold II initially entered into an alliance with Tippu Tib and later appointed him the governor of the Stanley Falls district (on the basis of a recommendation by Stanley). In 1891 Tippu Tib retired to Zanzibar Island, where he wrote his autobiography; however, his empire remained under the control of his son, Sefu. Ultimately, King Leopold II determined to put an end to the Arab Tib Empire, an economic rival. In October 1892 an expedition, led by Commandant Francis Dhanis and consisting mostly of 10,000 Congolese auxiliaries, was sent against the Tib Empire. In November a Belgian delegation met with Sefu to try to negotiate the release of two Belgian hostages. When the talks failed, the major fighting began. On November 23 the Belgians attacked Sefu's temporary fort at the Lomami River. The fort was completely destroyed, with 600 Arabs killed in the fort and another 2,000–3,000 killed when they tried to escape by jumping into the river. Sefu fled and was followed by Dhanis's troops, which had grown in number with the slaves captured from Sefu. The slavers city at Nyangwe was captured on March 5, 1893. Additional reinforcements joined the Belgians, who then attacked Sefu's luxurious capital city of Kasongo, which was easily captured. Additional Belgian armies were sent into the region and completed the destruction of the Tib Empire by February 1894.

This war neither ended the challenges to King Leopold II nor dampened the king's desire to extend his colony eastward to the Nile. In 1895 and 1897 the Batetela people rebelled against Belgian rule, though they were crushed in a genocidal slaughter by 1900. International pressure concerning the inhumane conditions in the Congo Free State led to the end of King Leopold's personal rule and the annexation of the area as a colony of Belgium, the Belgian Congo.

Coding: COW codes the Tippu Tib Empire as an autonomous entity from 1870 to 1894. Clodfelter (2002) refers to this as the "Arab War: 1892–94." Pakenham (1991) refers to it as an "Ivory War." Phillips and Axelrod (2005) do not cover this war.

Sources: Clodfelter (2002); Hochschild (1998); Pakenham (1991).

The Third British-Ashanti War of 1893–1894

Participants: United Kingdom vs. Ashanti
Dates: [ ]/[ ]/1893, to [ ]/[ ]/1894
Battle-Related Deaths: Ashanti—800; United Kingdom—200
Where Fought: Africa
Initiator: Ashanti
Outcome: United Kingdom wins
War Type: Imperial

Narrative: Even after two wars with the Ashanti kingdom of the central Gold Coast (extra-state war #311 in 1824–1826 and extra–state war #367 in 1873–1874), the British were still confined mostly to the coastal region of west Africa. The Ashanti had turned down a British offer of a protectorate in 1891, but the latter were still interested in extending their control into the Ashanti domain. In 1888 the British had helped arrange the accession of a new Ashanti ruler, King Prempeh I, hoping that the young king might be more open to British control. King Prempeh I, however, wished to restore Ashanti power and began raiding British territory in 1893. The British invaded Ashanti territory and defeated the king's forces by 1894, then forcing a protectorate on him. After further clashes in 1895–1896 (below the level of war), Prempeh was deported to the Seychelles and the protectorate firmly established. The final war against the Ashanti occurred in 1900 (extra-state war #417).

Coding: Clodfelter (2002) does not cover this war. Kohn (1986) and Phillips and Axelrod (2005) include it as the "Third Ashanti War."

Sources: Baden-Powell (1972); Edgerton (1995); Featherstone (1992a); Hernon (2002); Kohn (1986); Phillips and Axelrod (2005); Sivard (1991).

EXTRA-STATE WAR #399:

The Melilla War (or Rif War) of 1893–1894

Participants: Spain vs. Rif tribes
Dates: September 29, 1893, to March 5, 1894
Battle-Related Deaths: Rif tribes—1,500; Spain—1,000
Where Fought: Middle East
Initiator: Rif tribes
Outcome: Spain wins
War Type: Imperial

Narrative: The Rif tribesmen are a group of Muslim Berbers resident in the Rif Mountains in northern Morocco, very near the Straits of Gibraltar. This highland area thus lies somewhat distinct, to the north and west of the Atlas Mountain chain that runs across Morocco and Algeria. The location of the Rif brought the tribesmen into close proximity with the long-standing Spanish coastal port colonies at Ceuta and Melilla. Spain had controlled Melilla since 1497, and it had already endured an attack in 1774. Spain had also captured Tetuan as a result of the First Spanish-Moroccan War of 1859–1860 (inter-state war #31).

In 1893 the Spanish were in the midst of strengthening the fortifications at Melilla when 6,000 Rif warriors attacked the Spanish garrison of only 400 troops. The Spanish superiority in weapons contributed to an initial death toll of only 21 Spanish but 160 Rif. However, when a Spanish artillery shell struck a mosque in a village from which the Rif were organizing the siege, the war took on the broader sense and appeal of a jihad. The local outcry led to further recruitment of warriors, until between 12,000 and 20,000 were besieging the city. The attack on Melilla also fueled popular outrage in Spain, where ships and 3,000 troops were sent to reinforce the garrison. On October 28 the Spanish sent a column out in an attempt to dislodge the Rif, but their enemy's superior numbers led to serious losses among the Spanish. An additional three Spanish regiments arrived the next day and were able to temporarily push the Rif back. Nevertheless, the Rif maintained the siege, and as they strengthened their positions, it became more difficult to resupply the Spanish garrison. The Rif fighters were even able to seize and hold portions of the city's fortifications. In the beginning of November, Spain began a naval bombardment of the Rif positions, and at the end of the month another 7,000 Spanish reinforcements arrived. The Spanish were finally able to negotiate the Treaty of Fez (1894) directly with the sultan of Morocco. By the terms of the treaty, Spain was allowed to complete fortifications at Melilla. The sultan of Morocco agreed to pay an indemnity to Spain and to punish and suppress the Rif. Morocco would remain independent for another decade.

Melilla would again play an important role in the Second Spanish-Moroccan War of 1909–1910 (inter-state war #94). Both France and Spain continued to be interested in protecting and expanding their outposts in Morocco. In 1912 France established a protectorate over Morocco, with Spain retaining control of Ceuta and Melilla and gaining control of the Sahara possessions to the southwest.

Coding: Morocco was a member of the interstate system from 1847 to 1912. In this conflict, the sultan of Morocco was sympathetic to both sides, to the degree that he did not take military action against Spain but did not want to attack or suppress the Rif warriors, either. Thus, since the Moroccan government was not a party to this war, it is an extra-state war. Clodfelter does not cover this war. Kohn (1986) and Phillips and Axelrod (2005) call it the "Rif War" of 1893.

Sources: Brecke (1999); Jaques (2007); Kohn (1986); Pennell (2001); Phillips and Axelrod (2005); Sorokin (1937); Usborne (1936).

EXTRA-STATE WAR #400:
Mahdist-Italian War of 1893–1894

Participants: Italy vs. Mahdist Empire
Dates: December 21, 1893, to July 12, 1894
Battle-Related Deaths: Mahdist Empire—5,000; Italy—270
Where Fought: Africa
Initiator: Mahdist Empire
Winner: Italy
War Type: Imperial

Narrative: Muhammad Ahmad, who styled himself the Mahdi, or successor of the Prophet Muhammad, developed a substantial following in Sudan, which in the 1880s was ruled by the Egyptians. The Mahdi wanted to remove the foreign influences from Sudan, which ultimately led him to wage war against the Egyptians and Great Britain in 1881 (extra-state war #384). That war ended with the defeat of Gen. Charles Gordon and the British at Khartoum in 1885. The British and Egyptian forces then withdrew, leaving Sudan in control of the Mahdist Empire. Muhammad Ahmad died soon thereafter, and he was succeeded by Khalifa Abdallahi ibn Muhammad. The Mahdi's followers (also referred to as the Dervishes) then became involved in a war with Ethiopia (non-state war

#1559). In 1887 Ethiopia also confronted a war with Italy (extra-state war #392). Consequently, the Mahdist Empire's move eastward also brought it into contact with the Italian colony at Eritrea.

The Italians had established a colony in Eritrea in 1882. In its attempt to remove foreigners from the region, the Mahdist Empire's army of 11,000 left Kasala (in eastern Sudan, east of Khartoum) and invaded this coastal region. On December 21, 1893, at Agordat, the Mahdist Empire's army clashed with a force of 2,000 Italians. The Mahdist army was completely defeated at the Battle of Agordat on December 21 and then withdrew back into Sudan. In July 1894 the Italians went on the offensive and captured Kasala on July 12, ending this war. The British would resume their campaign against the Mahdist Empire from 1896 to 1899 (extra-state war #409), which led to the destruction of the Mahdist Empire.

Coding: The Mahdist Empire is coded as an autonomous entity from 1882 to 1898.

Sources: Clodfelter (2002); Jaques (2007); Zuljan (2003).

EXTRA-STATE WAR #401:
The Second Franco-Madagascan War of 1894–1895

Participants: France vs. Madagascar
Dates: June 16, 1894, to October 1, 1895
Battle-Related Deaths: France—6,000; Madagascar—2,000
Where Fought: Africa
Initiator: Madagascar
Outcome: France wins
War Type: Imperial

Narrative: In the previous extra-state war with Madagascar's Hova Dynasty (extra-state war #386), France gained a protectorate in the north of the island. By 1894 the French wished to gain additional territory and more control. Again the

Hova resisted, attacking the French in June 1894. The French responded by bombarding the coastal town of Tamatave on December 12, 1894. In February 1895 the French landed some 23,000 French and colonial troops at Majunga and marched toward the Hova capital of Tananarive. On June 29, 1895, the Madagascan army tried to stop the French advance at Tsarasoatra but was unsuccessful, suffering heavy losses. The French continued their offensive, routing the Madagascans at Andriba on August 22. After a brief French bombardment of Tananarive on September 30, 1895, the government of Madagascar surrendered, giving the whole of the island to France. The next year, the Madagascan queen was deposed and a French colonial government installed. It took the French another three years to establish control over most of the island.

Coding: Most of the French fatalities were the result of disease. As a result of this war, Madagascar, which had been coded as a French protectorate, becomes a direct French colony, a status that is retained until 1960. Clodfelter (2002) refers to this as "Conquest and Pacification of Madagascar" in 1894–99. Phillips and Axelrod (2005) refer to this as part of the "Madagascar Wars with France" of 1883–85 and 1894–99.

Sources: Bodart (1916); Brown (1979); Brown (2001a); Clodfelter (2002); Deschamps (1960); Jaques (2007); Kent (1976); Phillips and Axelrod (2005); Sorokin (1937).

EXTRA-STATE WAR #402:

The Second Dutch-Bali War of 1894

Participants: Netherlands vs. Bali
Dates: July [ ], 1894, to July [ ], 1894
Battle-Related Deaths: Bali—2,000; Netherlands—1,000
Where Fought: Asia
Initiator: Netherlands
Outcome: Netherlands wins
War Type: Imperial

Narrative: Since 1609 the Netherlands and its United East India Company had been spreading their influence through the area of what is now Indonesia. The growth of the Dutch colonial empire had occasionally provoked resistance, and the Dutch had been involved in wars with the Javanese (extra-state war #313), Bali (extra-state war #334), Bone (extra-state war #350), and Aceh (extra-state war #370).

One of the islands in the region is Lombok, which is located east across the Lombok Strait from Bali. The island is populated by the Sasak people, who are related to the Balinese, though the Sasak are predominantly Muslim while the Balinese are Hindu. The Dutch visited Lombok in 1674, settled on the eastern half of the island, and accommodated to the status quo by which the western portion of the island was ruled by a Hindu dynasty from Bali. The Sasak tired of Balinese rule, and a revolt began in Lombok in 1891. The Dutch intervened, at first imposing a blockade, and when that proved to be ineffective, in July 1894 they sent 2,400 Dutch and colonial troops in order to support the Sasak. On August 26 a Dutch contingent was attacked and routed near Cakranegara by Balinese forces in what came to be known as the "Lombok Treachery." Three months later the Dutch returned with a larger force to avenge their defeat. They burned Cakranegara and then defeated a more numerous Balinese army near the capital of Mataram on November 22, 1894. There the Balinese engaged in a *puputan*, a ritual suicidal assault, rather than surrender. This war enabled the Netherlands to establish direct control over the entire island.

Coding: Lombok is coded as an autonomous entity from 1816 to 1894. This is an imperial war, because the Dutch went beyond the status quo ante to firmly take over the entire island of Lombok. Covarrubias (1937) calls this the "Lombok War," and Clodfelter (2002) calls this the "Lombok Campaign" of 1894. Phillips and Axelrod (2005) do not cover it.

Sources: Clodfelter (2002); Covarrubias (1937); Jaques (2007); Ricklefs (1993); Schafer (1995).

EXTRA-STATE WAR #403:
The Portuguese–Gaza Empire War of 1895

Participants: Portugal vs. the Gaza Empire of Mozambique
Dates: Febuary 1, 1895, to December 28, 1895
Battle-Related Deaths: Gaza—2,000; Portugal—50
Where Fought: Africa
Initiator: Portugal
Outcome: Portugal wins
War Type: Imperial

Narrative: Portugal's interest in the region of Mozambique had begun with Vasco de Gama in 1498, and by 1510 the Portuguese had established trading outposts amid the Arab sultanates along the coast. The Portuguese gradually established forts and expanded their control in the region. The Berlin Conference held in 1884–1885 to discuss colonial issues preserved Portuguese rights in the region. Portugal approximately doubled its zone of control in Mozambique between 1885 and 1898, moving from the coastal strip and the banks of the Zambezi to control of the full country of Mozambique as we know it today. Frequently, the Portuguese had to confront the power of individually owned settlements (see extra-state war #393). The Portuguese had a "trans-Africa" dream of expanding their colonial holdings to link Mozambique in the east with Angola in the west. The Gaza Empire, an autonomous entity in the southern half of Mozambique and southeastern Zimbabwe, stood in the way of Portuguese expansionism. The Act of Berlin had included Gaza in the Portuguese territory. Despite earlier cooperation and treaties with the Portuguese, the Nguni kingdom of Gaza resisted Portuguese domination. The empire's last ruler, Gungunyane, laid siege to the Portuguese port of Lourenço Marques for a brief period in October 1894. In response the Portuguese sent reinforcements to Mozambique for an expedition against Gaza. In February

1895 the Portuguese were able to decisively defeat the Gazans in a battle at Marracuene (twenty miles from of Lourenço Marques). The Portuguese then dispatched three separate forces against Gaza. In November a Gazan force of 6,000 to 10,000 men was routed at Coolela. A Portuguese raid at Chaimite captured Gungunyane on December 28, 1895, thus ending the war. Gaza was not completely subdued, however, and it launched a revolt (not at war levels) in 1897. Gaza was again defeated by the Portuguese, and it ceased to exist as an autonomous entity in 1900.

Coding: Schafer (1995) classifies Gaza as the autonomous entity of "Shangane (Gaza Empire)" from 1819 to 1900. Clodfelter (2002) covers this war under "Portugal's Colonial Wars in Africa" (no start or end date to entry). Phillips and Axelrod (2005) do not cover it.

Sources: Azevedo (1991); Chilcote (1967); Clodfelter (2002); Duffy (1962); Duffy (1959); Hammond (1966); Schafer (1995); Vandervort (1998).

EXTRA-STATE WAR #404:
The Second Spanish-Cuban War of 1895–1898

Participants: Spain vs. Cuba
Dates: February 24, 1895, to April 21, 1898
Battle-Related Deaths: Spain—59,000; Cuba—20,000
Where Fought: W. Hemisphere
Initiator: Cuba
Outcome: Transformed into inter-state war #79
War Type: Colonial

Narrative: Christopher Columbus visited Cuba in 1492, and the Spanish conquest of Cuba began in 1511. Even though the British had briefly occupied Havana, Cuba was returned to the Spanish by the Treaty of Paris in 1763. It remained a Spanish possession while independence movements erupted throughout the Spanish Empire; however, in the nineteenth century,

Cuban discontent and desire for independence grew, leading to the First Spanish-Cuban (or Ten Years) War in 1868 (extra-state war #363). In this war the Spanish had had to expend a monumental effort to retain their colony in Cuba. The results of the war included Spanish promises of reform and greater autonomy for Cuba, which were never fully realized.

In the 1890s a set of forces combined to propel Cuba to independence. Two general factions existed within Cuba: one favored attaining Cuban autonomy from Spain by peaceful means; the other favored an armed revolution. A charismatic leader of the second group was José Martí, a writer who would later inspire Fidel Castro's revolution. Martí and other revolutionaries had fled to New York, where they organized the Revolutionary Cuban Party, and Martí's newspaper, *Pátria,* agitated for Cuban independence. On February 24, 1895, numerous demonstrations sparked uprisings within Cuba, beginning this war. Initially the revolutionary Cuban army was relatively small (4,500), but it swelled to 25,000 men by December 1895. At the time, the Spanish army numbered 180,000.

Martí did not arrive at the eastern side of Cuba until March 1895, and the Spanish deployed their forces to hunt down the revolutionary leaders. Martí was killed in an ambush on May 19, 1895, and subsequently became a rallying icon for his countrymen. On July 13 the revolutionaries defeated a royalist army at Peralajo. The revolutionaries sent two forces westward from their stronghold in the east across *la tracha* (the north-south trench that the Spanish had dug in the last war in an attempt to contain the revolutionaries in the eastern half of the island). They were successful in defeating the Spanish at Mal Tiempo on December 15; however, at Calimete on December 29 the Spanish were able to withstand the rebel charges. By January 1896 the revolutionaries were successful in spreading the revolution throughout the island. In February the Spanish replaced their captain-general with Valeriano Weyler, who attempted to reinvigorate the Spanish military. Weyler had been known for the brutalities inflicted on civilians during the last war. The imprisonment and death of tens of thousands of civilians in Weyler's concentration camps were widely reported in the Hearst newspapers in the United States. The American public was outraged, sent increased aid to the revolutionaries, and applied pressure on the American government to intervene.

Weyler was successful in reforming the Spanish military, which went on the offensive in February 1896. The Spanish were able to utilize their superior numbers to inflict stinging defeats on the revolutionary forces. By 1897, however, the war had begun to turn in the revolutionaries' favor. Negotiations between Spain and the United States led to the recall of General Weyler, and in early 1898 limited self-government was installed in Cuba. The United State also sent the U.S. battleship *Maine* to Havana to protect the Americans living in Cuba. On February 15, 1898, an explosion onboard the *Maine* led to the sinking of the ship and a loss of 270 American lives. The United States, fairly or not, blamed Spain. An ultimatum was issued to Spain by which Spain was to relinquish its sovereignty over Cuba. Fearing domestic discord, Spain rejected the demands, leading U.S. president McKinley to request that Congress authorize an invasion of Cuba. Congress went further and voted to recognize Cuban independence on April 19. The United States began a blockade of Cuba on April 22, and this date marks the transformation of the extra-state war into an inter-state war (#79) (which begins April 22, while the extra-state war ends on April 21), since the United States took over the bulk of the fighting. In reaction, Spain declared war on April 23, followed by a U.S. declaration two days later. By August 12, 1898, the inter-state war was over; Cuba became an occupied territory of the United States until 1902.

Coding: The Spanish-American War started on April 22, 1898; thus we end the Spanish-Cuban War on the previous day. This coding comes into effect since the Americans immediately assumed the bulk of the fighting against the Spanish. Clodfelter (2002) and Phillips and Axelrod (2005) call this "The Cuban War of Independence" of 1895–98.

Sources: Beals (1933); Carr (1982); Clarke (1906); Clodfelter (2002); LaFeber (1989); Morris (1970); Phillips and Axelrod (2005); Portell Vila (1949); Scheina (2003a); Smith (1965); Sorokin (1937); White (1909).

EXTRA-STATE WAR #405:
The Japan-Taiwanese War of 1895

Participants: Japan vs. Taiwanese
Dates: May 29, 1895, to October 21, 1895
Battle-Related Deaths: Taiwanese—7,760; Japan—4,800
Where Fought: Asia
Initiator: Taiwan
Outcome: Japan wins
War Type: Colonial

Narrative: Following Japan's victory over China in the First Sino-Japanese War, which ended in March 1895 (inter-state war #73), the island of Taiwan was ceded to Japan. When Japanese troops landed on the island on May 29, 1895, they were greeted with a large-scale rebellion by the Taiwanese. The Republic of Taiwan was declared, with its capital at Taipei. The Japanese continued their advance, and the capital fell in twelve days; however, an armed pirate group called the Black Flag kept the revolt going in the southern part of the island. Black Flag leader Liu Yung-fu, who had commanded military affairs in the south, was declared the president of the new Taiwanese government at Tainanfu, and he received weapons and assistance from China. Some 70,000 Japanese troops fought against a maximum Taiwanese force of 100,000, though their numbers declined rapidly as the Japanese advanced south. The Japanese southern campaign began in October 1895 with a three-pronged attack. Troops already on the island

marched southward, while others that had assembled on the Pescadores islands attacked from the sea. The fort of Takow was bombarded and easily captured on October 13. The Japanese fleet that arrived at Anping attempted to discuss surrender with Liu Yung-fu; however, Liu escaped aboard a British ship on October 18. Many of the Taiwanese surrendered as the Japanese occupied Anping on October 21. The same day, Japanese forces captured the southern capital of Tainanfu, thus ending the war. Attacks against the Japanese on Taiwan continued from 1896 to 1898 though at below war levels. Taiwan remained a Japanese colony until Japan's defeat in World War II in 1945.

Coding: Taiwan is coded as a part of China from 1816 to 1895 and then as a colony of Japan from 1895 to 1945.

Sources: Clodfelter (2002); Copper (1996); Davidson (1988); Kerr (1974); Kerr (1965); Roy (2003); Rubinstein (1999).

EXTRA-STATE WAR #406:
The Mazrui Rebellion of 1895–1896

Participants: United Kingdom vs. Mazrui clan of Kenya
Dates: July 3, 1895, to April 21, 1896
Battle-Related Deaths: Mazrui—800; United Kingdom—200
Where Fought: Africa
Initiator: Mazrui
Outcome: United Kingdom wins
War Type: Imperial

Narrative: By the eighteenth century, Arabs, particularly those from Oman, had displaced most of the Portuguese who had settled along the coast of East Africa, and the Mazrui, an Omani family, took over control of Mombasa from the Portuguese. Like the Portuguese, the Omani generally controlled only the coastal areas, though they shifted their capital to the nearby island of Zanzibar in 1839. By the later nineteenth century, both Britain and Germany wanted to expand their influence in the area. In 1885 Germany established a protectorate over the sultan of Zanzibar's coastal possessions, and in 1886 a border commission divided East Africa into a German sphere and a British sphere (in the north). To forestall their rivalry, Britain and Germany entered into the 1890 Helgoland-Zanzibar Treaty, by which Germany agreed not to interfere with British actions in what would become Kenya, while Germany focused on German East Africa, which would become Tanzania. Britain also began to extend its influence inland, particularly through the British East Africa Company and the Kenya-Uganda railroad. British expansionism, and in particular the actions of the East Africa Company, led to resistance from a number of local tribes, including the Mazrui. The Mazrui, led by Mbaruk bin Rashid (or Mbaruk of Gazi), had been involved in an uprising against the sultan of Zanzibar in 1882, in which the sultan was able to defeat the Mazrui with the assistance of Great Britain.

In 1895 the activities of the British East Africa Company precipitated the war. The sheik of the Takaungu (a branch of the Mazrui) had died, and the British East Africa Company appointed a man who was more supportive of the British than the rightful heir to succeed him as governor. Mbaruk then led the Mazrui in a rebellion against the British that entailed significant guerrilla warfare over nine months. The fighting was intensified by Mazrui fears that the rule of the British government would be harsher than that of the British East Africa Company (which the British had dissolved on July 1, 1895). On July 3, 1895, the British declared that the Mazrui were rebels, and they arrived at Gazi with warships and troops on July 24. Mbarak and the rebels fled to Mwele, where they established a fortress from which they could encourage attacks against the British along the coast. A 400-man British force captured Mwele, and the rebels fled. The Mazrui had some subsequent successes, including scattering a British force at Mgobani on October 16 and then at Mazeras (near Mombasa) in November. The rebels' success prompted other tribes to join in the fight against the British, and soon all of the British East Africa territory was in revolt. Ultimately, the British were forced to bring in troops from India, which arrived on December 30, 1895, to contribute to a two-pronged offensive to suppress the revolt. Despite initial loses to the rebels, the Indian forces advanced and defeated rebel groups on March 2 and March 6, 1896. Additional Indian reinforcements arrived on March 15 and advanced against the rebel stronghold at Mwele. When Mbaruk and 1,200 followers realized that the war was lost, they fled to German East Africa (Tanganyika), where they surrendered on April 21, 1896, and received asylum.

Coding: Kenya shifted from being a British protectorate to being a British colony in 1895, a status it retained until gaining independence in 1963. Britain was faced with a similar succession issue in Zanzibar, which led to the Anglo-Zanzibar War of 1896. This war has sometimes been referred to as the shortest war in history because it involved the British bombardment of the royal palace. A cease-fire was declared after thirty-seven minutes. Although neither Clodfelter (2002) nor Phillips and Axelrod (2005) include the Mazrui Rebellion, they both include the "Zanzibar War," which is not included here because of the limited number of fatalities.

Sources: Beachey (1996); Boahen (1985); Brantley (1981); Brecke (1999); Cutter (2007); Featherstone (1992a); Galbraith (1972); Gregory (1901); Ogot (1974); Richardson (1960a).

EXTRA-STATE WAR #407:

The Second Italian-Ethiopian War of 1895–1896

Participants: Italy vs. Ethiopia
Dates: December 7, 1895, to Ocotober 21, 1896
Battle-Related Deaths: Italy—9,000; Ethiopia—7,000

Where Fought: Africa
Initiator: Italy
Outcome: Ethiopia wins
War Type: Imperial

Narrative: After its relatively late unification, Italy had wanted to catch up to the other powers in developing a colonial empire. It began by securing a foothold along the African Red Sea coast at Eritrea in 1882. The first Italian attempt to expand this colonial domain was not successful. The Italian invasion of Ethiopia (in 1887) had been turned back by Ethiopian king Yohannes IV (see extra-state war #392). Italy had withdrawn its forces back into Eritrea. There, however, the Italians were able to withstand and defeat an attack in 1893 by the Mahdi army from Sudan that sought to eliminate foreigners from the region (extra-state war #400). Italy did not give up its interest in conquering Ethiopia, however. After the death of King Yohannes IV, who was killed while fighting the Mahdi in non-state war #1559, Menelik, an ally of Italy, assumed the throne. The Italians and Ethiopians signed the Treaty of Uccialli on May 2, 1889, but the terms of the treaty were interpreted differently by the parties. Italy maintained that the treaty gave it a protectorate over all of Ethiopia, an interpretation that the Ethiopians rejected.

In early 1895 the Italians were able to defeat rebel groups in the north Ethiopian province of Tigre. Later that year the Italians again sent an advance column into the Tigre province. Emperor Menelik's Ethiopian forces responded, defeating the Italian expedition at Amba Alagi on December 7, 1895, marking the start of the war. Buoyed by their victory, the Ethiopians advanced and besieged the small Italian garrison at Makele (capital of Tigre province) for six weeks. Although the Italians were able to repulse several assaults, they were ultimately forced to surrender on January 20, 1896. The Italians advanced with their main army of 20,000 troops to meet an Ethiopian army of 80,000 to 100,000

men at Adowa. The Italians apparently advanced prematurely instead of maintaining a defensive position. The Italian columns became separated and were annihilated by Emperor Menelik's forces on March 1, 1896. The timing of the battle was fortuitous for the Ethiopians, since they had been about to run out of food and soon would have had to withdraw. This battle was the biggest defeat of Europeans in an imperial war in the nineteenth century. Some saw this battle, along with the later Japanese victory over the Russians at Tsushima in 1905, as a signal that the European empires had finally overreached their resources. Fighting ended on October 21, and the Italians were forced to sue for peace. In the Treaty of Addis Ababa on October 26, 1896, Italy was able to retain its colony at Eritrea, though it had to recognize the independence of Ethiopia.

For a long time the Italian defeat in 1896 discouraged further attempts by Italy to colonize Ethiopia. Italy then shifted its colonial focus to Tripoli (Libya). Italy gained control of Libya and the Dodecanese as a result of an Italo-Turkish war in 1911 (inter-state #97). Italy under Mussolini would finally subdue Ethiopia as the result of inter-state war #127 in 1935, though Ethiopia's occupied status would last for only five years.

Coding: Not only did the Italian attack fail, but also, consequent to the Ethiopian victory, Ethiopia gained an enormous amount of "soft power" by being diplomatically recognized by the major European powers. As a result, by the COW coding system Ethiopia entered the interstate system on January 1, 1898, one of the earliest African entries. Consequently, any subsequent attack on Ethiopia would be an inter-state war. Jaques (2007) combines the entire period from the start of the 1887 war through this 1895 war as the "1st Italo-Ethiopian War."

Sources: Battaglia (1958); Berkeley (1935); Clodfelter (2002); Italy, Comitato per la Documentazione Dell'Opera Dell'Italia in Africa (1952); Jaques (2007); Kohn (1999); Marcus (1995); Phillips and Axelrod (2005); Schafer (1995); Vandervort (1998).

EXTRA-STATE WAR #409:
The Second British-Mahdi War of 1896–1899

Participants: United Kingdom vs. Mahdist Empire
Dates: June 7, 1896, to November 24, 1899
Battle-Related Deaths: Mahdist Empire—18,000; United Kingdom—1,200
Where Fought: Middle East
Initiator: United Kingdom
Outcome: United Kingdom wins
War Type: Imperial

Narrative: Egypt had gained control over Sudan in extra-state wars #307, #364, and #375. Then Great Britain obtained a protectorate over Egypt via conquest in inter-state war #65 in 1882. In the meantime the Sudanese under the Mahdi, Muhammad Ahmad, who wished to remove foreigners from the region, had rebelled against Egyptian and British influence. In extra-state war #384, Egypt and Britain were defeated by the Mahdist army. A British force under Gen. Charles "Chinese" Gordon was annihilated (and Gordon killed) at Khartoum. The Egyptians and British then withdrew from Sudan, leaving it in the control of the Mahdist Empire. Muhammad Ahmad died soon thereafter, and he was succeeded by Khalifa Abdallahi ibn Muhammad (Khalifa Abdullah), who continued the antiforeign crusade. The Mahdist army, also referred to as the Dervishes, then became involved in a war with Ethiopia (non-state war #1559) and was subsequently defeated in a brief conflict with the Italians at their colony in Eritrea (extra-state war #400).

Great Britain, then under Lord Salisbury's government, was unhappy with having lost control over Sudan. The British were wary of French and Italian designs on the region and were anxious to avenge Gordon's death and the humiliating British defeat at the hands of the Mahdist army. Therefore, in 1896, the British sent a large and elaborately organized expedition against the Mahdist Empire forces. Under the command of Sir Horatio Herbert (later Lord) Kitchener, an Anglo-Egyptian army of 26,000 advanced up the Nile toward Khartoum. To ensure necessary supplies, the British were accompanied by a flotilla of supply ships and were able to construct a railroad line as they advanced. The British encountered stiff resistance from the Mahdists; however, they were able to capture Firket on June 7, 1896, Dongola on September 21, 1896, and Abu Hamed on August 7, 1897. The British launched their first major assault against the numerically superior Mahdist army on April 8, 1898. At the Atbara River the British prevailed, forcing the retreat of 16,000 Mahdist warriors. A larger Mahdist army (50,000) attacked the British at Omdurman, just north of Khartoum on September 2, 1898. British weapons (including machine guns) led to the death of 11,000 Mahdi and an overwhelming British victory. The British and the Egyptians chased the Mahdist forces into Kordofan, where they besieged the Mahdi for over a year. Khalifa Abdullah was killed on November 24, 1899, thus ending the war.

Coding: The Mahdist Empire is coded as an autonomous entity that included Sudan from 1882 to 1898. As a result of this war, Sudan becomes a British colony, a status that it held until 1956.

Sources: Clodfelter (2002); Fabunmi (1960); Farwell (1967); Featherstone (1973); Halm (1996); Jaques (2007); Lewis (1987); Pakenham (1991); Phillips and Axelrod (2005); Powell (2003); Vandervort (1998); Williams (1907).

EXTRA-STATE WAR #410:
The Spanish-Philippine War of 1896–1898

Participants: Spain vs. Philippines
Dates: August 30, 1896, to May 1, 1898
Battle-Related Deaths: Spain—4,000; Philippines—4,000

Where Fought: Asia
Initiator: Philippines
Outcome: Merged or transformed into inter-state war #79
War Type: Colonial

Narrative: Among the European colonial powers, Spain lost the vast majority of its colonial holdings much earlier than the others. After losing most of the Americas, however, the Spanish still managed to retain the Philippines. The Spanish first visited the Philippines in 1521, in the company of Portuguese explorer Ferdinand Magellan, but Spanish colonization arguably began in 1564 with an expedition from New Spain (Mexico). At the time the Filipinos lived in small communities, with no central government, and the Spanish were gradually able to extend their control over the islands, though they had some difficulty with the Muslim Moros in the south. The Spanish also brought with them the Jesuits, and it was the growing power of the clergy that began to fuel the sentiments for independence.

The independence movement began not with the Moros but among the peoples of Spanish culture, the Filipino elite. Spanish injustices were highlighted in the poetry of José Rizal, who became a hero of the revolution by calling for Spanish reform. Rizal was arrested and exiled by the Spanish authorities in 1892. His arrest led to the creation of a revolutionary society, Katipunan, in Manila under the leadership of Andrés Bonifacio and Emilio Aguinaldo, mayor of the Luzon city of Cavite. The revolt began on August 30, 1896, when Bonifacio and Aguinaldo led a force of 800 revolutionaries in an attack against a Spanish depot at San Juan del Monte before heading toward Manila. Spanish forces routed the rebels, and the next day the Spanish governor declared a state of war. The rebels suffered another defeat three days later at Zapote Bridge. They did have some successes, defeating 500 Spanish troops at Imus on September 5, 1896, and at Binakayan on November 11, 1896.

Meanwhile, Rizal had been arrested again, and on December 30, 1896, Rizal was executed by a Spanish firing squad. This miscarriage of justice only served to further alienate the Filipinos and to intensify their revolutionary zeal. In early 1987 the Spanish began an offensive against a large rebel force (Aguinaldo and 5,000 rebels) at Dasmarinas, and the rebels were forced to retreat after suffering heavy loses. They were able to defeat a Spanish force at Puray on June 14, 1987, and as a result, in December, a truce was negotiated in which Spain promised reforms and Aguinaldo went into exile.

The extra-state war between Spain and the Filipinos ended at daybreak on May 1, 1898, when Adm. George Dewey's American fleet opened fire on the Spanish in Manila Bay. Dewey's opening salvo was the first gunfire in the Spanish-American War (inter-state war #79). Dewey's attack completely changed the composition of the fighting, since he sank the entire Spanish Far Eastern fleet with the loss of only one U.S. sailor, who died of a heart attack. The Battle of Manila Bay ended the war of independence as the United States took over the bulk of the fighting against the Spanish. The United States also brought Emilio Aguinaldo back to the Philippines from his exile in Hong Kong, and he organized a Filipino army that helped the United States defeat the Spanish. Ultimately, the Spanish-American War ended in a Spanish defeat on August 12, 1898. Instead of granting independence to the Philippines, the Treaty of Paris, which ended the Spanish-American War, transferred control over the Philippines from Spain to the United States.

Coding: Aguinaldo subsequently led a new revolt, this time against the United States in 1899 (extra-state war #414). The revolt was unsuccessful, and the Philippines remained as a colony of the United States from 1898 to 1942, when they were taken by Japan in World War II. The United States recovered the archipelago in 1945, and the Philippines was finally granted independence in 1946. Clodfelter (2002), Kohn (1999), and Phillips and Axelrod (2005) all describe the "Philippine Insurrection" of 1896-1898.

Sources: Agoncilla (1956); Anderson (1991); Clodfelter (2002); Kalaw (1925); Phillips and Axelrod (2005); Smith (1965); Zaide (1954).

EXTRA-STATE WAR #411:
The British–South Nigerian War of 1897

Participants: United Kingdom vs. South Nigeria
Dates: January 6, 1897, to February 25, 1897
Battle-Related Deaths: Nigeria—1,000; United Kingdom—20
Where Fought: Africa
Initiator: United Kingdom
Outcome: United Kingdom wins
War Type: Imperial

Narrative: The Portuguese were the first Europeans to visit Nigeria, in the late fifteenth century, though they were soon followed by the British, Dutch, and French. As a result of a Muslim jihad, a Muslim state was created in 1817 that controlled most of northern Nigeria. In 1861 Great Britain annexed the coastal city of Lagos, in a purported attempt to eliminate the slave trade there. The British gradually gained control of areas along the Niger River, partly through the efforts of Sir George Goldie, who acquired trading firms and signed treaties with many of the African leaders in the region. As a consequence, at the meeting of the great powers in Berlin (1884–1885) to discuss colonial issues, Britain was able to establish its claim to South Nigeria.

Goldie's firm was given a royal charter as the Royal Niger Company to administer the Niger River area; however, its activities were threatened by the Fulani emirates of Bida and Illorin. Consequently, in 1897 Britain organized the Niger-Sudan Expeditionary Force to deal with the tribal threats. This force was noteworthy in that it was entirely made up of native troops with British officers (no British troops). The

expedition started out from the confluence of the Niger and Benue rivers on January 6, 1897. Kabba was entered unopposed on January 13. The first major battle was fought at Bida (January 27), where the British faced the Nupe army of Emir Abubakr, which numbered approximately 10,000 warriors. The British were successful in routing the tribe, and then they moved on to Ilorin. There the British also decisively defeated the 10,000-man army of Emir Sulaymanu on February 16, 1897. By February 25 the expedition was completed. As a result of the war, Britain extended its colonial domain, incorporating Ilorin. The British would next attempt to extend their empire to North Nigeria in 1903 (extra-state war #422)

Coding: Clodfelter discusses this war as part of an entry entitled "Brassmen Rebellion: 1895."

Sources: Clodfelter (2002); *Columbia Encyclopedia* (1993); Featherstone (1992a); Jaques (2007); Oyewole and Lucas (2000); Pakenham (1991); Vandervort (1998).

EXTRA-STATE WAR #412:
The British-Pathan War of 1897–1898

Participants: United Kingdom vs. Pathan tribes
Dates: July 26, 1897, to March 7, 1898
Battle-Related Deaths: United Kingdom—1,100; Pathan tribes—[ ]
Where Fought: Asia
Initiator: Pathan tribes
Outcome: United Kingdom wins
War Type: Colonial

Narrative: The North-West Frontier of the British Empire in India had been a source of continual threats to British control since the mid-nineteenth century. At the conclusion of the Second British-Afghan War of 1878–1880 (extra-state war #379), the British had decided to withdraw their forces from Kabul and Kandahar; however, Russian expansionism in Central Asia, and in particular the Russo-Afghan War of

1885 (extra-state war #390), had renewed British interest and involvement in the region. In 1893 Britain and Afghanistan entered into an agreement to define the borders between them, but several of the local tribes, which had no say in the agreement, were unhappy with their placement within the British zone. In 1895 a British expedition (referred to as the Chitral Campaign) involved conflict with a number of the Pathan tribes (though the fatality level does not warrant its inclusion as a war). Some of the tribal chiefs were subsequently replaced by leaders more amenable to British rule.

In 1897 tribal discontent reappeared in the same region as the British attempted to establish forts there. The Waziri, the Swati, and the Afridi tribes combined against the British. The war began with an attack and a siege against the British garrison at the Malakand pass (which had been the site of a British victory in 1895). The "Mad Mullah of Swat" (Mullah Sadullah) instigated the attack on July 26, 1897. The garrison was relieved and the attackers were driven off on August 2, 1897. The British were similarly successful in defending the fort at Shabkadr on August 7; however, they were defeated by the Pathan at Landi Kotal after fierce fighting on August 24–25, and control of the strategic Khyber Pass also was lost. In order to regain control over the area, in October 1897 Britain decided to send a large army of 44,000 against the tribes. The mission, sometimes referred to as the Tirah campaign, confronted a force of 12,000 Afridi warriors at Dargai on October 18–20. Ultimately the British were able to crush the Afridi force and then went on to recapture Landi Kotal. During the late fall and winter the tribes repulsed several British attacks, and the British withdrew from the mountains to the plains. On March 7, 1898, however, the British recaptured the Khyber Pass. The Pathan sued for peace, thus ending the war.

Coding: Afghanistan is coded as an autonomous entity, but not an interstate system member, from 1855 to 1920. The term *Pathan* (or Pashtun or

Pushtun) refers to over sixty seminomadic tribes that inhabit the area of what is now Afghanistan and Pakistan. In 1901 Britain separated the region from India and created the semiautonomous North-West Frontier province, which joined Pakistan during the partition in 1947. Jaques (2007) refers to this war as the "Great Frontier Rising."

Sources: Clodfelter (2002); Featherstone (1973); Jaques (2007); Williams (1907).

EXTRA-STATE WAR #413:
The Hut Tax War of 1898

Participants: United Kingdom vs. Sierra Leone rebels
Dates: February [ ], 1898, to May [ ], 1898
Battle-Related Deaths: Sierra Leone rebels—1,600; United Kingdom—400
Where Fought: Africa
Initiator: Sierra Leone rebels
Outcome: United Kingdom wins
War Type: Colonial

Narrative: This war represents the resistance of the Temne and Mende peoples of the interior of Sierra Leone to a British tax.

The coastal portion of Sierra Leone emerged as a British colony in 1792. The British began to settle freed slaves there, and by the mid-nineteenth century they and their descendants were a majority in the colony. Then in 1885, when the European powers carved up Africa at the Treaty of Berlin, Britain was also given the interior portions of Sierra Leone. The coast remained a British colony, while the British established a "protectorate" over the indigenous tribes of the interior.

In 1896 the British decided to impose a tax on the interior, to reimburse the British for "protecting" it. This was the "hut tax," a fee imposed on each residence, a higher tax for larger huts and a lower fee for smaller huts. In the interior the Temne and Mende peoples opposed this hut tax. In the north the revolt was led by Bai Bureh (Temne ruler) and in the south by the Poro secret society. Along the upper reaches of the Little Scarcies River, Bai Bureh began a skilled campaign of military rebellion against the British. An initial British force formed from the West India regiment advanced into the Karene district in the north and was able to relieve some of the besieged forts. However, a larger expedition under Col. Edward Robert Prevost Woodgate and involving additional troops from England and Royal Navy ships was needed to quell the insurrection.

Incidentally, similar administrative and tax changes were imposed at the same time in another British holding in the area, Gambia. There, the rationale of the new regime was more patiently explained to the traditional rulers, and there was no tax war there.

Coding: Sierra Leone became independent of the British in 1961. Neither Clodfelter (2002) nor Phillips and Axelrod (2005) covers this war.

Sources: Catchpole and Akinjogbin (1983); *Columbia Encyclopedia* (1993); Fage (1969); Featherstone (1992a); Hernon (2002); James (1985); Kup (1975); Richardson (1948); Sivard (1991); Utting (1931).

EXTRA-STATE WAR #414:

The American-Philippine War of 1899–1902

Participants: United States vs. Philippines
Dates: February 4, 1899, to July 4, 1902
Battle-Related Deaths: Philippines—16,000;
  United States—4,500
Where Fought: Asia
Initiator: Philippines
Outcome: United States wins
War Type: Colonial

Narrative: The Philippines had begun revolting against Spanish colonial rule in 1896 (extra-state war #410). The independence movement was cut short by the Spanish-American War (interstate war #79), during which the United States became involved in hostilities in the Philippines.

The United States had even brought the Philippine independence leader Emilio Aguinaldo back to the Philippines from his exile in Hong Kong so that he could organize a Filipino army to help the United States overthrow the Spanish. With the Spanish defeat, the United States was faced with the question of what to do with the Spanish colonies of Cuba and the Philippines. In essence, the United States decided to keep them both. President McKinley said, "I ... went down on my knees and prayed Almighty God," and "it came to me this way ... they were unfit for self-government," but "we could not turn them over to France or Germany—our commercial rivals in the Orient—that would be bad business." So, "There was nothing left to do but educate the Filipinos, and uplift and civilize them" (quoted in LaFeber 1989, 200).

The Filipino revolutionaries had sought complete independence and refused to accept American annexation. On January 20, 1899, the Philippine Republic was proclaimed, with Aguinaldo as president. The next month the insurrectionists attacked an American post near Manila. The revolutionary army was repulsed by the numerically superior American army. For the next three years the revolutionaries launched numerous unsuccessful attacks against the Americans and suffered horrendous casualties; nevertheless, the Philippine rebel leader Aguinaldo proved to be a more effective fighter against the Americans than the Spanish had been. The Americans needed a larger army and more time to subdue the revolution. After two years of war, the Americans focused their efforts on capturing Aguinaldo, which was accomplished on March 23, 1901. The revolution continued, however, but under new leadership. The last of the rebel leaders finally concluded a treaty with the United States on May 6, 1902, though fighting continued till July 4.

In addition to the combatants, the war cost the lives of over 200,000 Philippine civilians. American brutality in the war and involvement in torture and massacres became a matter of popular discussion and debate in the United States. In the Second World War, Filipino forces fought alongside the United States against Japan. Aguinaldo, who had survived, collaborated with the Japanese. The Philippines did not gain its independence from the United States until 1946.

Coding: Clodfelter (2002) covers the "Filipino Insurrection" of 1899–1902, as do Phillips and Axelrod (2005), though they spell it as the "Philippine Insurrection."

Sources: Clodfelter (2002); Grunder and Livezey (1951); Heitman (1903); Kohn (1986); LaFeber (1989); Linn (2000); Phillips and Axelrod (2005); Storey and Lichauco (1926).

EXTRA-STATE WAR #415:
French Conquest of Chad of 1899–1900

Participants: France vs. Rabih az-Zubayr
Dates: July 17, 1899, to April 22, 1900
Battle-Related Deaths: Rabih az-Zubayr—900; France—125
Where Fought Africa
Initiator France
Outcome: France wins
War Type: Imperial

Narrative: Although France had earlier engaged in overseas colonization, the height of imperial expansionism began in the 1880s. The French government included deliberate imperialists, such as Jules Ferry, and the French pursued policies to increase their colonial empire, particularly in Asia, the Middle East, and Africa. In West Africa, France began with bases in Algeria and Senegal, and soon added new footholds on the Ivory Coast and Dahomey, to spread its influence toward Niger and Lake Chad. Before the outbreak of World War I, France would control most of northwest Africa.

From the sixteenth century the area of present-day Chad had been the locus of the Bornu, Wadai, and Bagirmi empires. By the early 1890s

the empires had been weakened by internal dissension and were thus vulnerable to outside intervention. Rabih az-Zubayr (Zobeir) was an African Arab soldier who had once served the Egyptian government in the Sudanese region of Bahr el-Ghazal. When the Mahdi took power in the Sudan (extra-state war #384), az-Zubayr refused to submit to the Mahdi, and he and his army of Dazingers (African slave-soldiers) headed west. By 1892 Rabih az-Zubayr had conquered Bagirmi, southeast of Lake Chad. Az-Zubayr, sometimes called the "Black Sultan," set up a slave trade state, which brought him in conflict with the French. In 1897 a French explorer advanced along Lake Chad and made a treaty with the emir of Bagirmi, establishing a French protectorate.

The French wanted to expand their area of control, and so in mid-1899 French armies from colonies in the north, west, and south advanced against az-Zubayr, who encountered a French expedition of 50 riflemen at Niellim on July 17, 1899. In the ensuing battle all but 3 of the French were killed, while az-Zubayr's force suffered 500 fatalities. To avenge this loss, in October the French from Fort Archambault sent an expedition against az-Zubayr at Kouno, where the Dazingers were badly beaten. The following year a combined French force, with troops from Congo, Algeria, and Niger, attacked at Kousséri on April 22, 1900. Az-Zubayr was captured and subsequently beheaded. This battle has also been referred to as the Battle on the Logone or the Battle of Lakhta. The French were able to consolidate their control over Chad, though az-Zubayr's son, Fader Allah, unsuccessfully led the Dazingers against the French in August 1901.

Coding: Bornu, Bagirmi, and Wadai are coded as autonomous entities from 1816 to 1892, 1892, and 1913, respectively.

Sources: Albrecht-Carrié (1958); Catchpole and Akinjogbin (1983); Decalo (1997); Jaques (2007); Kohn (1999); O'Brien (1999); Oliver and Atmore (1994); Richardson (1948).

EXTRA-STATE WAR #416:
The Second Boer War of 1899–1902

Participants: United Kingdom vs. Boer republics
Dates: October 11, 1899, to May 31, 1902
Battle-Related Deaths: United Kingdom—22,000;
 Boer republics—8,800
Where Fought: Africa
Initiator: Boer republics
Outcome: United Kingdom wins
War Type: Imperial

Narrative: The Boers had attacked the British in 1880–1881 and inflicted a rare defeat in a war on the British army (extra-state war #382). This episode was an important episode framing this 1899–1902 war.

Starting in the 1830s, the Boers, or descendants of the Dutch settlers of the Cape, had gradually moved inland to get away from the British, who were expanding their Cape Colony (in present-day South Africa). After moving north in the "Great Trek," the Boers established the Transvaal (South African Republic) and the Orange Free State as their own independent political entities. The Boers were at peace with the British for a time, but in 1877 Britain annexed the Transvaal, and the two parties were soon at war (extra-state war #382). As a result of the 1880–1881 war, on March 6, 1881, the British signed an armistice with Transvaal, giving it autonomy under British suzerainty. The discovery of diamonds near Kimberley and of gold in the Witwatersrand area of the south Transvaal in 1886 changed the status quo. Outsiders, mostly British, moved in to exploit the mineral wealth. Cecil Rhodes, the Cape Colony prime minister, provided imperial troops to protect British mining interests in the Transvaal. The Boers demanded that those troops be withdrawn, but the British just sent more troops to the Cape. Consequently, Transvaal and the Orange Free State declared war on Great Britain in October 1899.

Initially the British greatly underestimated the fighting ability of the Boers and anticipated a short war. As in the 1880–1881 war, however, the Boers were capable of fighting on a competitive level with the mighty British Empire, shocking the British as well as international opinion. The Boers began their offensive with attacks in both the east and west. In the east, the Boers invaded Natal on October 11, 1899, and on October 12 defeated the British at Laing's Nek, the site of a British defeat in the 1880 war, and then advanced to besiege the British forces at Ladysmith. Meanwhile, Transvaal general Piet Conje besieged Mafeking on October 13, 1899. This would become the most famous battle of the war. Col. Robert Baden-Powell, who would later utilize his fame to found the Boy Scouts, had been sent to Mafeking in September 1899 with orders to augment its defenses. Partially as a result of Baden-Powell's deceptions, the Boers felt that Mafeking was too heavily defended to assault it directly. Mafeking was able to survive the siege for 217 days. The exploits of the inhabitants of Mafeking were reported to the outside world by the first female war correspondent, Lady Sarah Wilson, the aunt of future prime minister Winston Churchill. Much later the relief of Mafeking would be depicted in the Shirley Temple film *The Little Princess*. In all, the Boers won a string of victories in 1899. Particularly in the "Black Week" of December 10–17, 1899, Britain's ineffective military strategy, plodding formations against mobile guerrilla tactics, led to British defeats and heavy casualties at the Modder River and Colenso.

In 1900, however, British reinforcements reversed the war's momentum. Ladysmith was relieved on February 28 (after a 118-day siege). The British then went on the offensive, capturing the Orange Free State capital of Bloemfontein on March 13, 1900. The British then invaded Transvaal and captured Johannesburg (May 31) and the capital, Pretoria, on June 5. The Boer defeat at Vlakfontein, on July 4, 1900, basically ended the formal resistance. This allowed Britain to annex the Transvaal and Orange Free State to South Africa. Nevertheless, bloody guerrilla fighting raged for another two years. Boer forces in the war peaked at about 40,000, and the British had to send an army of 448,000 to subdue them. Gen. Lord Horatio Kitchener utilized concentration camps and terrorism against the civilian population to subdue the Boers. By the Treaty of Vereeniging, on May 31, 1902, British sovereignty was finally recognized by the Boers. The British field commander won the war, but the public mood back home in Britain soured on the imperial adventures.

Coding: Transvaal is coded as an autonomous entity from 1852 to 1877 and from 1881 to 1900, while the Orange Free State is an autonomous entity from 1854 to 1900.

Sources: Belfield (1975); Clodfelter (2002); Dumas and Vedel-Peterson (1923); Featherstone (1992a); Pakenham (1994); Pemberton (1964); Phillips and Axelrod (2005); Thompson (2001); Warwick (1980); Williams (1907).

EXTRA-STATE WAR #417:
The Last Ashanti War of 1900

Participants: United Kingdom vs. Ashanti
Dates: April 2, 1900, to September 30, 1900
Battle-Related Deaths: Ashanti—1,000; United Kingdom—1,000
Where Fought: Africa
Initiator: Ashanti
Outcome: United Kingdom wins
War Type: Imperial

Narrative: The Ashanti (or Asante) had once controlled a large empire in West Africa (in what is now central Ghana). During the nineteenth century the Ashanti had fought three extra-state wars against the British: extra-state war #311 in 1824, #367 in 1873, and #398 in 1893. The Ashanti had been reduced to being vassals of the British but still retained their pride and autonomy. As long as they kept the "Golden Stool," upon which their kings were crowned and the symbol of the Ashanti nation, they remained unbowed. In early 1900 the British tried to take possession of the Golden Stool, and as a result this war is sometimes referred to as the "War of the Golden Stool." The Ashanti, led by Queen Yaa Asantewa, then launched a rebellion and laid siege to the British fort at Kumasi. The British were finally able to break out of the fort on June 23, 1900, and a "relief" column arrived in July, a month too late. The British then planned a West African expedition to pacify the Ashanti. In a major battle on September 30, 1900 at Aboasa, the Ashanti attacked the British forces, but because the British had machine guns, the rebellion was suppressed. The Ashanti kingdom was then formally annexed, and the queen was sent into exile.

Coding: Ghana is coded as a part of Sierra Leone and then as a colony of Britain from 1874 to 1957. Asante is coded as an autonomous entity until 1896 and then as occupied by Britain from then till 1901, at which time it is incorporated into Ghana.

Sources: Baden-Powell (1972); Catchpole and Akinjogbin (1983); Clodfelter (1992); Edgerton (1995); Featherstone (1992a); Hernon (2002); Phillips and Axelrod (2005); Richardson (1948); Zuljan (2003);

EXTRA-STATE WAR #419:
The Somali Rebellion of 1901–1904

Participants: Ethiopia, United Kingdom vs. Mohammad Abdullah Hassan's Dervishes
Dates: March 22, 1901, to April 21, 1904
Battle-Related Deaths: Dervishes—4,000; United Kingdom—400; Ethiopia—[ ]
Where Fought: Africa
Initiator: Mohammad Abdullah Hassan
Outcome: Ethiopia and United Kingdom win
War Type: Colonial

Narrative: In 1870 Egypt acquired a portion of the north coast of Somalia from the Ottoman Empire, though the Egyptians evacuated the area during the war with the Mahdi in Sudan (extra-state war #384). By this time Great Britain had established its colonial control over Egypt in 1882, and in 1884–1886 Britain utilized a series of treaties with the Somali tribes to establish British control in the region (British Somaliland), across the Red Sea from its port at Aden. In 1889 Italy also began its expansion in the area by creating a small protectorate in the central coastal region of Somalia. The other major threat to Somalia came from Ethiopia, under Emperor Menelik II. Ethiopia had also faced a war with the Mahdi (non-state war #1559) and was both concerned about the power of religious groups and desirous of expanding its territory eastward.

The major resistance to the expansionist plans of the foreign powers came from a religious leader, Sayyid Mohammad Abdullah Hassan, who would later be called the "Mad Mullah" by his opponents. After receiving religious training, Hassan returned from Mecca to Somalia, where he began to spread the religious teachings of a puritanical Sufi brotherhood called the Salihiyah. He also began referring to his followers as "Dervishes," or Muslims who adopted a life of poverty. Hassan soon became concerned about the growing influence of foreigners and Christians in Somalia and began amassing a well-organized army to confront them.

Hassan launched his first attack in September 1899 (with 1,500 warriors) against a group of British soldiers. In March 1900 an Ethiopian expedition was sent to capture Hassan, and in response, on March 4 Hassan's army attacked the Ethiopian garrison at Jijigato. In June 1900 he also launched raids into British Somaliland. Toward the end of 1900, Ethiopia suggested a joint British-Ethiopian offensive against Hassan, now known by the honorific title of sayyid. Between 1901 and 1904 the two countries conducted four major expeditions against the sayyid.

The first began on March 22, 1901, which marks the start of the war. A British force of 1,500 Somalis advanced from Burco while an Ethiopian army of 15,000 started from Harar in an attempt to crush the sayyid's army of 20,000 Dervishes. The forces opposing the mullah would grow to 16,000 British, African, and Indian troops. In a series of engagements, both sides inflicted heavy losses on their opponents. For example, the Dervishes ambushed a British patrol at Gumburu on April 17, 1903, causing heavy British casualties, and the following week the British inflicted terrible losses on the Dervishes at Daratoleh while suffering few of their own. A decisive victory for the British and Ethiopians occurred on January 10, 1904, at Jidballi, where some have claimed that 7,000 Dervishes were killed. Three months later two British ships attacked the sayyid's fortress at Illig (April 21, 1904). The sayyid fled into Italian Somaliland and sued for peace. In the Illig, or Pestalozza, agreement of March 1905, the sayyid committed to peace with Britain and Italy.

A second round of fighting began in 1908 and continued sporadically until a British attack by land, sea, and air on January 21, 1920, destroyed the sayyid's headquarters. He fled to Ethiopia, where he died on December 21, 1920, of influenza.

Coding: British Somaliland was a British protectorate from 1884 to 1940. Ethiopia was an autonomous entity (not an interstate system member) from 1855 to 1898 and then became a member of the interstate system in 1898, partially owing to its victory over Italy in 1896 (extra-state war #407). In an earlier version of the COW dataset, this war was coded as starting in 1899. Even though information on specific fatalities is limited, it does not appear that the war threshold of 1,000 battle-related deaths per year was met until the beginning of the joint British-Ethiopian expedition, which is now coded as the start of this war.

Sources: Clodfelter (1992); James (1985); Jaques (2007); Jardine (1923 and 1986); Kohn (1986); Phillips and Axelrod (2005); Schafer (1995).

EXTRA-STATE WAR #420:
The Bailundu Revolt of 1902–1903

Participants: Portugal vs. Bailundu of Angola
Dates: early 1902 to late 1903
Battle-Related Deaths: unknown
Where Fought: Africa
Initiator: Bailundu
Outcome: Portugal wins
War Type: Imperial

Narrative: In the late nineteenth century, Portugal had been involved in two wars in East Africa (extra-state wars #393 and #403). Now Portugal would face a series of three wars (extra-state wars #420, #421, and #430) in Angola in western Africa.

The Portuguese began to explore the area of what is now Angola in the fifteenth century, and they established a permanent settlement at Luanda in 1575. Generally, areas of Portuguese control were limited to the coastal zone. The entire region was heavily involved in the slave trade, with many slaves sent to work on the plantations in Brazil (another Portuguese colony). Although the Portuguese did attempt in the early nineteenth century to increase the area under their control, the major Portuguese expeditions were undertaken only after the great powers' conference in Berlin, which was held in 1884–1885 to discuss the distribution of colonies. The Berlin Conference recognized Portugal's dominance in Angola, though its borders were relatively undefined.

Although there were numerous distinct tribes in Angola, the three most prominent were the Ovimbundu, the Mbundu, and the Bakongo. The Mbundu kingdom was established in the center, and the Ovimbundu were south of them. The Ovimbundu were the most numerous, and within the Ovimbundu were a number of kingdoms, the most powerful of which was the kingdom of Bailundu. Beginning in the late nineteenth century Bailundu vigorously resisted the Portuguese encroachment. After 1886 Portugal began spreading its influence in Bailundu, and by the end of the century significant numbers of Portuguese had settled there. In 1902 the Bailundu king attempted to recover their lands and led an army made up of several ethnic groups, and estimated at 40,000 men, in a widespread rebellion against the Portuguese. The Portuguese responded by dispatching a large military force. The Portuguese offensive involved three major expeditions. A force of 400 Portuguese quickly defeated a group of rebels near Huambo. The other offensives marched inland in September, into Moxico, scattering the resistance, and by the end of 1903 the coalition had been defeated and Portuguese dominance affirmed. Nevertheless, Portugal would soon face opposition, and conduct two wars, in other parts of Angola.

Coding: Ovimbundu is coded as an autonomous entity until 1903, after which it is incorporated into Angola, which remains a Portuguese colony until 1975. The Ovimbundu were a major force behind the UNITA rebel army (see extra-state war #469).

Sources: Birmingham (2000); Brecke (1999); Broadhead (1992); Chilcote (1967); *Columbia Encyclopedia* (1993); Cutter (2007); Duffy (1962); Duffy (1959); Galbraith (1972); Roque (2003); Stearns (2001); Wilson (1975).

EXTRA-STATE WAR #421:
The Kuanhama Rebellion of 1902–1904

Participants: Portugal vs. Kuanhama of Angola
Dates: [ ]/[ ]/1902, to [ ]/[ ]/1904
Battle-Related Deaths: Portugal—2,000; Kuanhama—2,000
Where Fought: Africa
Initiator: Kuanhama
Outcome: Stalemate
War Type: Imperial

Narrative: While the Portuguese were engaged in a war in central Angola against Bailundu (extra-state war #420), they also faced resistance in southern Angola, which was one of the last areas of Portuguese Africa to be pacified. Although the Portuguese sent major expeditions to the region beginning in 1885, it took thirty years to exert full control. The situation was complicated by border disputes with Angola's neighbors. The Berlin Conference of 1885 had established most of the Portuguese colony's borders, but the southeastern border entailed disputes with France and Germany and was not settled until an Anglo-Portuguese agreement in 1891 and the arbitration of the king of Italy in 1895. The extension of Portuguese control over this area proceeded slowly, during expeditions in the late 1880s and 1890s, and was compromised by the fact that the Germans in South West Africa (Namibia) were engaged in gun running to the Kuanhama (Kwanhama) people who inhabited the region. The most serious revolt occurred among the Kuanhama between 1902 and 1904. In September 1904 the Portuguese suffered one of their most serious defeats when a Portuguese column lost over 300 men in a skirmish with the Kuanhama near the Kunene, along the border of the German South West African colony. The level of combat then declined, ending this war. The Kuanhama were influenced by the revolt of their neighbors, the Herero, who rebelled against Germany in 1904 (extra-state war #423), and violence resumed in Angola in 1905 and 1907.

Sources: Brecke (1999); Broadhead (1992); Chilcote (1967); *Columbia Encyclopedia* (1993); Cutter (2007); Duffy (1962); Duffy (1959); Galbraith (1972); Hammond (1966); Roque (2003); Stearns (2001); Wilson (1975); Zuljan (2003).

EXTRA-STATE WAR #422:
The British Conquest of Kano and Sokoto of 1903

Participants: United Kingdom vs. Kano and Sokoto
Dates: January 29, 1903, to July 27, 1903
Battle-Related Deaths: Kano and Sokoto—1,100; United Kingdom—[ ]

Where Fought: Africa
Initiator: United Kingdom
Outcome: United Kingdom wins
War Type: Imperial

Narrative: As a result of extra-state war #411, the United Kingdom had gained control over Ilorin and South Nigeria. Britain next turned to expanding its control in the north, and in January 1903 the British began a campaign against Kano and Sokoto. Kano and Sokoto were two of the Hausa/Fulani emirates that occupied much of northern Nigeria for centuries before the colonial conquest. Kano had been weakened in the earlier war and was thus the first target of the British campaign. The Kano Expeditionary Force seized Kano on February 3, 1903. The British then marched from Kano toward Sokoto. Meanwhile, a small British patrol repulsed a Kano force of 3,000 near Rawiya on February 25–26. Reaching Sokoto, the British were confronted by a powerful Fulani army on March 15, but British weaponry caused heavy casualties. Sultan Attahiru and his forces abandoned the capital and fled to Burmi. On July 27, 1903, heavy fighting resulted in the death of the sultan and several hundred of his followers, and the end of the great Fulani Empire. This war resulted in the expansion of the British Empire, though the British would face another war against Sokoto in 1906 (extra-state war #427).

Coding: Kano and Sokoto are both coded as autonomous entities, Kano until 1898 and Sokoto until 1903.

Sources: Catchpole and Akinjogbin (1983); Clodfelter (1992); Fage (1969); James (1985); Jaques (2007); Oliver and Atmore (1994).

EXTRA-STATE WAR #423
The Southwest African Revolt of 1904–1906

Participants: Germany vs. Herero and Nama
Dates: January 12, 1904, to May 4, 1906

Battle-Related Deaths: Herero and
    Nama—11,000; Germany—1,800
Where Fought: Africa
Initiator: Herero and Nama
Outcome: Germany wins
War Type: Colonial

Narrative: Germany was one of the last European powers to embark on a career of actual colonialism. After the Berlin Conference of 1884–1885, it claimed four areas of Africa. The present state of Namibia (formerly South West Africa) was one of these. This area had been inhabited by the Khoikhoi people (who were referred to as the Hottentots by the white South Africans). The remaining Khoikhoi were the Nama people. Another tribe in the region was the Herero, a Bantu people who had warred with the Khoikhoi in the past. As Germany tried to expand its control in the region, both the Herero and Nama people rebelled in 1904 against German rule. The Herero began the revolt in January 1904, subsequently ambushing German patrols at Owikokorero (March 13), Okakarui (April 3), and Onganjira (April 9). The Germans maintained the offensive until they marched on to Oviumbo, where, on April 13, Herero leader Samuel Haherero forced them to retreat. A second German expedition decisively defeated the Herero at the Waterberg mountains on August 11–12, 1904. Many of the Herero fled into the desert, where they were hunted down.

Meanwhile, the Herero were joined in the insurrection by the Nama, under the leadership of Hendrik Witbooi Tha Nama, who ambushed a German expedition at Freyer's Farm on August 30, 1904. Although the Nama suffered a defeat at Naris in December 1904, the following year they inflicted the most significant loss for the Germans during this war at Hartebeestmund on October 24, 1905. Soon thereafter, the Nama were defeated at Vaalgras (October 29). The final battle took place at Van Rooisvlei (inside British South Africa), where a German column defeated the Nama on May 4, 1906. Three days later the Nama leader, Jakob Morenga, surrendered.

Overall, it took the Germans almost another two years to completely suppress the revolt, in part through genocide of the Herero and Nama people. It has been estimated that 80 percent of the Herero and 50 percent of the Nama (about 75,000 people) died in mass killings and German concentration camps. The Germans would soon face a similar uprising by the Maji-Maji (extra-state war #426).

Coding: Phillips and Axelrod (2005) have two separate listings, one for the "Hottentot Uprising (1904–1907)" and one for the "Herero Uprising (1904–1907)."

Sources: Bley (1996); Bridgman (1981); Clodfelter (2002); Gewald (1999); Jaques (2007); Kohn (1999); Pakenham (1991); Phillips and Axelrod (2005); Vandervort (1998).

EXTRA-STATE WAR #424:
The Second Dutch-Achinese War of 1904–1907

Participants: Netherlands vs. Aceh
Dates: [ ]/[ ]/1904, to December [ ], 1907
Battle-Related Deaths: Netherlands—13,000;
    Achinese—11,200
Where Fought: Asia
Initiator: Aceh
Outcome: Netherlands wins
War Type: Colonial

Narrative: In 1873 the Netherlands launched a war to expand its colonial empire in the East Indies and to extend its control over the entire island of Sumatra by subduing the Achinese (extra-state war #370). The Dutch defeated the Achinese, and the sultanate of Aceh was annexed on January 24, 1874. Many of the Achinese, however, did not accept Dutch rule, and a guerrilla war endured for the next thirty years, albeit at below war fatality levels. Finally in 1903 the sultan of Aceh, who had tired of the fighting, signed a treaty with the Dutch, relinquishing sovereignty to the Netherlands. Nonetheless, the fighting increased to war level after that point.

Gradually the Dutch developed a new strategy, which involved building forts across the island. In 1907 the Dutch were able to defeat Achinese resistance.

Coding: Aceh (Atjeh) is coded as an autonomous entity from 1816 to 1903 and then as a part of the Dutch East Indies. Consequently, the war in 1904 is a colonial war. Although there was fighting in Aceh for almost the entire period of 1873 to 1914, it did not always reach the perquisite war level of 1,000 battle-related deaths per year. During the period 1878 to 1904, casualties were relatively low. Thus we code only the two periods of war: 1873 to 1878 and 1904 to 1908, when the battle-related deaths were highest. In 1949 Aceh became an autonomous province of Indonesia, and Achinese resistance to integration into Indonesia evolved into several civil wars starting in 1953. Clodfelter (2002) has an "Atjeh (Aceh) War: 1873–1914," while Phillips and Axelrod (2005) have an "Achinese War" of 1873 to 1907.

Sources: Clodfelter (2002); Kielstra (1883); Phillips and Axelrod (2005); Ricklefs (1993); Rose (1915); Vlekke (1960).

EXTRA-STATE WAR #425:
The Younghusband Expedition of 1904

Participants: United Kingdom vs. Tibet
Dates: March 31, 1904, to September 7, 1904
Battle-Related Deaths: Tibet—2,500; United Kingdom—300
Where Fought: Asia
Initiator: United Kingdom
Outcome: United Kingdom wins
War Type: Imperial

Narrative: The Tibetan "government" was a religious-political structure in which the "church" dominated the "state." In fact, it is estimated (Richardson 1984, 14) that monks constituted one-eighth of the population, so that as many as 400,000 individuals were part of this enormous, religious hierarchy. As such, they were each subordinate to the lamas, who were the leaders of the Tibetan church-state. Tibet had traditionally preferred a policy of isolationism but was gradually being forced into international affairs by the expansionist policies of Britain and Russia in Central Asia. The British, having secured India up to the Himalayas, wished to trade with Tibet. Tibet refused to agree on such matters as the right of passage of traders into their country or even what the borders were. In 1902 the Chinese government had proposed that a joint Chinese-Indian commission meet to discuss the frontier issues. In June 1903 Col. Francis Younghusband had been appointed to attend the meeting at the frontier, but the Chinese failed to arrive. The Dalai Lama, however, was apparently involved in communications with the Russians. Consequently, the British government in India felt that it had to make some sort of demonstration of force to get the Tibetans' attention and deter the Russians.

Britain sent Colonel Younghusband back to Tibet, this time with a small expeditionary force with orders to open negotiations on trade and border issues. When they encountered opposition, the expedition was reinforced by additional troops under Gen. James Macdonald. The war began when the expedition's advance was halted by a Tibetan force at Guru. There the Tibetans were roundly defeated on March 31, 1904. The British were similarly victorious at the Red Idol Gorge (April 9). Three days later the British arrived at Gyantse, which they besieged from April 12 to July 6, 1904. The arrival of British reinforcements enabled the British to finally storm the town and then move on toward Lhasa. The British reached Lhasa in August, but the Dalai Lama had apparently fled to Mongolia. Col. Younghusband was finally able to persuade the Tibetan officials to sign the Anglo-Tibetan Treaty on September 7, 1904.

Coding: Tibet was coded as a part of China from 1816 to 1848, then as an autonomous entity from 1848 to 1910. Tibet was occupied by China till 1912 (see extra-state war #435), then again becomes an autonomous entity till 1951, after which it is incorporated into China (see extra-state war #462). The Chinese, however, have held the view that Tibet was part of China throughout this entire period.

Sources: Biangyi (2005); Clodfelter (2002); Coates (2001); Phillips and Axelrod (2005); Richardson (1984); Richardson (1960a); Sorokin (1937); Williams (1907).

EXTRA-STATE WAR #426:
The Maji-Maji Revolt of 1905–1906

Participants: Germany vs. Maji-Maji rebels of Tanganyika
Dates: July 31, 1905, to June [ ], 1906
Battle-Related Deaths: Maji-Maji—5,400; Germany—3,440
Where Fought: Africa
Initiator: Maji-Maji
Outcome: Germany wins
War Type: Colonial

Narrative: The Portuguese explorer Vasco da Gama visited the Tanzanian coast, along the east coast of Africa, in 1498, where he came into contact with the Bantu people living there. Both the Portuguese and Arab traders from Oman established posts along the coast. As the scramble for Africa continued among the European powers, several German firms began signing treaties with some of the tribes in the interior of the region. Even though Germany was a latecomer to the game of colonial expansion, at the Berlin Conference of 1885, Germany claimed and began to occupy four colonies in Africa. German East Africa (now Tanzania) was one of these. The German East Africa Company governed the territory, and an agreement with Britain in 1890 added Rwanda and Burundi to German East Africa. Owing to the German East Africa Company's mismanagement, Germany took over direct control of the region and declared it a protectorate in 1891, though it took until 1898 for the Germans to establish control.

Opposition to the imposition of German rule had already led to uprisings in another of the German colonies, South West Africa, in 1904 (extra-state war #423). Similar protests against harsh German rule in German East Africa also provoked a rebellion there in July 1905. The rebellion began with small skirmishes in the Matumbu Hills near the coast, south of Dar es Salaam, before spreading west, then north and south. One of the rebels' grievances was the German attempt to force the tribes to grow cotton. The rebels were also influenced by a spiritual leader, Kinjikitile Ngwale, who encouraged the people to expel the Germans and promised that he could provide a potion, or "maji-maji," that would protect them from German bullets. This, of course, was untrue. Nonetheless, the first major assault against a small German fort at Kilosa on August 16, 1905, was a rebel victory. They then went on to besiege the Germans at Mahenge from August 30 to September 23. After lifting the siege, the Germans went on the offensive and attacked a force of 5,000 Ngoni tribesman at Namabengo on October 21, 1905. The rebels were destroyed not only by the German machine guns but also by a policy of destroying crops and starving the population. The Germans easily suppressed the remainder of the revolt by June 1906. German policy in German East Africa was similar to that in South West Africa, in that the Germans retaliated against the entire population, killing thousands. Estimates of the numbers of people who died as a result of German actions, disease, and starvation between October 1905 and June 1906 range from 75,000 to 300,000.

Coding: Determining the fatality figures for this war was difficult. The best-kept records were for the Germans, but even there, there is disagreement. For example, Clodfelter (2002) indicates German deaths at 422 added to deaths among their native personnel for a total of 3,422, whereas Phillips and Axelrod (2005) cite a total of 7,210. We accept Clodfelter's general analysis of the fatality ratios, though not quite his specificity.

Sources: Clodfelter (2002); *Columbia Encyclopedia* (1993); Iliffe (1967); Kohn (1999); Mann (2002); Pakenham (1991); Phillips and Axelrod (2005); Vandervort (1998).

EXTRA-STATE WAR #427:
Sokoto Uprising of 1906

Participants: United Kingdom vs. Mahdist rebels
Dates: January [ ], 1906, to March 10, 1906
Battle-Related Deaths: Mahdist rebels—2,000;
United Kingdom—80
Where Fought: Africa
Initiator: Mahdist rebels
Outcome: United Kingdom wins
War Type: Colonial

Narrative: Great Britain had gained control over South Nigeria as a result of extra-state war #411 in 1897 and over North Nigeria as a result of its war against Kano and Sokoto in 1903 (extra-state war #422). Not all of the inhabitants were happy with British rule. A Mahdi was an Islamic leader who claimed to be a descendant of the Prophet Muhammad and aimed to restore Islamic rule (thus frequently opposing foreign intervention). A Mahdist revolt broke out in Sokoto in northern Nigeria in early 1906, led by Dan Mafafao and Mallam Isa, who referred to himself as the prophet Jesus. A small British contingent, seeking to restore order, with three British officials and seventy black infantry was ambushed and massacred at Satiru. The ruling Fulani nobility of Sokoto also saw the Mahdist movement as a threat to their rule. Consequently, the Sultan of Sokoto supported a British expedition in March, which annihiliated the village of Satiru in retaliation, thus defeating the rebels.

Coding: Sokoto is coded as an autonomous entity from 1816 to 1903.

Sources: Catchpole and Akinjogbin (1983); Clodfelter (1992); Pakenham (1991); Zuljan (2003).

EXTRA-STATE WAR #429:
The Third British-Zulu War of 1906

Participants: United Kingdom vs. Zulu
Dates: March [ ], 1906, to July [ ], 1906

Battle-Related Deaths: Zulu—2,300; United
Kingdom—60
Where Fought: Africa
Initiator: Zulu
Outcome: United Kingdom wins
War Type: Colonial

Narrative: This was the last in a series of British wars against the Zulu people of the Natal region of South Africa. The first of the British-Zulu wars had occurred in 1838 (extra-state war #321) and had led to the British annexation of Natal to the Cape Colony. The second war, extra-state war #380 in 1879, ultimately enabled the British to annex Zululand in 1887. This region was also the site of some of the fighting in the two Boer Wars (extra-state wars #382 and #416). In 1906 the Zulu in Natal, under the leadership of Bambatha, made one final effort to expel the British from their territory. In February 1906 a disturbance had resulted from the refusal of several Zulu to pay a poll tax. Martial law was declared, and the British went on the offensive to stamp out the revolt. Overall, 12,000 Zulu would face 17,000 British troops. The first major action of the war took place at Bobe on May 5, 1906, where the advancing British troops were ambushed by the rebels. The Zulu were then beaten back, and they withdrew toward the Mome Gorge. Meanwhile, another Zulu force, under the leadership of Mehlokazulu, advanced to assist the rebellion in Natal. At Mpukonyoni the Zulu were intercepted by British forces and decisively defeated on May 28. Mehlokazulu then headed to meet Bambatha's force at the Mome Gorge. The Zulu were ultimately trapped in the Gorge, where they were attacked and slaughtered by the British. Both Bambatha and Mehlokazulu were killed. This defeat effectively ended the war, except for a few minor skirmishes.

Sources: Clodfelter (2002); Guy (2006); Jaques (2007); Pakenham (1991); Stuart (1913).

EXTRA-STATE WAR #430:
The Dembos War of 1907–1910

Participants: Portugal vs. the Dembos of Angola
Dates: [ ]/[ ]/1907, to [ ]/[ ]/1910
Battle-Related Deaths: Dembos—5,000; Portugal—100
Where Fought: Africa
Initiator: Portugal
Outcome: Portugal wins
War Type: Imperial

Narrative: The second-largest ethnic group in Angola was the Mbundu. The Mbundu kingdom was established in the north-central portion of Angola, and the Dembos (Ndembu) are part of the Mbundu people. The Portuguese came in contact with them when they established their settlement at Luanda in 1575, since the Dembos lived less than ninety-five miles northeast of there. The Dembos were involved in armed conflict with the Portuguese after 1850, though for the most part, Portuguese attempts to subjugate the Mbundu ended with a Portuguese victory in 1902. However, following wars against tribes in the center of Angola (extra-state war #420) and the south (extra-state war #421), the Portuguese wanted to further extend their control over the Dembos. Owing to the terrain, the Dembos campaign was probably the most difficult of the three wars. In 1907 Capt. João de Almeida led a force of 1,000 in an attempt to destroy the power of the Dembos. Between 1907 and 1910, there were numerous skirmishes between the Portuguese and the Dembos, though no real large-scale battles. Sustained fighting ended in 1910, but it took another seven years before Portugal completed its occupation.

Coding: The Dembos suffered most of the battle-related deaths. Many of the Portuguese deaths were from disease, though the development of new medicines also contributed to the Portuguese victory.

Sources: Broadhead (1992); *Columbia Encyclopedia* (1993); Duffy (1962); Duffy (1959); Hammond (1966); Riedinger (2007); Stearns (2001); Zuljan (2003).

EXTRA-STATE WAR #431:
Anti-Foreign Revolt of 1907

Participants: France vs. Sheikh Ma Al-Ainine
Dates: July 30, 1907, to [ ]/[ ]/1910
Battle-Related Deaths: Sheikh Ma Al-Ainine's army—3,000; France—[ ]
Where Fought: Africa
Initiator: France
Outcome: France wins
War Type: Imperial

Narrative: After the imperialists had come to power in France in the 1880s, the French began rapidly expanding their colonial empire in Asia, the Middle East, and Africa, involving the French in numerous wars. One of the foci of the French endeavors was northwest Africa. Ultimately, the French would expand their colonies from the north (Algeria), the west, and the south so that they would control almost the entire area before the outbreak of World War I. Early on the French had attempted to gain a foothold along the northwest coast in Morocco (see extra-state war #330 in 1844). In the 1890s they shifted further south, establishing colonies in Senegal, Dahomey, and Chad (extra-state wars #394, #395, #396, and #415). This war is the consequence of the French attempts to expand their influence into the area between the more northern and southern advances, into Mauretania (Mauritania).

Dutch, French, and English traders had all established outposts in what is now Mauretania in the fifteenth century, but the territory was controlled by a variety of tribes, and Europeans frequently sought to promote factional warfare as a means of deflecting attention away from themselves. After 1884 the French began moving northward, further into Mauretania, creating antiforeigner unity among the Mauretania tribes. The prominent leader of this movement was a religious leader, Sheikh Ma Al-Ainine (Mawlay Lahsin or Moulai Lahsin), who declared a holy war against the Europeans in 1895. The sheikh built his own fortress and began receiving assistance and weapons from the sultan of Morocco. Skirmishes between the French and the Mauretanian tribes continued, with some of the tribes going over to support the French, while others supported the sheikh. A defining moment of the conflict occurred in 1899. The French had become involved in a war against Rabih az-Zubayr in Chad (extra-state war #415). At one point the French attempted to secure their position by advancing across the Senegal River into southern Mauretania. There they were attacked by the forces of the emir of Adrar. Although the French withdrew back into Senegal, the emir of Adrar became one of the leaders of the anticolonial resistance movement. In 1903 France declared a protectorate over Mauretania, and it was incorporated into French West Africa the following year. In 1907 the French amassed troops for what they thought would be the final campaign into Mauretania's interior.

An additional catalyst for war was provided when a French force from Senegal landed in Casablanca (Morocco) in 1907. In response to anti-European riots there, the French butchered hundreds of Moroccan civilians on July 30, 1907. This episode fueled not only a civil war in Morocco but also attacks on French forces both in Morocco and Mauretania. The Moroccan sultan declared the struggle a holy war and sent troops to aid the rebels in Mauretania. Between 1907 and 1910 the French conducted a pacification program that resulted in the occupation of Adrar and the subjugation of most of the tribes. In the final battle the French defeated a combined force of 6,000 at Tadla. Ma Al-Ainine died at his base camp in Morocco, though his sons carried on the struggle against the French until 1934.

Coding: Adrar is coded as an autonomous entity until 1909. This war takes place at approximately the same time as a civil war in Morocco (intra-state war #646), in which France is also involved. After the French attack in Casablanca on July 30, 1907, the French then moved further inland, becoming involved in the Moroccan civil war. Hostilities would also reach war levels in 1912 and 1913 (extra-state wars #434 and #436).

Sources: Ashford (1962); Bennoune (1977); Burke (1972); Clodfelter (2002); Mercer (1976); Phillips and Axelrod (2005).

EXTRA-STATE WAR #432:

The Japan–Korean Guerrillas War of 1907–1910

Participants: Japan vs. Korean guerrillas
Dates: August 1, 1907, to August 16, 1910
Battle-Related Deaths: Korean guerrillas—17,600; Japan—136
Where Fought: Asia
Initiator: Korean guerrillas
Outcome: Japan wins
War Type: Colonial

Narrative: China and Japan went to war over control of Korea in 1894 (inter-state war #73). Japan's victory in that war ensured that Korea would come under Japan's sphere of influence, and in 1905 Japan established a protectorate over Korea. Right after the agreement to make Korea a protectorate was signed, the Japanese dissolved the Korean army. In August 1907 parts of the alienated military began a revolt against the occupiers. As the former military withdrew from Seoul, they were joined by the Righteous Army, which was formed by Korean literati and composed of mostly peasants. These units fought the Japanese for three years, and the Japanese responded with attacks against Korean civilians. Japanese repression created additional rebels; at peak strength the Koreans fielded 69,800 guerrillas, while Japan had two army divisions. In 1909 the Japanese resident general was assassinated, which precipitated Japan's complete annexation of Korea. We use August 16, 1910, the date of the Treaty of Annexation of Korea to Japan, as the end date of the war.

Coding: This is a colonial war because Korea, though not a colony, was a protectorate of Japan, and Koreans rebelled. Clodfelter (2002) refers to this as the "Japanese Subjugation of Korea: 1907–1911."

Sources: Clodfelter (2002); Hane (2000); Kim and Kim (1967); *Korea Past and Present* (1972); Korean Overseas Information Service (1987); Lee (1984); Oliver (1993); Schirokauer and Clark (2004)

EXTRA-STATE WAR #433:
The French Conquest of Wadai of 1909–1911

Participants: France vs. Wadai sultanate
Dates: May [ ], 1909, to late 1911
Battle-Related Deaths: Wadai—8,000;
France—4,000
Where Fought: Africa
Initiator: France
Outcome: France wins
War Type: Imperial

Narrative: France had begun its conquest of what is now Chad as a step in linking its colonial possessions in a broad expanse that would cross Africa from west to east, from the Atlantic to the Red Sea. In 1898 this plan had brought the French into conflict with Britain, which was trying to establish a colonial empire stretching the length of Africa from north to south. The result was the famous Fashoda Incident, when British and French expeditions confronted each other in the Upper Nile region. The ultimate result of the incident was that France had to give up its claim on the Upper Nile in exchange for part of the Sahara. France then focused on expanding its control in the central area instead, which included the regions of Bagirmi and Wadai in what is now Chad. In 1899 French expansionism led the French into a war (extra-state war #415)

against Rabih az-Zubayr, sometimes called the "Black Sultan", who had conquered Bagirmi, southeast of Lake Chad, and had established a slave trade state. In 1900 az-Zubayr was captured and subsequently beheaded, and the French were able to consolidate their control over Chad, though az-Zubayr's son, Fader Allah, unsuccessfully led the Dazingers against the French in August 1901.

Wadai was located further to the east of Lake Chad, in drier country than found around the lake. Wadai was, in fact, along the border of Sudan, which was controlled by Britain. The Wadai sultanate had existed for more than 400 years by the late nineteenth century. At that time Wadai came under the influence of the Senussi, an Islamic movement favoring the revitalization of Islam and the removal of foreigners. As France gradually occupied some of the outer provinces of Wadai, it raised the opposition of the Senussi. Wadai not only wanted the return of its territory, but also it refused to end the slave trade and would not allow the free passage of French explorers and traders. Consequently, France began moving it forces against Abéché in May 1909. Abéché was occupied by June. The French installed a puppet sultan, and the deposed sultan raised a revolt that lasted until 1911. At its peak this was a large war, with a maximum of 50,000 troops fighting on each side.

Coding: Wadai was an autonomous entity until 1913, when it became part of French Equatorial Africa.

Sources: Decalo, Thompson, and Adloff (1997); Kohn (1999); Phillips and Axelrod (2005); Schafer (1995); Zuljan (2003).

EXTRA-STATE WAR #434:
The French-Berber War of 1912

Participants: France vs. Berbers
Dates: March 31, 1912, to September 6, 1912
Battle-Related Deaths: Berbers—3,400;
France—200

Where Fought: Middle East
Initiator: Berbers
Outcome: France wins
War Type: Colonial

Narrative: Although Morocco had been the object of European colonization since the fifteenth century, European competition over Morocco was heightened in the mid-nineteenth century. France, Spain, and Germany were particularly interested in expanding their presence in Morocco. France had gone to war with Morocco in 1844 (extra-state war #330) and Spain fought against Morocco in 1859-1860 (inter-state war #31). Both France and Spain wanted to preclude German involvement in Morocco, and so in 1904 they entered into an agreement to partition Morocco between them. German objections led to the Algeciras Conference in 1906 to discuss the fate of Morocco. As a result German economic interests were protected, though Spain and France were accorded predominance in Morocco. At the time, Morocco was ruled by Abd al-Aziz IV, and the expansion of French influence met little resistance; however, opposition to foreign interference in Morocco was heightened by the French massacre of civilians at Casablanca in 1907. This led to wars, both within Morocco and between Morocco and the foreign powers. Abd al-Aziz was overthrown and replaced as sultan by his brother (Abd al-Hafid) in intra-state war #646 (1907–1908). Spain and Morocco went to war again in 1909 (inter-state war #94).

Abd al-Hafid (or Abd al-Hafiz) had a difficult time maintaining order in Morocco; he faced opposition to his rule, continued French interference, and the growing power of the antiforeigner movement. He was confronted in January 1911 by the Fez caids (local governors), and the sultan received French assistance to relieve the siege at Fez (though fatalities did not reach war level at this point). On July 1, 1911, the German warship *Panther* appeared at Agadir. This perceived threat encouraged France to come to terms with Germany. In November 1911 Germany dropped its opposition to a French protectorate in Morocco in exchange for French-controlled territory in Equatorial Africa. Within four months the continuing violence and opposition to his rule finally persuaded Sultan Abd al-Hafid to accept a French protectorate on March 30, 1912. As of March 31, 1912, the nature of the conflict shifted as the French clearly took over the bulk of the fighting against the Fez caids, thus beginning this extra-state colonial war between France and the Berbers.

By April, Fez was once again the scene of the fighting when Moroccan soldiers mutinied and joined the 15,000 rebels opposed to the sultan in a siege of the city. A French relief force arrived and destroyed the rebel camp on June 1, 1912. Meanwhile, in Cairo, Egyptian nationalists were planning to intervene in the fighting in Morocco as part of a broader Pan-Islamic resistance to French occupation in Algeria and Tunisia. They were hoping for a general uprising to take place after Ramadan in September 1912 and began sending arms to Berber rebel leader El Hiba. In reaction against the French protectorate and the French replacement of Sultan Abd el-Hafid by his brother Mulai Yusef, a new claimant to the throne, El Hiba seized Marrakesh on August 18. A 5,000-man French force met El Hiba's 10,000-man army near Sidi Ben Othman on September 6, 1912. Over 2,000 Moroccans were killed before the rebels withdrew and Marrakesh was relieved. This battle marked the end of the war; however, fighting would resume the next year with a new challenge to French rule (extra-state war #436).

Coding: Morocco is a member of the interstate system from 1847 to 1912, when it becomes a protectorate of France. France, not the government of Morocco, is the major combatant in the war against the Berbers, which determines the coding of this war as extra-state. The next war (extra-state war #436) in 1913–1915 is also extra-state, involving French and Spanish troops in a war against the Berbers. Clodfelter (2002) combines at least four of our wars together in the "French Conquest of Morocco: 1903–1914." Phillips and Axelrod (2005) apparently combine together our inter-state war between Spain and Morocco (war #94) and this current extra-state war (#434), and perhaps our intra-state war #646, as well, in their "Moroccan War (1907–1912)." However, they also identify the principal combatants as Morocco vs. France and Spain, plus Germany vs. France.

Sources: Abun-Nasr (1975); Bimberg (1999); Burke (1972); Chandler (1975); Clodfelter (2002); Harris (1913); Jaques (2007); La Porte (2004); MacLeod (1918); Mercer (1976); Phillips and Axelrod (2005); Schafer (1995).

EXTRA-STATE WAR #435:

The First Sino-Tibetan War of 1912–1913

Participants: China vs. Tibet
Dates: March [ ], 1912, to January [ ], 1913
Battle-Related Deaths: China—2,000; Tibet—[ ]
Where Fought: Asia
Initiator: Tibet
Outcome: Tibet wins
War Type: Colonial

Narrative: From the start of the COW system in 1816, China had exercised control over Tibet. In essence, China protected Tibet from foreign incursions and kept it relatively isolated from other states. The Manchu dynasty, however, had been in decline since the senility of Emperor Chien-lung in the early decades of the nineteenth century, and China was gradually carved up into European and Japanese spheres of influence. As the power of China waned, China's control over Tibet declined as well, and Tibet became relatively autonomous. This situation persuaded Great Britain to attempt to enter into a direct relationship with Tibet. The British ended up sending the Younghusband expedition to Tibet in 1903–1904, and the expedition fought its way to Lhasa, Tibet's capital, in order to extract diplomatic and trade agreements

(extra-state war #425). China's immediate response to the Younghusband expedition was a decision to reinforce its dominant position in Tibet (sometimes referred to as China's forward movement). In April 1906 China and Britain signed a treaty that reaffirmed China's responsibility for Tibet while supposedly protecting British trading rights. In 1910, however, China sealed the borders of Tibet, cutting trading ties with India. An "Imperial Resident" was appointed and a Chinese army was deployed to establish direct Chinese rule in Tibet. In February 1910 the Dalai Lama was deposed and fled to British India. The intensity of Chinese control did not endure, partially because of the difficulties for China caused by the First Nationalist revolution (intra-state war #657 in October to December 1911) but also because of the growing Tibetan resistance.

In December 1911 the Chinese troops in Tibet rebelled and replaced the Manchu administration with their own general, who was unable to maintain order against growing Tibetan opposition. Widespread rioting and looting began, which by March 1912 solidified into battles between the Tibetans and Chinese forces in Shigatse, Gyantse, and the capital of Lhasa. In July 1912 the new Chinese government dispatched an army for the relief of Lhasa, though it became involved in heavy fighting near Qamdo. In that same month, on July 24, 1912, the Dalai Lama returned from India. In August a truce was arranged with the assistance of a representative from Nepal. However, the Dalai Lama did not return to Lhasa until January 1913 after the withdrawal of the Chinese troops, which marks the end of the war. In October 1913 a conference among Britain, China, and Tibet was held in Simla (India) that divided Tibet into two sections: Outer Tibet, nearer to India, which would be autonomous, and Inner Tibet, closer to China, whose status was not clearly defined. Though the British and Tibetans accepted the proposal, China did not, leaving Tibet's status unresolved.

Coding: Tibet was never a state system member, but from 1848 to 1910 it was the type of autonomous entity we have called a protostate, since it lacked diplomatic recognition. The Chinese actions in 1910 changed Tibet's status to that of an occupied dependency. After this war Tibet then again becomes an autonomous entity until 1951, after which it is incorporated into China (see extra-state war #462). The Chinese, however, have held the view that Tibet was part of China throughout this entire period.

Sources: Christie (1976); *Columbia Encyclopedia* (1993); Grunfeld (1996); Palace (2004); Patterson (1960b); Patterson (1960a); Richardson (1984); Richardson (1962).

EXTRA-STATE WAR #436:

The Moroccan Berber War of 1913–1915

Participants: France, Spain vs. Berbers
Dates: March 26, 1913, to May 16, 1915
Battle-Related Deaths: Morocco—1,000; France—900; Spain—[ ]
Where Fought: Middle East
Initiator: France
Outcome: Conflict continues at below war level
War Type: Colonial

Narrative: After the Moroccan sultan had agreed to the establishment of the French protectorate over Morocco on March 30, 1912, Morocco ceased to be an independent member of the interstate system. France then took over the conduct of the war against the Berbers, who were opposed to both the sultan and the French protectorate (extra-state war #434). That war ended with the French defeating the Berber forces of Al Hiba on September 6, 1912. On November 27, 1912, France and Spain signed a new agreement, dividing Morocco into four zones. The French protectorate covered 90 percent of Morocco with Rabat as its capital, while the Spanish protectorate had its capital at Tetuán.

The French had replaced Sultan Abd al-Hafid, who had been linked to the antiforeigner movement) with his brother Mulai Yusef on August 13, 1912. The French appointed Gen. Louis-Hubert Lyautey to govern their protectorate, though the sultan continued to exercise authority in domestic affairs. General Lyautey proceeded to increase the size of the French military presence in Morocco to 32,000 troops. He also divided the French zone into five districts and began making plans to extend French influence from the cities into the interior, or the lawless "Blad Siba," which contained the Atlas Mountain regions inhabited by a number of Berber tribes. Although the vast majority of the Blad Siba was in the French protectorate, it also extended into the Spanish zone, as well. Thus this war involved both France and Spain fighting against the tribes that operated throughout this region.

The French began a campaign toward the Middle Atlas (inhabited by the Berber Zaian confederation) in March 1913. They initially were successful in capturing Casa Tadla on March 26 but were forced to retreat after facing fierce resistance at El Ksiba (June 8–10). Meanwhile, the Spanish were facing the most powerful caid (tribal leader) in the western portion of their zone, Ahmad ibn Muhammad Raisuli (El Raisuli). Raisuli had gained notoriety in 1904, when, as an element of his opposition to Moroccan sultan Abd al-Aziz, he had kidnapped a Greek American expatriate, Ion Percardis, leading to the "Percardis Incident," a confrontation between Morocco and the United States. Raisuli had no desire to submit to the Spanish protectorate and placed himself as the head of an open insurrection against the Spanish. In June 1913 the Spanish began military operations around Tetuán. Most of the Spanish offensives in 1914 involved small-scale encounters, and the Spanish were finally able to reach an agreement with Raisuli that granted him limited autonomy, though Raisuli continued to try to expand his area of influence.

Meanwhile, events in Europe had an impact on the war in Morocco. German agents arrived in the Spanish zone and began persuading some of the other caids to direct their attacks away from the Spanish and into the French zone. There a 14,000-man French force had won a victory at Khenifra (June 10–12, 1914). As the war in Europe progressed, 37 French battalions were withdrawn from Morocco and sent to Europe, which further emboldened the Berbers to increase their attacks throughout Morocco. Nonetheless, the French decided to attack the rebels at El Herri. Although the assault was initially successful, the tribesmen counterattacked and the French were decimated, suffering their worst defeat in Morocco on November 13, 1914. Sporadic fighting continued, including a costly battle on May 16, 1915 at Sidi Sliman. This date is coded as the end of the war. Fighting did continue in 1916 and 1917, though there is insufficient evidence on fatality levels to extend the war to this period. In November 1916 the French sent two separate expeditions against the Zaian confederation in a pincer movement, and by June 1917 they had generally succeeded in pacifying the central tribes. This situation would not last long, however. In 1921 war would break out between Spain and the Berbers inhabiting the Rif Atlas Mountains, and the war would involve France, as well, in 1925 (extra-state war #449).

Coding: Clodfelter (2002) combines a number of wars together in the "French Conquest of Morocco: 1903–1914." Phillips and Axelrod do not cover this war.

Sources: Abun-Nasr (1975); Bimberg (1999); Burke (1972); Chandler (1975); Clodfelter (2002); Harris (1913); Jaques (2007).

EXTRA-STATE WAR #437:
The Moro Rebellion of 1913

Participants: United States vs. the Moro
Dates: June 11, 1913, to October 22, 1913
Battle-Related Deaths: Moro—1,500; United
    States—50
Where Fought: Asia
Initiator: United States

Outcome: United States wins
War Type: Colonial

Narrative: The United States had gained control over the Philippines from Spain at the end of the Spanish American War (inter-state war #79). The Filipinos, who had tried to gain their independence from Spain (in extra-state war #410), were not pleased by the turn of events and staged a revolt against American control in 1899 (extra-state war #414). That war was fought mostly on the northern Philippine islands, Luzon in particular, and the southern islands were generally ignored. The Moro, the Muslim people of the southern islands of Mindanao and the Sulu archipelago, had largely escaped Spanish rule, as well; however, once the United States occupied the Philippines in 1898, it wanted to round out its control of the entire Philippine archipelago. In 1899 the United States negotiated a treaty with the sultan of Sulu, the head of the Moro, which recognized American sovereignty, but not all of the Moros agreed. From 1901 to 1913 various military campaigns were conducted to extend American control, and they encountered resistance but at below war levels. For instance, Phillips and Axelrod (2005) report that 600 Moros died in one battle (the fall of Bud Dajo) in 1906 alone.

In 1911 Gen. John Pershing (who would later gain fame during World War I and the U.S. war against Pancho Villa) returned to the Philippines to disarm the Moros. The Moros resisted briefly, but conflict died down until it resurfaced in 1913. In January more than 5,000 Moro retreated to Bagsak, an extinct volcano on the island of Jolo. When they would not leave, on June 11 Pershing launched a major offensive, against not only Bagsak but a number of other fortifications as well. General Pershing's forces captured several *cottas*, or Moro strongholds. Another group of Moros fortified themselves on Mount Talipao, where they were routed on August 13. The Moros returned to the area, where they were finally defeated and forced to surrender on October 22, 1913, which marks the end of the war.

Coding: Axelrod (2007), Kohn (1999), and Phillips and Axelrod (2005) all combine the skirmishes from 1901 to 1913.

Sources: Axelrod (2007); Byler (2005); Jaques (2007); Kohn (1999); Phillips and Axelrod (2005); Smythe (1973); Wiencek (2002).

EXTRA-STATE WAR #440:
The Second Sino-Tibetan War of 1918

Participants: China vs. Tibet
Dates: January 7, 1918, to August [ ], 1918
Battle-Related Deaths: China—1,000; Tibet—500
Where Fought: Asia
Initiator: China
Outcome: Stalemate
War Type: Imperial

Narrative: Ever since Tibet had expelled Chinese troops from the country in 1913 (extra-state war #435), tensions between the two had been high. The Simla Conference, organized by the British in India in 1913–1914, did not really settle the issues between Tibet and China. The conference proposed dividing Tibet into two zones: Outer Tibet, near India, and Inner Tibet, closer to China. China was allowed to station troops in Inner Tibet, though the Tibetan government at Lhasa would control the local government. Supposedly the autonomy of Outer Tibet was recognized, and China committed itself not to interfere in its internal affairs. However, in April 1914, two days after the agreement had been initialed by the three parties, the Chinese repudiated it. Consequently, Chinese forces continued to probe the undefined frontier between China proper and Inner Tibet. After the fall of Yuan Shih-kai (China's president from 1912 to 1916), China became involved in a civil war, the Southern China Revolt (intra-state war #675), and China entered into a period of warlord control of several of the outer provinces that bordered Tibet, including Sichuan and Yunnan. In January 1918 the warlord governor of Sichuan, Gen. P'eng Jih-sheng, took advantage of a skirmish between Chinese and Tibetan troops to launch a full-scale attack across the de facto border between China and Tibet (thus breaking the Simla truce). The Tibetans counterattacked, pushing the Chinese back beyond the upper Yangtze River. By April 1918 Gen. P'eng Jih-sheng was forced to surrender his garrison at Chamdo. The Tibetans continued their advance into China. A British consular official was able to mediate the dispute and reached two cease-fire agreements in August and October 1918. The agreements established a truce for a year (till October 1919).

The Chinese were suspicious of the agreement, since they saw Britain not as a neutral mediator but as favoring Tibet (which had received arms from India in 1914–1915). In May 1919 the Chinese put forward an alternative set of proposals in which autonomous Tibet was to recognize Chinese suzerainty. Talks broke down in August 1919. Britain took advantage of the resulting stalemate to open direct relations with Tibet, sending a delegation to the Dalai Lama in November 1920. Ultimately, the Tibetans had to give up their dream of conquering Inner Tibet and to agree to a partial withdrawal from the territorial gains they had made during the war. The agreed-upon line of control was almost the exact one of the Ch'ing dynasty period.

Coding: COW codes Tibet as being occupied by China from 1910 to 1912 and then as an autonomous entity from 1912 to 1951, after which it becomes integrated into China.

Sources: Christie (1976); *Columbia Encyclopedia* (1993); Grunfeld (1996); Patterson (1960b); Patterson (1960a); Richardson (1984).

EXTRA-STATE WAR #441:
The Caco Revolt of 1918–1920

Participants: United States vs. Caco rebels
Dates: October 17, 1918, to May 19, 1920
Battle-Related Deaths: Cacos—2,004; United
  States—98
Where Fought: W. Hemisphere
Initiator: Cacos
Outcome: United States wins
War Type: Colonial

Narrative: Haiti is located on the western half of the Caribbean island of Hispañola. After Columbus arrived at Hispañola in 1492, the Spanish settled the eastern half of the island (now the Dominican Republic). Spain ceded the western half (Haiti) to France in 1697. Although Spain also ceded the other half of the island to France in 1795, Spanish rule on the eastern half was restored in 1809. Meanwhile, in 1804, Haiti became the second country in the region to win independence (after the United States).

In 1904 President Teddy Roosevelt announced the "Roosevelt Corollary" to the Monroe Doctrine. According to this corollary, the United States had the right, in case of "wrongdoing" by Latin Americans, to the exercise of an "international police power." Under this policy the United States intervened in the Caribbean many times between 1904 and the early 1930s. One such case was Haiti, which was occupied by the United States from 1915 to 1934. One of the purposes of this doctrine was to deter European expansionism in the Western Hemisphere. In the case of Haiti, the United States was reacting to what it saw as undue influence by France and Germany, partially because of Haiti's debt to those countries. Turmoil was spreading in Haiti, and in 1914 all three countries landed troops in Haiti to protect their consulates. The final precipitant to American action occurred on July 28, 1915, when a Haitian mob killed the Haitian

president, Vilbrun Sam. The U.S. Marines landed that same day in an attempt to restore order. On August 12, 1915, the Haitian congress was coerced into signing the Haiti Treaty of 1915, which gave the United States extensive control. This began an occupation that lasted nineteen years. Even though the United States' occupying force supported an elected Haitian president, Philippe Sudre Dartiguenave, the intervention entailed the imposition of white U.S. Marines over a black indigenous population. As might be expected in such circumstances, Haitians were divided between those loyal to their president and acceptant of the marines on the one hand, and on the other, those supporting an opposition movement that wanted the United States out of Haiti.

The toughest opposition was from Haitian northern mountaineers named the Cacos. Cacos were rural bands of thieves and mercenaries who had ravaged Haiti throughout its century of unstable independence. The Cacos ultimately wanted to control Haiti, and they joined forces with the Bobo of the north to oppose American control. They were engaged in skirmishes against the American forces by October 1915. Low-level conflict continued until 1918, when a new Cacos revolt was led by Charlemagne Massena Peralte. The local gendarmerie was not able to quell the revolt, and in March 1919 the American Marines began to assist the gendarmerie in their fight against the rebels. Overall, the Cacos fielded about 5,000 fighters, from among an overall anti-U.S. rebellion of about 30,000 armed men. Against the Cacos, the U.S. fielded a Marine brigade of 1,500 troops, supported by 2,700 troops of the Haitian gendarmerie. Many of the rebels were emboldened by belief in voodoo and thought that it conveyed great powers on them. This led to disorganized and ill-fated operations. On October 7, 1919, Charlemagne's forces were repulsed in an attack on Port-au-Prince, and a month later, Charlemagne was killed. In January

1920, however, a new leader, Benoit Batraville, emerged, and the rebels went on a rampage in the capital. For the next few months the rebels engaged in numerous skirmishes in the capital and the countryside. Finally, in May 1920, the marines located the rebel camp and attacked, killing the Cacos chief. This ended the Cacos war and the marines succeeded in restoring order.

Coding: We code Haiti as an autonomous entity from 1816 and as a member of the interstate system from 1858 to 1915, after which it becomes an occupied territory of the United States. Hence, this war involving U.S. Marines versus Haitian Cacos rebels is an extra-state war. The Cacos suffered 2,004 fatalities, while the United States lost only 28 marines in battle, which is almost a 100 to 1 fatality ratio. Included in the U.S. death figure above are the deaths of seventy Haitian government gendarmes, fighting alongside the marines, who were also killed in combat. Clodfelter (2002) writes of the "Caco Revolt" of 1918–1920, while Phillips and Axelrod (2005) cover this war as the "Haitian Revolt" of 1918–1920."

Sources: Clodfelter (2002); Dupuy (1997); LaFeber (1989); Nicholls (1995); Phillips and Axelrod (2005); Scheina (2003b).

EXTRA-STATE WAR #442:

The Third British-Afghan War of 1919

Participants: United Kingdom vs. Afghanistan
Dates: May 3, 1919, to August 8, 1919
Battle-Related Deaths: United Kingdom—1,136; Afghanistan—1,000
Where Fought: Asia
Initiator: Afghanistan
Outcome: Compromise
War Type: Imperial

Narrative: The United Kingdom was concerned with securing its empire in India and had engaged in numerous wars along its lengthy northern border. Particularly in the northwest, Britain was concerned about the status of Afghanistan. To a good extent, Britain conceived of Afghanistan as a buffer between India and the expansionism of Russia in Central Asia. The First and Second British-Afghan wars (extra-state wars #322 in 1839 and #379 in 1878) were motivated by a desire to have a pro-British (or at least not a pro-Russian) ruler in power in Kabul. Britain's support of Afghanistan also led Britain into war with Persia, when Persia seized the Afghan city of Herat in 1855 (inter-state war #25). Meanwhile, Russian advances in Central Asia (extra-state wars #359, #361, #371, and #376) had brought Russia closer to Afghanistan. Despite the fact that Britain and Russia had signed an agreement guaranteeing the territorial integrity of Afghanistan, border clashes between Russia and Afghanistan became more common. Finally, in 1885, Russian troops attacked the Afghans and drove them out of the Panjdeh region (extra-state war #390). Although Britain considered a war with Russia at this point, instead the British negotiated an agreement under which Russia received the Panjdeh district in return for Afghan possession of the Zulfkan Pass. In 1893 Britain also forced Afghanistan to settle the border demarcation between Afghanistan and British India along what became known as the "Durand Line." Britain's growing influence in Afghanistan was also recognized in the 1907 Anglo-Russian agreement, which guaranteed the independence of Afghanistan under British influence. (This agreement was an integral part of the formation of the Triple Entente of Britain, France, and Russia.)

During World War I, Germany and the Ottoman Empire tried to fuel anti-British sentiments in Afghanistan, though Britain was able to keep Afghanistan neutral in the war through large subsidies. In 1919, however, Amir Amanullah Khan ascended the Afghan throne following the assassination of his father, Habibullah. He was backed by nationalists who wanted to free the country of British influence. On May 3, 1919, he declared a jihad and attacked across the Durand Line border into India, where he occupied the village of Bagh. His force of 10,000 soon faced a similarly sized force of Anglo/Indian troops. Initially the British troops were repulsed, but in their second attack they were able to defeat the Afghans and drive them out of India (May 9–11, 1919). The British then bombed Kabul and Jalalabad and launched an offensive into Afghanistan toward Dakka. There, on May 13–17, the Afghans were defeated, with heavy casualties on both sides. The British also attacked Spin Baldak on May 27 with similar results. In the final battle the Afghans attacked Thal in India but were repulsed on May 28. The Afghans then sued for peace, and an armistice was signed on May 31. The Treaty of Rawalpindi, signed on August 8, 1919, reaffirmed Afghan independence, but the Afghans promised to end raids along the border.

Coding: Afghanistan is coded as an autonomous entity until 1920. The Treaty of Rawalpindi gave Afghanistan full control over its foreign policy, which is a perquisite of COW interstate system membership. Afghanistan became a member of the interstate system the following year when it attained diplomatic recognition.

Sources: Albrecht-Carrié (1958); Clodfelter (2002); Dupree (1980); Jaques (2007); Kohn (1999); Molesworth (1962); Phillips and Axelrod (2005); Sorokin (1937).

EXTRA-STATE WAR #443:
The First British-Waziristan War of 1919–1920

Participants: United Kingdom vs. Waziristan tribes
Dates: May 26, 1919, to March [ ], 1920
Battle-Related Deaths: Waziristan tribes—1,600; United Kingdom—800
Where Fought: Asia
Initiator: Waziristan tribes
Outcome: United Kingdom wins
War Type: Imperial

Narrative: The term *Pathan* (or Pashtun or Pushtun) refers to over sixty seminomadic tribes

that inhabit the area of what is now Pakistan and Afghanistan. When trying to solidify its empire in British India, Britain had sent a multitude of expeditions into the region of the North-West Frontier along the Afghan border in attempts to subdue the tribes. Two of these had reached war levels, the Umbeyla Campaign in 1863 (extra-state war #357) and the British-Pathan War in 1897 (extra-state war #412). One of the difficulties had been that the border between British India and Afghanistan was not demarcated, and thus in 1893 Britain forced Afghanistan to agree to a demarcation along what was known as the Durand Line. Some of the tribes were unhappy with their placement within the British North-West Territory, which contributed to the outbreak of the 1897 war. Waziristan is a region within the general North-West Frontier area bordering Afghanistan; however, when the Durand Line was drawn, Waziristan became an independent territory, outside the bounds of effective British rule. Waziristan is generally divided into two parts, North Waziristan, which is inhabited by the Wazir tribes, and South Waziristan, which is home to the Mahsud.

The Third British-Afghan War (extra-state war #442) fanned the sentiments in Waziristan that the time was right to eliminate the vestiges of British control. In May 1919 the Wazir militia, serving with the British, revolted at Miranshah and Wana, starting the war. This war would be fundamentally different from the 1897 British war against the Pathan tribes because in 1919 most of the tribes had relatively modern weapons, and a number of their men had received military training while serving in British militias. Consequently, the fatalities would be higher. Within the first six months of the war, the tribes would stage over 100 raids against the British, frequently seizing weapons, and by June 1919 some areas had been cleared of British troops. It was not until November 1919, however, that the British developed plans for an offensive to subdue the tribes. A large UK force of 40,000 British and Indian troops, accompanied by another

40,000 noncombatants, advanced toward the Mahsud capital of Kaniguram. The armies met at Palosina on December 19–22, 1919, where both sides suffered heavy casualties. The Mahsud then withdrew toward a defensive position at Ahnai Tangi gorge. The battle there lasted a week, with fierce hand-to-hand combat in winter conditions. The British suffered 2,000 casualties, and the tribes had about 4,000 casualties, killed and wounded. The Mahsud kept retreating northward, where they sought aid from their Afghan allies, but the British maintained their offensive. Although the Mahsud never specifically sought an armistice, the significant fighting ceased as of the end of March 1920. Some order was restored, but another campaign was mounted by the British in 1936–1938 (extra-state war #455).

Coding: The fact that Waziristan was outside of British India makes this an imperial war. Waziristan became part of the semiautonomous North-West Frontier province, which joined Pakistan during the partition in 1947. Waziristan is now part of Pakistan's FATA, the Federally Administered Tribal Areas.

Sources: Ahmed (1991); Ahmed (1983); Beattie (2001); Caroe (1958); Clodfelter (2002); *Columbia Encyclopedia* (1993); De Watteville (1925); General Staff (1923); Molesworth (1962); Phillips and Axelrod (2005); Spain (1963); Williams (2005).

EXTRA-STATE WAR #444:
The Franco-Syrian War of 1920

Participants: France vs. Syrians
Dates: March [ ], 1920, to August 7, 1920
Battle-Related Deaths: France—3,500; Syria—[ ]
Where Fought: Middle East
Initiator: France
Outcome: France wins
War Type: Imperial

Narrative: During World War I, Great Britain was desirous of weakening one of its opponents, the Ottoman Empire. Thus the British considered an idea promoted by Sharif Husayn ibn Ali (the emir of Mecca) to encourage an Arab rebellion against the Ottomans. The proposal was discussed in the famous Husayn/McMahon correspondence of July 1915 to March 1916. In exchange for such an uprising, Husayn requested British support for an independent Arab state created from Ottoman territories (including the Arabian Peninsula, Greater Syria, and Iraq). Britain's agreement to Husayn's proposal led to the Arab Revolt, which began on June 10, 1916. During the final offensive of the revolt, which culminated in the seizure of Damascus in 1918, Husayn's forces were headed by his son, Amir Faysal (Faisal), who was assisted by Britain's famous T. E. Lawrence (Lawrence of Arabia). Faysal arrived in Damascus on October 1, 1918, and began establishing a ruling structure, which he assumed had British approval.

However, Britain had entered into other commitments, as well. The 1916 Sykes-Picot agreement between the United Kingdom and France established a plan for the division of the Arab territories of the Ottoman Empire between them. In March 1920 representatives from all parts of Syria met in Damascus and proclaimed an independent state of Syria with Faysal as its king. Despite pleas made by Faysal at the peace conference, the allies awarded Syria to France as a League of Nations mandate at the San Remo Conference in April 1920. Consequently France saw Faysal's actions in establishing an independent Syrian government as violating the terms of the peace treaty, and in June they issued an ultimatum to Faysal to accept their protectorate. Faysal attempted unsuccessfully to negotiate with the French commander in Beirut, Gen. Henri Gouraud. Instead, a few border clashes between the Syrians and the French convinced Gouraud of the need for military action. He sent an invasion force of 12,000 troops from Lebanon into Syria. On July 24, 1920, Faysal's army was defeated at Maisalun. On August 7, 1920, Gouraud entered Damascus and deposed the king, ending this war. Faysal then fled into exile (see extra-state war #445).

Coding: In September 1920 General Gouraud divided the mandate territory into four parts: Lebanon, Damascus, Aleppo, and Lattakia.

Sources: Cleveland (1994); Clodfelter (2002); Commins (2004); Jaques (2007); Lenczowski (1987); Tauber (1995).

EXTRA-STATE WAR #445:
The Iraqi-British War of 1920

Participants: United Kingdom vs. Iraq
Dates: June 5, 1920, to October 17, 1920
Battle-Related Deaths: Iraq—8,500; United
    Kingdom—1,040
Where Fought: Middle East
Initiator: Iraq
Outcome: United Kingdom wins
War Type: Colonial

Narrative: Similar to the preceding war (the Franco-Syrian War, #444), the Iraqi-British War had its origins in the decisions made by the great powers about the distribution of the former Ottoman Empire territories at the end of World War I. Great Britain had apparently entered into contradictory commitments. In order to persuade the Arab states, led by Sharif Husayn ibn Ali, the emir of Mecca, to revolt against the Ottomans, Great Britain had indicated its support for an independent Arab state that would include the territories of the Arabian Peninsula, Greater Syria, and Iraq. This commitment led to the outbreak of the Arab Revolt on June 10, 1916; however, Britain had entered into other commitments, as well. The 1916 Sykes-Picot agreement represented a commitment that the Arab territories would be divided between Britain and France. It was the latter agreement that was ratified by the San Remo Conference in April 1920.

At the end of World War I, Britain was in control of the provinces of Basra, Baghdad, and Mosul, which became the state of Iraq under the British mandate in 1920. However, a group of Iraqi nationalists met in Damascus and declared that Emir Abd Allah was the king of Iraq instead. Consequently, British attempts to impose its rule led to an uprising among the tribes along the Euphrates River in June 1920. The uprisings were extensive, and the British ended up deploying a force of 60,000 troops to confront as many as 130,000 Iraqis. The Iraqis began the war by attacking and destroying a British fort at Tel Afar (north of Baghdad) on June 5. An attack occurred south of Baghdad as well, where the insurgents besieged a garrison at Rumaithah from July 1 to July 20. Early successes on the part of the rebels led to the spread of the revolt to other areas, including Kurdistan. In response, the British dispersed a number of columns in order to try to dampen the widespread uprisings, and the British were generally victorious in heavy fighting. The last major battle took place at Kufah on October 17, 1920. Although the British were successful in defeating the uprising, they began to look for ways to reduce their presence in Iraq. Consequently, in 1921, they offered to make Faysal, who had been forced out of Damascus in the preceding war, the king of Iraq. Faysal agreed, and he was crowned king of Iraq on August 23, 1921.

Sources: Cleveland (1994); Clodfelter (2002); Jaques (2007); Marr (1985); Phillips and Axelrod (2005); Tauber (1995).

EXTRA-STATE WAR #446:
Conquest of Mongolia, 1920–1921

Participants: China, Russia vs. Baron von
    Ungern-Sternberg's White Army
Dates: October 10, 1920, to August 22, 1921
Battle-Related Deaths: China—4,000; White
    Army—1,000; Russia—[ ]
Where Fought: Asia
Initiator: White Army
Outcome: Russia wins
War Type: Imperial

Narrative: China had dominated Inner Mongolia and gained control over Outer Mongolia in the seventeenth century; however, in the following years both China and Russia vied for control of Outer Mongolia. Outer Mongolia remained part of China until the Chinese Revolution of 1911 (the First Nationalist war, intra-state war #657), when it took advantage of the chaos to declare its independence on November 11, 1911. Mongolia then enjoyed a period of autonomy, though it did accept Russian protection. The decline of Russian power as a result of the Russian Revolution (intra-state war #677) encouraged the Chinese government to reassert Chinese control in late 1919.

At this point Mongolia became the focus of a war that was a by-product of a Russian civil war between the "Reds," or the Russian Bolsheviks, and the "Whites," or the anti-Bolsheviks. The Bolsheviks were winning the war in both the west and the east, and by early 1920 most of the White forces in Siberia had been defeated. One of the White Russian armies was led by Baron Roman von Ungern-Sternberg, and in October 1920 the baron's small (3,000-man) army invaded Mongolia. The baron's motivation was apparently the restoration of the monarchies in Russia, Mongolia, and Manchuria. Owing to Chinese misrule, many Mongolians joined the baron's forces, including 60 Tibetan warriors sent by the Dalai Lama. The Chinese initially defeated Ungern-Sternberg in a ten-day battle at Huree (or Niislei Khuree) that began on October 26, 1920. However, on February 3, 1921, Ungern-Sternberg's force (now 5,000 soldiers) occupied Urga (now known as Ulan Bator, or Ulaan Baatar). The baron rescued Bogd Khan, the nominal ruler, or *khutuktu*, of Mongolia, from the Chinese and restored him to the throne. In reality, however, the baron ruled. In late March 1921, Ungern-Sternberg engaged in battle with a large Chinese force, in which 3,000 to 4,000 Chinese soldiers were killed. This led to the collapse of the Chinese army in Mongolia.

In late May 1921 the Russian Bolsheviks entered the war. Ungern-Sternberg's army crossed into Russia and captured several villages. Then the Red army routed the baron's troops and forced them back into Mongolia. On June 28, Red army units crossed into Mongolia to fight Ungern-Sternberg. The Russians captured Huree on July 5 and established a provisional revolutionary government there. Although Ungern-Sternberg had initially been welcomed by the Mongolians, his repressive measures made him increasingly unpopular, and some of his forces defected to the Russian provisional government. In late July the baron's forces suffered severe losses. Ungern-Sternberg was captured on August 22, which marks the end of the war. The provisional government declared the independence of Mongolia on September 14, 1921.

Coding: This war is coded as an extra-state war because it is ultimately a war against a nonstate actor (Baron von Ungern-Sternberg's White army) conducted by two interstate system members, China and Russia. Mongolia is coded as part of China till 1911 and as an autonomous entity from 1911 to 1919, after which it was occupied by China from 1919 to 1921. The Mongolian People's Republic then becomes a member of the interstate system in 1921.

Sources: Baabar (1999); Bauden (1989); Bisher (2005); Clodfelter (2002); Isono (1979); du Quenoy (2003).

EXTRA-STATE WAR #447:

The Italian-Sanusi War of 1923–1931

Participants: Italy vs. Sanusi tribe
Dates: March 23, 1923, to September 12, 1931
Battle-Related Deaths: Sanusi tribe—35,000; Italy—5,000
Where Fought: Middle East
Initiator: Sanusi tribe
Outcome: Italy wins
War Type: Colonial

Narrative: The Italians gained nominal control over Libya (Tripoli) in 1912 through the Treaty of Ouchy, which concluded the Italian-Turkish War (inter-state war #97); however, the Italians controlled only the coastal strip. This was especially true of the eastern region of Cyrenaica, which had been controlled by the Sanusi brotherhood since the 1840s. Revolt simmered on their part against the Italians basically from the first day of Italian rule. Resistance to Italian rule increased during World War I, when the tribe saw its efforts in opposition to Italy, which had killed 3,000 Italians between August 1914 and August 1915, as being in support of the Ottoman Empire. After the war the resistance to Italian control continued. The Italians did grant Cyrenaica limited autonomy under the Sanusi in exchange for the removal of the remaining Ottomans. In 1916 and 1917 agreements were signed establishing peaceful relations between Italy and the Sanusi.

After Benito Mussolini and the fascists came to power in Italy in 1923, however, the Italian policy toward the Sanusi changed. Italian control over all of Libya was seen as necessary, and thus Mussolini began major campaigns against the Sanusi leader, Omar Mukhtar (al-Mukhtar). On March 23, 1923, the Italians occupied the Sanusi capital of Ijdabiyya, marking the start of a war that would last eight years. The Sanusi themselves were divided into a faction that favored compromise and another led by Mukhtar, who promoted military resistance. The Sanusi engaged in guerrilla warfare, generally ambushing Italian expeditions that had ventured into their areas. In 1931 alone, the Sanusi engaged in over 250 such attacks. Therefore, the Italians adopted a new scorched earth policy, attacking civilians and placing over 85,000 Sanusi in concentration camps. In a final effort to defeat the Sanusi, the Italians attacked their stronghold at Al-Kufrah on September 12, 1931. The Sanusi were defeated, Omar Mukhtar was captured, and the war was thus effectively over. Mukhtar

was publicly executed on September 16. The remaining Sanusi leaders fled to Egypt, and Italian general Marshal Badoglio declared complete victory on January 24, 1932.

Coding: In addition to the battle-related deaths, an estimated 50 percent of the Sanusi population (100,000 people) died during this period, many in Italian concentration camps. Libya is coded as an autonomous entity until 1835, as a part of the Ottoman Empire until 1912, and as a colony of Italy until 1942. Cyrenaica and Tripolitania were united to form Libya in 1934. Phillips and Axelrod do not cover this war.

Sources: Abun-Nasr (1975); Clodfelter (2002); Ahmida (1994); Jaques (2007); Wright (1969).

EXTRA-STATE WAR #449:

The Rif Rebellion of 1921–1926

Participants: France, Spain vs. Rif tribes
Dates: June 1, 1921, to May 27, 1926
Battle-Related Deaths: Spain—50,000; France—10,000; Rif tribes—10,000
Where Fought: Middle East
Initiator: Spain
Outcome: France, Spain win
War Type: Colonial

Narrative: Morocco had suffered through numerous wars as the direct or indirect result of France and Spain attempting to extend their colonial rule over Morocco (see extra-state war #330 in 1844; inter-state war #31 in 1859; intra-state war #646 in 1907; inter-state war #94 in 1909; extra-state war #434 in 1912; and extra-state war #436 in 1913). The year 1921 would see the start of the largest rebellion against Spanish rule by the Rif Berbers of Spanish Morocco. It was a catastrophic disaster for the Spanish.

The Rif were Berber tribes living in the Rif section of the Atlas Mountains. At this time, there were two formidable Berber leaders: in the west was Ahmad ibn Muhammad Raisuli (El Raisuli), who had been instrumental in the 1913 war, and in the east was Mohammed ben Abd el-Krim el-Kettabi, one of the Rif's more educated leaders. Raisuli's power had been diminished by a defeat at the hands of the Spanish in July 1919. Thus the momentum shifted to Adb el-Krim in the east. Abd el-Krim's experiences had given him a hatred of Spanish rule, and in 1920 he began to organize an army to fight against the Spanish. The Spanish forces in Morocco were under the leadership of Maj. Gen. Manuel Fernandez Silvestre, who was not particularly capable and who seriously underestimated the Rif warriors. The initial 25,000 Spanish troops were allocated to a series of 144 small forts, and Silvestre's goal was to spread Spanish influence further into Rif territory. Abd el-Krim had warned the Spanish that if they crossed the Amekran River they risked a tribal uprising. On June 1, 1921, a small Spanish detachment of 200 men crossed the river. The native members of the expedition promptly mutinied, killing most of the Spanish officers, and thereby launched a massive uprising. Despite cautionary messages sent from the Spanish officers in the west, Silvestre sent another detachment into Rif territory to establish a new base at Igueriben, three miles south of the major Spanish fort at Anual. There they were again besieged by the Rif, who neutralized several attempts to relieve the fort. Igueriben was abandoned, and the Rif warriors then besieged Anual. When the 4,000 Spanish troops at Anual attempted to break the siege, they were decimated, Anual was stormed, and Silvestre killed.

The defeat at Anual led to a widespread Spanish panic. As the poorly trained Spanish soldiers abandoned the forts, most were killed. By August 1921, Abd el-Krim had driven most of the Spanish from Morocco, except for those at Melilla, but there Abd el-Krim halted the attack and withdrew to the mountains. This respite persuaded the Spanish to reassert their control. With reinforcements from Spain, the Spanish began to reclaim most of their former positions. In April 1922 the Spanish launched a new campaign against Raisuli, but then in May they adopted a policy of attempting to negotiate with Raisuli while utilizing the military against Raisuli's rival, Abd el-Krim. In one of the last engagements that year, the Spanish established a new outpost in Rif territory in November 1922. It was attacked by the Rif, but even though the Spanish suffered 2,000 fatalities, they held on. Meanwhile, Abd el-Krim began to establish the governmental structures for a Rif republic in the mountains. The November 1922 fatalities fueled a public debate within Spain between those who wanted to defeat the Rif versus those who wanted to abandon the colonial enterprise. The situation led to a coup by Gen. Miguel Primo de Rivera on November 13, 1923.

The general soon began to implement plans for a Spanish withdrawal from Morocco; however, as the troops withdrew to Tetuán, they were attacked, suffering significant losses. As Abd el-Krim's forces advanced, they came into contact with Raisuli. When Raisuli rejected Abd el-Krim's proposal to resume fighting the Spanish, Abd el-Krim had Raisuli captured, and he died not long thereafter. The prospects of the war were fundamentally altered on April 12, 1925, when Abd el-Krim attacked the French along the border between the Spanish and French zones. Initially the French posts fell to the Rif offensive, and Abd el-Krim had plans to capture Fez, but the French finally decided to cooperate with the Spanish in planning a coordinated attack against the Rif army. French fortunes reversed with the arrival of troop reinforcements and Gen. Henri-Philippe Pétain (hero of World War I). France and Spain assembled a force of 360,000 soldiers: 200,000 from Spain and 160,000 from France. A Spanish flotilla landed near the Rif headquarters on September 8, 1925. The Rif warriors fought fiercely but were driven back. On May 17, 1926, Abd el-Krim surrendered to the French and was sent into exile. France and Spain then restored their former colonial borders.

Coding: Fatality statistics for this war vary greatly, partially just because of the sheer number of fatalities and partially because some sources include deaths from disease, which we do, while others include civilian deaths, which we do not.

Sources: Bimberg (1999); Carr (1982); Chandler (1975); Clodfelter (2002); del Val (1920); Fontaine (1950); Furneaux (1967); Gabrielle (1953); Galey (1969); Harris (1927); Jacques (2007); Kohn (1999); *L'Afrique Francaise* (1926); La Porte (2004); Landau (1956); Payne (1967); Pennell (2001); Pennell (1982); Perry (1996); Phillips and Axelrod (2005); Sorokin (1937); Usborne (1936); Woolman (1968).

EXTRA-STATE WAR #450:
The Moplah Rebellion of 1921–1922

Participants: United Kingdom vs. Muslim Moplahs
Dates: August 20, 1921, to February [ ], 1922
Battle-Related Deaths: Muslim Moplahs—2,400; United Kingdom—50
Where Fought: Asia
Initiator: Muslim Moplahs
Outcome: United Kingdom wins
War Type: Colonial

Narrative: In the years after World War I, India was faced with a number of nationalist uprisings, partially fueled by the ideas of nationalism and self-determination espoused at the Paris Peace Conference. These ideas were also linked together with a growing focus on a jihad, or religious war, against foreign domination that was prevalent among Muslim communities. The Moplahs are a Muslim community of Malabar, which is now part of the Indian state of Kerala. In 1921 it was a remote area in the Madras residency. The Moplahs are descended from Arab settlers and Malayali-speaking converts to Islam. They had often revolted during the nineteenth century against Hindu landlords. Their rebellion in 1921 had two distinct components: a clash with British authorities resulting from dissatisfaction with British rule and a Muslim religious revival that erupted in anti-Hindu violence.

The revolt began on August 20, 1921, with Moplah attacks on British government property. British troops attempted to arrest the Moplah leaders, precipitating the first clashes and fatalities. There were relatively few British troops in the immediate area, so reinforcements were sent. A British detachment advanced to Tiruruangadi, where the Moplahs had taken refuge in a mosque. When the Moplahs fled the mosque, they dispersed in small groups, and British forces were divided into small columns to pursue them. After several months of small skirmishes, British reinforcements arrived and a more concerted offensive was begun in October. Order was restored by February 1922.

Coding: Simultaneously, civilian riots by the Moplahs against Hindus led to the death of approximately 3,000 Hindu civilians, and another 100,000 Hindus were driven from their homes.

Sources: Clodfelter (2002); Keep Military Museum (2000); Mansingh (2006); Wood (1987).

EXTRA-STATE WAR #451:
Franco-Druze War of 1925–1927

Participants: France vs. Druze
Dates: July 18, 1925, to May 27, 1927
Battle-Related Deaths: France—4,000; Druze—2,000
Where Fought: Middle East
Initiator: Druze
Outcome: France wins
War Type: Colonial

Narrative: The Druze constitute an offshoot of Shiia Islam that has long guarded its isolation in the Jebel Druze (mountains of Syria) and its independence. Syria had been part of the Ottoman Empire, and at the end World War I the Arabs had expected their independence and had begun to create a kingdom in Damascus under

King Faysal. However, Syria was then given to France as a League of Nations mandate, which precipitated the Franco-Syrian War of 1920 (extra-state war #444). The Druze resented this outside control and the abuses of the local governor, thus in July 1925 the Druze began a revolt against the French. Although this started as a relatively localized revolt, it soon spread throughout Syria as a rejection of the mandate system.

On July 18, 1925, the Druze under leader Sultan Pasha al-Atrash seized the town of Salkhad in southeast Syria. A French relief column of 200 troops was ambushed on July 21, suffering more than 50 percent fatalities. The French retreated to the Druze capital of Suwayda, which the French then destroyed. Fighting involving heavy losses continued throughout the region. The rebellion then spread to the north, where rebels seized the city of Hama. A French retaliatory bombardment on October 4–7, 1925, caused over 300 fatalities. Revolt then broke out in Damascaus itself, and the French were driven from the city in October. The French high commissioner's subsequent decision to heavily bombard the city caused 1,000 deaths and cost him his job. Fighting then spread to Lebanon, where 3,000 rebels besieged the French at Rashaya. A relief column arrived on November 24, just in time to avert its complete destruction. The French then launched a final offensive, recapturing Suwayda in April 1926. On May 7, 1926, the French then drove the rebels from Damascus, where aerial bombardment caused massive damage and casualties. The rebellion gradually wound down over the next year. On May 27, 1927, the French declared Lebanon a republic and the rebellion ended.

Coding: Our battle-related death figures do not include the estimated 2,000 civilians killed in the bombardments of Hama and Damascus.

Sources: Betts (1988); Cleveland (1994); Clodfelter (2002); Jaques (2007); Kohn (2007); Lenczowski (1987); Longrigg (1958); MacCallum (1928); Phillips and Axelrod (2005).

EXTRA-STATE WAR #452:
The Yen Bai Uprising of 1930–1931

Participants: France vs. Vietnamese Nationalists
Dates: February 9, 1930, to [ ]/[ ]/1931
Battle-Related Deaths: Vietnamese—1,000; France—1
Where Fought: Asia
Initiator: Vietnamese
Outcome: France wins
War Type: Colonial

Narrative: France had gained control of Vietnam through a series of wars (extra-state wars #349, #369, and #385). In the aftermath of World War I, a number of nationalist movements emerged, partially due to the nationalist and self-determination sentiments expressed at the Paris Peace Conference. The conference had particular impact on one Vietnamese émigré, Nguyen That Than, who arrived in Paris at the end of World War I. He drafted a letter to American president Woodrow Wilson requesting democratic reforms for Vietnam. He became involved in the French Socialist movement and studied revolutionary tactics in Moscow before becoming one of the founding members of the Indochina Communist Party (later the Vietnamese Communist Party) as Ho Chi Minh.

The oppressive nature of the French colonial government in Vietnam particularly helped to fuel a growing nationalist movement. In 1927 the Vietnamese Nationalist Party, referred to hereafter as VNQDD, was formed, and many Vietnamese military officers joined it, hoping for reforms. The French authorities, however, arrested a number of VNQDD members following the killing of a Frenchman, René Bazin, who was a recruiter of black market cheap labor, by a VNQDD member in 1929. Though the VNQDD had engaged in terrorist activities, it switched tactics to plan a general uprising initiated by a mutiny of the Vietnamese soldiers against their French officers at Yen Bai (Yenbay) in northern Vietnam. The mutiny took place on the night of

February 9–10, 1930. The French had been alerted about the mutiny and sent reinforcements, which easily put down the revolt and prevented it from spreading to other garrisons. The VNQDD leaders were captured and beheaded. This virtually destroyed the VNQDD, and many of its former members joined the new Indochina Communist Party. The sentiments of the uprising did spread, however, and the Communist Party led peasant revolts against the French the same year, partially staffed by those who had escaped from the French anti-VNQDD dragnet. In 1931 the 10,000-man French force in Vietnam succeeded in crushing these revolts.

Coding: The reported fatalities for this war were quite one-sided, with only one French death. The repercussions for the Vietnamese civilians were severe. The French subsequently instituted a reign of terror in which 50,000 Vietnamese civilians were imprisoned, 10,000 of whom died. This war was, of course, just a small precursor to the much larger revolution France faced in Vietnam after World War II (extra-state war #457).

Sources: Clodfelter (2002); Duiker (1976); Karnow (1983); Marr (1981); Phillips and Axelrod (2005); Rettig (2002); Richardson (1960a); Zuljan (2003).

EXTRA-STATE WAR #453:
Saya San's Rebellion of 1930–1932

Participants: United Kingdom vs. peasant rebels
Dates: December 22, 1930, to June [ ], 1932
Battle-Related Deaths: peasant rebels—1,000; United Kingdom—140
Where Fought: Asia
Initiator: peasant rebels
Outcome: United Kingdom wins
War Type: Colonial

Narrative: Burma, which had been an autonomous entity since 1555, came under British control as a result of three wars (extra-state wars #310 in 1823, #339 in 1852, and #387 in 1885). As of 1885, Burma became not just a colony but also part of British India. By 1930, however, Burma faced a number of problems. Burma was an agricultural, not industrial, society, so wealth was mostly in the hands of those who owned land. At the middle of the nineteenth century the Irawadi delta region was a sparsely populated region of swamp and jungle where rice was grown for subsistence. As Burma became part of British India, investors cleared land for rice cultivation, so that the area under cultivation grew sevenfold from 1870 to 1930. In the 1930s, as the effects of the world's Great Depression spread to Burma, many of the native Burmese lost their land to foreclosure on loans, and about half of the cultivated land wound up in the hands of absentee landlords. Burma was also challenged by the influx of workers from impoverished areas of India who swept in and offered to work for lower wages than would the native Burmese. These conditions, coupled with British inattention, made a revolt increasingly likely.

Consequently, Burma was shaken in 1930–1932 by an uprising against British rule, led by a former Buddhist monk named Saya San. As a monk, Saya San had worked among the Burmese peasants. When the British planned to institute a new tax in 1929, Saya San began urging the peasants to resist paying the tax and to work to force the British out of Burma. The British had tried to remove the vestiges of the Burmese monarchy and had transferred the Burmese throne to a museum in Calcutta. On October 30, 1930, however, Saya San organized his coronation as king of Burma. He established a royal palace on Alaungtang Hill in Tharawaddy, where he moved on December 21, 1930. There, the following day, he declared war against the British

Tharawaddy was a district inhabited by malcontents and had suffered significant economic problems. So when the revolts began, the British treated them as isolated minor incidents, instigated by an eccentric. However, despite the kingly dreams of Saya San, most of his followers wanted the recovery of their lands from Indian money-lenders. The generally reckless attacks by

Saya San's followers against the well-armed British were prompted partly by a belief in Saya San's invincibility and in the power of tattoos to protect one from bullets. The revolt soon spread from Tharawaddy to encompass twelve of Burma's forty districts, and it ultimately lasted eighteen months. The British finally had to bring in additional troops from India to suppress the revolt. In addition to the 3,000 rebels killed and wounded, 9,000 were captured and arrested, of whom 350 were put on trial and 128, including Saya San, were executed.

Although the rebellion was a failure, the rebel trials in particular led to a new generation of Burmese leaders who were instrumental in the 1937 separation of Burma from British India and its 1948 independence after a period of Japanese occupation.

Coding: Clodfelter (2002) concludes that 10,000 rebels were killed. This figure seems too high given the apparent number of rebels, or it may include large numbers of civilians. We follow Solomon, who describes 3,000 casualties, which would include approximately 1,000 fatalities. Phillips and Axelrod (2005) do not cover this war.

Sources: Callahan (2003); Clodfelter (2002); Hall (1981); Metcalf and Metcalf (2006); Phayre (2002); Phillips and Axelrod (2005); Solomon (1969).

EXTRA-STATE WAR #454:
The British-Palestinian War of 1936–1939

Participants: United Kingdom vs. Palestinians
Dates: April 20, 1936, to October [ ], 1936, and August [ ], 1937, to January [ ], 1939
Battle-Related Deaths: Palestinians—2,450; United Kingdom—126
Where Fought: Middle East
Initiator: Palestinians
Outcome: United Kingdom wins
War Type: Colonial

Narrative: Palestine was part of the Ottoman Empire from 1516 to 1918. At the end of World War I, the fate of Palestine was unclear, partially because of the competing British commitments. The Arabs had anticipated British support for Arab independence as the reward for their participation in the war against the Ottoman Empire. Yet the 1916 Sykes-Picot agreement between the United Kingdom and France had established a plan for the division of the Arab territories of the Ottoman Empire between them. At the San Remo Conference in April 1920, it was the latter agreement that prevailed, and France and Britain were awarded League of Nations mandates in the area (the French in the north in what is now Syria and Lebanon, and the British in the south, including Iraq, Transjordan, and Palestine). The Arabs had begun establishing an independent state of Greater Syria, under the leadership of King Faysal in Damascus. The Palestinians were divided in their view for the future of Palestine: whether to work toward an independent Palestinian state or to envision Palestine as part of a Greater Syria that would include Lebanon and possibly Iraq. By the end of 1920, however, it had become clear that an Arab Greater Syria was no longer an option (see extra-state war #444). The Palestinians then switched their focus to gaining their independence and dealing with another one of Britain's commitments, in this case to the Jewish community. In the 1917 Balfour Declaration, British foreign secretary Arthur Balfour had called for the establishment of a Jewish homeland in Palestine. In 1920 the Third Palestinian Arab Congress issued a statement proposing a halt in Jewish immigration to Palestine until its status had been resolved. The British refused to recognize this statement or subsequent Palestinian appeals. Meanwhile, Zionism and Jewish immigration into Palestine were increasing, especially as Jews fled Hitler's Germany. As a result the territory of Palestine went from being about 8 percent Jewish at the start of the mandate to nearly four times that by the time of this war. Although this immigration was legal, and the Jews pointed out that they were buying land, there was still a sense among many of the Palestinian Arabs that the Jews were gradually changing the nationality of the area.

Clashes between the Arabs and the Jews began in the 1920s and continued all through the years of the mandate. Britain's response was a series of studies and "White Paper" reports attempting to clarify Britain's role and to establish a balance between Palestinian and Zionist claims. Nevertheless, Britain's changing positions served to fuel Palestinian-British tensions. For instance, the 1930 Passfield White Paper had expressed concern over land availability and hinted at immigration restrictions; however, in 1931 the British policy, expressed in what the Arabs called the "Black Letter," committed Britain to promoting a Jewish homeland through further immigration and land settlement. Jewish immigration increased radically after 1933, and reports that the Jews were stockpiling weapons alarmed the Palestinians. In April 1936 local Arab leaders ordered a general strike, and on April 25 the Arab High Committee under the presidency of the mufti was created to direct the rebellion. The revolt had two major components. Partially, it was a civilian peasant revolt, and Arab atrocities against Jewish civilians became all too common. This triggered murderous retaliation by the Jewish group Irgun. Roads, telephone lines, and trains were disrupted, and a majority of banks and post offices were closed. The other part of the uprising was a simultaneous campaign of sabotage directed against the British governmental installations. What transformed this uprising into a war were the policies and actions of the British. British armed forces fought back, until the bulk of the fighting was clearly between them and the rebellious Palestinian forces. Initially the British had only minimal security forces at their disposal, so they also pursued a diplomatic track. The British were able to persuade the Arab High Committee to end the revolt in October 1936, after the death of 1,000 Arabs and 80 Jews, by offering to send another commission.

The commission, chaired by Lord Peel, issued a report in July 1937 in which it proposed the partition of Palestine into two separate states. (A third area, Jerusalem and Bethlehem, would have been neutralized as an international zone under the plan.) Upon the announcement of the report, the second, more violent stage of this war began. In August 1937 the mufti declared war on the British and the Jews. By summer 1938 several towns and much of the countryside were in the hands of the rebels. It reached a point where "the situation was such that civil administration and control of the country was, to all practical purposes, non-existent" (the British commander as quoted in Tessler 1994, 240). On September 2 the British cabinet made a decision to crush the Palestinian rebellion, and by September 22 the number of British troops in Palestine had been increased to 20,000. The Arab High Committee was outlawed. The British were able to restore order by January 1939. Britain ruled Palestine for another decade without a war, until the fight for Israeli independence (see non-state war #1572).

Coding: The period of October 1936 to August 1937 is coded as a break in the war due to the agreement between the British and the Arab High Committee. Calculating the battle-related deaths for the war was complicated by the existence of two simultaneous conflicts. As much as possible, the violence between the Jewish and Palestinian communities is not included in this war per se. We have also tried to exclude Arab civilian fatalities. Clodfelter (2002) calls this the "Arab Rising: 1936–1939" and reports 126 British deaths, 547 Jewish deaths, and 2,176 killed on the Arab side (including combatants and noncombatants). Cleveland (1994) describes deaths as more than 3,000 Arabs, 2,000 Jews, and 600 British. Nutting (1964) claims a total of 3,500 Arab deaths, 250 Jewish deaths, and 77 British deaths. He and Dimbleby (1980) both describe 1,000 Arabs killed in 1936 alone, and Dimbleby specifically notes that they were killed by the British. Smith (1992) is the only one who really tries to separate out civilian and combatant deaths, though he does so for only one year, 1938.

For that year he describes 292 Jewish, 69 British, and 1,700 Arab deaths, of which the official count is reportedly 1,138 combatants and 486 civilians. Clodfelter's numbers seem about midrange for the British and Jewish deaths and so will be adopted here; however, his figure seems low for the Arab deaths if it includes combatants and civilians. If we take Smith's ratio of combatant to total deaths of 70 percent and use Nutting's figure of 3,500 Arabs deaths, we end up with a figure of 2,450 Arab combatant deaths.

Sources: Cleveland (1994); Clodfelter (2002); Dimbleby (1980); Gerner (1991); Goldschmidt (1991); Morris (2001); Nutting (1964); Ovendale (1992); Phillips and Axelrod (2005); Smith (1992); Tessler (1994).

EXTRA-STATE WAR #455:

The Second British-Waziristan War of 1936–1938

Participants: United Kingdom vs. Pathan tribes
Dates: November 25, 1936, to January 8, 1938
Battle-Related Deaths: Pathan tribes—10,000; United Kingdom—200
Where Fought: Asia
Initiator: Pathan tribes
Outcome: United Kingdom wins
War Type: Imperial

Narrative: In attempting to secure British India from the endemic violence along its North-West Frontier, Britain in 1893 forced Afghanistan to agree to a demarcation of the border between India and Afghanistan along what would become known as the "Durand Line." Waziristan, an area in the middle of this border inhabited by Pathan (Pashtun, Pushtun) tribes, was not included in either Afghanistan or India, and thus was an independent territory, outside the bounds of effective British control. Waziristan is generally divided into two parts, North Waziristan, which is inhabited by the Wazir tribes, and South Waziristan, which is home to the Mahsud. In extra-state war #443, the British attempted to quell a rebellion by the Wazir and

Mahsud tribes against potential British rule. Although the war ended inconclusively, the British continued to try to expand their control into this region.

The war in 1936 was precipitated by a dispute over the marriage of a Muslim schoolteacher and an underage Hindu girl. A local mullah, Haji Mirza Ali Khan, the fakir of Ipi, inflamed the situation by asking for the return of the bride to her husband. The local tribal leaders appealed to Britain for assistance in controlling the fakir. The British decided to do so by building a road into the area where he had retreated. On November 25 two British brigades moved into the area to prepare for the roadwork, and they were attacked. A second, larger British expedition was dispatched, and the fakir fled into Mahsud territory, where he organized an army to harass the British. In response to their raids, the British launched a campaign with 37,000 troops, which seized the village of Arsal Kot, causing the Fakir to flee again. The Fakir was able to maintain a practice of attacking British columns until January 1938, when he retired to a series of caves along the Afghan border.

Coding: The only source to cite fatality statistics for the Pathan was Minahan's *Nations without States*, which claims over 10,000 Pathan deaths in this war.

Sources: Caroe (1958); Clodfelter (2002); Jaques (2007); Keesing's (1936, 1938); Minahan (2002); Spain (1963); Williams (2005).

EXTRA-STATE WAR #456:

The Indonesian War of 1945–1946

Participants: Netherlands, United Kingdom vs. Indonesia
Dates: November 10, 1945, to October 15, 1946
Battle-Related Deaths: Indonesia—3,600; United Kingdom—1,000; Netherlands—800
Where Fought: Asia
Initiator: Indonesia
Outcome: Compromise
War Type: Colonial

Narrative: The Dutch East Indies had been ruled by the Netherlands, at least in part, since the seventeenth century. The Dutch had expanded their control over the islands through several wars in the eighteenth and nineteenth centuries (extra-state wars #313, #334, #350, #370, and #402). The movement for independence for Indonesia began in the twentieth century, under the leadership of two organizations. In 1920 the Indonesian Communist Party (PKI) was formed, and then in 1927 the Indonesian Nationalist Party (PNI) emerged under the leadership of Achmed Sukarno. During World War II, Japan conquered most of Indonesia. At the end of the war, on August 17, 1945, independence advocates led by Sukarno and Muhammad Hatta proclaimed Indonesia an independent republic. The Dutch, however, did not recognize Indonesian independence, and in the fall Dutch troops aided by British forces landed to reclaim the Dutch colony.

On November 10, 1945, fighting broke out involving the Dutch and the British against the Indonesian People's Army, thus initiating the war. The costliest battle of the war took place at Surabaya, where in heavy fighting from November 10 to November 19 the British captured the city. Over the next year the Dutch were able to seize part of Indonesia, but much of the country remained under nationalist Indonesia control. The costs of the conflict led the parties to the agreement at Cheribon in October 1946, which ended the war. In the agreement the Dutch recognized the United States of Indonesia as a free state linked to the Dutch crown. Both sides were ultimately dissatisfied with the agreement, and the Dutch began a so-called police-level action in July 1947 to try to recover more territory. The fighting lasted until 1949, but it did not reach the requisite fatality levels to be included as a war.

Coding: Indonesia gained its independence and became a member of the COW interstate system in 1949.

Sources: Clodfelter (2002); Frederick (1989); Gebrandy (1950); Jaques (2007); Kahin (2003); Kahin (1952); Kohn (1999); Phillips and Axelrod (2005); Reid (1986); Wehl (1948); Wolf (1948); Woodman (1955).

EXTRA-STATE WAR #457:
The French-Indochina War of 1946–1954

Participants: France vs. Vietminh
Dates: November 20, 1946, to June 1, 1954
Battle-Related Deaths: Vietminh—175,000; France—94,500
Where Fought: Asia
Initiator: Vietminh
Outcome: Vietminh wins
War Type: Colonial

Narrative: France had colonized Vietnam in a series of wars in the late eighteenth and the nineteenth century (including extra-state wars #349, #369, and #385) and then incorporated it into its Colony of French Indochina in 1887. During World War II (inter-state war #139), Japan occupied Indochina, though it did allow the Vichy government in France to retain figurehead status until March 1945, when the Japanese ousted the French and created the autonomous state of Vietnam (consisting of Tonkin, Annam, and Cochin China) under the leadership of Bao Dai (the emperor of Annam). At the end of World War II, Japanese occupying forces in French Indochina surrendered to the Chinese in the north and British forces in the south. The British turned their sector of Vietnam back over to the French. Bao Dai's government collapsed fairly quickly, and the Vietminh, under the leadership of Ho Chi Minh, established a republic with its capital at Hanoi (within the Chinese zone). In opposition to colonialism, Ho Chi Minh had founded the Vietminh party, mixing Marxist and nationalist policies. France offered to recognize Vietnamese autonomy as part of the French Union, but the Vietminh insisted on full independence. War began in 1946 when the Nationalist Chinese who had occupied North Vietnam returned control to the French. The war began with a Vietminh attack on a French patrol boat in Haiphong harbor, and it quickly evolved into a long-running, bloody guerrilla war.

Once the Communists came to power in China in 1949, the Vietminh forces (led by Gen. Vo Nguyen Giap) had a source of supply and soldiery and were able to make advances throughout the countryside. That same year the French created a government under Bao Dai in a bid to gain popular support. In 1950 France concluded a treaty with Vietnam, offering it independence within the French Union. In general, the Western countries then recognized the Bao Dai government, while the Communist regimes recognized Ho Chi Minh's government in the north. Meanwhile, also in 1950, the war reached a general stalemate, with the French controlling the towns and the Vietminh the countryside, and France officially asked the United States for assistance in the war. Within four years the United States would be funding 80 percent of the French war costs; however, the French military position was deteriorating rapidly. The war culminated in the battle of Dienbienphu, a French base in the northwest of Vietnam between March 13 and May 7, 1954. The French, who had been frustrated enough by eight years of guerrilla war, lost a massive pitched battle at Dienbienphu. The U.S. secretary of state, John Foster Dulles, approached President Dwight Eisenhower with a plan to drop U.S. nuclear weapons on the Vietminh forces, but he was rebuffed by President Eisenhower. The French defeat at Dienbienphu led to the Geneva Conference, to negotiate a compromise settlement between the two warring sides. The war was temporarily resolved with the 1954 Geneva agreements, by which Vietnam was divided into northern and southern "regroupment" zones. Elections were to be held in 1956 to unify the country, but instead the regroupment zones

gradually became the states of North Vietnam and South Vietnam. The fighting eventually resumed as the Vietnamese War (intra-state war #748 and inter-state war #163), with the United States taking the South Vietnamese side and fighting against Ho Chi Minh. In that war the United States repeated a number of the mistakes of the French, and the Communists finally were able to take over all of Vietnam by 1975.

Coding: Our battle-related death figures do not include civilians killed during the war. Estimates of civilian fatalities range from 125,000 to 300,000.

Sources: Buttinger (1967); Cady (1954); Clodfelter (2002); Fall (1963); Hammer (1954); Karnow (1983); Keesing's (1954); O'Ballance (1964); Phillips and Axelrod (2005); Thompson (1968).

EXTRA-STATE WAR #459:
The Third Franco-Madagascan War of 1947–1948

Participants: France vs. Madagascar
Dates: March 29, 1947, to December 1, 1948
Battle-Related Deaths: Madagascar—11,200; France—1,000
Where Fought: Africa
Initiator: Madagascar
Outcome: France wins
War Type: Colonial

Narrative: The island of Madagascar had become a French colony in 1896 after two wars (extra-state wars #386 and #401). The conclusion of World War II caused a reshuffling, and demise, of many colonial empires. Thousands of Malagasy soldiers who had served in the French army in World War II returned to Madagascar and fueled the drive for independence. In 1946 cotier (coastal) ethnic groups began agitating against French rule, and the country's first political party was formed, advocating independence, the Democratic Movement for Malagasy Restoration (hereafter referred to as the

MDRM). On the night of March 29, 1947, as the party prepared for the first meeting of the national assembly, a number of nationalist attacks took place led by the Malagasy officers against French installations throughout the island. One such attack took place at a military camp at a railroad junction at Moramanga, where the French/Senegalese troops repulsed the insurgents and engaged in brutal reprisals. The MDRM was blamed for the attacks, and its leaders were arrested and jailed or executed. The uprising lasted twenty-one months. Ultimately, the French sent in reinforcements, and French troops under the leadership of Gen. Pierre Garbay, who would become known as the "butcher of Madagascar," managed to crush the rebellion by the end of 1948, with terrible Madagascan losses. It has been estimated that nearly 100,000 Madagascan civilians died during the war, while another 100,000 died from hunger or disease. The French lifted the state of emergency on December 1, 1948, which marked the end of the war.

Coding: In 1958 Madagascar achieved autonomy within the French community and independence in 1960, at which time it became a member of the COW interstate system.

Sources: Brown (2001); Ciment (2007); Clodfelter (2002); Deschamps (1960); Edgerton (2002); Jaques (2007); Kent (1976); Kohn (1999); Phillips and Axelrod (2005); Thompson and Adloff (1965).

EXTRA-STATE WAR #460:

The Malayan Rebellion of 1948–1957

Participants: United Kingdom vs. Malayan
   Communists
Dates: June 18, 1948, to August 31, 1957
Battle-Related Deaths: Malayan Communists—
   6,700; United Kingdom—2,400
Where Fought: Asia
Initiator: Malayan Communists
Outcome: United Kingdom wins
War Type: Colonial

Narrative: The United Kingdom had established settlements in Malay Peninsula in the late eighteenth and the early nineteenth century. By the 1870s the British dominated the peninsula, and by 1914 all of Malaya was under British control. During World War II the Japanese invaded Malaya, in 1941, and ruled until 1945, when Britain recovered its colony. During the Japanese occupation the primary opposition group was the Malayan Communist Party (MCP) and its Malayan People's Anti-Japanese Army (MPAJA), both of which were supported by the Chinese community. Chinese settlers had immigrated over the past two centuries and were prominent in rubber plantations and tin mines. When the British returned to power, they proposed a new government structure that would merge the federated and unfederated Malay states with the largely Chinese cities of Malacca and Penang, providing equal rights to all the inhabitants. The subsequent withdrawal of the proposed constitution angered the Chinese, and the mostly Chinese communist guerrillas began a revolt in June 1948.

The war began with attacks by the Chinese against the rubber plantations and tin mines, and the killing of thee European plantation managers persuaded the British to declare a state of emergency that would last for twelve years. The MCP and its military, the MPLA (Malayan People's Liberation Army), took the war to the jungles, where they would attack British forts. By 1950 the British realized that their tactics were not working, so they increased the size of the military and adopted the Briggs Plan, under which many Chinese were forced into resettlement areas. This gradually cut off new recruits, and by the time the Federation of Malay became independent in 1957, the war was mostly over. A coalition of ethnic political parties helped to assuage the grievances of the Chinese, though a few guerrillas remained active in the jungles along the border until 1960. Individuals in the Kennedy administration at the start of U.S. involvement in the Vietnam War turned to the

British success in Malaya as a model of how to defeat a communist insurgency in Southeast Asia.

Coding: Federated Malaya was a British colony from 1896 to 1942 and in 1946. It was incorporated into Malaysia in 1946 and became independent in 1957. Kohn (1999) and Phillips and Axelrod (2005) refer to this war as the "Malay Jungle Wars" of 1948–1960.

Sources: Andaya and Andaya (2001); Ciment (2007); Clodfelter (2002); Hall (1981); Kohn (1999); Phillips and Axelrod (2005);

EXTRA-STATE WAR #461:
The Indo-Hyderabad War of 1948

Participants: India vs. Hyderabad
Dates: September 13, 1948, to September 17, 1948
Battle-Related Deaths: Hyderabad—1,200; India—10
Where Fought: Asia
Initiator: India
Outcome: India wins
War Type: Imperial

Narrative: Hyderabad was one of several hundred princely states located within the Indian subcontinent that had a loose relationship with Britain. As independence approached in 1947, each of these was to accede to either India or Pakistan. Hyderabad, however, was an anomaly. This mostly Hindu state in the south of the subcontinent was ruled by a Muslim ruler, or nizam. He chose to join neither India nor Pakistan but to essentially maintain an independent existence. Tension built over the next year with a non-state war (#1571, the Hyderabad War of 1947–1948) breaking out in late summer between those who wanted to join India and the Razkars, the forces of the nizam. On September 13, 1948, India intervened in the war, which led to its transformation into this extra-state war. India invaded Hyderabad and in a four-day campaign conquered and annexed the state. Hyderabad was later divided among the linguistic states of Andhra Madhya, Pradesh, Tamil Nadu, and Karnataka.

Sources: Clodfelter (2002); Coplin (1997); Cross (1968).

EXTRA-STATE WAR #462:
The Third Sino-Tibetan War of 1950

Participants: China vs. Tibet
Dates: May [ ], 1950, to October 28, 1950
Battle-Related Deaths: China—10,000; Tibet—3,200
Where Fought: Asia
Initiator: China
Outcome: China wins
War Type: Imperial

Narrative: Tibet is extremely remote, and its international relations are traditionally limited, partly by its remoteness and partly by the dominant role played by China in Tibetan affairs. Tibet had been involved in war with Britain in 1904 over Britain's desire to gain access to Tibet (extra-state war #425) and in two extra-state wars with China over the status of their relationship, one in 1912 (extra-state war #435) and one in 1918 (extra-state war #440). Tibet also did engage in one non-state war (#1530, the Dogra-Tibet War), against Jammu, in 1841–1842. Moreover, Tibet's isolation contributed to its lack of diplomatic recognition, which meant that it was generally an autonomous entity and not a member of the interstate system. Tibet's autonomy had been reestablished when it fought against Chinese domination in 1912-1913 (extra-state war #435)

After the Chinese Communists were victorious in the Chinese Civil War (intra-state wars #710 and #725), China and its leader, Mao Zedong, turned their attention to securing China's border, which included restoring China's control over Tibet. In May 1950 Mao sent a Chinese force to capture Tibet. Most of the war consisted of the slow progress of a Chinese assault column of about 35,000 troops, opposed by only 8,500 Tibetan soldiers. Much of the fighting for Tibet was done by irregular forces of mountain tribes, not the regular Tibetan army. In the final offensive, begun on October 7, 1950, the Chinese were able to seize Chamdo and destroy most of Tibet's army, ending the fighting by October 28, 1950. The war resulted in an agreement (signed May 31, 1951) between the Tibetan theocracy and the Chinese government, in which Tibet was absorbed into China. Although only a couple of hundred Tibetan government troops died in battle in the war (the majority of the Tibetan deaths were among the tribal irregular forces), somewhere on the order of 1,000 times that (about 200,000 ethnic Tibetans) may have died in the Maoist-era repression and mass killing that followed (see Rummel 1994 for a general discussion).

Coding: Tibet was a part of China until 1848. It was then an autonomous entity until 1910, when it was occupied by China until 1912. Tibet then returned to the status of an autonomous entity until 1951, after which it was incorporated into China. Thus Tibet's next war with China would be an intra-state war. Intra-state war #741, the Tibetan Khamba Rebellion, took place in 1956–1959 and cost over 100,000 lives (the vast majority were civilians).

Sources: Ciment (2007); Clodfelter (2002); Richardson (1984); Rummel (1994); Schafer (1995); Sperling (2008).

EXTRA-STATE WAR #463:

The Franco-Tunisian War of 1952–1954

Participants: France vs. Tunisia
Dates: January 18, 1952, to July 31, 1954
Battle-Related Deaths: France—2,000;
   Tunisia—1,000
Where Fought: Middle East
Initiator: Tunisia
Outcome: Tunisia wins
War Type: Colonial

Narrative: Tunisia had been an autonomous entity for much of the 1,000 years previous to the late nineteenth century. The country was part of the COW interstate system from 1825 to 1881, when the French imposed a protectorate, and France and Tunisia then went to war (extra-state war #383). Over the next 75 years some 100,000 French settlers occupied much of the most fertile farmland. After World War I (inter-state war #106), a nationalist movement developed in Tunisia, with two primary organizations—the Destour (Constitutional) party was formed in 1920, and the more radical Neo-Destour party emerged in 1934 under the leadership of Habib Bourguiba. During World War II (inter-state war #139), Tunisia came under the control of Vichy France, and many of the battles of the war in North Africa were fought in Tunisia. While most of the Tunisian nationalists supported the Axis powers, Bourguiba and the Neo-Destour party gave their support to the Free French and their allies.

After the end of World War II, a desire for independence became more pronounced in Tunisia, and nationalist agitation began. In 1950 France made a proposal to give Tunisia a fair amount of autonomy; however, Prime Minister Muhammad Shanniq traveled to Paris to demand independence, a proposal that was rejected by the French on December 15, 1951. Agitation for independence led to the arrest of Bourguiba in January 1952, and his imprisonment precipitated a wave of violence against French rule and French settlers by an initial guerrilla force of 3,000 fighters. The guerrillas, or *fellagha*, were not organized by Neo-Destour, which claimed it did not approve of violence. The prospect of Tunisian independence was not popular with the French living in Tunisia, who formed their own guerrilla organization, the Red Hand. In March 1952 the French seized the bey of Tunis, after which the bey disavowed the nationalist struggle, and the French imposed martial law. Fighting between the French and *fellagha* was a guerrilla war that became increasingly intense, requiring the stationing in Tunisia of a French army of 70,000. The *fellagha,* under the leadership of Ben Youssef, planned a major offensive for fall 1954; however, the attack was averted and the course of the war changed when Pierre Mendés-France became French prime minister. Mendés-France adopted a new policy toward Tunisia, and on July 31, 1954, he flew to Tunisia to begin the negotiations by which the French were prepared to grant autonomy to Tunisia, which ended the war. In 1955 Bourguiba returned to Tunisia, and on March 20, 1956, Tunisia received its independence and Bourguiba became president of the National Constituent Assembly. In 1957 Bourguiba abolished the monarchy and became Tunisia's president. Ben Youssef opposed the agreement with the French and French actions in Algeria, and he continued guerrilla activities in southern Tunisia in 1956.

Coding: Tunisia was a French protectorate from 1881 until 1956.

Sources: Abun-Nasr (1975); Brecke (1999); *Columbia Encyclopedia* (1993); Entelis (1980); "Habib Bourguiba" (2000); Hourani (1991); Moore (1962); Morrow (1955); Sivard (1991); Stearns (2001).

EXTRA-STATE WAR #464:
The British–Mau Mau War of 1952–1956

Participants: United Kingdom vs. Mau Mau
Dates: October 20, 1952, to October [ ], 1956
Battle-Related Deaths: Mau Mau—16,500; United Kingdom—600
Where Fought: Africa
Initiator: Mau Mau
Outcome: British win
War Type: Colonial

Narrative: British East Africa (present-day Kenya) became a British protectorate in 1895 (see extra-state war #406). In 1920 the governmental administration changed, with the British inland territories becoming the Kenya colony, while the coastal strip became the Protectorate of Kenya. The Kikuyu are Kenya's largest ethnic group, constituting about one-quarter to one-fifth of the total population of Kenya. The Kikuyu were farmers in the fertile central highlands of Kenya. In the early twentieth century, there was a large influx of English settlers into Kenya, leading to competition for land between the settlers and the Kikuyu and Masai tribes. Starting in the 1920s and thereafter, a growing Kenyan political resistance movement developed, and in 1944 the Kenya African Union (KAU) was formed to work for a political system in which Africans had a voice. In 1947 Jomo Kenyatta (a Kikuyu) was chosen to be the KAU president. In 1950 the Kikuyu also organized a secret society for "land and freedom" (or mau mau), which was dedicated to using armed force to removing foreigners from Kenya. The British insisted on calling this group the Mau Mau.

In 1952, 30,000 Mau Mau, also under Kenyatta's leadership, began a campaign of vicious attacks against white settlers. On October 20, 1952, the British authorities declared a state of emergency and committed regular troops to fight alongside the Home Guard against the Mau Mau. The Mau Mau fled to camps in the forest where the Mau Mau men and women received military training. In 1953 the British jailed Jomo Kenyatta and other Kikuyu and Mau Mau leaders, and in June 1953 the British army of 10,000 British troops began a more coordinated campaign against the estimated 12,000 Mau Mau warriors. There were two guerrilla centers, one at Mount Kenya, led by Waruhiu Itote (a.k.a. General China), and the other in the Aberdare Mountains, led by Dedan Kimathi. The British utilized bombers and heavy artillery to try to drive the Mau Mau from their bases and toward the British troops. These attacks had some success in reducing the areas of resistance, and General China accepted an amnesty. After the failure of an expedition in 1955 to capture many Mau Mau, however, the British switched tactics from large-scale military expeditions to a reliance on guerrilla warfare conducted by small patrols called pseudogangs. The war became known for the brutality shown to captives on both sides. The British also targeted Nairobi, where they went through the city arresting Mau Mau supporters. By early 1956, only an estimated 1,500 Mau Mau remained in the forest, where they were starving and disease-ridden. By October 1956 the resistance had ended and Kenya was formally back under British control. In 1961 Kenya became independent, with Jomo Kenyatta its first president.

Coding: The fatalities in this war fell most heavily on the Mau Mau. Official reports indicate that 11,500 Mau Mau were killed by Kenya's security forces. This number does not include the large number of those who died of disease or those who died in detention camps; thus an estimate of 5,000 deaths has been added for a death total of 16,500. The British death total refers only to deaths among the security forces. It does not include the estimated 2,000 Kikuyu civilians who were loyal to the British who were killed or the deaths of the 26 Indian civilians and 32 white civilians. Oliver and Atmore (1994) list 3,000 to 30,000 Mau Mau "casualties."

Sources: Ciment (2007); Clodfelter (2002); Corfield (1960); Edgerton (2002); Maloba (1999); Odhiambo and Lonsdale (2003); Oliver and Atmore (1994); Phillips and Axelrod (2005); Rosberg and Nottingham (1966).

EXTRA-STATE WAR #465:
The Moroccan Independence War of 1953–1956

Participants: France, Spain vs. Morocco
Dates: August 20, 1953, to March 2, 1956
Battle-Related Deaths: France—2,000;
  Morocco—1,000

Where Fought: Middle East
Initiator: Morocco
Outcome: Morocco wins
War Type: Colonial

Narrative: In pursuit of colonial development (extra-state wars #330, #434), France had established a protectorate over Morocco in 1912. Challenges to French rule had been raised in 1913 and 1925 (extra-state wars #436 and #449). In the 1930s the nationalists created the Independence Party (Istiqlal), which began to pressure Sultan Muhammad V to end the French protectorate, though the French crushed the movement in 1937. During World War II, Morocco supported the Vichy French, until the allied forces landed there in 1942. After the war the independence movement in Morocco was strengthened by the support of the sultan, Muhammed V (Sidi Muhammad ben Yusuf). Anti-French riots took place in Tangier on March 30 and in Casablanca on December 8, 1952. The French response was a policy of trying to intimidate the nationalists and the sultan, and Istiqlal was outlawed. Finally, on August 20, 1953, the French removed Muhammad V from power and replaced him with Sultan Ben Arafa, who favored greater Moroccan autonomy under French control rather than independence. The overthrow of the popular Muhammad V unified Moroccan public opinion and was the stimulus for the resurrection of anti-French violence that began in 1953. The Moroccans engaged in a guerrilla warfare that generally targeted French government facilities and military installations; however, the uprisings also included attacks against French civilians, similar to the one in Oujda where Moroccans attacked French and other European residents in the streets.

For France, which had been weakened by World War II, 1954 was a critical year. The French colonial empire was under attack worldwide, most importantly in Indochina and

Algeria. Consequently, the new French government of Prime Minister Mendés-France opened negotiations with both Morocco and Tunisia in the hopes of resolving the conflicts without giving the colonies their full independence (see extra-state war #463). Fighting continued, however, and in August 1954 the French seized the Arab quarter of Fez, and in July 1955 there was fierce fighting in Casablanca. On August 20, 1955, hundreds of French were killed in attacks to commemorate the second anniversary of the removal of Muhammad V from power. At the same time, a conference began in France to discuss the situation in Morocco, and on September 12 the French approved a plan to pacify Morocco by reinstalling Muhammad V. On September 30, 1955, Sultan Ben Arafa resigned, and on October 31 Muhammad returned to power. Despite French expectations, the level of violence in Morocco only worsened. The newly formed Jaish-al-tahrir (Army of Liberation), which was created with the assistance of liberation groups in Cairo, began increased attacks, and in November the French authorities responded with orders to suppress all violence. The French initiative did not last long. On March 2, 1956, France terminated its protectorate, giving Morocco its independence and ending this war. In April 1956 Muhammad V went to Spain, where Gen. Francisco Franco agreed to yield Spanish control over the Rif areas of Morocco.

Coding: Moroccans refer to this war as "The Revolution of the King and the People" and celebrate it every August 20. Since the removal of Muhammad V was the stimulus for the anti-French violence, we use August 20, 1953, as the start day for this war. In contrast, Halstead (1969) utilizes the bombing of the market in Casablanca in December 1952 as the onset of the war.

Sources: Abun-Nasr (1975); *Chronicle of the 20th Century* (1987); Clodfelter (2002); Halstead (1969); Hourani (1991).

The Third Franco-Algerian War of 1954–1962

Participants: France vs. Algeria
Dates: November 1, 1954, to March 17, 1962
Battle-Related Deaths: France—18,000; Algeria—14,000
Where Fought: Middle East
Initiator: Algeria
Outcome: Algeria wins
War Type: Colonial

Narrative: France had gained control of Algeria in 1830 (see extra-state war #319), had expanded its zone of control in Algeria (see extra-state wars #324 and #345), and had in 1871 withstood a rebellion against its rule in Algeria (extra-state war #366). After that point the French pursued policies designed to link Algeria more closely to France, partly through giving Algerian land to European settlers and passing laws protecting European rights and partly by encouraging the Algerian Berbers to assimilate into French society and giving them greater status over the Arab population. As a result, at least 1 million French settlers held most of the arable land and all the political power in Algeria. Overall, the French saw their presence in Algeria as a *mission civilisatrice*, or a civilizing mission. France also incorporated Algeria legally and culturally into the French system to a degree not practiced with its other colonies. Thus while France was willing, sometimes reluctantly, to accept nationalism and decolonization in other parts of the French Empire, the French decided to strenuously resist any attempts at gaining independence for Algeria.

World War II fueled the nationalist movement in Algeria, leading to the creation of the Committee of Unity and Liberation and the subsequent National Liberation Front (FLN). Peaceful demonstrations for autonomy and/or independence took place in Algeria after the war, all to no avail. Thus in November 1954 the National Liberation Front, led by Ahmed Ben Bella, began the war for Algerian independence by launching simultaneous assaults on French army garrisons throughout the country. The result was an eight-year bloody guerrilla war that would lead to the fall of the French government, the return of Charles de Gaulle, and ultimately Algerian independence. Initially, the 3,000 rebels in the Army of National Liberation (ALN), the military arm of the FLN, appeared to be no match for the 60,000 French soldiers stationed in Algeria; however, the numbers in both the rebel and French armies would increase rapidly to peak levels of 60,000 ALN guerrillas and 500,000 French troops. During 1955 and 1956 the ALN utilized standard guerrilla tactics in attacks both in the countryside and the urban areas. As the ALN gained more experience in guerrilla warfare and its attacks became more successful, the French army responded with a harsher policy of repression and collective punishment. In 1957 and early 1958 the FLN began a campaign of terrorist bombings targeting the *colons,* or the French settlers in Algeria. These attacks led to increasing frustration among both the *colons* and the army about the course of the war. As a result, in May 1958 the French army sent tanks into Paris in an attempt to overthrow the French government. The arrival of Gen. Charles de Gaulle halted the coup attempt. Nevertheless, the Fourth Republic was dismantled and the new Fifth Republic was created with General de Gaulle as its executive. The military had supported de Gaulle because it assumed that he would pursue a harsher policy toward the Algerian nationalists; however, de Gaulle entered into negotiations with the FLN and concluded an agreement for a referendum on Algerian independence. A cease-fire was declared on March 17, 1962, ending the war. Algeria gained its independence on July 3, 1962.

Coding: Civilian deaths are not included in the battle-related deaths.

Sources: Ciment (2007); Clodfelter (2002); *Deadline Data* (1957, 1961, 1962); Feraoun (2000); Horne (1977); Phillips and Axelrod (2005); Pontecorvo and Solinas (1965); Roberts (2003); Schafer (1995); Stone (1997); Stora (2001); Windrow (1998).

EXTRA-STATE WAR #467:
The French-Cameroon War of 1957–1958

Participants: France vs. UPC (Union des Populations du Cameroon)
Dates: January 1, 1957, to January 5, 1958
Battle-Related Deaths: France—1,000; UPC—900
Where Fought: Africa
Initiator: Cameroon
Outcome: France wins
War Type: Colonial

Narrative: Cameroon, on the west coast of Africa, has a diverse population with over 150 different ethnic groups. Bantu-speaking people, such as the Douala, dominate along the southern coast, while such groups as the Fulani and the Bamileke live in the northern areas. Although a number of the colonial powers had developed settlements in what is now Cameroon, the dominant role of Great Britain was shifted to Germany in 1884, when Germany utilized a treaty with the Douala to declare a protectorate in the region. In 1911 Germany obtained additional territory in the area from France in exchange for Germany's yielding its interest in Morocco to France, and in 1913 Germany consolidated its control over the north. During World War I (inter-state war #106), Britain and France occupied the area, and at the conclusion of the war, the former French portion of Cameroon was reannexed by France to French Equatorial Africa and the remainder of Cameroon was divided into British and French zones, becoming League of Nations mandates. The United Nations assumed control over the mandates as trust territories in 1946.

After World War II (inter-state war #139), sentiment favoring independence spread in the French zone. In 1946 a Representative Assembly of Cameroun (ARCAM) was constituted and sent delegates to the French National Assembly.

In contrast, the UPC (Union des Populations du Cameroon) was formed on April 10, 1948, as a militant, proindependence party. The UPC refused to split from the French Communist party, and after several riots in 1955, the French authorities banned the UPC on July 13, 1955. The UPC went underground and began the war to gain independence from France. This was a guerrilla war, which dragged on even after France undertook steps that would lead toward granting Cameroon its independence. The heaviest fighting took place during 1957. On January 5, 1958, the government announced that French troops had crushed the Communist-led uprising, which marks the end of the war. Though France is classified as winning in terms of militarily defeating the UPC, the uprising was successful in persuading France to grant independence. France granted self-government to East Cameroon in 1957, internal autonomy in 1959, and independence on January 1, 1960. The British West Cameroon was divided into sectors (north and south), and in a UN-sponsored plebiscite in 1961, the north voted to join with Nigeria, while the southern portion voted to join with Cameroon. The British relinquished West Cameroon on October 1, 1961.

Coding: Deciding on fatality figures for the war is complicated by the fact that estimates range from thousands to hundreds of thousands, most of whom were civilians.

Sources: Clodfelter (2002); *Columbia Encyclopedia* (1993); Cutter (2007); DeLancey (2000); Schafer 1995.

EXTRA-STATE WAR #469:
The Angolan-Portuguese War of 1961–1974

Participants: Portugal vs. Angola
Dates: February 3, 1961, to October 14, 1974
Battle-Related Deaths: Angola—25,000;
 Portugal—4,000
Where Fought: Africa
Initiator: Angola

Outcome: Portugal withdraws and the fighting is transformed into non-state war #1581
War Type: Colonial

Narrative: Angola was a Portuguese colony for 400 years, from 1575 to 1975. Portugal fought three earlier wars as it extended its control in the area (extra-state wars #420, #421, and #430). In the post–World War II era, Portugal, under dictator Antonio de Oliveira Salazar, tried to buck the trend toward decolonization in Africa by insisting that its African colonies were really provinces of Portugal, despite the fact that the people had no political rights—even the 300,000 Portuguese settlers in Angola were mere subjects. The tactic worked to the extent that the Portuguese were the last major European power with colonies to leave the continent. Also unlike the other European powers, Portugal resisted giving up its colonies in the absence of an armed struggle (also see extra-state war #471).

At the time of the first uprising in Angola in February 1961, there were two nationalist movements operating in exile: the Marxist Popular Movement for the Rebellion of Angola (MPLA) and the National Front for the Liberation of Angola (FNLA), whose precursor was the UPA (Union of Angolan Peoples). The MPLA and the FNLA began a revolution against Portuguese rule in 1961. In 1966 a third revolutionary group, the Union for the Total Independence of Angola (UNITA), formed as a breakaway from the FNLA and opened a front in the south. Initially UNITA, led by Jonas Savimbi, launched major attacks on the Portuguese; however, by 1971 UNITA and Portugal entered into a "gentlemen's agreement" not to fight each other. The MPLA would not forgive UNITA for this betrayal, and in the future UNITA relied more on assistance from outside forces such as South Africa and the United States (see subsequent inter-state war #186 and intra-state wars #804 and #880). The war against Portugal was hindered by the conflicts among the rebel groups themselves. Portugal had 55,000 troops facing the Angolans, but in 1974 young army officers overthrew the regime in Portugal, and the new government appealed to the liberation movements in Angola to cease hostilities as a step toward independence. Portugal signed cease-fire agreements with each of the rebel groups in October 1974, the last on October 14, which marked the end of this war between the guerrillas and Portugal. As of the following day, fighting continued as a non-state war among the guerrilla groups themselves (non-state war #1581).

Coding: Although the parties agreed to separate cease-fires, fighting continued. On January 31, 1975, a transitional government was formed among the three revolutionary groups, and later that fall South Africa and Cuba begin to intervene, leading to inter-state war #186. On November 11, 1975, Angola gained its independence, became a member of the interstate system, and entered the inter-state war. As the role of the outside powers decreased, the fighting continued as an internationalized civil war, intra-state war #804. Clodfelter (2002) describes all the Portuguese wars in Africa (involving the three colonies of Angola, Guinea, and Mozambique) as one group, the "Wars of Independence in Portuguese Africa: 1961–1974." The conflict in Guinea-Bissau does not meet the COW war fatality level.

Sources: Bender (1978); Ciment (2007); Clodfelter (2002); Cook and Paxton (1998); Crocker (1992); Guimaraes (1998); Hodges (2001); Human Rights Watch (1989); Keesing's (1967, 1973, 1974); Legum (1981); Malaquias (2007); Phillips and Axelrod (2005); Windrich (1992).

EXTRA-STATE WAR #471:

The Mozambique-Portuguese War of 1964–1975

Participants: Portugal vs. Mozambique
Dates: September 25, 1964, to June 25, 1975
Battle-Related Deaths: Mozambique—10,000; Portugal—3,500
Where Fought: Africa
Initiator: Mozambique
Outcome: Mozambique wins
War Type: Colonial

Narrative: Portugal had engaged in two wars in its conquest of Mozambique (extra-state wars #393 and #403). After World War II, Portugal was faced with a growing independence movement in Mozambique. In 1962 the Front for the Liberation of Mozambique (FRELIMO) was formed and began training for war. Its first attack against Portugal occurred on September 25, 1964, at Chai in the north. The Portuguese military responded with a ruthless campaign against the guerrillas and the populace. Since Portugal was fighting simultaneous wars in Angola, Guinea-Bissau, and Mozambique, it did not have adequate resources for the war in Mozambique, and soon the guerrillas controlled much of the northern sector. Some 10,000 FRELIMO troops faced about 40,000 Portuguese. FRELIMO's leader, Eduardo Mondlane, was killed in 1969, and Marxist Samora Machel became the leader. FRELIMO's control continued to expand, and by the end of the war it controlled half the country. In 1974, however, a military coup in Portugal overthrew dictator Marcello Caetano, which ultimately led to Portugal's decision to abandon its colonial empire. Mozambique became independent on June 25, 1975.

Coding: Clodfelter (2002) describes all the Portuguese wars in Africa (involving the three colonies of Angola, Guinea, and Mozambique) as one group, the "Wars of Independence in Portuguese Africa, 1961–1974."

Sources: Ciment (2007); Clodfelter (2002); Edgerton (2002); Finnegan (1993); Hanlon (1984); Henriksen (1983); Isaacman (1983); Phillips and Axelrod (2005); Vines (1991).

EXTRA-STATE WAR #472:

The East Timorese War Phase 2 of 1975–1976

Participants: Indonesia vs. FRETILIN, UDT forces
Dates: October 16, 1975, to July 17, 1976
Battle-Related Deaths: FRETILIN, UDT forces—20,000; Indonesia—12,500

Where Fought: Asia
Initiator: Indonesia
Outcome: Transformed into intra-state war #806
War Type: Imperial

Narrative: In the fifteenth and sixteenth centuries, Portuguese explorers reached out for trade routes to Asia and the Spice Islands (the Moluccas). As a result, the eastern half of the island of Timor, which lies east of Java and north of Australia, became a Portuguese colony from 1566 to 1975. East Timor was militarily occupied by Japan during World War II but then reverted back to Portuguese control after the war. After the Portuguese military coup in 1974, Portugal became willing to relinquish its colonial empire. Thus the Revolutionary Front for the Independence of East Timor (FRETILIN) began agitating for independence for East Timor. The conflict that broke out in East Timor in 1975 and lasted through 1979 actually encompassed three distinct types of war. The first was a non-state war (#1582) between FRETILIN and the UDT (the Democratic Union) from August 11, 1975, to October 15, 1975. When Indonesia invaded East Timor on October 16, 1975, the war was transformed into this current extra-state war, and when Indonesian sovereignty was declared, the war was transformed again into an intra-state war (#806).

After achieving independence in 1949, Indonesia had tried to claim East Timor, a claim that Portugal had rejected; nevertheless, after the 1974 coup in Portugal, the new Portuguese government began planning to divest itself of its colonial empire. Thus Indonesia tried to take advantage of the declining Portuguese commitment to East Timor and of the disruption caused by the non-state war by attempting to capture East Timor militarily. The Indonesians seized Balibo on October 16, 1975, which marks the start of the war. During November, Indonesia launched several attacks against East Timor, prompting Portugal to seek UN intervention. On December 7, 1975, Indonesia conducted a full-scale invasion of East Timor with 10,000 troops. Vicious fighting continued in 1976, though at lower levels after February. In May an Indonesian-chosen East Timorese assembly voted to merge East Timor with Indonesia, and on July 17, 1976, Indonesian president Suharto declared that East Timor was an Indonesian province, which marks the end of the extra-state war. In the end, Indonesia found out that Timor was a bitter pill to swallow. Guerrilla warfare and brutality against civilians continued as a civil war between East Timor and Indonesia. A new burst of one-sided violence in 1999, which included rapes and murders by pro-Indonesian militia, provoked UN intervention. UN forces supervised an election in 2000, and East Timor gained its independence and became the first member to join the United Nations in the new millennium.

Coding: The portion of the conflict between October 16, 1975, and July 17, 1976, is coded as an extra-state war because it was a war between a system member (Indonesia) and nonstate entities outside its borders (FRETILIN and the UDT). The number of civilians killed during this phase of the conflict could be as high as 100,000.

Sources: Brecher and Wilkenfeld (1997); Chomsky (1979); Ciment (2007); Clodfelter (2002); *Facts on File World News Digest* (1975–1976); Gunn (1977); Jardine (1999); Jolliffe (1978); Keesing's (1975–1980); Phillips and Axelrod (2005); Smith (2003).

EXTRA-STATE WAR #473:
The Namibian War of 1975–1988

Participants: South Africa vs. SWAPO rebels of Namibia
Dates: October 17, 1975, to December 13, 1988
Battle-Related Deaths: SWAPO rebels of Namibia—19,000; South Africa—1,100
Where Fought: Africa
Initiator: South Africa
Outcome: SWAPO rebels of Namibia win
War Type: Colonial

Narrative: Today's Namibia (southwest Africa) has been a state system member since 1990 and was coded as a COW dependency for a century prior. From 1885 to 1915, it was a colony of Germany (see extra-state war #423). It was then occupied by South Africa and the United Kingdom in 1915 (in World War I, inter-state war #106), with the occupation continuing until 1922. From 1922 until 1966 it was a territory mandated to South Africa by the League of Nations and the United Nations, and from 1966 to 1990 it was a colony of South Africa.

The Namibian extra-state war was a struggle begun by Sam Nujoma of the Southwest African People's Organization (SWAPO) against South African control. In 1966 the United Nations had terminated South Africa's mandate, a decision the South Africans ignored. Growing opposition to South African rule also stemmed from the South African policy of developing "homeland" areas for black ethnic groups within Namibia. Low-level guerrilla warfare by SWAPO soon began but reached COW war levels only in 1975. That year Angola had gained its independence and was free to offer aid and sanctuary to SWAPO forces. South African offensives were designed not only to defeat SWAPO but also to overthrow Angola's leftist regime, involving South Africa in a war against Cuba and Angola (inter-state war #186). South Africa was also involved in the subsequent Angolan Control War (intra-state war #804), and its defeat in that war contributed to its willingness to accept a settlement on Namibia. The war ended with an agreement that South Africa would withdraw from the territory and elections would be held. Elections occurred in 1989, and Sam Nujoma was voted into power and an independent state of Namibia was established.

Coding: Schafer (1995) lists a COW territorial entity as "South West Africa (German West Africa; Namibia)." He also notes the existence of the port of Walvis Bay, which was a small British colony surrounded on all its land borders by German South West Africa. Walvis Bay was part of South West Africa from 1922 to 1977, then of South Africa. Its ambiguous status was an important part of the strategic considerations during the Namibian War. It was finally transferred from South Africa to Namibia in 1994.

Sources: Ciment (2007); Clodfelter (2002); Copson (1994); Di Pisani (1986); Katjavivi (1988); National Democratic Institute for International Affairs (1988); Phillips and Axelrod (2005); Schafer (1995); Soggot (1986).

EXTRA-STATE WAR #474:

The Western Sahara War of 1975–1983

Participants: Mauritania, Morocco vs. Algeria, Polisario rebels
Dates: December 11, 1975, to December 23, 1983
Battle-Related Deaths: Morocco—9,500; Polisario rebels—4,000; Mauritania—2,000; Algeria—500
Where Fought: Middle East
Initiator: Polisario rebels
Outcome: Fighting continues at below war level
War Type: Imperial

Narrative: Southwest of Morocco, on the African coast, lies the Western Sahara. With a population of under 100,000, it is a sparsely populated desert region. In square miles this contested area is about the size of Morocco. The area of what is now Western Sahara was a nonstate controlled territory in recent centuries. The Spanish first claimed the area in the 1860s but established effective control over the Spanish Sahara only in the 1930s. When Morocco became independent, as a state system member, in 1956, Spain retained control of Spanish Sahara. In late 1975 Spain, under pressure from Morocco, decided to withdraw from Spanish Sahara. The territory was renamed Western Sahara, and Spain ceded two-thirds to Morocco and one-third to Mauritania.

In December 1975 liberation groups in the Western Sahara called the Polisario Front then attacked both the Mauritanian and Moroccan zones (with the assistance of Algeria), seeking to establish the Saharan Arab Democratic Republic (SADR). Moroccan forces clashed directly with an Algerian army on January 27–29, 1976, bringing Algeria into the war. After Algeria recognized the Polisario's SADR, on March 6, 1976, it withdrew from active participation in the war, though it still provided assistance to the Polisario. Mauritania tired of the war in 1979 and withdrew from the Sahara, enabling Morocco to then control both zones. Eventually Morocco had more than 100,000 troops in the Sahara confronting 15,000 Polisario. The Polisario rebels continued their attacks against Morocco until 1983. Fighting continued at below war levels after that. A UN cease-fire was arranged in 1991. Since then the territory remains disputed, with Morocco controlling some areas and the Polisario the rest. About two dozen countries, many from the Arab League, recognize Moroccan sovereignty over the territory, whereas about twice that many, a large number of them African, recognize the Polisario government.

Coding: Morocco was involved in fifteen militarized interstate disputes (MIDs) in the 1970s and 1980s concerning the Western Sahara. Also within the time span of the extra-state war itself, there are nine more MIDs involving Morocco. Clodfelter (2002) calls this war the "Polisario Rebellion of 1976–1988." He mentions troops or volunteers fighting on the side of the Polisario from Algeria, Mauritania, Mali, and Niger, while Spain and France fight occasionally against the Polisario.

Sources: Ciment (2007); Clodfelter (2002); Cordesman (2004); Farsoun and Paul (1976); Hodges (1984); Keesing's (1975–1980); Lewis (1985); Marks (1976); Mercer (1976); Pazzanita and Hodges (1994); Schafer (1995); Zartman (1987); Zoubir (1990a); Zoubir (1990b).

EXTRA-STATE WAR #475:
The Khmer Insurgency of 1979–1989

Participants: Cambodia, Vietnam vs. Khmer Rouge
Dates: January 9, 1979, to September 25, 1989

Battle-Related Deaths: Vietnam—25,300; Cambodia—15, 000; Khmer Rouge—[ ]
Where Fought: Asia
Initiator: Vietnam
Outcome: Cambodia withdraws and fighting is transformed to intra-state war #857
War Type: Imperial

Narrative: In the late twentieth century, Cambodia and North Vietnam became involved in almost twenty years of conflict in wars of varying types and alignments. In inter-state war #176 (the Communist Coalition), North Vietnam, assisted by the Khmer Rouge, had fought against the conservative government of Cambodia, which was aided by the United States and South Vietnam. After North Vietnam withdrew from the fighting in Cambodia in 1971, the war continued as a civil war between the Cambodian government and the Khmer Rouge (intra-state war #785). The Khmer Rouge won the civil war, coming to power in April 1975. At the same time, the war in Vietnam (inter-state war #163) had ended with the victory of North Vietnam over the South. Within days the two victorious parties, Vietnam and the new Khmer Rouge government, were involved in conflict with each other (inter-state war #189). This war began primarily as a border war, though it ultimately led to the overthrow of the Pol Pot regime, which was responsible for killing over 1 million of its civilians in one of the worst mass killings in recorded history. Phnom Penh was captured on January 7, 1979, and the Vietnamese installed Heng Samrin as the chairman of the new Kampuchean People's Revolutionary Council on January 8, which marks the end of the inter-state war and the beginning of this extra-state war the next day).

Pol Pot and the other Khmer leaders fled from Phnom Penh into the west, and this war, between the Vietnamese army and its new Cambodian government ally against the Khmer Rouge, began with heavy fighting in the jungles in the west. The commitment to the Samrin regime created a long-lasting quagmire for

Vietnam, which did not remove its troops from Cambodia until 1989. The Cambodian resistance to the Vietnamese domination of Cambodia came both from the Khmer Rouge and from a number of smaller groups that formed mostly along the Thai-Cambodian border. The most significant of these was the Khmer People's National Liberation Front (KPNLF), which received assistance from Thailand. A second group, known as the Moulinaka, was loyal to the former ruler, Prince Sihanouk. The Khmer Rouge and the two non-Communist groups were united on June 22, 1982, into the Coalition Government of Democratic Kampuchea, though the Khmer Rouge played the dominant role. The resistance groups generally engaged in limited attacks from their bases in Thailand against the Vietnamese forces in Cambodia. In June 1980 a small Vietnamese force did attack in Thailand to punish the Thais for their support of the resistance. In November 1984 the Vietnamese launched a significant offensive against the resistance, causing many of the rebels to flee back into Thailand, where they also received assistance from the United States, China, and the Association of Southeast Asian Nations (ASEAN). The cycle of guerrilla warfare continued until 1989. The withdrawal of Vietnam's forces from Cambodia was completed by September 25, 1989, thus ending the extra-state war.

Coding: The coding of this overall conflict is determined by the changing role of the participants. Inter-state war #176 is transformed into intra-state war #785, which is followed by inter-state war #189, which is transformed into this extra-state war, and then back to an intra-state war (#857). This war is coded as an extra-state war because the bulk of the fighting was conducted by the Vietnamese army against two nonstate entities, the Khmer Rouge and the KPNLF. Clodfelter combines the inter-state and extra-state phases into the "Vietnamese-Cambodian War: 1977–1989." Kohn and Phillips and Axelrod divide the 1977–1998 period into

two wars, "The Kampuchean Civil War (1978–1998)" and the "Kampuchean-Thai Border War (1977–1995)."

Sources: Chanda (1988); Ciment (2007); Clodfelter (2002); Evans and Rowley (1990); Isaacs et al. (1987); Keesing's (1975–1980); Kohn (1999); Leighton (1978); *New York Times* (1975–1980); Phillips and Axelrod (2005).

EXTRA-STATE WAR #476:

The Soviet Quagmire of 1980–1989

Participants: Afghanistan, USSR vs. mujahideen
Dates: February 22, 1980, to February 15, 1989
Battle-Related Deaths: mujahideen—50,000;
USSR—40,000; Afghanistan—30,000
Where Fought: Asia
Initiator: mujahideen
Outcome: Transformed into intra-state war #851
War Type: Imperial

Narrative: Russia had developed an interest in Afghanistan in the nineteenth century as a function of Russian expansion into Central Asia, and the two entities had fought a war in 1885 (extra-state war #390). The USSR continued this interest, and in 1978 it began sending military troops and assistance to the leftist government of Afghanistan. By 1979 the USSR became directly involved in the war, aiding the government of Afghanistan in its civil war against the mujahideen (see intra-state war #812). In December 1979 the Soviets sent an additional 50,000 troops into Afghanistan and engineered a coup that placed Babrak Karmal in power on December 27, 1979. The number of Soviet troops in Afghanistan continued to increase, soon reaching a total of 85,000 troops; yet, throughout January 1980 most of the fighting against the mujahideen was still being done by the Afghan army. Increasingly, however, Afghan soldiers became reluctant to fight with the Soviets against fellow Afghans and deserted to join the opposition. The Afghan army declined from 100,000 to 40,000 men by 1980 and 30,000 by

1981. Consequently, the Soviets had to take over the bulk of the fighting from the Afghan government. This was evident during clashes in Kabul on February 22–24, 1980. When a system member (the USSR) is fighting against a non-state actor (the mujahideen) outside the system member's (Soviet) territory, the war is classified as an extra-state war. Thus February 22, 1980, marks the beginning of this extra-state war.

The rebels contained a number of elements who were fighting in response to the repressiveness of the Afghan government. The rebel groups were dispersed geographically, but they made several attempts at creating unity. The rival factions among the mujahideen created the Islamic Alliance for the Liberation of Afghanistan in 1980, but it quickly dissolved. In 1981 three of the groups united in the Islamic Unity of the Mujahideen of Afghanistan. Further attempts to institutionalize their cooperation in May 1982 also disintegrated. In April 1985 a new group, the Alliance of Seven, became more institutionalized, even opening an office in New York City. By relying on advanced weapons and an increase in troops to 104,000, the Soviets begin to tip the tide of war in their favor during 1981. The Soviet and Afghan forces launched a new offensive in April 1981 and laid siege to Kandahar in May. Heavy fighting took place in Kabul, as well. There are claims that the Soviets used chemical weapons during this period. Seeing this as part of the Cold War, the United States, Saudi Arabia, China, France, and Britain began funneling aid through Pakistan to arm and train elements of the mujahideen. An estimated 80,000 mujahideen were trained in Pakistan by the United States and Pakistan. The rebels were able to mount counteroffensives, and the Soviets continued to pour in more troops and material, and to suffer more casualties. The peak Soviet force numbered 115,000. The conflict soon evolved into a general stalemate.

In May 1986 Dr. Mohammed Najibullah replaced Karmal as general secretary of the People's Democratic Party of Afghanistan (PDPA), and a collective leadership team was created; however, by November of that year Karmal was relieved of all his posts. The new leadership attempted a policy of reconciliation, but the seven-party mujahideen alliance still demanded the complete withdrawal of Soviet troops. In 1988 the mujahideen were making advances but were hampered by a suspension of U.S. aid from December 1988 to July 1989, just as the Soviets were further increasing weapons shipments to the government. Meanwhile, the Soviets finally began to tire of their involvement in Afghanistan. In July 1987 Gorbachev proposed a transitional government for Afghanistan that would include the mujahideen. He finally proposed a Soviet withdrawal, which was incorporated into the 1988 Geneva Accords. The accords were signed between Pakistan and Afghanistan on April 14, 1988, with a Soviet and American guarantee. The troops withdrawals began on May 12, and by February 15, 1989, all the Soviet forces had withdrawn, marking the end of this extra-state war. Unfortunately, it did not mark the end of the fighting. Although many had assumed that the Afghan government would fall once the Soviet troops had departed, it did not do so. The fighting continued between the Afghan government and the mujahideen, and thus the war was transformed into an intra-state war (intra-state war #851).

Coding: This entire conflict involves numerous war classifications and war transformations depending on the types of war participants. It starts as an intra-state (civil) war #812; becomes this extra-state war as a result of Soviet involvement; returns to an intra-state war, #851, after the Soviets withdraw; then becomes inter-state war #225 as the allies attempt to overthrow the Taliban Afghan government; and reverts back to an extra-state war, #481, of the allies against al-Qaeda.

Sources: Dorronsoro (2005); Europa Yearbook (2005); Keesing's (1981).

EXTRA-STATE WAR #477:
The First PKK in Iraq of 1991–1992

Participants: Turkey vs. the Kurdistan Workers' Party (PKK)
Dates: August 4, 1991, to March 25, 1992
Battle-Related Deaths: PKK in Iraq—2,000; Turkey—300
Where Fought: Middle East
Initiator: Turkey
Outcome: Stalemate
War Type: Imperial

Narrative: The Kurdistan Workers' Party (PKK) was formed in 1974 in Ankara, Turkey, as an organization to promote Kurdish nationalism. In 1984 it began an armed struggle against Turkey (intra-state war #838) with the goal of securing an independent state of Kurdistan in an area that would comprise southeastern Turkey, northeastern Iraq, northeastern Syria, and northwestern Iran, areas in which the Kurdish population is the majority. After 1986 the level of conflict between Turkey and the PKK in the southeastern part of the country declined below war levels, until it flared up again in the 1990s (intra-state war #865). At that time the PKK began to shift its focus away from its activities in Turkey to a broader regional approach, specifically becoming involved with the issues of the Kurdish refugees in Iraq. Taking advantage of the disorder in Iraq as a result of the Iran-Iraq War (inter-state war #199), the PKK established bases in Iraq. At this point the struggle of the PKK against Turkey took on the characteristics of two different wars: the PKK activities in southeastern Turkey (intra-state); and attacks by Turkey against PKK elements based in Iraq. The latter conflict is an extra-state war, since it involved Turkey in a war with a nonstate entity outside its borders and it generally included Turkey getting permission from Iraq or the United States to launch its offensives.

During the Iran-Iraq War, Iraq signed a security act that allowed Turkey to conduct operations against the PKK in Iraq. In March 1991 Turkey reached an agreement with the Iraqi Kurds to jointly act against the PKK in Iraq. In May, related to the outcome of the Gulf War (inter-state war #211), the United States and its allies created a "safe zone" for the Kurds in northern Iraq. The allied forces began withdrawing from the area on July 12, 1991. In August 1991 Turkey launched an air attack against the PKK in Iraqi territory, starting this war. Turkey claimed that the attacks were in response to the increase in PKK activities within Iraq. Turkish ground forces also crossed the border into Iraq in an attempt to destroy the PKK bases there. Their attacks continued intermittently over the next seven months, though they were more prevalent in October 1991, January 1992, and March 1992. This offensive was unsuccessful in destroying the PKK and the war ended in March 1992.

Coding: Turkey launched similar attacks into Iraq, particularly in 1995 and 1996, though fatalities apparently did not reach war levels. Turkish activities were complicated by the fighting among the Kurdish groups within Iraq (see intra-state war #890, the Iraqi Kurd Internecine War). Consequently, Turkey launched a second war against the PKK in Iraq with the assistance of the Kurdistan Democratic Party (KDP) in 1997 (extra-state war #479).

Sources: Ciment (2007); Gunter (2003); Laizer (1996); Keesing's (1991, 1992).

EXTRA-STATE WAR #479:
Second PKK in Iraq of 1997

Participants: Turkey vs. the Kurdistan Workers' Party (PKK)
Dates: May 14, 1997, to June 14, 1997
Battle-Related Deaths: PKK in Iraq—2,500; Turkey—100
Where Fought: Middle East
Initiator: Turkey
Outcome: Stalemate
War Type: Imperial

Narrative: This war is a continuation of Turkey's attempt to destroy the Kurdish forces of the Kurdistan Workers' Party (PKK) and their bases in Iraq, begun in extra-state war #477 in 1991–1992. After the first war the PKK remained in Iraq, where it became involved in a war with the Iraqi Kurds in the Patriotic Union of Kurdistan (PUK), intra-state war #890, the Iraqi Kurd Internecine War in 1994–1995. In May 1997 Turkey made another attempt to defeat the PKK in Iraq, this time sending an estimated 50,000 troops into northern Iraq. The Turks remained there a month but were still unsuccessful in destroying the PKK.

Coding: In 2007 Turkey launched further attacks against the PKK, now reorganized as KADER or the KDK; however, these strikes apparently did not reach the war level threshold.

Sources: Ciment (2007); Clodfelter (2002); Gunter (2003); Yildiz (2007).

EXTRA-STATE WAR #480:
The Al Aqsa Intifada of 2000–2003

Participants: Palestinians vs. Israel
Dates: September 28, 2000, to September 9, 2003
Battle-Related Deaths: Palestinians—3,400; Israel—900
Where Fought: Middle East
Initiator: Palestinians
Outcome: Israel wins
War Type: Colonial

Narrative: When the Ottoman Empire was dismantled at the end of World War I, portions of Ottoman territory in the Levant were given as mandates by the League of Nations to France and the United Kingdom. The British mandate included Palestine, which Britain controlled until the end of World War II. At the end of the war, Britain was unable to maintain control of the region. Consequently, a series of wars were fought over control of Palestine: the 1947–1948 war between the Palestinians and the Jews (the Palestine War, non-state war #1572); the Arab-Israeli War of 1948–1949 (inter-state war #148); the Sinai War (inter-state war #155); the 1967 Six-Day War (inter-state war #169); the War of Attrition (inter-state war #172); and the Yom Kippur War of 1973 (inter-state war #181). Israel, which was founded in 1948, gained control of the Palestinian areas of the West Bank and Gaza Strip as a result of the 1967 war. Many Palestinians fled from Palestine into other Arab states, and this Palestinian diaspora contributed to three additional wars: Black September War in Jordan (intra-state war #780); the Second Lebanese War (intra-state War #801); and the War over Lebanon (inter-state war #205).

In the 1960s the Palestinians became increasing politicized, and a number of Palestinian organizations were formed, espousing different strategies for securing a Palestinian homeland. The most prominent was the Palestine Liberation Organization (PLO), led from 1969 to 2004 by Yasir Arafat. By the 1980s many Palestinians were discouraged by the Israeli occupation and the inability of the PLO to make progress toward securing a Palestinian homeland. This popular frustration exploded in December 1987 in a series of demonstrations and civil disobedience aimed at the Israelis. The Palestinians also began a campaign of low-level, "stone-throwing" attacks against the Israeli defense forces that became known as the intifada. This conflict did not reach a war level of fatalities.

A second intifada began on September 28, 2000, when Ariel Sharon marched to the al-Aqsa Mosque in Jerusalem. The Palestinians responded with increased armed attacks, and the Israelis responded with more military operations. In March 2002 Israel launched its largest military offensive in twenty years, Operation Defensive Shield, against the main cities in the West Bank and Gaza. The increased level of violence continued but declined after September 2003, marking the end of the war. Violent clashes have continued since then but not at war levels. The death of Arafat in November 2004 and the subsequent election of Mahmoud Abbas in 2005 brought a temporary lull in the fighting.

Coding: Although Israel occupies Palestine, Palestine is not within Israel's universally recognized borders, nor is it recognized as a member of the interstate system. Thus a war between Israel and the Palestinians is considered an extra-state war. Palestine is, however, an Israeli-occupied dependency, which makes this a colonial war.

Sources: Ciment (2007); Clodfelter (2002); Freedom House (2004); Gerner (1991); Global Security (2005); Kohn (1999); Phillips and Axelrod (2005); Project Plowshares (2004).

EXTRA-STATE WAR #481:
The Afghan Resistance of 2001–present

Participants: Afghanistan, Australia, Canada, France, Germany, United Kingdom, United States vs. al-Qaida, the Taliban

Dates: December 23, 2001–present

Battle-Related Deaths: al-Qaida, the Taliban—12,000; Afghanistan—1,600; United States—552; United Kingdom—110; Canada—88; Germany—25; France—12; Australia—6. (Fatality figures as of July 2008.)

Where Fought: Asia

Initiator: Afghanistan, Australia, Canada, France, Germany, United Kingdom, United States

Outcome: Ongoing

War Type: Imperial

Narrative: This war is the continuation of a conflict that began with the start of inter-state war #225, the Invasion of Afghanistan. This war was conducted by the United States and its allies against the Taliban government of Afghanistan, and it had as its goal the toppling of the Taliban regime. After the Taliban had been removed from power, which ended the inter-state phase of the war, the United States' goals for "Operation Enduring Freedom" evolved into capturing the remaining Taliban and al-Qaida leaders, who had been linked to the World Trade Center

attacks in New York City and at the Pentagon on September 11, 2001. Since the allies were no longer fighting against the government of a system member state but against nonstate entities outside their borders (the remaining members of the Taliban and their al-Qaida allies), the inter-state war was transformed into this extra-state war that begins when the Taliban are no longer the government of Afghanistan, on December 23, 2001. The new government of Afghanistan, the former Northern Alliance, is a minor participant in the war from the beginning, as well. Its limited role was partially dictated by the fact that the new government needed to rebuild its own military forces after the previous war.

After the Taliban were forced from power, they retreated into the countryside and began to regroup. Taliban and al-Qaida forces, estimated at 5,000 troops, established a base in northeastern Afghanistan, and on March 2, 2002, the coalition launched a major ground offensive, Operation Anaconda, to dislodge them. An estimated 400 Taliban were killed, but the conflict continued. Although the Taliban and al-Qaida forces had subsequently appeared to be in disarray, they were able to engage in increased fighting in June and July 2002. By February 2003 the Taliban were able to launch an offensive in five operational zones. The Taliban announced that their targets were not only the coalition forces but the Afghan government as well. The bulk of the fighting, however, was still conducted by the coalition forces. In 2003 the Afghan National Army (ANA) consisted of only 5,000–6,000 troops. The first battalion of Afghan National Guard (trained by the United States and France) was operational in April 2003, though the army was effectively limited to actions around Kabul.

March 19, 2003, marked the expansion of the related "War on Terrorism" with the start of the inter-state war to topple the regime in Iraq (inter-state war #227, Invasion of Iraq). The next day U.S.-led forces launched another major offensive in Afghanistan, Operation Viper, to combat the Taliban and al-Qaida fighters in southern Afghanistan around Kandahar. Although U.S. secretary of defense Donald Rumsfeld announced the end of the Afghan war on May 2, 2003—at the conclusion of the first phase of the Iraqi war—his comments were premature. The war in Afghanistan continued, and the coalition launched a number of major offensives, with limited success. Pakistan's armed forces also attacked the insurgents, mostly on its side of the Afghan-Pakistani border.

In July 2003 the new ANA began its first major anti-Taliban operation. On December 9, 2003, the United States launched a major ground offensive that became particularly controversial owing to the number of Afghan civilians killed in the attack. In 2004 al-Qaida demonstrated its resurgence with attacks in Europe, Kenya, Morocco, Saudi Arabia, and Iraq. That year, Pakistan also stepped up efforts to track down al-Qaida insurgents in its territory (see Waziristan War, intra-state war #932). The situation deteriorated for the coalition in 2004 as the Taliban increased the amount of territory under its control. There was a surge in violence in 2005 and 2006. In May 2006 the coalition launched its largest campaign since 2001. Operation Mountain Thrust was conducted primarily by troops from the United States, the United Kingdom, the Netherlands, and Canada and was aimed at quelling the violence before NATO-led forces would take over combat responsibility in southern Afghanistan from U.S. forces. Hostilities in Afghanistan increased in 2008 to the extent that American fatalities in Afghanistan exceed those in Iraq. The war is ongoing.

Coding Decisions: A difficulty in describing this war is in determining who the participants are. Not only do the participants and their levels of commitment change, but also the question of which states participate in the war is further clouded by the presence of the UN peacekeeping force. By 2002 there were sixty-eight countries included in the U.S.-led coalition, yet only a few contributed the requisite 1,000 troops to be considered COW war participants. The United States and the United Kingdom, which had been the major participants in the preceding inter-state war, were joined by France, Canada, and Australia. In 2002, 3,900 German troops joined the coalition, adding Germany as a war participant. Later that year, however, Australia removed its troops and thus ceased being a war participant.

Furthermore, at the end of inter-state war #225, the Bonn agreement of 2001 had included the decision to send an international peacekeeping force to Afghanistan. The UN Security Council authorized the deployment of an International Security Assistance Force (ISAF) to maintain security in Kabul, to assist in reconstruction, and to create the aforementioned Afghan National Army. Initially, nineteen countries contributed to the peacekeeping force. When the ISAF forces began arriving in January 2002, the contributors were predominantly western European, led by Britain. The major contributors were: Britain (1,863 troops), Germany (879), France (499), and Italy (357). Thus a number of the major participants were contributing forces to both the coalition and the ISAF; however, since the ISAF's mission was peacekeeping, the troops committed to the ISAF were not counted when considering which states were war participants.

However, the mission of the ISAF changed over time. On August 11, 2003, the North Atlantic Treaty Organization (NATO) assumed control over the ISAF peacekeeping force, which at that time consisted of 8,500 troops from thirty-seven countries. NATO subsequently pledged to increase the size of the ISAF to 10,000. On October 13, 2003, the Security Council agreed to an expansion of ISAF missions so that troops would be stationed outside of Kabul. This decision contributed to growing disagreements within NATO, since Canadian prime minister Jean Chrétien declined to deploy Canadian soldiers, which constituted nearly half of the ISAF, outside of Kabul. The split within NATO became even more problematic in 2005, when NATO began discussing altering its mission from peace and stability building to confronting the Taliban and al-Qaida. At a meeting on December 8, 2005, NATO agreed to keep its peacekeeping focus but to deploy NATO troops into the south and east, the sites of recent violence. In early 2006, NATO gradually took over responsibilities from the United States, with NATO members being increasingly involved in conflict. By June 2006, NATO agreed to double the size of the ISAF forces in southern Afghanistan, from 3,000 to 6,000, and to take over security operations (fighting) there from the United States. This incremental shift was problematic because the ISAF contingent was split into NATO countries that would fight and those that would not. This change in ISAF mission became even clearer when, after nine months of British command of the ISAF, an American general took control of both the U.S. and NATO forces on February 4, 2007, and declared that NATO troops would take an even more active role in fighting the insurgents. Thus, in terms of coding war participants, after December 8, 2005, countries that committed more than 1,000 troops to the NATO/ISAF contingent and allowed their troops to participate in fighting the insurgents are considered war participants. Therefore, the Netherlands, which had 1,700 troops, and aircraft, in the ISAF, is coded as a war participant, whereas Italy, which had contributed 1,950 troops, is not considered a war participant, because the Italian parliament does not allow the troops to take part in the battle against the Taliban insurgency.

Coding Notes: Many authors, including Phillips and Axelrod, combine these two wars (inter-state #225 and extra-state #481) into one, the United States' "War on Terrorism." Fatality figures frequently include the victims killed at the World Trade Center (see Uppsala Conflict Database). Pakistan is not listed as a member of the coalition, since its activities generally took place within Pakistan. It did, however, employ 60,000 troops and 55,000 paramilitary troops in 1,510 coalition-supportive operations along the Pakistani-Afghan border.

Sources: Barker (2006); BBC (2007); Center for Defense Information (2001, 2002); Clodfelter (2002); Coalition Public Awareness Working Group (2002); Conetta (2002); *Europa Yearbook* (2005); Global Security (2007); Iraq Coalition Casualty Count (2008); Islby (1989); Keesing's (2001); Project Ploughshares (2005); Straziuso

(2007); Uppsala Universitet (2004); Wiseman (2006); Wiseman (2005).

EXTRA-STATE WAR #482:
The Iraqi Resistance of 2003–present

Participants: Australia, Iraq, Italy, Netherlands, Poland, Republic of Korea, Spain, Ukraine, United Kingdom, United States vs. al-Qaida, Iraqi resistance
Dates: May 3, 2003–present
Battle-Related Deaths: al-Qaida, Iraqi resistance—20,000; Iraq—10,800; United States—3,985; United Kingdom—143; Italy—33; Poland—23; Ukraine—18; Spain—11; Netherlands—2; Republic of Korea—1; Australia—1. (Fatality figures as of July 2008.)
Where Fought: Middle East
Initiator: Australia, United Kingdom, United States
Outcome: Ongoing
War Type: Imperial

Narrative: After the September 11, 2001, al-Qaida attacks on New York and Washington, D.C., U.S. president George W. Bush announced that the United States would attack both the terrorists and the states that harbored them. Iraq was accused of granting haven to terrorists and of hiding weapons of mass destruction. Thus, on March 20, 2003, the United States and Great Britain invaded Iraq and had overthrown the Iraqi government of Saddam Hussein by April 10. This was inter-state war #227, the Invasion of Iraq.

Despite the assertion by President Bush that the mission of overthrowing the Iraqi regime was completed on May 2, 2003, conflict continued. Since the major parties to the conflict were the members of the U.S.-led coalition, confronting the Iraqi resistance fighters (instead of the Iraqi government), this war was transformed into this extra-state war. At this time there was no sovereign Iraqi government, and the Iraqi army had been dissolved after the inter-state war; thus the bulk of the fighting was conducted by the United States, the British, and their allies. The resistance movement, composed of various Sunni remnants of the old Iraqi army and elements of foreign al-Qaida fighters, grew rapidly. Saddam Hussein was captured in December 13, 2003. The war became increasingly complex as members of al-Qaida and other groups opposed to the U.S. occupation entered the conflict in Iraq. By late spring 2003, sniping incidents and bombings were killing American troops in small numbers. Even after June 2004, when the Iraqi government received sovereignty from the coalition, the bulk of the fighting was still waged by the allies. As the war dragged on into 2005 and 2006, especially after the bombing of the al-Askari shrine, much of the fighting consisted of conflicts between Sunnis and Shiites. In an attempt to gain control over Iraq, the United States instituted a "surge" policy in 2007 of sending in additional troops. While the initiative showed some gains as of 2008, the efficacy of this policy was not yet known and the war continued.

Coding: Accurate Iraqi death tolls since the insurgency began are difficult to ascertain partially because of the U.S. government's policy of not tracking opponent casualties. It is also difficult to separate Iraqi civilian deaths, which we do not include, from those of al-Qaida and other combatants. In November 2006 the Iraqi Ministry of Health estimated urban death tolls at 100,000 to 150,000. A report by Johns Hopkins in 2006 estimated that 655,000 Iraqis had died since the invasion. The Iraqi military had reached a size of 227,000 in November 2006. It is more difficult to assess the size of the resistance forces. One opposition group, the Mahdi Army, may have had 60,000 fighters in early 2007. Overall, it is estimated that there were some 200,000 opposition forces in early 2005.

Sources: BBC News (2007); Ciment (2007); "Coalition of the Willing" (2006); "Deaths from the War in Iraq" (2008); *Europa Yearbook* (2007); Freedom House (2007); Global Security (2005); Keesing's (2007, 2008); Ricks (2006).

Analyzing Extra-state Wars

Extra-state wars are much more common than inter-state wars, with 163 extra-state wars, compared with 95 inter-state wars, beginning between 1816 and 2007. Even so, extra-state wars do not occur that frequently. As Figure 4.1 indicates, 93 years have no extra-state war onsets and 58 years have only one.

The distribution of extra-state wars during our period of study is quite different from the pattern exhibited by inter-state wars. Since extra-state wars are by definition wars between members of the interstate system and nonsystem members, outside their borders, the existence of extra-state wars is heavily dependent on the prevalence of nonstate entities. Nonstate entities were most common in the early years of the interstate system, during the period of state formation. Such nonstate entities were the objects of the colonial enterprise, and thus extra-state wars were most common at the end of the nineteenth century, when imperialist sentiments had their widest support (see Figure 4.2).

This pattern is somewhat more visible when we combine our dates into decades (removing the wars from the first and last years—1816 and 2007—to make even decades). As Figure 4.3 shows, extra-state wars were almost nonexistent in the 1920s and 1930s; however, they revived with the drives for independence seen after World War II. An interesting recent development is the reemergence of extra-state wars in the late twentieth and the early twenty-first century as we begin to see a growing number of nonstate actors capable of waging war, such as al-Qaida. Relatedly, this overall pattern affects the types of extra-state wars that occur, as well. Extra-state wars consist of the following two types: colonial wars, between a state and a nonstate entity that is a colony, protectorate, or other form of dependency; and imperial wars, between a state and a nonstate entity that is not under its control. Imperial wars dominated in the later nineteenth and the early twentieth century, whereas colonial

FIGURE 4.1 **EXTRA-STATE WAR ONSETS BY NUMBER OF YEARS, 1816–2007 (NUMBER OF YEARS IN WHICH THE ONSET OF 0 THROUGH 5 EXTRA-STATE WARS OCCURRED)**

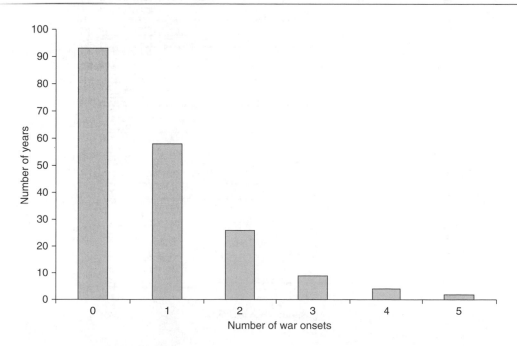

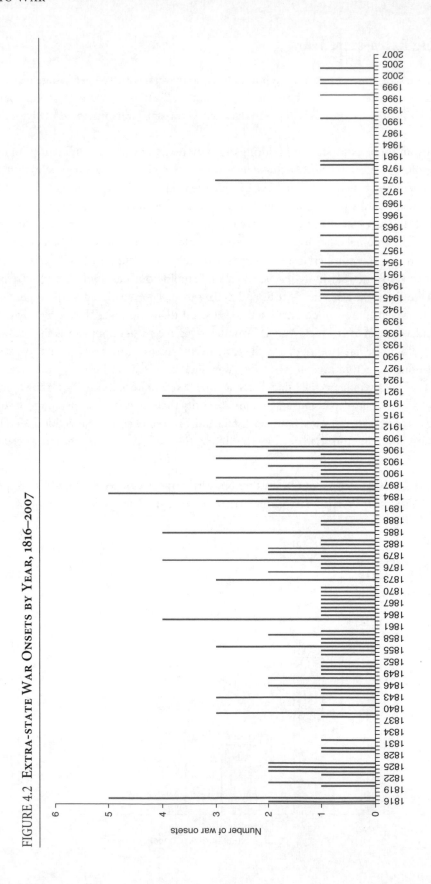

FIGURE 4.2 EXTRA-STATE WAR ONSETS BY YEAR, 1816–2007

FIGURE 4.3 **Extra-state War Onsets for All Extra-state Wars and Multiple State Extra-state Wars, 1817–2006 (Distribution by Decade)**

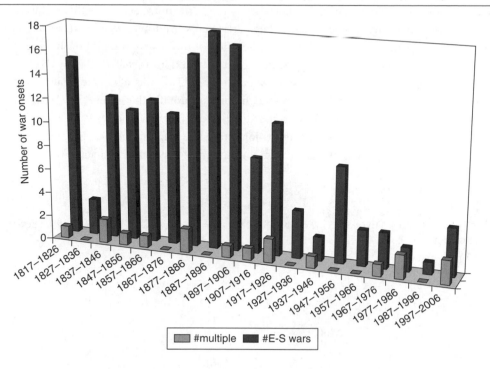

FIGURE 4.4 **Extra-state War Onsets by Region, 1816–2007**

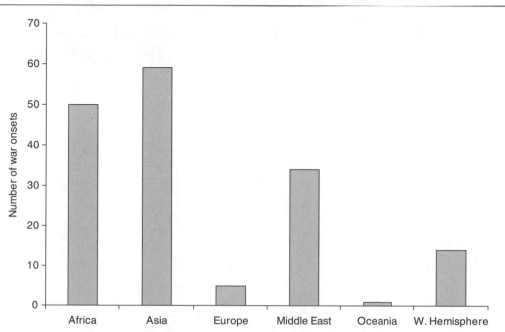

wars were more prevalent in the 1920s to 1970s. In the recent revival of extra-state wars, almost all of them are imperial wars, with the exception of the Al Aqsa Intifada (extra-state war #480). Another interesting feature of the trends in extra-state wars concerns the number of wars that involve only one state versus those that involve two or more state participants (multiple). While extra-state wars now are much less frequent than in the 1890s, the proportion of multiparty wars is now higher.

The nature of extra-state wars affects their regional distribution, as well. As Figure 4.4 reveals, Asia is the region where most of the extra-state wars occurred. This was also true of inter-state wars, though the number of extra-state Asian wars is more than double the number of Asian inter-state wars. Some of the other regions reflect greater differences. In terms of inter-state wars, the second most common war setting is Europe, whereas for extra-state wars it is Africa. Europe saw only five extra-state wars. By far, the least warlike region for both inter-state and extra-state wars is Oceania.

Notes

1. Melvin Small and J. David Singer, *Resort to Arms: International and Civil War, 1816–1980* (Beverly Hills, Calif.: Sage, 1982), 52.
2. Ibid.

CHAPTER FIVE

The Intra-state Wars

By Meredith Reid Sarkees

The largest category of war addressed in this volume is that of intra-state war, or wars that take place within the boundaries of a member of the interstate system. Intra-state war is also the dataset that has shown the most growth since the version published in Melvin Small and J. David Singer's *Resort to Arms*—increasing from 106 wars to the current 335 wars. Partially owing to the sheer magnitude of this data set, and partially because of an increasing interest in intra-state wars among the research community, CQ Press will publish a separate book within its Correlates of War series dedicated to this category: *A Guide to Intra-state Wars, 1816–2008*, by Jeffrey Dixon and Meredith Reid Sarkees. Consequently, fewer details about, and descriptions of, the intra-state wars will appear here than in the other war category chapters.

Defining Intra-state War

An intra-state war involves sustained combat between or among organized armed forces that takes place within the territorial boundaries of a state system member and leads to 1,000 battle-related deaths per year, or twelve-month period starting from the war onset. As described in Chapter 2, the expanded typology of wars includes three subcategories of intra-state war based on the nature of the war participants: civil war, regional internal war, and inter-communal war. All three categories must involve sustained combat between or among organized armed forces (there must be effective resistance by both sides) and thus do not include massacres of civilians (or genocide), though such activities frequently accompany intra-state wars, in particular, and are becoming increasingly common in inter-state wars as well. The key feature of intra-state wars that differentiates them from inter-state and extra-state wars is that military action generally takes place within the borders of the system member. The subsidiary classifications are based on the status of the war participants, or in other words, "who is fighting whom."

As described in Chapter 2, the same definition of the term *battle-related deaths,* and the requirement of 1,000 fatalities among the combatants per year, applies to all wars, including intra-state wars. Battle-related deaths are those that occur between or among the war participants, or combatants. Although some of the earlier intra-state war datasets included the deaths of civilians in civil wars, in order to maintain comparability among the datasets, we have undertaken a major initiative to exclude civilian fatalities, specifically in determining whether a particular incidence of combat should be considered a war. This is particularly difficult for intra-state wars, where it can be hard to distinguish combatants from civilians. Also governments are more likely to try to conceal the intentional or unintentional killing of civilians by claiming that the dead were combatants. Many historical reports indicate only total fatalities, without attempting to identify civilian deaths or separating out fatalities suffered by each war participant. However, there have been some new data-gathering projects that have provided valuable information on disaggregating fatality statistics, for example, CERAC (2008) concerning deaths in Colombia. Nevertheless, there are still significant areas of missing information in this regard, as is visible in some of the individual war descriptions. Included in this volume as wars are instances of combat in which it is believed that at least 1,000 battle-related deaths per year have occurred, based on descriptions of the sizes of the forces engaged or on descriptions of the individual battles, even if confidence in individual fatality statistics is not yet established.

When describing war duration, the general rules for all wars in terms of start dates, end dates, and breaks in the fighting apply to intra-state wars as well. These definitions become somewhat more significant in intra-state conflicts because civil wars frequently encompass periods when combat waxes and wanes. In particular, the Correlates of War (COW) Project codes the end of an intra-state war when there is a period of more than a year in which combat does not lead to 1,000 battle-related deaths. Similarly, cease-fire agreements can lead to periods of breaks within a war.

Civil Wars

The largest of the three intra-state war subcategories is that of civil wars. Civil wars as defined here must involve the active participation of the national government; specifically, the "bulk of the fighting" on one side has to be conducted by the national government of an interstate system member. Small and Singer defined civil war as sustained military conflict, "pitting the central government against an insurgent force capable of effective resistance."[1] The criteria for the national government to be classified as a war participant are the same as those for the other categories of war: that the state suffers 100 fatalities or commits 1,000 armed troops to combat. They also defined central government as those forces that were at the start of the war in de facto control of the nation's institutions, regardless of the legality or illegality of their claim.[2] This work accepts the further refinement of this definition suggested by Jeffrey Dixon, who also focuses upon the "institutions of governance and whichever party begins the war in possession of the institutions of governance (parliament, the palace, etc.) may be termed the government. When each side in a civil war controls an institution (i.e., Chile's Congressist rebellion, which pitted the President against Congress), then the executive or monarch's faction ought to be termed the government."[3] Control of the nation's institutions need not necessarily include control of the armed forces. Although a government can generally expect its armed forces to defend it, in a civil war the armed forces may actually be fighting against the government. In such cases the government must rely on civilian combatants or other branches of the civilian or military infrastructure that remain loyal.[4] Consequently, Small and Singer also included in the general category of "the government," or the side of the national government, all those—from national military forces to local police, and citizens—who enter the conflict in the name of that government.[5] This criterion would only become particularly difficult to apply in cases where two or more groups each claim to be fighting in support of the national government. Diplomatic recognition (or membership in the United Nations) is not a requirement for determining which group constitutes the national government. Although diplomatic recognition of a state is a requirement for an entity to be a member of the interstate system, that is not a de jure recognition (or approval) of a specific government. Thus it is possible for one party to be considered by COW as the government of a state owing to its control of the national institutions, while another party may be diplomatically recognized by other states or even retain the United Nations seat, as was the case when the Northern Alliance retained the UN seat for Afghanistan, despite the fact that the Taliban government was in control of the national institutions in Afghanistan.

In terms of classifying the other participant(s) in civil wars, Small and Singer required that the government is fighting against an internal insurgent force capable of "effective resistance." They developed a two-part definition of effective resistance; "a violent episode of sustained military combat shall be considered a civil war if (a) both sides are initially organized for violent conflict and prepared to resist the attacks of their antagonists, or (b) the weaker side, although initially unprepared, is able to inflict upon the stronger opponents at least five percent of the number of fatalities it sustains."[6] The effective-resistance criterion was specifically utilized to differentiate civil wars from massacres. The primary requirement is part (a), that each participant must have an organized armed force capable of engaging in sustained combat. However, application of this criterion alone would eliminate as civil wars such cases in which the nonstate actor is perhaps not initially well organized but relatively soon develops an armed organization. For example, the 1923 Agrarian Rising in Bulgaria was initially not considered to be a COW civil war, owing to organizational concerns, but it was later added to the civil war list (through the application of criterion b) when it became clear that the peasants became nominally organized and armed.[7] Referring to the other war participants as nonstate armed groups (NSAs) in this study has been useful to describe conflict participants, including rebel movements, progovernment militias, and community-based vigilante groups, as well as religious movements and foreign mercenaries.[8] A NSA is considered a war participant if it either commits 100 armed personnel to combat or suffers 25 battle-related deaths.

Initially, Small and Singer rejected further classifying or subdividing civil wars by the types of weapons or tactics used (overt vs. covert, or conventional military vs. guerrilla) or by the purposes and goals of the rebels. Requests from scholars, however, led COW to reconsider the issue. Despite the difficulty of ascertaining the objectives of political protagonists or most other entities, COW nonetheless concluded that motives and goals are the most relevant criteria for differentiating amongst the forms that civil war might take. COW adopted a minimalist categorization of the objectives of the nonstate participants, and in later versions of the dataset civil wars were grouped into two categories based on the apparent motives of the nonstate actors, as being either (1) conflicts for control of the central government; or (2) conflicts over local or regional interests. In category (1) for central control, the insurgent forces seek to overthrow the existing national regime and replace it with one that is more receptive to their material, cultural, or psychic interests. But at the more restricted local, provincial, or regional level, in category (2) the insurgents fight in order to modify the national regime's treatment of this particular region or group of people, to replace the local regime with a friendlier one, or to secede from the larger statewide political system in order to set up their own regime. In trying to make this distinction between local as separate from central government/statewide objectives, we not only recognize the ambiguities and uncertainties involved in the behavior of the different elements that make up the insurgency, but also we must recognize that their objectives are far from constant. These will change as the insurgent coalition changes in its composition and in the relative power of its constituent groups and as the fortunes of war fluctuate. It is this changeable nature of objectives that has dissuaded the project from trying to subdivide this category further. These two categories of civil war are identified as war types 4 and 5 in the overall schema (see Chapter 2, Table 2.1).

The category of civil wars is also the category in which wars are frequently internationalized and/or transformed into wars of a different type. Civil wars can become internationalized when a system member intervenes either (a) on the side of the regime of another state member fighting against insurgents within its territory; or (b) on the side of the insurgents. However, should the intervener subsequently take over the bulk of the fighting on behalf of the regime, the war then is transformed into an extra-state war between the intervener and a nonstate armed group outside its borders. If the intervener takes over the bulk of the fighting on behalf of the nonstate actor, the war becomes an inter-state war between the intervener and the state involved in the original civil war. In both these instances the civil war is coded as ending and a new inter-state or extra-state war is coded as beginning.

The final coding decision that especially affects civil wars is the issue of multiple simultaneous wars. In general, COW categorizes wars as mutually exclusive, utilizing the processes of war international-ization and war transformation to recode wars rather than having simultaneous wars of different types. It becomes more difficult, however, to distinguish separate wars when they take place within the confines of a state, to decide whether combat reflects (a) a single civil war involving many NSAs opposed to the central government; or (b) several simultaneous civil wars, each characterized by the same government fighting a different NSA or rebel group. The primary determinant in differentiation is the degree of coordination between/among the various NSAs. If a state is facing combat with a variety of NSAs that are coordinating their opposition, it is coded as one single civil war. If on the other hand the state is facing combat against multiple NSAs that are operating in geographically dis-tinct regions and are not coordinating their operations, then the conflict is coded as multiple wars, assuming that all the other criteria for a war are met. The key difficulties with this categorization are, of course, identifying all of the NSAs involved in the war and then determining how much coordina-tion existed between/among them. Although it is relatively easy to recognize evidence of coordination, such as common command structures, frequent meetings or communication among NSA leaders, and joint offensives, it is much more difficult to measure the absence of such coordination. Consequently, negative coordination criteria are utilized. In instances in which a state is engaged in combat with multiple NSAs, each of which is operating in a distinct geographic area, multiple wars will be consid-ered to exist unless there is specific evidence of coordination and cooperation between/among the NSAs. It should also be apparent that distinct civil wars will be coded if they occur within different states (against different state governments) even though the NSA may be identical in both cases.

Regional and Inter-communal Wars

The two other categories of intra-state wars, regional wars and inter-communal wars, also take place within the boundaries of a state interstate system member; however, they are in essence non-state wars in that neither of the major war participants conducting the bulk of the fighting on each side is the central government of the state. In virtually all respects, regional intra-state wars function like civil wars, but what gives them their distinct identity is that the major combatant on one side of the war is a local or regional government—not the national government—that is operating in its own inter-ests. The armed forces on this side of the war would be regional (similar to the New York State National Guard); however, as with civil wars, the side of the local or regional government would include all those that enter the conflict in the name of that government, from regional military forces to local police and citizens. The key difficulty in identifying these wars, and in differentiating them from civil wars, is in determining the purpose for which the regional government is fighting. If the regional government is fighting against an NSA for local issues, including the perpetuation of the regional government itself, then the war would be a regional intra-state war. On the other hand, a regional or local government could also be merely a participant in a civil war fighting alongside, or in the name of the national government, in a civil war opposing an NSA seeking local autonomy or independence. Conversely, the regional government could be a participant in a civil war against the national government if the regional government itself is seeking autonomy or independence. The extent to which regional governments have sufficient autonomy or latitude to act on their own is generally limited; thus the number of regional wars is quite small. Primary examples include wars conducted by Egypt while it was part of the Ottoman Empire. Although Egypt was involved in a number of wars at the behest of the Ottoman central government (thus classified as inter-state, extra-state, or civil wars), it also was involved in wars for its own benefit as it was attempting to break away from the Ottoman Empire, for example, the war in Lebanon in 1840, intra-state war #535, which is classified as a regional war.

Inter-communal wars also occur within the boundaries of a member of the interstate system, but neither of the major war participants conducting the bulk of the fighting on each side is a system member or a regional or local government. Inter-communal wars are becoming more common as advanced weapons technology boosts the probability that conflicts between/among NSAs will reach the requisite battle-death threshold for war. Regional wars are identified as war type 6 and inter-communal wars as war type 7 in the overall war typology (see Chapter 2, Table 2.1).

Table 5.1 consists of a list of the 335 intra-state wars. Each war will then be individually described with the pertinent basic data provided.

TABLE 5.1 LIST OF INTRA-STATE WARS IN CHRONOLOGICAL ORDER

Intra-state war number	War name	Page no	Intra-state war number	War name	Page no
500	First Caucasus War of 1818–1822	347	548	First Venezuelan War of 1848–1849	360
501	Sidon-Damascus War of 1820–1821	347	550	Viennese Revolt of 1848	360
502	First Two Sicilies War of 1820–1821	347	551	Milan Five-Day Revolt of 1848	361
503	Spanish Royalists War of 1821–1823	347	552	Second French Insurrection of 1848	361
505	Sardinian Revolt of 1821	348	553	Mayan Caste War Phase 2 of 1848–1855	361
506	Greek Independence War of 1821–1828	348	554	Hungarian War of 1848–1849	362
507	Egypt-Mehdi War of 1824	349	555	First Chilean War of 1851	362
508	Janissari Revolt of 1826	349	556	First Turco-Montenegrin War of 1852–1853	363
510	Miguelite War of 1828–1834	349			
511	First Murid War of 1830–1832	350	557	First Peru War of 1853–1855	363
512	First Albanian Revolt of 1830–1831	350	558	Puebla War of 1855–1856	363
513	First French Insurrection of 1830	350	560	Second Peru War of 1856–1858	364
515	Belgian Independence War of 1830	351	561	Mexican Reform War of 1858–1861	364
516	Egyptian Taka Expedition of 1831–1832	351	562	Second Turco-Montenegrin War of 1858–1859	365
517	First Polish War of 1831	351			
518	First Syrian War of 1831–1832	352	563	Second Venezuelan/Federalist War of 1859–1863	365
520	First Mexican War of 1832	352			
521	Egypt-Palestinian Anti-Conscription Revolt of 1834	352	565	Second Colombian War of 1860–1861	365
			566	Second Maronite-Druze War of 1860	366
522	First Carlist War of 1834–1840	353	567	Taiping Rebellion Phase 2 of 1860–1866	366
523	Second Murid War of 1834	353	568	Second Nien Revolt of 1860–1868	367
525	Cabanos Revolt of 1835–1837	353	570	Miao Revolt Phase 2 of 1860–1872	367
526	Farroupilha War of 1835–1845	354	571	Panthay Rebellion Phase 2 of 1860–1872	367
527	Texan War of 1835–1836	354			
528	First Bosnian War of 1836–1837	354	572	U.S. Civil War of 1861–1865	368
530	Third Murid War of 1836–1852	355	573	Third Buenos Aires War of 1861	368
531	Sabinada Rebellion of 1837–1838	355	575	Third Turco-Montenegrin War of 1861–1862	368
532	Druze Rebellion of 1837–1838	355			
533	Second Syrian War Phase 1 of 1839	356	576	Tungan Rebellion of 1862–1873	369
535	Lebanon Insurgency of 1840	356	577	Sioux-Minnesota War of 1862	369
536	First Colombian War of 1840–1842	356	578	Bolivian-Pérez Rebellion of 1862	370
537	Second Syrian War Phase 2 of 1840	357	580	Second Polish War of 1863–1864	370
538	First Argentina War Phase 2 of 1841–1842	357	581	Second Argentina War of 1863	370
			582	Xinjiang Muslim Revolt of 1864–1871	371
540	Second Bosnian War of 1841	358	583	First Cretan War of 1866–1867	371
541	Triangular Revolt of 1841	358	585	Yellow Cliff Revolt of 1866	371
542	Karbala Revolt of 1842–1843	358	586	Third Argentina War of 1866–1867	372
543	First Maronite-Druze War of 1845	359	587	Queretaro War of 1867	372
545	Mayan Caste War Phase 1 of 1847–1848	359	588	Meiji Restoration of 1868	372
546	Second Carlist War of 1847–1849	359	590	Third Venezuelan War of 1868–1871	373
547	Second Two Sicilies War of 1848–1849	360	591	Spanish Liberals War of 1868	373

(Continued)

TABLE 5.1 LIST OF INTRA-STATE WARS IN CHRONOLOGICAL ORDER

Intra-state war number	War name	Page no	Intra-state war number	War name	Page no
592	Guerre des Cacos of 1869	374	643	Bloody Sunday War of 1905–1906	387
593	Fourth Argentina War of 1870–1871	374	645	Romanian Peasant Revolt of 1907	387
595	Bolivia-Criollos War of 1870–1871	374	646	Overthrow of Abd el-Aziz of 1907–1908	388
596	Paris Commune War of 1871	374	647	Iranian Constitution War of 1908–1909	388
597	Third Carlist War of 1872–1876	375	648	Young Turks Counter-coup of 1909	389
598	Catonalist Uprising of 1874–1875	375	650	Second Albanian Revolt of 1910–1912	389
600	Fifth Argentina War of 1874	376	651	Asir-Yemeni Revolt of 1910–1911	389
601	Bosnia and Bulgaria Revolt of 1875–1876	376	652	Third Mexican War of 1910–1914	390
			656	Paraguay War of 1911–1912	390
602	Diaz Revolt of 1876	376	657	First Nationalists War of 1911	391
603	Defeat of Xinjiang Muslims of 1876–1877	377	658	Cuban Black Uprising of 1912	391
			670	Ecuadorian Civil War of 1912–1914	392
605	Third Colombian War of 1876–1877	377	671	Second Nationalists War of 1913	392
607	Satsuma Rebellion of 1877	378	672	China Pai-ling (White Wolf) War of 1914	392
608	Argentine Indians War of 1879–1880	378			
610	Fourth Buenos Aires War of 1880	378	673	Fourth Mexican War of 1914–1920	393
611	Haitian Civil War of 1883–1884	379	675	Southern China Revolt of 1916–1918	393
612	Fourth Colombian War of 1884–1885	379	676	Russia-Turkestan War of 1916–1917	393
613	Peru's National Problem of 1885	379	677	Russian Civil War of 1917–1921	394
616	First Yemeni Rebellion of 1890–1892	380	680	Finnish Civil War of 1918	394
617	Second Chilean War of 1891	380	681	Western Ukrainian War of 1918–1919	395
618	Zaili-Jinden Revolt of 1891	380	682	Sparticist Rising of 1919	395
620	Brazil Federalists War of 1893–1894	381	683	Hungary's Red Terror War of 1919–1920	396
621	Brazil Naval War of 1893–1894	381	685	First Chinese Warlord War of 1920	396
623	Tonghak Rebellion of 1894	381	686	Green Rebellion of 1920–1921	397
625	Third Peru War of 1894–1895	382	687	Gilan Marxists War of 1920–1921	397
626	Fifth Colombian War of 1895	382	688	Italian Fascist War of 1920–1922	397
627	Ecuador Liberals War of 1895	383	690	Kronstadt Rebellion of 1921	398
628	First Gansu Muslim War of 1895–1896	383	691	Basmachi in Turkestan War of 1921–1923	398
630	Druze-Turkish War of 1895–1896	383			
631	Second Cretan War of 1896–1897	384	692	Second Chinese Warlord War of 1922	398
632	Third Brazil-Canudos War of 1896–1897	384	693	Agrarian Rising of 1923	399
			695	De La Huerta Rebellion of 1923–1924	399
633	Fourth Venezuelan War of 1899	385	696	Honduran Conservative War of 1924	399
635	Second Yaqui War of 1899–1900	385	697	First Afghan Anti-Reform War of 1924–1925	400
636	Sixth Colombian (War of the 1,000 Days) of 1899–1902	385	698	Third Chinese Warlord War of 1925–1926	400
638	Fifth Venezuelan War of 1901–1903	386			
640	Ilinden War of 1903	386	700	Chinese Northern Expedition War of 1926–1928	401
641	First Uruguay War of 1904	386			
642	Second Yemeni Rebellion of 1904–1906	387	701	Cristeros Revolt of 1926–1929	401

(Continued)

TABLE 5.1 **LIST OF INTRA-STATE WARS IN CHRONOLOGICAL ORDER** (Continued)

Intra-state war number	War name	Page no	Intra-state war number	War name	Page no
702	Ethiopian Northern Resistance of 1928–1930	401	747	Iraq-Shammar War of 1959	415
			748	Vietnam War Phase 1 of 1960–1965	415
703	Second Gansu Muslim War of 1928–1930	402	750	First DRC (Zaire) War of 1960–1963	416
			751	First Laotian War of 1960–1962	416
705	Second Afghan Anti-Reform War of 1928–1929	402	752	First Iraqi Kurds War of 1961–1963	417
			753	Algerian Revolutionaries War of 1962–1963	417
706	Intra-Guomindang War of 1929–1930	403			
707	Escoban Rebellion of 1929	403	755	North Yemen War of 1962–1969	418
708	Ikhwan Revolt of 1929–1930	403	756	Second Laotian War Phase 1 of 1963–1968	418
710	Chinese Civil War Phase 1 of 1930–1936	404			
711	Xinjiang Muslim Revolt of 1931–1934	404	757	First Ogaden War of 1963–1964	419
712	Matanza War of 1932	404	758	First South Sudan War of 1963–1972	419
713	Aprista Revolt of 1932	405	760	Second DRC (Jeunesse) War of 1963–1965	420
715	Paulista Rebellion of 1932	405			
716	Fukien Revolt of 1934	405	761	First Rwanda War of 1963–1964	420
717	Spanish Miners War of 1934	406	762	Third DRC (Simba) Rebellion of 1964–1965	420
718	Spanish Civil War of 1936–1939	406			
720	Greek Civil War of 1944–1949	407	763	Zanzibar Arab-African War of 1964	421
721	Polish Ukrainians War of 1945–1947	407	765	Second Iraqi Kurds War of 1965–1966	421
722	Ukrainian Partisans War of 1945–1947	408	766	Dominican Republic War of 1965	421
723	Forest Brethren War of 1945–1951	408	767	First West Papua War of 1965–1969	422
725	Chinese Civil War Phase 2 of 1946–1950	408	768	First Uganda War of 1966	422
726	Taiwan Revolt of 1947	409	770	First Guatemala War of 1966–1968	422
727	Paraguay War of 1947	409	771	First Chad (FROLINAT) Rebellion of 1966–1971	423
728	Yemeni Imamate War of 1948	409			
730	Costa Rica War of 1948	410	772	Cultural Revolution Phase 1 of 1967	423
731	Seventh Colombian ("La Violencia") War of 1948–1958	410	773	Third Burmese War of 1967–1980	424
			775	Biafra War of 1967–1970	424
732	First Burmese War of 1948–1951	411	776	Cultural Revolution Phase 2 of 1967–1968	425
733	South Moluccas War of 1950	411			
735	Hukbalahap Rebellion of 1950–1954	412	777	Third Iraqi Kurds War of 1969–1970	425
737	Bolivia War of 1952	412	778	Naxalite Rebellion of 1970–1971	425
738	Indonesia-Darul Islam War of 1953	412	780	Black September War of 1970	426
740	Argentine Military War of 1955	413	781	Second Guatemala War of 1970–1971	426
741	Tibetan Khamba Rebellion of 1956–1959	413	782	Pakistan-Bengal War of 1971	427
			783	First Sri Lanka-JVP War of 1971	427
742	Indonesian Leftists War of 1956–1962	413	785	Khmer Rouge War of 1971–1975	427
743	First Lebanese War of 1958	414	786	First Philippine-Moro War of 1972–1981	428
745	Cuban Revolution of 1958–1959	414			
746	Second Burmese War of 1958–1960	415	787	Communist Insurgency of 1972–1973	428

(Continued)

TABLE 5.1 LIST OF INTRA-STATE WARS IN CHRONOLOGICAL ORDER

Intra-state war number	War name	Page no	Intra-state war number	War name	Page no
788	Eritrean Split of 1972–1974	429	831	Matabeleland War of 1983–1987	443
789	First Burundi War of 1972	429	832	Fourth Burmese War of 1983–1988	444
790	Philippines-NPA War of 1972–1992	430	833	Fourth Lebanese Civil War of 1983–1984	444
791	Rhodesia War of 1972–1979	430			
792	Baluchi Separatists War of 1973–1977	430	835	First Sri Lanka Tamil War of 1983–2002	445
793	Chilean Coup of 1973	431	836	Second South Sudan War of 1983–2005	445
795	Dhofar Rebellion Phase 2 of 1973–1975	431	837	Indian Golden Temple War of 1984	446
797	Fourth Iraqi Kurds War of 1974–1975	432	838	First Turkish Kurds War of 1984–1986	446
798	Eritrean War of 1975–1978	432	840	Fifth Iraqi Kurds War of 1985–1988	446
800	Argentine Leftists War of 1975–1977	432	842	South Yemen War of 1986	447
801	Second Lebanese War of 1975–1976	433	843	Holy Spirit Movement War of 1986–1987	447
802	Second West Papua War of 1976–1978	433			
803	Third Laotian War of 1976–1979	434	845	Second Sri Lanka-JVP War of 1987–1989	447
804	Angolan Control War of 1976–1991	434			
805	Second Ogaden War Phase 1 of 1976–1977	435	846	Inkatha-ANC War of 1987–1994	448
			847	Fifth Burmese War of 1988	448
806	East Timorese War Phase 3 of 1976–1979	435	848	First Somalia War of 1988–1991	449
			850	Fifth Lebanese War of 1989–1990	449
807	Third Lebanese War of 1978	436	851	Second Afghan Mujahideen Uprising of 1989–2001	450
808	Second Ogaden War Phase 3 of 1978–1980	436			
809	Third Guatemala War of 1978–1984	436	852	Third Chad (Déby Coup) War of 1989–1990	450
810	Saur Revolution of 1978	437			
811	Fourth DRC (Shaba) War of 1978	437	853	First Aceh War of 1989–1991	451
812	First Afghan Mujahideen Uprising of 1978–1980	438	854	Bougainville Secession War of 1989–1992	451
813	Overthrow of the Shah of 1978–1979	438	856	Eighth Colombian War of 1989–present	452
815	Sandinista Rebellion of 1978–1979	438	857	First Cambodian Civil War of 1989–1991	452
816	Anti-Khomeini Coalition War of 1979–1984	439	858	Romania War of 1989	452
817	El Salvador War of 1979–1992	439	860	First Liberia War of 1989–1990	453
818	Mozambique War of 1979–1992	440	861	Kashmir Insurgents War of 1990–2005	453
820	Second Chad (Habre Revolt) War of 1980–1984	440	862	Shiite and Kurdish War of 1991	454
			863	First Sierra Leone War of 1991–1996	454
822	Second Uganda War of 1980–1986	441	864	Croatian Independence War of 1991–1992	455
823	Nigeria-Muslim War of 1980–1981	441			
825	Hama War of 1981–1982	442	865	Second Turkish Kurds War of 1991–1999	455
826	Tigrean and Eritrean War of 1982–1991	442			
827	Shining Path War of 1982–1992	442	866	SPLA Division (Dinka-Nuer) War of 1991–1992	455
828	Contra War of 1982–1990	443			
			868	Jukun-Tiv War of 1991–1992	456

(Continued)

TABLE 5.1 **LIST OF INTRA-STATE WARS IN CHRONOLOGICAL ORDER** (Continued)

Intra-state war number	War name	Page no	Intra-state war number	War name	Page no
870	Second Somalia War of 1991–1997	456	907	Third Angolan War of 1998–2002	469
871	Georgia War of 1991–1992	457	908	Second Congo (Brazzaville) War of 1998–1999	470
872	Nagorno-Karabakh War of 1991–1993	457			
873	Dniestrian Independence War of 1991–1992	458	910	Moluccas Sectarian War of 1999–2000	470
			911	First Nigeria Christian-Muslim War of 1999–2000	471
875	Algerian Islamic Front War of 1992–1999	458			
			912	Second Aceh War of 1999–2002	471
876	Tajikistan War of 1992–1997	459	913	Oromo Liberation War of 1999	471
877	Bosnian-Serb Rebellion of 1992–1995	459	915	Second Chechnya War of 1999–2003	472
878	Second Liberia War of 1992–1995	460	916	Second Philippine-Moro War of 2000–2001	472
880	Angolan War of the Cities of 1992–1994	460			
881	Second Cambodian Civil War of 1993–1997	461	917	Guinean War of 2000–2001	472
			918	Third Burundi War of 2001–2003	473
882	Abkhazia Revolt of 1993–1994	461	920	Fourth Rwanda War of 2001	473
883	Second Burundi War of 1993–1998	462	921	First Nepal Maoist Insurgency of 2001–2003	474
885	South Yemeni Secessionist War of 1994	462			
886	Second Rwanda War of 1994	463	922	Fourth Liberia War of 2002–2003	474
888	First Chechnya War of 1994–1996	463	923	Ethiopian Anyuaa-Nuer War of 2002–2003	475
890	Iraqi Kurd Internecine War of 1994–1995	464			
			925	Côte d'Ivoire Military War of 2002–2004	475
891	Croatia-Krajina War of 1995	464	926	Third Philippine-Moro War of 2003	476
892	Third Liberia War of 1996	464	927	Darfur War of 2003–2006	476
893	Sixth Iraqi Kurds War of 1996	465	930	Third Aceh War of 2003–2004	476
895	Fifth DRC War of 1996–1997	465	931	Second Nepal Maoist War of 2003–2006	477
896	Third Rwanda War of 1997–1998	466	932	Waziristan War of 2004–2006	477
897	First Congo (Brazzaville) War of 1997	466	933	Second Nigeria Christian-Muslim War of 2004	478
898	Second Sierra Leone War of 1998–2000	466			
900	Kosovo Independence War of 1998–1999	467	935	First Yemeni Cleric War of 2004–2005	478
			936	Philippine Joint Offensive of 2005–2006	478
902	Guinea-Bissau Military War of 1998–1999	468	937	Fifth Chad War of 2005–2006	479
			938	Third Somalia War of 2006–2008	479
905	Africa's World War of 1998–2002	468	940	Second Sri Lanka Tamil War of 2006–present	480
906	Fourth Chad (Togoimi Revolt) War of 1998–2000	469			
			941	Second Yemeni Cleric War of 2007	480

Individual Descriptions of Intra-state Wars

INTRA-STATE WAR #500:
The First Caucasus War of 1818–1822

Participants: Russia vs. Chechens, Dhagestanis, Georgians
Dates: June 10, 1818, to [ ]/[ ]/1822
Battle-Related Deaths: Chechens, Dhagestanis, Georgians—6,000; Russia—5,000
Where Fought: Europe
Initiator: Chechens
Outcome: Russia wins
War Type: Civil for local issues

Narrative: The Russian Empire had conquered most of Georgia in 1801, and by 1814 most of Georgia had been pacified under imperial rule. The Russians, however, attempted to eliminate Georgian identity, and in 1818 the Georgians rebelled and were followed by the Chechens and Dhagestanis, who revolted later in the year. The Russian pacification campaign, begun in 1820, was temporarily successful in controlling the rebellion.

Source: Gvosdev (2000).

INTRA-STATE WAR #501:
The Sidon-Damascus War of 1820–1821

Participants: Sidon vs. Aleppo, Damascus
Dates: June [ ], 1820, to July 21, 1821
Battle-Related Deaths: Sidon—[ ]; Damascus, Aleppo —[ ] (Total Combatant Deaths: 1,000)
Where Fought: Middle East
Initiator: Sidon
Outcome: Aleppo, Damascus win
War Type: Regional internal

Narrative: A popular rebellion against taxation led to the ouster of Emir Bashir of Sidon as a result of a war waged by the valis of Damascus and Aleppo.

Sources: Farah (2000); Hitti (1962); Polk (1963); Richardson (1960a).

INTRA-STATE WAR #502:
The First Two Sicilies War of 1820–1821

Participants: Austria-Hungary, Two Sicilies vs. liberals
Dates: July 2, 1820, to March 23, 1821
Battle-Related Deaths: Austria-Hungary—[ ]; Two Sicilies—[ ]; liberals—[ ] (Total Combatant Deaths: 2,000)
Where Fought: Europe
Initiator: liberals
Outcome: Austria-Hungary, Two Sicilies win
War Type: Civil for central control

Narrative: After the Napoleonic Wars, liberalism began to spread throughout Europe. In the Two Sicilies soldiers began a rebellion against the reactionary King Ferdinand I. As the revolt spread, King Ferdinand appealed to Austria for assistance. Austrian forces defeated the Neapolitan rebels, enabling Ferdinand to reassert his power and rescind a promised constitution.

Sources: Berkeley (1932); Clodfelter (1992); Hearder (1977); Kohn (1999); Langer (1952); Phillips and Axelrod (2005); Shinn (1985); Smith (1968).

INTRA-STATE WAR #503:
The Spanish Royalists War of 1821–1823

Participants: Spain vs. Royalists
Dates: December 1, 1821, to April 6, 1823
Battle-Related Deaths: Spain—[ ]; Royalists—[ ] (Total Combatant Deaths: 1,500)

Where Fought: Europe
Initiator: Royalists
Outcome: Transformed into inter-state war #1
War Type: Civil for central control

Narrative: In 1820 a military rebellion had led to the creation of a constitutional monarch under a liberal government. King Ferdinand resisted this encroachment on his power, and the ensuing war pitted royalist guards against the troops and militia loyal to the constitutional authorities. The king appealed to the Holy Alliance for assistance. When France intervened (with the support of Austria, Prussia, and Russia), the war was transformed from a civil war into inter-state war #1 between France and Spain.

Sources: Campos y Serrano (1961); Carr (1982); Clarke (1906); Clodfelter (2002); Gambra (1972); Holt (1967); Hume (1900); Menendez Pidal (1968); Phillips and Axelrod (2005); Richardson (1960a); Smith (1965); Sorokin (1937); Urlanis (1960); Wright (1965).

INTRA-STATE WAR #505:
The Sardinian Revolt of 1821

Participants: Austria-Hungary, Sardinia vs. Carbonari
Dates: March 10, 1821, to May 8, 1821
Battle-Related Deaths: Austria-Hungary—[ ]; Sardinia—[ ]; Carbonari—[ ] (Total Combatant Deaths: 1,000)
Where Fought: Europe
Initiator: Carbonari
Outcome: Austria-Hungary, Sardinia win
War Type: Civil for central control

Narrative: After the Napoleonic Wars, the spread of liberalism threatened existing monarchies. King Victor Emmanuel I of Sardinia had refused to accept a constitutional monarchy, which ultimately led to a revolt by the Carbonari (freedom fighters). Victor Emmanuel was forced to abdicate in favor of his brother Charles Felix. Until Charles Felix was able to arrive, Victor Emmanuel's heir, Charles Albert became regent, and in order to

deter a war, he proclaimed a Spanish-type constitution. Opposing such reforms, Charles Felix asked for Austrian assistance, and the combined Austrian and Sardinian forces defeated the mutineers at the battle of Novara, restoring Charles Felix to power.

Sources: Berkeley (1932); Clodfelter (2002); Phillips and Axelrod (2005).

INTRA-STATE WAR #506:
The Greek Independence War of 1821–1828

Participants: Ottoman Empire vs. France, Greece, Russia, United Kingdom
Dates: March 25, 1821, to April 25, 1828
Battle-Related Deaths: Ottoman Empire—6,000; Greece—3,000; United Kingdom—80; Russia—60; France—40
Where Fought: Europe
Initiator: Greece
Outcome: Transformed into inter-state war #4
War Type: Civil for local issues

Narrative: Resistance to Ottoman rule arose in 1821 in several locations in the empire, including Greece. The Ottoman sultan Mahmud II was unable to subdue the Greeks and appealed to his vassal, Muhammad (Mehmed) Ali of Egypt for assistance. Egyptian forces, under Muhammad Ali's son, Ibrahim Pasha, landed in 1825. By June 5, 1827, almost all of Greece was again under Ottoman control. Support for Greek independence was widespread in Europe. The powers of Europe demanded an Egyptian withdrawal and an armistice. When these demands were rejected, the governments of Britain, France, and Russia tried to force mediation by sending warships to blockade the harbor of Navarino Bay. This war became an internationalized civil war when the Turco-Egyptians fired on the allied fleet. The allies destroyed the Ottoman fleet, ultimately gaining Greece its independence. Fighting did continue between the Greek rebels and the Turks in northern Greece. When Russia, which had designs on the Balkans, declared war on the Ottoman Empire and took over the bulk of the fighting from the Greeks, the civil war ended and inter-state war #4 began.

Sources: Albrecht-Carrié (1958); Anderson (1952); Clodfelter (2002); Crawley (1973); Crawley (1930); Palmer (1992); Papageorgiou (1985); Phillips (1897); Sonyel (1998); Woodhouse (1952).

INTRA-STATE WAR #507:
The Egypt-Mehdi War of 1824

Participants: Egypt vs. Mehdi army
Dates: March 20, 1824, to April [ ], 1824
Battle-Related Deaths: Egypt—[ ]; Mehdi army—[ ]
Where Fought: Middle East
Initiator: Mehdi army
Outcome: Egypt wins
War Type: Regional internal

Narrative: Muhammad (Mehmed) Ali, the governor of Egypt under the Ottoman Empire, faced a rebellion against his rule led by Seyh Ahmed, a religious leader who claimed to be a Mehdi, or descendant of the Prophet. The Mehdi united his followers and instigated a revolt by claiming that Muhammad Ali was an infidel. Muhammad Ali's troops defeated the rebels in a series of at least six fierce battles. This war is coded as a regional intra-state war because it was fought by a nonstate actor (the Mehdi army) against Egypt, which was acting on its own, not against the Ottoman Empire.

Source: Fahmy (2002).

INTRA-STATE WAR #508:
The Janissari Revolt of 1826

Participants: Ottoman Empire vs. Janissaries
Dates: June 14, 1826, to September 30, 1826
Battle-Related Deaths: Janissaries—6,000; Ottoman Empire—300
Where Fought: Middle East
Initiator: Janissaries

Outcome: Ottoman Empire wins
War Type: Civil for central control

Narrative: The Janissaries were the elite forces in the Ottoman military. They were made up mainly of Christian young men mainly from regions of southeast Europe conquered by the Ottomans who were raised as Muslims and trained as soldiers. Over time the Janissaries became a virtually ungovernable force, or state-within-a-state. In an attempt to reassert his control, Sultan Mahmud II in 1826 began to split the Janissaries up among various divisions of his newly created modern army. The Janissaries revolted, tried to storm the palace, and then retreated to their barracks, where they were crushed by artillery.

Sources: Atamian (1955); Clodfelter (2002); Deans (1854); Dumont (1963); Eversley (1917); Mathieu (1856); Palmer (1992); Phillips and Axelrod (2005); Richardson (1960a).

INTRA-STATE WAR #510:
The Miguelite War of 1828–1834

Participants: Portugal vs. constitutionalists, United Kingdom
Dates: July 11, 1828, to May 26, 1834
Battle-Related Deaths: Portugal—12,000; constitutionalists—8,000; United Kingdom—100
Where Fought: Europe
Initiator: constitutionalists
Outcome: Constitutionalists, United Kingdom win
War Type: Civil for central control

Narrative: In Portugal, Don Miguel was the leader of the absolutists in the royal family, who opposed the promulgation of a constitution, which his brother, Pedro I of Brazil and Portugal, had issued. Pedro abdicated in favor of his daughter, and Don Miguel was named the regent for Queen Maria II. Don Miguel was then proclaimed king in July 1828 by a subservient Cortes (parliament). Pedro abdicated his Brazilian throne and assembled a constitutionalist expedition from the Azores to reconquer the country with British assistance. In July 1833 Lisbon was taken by the constitutionalists under Pedro. Spain also intervened on the side of the constitutionalists (though not at levels to be considered a war participant), and the constitutionalists, with Spanish assistance, defeated Miguel's forces at Santarèm, Portugal, essentially ending the war.

Sources: Bollaert (1870); Clodfelter (1992); Phillips and Axelrod (2005); Richardson (1960a).

INTRA-STATE WAR #511:
The First Murid War of 1830–1832

Participants: Russia vs. Ghazi Muhammad
Dates: [ ]/[ ]/1830, to October 17, 1832
Battle-Related Deaths: Russia–1,000; Ghazi
    Muhammad—500
Where Fought: Europe
Initiator: Ghazi Muhammad
Outcome: Russia wins
War Type: Civil for local issues

Narrative: This is the first of three wars involving resistance to Russian rule in the Caucasus (around Dagestan and Chechnya) by the Murids, a Muslim religious movement. This rebellion was led by Ghazi Muhammad, who organized an army and began attacking Russian troops. The Russians dispatched 10,000 soldiers, who stormed the Murid fortress at Gimu in October 1832, killing Ghazi Muhammad and ending the rebellion. The Murids would revolt again in 1834 (intra-state war #523) and in 1836 (intra-state war #530).

Sources: Clodfelter (2002); Stone (2006).

INTRA-STATE WAR #512:
The First Albanian Revolt of 1830–1831

Participants: Ottoman Empire vs. Albanians
Dates: February [ ], 1830, to November [ ], 1831
Battle-Related Deaths: Albanians—10,000;
    Ottoman Empire–5,000

Where Fought: Europe
Initiator: Albanians
Outcome: Ottoman Empire wins
War Type: Civil for local issues

Narrative: The Albanians, a fiercely independent people, resisted Turkish control of their mainly mountaintop fortresses and towns. Once the Russo-Turkish War had ended in 1829, Sultan Mahmud II decided to suppress their disobedience. In August 1830, 500 beys (local government leaders) were massacred after being promised a reward for their loyalty. Over the next two years the Turks besieged and conquered many feudal castles belonging to Albanian leaders.

Source: Palmer (1992).

INTRA-STATE WAR #513:
The First French Insurrection of 1830

Participants: France vs. liberals
Dates: July 25, 1830, to July 29, 1830
Battle-Related Deaths: liberals–1,800; France—400
Where Fought: Europe
Initiator: liberals
Outcome: Liberals win
War Type: Civil for central control

Narrative: Charles X had been made king of France after the Napoleonic Wars. As a proponent of restoring absolute monarchy, he was resented by the middle classes. He dismissed the more liberal Chamber of Deputies in 1830, in response to their opposition to the reactionary Premier Jules de Polignac, a favorite of the king. A revolt promptly broke out in Paris, in late July 1830. Charles X fled and abdicated. The rebels, who were divided between liberal republicans and monarchists, then established a constitutional monarchy on July 30 with Louis-Philippe as king.

Sources: Beach (1971); Bertier de Sauvigny (1955); Bodart (1916); Clodfelter (1992); Leys (1955); Phillips and Axelrod (2005).

INTRA-STATE WAR #515:
The Belgian Independence War of 1830

Participants: Netherlands vs. Belgians
Dates: August 25, 1830, to November 4, 1830
Battle-Related Deaths: Belgians—600;
   Netherlands—500
Where Fought: Europe
Initiator: Belgians
Outcome: Belgians win
War Type: Civil for local issues

Narrative: The territory known today as Belgium had been controlled for centuries by other countries. In the aftermath of the Napoleonic Wars, the major powers agreed that Belgium should become part of the Netherlands. Both Flemings, who speak variations on Dutch, and Walloons, who speak French, chafed under the rule of William I and rose in rebellion in August 1830. A Dutch army of 9,000 was driven out of Brussels in late September, and independence was declared on October 4. The powers brokered a cease-fire, and in late December they declared that the United Kingdom of the Netherlands was dissolved. The following year the British and French also intervened to prevent William I from trying to recover Belgium, though fatalities did not reach war levels.

Sources: Clodfelter (1992); Langer (1952); Phillips and Axelrod (2005); Richardson (1960a).

INTRA-STATE WAR #516:
The Egyptian Taka Expedition of 1831–1832

Participants: Egypt vs. Hadendowa
Dates: [ ]/[ ]/1831, to [ ]/[ ]/1832
Battle-Related Deaths: Egypt—1,500;
   Hadendowa—[ ]
Where Fought: Middle East
Initiator: Egypt
Outcome: Hadendowa win
War Type: Regional internal

Narrative: In extra-state war #307, the Ottoman Empire, with its vassal Egypt, had established its control over most of Sudan in 1821. In the 1830s, Egypt had a powerful military, which it was using in support of Ottoman-instigated expeditions as well as for its own projects. Under Muhammad Ali, Egypt was trying to establish its independence from Ottoman rule and thus needed recruits for the army. The Egyptian governor-general of Sudan launched an expedition into Sudan to gain black recruits and subdue unrest in the region. The Egyptians were defeated by the Hadendowa tribe. This war is coded as a regional intra-state war rather than as a civil war, since Egypt, though it was a part of the Ottoman Empire, was acting on its own behalf and not at the behest of the sultan.

Sources: Hill (1970); Holt and Daly (2000); Mowafi (1981); Oliver and Atmore (2004).

INTRA-STATE WAR #517:
The First Polish War of 1831

Participants: Russia vs. Poles
Dates: February 7, 1831, to October 18, 1831
Battle-Related Deaths: Poles—20,000;
   Russia—15,000
Where Fought: Europe
Initiator: Poles
Outcome: Russia wins
War Type: Civil for local issues

Narrative: The once-autonomous kingdom of Poland had suffered through three partition agreements during the late eighteenth and the early nineteenth century. Russia had received the largest part, which was supposed to have a degree of independence within the Russian Empire. The Poles resented Russian rule, and a rebellion broke out on November 29, 1830, when junior Polish army officers occupied public buildings. As the rebels became increasingly radical, Russian tsar Nicholas I decided to send troops against the rebels in February 1831, starting the war. The first battles were won by the

Poles, and the Russians were stalemated at the Battle of Grochow. When spring arrived, however, Russian forces advanced, winning the battle of Ostroleka on May 26, and capturing Warsaw on September 8, 1831, after which the rebellion soon collapsed. Many of the deaths were due to disease. As a result of the war, the Polish constitution was suspended and Poland became more integrated into the Russian Empire.

Sources: Brzozowski (1833); Clodfelter (1992); Curtiss (1965); Gnorowski (1839); Grunwald (1955); Hordynsky (1832); Leslie (1956); Phillips and Axelrod (2005); Puzyrewsky (1893); Reddaway et al. (1941); Schiemann (1913); Stone (2006).

INTRA-STATE WAR #518:
The First Syrian War of 1831–1832

Participants: Ottoman Empire vs. Egyptians
Dates: October 1, 1831, to December 27, 1832
Battle-Related Deaths: Ottoman Empire—8,000; Egyptians—4,000
Where Fought: Middle East
Initiator: Egyptians
Outcome: Egyptians win
War Type: Civil for local issues

Narrative: The Ottoman Porte had promised Muhammad Ali, ruler of Egypt, control of Crete and Syria after providing Egypt's help during the Greek War of Independence. This promise was reneged upon, leading Muhammad Ali to send his son Ibrahim to seize Syria, which he successfully occupied in 1832. The Egyptians even entered Anatolia itself, decisively defeating the Ottoman army at Koniah in December 1832, ending the war. The Treaty of Kutahya of 1833 awarded Syria to Egypt.

Sources: Cattaui and Cattaui (1950); Clodfelter (1992); Dodwell (1931); Farah (2000); Florinsky (1953); Hitti (1962); Jaques (2007); Phillips and Axelrod (2005); Polites (1931); Polk (1963); Rood (2002); Sabry (1930); Sicker (1999); Williams (1907).

INTRA-STATE WAR #520:
The First Mexican War of 1832

Participants: Mexico vs. liberals
Dates: January 2, 1832, to December 11, 1832
Battle-Related Deaths: Mexico—[ ]; liberals—[ ] (Total Combatant Deaths: 4,000)
Where Fought: W. Hemisphere
Initiator: liberals
Outcome: Liberals win
War Type: Civil for central control

Narrative: After defeating the Spanish invasion of 1829 (extra-state war #317), Mexican liberals and conservatives turned to quarreling with each other. The conflict often took the form of personal conflicts, with this war featuring a contest between Anastasio Bustamante and the famous leader Antonio López de Santa Anna. Vice President Bustamante overthrew President Vicente Guerrero in December 1829, putting the conservatives back in power. Bustamante soon found himself in conflict with Santa Anna, the governor of Veracuz, who revolted in support of Guerrero. Bustamante's army was finally defeated at Posadas, forcing Bustamante's resignation. Santa Anna was elected president in January 1833.

Sources: Bravo Ugarte (1962); Jaques (2007); Schlarman (1950).

INTRA-STATE WAR #521:
The Egypt-Palestinian Anti-Conscription Revolt of 1834

Participants: Palestinians vs. Egypt
Dates: April 19, 1834, to October [ ], 1834
Battle-Related Deaths: Palestinians—1,500; Egypt—500
Where Fought: Middle East
Initiator: Palestinians
Outcome: Egypt wins
War Type: Regional internal

Narrative: As a result of the First Syrian War (intra-state war #518), Egypt was given control over greater Syria. The Egyptians subsequently raised taxes and tried to conscript Syrians into the Egyptian army, prompting an anti-conscription revolt in northern Palestine and Lebanon. It was soon suppressed, though opposition to Egyptian rule would resurface in 1837 in the Druze Rebellion (intra-state war #532).

Sources: Farah (2000); Hitti (1962); Nazzal and Nazzal (1997); Richardson (1960a).

INTRA-STATE WAR #522:
The First Carlist War of 1834–1840

Participants: France, Portugal, Spain, United Kingdom vs. Carlists
Dates: July 15, 1834, to July 15, 1840
Battle-Related Deaths: Spain–65,000; Carlists—60,000; France—7,700; United Kingdom—2,500; Portugal—50
Where Fought: Europe
Initiator: Carlists
Outcome: France, Portugal, Spain, United Kingdom win
War Type: Civil for central control

Narrative: Young Isabella II succeeded to the Spanish throne on the death of her father, Ferdinand VII, though her mother, Queen Maria Cristina, served as regent. Ferdinand's brother, Don Carlos, and his "Carlist" followers revolted, claiming that only males could rule under Salic law. The "Cristinos," supporting Maria Cristina, formed an alliance with Great Britain, France, and Portugal, which intervened in this war. The Carlists won several battles in the north until 1835, when the tide turned. Government forces and the British and French won battles at Terapegui and Huesca. Don Carlos fled into exile in 1839, and the war ended in 1840. The fatalities were the result of both vicious fighting and disease.

Sources: Bollaert (1870); Carr (1982); Clarke (1906); Clodfelter (1992); Harbottle and Bruce

(1971); Holt (1967); Hume (1900); Phillips and Axelrod (2005); Urlanis (1960).

INTRA-STATE WAR #523:
The Second Murid War of 1834

Participants: Russia vs. Shamil
Dates: September 26, 1834, to October 27, 1834
Battle-Related Deaths: Russia—[ ]; Shamil—[ ]
Where Fought: Europe
Initiator: Shamil
Outcome: Conflict continues at below war level
War Type: Civil for local issues

Narrative: The Murids (Caucasus Muslims) had revolted against Russian rule in 1830, when they were defeated and their leader killed. In 1834 a new leader, Imam Shamil, emerged and led a long-term rebellion against the Russians. This phase of the war ended when the imam's guerrilla forces merely withdrew into the forest. Attacks continued at below war levels until the next war, intra-state war #530.

Source: Stone (2006).

INTRA-STATE WAR #525:
The Cabanos Revolt of 1835–1837

Participants: Brazil vs. Cabanos
Dates: January 6, 1835, to May [ ], 1837
Battle-Related Deaths: Brazil—[ ]; Cabanos—[ ]
Where Fought: W. Hemisphere
Initiator: Cabanos
Outcome: Brazil wins
War Type: Civil for local issues

Narrative: During the first several decades of independence (1822), the central government of Brazil had lost control over the provinces. Five major provincial rebellions occurred during the 1830s, though only three reached war level (#525, #526, and #531). These wars broke out in various parts of the country. The Cabanos Revolt (also referred to as the Cabanagem Rebellion), began in the Pará province along the Amazon as a war between the rebels and the local government. Brazilian troops recaptured the area, ending the war in 1837. However, the conflict also involved native resentment against the Portuguese ruling class, and violence between these two groups continued until 1840. Up to 20 percent of the province's population died due to disease or violence during this conflict.

Sources: Bethell (1989); Chasteen (1994); Clodfelter (2002); Worcester (1973).

INTRA-STATE WAR #526:

The Farroupilha War of 1835–1845

Participants: Brazil vs. Farrapos
Dates: September 19, 1835, to March 1, 1845
Battle-Related Deaths: Brazil—[ ]; Farrapos—[ ]
   (Total Combatant Deaths: 10,000)
Where Fought: W. Hemisphere
Initiator: Farrapos
Outcome: Brazil wins
War Type: Civil for local issues

Narrative: This is the second of the Brazilian revolts in the 1830s (see also intra-state wars #525 and #531), and it was the longest and deadliest. The Farrapos ("ragamuffins") were a rebel group in the province of Rio Grande do Sol, the southern province of Brazil, which lies not far from Uruguay. There were three phases of this decade-long war. Initially, the provincial president was overthrown. This war evolved into a drive for provincial independence, sometimes called the War of the Ragamuffins, even though many of those involved were well-to-do. The rebels then invaded a nearby province and established the Rio Grande Republic. With support from neighboring Uruguay, which was not yet a state system member, the rebels continued the fight against the Brazilian government until they were defeated in 1845.

Sources: Barman (1988); Bethell (1989); Chasteen (1994); Clodfelter (2002).

INTRA-STATE WAR #527:

The Texan War of 1835–1836

Participants: Mexico vs. Texas
Dates: October 1, 1835, to April 22, 1836
Battle-Related Deaths: Mexico—1,500;
   Texas—700
Where Fought: W. Hemisphere
Initiator: Texas
Outcome: Texas wins
War Type: Civil for local issues

Narrative: By the 1830s settlers from the United States had begun to populate Texas in far greater number than the native Mexicans (approximately 25,000 U.S. colonists and 5,000 U.S. slaves versus 7,800 Mexicans). Under the existing agreement with the Mexican government, the settlers had to give up slavery, convert to Roman Catholicism, and become Mexican citizens. These onerous provisions contributed to the Texan desire for independence from Mexico. The Texans rebelled, attacked the Mexican army, and seized the Alamo in December 1835. In 1836 the Texans lost at the Alamo but dramatically reversed their fortunes under Sam Houston at the Battle of San Jacinto, securing Texan independence.

Sources: Alessio Robles (1945–1946); Axelrod (2007); Bancroft (1885); Callcott (1936); Clodfelter (1992); Phillips and Axelrod (2005); Scheina (2003a); Stephenson (1921).

INTRA-STATE WAR #528:

The First Bosnian War of 1836–1837

Participants: Ottoman Empire vs. Bosnians
Dates: [ ]/[ ]/1836, to [ ]/[ ]/1837
Battle-Related Deaths: Ottoman Empire—[ ];
   Bosnians—[ ] (Total Combatant Deaths: 1,000)
Where Fought: Europe
Initiator: Bosnians
Outcome: Ottoman Empire wins
War Type: Civil for local issues

Narrative: Bosnia had been an independent country until the late fifteenth century, when it was conquered by the Ottoman Empire. The Bosnians revolted several times against the Turks in the nineteenth century. The Ottomans created the "kapetanate," who ruled Bosnia for the sultan. When the sultan's Tanzimat reforms abolished their position, several kapetans rebelled. The rebels were soon defeated by the Ottomans.

Sources: Palmer (1992); Richardson (1960a); von Sax (1913).

INTRA-STATE WAR #530:
The Third Murid War of 1836–1852

Participants: Russia vs. Shamil
Dates: July [ ], 1836, to [ ]/[ ]/1852
Battle-Related Deaths: Russia—15,000; Shamil—[ ]
Where Fought: Europe
Initiator: Shamil
Outcome: Russia wins
War Type: Civil for local issues

Narrative: Although the Murids (the Caucus Muslims) had been unsuccessful in their previous revolts against Russian rule (intra-state wars #511 and #523), they had continued their opposition. Conflict at war level broke out again in 1836, under the leadership of Imam Shamil. The Russians besieged and captured the rebel stronghold at Ahulgo in 1839. Fighting continued during the 1840s, with armies on both sides numbering tens of thousands, but with no conclusive victory. By the 1850s the Russians dispatched 200,000 troops, which finally defeated the Murid army in 1852; however, Murid attacks continued on a limited scale until 1859.

Sources: Clodfelter (2002); Stone (2006).

INTRA-STATE WAR #531:
The Sabinada Rebellion of 1837–1838

Participants: Brazil vs. Bahian Sabinada
Dates: November 7, 1837, to March 13, 1838

Battle-Related Deaths: Bahian Sabinada—1,200; Brazil—600
Where Fought: W. Hemisphere
Initiator: Bahian Sabinada
Outcome: Brazil wins
War Type: Civil for local issues

Narrative: The third of the revolts in Brazil (see also intra-state wars #525 and #526) took place in Bahia province, in northeastern Brazil. The war began in Salvador, Brazil's second-largest city, and was led by newspaper editor Dr. Sabino Barroso. The army joined the rebellion and seized the city, whereupon Bahia was declared to be independent. Brazilian forces intervened, besieged Salvador, and ultimately defeated the rebellion.

Sources: Assunção (1999); Barman (1988); Bethell (1989); Clodfelter (2002); Kraay (1992); Worcester (1973).

INTRA-STATE WAR #532:
The Druze Rebellion of 1837–1838

Participants: Egypt vs. Druze
Dates: September 27, 1837, to August 22, 1838
Battle-Related Deaths: Egypt—15,000; Druze—[ ]
Where Fought: Middle East
Initiator: Druze
Outcome: Egypt wins
War Type: Regional internal

Narrative: Opposition to Egyptian rule continued in greater Syria. As with the earlier war (see intra-state war #521), the precipitant was Egyptian policies to conscript young men into Egypt's army. In this instance the Druze revolted and then destroyed two Egyptian expeditions in early 1838. Egypt had an ally in the Christians in Lebanon, and with the aid of the Christian army, Egypt was able to defeat the Druze, though the Egyptians sustained heavy losses. Opposition to Egyptian domination would lead to a widespread uprising in 1840 (intra-state war #535).

Sources: Clodfelter (2002); Farah (2000); Kisirwani (1980).

INTRA-STATE WAR #533:
The Second Syrian War Phase 1 of 1839

Participants: Ottoman Empire vs. Egypt
Dates: June 10, 1839, to June 24, 1839
Battle-Related Deaths: Ottoman Empire—2,000; Egypti—1,000
Where Fought: Middle East
Initiator: Egypt
Outcome: Egypt wins
War Type: Civil for local issues

Narrative: Through its defeat of the Ottoman Empire in the First Syrian War (intra-state war #518), Egypt had gained control over greater Syria. In 1838 Egypt ended its tribute payments to the Ottoman sultan and declared Egyptian independence. Sultan Mahmud II thereupon prepared an army and invaded Syria in 1839. The campaign did not go well for the Ottomans: the army was defeated at Nezib, and the fleet sent to fight Egypt in fact surrendered in Alexandria, which marks the end of this phase of the war. The major European powers became alarmed and tried to mediate the conflict. Egypt's Muhammad Ali refused their offer. The British then invaded Syria, which marks the start of the second phase of this conflict (intra-state war #537). In the meantime, the Egyptians were confronted with another uprising in Lebanon (intra-state war #535).

Sources: Clodfelter (2002); Farah (2000); Jaques (2007); Phillips and Axelrod (2005); Polk (1963).

INTRA-STATE WAR #535:
The Lebanon Insurgency of 1840

Participants: Lebanese Maronites vs. Amir Bashir, Egypt
Dates: May 27, 1840, to July 13, 1840
Battle-Related Deaths: Lebanese Maronites— 3,500; Amir Bashir, Egypt—1,000
Where Fought: Middle East
Initiator: Amir Bashir, Egypt

Outcome: Amir Bashir, Egypt win
War Type: Regional internal

Narrative: Opposition to Egyptian rule in greater Syria had led to wars in 1834 (intra-state war #521) and 1837 (intra-state #532). In response to the Ottoman invasion of Syria (intra-state war #533), Egypt stationed a large army in Syria. Having suffered severe losses to the Druze armies in the 1837 war, Egypt proposed disarming the Druze in 1840. This policy united the Druze and the Maronite Christians, whose joint army began seizing coastal towns from the Egyptians. In June the Egyptians landed reinforcements, and with the aid of Egypt's ally, Emir Bashir of Sidon, they were able to defeat the rebels.

Sources: Cbe (1993); Farah (2000); Farah (1967); Hitti (1962); Moosa (1986); Polk (1963); Richardson (1960a).

INTRA-STATE WAR #536:
The First Colombian War of 1840–1842

Participants: Colombia vs. progressives
Dates: July 15, 1840, to July 15, 1842
Battle-Related Deaths: Colombia—[ ]; progressives—[ ] (Total Combatant Deaths: 4,000)
Where Fought: W. Hemisphere
Initiator: progressives
Outcome: Progressives win
War Type: Civil for central control

Narrative: For most of the 1830s, Colombia was generally peaceful, under moderately conservative leaders. In 1837 conservative president José Ignacio de Márquez took over four almost-abandoned convents, which triggered a pro-clerical rebellion by the staunch conservatives in 1839. This revolt was defeated, though fatalities were not at a war level. After crushing the conservative revolt, the moderate government faced a new challenge, this time launched by the progressives, who wanted to remove the president.

Government forces lost the initial battles but finally won victories in October 1840 and April 1841. The rebellion collapsed within months. The defeat of the progressives led to a conservative restoration in which the Catholic Church regained powers (such as Ecclesiastical courts) that had been taken away as part of the South American campaign for independence under Bolivar.

Sources: Henao and Arrubla (1938); Richardson (1960a); Scheina (2003a).

INTRA-STATE WAR #537:

The Second Syrian War Phase 2 of 1840

Participants: Ottoman Empire, United Kingdom vs. Egypt
Dates: September 9, 1840, to November 27, 1840
Battle-Related Deaths: Egypt—19,000; Ottoman Empire—8,000; United Kingdom—14
Where Fought: Middle East
Initiator: United Kingdom
Outcome: Ottoman Empire, United Kingdom win
War Type: Civil for local issues

Narrative: Egypt sought to become independent of the Ottoman Empire, and in response the Ottomans attacked Egyptian-controlled Syria in the first phase of this war (intra-state war #533). This war ended with the Egyptian defeat of Ottoman forces in 1839. Fearing Egypt's growing power, the major European powers tried to mediate the conflict, and when Egypt's Muhammad Ali refused their offer, the European allies essentially renewed the conflict in 1840. The allied fleet, manned mostly by the British though periodically involving the Ottomans as well, bombarded the Egyptians in Beirut and cities along the coast. By November the Egyptians had been defeated and had agreed to return Syria to Ottoman control. Many scholars consider the Second Syrian War as one war from June 1839 to November 1840; however, since there was no sustained combat for over a year, between June 24, 1839, and September 9, 1940, we code the two phases as separate wars.

Sources: Anderson (1952); Cattaui and Cattaui (1950); Clodfelter (2002); Dodwell (1931); Farah (1967); Jaques (2007); Jochmus (1883); Jordan (1923); von Moltke (1935); Phillips and Axelrod (2005); Polites (1931); Sabry (1930); Temperly (1964).

INTRA-STATE WAR #538:

The First Argentina War Phase 2 of 1841–1842

Participants: Argentina vs. Unitarios
Dates: January 1, 1841, to December 6, 1842
Battle-Related Deaths: Unitarios—3,000; Argentina—300
Where Fought: W. Hemisphere
Initiator: Unitarios
Outcome: Argentina wins
War Type: Civil for central control

Narrative: Argentina had been embroiled in a series of military conflicts over unity since independence. The larger of these conflicts were non-state wars (#1503, #1513, #1518, #1527), since Argentina was not a member of the interstate system until 1841. In the last of these wars (#1527), a coalition of Unitarios, who favored a strong central government, and Uruguayan Colorados declared war in 1839 against federalist Juan Manuel de Rosas, the caudillo of the province of Buenos Aires. The war was ongoing on January 1, 1841, when Argentina, with Rosas as president, became a member of the interstate system. Thus the conflict was transformed into this intra-state war (phase 2). The federalist forces won a major engagement at Famaillá in September 1841 and crushed the Unitarios at the battle of Arroyo Grande on December 6, 1842, ending the war.

Sources: Acevedo (1934); Best (1960); Cady (1929); Crow (1971); Jaques (2007); Kirkpatrick (1931); Munro (1942); Scheina (2003a).

INTRA-STATE WAR #540:
The Second Bosnian War of 1841

Participants: Ottoman Empire vs. Bosnians
Dates: [ ]/[ ]/1841, to [ ]/[ ]/1841
Battle-Related Deaths: Ottoman Empire—[ ];
Bosnians—[ ] (Total Combatant
Deaths: 2,000)
Where Fought: Europe
Initiator: Bosnians
Outcome: Ottoman Empire wins
War Type: Civil for local issues

Narrative: In the First Bosnian War (intra-state war #528), the Bosnian kapetanate (or local administrators) revolted against the Ottomans when their positions were abolished in 1836–1837. Wider unrest among Bosnian Muslims followed the Gülhane Decree, which offered equality to Christians and Jews. The Second Bosnian War was precipitated in Travnik, where the governor was driven out of the city in 1840. The following year the Ottomans sent an army to suppress the rebellion.

Sources: Palmer (1992); Richardson (1960a).

INTRA-STATE WAR #541:
The Triangular Revolt of 1841

Participants: Mexico vs. military
Dates: September 4, 1841, to October 6, 1841
Battle-Related Deaths: Mexico—[ ]; military—[ ]
Where Fought: W. Hemisphere
Initiator: military
Outcome: Military wins
War Type: Civil for central control

Narrative: Mexican president Anastasio Bustamante had been forced from office as a result of the First Mexican war (intra-state war #520). After the Mexican loss in the Texan war (intra-state war #527), Bustamante was recalled from exile and reelected as president in 1837. He was confronted by a number of regional rebellions. The most serious of these was launched in August 1841 by Gen. Mariano Paredes y Arrillaga, the commander of the garrison of Jalisco State. Several regional caudillos and military garrisons joined the rebellion. In response, Bustamante offered a compromise by which a tripartite executive would be created. When this offer was rejected, he led his army to confront the rebel armies led by General Paredes and Gen. Antonio López de Santa Anna. The rebel victory forced Bustamante to resign again.

Sources: Costeloe (1988).

INTRA-STATE WAR #542:
The Karbala Revolt of 1842–1843

Participants: Ottoman Empire vs. Karbala
Dates: December 19, 1842, to January 13, 1843
Battle-Related Deaths: Karbala—3,000; Ottoman
Empire—1,600
Where Fought: Middle East
Initiator: Ottoman Empire
Outcome: Ottoman Empire wins
War Type: Civil for local issues

Narrative: Ottoman sultan Mahmud II was determined to impose greater centralized control over the Ottoman Empire. After regaining control of Syria from Egypt in 1840 as a result of the Second Syrian War (intra-state war #537), the Ottomans were particularly eager to extend their influence and reestablish control over Iraq. They were confronted by the growing power of urban gangs, which had increasingly taken control of the Shiite holy city of Karbala. The gangs wanted to keep the Ottomans out of Karbala, and in 1842 an Ottoman expedition was launched to retake the city. The Ottoman army besieged the city for a month before breaching its fortifications. The Turkish victory led to the deaths of 15 percent of the city's population.

Sources: Cole and Momen (1986).

INTRA-STATE WAR #543:
The First Maronite-Druze War of 1845

Participants: Maronites vs. Druze
Dates: April 30, 1845, to May 31, 1845
Battle-Related Deaths: Maronites—2,000;
Druze—1,000
Where Fought: Middle East
Initiator: Maronites
Outcome: Druze win
War Type: Inter-communal

Narrative: A result of the Second Syrian War (intra-state war #537) was the re-establishment of Ottoman control over Syria. Although the Ottomans would have preferred strong centralized control of the region, opposition by the European powers led to a situation in which local leaders maintained their jurisdiction. This situation heightened the tensions between the Druze and Christian Maronite communities. The Maronites, encouraged by France, wanted to force the Druze to leave Mount Lebanon, and they attacked in 1845. The Druze counterattacked and defeated the Maronites. Ottoman troops did not intervene. The issue of creating a viable administrative structure in mixed Druze-Christian areas was not resolved by the war.

Sources: Cbe (1993); Churchill (1862); Farah (2000); Firro (1992); Hitti (1962); Richardson (1960a); Traboulsi (2007).

INTRA-STATE WAR #545:
The Mayan Caste War Phase 1 of 1847–1848

Participants: Mayans vs. Yucatán
Dates: January 15, 1847, to August 16, 1848
Battle-Related Deaths: Yucatán—1,800;
Mayans—[ ]
Where Fought: W. Hemisphere
Initiator: Mayans

Outcome: Transformed into an intra-state, civil war #553
War Type: Regional internal

Narrative: The Caste War, based largely on racial divisions, was one of the bloodiest in Mexican and Latin American history. It is divided here into two distinct phases and two wars due to the nature of the participants. At the beginning of 1847, the province of Yucatán declared its independence from Mexico. Although this independence was not recognized, the Yucatán was clearly operating on its own and not in the interests of the central government at this point. Thus the subsequent war is coded as a regional war, not a civil war. The Maya Indians, who suffered under a repressive caste system, rebelled against the ruling Yucatán Ladinos (of European background). The Mayans attacked settlements in the interior and advanced on the Yucatán capital of Mérida, before halting their offensive for the planting season. The Yucatán had been unable to defeat the Mayans, so it ended its pursuit of independence and appealed to the Mexican government for assistance. Mexican agreement and the sending of Mexican forces in August ended this regional war between two nonstate actors and transformed it into its second phase, a civil war (intra-state war #553).

Sources: Angel (1993); Clodfelter (2002); Scheina (2003a).

INTRA-STATE WAR #546:
The Second Carlist War of 1847–1849

Participants: Spain vs. Carlists
Dates: May 15, 1847, to May 1, 1849
Battle-Related Deaths: Carlists—7,000;
Spain—3,000
Where Fought: Europe
Initiator: Carlists
Outcome: Spain wins
War Type: Civil for central control

Narrative: The First Carlist War (intra-state war #522) in 1835 had involved Don Carlos and his "Carlist" followers trying to seize the throne of Spain from regent Maria Cristina, supported by the "Cristinos." Queen Isabella II ascended to the throne in 1843, prompting a second Carlist revolt, this time in the name of Don Carlos's son, Don Carlos II. The Second Carlist War began with guerrilla attacks, which later led to several major engagements with 50,000 government troops facing 10,000 Carlists. Don Carlos II was detained by the French and so never joined the war. Without him, the war ended with a Carlist defeat.

Sources: Bollaert (1870); Clarke (1906); Godechot (1971); Holt (1967); Phillips and Axelrod (2005); Smith (1965).

INTRA-STATE WAR #547:

The Second Two Sicilies War of 1848–1849

Participants: Two Sicilies vs. liberals
Dates: January 12, 1848, to May 15, 1849
Battle-Related Deaths: Two Sicilies—1,500; liberals—[ ]
Where Fought: Europe
Initiator: liberals
Outcome: Two Sicilies win
War Type: Civil for central control

Narrative: The revolutions of 1848, which involved liberal opposition to monarchical rule, hit many countries in Europe, including several states in Italy. In the Two Sicilies (consisting of Sicily and Naples), the revolt began in Sicily. When King Ferdinand was unable to get Austrian assistance, he agreed to a liberal constitution, which stopped the fighting. The liberals in Naples were also motivated to act, however, and fighting resumed. The revolutionary movement was ultimately defeated, and Sicily was reconquered in May 1849.

Sources: Clodfelter (1992); Godechot (1971); King (1899); Orsi (1914).

INTRA-STATE WAR #548:

The First Venezuelan War of 1848–1849

Participants: Venezuela vs. conservatives led by former president José Antonio Páez
Dates: February 4, 1848, to August 15, 1849
Battle-Related Deaths: Venezuela—1,500; Páez-led conservatives—[ ]
Where Fought: W. Hemisphere
Initiator: Páez-led conservatives
Outcome: Venezuela wins
War Type: Civil for central control

Narrative: José Antonio Páez was the most powerful caudillo to emerge from the Venezuelan wars of independence. He then influenced Venezuelan politics for decades. In 1847 Páez supported the semi-liberal presidency of Josè Tedeo Monagas; however, when Monagas supported an attack on the Congress, Páez abandoned this alliance and led a revolt. Other regional caudillos joined the fray on one side or the other. The conflict lasted until 1849, when the liberals and Monagas won the war. Monagas then dominated the country for over a decade, while Páez accepted exile in the United States in 1850.

Sources: Clodfelter (2002); Phillips and Axelrod (2005); Scheina (2003a).

INTRA-STATE WAR #550:

The Viennese Revolt of 1848

Participants: Austria vs. Viennese
Dates: March 13, 1848, to October 31, 1848
Battle-Related Deaths: Viennese—3,000; Austria—249
Where Fought: Europe
Initiator: Viennese
Outcome: Austria wins
War Type: Civil for central control

Narrative: The overthrow of Louis-Philippe in France led to liberal revolts in several other European states. In Vienna an urban uprising took place on March 13, 1848. The emperor fired the long-serving foreign minister, Prince Fürst von Metternich, and promised a liberal constitution. The government subsequently tried to stop the liberalization process by dissolving the Reichstag, but public outcry led the government to allow the legislature to reassemble. Meanwhile, Austria faced similar revolts in Milan and Hungary (intra-state wars #551 and #554). Further revolutionary activity in Vienna was brutally suppressed in October, ending the war. Ultimately, however, Emperor Ferdinand I succumbed to liberal pressures and abdicated in favor of his nephew Franz Joseph.

Sources: Bodart (1916); Cayley (1856); Clodfelter (2002); Droz (1957); Godechot (1971); Macartney (1968); Maurice (1887); Phillips and Axelrod (2005); Sorokin (1937).

INTRA-STATE WAR #551:
The Milan Five-Day Revolt of 1848

Participants: Austria vs. Milan
Dates: March 18, 1848, to March 23, 1848
Battle-Related Deaths: Austria—600; Milan—430
Where Fought: Europe
Initiator: Milan
Outcome: Transformed into inter-state war #10
War Type: Civil for local issues

Narrative: The 1848 liberal revolutionary movement spread from the Two Sicilies (intra-state war #547) to other parts of Italy. Milan was under the control of Austria and the Milanese revolted against the Austrian garrison. The revolt was successful in obtaining a brief period of independence for Milan, until Austria reasserted its control (see inter-state war #10).

Sources: Clodfelter (2002); Macartney (1968); Phillips and Axelrod (2005).

INTRA-STATE WAR #552:
The Second French Insurrection of 1848

Participants: France vs. Radicals
Dates: June 23, 1848, to June 26, 1848
Battle-Related Deaths: Radicals—1,600; France—1,200
Where Fought: Europe
Initiator: Radicals
Outcome: France wins
War Type: Civil for central control

Narrative: The liberal revolutionary movement of 1848 led to two rebellions in France, but only the latter qualified as a war. There was a general feeling that King Louis-Philippe's government had failed to solve the problems created by the 1846–1847 depression. Moderate Republicans and the Radicals instigated uprisings that ultimately toppled the king in February 1848, though there were insufficient fatalities for this to be considered a war. A Second Republic was declared, which satisfied the moderates, but it failed to really address workers' grievances. Thus the Radicals rebelled against the Republican government in June. The rebellion was brutally suppressed by the government.

Sources: Bodart (1916); Cayley (1856); Clodfelter (2002); Godechot (1971); Phillips and Axelrod (2005); Robertson (1952).

INTRA-STATE WAR #553:
The Mayan Caste War Phase 2 of 1848–1855

Participants: Mexico vs. Yucatán Maya
Dates: August 17, 1848, to March 4, 1855
Battle-Related Deaths: Mexico—[ ]; Yucatán Maya—[ ]

Where Fought: W. Hemisphere
Initiator: Mexico
Outcome: Mexico wins
War Type: Civil for local issues

Narrative: The is the second phase of the Mayan Caste War. The first phase (intra-state war #545) was a regional war in that it was a revolt of the Mayans against the Mexican province of Yucatán, which had tried to become independent from Mexico. After the Yucatán officials realized that they could not contend with the revolt, they asked for the assistance of the Mexican government and ended their move toward independence. When the Mexican government assented and sent troops to fight the Mayans, the war was thus transformed into a different category of war, this civil war of the central government against an internal armed group. Heavy fighting resumed late in 1848 and lasted for another seven years. The war essentially became stalemated, with battles being won by both sides, while fighting and disease decimated the population. Finally the Yucatán government declared that it had defeated the rebellion in 1855, thus ending this war. Limited fighting continued, however, for another ten years. The Yucatán also became involved in the Mexican Reform War of 1858 (intra-state war #561).

Sources: Angel (1997); Angel (1993); Bodart (1916); Cayley (1856); Clodfelter (1992); Godechot (1971); Hamnett (1999); Parkes (1960); Reed (2001); Robertson (1952); Scheina (2003a).

INTRA-STATE WAR #554:
The Hungarian War of 1848–1849

Participants: Austria, Russia vs. Hungary
Dates: September 9, 1848, to August 13, 1849
Battle-Related Deaths: Austria—46,000; Hungary—20,000; Russia—14,500
Where Fought: Europe
Initiator: Hungary
Outcome: Austria, Russia win
War Type: Civil for local issues

Narrative: The liberal European revolutions of 1848 also spread to Hungary. On March 3, 1848, Hungarian nationalist Louis Kossuth denounced the Hapsburg regime, and an independent Hungarian government was established. Initially Austria utilized a Croatian army in an unsuccessful attempt to suppress the rebellion. The Hungarian army repelled the invaders and advanced into Austria itself; however, the Austrian army, which had just defeated the Viennese revolt (intra-state war #550), was able to stop the Hungarian advance. In July 1849 the Russians intervened on the side of the Austrians, and the rebellion was defeated within a month after the Austrians victory over Hungarian forces at the Battle of Temesván.

Sources: Albrecht-Carrié (1958); Bodart (1916); Clodfelter (1992); Curtiss (1965); Headley (1852); Macartney (1968); Phillips and Axelrod (2005).

INTRA-STATE WAR #555:
The First Chilean War of 1851

Participants: Chile vs. liberals
Dates: September 5, 1851, to December 15, 1851
Battle-Related Deaths: liberals—2,500; Chile—1,500
Where Fought: W. Hemisphere
Initiator: liberals
Outcome: Chile wins
War Type: Civil for central control

Narrative: Chile, like most Latin American states, was dominated politically by the rivalry between conservative landowners and liberal commercial interests. The role of the Catholic Church was also disputed between the two sides. In Chile's case, the conservatives had controlled the country since independence. In 1850 the liberals believed they had a chance to win the presidency, but conservative control of the electoral machinery prevented this. In September 1851, the liberals rebelled in both the south and north of Chile. Former president Manuel Bulnes led the government forces opposed by liberal general José María de la Cruz, who was the losing candidate in 1850. After the major battle of the war, Loncomilla, at the end of November the government gradually defeated the liberals by mid-December. A general amnesty was declared, and a new civil code was written.

Sources: Bernstein (1965); Clodfelter (2002); Davis (1968); Richardson (1960a); Scheina (2003a); Williams et al. (1955).

INTRA-STATE WAR #556:

The First Turco-Montenegrin War of 1852–1853

Participants: Ottoman Empire vs. Montenegro, Hercegovina
Dates: December 2, 1852, to March 13, 1853
Battle-Related Deaths: Ottoman Empire—[ ]; Montenegro, Hercegovina—[ ] (Total Combatant Deaths: 6,500)
Where Fought: Europe
Initiator: Turkey
Outcome: Montenegro, Hercegovina win
War Type: Civil for local issues

Narrative: Montenegro followed other parts of the Ottoman Empire in trying to assert its independence (for instance, see the Bosnian wars, intra-state wars #528 and #540). This war was triggered when Daniela II, the prince-bishop of Montenegro, separated the offices of prince and bishop, creating a hereditary monarchy and thus violating his authority as a vassal of the Ottomans. The Turks sent troops but were forced to retreat after several losses. Austria put troops on the Bosnian border, and Russia added pressure for the Ottomans to withdraw. The Ottomans did withdraw from Montenegro in 1853; however, Montenegro's status was not resolved, leading to a second war in 1858 (intra-state war #562).

Sources: Clodfelter (1992); Frilley and Wlahovitj (1876); Gopcevic (1877); Kohn (1999); Markham

(1968); Palmer (1992); Phillips and Axelrod (2005); Pike (1967); Richardson (1960a).

INTRA-STATE WAR #557:

The First Peru War of 1853–1855

Participants: Peru vs. liberals
Dates: December 21, 1853, to January 7, 1855
Battle-Related Deaths: Peru—[ ]; liberals—[ ] (Total Combatant Deaths:—4,000)
Where Fought: W. Hemisphere
Initiator: liberals
Outcome: Liberals win
War Type: Civil for central control

Narrative: This war was precipitated by personal rivalries as well as controversy over the treatment of blacks and Indian descendents of the Incas. Raymon Castilla, Peru's president from 1846 to 1851, initiated a policy of trying to pay down the internal debt. His successor, José Rufino Echenique, had an administration noted for graft, and it paid numerous fraudulent claims for government compensation. This issue, along with resistance to a tax imposed on the Indians led to widespread uprisings fueled by the liberals. Despite early losses the rebel army advanced toward Lima, emancipating black slaves along the way. They defeated Echenique's forces at the battle of La Palma. Echenique fell from power, and Castilla returned as president in 1855.

Sources: Basadre (1940); Marett (1969); Markham (1968); Munro (1942); Pike (1967).

INTRA-STATE WAR #558:

The Puebla War of 1855–1856

Participants: Mexico vs. Puebla
Dates: December 11, 1855, to March 21, 1856
Battle-Related Deaths: Puebla—3,000; Mexico—600
Where Fought: W. Hemisphere
Initiator: Military
Outcome: Mexico wins
War Type: Civil for central control

Narrative: This war began as a conservative defense of religion and as a reaction against liberal measures that had been adopted in Mexico. The liberal Plan of Ayutla (1853–1855) led to the final overthrow of the venerable Gen. Antonio López de Santa Anna. Subsequent military reorganization plans attempted to decrease the power of the military and thus fostered a number of low-level military revolts. The government initially was able to defeat these with the national guard, but the rebellion continued to grow. The rebels established a base at Puebla, where they were ultimately defeated by an enlarged Mexican army. The government could thus continue the policies that characterized the liberal period known as La Reforma.

Sources: Broussard (1979); Hamnett (2001).

INTRA-STATE WAR #560:
The Second Peru War of 1856–1858

Participants: Peru vs. conservatives
Dates: October 31, 1856, to March 7, 1858
Battle-Related Deaths: Peru—[ ]; conservatives—[ ] (Total Combatant Deaths: 3,000)
Where Fought: W. Hemisphere
Initiator: conservatives
Outcome: Peru wins
War Type: Civil for central control

Narrative: Peruvian president Raymon Castilla returned to power in Peru for a second term in 1855 as a consequence of his victory in the first Peruvian civil war (intra-state war #557). Thus empowered, the parliamentary liberals launched a program of reforms, an essential component of which was to reduce the power of the Roman Catholic Church. The measures aroused a new conservative movement, and even President Castilla was unhappy with the proposed restrictions of presidential power. After the new constitution was adopted in 1856, the conservatives rose in revolt. The conservatives finally surrendered after an eight-month siege at Arequipa.

Even though the conservatives were defeated, an element of their program was achieved when Castilla disbanded the liberal assembly.

Sources: Basadre (1940); Marett (1969); Markham (1968); Munro (1942); Pike (1967).

INTRA-STATE WAR #561:
The Mexican Reform War of 1858–1861

Participants: Mexico vs. liberals
Dates: February 15, 1858, to January 1, 1861
Battle-Related Deaths: Mexico—[ ]; liberals—[ ] (Total Combatant Deaths: 8,000)
Where Fought: W. Hemisphere
Initiator: liberal
Outcome: Liberals win
War Type: Civil for central control

Narrative: The conservative challenge to the liberal military reforms in Mexico was defeated in 1856 (intra-state war #558). The reform movement continued, promulgating an 1857 constitution that challenged the power of the Roman Catholic Church. In response, the conservatives launched a revolution. They forced President Ignacio Comonfort to resign and installed Gen. Felix Zuloaga as president. The liberals created an alternative government at Veracruz under the leadership of Benito Juárez and launched a war against the conservatives. For the first two years the conservatives won the most battles, notably the battle of Ahualulco de los Piños, on October 29, 1858. The liberals, however, had some aid from the United States, and by 1860 the momentum of the conflict had turned in their favor. By January 1861 the conservatives had been defeated; Juárez assumed power in Mexico City on January 11, 1861. Conservative opposition remained, and the more reactionary among them sought the assistance of France's Napoleon III, which led to the Franco-Mexican War in 1862 (inter-state war #40).

Sources: Clodfelter (1992); Davis (1968); Hamnett (2001); Jensen (1953); Kohn (1999);

Meyer et al. (2003); Miller (1985); Richardson (1960a).

INTRA-STATE WAR #562:
The Second Turco-Montenegrin War of 1858–1859

Participants: Ottoman Empire vs. Montenegrins
Dates: May 4, 1858, to June 1, 1859
Battle-Related Deaths: Ottoman Empire—3,000;
    Montenegrins—1,400
Where Fought: Europe
Initiator: Montenegrins
Outcome: Montenegrins win
War Type: Civil for local issues

Narrative: Montenegro had gained limited autonomy from the Ottoman Empire as a result of the First Turco-Montenegrin War (intra-state war #556) in 1852 and pressure applied by Austria and Russia. Montenegro's ultimate status had not been determined by the war, and the great powers attempted to promote a settlement in 1857 by which Montenegro would gain additional territory but would still remain part of the Ottoman Empire. The Montenegrins rejected the settlement and launched an attack on Turkish forces in 1858 with the help of Hercegovina. The Montenegrins were victorious in forcing Turkish withdrawal, though Montenegro's status was still not determined; the two parties would go to war again in 1861 (intra-state war #575).

Sources: Clodfelter (1992); Frilley and Wlahovitj (1876); Gopcevic (1877); Roberts (2007); Stevenson (1971).

INTRA-STATE WAR #563:
The Second Venezuelan/Federalist War of 1859–1863

Participants: Venezuela vs. liberals
Dates: February 1, 1859, to May 23, 1863
Battle-Related Deaths: Venezuela—15,000;
    liberals—5,000

Where Fought: W. Hemisphere
Initiator: liberals
Outcome: Liberals win
War Type: Civil for central control

Narrative: Venezuela was ruled by the Monagas brothers from 1846. In 1854 they abolished slavery and in 1857 promoted a new constitution, which led to widespread opposition from both liberals and conservatives. The Monagas oligarchy was overthrown in 1858. The conservatives assumed power and a war erupted between the conservatives (also called the constitutionists) and the liberals (or federalists). The conservatives were initially successful. Their government changed hands a number of times until José Antonio Páez, who was a former president, came back from exile in 1861. The liberals continued to battle against his authoritarian repression until they were successful in overthrowing him in 1863.

Sources: Clodfelter (2002); Gilmore (1964); Munro (1942); Phillips and Axelrod (2005); Scheina (2003a); Stearns (2001); Williams et al. (1955); Wise (1951).

INTRA-STATE WAR #565:
The Second Colombian War of 1860–1861

Participants: Colombia vs. liberals
Dates: May 15, 1860, to July 18, 1861
Battle-Related Deaths: Colombia—[ ]; liberals—[ ]
    (Total Combatant Deaths: 2,500)
Where Fought: W. Hemisphere
Initiator: liberals
Outcome: Liberals win
War Type: Civil for central control

Narrative: During the nineteenth century, Colombian politics was dominated by the rivalry between the liberals, who promoted local government and the separation of church and state, and the conservatives, who favored a strong central government and preservation of rights for the

Roman Catholic Church. In 1858 conservative president Mariano Ospina promulgated a constitution that included some of the liberal principles. Consequently, the republic's provinces gradually became more independent, and when the central government tried to reassert control by bringing local militias under central control, civil war broke out. Four of the provinces declared independence and chose Gen. Tomas Cypriano de Mosquera, the liberal governor of Cauca province, to lead their army against the central government. Mosquera defeated the Colombian army on July 18, 1861, ending the war, though some fighting continued throughout the next year. Ospina was deposed and Mosquera declared the provisional president.

Sources: Clodfelter (2002); Henao and Arrubla (1938); Kohn (1999); Munro (1942); Phillips and Axelrod (2005); Richardson (1960a); Scheina (2003a).

INTRA-STATE WAR #566:

The Second Maronite-Druze War of 1860

Participants: Maronites vs. Druze
Dates: May 26, 1860, to July 12, 1860
Battle-Related Deaths: Maronites—8,000; Druze—1,500
Where Fought: Middle East
Initiator: Maronites
Outcome: Druze win
War Type: Inter-communal

Narrative: In 1845 the Druze had defeated the Maronites in a war over control of Mount Lebanon (intra-state war #543). Hostility remained between the two groups, and in 1860 they began to prepare for war. Although there is disagreement over who started the war, it appears that the Maronites declared war on May 21, 1860, and launched an attack on May 26. The Maronites had a larger army, but the Druze were successful, and their victories precipitated a large-scale massacre of Maronite civilians in Beirut and

Damascus. Initially, the Ottoman troops in the region refused to intervene. Consequently, France sent a military contingent to Beirut. Before the French disembarked, however, Ottoman reinforcements arrived and restored order.

Sources: Clodfelter (2002); Dau (1984); Farah (2000), Hitti (1962); Makdisi (2000); Moosa (1986); Palmer (1992); Richardson (1960a).

INTRA-STATE WAR #567:

The Taiping Rebellion Phase 2 of 1860–1866

Participants: China, United Kingdom vs. Taiping army
Dates: October 25, 1860, to February 9, 1866
Battle-Related Deaths: Taiping army—85,000; China—26,000; United Kingdom—25
Where Fought: Asia
Initiator: Taiping army
Outcome: China, United Kingdom win
War Type: Civil for central control

Narrative: The rebellion by the Taiping religious movement was fought for ten years as a non-state war (Taiping Rebellion Phase 1, war #1534). When China entered the interstate system in 1860, the rebellion was transformed into this intra-state war. By 1860 the Taiping capital of Nanking was surrounded by Manchu forces. The Taiping army broke the siege and resumed the offensive, advancing on Shanghai in 1862. Shanghai was defended by a foreign force, including British troops, which entered the war repulsing the Taiping attack. The Chinese imperial forces then went on the offensive, reconquering much of China. The Taiping army in Nanking was defeated in July 1864, and the remaining Taiping armies were defeated by February 1866.

Sources: Chu (1966); Clodfelter (2002); Elleman (2001); Franke (1970); Gregory (1959); Jen Yu-wen (1973); Lin-le (1866); Michael (1957); Pelissier (1963); Phillips and Axelrod (2005); Spielmann (1900); Teng (1963); Wilson (1868).

INTRA-STATE WAR #568:
The Second Nien Revolt of 1860–1868

Participants: China vs. Nien
Dates: October 25, 1860, to August 16, 1868
Battle-Related Deaths: China—[ ]; Nien—[ ]
  (Total Combatant Deaths: 75,000)
Where Fought: Asia
Initiator: Nien
Outcome: China wins
War Type: Civil for local issues

Narrative: The war of the Nien began in 1855 as a non-state war against local Han officials in Anhui and Hunan provinces in central China (non-state war #1539). The Nien briefly allied with the Taiping in their rebellion (non-state war #1534). The Nien war ended temporarily in 1858 when one of the Nien leaders defected to the growing imperial army. In 1860 the Nien renewed their war under new leadership, and since China became a member of the interstate system in 1860, the war is transformed into this intra-state war. The Nien posed a significant threat to the central government and were able to continue fighting for two more years after the government defeated the Taiping (intra-state war #567). The Nien utilized guerrilla warfare, frequently involving female soldiers. During the 1860s the major Nien forts were surrounded and reduced. In 1868 a 50,000-soldier Chinese army finally defeated the Nien.

Sources: Chiang (1954); Clodfelter (2002); Elleman (2001); Phillips and Axelrod (2005); Teng (1961).

INTRA-STATE WAR #570:
The Miao Revolt Phase 2 of 1860–1872

Participants: China vs. Miao
Dates: October 25, 1860, to May 1, 1872
Battle-Related Deaths: China—[ ]; Miao—[ ]
  (Total Combatant Deaths: 75,000)
Where Fought: Asia
Initiator: Miao
Outcome: China wins
War Type: Civil for local issues

Narrative: The Miao ethnic group lives in southwest China, particularly Guizhou province. In 1855, aided by the White Lotus Society, they rebelled against local Han officials (non-state war #1539). When China became a member of the interstate system in 1860, the war was transformed into this intra-state war. During the early 1860s the Miao made gains, while the imperial government focused on defeating the Taiping Rebellion (intra-state war #567). Many of the Miao were killed by disease, however. In 1866 the province of Hunan provided military assistance to Guizhou, leading to government victories. The Chinese became increasingly successful after their defeat of the Taipings in 1866, and within six years the Miao rebellion was brought to an end.

Sources: Clodfelter (2002); Jenks (1994); Teng (1961).

INTRA-STATE WAR #571:
The Panthay Rebellion Phase 2 of 1860–1872

Participants: China vs. Muslims (Hui)
Dates: October 25, 1860, to December 26, 1872
Battle-Related Deaths: China—[ ]; Muslims (Hui)—[ ]
Where Fought: Asia
Initiator: Muslims
Outcome: China wins
War Type: Civil for local issues

Narrative: This war began in 1856 as a non-state armed conflict between Muslims and Han officials in the Chinese province of Yunnan (non-state war #1541). The non-state war was transformed into this civil war when China became a member of the interstate system in 1860. The rebels created an independent Panthay (or Pingnan) kingdom that controlled half of Yunnan by 1868. After the Chinese defeated the Taipings (intra-state war #567), they named a new governor of Yunnan and began to devote more resources to defeating the Panthay. In response the Panthay unsuccessfully sought British assistance. Imperial troops captured the Panthay capital, ending the rebellion in 1872.

Sources: Atwill (2003); Elleman (2001).

INTRA-STATE WAR #572:
The U.S. Civil War of 1861–1865

Participants: United States vs. Confederacy
Dates: April 10, 1861, to April 9, 1865
Battle-Related Deaths: United States—360,000; Confederacy—258,000
Where Fought: W. Hemisphere
Initiator: Confederacy
Outcome: United States wins
War Type: Civil for local issues

Narrative: The United States was divided over the slavery issue, and the issue was polarized by events in the 1850s, including the Dred Scott decision and John Brown's raid on Harpers Ferry. The Republican Party, which emerged as the party opposed to the spread of slavery, won the 1860 presidential election. The Southern states refused to accept Republican Abraham Lincoln as their president and, beginning with South Carolina, began to secede from the United States, creating the Confederate States of America. The war began with an attack by the Confederate army on the federal Fort Sumter in Charleston, South Carolina. In the early years the North suffered from poor military leadership and the Confederates won victories at Bull Run, the Shenandoah Valley, and Chancellorsville, before being turned back at Gettysburg. Northern economic superiority gradually wore down the South, which ultimately suffered defeat through a war of attrition.

Sources: Bodart (1916); Carrere (1972); Clodfelter (1992); Dumas and Vedel-Peterson (1923); Morris (1970).

INTRA-STATE WAR #573:
The Third Buenos Aires War of 1861

Participants: Argentina vs. Buenos Aires
Dates: August 20, 1861, to December 2, 1861
Battle-Related Deaths: Argentina—500; Buenos Aires—500
Where Fought: W. Hemisphere
Initiator: Buenos Aires
Outcome: Buenos Aires wins
War Type: Civil for local issues

Narrative: The First Buenos Aires War was a non-state war (#1503) between the independent entity of Buenos Aires and the united provinces of Argentina in 1820. Buenos Aires remained independent, while Argentina became a member of the interstate system in 1841. Fighting at below war levels took place between Buenos Aires and Argentina in 1852, after which Buenos Aires maintained its independence. However, a second war in 1859 (extra-state war #351) led to the defeat of Buenos Aires and its incorporation into Argentina. A difference of opinion remained over whether Buenos Aires (favored by the centralists) or the provinces (favored by the federalists) would dominate Argentina. This civil war started when Buenos Aires, under the leadership of Bartolomé Mitre, sent its forces against federalist Argentina. At the battle of Pavón, the Buenos Aires army was victorious. Mitre then formed a new national government, and the capital was moved to Buenos Aires.

Sources: Bunkley (1950); Clodfelter (2002); Jaques (2007); Kohn (1999); Phillips and Axelrod (2005); Scheina (2003a); Scobie (1955).

INTRA-STATE WAR #575:
The Third Turco-Montenegrin War of 1861–1862

Participants: Turkey vs. Montenegro
Dates: December [ ], 1861, to August 31, 1862
Battle-Related Deaths: Ottoman Empire—[ ]; Montenegro—[ ] (Total Combatant Deaths: 3,500)

Where Fought: Europe
Initiator: Ottoman Empire
Outcome: Compromise
War Type: Civil for local issues

Narrative: As with the two preceding wars (intra-state wars #556 and #562), this war involved Montenegro's desire for independence from the Ottoman Empire and the Ottoman's desire to reassert control. Montenegro's status was still undetermined, though the Ottomans had been forced to withdraw, partially owing to great power pressure. When Montenegrin leader Danilo II was assassinated in 1860, the Ottoman Empire took advantage of the ensuing disorder to try to reassert its control. The Ottomans quickly occupied most of Montenegro, but they were unable to capture the capital. Montenegro's status would again become an issue in the revolts in 1875 (intra-state war #601).

Sources: Clessold (1966); Clodfelter (1992); Kohn (1999); Phillips and Axelrod (2005); Richardson (1960a).

INTRA-STATE WAR #576:
The Tungan Rebellion of 1862–1873

Participants: China vs. Muslims in Sinkiang
Dates: May [ ], 1862, to October 24, 1873
Battle-Related Deaths: China—[ ]; Muslims in Sinkiang—[ ]
Where Fought: Asia
Initiator: Muslims in Sinkiang
Outcome: China wins
War Type: Civil for local issues

Narrative: China is considered to have become a member of the interstate system in 1860, at which time it was involved in four major rebellions (intra-state wars #567, #568, #570, and #571). The Taiping religious revolt (non-state war #1534 and intra-state war #567) was the most significant of these, and it sparked several other rebellions, including this one by the Tungan Muslims in northwest China. The Muslims, and particularly a militant group called the Xinjiao, led by Ma Hualong, rebelled in 1862 and by 1864 controlled most of Shaanxi and Gansu provinces. The central Chinese government launched a major offensive against the Tungan in 1867 with an army that soon numbered 100,000 soldiers. Initially the Tungan in Shaanxi were defeated or fled to Gansu. The Chinese continued their advance, and finally in 1873 the last Muslim stronghold of Suzhou was captured and the remaining Muslim troops were executed.

Sources: Elleman (2001); Lipman (1984).

INTRA-STATE WAR #577:
The Sioux–Minnesota War of 1862

Participants: Santee Sioux vs. settlers, militia
Dates: August 17, 1862, to September 26, 1862
Battle-Related Deaths: settlers, militia—851; Santee Sioux—217
Where Fought: W. Hemisphere
Initiator: Santee Sioux
Outcome: Settlers, militia win
War Type: Regional internal

Narrative: The Santee Sioux Indians in Minnesota felt themselves threatened by the growing influx of European settlers. In 1862 a crop failure made the Sioux increasingly dependent on rations from the United States government, and when these were not forthcoming, the Sioux began attacking the settlements. The local militia, reinforced by the Minnesota infantry, met the Sioux in several battles, finally defeating them at the Battle of Wood Lake. Although the uprising by the Santee Sioux was over, warfare between the United States and other Sioux tribes continued, but at below war levels. This war is coded as a regional war and not a civil war, because the fighting was done by the local militia and Minnesota troops rather than by the U.S. government. ,

Sources: Axelrod (2007); Clodfelter (1992); Kessel and Wooster (2005); Richardson (1960a).

INTRA-STATE WAR #578:
The Bolivian-Pérez Rebellion of 1862

Participants: Bolivia vs. forces of Gregorio Pérez
Date: September 15, 1862
Battle-Related Deaths: Boliva—[ ]; forces of Gregorio Pérez—[ ] (Total Combatant Deaths: 1,000)
Where Fought: W. Hemisphere
Initiator: forces of Gregorio Pérez
Outcome: Bolivia wins
War Type: Civil for central control

Narrative: Bolivia is a country about which it used to be said that there had been more rebellions than years of independence. That adage seemed true during the middle of the nineteenth century, when Bolivia experienced a number of rebellions, though most did not reach war levels. Gen. José María de Achá had come to power in a coup in 1861, and in March 1862, Gen. Gregorio Pérez had helped him suppress a further rebellion. By September 1862, however, General Pérez had decided to rebel. The Bolivian government forces defeated the rebels in a one-day battle.

Source: Scheina (2003a).

INTRA-STATE WAR #580:
The Second Polish War of 1863–1864

Participants: Russia vs. Poles
Dates: January 22, 1863, to April 19, 1864
Battle-Related Deaths: Russia—10,000; Poles—6,500
Where Fought: Europe
Initiator: Poles
Outcome: Russia wins
War Type: Civil for local issues

Narrative: The once-independent entity of Poland had been partitioned among Russia, Austria, and Prussia, with Russia gaining the largest portion. Although Poland initially had a degree of independence within the empire, it was lost as a result of the first Polish rebellion (intra-state war #517). After coming to the Russian throne in 1856, Czar Alexander attempted to develop a better relationship with the Poles, but his limited reforms failed to dampen the Polish desire for independence. Marquis Aleksander Wielopolski, the local administrator in Poland, tried to force Polish youth into the army, and this led to open rebellion in January 1863. The Poles conducted guerrilla warfare against the numerically superior Russian forces for over a year; however, the rebellion was ultimately suppressed. Poland lost all elements of self-government, and Russia implemented a strict policy of Russification.

Sources: Clodfelter (1992); Edwards (1865); Florinsky (1953); Leslie (1963); Phillips and Axelrod (2005); Reddaway (1941).

INTRA-STATE WAR #581:
The Second Argentina War of 1863

Participants: Argentina vs. Montoneros
Dates: April 2, 1863, to November 12, 1863
Battle-Related Deaths: Argentina—[ ]; Montoneros—[ ] (Total Combatant Deaths: 2,500)
Where Fought: W. Hemisphere
Initiator: Montoneros
Outcome: Argentina wins
War Type: Civil for central control

Narrative: Argentina had faced a series of wars for control of the country. For example, in 1841 (intra-state war #538), the federalists, who favored provincial control, defeated the unitarians, who preferred a centralized government. In 1861 (intra-state war #573), however, Buenos Aires and Gen. Bartolomé Mitre defeated the federalist government and established a united Argentina under Buenos Aires control. The constitution was then amended to permit central government intervention in the provinces.

The leftist Montoneros opposed such a concentration of power and launched a rebellion under the leadership of Angel Vicente Peñaloza, a caudillo of La Rioja province. Peñaloza was able to capture the city of Córdoba but was ultimately defeated by government forces. The issue of the degree of governmental control was unresolved and would lead to war again in three years (intra-state war #586).

Sources: Best (1960); Kirkpatrick (1931); McLynn (1980).

INTRA-STATE WAR #582:
The Xinjiang Muslim Revolt of 1864–1871

Participants: China, Russia vs. Muslims
Dates: July [ ], 1864, to July 3, 1871
Battle-Related Deaths: China—[ ]; Muslims—[ ]; Russia—[ ]
Where Fought: Asia
Initiator: Muslims
Outcome: Muslims win
War Type: Civil for local issues

Narrative: Xinjiang is the largest province in northwest China (north of Tibet). It was the site of several non-state wars between China and Muslims of Central Asia (wars #1508, #1515, #1533, #1543). In this instance three armies of Muslim warriors, under the overarching leadership of Yakub Beg, launched a war in order to drive the Ch'ing out of the province and to create an independent Muslim state. The Muslims were successful in gaining control of much of Xinjiang. Russia intervened in the war in 1871 against the Muslims, and its capture of the city of Ili marked the end of the fighting. The Chinese government was occupied with other rebellions at the time, and, therefore, fighting did not resume until 1876 (intra-state war #603).

Sources: Clodfelter (1992); Elleman (2001); Kohn (1999); Phillips and Axelrod (2005).

INTRA-STATE WAR #583:
The First Cretan War of 1866–1867

Participants: Ottoman Empire vs. Cretans
Dates: May 29, 1866, to February 22, 1867
Battle-Related Deaths: Ottoman Empire—[ ]; Cretans—[ ] (Total Combatant Deaths: 10,000)
Where Fought: Europe
Initiator: Cretans
Outcome: Ottoman Empire wins
War Type: Civil for local issues

Narrative: Crete, which is the southernmost island of Greece, had long suffered under Ottoman attempts to suppress Christianity. In 1858 the Porte had promised to institute several reforms, the most important of which would have given Christianity equal standing with Islam. By 1866, however, this had not been done, and many Cretans rose in revolt, seeking independence or unity with Greece. Initially the Cretans were successful in defeating the Ottoman garrison of Turkish and Egyptian soldiers; however, reinforcements arrived from the Turkish mainland, and they soon defeated the rebellion.

Sources: Clodfelter (1992); Florinsky (1953); Gerolymatos (2002); Phillips and Axelrod (2005); Williams (1907).

INTRA-STATE WAR #585:
The Yellow Cliff Revolt of 1866

Participants: China vs. Zhang Jizhong's followers
Dates: October [ ], 1866, to October [ ], 1866
Battle-Related Deaths: China—[ ]; Zhang Jizhong's followers—[ ]
Where Fought: Asia
Initiator: Zhang Jizhong's followers
Outcome: China wins
War Type: Civil for local issues

Narrative: Throughout the mid-nineteenth century, revolts flared in many parts of China. One of the lesser known is called the Yellow Cliff

Revolt. Zhang Jizhong had established a religious community, known as Taizhou, in a valley surrounded by yellow cliffs in the eastern province of Shandong. Zhang sought to protect his community from the ravages of the Nien war (intra-state war #568). When a local government official sent an investigative mission to Taizhou, it was attacked, starting this war. The government ordered a full-scale invasion of the community. Thousands died in the battle and by falling from the cliffs. In the end, two hundred disciples, along with Zhang Jizhong, immolated themselves rather than be captured.

Source: Perry and Chang (1980).

INTRA-STATE WAR #586:
The Third Argentina War of 1866–1867

Participants: Argentina vs. Montoneros
Dates: December 15, 1866, to October 15, 1867
Battle-Related Deaths: Argentina—[ ];
    Montoneros—[ ] (Total Combatant
    Deaths: 2,500)
Where Fought: W. Hemisphere
Initiator: Montoneros
Outcome: Argentina wins
War Type: Civil for central control

Narrative: The Montonero leftists were opposed to the centralist constitution for Argentina that had been promoted by President Bartolomé Mitre. In 1863 the Montoneros had launched an unsuccessful rebellion from La Rioja province (intra-state war #581). Subsequently, Argentina had become involved in the Paraguayan, or Lopez, War (inter-state war #49). The war meant increased hardships for the gauchos, and anti-war sentiments fueled a second Montonero rebellion in 1866. As in the earlier war, the rebellion began in La Rioja, this time led by Felipe Varela. In this war, however, five other provinces joined the revolt, and Varela received assistance from Chile and Brazil. Nevertheless, this war too ended in a government victory.

Sources: Best (1960); Clodfelter (2002); Kirkpatrick (1931).

INTRA-STATE WAR #587:
The Queretaro War of 1867

Participants: Mexico vs. liberals
Dates: February 6, 1867, to May 14, 1867
Battle-Related Deaths: Mexico—1,500;
    liberals—1,000
Where Fought: W. Hemisphere
Initiator: liberals
Outcome: Liberals win
War Type: Civil for central control

Narrative: This is a brief war that takes place after the end of the Franco-Mexican War (inter-state war #40). That war was the result of France's desire to expand its influence in Mexico. The French prevailed in the war and installed Austrian archduke Maximilian as emperor of Mexico. Fighting between the Mexican and French armies continued until the French withdrawal, which was completed by February 5, 1867. With the French troops gone, the inter-state war ended and the remaining fighting was transformed into this civil war between Maximilian's troops and those of the liberal government. The major battle took place at Querétaro, where imperial troops were surrounded by the Mexican Republicans in March. Maximilian was unable to regain support from France, and Querétaro fell after a two-month siege. Maximilian was captured and executed on June 19, 1867.

Sources: Clodfelter (1992); Gilmore (1964); Hamnett (2001); Jaques (2007); Rondon Marquez (1944).

INTRA-STATE WAR #588:
The Meiji Restoration of 1868

Participants: Japan vs. Tokugawa
Dates: January 3, 1868, to July 4, 1868
Battle-Related Deaths: Japan—[ ]; Tokugawa—[ ]
    (Total Combatant Deaths: 3,000)

Where Fought: Asia
Initiator: Japan
Outcome: Japan wins
War Type: Civil for central control

Narrative: Japan had been ruled by the Tokugawa shogunate since the early seventeenth century. By the mid-nineteenth century, the Shogunate was being weakened both by internal challengers and by pressure from Western countries (see the Shimonoseki War in 1863–1864, extra-state war #356). Some of the Japanese nobles wanted to remove the shogun and restore the power of the emperor. In 1867 the shogun resigned, and on January 3, 1868, forces of several of the daimyo (or local semifeudal units) seized the imperial capital of Kyoto from the Tokugawa troops. This new imperial army began a campaign to defeat the remaining Tokugawa forces. Edo (now Tokyo) was captured, and the remaining Tokugawa were defeated in a battle nearby on July 4, 1868.

Sources: Clodfelter (1992); Craig (1961); Fairbank et al. (1960); Hall (1968); Phillips and Axelrod (2005); Richardson (1960a).

INTRA-STATE WAR #590:
The Third Venezuelan War of 1868–1871

Participants: Venezuela vs. conservatives
Dates: January 11, 1868, to January 7, 1871
Battle-Related Deaths: Venezuela—[ ]; conservatives—[ ] (Total Combatant Deaths: 3,000)
Where Fought: W. Hemisphere
Initiator: conservatives
Outcome: Conservatives win
War Type: Civil for central control

Narrative: Like many Latin American states, Venezuela throughout the nineteenth century suffered through episodes of liberal-conservative fighting, and violent uprisings by regional caudillos (see intra-state wars #548 and #563). At the end of the last war, in 1863, the federalists

(liberals) had come to power, and in this war, sometimes called the Blue Revolution, federalist president Ezequiel Bruzual faced a rebellion by the conservatives led by José Tadeo Monagas. The war had two phases, and the period in-between, from August 1868 to August 1869, is coded as a break in the war. In the first phase Bruzual was defeated and Monagas became president. Monagas died after a short period and was succeeded by his son. In the second phase the federalists, under Gen. Antonio Guzmán Blanco, renewed the fighting and ultimately overthrew Monagas in 1870, though sporadic fighting continued till the following year.

Sources: Gilmore (1964); Phillips and Axelrod (2005); Rondon Marquez (1944); Scheina (2003a).

INTRA-STATE WAR #591:
The Spanish Liberals War of 1868

Participants: Spain vs. liberals
Dates: September 18, 1868, to September 29, 1868
Battle-Related Deaths: Spain—[ ]; liberals—[ ] (Total Combatant Deaths: 1,600)
Where Fought: Europe
Initiator: liberals
Outcome: Liberals win
War Type: Civil for central control

Narrative: Queen Isabella II had become increasingly autocratic, which had led some of her ministers to try to oust her in July 1868. The coup attempt failed, but opposition to her reign continued. A revolutionary proclamation was issued, and rebels within the navy seized Cádiz on September 18, 1868. The rebellion spread, with uprisings occurring throughout Spain. The queen returned from a trip to France in time to see the Spanish Royal Army defeated by the rebels in the battle of Alcolea, near Cordóba on September 28, 1868. Isabella was deposed the next day, ending the war, and fled back to France.

Sources: Bollaert (1870); Carr (1982); Clarke (1906); Phillips and Axelrod (2005); Sorokin (1937).

INTRA-STATE WAR #592:
The Guerre des Cacos of 1869

Participants: Haiti vs. black peasants
Dates: February [ ], 1869, to December 18, 1869
Battle-Related Deaths: Haiti—[ ]; black
   peasants—[ ]
Where Fought: W. Hemisphere
Initiator: black peasants
Outcome: Black peasants win
War Type: Civil for central control

Narrative: Haiti was the first Latin American country to win its independence, from France in 1804. Soon after gaining its independence, Haiti was divided into a black-controlled north and a mulatto-dominated south. Although the two parts were later united, hostility remained between the blacks and mulattoes. Subsequently, Haiti suffered from numerous coups and revolts, many related to racial issues between the black peasants and the government, which was controlled by the mulattos. One of these occurred in 1869, when a revolt by black peasants, known as cacos, precipitated widespread uprisings against the government. The government unsuccessfully battled two rebel armies, one in the north, under the leadership of Jean Nissage-Saget, and one in the south. Finally the rebels captured the capital of Port-au-Prince and installed Nissage-Saget as president.

Source: Clodfelter (2002).

INTRA-STATE WAR #593:
The Fourth Argentina War of 1870–1871

Participants: Argentina vs. Entre Rios province
Dates: May 20, 1870, to March 13, 1871
Battle-Related Deaths: Argentina—[ ]; Entre Rios
   province—[ ] (Total Combatant Deaths: 1,500)
Where Fought: W. Hemisphere
Initiator: Entre Rios province
Outcome: Argentina wins
War Type: Civil for local issues

Narrative: The second and third civil wars in Argentina (intra-state wars #581 and #586) had involved rebellions by the leftist Montoneros, originating in La Rioja province. Both of these revolts had been suppressed by the government. In this war the rebellion began in Entre Rios province. The government sent forces to reassert its control, and again the Argentine government triumphed over a regional caudillo.

Sources: Best (1960); Clodfelter (2002); Phillips and Axelrod (2005).

INTRA-STATE WAR #595:
The Bolivia-Criollos War of 1870–1871

Participants: Bolivia vs. *criollos*
Dates: November 24, 1870, to January 15, 1871
Battle-Related Deaths: Bolivia—[ ]; *criollos*—[ ]
   (Total Combatant Deaths: 1,087)
Where Fought: W. Hemisphere
Initiator: *criollos*
Outcome: *Criollos* win
War Type: Civil for central control

Narrative: In 1865 Gen. Mariano Melgarejo overthrew President Manuel Belzú, and established an increasingly repressive regime. This prompted a number of rebellions, though the one that reached war levels occurred in 1870. In November a group of *criollos* (native-born Bolivians of Spanish descent) allied with Col. Hilarión Daza and persuaded elements within the army to rebel. Despite initial losses the rebels finally prevailed and Melgarejo fled into Patagonia.

Source: Scheina (2003a).

INTRA-STATE WAR #596:
The Paris Commune War of 1871

Participants: France vs. Communards
Dates: April 2, 1871, to May 29, 1871

Battle-Related Deaths: Communards—25,000; France—879
Where Fought: Europe
Initiator: Communards
Outcome: France wins
War Type: Civil for central control

Narrative: France's defeat in the Franco-Prussian War (inter-state war #58), which ended on February 26, 1871, led to the end of the reign of Emperor Napoleon III and the creation of the Third French Republic. Refusing to accept the terms of the peace treaty negotiated by the monarchist Assembly, leading French dignitaries organized an independent republican French government called the Commune of Paris. The Communard troops occupied the streets of Paris, leading the French government to send an army against the Commune. Thousands were killed in combat as well as in massacres, before the Communards were finally overwhelmed. A conservative republican government, representing neither Napoleon's antirepublican forces nor the radical Communards, resulted.

Sources: Bodart (1916); Carrere (1972); Clodfelter (1992); Phillips and Axelrod (2005); Richardson (1960a); Sorokin (1937); Urlanis (1960).

INTRA-STATE WAR #597:
The Third Carlist War of 1872–1876

Participants: Spain vs. Carlists
Dates: April 20, 1872, to February 20, 1876
Battle-Related Deaths: Carlists—43,000; Spain—7,000
Where Fought: Europe
Initiator: Carlists
Outcome: Spain wins
War Type: Civil for central control

Narrative: After Queen Isabella was overthrown in intra-state war #591, Duke Amadeus was elected king. The Carlists, who had supported claims to the throne by the family of Don Carlos in two earlier rebellions (intra-state wars #522 and #546), rose again in revolt, this time in support of Don Carlos III. Opposition forced Amadeus to abdicate in 1873, and Spain's first republic was proclaimed; however, the Carlists continued their rebellion, and with support of the Basques they seized power in the north. The continuing warfare led to the collapse of the republic, which was replaced by a military dictatorship. Ultimately, the Bourbon monarchy was restored under Isabella's son, Alfonso XII. His army was finally able to defeat the Carlists in 1876, and Don Carlos fled to France.

Sources: Clarke (1906); Clodfelter (1992); Harbottle and Bruce (1971); Holt (1967); Phillips and Axelrod (2005); Richardson (1960a); Sorokin (1937).

INTRA-STATE WAR #598:
The Catonalist Uprising of 1874–1875

Participants: Spain vs. rebel cities (cantons)
Dates: [ ]/[ ]/1874, to January [ ], 1875
Battle-Related Deaths: Spain—[ ]; rebel cities (cantons)—[ ] (Total Combatant Deaths: 2,000)
Where Fought: Europe
Initiator: rebel cities (cantons)
Outcome: Spain wins
War Type: Civil for local issues

Narrative: While Spain was in the midst of the Third Carlist War (intra-state war #597), it was also confronted by a rebellion in many of its cities that was led by leftist social revolutionaries. Cities such as Valencia, Seville, and Cartagena declared themselves to be independent and created governments to implement social reforms. The Spanish government sent troops to reassert its control. The cities did not create a united front, and though they individually engaged in heavy fighting, the government was able to conquer them one by one. The rebellion ended with the defeat of Cartagena, which required a long siege and a naval blockade.

Source: Clodfelter (2002).

INTRA-STATE WAR #600:
The Fifth Argentina War of 1874

Participants: Argentina vs. Mitre-led rebels
Dates: September [ ], 1874, to November 6, 1874
Battle-Related Deaths: Argentina—[ ]; Mitre-led rebels—[ ] (Total Combatant Deaths: 1,000)
Where Fought: W. Hemisphere
Initiator: Mitre-led rebels
Outcome: Argentina wins
War Type: Civil for central control

Narrative: Liberal Bartolomé Mitre had ruled Argentina from 1862 to 1868, when he lost the election to Domingo Faustino Sarmiento. Although Sarmiento was one of the famous reformers in South American history, he had been an ineffective leader. Mitre ran for the presidency again in 1874 and lost to Nicolás Avellaneda in what Mitre claimed was a rigged election. Mitre immediately led a rebellion. Federal troops defeated the rebellion at Buenos Aires on November 6, 1874, and forced Mitre to surrender, ending his contention for national domination.

Sources: Herring (1966); Kohn (1999); Phillips and Axelrod (2005).

INTRA-STATE WAR #601:
The Bosnia and Bulgaria Revolt of 1875–1876

Participants: Ottoman Empire vs. Bosnia, Bulgaria
Dates: June 30, 1875, to June 29, 1876
Battle-Related Deaths: Ottoman Empire—6,000; Bosnia, Bulgaria—3,000
Where Fought: Europe
Initiator: Bosnia, Bulgaria
Outcome: Transformed into extra-state war #373
War Type: Civil for local issues

Narrative: The Balkan provinces of the Ottoman Empire were restive under Ottoman rule, and wars for independence had broken out in Greece (intra-state war #506), Albania (intra-state war #512), Bosnia (intra-state wars #528 and #540), Montenegro (intra-state wars #556, #562, and #575), and Crete (intra-state war #583). Much of this unrest culminated in 1875, when Christian peasants in Hercegovina rebelled against Ottoman rule. The revolt quickly spread to Bosnia and then, in spring 1876, to Bulgaria. There, a riot in Salonkia led to the massacre of Christians by Turkish irregulars, which aroused sympathy for the rebels in Europe. Ottoman efforts to suppress the rebellion led the rebels to appeal to Serbia for assistance. At this point Serbia was an independent autonomous entity though not a member of the interstate system. Thus when Serbia declared war on the Ottoman Empire on June 30, 1876, and took over the bulk of the fighting from the rebellious provinces, this civil war ended (as of the preceeding day) and the fighting was transformed into extra-state war #373. That war lasted less than a year, until Russia intervened and the war was transformed again into the Second Russo-Turkish War (interstate war #61). The Treaty of Berlin at the end of that war recognized Montenegro's independence and gave some autonomy to Bulgaria.

Sources: Allen and Muratoff (1953); Clodfelter (2002); Dumas and Vedel-Peterson (1923); Finkel (2005); Florinsky (1953); Gerolymatos (2002); Hentea (2007); Hozier (1878); Langer (1931); *London Times* (1875–1876); MacKenzie (1967); Palmer (1992); Palmer (1992); Phillips and Axelrod (2005); Richardson (1960a); Schafer (1995); Seton-Watson (1952); von Sax (1913); Stavrianos (1958); Sumner (1937); von Sternegg (1866–1889); Williams (1907).

INTRA-STATE WAR #602:
The Diaz Revolt of 1876

Participants: Mexico vs. rebels
Dates: March [ ], 1876, to November 23, 1876
Battle-Related Deaths: Mexico—1,900; rebels—[ ]
Where Fought: W. Hemisphere
Initiator: rebels

Outcome: Rebels win
War Type: Civil for central control

Narrative: In the Mexican presidential election of 1871, liberal president Benito Juárez defeated two contenders, including Porfirio Díaz, who had supported Juárez in the recent war against the French (inter-state war #40). Seeing the election results as fraudulent, Díaz staged the unsuccessful La Noria insurrection in 1871–1872. After the 1876 elections Díaz again raised the flag of rebellion. The war began in the northeast and soon spread to the southeast. The decisive battle was fought in mid-November at Tecoac, where Díaz defeated the government forces. Díaz seized power and thus beginning his long dictatorship, which lasted until the Third Mexican War in 1910 (intra-state war #652).

Sources: Clodfelter (1992); Kohn (1986).

INTRA-STATE WAR #603:
The Defeat of Xinjiang Muslims of 1876–1877

Participants: China vs. Muslims
Dates: April [ ], 1876, to December 1, 1877
Battle-Related Deaths: China—[ ]; Muslims—[ ]
Where Fought: Asia
Initiator: China
Outcome: China wins
War Type: Civil for local issues

Narrative: The revolt of the Xinjiang Muslims began in 1864 (intra-state war #582). The Muslims gained control over most of Xinjiang while the Chinese government was focused on rebellions elsewhere. The intervention of Russia halted the fighting in 1871. Finally, in 1876, the Chinese government decided to reassert its control and sent an army of 100,000 soldiers under Gen. Zuo Zongtang (or Tso Tsung-t'ang) to recapture the area. Gen. Zuo Zongtang had recently defeated the Tungan Muslim rebellion in Shaanxi and Gansu provinces (intra-state war

#576). In Xinjiang his 90,000 soldiers faced a rebel force of 45,000 under Yakub Beg. The rebels were first defeated in the north, and they retreated westward. The rebel stronghold, Turfan, was captured on May 16, 1877. Yakub Beg died later that month, and by the end of the year the remaining Muslim forces had been defeated. Half of the Muslims in Xinjiang may have died as a result of the events of these two wars.

Sources: Clodfelter (2002); Elleman (2001).

INTRA-STATE WAR #605:
The Third Colombian War of 1876–1877

Participants: Colombia vs. conservatives
Dates: July 26, 1876, to July 1, 1877
Battle-Related Deaths: Colombia—2,100; conservatives—1,770
Where Fought: W. Hemisphere
Initiator: conservatives
Outcome: Colombia wins
War Type: Civil for central control

Narrative: As in many Latin American states, politics in Colombia in the nineteenth century was dominated by the rivalry between liberals and conservatives. The liberals controlled the presidency from 1861, and under their lax rule several provinces gained virtual independence. The most serious rebellion during this period was staged by the conservatives, who controlled the provinces of Cauca, Antioquia, and Tolima. The conservatives began the war by seizing control of the city of Palmira. The government dispatched an army, and major battles were fought at Los Chancos, the site of a liberal victory; Garrapata, which ended in a draw; La Donjuana, another liberal victory; and Manizales, yet another liberal victory and one that ended the war.

Sources: Henao and Arrubla (1938); Posada-Carbo (1994); Richardson (1960a); Scheina (2003a).

INTRA-STATE WAR #607:
The Satsuma Rebellion of 1877

Participants: Japan vs. Satsumas
Dates: January 29, 1877, to September 24, 1877
Battle-Related Deaths: Satsumas—10,000;
   Japan—7,000
Where Fought: Asia
Initiator: Satsumas
Outcome: Japan wins
War Type: Civil for local issues

Narrative: In the mid-nineteenth century, Japan was dominated by a conflict between the old order and movements toward modernization. In particular, during the war of the Meiji Restoration (intra-state war #588), the feudal system of the shogunate was destroyed with the return to rule by the emperor, who was supported by the peasants. This war represents the last attempt by the old feudal elements to defeat modernization. The samurai army of the Satsuma clan on Kyushu rebelled in January 1877. A rebel force numbering 15,000 laid siege to the imperial castle at Kumamoto for almost two months, but the siege was finally broken by the arrival of a 50,000-troop imperial relief column. After suffering several additional defeats, the rebels retreated to their base at Kagoshima Castle. There, rebel leader Saigo Takamori committed suicide, and his remaining troops recklessly charged enemy lines, thus ending this anti-Meiji revolt.

Sources: Buck (1973); Clodfelter (1992); Mounsey (1879); Richardson (1960a).

INTRA-STATE WAR #608:
The Argentine Indians War of 1879–1880

Participants: Argentina vs. Indians
Dates: April 6, 1879, to July 8, 1880
Battle-Related Deaths: Indians—1,500;
   Argentina—200
Where Fought: W. Hemisphere
Initiator: Argentina
Outcome: Argentina wins
War Type: Civil for local issues

Narrative: The united provinces of Argentina went to war with the Ranqueles tribes of Indians in central Argentina in 1833, primarily over control of the Pampas grasslands (non-state war #1518). Since then the Indians had engaged in periodic attacks on Argentine towns and the Argentine army. Once the Argentine government had defeated the 1874 rebellion (intra-state war #600), its attention was oriented toward trying to control the Ranqueles permanently. Julio A. Roca, the minister of war, personally directed the five-pronged offensive, also referred to as the "Conquest of the Desert," which aimed at permanently seizing Indian territory. Roca advanced with a 6,000-troop army, defeated the Indian warriors, and drove the Indians from the Pampas and into Patagonia. Hunger and disease caused many fatalities on both sides.

Sources: Hasbrouck (1935); Perry (1972); Richardson (1960a); Scheina (2003a).

INTRA-STATE WAR #610:
The Fourth Buenos Aires War of 1880

Participants: Argentina vs. Buenos Aires
Dates: June 21, 1880, to July 21, 1880
Battle-Related Deaths: Buenos Aires—800;
   Argentina—400
Where Fought: W. Hemisphere
Initiator: Buenos Aires
Outcome: Argentina wins
War Type: Civil for local issues

Narrative: The city and province of Buenos Aires had fought a series of wars with the provinces of Argentina over which would control Argentina and over the degree of control the government would have. In 1880 Julio Roca, the minister of war who had won the previous year's Indian War (intra-state war #608), was elected as the incoming president. The *porteños* (citizens of the city of Buenos Aires), who had backed the candidacy of their own governor, refused to accept the result and staged an armed rebellion, forcing President Nicolás Avellaneda from office. Roca led an army against Buenos Aires and defeated the *porteños*, thus securing his presidency.

Sources: Akers (1930); Clodfelter (2002); Langer (1968); Richardson (1960a).

INTRA-STATE WAR #611:
The Haitian Civil War of 1883–1884

Participants: Haiti vs. republicans
Dates: March 27, 1883, to January 8, 1884
Battle-Related Deaths: Haiti—8,000; republicans—100
Where Fought: W. Hemisphere
Initiator: republicans
Outcome: Haiti wins
War Type: Civil for central control

Narrative: Although politics in Haiti was dominated by the conflict between the blacks, generally peasants, and the mulattoes, who frequently controlled the government, it also was divided along ideological lines between republicans and reactionaries. The republican government was overthrown by the reactionaries in 1867. In March 1883, republican exiles led by Jean-Pierre Boyer-Bazelais invaded from Jamaica, to challenge the regime of President Lysius Salomon. They landed and easily captured Miragoane, since the government garrison had fled. Revolts also occurred in other southern cities, though they were gradually suppressed, as was an attempted coup staged in Port-au-Prince, which led to the burning of the city. The government troops besieged Miragoane, where many of the rebels and civilians died of disease. The rebels held the city until January 1884, when Miragoane was stormed and the survivors executed.

Sources: Clodfelter (2002); Heinl (1996); Rodman (1954).

INTRA-STATE WAR #612:
The Fourth Colombian War of 1884–1885

Participants: Colombia vs. liberals
Dates: November 15, 1884, to August 26, 1885
Battle-Related Deaths: liberals—700; Colombia—300
Where Fought: W. Hemisphere
Initiator: liberals
Outcome: Colombia wins
War Type: Civil for central control

Narrative: Liberals controlled the national government of Colombia after 1861. In the Third Colombian War of 1876–1877 (intra-state war #605), the liberals defeated the rebellion instigated by the conservatives in several of the provinces. In the 1880 election the liberals maintained control when Rafael Núñez won the presidency; however, Núñez soon created the National Party in an attempt to appeal to moderates within both the conservatives and the liberals. This alienated the liberals, and in 1884 they raised an army and rebelled against Núñez. Over the next nine months they lost most of the engagements, and the government declared victory in August 1885.

Sources: Henao and Arrubla (1938); Munro (1942); Richardson (1960a); Scheina (2003a).

INTRA-STATE WAR #613:
Peru's National Problem of 1885

Participants: Peru vs. Indians
Dates: March 2, 1885, to May 25, 1885
Battle-Related Deaths: Indians—2,000; Peru—200
Where Fought: W. Hemisphere
Initiator: Indians
Outcome: Peru wins
War Type: Civil for local issues

Narrative: Peru suffered a significant loss in the War of the Pacific (inter-state war #64, 1879–1883) of Peru and Bolivia against Chile. At the end of the war Gen. Miguel Iglesias abandoned the Peruvian resistance to make peace with Chile, and consequently as Chile withdrew from Peru, it recognized Iglesias as the president of Peru. Peru then entered a period of political upheaval against the Iglesias regime, partially led by Gen. Andrés Avelino Cáceres, who had led a resistance army in the fight against Chile. One element of the resistance was an uprising staged by the indigenous people. The Indian uprising, led by Pedro Pablo Atusparia, began over the issue of taxation, though it broadened to include removal of Iglesia officials. The Indians succeeded in defeating government forces at Yungay, where they were joined by troops that supported Cáceres. In response, the government launched its Northern Pacification Force, which killed thousands of Indian combatants and peasants.

Source: Thurner (1997).

INTRA-STATE WAR #616:

The First Yemeni Rebellion of 1890–1892

Participants: Ottoman Empire vs. forces of Zaidi imam
Dates: April [ ], 1890, to September [ ], 1892
Battle-Related Deaths: Ottoman Empire—[ ]; forces of Zaidi imam—[ ]
Where Fought: Middle East
Initiator: forces of Zaidi imam
Outcome: Ottoman Empire wins
War Type: Civil for local issues

Narrative: In 1872 the Ottoman Empire had reasserted its control over Asir and Yemen (see extra-state war #365); however, opposition to Ottoman rule by the Yemeni tribes continued at below war levels. In 1890 the Zaidi imam Yahya tried to unite the opposition into an armed insurrection against the Ottomans. On two occasions the Yemenis besieged the Ottomans at the capital of Sanaa. Ottoman reinforcements from Hodeida ultimately relieved the city and defeated the rebels.

Sources: Baldry (1976); Farah (2002).

INTRA-STATE WAR #617:

The Second Chilean War of 1891

Participants: Chile vs. Congressists
Dates: January 7, 1891, to August 29, 1891
Battle-Related Deaths: Chile—1,000; Congressists—700
Where Fought: W. Hemisphere
Initiator: Congressists
Outcome: Congressists win
War Type: Civil for central control

Narrative: This war was the most serious civil conflict in Chile in the nineteenth century. Reformist president José Manuel Balmaceda squared off against an oligarchy-dominated Congress. Chile's finances, which had been depleted by the War of the Pacific (inter-state war #64), were further strained by Balmaceda's reform program, and the Congress rebelled against him. By May the rebels had captured the entire north of the country. On August 20 the Congressists army began its campaign against Santiago. Two major battles were fought near Valpariso, both of them government defeats, which ended the fighting. Balmaceda took his own life on September 18.

Sources: Akers (1930); Bernstein (1965); Blakemore (1965); Clodfelter (2002); Harbottle and Bruce (1971); Phillips and Axelrod (2005); Richardson (1960a); Scheina (2003a).

INTRA-STATE WAR #618:

The Zaili-Jindan Revolt of 1891

Participants: China vs. Zaili, Jindan sects
Dates: November 11, 1891, to December 27, 1891
Battle-Related Deaths: Zaili, Jindan sects—10,000; China—500

Where Fought: Asia
Initiator: Zaili, Jindan sects
Outcome: China wins
War Type: Civil for local issues

Narrative: The Taoist White Lotus movement dates to the thirteenth century. In the late nineteenth century, sects related to it flourished in north China and Manchuria. In the winter of 1891 the Zeili and Jindan sects rebelled in Jehol in Inner Mongolia over issues of taxation, government suppression, and the influx of foreigners. The government sent 10,000 troops, and within two months this force had defeated the insurgents. Twenty thousand sect members—combatants and civilians—died in the process.

Source: Shek (1980).

INTRA-STATE WAR #620:
The Brazil Federalists War of 1893–1894

Participants: Brazil vs. Rio Grande do Sul
Dates: February 2, 1893, to August 31, 1894
Battle-Related Deaths: Brazil—[ ]; Rio Grande do Sul—[ ] (Total Combatant Deaths: 1,500)
Where Fought: W. Hemisphere
Initiator: Rio Grande do Sul
Outcome: Brazil wins
War Type: Civil for local issues

Narrative: Two separate rebellions occurred in Brazil in 1893. The first involved the federalists, who wanted greater autonomy from the centralist Republican government. In February the federalists in the southern province of Rio Grande do Sul, who were known as Maragatos, began attacking government troops. The rebels, with a peak strength of 6,000 men, defeated government troops at Rio Negro in late November 1893. Meanwhile, the second war (intrastate war #621) began with a naval revolt. After suppressing that rebellion, more government forces were available to fight against the federalists. In the war's biggest battle, on June 29, 1894,

at Paso Fundo, the federalists were defeated. Their leader was killed on August 10, 1894, and the war soon ended.

Sources: Bello (1966); Clodfelter (2002); Davis (1968); Love (1971); Schneider (1991).

INTRA-STATE WAR #621:
The Brazil Naval War of 1893–1894

Participants: Brazil vs. Naval Royalists
Dates: September 6, 1893, to April 16, 1894
Battle-Related Deaths: Brazil—[ ]; Naval Royalists—[ ] (Total Combatant Deaths: 1,000)
Where Fought: W. Hemisphere
Initiator: Naval Royalists
Outcome: Brazil wins
War Type: Civil for central control

Narrative: The second war that confronted Brazil in 1893 involved a revolt by the navy (see the earlier war, intra-state war #620). At the time, the president was Floriano Peixoto, and his attempts to consolidate the power of the central government were unpopular with the military, especially with Adm. Custodio Mello, who wanted to replace the president. Mello led much of the Brazilian navy into rebellion, though segments of the navy remained loyal, along with almost all of the army. For six months there were skirmishes between rebel ships and loyal batteries on shore. After an unsuccessful rebel assault on the government arsenal at Niteroi, most of the fleet surrendered in mid-March 1894. The rebel flagship *Aquidaban* was sunk on April 16, ending this war. Some of the rebels who escaped capture joined the federalist rebellion (intra-state war #620).

Sources: Bello (1966); Clodfelter (2002); Davis (1968); Martin and Lovett (1968); Schneider (1991); Smith (1970).

INTRA-STATE WAR #623:
The Tonghak Rebellion of 1894

Participants: Japan, Korea vs. Tonghak Society
Dates: February 29, 1894, to November 28, 1894

Battle-Related Deaths: Japan—[ ]; Korea—[ ];
  Tonghak Society—[ ]
Where Fought: Asia
Initiator: Tonghak Society
Outcome: Korea, Japan win
War Type: Civil for central control

Narrative: The Tonghak Society arose in Korea in the mid-nineteenth century, and it opposed the feudal system, with its oppression of the peasants. In 1894 the Tonghaks raised a peasant army and launched an attack against the Yi dynasty. The Korean government was unable to quell the disturbances, and the first phase of the war ended with a negotiated agreement between the government and the rebels. The Korean government had asked for Chinese and Japanese help in confronting the 100,000 rebels. In early May both nations sent troops, which led in late July to the First Sino-Japanese War (inter-state war #73), in which Korea's "allies" were fighting each other over the future of Korea. Consequently, the Tonghak broke the cease-fire and started the second phase of their rebellion against the government of Korea, though this time the Tonghak also opposed the growing Japanese influence. In October the Japanese intervened in the civil war to support the government of Korea, which was then able to defeat the Tonghak.

Sources: "Chronology of the Peasant War" (1994); Clodfelter (2002); Jae-gon (1994); Phillips and Axelrod (2005); Young-hee (1994).

INTRA-STATE WAR #625:
The Third Peru War of 1894–1895

Participants: Peru vs. liberals
Dates: October 15, 1894, to March 19, 1895
Battle-Related Deaths: Peru—[ ]; liberals—[ ]
  (Total Combatant Deaths: 4,000)
Where Fought: W. Hemisphere
Initiator: liberals
Outcome: Liberals win
War Type: Civil for central control

Narrative: At the conclusion of Peru's war with the Indians (intra-state war #613), Gen. Andrés Avelino Cáceres marched his troops to the capital and demanded a presidential election. Cáceres was elected president the following year, 1886. José Nicolás de Piérola had briefly been president of Peru but had left office owing to his failures against the Chilean invaders in the War of the Pacific (inter-state war #64). In the fall of 1894, Piérola, who was then the leader of the Civilista Party, staged a revolt against Cáceres. The rebels won the war by the following spring. As president, Piérola fostered development for the war-torn nation.

Sources: Gonzales (1987); Pike (1967).

INTRA-STATE WAR #626:
The Fifth Colombian War of 1895

Participants: Colombia vs. liberals
Dates: January 22, 1895, to March 15, 1895
Battle-Related Deaths: liberals—800;
  Colombia—400
Where Fought: W. Hemisphere
Initiator: liberals
Outcome: Colombia wins
War Type: Civil for central control

Narrative: This war continued the pattern of earlier conflicts in Colombia that revolved around the enduring feud between conservatives and liberals. In January 1895 the liberals launched a revolt in several provinces against the government of President Miguel Antonio Caro. The government's counteroffensive confronted both the liberals and irregular forces from Venezuela and Mexico. Battles during the war, including the crucial engagements of Enciso and Capitanejo, involved between 1,500 and 2,500 men on each side. The liberals lost both of these important battles, and the war.

Source: Scheina (2003a).

INTRA-STATE WAR #627:
The Ecuador Liberals War of 1895

Participants: Ecuador vs. liberal caudillos
Dates: February 18, 1895, to September 22, 1895
Battle-Related Deaths: Ecuador—900; liberal
     caudillos—100
Where Fought: W. Hemisphere
Initiator: liberal caudillos
Outcome: Liberal caudillos win
War Type: Civil for central control

Narrative: In Ecuador the struggle between liberals and conservatives was compounded by the rivalry between the highland capital of Quito, controlled by the conservative government, and the port city of Guayaquil. In 1895 liberal Eloy Alfaro led 3,000 rebels from Guayaquil against the government in Quito. Alfaro's forces defeated the 2,350 government troops on August 14–15. Though a more moderate regime came to power, the liberals continued fighting until Alfaro came to power. He served as president until 1901 and then again from 1907 to 1911, during which time many of his reforms restricted the powers of the church.

Source: Clodfelter (2002).

INTRA-STATE WAR #628:
The First Gansu Muslim War of 1895–1896

Participants: China vs. Gansu Muslims
Dates: April [ ], 1895, to April [ ], 1896
Battle-Related Deaths: China—[ ]; Gansu
     Muslims—[ ] (Total Combatant Deaths: 10,000)
Where Fought: Asia
Initiator: Gansu Muslims
Outcome: China wins
War Type: Civil for local issues

Narrative: This is another of the little-known wars that killed tens of thousands of people in China during the last half of the nineteenth century. This one occurred in Gansu (Kansu) province, which is located in northwest China along the upper reaches of the Yellow River. The war originated in disputes among rival Muslim sects. After their defeat in the Tungan Rebellion (intra-state war #576), many of the Muslim Ma family of warlords had remained in Gansu and had accommodated themselves to government rule. The Salar Muslims had greater ties to the Sufi movement in Central Asia and the Middle East. The two groups accused each other of misleading the people and appealed to local governmental officials for relief. The government's failure to act led the Salar into open rebellion. The government finally acted and sent troops to suppress the rebellion. War would return to the region in 1928 (intra-state war #703).

Source: Lipman (1984).

INTRA-STATE WAR #630:
The Druze-Turkish War of 1895–1896

Participants: Ottoman Empire vs. Druze
Dates: October [ ], 1895, to [ ]/[ ]/1896
Battle-Related Deaths: Ottoman Empire—[ ];
     Druze—[ ] (Total Combatant Deaths: 1,000)
Where Fought: Middle East
Initiator: Druze
Outcome: Ottoman Empire wins
War Type: Civil for local issues

Narrative: The Druze are a group of people who live in Lebanon and Syria and who constitute an offshoot of Shia Islam. They had been involved in two wars with the Maronites over control of Lebanon (intra-state wars #543 and #566). In this war the Druze fought against the Ottomans, who had regained control of the region from Egypt as a result of Second Syrian War (intra-state war #537). The Druze revolt against the Ottomans broke out in October 1895, originating in a quarrel between Druze and other Muslims in the Hawran region. Government troops were sent to restore order but made little headway during the winter. An agreement reflecting this stalemate was reached in February 1896; however, mistreatment of the Druze increased, and in early 1896 a revolt began again. Initially, Ottoman troops were defeated, but large reinforcements succeeded in pushing back the Druze. Some accepted the Ottoman terms to surrender in August, but others continued fighting until early 1897.

Sources: Betts (1988); Firro (1992).

INTRA-STATE WAR #631:
The Second Cretan War of 1896–1897

Participants: Ottoman Empire vs. Cretan Muslims
Dates: March 10, 1896, to February 14, 1897
Battle-Related Deaths: Ottoman Empire—[ ]; Cretan Muslims—[ ] (Total Combatant Deaths: 1,000)
Where Fought: Europe
Initiator: Cretan Muslims
Outcome: Transformed into inter-state war #76
War Type: Civil for local issues

Narrative: The Cretans had rebelled twice before against Ottoman rule: during the Greek War of Independence of 1821–1828 (intra-state war #506) and in the First Cretan War, in 1866 (intra-state war #583). In 1894 the Christians in Crete formed a committee called Epitropi, which desired independence or union with Greece. Epitropi soon became a revolutionary organization, encouraged by a similar movement in Greece. The replacement of the Christian governor of Crete by a Muslim infuriated the Christian community, and a large-scale rebellion broke out when the governor demanded that the Epitropi be disbanded. Ottoman forces on the island moved to suppress the revolt. Fighting temporarily subsided in August, when the great powers persuaded the Ottoman Empire to institute reform measures. When fighting resumed, the Greek government decided to intervene. On February 15, 1897, the Greeks announced their plan to militarily occupy Crete. The Greeks thus took over the bulk of the fighting, and the war was transformed into the Greco-Turkish War (inter-state war #76).

Sources: Clodfelter (1992); Ekinci (2006); Palmer (1992); Phillips and Axelrod (2005); Williams (1907).

INTRA-STATE WAR #632:
The Third Brazil-Canudos War of 1896–1897

Participants: Brazil vs. Canudos
Dates: October 1, 1896, to October 5, 1897
Battle-Related Deaths: Canudos—3,000; Brazil—2,200
Where Fought: W. Hemisphere
Initiator: Brazil
Outcome: Brazil wins
War Type: Civil for local issues

Narrative: This war took place in the Bahia province, in northeastern Brazil. A cult that combined Catholicism with ancient Indian beliefs was established in the region by Antonio Maciel, whose fanatical ideas soon claimed a large following among the peasantry. Maciel the Conselheiro (counselor) created a theocratic state that was centered at Canudos, 300 miles northwest of Salvador. The government of Brazil saw the cult as monarchists who posed a threat to the new republic and in 1896 decided to eliminate it. Several expeditions were sent to Canudos, though they generally failed to defeat the cult because of a lack of sufficient troops. Finally, in 1897, Canudos was besieged and the Conselheiro was killed in the final assault.

Sources: Akers (1930); Bello (1966); Clodfelter (2002); Cunha (1944); Davis (1968); Levine (1988); Madden (1993).

INTRA-STATE WAR #633:
The Fourth Venezuelan War of 1899

Participants: Venezuela vs. Castro-led rebels
Dates: May 24, 1899, to October 22, 1899
Battle-Related Deaths: Venezuela—1,200;
　Castro-led rebels—900
Where Fought: W. Hemisphere
Initiator: Castro-led rebels
Outcome: Castro-led rebels win
War Type: Civil for central control

Narrative: Venezuela had been controlled by the dictatorships of Antonio Guzmán Blanco from 1870 to 1888 and Gen. Joaquín Crespo from 1894 to 1898. Crespo then engineered the election of Gen. Ignacio Andrade as his successor. Objecting to Andrade's rule, caudillo Cipriano Castro began what was referred to as the "Revolution of Liberal Restoration" in late May 1899. Castro defeated government troops as his army marched toward Caracas. At the decisive battle of Tocuyito, on September 13, 1899, the 2,000-strong rebel army entrapped the 4,000 government troops. Andrade fled the country, and Castro was elected president.

Sources: Clodfelter (2002); Jaques (2007); Scheina (2003a).

INTRA-STATE WAR #635:
The Second Yaqui War of 1899–1900

Participants: Mexico vs. Yaqui Indians
Dates: July 21, 1899, to January 18, 1900
Battle-Related Deaths: Yaqui Indians—1,500;
　Mexico—100
Where Fought: W. Hemisphere
Initiator: Yaqui Indians
Outcome: Mexico wins
War Type: Civil for local issues

Narrative: Both the province of Yucatan and the Mexican government had fought against the Yaqui Indians in the Caste War (intra-state wars #545 and #553). Although the Yaqui were defeated, they continued their opposition to their mistreatment, particularly waging a guerrilla war in the 1880s. In July 1899 Yaqui chiefs demanded that all Mexicans leave Yaqui land. In the ensuing conflict some 3,000 Yaqui fighters faced at least 1,000 Mexican troops, yet they suffered numerous defeats. The largest battle was fought on January 18, 1900, and resulted in a Mexican victory. This ended the war, though small skirmishes continued.

Sources: Clodfelter (1992); Hu-DeHart (1984); Scheina (2003a).

INTRA-STATE WAR #636:
The Sixth Colombian (War of the 1,000 Days) of 1899–1902

Participants: Colombia vs. liberals
Dates: October 17, 1899, to November 21, 1902
Battle-Related Deaths: liberals—53,000;
　Colombia—47,000
Where Fought: W. Hemisphere
Initiator: liberals
Outcome: Colombia wins
War Type: Civil for central control

Narrative: This war represents the culmination of almost a century of battles between the liberals and conservatives in Colombia. After 1861 the liberals had dominated through the 1863 constitution; however, they lost power in the 1880s, and the 1886 constitution was more conservative, giving increased power to the president. The liberals, who objected to governmental policies, attempted a brief, unsuccessful revolt in 1895 (intra-state war #626). By 1899 the liberals thought their prospects had improved, and they launched a rebellion in Santander province. With the exception of a major liberal victory at La Laja Bridge in December, however, the conservatives won most of the battles. Consequently, the liberals shifted to a guerrilla war. In the fall of 1902 the liberals' top guerrilla leader, Cesáreo Pulido, was captured and executed. The war continued until November when rebel general Benjamin Herrera signed what was called the Wisconsin Treaty (so named for the American ship on which it was signed).

Sources: Bergquist (1978); Clodfelter (2002); Demarest (2001); Galbraith (1953); Henao and Arrubla (1938); Phillips and Axelrod (2005); Scheina (2003a); Wood (1968).

INTRA-STATE WAR #638:
The Fifth Venezuelan War of 1901–1903

Participants: Venezuela vs. Matos-led rebels
Dates: December 29, 1901, to July 19, 1903
Battle-Related Deaths: Matos-led rebels—3,000; Venezuela—1,000
Where Fought: W. Hemisphere
Initiator: Matos-led rebels
Outcome: Venezuela wins
War Type: Civil for central control

Narrative: After seizing power in 1899 (intra-state war #633), Cipriano Castro became increasingly dictatorial, and by December 1901 he faced a rebellion launched by Gen. Manuel Matos called the "Liberation Rebellion." Government forces, under the leadership of Juan Vincente Gómez, went on the offensive, defeating the rebels in most of their engagements, including the battle at La Victoria, where 6,000 government troops defeated 14,000 rebels. The final rebel stronghold on the Orinoco River was lost in July 1903, ending the war. Gómez later betrayed Castro by overthrowing the dictator in 1908 and heading his own despotic regime until 1935.

Sources: Clodfelter (2002); Scheina (2003a); Singh (1999).

INTRA-STATE WAR #640:
The Ilinden War of 1903

Participants: Ottoman Empire vs. IMRO rebels
Dates: August 2, 1903, to November 2, 1903

Battle-Related Deaths: Ottoman Empire—5,330; IMRO rebels—1,000
Where Fought: Europe
Initiator: IMRO rebels
Outcome: Ottoman Empire wins
War Type: Civil for local issues

Narrative: Throughout the nineteenth century the Ottoman Empire had been losing control of its Christian-inhabited territories of the Balkans. In Macedonia the Internal Macedonia Revolutionary Organization (IMRO) was founded in 1893 with the goal of gaining autonomy for Macedonia. In August 1903 IMRO launched a revolt, which took its name from the day the revolt was launched, St. Elijah's Day (Ilinden). The IMRO began attacking Turkish troops in the region, and initially the rebels were successful in capturing several provinces; however, the Turks sent 351,000 troops to try to put down 27,000 resistance fighters. The Turks won the war and then retaliated by destroying 200 villages.

Sources: Anastasoff (1977); Clodfelter (1992); Georgieva and Konechni (1998); Gerolymatos (2002); Glenny (1999); Hupchick (2002); Karpat (1972); Palmer (1992).

INTRA-STATE WAR #641:
The First Uruguay War of 1904

Participants: Uruguay vs. Blancos
Dates: January 1, 1904, to September 1, 1904
Battle-Related Deaths: Uruguay—[ ]; Blancos—[ ] (Total Combatant Deaths: 1,000)
Where Fought: W. Hemisphere
Initiator: Blancos
Outcome: Uruguay wins
War Type: Civil for central control

Narrative: This war continued the struggle between the liberal Colorados and the conservative Blancos that had plagued Uruguay since the 1830s. In this case, the liberal president José Batlle y Ordóñez faced a conservative rebellion in January 1904. Two major battles occurred, both of which were government victories.

The Battle of Tupambae on June 22–24 was the bloodiest battle in Uruguay's history, resulting in 2,300 casualties. Batlle thus won the war and went on to become one of the great reformers in Latin American history.

Sources: Acevedo (1934); Clodfelter (1992); Rodriguez Herrero (1934).

INTRA-STATE WAR #642:

The Second Yemeni Rebellion of 1904–1906

Participants: Ottoman Empire vs. forces of Imam Yahya
Dates: November 8, 1904, to January 10, 1906
Battle-Related Deaths: Ottoman Empire—30,000; forces of Imam Yahya—[ ]
Where Fought: Middle East
Initiator: Yemen
Outcome: Stalemate
War Type: Civil for local issues

Narrative: By 1871 the Ottoman Empire had reasserted its control over Yemen and Asir (extra-state war #365). Opposition to Ottoman rule had continued, leading to war in 1890 (intra-state war #616). In 1904 the Yemeni Zaidi imamate passed to Yahya Muhammad Hamid al-Din who began a revolt in northern Yemen as a challenge to the secular Ottoman regime. The rebels laid siege to the garrison at Sanaa in December, leading to starvation in the city. After four months the city, which had lost half its population, surrendered on April 19, 1905. An Ottoman counterattack was delayed by the spread of typhoid fever among the troops stationed at Hodeida. The numerically superior Ottoman troops recaptured Sanaa in August; however, Ottoman attempts to capture the imam or to spread their control into the northern tribal areas met with defeat. The Ottoman campaign against Yemen ended in January 1906; nevertheless, war would break out again in 1910 (intra-state war #651).

Sources: Baldry (1976); Dresch (2000); Farah (2002); Kuneralp (1987).

INTRA-STATE WAR #643:

The Bloody Sunday War of 1905–1906

Participants: Russia vs. workers/peasants
Dates: January 22, 1905, to January 1, 1906
Battle-Related Deaths: Russia—1,500; workers/peasants—[ ]
Where Fought: Europe
Initiator: workers/peasants
Outcome: Russia wins
War Type: Civil for central control

Narrative: Popular discontent confronted Russia's Romanov dynasty at the start of the twentieth century, but it took Russia's participation, and ultimate defeat, in the Russo-Japanese War (inter-state war #85) to galvanize this discontent into an open mass rebellion. On January 22, 1905, workers marched to the Winter Palace to ask the czar for bread and reform. They were attacked by government soldiers in what became known as the "Bloody Sunday" massacre. The massacre precipitated riots and clashes between armed workers and government soldiers in many parts of the country, including in Moscow in mid-December. The rebellion was suppressed by January 1906, though revolutionary sentiment would flare again in 1917 (intra-state war #677).

Sources: Clodfelter (1992); DeFronzo (1996); Goldstone (1998); Harcave (1964); Moorehead (1958).

INTRA-STATE WAR #645:

The Romanian Peasant Revolt of 1907

Participants: Romania vs. peasants
Dates: March 15, 1907, to April 30, 1907
Battle-Related Deaths: Romania—2,000; peasants—[ ]

Where Fought: Europe
Initiator: peasants
Outcome: Romania wins
War Type: Civil for central control

Narrative: Between the end of the Crimean War in 1856 (inter-state war #22) and the Congress of Berlin in 1878 at the end of the Second Russo-Turkish War (inter-state #61), Romania gradually gained its independence from the Ottoman Empire. Independence did not solve all of Romania's problems, however, and in 1907 it was confronted with a true peasant rebellion. The peasants of northern Moldavia rebelled against their perceived oppressors, including absentee landlords and Jewish moneylenders. The government put down the rebellion ruthlessly, killing a total of 11,000 peasants, both rebels and civilians.

Sources: Clodfelter (1992); Richardson (1960a); Stavrianos (1958).

INTRA-STATE WAR #646:
The Overthrow of Abd el-Aziz of 1907–1908

Participants: Morocco, France vs. forces of Mulai Abd el-Hafid
Dates: August 1, 1907, to September 1, 1908
Battle-Related Deaths: forces of Mulai Abd el-Hafid—800; Morocco—400; France—200
Where Fought: Middle East
Initiator: forces of Mulai Abd el-Hafid
Outcome: Forces of Mulai Abd el-Hafid win
War Type: Civil for central control

Narrative: In 1907 Morocco was ruled by Sultan Abd el-Aziz. The sultan had become unpopular, partially because of his European proclivities and reliance on France. For a long period France had been trying to expand its influence in Morocco (France's first war with Morocco had occurred in 1844, extra-state war #330), and the sultan had agreed to the landing of French troops in Casablanca to counteract antiforeign riots. A secret organization, Hafiziya,

had been formed to work toward the sultan's ouster, and it joined with local religious leaders and the sultan's older brother, Mulai Abd el-Hafid, in launching a rebellion against the sultan. Initially the French were not involved in the civil war; however, they finally came to the sultan's aid. Although the French had some successes against the rebels, Mulai Abd el-Hafid was ultimately successful in defeating the sultan's troops and replacing him.

Sources: Ashmead-Bartlett (1910); Burke (1976); Burke (1972); Chandler (1975); Clodfelter (2002); Cooke (1972); Dunn (1981); Freeman-Grenville (1973); Harris (1913); Mercer (1976); Phillips and Axelrod (2005); "Recent Distrubances in Morocco" (1907); Richardson (1960a); Usborne (1936).

INTRA-STATE WAR #647:
The Iranian Constitution War of 1908–1909

Participants: Iran, Russia vs. constitutionalists
Dates: June 23, 1908, to July 17, 1909
Battle-Related Deaths: Russia—100; Iran—[ ]; constitutionalists—[ ] (Total Iranian Combatant Deaths: 1,000)
Where Fought: Middle East
Initiator: constitutionalists
Outcome: Constitutionalists win
War Type: Civil for central control

Narrative: Persia was ruled by the Qajar shah, Muhammed Ali Shah, who wished to retain his dictatorial powers. The people, and the Democratic Party in the National Assembly, wanted greater freedom under some form of constitutional rule. In 1906 a general strike forced the shah to grant a constitution with parliamentary government. In 1908, however, the Russian czar encouraged the shah to repudiate the constitution and dissolve the National Assembly. In response, the city of Tabriz revolted in support of the constitution. When the shah's army laid siege to Tabriz, the Russians intervened and sent a column to assist the shah. The various revolutionaries joined to march against the capital, taking Tehran in July 1909 and overthrowing the shah.

Sources: Browne (1966); Clodfelter (1992); Lenczowski (1987); Wilbur (1963).

INTRA-STATE WAR #648:
The Young Turks Counter-coup of 1909

Participants: Ottoman Empire vs. antigovernment troops
Dates: April 14, 1909, to April 28, 1909
Battle-Related Deaths: Ottoman Empire—[ ]; antigovernment troops—[ ] (Total Combatant Deaths: 6,000)
Where Fought: Middle East
Initiator: antigovernment troops
Outcome: Ottoman Empire wins
War Type: Civil for central control

Narrative: At the beginning of the twentieth century, the Ottoman Empire was in rapid decline. In 1908 the "Young Turk" officers of the Ottoman army intervened in order to save the empire by demanding a return to constitutional rule. Unexpectedly, Sultan Abdul-Hamid agreed to their demands to permit reforms and to create a Young Turk government with Huscyin Hilmi (or Hussein Hilmi) as grand vizier. The sultan secretly tried to undermine this situation, and in April 1909 troops of the Albanian First Army Corps staged a coup against the Young Turks and demanded a fundamentalist regime. The sultan acceded to the coup, and Hilmi was deposed. In defense of the Young Turks, the garrison in Salonika (in what is now northeastern Greece) sent troops under Mustafa Kemal (later Ataturk) to seize Constantinople and overthrow the sultan.

Sources: *Chronicle of the 20th Century* (1987); Langer (1952); Palmer (1992); Phillips and Axelrod (2005); *New York Times Index* (1909).

INTRA-STATE WAR #650:
The Second Albanian Revolt of 1910–1912

Participants: Ottoman Empire vs. Albania
Dates: March [ ], 1910, to October 16, 1912
Battle-Related Deaths: Ottoman Empire—[ ]; Albania—[ ]
Where Fought: Europe
Initiator: Albania
Outcome: Transformed into inter-state war #100
War Type: Civil for local issues

Narrative: Albania was one of the last Ottoman territories in the Balkans to gain its independence. Contrary to its earlier commitments, the new Young Turk government imposed new taxes on Albania, precipitating a series of attacks against Ottoman garrisons. Initially, it took 40,000 Ottoman troops to suppress the revolt. The rebels resumed their attacks in March 1911, and the Turks won another brief pause in the fighting by promising Albanian autonomy. However, the Albanians once again resumed fighting and captured Pristina (in present-day Kosovo). This war was ultimately subsumed into the First Balkan War later in 1912 (inter-state war #100), and Albania obtained its independence at the conclusion of this conflict.

Sources: Clodfelter (2002); Phillips and Axelrod (2005).

INTRA-STATE WAR #651:
The Asir-Yemen Revolt of 1910–1911

Participants: Ottoman Empire vs. Yemen, Asir
Dates: October 15, 1910, to October 9, 1911
Battle-Related Deaths: Ottoman Empire—7,000; Yemen, Asir—2,000
Where Fought: Middle East
Initiator: Yemen, Asir
Outcome: Stalemate
War Type: Civil for local issues

Narrative: Although the Ottomans had been able to defeat the uprising in Yemen in 1904 (intra-state war #642), they had been unable to capture the Zaidi imam Yahya, who continued low level attacks against the Ottoman forces. Meanwhile, the Ottomans were also facing disturbances led by Sayyid Muhammad in Asir. The Ottomans and Asiris had reached an agreement in June 1910, but by October the Asiris and Yemenis had resumed their attacks, coordinated as a result of an agreement between Sayyid Muhammad and Imam Yahya. As in the earlier war (#642), the imam besieged Sanaa, and the Ottomans had to send reinforcements to relieve the city in April 1911. At this point the conduct of the war was affected by the outbreak of the war between Italy and Turkey (inter-state war #97). In the summer of 1911, Italy not only provided arms to the Asiris but also bombarded the Turks at al-Qunfidah in aid of the Asiris. The fighting in Asir thus was subsumed into the Italo-Turkish War. At that point Imam Yahya concluded a treaty with the Turks, ending this war. In 1912 the imam declared a jihad against the Italians and even assisted the Turks in their attacks against Asir.

Sources: Baldry (1976); Farah (2002).

INTRA-STATE WAR #652:
The Third Mexican War of 1910–1914

Participants: Mexico vs. liberals, radicals
Dates: November 20, 1910, to July 15, 1914
Battle-Related Deaths: Mexico—56,250; liberals, radicals—37,500
Where Fought: W. Hemisphere
Initiator: liberals, radicals
Outcome: Liberals, radicals win
War Type: Civil for central control

Narrative: The Mexican Revolution was originally treated by Small and Singer as one civil war from 1910 to 1920, while others have divided it into four separate phases. Here it is divided into two distinct wars, the Third and Fourth Mexican wars (intra-state wars #652 and #673). On November 20, 1910, a revolt led by Francisco Madero was launched against Porfirio Díaz. Madero was soon joined by the armies of Pancho Villa and Emiliano Zapata. By May 24, 1911, Díaz resigned and Madero was elected president. Madero's moderate regime did not deliver the more revolutionary reforms desired by Zapata, who resumed attacks on the Mexican government forces. The revolt spread throughout the north. Gen. Victoriano Huerta, who led Madero's forces, conducted several successful campaigns against the rebels; however, Huerta betrayed his chief, arresting and killing him in 1913. The rebels, including Zapata, Venustiano Carranza, Álvaro Obregón, and Plutarco Elías Calles, converged on Mexico City, where Huerta's forces were defeated in heavy fighting in July 1914. This war ended with Huerta's defeat, after which Carranza became president. The next war began later that year.

Sources: Clodfelter (2002); Cumberland (1968); Jensen (1953); McCaa (2003); McHenry (1962); Phillips and Axelrod (2005); Scheina (2003b); Wright (1965).

INTRA-STATE WAR #656:
The Paraguay War of 1911–1912

Participants: Paraguay vs. radicals
Dates: July 15, 1911, to May 11, 1912
Battle-Related Deaths: Paraguay—4,000; radicals—1,000
Where Fought: W. Hemisphere
Initiator: radicals
Outcome: Radicals win
War Type: Civil for central control

Narrative: Paraguay had been ruled by three long-term dictatorships from 1814 until 1870. Paraguay's loss in the Lopez War against Brazil and Argentina (inter-state war #49) in 1870 began a period of internal conflict and short-term leaders. In 1911 the cívico and radical factions battled each other. President Liberato

Rojas and Maj. Albino Jara, who led the cívico faction, faced a rebellion by the radical liberals, led by Eduardo Schaerer and former president Manuel Gondra. In the final battle of the war, Jara's forces were ambushed at Paraguari. Jara was slain, and Schaerer then assumed the presidency.

Source: Warren (1949).

INTRA-STATE WAR #657:
The First Nationalists War of 1911

Participants: China vs. National Revolutionary Alliance
Dates: October 11, 1911, to December 31, 1911
Battle-Related Deaths: China—800; National Revolutionary Alliance—200
Where Fought: Asia
Initiator: National Revolutionary Alliance
Outcome: National Revolutionary Alliance wins
War Type: Civil for central control

Narrative: At the beginning of the twentieth century, the Ch'ing dynasty was ruled by a weak, young emperor who was dominated by the empress dowager. A number of revolutionary societies arose, some of which highlighted the differences between the Han Chinese and the ruling Manchu elite. A group called the National Revolutionary Alliance emerged that combined the Nationalist movement led by Sun Yat-sen (Sun Zhongshan) with secret military societies. These dissident army soldiers began the war when they seized the city of Wuchang and declared war against the dynasty. This initiated rebellions all over the country. Soon much of China was in the hands of the nationalist revolutionaries, and they declared their occupied areas a republic. An advisory assembly to the throne recalled former regent Yüan Shih-k'ai as prime minister in an attempt to restore order. His army did take several cities from the republicans, but he was unable to stop the advance of the revolutionary movement. The fighting ended in December 1911 when the republicans

convened a conference at their capital, Nanking, and elected Sun Yat-sen as provisional president. In January 1912 Sun offered the presidency to Yüan Shih-k'ai, who then encouraged the emperor to abdicate on February 12, 1912.

Sources: Clubb (1964); Elleman (2001); Franke (1970); Li (1956); Lipman (1984); MacNair (1931); McAleavy (1968); Mende (1961); Phillips and Axelrod (2005); Pritchard (1951).

INTRA-STATE WAR #658:
The Cuban Black Uprising of 1912

Participants: Cuba vs. Patri do Indepentente
Dates: May 20, 1912, to June 27, 1912
Battle-Related Deaths: Patri do Indepentente—1,000; Cuba—50
Where Fought: W. Hemisphere
Initiator: Patri do Indepentente
Outcome: Cuba wins
War Type: Civil for local issues

Narrative: Despite the end of slavery in Cuba in 1880, blacks were still discriminated against in Cuban society and politics. Even the establishment of the Cuban Republic did not ensure black political participation. Consequently in 1907, the Association of Black Independents (Patri do Indepentente) was created with the goal of ending inequities. The association was unable to gain approval as a political party by the Congress and thus launched a series of strikes and revolts against the 5,000-troop army of President José Gómez. The rebels, although numbering 10,000, were poorly armed. The blacks were accused of causing a race war against whites, and a number of white militias were created. Both government forces and the militias conducted punitive expeditions, which killed both rebels and civilians. The revolt ended after the death of rebel leader Evaristo Estenóz on June 26.

Sources: Clodfelter (1992); Gerome (1997); Helg (1995); Nodal (1986).

INTRA-STATE WAR #670:
The Ecuadorian Civil War of 1912–1914

Participants: Ecuador vs. Esmeraldas province
Dates: [ ]/[ ]/1912, to [ ]/[ ]/1914
Battle-Related Deaths: Ecuador—[ ]; Esmeraldas province—[ ]
Where Fought: W. Hemisphere
Initiator: Esmeraldas province
Outcome: Ecuador wins
War Type: Civil for local issues

Narrative: Liberal Eloy Alfaro came to power in Ecuador in 1895 at the conclusion of a revolt by Ecuadorian liberals (intra-state war #627). Alfaro became increasingly authoritarian, which alienated his fellow liberals, who then launched a revolt (below war level) against him, sometimes called the War of the Generals. Alfaro was driven from office and killed. The next liberal president, Leonidas Plaza, faced rebellion in the northern province of Esmeraldas. The government was able to defeat the insurrection, though much of the province was destroyed in the process.

Source: Clodfelter (2002).

INTRA-STATE WAR #671:
The Second Nationalists War of 1913

Participants: China vs. republicans
Dates: July 12, 1913, to September 1, 1913
Battle-Related Deaths: China—[ ]; republicans—[ ] (Total Combatant Deaths: 5,000)
Where Fought: Asia
Initiator: republicans
Outcome: China wins
War Type: Civil for central control

Narrative: The Chinese Revolution overthrowing the Ch'ing dynasty occurred in 1911 (intrastate war #657). Gen. Yüan Shih-k'ai was selected as provisional president of China by the National Assembly after the resignation of revolutionary leader Sun Yat-sen. Ultimately, Yüan Shih-k'ai and Sun Yat-sen could not agree on the way to govern China, and in July 1913 six southern provinces led by Sun Yat-sen's revolutionary republicans declared their independence from Beijing. Yüan's forces quickly succeeded in quashing this rebellion. Sun fled to Japan, where he reorganized his party as the Zhongguo Gemingdang (Guomindang). The parties would go to war again in 1916 (intra-state war #675).

Sources: Clubb (1964); Elleman (2001); Franke (1970); Li (1956); MacNair (1931); McAleavy (1968).

INTRA-STATE WAR #672:
The China Pai-ling (White Wolf) War of 1914

Participants: China vs. Pai-ling
Dates: March 15, 1914, to September 15, 1914
Battle-Related Deaths: China—[ ]; Pai-ling—[ ] (Total Combatant Deaths: 5,000)
Where Fought: Asia
Initiator: Pai-ling
Outcome: China wins
War Type: Civil for local issues

Narrative: President Yüan Shih-k'ai had just defeated the Nationalist rebellion in the south (intra-state war #671) when he faced new rebellion in the northwest. The Pai-ling, under the leadership of the White Wolf, were a group of bandits who attacked towns and kidnapped foreigners. The British and American governments appealed to Yüan Shih-k'ai to remove the bandit threat, and he dispatched several brigades against them. Initial attempts to apprehend the White Wolf were unsuccessful; however, in April the Eighth Division, which had been specially trained, entered the conflict. The bandits were decisively defeated, and White Wolf was killed.

Sources: Chesneaux (1973); Li (1956); Lipman (1984); Richardson (1960a); Sheridan (1966).

INTRA-STATE WAR #673:
The Fourth Mexican War of 1914–1920

Participants: Mexico, United States vs.
   conventionists
Dates: November 19, 1914, to July 28, 1920
Battle-Related Deaths: Mexico—18,750;
   conventionists—12,500; United States—15
Where Fought: W. Hemisphere
Initiator: conventionists
Outcome: Mexico, United States win
War Type: Civil for central control

Narrative: Venustiano Carranza had become president as a result of the first phase of the Mexican revolution (intra-state war #652); however, the former revolutionary allies began to fight among themselves. The more radical leaders, including Pancho Villa and Emiliano Zapata (also referred to as the conventionists), rebelled against the leadership of the moderates, or constitutionalists, including Carranza and Álvaro Obregón. In November 1914 Carranza and the constitutionalists fled Mexico City and established their capital at Vera Cruz. Fighting flared up all over the country, but the major battles involved Villa and Obregón and centered on Mexico City, which changed hands several times. By mid-1915 the rebels were being defeated, and the warfare devolved into more of a guerrilla war. Villa's activities in the north led the United States to intervene in the war against him after Villa attacked Columbus, New Mexico. In elections in 1917, Carranza was reaffirmed as president; nevertheless, fighting continued. Carranza then faced another threat as his ally Obregón deserted him and joined the revolt. Carranza fled Mexico City on May 7. Villa negotiated a settlement with provisional president Adolfo de la Huerta in July 1920, and Obregón was elected president the following year.

Sources: Clodfelter (1992); Cumberland (1968); Jensen (1953); McHenry (1962); Phillips and Axelrod (2005); Scheina (2003b); Wright (1965).

INTRA-STATE WAR #675:
The Southern China Revolt of 1916–1918

Participants: China vs. Yunnan rebels
Dates: January [ ], 1916, to November 17, 1918
Battle-Related Deaths: China—[ ]; Yunnan
   rebels—[ ] (Total Combatant Deaths: 2,500)
Where Fought: Asia
Initiator: Yunnan rebels
Outcome: China wins
War Type: Civil for local issues

Narrative: In July 1913 six southern provinces led by Sun Yat-sen's revolutionary republicans unsuccessfully attempted to become independent from the Chinese government of Yüan Shih-k'ai (intra-state war #671). Yüan Shih-k'ai was becoming increasingly unpopular, and in 1915 he proposed a plan to restore dynastic rule, with himself on the throne. Once again, Sun Yat-sen declared his opposition and encouraged the provinces to revolt. In 1916 Yunnan, under governor T'ang Chi-yao, seceded and was followed by seven more provinces in the south and west. Yüan Shih-k'ai died in June 1916, and Vice-President Li Yüan-hung became acting president. Soon thereafter, the navy, wanting to protect the republic, joined the revolt. In 1917 the Manchu emperor was briefly restored to power, which fueled further provincial attacks. In September Sun Yat-sen took over leadership of the movement in the south; however, the southern factions were not united, and Sun resigned in 1918. The southern provinces then ended their rebellion and entered into peace talks with the central government.

Sources: Chien-Nung (1956); Linebarger (1941); Phillips and Axelrod (2005); Richardson (1960a).

INTRA-STATE WAR #676:
The Russia-Turkestan War of 1916–1917

Participants: Russia vs. Kazaks, Kirghiz
Dates: July 4, 1916, to February 27, 1917

Battle-Related Deaths: Kazaks, Kirghiz—1,000; Russia—350
Where Fought: Europe
Initiator: Kazaks, Kirghiz
Outcome: Russia wins
War Type: Civil for local issues

Narrative: In the middle of World War I, Russia issued a decree that non-Russian people, including the Kirghiz and related Muslim peoples in Turkestan, who had been exempt from military service, were now to be conscripted into Russia's military and its accompanying labor force. The people of Turkestan rebelled and began attacking local Russian officials and civilians. The Russian army was then sent in and easily ended the revolt. While thousands of Muslims were killed, hundreds of thousands were either incarcerated or sought refuge in China.

Sources: Bremer and Taras (1993); Clodfelter (1992); Seton-Watson (1967); Soucek (2000).

INTRA-STATE WAR #677:
The Russian Civil War of 1917–1921

Participants: USSR vs. anti-Bolsheviks, Finland, France, Japan, United Kingdom, United States
Dates: December 9, 1917, to March 18, 1921
Battle-Related Deaths: USSR—475,000; anti-Bolsheviks—325,000; Japan—1,500; United Kingdom—350; United States—275; Finland—50; France—50
Where Fought: Europe
Initiator: anti-Bolsheviks
Outcome: USSR wins
War Type: Civil for central control

Narrative: In March 1917 Russia's Czar Nicholas II was overthrown, and by November 1917 the Bolsheviks, led by Vladimir Lenin, had seized power. Opposition to the new regime soon spread, and a revolt of the Don Cossacks on December 9, 1917, initiated this long, bloody conflict. The Whites, or anti-Bolsheviks, went on the offensive, launching the first and second Kuban campaigns (campaigns in the Kuban region) during early 1918. Other countries, fearing the spread of Marxism, also began to intervene. The Japanese occupied Vladivostok in December 1917. The French sent forces to the Ukraine, and a British-American-French expedition occupied Murmansk, in order to support the Whites. The Czech legion, comprising 50,000 men, marched westward along the Trans-Siberian Railroad. As the Whites advanced into Russia, an anti-Soviet government was established at Omsk in the fall of 1918. Meanwhile, World War I (inter-state war #106) ended, and the Bolshevik Red Army, rebuilt by Leon Trotsky, retook the offensive. In addition to fighting the Whites, the Bolsheviks tried to reoccupy the Baltic States and became involved in a war with Poland (see inter-state wars #107, #108, and #109). Many of the foreign interveners withdrew from the war by early 1920. The Red Army then defeated the Whites in the Crimea, basically ending the war, though some fighting continued into 1921. Although some researchers divide the Russian Civil War into several different wars, since there was cooperation among the various White armies, we consider this to be one civil war.

Sources: Baerlein (1971); Bradley (1963); Brinkley (1966); Clodfelter (2002); Dupuy and Dupuy (1970); Goldstone (1998); Heflin (1970); Liebman (1970); Phillips and Axelrod (2005); Silverlight (1970); Stewart (1933); Urlanis (1960); Yanaga (1949).

INTRA-STATE WAR #680:
The Finnish Civil War of 1918

Participants: Finland, Germany vs. Red Guard, USSR
Dates: January 28, 1918, to May 16, 1918
Battle-Related Deaths: Red Guard—8,500; Finland—5,300; Germany—950; USSR—400
Where Fought: Europe
Initiator: Red Guard

Outcome: Finland, Germany win
War Type: Civil for central control

Narrative: Finland had been under Russia control since 1809. Finland declared its independence in December 1917 under the moderate leadership of Pehr Evind Svinhufvud. Svinhufvud was determined not to share power with the Social Democrats, and Finland was soon divided along ideological lines. By January 1918 war had erupted between the Finnish security force (the White Guard) and the Red Guards established by the Social Democrats. The Red Guard was numerically superior, being able to mobilize 140,000 troops, and it was assisted by 10,000 Bolshevik troops that had remained in the country. The White Guard forces numbered at most 80,000 men, though in April Germany also sent 12,000 troops to their assistance. The Whites, however, also had professional military leadership, including Carl Gustaf von Mannerheim. The Whites defeated the Reds at the decisive battle at Tampere on April 6. Meanwhile, the German troops advancing toward Helsinki destroyed the remaining Socialist strongholds in the south. What followed after the conclusion of the war has been called the White Terror, during which Red prisoners were executed, starved, or massacred.

Sources: Clodfelter (2002); Gerrard (2000); Kohn (1999); Langer (1952); Siaroff (1999); Singleton (1989); U.S. Library of Congress (2008); Wuorinen (1965).

INTRA-STATE WAR #681:
The Western Ukrainian War of 1918–1919

Participants: Ukraine Poles vs. Ukrainians
Dates: November 1, 1918, to February 13, 1919
Battle-Related Deaths: Ukraine Poles—[ ];
    Ukrainians—[ ] (Total Combatant
    Deaths: 1,000)
Where Fought: Europe
Initiator: Poles

Outcome: Transformed into inter-state war #109
War Type: Regional internal

Narrative: Toward the end of World War I, the Western Ukraine declared itself to be an independent republic. The region was also inhabited by a significant number of Poles (39 percent), who responded to the declaration by forming their own army and launching a rebellion in the city of Lviv. Polish attacks drove back the smaller Ukrainian forces. The battle lines soon stabilized with the Poles occupying the western portion of the city, from which a rail line brought supplies from Poland. Fighting continued until the war was subsumed into the Russo-Polish War (inter-state war #109).

Sources: Brecke (1999); Clodfelter (2002); Hupchick and Cox (2001); Kubijovyč (1963); Prazmowska (2004); Sullivant (1962).

INTRA-STATE WAR #682:
The Sparticist Rising of 1919

Participants: socialists vs. German Freikorps
Dates: January 6, 1919, to May [ ], 1919
Battle-Related Deaths: socialists—2,100; German
    Freikorps—70
Where Fought: Europe
Initiator: socialists
Outcome: German Freikorps wins
War Type: Inter-communal

Narrative: Following Germany's defeat in World War I, there was a fear among Germany's ruling elite that the country faced the possibility of a Bolshevik uprising. To prevent such an occurrence, popular demonstrations were dispersed by the military. The ruling Council also fired the police chief of Berlin, who was a Socialist, and his dismissal became the precipitant for an uprising led by the radical Spartacus League. The German Freikorps, a band of ex-military officers and mercenaries, responded to the uprising, capturing and killing Spartacus League founders Rosa Luxembourg and Karl Liebknecht. The

Freikorps attacked the demonstrations in Berlin and then went on to suppress a revolt in Bavaria as well.

Sources: Clodfelter (1992); Phillips and Axelrod (2005); Waldman (1958).

INTRA-STATE WAR #683:
Hungary's Red Terror War of 1919–1920

Participants: Hungary vs. anti-Communists
Dates: March 25, 1919, to February 15, 1920
Battle-Related Deaths: Hungary—1,000; anti-Communists—500
Where Fought: Europe
Initiator: anti-Communists
Outcome: Anti-Communists win
War Type: Civil for central control

Narrative: The dual monarchy of Austria-Hungary dissolved in the aftermath of its defeat in World War I (inter-state war #106). Prime Minister Count Mihály Károlyi proclaimed Hungarian independence on November 16, 1918. Károlyi faced harsh demands by the victorious Allies and resigned in protest. In effect, he surrendered the government to Communist leader Béla Kun. Kun declared the creation of the Hungarian Soviet Republic in March 1919 and immediately created the Hungarian Red Army, which he utilized on the domestic front to force nationalization of Hungary's estates. Kun's policies immediately provoked a counterrevolution against him. The Communist government's effort to establish itself was further complicated when it was invaded by Romania and Czechoslovakia (inter-state war #112). Kun responded to the domestic revolt with arbitrary violence. He fled when the Romanians and Czechs troops arrived in Budapest on August 4. The leader of the counterrevolutionaries, Adm. Miklós Horthy de Nagybánya, ended the war and then became head of state in March 1920.

Sources: Adám (1993); Clodfelter (2002); Heflin (1970); Hentea (2007); Hupchick and Cox (2001);

Goldstone (1998); Jasci (1969); Kiritzesco (1934); Kohn (1999); Phillips and Axelrod (2005); Volgyes (1971).

INTRA-STATE WAR #685:
The First Chinese Warlord War of 1920

Participants: Anhui army vs. Chihli, Fengtien
Dates: July 14, 1920, to July 19, 1920
Battle-Related Deaths: Anhui army—[ ]; Chihli, Fengtien—[ ]
Where Fought: Asia
Initiator: Chihli, Fengtien
Outcome: Chihli, Fengtien win
War Type: Inter-communal

Narrative: Yüan Shih-k'ai's death in 1916 led to the "warlord" period (1920–1927), in which China was dominated by regional military leaders who engaged in a series of wars with one another. Overall, there were approximately 1,300 warlords, and they were involved in hundreds of conflicts; however, most of them did not entail war-level fatalities. Three separate warlord wars are included here (intra-state wars #685, #692, and #698). The chief objective of most of the warlords in these conflicts was to take control of Beijing. In this war Duan Qirui, who led the Anhui clique, fought against the Chihli clique, led by Feng Guozhang, who was allied with the Fengtien army, led by Chang Tso-lin. Duan Qirui had been the prime minister, though his opposition to peace between the north and the south after the Southern China Revolt (intra-state war #675) led to his resignation in 1918. The warlords of the Chihli clique and the Fengtien army wanted Duan to return control of his army to the ministry of war, and when he refused, they launched this war. Duan's army was quickly defeated, and the former prime minister was forced to flee.

Sources: Ch'en (1968); Chien-Nung (1956); Elleman (2001); Richardson (1960a); Schurmann and Schell (1967).

INTRA-STATE WAR #686:
The Green Rebellion of 1920–1921

Participants: USSR vs. peasants in Ta
Dates: August [ ], 1920, to August [ ], 1921
Battle-Related Deaths: peasants in Ta—5,000;
USSR—1,700
Where Fought: Europe
Initiator: peasants in Ta
Outcome: USSR wins
War Type: Civil for local issues

Narrative: Even after enduring civil war for over three years (intra-state war #677), the new Soviet Union continued to face more rebellions over local issues. One of these began in August 1920 in the Tambov province (southeast of Moscow) and was known as the Green Rebellion, since it concerned landownership. Russian peasants, fearing that their dreams of landownership would be dashed by the new Soviet regime, rebelled against Bolshevik forces. Although the Greens had 21,000 troops, they were attacked by Trotsky's new Soviet army, which defeated them within a year.

Source: Clodfelter (2002).

INTRA-STATE WAR #687:
The Gilan Marxists War of 1920–1921

Participants: Iran vs. SSRI, USSR
Dates: August 10, 1920, to November 11, 1921
Battle-Related Deaths: Iran—[ ]; SSRI—[ ];
USSR—[ ] (Total Combatant Deaths: 1,500)
Where Fought: Middle East
Initiator: SSRI
Outcome: Iran wins
War Type: Civil for central control

Narrative: At the end of the Russian Civil War (intra-state war #677), the Soviet fleet landed in May 1920 at the Iranian Caspian port of Enzeli, from which the Soviets soon extended their control over northern Iran. The Soviets came into contact with Kuchik Khan, the leader of a local

rebel group, the Jangalis ("Men of the Jungle"). The Jangalis had arisen among the small landholders in northern Iran during World War I. After the war they became influenced by Marxist ideology and were able to expand their influence in Gilan province. There the Soviets helped Mirza Kuchik Khan (or Kuchak Khan) establish the Soviet Socialist Republic of Iran (SSRI). In August 1920 the SSRI began assembling weapons and threatened to launch an offensive against Teheran. Iranian government troops responded and attacked the SSRI and Soviet troops at Manjil. The numerically superior Iranian troops, who were aided by the British, quickly defeated the SSRI forces. This war helped to spark the coup by Reza Khan Mirpanj, who overthrew the Qajar dynasty on February 21, 1921. Soon he also sent troops against the SSRI, and by November 11, 1921, the revolt was over, and the rule of the central Iranian government was again established over the region.

Sources: Chaqueri (1995); Lenczowski (1987).

INTRA-STATE WAR #688:
The Italian Fascist War of 1920–1922

Participants: Blackshirts vs. leftists
Dates: October [ ], 1920, to October 1, 1922
Battle-Related Deaths: leftists—3,000;
Blackshirts—300
Where Fought: Europe
Initiator: Blackshirts
Outcome: Blackshirts win
War Type: Inter-communal

Narrative: In March 1919 Benito Mussolini founded the fascist movement, with its Blackshirt military. The fascists were angered over the growing power of socialism and the economic dislocations in postwar Italy. This war involved a conflict between the Blackshirts and the leftists (that included liberals and socialists), and originated when the socialists seized factories and land in the countryside. The fascists intervened to protect the landlords and the factory owners, and over the course of two years, the fascists and leftists engaged in a series of attacks and riots. The fascists ultimately destroyed most of the leftist strongholds, while government forces did not intervene.

Sources: Clodfelter (1992); Goldstone (1998); Phillips and Axelrod (2005).

INTRA-STATE WAR #690:

The Kronstadt Rebellion of 1921

Participants: USSR vs. sailors
Dates: March 7, 1921, to March 18, 1921
Battle-Related Deaths: USSR—2,000; sailors—600
Where Fought: Europe
Initiator: sailors
Outcome: USSR wins
War Type: Civil for local issues

Narrative: The giant Russian naval base at Kronstadt near St. Petersburg was one of the major Russian naval facilities. The sailors at the base had played pivotal roles in the Russian civil wars in 1905 and 1917 (intra-state wars #643 and #677). By 1921, however, many of these revolutionary sailors had come to the conclusion that the new Soviet government had betrayed their ideals. In March 1921, 10,000 of them rebelled, though the number of revolutionaries soon reached 27,000 with the addition of additional seamen, allied soldiers, and civilians. A force of 45,000 Bolshevik troops moved against the rebels. The first Soviet attack was repulsed, but the Soviets soon succeeded in taking Kronstadt.

Sources: Clodfelter (2002); Phillips and Axelrod (2005).

INTRA-STATE WAR #691:

The Basmachi in Turkestan War of 1921–1923

Participants: USSR vs. Basmachi/Enver Pasha
Dates: November 10, 1921, to July [ ], 1923

Battle-Related Deaths: Basmachi/Enver Pasha—2,500; USSR—1,000
Where Fought: Europe
Initiator: Basmachi/Enver Pasha
Outcome: USSR wins
War Type: Civil for local issues

Narrative: Another challenge to the new Soviet regime took place in central Asia and involved the Basmachi. The Basmachi was an Islamic movement that opposed the societal changes implemented by the Bolsheviks. The Basmachi movement had been relatively dispersed; however, it was revitalized and centralized in the fall of 1921 by Enver Pasha (former leader of the Young Turk movement in the Ottoman Empire), who saw the Basmachi as a possible tool in a Pan-Turk confederation. Enver Pasha reformed and strengthened the Basmachi army of over 20,000 men and then launched a jihad against Soviet rule. Initially the Basmachi were successful in conquering most of Bokhara; however, the Soviets responded in 1922 with an offensive aimed at killing Enver Pasha. By August Enver was dead. Fighting continued under the leadership of Basmachi leader Selim Pasha, but the Basmachi suffered a series of defeats, and Selim Pasha fled in 1923.

Sources: Clodfelter (2002); Olcott (1981); Ritter (1985).

INTRA-STATE WAR #692:

The Second Chinese Warlord War of 1922

Participants: Chihli army vs. Fengtien army
Dates: April 8, 1922, to May 5, 1922
Battle-Related Deaths: Chihli army—[ ]; Fengtien army—[ ]
Where Fought: Asia
Initiator: Fengtien army
Outcome: Chihli army wins
War Type: Inter-communal

Narrative: The alliance of the Chihli clique and the Fengtien army had defeated the Anhui clique led by former prime minister Duan Qirui (intra-state war #685). The alliance between the two warlord armies had been one of convenience, however, and the two factions were soon battling each other for control of the north. The Chihli faction was now controlled by Wu P'ei-fu, while Chang Tso-lin was still the warlord of the Feng-tien army. The Chihli were victorious in this short war. As a result of the Fengtien loss, the president ordered Chang Tso-lin to be deprived of his rank and to remove his troops from the capital. Chang then merely returned to his base in Manchuria, where he worked to rebuild his army.

Sources: Chien-Nung (1956); Elleman (2001); Sheridan (1966).

INTRA-STATE WAR #693:
The Agrarian Rising of 1923

Participants: Bulgaria vs. Agrarian League
Dates: September 23, 1923, to September 28, 1923
Battle-Related Deaths: Bulgaria—[ ]; Agrarian League—[ ] (Total Combatant Deaths: 3,000)
Where Fought: Europe
Initiator: Agrarian League
Outcome: Bulgaria wins
War Type: Civil for central control

Narrative: In Bulgaria, Aleksandur Stamboliyski founded the peasant-based Agrarian League after World War I. This party campaigned in favor of an agrarian revolution and reform. The party also formed a paramilitary organization known as the Orange Guards. Stamboliyski's Agrarians won the 1920 election, but he was overthrown and murdered on June 8, 1923, by forces of the Right, which then banned the Agrarians. In September the Agrarians, with the help of Yugoslavia, began an armed rebellion against the government. It was suppressed with great severity by government forces.

Sources: Clodfelter (1992); Crampton (1987).

INTRA-STATE WAR #695:
The De La Huerta Rebellion of 1923–1924

Participants: Mexico vs. Huerta-led rebels
Dates: December 4, 1923, to February [ ], 1924
Battle-Related Deaths: Mexico—[ ]; Huerta-led rebels—[ ] (Total Combatant Deaths: 7,000)
Where Fought: W. Hemisphere
Initiator: Huerta-led rebels
Outcome: Mexico wins
War Type: Civil for central control

Narrative: When one of the victors of the Mexican Civil War (intra-state war #673), Álvaro Obregón, was finishing his presidential term, he chose his loyal lieutenant, Plutarco Elías Calles, to succeed him. Conservatives opposed the radical Calles and revolted in a barracks uprising. Much of the Mexican army followed the rebels, who were led by the minister of finance, Adolfo de la Huerta. An estimated 24,000 conservative civilians also joined the revolt as armed combatants. The insurgents won some victories, especially in Vera Cruz, Jalisco, and Oaxaca. From there they marched on the capital. But Obregón rallied the north, where his strength was. Also the United States sent arms to aid the Obregón government. The tide then turned, with the rebels being defeated soundly at Esperanza.

Sources: Clodfelter (1992); Scheina (2003b).

INTRA-STATE WAR #696:
The Honduran Conservative War of 1924

Participants: Honduras vs. conservatives
Dates: February 9, 1924, to March 31, 1924
Battle-Related Deaths: Honduras—[ ]; conservatives—[ ] (Total Combatant Deaths: 1,000)
Where Fought: W. Hemisphere
Initiator: conservatives
Outcome: Conservatives win
War Type: Civil for central control

Narrative: Honduras was long one of the most unstable states in Central America. In 1919 liberal Rafael López Gutiérrez launched an insurrection against President Francisco Bertrand, an incident during which the U.S. Marines were landed to keep order. Gutiérrez became president the following year. When the 1923 elections produced no clear winner, Gutiérrez declared a dictatorship. The conservatives led by Tiburcio Carías Andino revolted in 1924. In March the rebels occupied the capital and Gutiérrez was killed. The United States again landed more troops but did not become a formal intervener in the war, though it did promote a pact by which neighboring states agreed to stop providing bases for insurgents. A provisional president was chosen, and a new constitution was written.

Source: Stearns (2001).

INTRA-STATE WAR #697:
The First Afghan Anti-Reform War of 1924–1925

Participants: Afghanistan vs. Khost rebels (antireformists)
Dates: March 15, 1924, to January 15, 1925
Battle-Related Deaths: Afghanistan—[ ]; Khost rebels (antireformists)—[ ] (Total Combatant Deaths: 1,500)
Where Fought: Asia
Initiator: Khost rebels (antireformists)
Outcome: Afghanistan wins
War Type: Civil for central control

Narrative: In 1919 Amanullah became emir of Afghanistan. He began to promulgate reforms in this deeply traditional society and relied on German technical assistance for many of his programs. These reforms antagonized religious leaders and led to two uprisings, this one in 1924 and another in 1928 (intra-state war #705). In 1924 a rebellion was begun in April in Khost province by the Mangal tribe. The "Lame

Mullah" had prompted the revolt against what he saw as the anticlerical components of a new civil code. It took the government ten months to suppress the revolt.

Sources: Fletcher (1965); Fraser-Tyler (1967); Gregorian (1969); Lenczowski (1987).

INTRA-STATE WAR #698:
The Third Chinese Warlord War of 1925–1926

Participants: Feng Yuxiang army vs. Chang Tso-lin army
Dates: October 15, 1925, to April 20, 1926
Battle-Related Deaths: Feng Yuxiang army—[ ]; Chang Tso-lin army—[ ]
Where Fought: Asia
Initiator: Chang Tso-lin army
Outcome: Chang Tso-lin army wins
War Type: Regional internal

Narrative: Wu P'ei-fu's Chihli faction had defeated Chang Tso-lin's Fengtien army in the Second Chinese Warlord War (intra-state war #692). Chang had then retreated to his base in Manchuria, where he rebuilt his army. In 1924 Chang Tso-lin formed an alliance with former Chihli leader Feng Yuxiang and his Guominjun army. Their armies advanced to Beijing and removed the Manchu emperor Puyi from power. They asked former prime minister Duan Qirui to form a new government. Duan tried to come to terms with the Nationalist Guomindang (Kuomintang), but Sun-Yat-sen's death in 1925 derailed the initiative. Duan had no army of his own and instead relied on Feng Yuxiang's Guominjun. In a shift in warlord alliances, Chang Tso-lin now allied with Wu P'ei-fu, and they attacked Feng Yuxiang's Guominjun. By early in the next year, Feng Yuxiang's forces had been completely routed and Duan Qirui removed from power.

Sources: Chien-Nung (1956); Elleman (2001); Sheridan (1966).

INTRA-STATE WAR #700:

The Chinese Northern Expedition War of 1926–1928

Participants: warlord government vs.
Guomindang, Japan
Dates: July 1, 1926, to June 30, 1928
Battle-Related Deaths: warlord government—
78,000; Guomindang—48,000; Japan—500
Where Fought: Asia
Initiator: Guomindang
Outcome: Guomindang, Japan win
War Type: Civil for central control

Narrative: After his defeat in the Third Warlord War (intra-state war #698), Feng Yuxiang allied his Guominjun forces with the Nationalist Guomindang (Kuomintang), now controlled by Chiang Kai-shek. The Nationalists, who had established a rival government in the south, wanted to unite China under Nationalist leadership. Thus in July 1926 the Guomindang-Guominjun army began their northern offensive against the government in Beijing, and the warlords protecting it. By spring 1927 the Nationalists controlled the country south of the Yangtze River. The growing threat to the government in Beijing led Japan to intervene, sending troops to protect Japanese interests, which led to skirmishes with government forces. The Nationalists continued their advance and were ultimately successful in overthrowing the government in Beijing.

Sources: Brecher and Wilkenfeld (1997); Chi (1969); Chien-Nung (1956); Clodfelter (1992); Elleman (2001); Johnson (1976); McAleavy (1968); Richardson (1960a); Takeuchi (1935).

INTRA-STATE WAR #701:

The Cristeros Revolt of 1926–1929

Participants: Mexico vs. Cristeros
Dates: August 31, 1926, to June 21, 1929
Battle-Related Deaths: Mexico—6,000;
Cristeros—4,000

Where Fought: W. Hemisphere
Initiator: Cristeros
Outcome: Compromise
War Type: Civil for central control

Narrative: The liberal forces that had won the Mexican Revolution (intra-state war #652) had repressed the Catholic Church, believing that it had too much control over Mexican society. This had prompted two conservative rebellions (intra-state wars #673 and #695). The subsequent regime of President Plutarco Elías Calles was vehemently anticlerical, which precipitated a Catholic rebellion by the Cristeros. The rebellion began in the western provinces, and by 1929 the Cristeros controlled most of the region. Despite its superiority in weapons, the government was unable to militarily defeat the Cristeros. In order to try to end the war, the government of President Emilio Portes Gil removed many of the restrictions on the church. Most of the Cristeros then laid down their arms.

Sources: Bailey (1974); Clodfelter (1992); Cumberland (1972); Munro (1942); Parkes (1960); Phillips and Axelrod (2005); Scheina (2003b); Schlarman (1950).

INTRA-STATE WAR #702:

The Ethiopian Northern Resistance of 1928–1930

Participants: Ethiopia vs. Northern Resistance
Dates: August [ ], 1928, to April [ ], 1930
Battle-Related Deaths: Ethiopia—[ ]; Northern
Resistance—[ ] (Total Combatant
Deaths: 2,000)
Where Fought: Middle East
Initiator: Northern Resistance
Outcome: Ethiopia wins
War Type: Civil for local issues

Narrative: Ethiopia's ruler Lij Iyasu had angered many of his subjects by siding with the Central Powers in World War I (inter-state war #106). Lij Iyasu, a grandson of Emperor Menelik II, was

401

overthrown in 1916, and power was transferred to Empress Zawditu, a daughter of Menelik II, with Ras Tafari Makonnen as regent. In 1928, in the northeastern provinces, the Raya and the Azebo Oromo peoples began a series of raids against the Anfar people. This led to a violent clash with the troops of the local governor. Perceiving these growing conflicts as a threat to the central government, Tafari decided to act and sent an expedition against the Oromo. The government forces suffered several defeats in 1929. The empress's estranged husband, Ras Gugsa Welle (Wale) was opposed to the growing influence of Tafari, and he tried to take advantage of the situation to unite the Oromo and Tigreans in a broad resistance army. The armies met in battle in March 1930. Ras Gugsa's allies deserted him, and he was killed. The government was then able to defeat the remaining rebels. When Zawditu died in 1930, Tafari was crowned as Haile Selassie.

Source: McCann (1985).

INTRA-STATE WAR #703:
The Second Gansu Muslim War of 1928–1930

Participants: China vs. Gansu Muslims
Dates: [ ]/[ ]/1928, to [ ]/[ ]/1930
Battle-Related Deaths: China—[ ]; Gansu
  Muslims—[ ]
Where Fought: Asia
Initiator: Gansu Muslims
Outcome: China wins
War Type: Civil for local issues

Narrative: The First Gansu Muslim War, in 1895 (intra-state #628), had begun as an intra-Muslim conflict between the Salar and the Ma families, and the government became involved to suppress the conflict. In 1928 another member of the Ma family, Ma Zhongying, gathered a force of thousands of discontented Muslims and began attacking local Hans and Han officials. Their initial goal had been to maintain a degree

of regional independence, however, the central government needed the manpower and resources of the region, and thus needed to retain control. The unity of the Muslims began to break down, partially owing to personality conflicts. The war ceased when many of the Muslims ended their rebellion and instead joined the Guomindang as it fought against the warlords (intra-state war #706) and prepared for the war with the Communists (intra-state war #710).

Source: Lipman (1984).

INTRA-STATE WAR #705:
The Second Afghan Anti-Reform War of 1928–1929

Participants: Afghanistan vs. Habibullah
  (antireformists)
Dates: November 10, 1928, to October 15, 1929
Battle-Related Deaths: Afghanistan—7,500;
  Habibullah (antireformists)—7,500
Where Fought: Asia
Initiator: Habibullah (antireformists)
Outcome: Afghanistan wins
War Type: Civil for central control

Narrative: Amanullah Khan attempted to institute liberal reforms in Afghanistan, leading to clerical opposition in the First Anti-Reform War in 1924 (intra-state war #697). Although the government was able to defeat the earlier rebellion, opposition to Amanullah continued. In 1928 reactionary tribal chiefs rebelled, encouraged by the mullahs. On January 17 they took Kabul, forcing Amanullah into exile. The rebel chief seized the crown as Habibullah Khan and began a reign of terror. This prompted the formation of a counterrevolutionary army, led by Muhammad Nadir Khan. The rebels won a decisive victory at Charasih in early October 1929. The usurping king, Habibullah Khan, was captured and killed, and Nadir Khan became king of Afghanistan.

Sources: Clodfelter (1992); Fletcher (1965); Fraser-Tyler (1967); Gregorian (1969); Lenczowski

(1987); Phillips and Axelrod (2005); Richardson (1960a).

INTRA-STATE WAR #706:
The Intra-Guomindang War of 1929–1930

Participants: China vs. warlords
Dates: March 1, 1929, to November 4, 1930
Battle-Related Deaths: China—[ ]; warlords—[ ]
   (Total Combatant Deaths: 75,000)
Where Fought: Asia
Initiator: warlords
Outcome: China wins
War Type: Civil for central control

Narrative: The Nationalists had come to power at the end of their Northern Campaign (intra-state war #700), partially as a result of their alliance with several of the warlord armies. The victorious Guomindang (Kuomintang)–Guominjun alliance, however, soon fractured. Warlords Yan Xishan, Feng Yuxiang, and Li Zongren issued an anti–Chiang Kai-shek declaration and went to war with Chiang's Guomindang. The rebels launched a three-pronged assault in what was also known as the "Central Plains War." Both sides commanded armies in excess of 500,000 troops, and both secured victories in costly battles. The tide was turned in the government's favor in September when Manchurian warlord Chang Tso-lin and his army entered the war on the side of the government. The armies of the rebellious warlords soon withdrew from the war.

Sources: Clubb (1964); MacNair (1931); McAleavy (1968).

INTRA-STATE WAR #707:
The Escoban Rebellion of 1929

Participants: Mexico vs. Escoban-led rebels
Dates: March 3, 1929, to May 4, 1929
Battle-Related Deaths: Escoban-led rebels—1,600; Mexico—400
Where Fought: W. Hemisphere
Initiator: Escoban-led rebels
Outcome: Mexico wins
War Type: Civil for central control

Narrative: This was the final rebellion emanating from the Mexican Revolution. Liberal President Plutarco Elías Calles had already withstood a conservative challenge to his rule from the Cristeros (intra-state war #701). This new rebellion occurred from within the military, when former general Gonzálo Escobar initiated the war in early March 1929. About 30,000 troops and armed civilians joined his rebellion. Most of the Mexican army remained loyal to the government. In the decisive battle 9,000 federal troops easily defeated 8,000 rebels.

Sources: Clodfelter (1992); Scheina (2003b).

INTRA-STATE WAR #708:
The Ikhwan Revolt of 1929–1930

Participants: Saudi Arabia vs. Ikhwan
Dates: March 30, 1929, to October 10, 1930
Battle-Related Deaths: Ikhwan—5,000; Saudi Arabia—500
Where Fought: Middle East
Initiator: Ikhwan
Outcome: Saudi Arabia wins
War Type: Civil for central control

Narrative: Ibn Saud had finished uniting most of the Arabian Peninsula with the conquest of the Hejaz in 1925 (see non-state wars #1567 and #1568). On January 28, 1926, he became king of the United Kingdom of Najd and Hejaz, and Saudi Arabia became a member of the interstate system in 1927. Ibn Saud had come to power with the assistance of the Ikhwan, which was a paramilitary group of religious warriors; however, the Ikhwan became disenchanted with Ibn Saud because he was not as fervent a Wahhabi leader as they had hoped he would be. The main battle was at Sibillah on March 30, 1929, when the Saudi army of 30,000 defeated 10,000 Ikhwan.

Sources: Aburish (1995); Clodfelter (1992); Lacey (1981); Lenczowski (1987).

INTRA-STATE WAR #710:
The Chinese Civil War Phase 1 of 1930–1936

Participants: China vs. Communists
Dates: November 15, 1930, to December 31, 1936
Battle-Related Deaths: Communists—300,000; China—200,000
Where Fought: Asia
Initiator: Communists
Outcome: Stalemate
War Type: Civil for central control

Narrative: The Nationalist Guomindang (Kuomintang) and the Communists had turned from allies into long-term rivals for the control of China. Their united front had disintegrated in 1927, when conflicts between the two groups erupted in Shanghai and during the Communists' Autumn Harvest Campaign. After coming to power at the end of the Northern Expedition (intra-state war #700), the Guomindang began a series of campaigns, called Extermination Campaigns, in 1930. The Communists were able to hold their positions through the first four campaigns; however, during the fifth campaign, government forces came close to encircling the Communists. Consequently, the Communists decided to withdraw and begin the Long March to take the army to the north. They emerged at the end of the 6,000-mile trek with only 50,000 troops of the 200,000 who had set out. Fighting continued until 1936, when the two parties signed a united front agreement to respond to the growing Japanese threat. The Chinese Civil War went into hiatus until it revived (as intra-state war #725) at the end of World War II.

Sources: Clodfelter (1992); Clubb (1964); Elleman (2001); Isaacs (1961); McAleavy (1968); Phillips and Axelrod (2005); T'ang (1934); Wilson (1971).

INTRA-STATE WAR #711:
The Xinjiang Muslim Revolt of 1931–1934

Participants: China, USSR vs. central Asian rebels
Dates: February [ ], 1931, to August [ ], 1934
Battle-Related Deaths: central Asian rebels—10,000; China—10,000; USSR—1,000
Where Fought: Asia
Initiator: central Asian rebels
Outcome: China, USSR win
War Type: Civil for local issues

Narrative: China had long attempted to control the western area of Xinjiang (or East Turkestan). During periods of central government weakness, many regions within the area would typically attempt to revolt and break away. While the Chinese government was occupied with its war against the Communists (intra-state war #710), a weak Chinese governor was in charge of Xinjiang. The local Uighur and Tungan peoples rose in revolt against the local officials and ultimately declared their intent to secede. Although the rebels were successful in capturing much of the province, the Chinese government finally launched a pacification campaign, which, with assistance from the Soviet Union, was able to suppress the rebellion.

Sources: Starr (2004); Tyler (2004).

INTRA-STATE WAR #712:
The Matanza War of 1932

Participants: El Salvador vs. leftists
Dates: January 20, 1932, to January 29, 1932
Battle-Related Deaths: leftists—2,500; El Salvador—100
Where Fought: W. Hemisphere
Initiator: leftists

Outcome: El Salvador wins
War Type: Civil for central control

Narrative: El Salvador was ruled by the tyranni-cal government of Gen. Maximiliano Hernández Martínez. His rule, along with the great disparity in the distribution of wealth within the country, led to increasing opposition from the Commu-nist Party. The Communists aimed to overthrow the government and began organizing members of the military and peasantry for a revolt in January 1932. On January 22, 16,000 Salvadoran peasants, led by Augustíne Farabundo Martí, rebelled. The rebels attacked several towns but were totally unsuccessful. The government undertook a series of massacres called the Matanza, killing thousands of peasants.

Sources: Anderson (1971); Ching and Tilley (1998); Clodfelter (1992); Phillips and Axelrod (2005); Scheina (2003b); White (1973).

INTRA-STATE WAR #713:
The Aprista Revolt of 1932

Participants: Peru vs. Aprista rebels
Dates: May 7, 1932, to July 17, 1932
Battle-Related Deaths: Aprista rebels—1,000; Peru—100
Where Fought: W. Hemisphere
Initiator: Aprista rebels
Outcome: Peru wins
War Type: Civil for central control

Narrative: Founded by Victor Haya de la Torre, the Popular Alliance for Revolution in the Americas (APRA), or Aprista Party, was one of the more serious reformist parties in South America. Torre had a rancorous rivalry with the then-current Peruvian caudillo Luis Sánchez Cerro. After a bitterly contested presidential elec-tion, which Torre lost, the Apristas initiated civil disturbances to try to prevent Sánchez Cerro's inauguration. In March an Aprista member attacked the president. Torre was arrested,

precipitating the revolt, which began within the navy and spread to several towns as workers and students joined the insurrection. The rebels cap-tured the city of Trujillo, but it was retaken by the government forces in house-to-house fighting. The Apristas were soon defeated, and hundreds of Apristas were executed by the government.

Sources: Clodfelter (2002); Scheina (2003b).

INTRA-STATE WAR #715:
The Paulista Rebellion of 1932

Participants: Brazil vs. Paulistas
Dates: June 9, 1932, to August 31, 1932
Battle-Related Deaths: Brazil—[ ]; Paulistas—[ ] (Total Combatant Deaths: 5,000)
Where Fought: W. Hemisphere
Initiator: Paulistas
Outcome: Brazil wins
War Type: Civil for central control

Narrative: Brazilian politics often revolved around rivalry between the major states, includ-ing São Paulo and Minais Gerais. At the time of this revolt, the authoritarian regime of President Getúlio Vargas, who had come to power by revo-lution in 1930, was disliked by the Paulistas (of São Paulo). On July 9, 1932, the Paulistas rebelled. Anticipated assistance from other prov-inces never materialized. Vargas's 100,000 troops were able to surround and capture the city.

Sources: Bello (1966); Bernstein (1965); Clodfelter (1992); Richardson (1960a); Scheina (2003b); Young (1967).

INTRA-STATE WAR #716:
The Fukien Revolt of 1934

Participants: China vs. 19th Route Army
Dates: January 5, 1934, to January 15, 1934
Battle-Related Deaths: China—[ ]; 19th Route Army—[ ]
Where Fought: Asia
Initiator: 19th Route Army

Outcome: China wins
War Type: Civil for central control

Narrative: While the Guomindang (Kuomintang) was concentrating on its conflict with the Communists (intra-state war #710), opposition to the Guomindang rose from another source as well. The Guomindang's 19th Route Army had defended Shanghai from the Japanese in 1932, after which it was assigned to the city of Fukien. Although the army had previously fought against the Communists, it had begun talks with them in terms of creating a united front against Japan. The 19th Route Army became disenchanted with the lack of Guomindang measures against the Japanese, and in November of 1933 they established a People's Revolutionary Government in Fukien. The Guomindang sent troops to the region in January. A combination of air attacks and a ground assault defeated the Fukien forces within ten days.

Sources: Litten (1988); Thornton (1982).

INTRA-STATE WAR #717:
The Spanish Miners War of 1934

Participants: Spain vs. Asturian miners
Dates: October 4, 1934, to October 8, 1934
Battle-Related Deaths: Asturian miners—1,051;
    Spain—284
Where Fought: Europe
Initiator: Asturian miners
Outcome: Spain wins
War Type: Civil for local issues

Narrative: This war is a conflict that was a prelude to the Spanish Civil War of 1936–1939 (intra-state war #718). After the Spanish monarchy was deposed in 1931, Spanish politics had been dominated by a bitter rivalry between the Left and the Right. In October 1934 this rivalry led to war, when various groups of separatists, leftists, and anarchists rebelled in Madrid, Barcelona, and the province of Asturias. The conservative government in Madrid dispatched troops under Gen. Francisco Franco to subdue the revolt. The revolts were quickly squelched, except for that in Asturias. There, 70,000 miners had seized key positions. In heavy fighting the miners were defeated within days amid reports of torture by Franco's troops.

Sources: Clodfelter (1992); Phillips and Axelrod (2005); Oliviera (1946); Thomas (1961).

INTRA-STATE WAR #718:
The Spanish Civil War of 1936–1939

Participants: Spain vs. Falange, Germany, Italy,
    Portugal
Dates: July 18, 1936, to March 29, 1939
Battle-Related Deaths: Spain—286,000;
    Falange—174,000; Italy—4,000; Portugal—
    2,000; Germany—300
Where Fought: Europe
Initiator: Falange
Outcome: Falange, Germany, Italy, Portugal win
War Type: Civil for central control

Narrative: Since 1931, Spain's centrist republic had been thrown into turmoil by the strife between the extreme Right and Left. The leftist popular front won the 1936 elections and continued to institute secular reforms. The Falange Party, led by Gen. Francisco Franco, plotted military rebellion. A revolt by army officers in Melilla in Spanish Morocco on July 17, 1936, led to revolts at garrisons around Spain, and the rebels soon threatened Madrid. The loyalists fortified the city with the help of foreign volunteers. Great Britain and France initiated a policy of nonintervention, whereas Germany, Italy, and Portugal sent troops to aid the Falange. Madrid capitulated after a twenty-eight-month siege. At that point Franco was named chief of the Spanish state by the insurgents, and his autocratic rule lasted for four decades.

Sources: Carr (1982); Clodfelter (1992);
Coverdale (1975); Payne (1970); Phillips and
Axelrod (2005); Thomas (1961); Urlanis (1971).

INTRA-STATE WAR #720:

The Greek Civil War of 1944–1949

Participants: Greece, United Kingdom vs.
    Communists
Dates: December 3, 1944, to January 16, 1949
Battle-Related Deaths: Communists—50,000;
    Greece—17,970; United Kingdom—237
Where Fought: Europe
Initiator: Communists
Outcome: Greece, United Kingdom win
War Type: Civil for central control

Narrative: During World War II (inter-state war
#139), Communists in Greece had been promi-
nent in the resistance against the Germans. In
September 1944, however, the British had liberated Greece from the Nazis and restored the
prewar Greek government. Although the Communist National Liberation Front (EAM) party
was included in the government, a faction of its
military wing, the National Popular Liberation
Army (ELAS), resisted cooperating with the
British-backed government and confronted government and British troops in December 1944.
A truce among the parties that concluded in
February 1945 lasted a year and is coded as a
break in the war. Fighting resumed the following
year, and in May 1946 Communist rebels, supported by the neighboring Marxist-Leninist
states, began a general revolt against the Greek
government. Owing to declining British support, the United States began to send substantial
amounts of aid to the government, enabling it to
go on the offensive and defeat the Communists
in 1949.

Sources: Cady and Prince (1966); Clodfelter
(1992); Heflin (1970); O'Ballance (1966a); Phillips
and Axelrod (2005); Richardson (1960a); Taylor
and Hudson (1972); Wood (1968); Wright (1965).

INTRA-STATE WAR #721:

The Polish Ukrainians War of 1945–1947

Participants: Poland, USSR vs. Ukrainian Partisan
    Army (UPA)
Dates: May 8, 1945, to November 18, 1947
Battle-Related Deaths: Poland—11,000; UPA—
    8,700; USSR—5,000
Where Fought: Europe
Initiator: UPA
Outcome: Poland, USSR win
War Type: Civil for local issues

Narrative: Although the Ukraine had been part
of the Soviet Union, many Ukrainians sought
their own state. During World War II (inter-state
war #139) the Ukrainian Partisan Army (UPA)
fought for autonomy or independence against
the Germans, Soviets, and Poles. The end of
World War II marked the start of two separate
Ukrainian wars, including this one fought in
Poland and another fought in the Soviet Union
(intra-state war #722). At the end of the Russo-
Polish war (inter-state war #109), the Peace of
Riga in 1921 divided the territory of Ukraine
between the Soviet Union and Poland, with the
Ukrainians in western Galacia incorporated into
Poland. During World War II (inter-state war
#139), the Soviet Union occupied Galacia, and
the UPA resistance against the USSR, Germany,
and Poland is included within World War II. The
overall strength of the UPA in Poland in 1944
was 40,000 guerrillas. However, Soviet forces
also remained in Poland at the end of the war
(May 7, 1945), and the continuing UPA resistance is coded as this civil war fought in Poland
against Polish and Soviet troops. The UPA fought
for independence and to prevent ethnic Ukrainians from being deported to the USSR. The
Polish government forces gradually defeated the
UPA, subduing the army by November 1947.

Sources: Clodfelter (2002); *New York Times Index*
(1947).

INTRA-STATE WAR #722:

The Ukrainian Partisans War of 1945–1947

Participants: USSR vs. UPA
Dates: May 8, 1945, to December 31, 1947
Battle-Related Deaths: USSR—35,000; UPA—[ ]
Where Fought: Europe
Initiator: UPA
Outcome: USSR wins
War Type: Civil for local issues

Narrative: The Ukraine had been part of the Soviet Union prior to World War II (inter-state war #139); however, many Ukrainians sought an independent state. The Ukrainian Partisan Army (UPA) first began operations in 1942 against the Germans and then expanded to include fighting against the Soviets as the war wound down. The day after the end of World War II marks the start of this separate war, in which the UPA fought against the Soviet army and the NKVD (the Soviet secret police) within the Ukraine. The UPA in the Ukraine at its height had 90,000 men who engaged in a guerilla war, causing the deaths of over 35,000 Soviet troops. Although most of the fighting ended in 1947, limited attacks continued until 1954.

Sources: Clodfelter (2002); Magocsi (1996); Rieber (2003); Wilson (2000).

INTRA-STATE WAR #723:

The Forest Brethren War of 1945–1951

Participants: USSR vs. Baltic guerrillas
Dates: May 8, 1945, to December 31, 1951
Battle-Related Deaths: Baltic guerrillas—17,700; USSR—14,700
Where Fought: Europe
Initiator: Baltic guerrillas
Outcome: USSR wins
War Type: Civil for local issues

Narrative: All along the western borderlands of the Soviet Union, local guerrilla forces emerged during World War II (inter-state war #139) to oppose first the Germans and then the return of the Soviets. In the Baltic States (Estonia, Latvia, and Lithuania), they were known as the Forest Brethren (or Brothers). Fierce fighting occurred primarily in Lithuania between the Soviet army and the Brethren for the first two and a half years after the end of the World War (May 7, 1945), and then continued at lower levels. By 1951 the Soviets had crushed the partisans, though suffering heavy losses themselves.

Sources: Clodfelter (2002); Kaszeta (1988); Kuodytė and Tracevskis (2006); Nahaylo and Swobodo (1990); Raun (1987); Stašaitis (2000).

INTRA-STATE WAR #725:

The Chinese Civil War Phase 2 of 1946–1950

Participants: China vs. Communists
Dates: March 15, 1946, to April 21, 1950
Battle-Related Deaths: Communists—872,400; China—327,600
Where Fought: Asia
Initiator: Communists
Outcome: Communists win
War Type: Civil for central control

Narrative: As Japanese forces began to withdraw from China at the end of World War II (inter-state war #139), the Nationalist Guomindang and Communist forces took the opportunity to resume their struggle (see Phase 1 in 1930, intra-state war #710). The Nationalist forces were flown from their redoubt near Chungking to major cities in China with the help of the United States. Meanwhile, the Russians provided weapons to the Chinese Communists. The Chinese Communists, though based in the countryside, began to surround Nationalist garrisons in cities. The Nationalists, weakened by corruption among its military leaders and dissertions of the soldiers, were unable to garner popular support.

The Guomindang (Kuomintang) suffered a cascading series of defeats, from the north toward the south. In 1948 the Communists crossed the Yangtze, and Shanghai fell in May, Canton in October, and Chungking in November. The Nationalists had no recourse except to flee to Formosa (Taiwan), where they set up a government in exile, in December 1949. The Communists set up their own regime, the People's Republic of China, in Peking in October 1949. The final remnants of the Nationalist forces were defeated in early 1950.

Sources: Cady and Prince (1966); Clodfelter (1992); Clubb (1964); Elleman (2001); Kende (1971); McAleavy (1968); Phillips and Axelrod (2005); Taylor and Hudson (1972); Thornton (1982); Wright (1965).

INTRA-STATE WAR #726:

The Taiwan Revolt of 1947

Participants: China vs. Taiwanese
Dates: February 28, 1947, to March 21, 1947
Battle-Related Deaths: Taiwanese—1,000; China—250
Where Fought: Asia
Initiator: Taiwanese
Outcome: China wins
War Type: Civil for local issues

Narrative: Taiwan (or Formosa) had been acquired by Japan in 1895 as a result of the First Sino-Japanese War (over Korea) of 1894–1895 (inter-state war #73). In the aftermath of World War II (inter-state war #139), the island was returned to Chinese control; however, since the Taiwanese see themselves as different from the mainland Chinese, they chafed under rule by the Chinese Guomindang (Kuomintang). The revolt began in Taipei on February 28, 1947, and spread to other areas of the island. Ultimately, 80,000 Guomindang troops faced the rebels, who were crushed within weeks.

Sources: Clodfelter (1992); Kerr (1965).

INTRA-STATE WAR #727:

The Paraguay War of 1947

Participants: Paraguay vs. leftists
Dates: March 7, 1947, to August 20, 1947
Battle-Related Deaths: Paraguay—[ ]; leftists—[ ] (Total Combatant Deaths: 4,000)
Where Fought: W. Hemisphere
Initiator: leftists
Outcome: Paraguay wins
War Type: Civil for central control

Narrative: Since 1940, Gen. Higinio Morinigo had ruled Paraguay as a dictator. During the 1940s, Paraguay had frequent strikes, riots, and other violent disturbances sponsored by the liberals. Morinigo retained his position with the strong support of the military, which received 45 percent of national income in Paraguay. Although he allowed limited reforms in 1946, including the resumption of political party activities, the liberal Febreristas resigned from the cabinet in 1947. Under the leadership of Rafael Franco, the leftists attempted to seize power, leading to a five-month civil war, in which they were defeated. Morinigo remained in office until he was overthrown in a military coup in 1948.

Sources: Cady and Prince (1966); Cardoza (1949); Clodfelter (2002); Phillips and Axelrod (2005); Scheina (2003b); Warren (1949).

INTRA-STATE WAR #728:

The Yemeni Imamate War of 1948

Participants: Yemen vs. anti-imam coalition
Dates: February 17, 1948, to March 20, 1948
Battle-Related Deaths: Yemen—[ ]; anti-imam coalition—[ ] (Total Combatant Deaths: 4,000)
Where Fought: Middle East
Initiator: anti-imam coalition
Outcome: Yemen wins
War Type: Civil for central control

Narrative: Yemen was a deeply conservative society, ruled by Zaidi imams, and with regions dominated by semiautonomous tribes. Imam Yahya had been imam since 1904, and his son Ahmad was crown prince. Imam Yahya tried to isolate Yemen from the deleterious effects of modernization; however, outside influences began to trickle into Yemen, some from the nearby British colony at Aden and some from the few Yemenis who went abroad for education or employment. Such foreign ideas contributed to a growing opposition movement in Yemen. In 1948, a coalition of opposition groups decided to remove the imam from power. On February 17, 1948, the imam was murdered by "reformers," who then raised a revolt among the army. The rebels failed to kill Ahmad, and he rallied the tribes to his cause. In just over a month the rebels were defeated.

Sources: Burrowes (1987); Cady and Prince (1966); Ingrams (1963); O'Ballance (1970); Stearns (2001); Wenner (1991).

INTRA-STATE WAR #730:
The Costa Rica War of 1948

Participants: Costa Rica vs. National Union Party
Dates: March 12, 1948, to April 17, 1948
Battle-Related Deaths: Costa Rica—1,500; National Union Party—500
Where Fought: W. Hemisphere
Initiator: National Union Party
Outcome: National Union Party wins
War Type: Civil for central control

Narrative: The end of World War II (inter-state war #139) precipitated unrest and a number of wars. Even Costa Rica, which had a history of being relatively free of violent internal conflict, was affected. The 1948 presidential electoral contest was particularly strident. Although Otilio Ulate was initially declared the winner, the results were declared invalid by Congress. Civil war broke out, initiated by Ulate's followers (the National Union Party) led by Col. José "Pepe" Figueres Ferrer. The government forces

were aided by the followers of other candidate, Rafael Calderón Guardia. As Figueres's "Army of National Liberation" gained adherents, it went on the offensive and soon controlled most of the country. The president fled, and a junta that included Figueres ruled until Ulate was inaugurated that fall.

Sources: Bell (1971); Cady and Prince (1966); Clodfelter (1992); Phillips and Axelrod (2005); Scheina (2003b).

INTRA-STATE WAR #731:
The Seventh Colombian ("La Violencia") War of 1948–1958

Participants: Colombia vs. liberals
Dates: April 9, 1948, to August 7, 1958
Battle-Related Deaths: liberals—20,000; Colombia—9,800
Where Fought: W. Hemisphere
Initiator: liberals
Outcome: Colombia wins
War Type: Civil for central control

Narrative: In 1930 the liberals came to power in Colombia and initiated a reform agenda that exacerbated the conflict between the liberals and conservatives. In the 1946 presidential election, the liberals split, putting forward two candidates, which allowed the conservatives to capture the presidency. This war began when the popular liberal leader, Jorge Eliécer Gaitán, was assassinated on April 9, 1948. The murder sparked a long period of conflict known as La Violencia. The major participants in the conflict were the government, the liberal and conservative partisans, and general bandits. In terms of analyzing this conflict as a war, we have tried to avoid including activities and fatalities caused by the bandits and have attempted to focus instead on the combat between the government forces and the partisans. The initial attack was led by the liberal partisans, who attacked government installations, and the army was brought in to suppress the rebellion. Especially as the violence spread throughout the countryside, government forces became increasingly aligned with the conservatives when liberal brigades deserted, some joining the liberal partisans. In 1950 the government sent a military expedition to destroy the liberal strongholds in the plains. In 1958 the liberals and conservatives reached an agreement to establish the United Front. Although some fighting continued after that, it was at below war levels. In *Resort to Arms*, Small and Singer coded two separate wars in Colombia, one in 1948 and the other from 1949 to 1962. Since new evidence indicates that the fighting continued at war level in 1948–1949, we have combined them here.

Sources: Cady and Prince (1966); Clodfelter (1992); Kohn (1999); Huntington (1962); Kende (1971); Maullin (1973); Mydans and Mydans (1968); Petras (1968); Phillips and Axelrod (2005); Rummel (1972); Scheina (2003b); Taylor and Hudson (1972); Wood (1968).

other disaffected group was the Communists, who were denied a place in the government. The Communists began civil disobedience measures in March 1848; however, the war began with the Karens demand for independence in August. Working together in an informal alliance, the Karen National Defense Organization (KNDO) and the Communists soon controlled much of southern Burma. The government launched counteroffensives in 1949 and 1950 that regained control of the country. For the most part the Communists had been suppressed, and the government entered into an agreement with the Karens in 1951. War would resume in 1958 (intra-state war #746).

Sources: Cady (1958); Cady (1953); Cady and Prince (1966); Ciment (2007); Clodfelter (2002); Donnison (1970); Fearon and Laitin (2006); Phillips and Axelrod (2005); Taylor and Hudson (1972); Tinker (1957); Wood (1968).

INTRA-STATE WAR #732:
The First Burmese War of 1948–1951

Participants: Burma vs. Karens, Communists
Dates: August 15, 1948, to July 31, 1951
Battle-Related Deaths: Burma—[ ]; Karens, Communists—[ ] (Total Combatant Deaths: 8,000)
Where Fought: Asia
Initiator: Karens, Communists
Outcome: Burma wins
War Type: Civil for local issues

Narrative: Burma consists of a population that is about 60 percent Burman, with the rest belonging to various ethnic minorities including the Shan, Karen, Kachin, and Chin. When Burma gained its independence from Britain in 1948, the Karens objected to the fact that the Shan, Kachin, and Karenni tribes were granted semi-autonomous regions, while they were not. The

INTRA-STATE WAR #733:
The South Moluccas War of 1950

Participants: Indonesia vs. Moluccans
Dates: May 31, 1950, to November 3, 1950
Battle-Related Deaths: Indonesia—[ ]; Moluccans—[ ] Total Combatant Deaths: 5,000)
Where Fought: Asia
Initiator: Moluccans
Outcome: Indonesia wins
War Type: Civil for local issues

Narrative: As Indonesia gained its independence in 1949, the inhabitants of the South Moluccas wanted their own state. They declared their independence on April 26, 1950. Indonesia was not prepared to let them secede and therefore launched an offensive in September, deploying 20,000 troops, which soon suppressed the rebellion.

Sources: Armstrong (2004); Clodfelter (2002); Kahin (1952); Kosut (1967).

INTRA-STATE WAR #735:
The Hukbalahap Rebellion of 1950–1954

Participants: Philippines vs. Huks
Dates: November 1, 1950, to May [ ], 1954
Battle-Related Deaths: Huks—9,700;
  Philippines—1,600
Where Fought: Asia
Initiator: Huks
Outcome: Philippines wins
War Type: Civil for central control

Narrative: While under Japanese occupation in World War II, many Filipinos joined Communist-led anti-Japanese organizations called Hukbalahap, or the Huks. When the Philippines was granted independence in 1946, the Huks were excluded from the government. The Huks then retreated to the jungles and began a rebellion in 1948. The height of their insurgency came during 1950, with a Huk victory in Tarlac Province, where fighting attained war level by COW standards. Increased military assistance from the United States and a new counterinsurgency strategy developed by the minister of defense, Ramon Magsaysay, enabled the government to defeat the Huks.

Sources: Bashore (1962); Cady and Prince (1966); Ciment (2007); Clodfelter (2002); Hammer (1962); Kerkvliet (1977); Kohn (1999); Phillips and Axelrod (2005); Taylor and Hudson (1972); Tirona (1962); Vinacke (1956); Wood (1968).

INTRA-STATE WAR #737:
The Bolivia War of 1952

Participants: Bolivia vs. leftists
Dates: April 8, 1952, to April 11, 1952
Battle-Related Deaths: Bolivia—[ ]; leftists—[ ]
  (Total Combatant Deaths: 1,500)
Where Fought: W. Hemisphere
Initiator: Leftists
Outcome: Leftists wins
War Type: Civil for central control

Narrative: The Revolutionary Nationalist Movement (MNR) had briefly been in power in the mid-1940s but was outlawed in 1946. The MNR still had many adherents in Bolivia owing to its support for land reform. In the presidential election of 1951, the MNR candidate, Victor Paz Estenssoro, won a plurality of the votes. In order to prevent an MNR victory, the president ceded power to a military junta. The MNR then led a revolt against the government. The MNR was successful in overthrowing the junta, and Paz Estenssoro was recalled from exile to assume the presidency.

Sources: Alexander (1958); Cady and Prince (1966); Ciment (2007); Clodfelter (2002); Goldstone (1998); Kohn (1999); Malloy (1970); Phillips and Axelrod (2005); Scheina (2003b); Selbin (1993); Taylor and Hudson (1972); Wright (1965).

INTRA-STATE WAR #738:
The Indonesia-Darul Islam War of 1953

Participants: Indonesia vs. Darul Islam
Dates: September 20, 1953, to November 23, 1953
Battle-Related Deaths: Indonesia—1,700; Darul Islam—1,000
Where Fought: Asia
Initiator: Darul Islam
Outcome: Indonesia wins
War Type: Civil for central control

Narrative: When Indonesia gained its independence in 1949, it was confronted with several rebellions. One was conducted by a radical Islamic movement called Darul Islam. Darul Islam wanted Indonesia to abandon the idea of a secular state and to create an Islamic state. Darul Islam conducted a low-level revolt from 1949 onward, but the conflict did not become a war until it spread from its base in West Java to Aceh. In 1949 Islamic Aceh had been incorporated into Christian-dominated North Sumatra province. In reaction, in 1953 Teungku David

Beureueh, who was the military governor of Aceh from 1945 to 1953, declared that Aceh should instead be part of the Islamic state to be led by Darul Islam. Rebel attacks reached war level after a major revolt in September. In November, the Indonesian government launched an offensive that was able to contain the revolt, ending the war. Conflict did continue at below war levels until 1963, when Aceh was re-created as a province with a special provision for Islamic law. War would return in 1989 (intra-state war #853).

Sources: Armstrong (2004); Cady and Prince (1966); Cribb (1999); Kingsbury (2007); Kosut (1967); Lowry (1996); Tan (2000).

INTRA-STATE WAR #740:
The Argentine Military War of 1955

Participants: Argentina vs. military
Dates: June 15, 1955, to September 19, 1955
Battle-Related Deaths: Argentina—[ ]; army—[ ]
(Total Combatant Deaths: 3,000)
Where Fought: W. Hemisphere
Initiator: military
Outcome: Army wins
War Type: Civil for central control

Narrative: Juan Perón was a populist president and dictator who had ruled Argentina since 1946. His demagogic style appealed especially to the urban workers and poor, but his meddling in the economy created monetary chaos. He eventually made enemies of the Roman Catholic Church, other conservative groups, and the military. When Perón's popular wife, Eva, died in 1952, much of his support began to evaporate and he became even more radical. In June 1955, when Perón deported two bishops, the Vatican excommunicated him. That same day the navy and the air force launched a rebellion against Perón. The army generally stayed loyal and was initially able to suppress the rebellion; however, the rebels launched a second wave of attacks in September. Perón fled to Paraguay and on to Spain.

Sources: Clodfelter (2002); Phillips and Axelrod (2005); Rummel (1972); Scheina (2003b); Taylor and Hudson (1972).

INTRA-STATE WAR #741:
The Tibetan Khamba Rebellion of 1956–1959

Participants: China vs. Khamba Tibetans
Dates: March 1, 1956, to April 14, 1959
Battle-Related Deaths: Khamba Tibetans—12,000; China—4,000
Where Fought: Asia
Initiator: Khamba Tibetans
Outcome: China wins
War Type: Civil for local issues

Narrative: In 1951 the Dalai Lama's government of Tibet and the new People's Republic of China signed an accord reaffirming Tibet's existing political system. Since Outer Tibet was the focus of this status quo arrangement, the Chinese attempted to impose reforms on Inner Tibet, where the Khamba people lived. The Khamba objected to the Chinese plans and rose in revolt in defense of Tibetan religious institutions. The conflict began with Khamba attacks on Chinese officials. The attacks became more widespread, finally threatening Lhasa, the capital. The Chinese finally deployed an army of almost 70,000 troops to defeat the rebellion. The Dali Lama fled to India.

Sources: Clodfelter (1992); Norbu (1979); Patterson (1960a, 1960b); Richardson (1960a); Thomas (1959).

INTRA-STATE WAR #742:
The Indonesian Leftists War of 1956–1962

Participants: Indonesia vs. leftists
Dates: December 15, 1956, to June 4, 1962
Battle-Related Deaths: leftists—23,500; Indonesia—3,700

Where Fought: Asia
Initiator: leftists
Outcome: Indonesia wins
War Type: Civil for central control

Narrative: After gaining independence in 1949, Indonesia was confronted by opposition not only from a conservative Muslim movement (intra-state war #738) but also from its widespread islands. The government of Achmed Sukarno had become extremely authoritarian by the late 1950s. Leftist military officers, often representative of local ethnic groups, conducted a number of revolts in such widespread islands as Sumatra, Celebes, and Borneo, which all declared a desire for independence. Sukarno's army was able to put down these revolts, even though the United States was secretly dropping arms to the rebels.

Sources: Brackman (1963); Britton and Nixon (1975); Cady and Prince (1966); Clodfelter (2002); Cribb (1999); Feith (1964); Kohn (1999); Kosut (1967); Lowry (1996); Phillips and Axelrod (2005); Rummel (1972); Stearns (2001); Taylor and Hudson (1972).

INTRA-STATE WAR #743:
The First Lebanese War of 1958

Participants: Lebanon, United States vs. National Front
Dates: May 9, 1958, to September 15, 1958
Battle-Related Deaths: Lebanon—[ ]; National Front—[ ] (Total Lebanese Combatant Deaths: 1,400; United States—1)
Where Fought: Middle East
Initiator: National Front
Outcome: Lebanon, United States win
War Type: Civil for central control

Narrative: According to the National Pact, the president of Lebanon was to be a Christian, the prime minister a Sunni Muslim, and the speaker of Parliament a Shiite. Lebanon's religious diversity also promoted a policy of nonalignment, whereby Lebanon avoided alliances with either the West or the Arab East. Camille Chamoun, elected president in 1952, began to violate this unwritten rule by seeking closer ties to the West. This alienated the Muslim population, and Muslim groups united as the National Front in rebellion against Chamoun's government. In May 1958, there was major fighting in Beirut and Tripoli, and as the rebels (aided by the United Arab Republic) became increasingly successful, Chamoun asked the United States for help. President Dwight D. Eisenhower dispatched the Sixth Fleet, sending troops to Lebanon in July. Within two months the Lebanese and American troops had control of the situation, and Chamoun stepped aside, allowing Gen. Faud Chehab to become president.

Sources: Agwani (1965); Cady and Prince (1966); Clodfelter (2002); Lenczowski (1987); Nantet (1963); Phillips and Axelrod (2005); Rabinovich (1985).

INTRA-STATE WAR #745:
The Cuban Revolution of 1958–1959

Participants: Cuba vs. Castroites
Dates: May 24, 1958, to January 2, 1959
Battle-Related Deaths: Cuba—2,000; Castroites—1,000
Where Fought: W. Hemisphere
Initiator: Castroites
Outcome: Castroites win
War Type: Civil for central control

Narrative: Fidel Castro returned to Cuba in 1956 and assembled an armed guerrilla force in opposition to the unpopular government of Fulencio Batista. Although the rebels launched attacks against government forces in 1957, war-level hostilities did not begin until the following year. In April 1959 Castro called for a general strike. When that failed to materialize, the government launched a series of attacks against the guerrillas. The rebels began their major offensive in August, and the final advance began in

November. Batista fled in January 1959, and the rebels entered Havana.

Sources: Cady and Prince (1966); Clodfelter (2002); Mydans and Mydans (1968); Phillips and Axelrod (2005); Scheina (2003b); Taylor and Hudson (1972); Wood (1968).

INTRA-STATE WAR #746:
The Second Burmese War of 1958–1960

Participants: Burma vs. Karens, Communists
Dates: November [ ], 1958, to April [ ], 1960
Battle-Related Deaths: Karens, Communists—2,300; Burma—850
Where Fought: Asia
Initiator: Karens, Communists
Outcome: Conflict continues at below war level
War Type: Civil for central control

Narrative: In the First Burmese War (intra-state war #732), the government defeated a rebellion by the Communists allied to the Karens in 1951. Fighting between the government and these two groups reignited in 1958. Subsequently, Burma's Prime Minister U Nu offered concessions to the two rebel groups, which aroused concerns within Burma's military. The military staged a coup, replacing U Nu with Gen. U Ne Win. Fighting between the government and the rebels declined to below war levels after that.

Sources: Cady (1958); Cady and Prince (1966); Ciment (2007); Clodfelter (2002); Donnison (1970); Fearon and Laitin (2006); Phillips and Axelrod (2005); Taylor and Hudson (1972); Tinker (1957); Wood (1968).

INTRA-STATE WAR #747:
The Iraq-Shammar War of 1959

Participants: Iraq vs. Shammar tribe, pro-Western officers
Dates: March 6, 1959, to March 10, 1959
Battle-Related Deaths: Iraq—[ ]; Shammar tribe, pro-Western officers—[ ] (Total Combatant Deaths: 2,000)

Where Fought: Middle East
Initiator: Shammar tribe, pro-Western officers
Outcome: Iraq wins
War Type: Civil for central control

Narrative: In 1958 King Faisal II was overthrown by a revolutionary coup, and Premier Abdul Karim Qasim (Abdel Karim Kassem) began efforts to consolidate his power. Two major opposition groups were the Communists and the Nasserites, the latter of whom favored union with Egypt. Increasing Communist agitation prompted a dissident army faction in Mosul to act. The garrison, which was allied with the local Shammar tribe, seized power in Mosul and declared a revolt against Kassem's regime. Government forces, aided by the local Kurdish tribes, launched a counterattack that quickly defeated the rebels. In the aftermath of the war the Communists gained strength and a rally in Kirkuk in July 1959 led to widespread civilian bloodshed.

Sources: Ciment (2007); Lenczowski (1987); O'Ballance (1973); Taylor and Hudson (1972).

INTRA-STATE WAR #748:
The Vietnam War Phase 1 of 1960–1965

Participants: Republic of Vietnam, United States vs. NLF
Dates: January 1, 1960, to February 6, 1965
Battle-Related Deaths: NLF—76,900; Republic of Vietnam—23,300; United States—506
Where Fought: Asia
Initiator: NLF
Outcome: Transformed into inter-state war #163
War Type: Civil for central control

Narrative: After the French colonial rule in Vietnam had been defeated (extra-state war #457), the Geneva Accords divided Vietnam at the 17th parallel into two disparate districts. Although this division was supposed to be temporary, the southern sector soon solidified as the Republic of Vietnam. South Vietnam's Communists, the Viet Cong, launched a civil war against the government. Guerrilla activities began in 1958, though the conflict does not cross our war-severity threshold until 1960, the year in which the rebels took the name the National Liberation Front (NLF). The United States had some 800 "advisers" in South Vietnam. However, the United States is not coded as an intervener in the war until 1961, by which time there were a sufficient number of these advisers assisting the Saigon government against the NLF for the United States to be considered a war participant (a minimum of 1,000). Thus the civil war phase of the Vietnam conflict continued until February 6, 1965. On February 7, 1965, after the NLF attack on Pleiku, the United States started to bomb North Vietnam and thus converted the war into an inter-state war (#163).

Sources: Alcock and Lowe (1970); Baldwin (1972); Bourne (1970); Buttinger (1967); Chomsky (1971); Ciment (2007); Clodfelter (2002); Cooper (1970); Gettleman (1970); Grant (1970); Herr (1977); Herring (1979); Kahin and Lewis (1969); Kende (1971); Leitenberg and Burns (1973); Phillips and Axelrod (2005); Pike (1966); Taylor and Hudson (1972); Turner (1975); U.S. Senate (1969).

INTRA-STATE WAR #750:

The First DRC (Zaire) War of 1960–1963

Participants: Zaire vs. Katanga, leftists, Belgium
Dates: July 4, 1960, to January 14, 1963
Battle-Related Deaths: Zaire—[ ]; Katanga, leftists—[ ] (Total DRC Combatant Deaths: 9,000; Belgium—50)
Where Fought: Africa
Initiator: Katanga, leftists
Outcome: Zaire wins
War Type: Civil for local issues

Narrative: The Belgian Congo was one of the most misruled colonies in Africa. Belgian rule collapsed after riots in 1959, and the Congo was

granted independence on June 30, 1960. Though initially known as the Republic of Congo, in order to differentiate it from its neighbor of the same name, it is currently referred to as the Democratic Republic of Congo (DRC). The leadership of the country was not entirely prepared to lead the new state, and President Joseph Kasavubu and Premier Patrice Lumumba had radically different political agendas. In early July, Moise-Kapenda Tshombe, head of Katanga province, declared its independence and started the war. Lumumba asked for Soviet help, which led to his ouster and death in circumstances that suggested the complicity of Belgium and the United States. Kasavubu sought the deployment of UN peacekeepers to aid the government, while Belgium briefly intervened against the government to protect Europeans resident in the country. The forces of the United Nations did actively intervene in the war, helping to defeat Tshombe and reunify the Congo; however, another war would begin within months (intra-state war #760).

Sources: Bercovitch and Fretter (2004); Cady and Prince (1966); Ciment (2007); Clodfelter (2002); Cutter (2007); Meredith (2005); Mydans and Mydans (1968); Lefever (1972); Oliver and Atmore (2004); Phillips and Axelrod (2005); Stearns (2001); Taylor and Hudson (1972); Van Nederveen (2001).

INTRA-STATE WAR #751:

The First Laotian War of 1960–1962

Participants: Laos vs. Democratic Republic of Vietnam, Pathet Lao
Dates: October 15, 1960, to July 15, 1962
Battle-Related Deaths: Laos—4,000; Pathet Lao—1,000; Democratic Republic of Vietnam—[ ]
Where Fought: Asia
Initiator: Pathet Lao
Outcome: Compromise
War Type: Civil for central control

Narrative: After gaining its independence from France, Laos was consumed by the rivalry among the royalist conservative government, the Marxist Pathet Lao, and neutralists. The Pathet Lao started the conflict against the Royal Lao Army in 1959, but it did not reach war level until 1960. Most of the fighting took place on the Plain of Jars in north-central Laos. The Communist offensive gradually gained control over most of the northeast, which prompted the United States to increase its military assistance to the government. At this point North Vietnam directly intervened in the war on the side of the insurgents. A cease-fire in 1961 briefly stopped the fighting, and an international conference in Geneva tried to reach a settlement. The government soon resumed the hostilities, leading to its defeat at Nam Tha in early 1962. In June the parties agreed to form a coalition government, and in July a meeting in Geneva provided international guarantees for neutrality. Nevertheless, Laos was destined to remain embroiled in fighting between Communist and anti-Communist forces, and war resurfaced less than a year later (intra-state war #756).

Sources: Adams and McCoy (1970); Cady and Prince (1966); Chomsky (1971); Clodfelter (2002); Gettleman (1970); Isaacs et al. (1987); Langer and Zaslof (1970); Mydans and Mydans (1968); Phillips and Axelrod (2005); Taylor and Hudson (1972); Wood (1968); Zhang (2002).

INTRA-STATE WAR #752:
The First Iraqi Kurds War of 1961–1963

Participants: Iraq vs. Kurds
Dates: September 11, 1961, to November 22, 1963
Battle-Related Deaths: Kurds—2,000; Iraq—500
Where Fought: Middle East
Initiator: Kurds
Outcome: Stalemate
War Type: Civil for local issues

Narrative: The Kurds, some of whom live in northern Iraq, were desirous of having an independent state and created the Kurdish Democratic Party (KDP). President Abdul Karim Qasim (Abdel Karim Kassem) had initially promised the Kurds a degree of autonomy, but when KDP leader Mullah Mustafa Barzani began to assert control over the region, war broke out. The Kurds attacked an Iraqi military column in September 1961, starting the war. The Iraqis retaliated, and in combat over the next two years, they generally gained control over the cities, but even government bombing campaigns were unable to defeat the Kurds in their mountain strongholds. In addition to the combatants, thousands of civilians were killed. The war ended when the new Baath government announced that it would seek a negotiated settlement to the war. A cease-fire was signed in February 1964 that generally held until fighting resumed in 1965 (intra-state war #765).

Sources: Bercovitch and Fretter (2004); Ciment (2007); Clodfelter (2002).

INTRA-STATE WAR #753:
The Algerian Revolutionaries War of 1962–1963

Participants: Algeria vs. ALN
Dates: July 28, 1962, to January 15, 1963
Battle Related Deaths: Algeria—800; ALN—700
Where Fought: Middle East
Initiator: ALN
Outcome: ALN wins
War Type: Civil for central control

Narrative: Algeria gained its independence from France in 1962 after an eight-year war (extra-state war #466). That war had been launched by the Algerian National Liberation Front (FLN). During the war the FLN established a provisional government, which soon came under the leadership of Ben Yusuf Ben Khedda. Ben Khedda formed the first Algerian government after independence. He soon faced growing opposition from the more radical Ahmed Ben

Bella, who had the support of the National Liberation Army (ALN), which was under the leadership of Houari Boumédienne. The ALN opposed the FLN's more centralized government and initiated a war for control of the new government. Elections held in September chose Ben Bella as resident, though clashes with the FLN continued into the next year. In addition to the combatants, up to 45,000 civilians died as a result of the war.

Sources: Cady and Prince (1966); Ciment (2007); Clodfelter (2002); Horne (1977); Keesing's (1962); Ottaway (1970); Stearns (2001); Stone (1997).

INTRA-STATE WAR #755:
The North Yemen War of 1962–1969

Participants: Egypt/United Arab Republic, Yemen Arab Republic vs. Royalists
Dates: November 15, 1962, to September 3, 1969
Battle-Related Deaths: Egypt/United Arab Republic—10,000; Yemen Arab Republic—[ ]; Royalists—[ ] (Total Combatant Deaths: 100,000)
Where Fought: Middle East
Initiator: Royalists
Outcome: Yemen, Egypt win
War Type: Civil for central control

Narrative: Yemen had been under the rule of the Zaidi imams, who had tried to preserve their traditional society by limiting outside influences. This conservatism led to war in 1948 (intra-state war #728). Opposition to the imam's rule resurfaced in late September 1962, when the imam was overthrown by the military and a republic proclaimed under the leadership of Abdullah al-Sallal. The imam fled to the interior, where he was able to persuade loyal tribes to launch a war against the new regime. Shortly thereafter Egypt sent troops to assist the Yemeni government. The war evolved into a general stalemate. Even after the withdrawal of Egypt's 55,000 troops in 1967, the royalists were unable

to defeat the government. When the government finally broke the rebels' siege of Sanaa, the rebellion soon collapsed.

Sources: Burrowes (1987); Cady and Prince (1966); Clodfelter (2002); Keesing's (1963); Mydans and Mydans (1968); O'Ballance (1970); Phillips and Axelrod (2005); Taylor and Hudson (1972); Wenner (1991); Wood (1968).

INTRA-STATE WAR #756:
The Second Laotian War Phase 1 of 1963–1968

Participants: Laos, United States vs. Democratic Republic of Vietnam, Pathet Lao
Dates: March 19, 1963, to January 12, 1968
Battle-Related Deaths: Laos—11,250; Pathet Lao—7,250; Democratic Republic of Vietnam—2,250; United States—200
Where Fought: Asia
Initiator: Pathet Lao
Outcome: Transformed into inter-state war #170
War Type: Civil for central control

Narrative: The Laotian government and the Communist Pathet Lao had ended their first war (intra-state war #751) by forming a coalition government. In early 1963 the coalition collapsed and the fighting resumed. The North Vietnamese continued to increase the level of their commitment to the Pathet Lao throughout 1963. The Communists continued to expand their control, and by the end of 1963 the Pathet Lao controlled two-thirds of the country. In 1964, another Pathet Lao brought them to within ninety miles of Vientienne. In May 1964 the United States began reconnaissance flights over Laos and soon was bombing Pathet Lao positions, thus making the United States an intervener in the war. As the intensity of the war in Vietnam increased (inter-state war #163), so did the commitments of the United States and North Vietnam to the war in Laos. By 1968 the North Vietnamese had 200,000 troops in Laos. The biggest victory of the Pathet Lao/North

Vietnamese offensive occurred at Nam Bac, where the government's garrison was overrun in January 1968. At this point the United States and North Vietnam take over the bulk of the fighting, ending this civil war and transforming it into the "second phase" of this war, inter-state war #170.

Sources: Adams and McCoy (1970); Brown (2001b); Chomsky (1971); Clodfelter (2002); Gettleman et al. (1970); Girling (1970); Isaacs et al. (1987); Keesing's (1970–1974); Langer (1968); Langer and Zasloff (1970); Mydans and Mydans (1968); Simmonds (1973); Taylor and Hudson (1972); Wood (1968); Wright (1965); Zhang (2002).

INTRA-STATE WAR #757:

The First Ogaden War of 1963–1964

Participants: Ethiopia vs. Ogaden, Somalia
Dates: June [ ], 1963, to March 30, 1964
Battle-Related Deaths: Ethiopia—[ ]; Ogaden—[ ]; Somalia—[ ]
Where Fought: Africa
Initiator: Ogaden
Outcome: Ethiopia wins
War Type: Civil for local issues

Narrative: The Somali people inhabit not only Somalia but also areas of Djibouti, the eastern Ogaden region of Ethiopia, and northern Kenya. After attaining its independence from Britain in 1960, Somalia began efforts to liberate the Somalis living in the Ogaden region of Ethiopia. In June 1963 the Ogaden, with Somali encouragement, began a rebellion against Ethiopia. In November, Somalia sent troops to assist the rebels. Ethiopia retaliated with air strikes, both in the Ogaden and against Somalia in January 1964. At that point Sudan mediated a cease-fire, which generally stopped the fighting. War would resume in 1976 (intra-state war #805).

Sources: Bercovitch and Fretter (2004); Ciment (2007); Cordesman (1993); Meredith (2005).

INTRA-STATE WAR #758:

The First South Sudan War of 1963–1972

Participants: Sudan vs. Anya-Nya
Dates: October 1, 1963, to February 28, 1972
Battle-Related Deaths: Sudan—[ ]; Anya-Nya—[ ]
 (Total Combatant Deaths: 100,000)
Where Fought: Africa
Initiator: Anya-Nya
Outcome: Compromise
War Type: Civil for local issues

Narrative: The animist and Christian black ethnic groups in southern Sudan chafed under a government dominated by the Muslim Arab peoples of northern Sudan. Gen. Ibrahim Abboud, who had come to power as the result of a military coup in 1958, began the process of trying to extend Arab control. In the late 1950s black resistance turned into an organized, rebellious armed movement. They called themselves the Land Freedom Army, or the Anya-Nya ("snake venom"). It also evolved into a broader movement, the Sudan African National Union (SANU) in 1963. Under the leadership of Emilio Tafeng, SANU began a rebellion. The Sudanese army was increased in the south to 20,000 and received assistance from Egypt. The guerrillas, who numbered around 10,000 at their peak, received assistance from Israel. This was a vicious war, destroying huge areas of southern Sudan. In addition to the combatants, as many as 400,000 civilians died. After Col. Gaafar Mohammed Nimeiry seized power in 1969, he began negotiations with the rebels. This war finally ended with a negotiated peace, which granted the south some autonomy. Promises of autonomy were never realized, however, and within a little more than a decade, war resumed (intra-state war #836).

Sources: Clodfelter (2002); Cordesman (1993); Edgerton (2002); Eprik (1972); Johnson (2003); Meredith (2005); Taylor and Hudson (1972); Wood (1968).

INTRA-STATE WAR #760:
The Second DRC (Jeunesse) War of 1963–1965

Participants: Congo vs. Jeunesse warriors
Dates: October [ ], 1963, to January 1, 1965
Battle-Related Deaths: Congo—[ ]; Juenesse warriors—[ ] (Total Combatant Deaths: 9,000)
Where Fought: Africa
Initiator: Jeunesse warriors
Outcome: Congo wins
War Type: Civil for local issues

Narrative: The first Democratic Republic of Congo (DRC) war (intra-state war #750), which ended in January 1963, had involved Katanga's attempt to secede. Later that year another revolt broke out in Kwilu province, begun by a group calling themselves the Jeunesse ("young warriors"). Under the leadership of Maoist Pierre Mulele, the Jeunesse began attacks against government forces, interspersed with urban guerrilla actions and terrorism. Even though the rebels were poorly armed, it took the government over a year to crush their revolt.

Sources: Clodfelter (2002); Meredith (2005); Phillips and Axelrod (2005).

INTRA-STATE WAR #761:
The First Rwanda War of 1963–1964

Participants: Rwanda vs. Watusi
Dates: November 15, 1963, to February 6, 1964
Battle-Related Deaths: Watusi—900; Rwanda—100
Where Fought: Africa
Initiator: Watusi
Outcome: Rwanda wins
War Type: Civil for central control

Narrative: During the final years of Belgium's control over Rwanda, the Social Revolution broke out between the Hutu and the Tutsi peoples (non-state war #1574). The Hutu prevailed, the Tutsi king was deposed, and Rwanda became a republic when it attained its independence from Belgium in 1962. At that point approximately 140,000 Tutsi fled to nearby countries. In 1963 the Tutsi émigrés invaded Rwanda to try to oust the Hutu-dominated regime. The Tutsi launched a five-pronged invasion but were easily repulsed by government forces. Conflict between the Hutu and Tutsi was reignited in the Second Rwanda War (intra-state #886) and the ensuing genocide of 1994.

Sources: "Atlantic Report: Rwanda" (1964); Ciment (2007); Clodfelter (2002); Cutter (2007); Edgerton (2002); Lemarchand (1970); Meredith (2005); Phillips and Axelrod (2005); Taylor and Hudson (1972).

INTRA-STATE WAR #762:
The Third DRC (Simba) Rebellion of 1964–1965

Participants: Belgium, DRC vs. Gbenye followers
Dates: January 1, 1964, to September 14, 1965
Battle-Related Deaths: Gbenye followers—4,000; DRC—250; Belgium—4
Where Fought: Africa
Initiator: Gbenye followers
Outcome: Belgium, DRC win
War Type: Civil for central control

Narrative: While the Democratic Republic of Congo (DRC) was involved with the Jeunesse revolt in Kwilu province (intra-state war #760), a second revolution, led by Christophe Gbenye, broke out in the same region. The rebels were called the Simbas ("Lions"), and they quickly defeated the government army and established control over the northeast, capturing Stanleyville in August 1964. Moise-Kapenda Tshombe, the former Katangan secessionist leader (see intra-state war #750), was recalled from exile to become premier and to deal with the rebellion. The U.S. Air Force assisted in transporting Belgian troops who parachuted into Stanleyville in November (thus making Belgium a participant in the war).

The Simbas received help from Cuba, Algeria, and Egypt but were defeated in 1965.

Sources: Clodfelter (2002); Van Nederveen (2001).

INTRA-STATE WAR #763:

The Zanzibar Arab-African War of 1964

Participants: Zanzibar Arab government vs. Okello-led Africans
Dates: January 12, 1964, to January 15, 1964
Battle-Related Deaths: Zanzibar—[ ]; Okello-led Africans—[ ]
Where Fought: Africa
Initiator: Okello-led Africans
Outcome: Okello-led Africans win
War Type: Civil for central control

Narrative: Sultan Sayyid Said of Oman became sultan of Zanzibar as a result of non-state war #1514. Through an agreement with Germany, Britain gained a protectorate over Zanzibar in 1890, though it maintained the Arab ruling structure until granting Zanzibar its independence in December 1963. In 1964 the government of Sultan Jamshid ibn Abdullah was challenged by a leftist revolt by the majority African population led by Joseph Okello. After the brief fighting, during which thousands of Arab civilians also were killed, the sultan fled and a republic was established under the leadership of Abeid Karume, leader of the Afro-Shirazi Party (ASP). Karume then began suppressing the Arab elite.

Sources: Clodfelter (2002); Cutter (2007); Meredith (2005).

INTRA-STATE WAR #765:

The Second Iraqi Kurds War of 1965–1966

Participants: Iraq vs. Kurds
Dates: April 3, 1965, to June 21, 1966
Battle-Related Deaths: Kurds—2,500; Iraq—500

Where Fought: Middle East
Initiator: Iraq
Outcome: Compromise
War Type: Civil for local issues

Narrative: The First Iraqi Kurds revolt ended in a stalemate and a cease-fire agreement signed by the new Baathist regime (intra-state war #752). The government's refusal to make further concessions to the Kurds prompted the Kurds to establish a Revolutionary Council in October 1964, which soon had control over most of Kurdistan. As the Kurds became increasingly autonomous, the Iraqi government decided it had to reassert control and launched an offensive against the Kurds in April 1965. A cease-fire was arranged after the army lost several battles against the Kurdish Peshmerga. The fighting had ended in a stalemate, and in the subsequent agreement the Kurds were recognized as part of a binational state and their rights were to be ensured. The two parties would go to war again in 1969 (intra-state war #777).

Sources: Bercovitch and Fretter (2004); Clodfelter (2002); Keesing's (1954–1966).

INTRA-STATE WAR #766:

The Dominican Republic War of 1965

Participants: Dominican Republic, United States vs. leftists
Dates: April 25, 1965, to September 6, 1965
Battle-Related Deaths: Dominican Republic—[ ]; leftists—[ ] (Total Dominican Combatant Deaths: 3,000; United States—27)
Where Fought: W. Hemisphere
Initiator: leftists
Outcome: Conflict continues at below war level
War Type: Civil for central control

Narrative: On September 25, 1963, a military junta staged a coup against leftist president Juan Bosch. Popular resistance to the junta spread, and in April 1965 pro-Bosch army troops (constitutionalists) revolted against the two-year-old government. In order to forestall what he believed would be a Communist takeover, U.S. president Lyndon Johnson sent in thousands of U.S. troops on April 28, 1965, to intervene on the side of the government. The government and American troops gradually retook constitutionalist positions. The Organization of American States (OAS) tried to arrange a truce in May, but order was not fully restored until September.

Sources: Bercovitch and Fretter (2004); Cady and Prince (1966); Carey (1972); Ciment (2007); Clodfelter (2002); Gleijeses (1978); Mydans and Mydans (1968); Phillips and Axelrod (2005); Scheina (2003b); Taylor and Hudson (1972); Wood (1968).

INTRA-STATE WAR #767:

The First West Papua War of 1965–1969

Participants: Indonesia vs. OPM, West Papua
Dates: July 26, 1965, to September 17, 1969
Battle-Related Deaths: Indonesia—[ ]; OPM, West Papua—[ ] (Total Combatant Deaths: 3,000)
Where Fought: Asia
Initiator: OPM, West Papua
Outcome: Stalemate
War Type: Civil for local issues

Narrative: West Irian (Irian Jaya) occupies the western half of the island of New Guinea, while Papua New Guinea occupies the eastern half. The Dutch ceded West Irian to Indonesia in 1963 with the stipulation that Indonesia prepare it for independence. Instead, Indonesia tried to extend its control over the area. Consequently, the Free Papua Movement (OPM) began a rebellion. After early victories government troops were forced to draw back in the faced of determined resistance. The rebels captured Manokwari in January 1967, where a Free Papuan State was declared. The conflict ended in a stalemate in 1969, when the United Nations conducted a referendum in West Irian that approved Indonesia's

annexation of the region. War would return in 1976 (intra-state war #802).

Sources: Bercovitch and Fretter (2004); Ciment (2007); Elmslie (2003); Facts on File (1969); Minahan (1996); Project Ploughshares (2000).

INTRA-STATE WAR #768:

The First Uganda War of 1966

Participants: Uganda vs. Baganda tribe
Dates: May 23, 1966, to June 1, 1966
Battle-Related Deaths: Uganda—[ ]; Baganda tribe—[ ] (Total Combatant Deaths: 1,000)
Where Fought: Africa
Initiator: Baganda tribe
Outcome: Uganda wins
War Type: Civil for local issues

Narrative: Uganda attained its independence from Britain in 1962. At that point Milton Obote became prime minister, with Mutesa II, the traditional *kabaka*, or king, of the Baganda tribe, as a ceremonial president. Obote, however, saw the *kabaka* as a rival for power in Uganda, and in April 1966, Obote had him removed from office. The Baganda parliament then launched a rebellion. The revolt lasted just over a week, and it was suppressed by Obote's government. The *kabaka* went into exile in London.

Sources: Brogan (1998); Ciment (2007); Edgerton (2002); Gukiina (1972); Meredith (2005); Taylor and Hudson (1972); Young (1966).

INTRA-STATE WAR #770:

The First Guatemala War of 1966–1968

Participants: Guatemala, United States vs. leftists
Dates: October [ ], 1966, to August [ ], 1968
Battle-Related Deaths: leftists—800; Guatemala—200; United States—28
Where Fought: W. Hemisphere
Initiator: leftists
Outcome: Guatemala, United States win
War Type: Civil for central control

Narrative: After the overthrow of President Jacobo Arbenz Guzmán's government in 1954, Guatemala was ruled by a succession of right-wing military dictators. In response, leftist revolutionary organizations were formed, including the Revolutionary Armed Forces (FAR) and the Revolutionary Movement. In July 1966 Julio César Méndez Montenegro became president and tried unsuccessfully to reach an agreement with the leftists. FAR, now under the leadership of César Montes, began a series of attacks throughout the countryside against the government. Forces from the United States helped the Guatemalan government pursue the rebels. The leftists were also attacked by rightist paramilitary organizations, including the White Hand, a Guatemalan militia group. By 1968 the level of violence had dropped below war level, though war would return two years later (intra-state war #781).

Sources: Bercovitch and Fretter (2004); Clodfelter (2002); LaFeber (1993); Scheina (2003b).

INTRA-STATE WAR #771:
The First Chad (FROLINAT) Rebellion of 1966–1971

Participants: Chad, France vs. FROLINAT rebels
Dates: November [ ], 1966, to June 16, 1971
Battle-Related Deaths: FROLINAT rebels—3,000; Chad—500; France—50
Where Fought: Africa
Initiator: FROLINAT rebels
Outcome: Chad, France win
War Type: Civil for local issues

Narrative: Chad, one of the poorest nations in the Sahelian region of Africa, has a population that is split between Christians and animist blacks in the south and Muslims in the north. Strife, either political or military, has been endemic in Chad since it gained its independence from France in 1960. The first president, François Tombalbaye, was from the south. In 1963 he outlawed all political parties except his own and gradually removed all the northerners

from the government. In response the National Liberation Front of Chad (FROLINAT) was created with the goal of removing Tombalbaye from power. In November 1966 FROLINAT launched a rebellion in the northern part of the country. Its successes in defeating government forces within the first two years led the French to intervene to support the government. France withdrew its forces by June 1971, by which time the government had suppressed the rebellion.

Sources: Bercovitch and Fretter (2004); Ciment (2007); Clodfelter (2002); Cutter (2007); Nolutshungu (1996).

INTRA-STATE WAR #772:
The Cultural Revolution Phase 1 of 1967

Participants: Red Guard vs. regional military
Dates: January 9, 1967, to September 4, 1967
Battle-Related Deaths: Red Guard—[ ]; regional military—[ ]
Where Fought: Asia
Initiator: regional military
Outcome: Transformed into an intra-state, civil war #776
War Type: Regional internal

Narrative: The Communists had come to power through the Chinese Civil War (intra-state war #725). In order to recapture the spirit of that earlier time, Mao Tse-tung (Mao Zedong) launched the Great Proletarian Cultural Revolution in April 1966. The primary proponents of the revolution were the Red Guard, and its targets were the remaining reactionary elements in Chinese society, sometimes referred to as the "Four Olds." In its initials stages, Red Guard (frequently students) engaged in demonstrations, political reeducation, and condemnation of the entrenched bureaucracy. The war itself began in January 1967, when the Red Guard was ordered to seize power in the provinces. Clashes between the Red Guard and the military forces of its more conservative opponents, sometimes called the

Scarlet Guards, continued throughout the year. This phase of the Cultural Revolution is coded as a regional internal war because it involved attacks by the nongovernmental Red Guard against the regional military forces, which were acting on their own against the interests of the central government. As the level of violence increased, however, Mao decided to terminate the revolution by force. When Mao ordered the People's Liberation Army (PLA) to attack the Red Guard in September 1967, the war was transformed into a civil war, involving the forces of the central government (see intra-state war #776).

Sources: An (1972); Cheng (1972); Clodfelter (2002); Phillips and Axelrod (2005); Taylor and Hudson (1972); Thornton (1982); Walder and Su (2003).

INTRA-STATE WAR #773:

The Third Burmese War of 1967–1980

Participants: Burma vs. Karens, Communists
Dates: June [ ], 1967, to October 22, 1980
Battle-Related Deaths: Karens, Communists— 22,400; Burma—6,800
Where Fought: Asia
Initiator: Karens
Outcome: Conflict continues at below war level
War Type: Civil for local issues

Narrative: The Second Burmese War (intra-state war #746) had involved fighting against the central government by the Karens and the Communists. The war ended in 1960, though conflict between the groups continued at below war levels. Since the Communist Chinese government was suspected of aiding the Karens, anti-Chinese rioting took place in Rangoon in June 1967, which corresponded to the increased level of attacks by the Karens and Communists that marked the start of this war. In March 1970 the Communists seized the northern town of Kyokuk. A government counterattack led to a government victory at Luchin in 1971, and further battles involved

increased fatalities. In 1976 the National Democratic Front was formed among nine ethic groups, including the Karens, to promote demands for autonomy. During the remainder of the 1970s the war continued, but fatality levels began to decline as the Chinese decreased their level of support for the rebels. U Ne Win's reelection as president in 1978, however, prompted bloody clashes between the Communists and the government. Conflict declined below war levels after 1980, but war would resume again in 1983 (intra-state war #832).

Sources: Brogan (1998); Clodfelter (2002); Kohn (1999); Phillips and Axelrod (2005); Stearns (2001).

INTRA-STATE WAR #775:

The Biafra War of 1967–1970

Participants: Nigeria vs. Biafrans
Dates: July 6, 1967, to January 12, 1970
Battle-Related Deaths: Nigeria—[ ]; Biafrans—[ ] (Total Combatant Deaths: 45,000)
Where Fought: Africa
Initiator: Nigeria
Outcome: Nigeria wins
War Type: Civil for local issues

Narrative: Nigeria has three major tribal groups, the Yoruba, the Hausa, and the Ibo. When Nigeria attained its independence in 1960, politics centered on the rivalry among these three groups. The predominantly Catholic Ibo from the eastern region made up most of the government officials. In 1966 a coup d'etat led to rioting and attacks on the Ibo by the predominantly Muslim Hausa. Thousands died, and many tens of thousands of Ibo fled eastward. Furthermore, in May 1967 the government announced a redistricting plan that would have reduced the relative influence of the Ibo. Consequently, on May 30, 1967, the Ibo in three eastern states, under the leadership of Lt. Col. (later General) Chukwuemeka Odumegwu Ojukwu declared the independence of the Republic of Biafra. Initially,

Nigeria established a quarantine around the breakaway region, but in July Nigerian troops invaded Biafra. They made slow progress at first. A Biafran counteroffensive almost reached the Nigerian capital of Lagos before being repulsed. After failed peace talks in 1968, the government gradually suppressed the Biafran resistance.

Sources: Ciment (2007); Clendenen (1972); Clodfelter (2002); Cutter (2007); Edgerton (2002); Meredith (2005); Phillips and Axelrod (2005); Taylor and Hudson (1972).

INTRA-STATE WAR #776:

The Cultural Revolution Phase 2 of 1967–1968

Participants: China vs. Red Guard
Dates: September 5, 1967, to September 1, 1968
Battle-Related Deaths: China—[ ]; Red Guard—[ ] (Total Combatant Deaths: 50,000)
Where Fought: Asia
Initiator: Red Guard
Outcome: China wins
War Type: Civil for central control

Narrative: As the first phase of the Cultural Revolution (intra-state war #772), and its Red Guard proponents, became increasingly violent, Mao Tse-tung decided that the Cultural Revolution had to be stopped. On September 5, 1967, Mao ordered the People's Liberation Army (PLA) to disarm the Red Guard and to fight them if they resisted. This transformed the war into a civil war, involving the forces of the central government. Battles between the two parties continued for another year. Gradually the Cultural Revolution, which had been supported by the more radical wing of the Communist Party, led by the "Gang of Four" (including Mao's wife, Chiang Ching), was ended by the moderate faction under Chou En-lai. Total deaths for combatants and civilians during both phases of the Cultural Revolution exceeded 340,000.

Sources: An (1972); Cheng (1972); Clodfelter (2002); Phillips and Axelrod (2005); Taylor and

Hudson (1972); Thornton (1982); Walder and Su (2003).

INTRA-STATE WAR #777:

The Third Iraqi Kurds War of 1969–1970

Participants: Iraq vs. Kurds
Dates: January 3, 1969, to March 11, 1970
Battle-Related Deaths: Kurds—3,200; Iraq—800
Where Fought: Middle East
Initiator: Iraq
Outcome: Compromise
War Type: Civil for local issues

Narrative: The second war between Iraq and the Kurds had ended with a cease-fire in 1966 (intra-state war #765). The twelve-point program adopted at that time provided some autonomy to the Kurds. However, in July 1968 a coup brought Gen. Hassan al-Bakr to power, and the Kurds began to complain about the regime's failure to implement the twelve-point program. In 1969 the government sent 60,000 troops against the Kurds, who responded with an attack on the Kirkuk oil facilities in March 1969, putting much of Iraq's oil production out of production for some days. Saddam Hussein was involved in conducting secret talks between the Baathist government and the Kurds. In March 1970 the war ended when the government again guaranteed Kurdish rights.

Sources: Bercovitch and Fretter (2004); Brogan (1998); Keesing's (1970); Tripp (2000).

INTRA-STATE WAR #778:

The Naxalite Rebellion of 1970–1971

Participants: India vs. Naxalite Marxists
Dates: February [ ], 1970, to November [ ], 1971
Battle-Related Deaths: Naxalite Marxists—2,000; India—100
Where Fought: Asia

Initiator: Naxalite Marxists
Outcome: India wins
War Type: Civil for local issues

Narrative: The Naxalbar area in the Indian state of West Bengal was the location of a movement of landless peasants in 1967. The Naxalite name was later taken by Marxist guerrillas who operated in east Indian states such as West Bengal and Andra Pradesh and who believed in the necessity of a violent revolution to address social disparities. In 1969 the radicals launched a number of attacks on government installations in the region; however, war-level hostilities emerged in early 1970, when the government began an offensive against the rebels. By the next year the Naxalite movement had been severely weakened, and hostilities ceased as a Communist government was elected in West Bengal that granted many of the peasant demands. Starting in the 1980s the Naxalites resumed their attacks in a number of Indian states, but death totals have been below war level.

Sources: Brogan (1998); Clodfelter (2002).

INTRA-STATE WAR #780:
The Black September War of 1970

Participants: Jordan vs. Palestinians, Syria
Dates: September 13, 1970, to September 24, 1970
Battle-Related Deaths: Palestinians—2,690; Jordan—750; Syria—100
Where Fought: Middle East
Initiator: Jordan
Outcome: Jordan wins
War Type: Civil for central control

Narrative: Large numbers of Palestinians fled to Jordan as the result of the Israeli victory in the Six-Day War (inter-state war #169) and its occupation of the West Bank. The Palestinian guerrillas in the refugee camps posed a challenge to Jordan's King Hussein, partially because the guerrillas' attacks against Israel led to Israeli retaliation against Jordan. Military clashes between Jordan and the Palestinians began in early 1970. In September 1970 the guerrillas hijacked three airliners, which they subsequently detonated. King Hussein decided that he had to deal with the Palestinian threat to his control in Jordan, and he ordered his 52,000-troop army and 2,000-troop air force to attack the 20,000 Palestinian guerrillas (fedayeen). The Syrians intervened on September 20 to assist the Palestinians, but their tanks were repelled. The fighting was over by September 24, and on September 27, President Gamal Abdel Nasser brokered a cease-fire. Most of the fedayeen then left Jordan for Syria.

Sources: Cleveland (1994); Clodfelter (2002); Higham (1972); Lenczowski (1987); Snow (1972).

INTRA-STATE WAR #781:
The Second Guatemala War of 1970–1971

Participants: Guatemala vs. leftists
Dates: November 15, 1970, to September 15, 1971
Battle-Related Deaths: leftists—950; Guatemala—50
Where Fought: W. Hemisphere
Initiator: Guatemala
Outcome: Guatemala wins
War Type: Civil for central control

Narrative: The First Guatemala War (intra-state war #770) was a revolt by the leftist Revolutionary Armed Forces (FAR) against Guatemala's military dictatorship. Even though the rebels were defeated in 1968, low-level conflict continued. The election of right-wing Col. Carlos Araña Osorio to the presidency in May 1970 led to renewed warfare. Araña declared martial law and vowed to eliminate all the guerrillas. The guerrillas retaliated, but they were crushed and rebel leader Marco Antonio Yon Sosa was killed.

Sources: Bercovitch and Fretter (2004); Clodfelter (2002); Crow (1971); Keesing's (1971–1972); LaFeber (1993); Scheina (2003b); Taylor and Hudson (1972).

INTRA-STATE WAR #782:
The Pakistan-Bengal War of 1971

Participants: Pakistan vs. Bengalis
Dates: March 25, 1971, to December 2, 1971
Battle-Related Deaths: Pakistan—2,500;
Bengalis—[ ]
Where Fought: Asia
Initiator: Pakistan
Outcome: Transformed into
inter-state war #178
War Type: Civil for local issues

Narrative: The partition of British India in 1947 created Pakistan as a Muslim state, which consisted of two geographically separated parts, East and West Pakistan. East Pakistan (or East Bengal) was more populous, but the political elite in West Pakistan dominated the state. In East Bengal the Awami League was the political party that generally favored independence, and as it became increasingly powerful, the Pakistani government decided to act. On March 25, 1971, the Pakistani military seized members of the Awami League. The Bengali military resisted, and fighting between the two armies became increasingly vicious. As refugees fled into India, the Indian government appealed for assistance. Pakistan then launched a preemptive attack on India, which thus ended this civil war and transformed it into the Bangladesh War between India and Pakistan (inter-state war #178). East Bengal ultimately declared its independence as the new state of Bangladesh.

Sources: Ayoob and Subrahmanyam (1972); Bercovitch and Fretter (2004); Brogan (1998); Clodfelter (2002); Facts on File (1972); Payne (1973); Phillips and Axelrod (2005).

INTRA-STATE WAR #783:
The First Sri Lanka-JVP War of 1971

Participants: Sri Lanka vs. JVP
Dates: April 6, 1971, to May 16, 1971
Battle-Related Deaths: JVP—4,000;
Sri Lanka—53
Where Fought: Asia
Initiator: JVP
Outcome: Sri Lanka wins
War Type: Civil for central control

Narrative: The Janatha Vimukthi Peramuna (JVP), or People's Liberation Front, was created in Sri Lanka in 1967 as a Marxist organization dedicated to armed struggle. It really only became well known in Sri Lanka during the 1970 election campaign, when it urged the masses to support the United Front of moderate leftist Sirimavo Bandaranaike. Bandaranaike, the world's first female prime minister in 1960–1965, was seeking reelection to that office. The United Front won the election, but ultimately Bandaranaike's policies were not radical enough for the JVP. In April 1971 the JVP hoped to launch a radical revolution and began with widespread attacks against ninety-two police stations, of which thirty-five were captured. Bandaranaike was able to mobilize the military, which, with assistance from a number of foreign countries, was able to defeat the rebels.

Sources: Bush (2003); Clodfelter (2002); Gunaratna (2001); Keesing's (1971–1972).

INTRA-STATE WAR #785:
The Khmer Rouge War of 1971–1975

Participants: Cambodia, United States vs. Khmer Rouge
Dates: July 3, 1971, to July 17, 1975
Battle-Related Deaths: Cambodia—45,000; Khmer Rouge—40,000; United States—375
Where Fought: Asia
Initiator: Khmer Rouge
Outcome: Khmer Rouge wins
War Type: Civil for central control

Narrative: As the Vietnam War (inter-state war #163) raged, Prince Sihanouk of Cambodia maintained a neutralist regime, even in the face of U.S. bombing raids against the Viet Cong sanctuaries in Cambodia. In March 1970 Sihanouk was overthrown in a coup led by Lon Nol. This sparked the outbreak of inter-state war #176, which involved North Vietnam, aided by the Communist Khmer Rouge, against Cambodia, which was aided by the United States and South Vietnam. The inter-state war continued until July 2 1971, at which time the withdrawal of North Vietnamese forces transformed the war into this civil war (starting the next day) between Cambodia, still aided by the United States, and the Khmer Rouge. The United States ended its participation in the war in 1973, after which the Khmer Rouge launched an offensive to capture the capital, which it did by 1975, ending this war. It then instituted one of the most genocidal regimes in history—and the deadliest on a per capita basis in the twentieth century (see Rummel 1994 for statistical documentation). This oppression continued until the Khmer Rouge was expelled from power when its former ally, North Vietnam, invaded in 1977 (inter-state war #189).

Sources: Bercovitch and Fretter (2004); Caldwell and Tan (1973); Clodfelter (2002); Far Eastern Economic Review (1970–1972); Isaacs et al. (1987); Keesing's (1970–1975); Leifer (1975); Leitenberg and Burns (1973); Phillips and Axelrod (2005); Rummel (1994); Suhrke (1971).

INTRA-STATE WAR #786:
The First Philippine-Moro War of 1972–1981

Participants: Philippines vs. MNLF Moros
Dates: January 1, 1972, to April 19, 1981
Battle-Related Deaths: MNLF Moros—20,000; Philippines—10,000
Where Fought: Asia
Initiator: MNLF Moros

Outcome: Philippines wins
War Type: Civil for local issues

Narrative: The Moro are Philippine Muslims of the southern island of Mindanao. The Moro had resented and frequently resisted rule by the regime in the northern capital of Manila, especially as Christian settlers moved in increasing numbers to the south, displacing many Moro residents. Ferdinand Marcos was elected president in 1965, and he greatly expanded his powers as he dealt with internal unrest. He declared martial law in 1972 and almost immediately faced a major revolt by the Moro, who were seeking independence. Seven thousand guerrillas of the Moro National Liberation Front (MNLF) were soon in the field in Mindanao and Sulu. The guerrillas controlled the capital of Sulu for two days in 1974. In December 1976 a cease-fire halted the fighting briefly, but it soon broke down. The war gradually subsided as the government increased its aid to the region. The MNLF resumed significant attacks in 2000 (intra-state war #916).

Sources: Clodfelter (2002); Keesing's (1972–1981); Kohn (1999); *Philippines Information Bulletin* (1974); Muslim and Cagoco-Guiam (2002); Phillips and Axelrod (2005); Suhrke and Noble (1977a, 1977b); Tan (2000).

INTRA-STATE WAR #787:
The Communist Insurgency of 1972–1973

Participants: Thailand vs. Communists
Dates: January [ ], 1972, to October 15, 1973
Battle-Related Deaths: Thailand—1,500; Communists—700
Where Fought: Asia
Initiator: Communists
Outcome: Stalemate
War Type: Civil for central control

Narrative: A low-level Communist insurgency in the northeast of Thailand began in 1965. At first the Communist attacks were kidnapping or assassinating government officials; however, their activities increased in frequency and intensity as the number of American military personnel stationed in the country grew (37,000 in 1968). The conflict incurred war-level fatalities after a government offensive in January 1972, in which 10,000 Thai troops attacked the 2,500 guerrillas who were based near Laos. Major fighting ended in October 1973 when a popular revolt overthrew the military government. Hostilities did resume at subwar levels when the military returned to power in 1976.

Sources: Ciment (2007); Clodfelter (2002); Morell (1972); Race (1975); Race (1974).

INTRA-STATE WAR #788:
The Eritrean Split of 1972–1974

Participants: ELF vs. EPLF
Dates: February [ ], 1972, to [ ]/[ ]/1974
Battle-Related Deaths: ELF—[ ]; EPLF—[ ]
   (Total Combatant Deaths: 3,000)
Where Fought: Africa
Initiator: ELF
Outcome: Stalemate
War Type: Inter-communal

Narrative: Eritrea sought independence from Ethiopia. In 1961 the Eritrean Liberation Front (ELF) began a low-level guerrilla war against the Ethiopian government. In 1970 a group of ELF members split from the group and created a rival organization, the Eritrean Popular Liberation Front (EPLF). Although both organizations shared a Marxist orientation and the goal of independence, they were soon involved in skirmishes against each other. The conflict reached war level in 1972. The ELF and the EPLF stopped their infighting as the war with Ethiopia approached (intra-state war #798), and the EPLF gradually became the primary revolutionary organization.

Sources: Brogan (1998); Clodfelter (2002).

INTRA-STATE WAR #789:
The First Burundi War of 1972

Participants: Burundi vs. Hutu
Dates: April 29, 1972, to May 25, 1972
Battle-Related Deaths: Hutu—1,500;
   Burundi—500
Where Fought: Africa
Initiator: Hutu
Outcome: Burundi wins
War Type: Civil for central control

Narrative: Like Rwanda to the north, Burundi became independent in 1962 when the Belgian Trusteeship of Ruanda-Urundi was divided. Also as in Rwanda, postindependence politics was dominated by the Tutsi/Hutu rivalry. A Tutsi kingdom had taken over in Burundi from the departing Belgians, though a coup in 1966 brought the army to power. Once in office, Tutsi officer Capt. Michel Micombero began to remove the Hutu from the government. This precipitated an attack in April 1972 against government installations by the Hutu (including some who wanted to restore the monarchy), who received some assistance from rebels in Zaire. The actual rebellion was fairly limited, and the government forces were able to defeat the rebels within a month. However, the government forces then proceeded to launch mass attacks against Hutu civilians in which approximately 150,000 people were killed. Conflict between the Hutu and Tutsi continued periodically for the next twenty years, when a second civil war broke out in 1993 (intra-state war #883).

Sources: Bentley and Southall (2005); Ciment (2007); Clodfelter (2002); Cutter (2007); Edgerton (2002); Eggers (1997); Lemarchand (2004); Lemarchand (1994); Lemarchand (1975); Marchak (2003); Melady (1974); Meredith 2005); Ndarubagiye (1996); Phillips and Axelrod (2005); Rwantabagu (2001); Scherrer 2002).

INTRA-STATE WAR #790:
The Philippines-NPA War of 1972–1992

Participants: Philippines vs. NPA
Dates: October 1, 1972, to December 31, 1992
Battle-Related Deaths: NPA—22,000;
    Philippines—9,000
Where Fought: Asia
Initiator: NPA
Outcome: Stalemate
War Type: Civil for central control

Narrative: The social inequality in the Philippines that had fueled the Huk rebellion in 1950 (intra-state war #735) had continued to worsen with time. Economic disparity led to the emergence of a Communist group, the New People's Army (NPA), which was formed in 1969 as the military wing of the Communist Party of the Philippines (PKP). Under the leadership of José Maria Sison, the NPA began a long-lasting rebellion against the Philippine government, under the Marcos regime. Fighting was particularly intense in the 1980s, when the NPA had 20,000 guerrillas. The Aquino government continued the war after Marcos was deposed in 1986. In 1992 the National Unification Commission established a peace process, which ended the major fighting. Despite several attempts at negotiating a settlement, however, the peace process stalled, and clashes between the government and the NPA have continued at sub-war levels.

Sources: Clodfelter (2002); Keesing's (1972–1981); Phillips and Axelrod (2005); Project Ploughshares (2000).

INTRA-STATE WAR #791:
The Rhodesia War of 1972–1979

Participants: Rhodesia vs. Patriotic Front
Dates: December 28, 1972, to December 28, 1979
Battle-Related Deaths: Patriotic Front—10,000;
    Rhodesia—1,000

Where Fought: Africa
Initiator: Patriotic Front
Outcome: Patriotic Front wins
War Type: Civil for central control

Narrative: In November 1965 the white-controlled Rhodesian Front declared unilateral independence from Britain in order to maintain white domination of what had been the British colony of Southern Rhodesia. The new government under the leadership of Prime Minister Ian Smith established a system whereby Rhodesia's 240,000 whites ruled over its 4,000,000 blacks. The blacks began to create resistance organizations, loosely linked together in the Patriotic Front. The more moderate group was the Zimbabwe African People's Union (ZAPU) led by Joshua Nkomo, while the Zimbabwe African National Union (ZANU) led by Robert Mugabe favored a more radical approach and tactics. Guerrilla attacks by black forces began in 1967 but reached war levels only in 1972. After 1975 the rebels had access to bases in Mozambique, which helped their cause, and their strength grew to 20,000 by 1976. The Rhodesian military was successful in most direct engagements but was depleted by white emigration. Smith also faced international pressure to reach a negotiated settlement. He finally created a black government and left Rhodesia in control of Bishop Abel Muzorewa. Negotiations led to a new government, and in 1980, Robert Mugabe was elected prime minister of what had become Zimbabwe.

Sources: Clodfelter (2002); Edgerton (2002); Meredith (2005); Phillips and Axelrod (2005); Preston (2004).

INTRA-STATE WAR #792:
The Baluchi Separatists War of 1973–1977

Participants: Pakistan vs. Baluchi rebels
Dates: January 23, 1973, to July [ ], 1977
Battle-Related Deaths: Baluchi rebels—5,300;
    Pakistan—3,300

Where Fought: Asia
Initiator: Baluchi rebels
Outcome: Pakistan wins
War Type: Civil for local issues

Narrative: The Baluchi make up one of the major ethnic groups in Pakistan, living in Baluchistan, which is Pakistan's largest and least populated province. They generally favored the creation of their own state, and in 1973 they launched a rebellion against the Pakistani government. Pakistan, under the leadership of Zulfikar Ali Bhutto, sent a 70,000-troop army to suppress the 55,000 tribal guerrillas. The shah of Iran, who feared that the war might spread to the Baluchi living in Iran, provided advanced weapons, including helicopters, to the Pakistani government, enabling it to defeat the rebels.

Sources: Brogan (1998); Clodfelter (2002).

INTRA-STATE WAR #793:
The Chilean Coup of 1973

Participants: Chile vs. Pinochet led military
Dates: September 11, 1973, to September 15, 1973
Battle-Related Deaths: Pinochet led military—
    3,000; Chile—400
Where Fought: W. Hemisphere
Initiator: Pinochet led military
Outcome: Pinochet led military wins
War Type: Civil for central control

Narrative: Salvador Allende became the first freely elected Marxist president in Latin America in 1970. In the election Allende won a plurality of the vote, though not a majority. Thus the United States began lobbying the opposition to try to prevent Allende from taking office. Allende was nonetheless inaugurated, and his policies soon provoked opposition by conservative groups and nervousness on the part of the armed forces. His government nationalized American-owned mining interests, further alienating the United States, which then increased its programs aimed at undermining Chile's economy and the

regime. On September 11, 1973, the military staged a coup. Fighting occurred between the military and the forces of the Movement of the Revolutionary Left (MIR), which was a member of the Popular Unity Coalition along with Allende's Socialist Party. Allende either was murdered or committed suicide. Gen. Augusto Pinochet, the military strongman who led the coup, then ruled Chile as a dictator for a decade and a half, until Patricio Aylwin was elected president in December 1989.

Sources: Ciment (2007); Clodfelter (2002); Scheina (2003b).

INTRA-STATE WAR #795:
The Dhofar Rebellion Phase 2 of 1973–1975

Participants: Iran, Oman, United Kingdom vs.
    PFLOAG
Dates: October [ ], 1973, to December 11, 1975
Battle-Related Deaths: PFLOAG—2,500;
    Oman—370; Iran—100;
    United Kingdom—35
Where Fought: Middle East
Initiator: Oman
Outcome: Iran, Oman, United Kingdom win
War Type: Civil for local issues

Narrative: This war is a continuation of non-state war #1577, the Oman-Dhofar War, which began in 1968. Dhofar, seeking independence, went to war with Oman. The conflict was a non-state war, since Oman was an autonomous entity but not a member of the interstate system at the time. That war ended in July 1970 when the sultan was overthrown. There was a general hiatus in the fighting, during which Oman became a state system member (October 7, 1971), after which point the conflict is coded as a civil war between Dhofar and Oman. The new sultan began building up his armed forces and was aided by troops from Iran and the United Kingdom. The Dhofar guerrillas of the Popular Front for the Liberation of the Occupied Arabian Gulf

(PFLOAG) received assistance from China and the People's Democratic Republic of Yemen. The foreign assistance helped Oman launch a new offensive against the PFLOAG in 1973, and the sultan declared on December 11, 1975, that the rebels had been defeated.

Sources: Beckett (2001); Clodfelter (2002); Cordesman (1997); Cordesman (1993); Lenczowski (1987); Metz (1994); Minahan (1996).

INTRA-STATE WAR #797:

The Fourth Iraqi Kurds War of 1974–1975

Participants: Iraq vs. Iran, Kurds
Dates: March 18, 1974, to April 3, 1975
Battle-Related Deaths: Kurds—13,000; Iraq—7,000; Iran—[ ]
Where Fought: Middle East
Initiator: Iraq
Outcome: Iraq wins
War Type: Civil for local issues

Narrative: In 1970, at the end of the Third Iraqi Kurds War (intra-state war #777), Iraq had offered the Kurds an agreement that included limited autonomy. The two sides could not agree on the final terms, however, and when Kurdish Democratic Party (KDP) leader Mullah Mustafa Barzani rejected Iraq's final offer, Iraq launched another offensive against the Kurds in 1974. The Kurds, with 100,000 troops and militiamen initially were able to resist the attack of Iraq's 100,000-troop army, especially during the period in which they were aided by Iran (and secretly the CIA). Nevertheless, after Iranian and U.S. aid was withdrawn, the Kurds were quickly defeated.

Sources: Brogan (1998); Clodfelter (2002).

INTRA-STATE WAR #798:

The Eritrean War of 1975–1978

Participants: Cuba, Ethiopia vs. EPLF
Dates: January 31, 1975, to December [ ], 1978

Battle-Related Deaths: EPLF—6,400; Ethiopia—6,100; Cuba—[ ]
Where Fought: Africa
Initiator: EPLF
Outcome: Cuba, Ethiopia win
War Type: Civil for local issues

Narrative: Eritrea and Ethiopia had been colonial possessions of Italy. After World War II (inter-state war #139), the United Nations decided to create a federation between the two, which lasted until Eritrea voted to become part of Ethiopia in 1962. Resistance to Ethiopian rule led to the development of the Eritrean Liberation Front (ELF) and the Eritrean People's Liberation Front (EPLF), which went to war against each other in 1972 (intra-state war #788). In 1974, Emperor Haile Selassie was overthrown by a Marxist military coup by the Dergue led by Col. Mengistu Haile Mariam. The Eritreans decided to take advantage of Ethiopia's internal disorder to launch a struggle for independence. Initially the rebels were successful in gaining control of 85 percent of Eritrea. After Ethiopia's 1977 victory over Somalia in the Ogaden War (intra-state war #805), however, Ethiopian troops with the assistance of Cuba launched a major offensive that defeated the Eritreans. Nevertheless, the Eritreans would go to war again against Ethiopia in 1982 (intra-state war #826).

Sources: Brogan (1998); Ciment (2007); Clodfelter (2002); Cordesman (1993); Cousin (1997); Cutter (2007); Keesing's (1974–1980); Lefebvre (1996); Meredith (2005); Tareke (2002).

INTRA-STATE WAR #800:

The Argentine Leftists War of 1975–1977

Participants: Argentina vs. Montoneros, ERP
Dates: February [ ], 1975, to March [ ], 1977
Battle-Related Deaths: ERP, Montoneros—2,600; Argentina—250
Where Fought: W. Hemisphere
Initiator: Montoneros, ERP

Outcome: Argentina wins
War Type: Civil for central control

Narrative: Populist president Juan Perón was overthrown in 1955 by a military dictatorship. In opposition to the dictatorship, two major leftist groups were founded: the Montoneros, which supported the return of Perón, and the Marxist People's Revolutionary Army (ERP). The government allowed Perón to return and resume his presidency, but as he began to favor the military, the leftists resumed their opposition. This was particularly true after Isabel Perón assumed the presidency in 1974. The leftist attacks reached war level in 1975, and the government responded with a major offensive from February to April. Isabel Perón's inability to defeat the leftists led to her removal from power in 1976 by the military. The military's repressive tactics led not only to the defeat of the rebels but also to the deaths and disappearances of thousands of civilians.

Sources: Clodfelter (2002); Phillips and Axelrod (2005); Scheina (2003b).

INTRA-STATE WAR #801:

The Second Lebanese War of 1975–1976

Participants: Phalange, Syria vs. Lebanese National Movement
Dates: April 13, 1975, to November 15, 1976
Battle-Related Deaths: Syria—500; Phalange—[ ]; Lebanese National Movement—[ ] (Total Lebanese Combatant Deaths: 25,000)
Where Fought: Middle East
Initiator: Lebanese National Movement
Outcome: Compromise
War Type: Inter-communal

Narrative: In 1975 Lebanon faced a number of problems, including the presence of thousands of Palestinian refugees living in camps in the south and disputes over political control of the country by its various religious populations, including the Maronites, the Sunnis, and the Shia community. Tensions were also fueled by the arrival of the Palestine Liberation Organization (PLO), following its expulsion from Jordan in 1970 (intra-state war #780). Although there were attacks between and among the various armed groups, the war erupted in 1975 with the Palestinian attack in Beirut against the Christian Phalange, which was soon supported by the militia of the National Liberals. By June full-scale war divided the country into two general camps: Christians versus Muslims. This war is coded as an inter-communal war, rather than a civil war, because the forces of the Lebanese government were not involved in the fighting; the government had decided to create a nonpoliticized army for fear that the army's intervention in the conflict on one side or the other would split the ruling coalition. The army's activities during this period were supposedly only neutral interventions to stop the fighting. In 1976 Syria decided to intervene. Syria had previously supported the Palestinian and Muslim groups, but in 1976, Syria intervened against its traditional allies in support of the Maronites. With Syrian support the Maronites went on the offensive. The Christians were on the verge of victory, but a settlement urged by Saudi Arabia ended the war.

Sources: Ciment (2007); Clodfelter (2002); Goldschmidt (1991); Haley and Snider (1979); Lenczowski (1987); Meo (1977); Phillips and Axelrod (2005); Rabinovich (1985); Salibi (1976).

INTRA-STATE WAR #802:

The Second West Papua War of 1976–1978

Participants: Indonesia vs. OPR, West Papua
Dates: January 1, 1976, to April 14, 1978
Battle-Related Deaths: OPR, West Papua—2,000; Indonesia—100
Where Fought: Asia
Initiator: OPR, West Papua
Outcome: Stalemate
War Type: Civil for local issues

Narrative: The First West Papua War (intra-state war #767) was a revolt by the Free Papua Movement (OPM) seeking independence for West Irian from Indonesia. The conflict ended in a stalemate in 1969, when the United Nations conducted a referendum in West Irian that approved Indonesia's annexation of the region. The OPM conducted small-scale armed attacks after that point, and the conflict flared into war again in 1976. In 1977 Indonesia launched a major offensive against the guerrillas. Conflict continued to escalate, with widespread OPM attacks on government installations. The OPM also attempted to interfere with local mining operations, provoking Indonesian bombing raids. Overall, an estimated 10,000 OPM guerrillas battled roughly 15,000 to 20,000 Indonesian troops. There was no clear-cut conclusion to the war, though factional fighting within the OPM weakened its level of activity.

Sources: Bercovitch and Fretter (2004); Ciment (2007); Elmslie (2003); Emmerson (1999); Foster (2003); Keesing's (1977); Lowry (1996); Minahan (2002); Project Ploughshares (2004).

INTRA-STATE WAR #803:

The Third Laotian War of 1976–1979

Participants: Laos, Vietnam vs. Hmong
Dates: January [ ], 1976, to May [ ], 1979
Battle-Related Deaths: Hmong—5,000; Laos—1,000; Vietnam—1,000
Where Fought: Asia
Initiator: Hmong
Outcome: Laos, Vietnam win
War Type: Civil for local issues

Narrative: The second war between the government of Laos and the Communist Pathet Lao, which encompassed two phases (intra-state war #756 and inter-state war #170), led to the creation of a coalition government, which evolved in 1975 into a government dominated by the Pathet Lao. During the war the United States

had recruited many of the Hmong people to become involved in the war in support of the Laotian monarchy. Thus, suitably trained, the Hmong launched an attack in 1976 against the Pathet Lao government. Vietnam, which still had troops stationed in Laos, soon entered the war against the Hmong. A joint Laotian-Vietnamese offensive in 1977–1978, which included the use of chemical warfare, defeated the rebels.

Sources: Brown and Zasloff (1980); Clodfelter (2002); Keesing's (1975–1981); Phillips and Axelrod (2005); Valdes (1979).

INTRA-STATE WAR #804:

The Angolan Control War of 1976–1991

Participants: Angola, Cuba vs. South Africa, UNITA
Dates: February 13, 1976, to May 15, 1991
Battle-Related Deaths: Cuba—5,500; South Africa—800; Angola—[ ]; UNITA—[ ]
Where Fought: Africa
Initiator: UNITA
Outcome: Compromise
War Type: Civil for central control

Narrative: In 1975, as Angola was poised to become independent of Portugal (as a result of extra-state war #469), three guerrilla groups vied for control of Angola: (1) the Popular Movement for the Liberation of Angola (MPLA), around Luanda, the capital; (2) the National Front for the Liberation of Angola (FNLA), in the north, among the Kongo people; and (3) the National Union for the Total Independence of Angola (UNITA) in the center and south. A non-state war erupted among these groups in the months preceding independence (non-state war #1581); however, none of the parties was victorious. Consequently, when independence day arrived, on November 11, 1975, there were declarations of two separate governments: the People's Republic of Angola formed by the MPLA in Luanda; and the Social Democratic Republic of Angola formed by the FNLA and UNITA in Huambo. The MPLA government was recognized as the new government of Angola, and the enduring conflict transformed into this civil war. The war internationalized when Cuba immediately entered the war on the side of the government. South Africa announced that it had withdrawn all of its forces by March 27, 1976, but continued to intervene in support of UNITA. The MPLA and the Cubans defeated the FNLA and UNITA in pitched battles. Thereafter, the war degenerated into a lengthy guerrilla conflict, with Jonas Savimbi, the UNITA leader, continuing the war in the south with U.S. matériel aid. In August 1988 a cease-fire agreement involved pledges that foreign forces would withdraw. Fighting ceased on May 15, 1991, and on May 31, 1991, UNITA and the MPLA-led government negotiated a power-sharing arrangement. Unfortunately, the next war broke out within months (intra-state war #880).

Sources: Bercovitch and Fretter (2004); Clodfelter (2002); Cutter (2007); Human Rights Watch (1994); Keesing's (1975–1980); Malaquias (2007); Phillips and Axelrod (2005); Valdes (1979).

INTRA-STATE WAR #805:

The Second Ogaden War Phase 1 of 1976–1977

Participants: Cuba, Ethiopia vs. Somalia, WSLF
Dates: July 1, 1976, to July 22, 1977
Battle-Related Deaths: WSLF—20,000; Ethiopia—9,000; Somalia—1,900; Cuba—1,500
Where Fought: Africa
Initiator: WSLF
Outcome: Transformed into inter-state war #187
War Type: Civil for local issues

Narrative: In 1963 the Ogaden launched a move for independence from Ethiopia in the First Ogaden War (intra-state war #757). The war was ended by cease-fire, which stopped the fighting but did not resolve the issues of Ogaden independence. The Second Ogaden War, which

started in 1976, had three distinct phases, which basically consisted of two periods of intra-state war separated by an inter-state war in the interim period. In 1976 the Dergue government of Ethiopia was already involved in a war with Eritrea (intra-state war #798). The revolutionary group in the Ogaden, the Western Somali Liberation Front (WSLF), decided to take advantage of Ethiopia's preoccupation with Eritrea to relaunch its war of independence. The WSLF had been trained in Somalia and had the support of Somali troops, while Cuba supported the Ethiopian government. Although the WSLF initially made some military gains, when its advance stalled, Somalia launched a full-scale invasion of its own. This thus transformed the conflict into an inter-state war (#187). The conflict would revert to a civil war again in 1978 (intra-state war #808).

Sources: Ciment (2007); Cordesman (1993); Cutter (2007); Keesing's (1975–1980).

INTRA-STATE WAR #806:

The East Timorese War Phase 3 of 1976–1979

Participants: Indonesia vs. FRETILIN
Dates: July 18, 1976, to May 26, 1979
Battle-Related Deaths: Indonesia—1,800; FRETILIN—[ ]
Where Fought: Asia
Initiator: FRETILIN
Outcome: Indonesia wins
War Type: Civil for local issues

Narrative: The war for control over East Timor had three distinct phases: the first was a non-state war involving the Revolutionary Front for the Independence of East Timor (FRETILIN) and the Timorese Popular Democratic Association, East Timor (APODETI) against the Timorese Democratic Union (UDT) (non-state war #1582). When Indonesia intervened in the war, it became an extra-state war (#472). In July 1976, Indonesia annexed East Timor as a province, which transformed the war into this intra-state war. Following Indonesia's annexation, the armed resistance against Indonesia was continued by FRETILIN, which favored Timorese independence. By the end of 1977, FRETILIN's forces were contained, and in 1979 a government offensive defeated the resistance. East Timor finally became independent in 2003 with help from the UN.

Sources: Armstrong (2004); Clodfelter (2002); Emmerson (1999); Lisbon Correspondent (1979); Lowry (1996); McCrum (1994); Xinhua General Overseas News Service (1977).

INTRA-STATE WAR #807:

The Third Lebanese War of 1978

Participants: Israel, Maronite militias vs. PLO, Shiite militia, Syria
Dates: February 1, 1978, to October 4, 1978
Battle-Related Deaths: Maronite militias—1,500; PLO, Shiite militia—800; Syria—800; Israel—[ ]
Where Fought: Middle East
Initiator: PLO, Syria
Outcome: Stalemate
War Type: Inter-communal

Narrative: Syrian intervention had ended the war in Lebanon in 1976 (intra-state war #801); however, violence between the Christian and Muslim militias continued to erupt. Syria had intervened in the last war to assist the Maronites, but in this war the Syrians switched sides. In early 1978, Syria helped to form an alliance between the Palestine Liberation Organization (PLO) and the Shiite forces and then encouraged them to attack the Maronite militias. As the fighting spread, Israel invaded southern Lebanon. The worst fighting of the war took place when the Syrians bombarded the Maronites in East Beirut. A cease-fire finally stopped the fighting. This war is coded as an inter-communal war, since Lebanon's army had disintegrated.

Sources: Ciment (2007); Clodfelter (2002); Lenczowski (1987); Phillips and Axelrod (2005); Rabinovich (1985).

INTRA-STATE WAR #808:

The Second Ogaden War Phase 3 of 1978–1980

Participants: Cuba, Ethiopia vs. Ogaden (WSLF), Somalia
Dates: March 10, 1978, to December 3, 1980
Battle-Related Deaths: Ogaden—20,000; Ethiopia—2,000; Somalia—2,000; Cuba—[ ]
Where Fought: Africa
Initiator: Ogaden
Outcome: Cuba, Ethiopia win
War Type: Civil for local issues

Narrative: The overall conflict over the Ogaden is coded into three distinct phases. It began as the Ogaden War Phase 1, intra-state war #805, a civil war between Ethiopia and the Ogaden Western Somali Liberation Front (WSLF) rebels. The war was then transformed into an inter-state war (#187) between Ethiopia and Somalia by the invasion of Somali troops. Finally, the war was transformed into this civil war by the withdrawal of Somalia from the fighting in March 1978. The WSLF continued to engage the Ethiopian and Cuban troops in fierce battles. In response, the Ethiopian government launched Operation Lash in August 1980. Approximately 60,000 Ethiopian and Cuban troops advanced against the WSLF forces. Somalia intervened briefly in November to attempt to assist the faltering rebels, but they were soon driven back into Somalia. The WSLF was ultimately defeated.

Sources: Bercovitch and Fretter (2004); Clodfelter (2002); Tareke (2002).

INTRA-STATE WAR #809:

The Third Guatemala War of 1978–1984

Participants: Guatemala vs. Indians, leftists
Dates: March 12, 1978, to April 13, 1984
Battle-Related Deaths: Indians, leftists—4,750; Guatemala—1,250
Where Fought: W. Hemisphere

Initiator: Guatemala
Outcome: Guatemala wins
War Type: Civil for central control

Narrative: Leftist opposition to Guatemala's military dictatorship had been crushed in 1971 (intra-state war #781); however, the leftist movement reemerged in the late 1970s, sometimes involving progressive Catholic clergy. The Democratic Front Against Repression (FDCR), a broad coalition of opposition groups, was created that included the older Revolutionary Armed Forces (FAR) along with newer groups, such as the Guerrilla Army of the Poor (EGP), which had a large Mayan membership. The government launched a brutal war against the opposition, aimed at depopulating the areas that supported the rebels. The guerrillas were unable to protect the population, and an estimated 100,000 civilians were killed or disappeared during the campaign. By 1984 the fighting had ceased and the government had extended its control into Mayan areas.

Sources: Clodfelter (2002); Costello (2002); BBC News (2002); Hunt (2002); LaFeber (1993).

INTRA-STATE WAR #810:
The Saur Revolution of 1978

Participants: Afghanistan vs. leftist military
Dates: April 27, 1978, to April 28, 1978
Battle-Related Deaths: Afghanistan—1,800; leftist military—1,200
Where Fought: Asia
Initiator: leftist military
Outcome: Leftist military wins
War Type: Civil for central control

Narrative: This war is the first in a succession of five wars that confronted Afghanistan after 1978. Afghanistan had been ruled by a monarchy until 1973, when King Mohammad Zahir Shah was overthrown in a bloodless coup by his cousin Mohammed Daoud, who had served as prime minister. Daoud established an increasingly authoritarian state, which led to growing Marxist resistance. The primary Marxist factions

were the Khalq ("Masses"), headed by Nur Muhammad Taraki and Hafizullah Amin, and the Parcham ("Flag") faction, headed by Babrak Karmal. Marxist elements in the military, aided by the Soviet Union, launched a revolt against Dauod. In this thirty-six-hour war, Daoud was killed and Taraki was installed as president of the Revolutionary Council of Afghanistan.

Sources: Arnold (1983); Clodfelter (2002); Dorronsoro (2005); *Europa Yearbook* (2005); Evans (2002); Human Rights Watch (2001); Keesing's (1978, 1979).

INTRA-STATE WAR #811:
The Fourth DRC (Shaba) War of 1978

Participants: Belgium, DRC, France vs. FNLC
Dates: May 1, 1978, to June 6, 1978
Battle-Related Deaths: FNLC—900; DRC—100; France—5; Belgium—[ ]
Where Fought: Africa
Initiator: FNLC
Outcome: DRC, Belgium, France win
War Type: Civil for central control

Narrative: The province that was called Katanga back in the 1960s was known as Shaba in 1978. Katanga had unsuccessfully tried to secede from the Democratic Republic of Congo (DRC) in 1960 (intra-state war #750), and many of the former rebels had fled into Angola. When the DRC government (then called Zaire) sent troops to intervene in the war in Angola in 1975 (inter-state war #186), it aroused the National Front for the Liberation of the Congo (FNLC), which consisted of Katangan army troops who had fled to Angola. In May 1978 the FNLC invaded Shaba province. Numbering about 4,000, the rebels seized the mining city of Kolwezi on May 12, taking about 2,500 European hostages. The DRC (Zairean) army began a counterattack a week later, and French and Belgian paratroopers landed in Kolwezi to rescue the hostages. At that point the FNLC began withdrawing. Most of the hostages were rescued, except for 131 Europeans, who were killed.

Sources: Brogan (1998); Clodfelter (2002); Cutter (2007); Stearns (2001); Van Nederveen (2001).

INTRA-STATE WAR #812:
The First Afghan Mujahideen Uprising of 1978–1980

Participants: Afghanistan, Russia vs. mujahideen
Dates: September 1, 1978, to February 21, 1980
Battle-Related Deaths: mujahideen—21,200; Afghanistan—11,800; Russia—2,000
Where Fought: Asia
Initiator: mujahideen
Outcome: Transformed into extra-state war #476
War Type: Civil for central control

Narrative: In the Saur Revolution (intra-state war #810), the Marxists had come to power and installed Muhammad Taraki as president of the Revolutionary Council. Soon thereafter Muslim tribal fighters began uncoordinated attacks against the new regime. The rebels formed the anti-Communist National Rescue Front in July, and large-scale fighting began in September with uprisings in Hazarajat. The revolt began in the mountains, which were soon under rebel control. The strength of the rebel mujahideen grew from 30,000 to 200,000. In the spring of 1979 the mujahideen proclaimed their intention of overthrowing the Marxist government. At this point the Soviet Union intervened to assist the government. In September 1979 President Taraki was overthrown, killed, and replaced by Hafizullah Amin. The Soviet Union engineered another coup in December 1979, placing Babrak Karmal of the Parchams in power. As the Afghan army became increasingly reluctant to fight with the Soviets against fellow Afghans, the Soviet army took over the bulk of the fighting, especially in clashes in Kabul in February 1980. Thus the civil war ends as the fighting is transformed into the Soviet Quagmire (extra-state war #476).

Sources: Arnold (1983); Clodfelter (2002); Dorronsoro (2005); *Europa Yearbook* (2005); Evans (2002); Human Rights Watch (2001); Keesing's (1978, 1979); Uppsala Universitet (2004).

INTRA-STATE WAR #813:
The Overthrow of the Shah of 1978–1979

Participants: Iran vs. anti-shah coalition
Dates: September 3, 1978, to February 11, 1979
Battle-Related Deaths: anti-shah coalition—1,000; Iran—100
Where Fought: Middle East
Initiator: Iran
Outcome: Anti-shah coalition wins
War Type: Civil for central control

Narrative: Reza Shah Pahlavi had been returned to the throne of Iran in a CIA-backed coup in 1953. The shah began a program of modernization, called the White Revolution, which prompted increasing opposition to his rule within both the Left and the religious clerics on the Right. Beginning in late 1977 street protests were erupting on a regular basis. The war began in September 1978 when a group of demonstrators were attacked by the government. On January 16, 1979, the shah left the country. The succeeding government engaged in heavy fighting on February 10, but as army troops deserted, the government surrendered on February 11 to Ayatollah Khomeini.

Sources: Ciment (2007); Clodfelter (2002); Hiro (1996); Lenczowski (1987); Phillips and Axelrod (2005).

INTRA-STATE WAR #815:
The Sandinista Rebellion of 1978–1979

Participants: Nicaragua vs. Sandinistas
Dates: September 9, 1978, to July 18, 1979
Battle-Related Deaths: Sandinistas—3,000; Nicaragua—1,000

Where Fought: W. Hemisphere
Initiator: Sandinistas
Outcome: Sandinistas win
War Type: Civil for central control

Narrative: The Somozas had misruled Nicaragua since the 1930s. The regime had become increasingly corrupt, leading to opposition from the Sandinista National Liberation Front (FSLN) starting in the late 1960s. Repressive measures taken by the government and rightist militias, including the January 1978 murder of popular newspaper editor Pedro Chamorro, precipitated popular demonstrations and FSLN attacks. The war began in September 1978 when the FSLN seized several cities in an attempt to instigate a widespread rebellion. The cities were soon recaptured by the government, and the Sandinistas withdrew to their bases in Costa Rica, where they received weapons and training from Cuba. The next major FSLN campaign began in January 1979, with the FSLN gradually seizing towns as they advanced on Managua. Under international pressure President Anastasio ("Tachito") Somoza Debayle resigned in July, and the war ended in a Sandinista victory.

Sources: Clodfelter (2002); Phillips and Axelrod (2005); Scheina (2003b).

INTRA-STATE WAR #816:
The Anti-Khomeini Coalition War of 1979–1984

Participants: Iran vs. Anti-Khomeini Coalition
Dates: February 12, 1979, to March [ ], 1984
Battle-Related Deaths: Iran—[ ]; Fedayeen Khalq, Kurds—[ ] (Total Combatant Deaths: 20,000)
Where Fought: Middle East
Initiator: Anti-Khomeini Coalition
Outcome: Iran wins
War Type: Civil for central control

Narrative: Following the overthrow of Shah Pahlavi II in 1979 (intra-state war #813), the new Islamic republic immediately faced opposition

from a variety of groups, herein referred to as the "Anti-Khomeini Coalition." The Coalition included Marxist groups, such as the Tudeh Party and the Fedayeen Khalq; elements in the army; unemployed workers; supporters of the former shah; the Kurds; and the Baluchis. The war began with fighting in Tabriz led by the former shah's supporters. The Kurds then began an uprising, and battles occurred in Teheran involving the Fedayeen Khalq. The government was able to suppress most of the rebellion by 1981; however, the Kurds continued fighting until 1984.

Sources: Brogan (1998); Clodfelter (2002); Lenczowski (1987); Phillips and Axelrod (2005).

INTRA-STATE WAR #817:
The El Salvador War of 1979–1992

Participants: El Salvador vs. Salvadorean Democratic Front
Dates: July 1, 1979, to February 1, 1992
Battle-Related Deaths: El Salvador—[ ]; Salvadorean Democratic Front—[ ] (Total Combatant Deaths: 25,000)
Where Fought: W. Hemisphere
Initiator: Salvadorean Democratic Front
Outcome: Compromise
War Type: Civil for central control

Narrative: El Salvador was ruled by a handful of families who controlled vast land and commercial wealth. This made the country ripe for revolution in the 1970s, and a coup was attempted in 1972. Leftist guerrillas, led by the People's Revolutionary Army, engaged in limited attacks against the government in 1978 and early 1979. The attacks reached war level in the summer of 1979, fueled by the success of the Sandinista Revolution in Nicaragua (intra-state war #815). Cuba hosted a meeting of the various Salvadorean revolutionary groups in May 1980 and encouraged them to create the united Farabundo Martí National Liberation Front (FMLN), to which Cuba provided weapons. By the early

1980s the guerrillas controlled about a third of the country. In January 1981 the FMLN launched a major offensive, which gained the group international recognition. Because a rebel victory looked possible, the United States increased its aid to the Salvadorean government. The government was still unable to defeat the FMLN, and by 1989 the two sides were deadlocked. A compromise settlement in 1992 attempted to reintegrate the rebels back into society.

Sources: Clodfelter (2002); Scheina (2003b).

INTRA-STATE WAR #818:
The Mozambique War of 1979–1992

Participants: Mozambique, Tanzania, Zimbabwe vs. Renamo
Dates: October 21, 1979, to October 4, 1992
Battle-Related Deaths: Zimbabwe—500; Tanzania—50, Mozambique—[ ]; Renamo—[ ]
Where Fought: Africa
Initiator: Renamo
Outcome: Mozambique, Tanzania, Zimbabwe win
War Type: Civil for central control

Narrative: In 1975 Mozambique became independent under the tutelage of the Marxist Front for the Liberation of Mozambique (FRELIMO). The one-party regime imposed nationalization, and as a result, rampant discontent grew during the late 1970s. In 1979 the anti-Communist Mozambican National Resistance (MNR, or Renamo) began major attacks against the regime. Part of Renamo's original support came from the Rhodesian government, and Renamo also received covert aid from South Africa; however, after Rhodesia became Zimbabwe (see intra-state war #791), Zimbabwe switched to supporting the FRELIMO government. A defense agreement between Zimbabwe and Mozambique in 1982 led to the deployment of Zimbabwean troops, and Tanzanian troops also intervened.

Renamo continued its violent attacks but was unable to defeat the government forces. On October 4, 1992, a cease-fire was signed and Renamo joined the political process.

Sources: Brogan (1998); Ciment (2007); Clodfelter (2002); Cutter (2007); Meredith (2005); Phillips and Axelrod (2005); Uppsala Universitet (1995c).

INTRA-STATE WAR #820:
The Second Chad (Habré Revolt) War of 1980–1984

Participants: Chad, Libya vs. FAN, France
Dates: March 22, 1980, to September [ ], 1984
Battle-Related Deaths: Chad—3,500; FAN—1,500; Libya—1,000; France—200
Where Fought: Africa
Initiator: FAN
Outcome: FAN, France win
War Type: Civil for local issues

Narrative: In 1966 Chad was confronted by the National Liberation Front of Chad (FROLINAT) rebellion (intra-state war #771). Chad, with the assistance of France, defeated the rebels in 1971; however, FROLINAT under the leadership of Hissène Habré continued to be a major force in Chadian politics. The group split in two when Habré formed the Armed Forces of the North (FAN). FROLINAT continued to launch attacks against the government from Libya and was also involved in fighting against FAN. The FROLINAT leader in the north, Goukouni Oueddei, seized power in March 1979, and there was an attempt at creating a coalition government with Habré as defense minister. The coalition was unstable, and in March 1980 Habré's forces attacked the government. Libyan troops intervened in December, enabling Goukouni's forces to drive Habré into Sudan. Libya ultimately withdrew its forces from Chad in October 1981, though they returned in 1983. Meanwhile, Habré's forces launched an offensive and seized power in 1982. Goukouni fled to Libya and then launched a new offensive with Libyan support. France sent troops to aid Habré, and the rebel offensive was stopped. The ensuing settlement called for the removal of foreign troops; however Libyan forces remained and began to expand their presence in the Aouzou Strip. This set the stage for the war over the Aouzou Strip in 1986 (inter-state war #207).

Sources: Amoo (2003); Bercovitch and Fretter (2004); Brogan (1998); Ciment (2007); Clodfelter (2002); Cordesman (2004); Mays (2003); Meredith (2005); Nolutshungu (1996); Phillips and Axelrod (2005); Project Ploughshares (2000, 2004).

groups immediately formed, including the National Resistance Army (NRA), led by former defense minister Yoweri Museveni. The NRA began attacks against the government. Obote launched a major offensive against the NRA, but the NRA soon controlled the south and west. A coup led to the removal of Obote in 1985. The new government under Tito Okello was then overthrown by the Museveni's NRA in January 25, 1986. Control over the entire country was secured in March, ending the war.

Sources: Ciment (2007); Clodfelter (2002); Edgerton (2002); Jackson (2002); Katumba-Wamala (2000); Southall (1980).

INTRA-STATE WAR #822:
The Second Uganda War of 1980–1986

Participants: Uganda vs. National Resistance Army
Dates: December 8, 1980, to March 19, 1986
Battle-Related Deaths: Uganda—40,000; National Resistance Army—6,000
Where Fought: Africa
Initiator: National Resistance Army
Outcome: National Resistance Army wins
War Type: Civil for local issues

Narrative: Milton Obote's government was overthrown in 1971 by former Ugandan military leader Idi Amin, who then established one of the world's most repressive regimes. Faced with growing opposition, Amin tried to garner popular support by invading Tanzania in 1978 (inter-state war #190). Not only was Tanzania able to repel the invasion, but also it then launched a counterattack against Uganda that overthrew Amin. The Uganda National Liberation Front (UNLF) was created to serve as a temporary government pending elections in December. Obote was then returned to power in what some claimed was a rigged election. Several resistance

INTRA-STATE WAR #823:
The Nigeria-Muslim War of 1980–1981

Participants: Nigeria vs. Muslim fundamentalists
Dates: December 18, 1980, to January 1, 1981
Battle-Related Deaths: Muslim fundamentalists—1,000; Nigeria—50
Where Fought: Africa
Initiator: Muslim fundamentalists
Outcome: Nigeria wins
War Type: Civil for local issues

Narrative: After general elections in July 1979, Nigeria was returned to civilian rule under President Alhaji Shehu Shagari; however, that did not end the many conflicts within society, in particular those involving religion. The Al Masifu sect led by Alhaji Muhammadu Marwa Maitatsine wanted to purify Islam and began intimidating citizens in Kano province. The governor finally ordered the sect to leave the province. The sect refused and instead on December 18, 1980, attacked a group of Muslims praying in a mosque. The sect repulsed an intervention by the local police, and the governor called for military assistance. An attack by the army and air force forced the Al Masifu to flee Kano city, although fighting continued in a nearby village.

Sources: Agi (1998); Ciment (2007); Clark (1987); Clodfelter (2002); Falola (1998); Falola and Heaton (2008); Udoidem (1997).

INTRA-STATE WAR #825:

The Hama War of 1981–1982

Participants: Syria vs. Muslim Brotherhood
Dates: November [ ], 1981, to February 23, 1982
Battle-Related Deaths: Muslim Brotherhood—
  2,000; Syria—1,000
Where Fought: Middle East
Initiator: Muslim Brotherhood
Outcome: Syria wins
War Type: Civil for central control

Narrative: The Baath Party and its Alawi-dominated military controlled Syrian politics since 1963. In the late 1970s, President Hafez al-Assad's government was facing criticism for its policies on a number of fronts. Among the few groups to openly challenge the regime was the Muslim Brotherhood, whose members opposed the secular nature of the Baathist regime. Strikes and demonstrations in Aleppo in late 1979 and early 1980 led to the deaths of hundreds of demonstrators when the army surrounded the city. The conflict reached war level in late 1981, when the Brotherhood bombed a military headquarters in Damascus. The most serious conflict of the war took place in the city of Hama in February 1982. The Brotherhood seized control of the city and tried to instigate a widespread uprising against the government. The Syrian military responded with a major assault. President Assad sent in between 9,000 and 12,000 troops to crush the revolt. The rebels held out for three weeks before the Syrian tanks destroyed both the rebellion and the city. In addition to the combatants, another 17,000 civilians died in the conflict.

Sources: Cleveland (1994); Clodfelter (2002); Hiro (2003); Keesing's (1982); Stearns (2001).

INTRA-STATE WAR #826:

The Tigrean and Eritrean War of 1982–1991

Participants: Ethiopia vs. Eritrea, Tigray
Dates: January 23, 1982, to May 28, 1991
Battle-Related Deaths: Eritrea, Tigray—65,000;
  Ethiopia—10,000
Where Fought: Africa
Initiator: Eritrea, Tigray
Outcome: Eritrea, Tigray win
War Type: Civil for local issues

Narrative: The Eritrean independence movement was defeated by Ethiopia with the assistance of Cuba in 1978 (intra-state war #798). Groups within the adjacent province of Tigray also sought independence and created the Tigray People's Liberation Front (TPLF) in 1975. The TPLF, with support from the Eritrean People's Liberation Front (EPLF), engaged in low-level attacks against the government after 1976. In 1982 the Ethiopian Dergue government decided to develop a plan to finally eliminate the rebels; however, a preemptive attack by the rebels against Asmara started the war. On February 15 the government launched Operation Red Star on three fronts against Tigray and Eritrea. The rebels were seriously outnumbered—the government deployed almost 137,000 troops to rebels numbering 22,000–35,000. Early government advances were finally halted by the rebels. A rebel offensive was launched in March 1988, which led to the collapse of the Ethiopian army in 1991. The rebels overthrew the Mengistu government. The EPLF then took control of Eritrea, which achieved independence in May 1993.

Sources: Brogan (1998); Ciment (2007); Phillips and Axelrod (2005); Tareke (2002).

INTRA-STATE WAR #827:

The Shining Path War of 1982–1992

Participants: Peru vs. Shining Path, TARM
Dates: March 4, 1982, to September 12, 1992

Battle-Related Deaths: Shining Path, TARM—12,000; Peru—4,000
Where Fought: W. Hemisphere
Initiator: Shining Path
Outcome: Peru wins
War Type: Civil for central control

Narrative: In 1980 the Sendero Luminoso ("Shining Path") began a revolt against the Peruvian establishment, though the fighting did not reach war level until 1982. The movement, which had been founded by Abimael Guzmán, had an ideology that was an amalgam of Maoist-style communism and Quechua tribalism. Shining Path activities began around Ayacucho, in the south, where the last major battle for Peruvian independence had been fought against the Spanish (extra-state war #312). Guzmán's strategy anticipated a long-term guerrilla war. The Shining Path was joined by a small armed force from the Tupac Amarú Revolutionary Movement (TARM). In addition to battles between the rebels and the government forces, the war entailed massacres of civilians by both sides. In 1990 newly elected president Alberto Fujimori intensified the war. The capture of Guzmán in 1992 effectively ended the war, though limited attacks did occur later.

Sources: Clodfelter (2002); Project Ploughshares (2000); Scheina (2003b).

INTRA-STATE WAR #828:
The Contra War of 1982–1990

Participants: Nicaragua vs. Contras
Dates: March 18, 1982, to April 19, 1990
Battle-Related Deaths: Contras—25,200; Nicaragua—7,000
Where Fought: W. Hemisphere
Initiator: Contras
Outcome: Stalemate
War Type: Civil for central control

Narrative: The Sandinista National Liberation Front had overthrown the Somoza regime in Nicaragua in 1979 (intra-state war #815). The Sandinista's reforms engendered opposition among a variety of groups, including supporters of the former Somoza regime (Somocistas), the privileged elites, the Miskito Indians, and the Democratic Revolutionary Alliance. The counterrevolutionaries were collectively referred to as the Contras, and they received significant assistance from the United States in their attempt to overthrow the Sandinista government. The Contras waged a guerrilla war that targeted not only the government but also the Sandinista's civilian supporters. The conflict reached war level after the Contras began major operations in 1982. The Sandinistas were voted out of office in February 1990, and a peace deal was finally brokered by President Óscar Arias Sánchez of Costa Rica, ending the war in April.

Sources: Clodfelter (2002); LaFeber (1993); Phillips and Axelrod (2005); Selbin (1993).

INTRA-STATE WAR #831:
The Matabeleland War of 1983–1987

Participants: Zimbabwe vs. ZAPU
Dates: January [ ], 1983, to December 27, 1987
Battle-Related Deaths: Zimbabwe—[ ]; ZAPU—[ ] (Total Combatant Deaths: 10,000)
Where Fought: Africa
Initiator: Zimbabwe
Outcome: Zimbabwe wins
War Type: Civil for central control

Narrative: Black majority rule had come to Rhodesia (later Zimbabwe) as a result of a war between the white government and black resistance organizations, primarily the Zimbabwe African People's Union (ZAPU), led by Joshua Nkomo, and the Zimbabwe African National Union (ZANU), led by Robert Mugabe (intra-state war #791). Initially, in 1980 a coalition government was created that included Nkomo but was headed by Mugabe. The former rebels soon quarreled over Mugabe's avowed goal of creating a one-party state under the leadership of his ZANU party. Mugabe developed his own personal army in preparation for a showdown. In 1982 Nkomo was removed from the government because Mugabe blamed him for growing unrest in Matabeleland (in southwestern Zimbabwe), which was ZAPU's base. In January 1983, Mugabe sent his new brigade into Matabeleland, where it attacked ZAPU officials and civilians. A similar offensive in 1984 was referred to as the Gukurahundi ("Strong Wind"). Gradually ZAPU was worn down. The December 1987 Unity Accord merged ZANU and ZAPU. In addition to the combatants, an estimated 10,000 civilians were killed.

Sources: Ciment (2007); Clodfelter (2002); Cutter (2007); Meredith (2005).

INTRA-STATE WAR #832:
The Fourth Burmese War of 1983–1988

Participants: Burma vs. Karens, Kachin rebels
Dates: Feburary 1, 1983, to January [ ], 1988
Battle-Related Deaths: Burma—2,800; Karens, Kachin rebels—1,200
Where Fought: Asia
Initiator: Kachin rebels
Outcome: Burma wins
War Type: Civil for local issues

Narrative: The Karens, and the Karen National Liberation Front (KNLA), had been in almost constant rebellion against the Burmese government since 1948, with wars in 1948, 1958, and 1967 (intra-state wars #732, #746, and #773). Hostilities increased again in 1983, and in 1984 the government launched a new offensive in which government troops captured two of the Karen strongholds. In 1987 a second major offensive included attacks against the Kachin rebels in the north, and government victories succeeded in ending hostilities, though they also

set the stage for the prodemocracy revolt (intra-state war #847).

Sources: Bercovitch and Fretter (2004); Brogan (1998); Clodfelter (2002); Steinberg (1990).

INTRA-STATE WAR #833:
The Fourth Lebanese Civil War of 1983–1984

Participants: France, Lebanon, United States vs. Shiites, Druze
Dates: April 18, 1983, to February 29, 1984
Battle-Related Deaths: Lebanon—[ ]; Shiites, Druze—[ ] (Total Lebanese Combatant Deaths: 2,000); United States—273; France—95
Where Fought: Middle East
Initiator: Druze
Outcome: Shiites, Druze win
War Type: Civil for central control

Narrative: In 1982 Israel wanted to stop the shelling of its country by the Palestine Liberation Organization (PLO) from bases in southern Lebanon and consequently went to war with Syria and the PLO (inter-state war #205). As a result the PLO was forced to leave Lebanon for its new base in Tunisia. That did not, however, end the conflict in Lebanon. The Druze and Shiites were unhappy with their treatment by the Maronite-run government, which had bulldozed Shiite settlements in Beirut in 1982. In 1983 they rebelled. The war began on April 18, when the U.S. embassy in Beirut was bombed. Throughout the rest of the year the Shia Amal forces, allied with the Druze, fought against the Christian Phalange and the Lebanese army. The conflict also included the use of a truck bomb against the American and French headquarters, killing 241 marines in October. In response France and the United States launched air attacks against Druze and Syrian positions in December. In February 1984 the Shiites captured West Beirut. At that point the Lebanese army had virtually ceased to exist. Lebanese president

Amine Pierre Gemayel traveled to Damascus, where on February 29, 1984, he agreed to most of Syria's demands.

Sources: Ciment (2007); Clodfelter (2002); Phillips and Axelrod (2005); Rabinovich (1985).

INTRA-STATE WAR #835:
The First Sri Lanka Tamil War of 1983–2002

Participants: India, Sri Lanka vs. Tamils
Dates: July 25, 1983, to January 22, 2002
Battle-Related Deaths: Tamils—17,000; Sri Lanka—8,500; India—1,155
Where Fought: Asia
Initiator: Tamils
Outcome: Compromise
War Type: Civil for local issues

Narrative: Since gaining its independence from Britain in 1948, Sri Lanka has been dominated by the Sinhalese majority, most of whom are Buddhist. The Tamils, who generally live in the north and the east coast of the island, are largely Hindu. The Sinhalese government passed a series of laws to benefit the Sinhalese and disadvantage the Tamils. Consequently, the Tamils created the Liberation Tigers of Tamil Eelam (LTTE) to pursue an independent Tamil state. In July 1983 the LTTE launched a rebellion against the Sri Lankan government, utilizing both guerrilla war tactics and direct military confrontations. In 1987 India intervened, apparently to stop the fighting but became militarily involved on the side of the government in the offensive to recapture Jaffna. The Indians troops left in 1990, but the war continued until negotiations created a cease-fire in February 2002, whereby the Tamils maintained a degree of autonomy. Unfortunately, the underlying political issues facing Tamil-Sinhalese relations were never resolved, and the country returned to war in 2006 (intra-state war #940).

Sources: Bercovitch and Fretter (2004); Bloom (2003); Bush (2003); Clodfelter (2002); Gunaratna (1998); Project Ploughshares (2000, 2004); Rudolph (2003); de Silva (1998); World Alliance for Peace in Sri Lanka (2005).

INTRA-STATE WAR #836:
The Second South Sudan War of 1983–2005

Participants: Sudan vs. SPLA-Garang faction
Dates: November 17, 1983, to January 10, 2005
Battle-Related Deaths: Sudan—[ ]; SPLA-Garang faction—[ ]
Where Fought: Middle East
Initiator: SPLA-Garang faction
Outcome: Compromise
War Type: Civil for central control

Narrative: The conflict between Sudan's Arab/Muslim north and the black/animist south led to a lengthy war in 1963 (intra-state war #758). An even longer war broke out in 1983 after Gen. Gaafar Nimeiry, who became military ruler in 1969, declared an Islamic republic. The Sudan People's Liberation Army (SPLA) demanded the end of the imposition of Sharia law (code of law based on the Koran) in the south. Although the south preferred to secede from Sudan, the SPLA's stated goal was to overthrow the government. The Dinka-dominated SPLA launched the rebellion in 1983 and soon dominated most of the south. The SPLA was on the verge of victory when the war stopped as the SPLA split in two. The period from August 27, 1991, to April 15, 1992, is coded as a break in this war, while the two SPLA factions fought against each other (intra-state war #866). In April 1992 the government decided to take advantage of the infighting by launching a new offensive against the SPLA. The stalemate was finally broken by negotiations, resulting in a peace agreement in January 2005, which gave the SPLA representation in the government.

Sources: Brogan (1998); Cheeseboro (2001); Clodfelter (2002); Collins (1999); Cordesman (1993); Cutter (2007); Hutchinson (2001); Johnson (2004); Project Ploughshares (2004).

INTRA-STATE WAR #837:
The Indian Golden Temple War of 1984

Participants: India vs. Sikhs
Dates: June 1, 1984, to July 30, 1984
Battle-Related Deaths: Sikhs—1,200; India—700
Where Fought: Asia
Initiator: India
Outcome: Stalemate
War Type: Civil for local issues

Narrative: Many of the Sikhs living in India's state of Punjab favored a separate Sikh homeland and created Akali Dal as a political party to pursue that goal. Starting in August 1982 Akali Dal organized daily demonstrations at the primary Sikh shrine, the Golden Temple. Akali Dal then expanded its tactics to include attacks against the police and Hindus, which prompted Pakistan to provide it with covert assistance. The war started when the Sikhs occupied the Golden Temple in the hopes that this would start a widespread rebellion. Having learned of the Sikh-Pakistan connection, Prime Minister Indira Gandhi was under pressure to act. Indian forces surrounded the Temple and on June 4 launched an assault called Operation Blue Star. Although the temple's defenders were well armed, they were soon routed. Violence continued throughout Punjab for another month, including revolts by Sikh soldiers. On October 31, Gandhi was assassinated by two of her bodyguards who were Sikh militants.

Sources: Ciment (2007); Clodfelter (2002); Phillips and Axelrod (2005).

INTRA-STATE WAR #838:
The First Turkish KurdsWar of 1984–1986

Participants: Turkey vs. Kurds, PKK
Dates: August 14, 1984, to March [ ], 1986
Battle-Related Deaths: Kurds, PKK—9,000; Turkey—1,500
Where Fought: Middle East

Initiator: Kurds, PKK
Outcome: Conflict continues at below war level
War Type: Civil for local issues

Narrative: The Kurds are a sizable minority in Turkey, about 23 percent of the population. Suppression of the Kurds by the government had begun in 1925, which led to the Kurdish desire for a separate Kurdistan. A number of Kurdish parties and armed groups were created, including the Workers' Party of Kurdistan (PKK) in 1978. As the PKK began engaging in terrorist activities, the Turkish government attempted to suppress the group. Even though the PKK had suffered severe losses, in August 1984 it officially began a major offensive against the government in the southeastern provinces. In response, the government launched Operation Comfort to track down the rebels. The Turkish manhunt lasted until early 1986, after which the conflict continued but at below war level.

Sources: Brogan (1998); Ciment (2007); Clodfelter (2002); Gunter (2003); O'Ballance (1996); Phillips and Axelrod (2005).

INTRA-STATE WAR #840:
The Fifth Iraqi Kurds War of 1985–1988

Participants: Iraq vs. Iran, Kurds
Dates: January [ ], 1985, to September 6, 1988
Battle-Related Deaths: Iraq—[ ]; Kurds—[ ]; Iran—[ ]
Where Fought: Middle East
Initiator: Kurds
Outcome: Iraq wins
War Type: Civil for local issues

Narrative: The previous war between Iraq and the Kurds (intra-state war #797) had ended in a defeat for the Kurds in 1975. In 1980 Iraq became involved in a long war with Iran (inter-state war #199). In the course of the war Iran invaded northern Iraq, where it received assistance from the Kurds. This situation prompted Iraq to reach an agreement with the Kurds in

1984, but when the agreement broke down, the Kurds launched a new offensive against Iraq in early 1985 with the help of Iran. The Kurds made significant gains in territory; however, immediately following the end of the Iran-Iraq War, Iraq attacked the Kurds and in one such assault killed 4,000 Kurds in a chemical weapons attack on Halabja in 1988. The Kurds were defeated, and 60,000 Kurds fled to refugee camps in Turkey and Iran.

Sources: Bercovitch and Fretter (2004); Brogan (1998); Ciment (2007); Cleveland (1994); Leezenberg (2004); Phillips and Axelrod (2005); Project Ploughshares (2005).

INTRA-STATE WAR #842:

The South Yemen War of 1986

Participants: PDRY vs. leftist factions
Dates: January 13, 1986, to January 29, 1986
Battle-Related Deaths: leftist factions—8,800; PDRY—4,200
Where Fought: Middle East
Initiator: PDRY ·
Outcome: Leftist factions win
War Type: Civil for central control

Narrative: South Yemen gained its independence from Britain in 1967. Its Socialist government was overthrown in 1969 by a more radical group, which renamed the country the People's Democratic Republic of Yemen (PDRY). Abd al-Fattah Ismail seized power in 1978, serving as president, with Ali Nasser Muhammed as his prime minister. Conflict soon developed between the two men, since Ali favored a Chinese revolutionary model, while Ismail favored the Soviet alternative. Ismail resigned, or was forced to resign, in 1980 and was replaced as president by Ali, who pursued less radical policies. In 1985 Ali's popularity within the Central Committee was declining, and Ismail was readmitted to the Central Committee. Ali decided that decisive measures were necessary. At a meeting of the Politburo on January 13, 1986, a gun battle occurred and several members were killed, including Ismail. Ali fled the capital and gathered an army for an attack on the leftist factions. In the end, Ali's force was defeated in heavy fighting.

Sources: Clodfelter (2002); Congressional Quarterly (1994); Cordesman (1993); Ismael and Ismael (1986); Phillips and Axelrod (2005).

INTRA-STATE WAR #843:

The Holy Spirit Movement War of 1986–1987

Participants: Uganda vs. HSMF
Dates: August [ ], 1986, to October [ ], 1987
Battle-Related Deaths: HSMF—5,000; Uganda—2,000
Where Fought: Africa
Initiator: HSMF
Outcome: Uganda wins
War Type: Civil for central control

Narrative: The Holy Spirit Movement was a religious sect in northern Uganda headed by Alice Lakwena. Lakwena was convinced that she had to overthrow the government of Yoweri Museveni in order to remove wrongdoing from society. She recruited an army, the Holy Spirit Mobile Force (HSMF), which ultimately had approximately 10,000 soldiers. The warriors were coated with special oils to protect them from bullets. The HSMF marched toward Kampala, winning a victory at Kilak Corner in November 1986; however, they were defeated in heavy fighting at Jinja the following year.

Sources: Ciment (2007); Cline (2003); Clodfelter (2002); Dunn (2007); Edgerton (2002); Jackson (2002).

INTRA-STATE WAR #845:

The Second Sri Lanka-JVP War of 1987–1989

Participants: Sri Lanka vs. JVP
Dates: July 29, 1987, to December 29, 1989

Battle-Related Deaths: Sri Lanka—[ ]; JVP—[ ]
Where Fought: Asia
Initiator: JVP
Outcome: Sri Lanka wins
War Type: Civil for central control

Narrative: The long-running war between the Sri Lankan government and the Liberation Tigers of Tamil Eelam (LTTE) had begun in 1983 (intra-state war #835). In 1987 the Indo-Lanka Accord, which allowed India to intervene, supposedly to stop the fighting, became the focal point of the opposition to the Sri Lankan government espoused by the Marxist Janatha Vimukthi Peramuna (JVP). The JVP launched a series of guerrilla attacks against government installations and civilians throughout the country. As the violence approached the capital, the government declared a state of emergency. After April 1989, the JVP increased its attacks against the government; however, as the conflict made life more difficult for the citizens, popular support for the JVP declined. In 1989 the police and the army joined forces in an offensive that defeated the JVP.

Sources: Clodfelter (2002); Gunaratna (2001).

INTRA-STATE WAR #846:
The Inkatha-ANC War of 1987–1994

Participants: IFP vs. ANC
Dates: December 20, 1987, to April 26, 1994
Battle-Related Deaths: IFP—[ ]; ANC—[ ] (Total Combatant Deaths: 20,000)
Where Fought: Africa
Initiator: IFP
Outcome: Stalemate
War Type: Inter-communal

Narrative: In 1987 South Africa was still under an apartheid system that privileged the white minority over the black majority. The military wing of the African National Congress (ANC) conducted guerrilla attacks against the government. But it was also involved in fighting with the Inkatha Freedom Party (IFP), led by Zulu chief Mangosuthu Buthelezi. The two groups were competing for control of the black population, and the more conservative Inkatha wanted to ensure that the leftist ANC would not come to power once apartheid ended. The inter-communal war began with attacks by the IFP, apparently encouraged by the South African government, against the ANC in Natal province. The fighting spread throughout the country and continued until the presidential election in 1994, in which the ANC's Nelson Mandela was elected.

Sources: Berkeley (2001); Ciment (2007); Clodfelter (2002); Keesing's (1987–1994); Kohn (1999); Meredith (2005); Ottaway (1993); Project Ploughshares (2002); Thompson (2001).

INTRA-STATE WAR #847:
The Fifth Burmese War of 1988

Participants: Burma vs. prodemocracy movement
Dates: March [ ], 1988, to October 3, 1988
Battle-Related Deaths: Burma—[ ]; prodemocracy movement—[ ] (Total Combatant Deaths: 3,000)
Where Fought: Asia
Initiator: prodemocracy movement
Outcome: Burma wins
War Type: Civil for central control

Narrative: In Burma the government of U Ne Win not only faced continuing opposition from the Karens and the Communists but rising urban unrest as well. Opposition to the government was fueled by a worsening economic situation and by the government's resistance to democratic reforms. The war began with riots mostly by students in Rangoon, which were brutally dispersed by government troops. U Ne Win resigned, and on September 9, 1988, former prime minister U Nu announced the creation of a new government that would involve a new party, the National League for Democracy, which included noted democracy advocate Aung San

Suu Kyi. On September 24, the military staged a coup, overthrowing the provisional government. The military then created a new government called the State Law and Order Restoration Council (SLORC), which changed the name of the country to the Union of Myanmar. The SLORC also had the army attack the prodemocracy protestors. The army's suppression of a general strike led by the prodemocracy movement in October ended the war; however, members of the movement continued their activities by other means.

Sources: Brogan (1998); Ciment (2007); Keesing's (2006); Phillips and Axelrod (2005); Project Ploughshares (2008); Tilman (1987).

INTRA-STATE WAR #848:
The First Somalia War of 1988–1991

Participants: Somalia vs. rebel clans
Dates: May 26, 1988, to January 26, 1991
Battle-Related Deaths: Somalia—[ ]; rebel clans [ ] (Total Combatant Deaths: 5,000)
Where Fought: Africa
Initiator: rebel clans
Outcome: Rebel clans win
War Type: Civil for central control

Narrative: Somalia had been ruled since 1969 by Muhammad Siad Barre. Barre had originally had the support of the Soviet Union; however, after Somalia tried to capture the Ogaden from Ethiopia (intra-state war #805 and inter-state war #187), the USSR switched to supporting Ethiopia. Somalia's loss in that war in 1978 led to a flood of refugees from the Ogaden into Somalia. The refugees also included a number of Somalis who had participated in the war. Some were members of the Somali National Movement (SNM), which in May 1988 began a rebellion against the Somali government. The SNM was only one of the four clan-based rebel groups that ultimately confronted the government as the rebellion spread throughout the country:

also involving the Somali National Alliance (SNA), the Somali Salvation Alliance (SSA), and the United Somali Congress (USC). In 1990 the rebels besieged the capital of Mogadishu. Siad Barre finally fled the country in January 1991, ending this war. Somalia was left in a state of total anarchy, and warfare would resume in November 1991 (intra-state war #870).

Sources: Bercovitch and Fretter (2004); Brogan (1998); Clodfelter (2002); Cordesman (1993); Cutter (2007); Project Ploughshares (2000).

INTRA-STATE WAR #850:
The Fifth Lebanese War of 1989–1990

Participants: Lebanon vs. militias, Syria
Dates: February [ ], 1989, to October 13, 1990
Battle-Related Deaths: militias—2,500; Syria—150; Lebanon—[ ]
Where Fought: Middle East
Initiator: Lebanon
Outcome: Militias, Syria win
War Type: Civil for central control

Narrative: The last Lebanese war had involved the government of Lebanon (aided by France and the United States) fighting against the Druze and Shiites in 1983 (intra-state war #833). The fighting had ended in 1984 with the Shiite occupation of West Beirut and the virtual destruction of the Lebanese army. Syria continued to interfere in Lebanon, particularly to stop the fighting between Amal and Hezbollah in 1988. In 1989 Gen. Michel Aoun of the rebuilt Lebanese army decided to confront the power of the militias and the Shiite-Syrian alliance. Aoun first clashed with the Maronite militia (the Lebanese Forces) and was successful in driving them out of their headquarters in Beirut. He then confronted the Druze and Shiite militias, which were aided by Syria. Aoun was initially successful in battles with the militias; however, at that point Syria launched an attack against the Lebanese army and forced its surrender in 1990.

Nevertheless, the militias did agree to withdraw from Beirut.

Sources: Brogan (1998); Ciment (2007); Clodfelter (2002); Congressional Quarterly (1994); Phillips and Axelrod (2005).

INTRA-STATE WAR #851:
The Second Afghan Mujahideen Uprising of 1989–2001

Participants: Afghanistan vs. mujahideen
Dates: February 16, 1989, to October 6, 2001
Battle-Related Deaths: Afghanistan—[ ]; mujahideen—[ ] (Total Combatant Deaths: 15,000)
Where Fought: Asia
Initiator: mujahideen
Outcome: Transformed into inter-state war #225
War Type: Civil for central control

Narrative: After the Soviets withdrew from their quagmire conflict in Afghanistan (extra-state war #476) in February 1989, the conflict reverted back to this civil war between the government of Afghanistan and the mujahideen. It had been assumed that the government of Mohammed Najibullah would not last without Soviet support; however, it was aided by the fact that it was opposed by fifteen different rebel groups that frequently fought among themselves. In March 1989 the mujahideen launched a major attack on the capital, but they were repulsed. Najibullah stayed in power for three years, but on April 19, 1992, the army forced him from office and allowed the mujahideen to take the capital. The war was not over yet, however. The rebel factions fought among themselves. A fundamentalist Muslim group called the Taliban captured the capital on September 27, 1996, and continued the fighting as it attempted to extend its control to the countryside. Its opponent was the various other mujahideen groups now allied into the United Islamic Front for the Salvation of Afghanistan, or the Northern Alliance. The Taliban launched major offensives that gave it control of 95 percent of the country by the end of 2000. The Taliban's success contributed to the decision of the United States and its allies to intervene in the conflict to support the Northern Alliance. As the United States and the United Kingdom took over the bulk of the fighting against the Taliban, the civil war ended on October 6, 2001, and the new inter-state war (#225) was begun on October 7, 2001.

Sources: Brogan (1998); Center for Defense Information (2001); Clodfelter (2002); Dorronsoro (2005); *Europa Yearbook* (2005); Human Rights Watch (2001); Phillips and Axelrod (2005); Project Ploughshares (2000); Uppsala Universitet (2004).

INTRA-STATE WAR #852:
The Third Chad (Déby Coup) War of 1989–1990

Participants: Chad vs. Déby's MPS
Dates: March [ ], 1989, to December 4, 1990
Battle-Related Deaths: Chad—3,000; Déby's MPS—800
Where Fought: Africa
Initiator: Déby's MPS
Outcome: Déby's MPS wins
War Type: Civil for central control

Narrative: Hissène Habré came to power in 1982 during a war against the National Liberation Front of Chad (FROLINAT) leader Goukouni Oueddei (intra-state war #820). Both France and Libya had intervened in that war, and at the conclusion of the fighting, both had agreed to remove their forces. Libyan forces remained, however, and expanded their presence in the Aouzou Strip, which led to the war between Libya and Chad (inter-state war #207). Although Libya lost the war in 1987, it continued to intervene in Chad, in particular by supporting Idriss Déby in his attempt to overthrow Habré. The war began in March 1989 with Déby's forces making raids into Chad from their base in Sudan. In November 1990 Déby led his

2,000-troop army, the Patriotic Salvation Movement (MPS), against the 30,000-troop Chadian army. Within three weeks Déby's forces succeeded in capturing the capital, N'Djamena, where Déby took control.

Sources: BBC News (2006); Brogan (1998); Ciment (2007); Clodfelter (2002); Cutter (2007); Hall (2000); Keesing's (1989, 1990); Nolutshungu (1996).

INTRA-STATE WAR #853:
The First Aceh War of 1989–1991

Participants: Indonesia vs. GAM
Dates: June [ ], 1989, to June [ ], 1991
Battle-Related Deaths: Indonesia—[ ]; GAM—[ ] (Total Combatant Deaths: 2,000)
Where Fought: Asia
Initiator: GAM
Outcome: Indonesia wins
War Type: Civil for local issues

Narrative: Aceh is located in north Sumatra, Indonesia. Aceh had been promised a special autonomous status when Indonesia attained independence from the Dutch in 1949. When Aceh's autonomy was not maintained, Aceh joined the Darul Islam revolt against Indonesia in 1953 (intra-state war #738). Indonesian rule under General Suharto was particularly harsh in Aceh, leading to the creation of the secessionist Free Aceh Movement (GAM) in 1976. Between 1976 and 1989, GAM expanded its forces, some of whom received military training in Libya. It also undertook low-level guerrilla operations against the government. The GAM rebellion reached war level after mid-1989. Indonesian security forces responded brutally, and by mid-1991 the rebellion was largely suppressed. Hostilities would flare into war again in May 1999 (intra-state war #912).

Sources: Clodfelter (2002); GlobalSecurity.org (2005); Kingsbury (2007); Lowry (1996); Mallay (1999); Stearns (2001); Tan (2000).

INTRA-STATE WAR #854:
The Bougainville Secession War of 1989–1992

Participants: Papua New Guinea vs. BRA
Dates: July 14, 1989, to September [ ], 1992
Battle-Related Deaths: Papua New Guinea—[ ]; BRA—[ ] (Total Combatant Deaths: 3,000)
Where Fought: Asia
Initiator: Papua New Guinea
Outcome: Conflict continues at below war level
War Type: Civil for local issues

Narrative: Papua New Guinea was a mandate of Australia until it attained its independence in 1975. It consists of the eastern half of the island of New Guinea as well as a string of islands in the Solomon Sea, including Bougainville. Australian firms remaining on the island were seen as expropriating Bougainville's riches for their own benefit and for that of the central government of Papua New Guinea. In 1988 a secessionist movement was created in Bougainville and led by the Bougainville Revolutionary Army (BRA). The BRA began sabotaging the Australian mines in May 1989, and the war began in July when the government declared a state of emergency and launched a brutal campaign to suppress the BRA. The government withdrew its troops from the island in March 1990 but then blockaded the island when Bougainville declared its independence. The government forces soon returned to Bougainville and launched further major offensives in 1991 and 1992. Fighting dropped below war levels after a September 1992 government attack that also targeted Bougainville's supporters in the Solomon Islands. A peace agreement was reached in 2001 that granted Bougainville limited autonomy. An estimated 20,000 people died during the overall period of hostilities (1989–2001), though the vast majority of these were civilians.

Sources: Bercovitch and Fretter (2004); Clodfelter (2002); Keesing's (1989, 1998, 2005).

INTRA-STATE WAR #856:

The Eighth Colombian War of 1989–present

Participants: Colombia vs. drug lords, FARC
Dates: August 19, 1989–present
Battle-Related Deaths: drug lords, FARC—17,681; Colombia—10,480
Where Fought: W. Hemisphere
Initiator: drug lords, FARC
Outcome: Ongoing
War Type: Civil for local issues

Narrative: The instability in Colombia encouraged the growth of nonstate actors who are capable of conducting warfare. Starting in the 1980s, Colombia was confronted with rising conflict involving the illegal drug industry, the Marxist Revolutionary Armed Forces of Colombia (FARC), and a variety of paramilitary groups allied together as the United Self-Defense Groups of Colombia (AUC). Both the drug industry and FARC had their own motives for combating government forces; however, the parameters of the conflict changed in May 1982 when FARC decided to use profits from the drug trade to finance its operations against the government. As a result FARC was able to increase the size of its army and the deadliness of its attacks. War-level fatalities began in mid-1989 when drug lord Pablo Escobar Gaviriahad ordered a number of government officials murdered. The government then launched a major offensive against the drug industry. As FARC also increased its attacks on the government, the paramilitary AUC became more involved in the fighting against the rebels on the government's behalf. By 1999 the insurgents controlled large segments of Colombia. The war is still ongoing, and by the end of 2007, in addition to the combatants, 14,966 civilians have been killed as well (CERAC 2008).

Sources: CERAC (2008); Clodfelter (2002); Manwaring (2002); Project Ploughsares (2008); Restrepo et al. (2004); Restrepo et al. (2003); Richani (2005); Scheina (2003b); United States Institute of Peace (2004).

INTRA-STATE WAR #857:

The First Cambodian Civil War of 1989–1991

Participants: Cambodia vs. Khmer Rouge, KPNFL
Dates: September 26, 1989, to October 23, 1991
Battle-Related Deaths: Cambodia—[ ]; Khmer Rouge, KPNFL—[ ]
Where Fought: Asia
Initiator: Khmer Rouge, KPNFL
Outcome: Compromise
War Type: Civil for central control

Narrative: Vietnam and Cambodia went to war in 1977, at the conclusion of which Vietnam had ousted the genocidal Khmer Rouge regime (inter-state war #189). Vietnamese forces remained in the country to fight the remnants of the Khmer Rouge (extra-state war #475). When the Vietnamese forces withdrew from Cambodia in September 1989, the Cambodian government took over the bulk of the fighting against the Khmer Rouge and the fighting was transformed into this civil war. The Khmer Rouge and the rebel Khmer People's National Liberation Front (KPNLF) attacked, hoping to increase their territory as the Vietnamese left. The Vietnamese departure also prompted a flurry of diplomatic activity. Under UN auspices a peace treaty was signed on October 23, 1991, which created a coalition government that included Khmer representation. Peace was attained for a short while, but war resumed in1993 (intra-state war #881).

Sources: Brogan (1998); Ciment (2007); Clodfelter (2002); Phillips and Axelrod (2005).

INTRA-STATE WAR #858:

The Romania War of 1989

Participants: Romania vs. anti-Ceauşescu rebels
Dates: December 18, 1989, to December 26, 1989
Battle-Related Deaths: anti-Ceauşescu rebels—700; Romania—300
Where Fought: Europe

Initiator: anti-Ceaușescu rebels
Outcome: Anti-Ceaușescu rebels win
War Type: Civil for central control

Narrative: Communist president Nicolae Ceaușescu had misruled this impoverished nation since 1974. The 1989 movement toward democracy that spread throughout eastern Europe arrived in Romania as well, and only in Romania did the collapse of the Communist regime lead to war. The conflict began in Timișoara, where a Calvinist pastor was being removed from his position by the government because of his criticism of the regime. This precipitated large antigovernment demonstrations on December 16 and 17 at which government forces opened fire on the protestors. The war began the following day: the government arranged a progovernment rally in Bucharest, which was attacked by protestors. This led to the defection of major segments of the armed forces either in support of the protestors or to a position of neutrality. Ceaușescu fled on December 22, while the dissident officers seized power. The state Securitate and loyal army units then launched counterrevolutionary attacks against the protestors and the forces of the new government. Ceaușescu was captured and executed, and the fighting ceased shortly afterward.

Sources: Clodfelter (2002); Hall (2000).

INTRA-STATE WAR #860:
The First Liberia War of 1989–1990

Participants: Liberia, Nigeria vs. NPFL
Dates: December 24, 1989, to November 28, 1990
Battle-Related Deaths: Liberia—[ ]; NPFL—[ ];
    Nigeria—0
Where Fought: Africa
Initiator: NPFL
Outcome: NPFL wins
War Type: Civil for central control

Narrative: Samuel K. Doe seized power in Liberia through a coup in 1980. Doe, who became a ruthless dictator, was elected president in 1985 in what many claimed were rigged elections. This mobilized the antigovernment opposition. At the end of 1989, Charles Taylor's National Patriotic Front of Liberia (NPFL) invaded Liberia from its base in Côte d'Ivoire. By September 1990 his forces controlled much of the country. Taylor's advance was halted by the intervention of the Economic Community of West African States (ECOWAS) forces, which included a large number of Nigerian troops. Doe was killed on September 10, yet Doe's supporters, aided by Nigeria, attacked Taylor's army. A cease-fire on November 28 ended the war; however fighting continued at below war level. Warfare would resume two years later (intra-state war #878).

Sources: Ciment (2007); Clodfelter (2002); Edgerton (2002); GlobalSecurity.org (2005); Meredith (2005); Uppsala Universitet (2004).

INTRA-STATE WAR #861:
The Kashmir Insurgents War of 1990–2005

Participants: India vs. Kashmiri guerrillas
Dates: September 19, 1990, to October 8, 2005
Battle-Related Deaths: Kashmiri guerrillas—
    21,700; India—6,000
Where Fought: Asia
Initiator: Kashmiri guerrillas
Outcome: Conflict continues at below war level
War Type: Civil for local issues

Narrative: The dispute over control of Muslim Kashmir has been a main cause of the hostility and warfare between India and Pakistan (interstate wars #147 and #166). Kashmir was divided into a Pakistani-controlled sector and one controlled by India. The Muslims in the Indian sector became increasing unhappy with Indian rule and, seeking either independence or union with Pakistan, created the Jammu Kashmir Liberation Front (JKLF). The JKLF began low-level guerrilla attacks against India in 1988; these flared into war in 1990. The fifteen year war involved as many as 140 Kashmiri groups fighting against India, which stationed 150,000 to 500,000 troops in the region. Hostilities there also contributed to the outbreak of the Kargil War between India and Pakistan in 1999 (inter-state war #223). The level of hostilities increased in 2000 and 2001 but then declined to below war level in October 2005 in the wake of an earthquake in Pakistani-controlled Kashmir.

Sources: Clodfelter (2002); Evans (2000); Hall (2000); Keesing's (2001–2006); Kohn (1999); Project Ploughshares (2000); Swami (2005).

INTRA-STATE WAR #862:
The Shiite and Kurdish War of 1991

Participants: Iraq vs. Kurds, Shiites
Dates: March 1, 1991, to March 31, 1991
Battle-Related Deaths: Iraq—[ ]; Shiites, Kurds—[ ]
Where Fought: Middle East
Initiator: Shiites
Outcome: Iraq wins
War Type: Civil for local issues

Narrative: In the wake of Iraq's 1991 loss in the Gulf War (inter-state war #211), Shiites in the south thought the Baathist regime of Saddam Hussein was about to fall. They decided to take advantage of the situation and launch a rebellion in pursuit of greater autonomy. They seized the major cities in the south, including Basra. Their example was followed by the Kurds, who then seized all of Kurdistan in the north. Hussein responded by dispatching the Republican Guard, which had survived the war, to suppress the rebellion. The south was attacked first, and the Shiites were decimated. The Republican Guard then moved north, where they again suppressed the rebels and then captured Kirkuk by the end of March, which ended the war. An estimated 750,000 Kurds fled into the mountains

and into Turkey. This war led the United Nations to create "no-fly zones" in both southern and northern Iraq.

Sources: Brogan (1998); Cleveland (1994); Clodfelter (2002); Kohn (1999); Phillips and Axelrod (2005); Project Ploughshares (2004).

INTRA-STATE WAR #863:
The First Sierra Leone War of 1991–1996

Participants: Sierra Leone vs. RUF
Dates: March 23, 1991, to April 23, 1996
Battle-Related Deaths: Sierra Leone—[ ]; RUF—[ ]
(Total Combatant Deaths: 20,000)
Where Fought: Africa
Initiator: RUF
Outcome: Sierra Leone wins
War Type: Civil for central control

Narrative: In 1985 the collapse of the economy in Sierra Leone contributed to the coup that brought Gen. Joseph Saidu Momoh to power. He tried unsuccessfully to implement an economic reform program with the World Bank. A rebel movement known as the Revolutionary United Front (RUF), under the leadership of Foday Sankoh, had been based in Liberia, where it had been aided by that country's leader, Charles Taylor. In 1991 the RUF crossed into Sierra Leone and began a war to overthrow the government by using its teenage soldiers to terrorize the population. Meanwhile President Momoh was overthrown in a coup that brought Capt. Valentine Strasser to power. Both Strasser and Sankoh seemed primarily interested in exploiting Sierra Leone's diamond wealth; however, Strasser did recruit a mercenary army to drive the RUF out of the capital. Despite RUF intimidation tactics, Ahmed Tejan Kabbah won a democratic election in 1996. He signed a peace agreement with the RUF in April that stopped the civil war, though RUF continued terrorizing citizens. War would resume in 1998 (intra-state war #898).

Sources: Ciment (2007); Clodfelter (2002); Edgerton (2002); Meredith (2005).

INTRA-STATE WAR #864:

The Croatian Independence War of 1991–1992

Participants: Yugoslavia vs. Croatia
Dates: May 2, 1991, to January 2, 1992
Battle-Related Deaths: Yugoslavia—[ ]; Croatia—[ ]
Where Fought: Europe
Initiator: Yugoslavia
Outcome: Croatia wins
War Type: Civil for local issues

Narrative: By 1989 the conflict between Yugoslavia and its constituent republics was worsening. Both Slovenia and Croatia held free elections in April 1990, with Croatia electing Franjo Tudjman as president. Tudjman began removing Serbs from government positions and provoking disputes with the Yugoslav government. Croatia also began importing arms and building its own military in preparation for independence. The war began with cross-border skirmishes in which Croatian police were killed on May 2, 1991. The dissolution of Yugoslavia began with the declarations of independence by Slovenia and Croatia on June 25, 1991. While Slovenia achieved independence with little fighting, Yugoslavia was determined to fight for Croatia. The Yugoslav government launched an invasion of Croatia, and Dubrovnik was shelled. Serbs living in Croatia set up an independent republic in Krajina from which they expelled the Croats. The United Nations arranged a cease-fire on January 2, 1992, and Croatia's independence was recognized two weeks later. Nevertheless, Croatia would go to war with Krajina in 1995 (intra-state war #891).

Sources: Bassiouni (1992); Brogan (1998); Ciment (2007); Clodfelter (2002); Uppsala Universitet (1995b).

INTRA-STATE WAR #865:

The Second Turkish Kurds War of 1991–1999

Participants: Turkey vs. PKK
Dates: July 10, 1991, to February 16, 1999
Battle-Related Deaths: Turkey—3,500; Kurds, PKK—13,000
Where Fought: Middle East
Initiator: Kurds, PKK
Outcome: Stalemate
War Type: Civil for local issues

Narrative: The desire for autonomy or independence led the Kurds in Turkey to create the Workers' Party of Kurdistan (PKK) in 1978. The PKK attacks against Turkey reached the level of a war in 1984 (intra-state war #838). The war lasted until early 1986, after which the conflict continued but at below war level. By 1991 the conflict had again reached the level of an intra-state war; however, this time the PKK began to shift its focus to a broader regional approach and established bases in Iraq. Thus the struggle of the PKK against Turkey took on the characteristics of two different wars: the intra-state PKK activities in southeastern Turkey and attacks by Turkey against PKK elements based in Iraq (see extra-state wars #477 and #479). The PKK war inside Turkey reached war-level fatalities in 1991 partly as a repercussion of the Gulf War (inter-state war #211), since Iraq sent aid to the PKK for operations in Turkey at that point. The war continued until 1999, when PKK leader Abdullah Ocalan was captured.

Sources: Brogan (1998); Clodfelter (2002); Keesing's (1990–1993); Kutschera (1994); McKiernan (1999); O'Ballance (1996); Project Ploughshares (2000); Yavuz (2001).

INTRA-STATE WAR #866:

The SPLA Division (Dinka-Nuer) War of 1991–1992

Participants: Garang faction vs. Nuer faction
Dates: August 28, 1991, to November [ ], 1992

Battle-Related Deaths: Garang faction—[ ]; Nuer faction—[ ] (Total Combatant Deaths: 1,200)
Where Fought: Africa
Initiator: Nuer faction
Outcome: Conflict continues at below war level
War Type: Inter-communal

Narrative: This war takes place in the midst of the war between Sudan and the Sudan People's Liberation Army (SPLA) (intra-state war #836). In 1983 Sudan's leader, Gen. Gaafar Nimeiry, declared his intention to transform Sudan into an Islamic republic. At that point the SPLA launched a rebellion (#836). The SPLA was on the verge of victory, when it split in two and this war resulted. One of the SPLA factions was led by John Garang, a Dinka, who wanted the creation of a secular Sudan. The other faction was headed by Reik Machar, a Nuer, who favored secession. Machar launched a coup attempt against Garang, whom he accused of being dictatorial. The resulting war involved not only conflict between the two factions but also raids on Dinka and Nuer tribal members. When he was close to losing the war, Machar received weapons from the Sudanese government, which was happy to see this internecine conflict between its opponents. The two factions temporarily agreed to suspend their conflict during peace talks led by the Organization of African Unity (OAU) in May 1992, and the conflict declined to below war level after November. Meanwhile, in April 1992, the government decided to take advantage of the infighting by launching a new offensive against the SPLA, thus resuming war #836.

Sources: Clodfelter (2002); Collins (1999); Cordesman (1993); Cutter (2007); Hutchinson (2001); Iyob and Khadiagala (2006); Johnson (2004).

INTRA-STATE WAR #868:
The Jukun-Tiv War of 1991–1992

Participants: Jukun vs. Tiv
Dates: October [ ], 1991, to March [ ], 1992

Battle-Related Deaths: Jukun—[ ]; Tiv—[ ]
Where Fought: Africa
Initiator: Tiv
Outcome: Stalemate
War Type: Inter-communal

Narrative: The Jukun are an ethnic group clustered in the Taraba province of eastern Nigeria. To the southwest lies the adjacent province of Benue, where many Tiv live. After Nigeria gained its independence in 1960, the Jukun and Tiv peoples engaged in periodic skirmishes, partially because the minority Jukun, who dominated politics in the region, feared the potential political power of the majority Tiv. Conflict began in 1990 between Jukun and Tiv political factions, but it reached inter-communal war level in October 1991 as a result of government plans to create a new administrative district that would be placed within an area either dominated by the Junkun or populated by the Tiv. In February the Nigerian government unsuccessfully attempted to arrange a cease-fire between the Jukun and Tiv leaders. Finally, in March, the presence of government forces was successful in ending the war.

Sources: Facts on File (1991–1992); Keesing's (1991–1992); Maier (2000).

INTRA-STATE WAR #870:
The Second Somalia War of 1991–1997

Participants: Australia, France, Italy, Nigeria, Pakistan, Somalia, United States vs. Aideed faction
Dates: November [ ], 1991, to January [ ], 1997
Battle-Related Deaths: Somalia—[ ]; Aideed faction—[ ](Total Somali Combatant Deaths: 32,000); United States—44; Pakistan—24; France—2; Australia—[ ]; Italy—[ ]; Nigeria—[ ]
Where Fought: Africa
Initiator: Aideed faction
Outcome: Compromise
War Type: Civil for central control

Narrative: The disintegration of Somalia began with Somalia's 1978 loss in the two-phases of the Second Ogaden War (intra-state war #805 and inter-state war #187). Violence then spilled into Somalia itself, precipitating a civil war in 1988 (intra-state war #848), which ended in the defeat of the government of Muhammad Siad Barre. The war left Somalia in a state of total anarchy, as factional fighting within the winning coalition soon broke out. The United Somali Congress (USC), which controlled the capital, proclaimed Ali Mahdi Mohammed as president. The Somali National Movement (SNM) seized control in the north and declared its independence. Barre and his followers controlled the south. The failure of an attempt to create a unity government in October 1991 precipitated conflict at war level in November. The USC split into an Aideed faction and the Mahdi faction that controlled the capital. As the fighting between the Aideed and Mahdi factions became more intense, the United Nations sent a peace-keeping mission into Somalia, which became involved in the fighting. International attempts to end the conflict failed. In January 1997, however, the leaders of the Aideed and Mahdi factions agreed to the terms of a cease-fire, which ended the war, though some low-level conflict persisted among the clans.

Sources: Australian War Memorial (1992); Bercovitch and Fretter (2004); Ciment (2007); Clodfelter (2002); Cordesman (1993); Cutter (2007); Human Rights Watch (1994); Project Ploughshares (2005); United Nations (1997).

INTRA-STATE WAR #871:
The Georgia War of 1991–1992

Participants: Georgia vs. reform movement
Dates: December 26, 1991, to March [ ], 1992
Battle-Related Deaths: Georgia—[ ]; reform—[ ]
   (Total Combatant Deaths: 5,000)
Where Fought: Europe
Initiator: reform
Outcome: Reform wins
War Type: Civil for central control

Narrative: In March 1991 Georgia voted to secede from the Soviet Union, and in May Zviad Gamsakhurdia was elected as its president. Opposition to his autocratic rule developed fairly quickly. Abkhazia and South Ossetia began agitating for independence. Prodemocracy protestors and the national guard rioted against his leadership, while others, such as Eduard Shevardnadze, former Soviet foreign minister, urged that Georgia remain tied to the USSR. Georgia became independent after the collapse of the USSR on December 26, 1991, and war broke out immediately, led by national guard leader Tengiz Kitovani. In January 1992 Gamsakhurdia fled and military rule was established; however, the fighting continued. By March the national guard, with Russian assistance, had restored order. Shevardnadze was invited back to head the new provisional government. The independence movement in Abkhazia would lead to war in 1993 (intra-state war #882).

Sources: Bercovitch and Fretter (2004); Ciment (2007); Kaufman (2001).

INTRA-STATE WAR #872:
The Nagorno-Karabakh War of 1991–1993

Participants: Azerbaijan vs. Armenia, Nagorno-Karabakh
Dates: December 26, 1991, to February 5, 1993
Battle-Related Deaths: Azerbaijan—7,000; Nagorno-Karabakh—3,000; Armenia—1,000
Where Fought: Europe
Initiator: Nagorno-Karabakh
Outcome: Transformed into inter-state war #216
War Type: Civil for local issues

Narrative: Nagorno-Karabakh is generally Christian and ethnically Armenian. It was incorporated into the Russian Empire in the early nineteenth century along with Armenia and Muslim Azerbaijan. Until 1920, Nagorno-Karabakh was considered a part of Armenia, but in 1921, Russia gave the region to Azerbaijan. From the 1950s onward the Armenians living in Nagorno-Karabakh petitioned Moscow to be annexed to Armenia. In September 1991, as the Soviet Union disintegrated, Nagorno-Karabakh declared independence from the USSR, and ultimately from Azerbaijan as it became independent on December 26, 1991, marking the start of this war. In January 1992 Azerbaijani forces attacked the capital of Nagorno-Karabakh, but the forces of Nagorno-Karabakh, with the assistance of Armenia, then went on the offensive and captured the last Azeri stronghold in the region (Shusha) on May 8. Most important, on May 18, Nagorno-Karabakh captured Lachin, which created a land link, the "Lachin Corridor," between Nagorno-Karabakh and Armenia. In June 1992 the tide turned when Azerbaijani forces, under new president Abulfaz Elchibey, launched a major offensive. Armenia then came to the aid of Nagorno-Karabakh, taking over the bulk of the fighting against Azerbaijan in a major offensive on February 6, 1993. This marks the beginning of inter-state war #216 (with this civil war ending the preceding day). That war became virtually a stalemate, and a cease-fire was signed on May 12, 1994, which ended the war but left the ultimate status of Nagorno-Karabakh unresolved.

Sources: Bercovitch and Fretter (2004); Brogan (1998); Clodfelter (2002); Croissant (1998); Kaufman (2001).

INTRA-STATE WAR #873:
The Dniestrian Independence War of 1991–1992

Participants: Moldova vs. Dniestria
Dates: December 26, 1991, to July 2, 1992
Battle-Related Deaths: Moldova—[ ]; Dniestria—[ ] (Total Combatant Deaths: 1,000)
Where Fought: Europe
Initiator: Dniestria
Outcome: Compromise
War Type: Civil for local issues

Narrative: When the Soviet Union annexed Moldova from Romania in 1940, the region now known as Transdniestria was detached from the Ukraine and given to Moldova. As the Soviet Union began to lose control in 1990, the residents of Transdniestria signaled a desire to secede from Moldova and either become independent or join Russia. Moldova became a member of the interstate system on December 26, 1991, and the conflict evolved into full-scale war. The Dniestrian secessionists received assistance from the Russian Fourteenth Army, which was still stationed in the region. By July 1992 Moldova had lost control of the region. An accord, signed on July 21, 1992, gave Dniestria semiautonomous status within Moldova. In effect, Transdniestria is essentially an unrecognized but independent entity, supported by the presence of Russian troops.

Sources: Bercovitch and Fretter (2004); Kaufman (2001); Kaufman (1997); King (2000); Minahan (2002).

INTRA-STATE WAR #875:
The Algerian Islamic Front War of 1992–1999

Participants: Algeria vs. Islamic opposition
Dates: February 7, 1992, to June [ ], 1999
Battle-Related Deaths: Algeria—[ ]; Islamic opposition—[ ]
Where Fought: Middle East
Initiator: Algeria
Outcome: Compromise
War Type: Civil for central control

Narrative: After gaining independence from France in 1962, Algeria's government was dominated by the military. In the 1972 national charter, the National Liberation Front (FLN) government described the regime as Socialist, with Islam as the state religion. There was little opposition to the regime until the early 1980s, when Islamic groups tried to develop autonomy from the state. Riots in 1988 persuaded President Chadli Benjedid to end the one-party system. The major contender for power was the Islamic Salvation Front (FIS), which promoted the creation of an Islamic state. The two groups participated in the first round of national elections, held on December 26, 1991. The elections resulted in a major FIS victory. To prevent the FIS from coming to power, the military staged a coup on January 11, 1992. The military then began an effort to destroy the FIS. Algeria entered a period of violence, in which the FIS targeted not only governmental forces but civilians as well. The FIS increasingly lost control over armed rebel groups such as the Armed Islamic Group (GIA), which kept fighting despite a cease-fire agreement in 1997. In 1999 the new president, Abdelaziz Bouteflika, offered an amnesty program to the rebels. Although the GIA vowed to prolong the conflict, fighting between the government and the rebels dropped below war level at this point. Violence has continued but is directed mostly at civilians.

Sources: Brogan (1998); Ciment (2007); Clodfelter (2002); Meredith (2005); Mortimer (1996); Project Ploughshares (2004).

INTRA-STATE WAR #876:

The Tajikistan War of 1992–1997

Participants: Russia, Tajikistan vs. United Tajik Opposition
Dates: May 1, 1992, to June 27, 1997
Battle-Related Deaths: Tajikistan—[ ]; United Tajik Opposition—[ ] (Total Tajik Combatant Deaths: 20,000); Russia—[ ]
Where Fought: Asia
Initiator: United Tajik Opposition
Outcome: Compromise
War Type: Civil for central control

Narrative: The breakup of the Soviet Union in 1991 led to the independence of its constituent republics, including Tajikistan. Unlike some of the other republics, Tajikistan wanted to keep its ties with Russia, and it retained its Communist leadership. Opposition to the government soon

developed among those who sought democratic reforms and those who favored the creation of an Islamic republic. The conflict escalated to war level when progovernment militias attacked rebel bases in the south. The rebel forces, which were increasingly dominated by Islamic groups, made significant gains in the south and briefly occupied the capital of Tajikistan, Dushanbe. In March 1993 the rebels attacked the 25,000 Russian troops stationed in Tajikistan, making Russia a participant in the war. The government began to regain control of the country with help from Russia. Meanwhile, the Islamic rebels in the south received assistance from the mujahideen forces in Afghanistan. In December 1996 President Imomali Rakhmonov's government signed a cease-fire agreement with the United Tajik Opposition, which ended the war and gave the rebels 30 percent of government positions.

Sources: Bercovitch and Fretter (2004); Ciment (2007); Curtis (1997); Dawisha (1997); Project Ploughshares (2000).

INTRA-STATE WAR #877:

The Bosnian-Serb Rebellion of 1992–1995

Participants: Bosnia, Croatia, United States vs. Bosnian Serbs, Croatia
Dates: June 6, 1992, to December 14, 1995
Battle-Related Deaths: Bosnia—27,500; Bosnian Serbs—18,543; Croatia—185; United States—0
Where Fought: Europe
Initiator: Bosnian Serbs
Outcome: Bosnia, Croatia, United States win
War Type: Civil for local issues

Narrative: The European Community (EC) recognized the independence of Bosnia-Hercegovina on April 7, 1992 (making Bosnia a COW system member on that date). It also marked the beginning of inter-state war #215, involving the Yugoslav Army (the JNA) and the Bosnian Serbs. Under international pressure most of the JNA forces withdrew from Bosnia by June 5, 1992, ending the inter-state war. The fighting then continued the next day as this internationalized civil war pitting the Bosnian Muslim government against the Bosnian Serbs, who wanted to secede. Croatia also intervened, at one point assisting the Bosnians and at another time assisting the Serbs. In December 1994 former U.S. president Jimmy Carter was instrumental in persuading the parties to adopt a cease-fire, which lasted only about three months (and is coded as a break in the war from December 31, 1994, to March 20, 1995). In an attempt to end the conflict after fighting resumed, the North Atlantic Treaty Organization (NATO) began Operation Deliberate Force, a bombing campaign against the Bosnian Serbs conducted primarily by the United States. Fighting continued until the Dayton Peace Agreement, signed on December 14, 1995. This war involved "ethnic cleansing" against civilians, which led to the deaths of over 300,000 people, though the actual number of fatalities will probably never be known.

Sources: Clodfelter (2002); Hellenic Resources Network (2006); Human Rights Watch (2000); Mosley (2000); NATO (2002); Tabeau and Bijak (2005); Williams (2001).

INTRA-STATE WAR #878:
The Second Liberia War of 1992–1995

Participants: Liberia, Nigeria vs. NPFL, ULIMO
Dates: October 15, 1992, to August 19, 1995
Battle-Related Deaths: Liberia—[ ]; NPFL, ULIMO—[ ]; Nigeria—[ ]
Where Fought: Africa
Initiator: NPFL, ULIMO
Outcome: Compromise
War Type: Civil for central control

Narrative: The previous intra-state war in Liberia (#860) involved a 1989 attempt to overthrow the government by Charles Taylor's National Patriotic Front of Liberia (NPFL). Taylor's offensive was

stopped by the intervention of the Economic Community of West African States (ECOWAS), primarily with troops from Nigeria. A cease-fire on November 28, 1990, ended the fighting. In the interim the United Liberation Movement of Liberia for Democracy (ULIMO) was created by the followers of former President Samuel K. Doe. In October 1992 this war started when the NPFL attacked the ECOWAS forces, or Monitoring Group (ECOMOG), defending the government (thus making Nigeria a war participant). ULIMO then began its attacks on the NPFL, and the fighting evolved into a general stalemate. This war ended in a power-sharing arrangement, the Abuja Accord, that created the six-member Council of State, which included representatives of all the warring factions.

Sources: Bercovitch and Fretter (2004); Ciment (2007); Clodfelter (2002); DeGeorge (2001).

INTRA-STATE WAR #880:
The Angolan War of the Cities of 1992–1994

Participants: Angola vs. UNITA
Dates: October 28, 1992, to November 15, 1994
Battle-Related Deaths: Angola—[ ]; UNITA—[ ]
Where Fought: Africa
Initiator: UNITA
Outcome: Compromise
War Type: Civil for central control

Narrative: Angola's first civil war (intra-state war #804) had lasted for fifteen years (1976–1991). It ended in a power-sharing arrangement between the Popular Movement for the Liberation of Angola (MPLA) government and the National Union for the Total Independence of Angola (UNITA) rebels led by Jonas Savimbi. The government held elections in 1992, and when UNITA lost by a narrow margin, it launched another war. Most of the fighting took place in the cities. At first UNITA was driven out of the capital of Luanda, but then it captured the provincial capital of Huambo after a two-month siege in March 1993 and soon controlled two-thirds of the country. South African mercenaries joined the war on the side of the government and helped it stop the rebel advance. The war ended in 1994 in another power-sharing agreement, which was to be overseen by the United Nations. This war caused horrendous destruction, and the estimates of the number of civilians killed ranges from 80,000 to 300,000.

Sources: Bercovitch and Fretter (2004); Clodfelter (2002); DeGeorge (2001); Keesing's (1993, 1994); Malaquias (2007); Meredith (2005); Phillips and Axelrod (2005); Project Ploughshares (2000).

INTRA-STATE WAR #881:
The Second Cambodian Civil War of 1993–1997

Participants: Cambodia vs. Khmer Rouge
Dates: January 29, 1993, to July 1, 1997
Battle-Related Deaths: Cambodia—[ ]; Khmer Rouge—[ ] (Total Combatant Deaths: 15,000)
Where Fought: Asia
Initiator: Khmer Rouge
Outcome: Cambodia wins
War Type: Civil for central control

Narrative: The genocidal Khmer Rouge regime was ousted from power by Vietnam (inter-state war #189), which then kept forces in Cambodia and fought against the remnants of the Khmer Rouge (extra-state war #475). When the Vietnamese forces withdrew from Cambodia in September 1989, the Cambodian government continued the fight against the Khmer Rouge in the first civil war (intra-state war #857). The war ended in 1991 through a UN-sponsored treaty, which created a coalition government that included Khmer representation. Peace lasted less than two years. The war began anew in January 1993, when the Khmer Rouge launched attacks against the government prior to UN-sponsored elections in May 1993, in which the Khmer Rouge

refused to participate. The elections ultimately produced a new coalition government between the royalists led by Prince Norodom Ranariddh and the Communists led by Hun Sen. Fighting continued between the Khmer Rouge and the now-allied Communist and royalist army until 1997, when Hun Sen seized full power through a coup in Phnom Penh. The prince fled and joined his forces to the Khmer Rouge; however, by then the Khmer Rouge had been so weakened by defections that the fighting dropped below war level at this point.

Sources: Bercovitch and Fretter (2004); Ciment (2007); Project Ploughshares (2000).

INTRA-STATE WAR #882:
The Abkhazia Revolt of 1993–1994

Participants: Georgia vs. Abkhazia
Dates: August 18, 1993, to April 14, 1994
Battle-Related Deaths: Georgia—5,000; Abkhazia—3,000
Where Fought: Europe
Initiator: Georgia
Outcome: Abkhazia wins
War Type: Civil for local issues

Narrative: As Georgia became independent of the Soviet Union in December 1991, its government faced independence movements in South Ossetia and Abkhazia and a reform movement that ultimately succeeded in overthrowing the government (intra-state war #871). Although the fighting in South Ossetia did not reach war level, war began in Abkhazia in 1993. In response to the Abkhazian reinstatement of the 1925 Abkhaz constitution, Georgia sent national guard troops into Abkhazia. At first the government troops were successful, but an Abkhaz offensive enabled the troops to reoccupy all of Abkhazia by the end of September. The war ended with a cease-fire agreement in April 1994 that included the stationing of Russian peacekeepers and semiautonomy for Abkhazia. In addition to the combatants, 20,000 civilians died in this war. An additional 250,000 Georgians living in Abkhazia were displaced.

Sources: Bercovitch and Fretter (2004); Ciment (2007); Kaufman (2001); Demetriou (2002); Toft (2003).

INTRA-STATE WAR #883:
The Second Burundi War of 1993–1998

Participants: Burundi vs. Tutsi army
Dates: October 21, 1993, to June [ ], 1998
Battle-Related Deaths: Burundi—[ ];
   Tutsi army—[ ]
Where Fought: Africa
Initiator: Tutsi army
Outcome: Conflict continues at below war level
War Type: Civil for central control

Narrative: The First Burundi War (intra-state war #789) concerned an attack by the Hutu against the Tutsi government, which then led to widespread violence against the Hutu. Conflict between the Hutu and Tutsi continued periodically for the next twenty years, though it tended to involve the murder of civilians rather than attacks against the government. This war broke out in October 1993 when Tutsi army troops murdered Hutu president Melchior Ndadaye, and involved the Tutsi-dominated military against Hutu rebels. In addition to the combatants, 50,000 civilians were killed in the next few months alone. In 1994 a coalition government was formed, but the events next door in Rwanda, where extremist Hutu killed hundreds of thousands of Tutsi, prevented a cessation of hostilities. Intense fighting continued in 1995. The army staged a coup in 1996 against the Hutu president, and Pierre Buyoya, a Tutsi, was installed as president. The fighting continued, at this stage with the National Council for the Defense of Democracy (CNDD) leading the Hutu attacks against the government. In June 1998 a transitional constitutional act was passed that gave the Hutu greater representation in the parliament. This and the related cease-fire reduced the level of fighting below war levels. The

more extremist Hutu militias continued their attacks and also engaged in fighting among themselves. Fighting at war levels would resume in 2001 (intra-state war #918).

Sources: Bercovitch and Fretter (2004); Ciment (2007); Clodfelter (2002); Cutter (2007); Dougherty (2004); Home Office (2004); Lemarchand (2004); Phillips and Axelrod (2005); Project Ploughshares (2000); Reyntjens (2000); Tripp (2005).

INTRA-STATE WAR #885:
The South Yemeni Secessionist War of 1994

Participants: Yemen vs. South Yemen
Dates: February 21, 1994, to July 7, 1994
Battle-Related Deaths: Yemen—[ ]; South
   Yemen—[ ] (Total Combatant Deaths: 7,000)
Where Fought: Middle East
Initiator: South Yemen
Outcome: Yemen wins
War Type: Civil for local issues

Narrative: After over twenty years of rivalry, the Marxist state of the People's Democratic Republic of Yemen (South Yemen) agreed to unite with the more conservative Republic of Yemen (North Yemen) in 1990. The new government was led by Vice President Ali Salim al-Beidh from the south, and President Ali Abdullah Salih from the north. Al-Beidh and Salih soon disagreed over oil profits and the responsibility for the murder of several members of the south's Yemeni Socialist Party. In 1993 al-Beidh left the capital of Sanaa, thus effectively shutting down the government. The war began in 1994 with skirmishes between the armies of the north and the south. In May al-Beidh declared South Yemen's independence, prompting an invasion by the northern army. Despite the south's superiority, in weaponry, the northern army's numerical superiority enabled it to capture Aden in July, which ended the fighting.

Sources: Bercovitch and Fretter (2004); Congressional Quarterly (1994); Keesing's (1994).

INTRA-STATE WAR #886:
The Second Rwanda War of 1994

Participants: Rwanda vs. Patriotic Front
Dates: April 6, 1994, to July 18, 1994
Battle-Related Deaths: Rwanda—[ ]; Patriotic Front—[ ]
Where Fought: Africa
Initiator: Patriotic Front
Outcome: Patriotic Front wins
War Type: Civil for central control

Narrative: The Rwanda Patriotic Front (RPF) had been organized in Uganda to represent Tutsi who had been driven there by the civil war in 1963 (intra-state war #761) and the subsequent killings of Tutsi civilians. Starting in 1991 the RPF began a low-level guerrilla war against Rwanda, which the RPF accused of conducting a genocide against the Tutsi. An RPF offensive advanced on the capital while also engaging in the murder of Hutu civilians. Under international pressure Rwanda's Hutu president Juvénal Habyarimana signed the 1993 Arusha Accords with the RPF, by which Rwanda's Hutu government was to cede some power to the Tutsi. On April 6, President Habyarimana and President Cyprien Ntaryamira of Burundi were killed when their plane exploded on the return from a conference in Tanzania. The guilty party was the extremely anti-Tutsi element of the Hutu palace guard, who opposed any compromise with the Tutsi. The result was in essence two conflicts: a well-planned killing spree by the Hutu army and Hutu death squads against Tutsi civilians, and a civil war between the Rwandan government and the RPF. The RPF began a three-pronged offensive and ultimately captured the capital in July and soon controlled the entire country. The RPF came to power and ended the genocide that may have killed almost 1 million civilians. War would return in 1997 (intra-state war #896).

Sources: Ciment (2007); Clodfelter (2002); Cutter (2007); International Crisis Group (2001); Keesing's (2000); Meredith (2005); Phillips and Axelrod (2005); Tripp (2005); Twagilimana

(2003); United States Institute of Peace (2002); Walker (2005).

INTRA-STATE WAR #888:
The First Chechnya War of 1994–1996

Participants: Russia vs. Chechnya
Dates: December 11, 1994, to August 31, 1996
Battle-Related Deaths: Chechnya—6,000; Russia—4,000
Where Fought: Europe
Initiator: Chechnya
Outcome: Chechnya wins
War Type: Civil for local issues

Narrative: Just prior to the fall of the Soviet Union, the Chechens declared their independence, which precipitated a brief conflict in 1991. In 1994 Russia's president Boris Yeltsin decided to take a more proactive stance against Chechnya and helped to create the Chechen Interim Council (IC) to oppose Chechen president Dzhokhar Dudayev. In September 1994 an armed conflict broke out between Dudayev's forces and those of the IC, which was defeated. In November Yeltsin issued an ultimatum, and when Dudayev's forces refused to capitulate, Russia attacked. Approximately 40,000 Russian troops crossed into Chechnya and attacked the capital, Grozny, capturing the city in February 1995 after weeks of heavy fighting. For the next eighteen months an intense guerrilla war was fought in the Caucasus Mountains. Dudayev was killed, and Aslan Maskhadov succeeded him as the chief Chechen leader. In August 1996 the Chechens recaptured Grozny. At this point the Russians agreed to a negotiated settlement, in which Russia granted Chechnya autonomy but not formal independence, withdrawing its troops by January 1997. In addition to the combatants, 60,000 Chechen civilians were killed during the war.

Sources: Ayers (2001); Blank and Tilford (1995); Ciment (2007); Clodfelter (2002); Perovic (2006); Project Ploughshares (2000).

INTRA-STATE WAR #890:
The Iraqi Kurd Internecine War of 1994–1995

Participants: PUK vs. KDP
Dates: December 20, 1994, to August 11, 1995
Battle-Related Deaths: PUK—[ ]; KDP—[ ]
Where Fought: Middle East
Initiator: KDP
Outcome: Stalemate
War Type: Inter-communal

Narrative: In the wake of Iraq's 1991 loss in the Gulf War (inter-state war #211), Shiites in the south and the Kurds in the north launched a war for regional autonomy (intra-state war #862). The Kurds briefly declared an independent Kurdistan, but they were soon defeated by Iraq's Republican Guard. The cease-fire left the status of the Kurds unresolved. In May 1992 the Kurds held their first general elections, and the two major contenders were Massoud Barzani's Kurdistan Democratic Party (KDP) and the Patriotic Union of Kurdistan (PUK) of Jalal Talabani. While the two parties created a coalition government, within two years they were at war with each other over which group would ultimately claim the mantle of leadership of the Kurds. Fighting began when a PUK official refused to obey Barzani's orders. A cease-fire was brokered by the Western powers that ended the war in August 1995. A year later the PUK advanced into KDP territory, and Barzani requested the assistance of the Iraqi government, which sent troops into PUK territory (intra-state war #893).

Sources: Brogan (1998); Facts on File (1994, 1995); Gunter (1996); Kohn (1999); Project Ploughshares (2004); Tripp (2000).

INTRA-STATE WAR #891:
The Croatia-Krajina War of 1995

Participants: Croatia vs. Krajina Serbs
Dates: May [ ], 1995, to November [ ], 1995
Battle-Related Deaths: Croatia—[ ]; Krajina Serbs—[ ]
Where Fought: Europe
Initiator: Krajina Serbs
Outcome: Croatia wins
War Type: Civil for local issues

Narrative: Following Croatia's war for independence (intra-state war #864), Croatia attained its independence from Yugoslavia; however, Croatia itself contained several Serb dominated areas, including Western Slovenia and Krajina. During that war the Serbs of Krajina declared a Serb Republic of Krajina, and the area was patrolled by UN forces after 1992. In January 1993 clashes began to erupt between the Croatian army and Krajina Serb forces. In May 1995 this war started when Croatia sent forces to regain control over Western Slovenia. Then in August it launched "Operation Storm" against Krajina. The Croats were able to gain control of Krajina in heavy fighting in which Krajina was supported by Yugoslavia. The agreement of understanding that concluded the war included provisions for the return of UN forces, followed by complete control under the central Croatian government by 1998. Croatian general Ante Gotovina was charged with crimes against humanity for actions taken against the Serb community in the wake of the war.

Sources: Amnesty International (2004); Bercovitch and Fretter (2004); Ciment (2007); Gagnon (2004); Keesing's (1993, 1994); Ramet (2005).

INTRA-STATE WAR #892:
The Third Liberia War of 1996

Participants: Liberia vs. NPFL
Dates: April 5, 1996, to August 20, 1996
Battle-Related Deaths: Liberia—[ ]; NPFL—[ ]
(Total Combatant Deaths: 3,000)
Where Fought: Africa
Initiator: NPFL
Outcome: Compromise
War Type: Civil for central control

Narrative: The previous war in Liberia (intra-state war #878) ended in 1995 with a power-sharing arrangement, the Abuja Accord, which created the six-member Council of State that included representatives from all the warring factions. In April 1996 serious fighting again erupted in Monrovia as the coalition split apart. The National Patriotic Front of Liberia (NPFL) forces of Charles Taylor fought against the government forces. During the fighting Taylor's forces gained control over more territory; however, when the troops from the Economic Community of West African States Monitoring Group (ECOMOG) were attacked, Nigeria, the primary supplier of ECOMOG troops, called for another cease-fire, and a new peace accord was signed in August. The militia leaders all agreed to form their groups into political parties that would compete in an upcoming election. In the July 1997 elections, Charles Taylor's National Patriotic Party won.

Sources: Ciment (2007); Clodfelter (2002); Cutter (2007); Howe (1997); Meredith (2005).

INTRA-STATE WAR #893:
The Sixth Iraqi Kurds War of 1996

Participants: Iraq vs. PUK
Dates: August 31, 1996, to October 23, 1996
Battle-Related Deaths: Iraq—[ ]; PUK—[ ]
    (Total Combatant Deaths: 1,500)
Where Fought: Middle East
Initiator: PUK
Outcome: Stalemate
War Type: Civil for local issues

Narrative: Factional fighting between the PUK (Patriotic Union of Kurdistan) and the KDP (Kurdish Democratic Party) wracked the region of northern Iraq during the mid-1990s (intra-state war #890). A cease-fire was brokered by the Western powers that ended the war in August 1995. A year later this war began when the PUK, aided by Iran, advanced into KDP territory. The KDP's leader, Massoud Barzani, requested the assistance of the Iraqi government, which sent troops against the PUK. Initially, the Iraqi and KDP forces made advances, capturing much of the PUK's territory, including Irbil, Sulaymania, and Dukan in September. In October a PUK counteroffensive regained some of its territory, including Sulaymania. On October 23, 1996, the two sides agreed to a cease-fire, and Iraqi forces withdrew.

Sources: Brogan (1998); Project Ploughshares (2000).

INTRA-STATE WAR #895:
The Fifth DRC War of 1996–1997

Participants: DRC vs. Angola, ADFL, Rwanda, Uganda
Dates: October 8, 1996, to May 17, 1997
Battle-Related Deaths: DRC—[ ]; ADFL—[ ]
    (Total DRC Combatant Deaths: 4,000);
    Uganda—[ ]; Angola—[ ]; Rwanda—[ ]
Where Fought: Africa
Initiator: ADFL
Outcome: Angola, ADFL, Rwanda, Uganda win
War Type: Civil for central control

Narrative: Over a million Hutu refugees fled from the 1994 genocide in Rwanda into the Democratic Republic of Congo (then called Zaire). This change in the racial mix in the DRC led to unrest there as well. By 1996 Congo's Kivu province had begun advocating the removal of the Congolese Tutsi population. In response the Tutsi created the Alliance of Democratic Forces for the Liberation of Congo-Zaire (ADFL). In October the ADFL launched a rebellion against the Congolese government. Under the leadership of Laurent Kabila, and with the assistance of Rwanda and Uganda, the ADFL was successful in capturing much of eastern Zaire by March 1997. Many of the Rwandan refugees fled back to Rwanda, while others were killed by the ADFL. Angola also intervened on the side of the rebels as the ADFL continued its offensive, overthrowing in May the regime of President Mobutu Sese

Seko, who had ruled Zaire since 1965. Kabila, as the new ruler, switched the name of the country back to the Democratic Republic of Congo.

Sources: Bercovitch and Fretter (2004); Brogan (1998); Ciment (2007); Clodfelter (2002); Meredith (2005); Pitsch (2001); Project Ploughshares (2000); Prunier (2004); Reed (1999); Stearns (2001).

INTRA-STATE WAR #896:
The Third Rwanda War of 1997–1998

Participants: Rwanda vs. Hutu rebels
Dates: March 17, 1997, to October 30, 1998
Battle-Related Deaths: Hutu rebels—3,000; Rwanda—300
Where Fought: Africa
Initiator: Hutu rebels
Outcome: Rwanda wins
War Type: Civil for central control

Narrative: Rwandan Tutsi exiles who had fled into Uganda created the Rwanda Patriotic Front (RPF), which returned and captured control of Rwanda in 1994 (intra-state war #886). Meanwhile Rwanda endured a period of genocide, during which Hutu militias murdered thousands of civilians, mostly Tutsi. The remnants of the Rwandan army and at least 1 million Hutu fled into the Democratic Republic of Congo (DRC; Zaire), contributing to the war there (intra-state war #895). The Hutu in the DRC included the Interahamwe militia and the Army for the Liberation of Rwanda (ALIR). In March 1997, the Hutu launched a significant series of attacks against the Tutsi in northwest Rwanda, marking the start of this war. Conflict continued throughout the year, often involving the killing of thousands of civilians. Significant attacks occurred in January 1998, and in March the Hutu strikes spread to southeast Rwanda. The Hutu were unable to overthrow the Tutsi government. Fatality levels tapered off after the end of October 1998, marking the end of the war. Fighting resumed in 2001 (intra-state war #920).

Sources: Bercovitch and Fretter (2004); Cutter (2007); Jackson (2004); Keesing's (1997, 1998); Reyntjens (2000).

INTRA-STATE WAR #897:
The First Congo (Brazzaville) War of 1997

Participants: Republic of Congo vs. Angola, FDU (Cobra militia)
Dates: June 5, 1997, to October 15, 1997
Battle-Related Deaths: Congo—[ ]; FDU (Cobra militia)—[ ] (Total Congo Combatant Deaths: 4,000); Angola—[ ]
Where Fought: Africa
Initiator: FDU (Cobra militia)
Outcome: Angola, FDU (Cobra militia) win
War Type: Civil for central control

Narrative: In 1979 Marxist Denis Sassou-Nguesso became president of the Republic of Congo. Elections in 1992 brought Pascal Lissouba to power as president, and Sassou-Nguesso retired, though his Congolese Labor Party (PCT) remained in the coalition government. In June 1997, Sassou-Nguesso staged a revolt to overthrow President Lissouba. With the assistance of Angola, Sassou-Nguesso's Cobra militia forces seized the capital in October; Lissouba fled. Fighting resumed a year later (intra-state war #908).

Sources: Bercovitch and Fretter (2004); Ciment (2007); Clodfelter (2002); Cutter (2007); Project Ploughshares (2000); Stearns (2001).

INTRA-STATE WAR #898:
The Second Sierra Leone War of 1998–2000

Participants: Sierra Leone vs. Ghana, Guinea, Kabbah faction, Nigeria, United Kingdom
Dates: February 6, 1998, to November, 10, 2000
Battle-Related Deaths: Sierra Leone—[ ]; Kabbah faction—[ ]; Nigeria—[ ]; Ghana—[ ]; Guinea—[ ]; United Kingdom—9

Where Fought: Africa
Initiator: Kabbah faction
Outcome: Kabbah faction wins
War Type: Civil for central control

Narrative: In 1991 a brutal uprising by the Revolutionary United Front (RUF) began in Sierra Leone (intra-state war #863). A cease-fire was negotiated on December 1, 1996. Conflict resumed the following spring at below war level, and President Ahmed Tejan Kabbah was ousted in May 1997 by a military faction led by Maj. Paul Koroma. The coup leaders created the Armed Forces Revolutionary Council (AFRC) and invited the RUF to join the new military government. This war began in February 1998 when the Economic Community of West African States Monitoring Group (ECOMOG) troops from Guinea, Ghana, and Nigeria undertook direct military action and overthrew the AFRC/RUF government. The civilian Kabbah government was returned to power on March 10, 1998. The war continued, now with the AFRC and the RUF fighting against the Kabbah government and the ECOMOG troops. In January 1999 there was fierce fighting around Freeport, involving not only the RUF and ECOMOG but also progovernment irregulars known as the Kamajors. Meanwhile the Kabbah government and the leadership of the RUF had entered tentative cease-fire discussions. The two parties reached a peace agreement in Lomé, Togo on July 7, 1999. The agreement collapsed in May 2000 when RUF returned to fighting the government (the period from July 1999 to May 2000 is coded as a break in the war). The conflict was further exacerbated by the arrival in May 2000 of a contingent of British paratroopers in aid of the current government. A new cease-fire agreement, brokered by the Economic Community of West African States (ECOWAS), was signed on November 10, 2000, ending the war.

Sources: BBC News (1999, 2000); Bercovitch and Fretter (2004); Ciment (2007); Clodfelter (2002); Edgerton (2002); Ero (2000); Keesing's (1998,

1999); Khobe (2000); Meredith (2005); Project Ploughshares (2002).

INTRA-STATE WAR #900:

The Kosovo Independence War of 1998–1999

Participants: Yugoslavia vs. KLA
Dates: February 28, 1998, to March 23, 1999
Battle-Related Deaths: KLA—800;
   Yugoslavia—400
Where Fought: Europe
Initiator: Yugoslavia
Outcome: Transformed into inter-state war #221
War Type: Civil for local issues

Narrative: Kosovo was an area of Yugoslavia that was heavily populated by ethnic Albanians. It had been relatively autonomous within Yugoslavia until Yugoslavia revoked that status in 1990. In 1992 a vote within Kosovo expressed a desire for independence from Yugoslavia and perhaps unity with Albania. When Yugoslavia (Serbia) resisted the Kosovar demands, a number of Kosovars created the Kosovo Liberation Army (KLA) to fight for independence. In 1996 and 1997 the conflict involved only brief exchanges of gunfire; however, on February 28, 1998, the Serbian government launched a major assault against the KLA stronghold in the Drenicia Valley, which marks the beginning of the war. In March 1998 the KLA counterattacked, gaining control over a third of Kosovo by July. In August, a Yugoslav offensive retook most of the territory, during which thousands of Kosovar civilians were killed in a program of ethnic cleansing. As a result the North Atlantic Treaty Organization (NATO) began bombing Kosovo and Serbia in an attempt to drive the Serb forces from the area. Since at this stage NATO takes over the bulk of the fighting against Yugoslavia, this intra-state war ends and an inter-state war (#221) begins.

Sources: BBC News (1999a); BBC News (1999b); BBC News (1999c); CNN (1999); CNN (1998); Congressional Research Service (2000);

Congressional Research Service (1998); Daalder and O'Hanlon (2000); Haglund and Sens (2000); Human Rights Watch (2001); Human Rights Watch (2000); Independent International Commission on Kosovo (2000); Jane's Defense (1999); Jones (2000); Judah (2000); Kostakos (2000); Lampe (2000); Loeb (1999); Mennecke (2004); Miller (2007); NATO (1999); Project Ploughshares (2005); Waller et al. (2001); Youngs et al. (1999).

INTRA-STATE WAR #902:
The Guinea-Bissau Military War of 1998–1999

Participants: Guinea-Bissau, Guinea, Senegal vs. Mané junta
Dates: June 7, 1998, to May 6, 1999
Battle-Related Deaths: Guinea-Bissau—[ ]; Mané junta—[ ] (Total Guinea-Bissau Combatant Deaths: 2,000); Senegal—[ ]; Guinea—[ ]
Where Fought: Africa
Initiator: Mané junta
Outcome: Mané junta wins
War Type: Civil for central control

Narrative: Guinea-Bissau faced public discontent over government corruption and military opposition to the government's policies concerning a rebellion in Senegal. The final straw was the dismissal of Gen. Ansumane Mané, and when troops arrived to arrest him, fighting broke out. Mané formed a junta that called for President João Bernardo Viera to resign, and it soon had the support of 90 percent of the military. Fighting began on June 7, 1998, and lasted for almost a year. Both Senegal and Guinea sent in troops to assist the faltering government. Mediation efforts by the Community of Portuguese-Speaking Countries (CPLP) and the Economic Community of West African States (ECOWAS) led to ceasefire agreements that soon dissolved. President Viera was overthrown on May 6, 1999 (ending

the war), and on May 10, 1999, he signed an unconditional surrender.

Sources: Ciment (2007); Cutter (2007); IRIN (1998); Keesing's (1998, 1999); Project Ploughshares (2004).

INTRA-STATE WAR #905:
Africa's World War of 1998–2002

Participants: Angola, Chad, Democratic Republic of Congo, Namibia, Sudan, Zimbabwe vs. MLC, RCD, et al.
Dates: August 2, 1998, to December 17, 2002
Battle-Related Deaths: Democratic Republic of Congo—[ ]; RCD, MLC, et al.—[ ]; Zimbabwe—[ ]; Rwanda—[ ]; Chad—[ ]; Sudan—[ ]; Burundi—[ ]; Uganda—[ ]; Angola—[ ]; Namibia—[ ]
Where Fought: Africa
Initiator: MLC, RCD, et al.
Outcome: Compromise
War Type: Civil for central control

Narrative: A cluster of intra-state wars occurred in the Great Lakes region of Africa during the 1990s affecting Uganda, Rwanda, Burundi, and Democratic Republic of Congo. In 1996 the forces of the Rwandan government attacked Rwandan Hutu who had fled into Zaire (Democratic Republic of Congo), and the Rwandan forces, aided by Angola and Uganda, supported the Alliance of Democratic Forces for the Liberation of Congo-Zaire (ADFL), a rebel group led by Laurent Kabila, in overthrowing the government of Mobutu Sese Seko in 1997 (intra-state war #895). When President Kabila ordered the Rwandans to leave the DRC, some of Kabila's former allies along with other disaffected groups formed a united political unit, the Congolese Rally for Democracy (RCD), with the goal of unseating the president. The war began in August 1998, and within a month nine countries became involved in the most widespread war in the continent's modern history. Initially the rebel forces, aided by Rwanda, Uganda, and Burundi had military success. They were later joined by a new rebel group, the Congolese Liberation Movement (MLC). The DRC government was aided by Chad, Angola, Sudan, Zimbabwe, and Namibia. By March 1999 the rebel groups controlled one-third of the country. Kabila was assassinated in January 2001 and replaced as president by his son, Joseph Kabila. The fighting continued but began to abate with the July 22, 2002, Pretoria Accord, in which Uganda and Rwanda agreed to withdraw their forces. The war concluded with a December 2002 agreement, and the new government created on June 30, 2003, included both Kabila and members of the rebel groups.

Sources: Bercovitch and Fretter (2004); Ciment (2007); Clodfelter (2002); Coghlan et al. (2004); Crossette (2000); Cutter (2007); Edgerton (2002); GlobalSecurity.org (2005); International Rescue Committee (2004); Pitsch (2001); Project Ploughshares (2004); Prunier (2004); Swarns (2001); Tripp (2005); Tull (2007).

INTRA-STATE WAR #906:
The Fourth Chad (Togoimi Revolt) War of 1998–2000

Participants: Chad vs. MDD, MDJT
Dates: October 16, 1998, to April 28, 2000
Battle-Related Deaths: Chad—[ ]; MDD, MDJT—[ ] (Total Combatant Deaths: 1,500)
Where Fought: Africa
Initiator: MDD, MDJT
Outcome: Conflict continues at below war level
War Type: Civil for central control

Narrative: Idriss Déby and his Patriotic Salvation Movement (MPS) came to power in 1990 as a result of the previous war in Chad (intra-state war #852). In October 1998 Déby was confronted with a revolt in the north led by former defense minister Youssouf Togoimi, who led the Movement for Democracy and Justice in Chad (MDJT). The war was waged mostly as a guerrilla war in the Tibesti region, where the rebels attacked government military installations. In February 2000 the MDJT formed an alliance with two other rebel groups: the Movement for Unity and the Republic (MUR) and the Democratic Revolutionary Council (CDR). The rebels launched several attacks against government positions, with a major one occurring in April 2000. After that the conflict continued but at below war level. Libya was able to mediate a peace settlement that was signed in 2002, and some of the rebels were integrated into Chad's army. Togoimi died later that year.

Sources: BBC News (1998–2002); Ciment (2007); Cutter (2007); Frère, (2007); Keesing's (1998–2003); Nolutshungu (1996); Project Ploughshares (2005); Project Ploughshares (2000).

INTRA-STATE WAR #907:
The Third Angolan War of 1998–2002

Participants: Angola vs. UNITA
Dates: December 4, 1998, to February 22, 2002
Battle-Related Deaths: Angola—[ ]; UNITA—[ ] (Total Combatant Deaths: 16,000)
Where Fought: Africa
Initiator: Angola
Outcome: Angola wins
War Type: Civil for central control

Narrative: The previous war in Angola (intra-state war #880) between the Popular Movement for the Liberation of Angola (MPLA) government and the National Union for the Total Independence of Angola (UNITA) rebels ended with a 1994 power-sharing agreement that was to be overseen by the United Nations. The UN concluded that UNITA's Jonas Savimbi was obstructing the peace process, and in 1997 the UN voted to impose sanctions on UNITA. Both UNITA and the government continued to augment their militaries, and by December 1998 the government felt it was in a strong enough position to launch an offensive against UNITA. In early 1999, UNITA counterattacked and advanced near the capital. By late 1999 the heavy fighting had displaced 4 million people. The government's offensive sapped UNITA's strength, forcing the rebels to resort to guerrilla tactics. Government forces killed Savimbi on February 22, 2002, thus ending the war. On April 4, 2002, the two sides signed a peace agreement.

Sources: Bercovitch and Fretter (2004); Ciment (2007); Cutter (2007); Harden (2001); Keesing's (1997–1999); Kohn (1999); Malaquias (2007); Meredith (2005); Project Ploughshares (2003).

INTRA-STATE WAR #908:
The Second Congo (Brazzaville) War of 1998–1999

Participants: Republic of Congo (Brazzaville) vs. Cocoye and Ninja militias,
Dates: December 15, 1998, to November 16, 1999
Battle-Related Deaths: Congo (Brazzaville)—[ ]; Cocoye and Ninja militias—[ ] (Total Combatant Deaths: 2,100)
Where Fought: Africa
Initiator: Cocoye and Ninja militias
Outcome: Congo (Brazzaville) wins
War Type: Civil for central control

Narrative: Conflict in the Congo broke out between rival presidential contenders in 1997 (intra-state war #897). Assisted by Angola, the Cobra militia, supporting Denis Sassou-Nguesso, gained control of the government by October 1997, ending the war. A forum on reconciliation was held in January 1998, but the talks were unable to either reduce tensions between the groups or avert the outbreak of a second war. The supporters of former president Pascal Lissouba launched a major strike against Brazzaville in December 1998. The rebel forces, including Ninja and Cocoye militias, were concentrated in the center of the country, and the government and Cobra militia attacked them there. Attacks continued throughout the early part of 1999. The rebels were unable to defeat the government, and the conflict began to decline toward the end of the

year. On November 16, 1999, the Pointe-Noire Peace agreement was signed by all the parties, and the process of disarming the militias began in early 2000.

Sources: Bercovitch and Fretter (2004); Cutter (2007); Project Ploughshares (2006); Stearns (2001); Uppsala Universitet (2002).

INTRA-STATE WAR #910:
The Moluccas Sectarian War of 1999–2000

Participants: Laskar Jihad vs. FKM, RMS
Dates: January [ ], 1999, to August 22, 2000
Battle-Related Deaths: Laskar Jihad—[ ]; FKM, RMS—[ ] (Total Combatant and Civilian Deaths: 3,800)
Where Fought: Asia
Initiator: Laskar Jihad
Outcome: Conflict continues at below war level
War Type: Inter-communal

Narrative: Within Indonesia the Moluccas, formerly known as the Spice Islands, lie east of Sulawesi (Celebes). During the regime of President Suharto, Indonesia adopted a policy of transmigration, by which the government encouraged migration of people from Java to the less populated islands, including the Moluccas. Conflict developed between the Christian and the Muslim migrants, particularly the members of the Laskar Jihad. The primary Christian groups were the Maluku Sovereignty Front (FKM) and the Republic of South Maluka (RMS). The Muslims attacked the Christians in Ambon in January 1999, and most of the fighting took place here. The level of violence increased during the summer months, and it encompassed not only fighting between the militias but also attacks on civilians, sometimes involving forced conversions. The Indonesian military did not intervene to protect the Christians and may actually have helped the Muslims. An upsurge in violence in August 2000 caused 100,000 people to flee their homes.

Sources: Armstrong (2004); Clodfelter (2002); Facts on File (1999, 2000); GlobalSecurity.org (2005); Minahan (2002); Project Ploughshares (2004); Wayman and Tago (2009).

INTRA-STATE WAR #911:
The First Nigeria Christian-Muslim War of 1999–2000

Participants: Christian Tarok vs. Muslim Fulani
Dates: May [ ], 1999, to May 31, 2000
Battle-Related Deaths: Christian Tarok—[ ]; Muslim Fulani—[ ] (Total Combatant Deaths: 2,000)
Where Fought: Africa
Initiator: Muslim Fulani
Outcome: Christian Tarok wins
War Type: Inter-communal

Narrative: Nigeria is generally divided into a Muslim-dominated north and a Christian south. The country had been ruled for fifteen years by a military dictatorship from the north, and tensions between the two groups were heightened by Muslim attempts to increasingly apply Sharia law. In 1999 Olusegun Obasanjo, a southern Christian, was elected as president in May, which precipitated attacks by the Muslim Fulani against the Christian Tarok. Fighting peaked in May 2000, after which the level of conflict declined; however, the fighting would return to war level in 2004 (intra-state war #933).

Sources: Ciment (2007); Project Ploughshares (2004).

INTRA-STATE WAR #912:
The Second Aceh War of 1999–2002

Participants: Indonesia vs. GAM
Dates: May 3, 1999, to December 9, 2002
Battle-Related Deaths: GAM—3,500; Indonesia—330
Where Fought: Asia
Initiator: GAM
Outcome: Compromise
War Type: Civil for local issues

Narrative: The movement supporting Aceh's independence from Indonesia had been suppressed in 1991 (intra-state war #853). A second phase of the conflict began in May 1998 after the resignation of General Suharto and Indonesia's allowance of an independence referendum in East Timor. Hoping for similar moves toward independence for Aceh, the Free Aceh Movement (GAM) increased its attacks against government troops the following year, starting this war. In this instance, however, the government's goal was to suppress GAM, and it moved troops into the region and began an offensive against the group. The fighting created a flow of 100,000 refugees and the massacres of civilians. In July 2001 new president Megawati Sukarnoputri proposed autonomy for the region. A peace treaty was signed in December 2002, ending this war. Nevertheless, war would resume in 2003 (intra-state war #930).

Sources: Armstrong (2004); Ciment (2007); Clodfelter (2002); International Crisis Group (2002); Kingsbury (2007); Project Ploughshares (2004); Tan (2000).

INTRA-STATE WAR #913:
The Oromo Liberation War of 1999

Participants: Ethiopia vs. OLF
Dates: May 30, 1999, to August 18, 1999
Battle-Related Deaths: OLF—800; Ethiopia—200
Where Fought: Africa
Initiator: OLF
Outcome: Ethiopia wins
War Type: Civil for local issues

Narrative: The Oromo are the largest ethnic group in Ethiopia, approximately 32 percent of the population, though they saw themselves as targets of government discrimination. Consequently, the Oromo Liberation Front (OLF) was formed in 1973, seeking Oromo independence. The OLF was largely driven from the country in 1992, principally to Somalia and Eritrea, both of which have utilized the OLF to destabilize the

Ethiopian government. Clashes between the Ethiopian government and the OLF reached war status in May 1999. Conflict was particularly fierce in August 1999 when the government claimed to have destroyed the OLF; however, low-level conflict did continue after that point.

Sources: ABO/OLF (2005); Ciment (2007); Cordesman (1993); Cutter (2007).

INTRA-STATE WAR #915:
The Second Chechnya War of 1999–2003

Participants: Russia vs. Chechnya
Dates: August 7, 1999, to October 3, 2003
Battle-Related Deaths: Chechnya rebels—15,000; Russia—5,000
Where Fought: Europe
Initiator: Chechnya
Outcome: Russia wins
War Type: Civil for local issues

Narrative: Chechnya and Russia went to war in December 1994 over Chechnya's desire for independence (intra-state war #888). The Russians were unable to defeat the Chechens during the almost two-year war, and as a result Chechnya was granted limited autonomy. The Second Chechnya War concerned Russia's attempt to regain control over Chechnya but began in response to Chechnya attacks on the Russian province of Dagestan in August 1999. In response, Russia's new president, Vladimir Putin, adopted a hard line against Chechnya and began a bombing campaign against the Chechen capital of Grozny. The Russians pushed the Chechens out of Dagestan after severe fighting, and in 2000 the Russians took control of Grozny. Russia established a new Chechen government, which was overwhelmingly elected in October 2003. The war ended at this point, though low-level guerrilla attacks continued after this date.

Sources: Bercovitch and Fretter (2004); Ciment (2007); Project Ploughshares (2004); Thomas (2001).

INTRA-STATE WAR #916:
The Second Philippine-Moro War of 2000–2001

Participants: Philippines vs. MILF
Dates: April 23, 2000, to June 22, 2001
Battle-Related Deaths: Philippines—[ ]; MILF—[ ] (Total Combatant Deaths: 2,700)
Where Fought: Asia
Initiator: Philippines
Outcome: Compromise
War Type: Civil for local issues

Narrative: In 1972 the Philippine government faced an uprising by the Muslim Moros, who opposed Christian settlements in Mindanao (intra-state war #786). The war gradually subsided as the government increased its aid to the region. During that war the primary rebel group was the Moro National Liberation Front (MNLF). In 1977 the more radical Moro Islamic Liberation Front (MILF) split from the MNLF and placed more emphasis on the desire to create an Islamic state. In April 2000 Philippine president Joseph Estrada launched this war with an offensive against the MILF. Peace talks were scheduled for August 15, 2000; however, the MILF withdrew. President Estrada was deposed in January 2001, and his successor, Gloria Macapagal-Arroyo, ended the military offensive on February 9. A cease-fire was declared on April 2, though violations continued, and a peace agreement between the government and the MILF was signed on June 22, 2001. War would resume in 2003 (intra-state war #926).

Sources: BBC News (2005); Ciment (2007); Keesing's (2000, 2001); Project Ploughshares (2005).

INTRA-STATE WAR #917:
The Guinean War of 2000–2001

Participants: Guinea vs. RFOG
Dates: September 11, 2000, to April [ ], 2001

Battle-Related Deaths: Guinea—[ ]; RFDG—[ ]
Where Fought: Africa
Initiator: RFDG
Outcome: Stalemate
War Type: Civil for central control

Narrative: Lasana Conte came to power in Guinea through a bloodless coup in 1984 and was ultimately elected president in 1995; however, Conte also ushered in a period of civil unrest and government repression. The situation in Guinea was further destabilized by its proximity to Liberia and Sierra Leone, whose civil wars (intra-state wars #892 and #898) led to the presence of approximately 500,000 refugees living in Guinea. In particular, Guinea harbored a Liberian rebel group while anti-government Guinean rebels were based in Liberia. On September 11, 2000, a major Guinean rebel group, the Rally of Democratic Forces of Guinea (RFDG), launched a series of attacks against Guinean government forces from its base in Liberia, starting the war. In response, starting on September 22, Guinean forces launched an offensive that targeted both the RFDG and Liberian forces. Heavy fighting was reported in December 2000 and from January to March 2001. An ECOWAS meeting in April was able to deter a full-scale war between Guinea and Liberia and ended this civil war as well.

Sources: BBC News (2005); Bercovitch and Fretter (2004); Keesing's (2000, 2001); Onishi (2001); Project Ploughshares (2004).

INTRA-STATE WAR #918:
The Third Burundi War of 2001–2003

Participants: Burundi vs. FNL
Dates: March 21, 2001, to October 8, 2003
Battle-Related Deaths: FNL—3,000;
    Burundi—150
Where Fought: Africa

Initiator: FNL
Outcome: Compromise
War Type: Civil for central control

Narrative: In the midst of the last war in Burundi (intra-state war #883, from 1993 to 1998), the army staged a coup in 1996, replacing the Hutu president with a Tutsi, Pierre Buyoya. The fighting continued, with the Hutu National Council for the Defense of Democracy (CNDD) leading the attacks against the government. In June 1988 a compromise agreement gave the Hutu greater representation in the parliament, and the related cease-fire reduced the level of fighting below war levels. The more extremist Hutu militias did continue their attacks but were also engaged in fighting among themselves. The National Liberation Front (FNL or FROLINA), which was the armed wing of the Party for the Liberation of the Hutu People (PALIPEHUTU), were excluded from the peace process and utilized that opportunity to increase their attacks on the government in March 2001, starting this war. The government responded with an offensive that attempted to reverse the rebel gains. The rebels launched attacks around the capital of Bujumbura in December, which continued for the next two years. An October 2003 cease-fire led to the November 16 agreement that brought most of the rebel soldiers into the Burundi armed forces. In addition to the combatants, thousand of civilians had been killed in the war. The FNL continued its attacks on the government at below war level.

Sources: Ciment (2007); Cutter (2007); Home Office (2004); IRIN (2001); Phillips and Axelrod (2005); Project Ploughshares (2004).

INTRA-STATE WAR #920:
The Fourth Rwanda War of 2001

Participants: Rwanda vs. ALIR
Dates: May 21, 2001, to September 4, 2001
Battle-Related Deaths: ALIR—1,800; Rwanda—[ ]
Where Fought: Africa

Initiator: ALIR
Outcome: Rwanda wins
War Type: Civil for central control

Narrative: During the previous war in Rwanda (intra-state war #896 in 1997 to 1998), the Hutu were unable to overthrow the Tutsi government, and fatality levels in the fighting declined below war level at the end of October 1998. Many Rwandan Hutu had fled into the Democratic Republic of Congo (DRC), where several organizations that were hostile to the Rwandan government, referred to as the Interahamwe, were based, including the Democratic Forces for the Liberation of Rwanda (FDLR) and the Army for the Liberation of Rwanda (ALIR). These groups were encouraged by the DRC to return to Rwanda, and as they did, they were intercepted by the Rwandan army. This war commenced in May 2001, and the rebel forces were defeated by September 4.

Sources: Bercovitch and Fretter (2004); Ciment (2007); Human Rights Watch (2001); Project Ploughshares (2004).

INTRA-STATE WAR #921:
The First Nepal Maoist Insurgency of 2001–2003

Participants: Nepal vs. CPN
Dates: November 23, 2001, to January 29, 2003
Battle-Related Deaths: CPN—3,100; Nepal—680
Where Fought: Asia
Initiator: CPN
Outcome: Stalemate
War Type: Civil for central control

Narrative: In 1994 the ruling Nepali Congress Party was defeated by the United Marxist and Leninist Party (UML), which made Nepal the world's first Communist monarchy. One Communist faction, the Communist Party of Nepal (CPN), was excluded, however, and in 1996 it declared a goal of creating a Maoist revolution.

Violence was directed against the government and civilians but was at below war-level fatalities. Following the massacre of Nepal's royal family on June 1, 2001, the new king, Gyanendra, adopted a hard-line toward the rebels. CPN attacks on November 23 were met by a more aggressive army. Fighting continued to escalate throughout 2002, until the pattern of almost daily clashes was ended by a cease-fire in 2003.

Sources: Bercovitch and Fretter (2004); Ciment (2007); Clodfelter (2002); GlobalSecurity.org (2005); Keesing's (2001–2003); Marks (2003); Onesto (2005); Project Ploughshares (2000); Vaughn (2005).

INTRA-STATE WAR #922:
The Fourth Liberian War of 2002–2003

Participants: Liberia vs. LURD, MODEL
Dates: February [ ], 2002, to August 11, 2003
Battle-Related Deaths: Liberia—[ ]; LURD, MODEL—[ ] (Total Combatant Deaths: 3,000)
Where Fought: Africa
Initiator: LURD, MODEL
Outcome: LURD, MODEL win
War Type: Civil for central control

Narrative: Charles Taylor's desire to rule Liberia had contributed to three earlier wars in that country (intra-state wars #860, #878, and #892) before Taylor was elected president in 1997. Conflict continued, and two rebel groups, Liberians United for Reconciliation and Democracy (LURD) and Movement for Democracy in Liberia (MODEL), began attempts to oust Taylor from power in 1999 with the assistance of Guinea. The rebels launched a major offensive in February 2002, which marks the start of the war. The rebels soon controlled over 60 percent of the country. Government forces counterattacked, and by October 2002 Taylor had reoccupied most of the country's territory. By November 2002 the conflict had created nearly

130,000 internally displaced persons (IDPs), as well as 230,000 refugees in bordering states. By May 2003 the rebel forces had neared the capital. On August 11, 2003, Taylor relinquished power and was granted asylum in Nigeria. A peace agreement was signed on August 18 in Accra.

Sources: BBC News (2003); Bercovitch and Fretter (2004); Ciment (2007); GlobalSecurity.org (2005); International Crisis Group (2002); Keesing's (2003–2004); Project Ploughshares (2005); Reno (2007).

INTRA-STATE WAR #923:

The Ethiopian Anyuaa-Nuer War of 2002–2003

Participants: Anyuaa vs. Nuer
Dates: August [ ], 2002, to January [ ], 2003
Battle-Related Deaths: Anyuaa—[ ]; Nuer—[ ]
(Total Combatant Deaths: 1,500)
Where Fought: Africa
Initiator: Nuer
Outcome: Conflict continues at below war level
War Type: Inter-communal

Narrative: Competition over scarce resources in Ethiopia led to conflict between the Anyuaa (Anuak) and the Nuer peoples. Tensions between the two were exacerbated by a government policy that encouraged the resettlement of Nuer refugees from Sudan into Anyuaa territory. Warfare began in 2002 with Nuer attacks against the Anyuaa. The fighting, which also targeted civilians, was mostly ended in January 2003 with the arrival of government troops.

Sources: Project Ploughshares (2005).

INTRA-STATE WAR #925:

The Côte d'Ivoire Military War of 2002–2004

Participants: Côte d'Ivoire, France vs. MJP, MPCI, MPIGO

Dates: September 19, 2002, to November 16, 2004
Battle-Related Deaths: MJP, MPCI, MPIGO—2,500; Côte d'Ivoire—200; France—9
Where Fought: Africa
Initiator: MJP, MPCI, MPIGO
Outcome: MJP, MPCI, MPIGO win
War Type: Civil for central control

Narrative: During Côte d'Ivoire's first coup, Gen. Robert Guei overthrew President Henri Konan Bédié in 1999. Guei promised open elections, but when prospects seemed to favor his opponent, Guei canceled the elections and proclaimed himself the winner. Popular uprisings forced Guei to flee, and his opponent, Laurent Gbagbo became president. The year 2001 was marred by numerous coup attempts. The coup attempt that began this war started on September 19, 2002, when the army, instigated by followers of Guei, conducted three major attacks against the government. The main rebel group was the Patriotic Movement of Ivory Coast (MPCI), but two new rebel groups had emerged, the Ivorian Popular Movement of the Great West (MPIGO) and the Movement for Justice and Peace (MJP). In opposition, the Front for the Liberation of the Great West (FLGO) was created as a militia to fight with the government forces when the government launched an attempt to retake rebel-held areas in the west on November 30. To support the government, France entered the fighting in December 2002. On February 27, 2004, the United Nations established a new peacekeeping force, the UN Operations in the Côte d'Ivoire (UNOIC), and with UN encouragement, the Accra Agreement was signed on July 31, 2004, in an attempt to restart the peace process. November marked an escalation in the conflict, but riots on November 16, 2004, marked the end of the major hostilities. A general cease-fire was negotiated in April 2005.

Sources: Baégas and Marshall-Fratani (2007); BBC News (2006); Bercovitch and Fretter (2004); GlobalSecurity.org (2005); Project Ploughshares (2004).

INTRA-STATE WAR #926:
The Third Philippine-Moro War of 2003

Participants: Philippines vs. ASG, MILF
Dates: February 11, 2003, to July [ ], 2003
Battle-Related Deaths: ASG, MILF—590;
    Philippines—410
Where Fought: Asia
Initiator: Philippines
Outcome: Conflict continues at below war level
War Type: Civil for local issues

Narrative: After Gloria Macapagal-Arroyo became president of the Philippines, an attempt was made to come to terms with the Muslim Moro rebel movement, and a peace agreement between the government and the Moro Islamic Liberation Front (MILF) was signed on June 22, 2001 (intra-state war #916). Meanwhile a more radical Islamic group, Abu Sayyaf (ASG), was formed that began seizing Western hostages. The government, with the assistance of the United States, deployed troops to contain Abu Sayyaf, though attacks were at below war level. There were links between the MILF and Abu Sayyaf, with some rebels claiming dual membership. The cease-fire between the MILF and the government broke down in February 2003 as the government launched major attacks in February and June 2003. After July the fighting continued but at below war level.

Sources: Ciment (2007); Keesing's (2002–2003).

INTRA-STATE WAR #927:
The Darfur War of 2003–2006

Participants: Sudan vs. SLA, JEM
Dates: February 26, 2003, to December 11, 2006
Battle-Related Deaths: Sudan—[ ]; SLA, JEM —[ ]
Where Fought: Middle East
Initiator: SLA
Outcome: Stalemate
War Type: Civil for local issues

Narrative: Arab nomads and black African farmers from such ethnic groups as the Zaghawa and Fur had long feuded over land and water rights in the Darfur region of Sudan. During the civil war of Sudan against the Sudan People's Liberation Army, or SPLA (intra-state war #836), the government began arming Arab militias, known as the Janjaweed. Two non-Arab groups emerged, seeking autonomy for Darfur: the Sudan Liberation Army (or SLA, formerly known as the Darfur Liberation Movement) and the Justice and Equity Movement (JEM). The SLA, and later the JEM, began attacking government targets in February 2003. In its fight against the rebels, the Sudanese government utilized the Janjaweed to attack rebel bases. The Janjaweed began indiscriminate attacks on civilians, leading to one of the worst humanitarian crises in recent times. At least 2.5 million people had been displaced, and an estimated 200,000–400,000 civilians have died. The Darfur Peace Agreement between Sudan and the SLA was signed on May 5, 2006, though fighting continued until December. After that the war ended; still, the level of the attacks against the civilians remained high.

Sources: BBC News (2004); Cutter (2007); Johnson (2004); Keesing's (2006); Kessler (2006); Project Ploughshares (2008); Timberg (2006).

INTRA-STATE WAR #930:
The Third Aceh War of 2003–2004

Participants: Indonesia vs. GAM
Dates: May 18, 2003, to November 18, 2003
Battle-Related Deaths: GAM—1,400;
    Indonesia—150
Where Fought: Asia
Initiator: Indonesia
Outcome: Indonesia wins
War Type: Civil for local issues

Narrative: Although the Indonesian government had attempted to defeat the Free Aceh Movement (GAM), new president Megawati Sukarnoputri signed a peace treaty in December 2002 that provided some autonomy for the region and that ended the war (intra-state war #912). The peace agreement collapsed, however, and war reemerged in May 2003 when the government launched a major offensive that caused significant damage to GAM. After November 2003, conflict returned to below war levels, thus ending the war. The December 2004 tsunami, which killed an estimated 100,000 people in Aceh, became a major impetus for peace. The Helsinki Accord was signed in August 2005, ending the conflict as GAM surrendered its weapons.

Sources: Bercovitch and Fretter (2004); Kingsbury (2007); Project Ploughshares (2007).

INTRA-STATE WAR #931:
The Second Nepal Maoist War of 2003–2006

Participants: Nepal vs. CPN
Dates: August 27, 2003, to April 26, 2006
Battle-Related Deaths: CPN—5,770; Nepal—1,260
Where Fought: Asia
Initiator: CPN
Outcome: Compromise
War Type: Civil for central control

Narrative: The Communist Party of Nepal (CPN) launched a Maoist revolution in Nepal in 1996, though it did not reach war level until 2001 (intra-state war #921).The war was ended by a cease-fire agreement in January 2003. Fighting resumed in the fall of 2003 when the CPN attacked army officers in Kathmandu. Although the government claimed some successes in battles against the CPN, the latter established its control in areas in both eastern and western Nepal. The CPN issued a unilateral cease-fire on September 3, 2005, and in November 2005 it entered into an agreement with the other dissident groups in an attempt to force the king's resignation. Nevertheless, the war raged on until a truce was finally agreed to in April

2006, with the final peace agreement in November. The Maoists entered the political process and began steps to limit the power of the king.

Sources: Ciment (2007); Keesing's (2003–2005); Project Ploughshares (2005).

INTRA-STATE WAR #932:
The Waziristan War of 2004–2006

Participants: Pakistan, United States vs. Waziri tribes
Dates: February 20, 2004, to September 5, 2006
Battle-Related Deaths: Waziri tribes—1,800; Pakistan—1,200; United States—[ ]
Where Fought: Asia
Initiator: United States, Pakistan
Outcome: Waziri tribes win
War Type: Civil for local issues

Narrative: North and South Waziristan are part of Pakistan's Federally Administered Tribal Areas (FATA). They are mountainous regions along Pakistan's border with Afghanistan in which the Pakistani government has had little control, leaving local tribal leaders to govern. The allied countries' invasion of neighboring Afghanistan in 2001, which overthrew its Taliban government (inter-state war #225), created additional problems for Pakistan's government. The Taliban continued its war against the allies in conjunction with al-Qaida (extra-state war #481). The Taliban and al-Qaida recruited heavily among their fellow Pushtun in Waziristan and created bases in Waziristan. The United States pressured the Pakistani government of President Pervez Musharraf to intervene, and in February 2004 the two countries launched an offensive into the region. The attacks were conducted at intervals for the next two years and were largely ineffective. In September 2006 the Pakistan government announced that it had signed an agreement with the Waziri tribes to stop the fighting if the tribes agreed to remove the foreign forces. Despite the agreement, hostilities would later resume.

Sources: BBC News (2004); International Institute for Strategic Studies (2003); Project Ploughshares (2008); Project Ploughshares (2005); Roggio (2006).

INTRA-STATE WAR #933:
The Second Nigeria Christian-Muslim War of 2004

Participants: Christian Tarok vs. Muslim Fulani
Dates: March [ ], 2004, to September 16, 2004
Battle-Related Deaths: Christian Tarok—[ ]; Muslim Fulani—[ ] (Total Combatant Deaths: 1,650)
Where Fought: Africa
Initiator: Muslim Fulani
Outcome: Stalemate
War Type: Inter-communal

Narrative: The election of a southern Christian as Nigeria's president precipitated attacks by Nigeria's Muslim Fulani against the Christian Tarok between 1999 to 2000 (intra-state war #911). Fighting peaked in May 2000, after which the level of conflict declined. In 2004 Muslim attacks again produced war-level fatalities. In an attempt to stem the rising inter-communal conflict, Nigeria's government declared a state of emergency and outlawed the extremist Muslim group the Council of Ulamma. The government's measures reduced the level of violence and ended this war in September 2004. In addition to the fatalities within the Muslim and Christian militias, as many as 50,000 civilians may have been killed in the fighting since 1999.

Sources: Ciment (2007); Project Ploughshares (2004).

INTRA-STATE WAR #935:
The First Yemeni Cleric War of 2004–2005

Participants: Yemen vs. Zaidi Muslims
Dates: June 21, 2004, to April 8, 2005

Battle-Related Deaths: Zaidi Muslims—1,350; Yemen—900
Where Fought: Middle East
Initiator: Zaidi Muslims
Outcome: Yemen wins
War Type: Civil for central control

Narrative: Much of Yemen remains under the control of various tribes, over which the central government has been trying to extend its control. This lack of governmental control has led Yemen into being a haven for foreign terrorists. In 2004 Yemen experienced conflict in the northwest between the government and the followers of Hussein al-Houthi, a cleric of the Zaidi sect, a branch of Shia Islam. President Ali Abdallah Salih accused the cleric of establishing an armed force and of trying to overthrow the government. The war began on June 21, 2004, when the government tried to disarm the rebels. When the rebels resisted, the government used heavy weapons to try to dislodge the rebels from their stronghold. On September 10 the government killed al-Houthi, yet the rebels continued their activities under the leadership of the cleric's father, Badr al-Din. The government was successful in suppressing the major clashes by April 8, 2005. War-level fighting would resume two years later (intra-state war #941).

Sources: BBC News (2005); Keesing's (2004–2005); Project Ploughshares (2008).

INTRA-STATE WAR #936:
The Philippine Joint Offensive of 2005–2006

Participants: Philippines vs. MILF, NPA
Dates: January 17, 2005, to January 11, 2006
Battle-Related Deaths: MILF, NPA—2,100; Philippines—723
Where Fought: Asia
Initiator: Philippines
Outcome: Conflict continues at below war level
War Type: Civil for local issues

Narrative: The Philippines had confronted two different rebellions. One was launched by the leftists, including the New People's Army (NPA), the armed wing of the Philippine Communist Party, (see intra-state war #790). The second war involved militant Muslim groups, including the MNLF (Moro National Liberation Front), MILF (Moro Islamic Liberation Front), and Abu Sayyaf (intra-state wars #786, #916, and #926). After becoming president, Gloria Macapagal-Arroyo had tried to come to terms with the Muslim Moros, but the cease-fires did not hold. Consequently, President Arroyo hoped to finally defeat both rebellions through a major offensive in 2005. Heavy fighting persuaded the MILF to enter peace negotiations in April; however, these made little progress and fighting continued. The government similarly launched attacks against the NPA. Although the government was unsuccessful in destroying the NPA, the redeployment of troops in June 2006 did serve to bring the level of fighting below war level.

Sources: Keesing's (2004–2005); Project Ploughshares (2008).

INTRA-STATE WAR #937:

The Fifth Chad War of 2005–2006

Participants: Chad vs. FUDC
Dates: December 18, 2005, to December 20, 2006
Battle-Related Deaths: FUDC—1,000; Chad—100
Where Fought: Africa
Initiator: FUDC
Outcome: Chad wins
War Type: Civil for central control

Narrative: In 2000 Chad's president Idriss Déby and his Patriotic Salvation Movement (MPS) defeated a revolt by former defense minister Youssouf Togoïmi, who led the Movement for Democracy and Justice in Chad (MDJT) (intra-state war #906). Opposition to Déby continued,

leading to the formation of two new rebel groups—the Platform for Change, National Unity and Democracy (SCUD) and the Rally for Democracy and Change (RFD). In 2005 constitutional reforms were approved that increased the power of the president. This produced calls from SCUD and the RFD for Déby's resignation and an increase in their attacks on the government in December 2005. In 2006 eight rebel groups united to form the United Front for Democratic Change (FUDC), funded by Sudan. In spring 2006 the FUDC began an offensive to try to overthrow Déby. In the fall, rebel attacks reached N'Djamena before being beaten back in December. The FUDC then fragmented, and some of the rebels joined Chad's army.

Sources: BBC News (2005); Cutter (2007); Keesing's (2005–2006); Maliti (2008); Project Ploughshares (2008).

INTRA-STATE WAR #938:

The Third Somalia War of 2006–2008

Participants: Ethiopia, Somalia, United States vs. Eritrea, SCIC
Dates: March 6, 2006, to June 11, 2008
Battle-Related Deaths: Somalia—[ ]; SCIC—[ ]; Ethiopia—[ ]; Eritrea—[ ]; United States—[ ]
Where Fought: Africa
Initiator: SCIC
Outcome: Ethiopia, Somalia, United States win
War Type: Civil for central control

Narrative: Between 1991 and 1996, Somalia suffered through an internationalized civil war (intra-state war #870), during which the United Somali Congress (USC) split into an Aideed faction and the Mahdi faction that controlled the capital. In January 1997 the leaders of the Aideed and Mahdi factions agreed to the terms of a cease-fire, which ended the war, though some low-level conflict persisted among the other clans. International efforts to end the conflict led to the creation in 2000 of a Somali Intergovernmental Authority on Development (IGAD) in Djibouti, which transformed into the Transitional National Government (TNG). In 2005 the TNG began to gain control in Somalia; however, it was confronted by the Supreme Council of Islamic Courts (SCIC), which also wanted to establish control over the country and to impose Sharia law. In March 2006 the SCIC began an offensive against the TNG and soon controlled most of the country. Ethiopia intervened to aid the TNG, while Eritrea provided assistance to the SCIC. In December 2006 government and Ethiopian forces, aided by U.S. air strikes, began an advance against SCIC forces in 2007. The TNG was successful in extending its control, and a cease-fire on June 11, 2008, ended most of the fighting.

Sources: Bercovitch and Fretter (2004); Ciment (2007); Cloud (2007); Cutter (2007); Gettleman (2006); Keesing's (2006); Mbaria (2007); Project Ploughshares (2008).

INTRA-STATE WAR #940:
The Second Sri Lanka Tamil War of 2006–present

Participants: Sri Lanka vs. LTTE
Dates: October 11, 2006–present
Battle-Related Deaths: Sri Lanka—[ ]; LTTE—[ ]
Where Fought: Asia
Initiator: Sri Lanka
Outcome: War ongoing
War Type: Civil for local issues

Narrative: The long-running war between the Liberation Tigers of Tamil Eelam (LTTE) and the Sri Lankan government (intra-state war #835) ended with a cease-fire in February 2002. Despite international mediation attempts, however, no peace treaty was signed and the Tamil concerns were not addressed. The situation was exacerbated by the 300,000 Tamils who were displaced by the war and by the government's failure to provide assistance to the Tamil areas that were hard hit by the December 2004 tsunami. The

LTTE also faced the desertion of the Karuna faction, purportedly encouraged by the government. In January 2006 a series of small-scale attacks mostly targeting civilians were conducted by both the government and the LTTE. The conflict escalated to war with the October 2006 offensive launched by the government against the LTTE forces at the Jaffna Peninsula.

Sources: BBC News (2006); International Institute for Strategic Studies (2006); Keesing's (2006); Project Ploughshares (2008); Project Ploughshares (2005); Refugees International (2006).

INTRA-STATE WAR #941:
The Second Yemeni Cleric War of 2007

Participants: Yemen vs. Zaidi Muslims
Dates: January 29, 2007, to June 16, 2007
Battle-Related Deaths: Zaidi Muslims—2,000; Yemen—1,500
Where Fought: Middle East
Initiator: Zaidi Muslims
Outcome: Stalemate
War Type: Civil for central control

Narrative: In 2004 Yemen conducted a war (intra-state # 935) against the followers of Hussein al-Houthi, a cleric of the Zaidi sect, a branch of Shia Islam. President Ali Abdallah Salih accused the cleric of trying to overthrow the government. During the war the government killed al-Houthi, though the war continued under the leadership of the cleric's father, Badr al-Din. The war ended as fighting died down in April 2005. In 2006 the government released 600 members of the rebel group Shabab al-Moumineen ("Believing Youth"), who had been detained in the earlier war. In January 2007, attacks by the rebels began this war. The government then began a campaign against them involving 30,000 troops but was unable to subdue the rebels. With the assistance of Qatar, a cease-fire was negotiated in June 2007.

Sources: AlJazeera (2007); Project Ploughshares (2008).

Analyzing Intra-state Wars

Civil wars are by far the most common type of intra-state war, constituting 307 of the 335 intra-state wars. Of these, 175 are war type 4, for control of the central government, while 132 concern local issues (war type 5). There are only 11 regional wars (war type 6) and 17 inter-communal wars (war type 7). Partially because of the larger number of intra-state wars when compared with the other categories of war, we see some slightly different distribution patterns. As Figure 5.1 shows, there are still a significant number of years that experience no intra-state war onsets; however, there are also a number of years that have large numbers of wars, with the highest number being ten onsets in a given year.

The intra-state wars also have different distributions over the time span of 1816 to 2007. There were no intra-state war onsets during most of World War II, 1937 to 1943; however, intra-state wars became much more common in the later half of the twentieth century, with the highest number of intra-state war onsets (ten in a year) occurring in 1991 (see Figure 5.2).

The overall pattern is perhaps more visible when war onsets are combined into ten-year periods (the wars in the two end years, 1816 and 2007, have been excluded to yield nineteen decades) (see Figure 5.3). This figure also shows another interesting trend, the increasing number of intra-state wars that are internationalized by the outside intervention of one or more other system members. This reflects an increased willingness of states to become involved in wars within other countries over the past fifty years and perhaps a corresponding diminution in the concept of sovereignty.

Finally, in examining the onsets of intra-state war by geographic region, a much more even distribution is apparent than that which appeared in other categories, with the exception of Oceania, which experienced no intra-state wars.

FIGURE 5.1 Intra-state War Onsets by Number of Years, 1816–2007 (Number of Years in Which the Onset of 0 through 10 Intra-state Wars Occurred)

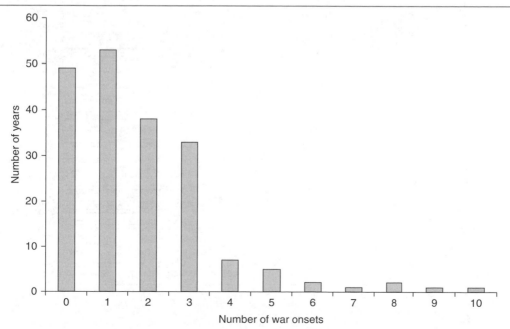

FIGURE 5.2 INTRA-STATE WAR ONSETS BY YEAR, 1816–2007

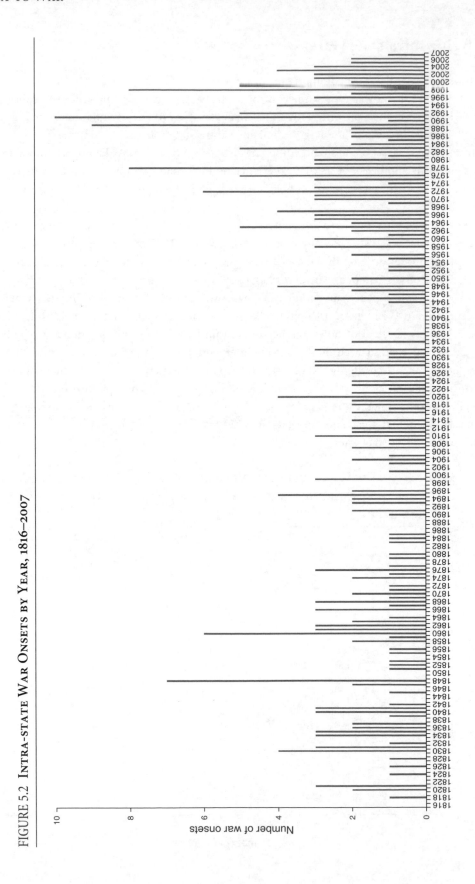

FIGURE 5.3 **INTRA-STATE WAR AND INTERNATIONALIZED INTRA-STATE WAR ONSETS, 1817–2006 (DISTRIBUTION BY DECADE)**

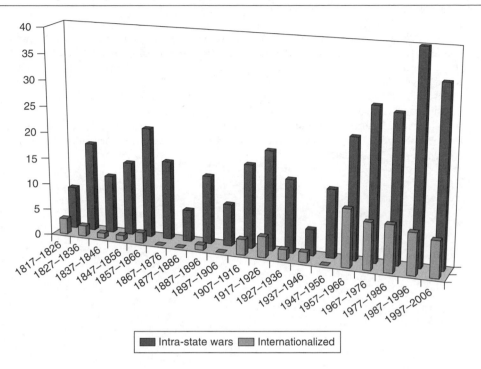

FIGURE 5.4 **INTRA-STATE WAR ONSETS BY REGION, 1816–2007**

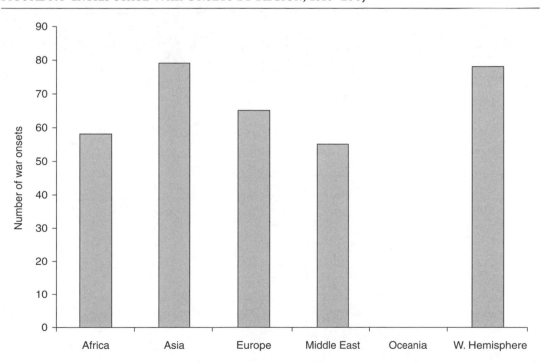

Notes

1. Melvin Small and J. David Singer, *Resort to Arms: International and Civil War, 1816–1980* (Beverly Hills, Calif.: Sage, 1982), 216 (hereafter cited as *Resort*).
2. Small and Singer, *Resort*, 213.
3. Jeffrey Dixon, "Suggested Changes to the COW Civil War Dataset 3.0" (paper presented at the annual meeting of the International Studies Association, Portland, Ore., February 25–March 1, 2003), 4.
4. Small and Singer, *Resort*, 214.
5. Small and Singer, *Resort*, 213.
6. Small and Singer, *Resort*, 215.
7. Dixon, "Suggested Changes to the COW Civil War Dataset 3.0," 10.
8. Malian Ministry of Foreign Affairs and International Cooperation, "Mapping of Non-State Armed Groups in the ECOWAS Region" (paper presented at the 6th Ministerial Meeting of the Human Security Network, Bamako, Mali, May 27–29, 2004), 26.

CHAPTER SIX

The Non-state Wars

Previously, the Correlates of War (COW) Project has examined only wars that involved the government of a member of the interstate system (a state) in one form or another. The inclusion of non-state wars in the data presented here represents an attempt to broaden our understanding of war by including wars between or among nonstate entities. Such entities include governments of other types of geopolitical units (GPUs), such as dependencies or nonstate autonomous entities, that do not meet the criteria of system membership. They also might involve nonterritorial entities (NTEs) or nonstate armed groups (NSAs) that have no defined territorial base. From a state-centric theoretical perspective, wars between or among non-state actors fall into four general categories (see Table 2.1). Two of these types take place within existing system members—regional internal wars (war type 6, of which there are eleven in our data) and inter-communal wars (war type 7, of which there are twenty)—and thus are included along with civil wars in the broader category of intra-state wars (see Chapter 5). The remaining two classifications, wars between or among nonstate entities that take place in nonstate territory (war type 8, of which we have sixty-one) and wars between NSAs that take place across state borders (war type 9, of which we have identified one), are the focus of the discussion here.

In the first class, in nonstate territory, combat takes place in territory that is not part of the territory of a member of the interstate system. Such territory could be a dependency, a nonstate autonomous entity (which does not meet the criteria of system membership), or a theoretically uninhabited territory. Such conflicts were common in territories that were in pre-state-formation periods. The second category, across state borders, involves wars that take place across the borders of existing states but do not involve the state or regional governments in the conflict.

Identifying such non-state wars involves many of the same difficulties experienced while identifying extra-state and intra-state wars, in terms of both describing the nonstate participants in the war and recording the battle-related deaths. When discussing civil wars, Correlates of War scholars Melvin Small and J. David Singer established the requisite condition that the government must be fighting against an internal insurgent force capable of "effective resistance." They then developed two alternative criteria for defining effective resistance: "(a) both sides are initially organized for violent conflict and prepared to resist the attacks of their antagonists, or (b) the weaker side, although initially unprepared, is able to inflict upon the stronger opponents at least five percent of the number of fatalities it sustains."[1] The effective resistance criteria were specifically utilized to differentiate wars from massacres, one-sided state killings, or general riots by unorganized individuals. For a state to be considered a participant in any class of war, the minimum requirement is that it has to either commit 1,000 troops to the war or suffer 100 battle-related deaths. Since nonstate armed groups are generally smaller than states and have fewer resources than states, we have adopted a more minimalist requirement for an NSA to be considered a war participant. An NSA can be considered a war participant if it either commits 100 armed personnel to the war or suffers 25 battle-related deaths. Thus non-state wars involve combat between two or more nonstate armed groups that are organized for combat, are capable of effective resistance, and commit a minimum of 100 troops to the war or suffer 25 battle-related deaths. Admittedly, this lower level to qualify as a war participant may make it more complicated to identify all of the participants in a non-state war; however, so far most of the non-state wars generally involve combat between two major nonstate actors.

The same battle-related death definition of war as involving sustained combat with 1,000 battle-related deaths between/among the combatants per year applies to all wars, including non-state wars; however, as with civil wars it is often difficult to ascertain battle-related deaths in non-state wars. Nonstate armed groups may or may not wear identifying clothing, so it may be more difficult for observers to distinguish combatant deaths from civilians who may have been killed. Similarly, it is frequently difficult to separate wars (or actions by NSAs) from general riots that may result from, or occur along with, armed group actions. Consequently, historians frequently report fatality and casualty numbers that include the deaths of noncombatants. Nevertheless, we have attempted to report only battle-related deaths among the combatants, frequently by making judgments on fatalities related to the reported sizes of the combatant forces, if available.

Table 6.1 lists the sixty-two non-state wars that have been identified to date. Since this dataset is in its initial release, it is assumed that there are a number of non-state wars that have not yet been identified. It is hoped that colleagues in the research community will be willing to report any potential war candidates. Individual descriptions of the wars follow the table.

TABLE 6.1 LIST OF NON-STATE WARS IN CHRONOLOGICAL ORDER

Non-state war number	War name	Page no	Non-state war number	War name	Page no
1500	First Maori Tribal War of 1818–1824	488	1539	Han-Nien War of 1855–1858	511
1501	Shaka Zulu-Bantu War of 1819–1828	488	1540	Filibuster War of 1856–1857	512
1502	Burma-Assam War of 1819–1822	489	1541	Han-Panthay War Phase 1 of 1856–1860	513
1503	Buenos Aires War of 1820	489			
1505	Second Maori Tribal War of 1821–1823	490	1542	First Zulu Internecine War of 1856	514
1506	Siam-Kedah War of 1821	491	1543	Kucha and Khoja Uprising of 1857	514
1508	China-Kashgaria War of 1825–1828	491	1544	First Boer-Basuto War of 1858	515
1509	Mexico-Yaqui Indian War of 1825–1827	492	1545	First Ethiopian War of 1858–1861	516
1510	Central American Confederation War of 1826–1829	493	1546	Second Tukulor War of 1860–1862	517
			1548	Transvaal War of 1862–1864	517
1511	Viang Chan-Siamese War of 1826–1827	494	1550	Central American War of 1863	518
			1551	First Australian Aboriginal War of 1864–1865	518
1512	Peru-Gran Colombia War of 1828–1829	494			
			1552	Second Boer-Basuto War of 1865–1866	519
1513	Argentine War for Unity of 1829–1831	495	1553	Second Ethiopian War of 1868–1872	520
1514	Sayyid Said War of 1829–1830	496	1554	Uruguay Colorados-Blancos War of 1870–1872	521
1515	China-Kokand War of 1830–1831	497			
1516	Siam-Cambodia-Vietnam War of 1831–1834	497	1556	Second Zulu Internecine War of 1883–1884	521
1518	Argentina-Ranqueles Indian War of 1833–1834	498	1557	Oman-Ibadi War of 1883–1884	522
			1558	Second Australian Aboriginal War of 1884–1894	523
1520	Bolivia Conquest of Peru in 1835–1836	498			
1521	Boer-Matabele War of 1836–1837	499	1559	Ethiopia-Mahdi War of 1885–1889	524
1523	Dissolution of the Bolivia-Peru Confederation of 1837–1839	500	1560	German East Africa Company War of 1888–1889	525
1524	Persian Siege of Herat of 1837–1838	500	1561	Rabih Zubayr-Bornu War of 1893	526
1525	Boer-Zulu War of 1838	501	1567	First Nejd-Hejaz War of 1919	526
1527	Anti-Rosas War of 1839–1840	502	1568	Second Nejd-Hejaz War of 1924–1925	527
1528	Dissolution of the Central American Confederation of 1839–1840	503	1570	Partition Communal War of 1946–1947	528
1530	Dogra-Tibet War of 1841–1842	504	1571	Hyderabad War of 1947–1948	529
1531	First Haiti-Santo Domingo War of 1844–1845	504	1572	Palestine War of 1947–1948	529
			1573	Cheju Rebellion of 1948–1949	530
1533	War of Seven Khojas of 1847–1848	506	1574	Rwandan Social Revolution of 1959–1962	531
1534	Taiping Rebellion Phase 1 of 1850–1860	507			
			1577	Dhofar Rebellion Phase 1 of 1968–1971	532
1535	First Tukulor War of 1852–1854	508			
1536	Kashmir-Dards of Chilas War of 1852	509	1581	Angola Guerrilla War of 1974–1975	533
1537	Han-Miao War Phase 1 of 1854–1860	509	1582	East Timorese War Phase 1 of 1975	534
1538	Second Haiti-Santo Domingo War of 1855–1856	510	1594	Hema-Lendu War of 1999–2005	535

Individual Descriptions of Non-state Wars

NON-STATE WAR #1500:
The First Maori Tribal War of 1818–1824

Participants: Te Rauparaha's Ngati Toa vs. Ngati Ira, Ngai Tahu, Rangitikei, Taranaki, and Waikato
Dates: [ ]/[ ]/1818, to [ ]/[ ]/1824
Battle-Related Deaths: Ngati Ira, Ngai Tahu, Rangitikei, Taranaki, Waikato—6,000; Te Rauparaha's Ngati Toa—1,500
Where Fought: Oceania
Initiator: Te Rauparaha's Ngati Toa
Outcome: Te Rauparaha's Ngati Toa win
War Type: In nonstate territory

Narrative: New Zealand was one of the later areas to receive European settlers, and by the beginning of the nineteenth century, the Europeans who lived on the islands of New Zealand were still relatively few. The Europeans who came, however, did bring with them modern weapons, such as rifles, which changed the nature of the warfare among the Maori tribes. This precipitated a period (roughly 1805 to 1840) of increasingly deadly tribal warfare, which some have referred to as the "Musket Wars." Although there were numerous instances of tribal conflict over land or tribal honor, we are including two particular campaigns: one by the Ngati Toa tribe under the leadership of Te Rauparaha and one by the Nga Phuhi tribe under Hongi Hika (nonstate war #1505). Both Te Rauparaha and Hongi Hika provided leadership for wide-ranging combat that appears to meet the war-level threshold of 1,000 battle-related deaths per year.

According to the first (1966) edition of *An Encyclopaedia of New Zealand* (McLintock 2005), "The Maori leader responsible for the greatest slaughter in the early nineteenth century was undoubtedly Te Rauparaha, a chief of the Ngati Toa tribe of the Kawhia district." Between 1818 and 1820, the Ngati Toa joined with a few allied tribes for a collective campaign against their enemies. Their *taua*, or war party, was large and was successful in virtually all its battles during this two-year expedition. On subsequent expeditions until 1824, Te Rauparaha ultimately defeated the Taranaki, Ngai Tahu, Waikato, Ngati Ira, and Rangitikei tribes. Though the level of warfare declined after this point, Te Rauparaha continued to attack neighboring tribes, and by 1828 he controlled most of the east coast of the north island.

Coding: The battle-related death figures cited above are approximations, based on some limited information about the individual battles and on our attempts to isolate the fatality levels of combatants from those of civilians. It has been estimated that up to 200,000 people, or 50 percent of the Maori, died between 1805 and 1840 from the combined causes of warfare, genocide, and European diseases (Pool 1973). Estimates of those who died in war range from 20,000 to 80,000, though those figures include civilians as well as combatants (Vayda 1970).

Sources: Blick (1988); Clodfelter (2002); Langer (1952); McLintock (2005); Pool (1973); Stearns (2001); Tregar (1890); Vayda (1970).

NON-STATE WAR #1501:
The Shaka Zulu-Bantu War of 1819–1828

Participants: Shaka Zulu vs. Bantu
Dates: [ ]/[ ]/1819, to September 24, 1828
Battle-Related Deaths: Bantu—40,000; Zulu–20,000
Where Fought: Africa
Initiator: Zulu

Outcome: Zulu win
War Type: In nonstate territory

Narrative: In 1816 Shaka became chief of the Zulu tribe, and he was known for revolutionizing warfare in southern Africa by inventing the assegai, a light javelin. Shaka's militarized kingdom spread destruction throughout southeastern Africa in an ever-widening arc of warfare known as Mfecane, or "the Crushing." This war began with the Battle of Gqoli Hill, where the Zulu defeated a larger Ndwandwe army. The Zulu armies then conducted a series of attacks against many of the other Bantu tribes in the area. The Zulu were successful in expelling many of the Bantu, who in turn displaced other tribal groups as far away as modern Tanzania. Only Shaka's assassination in September 1828 ended this decade of bloodshed.

The maximum number of troops on the Zulu side has been estimated at between 30,000 (by Phillips and Axelrod) and 100,000 (by OnWar. com). Estimates for the number of Bantu troops are similar. The numbers of battle-related deaths testify to the substantial severity of this war. Clodfelter does not cover this war. Phillips and Axelrod (2005) have two separate entries, "Shaka Zulu's Wars of Expansion" of 1819–1828, and the "Zulu Civil War" of 1817–1819.

Sources: Brecke (1999); Davidson (1972); Davis (2006); Deflem (1999); Fage and Oliver (1976); Hallett (1970); Kohn (1999); Morris (1998); Phillips and Axelrod (2005); Saunders and Soothey (2000); Thompson (2001); Wilson (1975).

NON-STATE WAR #1502:

The Burma-Assam War of 1819–1822

Participants: Burma vs. Assam
Dates: [ ] /[ ]/1819, to [ ]/[ ]/1822
Battle-Related Deaths: Burma—[ ]; Assam—[ ]
   (Total Combatant and Civilian Deaths: 26,000)
Where Fought: Asia
Initiator: Burma

Outcome: Burma wins
War Type: In nonstate territory

Narrative: In 1817 unrest in Assam led one of its ruling factions to request Burmese intervention. After twice trying to impose a candidate as rajah, the Burmese decided on military action. In 1819 Burma sent Gen. Maha Bandula with a force of 8,000 troops, which grew to over 10,000, through the Himalayas. The Burmese defeated the Assam army at the Battle of Kathalguri, and Burma then assumed control over Assam, though the Assam king remained as titular ruler. This attachment of Assam to Burma lasted only five years. When two Assamese pretenders to the throne raised forces to oppose the Burmese, the Burmese troops pursued these forces into British territory in early 1822. This helped lead to extrastate war #310, the First British-Burmese War, in 1823. With Britain's victory in 1826, Assam became part of India (then a British colony).

Coding: Burma was an autonomous entity from 1753 until 1885, and Assam (today part of India) was an autonomous entity from 1492 until 1819. In 1819 Assam became part of Burma as a result of this war. After this loss of independence, Assam never regained its autonomous status. This war is between two nonstate GPUs, though one entity (Burma) eventually attained statehood, while Assam did not. Neither Clodfelter (2002) nor Phillips and Axelrod (2005) specifically cover this war; however, they both cover the First Anglo-Burmese War of 1824–1826, and in the process they describe Burmese intrusions that we have described as the events that triggered that Anglo-Burmese War.

Sources: Brecke (1999); Bruce (1973); Cady (1958); Hall (1981); Hernon (2002); Schafer (1995); Thant (2001).

NON-STATE WAR #1503:

The Buenos Aires War of 1820

Participants: Buenos Aires vs. provinces
Dates: January 8, 1820, to February 23, 1820
Battle-Related Deaths: Buenos Aires—1,200;
   provinces —[ ]

Where Fought: Western Hemisphere
Initiator: provinces
Outcome: Provinces win
War Type: In nonstate territory

Narrative: While under Spanish colonial rule, the territories of Argentina, Uruguay, Paraguay, and briefly Bolivia were united in the Viceroyalty of Río de la Plata, with its capital at Buenos Aires. The disintegration of the viceroyalty led to the creation of the United Provinces of South America in 1810. Within the United Provinces, political sentiment was divided, however, between those who wished the provinces to remain united (Unitarians) and those who opposed continued domination by Buenos Aires (the Federalists). In 1815 the provinces in the northeast (including Banda Oriental, now Uruguay) broke away from the United Provinces and created the Federal League (Liga Federal) under the leadership of José Gervasia Artigas. In 1816 the Congress of Tucumán proclaimed that the United Provinces of South America were independent of Spanish rule. In 1819 the Congress of the United Provinces, reflecting the Unitarian position, created a strong central government in the city of Buenos Aires, controlled by those known as the *porteños*. This move was opposed by the provinces that preferred a more federal distribution of power, including Tucumán, and the provinces in the Federal League. As Buenos Aires attempted to expand the scope of its control, the military in the provinces began to revolt, starting the war. Buenos Aries was at a disadvantage, since part of its army under José de San Martín was gone, fighting the Spanish in Chile. The revolt spread throughout a number of provinces, and it culminated in a battle at Cepeda, where 1,600 troops from the provinces of Santa Fé, Entre Ríos, Salta, and Tucumán confronted and defeated 2,000 *porteños*. The Treaty of Pilar, signed on February 23, 1820, created a loose federation. It also led to the dissolution of the Federal League later that year.

Disagreements over the desired degree of unity for the region would continue to bedevil the parties within Argentina and the broader region and would contribute to a number of wars, including non-state war #1513, the Argentine War for Unity of 1829–1831; non-state war #1518, the war against the native Indian tribes; non-state war #1527, the war against General Rosas; extra-state war #327, the Uruguay War of 1843–1851; and extra-state war #351, the Argentine-Buenos Aires War of 1859. Although Buenos Aires lost this war, it eventually overcame provincial opposition to become the capital of a united Argentina, which joined the interstate system in 1841.

Coding: Neither Clodfelter (2002) nor Phillips and Axelrod (2005) include this particular war. Lemke (2006) identified twenty territorial entities in the La Plata region in 1810–1862, and found ten wars (as we would define war) between those entities. Lemke found this war to be one of the ones with the fewest battle-related deaths.

Sources: Brecke (1999); Lemke (2006); Schafer (1995); Scheina (2003a); Wright and Nekhom (1978).

NON-STATE WAR #1505:

The Second Maori Tribal War of 1821–1823

Participants: Hongi Hika's Nga Phuhi vs. Ngati Maru, Ngati Paoa, Te Arawa, Waikato River Maori
Dates: September [ ], 1821, to [ ]/[ ]/1823
Battle-Related Deaths: Ngati Maru, Ngati Paoa, Te Arawa, and Waikato River Maori—2,000; Hongi Hika's Nga Phuhi—500
Where Fought: Oceania
Initiator: Hongi Hika's Nga Phuhi
Outcome: Hongi Hika's Nga Phuhi win
War Type: In nonstate territory

Narrative: Along with non-state war #1500, this war is part of the so-called Musket Wars among the Maori tribes of New Zealand. The possession of rifles enabled certain tribes to attack and conquer their neighboring tribes with more fatalities than had been common in the past.

One particular tribal chief, Hongi Hika, understood the potential of the new weapons and even traveled to England in 1820 in the hopes of obtaining additional guns. Having achieved his objective, he returned to New Zealand and launched an offensive against the neighboring tribes in 1821. The expedition was successful from his point of view, enabling him to cause relatively high numbers of death while having his army remain unscathed. Reportedly, there were two major differences between Hongi Hika's war and that of Te Rauparaha (non-state war #1500): Hongi Hika was not interested in conquering land, and Hongi Hika adopted an explicit policy of genocide.

Coding: The battle-related death figures cited above are approximations, based on some limited information about the individual battles and on our attempts to isolate the fatality levels of combatants from those of civilians. It has been estimated that up to 200,000 people, or 50 percent of the Maori, died between 1805 and 1840 of warfare, genocide, and European diseases (Pool 1973). Estimates of the number who died in the war range from 20,000 to 80,000, though those figures include civilians as well as combatants.

Sources: Blick (1988); Clodfelter (2002); Langer (1952); McLintock (2005); Pool (1973); Stearns (2001); Tregar (1890); Vayda (1970).

NON-STATE WAR #1506:
The Siam-Kedah War of 1821

Participants: Siam vs. Kedah
Dates: November [ ], 1821, to December [ ], 1821
Battle-Related Deaths: Siam–[ ]; Kedah—[ ]
   (Total Combatant and Civilian Deaths:
   up to 21,000)
Where Fought: Asia
Initiator: Siam
Outcome: Siam wins
War Type: In nonstate territory

Narrative: Siam (now known as Thailand) was one of the few entities in Asia to retain its independence throughout the period of European colonialism, and it was an autonomous entity until it became a member of the interstate system in 1887. In the early nineteenth century, Siam was interested in expanding its influence, which led to its involvement in several wars. At this point Siam particularly tried to revive its claims to the Malay states to Siam's south. One such state was Kedah, which was also an autonomous entity. The sultan of Kedah had angered the king of Siam when he had ceded territory to Great Britain (Pinang in 1786 and Port Wellesley in 1800). In 1818 the king of Siam ordered the sultan of Kedah to make up for the lost territory by invading the neighboring state of Perak, which also bordered Siam. Even though Kedah was successful in conquering Perak, it was not sufficient to appease the king. In 1821 the sultan of Kedah was ordered to come to Bangkok to answer charges. When he refused, Siam invaded, starting this war. In a bloody contest, Siam defeated Kedah, the sultan was forced into exile, and Kedah became part of Siam. In 1909 Siam surrendered Kedah to Great Britain.

Coding: Determining the battle-related deaths for this war was problematic. A number of sources refer to the war as "bloody" and Hall (1981) remarks that Siam "laid waste" to Kedah as part of the campaign. The only figure we found indicated 21,000 deaths, though that number probably includes a number of massacred civilians. Neither Clodfelter nor Phillips and Axelrod cover this war.

Sources: Andaya and Andaya (2001); Andaya and Andaya (1982); Brecke (1999); Hall (1981); Kennedy (1962); Richardson (1960a); Schafer (1995); Smith (1967); Wyatt (2003); Wyatt (1984).

NON-STATE WAR #1508:
The China-Kashgaria War of 1825–1828

Participants: China vs. Kokand and Kashgaria
   Muslim rebels
Dates: [ ]/[ ]/1825, to [ ]/[ ]/1828
Battle-Related Deaths: China—[ ]; rebels—[ ]
Where Fought: Asia

Initiator: China
Outcome: China wins
War Type: In nonstate territory

Narrative: Kashgaria is the portion of what was then the Chinese province of Singkiang (now transliterated as Xinjiang) lying to the south of the Tien Shan mountains. Kashgaria was periodically controlled by China but was an autonomous entity from 1678 to 1759. In 1759 it was conquered once again by the Chinese emperor Chien Lung, and in the 1820s Kashgaria was loosely controlled by China. To the west, Kokand was an autonomous entity that wanted special trading privileges in Kashgaria. When the Chinese refused this request, a jihad was declared against China by Jahangir (a Khoja, or trader who converted to Islam), who led a small army of his followers from Kokand and the Kirghiz tribes (some of which lived in Kokand territory) against China in 1820. At that time, Jahangir's forces were routed by the Chinese, though he continued low-level attacks for several years.

However, in 1825 a Chinese massacre of a Kirghiz (Muslim) camp caused a widespread uprising against Chinese rule begun by the Kirghiz who trapped and destroyed the initial Chinese force. In aid of his allies, Jahangir again led an army from his base in Kokand against the Chinese. He was aided by a Kokand army led by Muhammad Ali Khan (Kokand's ruler) and forces from the Kashgar, Kirghiz, and Kazakh tribes in Kashgaria. Jahangir's army surrounded the Chinese forces at Kashgar. After a siege in which thousands of Jahangir's troops were killed, the Chinese army was annihilated. Jahangir established his rule in Kashgar, and the forces of Kokand withdrew. In 1827, in an attempt to reconquer the area, China fielded an army of 22,000 troops, compared with 20,000 for the rebels. After heavy fighting Jahangir fled from Kashgar and the Chinese reasserted their control. In 1828 Jahangir was captured and sent to Peking, where he was executed.

Coding: This war is coded as a non-state war because China, Kokand, and Kashgaria are not members of the interstate system at this time. China does not become a state system member until 1860. Kashgaria would become autonomous once again from 1863 to 1878, during a period of weakness in the Chinese dynastic cycle. Although this was a substantial war, with large numbers of troops on each side, we have been unable to locate adequate fatality statistics. Clodfelter (2002) very briefly reviews "Campaigns in Kashgaria" of 1825–1831 and claims that the fatalities on both sides totaled 40,000 for the entire six-year period, which would include this war and non-state war #1515. Phillips and Axelrod do not include this war.

Sources: Clodfelter (2002); Fairbank (1992); Minahan (1996); Morse (1966); Saray (2003); Schafer (1995); Twitchett and Fairbank (1978).

NON-STATE WAR #1509:

The Mexico-Yaqui Indian War of 1825–1827

Participants: Mexico vs. Yaqui Indians
Dates: October 25, 1825, to April 13, 1827
Battle-Related Deaths: Mexico—[ ]; Yaqui Indians—[ ] (Total Combatant Deaths: 3,000)
Where Fought: Western Hemisphere
Initiator: Mexico
Outcome: Compromise: the Yaqui win some autonomy
War Type: In nonstate territory

Narrative: The Yaqui Indians lived in northern Mexico. Although they had generally cooperated with the Mexican authorities, in the 1820s they began to develop a greater sense of autonomy. This was partially due to the work of Juan Ignacio Jusacamea, later known as Juan Banderas, who promoted the idea of an Indian military confederation and who began to assemble an Indian army. The event that precipitated this war in 1825 was the attempt of the Mexicans to draft Yaqui men to serve in the war against the Apache. When the Yaqui declined, the Mexicans sent a small contingent to force compliance, causing a battle in which a number of Yaqui were killed. The Yaqui responded by attacking nearby Mexican towns. The number of recruits to the Yaqui army grew steadily, and though the rebels generally conducted guerrilla-style attacks, they were able to defeat a Mexican force in a battle in June 1826. However, Banderas was unsuccessful in attracting the other Indian nations to join the Yaqui revolt. The Mexicans had few resources and had initially committed 800 troops to fight an estimated 3,000 Yaqui. Nevertheless, as the war dragged on, both sides grew weary of conflict. Thus on November 17, 1826, the Mexicans offered an amnesty to the rebels, with Banderas finally surrendering on April 13, 1827, marking the end of the war. Banderas launched another rebellion in 1830, though at below war-level hostilities. He was finally captured and executed in January 1833.

Coding: Mexico became an autonomous entity in 1821 (see extra-state war #304, the War of Mexican Independence). Yet Mexico did not become a state system member until 1831 (see extra-state war #317, the Spanish war of the Reconquest of Mexico, a war lost by Spain). Thus this current war is a non-state war because it occurred during this decade of Mexican autonomy. Clodfelter (2002) covers wars against two Indian tribes under "Yaqui-Mayo Wars" of 1825–1926. Phillips and Axelrod do not cover this war.

Sources: Clodfelter (2002); Hu-DeHart (1984); Schafer (1995); Scheina (2003a); Spicer (1980).

NON-STATE WAR #1510:
The Central American Confederation War of 1826–1829

Participants: conservative Confederation vs. liberals
Dates: [ ]/[ ]/1826, to April 12, 1829
Battle-Related Deaths: conservative Confederation—2,000; liberals—1,300
Where Fought: Western Hemisphere
Initiator: liberals
Outcome: Liberals win
War Type: In nonstate territory

Narrative: While they were under Spanish rule, Costa Rica, El Salvador, Guatemala, Honduras, and Nicaragua had been administratively united. After they received their independence in 1821, they decided to unite again into the Central American Confederation in 1825. However, ideological differences between the conservatives (mainly from Guatemala) and liberals (from El Salvador and Honduras), partially over the role of the Roman Catholic Church, fueled immediate disagreements within the Confederation. As the leadership of the Confederation became more conservative, the liberals attempted a coup in 1826. The conservative government suppressed the coup and launched an offensive in May 1827 against the liberal government in San Salvador, which was besieged for a month. The Confederation subsequently overthrew the liberal president of Honduras in November. The president's nephew, Gen. Francisco Morazán, led the liberal counterattack, liberating Honduras and then El Salvador in October 1828. Morazán then marched toward the Confederation capital at Guatemala City, which surrendered after a two-month siege on April 12, 1829. Morazán was named the new Confederation president, and he moved the capital to San Salvador. The conflicts between the conservatives and liberals remained, and they led to a second war in 1839 (non-state war #1528), which led to the dissolution of the Confederation.

Coding: Both Clodfelter (2002) and Phillips and Axelrod (2005) combine our two wars (non-state wars #1510 and #1528) together as "Central American Wars" of 1822–1839 and "Central American Federation Civil Wars," respectively. The battle-related death figures reported above are extrapolations from the totals provided by Clodfelter (2002), though as Scheina points out, these figures are probably understatements, since they apparently do not include deaths from disease.

Sources: Clodfelter (2002); Jaques (2007); Phillips and Axelrod (2005); Richardson (1960a); Scheina (2003a).

NON-STATE WAR #1511:
The Viang Chan-Siamese War of 1826–1827

Participants: Viang Chan (Vientiane) vs. Siam
Dates: []/[ ]/1826, to May 15, 1827
Battle-Related Deaths: Viang Chan—24,000; Siam—7,000
Where Fought: Asia
Initiator: Viang Chan
Outcome: Siam wins
War Type: In nonstate territory

Narrative: In 1826 the area of modern Laos was divided into three city-states: Viang Chan (Vientiane), Luang Prabang, and Champassak. All three had been invaded by neighboring Siam in 1778, and since then, even though they retained some autonomy and their kings, they were under Siam's control. Viang Chan's king at the time, Chao-Anou, desired to break away from Siam's control. In 1826 a false rumor of a pending British attack on Siam triggered Chao-Anou's rebellion. He sent three armies into Siam on the pretext of providing military assistance to Siam. Since the Siamese were caught off guard, the Viang Chan armies successfully advanced into Siam. The Siamese rallied their forces, however, and after the decisive battle of Nong-Boua Lamp'ou, in northern Siam, the Siamese launched a counteroffensive. They forced their way across the Mekong River and devastated Viang Chan, ending the war in 1827. In 1828 Chao-Anou did make an attempt to return to power with the assistance of troops from Vietnam, but he was captured by the Siamese and executed. As a result of this war, Vientiane was controlled by Siam from 1828 until 1893, when France annexed it to French Indochina.

Coding: This war is coded as a non-state war because neither Siam nor Viang Chan was a member of the interstate system. Siam was an autonomous entity and did not become a state system member until 1887 and named Thailand in 1938. Both Clodfelter (2002) and Phillips and Axelrod (2005) include a "Siamese-Laotian War" of 1826–1829.

Sources: Clodfelter (2002); Dobby (1973); Evans (2002); Hall (1981); Manich (1967); Phillips and Axelrod (2005); Schafer (1995); Stuart-Fox (1997); Toye (1968); Wyatt (1984).

NON-STATE WAR #1512:
The Peru-Gran Colombia War of 1828–1829

Participants: Peru vs. Gran Colombia
Dates: July 3, 1828, to February 28, 1829
Battle-Related Deaths: Peru—3,500; Gran Colombia—1,000
Where Fought: Western Hemisphere
Initiator: Peru
Outcome: Gran Colombia wins
War Type: In nonstate territory

Narrative: During five years of fairly continuous fighting, from 1817 to 1822, Simón Bolívar had been instrumental in securing independence for Venezuela, Colombia, and Ecuador from Spain (extra-state wars #303 and #308). The three then merged into a new autonomous entity called Gran Colombia. Bolívar had also helped secure the independence of Peru and Upper Peru, the latter of which was named Bolivia in his honor (in extra-state war #312). Consequently, Bolívar hoped to join Peru and Bolivia to Gran Colombia; however, nationalists in Peru wanted to maintain their independence and perhaps even restore Bolivia to Peru's control. Peru also had designs on Ecuador. On April 18, 1828, Peru sent troops into Bolivia and demanded the removal of the Gran Colombian forces that had been stationed there. In July Peru and Bolivia signed a treaty, and sent troops against Gran Colombia. The ensuing war involved both sea battles and land engagements, many of which took place in what is now Ecuador. Although the sea battles were important, the land conflict was decisive. Gran Colombia had a 4,200-man army in Ecuador, commanded by Antonio Sucre. On February 26, 1829, Sucre forced a battle at the narrow defile of Portete de Tarqui, where the Peruvians were unable to deploy their larger army. Gran Colombia suffered 360 deaths in action, while Peru lost between 600 and 1,500 in this, the largest battle of the war. Peru conceded defeat the next day, and in the Treaty of Girón of February 28, Peru had to evacuate any of the disputed territory.

Coding: Gran Colombia existed as an autonomous entity, though not a member of the interstate system, until 1830, when Bolívar resigned as president. At that juncture it broke apart, without a civil war, into present-day Ecuador, Venezuela, and Colombia. Of these three, Ecuador did not enter the COW interstate system until 1854, but Colombia qualified almost immediately in 1831, followed by Venezuela in 1841. Peru became a member of the system in 1839. Clodfelter (2002) has a short entry on the "Peruvian-Colombian War" of 1827–1829, while Phillips and Axelrod do not cover this war.

Sources: Brecke (1999); Clodfelter (2002); Schafer (1995); Scheina (2003a).

NON-STATE WAR #1513:
The Argentine War for Unity of 1829–1831

Participants: Unitarians vs. provinces
Dates: April 26, 1829, to November 30, 1831
Battle-Related Deaths: Unitarians—[ ];
    provinces—[ ] (Total Combatant Deaths: 5,426)
Where Fought: Western Hemisphere
Initiator: Unitarians
Outcome: Provinces win
War Type: In nonstate territory

Narrative: The 1820s were a decade of war for the United Provinces of South America. The United Provinces had secured its independence from Spain in 1816 but soon became involved in a number of conflicts involving its composition and its relationship to its neighbors (see non-state war #1503 and extra-state war #315). Non-state war #1503 had concerned the issue of the

relationship between the provinces and the central government in Buenos Aires. The *porteños,* or people of the port of Buenos Aires, favored a strong central government based in Buenos Aires (which was known as the Unitarian position). Those opposing were the Federalists, favoring a loose confederation of provinces. The provinces had prevailed in that war, and the 1820 Treaty of Pilar created a loose federation. The change in name from the United Provinces of South America to the "Republic of Argentina" was reflected in a new constitution, adopted on December 24, 1826. After fighting against Brazil (in extra-state war #315 from 1826 to 1828), Gen. Juan Lavalle seized power in Buenos Aires in December 1828. He and the Unitarians engaged in several skirmishes with the provinces that month; however, the major challenge to Lavalle was raised in April 1829 by the caudillos of the provinces of Entre Rios and Buenos Aires, Estanislao López and Juan Manuel de Rosas. The provinces defeated Lavalle, and Rosas took over control of the city of Buenos Aires. Rosas remained the caudillo of the province of Buenos Aires, though he generally functioned as the leader of Argentina, which had no real federal structure at this time. Nevertheless, this did not end the Unitarian movement, and in fact led to this war.

Unitarian forces under Gen. Juan Paz rebelled against Rosas. With an army that initially numbered only 1,000 men, Paz won several battles near Córdoba and went on to defeat provincial armies of 1,600 at San Roque and 5,000 at La Tablada. Owing to the Unitarian successes, Paz's army swelled from 1,000 to 4,000 during the period of April 1829 to February 1830. Paz by then controlled nine interior provinces, which he organized into the Unitarian League. The coastal areas including Buenos Aires, referred to as the "Littoral League," remained in the sphere of Rosas and his allies. In May 1831 General Paz was captured, and without his leadership the Unitarians lost the battle of Ciudadela de Tucumán in November 1831, ending this war.

Rosas remained in power from 1829 to 1852 and involved Argentina in another series of wars, including non-state war #1510 (the war against the native Indian tribes); non-state war #1527 (the war against General Rosas); extra-state war #327 (the Uruguay War of 1843–1851); and extra-state #351 (the Argentine-Buenos Aires War of 1859). Buenos Aires eventually overcame provincial opposition to become the capital of a united Argentina, which joined the interstate system in 1841.

Coding: This is a substantial war, with a maximum troop strength of 4,000 on the Unitarian side and 5,000 on the Provincial side, and over 1,000 soldiers died in the 1830 battle of Oncativo alone. Lemke (2006) divides the fighting into the 1829–1830 phase, with 4,004 battle-dead, and the 1831 phase, with 1,422 battle-deaths. Lemke also provides additional information on the Argentine provinces. While Schafer (1995) recognizes only Buenos Aires, Córdoba, Corrientes, and San Juan as autonomous entities, Lemke identifies twenty provinces and entities, including Entre Rios and the Pampas tribes. Clodfelter (2002) includes an "Argentine Unitarian-Federalist War" of 1828–1831, while Phillips and Axelrod do not.

Sources: Clodfelter (2002); Lemke (2006); Sarmiento (1971); Schafer (1995); Scheina (2003a); Wright and Nekhom (1978).

NON-STATE WAR #1514:

The Sayyid Said War of 1829–1830

Participants: Sayyid Said army vs. Mombasa
Dates: December 18, 1829, to May 9, 1830
Battle-Related Deaths: Mombasa—[ ]; Sayyid Said army—[ ] (Total Combatant Deaths: 1,000)
Where Fought: Africa
Initiator: Sayyid Said
Outcome: Sayyid Said wins
War Type: In nonstate territory

Narrative: Sayyid Said (or Sultan bin Ahmad Al Bu Saidi) was the ruler of Muscat (Oman) from 1806 to 1856. He was interested in trade with East Africa and in restoring Muscat's domination of the seacoast, which was being threatened both by pirates and by expanding European influence. Sayyid Said possessed both an adequate army, with French advisers, and a navy that had been provided to him by the British. He began to deepen his engagement in the region by expanding trade with the island of Zanzibar, and he also established new trade links with the African interior. In 1817 Sayyid Said sent thirty ships to East Africa in an attempt to lessen the domination of the Mazaria tribe near Mombasa, a town on the mainland near Zanzibar. Initially the sultan only wanted more indirect influence, through trade, in the region; however, he began to think of asserting more direct control. In January 1828 the sultan launched a brief military expedition against Mombasa, which ended with the Mazaria recognizing his preeminence and allowing a Muscat garrison in Mombasa. Nevertheless, the Mazaria renounced this agreement once the sultan had returned to Muscat. In 1829 Sayyid Said decided to begin moving his base of operations to Zanzibar, where he had a new palace built. This war, which was his second expedition against Mombasa and the Mazaria tribe, began in December 1929. Initially the results of the offensive were the same, with initial concessions from the Mazaria, followed by disavowal. By 1830, however, the sultan established control over Zanzibar and the Mombasa coast. Under Sayyid Said's leadership, Zanzibar flourished as a center for trade for all East Africa. In 1840 Sayyid Said moved permanently to Zanzibar, becoming sultan of Zanzibar.

Coding: Zanzibar's domination in East Africa brought it into increasing conflict with the expanding European colonial empires, particularly the Germans and the British (see non-state war #1560 and extra-state war #406).

Sources: Bhacker (1992); Davies (1997); Lea (2001); Nicolini (2004); Oliver and Atmore (1994); Richardson (1960a).

NON-STATE WAR #1515:
The China-Kokand War of 1830–1831

Participants: Kokand vs. China
Dates: September [ ], 1830, to November [ ], 1831
Battle-Related Deaths: China—[ ]; Kokand—[ ]
Where Fought: Asia
Initiator: Kokand
Outcome: Kokand wins
War Type: In nonstate territory

Narrative: During the early nineteenth century, the Khanate of Kokand was the main rival of the Khanate of Bukhara for primacy in what would later become Russian Central Asia. In an endeavor to control trade routes, Kokand also wanted to extend its influence into Kashgaria, which had been conquered by China in 1759. The degree of China's control over Kashgaria had fluctuated, and in the 1820s, Muslim tribes, including some from Kokand, had attempted to assert control in Kashgaria (see non-state war #1508 in 1825). The Ch'ing government wanted to prevent a trade monopoly by Kokand and periodically placed an embargo on Kokand's goods. In response, in the fall of 1830, Kokand decided to send an army of an estimated 7,000 to 10,000 troops under the leadership of commander-in-chief Hakk Kuli (Haqq Quli Mingbashi) into Kashgaria. In a three-pronged offensive, the Kokand army defeated the Chinese at Min-Yol and similarly conquered the Chinese garrison at Kashgar. The garrison at Yarkand was better able to prepare its defense and mobilized 5,000 troops, who repelled the invaders. Finally, a disturbance between Kokand and Bukhara forced the khan of Kokand to recall his army. The Chinese began organizing a retaliatory offensive in early 1831; however, the trade issues were resolved by negotiations in the fall. By the end of the year Kokand's trade had been resumed.

Coding: Kokand is coded as the winner in the war because it gained its goal of resuming trade.

China did gain to the extent that the invaders withdrew and it was able to maintain some semblance of control over Kashgaria; however, in its weakening condition China could not expand its control westward. Although this was a substantial war, with large numbers of troops on each side, we have been unable to locate adequate fatality statistics. Clodfelter (2002) very briefly reviews "Campaigns in Kashgaria" of 1825–1831 and claims that the fatalities on both sides totaled 40,000 for the entire six-year period, which would include this war as well as war #1508. Phillips and Axelrod do not include this war.

Sources: Clodfelter (2002); Fairbank (1978); Palmer (1957); Richardson (1960a); Saray (2003); Twitchett and Fairbank (1978).

NON-STATE WAR #1516:
The Siam-Cambodia-Vietnam War of 1831–1834

Participants: Siam vs. Cambodia, Vietnam
Dates: [ ]/[ ]/1831, to [ ]/[ ]/1834
Battle-Related Deaths: Siam—[ ]; Cambodia, Vietnam—[ ] (Total Combatant and Civilian Deaths: 22,000)
Where Fought: Asia
Initiator: Siam
Outcome: Cambodia, Vietnam win
War Type: In nonstate territory

Narrative: In 1831 Cambodia was an autonomous entity caught between the growing colonial empires, with Britain expanding its influence in Burma and France spreading its interests in Vietnam. Cambodia was also caught between two powerful neighbors, Siam and Vietnam, both of which had designs on Cambodia. In 1802, Cambodia had adopted a policy of paying tribute to Siam and Vietnam and accepting guidance from both states. This policy became problematic in 1812 when both Siam and Vietnam sent troops into Cambodia to support rival claimants (the king and his brother) to the Cambodian throne. King Ang Chan was able to regain his throne with the assistance of Vietnam, ruled by Emperor Minh Mang, and then became a Vietnamese vassal. The Siamese king, Rama II, withdrew his promotion of the usurper but continued to hold Cambodian territory. In 1831 the Siamese invaded Cambodia again. The Siamese commander P'ya Bodin (who had recently conquered Laos in non-state war #1511) was dispatched to seize Cambodia. He quickly took the key cities and won a major victory over the Cambodians at Kompong-Chnang, which caused King Ang Chan to flee to Vietnam. Siam's rule was brief, and a popular uprising against Siam began in Cambodia. The Vietnamese followed with a major counterattack in 1833. Emperor Minh Mang sent 15,000 troops to liberate the Mekong Delta from the Siamese invaders. The success of this operation not only led to the defeat and withdrawal of Siam's forces, but it also meant that Cambodia came under Vietnam's complete control. This lasted for seven years, until the resistance by the Cambodians persuaded the Vietnamese to accept a return to the 1802 practice of shared Siamese and Vietnamese control.

Coding: With 22,000 battle-related deaths, it is one of the more severe non-state wars. Clodfelter (2002) has an entry grouping "Siamese-Vietnamese Wars: 1811–45." Phillips and Axelrod (2005) have a "Siamese-Cambodian War" of 1831–1834.

Sources: Clodfelter (2002); Hall (1981); Kohn (1999); Paloczi-Horvath (1995); Phillips and Axelrod (2005); Schafer (1995); Wyatt (1984).

NON-STATE WAR #1518:

The Argentina-Ranqueles Indians War of 1833–1834

Participants: Argentina vs. Ranqueles Indians
Dates: March 16, 1833, to March 25, 1834
Battle-Related Deaths: Ranqueles Indians—
   6,000; Argentina—[ ]
Where Fought: Western Hemisphere
Initiator: Argentina
Outcome: Argentina wins
War Type: In nonstate territory

Narrative: During the 1820s the United Provinces of South America (which became the Republic of Argentina in 1826) was engaged in several conflicts over the degree of centralization suitable for the country (see earlier non-state wars #1503 and #1513 as well as extra-state war #315). During the periods of conflict in northern Argentina, the issue of the Argentine Indians and the control of the Pampas (the rich grassland area of Argentina) had been downplayed. However, after General Rosas came to power in the Argentine War for Unity in 1829–1831 (non-state war #1513), conflict in the northerly portions of Argentina subsided as the Unitarians and Federalists moved toward unity. The Rosas government then decided to attack the Indians to the south. The Argentine army of 3,800 troops was split into a three-prong offensive that drove the native Argentines south to the Colorado River. Although the major offensive ended in 1834, for the next forty years the Indians retaliated by engaging in a series of attacks against the army and border towns. The Argentine government did conduct a number of ineffective campaigns against Indians, at below war-level hostilities; however, in 1879–1880, another war, intra-state #608, was fought against the Patagonian Indians.

Coding: Neither Clodfelter nor Phillips and Axelrod cover this war.

Sources: Richardson (1960a); Scheina (2003a); Sulé (2003).

NON-STATE WAR #1520:

The Bolivia Conquest of Peru in 1835–1836

Participants: Bolivia vs. Peru
Dates: June 16, 1835, to February 7, 1836
Battle-Related Deaths: Peru—[ ]; Bolivia—[ ]
Where Fought: Western Hemisphere
Initiator: Bolivia
Outcome: Bolivia wins
War Type: In nonstate territory

Narrative: In 1829, at the end of the Peru-Gran Colombia War (non-state war #1512), Peru's plans for unity with Bolivia had been defeated; however, the goal of unity remained paramount among circles in both Peru and Bolivia. The debate over whether Peru should declare war on Bolivia divided the Peruvian government and precipitated an armed conflict in Peru in 1834. When Peru's liberal president Luis José de Obregoso was overthrown on February 23, 1835, Bolivia's president, Andrés de Santa Cruz, saw this as an opportunity to ensure the Bolivian conception of unity, and he entered into an agreement with Obregoso to cooperate in support of confederation. On June 16, 1835, a Bolivian force of 5,000 troops crossed into Peru, where they met a Peruvian force under former president Agustín Gamarra. Gamarra's force of 4,000 soldiers and 6,000 poorly armed Indians was defeated at Yanacocha on August 1. Gamarra fled the country, and the war was continued by conservative general Felipe Santiago de Salaverry. The armies of Salaverry and Santa Cruz met at the decisive battle of Socabaya on February 7, 1836. Salaverry's army was defeated, and Salaverry himself was executed. As a result the Bolivian plan for the confederation of Peru and Bolivia was implemented.

Coding: Both South Peru and North Peru declared themselves to be independent countries, and they united together with Bolivia to create the Bolivia-Peru Confederation, or the Confederation of the Andes. The Confederation existed for three years, until its dissolution in non-state war #1523.

Sources: Jaques (2007); Scheina (2003a).

NON-STATE WAR #1521:
The Boer-Matabele War of 1836–1837

Participants: Boer Trekkers vs. Matabele
Dates: August 15, 1836, to November 12, 1837
Battle-Related Deaths: Matabele—3,000; Boers—350

Where Fought: Africa
Initiator: Matabele
Outcome: Boers win
War Type: In nonstate territory

Narrative: The Boers were the rural descendants of Dutch colonists who had come to the Cape (southern tip of Africa) with the Dutch East India Company starting in 1650. When the British took the Cape a century and a half later, the Boers began to move out in what became known as the Great Trek. The Boers objected to British rule in general and specifically to the British outlawing of the slave trade. The Boers moved north in two columns, both of which came into contact with black south African tribes. One group led by Piet Retief headed eastward toward Natal, where it came in conflict with the Zulu (non-state war #1525). The other Boer group following A. H. Potgeiter, headed toward the Transvaal, where it encountered the Matabele (or Ndebele) people.

The Matabele had been battling encroachments by the Griquas and Zulu and preemptively decided to eliminate the new threat of the Boer invaders. On August 15, 1836, a Matabele expedition became aware of a group of Boers preparing a settlement on Matabele land. The warriors attacked and destroyed several different Boer contingents. In October a force of 5,000 Matabele attacked the Boers near the Vaal River, in a spot that later would be called "the Hill of the Fight" (Lye 1969, 94). The whites survived this assault by forming a circle with their wagons. During the rest of the year the Boers went on the offensive, defeating the Matabele and finally driving them north into what is now Zimbabwe, where they are the second-largest ethnic group.

Coding: Neither Clodfelter (2002) nor Phillips and Axelrod (2005) cover this war.

Sources: Crais (1992); Davidson (1972); Davis (2006); Fage and Oliver (1976); Hallett (1970); Lye (1969); Richardson (1960a); Thompson (1995).

NON-STATE WAR #1523:

The Dissolution of the Bolivia-Peru Confederation of 1837–1839

Participants: Argentina, Chile vs. the Bolivia-Peru Confederation
Dates: September 15, 1837, to January 20, 1839
Battle-Related Deaths: Peru, Bolivia—1,500; Chile—1,400; Argentina—100
Where Fought: Western Hemisphere
Initiator: Chile
Outcome: Chile wins
War Type: In nonstate territory

Narrative: For many of the colonial years Bolivia had been part of the Viceroyalty of Peru. In 1824, in extra-state war #312, Peru and Bolivia had gained independence from Spain as separate countries. In 1835 Bolivia mounted an expedition to conquer Peru and reunite the two countries (non-state war #1520). This effort temporarily succeeded, and the Bolivia-Peru Confederation, or the Confederation of the Andes, was created in October 1836. Chile and Argentina, however, felt threatened by the emergence of a larger country to their north, and thus they decided to attack into Bolivia-Peru to break up the fledgling confederation. In the initial stages of the conflict, Chile seized three Peruvian ships in August 1836. Chile then declared war on December 28, 1836, followed by Argentina on May 19, 1837. Sustained combat (and thus the war) began in September when a large contingent of Chilean forces was dispatched. The Chileans landed and were besieged at Arequipa (in Peru) by the forces of Marshal Andrés Santa Cruz, the Bolivian president, who had assumed the title of Protector of the Confederation. The invaders were weakened by smallpox and withdrew in November 1837 after signing the Treaty of Paucarpata. Chile subsequently repudiated the treaty, and the Chilean navy, which had blockaded the port of Callao, went on the offensive against the Confederation ships in January 1838. Meanwhile, Argentina had sent two armies

into Bolivia in April 1838, where they engaged in several skirmishes along the border. On June 24, 1838, Bolivian and Argentine forces met at the Battle of Montenegro, and when the troops from the Argentina were defeated, Argentina withdrew from the war. Chile established a base in northern Peru, where the Chilean forces met the Bolivian army of Santa Cruz in several engagements before the final confrontation at Yungay on January 20, 1939. In a bloody battle the Bolivians were defeated. Santa Cruz fled to Ecuador, and the Confederation came to an end. The idea of Peru-Bolivian unity remained, and conflict in the region returned in 1841 when the dictator of Peru, Agustín Gamarra, invaded Bolivia to try to incorporate it into Peru (extra-state war #325).

Coding: Many authors start this war on December 28, 1836, with the Chilean declaration of war; however, we start the war when Chilean troops were sent to Peru. Peru and Chile enter the state system in 1839 and Bolivia in 1848. Clodfelter calls this the "War of the Peruvian-Bolivian Confederation" of 1836–1839, as do Phillips and Axelrod.

Sources: Brecke (1999); Clodfelter (2002); Jaques (2007); Phillips and Axelrod (2005); Schafer (1995); Scheina (2003a).

NON-STATE WAR #1524:

The Persian Siege of Herat of 1837–1838

Participants: Persia vs. Herat
Dates: November 22, 1837, to September 9, 1838
Battle-Related Deaths: Persia—1,700; Herat—[ ]
Where Fought: Asia
Initiator: Persia
Outcome: Herat wins
War Type: In nonstate territory

Narrative: In the 1830s, Central Asia was the object of expansionist designs by Great Britain, Russia, and Persia. The area of Afghanistan was not yet unified and consisted of regions controlled by tribes and autonomous entities at

Kabul and Kandahar in the east and Herat in the northwest. Herat had been an important stop on the trade routes from China to Europe and India to Persia. It had also been at one time part of the Persian Empire, and Persia still had an interest in Herat because of historical and linguistic ties. The Persian Qajar dynasty of Muhammad Shah was waning, but he saw an opportunity to expand into a similarly weakened Afghanistan. At the urging of Russian czar Nicholas I, the Persian army of 40,000 troops, accompanied by Russian advisers, in November 1837 invaded Herat, which was defended by 4,000 troops under Vizier Yar Muhammad. Alarmed at the possibility of Russian influence in the region, the British assisted Herat during the nine-month siege. Capt. Eldred Potter of the British East India Company entered Herat in disguise and organized the city's defenses. The Persians conducted an assault on Herat on June 24, 1838, which was repulsed with heavy Persian losses. The British also occupied Kharg Island in the Persian Gulf and prepared an army in India for possible intervention. Consequently, the Qajar shah was persuaded to end the siege and return to Persia, ending the war. Herat was later captured by the Persians in 1852 but reconquered by the Afghans in 1863.

Coding: Herat is coded as an autonomous entity from 1819 to 1863; Persia is coded as an autonomous entity from 1816 until it becomes a member of the interstate system in 1855. Clodfelter (2002) has a "Persian-Afghan War" of 1836–1838, as do Phillips and Axelrod (2005).

Sources: Brecke (1999); Dupree (1973); Dupuy and Dupuy (1970); Jaques (2007); Richardson (1960a); Schafer (1995); Sivard (1991); Tanner (2002).

NON-STATE WAR #1525:
The Boer-Zulu War of 1838

Participants: Boer Trekkers vs. Zulu
Dates: February 6, 1838, to December 20, 1838
Battle-Related Deaths: Zulu—3,000; Boers—700

Where Fought: Africa
Initiator: Zulu
Outcome: Boers win
War Type: In nonstate territory

Narrative: The Correlates of War Project recognizes the Zulu as an autonomous entity starting in 1818, when they came together under the leadership of Shaka. The Zulu, located near Natal, soon thereafter faced two-pronged white pressure, from the British and the Boers. The Boers were the descendants of Dutch colonists who had come to the Cape starting in 1650. When the British took over the Cape in 1806, the Boers moved north in a migration known as the Great Trek of 1836. The Boer Trekkers moved north in two columns, both of which came into contact with black south African tribes. One group, following A. H. Potgeiter, headed toward the Transvaal and fought the Matabele (nonstate war #1521) in 1836–1837.

The other Boer group, led by Piet Retief, headed eastward toward Natal, along the Indian Ocean, where they encountered the Zulu. Initially, the Boers tried to negotiate a treaty with the Zulu, in which the Zulu would cede them the Natal area as a new Boer homeland. Although the Zulu at first seemed to agree, they used a ceremonial occasion as a trap to slaughter the Boer negotiators on February 6, 1838, which starts this war. Further Zulu attacks on the Boers ensued. The Zulu were then distracted by the arrival of a very large contingent of the British army on April 17, 1838. The Zulu managed to wipe out most of the British force in the First British-Zulu War (extra-state war #321). The Boers, impressed by this Zulu victory, tried to negotiate a settlement that would have been favorable to the Zulu, but the Zulu were now determined to continue the war against the Boers. In a sharp reversal, a Boer force won a major victory against a Zulu army of 12,000–16,000 warriors at a battle near the Ncome River in December 1838. Many of the fleeing Zulu jumped into the Ncome, where they were

slaughtered by the Boers. The Ncome was thereafter referred to as the Blood River and this
battle as the Battle of Blood River. The Zulu
then withdrew, ending the war.

After suffering devastating losses, including
many Zulu in the victory over the British column, the Zulu split politically. One Zulu leader,
Mpande, emerged as a seeker of peace with the
Boers, but his brother Dingaan urged further
warfare. The Boers agreed to cooperate with
Mpande. Mpande and Dingaan met in combat
in January 1840, at the Battle of Marango,
which was over before the Boer contingent
arrived. Dingaan's defeated contingent withdrew north into Swaziland. In an agreement
between Mpande's Zulu and the Boers, the
latter were able to establish a state in southern
Natal for three years. In 1843 the British
annexed this Afrikaner Republic of Natal to
the Cape Colony. The British would confront
the Zulu again in 1879 (extra-state war #380).
Many of the Boers then moved on to Transvaal
and the Orange Free State. This migration
would lead to wars with the British, notably
the First Boer War of 1880 (extra-state war
#382) and the Second Boer War of 1899–1902
(extra-state war #416).

Coding: Clodfelter (2002) describes this as the
"Boer-Zulu War" of 1838. Phillips and Axelrod
(2005) agree with the label but continue the war
to 1840.

Sources: Clodfelter (2002); Featherstone (1973);
Knight (2003); Kohn (1999); Oliver and Atmore
(1994); Phillips and Axelrod (2005); Stearns
(2001); Vandervort (1998); Williams (1907).

NON-STATE WAR #1527:
The Anti-Rosas War of 1839–1840

Participants: Anti-Rosas Allies vs. Rosas'
Federalist Army
Dates: February 24, 1839, to December 31, 1840
Battle-Related Deaths: Anti-Rosas Allies—2,500;
Rosas Federalist Army—500
Where Fought: Western Hemisphere

Initiator: Anti-Rosas Allies (Unitarians and
Colorados)
Outcome: Transformed into intra-state war #538
War Type: In nonstate territory

Narrative: The Argentine War for Unity of
1829–1831 (non-state war #1513) concerned the
relationship between the autonomous city of
Buenos Aires and the remaining Argentine provinces. The *porteños,* or people of the port of
Buenos Aires, favored a strong central government based in Buenos Aires, and this was known
as the Unitarian position. Those opposing were
the Federalists, favoring a loose confederation of
provinces. During the war a Federalist, Juan
Manuel de Rosas, the caudillo of the province of
Buenos Aires, and his allies gained control of the
coastal areas including Buenos Aires, creating
the "Littoral League." The Federalists defeated
the Unitarians in November 1831, and Rosas
remained in power.

The Unitarians then focused their attention
on events in Uruguay, where a conflict was raging
between the Blancos, headed by Manuel Oribe,
and the Colorados, headed by Fructuoso Rivera.
The Unitarians formed an alliance with Rivera,
who captured Montevideo on October 24, 1838.
Oribe fled to Argentina, where Rosas gave him a
military command. The Unitarians then
announced the creation of a government in exile
in Montevideo, and it, along with Rivera's Uruguay, declared war against Rosas (not against
Argentina) on February 24, 1839, which marks
the start of this war. Fighting commenced along
Argentina's coast, where the provincial governors
were divided among the Unitarians and Federalists. The governor of Corrientes was defeated and
killed at Pago Largo by the Federalists in March.
On September 2 a Unitarian force headed by
Gen. Juan Lavalle, whom Rosas had deposed
from Buenos Aires in 1829, landed in Entre Rios.
The Unitarians initially had some battle successes, including at Yerua on September 22, 1839;.
however, the Federalist forces of Gen. Pascual
Echague, governor of Entre Rios, defeated Lavalle

at Sauce Grande on July 16, 1840. Although the fighting continued, this war is ended on December 31, 1840 (see coding rules below).

Coding: Argentina entered the COW interstate system as of January 1, 1841, with Rosas as head of state. Thus the war against him became an intra-state civil war at that point, the First Argentina Phase 2, intra-state war #538.

Sources: Jaques (2007); Scheina (2003a).

NON-STATE WAR #1528:

The Dissolution of the Central American Confederation of 1839–1840

Participants: conservatives vs. liberals
Dates: March 19, 1839, to March 21, 1840
Battle-Related Deaths: liberals—2,000; conservatives—1,700
Where Fought: Western Hemisphere
Initiator: conservatives
Outcome: Conservatives win
War Type: In nonstate territory

Narrative: Once part of the Viceroyalty of New Spain (ruled from Mexico), Costa Rica, El Salvador, Guatemala, Honduras, and Nicaragua had been administratively united. After they received their independence in 1821, they decided to unite again in a Central American Confederation in 1825. However, ideological differences between the conservatives (mainly from Guatemala) and the liberals (from El Salvador and Honduras) led to war in 1826 (non-state war #1510). As a result of the liberal victory in the war, Gen. Francisco Morazán was named the new Confederation president, and he moved the capital to San Salvador. Nevertheless, the conflicts between the liberals and conservatives continued as they vied for control both of the Confederation as a whole and of the provinces. In terms of the Confederation, the conflict ultimately evolved into a struggle for control between Morazán and the conservative Rafael Carrera, who had been a soldier in the liberal Guatemalan army but had deserted and forged his own army among the Indians and peasants. In March 1838 Carrera's army was conducting guerrilla operations against the government in Guatemala City. The city requested assistance from Morazán, who led 1,000 Salvadoran troops to Guatemala. While Morazán was thus occupied, the Confederation began to dissolve, with Nicaragua seceding in April 1838. Morazán then returned to San Salvador in an attempt to stop the Confederation's disintegration. Meanwhile, the conservatives came to power in Guatemala, and they finally reached an agreement with Carrera, giving him a position as a military commander.

In 1839 Carrera formed a conservative alliance with Honduras and Nicaragua against Morazán. The war began on March 19, 1839, when conservative forces from Honduras and Nicaragua invaded El Salvador and defeated Morazán at Jicaral. Liberal forces were successful in routing the invaders at Espiritu Santo in April. They then went on the offensive under Gen. José Trinidad, who invaded Honduras, seizing the capital in September. The army under Morazán then reentered Guatemala and seized the capital; however, the tide had turned against the liberals. On March 19, 1840, a counterattack led by Carrera surrounded the liberals in Guatemala City. After fighting for three days, Morazán escaped the encirclement and fled on March 21, which ends the war. Morazán was forced into exile, though he made a final attempt to reestablish the Confederation in 1842 by defeating the government of Costa Rica. Morazán was ultimately overthrown and executed on September 15, 1842.

Coding: Clodfelter (2002) treats this as part of "Central American Wars" of 1822–1839. Similarly, Phillips and Axelrod (2005) devote a general passage to "Central American Federation Civil Wars of 1826–1829 and 1838–1840." COW sees these as two distinct wars, separated by almost a decade without war. We also do not include the period of conflict in 1838 (prior to this war) between Guatemala and Carrera's Indian army.

The battle-related death figures reported above are extrapolations from the totals provided by Clodfelter (2002), though as Scheina points out, these figures are probably understatements, since they apparently do not include deaths from disease.

Sources: Brecke (1999); Clodfelter (2002); Jaques (2007); Phillips and Axelrod (2005); Scheina (2003a); Woodward (1985).

NON-STATE WAR #1530:
The Dogra-Tibet War of 1841–1842

Participants: Jammu vs. Tibet
Dates: May [ ], 1841, to October 17, 1842
Battle-Related Deaths: Jammu—3,000; Tibet—1,000
Where Fought: Asia
Initiator: Jammu
Outcome: Compromise
War Type: In nonstate territory

Narrative: This war is called the Dogra-Tibet War in recognition of the fact that the Dogra was the ethnic group of the Hindu rulers of Jammu. Jammu was a princely political entity, which since the sixteenth century was part of Jammu and Kashmir. This area has long been a region of boundary disputes and warfare, since it shares borders with Afghanistan, China, and Tibet. During India's colonial period, this area constituted the northernmost of all the territories claimed by India. Since the partition of India and Pakistan, this area has been the site of competing claims by India and Pakistan.

In 1840 a disruption of the wool and tea trade had caused economic harm to Jammu. An alternative trade route had been developed as a result of a British endeavor to export opium through Tibet. Thus the Dogra concluded that a solution would be to capture western Tibet, thereby disrupting the newer route. Consequently, in May 1841 the Dogra sent an army of 6,000 men into Tibet in a three-pronged offensive. The Dogra army advanced into Tibet. The British, eager to maintain their own trade route, persuaded the Sikh rulers in Kashmir to order the Dogra commander to withdraw his forces, but the order had no effect. Similarly, the Ch'ing (Chinese) garrison in Tibet was powerless to stop the conflict. The Tibetans themselves, however, mounted a resistance to the invasion. The Dogra army was weakened by the increasing cold and by the reduction of supplies that reached them through the long supply lines. The Tibetans met the Dogra army in December 1841 and were able to kill the Dogra commander, Zorawar Singh, and repulse the army. The Tibetans, aided by China, advanced into Ladakh, where they were stopped by the Dogra army. The Dogra launched a second, larger expedition of 8,000 troops in 1842, which defeated the Tibetans at the Battle of Chushul in August, and continued hostilities in September. The war was ended in October 1842 with the signing of a treaty of peace at Leh. The outcome was an arranged territorial compromise. The Dogra renounced all claims to Tibet proper, but the Tibetans accepted Dogra supremacy over the region of Ladakh. Probably the most significant long-term outcome was the transfer of Ladakh from the Chinese orbit to that of the Indian subcontinent. This would be reversed in 1962, as an outcome of the Sino-Indian Assam war (inter-state war #160).

Coding: Four years later (1846) Jammu would buy Kashmir as a result of the First British-Sikh War (extra-state war #331). Developments in Kashmir would lead to another war for Gulab Singh, this one involving Kashmir (non-state war #1536). Neither Clodfelter (2002) nor Phillips and Axelrod (2005) cover this war.

Sources: Brecher (1953); Brecke (1999); Lamb (1960); Shakabpa (1967); Twitchett and Fairbank (1978).

NON-STATE WAR #1531:
The First Haiti-Santo Domingo War of 1844–1845

Participants: Santo Domingo vs. Haiti
Dates: February 27, 1844, to December 21, 1845

Battle-Related Deaths: Haiti—[ ]; Santo
   Domingo—[ ]
Where Fought: Western Hemisphere
Initiator: Santo Domingo
Outcome: Santo Domingo wins
War Type: In nonstate territory

Narrative: This war takes place on the large
Caribbean island of Hispañola. Today, the island
contains the Dominican Republic on the eastern
side, while the western region is Haiti. Spain's
activities on the island had begun with Christopher Columbus (1492) and his brother, Bartholomew Columbus, who founded the city of
Santo Domingo in 1496. The city became the
seat of the Spanish Captaincy-General of Santo
Domingo, which covered the Spanish Caribbean
islands. In 1697 the Spanish, who were unable to
control the whole island, ceded the western one-
third of the island to France. In 1795 the Spanish
gave up the whole island to the French. Spanish
control over the eastern portion was restored
after a rebellion against the French in 1808–
1809. The Spanish were ousted in 1821, and by
1822 the Haitians controlled the whole island.

In the 1830s a revolutionary movement began
in Santo Domingo against Haitian domination.
Juan Pablo Duarte organized La Trinitaria, a
secret society devoted to promoting independence. Duarte and the members of La Trinitaria
were able to gain the support of two Haitian
military regiments that consisted of Dominicans. They took advantage of a Haitian rebellion
against its dictator, Jean-Pierre Boyer, to begin
their own revolution by capturing the city of
Santo Domingo on March 24, 1843. The new
Haitian president, Charles Hérard, sent troops
to restore order in Santo Domingo. La Trinitaria's two regiments switched their allegiance to
Hérard, and Duarte was forced to flee to exile
in Venezuela. In an attempt to ameliorate the
opposition in Santo Domingo, Hérard implemented a number of reforms; however, by that
time the Dominicans had become committed
to independence. Among the Dominicans were
three general opposition groups with differing

goals. One group favored seeking Spanish assistance to combat the Haitians, while a second
favored seeking French assistance. The Trinitarios wanted complete independence without
relying on foreign assistance. The pro-French
contingent planned a coup against the Haitians
for April 25, 1844.

Meanwhile, the remaining members of La
Trinitaria continued to plan a rebellion, and on
January 16, 1844, they issued a call for a rebellion in pursuit of independence from Haiti.
They decided to preempt the pro-French plans,
and the war begins with the Trinitarios' seizure
of the fortress in Santo Domingo on February
27, 1844. However, the more conservative pro-
French faction took control of the revolutionary
junta in March. Hérard decided to subdue the
revolution and on March 7, 1844, Hérard sent a
30,000-man army in a three-pronged attack
against the rebels. Initially most of the fighting
consisted of skirmishes won by the Haitians;
however, on March 19 the rebel forces under
Gen. Pedro Santana defeated a Haitian force at
the Battle of Azua. The rebels were also victorious against a second Haitian army under Gen.
Jean Louis Pierrot in the Battle of Santiago on
March 30. The rebels were similarly successful in
naval battles. Meanwhile the Trinitarios arranged
to repatriate Juan Pablo Duarte on March 15.
Duarte and Santana disagreed over war strategy,
with Santana favoring a more defensive strategy
while seeking French assistance. The clash
prompted the Trinitarios to stage a coup, seizing
control of the revolutionary movement in June.
When the Trinitarios attempted to replace Santana as military commander, he removed his
army to Santo Domingo where he proclaimed
himself president. Santana arranged for the
arrest of the leaders of the Trintarios and sent
them into exile.

Meanwhile, as a consequence of the Haitian
losses, President Hérard was overthrown on May
3, 1844, which led to a temporary lull in hostilities. The new president, Gen. Phillipe Guerrier,
died within eleven months and was replaced on

April 16, 1845, by Gen. Jean Louis Pierrot, who resumed the war against the rebels in 1845. The Dominicans responded with an attack into Haiti in June, but they were repulsed. Subsequent Haitian offensives in September and October were defeated. The Haitian fleet was no more successful. A Haitian squadron carrying troops was driven aground on December 21, 1845, and the admiral was captured by the rebels. This marks the end of this war. When Pierrot tried to begin a new campaign in 1846, he was overthrown on February 27.

Coding: Clodfelter (2002, 338) claims that there are no accurate battle-death statistics available for this war though he does argue that fatalities were high for both parties and that Haitian losses were probably twice as high as the Dominicans' losses. The war is coded as a victory for Santo Domingo, since the Haitians were expelled from the east and the Dominican Republic was proclaimed in 1844; however, the issue of the relationship of Haiti and the Dominican Republic was not resolved. Haiti would attack the Dominican Republic in 1849, though the conflict did not reach war-level fatalities. The two parties would go to war again in 1855 (non-state war #1538). In 1861 the Dominican Republic fell back under Spanish colonial control, thus COW codes the Dominican Republic as an autonomous entity from 1844 to 1861. Clodfelter (2002) combines a series of wars together in an entry on "Haitian-Dominican Wars: 1844, 1845, 1849, 1854–56." Phillips and Axelrod have an entry for "Santo Domingo, Uprising in 1844."

Sources: Bird (1971); Clodfelter (2002); Heinl (1996); Moya Pons (1995); Phillips and Axelrod (2005); Scheina (2003a).

NON-STATE WAR #1533:
The War of the Seven Khojas of 1847–1848

Participants: Khojas vs. China
Dates: [ ]/[ ]/1847, to January [ ], 1848
Battle-Related Deaths: Khojas—[ ]; China—[ ]
Where Fought: Asia

Initiator: Khojas
Outcome: China wins
War Type: In nonstate territory

Narrative: This is the third non-state war to in some way involve the Central Asian Khanate of Kokand and China (see non-state wars #1508 and #1515), though in this case Kokand was not a war participant. Kokand was interested in expanding its influence eastward into Chinese Turkestan (Kashgaria and Xinjiang) primarily in order to control trade routes. Kokand was a base for the Khojas, who were traders in the region who had converted to Islam. The activities of the Khojas had contributed to the two earlier wars and, as a result, in the 1831 agreement between China and Kokand, which ended the 1830–1831 war (non-state war #1515), Kokand gained control over the trade in the region but had to pledge to prevent the Khojas from leaving Kokand's territory.

However, in the spring of 1847, seven of the Khoja leaders organized a unified army that included Kokandis, émigré Kashgaris, and Kirghiz, under the leadership of Katta Tora (Muhammad Amin). The Khoja army marched into Kashgaria, defeating the Chinese at Min-Yol. The Chinese retreated to Kashgar, where the 3,000 Chinese troops were besieged at the fort when substantial numbers of the populace joined in the fighting. Other locals, however, recalled the defeat of the invasion led by Jahangir (non-state war #1508) and remained on the sidelines. The Khoja army overwhelmed the Chinese and occupied Kashgar, proclaiming Katta Tora as Khan (ruler). China sent reinforcements, committing up to 10,000 soldiers in this campaign. The Chinese force won a series of engagements, and the invaders retreated to Kokand. Along with them went up to 100,000 Kashgari civilians, most of whom died from exposure to the cold (Richardson 1960a, 81).

Coding: The Khojas and China would fight one more war in 1857 (non-state war #1543). By 1865, however, Kokand was fully incorporated into

Russian control (see extra-state war #359). Thus czarist conquests in Central Asia brought the era of Chinese-Muslim wars involving Kokand to a close. Neither Clodfelter nor Phillips and Axelrod cover this war.

Sources: Brecke (1999); Richardson (1960a); Saray (2003); Twitchett and Fairbank (1978).

NON-STATE WAR #1534:
The Taiping Rebellion Phase 1 of 1850–1860

Participants: Taiping rebels vs. China
Dates: December [ ], 1850, to October 24, 1860
Battle-Related Deaths: China—290,000; Taiping rebels—240,000
Where Fought: Asia
Initiator: China
Outcome: Transformed into intra-state war #567
War Type: In nonstate territory

Narrative: The Taiping (or T'ai P'ing) movement began as a predominantly religious movement, founded by Hung Hsiu-ch'uan, who had had visions that he connected to the Christian Gospels. Thus Hung Hsiu-ch'uan's teachings were a variant of Christianity, though he ultimately earned the condemnation of the majority of Christian missionaries in China. Hung Hsiu-ch'uan began by doing missionary work among his own clan, the Hakka, and in 1846 developed a following, referred to as the Society of God Worshippers. As Hung Hsiu-ch'uan's popularity grew, he began condemning all existing religions, criticisms that the Manchu government considered to be subversive. The war began in December 1850 when the government issued orders for Hung Hsiu-ch'uan's arrest and for the suppression of his followers. His followers in Guangxi province resisted and took up arms against the government. The rebels were successful in limited engagements with provincial troops, and they were able to capture the small city of Yung An, where, in 1851, Hsiu-ch'uan proclaimed the Great Peaceful Heavenly

Dynasty (or the T'ai P'ing T'ien Kuo), with himself as the Heavenly King (or T'ien Wang) (Fitzgerald 1967, 574). From the base in Yung An, the rebels announced an anti-Manchu revolution and began spreading northward, capturing virtually all the cities in their path including the southern capital of Nanking on March 8, 1853. At this stage, the Taiping army consisted of 750,000 soldiers, which caused over 30,000 deaths in the battle for Nanking alone. In Nanking, T'ien Wang settled and began creating an administrative apparatus. The Taiping were also noted for their relatively equal treatment of women, even including female soldiers in their armies. Though the Taiping continued to send out military expeditions, they were unsuccessful in expanding their influence into northern China. They were, however, able to able to withstand three sieges and to hold Nanking for eleven years. The warfare continued incessantly from 1856 to 1859.

Ultimately, the Taiping Rebellion was suppressed as a result of foreign intervention in China. The latter years of the rebellion overlapped with the Second Opium War (or the Arrow War, extra-state war #343), from 1856 to 1860, during which France and Great Britain went to war with China to secure trade access to China. The Manchu government in essence utilized the issue of the opium trade, which the Western powers favored and which the Taiping did not, to divide its opponents. As a result, the Manchus were able to grant improved trade concessions to France and Britain in exchange for their assistance in fighting the Taiping. French and British troops aided the Manchu government to defend Shanghi in August 1860.

Coding: China becomes a member of the interstate system on October 25, 1860, thus this non-state war ends at that point and the fighting is transformed into a civil war (intra-state war #567), which continues until 1866. The Taiping Rebellion was one of the world's deadliest wars, primarily due to the number of civilians killed. Overall fatality estimates for combatants and civilians have ranged from 9 to 40 million lives lost, with Clodfelter (2002) estimating 20 million. Traditionally, COW has estimated 2 million combatant and civilian deaths for the three-and-a-half-year intra-state phase in the 1860s, and, accepting the overall 20 million figure would leave the remainder (as many as 18 million deaths) for the ten-year non-state phase. Battle-related death estimates for combatants for each side also are uncertain. As Clodfelter (2002, 256) notes, most of the civilian deaths during this period were due to disease and starvation. He concludes that combatant battle-related deaths numbered in the hundreds of thousands, since this was not a war of large-scale battles. The battle-related death figures cited above follow Clodfelter's treatment and are derived from attempts to combine the statistics from individual battles. These figures may also be underestimates because they probably do not include combatant fatalities from disease. However, the ratio of deaths between the parties does reflect the higher fatality level for the Chinese government during the first non-state phase when the Taiping were winning the war. The Taiping suffered more deaths than the Chinese in the second intra-state war phase.

Sources: Clodfelter (2002); Elleman (2001); Fitzgerald (1967); Michael and Chang (1966–1971); Phillips and Axelrod (2005); Spence (1996); Stearns (2001); Yu (2002).

NON-STATE WAR #1535:
The First Tukulor War of 1852–1854

Participants: Tukulor vs. Malinke, Bambara
Dates: [ ]/[ ]/1852, to [ ]/[ ]/1854
Battle-Related Deaths: Malinke, Bambara—6,000; Tukulor—4,000
Where Fought: Africa
Initiator: Tukulor
Outcome: Tukulor win
War Type: In nonstate territory

Narrative: The Tukulor inhabited an area called Tekrur, in West Africa along the Senegal River, in what is now Guinea. In the eleventh century they converted to Islam and extended their influence northward into Morocco. The Mali Empire conquered Tekrur in the fourteenth century and remained dominant until the mid-nineteenth century. In 1826 a Tukulor cleric named Umar Tal went to Mecca and was initiated into an Islamic brotherhood (Tijaniyya). This gave him the honorific name al-Hajj Umar. He wanted to restore the purification of Islam in western Africa and to revive the importance of Tekrur by waging a jihad. In the 1850s, al-Hajj Umar began to attack and conquer a number of neighboring entities and thus plunged the region now known as Mali into a decade-long period of warfare.

In 1852 Umar began the war by moving northward, where he successfully attacked the relatively small Malinke tribe. This victory prompted many followers to join the jihad. When Umar next turned westward to attack the "pagan" Bambara tribe, he fielded an army of 50,000, compared with the 10,000 troops of the Bambara and this war ends as a Tukulor victory. After conquering the Bambara, Umar planned to spread his influence further westward; however, this brought him into conflict with the French, who were trying to expand their colonial empire eastward from Saint-Louis, on the Atlantic coast. The jihad then becomes an extra-state war (#340) of the Tukulor against the French from 1854 to 1857. At the conclusion of that war, Umar Tal realized that he had to forgo westward expansion, and he shifted to attacking the Segu and Masina tribes in the east in the Second Tukulor War of 1860–1862 (non-state war #1546).

Coding: Clodfelter (2002) does not cover this war. Phillips and Axelrod (2005) briefly discuss this war in the context of the "Tukulor-French Wars (1854–1864)."

Sources: Fage (1969); Oliver and Atmore (1981); Phillips and Axelrod (2005); Robinson (1988); Stearns (2001); Vandervort (1998).

NON-STATE WAR #1536:
The Kashmir-Dards War of 1852

Participants: Jammu and Kashmir vs. Dards
Dates: spring 1852 to [ ]/[ ]/1852
Battle-Related Deaths: Jammu and Kashmir—
[1,600]; Dards—[400]
Where Fought: Asia
Initiator: Dards
Outcome: Dards win
War Type: In nonstate territory

Narrative: This war took place in the northern reaches of what is now Pakistan, in the region of Gilgit. To the south of Gilgit lies Kashmir. Prior to 1846, Kashmir and Gilgit had been ruled by the Sikhs of Punjab. Gilgit was inhabited by the Dards ethnic group, and in the 1840s, the Dards in the area of Chilas had launched raids into the Astore Valley and captured many of its residents as slaves. This prompted an expedition in 1842 by Punjab to restore order in the region. In 1846, as a result of the First British-Sikh War of 1845–1846 (extra-state war #331), Britain conquered Punjab, and Kashmir and Gilgit were sold to the Hindu ruler (maharaja) of Jammu, Gulab Singh, (in recognition of his assistance during the war), thus creating the modern state of Jammu and Kashmir.

Though Gulab Singh had defined the eastern border of his domain with Tibet in 1842 (non-state war #1530), the northern border of Kashmir was undefined, especially in the northern area of Gilgit. Gulab Singh had some difficulty in establishing control in Kashmir. Consequently he asked for British assistance, and Britain sent an army of 10,000 soldiers which intimidated the Kashmiris into submission. Gulab Singh also sent troops to take possession of Gilgit. However, the initial period of stability did not last. In 1848 the rajas of Hunza and Yasin Raja defeated the Kashmiri forces and seized Gilgit. Though Gulab Singh's Dogra (ethnic group) army soon regained control, a second uprising began in 1852. Gaur Rahman, the raja of Yasin, surrounded two forts occupied by Gulab Singh's forces. A relief column of 1,200 men led by Bhup Singh was trapped by the Dards and annihilated. Other efforts to relieve the forts also met with disaster. Gaur Rahman thus expelled the Jammu and Kashmir forces and ruled Gilgit for the next eight years until Jammu and Kashmir reestablished control in 1860.

Coding: Neither Clodfelter nor Phillips and Axelrod cover this war.

Sources: Brecher (1953); Brecke (1999); Bamzai (1994); Drew (1877); Kadian (1993); Richardson (1960a).

NON-STATE WAR #1537:
The Han-Miao War Phase 1 of 1854–1860

Participants: Han vs. Miao
Dates: March 24, 1854, to October 24, 1860
Battle-Related Deaths: Han—[ ]; Miao—[ ]
Where Fought: Asia
Initiator: Miao
Outcome: Transformed to intra-state war #570
War Type: In nonstate territory

Narrative: During the 1850s the Han Ch'ing government of China faced a number of serious threats. The most critical domestic threat was that posed by the Taiping Rebellion, which had begun in 1850 in the southeastern province of Guangxi (non-state war #1534). Though the Taiping Rebellion had begun primarily as a religious-based challenge to imperial rule, discontent with the central government arose at this time from other sources, as well. The population explosion in China fueled migration and competition for territory and resources, while natural disasters and repressive governmental policies all contributed to discontent in a number of provinces. In 1854 a rebellion was launched in the southern province of Guizhou. This rebellion has come to be referred to as the Miao Rebellion, named after one of the primary ethnic group participants. However, as Robert Jenks has argued (1994, 3), this title is misleading in that it highlights ethnic differences and ignores the collaborative roles that other ethnic and religious groups, including disgruntled Han and the White Lotus Society, played in the revolt throughout Guizhou.

The rebellion was launched by Yang Yuanbao, who was angered by the increased taxation imposed on the poor by the province to fund the war against the Taiping. Although Yang Yuanbao was soon arrested and died in prison, the challenge to the government was continued by a growing number of rebels. On September 27, 1854, the rebels, under the leadership of Yang Longxi, seized control of the city of Tongzi. Many of the government troops had been sent to fight the Taiping, and the rebels were able to conduct attacks throughout the province. Yang Longxi was killed in 1855, but the rebellion continued to grow, fueled by growing poverty among the people. Many of the towns were besieged by the rebels for extended periods, and even though reinforcements of imperial troops were sent from nearby provinces, they were unable to deal with the widespread rebellion. The government officials were also concerned that the Muslim rebellion that had broken out in 1856 in neighboring Yunnan province (nonstate war #1541) might spread to Guizhou, as well. In 1857 and 1858 groups called the White Signals and the Yellow Signals, owing to the colors of their flags and turbans, joined the rebellion. They relied more on hit-and-run tactics, as opposed to the Miao preference for seizing territory. By 1860 the provincial capital was being threatened by the rebels.

Coding: This non-state war ends on October 24, 1860. China becomes a member of the COW interstate system on October 25, partially as a result of the Second Opium War (extra-state war #343), by which Britain and France gain expanded trading rights in China. Thus after this point, wars against the Chinese government are intra-state civil wars. The fighting involving the China

and the Miao continued (intra-state war #570). As with the other wars involving China during this period, there are rarely any reliable battle-related death figures for combatants. Jenks (1994) notes that one estimate is that 4.9 million deaths could be attributed to the Miao revolt over the entire 1854–1873 period. Most of these deaths would, of course, have been among civilians, not combatants, but the total reveals something about the severity of this war.

Sources: Clodfelter (2002); Elleman (2001); Jenks (1994); Phillips and Axelrod (2005).

NON-STATE WAR #1538:

The Second Haiti-Santo Domingo War of 1855–1856

Participants: Haiti vs. Dominican Republic
Dates: November [ ], 1855, to January 27, 1856
Battle-Related Deaths: Haiti—[ ]; Dominican Republic—[ ]
Where Fought: Western Hemisphere
Initiator: Haiti
Outcome: Dominican Republic wins
War Type: In nonstate territory

Narrative: Haiti and Santo Domingo shared the island of Hispaniola. Between 1822 and 1844 the smaller nation of Haiti controlled its larger neighbor; however, as a result of the First Haiti-Santo Domingo War (non-state war #1531), Santo Domingo won its independence and the creation of the Dominican Republic was declared in 1844. Nevertheless, Haiti was not reconciled to its loss and invaded the Dominican Republic again in 1849 in an unsuccessful attempt to regain its former territory (though fatality levels were insufficient for a war classification). Haiti again attempted to reassert its control in this 1855–1856 war.

In the 1850s the United States was in the throes of expansionist fervor, primarily for economic reasons. It was advocated that the United States should gain control of the Caribbean islands in general, though the Dominican Republic was often specifically mentioned, in order to control its commerce. There was also a faction that advocated colonization in the Caribbean as a means to address the slavery issue. Consequently, Emperor Faustian I of Haiti (Soulouque) was concerned about the possible outcome of annexation talks between the Dominican and U.S. governments. Thus he purportedly ordered the invasion of the Dominican Republic in 1855 in order to avoid a possible annexation of all or part of it by the slaveholding United States. The attack was also timed to occur while the British and French were distracted by the Crimean War. Haitian troop strength may have reached 30,000. Similarly to the 1844 war, the Haitian army invaded the Dominican Republic from the north, center, and south. The northern and southern columns were both defeated on the same day, December 22, 1856. Haitian losses totaled 695 men in the south alone. The Dominicans were also victorious in the Battle of Sabana Larga, which was a contest between approximately 8,000 Dominicans and 22,000 Haitians on January 27, 1856, in which thousands died. Following this decisive battle the Haitians retreated from the Dominican Republic and the war ended.

Coding: In order to emphasize the linkage between this war and the 1844 war, we have referred to this war as the Second Haiti-Santo Domingo War, even though the name the Dominican Republic had been adopted by this time. In 1861 the Dominican Republic fell back under Spanish colonial control; thus we code the Dominican Republic as an autonomous entity from 1844 to 1861. Santo-Domingo would chafe under Spanish rule, however, and war broke out again in 1863 (extra-state war #353).

Clodfelter (2002, 338) claims that there are no accurate battle-death statistics available for this war. He does argue that fatalities were high for both parties and that Haitian losses were probably twice as high as those for the Dominicans. Clodfelter (2002) combines a series of wars together in an entry on "Haitian-Dominican Wars: 1844, 1845, 1849, 1854–56." Phillips and Axelrod do not include this war.

Sources: Clodfelter (2002); LaFeber (1994); Scheina (2003a).

NON-STATE WAR #1539:

The Han-Nien War of 1855–1858

Participants: Han vs. Nien
Dates: [ ]/[ ]/1855, to [ ]/[ ]/1858
Battle-Related Deaths: Han—[ ]; Nien—[ ]
Where Fought: Asia
Initiator: Nien
Outcome: Stalemate
War Type: In nonstate territory

Narrative: The Nien lived in Anhui province, and though they were generally farmers, they also engaged in banditry and salt smuggling. Anhui province was subject to frequent natural disasters, and in the early 1850s floods caused hardships among the peasants and resentment toward the rich. This dissatisfaction was later fueled by the arrival of the Taiping religious movement (see non-state war #1534). In 1854 some of the Nien joined the Taiping army when it took control of northern Anhui; however, in 1855 the Nien took advantage of the Han (Ch'ing) government's preoccupation with the Taiping to establish their own rebel movement. At this time the Nien were led by Zhang Luoxing, who united the four Nien bands into the "Nien League." The Nien army also adopted the title Da Han, or "Great Chinese" (Elleman 2001, 59). Han forces defeated the Nien in 1855; nevertheless, by the following year the Nien had over 1 million followers. The Nien also allied with the Taiping at that point, and the two armies launched a combined offensive into Henan province in 1856–1857. The attack was repulsed by imperial forces. In 1858 one of the Nien bands broke with the Taiping and joined the Manchu army. The bulk of the Nien forces withdrew from the fighting and returned to Anhui, which marks the end of this war.

Coding: The Nien resumed their fight against the Ch'ing government in 1860. By October of that year, however, China is considered to have become a member of the COW interstate system, so the second phase of the conflict between the Nien and the Chinese government is thus a civil war (intrastate war #568).

Sources: Clodfelter (2002); Elleman (2001); Stearns (2001).

NON-STATE WAR #1540:

The Filibuster War of 1856–1857

Participants: Nicaragua vs. Costa Rica, Honduras, Guatemala, and El Salvador
Dates: February 26, 1856, to May 1, 1857
Battle-Related Deaths: Central American Allies—6,700; Walker's Nicaragua—1,000
Where Fought: Western Hemisphere
Initiator: Costa Rica
Outcome: Central American Allies win
War Type: In nonstate territory

Narrative: After achieving their independence from Spain, Costa Rica, El Salvador, Guatemala, Honduras, and Nicaragua combined to form the Central American Confederation in 1825. Ideological differences between the liberals and conservatives, however, led to the destruction of the Confederation in 1840 (non-state war #1528). The ideological conflict continued within Nicaragua, with the liberals based at Leon and the conservatives at Granada. Politics in Nicaragua were also disrupted by Great Britain and the United States, which along with American industrialist Cornelius Vanderbilt, were interested in gaining access to Nicaragua as the location of a possible transisthmian canal. In 1855 the conflict between the conservatives and liberals had becomes more severe, and the liberals approached William Walker for assistance. Walker was a "filibuster," an American soldier of fortune who had created a personal army in an attempt to spread democracy to Mexico. He agreed to become involved and sailed from San Francisco to Nicaragua with fifty-six men to fight as mercenaries for the liberals. With the assistance of Vanderbilt,

Walker expanded his army and seized control in Granada on October 13, 1855. Becoming the generalissimo of the army, Walker essentially ran the country through the figurehead president Patricio Rivas, a moderate conservative.

During 1855 and 1856, Walker alienated his benefactor by planning to take control of Vanderbilt's Accessory Transit (railroad) Company, and Vanderbilt began to promote a revolution against Walker. On February 26, 1856, Costa Rica declared war on Nicaragua, supported by a $100,000 loan from Peru and financial support from Vanderbilt. Nicaraguan president Rivas immediately declared war on Costa Rica in return. Costa Rican president Juan Rafael Mora led his army against Walker's forces in battle in March 1856. On April 11 approximately 2,500 to 4,000 Costa Ricans defeated Walker's approximately 550–600 filibusters, with 150 Costa Ricans and 58 filibusters killed. Proving far more deadly than the battle itself, an epidemic of cholera afterward wiped out all but 400 remaining members of the Costa Rican army. Walker had himself selected as president of Nicaragua on June 29, 1856. Although American minister to Nicaragua John H. Wheeler recognized the new government, President Franklin Pierce overrode that decision. Walker responded by repealing Nicaragua's constitution of 1838, thereby opening the country to slavery in order to gain support from proslavery elements in the United States.

El Salvador, Guatemala, and Honduras banded together to oust Walker in late 1856, attacking Walker's capital, Granada, with approximately 4,000 troops. The city was defended by only 277 men, and after a seventeen-day battle, the 111 surviving filibusterers fled. Naval forces, controlling the seas and waterways, played a smaller yet still important role in the fighting. A filibuster schooner sank a Costa Rican brig off San Juan de Sur, resulting in the death of 74 of the 115 men aboard the vessel. In a typical land battle, Walker checked 2,000 Guatemalan troops with 400 men on March 16, 1857. In spite of this victory, the overwhelming strength of the allies soon forced him to fall back to Rivas. After the filibusters' numbers dwindled to only 300 men fit for action, Walker fled on May 1, 1857. Overall, Walker's Nicaragua had committed 2,578 troops to the war against the allies' 17,800. In 1860 Walker was captured by the British while trying to intervene in Honduras. They turned him over to the Hondurans, who put Walker before a firing squad. In modern-day Central America, Walker's name lives on and is synonymous with North American arrogance and avarice.

Coding: Of the Central American battle-related deaths, 5,000 were from disease. Clodfelter (2002) addresses the "Filibuster War: 1856–57," while Phillips and Axelrod (2005) call it "Walker's Invasion of Nicaragua (1855–1857)."

Sources: Brecke (1999); Clodfelter (2002); LaFeber (1994); Richardson (1960a); Scheina (2003a).

NON-STATE WAR #1541:
The Han-Panthay War Phase 1 of 1856–1860

Participants: Han vs. Yunnan Muslims
Dates: May 19, 1856, to October 24, 1860
Battle-Related Deaths: Han—[ ]; Yunnan Muslims—[ ]
Where Fought: Asia
Initiator: Han officials
Outcome: Transformed into intra-state war #571
War Type: In nonstate territory

Narrative: Yunnan province is located in southwest China. The Muslims there (also referred to as the Hui or the Panthay by the British) were a minority group, and they felt that they had been discriminated against by the government taxation policies and by the recent influx of majority Han Chinese immigrants, which even had private militias called *tuanlian* that were dedicated to eliminating Muslims (Elleman 2001, 64). Beginning in the 1830s the militias, with the consent of the government officials, began attacks on Muslims in the area. In 1853 the Yunnan governor issued a declaration to all government officials to eliminate the Muslims from the province. The specific precipitant of this war was a massacre of 4,000 to 7,000 Muslims in the Yunnan city of Kunming on May 19, 1856. The massacre was conducted by imperial officials, Han militias, and the Han townspeople. Official orders were issued to burn the mosques and exterminate all Muslims. What the Han had not anticipated was the intensity of the Muslim resistance. In September 1856 the Muslims under the leadership of Du Wenxiu seized the city of Dali, where they established a "Kingdom of the Pacified South," with Du Wenxiu as its sultan. The Panthay continued their rebellion, seizing a growing number of cities throughout the southern and eastern regions of the province. The local officials simply did not have enough troops to cope with the attacks by the Muslim army, which numbered 350,000 by 1868. Unlike the Nien, who had begun a rebellion in 1855 (non-state war #1539), the Panthay had a broader political goal of creating an independent Muslim state, though one that also maintained its Han heritage.

Coding: This non-state war ends on October 24, 1860. China becomes a member of the COW interstate system on October 25, partially as a result of the Second Opium War (extra-state war #343), by which Britain and France gained expanded trading rights in China. Thus after this point, wars against the Chinese government are intra-state civil wars. The fighting involving the China and the Panthay continues in intra-state war #571. We have kept the term Panthay in the name of this war, despite the fact that it was not one used by the Muslims themselves. As Atwill (2003, 1079) argues, the term Panthay was mistakenly applied by the British; however, since it is widely recognized in terms of this war, creating a different title would cause more ambiguity than clarity. Clodfelter (2002) only briefly addresses this war, and Phillips and Axelrod (2005) only mention it in one short essay on all the "Chinese Revolts (1865–1881)."

Sources: Atwill (2003); Clodfelter (2002); Elleman (2001); Phillips and Axelrod (2005); Stearns (2001).

NON-STATE WAR #1542:

The First Zulu Internecine War of 1856

Participants: Mbuyazi's faction vs. Cetshwayo's faction
Dates: December 2, 1856
Battle-Related Deaths: Mbuyazi's faction—5,000; Cetshwayo's faction—[ ]
Where Fought: Africa
Initiator: Mbuyazi's faction
Outcome: Cetshwayo's faction wins
War Type: In nonstate territory

Narrative: The Zulu had created a large empire in southern Africa, in what is now the KwaZulu/Natal province of South Africa, beginning in 1819 (non-state war #1501). Since then the tribe and its territory had been reduced via conflicts with the Boers and British (non-state war #1525 and extra-state war #321). This internal war weakened them further, thus preparing the way for further defeats at the hands of the Europeans and final annexation by the British in the Second British-Zulu war in 1879 (extra-state war #380).

King Mpande of the Zulu had delayed naming an heir lest that undermine his own kingship. Furthermore he sought to pit the contenders against each other. Two of his sons, half-brothers Cetshwayo (or Cetewayo) and Mbuyazi (or Mbulazi), were the most likely to succeed their father. Each man recruited supporters from among the Zulu chiefs. The contenders decided to settle the succession issue in a one-day battle. The two factions clashed at the Battle of the Thukela River on December 2, 1856. Cetshwayo's army of 15,000 to 20,000 was three times that of Mbuyazi (Knight 1998, 59). Although Mbuyazi's forces initially held their positions, they were gradually forced to retreat by Cetshwayo's advance. As they approached the Thukela River, the warriors became entangled in their fleeing civilian supporters, virtually all of whom were killed by Cetshwayo's forces. This battle, later known as the Battle of 'Ndondakusuka

("the place of bones"), was one of the bloodiest battles in Zulu history. With his victory, Cetshwayo secured his position as Mpande's successor, though he did not take the throne itself until the death of his father by natural causes, sixteen years later. When the British invaded Zululand in 1879, Cetshwayo, having by then acceded to the throne, opposed them (in extra-state war #380).

Coding: Knight (1998, 65) concludes that 10,000 to 15,000 noncombatants were killed during the war. He also indicates that figures for losses among Cetshwayo's forces are unknown. Clodfelter's (2002) estimate of 3,000 total deaths seems conservative. Clodfelter does not have a separate entry on this civil war but discusses it under the heading "Zulu War: 1879," which focuses mainly on our extra-state war #380. Phillips and Axelrod (2005) have the "Zulu Civil War" of 1856.

Sources: Brownstone and Frank (1994); Clodfelter (2002); Knight (1998); Knight (1995); Kohn (1999); Phillips and Axelrod (2005); Sivard (1991).

NON-STATE WAR #1543:

The Kucha and Khoja Uprising of 1857

Participants: Kucha and Khoja rebels vs. China
Dates: [ ]/[ ]/1857, to September [ ], 1857
Battle-Related Deaths: Kucha—[ ]; Khoja—[ ]; China—[ ] (Total Combatant Deaths: 2,500)
Where Fought: Asia
Initiator: Kucha rebels
Outcome: China wins
War Type: In nonstate territory

Narrative: The Xinjiang region in westernmost China had experienced varying levels of Chinese control for 2,000 years. Xinjiang includes Kashgaria, the site of three previous non-state wars (#1508, #1515, and #1533), and Kucha, which is halfway across the Trim Basin toward China, farther east than Kashgaria. The outbreak of this war in Kucha reflects the sense that the western unrest had spread closer to China's heartland.

At the time of this war the Ch'ing dynasty was being weakened by such internal conflicts as the Taiping Rebellion (non-state war #1534) and revolts by the Miao, the Nien, and the Panthay (non-state wars #1537, #1539, and #1541), as well as by European encroachment (the Second Opium War, extra-state war #343). Thus the Kucha saw an opportunity to promote their independence, and they were aided by the Khojas (traders who had converted to Islam) based in Kokand.

The Kucha people were divided between Muslims and non-Muslims; however, the Muslims in particular had become disenchanted with Han Ch'ing rule, especially after thirty of the local Muslims were executed in 1855. Consequently, a Kucha uprising broke out in early 1857. The Ch'ing got the uprising under control quickly, but in May the Khojas, under the command of Wali Khan Tore, crossed the Chinese border and marched on Kashgar. The Khojas occupied Kashgar for approximately four months, during which time Wali Khan Tore proclaimed himself ruler of Kashgar. The Khoja army also beseiged Yarkand for seventy days, until Ch'ing relief forces arrived. By that time, the Khoja forces around Yarkand may have numbered up to tens of thousands. Nevertheless, in September the Ch'ing army defeated the Khojas, who retreated into Kokand, where Wali Khan Tore was given asylum by Khudayar Khan, the ruler of Kokand.

Coding: Kokand was not a direct participant in this war, though the Khojas were aided by leading Kokand citizens. By 1865 Kokand was fully incorporated into Russian control (extra-state war #359). Hence, czarist conquests in Central Asia brought to a close the era of Chinese-Muslim wars involving Kokand. This war is in neither Clodfelter (2002) nor Phillips and Axelrod (2002).

Sources: Fairbank (1978); Richardson (1960a); Saray (2003).

NON-STATE WAR #1544:

The First Boer-Basuto War of 1858

Participants: Boers (of the Orange Free State) vs. the Basuto
Dates: [ ]/[ ]/1858, to [ ]/[ ]/1858
Battle-Related Deaths: Basuto—[ ]; Boers—[ ]
Where Fought: Africa
Initiator: Boers
Outcome: Stalemate
War Type: In nonstate territory

Narrative: The Basuto (also referred to as the Sotho) emerged from the Bantu-speaking tribes that were scattering during the consolidation of power by Shaka Zulu (non-state war #1501). The Basuto were brought together under the leadership of Moshoeshoe, who founded a kingdom in what is now Lesotho in 1820; however, Moshoeshoe faced continuing threats from the Zulu as well as the British and the Boers. In the Great Trek, one of the Boer expeditions had headed eastward toward Natal, where they came in conflict with the Zulu (non-state war #1525). After the war the Boers were able to establish dominance over the area, founding the Afrikaner Republic of Natal in southern Natal. A scant three years later, in 1843, the British annexed the settlement to the Cape Colony. Many of the Boers then moved westward, north of the Orange River. In 1848 Britain annexed this region as the Orange River Sovereignty. At this point the Basuto were loosely allied to the British, and Moshoeshoe made continued appeals to the British for assistance in halting the Boer advance. Nevertheless, the British in essence gave two-thirds of the Basuto land to the Orange Free State. The British were unable to establish effective control over the Sovereignty, and they ultimately recognized the independence of the Transvaal in 1852 and the Orange Free State in 1854, both controlled by the Boers.

Under the terms of the British-Boer Sand River Convention, weapons were not to be supplied to the native inhabitants, and the Boers began a policy of seizing Basuto weapons. In general, the Boers of the Orange Free State would allocate territory that had been taken from the tribes to those tribes that were peaceful and accepted Boer rule. Otherwise, it was a policy of severity. Conflict between the Boers and Moshoeshoe's Basuto began in 1852 in response to the Boers' continued expansion and seizure of Basuto land. The two parties battled at below war levels from 1853 to 1854. In 1858 the spark for the Boer-Basuto war was the seizure of a number of Boer cattle by the Basuto. The Boers then launched a raid into Basuto land, triggering this war, and Moshoeshoe responded by declaring war on the Boers. The war took the form of cross-territory raids. Since the Basuto had a large army, they were generally able to hold on to their territory, even though Boers from Transvaal arrived to provide assistance to the Orange Free State. Paul Kruger, the future president of the South African Republic, finally assisted the Basuto in negotiating an agreement to end the war. The period of 1862 to 1864 involved a conflict among the Boers in Transvaal (nonstate war #1548). However, in 1865, war between the Boers and the Basuto would reemerge (nonstate war #1552).

Coding: The Boers would also be involved in two wars with the British, the First Boer War of 1880–1888 (extra-state war #382) and the Second Boer War of 1899–1902 (extra-state war #416). Clodfelter (2002) includes only one sentence about this war in an entry called "Basuto Wars: 1852–81." Cutter (2007) and Phillips and Axelrod (2005) refer to one "Basuto War" that lasts from 1856 to 1868, or 1858 to 1868, respectively. Especially because of the intervening war among the Boers in 1862–1864, we divide this period into two separate wars, the First and then a Second Boer-Basuto War in 1865–1866 (non-state war #1552).

Sources: Clodfelter (2002); Coplan and Quinlan (1997); Cutter (2007); Kruger (1902); Phillips and Axelrod (2005); Sillery (1952).

NON-STATE WAR #1545:

The First Ethiopian War of 1858–1861

Participants: Ethiopia vs. provincial princes
Dates: [ ]/[ ]/1858, to January [ ], 1861
Battle-Related Deaths: Tigray—[ ]; Ethiopia—[ ] (Total Combatant Deaths: 2,000)
Where Fought: Africa
Initiator: provincial princes
Outcome: Ethiopia wins
War Type: In nonstate territory

Narrative: For many centuries Ethiopia had rotated between having a centralized government and being divided among several regional polities. In 1855 Tewodros (Theodore) II reunited Ethiopia after a long period of disunion; however, fractures within his rule began appearing by 1858. Two provincial leaders, Wagshum Gebre Medhim of Lasta and Neguse Welde Mikail of Tigray and Begemdir, rebelled. After defeating the rebels, Tewodros was faced with uprisings in Welo and Showa (Shoa). He fought the rebels in Welo for one and a half years but easily overcame the resistance in Showa. Meanwhile Mikail reentered the fray by attacking Tigray. Conflicts in other regions prevented the emperor from dealing with this threat until January 1861. Eventually, the main opposition leaders including Mikail were defeated and killed, thus ending the war.

Warfare in Ethiopia continued, however. In 1867, Ethiopia went to war with Britain (extra-state war #362), and as a result Ethiopia faced a second revolt in the provinces (non-state war #1553) in 1868. The forces of the Mahdi attacked Ethiopia in 1885 (non-state war #1559), and Italy began its attempt to conquer Ethiopia in 1887 (extra-state war #392).

Coding: This war is in neither Clodfelter (2002) nor Phillips and Axelrod (2005).

Sources: Bahru Zewde (1991); Brecke (1999); Marcus (2001); Nelson and Kaplan (1981); Richardson (1960a).

NON-STATE WAR #1546:

The Second Tukulor War of 1860–1862

Participants: al-Hajj Umar's Tukulor vs. Masina, Segu

Dates: [ ]/[ ]/1860, to March 16, 1862

Battle-Related Deaths: Masina, Segu—[ ]; Tukulor—[ ] (Total Combatant and Civilian Deaths: 70,000)

Where Fought: Africa

Initiator: Tukulor

Outcome: Tukulor win

War Type: In nonstate territory

Narrative: Al-Hajj Umar was a Tukulor cleric who decided to conduct a jihad to restore the purification of Islam in western Africa and thereby also restore the importance of the Tukulor. In 1852 Umar began the war by moving northward from his territory in present-day Mali against the Malinke tribe (in the First Tukulor War, non-state war #1535). As he then advanced westward, against the Bambara people, Umar came in contact with the French, who were attempting to expand their colonial empire eastward from Saint-Louis, on the Atlantic coast. The resulting war between the Tukulor and the French (extra-state war #340) lasted from 1854 to 1857. At the conclusion of that war, Umar Tal realized that he had to forgo westward expansion, and he shifted to attacking the Segu and Masina tribes in the east, which is this non-state war phase. Both Segu and Masina were quickly conquered by the Tukulor, and al-Hajj Umar extended his empire to incorporate Timbuktu. Umar was killed in battle in 1864, whereupon the Tukulor Empire was divided among his sons. Thus weakened, the empire was vulnerable to further French colonial expansion in the 1890s.

Coding: Clodfelter (2002) does not cover this war. Phillips and Axelrod (2005) briefly discuss this war in the context of the "Tukulor-French Wars (1854–1864)."

Sources: Fage (1969); Oliver and Atmore (1981); Robinson (1988); Stearns (2001); Vandervort (1998).

NON-STATE WAR #1548:

The Transvaal War of 1862–1864

Participants: Regional governments in Transvaal vs. Transvaal central government

Dates: April [ ], 1862, to January [ ], 1864

Battle-Related Deaths: regional governments— 3,000; Transvaal central government—3,000

Where Fought: Africa

Initiator: regional governments

Outcome: Transvaal central government wins

War Type: In nonstate territory

Narrative: The 1830's Great Trek by the Boers resulted in the creation of several autonomous political systems in the interior of what is now South Africa. The most enduring of these were Transvaal and the Orange Free State. Britain had seized these territories as the Orange River Sovereignty in 1848, but when it was unable to establish order, it gave independence to Transvaal in 1852 and the Orange Free State in 1854. In 1856 the South African Republic was established in Transvaal, with Marthinus Pretorius as its president. When he also accepted the presidency of the neighboring Orange Free State, he was forced out of his original office. His replacement, too, was essentially forced out in an internal coup led by Stephanus Schoeman. While backed up by 150 armed men, Schoeman forced the Executive Council to appoint him the new acting president. Schoeman, however, soon faced rebellion by Paul Kruger, who rose to prominence later in the period as the leader of the Boer resistance against the British. Each side had about 10,000 troops in the ensuing conflict. In January 1864 Pretorius helped to broker a deal among these rival regional leaders. As a reward, Pretorius again became president.

Coding: This war is in neither Clodfelter (2002) nor Phillips and Axelrod (2005).

Sources: Davenport and Saunders (2000); Kohn (1999); Kruger (1902).

NON-STATE WAR #1550:
The Central American War of 1863

Participants: Guatemala, Nicaragua vs. El
   Salvador, Honduras
Dates: January 23, 1863, to November 15, 1863
Battle-Related Deaths: Guatemala and
   Nicaragua—[ ]; El Salvador and Honduras—[ ]
Where Fought: Western Hemisphere
Initiator: Guatemala
Outcome: Guatemala, Nicaragua win
War Type: In nonstate territory

Narrative: While under Spanish colonial rule,
Costa Rica, El Salvador, Guatemala, Honduras,
and Nicaragua had been administratively united.
After they received their independence in 1821,
they decided to unite again in a Central American Confederation in 1825. Ideological differences between the conservatives and liberals,
however, led to war in 1826, which was concluded with a liberal victory (non-state war
#1510). The conservative challenge, raised by
Gen. Francisco Rafael Carrera of Guatemala,
was instrumental in destroying the Central
American Confederation in 1839 (non-state war
#1528). Subsequently, Carrera tried to impose
conservative governments on other Central
American countries through a series of localized
invasions. The conflict between the liberals and
the conservatives was also at the base of the Filibuster War in Nicaragua in 1856 (non-state war
#1540), which led to the establishment of a con-
servative government in Nicaragua.

Gerardo Barrios, who had been a compatriot
of Carrera's, was elected as president of El Salvador; however, he soon began implementing
liberal policies. Then a liberal, Victoriano Castellanos, became president in Honduras, as well.
Thus Carrera, and ultimately his conservative
ally Nicaragua, decided to act. Carrera began
this war in January 1863 with an invasion of El
Salvador in an attempt to oust its liberal regime.
His forces of 6,500 were defeated by 5,500 troops
at the battle of Ocotepeque in late February
1863. Other, smaller incursions were only slightly

more successful. The war then spread when El
Salvador formed an alliance with Honduras to
oppose the Guatemala-Nicaragua pact. The two
liberal allies invaded Nicaragua in April 1863
but were defeated by 1,500 Nicaraguans. Carrera
then invaded El Salvador again and besieged San
Salvador for four months, at the end of which
liberal president Barrios fled the country and
was replaced by a conservative regime. Similarly
the president of Honduras was overthrown by a
conservative in the aftermath of the conflict.

Coding: The number of total deaths for all
participants is unknown, but Guatemala lost 900
in one battle (Ocotepeque). Guatemala and
Nicaragua are coded as the victors, since liberal
governments were forced out of El Salvador and
Honduras. This war is in neither Clodfelter (2002)
nor Phillips and Axelrod (2005).

Sources: Scheina (2003a); Woodward (1993).

NON-STATE WAR #1551:
The First Australian Aboriginal War of 1864–1865

Participants: Aborigines vs. white settlers
Dates: December 18, 1864, to December 18, 1865
Battle-Related Deaths: Aborigines—890; white
   settlers—110
Where Fought: Oceania
Initiator: white settlers
Outcome: Conflict continues at below war level
War Type: In nonstate territory

Narrative: When European settlers began arriving in Australia, their initial contacts with the
Aborigines, or native peoples, were generally
peaceful. As the settlers' economy developed,
however, its reliance on livestock that roamed
over large tracts of land led to conflicts with the
way of life of the indigenous people. Settlers
seized land without authorization. Aboriginal
seizures of livestock became more common, and
the settlers increasingly engaged in punitive
attacks. Official British policy at the time had
dual recommendations for treating the native

peoples, on one hand humanely, while simultaneously forbidding the settlers from conceding any of their property. In the late 1830s, as the settlers continually expanded the scope of their settlements, the indigenous communities began to offer greater resistance to encroachments on their land. Though violence between the two parties lasted for over 150 years, the increased level of violence endured for over 60 years, generally described as occurring between 1840 and 1901. Conflict largely consisted of skirmishes and retaliatory raids that resulted in few deaths. However, assessing the level of violence in this case is contentious. Older scholarship tended to downplay the level of violence and degree of Aboriginal coordination and to highlight the image of Aboriginal people as victims. More recent scholarship has included discussions of Aboriginal agency in ways that indicate they would qualify as a nonstate armed group, and thus as a potential war participant (Broome 2005). Similarly, Gat (1999) analyzed the warfare tactics used by the Aborigines and concluded that they utilized both small-scale raids and large battles. Consequently, we have included as wars two periods in which the level of fatalities would seem to reach war levels.

In 1864–1865 much of the violence took place in Queensland. For instance, on December 18, 1864, a skirmish took place at Cape York Peninsula between the Aborigines and a group of settlers who were beginning a trek to establish a new settlement near Mitchell River. This was reported to be one of the first instances in which the Aborigines engaged in a limited pitched battle. The settlers reported that attacks by Aborigines continued for the entire three-month trek but increased as they neared their destination. In April 1865 similar confrontations took place in Western Australia as well.

Coding: Evaluating the battle-related deaths for this war was complicated, owing to both the disagreements among scholars about the number of fatalities and the fact that the deaths occurred over a long time period. We began with the estimate cited in Broome (2005) of 2,500 Europeans and 20,000 Aborigines killed between 1840 and 1894, and then used the listing of battles by Coulthard-Clark (2001) to identify the periods of the most intense conflict. Thus we have coded the period of 1864–1865 and 1884–1894 as nonstate wars #1551 and #1558. Clodfelter includes a brief entry for the "Australian Aboriginal Wars: 1830–1901." Phillips and Axelrod (2005) do not discuss the war in Australia, though they do include an entry for the conflict between the Aborigines and the settlers in Tasmania in 1804–1830.

Sources: Broome (2005); Broome (2002); Clodfelter (2002); Coulthard-Clark (2001); Gat (1999); Kirkby (1984).

NON-STATE WAR #1552:

The Second Boer-Basuto War of 1865–1866

Participants: Boers (of the Orange Free State) vs. the Basuto
Dates: June 9, 1865, to April 3, 1866
Battle-Related Deaths: Boers—[ ]; Basuto—[ ] (Total Combatant Deaths: 1,200)
Where Fought: Africa
Initiator: Boers
Outcome: Boers win
War Type: In nonstate territory

Narrative: The Basuto were one of the tribes to emerge out of the chaos of the Mfecane ("the crushing"), through which the Zulu were expanding their empire (see non-state war #1501). In 1820 the Basuto were able to retreat to high country and establish relatively effective defenses in what is now Lesotho under the leadership of King Moshoeshoe. However, Basuto territory was threatened by the Boers who were emigrating from Natal. In 1848 Britain annexed this region as the Orange River Sovereignty and in essence gave two-thirds of the Basuto land to the Boers. The British were unable to establish effective control over the Sovereignty, and they ultimately recognized the independence of the Transvaal in 1852 and the Orange Free State in

519

1854, both controlled by the Boers. The Boer government of the Orange Free State, soon came into conflict with the Basuto (or Sotho), and the First Boer-Basuto War erupted in 1858 (non-state war #1544).

At the conclusion of the first war, the Basuto had been able to retain their territory; Boer expansionism, however, did not cease. In 1865 a Boer family was murdered, and the Orange Free State decided to launch a major offensive against the Basuto. War began in June 1865, and the Orange Free State requested additional troops from Transvaal. In an initial engagement, 3,000 Basuto aided by 4,000 Zulu decimated a Free State encampment, until they were driven off by the Transvaal reinforcements. The Boers continued their advance into Basuto territory, where they encountered 20,000 Basuto warriors. The Boers gained the advantage because of their possession of modern weapons. Moshoeshoe appealed to the British for assistance, and the British helped negotiate the Treaty of Thaba Bosiu, by which much of the Basuto territory was ceded to the Orange Free State. This marks the end of the war. Nevertheless, the disputes did not end, aggravated by the discovery of gold and diamonds in the region. In 1868 the Basuto again asked for British assistance, and the British merely annexed the Basuto territory to the Cape Colony in 1871 under the pretext of protecting it. Finally, in 1966, Basutoland became the independent entity of Lesotho.

Coding: The Boers were subsequently involved in two wars with the British, the First Boer War of 1880–1881 (extra-state war #382) and the Second Boer War of 1899–1902 (extra-state war #416). Clodfelter (2002) includes only one sentence about this war in an entry called "Basuto Wars: 1852–81." Cutter (2007) and Phillips and Axelrod (2005) refer to one "Basuto War" that lasts from 1856 to 1868, or 1858 to 1868, respectively. Especially because of the intervening war among the Boers in 1862–1864, we divide this period into two separate wars, the First and then a Second Boer-Basuto War in 1865–1866.

Sources: Clodfelter (2002); Cutter (2007); Haliburton (1977); Kruger (1902); Phillips and Axelrod (2005); Sanders (1975); Thompson (1975); Williams (1907).

NON-STATE WAR #1553:
The Second Ethiopian War of 1868–1872

Participants: Ethiopia vs. Tigray
Dates: April 13, 1868, to January 21, 1872
Battle-Related Deaths: Ethiopia—30,000; Tigray—5,000
Where Fought: Africa
Initiator: Ethiopia
Outcome: Tigray wins
War Type: In nonstate territory

Narrative: In 1855 Ras Kassa Hailu came to power in Ethiopia as Emperor Tewodros II. His primary goal was to restrict the power of the local princes (or kings) and to create a unified Ethiopia. Tewodros was able to defeat the challenges to his rule that arose in the provinces in 1858 (non-state war #1545); however, in 1867 Emperor Tewodros confronted a more serious threat when Ethiopia was invaded by British forces (extra-state war #362). Rather than be captured by the British, Tewodros committed suicide on April 13, 1868. Ethiopia was once again fractured along regional lines, as provincial leaders vied for control of the state. Tekla Giorgis, the king of Lasta, assumed power in the central highlands as Tewodros's successor, partially by coming to an agreement with the ruler of Showa. Tekla Giorgis also attempted to gain the support of the governor of Tigray, Dejazmatch Kassa (Kasa Mercha) but was rebuffed, since Dejazmatch Kassa wanted the throne for himself. As a result, Tekla Giorgis's Ethiopia invaded Tigray. Although Tekla Giorgis had 60,000 troops, Dejazmatch Kassa prevailed with a smaller, 12,000-man army, in large part because his forces had European weapons and training.

Dejazmatch Kassa was crowned the ruler of Ethiopia as Emperor Yohannis IV on January 21, 1872.

Coding: Clodfelter (2002) does not cover this war. Phillips and Axelrod (2005) describe it as the "Ethiopian Civil War (1868–1872)."

Sources: Lea (2001); Lewis (1987); Marcus (2001); Marcus (1975); Nelson and Kaplan (1981); Phillips and Axelrod (2005); Richardson (1960a).

NON-STATE WAR #1554:
The Uruguay Colorados-Blancos War of 1870–1872

Participants: Blancos vs. Colorados
Dates: March 5, 1870, to April 6, 1872
Battle-Related Deaths: Blancos—[ ]; Colorados—[ ] (Total Combatant Deaths: 3,000)
Where Fought: Western Hemisphere
Initiator: Blancos
Outcome: Colorados win
War Type: In nonstate territory

Narrative: Uruguay had a bloody history during the nineteenth century. Much of the fighting revolved around the rivalry between the country's two major parties, the Colorados (Reds) and Blancos (Whites). Classifying the Uruguayan factions this way originated in 1836 when Uruguayan president Gen. Manuel Oribe faced a rebellion by former president Fructuoso Rivera. Oribe wanted his followers to identify themselves by wearing white, and Rivera responded by having his supporters wear red. The social class base of the two parties also aligned with these colors, with the Blancos (Whites) as the more conservative agricultural interests and the Colorados (Reds) representing intellectuals, "have-nots," and émigrés. Colorados thus tended to be more concentrated around Montevideo, which was the principal port and the capital.

In 1868 the Blancos and the Colorados contested for the presidency of Uruguay. The Blancos staged a coup against the Colorados president, though the Blancos were ultimately captured and a new Colorados president, Gen. Lorenzo Batlle, was installed. The Blancos were unhappy with this state of affairs and launched this war against the government on March 5, 1870. The revolt, led by Blanco colonel Timteo Aparicio Saravia, is sometimes known as La Revolución de las Lanzas, or the Revolution of the Spears. The first major battle, at Severino, resulted in a victory for Saravia on September 12. A battle near Montevideo later that month resulted in heavy casualties on both sides. The Blancos army grew to have 5,000 troops, though it opposed 7,000 Colorado forces. On December 25 the Colorados emerged victorious at the Battle of Sauce, which cost 1,000 lives. Further defeats led Saravia to resort to guerrilla warfare, which extended the war into 1872. Finally, a truce was signed in April 1872 by which the nation's provinces were divided between the two parties, with the Blancos in the north (farthest away from the coast) and the Colorados in the center and south (near Montevideo and the La Plata estuary).

Coding: This war is in neither Clodfelter (2002) nor Phillips and Axelrod (2005).

Sources: Brecke (1999); Scheina (2003a).

NON-STATE WAR #1556:
The Second Zulu Internecine War of 1883–1884

Participants: Cetshwayo/Dinizulu faction (Usuthu) vs. Zibhebhu faction (Mandlakazi)
Dates: March 28, 1883, to June 4, 1884
Battle-Related Deaths: Cetshwayo faction— 4,500; Zibhebhu faction—1,000
Where Fought: Africa
Initiator: Cetshwayo faction
Outcome: Cetshwayo faction wins
War Type: In nonstate territory

Narrative: In the bloody Battle of 'Ndondaku-suka in 1856 (in the First Zulu Internecine War, non-state war #1542), Cetshwayo defeated his brother, Mbuyazi, for the right to inherit the leadership of the Zulu from their father, Mpande. Mpande died in 1872, and Cetshwayo was crowned in Natal in 1873. By 1879 Cetshwayo was involved in a war with the British (extra-state war #380). The Zulu were defeated, and Cetshwayo was imprisoned for almost four years before being allowed to return home. In trying to eliminate the threat posed by the Zulu, the British devised a divide-and-conquer strategy, which divided the Zulu into thirteen chiefdoms. This policy ended up being particularly divisive in that it penalized the chiefs who had remained loyal to Cetshwayo. One of the emerging Zulu leaders was Zibhebhu (Zibelu), who sheltered much of Cetshwayo's family while he was imprisoned. Competition grew among the thirteen chiefs, and from prison Cetshwayo tried to persuade the British that the only way to restore order was to reinstate him as head of the Royal House. The British ultimately allowed Cetshwayo to visit Britain in 1882 to plead his case before Queen Victoria. As a result, Cetshwayo returned to Zululand as king on January 10, 1883.

Trouble began almost immediately between Cetshwayo and the other claimants to Zulu leadership, especially Zibhebhu. During March 1883, Cetshwayo's supporters assembled a 5,000-warrior army (uSuthu). The uSuthu attacked into Zibhebhu territory, where they were defeated by an army one-third their size. Cetshwayo then raised a larger army and marched into Zibhebhu territory again on July 29, 1883. Cetshwayo was defeated again and died in 1884. He was succeeded by his sixteen-year-old son, Dinizulu. Dinizulu was able to gather an army of 7,000, with support of 120 Transvaal Boers, to oppose Zibhebhu's 3,000. The forces met at the Battle of Tshaneni on June 4, 1884, and Dinizulu was able to win final victory in the showdown with Zibhebhu's army. The need for outside support was perhaps an indicator of the gradual decline of the Zulu vis-à-vis outsiders. In May 1877 Zululand became a British colony, and in 1889 Dinizulu was arrested and exiled to St. Helena.

Coding: The Boers are not coded as participants in the war, since apparently only 70 of them participated in the fighting and they suffered no casualties. However, in repayment for their support of Dinizulu, the Boers demanded and received a large portion of Zulu territory. The total number of combatant and civilian deaths in this war may be as high as 51,000. Clodfelter (2002) does not have a separate entry on this civil war but discusses it briefly under the heading "Zulu War: 1879." Phillips and Axelrod (2005) discuss the "Zulu Civil War" of 1856.

Sources: Guy (1974); Knight (1998); Kohn (1999); Phillips and Axelrod (2005); Richardson (1960a); Sivard (1991).

NON-STATE WAR #1557:
The Oman-Ibadi War of 1883–1884

Participants: Oman vs. Ibadi
Dates: October [ ], 1883, to [ ]/[ ]/1884
Battle-Related Deaths: Oman—[ ]; Ibadi—[ ]
  (Total Combatant Deaths: 1,000)
Where Fought: Middle East
Initiator: Ibadi
Outcome: Oman wins
War Type: In nonstate territory

Narrative: Oman (also known as "Muscat and Oman") constitutes the eastern tip of the Arabian Peninsula. It was a Portuguese colony from 1508 to 1650, and it was occupied by Iran for six years in the 1740s, after which it was an autonomous entity. In 1829 the sultan of Muscat, Sayyid Said, established a coastal empire in eastern Africa (non-state war #1514) and he also became the sultan of Zanzibar. At that point Muscat and Oman was the most powerful state in Arabia, with an empire that included, in addition to Zanzibar, much of the coast of Persia and Baluchistan (now Pakistan). Upon Sultan Said's death in 1856, a dispute arose among his sons over the allocation of his empire among them, resulting in the division of the sultanates of Zanzibar and Muscat (Oman), with Majid becoming sultan of Zanzibar, Thuwaini becoming ruler of Muscat, and Turki as wali of Sohar.

The area of Muscat and Oman was not entirely united, with some of the cities not joining Oman until 1929. This was partially due to the differences between the coastal and the interior areas. In 1883 the sultan of Muscat and Oman, Sultan Turki bin Said bin Sultan, faced a revolt in the interior of Oman led by members of the Ibadi Muslim sect. The Ibadi, following the teachings of a mystic, Shaykh Said ibn Khalfan al-Khalili (1811–1870), preferred religious rule by the imam of Oman to that of the sultan and thus had begun attacking the sultan's forces in 1874. This war began in October 1883 with a more serious attack by a larger Ibadi army against Sultan Said Turki's forces in the capital, Muscat. The war was brief, and a bribe from the government, as well as gunfire from a British warship, helped dissuade the Ibadi forces and allowed the sultan's forces to prevail. This was not the end of the religious movement, however. Another revolt began in 1913, during which the British protected the sultan. Seven years later the British arranged the Treaty of Seeb, which attempted to create separate domains for the "Sultan of Muscat and Oman" and for the "Imam of the Muslims," who ruled the interior (Hoffman 2008, 6).

Coding: Oman was a British protectorate from 1892 until 1971, after which it becomes a member of the COW interstate system. Since Oman is not a system member in 1883, this war is between two nonstate actors. Oman would become involved in another non-state war, against Dhofar (see non-state war #1577), eighty-five years later. Neither Clodfelter (2002) nor Phillips and Axelrod (2005) cover this war.

Sources: Bhacker (1992); Brecke (1999); Hoffman (2008); Kostiner (2000); Landen (1967); Richardson (1960a); Ripenburg (1998); Schafer (1995); Townsend (1977).

NON-STATE WAR #1558:
The Second Australian Aboriginal War of 1884–1894

Participants: Aborigines vs. white settlers
Dates: August [ ], 1884, to November 16, 1894
Battle-Related Deaths: Aborigines—8,900; white settlers—1,100
Where Fought: Oceania
Initiator: white settlers
Outcome: Conflict continues at below war level
War Type: In nonstate territory

Narrative: When European settlers began arriving in Australia, their initial contacts with the Aborigines, or native peoples, were generally peaceful. As the settlers' economy developed, however, its reliance on livestock that roamed over large tracts of land threatened the indigenous peoples' way of life. Settlers seized land without authorization. Aboriginal seizures of livestock became more common, and the settlers increasingly engaged in punitive attacks. Increased levels of violence endured for over sixty years, generally described as occurring between 1840 and 1901. Within these years, we have identified two periods in which fatality levels appear to have exceeded the 1,000 battle-related deaths per year: 1864–1865 (non-state war #1551) and this war between 1884 and 1894.

As the technology of warfare advanced, so did the fatality levels, thus confrontations between the Aborigines and the settlers between 1884 and 1894 may have been the deadliest. In August 1884 a costly confrontation took place at a settlement at Reservoir in the Northern Territory. Later that year Battle Mountain was the site of a classical battle between a group of an estimated 600 Kalkadoon warriors and a large force of police, leading to over 200 deaths. Such conflicts continued throughout Australia for the next ten years, though they seemed to taper off after a confrontation in November 1894 in the Northern Territory led by Jandamarra.

Coding: Evaluating the battle-related deaths for this war was complicated, owing to both the disagreements among scholars about the number of fatalities and the fact that the deaths occurred over a long time period. We began with the estimate cited in Broome (2005) of 2,500 Europeans and 20,000 Aborigines killed between 1840 and 1894, and then used the listing of battles by Coulthard-Clark (2001) to identify the periods of the most intense conflict. Thus we have coded the period of 1864–1865 and 1884–1894 as non-state wars #1551 and #1558. Clodfelter includes a brief entry for the "Australian Aboriginal Wars: 1830–1901." Phillips and Axelrod (2005) do not discuss the war in Australia, though they do include an entry for the conflict between the Aborigines and the settlers in Tasmania in 1804–1830.

Sources: Broome (2005); Broome (2002); Clodfelter (2002); Coulthard-Clark (2001); Gat (1999); Kirkby (1984).

NON-STATE WAR #1559:
The Ethiopia-Mahdi War of 1885–1889

Participants: Ethiopia vs. Mahdist army
Dates: May [ ], 1885, to March 12, 1889
Battle-Related Deaths: Ethiopia—15,000; Mahdist army—15,000
Where Fought: Africa
Initiator: Ethiopia
Outcome: Mahdist army wins
War Type: In nonstate territory

Narrative: Muhammad Ahmad, who styled himself the Mahdi, or successor of the Prophet Muhammad, developed a substantial following in Sudan in the 1880s. The Mahdi wanted to remove what he perceived to be foreign influences from Sudan and ultimately the entire region (including the British, Egyptians, Italians, and Ethiopians). The Mahdi gathered a large army and declared war against the British and the Egyptians in August 1881 (extra-state war #384). The war ended in 1885, most notably with the massacre of the British troops, led by Gen. Charles Gordon, at Khartoum; however, while the Anglo-Egyptian forces retreated from central Sudan, the Mahdist army also defeated British forces along the Red Sea on March 22, 1885. This expedition brought the Mahdist army into contact with Ethiopia.

The Mahdi wrote Ethiopian emperor Yohannes a letter suggesting that the emperor should welcome Mahdist rule or face attack. The emperor did not reply, and instead in May 1885, 30,000 Ethiopians attacked the Sudanese city of Gallabat (al-Qallabat), killing 6,000 Sudanese. The Mahdi died in June 1885, though his mission was continued by his disciple Khalifa Abdullahi, who sent an army toward Ethiopia, though a major invasion never materialized at that point. The Ethiopians were then faced with an additional challenge as the Italians began their excursions into Ethiopia from their Red Sea posts. On January 26, 1887, an Italian regiment was annihilated by 15,000 Ethiopians at Dogali (the First Italian-Ethiopian War, extra-state war #392). The Italians withdrew in March 1887. In early 1887 the Ethiopians again occupied the Sudanese town of Gallabat, and in retaliation, in July 1887, the Mahdist army (with 60,000–80,000 troops) advanced into Ethiopia, where it crushed the Ethiopian army at Debra Sina. The Mahdist army then withdrew to Gallabat. Meanwhile, Yohannes mobilized another army, and on March 9, 1889, over 100,000 Ethiopians attacked the Mahdist army at Gallabat. Although the Ethiopians initially forced the Mahdist army to retreat, Emperor Yohannes was killed in the battle. The news of the emperor's death demoralized the Ethiopian troops, who scattered and were massacred when the Mahdist army counterattacked, which marked the end of the war.

Coding: The Mahdist forces would later fight against Italy in 1893 (extra-state war #400). The British then resumed their campaign against the Mahdi from 1896 to 1899 (extra-state war #409). Clodfelter (2002) includes the "Mahdist-Abyssinian War: 1884–1889." Phillips and Axelrod do not cover this war.

Sources: Clodfelter (2002); Jaques (2007); Lewis (1987); Pakenham (1991).

NON-STATE WAR #1560:
The German East Africa Company War of 1888–1889

Participants: German East Africa Company vs. Arabs, Swahili
Dates: September [ ], 1888, to May [ ], 1889
Battle-Related Deaths: Arabs, Swahili—[ ]; German East Africa Company—[ ]
Where Fought: Africa
Initiator: Arabs, Swahili
Outcome: German East Africa Company
War Type: In nonstate territory

Narrative: By 1829 Sultan Sayyid Said had established Omani control of the East African coast near the island of Zanzibar and had ultimately become the sultan of Zanzibar as well (non-state war #1514). The Germans, too, were interested in gaining economic interests in the area, specifically under the auspices of the Society for German Colonization, which later became the German East Africa Company. In 1884 the company purchased a large amount of land (in what is now Tanganyika) from the local chiefs. When company officials arrived in 1887, they initially tried to establish good relations with the sultan of Zanzibar, and in April 1888 he agreed to turn over the administration of the southern coastal region to the company as long as it recognized his dominion. Difficulties began at that point. The brutality of the German East Africa Company officials and militia soon alienated the Arabs and the Swahili who lived in the area. The specific precipitant of the war was Emil von Zelewski, who was one of the most notorious of the company officials.

In August 1888 Zelewski sailed into the port of Pangani and announced that he was taking over control of the town. The Wali of the town refused to comply. Zelewski demanded that the sultan affirm their agreement and support him militarily. However, in September 1888 Arabs under the leadership of Abushiri ibn Salim al Harthi began a revolt against the company. The Arabs were aided by local Swahili chiefs, who sent 6,000 troops to Pangani. The sultan's forces did come to Pangani, though they refused to arrest the local leaders who had defied the Germans, and they soon returned to Zanzibar. The rebels before long had an army of over 20,000 men, and they began attacking the Germans and company holdings. The rebels were divided on their ultimate goals; some wanted to restore the rule of the sultan, while others saw the sultan as having betrayed them in signing the agreements with the German company in the first place. By November 1888, Abushiri began to lose control of rebels around Pangani, so he marched south with 2,000 troops and launched a new offensive aimed at isolating the Germans at Bagamoyo. Meanwhile, over 1,000 Swahili besieged the company compound at Dar-es-Salaam, the only major post still head by the Germans. The Germans had superior weapons, and the rebels could not break into the compound. In April 1889, Abushiri accepted a truce, though he conducted another assault against Bagamoyo in May. That same month the German government authorized German explorer Maj. Hermann von Wissman to assemble a force of mercenaries to assist the company in restoring order in company territory. Wissman then launched a series of attacks, killing thousands of Arabs and Swahili. By 1890 the rebellion was suppressed. Once the area had been pacified, the German government revoked the company's charter and made the territory into a direct German protectorate in 1891.

Coding: This war is coded as a non-state war because the conflict was conducted by nonstate armed groups (the Arab and Swahili forces) and directed at the German East Africa Company and German mercenaries, not the German government itself, though at the end the mercenaries were acting at the government's behest.

Sources: Edgerton (2002); Kohn (1999); Oliver and Atmore (1994); Pakenham (1991); Phillips and Axelrod (2005).

NON-STATE WAR #1561:
The Rabih Zubayr-Bornu War of 1893

Participants: Rabih Zubayr's army vs. Bornu
Dates: [ ]/[ ]/1893, to [ ]/[ ]/1893
Battle-Related Deaths: Rabih Zubayr's army—[ ];
   Bornu—[ ] (Total Combatant Deaths: 4,000)
Where Fought: Africa
Initiator: Rabih Zubayr's army
Outcome: Rabih Zubayr's army wins
War Type: In nonstate territory

Narrative: Bornu was an autonomous Muslim state on the southwest side of Lake Chad, in what is now Nigeria. By the early 1890s it had been weakened by internal dissension, leaving it vulnerable to outside intervention. Rabih Zubayr (Zobeir), an African Arab soldier who had once served the Egyptian government in the Sudanese region of Bahr el-Ghazal, refused to submit to the Mahdi when the latter took power in the Sudan (extra-state war #384). Rabih led his army of Dazingers (African slave soldiers) westward from Sudan to establish his own empire. In 1887, Rabih attempted to conquer the kingdom of Waddai (in what is now southern Chad) but failed. In 1892 he was able to occupy Bagrimi, southeast of Lake Chad, and then in 1893 he shifted his focus to Bornu, beginning this war. In 1893 Rabih's 3,000-man force faced the Bornu army, led by Moman Tar, Shehe Hashim, and Shehu Kiari. Rabih's army was victorious and seized the Bornu capital of Kukawa. Rabih, sometimes called the "Black Sultan," then established a slave-trading empire. His "empire" was later dispatched by the French in 1899–1900 (extra-state war #415). The area was divided among Great Britain, France, and Germany. Today, Bornu is a regional state within Nigeria.

Coding: Clodfelter (2002), Phillips and Axelrod (2005), and Kohn (1999) all have entries on the "French Conquest of Chad," which Clodfelter dates from 1897 to 1901, while Phillips and Axelrod and Kohn extend it from 1897 to 1914.

These correspond to our extra-state war #415, the French Conquest of Chad, during which French forces capture and kill Rabih Zubayr. They all mention in passing, but do not discuss as a separate war, the preceding period in 1893, during which Rabih Zubayr fought against Bornu to gain control of this region.

Sources: Brecke (1999); Catchpole and Akinjogbin (1983); Decalo (1987); Oliver and Atmore (1994); Richardson (1960a); Sivard (1991).

NON-STATE WAR #1567:
The First Nejd-Hejaz War of 1919

Participants: Nejd vs. Hejaz
Dates: May 25, 1919
Battle-Related Deaths: Hejaz—4,000; Nejd—[ ]
Where Fought: Middle East
Initiator: Nejd
Outcome: Nejd wins
War Type: In nonstate territory

Narrative: Nejd and Hejaz were autonomous entities located within present-day Saudi Arabia. Since the eighteenth century, Nejd had been the home of the Wahhabi sect of Islam, which had engaged in a war with the Ottomans and Egyptians in 1816 (extra-state war #301). The Nejd ruler had been exiled from the area by the rulers of the capital, Riyadh, but his son, Abdul Aziz ibn Saud, had returned in 1901 to conquer the city, giving him control over Nejd. Hejaz, located in the northwestern sector of the Arabian Peninsula along the Red Sea coast, is the home of the holy cities of Mecca and Medina. Hejaz had been attacked by the Wahhabis in 1817, but after order was restored by the Ottomans (extra-state war #301), the Hejaz gradually came under direct Ottoman rule (1841–1916). In 1916 the independence of Hejaz was proclaimed by Husayn (Hussein) ibn Ali, the sharif of Mecca, who along with Lawrence of Arabia (T. E. Lawrence) had been instrumental in destroying Ottoman authority during World War I (inter-state war #106).

Border conflicts persisted between Hejaz and Nejd, and during World War I, Britain used its influence to discourage war. Abdul Aziz ibn Saud, however, wanted to expand his empire and used the Ikhwan, a paramilitary religious sect, to attack the Hejazi forces near the southern city of Turaba, southeast of Mecca, on May 25, 1919. In a fierce battle the Ikhwan inflicted a severe defeat on the Hejaz army, commanded by Emir Abdullah. Hostilities subsided, until they flared again five years later in the Second Nejd-Hejaz War of 1924–1925 (non-state war #1568).

Coding: Clodfelter (2002) has one entry in which he combines the "Hejaz War: 1919–25, and Ikhwan Rebellion: 1929–30" (our non-state wars #1567 and #1568 and intra-state war #708). These wars are not covered by Phillips and Axelrod.

Sources: Clodfelter (2002); Lenczowski (1987); Richardson (1960a); Schafer (1995).

NON-STATE WAR #1568:
The Second Nejd-Hejaz War of 1924–1925

Participants: Nejd vs. Hejaz
Dates: September 4, 1924, to December 23, 1925
Battle-Related Deaths: Nejd—[ ]; Hejaz[ ]
Where Fought: Middle East
Initiator: Nejd
Outcome: Nejd wins
War Type: In nonstate territory

Narrative: Nejd and Hejaz were autonomous entities located within present-day Saudi Arabia. Nejd, the home of the Wahhabi sect of Islam, was ruled after 1901 by Abdul Aziz ibn Saud. Hejaz, located along the Red Sea coast of the Arabian Peninsula, is the home of the holy cities of Mecca and Medina. Hejaz had been attacked by the Wahhabis in 1817, but after order was restored by the Ottomans (extra-state war #301), the Hejaz gradually came under direct Ottoman rule (1841–1916). In 1916 the independence of Hejaz was proclaimed by Husayn (Hussein) ibn Ali, the sharif of Mecca. Border conflicts between

Nejd and Hejaz flared up during World War I (inter-state war #106), though Britain used its influence to dampen the possibility of war between the two. Abdul Aziz ibn Saud, however, wanted to expand his empire and utilized the Ikhwan, a paramilitary religious sect, as his army. In their first major encounter the Ikhwan defeated the Hejazi forces near the southern city of Turaba, southeast of Mecca, on May 25, 1919 (non-state war #1567). Tensions subsided but then gradually returned. Ibn Saud was committed to expanding his territory and was putting pressure on his borders with Iraq, Transjordan, and Hejaz, attacking its railroad in 1922. Husayn likewise had a disagreement with Great Britain over promises Britain had made to him in exchange for his help against the Ottomans in World War I (see the discussions in extra-state wars #444 and #445). Husayn also alienated other Arab leaders when he proclaimed himself to be "King of the Arab Countries" in October 1916 and then the caliph in 1924.

An international conference met in Kuwait in early 1924 to discuss a resolution of the Hejaz-Nejd issues; however, talks were suspended in mid-March when Ibn Saud sent an expedition into Iraq. Finally, he launched a major invasion of Hejaz. The Ikhwan attacked the city of Taif (seventy miles from Mecca) on September 4, 1924, and massacred 3,000 civilians. At that point Great Britain considered intervening but in the end sent Ibn Saud a message in late September that indicated Britain would not intervene. The Ikhwan then moved on toward Mecca. On October 3, Husayn abdicated in favor of his son, Ali. Mecca fell to Ibn Saud on October 13, and Ali and the Hejaz forces withdrew to the Hashemite stronghold of Jedda, where they held out for a year. A new offensive was launched by Ibn Saud in late 1925. Medina succumbed on December 5, 1925, and Jedda fell on December 23, ending the war. On January 8, 1926, Ibn Saud was proclaimed king of Hejaz and sultan of the Nejd, thus uniting most of the Arabian Peninsula into a single state.

Coding: Abdul Aziz ibn Saud is seen as the father of Saudi Arabia. Partially as a consequence of the Second Nejd-Hejaz War and the unity of Nejd and Hejaz, Saudi Arabia becomes a member of the interstate system on May 20, 1927. In 1929, however, the Ikhwan launched a rebellion against Ibn Saud because he was not as conservative as they had expected (intra-state war #708).

Sources: Lenczowski (1987); Paris (2003); Richardson (1960a); Schafer (1995).

NON-STATE WAR #1570:
The Partition Communal War of 1946–1947

Participants: Muslims vs. Hindus, Sikhs
Dates: August 16, 1946, to August [ ], 1947
Battle-Related Deaths: Muslims—[ ]; Hindus—[ ];
  (Total Combatant and Civilian Deaths: 225,000–500,000)
Where Fought: Asia
Initiator: Muslims
Outcome: Muslims
War Type: In nonstate territory

Narrative: The steady move toward decolonization began at the end of World War II (interstate war #139). Great Britain, which had fought so many wars to develop and protect its empire in India, finally decided to end its 190-year rule of the country by 1947. The movement favoring Indian independence was prompted by the nonviolent "Quit India" campaign of Mohandas Gandhi. One particularly complex issue that confronted Britain was how to create a system that would facilitate the cooperation of India's Hindu majority with the smaller religious groups, especially the Muslims. Both the Hindus and Muslims created political organizations to promote their perspectives. The Muslim League had been created in 1906 and experienced an increase in membership as independence neared, as it supported the creation of an independent Muslim state. In contrast, Hindu organizations, such as Hindu Mahasabha, espoused opposition to partition. Britain proposed that India become a federal state, with three major territories corresponding to the major religious groups. In the summer of 1946 Britain's plan collapsed because it failed to get the support of the Congress Party. Leaders of the Muslim League were infuriated and called on Muslims to engage in direct action to create a Muslim state.

Conflict between the Hindus and Muslims began on August 16–20, 1946, with the "Great Calcutta Killing," which led to 6,000 deaths. The British ultimately decided that the only way to resolve the issue was to partition India into two separate states, India, which would be predominantly Hindu, and Pakistan, which would be Muslim. Violence between the Hindus and Muslims continued through the next year, peaking around the date of partition, August 14, 1947, especially in Punjab, a state that would be divided between India and Pakistan. The partition plan, which had not yet established the exact border between India and Pakistan, combined with enduring violence to prompt a massive exodus of Muslim refugees fleeing to Pakistan and Hindus fleeing into India. Violence continued after August at a lower level and generally subsided after the assassination of Mohandas Gandhi on January 30, 1948.

Coding: A difficulty in describing and coding this war arises over the question of whether this was a war or simply mob violence. Phillips and Axelrod (2005) refer to this as the "Indian Civil War (1947–1948)," while Clodfelter (2002) has an entry for the "Partition Riots: 1946–47." We have concluded that there was sufficient organization among the religious groups to consider them as nonstate armed groups and that the Muslim call for "direct action" implies an element of coordination. However, there is no doubt that there also was significant violence against noncombatants. We have not been able to discern or construct an adequate way in which to separate out the combatant deaths from the overall death toll. Clodfelter indicates that the total death toll might be 500,000, while Phillips and Axelrod and Ciment (2007) indicate that it might be as high as one million. The Muslims are coded as the winners to the extent that a separate Muslim state was created.

Sources: Ciment (2007); Clodfelter (2002); Phillips and Axelrod (2005); Richardson (1960a).

NON-STATE WAR #1571:
The Hyderabad War of 1947–1948

Participants: Communists, Telenganans vs. Razakars (allied to the Nezam) of the Muslimeem Party
Dates: August 15, 1947, to September 12, 1948
Battle-Related Deaths: Communists—[ ]; Telenganans—[ ]; Razakars—[ ] (Total Combatant Deaths—4,000)
Where Fought: Asia
Initiator: Telenganans
Outcome: Transformed into extra-state war #461

Narrative: As the British prepared to withdraw from the Indian subcontinent in 1947, each of the several hundred princely entities was supposed to chose accession to either India or Pakistan. Hyderabad, a state in interior southern India, provided one of the largest problems to that process. Its nizam, Mir Osman Ali Khan, was a Muslim ruling a mainly Hindu population. He refused to choose the new state to which he would accede, hoping that he would then became the ruler of an independent entity.

At the time, the nizam was also facing an internal challenge to his rule within Hyderabad. The Telenganans, the people of the Telugu-speaking regions of Hyderabad, were rural people who had begun to unite in opposition to the continued rule by the wealthy. The Telenganans were supported by the Communist party and the left-wing Andhra Mahasabha movement. Although the Telenganans' primary goal was the removal of the nizam, they also favored joining India. The movement was relatively small at the beginning, but the peasants soon had militias with over 12,000 members. In opposition to the Telenganans, the ruling class (including the nizam) created a private Islamic militia called

the Razakars—which ultimately had 200,000 members—to resist Indian pressure. The conflict between the two groups began with isolated attacks in 1946, involving few fatalities; however, war began in August 1947 and lasted a year. As the war dragged on, the Razakars launched a reign of terror throughout Hyderabad. The growing violence of the Razakars, and the nizam's unwillingness to restrain them, represented a threat to Hyderabad's neighbors and thus became one of the motivations for India's intervention. This war ended on September 12, and was transformed by the invasion of Hyderabad by India on September 13, 1948, into the Indo-Hyderabad War (extra-state war #461).

Coding: Clodfelter does not cover this war but does discuss the subsequent Indian "Conquest of Hyderabad: 1948." Phillips and Axelrod do not cover it.

Sources: Clodfelter (2002); Guha (2007); Luther (2000); Menon (1998); Menon (1956); Metcalf and Metcalf (2006); Minahan (2002); Welch (1980).

NON-STATE WAR #1572:
The Palestine War of 1947–1948

Participants: Arabs vs. Zionists
Dates: November 29, 1947, to May 14, 1948
Battle-Related Deaths: Arabs—991; Zionists—895
Where Fought: Middle East
Initiator: Zionists
Outcome: Transformed into inter-state war #148
War Type: In nonstate territory

Narrative: As a consequence of the dismemberment of the Ottoman Empire at the end of World War I (inter-state war #106), Palestine was awarded to Great Britain as a mandate under the auspices of the League of Nations. Britain maintained control of Palestine during World War II (inter-state war #139). The years of the war also saw the growth of the Zionist movement. At the meeting of the World Zionist

Congress in New York in May 1942, a resolution was passed supporting the creation of a Jewish state in Palestine based on the pledge of support offered by Great Britain in the Balfour Declaration of 1917. After that point clashes between the Zionists and the British in Palestine increased. The violence was frequently conducted by the Palmach, an elite branch of the Haganah. As World War II ended, and the implications of the Holocaust became more broadly known, Jewish immigration to Palestine increased. Britain finally admitted that it could no longer manage the situation in Palestine and transferred its authority to the United Nations on April 2, 1947, though its mandate was to end on May 15, 1948. On November 29, 1947, the United Nations passed a resolution calling for the division of Palestine into a Jewish state and an Arab state. The declaration immediately led to an increase in violence in Palestine and thus the start of this war.

Fighting between the Zionists and the Arabs increased in its level of hostility, and fatalities, between November 29, 1947, and May 14, 1948. During this period the well-armed Zionist forces increased the territory under their control. The fighting involved approximately 35,000 Jews (in the Irgun, Stern Gang, and Haganah) fighting against 35,000 Palestinian Arabs and 6,000–7,000 allied fighters from the Arab Liberation Army, who began entering Palestine in January 1848. This phase of the conflict was almost a stalemate. In early fighting the Arab forces cut off Jerusalem from Tel Aviv, causing a lack of food in Jerusalem. In April, however, the Jewish forces secured a series of victories, regained the entire Tel Aviv–Jerusalem road, and established Jewish control over most of the land given to the Jewish state by the UN Partition Plan.

Coding: This war ends the day before the declaration of the Israeli state, at which point Israel becomes a member of the COW interstate system. This war is then transformed into an inter-state war between Israel and the Arab states. Clodfelter (2002) includes both the non-state and

inter-state wars in one overall "Israeli War of Independence: 1947–49." Phillips and Axelrod (2005), while dealing with general history back to the Balfour Declaration, basically skip the non-state war and focus instead on the "Arab-Israeli War (1948–1949)."

Sources: Gelber (2006); Gerner (1991); Lenczowski (1987); Milstein (1997); Morris (2001); Richardson (1960a); Tessler (1994).

NON-STATE WAR #1573:
The Cheju Rebellion of 1948–1949

Participants: Communist rebels, rebel military vs. South Korean police, loyal army soldiers
Dates: April 3, 1948, to May [ ], 1949
Battle-Related Deaths: Communists, rebel military—26,000; government, civilians—17,000
Where Fought: Asia
Initiator: Communists
Outcome: South Korea wins
War Type: In nonstate territory

Narrative: In 1945, at the end of World War II (inter-state war #139), the northern half of Korea was occupied by Soviet forces, while the United States had control in the south. This arbitrary division thus set the stage for the emergence of a Communist state in the north and a non-Communist state in the south. This war represents an attempt to establish a Communist presence in the southern island of Cheju, as well. Thus this war was seen as a threat to the nascent South Korea from within, by rebels espousing the Marxist-Leninist creeds of nascent North Korea.

The precipitant of this war was the plan sponsored by the United Nations to create a separate South Korean government and to hold general elections on May 10, 1948, actions that opponents felt might reify the status quo. At first Communist guerrillas initiated what they called the "February 7 National Salvation Struggle," which aimed at disrupting the United Nations plans for the elections. Their actions began as strikes and vandalism, leading to the arrest of over 8,000 people. In March the South Korean Labor Party (SKLP) decided to switch to a strategy of direct force to conquer the island.

On April 3, 1948, over 3,000 Communists, operating in collusion with Communists within the South Korean constabulary units, rebelled and launched attacks on local police stations in northern Cheju Island, the largest island in Korea, located in the Yellow Sea to the south of the Korean peninsula. Although the rebellion started in the northern region of the island, it expanded as the guerrillas were joined by other islanders who were displeased with the American military government, local Koran authorities, and the election plans. At first the American military governor tried to defeat the rebellion by relying on the local police, but when that proved to be ineffective, he requested the assistance of two South Korean army regiments. The army was somewhat successful in suppressing the rebellion; however, in October a large-scale revolt broke out again throughout Cheju. The rebels were also joined by an uprising in the military. In what is called the Yosu-Sunch'on Rebellion, military forces located at Yosu, on the southern mainland, who were going to be deployed to suppress the rebellion at Cheju, revolted on October 19, 1948, in the hopes of spreading resistance throughout the military. The military resisters were joined by the local Communists, and they began to spread the rebellion inland. The military soon restored order at Yosu, but the rebels continued guerrilla operations. Similar military rebellions broke out at Taegu in November, and at Och'on airfield on January 3, 1949. The rebellion was defeated by May 1949, though sporadic guerrilla activities continued until 1950.

Coding: This war is coded as a non-state war because Korea is militarily occupied, and thus it is considered a dependency and not a member of the interstate system at this time. The death toll in this conflict is highly uncertain and varies from source to source. One report has it that 15,000

people were killed by the Communists. Somewhere between 20,000 and 30,000 of the rebels were killed. Of the around 2,000 insurgents who were captured in the fighting, 250 were executed and the rest sentenced to prison for varying lengths of time. According to the ROK (Republic of Korea) government count, 27,719 deaths occurred during the yearlong war.

Neither Clodfelter (2002) nor Phillips and Axelrod (2005) cover this war as a separate war. Clodfelter, however, mentions it in his opening paragraph on the "North Korean Invasion: 1950."

Sources: Clodfelter (2002); Korean Institute of Military History (2000); Millett (2005); Nahm and Hoare (2004); Oh (1999); Pratt and Rutt (1999); Richardson (1960a).

NON-STATE WAR #1574:

The Rwandan Social Revolution of 1959–1962

Participants: Hutu vs. Tutsi
Dates: October 19, 1959, to July 1, 1962
Battle-Related Deaths: Hutu—[ ]; Tutsi—[ ]
   (Total Combatant and Civilian Deaths: 5,000 to 20,000)
Where Fought: Africa
Initiator: Hutu
Outcome: Hutu victory
War Type: In nonstate territory

Narrative: Rwanda was an autonomous entity from 1492 until 1891, when it became part of German East Africa. After Germany's defeat in World War I, Rwanda was united with Burundi as RwandaBurundi. This larger entity became a mandated territory to Belgium under the League of Nations, and subsequently a trust territory of the United Nations. This war of 1959–1962 occurred in the final years of Belgian control, before Rwanda's independence in 1962. Although the Belgian authorities did try to combat the violence, the fighting was basically between the Hutu and the Tutsi peoples.

The roots of the conflict include elements of Belgian and German colonial policies that fostered antagonism between Hutu and Tutsi. The Tutsi, numbering about 10 percent to 15 percent of the population, were favored by the Belgians during the colonial period. A Tutsi king was effectively the local government under the Belgians, and this fueled resentment on the part of the Hutu majority. As independence from Belgium neared, the polarization in the country increased. In 1957 the High Council of Rwanda, which was composed entirely of Tutsi, published its views on the steps necessary in preparing for independence, which include rule by the Tutsi elite. In response a group of Hutu leaders released its "Manifesto of the Bahutu," which urged that independence be delayed until a more equitable government could be established. Nyrop et al. (1969, 18) argue that this statement represents the first indication of organized Hutu resistance. Another Hutu organization, the Association for the Betterment of the Masses (APROSOMA), was formed the same year.

During 1959 an increasing number of political parties were formed, of which the Party of the Hutu Emancipation Movement (PARME-HUTU) is of particular note in that its espoused goal was the termination of Tutsi domination. This war starts in October 1959 when the Hutu organizations launched the Rwandan Social Revolution. The majority Hutu rose up and attacked the Tutsi and the Twa (pygmy allies of the Tutsi). The Tutsi faired so badly that 150,000, or about one-third of their population, fled into exile as a consequence of the fighting and repression. This reduced the Tutsi share of Rwanda's population to about 10 percent. Not surprisingly, the Hutu, with 85 percent to 90 percent of the population, won the UN-supervised referendum in 1961, leading to independence. Rwanda became an independent country on July 1, 1962, which marks the end of this war. Tranquility was short-lived. Exiled Tutsi invaded Rwanda in 1963, and violence continued back and forth for decades, eventually even spilling over into Burundi and the Congo.

Coding: Phillips and Axelrod (2005) cover the 1959–1961 "Ruandan (Rwandan) Civil War." Clodfelter (2002) only briefly mentions this war in a composite entry for "Buhutu Uprisings in Burundi and Rwanda: 1972, 1988, 1990–."

Sources: Ciment (2007); Clodfelter (2002); Mamdani (2002); Meredith (2005); Nyrop et al. (1969); Phillips and Axelrod (2005); Schafer (1995).

NON-STATE WAR #1577:

The Dhofar Rebellion Phase 1 of 1968–1971

Participants: Dhofar rebels vs. Oman government
Dates: September [ ], 1968, to October 6, 1971
Battle-Related Deaths: PFLOAG, NDFLOAG—[ ]; Oman—[ ] (Total Combatant Deaths: 5,000)
Where Fought: Middle East
Initiator: Dhofar rebels
Outcome: Stalemate
War Type: In nonstate territory

Narrative: Oman (also known as Muscat and Oman) has had the longest history of independence in the Arab world, being an autonomous entity almost continuously from 1650 to the present, though it did not become a state system member until 1971. Oman was also a powerful trading country that controlled coastal areas from East Africa to Gwador (in modern-day Pakistan) (see non-state war #1514). It faced some internal challenges, however. There was a long-running dispute between Oman and Inner Oman, whose people adhered to the Ibadi sect of Islam. The two parties went to war in 1883 (non-state war #1557), and conflict flared up again in 1913 and 1957, though at below war levels.

A second area of conflict occurred in the western province of Dhofar. The conflict derived from the differences between the people of the interior mountains (jebalis) and the sultan's coastal people. The hostilities that began in 1964 were at first conducted by the Dhofar Liberation Front (DFL) and were related to the government's discriminatory practices and the jebalis' desire for representation in government. In September 1968, however, power within the DFL shifted to a Marxist faction, and both the rationale and tactics of the uprising changed to a broader opposition to imperialism. Correspondingly, the rebels changed their name to the Popular Front for the Liberation of the Occupied Arabian Gulf (PFLOAG). This shift marks the start of the war. The events in Oman were also linked to the Cold War. In 1967 the former British colony in nearby Aden emerged as the Marxist-Leninist "People's Democratic Republic of Yemen (PDRY)." As the only Communist country in the region, it developed ties with the People's Republic of China, and soon the Chinese were funding and supplying weapons to both the PDRY and the PFLOAG. The war at this stage was basically a rural guerrilla war. In 1970 the fighting expanded toward the capital of Muscat with the arrival of a new opposition group, the National Democratic Front for the Liberation of Oman and the Arab Gulf (NDFLOAG). NDFLOAG, which was funded by the Iraqi Baathists, adopted more of an urban terrorism campaign strategy. Within the year, however, most of its leadership and members had been captured or killed. The remaining rebels were absorbed into PFLOAG.

Coding: This war ends on October 6, 1971. As of the following day, Oman becomes a member of the COW interstate system; thus the subsequent Dhofar Rebellion Phase 2 from 1973 to 1975 is classified as an intra-state war (#795). It has been estimated that 10,000 combatants and civilians died during the course of the two wars. Clodfelter (2002) calls this the "Dhofar Rebellion" of 1966–1976. This war is not covered by Phillips and Axelrod.

Sources: Clodfelter (2002); Graz (1990); Landen (1967); Lenczowski (1987); Metz (1994); O'Neill (1980); Outram (2004); Ripenburg (1998); Schafer (1995); Townsend (1977).

NON-STATE WAR #1581:
The Angola Guerrilla War of 1974–1975

Participants: FLNA, UNITA vs. MPLA
Dates: October 15, 1974, to October 22, 1975
Battle-Related Deaths: FLNA—[ ], MPLA—[ ]; UNITA—[ ];
Where Fought: Africa
Initiator: MPLA
Outcome: Transformed into inter-state war #186
War Type: In nonstate territory

Narrative: Angola was a Portuguese colony for 400 years, from 1575 to 1975. Portugal fought three earlier wars as it extended its control in the area in 1902–1910 (extra-state wars #420, #421, and #430). In the post–World War II era, Portugal was the last major European power with colonies in Africa, and Portugal resisted giving up its colonies in the absence of an armed struggle (also see the war in Mozambique extra-state war #471).

In February 1961 the war for Angolan independence began (extra-state war #469). At the time there were two nationalist movements operating in exile: the Marxist Popular Movement for the Rebellion of Angola (MPLA) and the National Front for the Liberation of Angola (FNLA). Their war against Portugal was hampered by conflict among the rebel groups. In 1966 a third revolutionary group, National Union for the Total Independence of Angola (UNITA), formed as a breakaway from the FNLA. Initially UNITA, led by Jonas Savimbi, launched major attacks on the Portuguese; however, by 1971 UNITA and Portugal entered into a "gentleman's agreement" not to fight each other. The MPLA would not forgive UNITA for this betrayal. Then in April 1974 young army officers overthrew the regime in Portugal, and the new government appealed to the liberation movements in Angola to cease hostilities as a step toward independence. Portugal signed cease-fire agreements with each of the rebel groups in October 1974, the last on October 14, which marked the end of the extra-state war between the guerrillas and Portugal. As of the following day, fighting continued as this non-state war among the guerrilla groups themselves.

Toward the end of 1974, the FNLA was the strongest of the three guerrilla groups, having more than twice as many troops as the MPLA. UNITA was the weakest, with only 1,000 troops. Sporadic attacks occurred among the groups. Portugal was desirous of creating a government in Angola before it was going to grant independence in November 1975. Therefore, the guerrilla groups began to come to terms among themselves: The MPLA signed a cease-fire with UNITA on December 18, 1974, and with the FNLA on January 5, 1975. The leaders of the three rival groups met in January 1975, agreed to form a coalition government (on January 15, 1975), and promised to hold elections before the country's upcoming day of independence in November. The spirit of cooperation did not last long, however. February 1975 saw a revival of the war when the MPLA attacked the FNLA. Initially the war involved only the MPLA and FNLA, while UNITA stayed out of the fray; however, in June 1975 UNITA once again entered the fighting on the side of the FNLA. The Angolan war soon assumed international dimensions, as the United States and South Africa aided the FNLA, while the MPLA received massive aid from Cuba and Russia. By September 1975 the MPLA was winning in that it controlled many of the major cities. This prompted South African forces to directly enter the war. This non-state war thus ends on October 22, 1975, and the fighting is transformed into inter-state war #186, which starts the next day.

Coding: A turning point came on October 23, 1975, when South African forces directly entered the war, and the bulk of the fighting was taken

over by South Africa and Cuba, which makes the fighting an inter-state war (#186). On November 11, 1975, Angola gained its independence, immediately became a member of the interstate system, and became a participant in the inter-state war. The inter-state war ended on February 12, 1976, as the Angola government took over the bulk of the fighting, and the conflict continued as intra-state war #804. Clodfelter (2002) describes all the Portuguese wars in Africa—involving the three colonies of Angola, Guinea, and Mozambique—as one group, the "Wars of Independence in Portuguese Africa: 1961–1974." The conflict in Guinea-Bissau does not meet the COW fatality level necessary to be classified as a war.

Sources: Bender (1978); Ciment (2007); Clodfelter (2002); Crocker (1992); Guimaraes (1998); Hodges (2001); Hodges (1978); Keesing's (1974, 1975); Legum (1981); Legum (1978); Meredith (2005); Windrich (1992).

NON-STATE WAR #1582:

The East Timorese War Phase 1 of 1975

Participants: FRETILIN vs. UDT (and APODETI)
Dates: August 11, 1975, to October 15, 1975
Battle-Related Deaths: APODETI—[ ]; FRETILIN—[ ]; UDT—[ ] (Total Combatant Deaths: 3,000)
Where Fought: Asia
Initiator: UDT
Outcome: Transformed into extra-state war #472
War Type: In nonstate territory

Narrative: In the fifteenth and sixteenth centuries, Portuguese explorers reached out for trade routes to Asia and the Spice Islands. As a result the eastern half of the island of Timor, which lies east of Java and north of Australia, became a Portuguese colony from 1566 to 1975. After the Portuguese military coup in 1974, Portugal became willing to relinquish its colonial empire. Thus, the Revolutionary Front for the Independence of East Timor (FRETILIN) began agitating for independence for East Timor. The conflict that broke out in East Timor in 1975 and lasted through 1979 actually encompassed three distinct types of war. The first was this non-state war between FRETILIN and the Democratic Union (UDT) from August 11, 1975, to October 15, 1975. When Indonesia invaded East Timor on October 16, 1975, the war was transformed into an extra-state war (#472), and when Indonesian sovereignty was declared, the war was transformed again, this time into an intra-state war (#806).

After the Portuguese revolution, the new government permitted the development of political parties in East Timor, and three emerged fairly quickly. the Timorese Popular Democratic Association (APODETI) was created in May 1974 to promote the unification of East Timor with Indonesia, which already controlled the western half of the island of Timor. The UDT consisted mostly of Portuguese colonists, and FRETILIN was Marxist in orientation. In January 1975 FRETILIN and the UDT formed an alliance while local elections were being held. The results of the elections went against APODETI and unification with Indonesia. On August 10, however, the UDT, fearing FRETILIN domination, began to promote the Indonesian option, and ultimately staged a coup. The UDT seized key installations in the capital of Dili, and a war between FRETILIN and the UDT ensued. The Portuguese had only 400 troops on the island, and they abstained from involvement in the fighting. By August 30, FRETILIN claimed that it controlled most of East Timor, even though forces from APODETI were assisting the UDT. By September 9, FRETILIN had captured the capital and the UDT forces were retreating into Indonesia. On September 13, Indonesia indicated its willingness to intervene, should Portugal not object. Meanwhile Portugal arranged peace talks among the war participants for September 20.

Coding: This war is coded as ending on October 15, 1975. On October 16, Indonesia instituted a naval blockade of East Timor. Indonesia's entry into the war changed it from a non-state war into an extra-state war (#472) between a state and a nonstate armed group.

Sources: Brecher and Wilkenfeld (1997); Chomsky (1979); Ciment (2007); Clodfelter (2002); *Facts on File* (1975–1976); Gunn (1977); Jardine (1999); Jolliffe (1978); Keesing's (1975–1980); Phillips and Axelrod (2005); Smith (2003).

NON-STATE WAR #1594:

The Hema-Lendu War of 1999–2005

Participants: Hema vs. Lendu
Dates: June [ ], 1999, to March [ ], 2005
Battle-Related Deaths: Lendu—[ ]; Hema—[ ]
   (Total Combatant and Civilian Deaths: 60,000)
Where Fought: Africa
Initiator: Lendu
Outcome: Stalemate
War Type: Across state borders

Narrative: While the Democratic Republic of Congo (DRC) was being ravaged by Africa's World War (intra-state war #905), a non-state war was also raging in the Ituri district of the DRC. The war was a conflict between the Hema and the Lendu peoples and their related militias, and some of the origins of the conflict derive from the colonial period during which the DRC was under Belgian control. The Hema have an economy that is primarily dependent on livestock, which requires large amounts of land. The Lendu, on the other hand, are farmers, who were not particularly inclined to yield their land to the Hema. The Lendu believed that the Belgian authorities favored the Hema, a policy that they saw as being continued in the DCR. The conflict between the groups has recently been heightened by the presence of gold in the region. Although the groups had clashed earlier, the escalation of violence in 1999 marks the start of the war.

The Union des Patriotes Congolais (UPC) claims to be defending the Hema, while the

Résistance Patrique d'Ituri (FRPI) and the Front Nationaliste et Intégrationniste (FNI) supported the Lendu. The government of Uganda denies involvement in the war, but Uganda factions were reported to be assisting the Hema as well. The war began in 1999 when the Ugandan army created a new provincial structure in Ituri and named a Hema as the new governor. Perceiving collusion between the Hema and the Ugandan authorities, the Lendu attacked Hema institutions. The Ugandans did nothing to stop the fierce fighting and indeed provided military training to both sides. Some of the fighting crossed the border into Uganda, along with 8,000 refugees. After the Uganda army evacuated the town of Bunia in 2003, significant fighting between the Hema and Lendu took place there. In the beginning of 2003, a UN peacekeeping force (Mission of the United Nations Organisation in the Democratic Republic of the Congo, or MONUC) was dispatched to the region in the context of the conclusion of Africa's World War (intra-state war #905); however, the peace settlement did not apply to the militias, and fighting between the Hema and Lendu revived again at the end of the year. Even though the United Nations was unable to stop the fighting, the level of fatalities apparently declined in 2005, which marks the end of this war.

Coding: This war is coded as a non-state war, with a war type of "across state borders" because this conflict is seen as transcending the boundaries of a state in a couple of ways. Both Rwanda and Uganda have been backing the rival militias, in what some see as a proxy war. This support has also meant that military engagements have migrated back and forth across the Uganda-DCR border. Determining the battle-related deaths for this war has so far proved to be impossible. It has been estimated that 60,000 people (combatants and civilians) have died in the fighting during this period. Thus it would seem likely that 1,000 combatants have died per year. The Uppsala Conflict Data Project codes a best estimate of deaths of 2,394 in 2002 and 1,875 in 2003, though their figures include civilians killed during the war.

Sources: BBC News (2002); Human Rights Watch (2003); IRIN (2005); IRIN (2004); IRIN (1999); Meredith (2005); Tripp (2005); Uppsala Universitet (2003).

Analyzing Non-state Wars

There are sixty-two non-state wars in the dataset. Of these, sixty-one fall into war type 8 (that is, they take place in nonstate territory) and only one (non-state war #1594) is in war type 9 (takes place across state borders). The definitional characteristics of non-state wars are such that they produce distributional patterns that are different from the other categories of war.

As Figure 6.1 shows, non-state wars are fairly rare, with the overwhelming number of years (144 out of 192, or 75 percent) having no non-state war onsets (though that may also be a function of the preliminary nature of this dataset).

Figure 6.2 reveals the distribution of non-state wars over time, and here the impact of the definition of non-state wars is readily visible. Virtually all of the non-state wars (sixty-one of the sixty-two wars) occurred in nonstate territory, which generally is territory that is in prestate-formation phases, or territory that is a dependency. Thus the vast majority of non-state wars occurred prior to 1870, when extensive geographical areas were not yet incorporated into system members. This was also the period in which there were numerous nonstate territorial entities with the capability to engage in war. As geopolitical units increasingly formed into states (becoming members of the COW interstate system) and as colonies and other dependencies gained their autonomy and became system members, the territory in which such non-state wars could take place became more limited—thus the number of non-state wars declined. This pattern is similar to that for extra-state wars (see Chapter 4), which also by definition require the existence of nonstate actors outside of system member borders.

FIGURE 6.1 **Non-state War Onsets by Number of Years, 1816–2007 (Number of Years in Which the Onset of 0, 1, 2, or 3 Non-state Wars Occurred)**

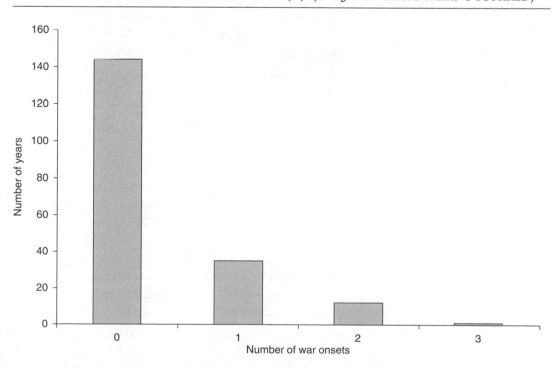

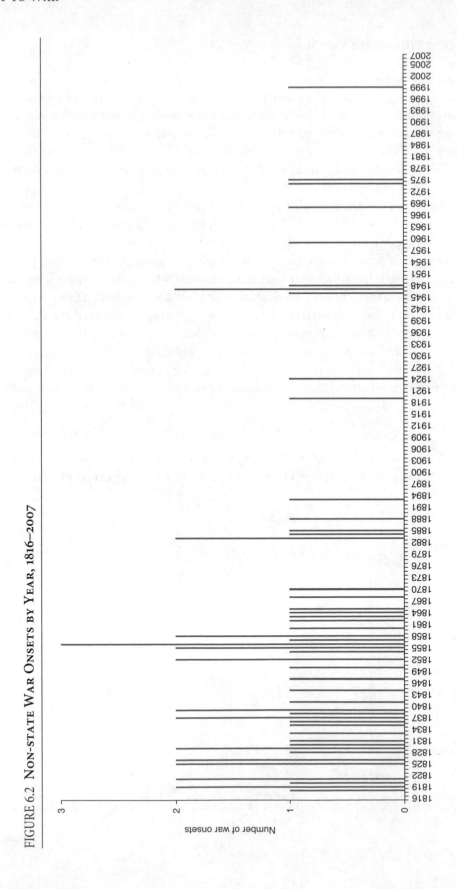

FIGURE 6.2 NON-STATE WAR ONSETS BY YEAR, 1816–2007

FIGURE 6.3 NON-STATE WAR ONSETS BY DECADE, 1817–2006

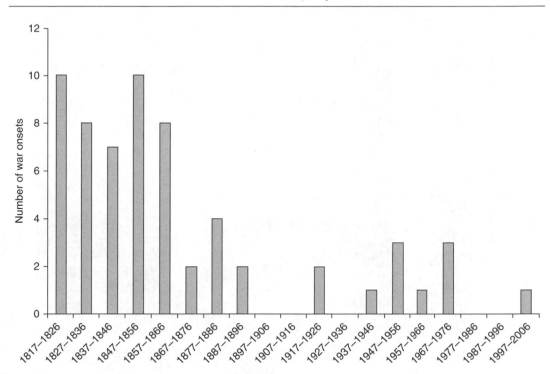

The pattern of decline in non-state wars is visible in Figure 6.3, which examines the number of non-state war onsets per decade. This pattern might portend the demise of non-state wars. However, there are countervailing trends as well. As Sarkees and Singer have argued, there is evidence of the growing power and efficacy of nonstate actors, particularly as they attain the capabilities to wage war.[2] The significant increase in the number of intra-state wars, including those that involve nonstate actors within states (see Chapter 5), and the revival of extra-state wars (see Chapter 4), both of which involve nonstate actors, provide some indication that the category of non-state wars may continue in the future as well.

Finally, in looking at the distribution of non-state wars by region in Figure 6.4, we see that Africa, Asia, and the Western Hemisphere are the most common locations for these wars. There are some differences in these distributions over time. The non-state wars in the Western Hemisphere tended to occur during the early years of the nineteenth century, whereas the non-state wars began to occur more frequently in Africa and Asia in the latter half of the nineteenth century, perhaps as colonial empires lingered there later. The relatively early development of the state system in Europe has apparently so far precluded non-state wars there. In contrast, non-state wars have been more common in Oceania than have other types of wars.

FIGURE 6.4 NON-STATE WAR ONSETS BY REGION, 1816–2007

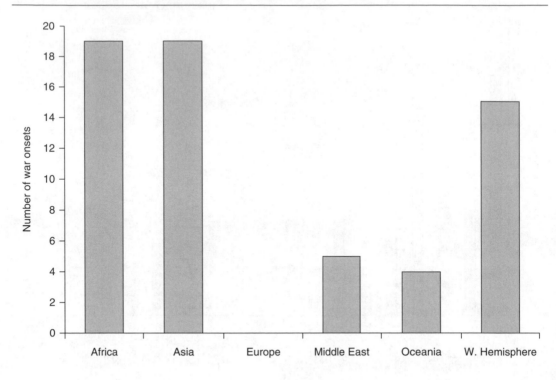

NOTES

1. Melvin Small and J. David Singer, *Resort to Arms: International and Civil War, 1816–1980* (Beverly Hills, Calif.: Sage, 1982), 215.
2. Meredith Reid Sarkees and J. David Singer. "Armed Conflict Past and Future: A Master Typology?" (paper presented at the European Union Conference on Armed Conflict Data Collection, Uppsala, Sweden, June 2001).

CHAPTER SEVEN

What Do We Know about War?

By Meredith Reid Sarkees

> War fosters an impossible collection of opposites: murder, soldierly comradeship, torture, religious conviction, the destruction of the earth, patriotism, annihilation, hope for immortal glory. Wartime seems to propel life to its most vivid, most meaningful level. Engaged in the activity of destruction, its soldiers and its victims discover a profound sense of existing, of being human. The mind withdraws from this paradox, and, indeed, few writers have taken on the task of unlocking the baleful, intoxicating, and necessary force that is war. Instead, the bare fact that war has dominated human history since the earliest records and seems always ready to break out is ignored, condemned, or lamented.[1]

As psychologist James Hillman noted above, from his book titled *A Terrible Love of War*, attempts to understand war are made more difficult by the fact that the specific linkage between humankind and war is complex and still a matter of significant contestation: some see the propensity to engage in war as biologically determined, while others see the practice of warfare as an historical or cultural construct. Views on war range from overwhelmingly negative to enthusiastically supportive (even if only in utilitarian terms). A plethora of peace groups, including the Women's International League for Peace and Freedom (WILPF), have as their ultimate goal "the prevention and eradication of war."[2] In contrast, some opine that we need to "Give War a Chance" as a means of confronting global evil.[3] Meanwhile, others argue that the enduring attraction of war is due to the fact that "it can give us what we long for in life. It can give us purpose, meaning, a reason for living."[4] In order to grapple with the complexity of war, Hillman argues that we need to get at its myths, to "recognize that war is a mythical happening."[5] It is the myths about war that have combined to make war seem as "normal."[6] Hillman finds proof of war's normalcy in its constancy throughout history, its ubiquity over the globe, and in its acceptability.[7] The standards of normality can derive from theology, the law, medicine, philosophy, education, or the culture of society, and are in essence our beliefs.[8] Such beliefs are "enfolded together in the great bed of myth" that leads to the "deceptive rush to war."[9] The importance of myths is also addressed by Beatrice Heuser and Cyril Buffet, who highlight the ways in which myths are utilized in the context of recommendations for future governmental policies.[10] Though they focus upon the origins of myths in untrue representations of historical events, they similarly emphasize the ways in which myths are deliberately used to provide a moral argument that takes the place of rational justification.[11] To a great extent, such myths overlay our discussions of war and bedevil our attempts at more completely comprehending the role of war in human history, its complexities, its endurance, and the ways in which it is evolving.

Though it is not possible to comprehensively discuss the roles and implications of myths within the confines of this chapter, it is important to briefly address the origins of beliefs about war in order to understand the competing perspectives on war and the resultant perceptions about the ways in which war may or may not be changing. Hillman argues that it is necessary to examine war in terms of the complexity of the beliefs about war that originate in theology, psychology, and philosophy and the ways in which they interact.[12] Beliefs about war developed in each of these areas will be briefly discussed within the overall parameters of the contestations concerning the evolution of war and the empirical findings about war.

War and Religion

Hillman devoted an entire chapter to the subject "Religion Is War."[13] Religion is characterized by the belief in the "absolute superiority in the object of that belief."[14] Monotheistic faiths see one particular god as supreme, consequently others who believe in a different god "exhibit in their very existence a denial of the complete truth of your god. It is a necessity of your truth and your faith to war against them, because . . . their existence places in essential doubt the foundations of your belief in your god."[15] Religion becomes the justification for wars of conquest and conversion, and god is seen as taking sides in the battle. However, monotheistic faiths have also struggled with reconciling competing religious teachings, for instance Scriptures that tell people not to kill and to turn the other cheek are contrasted to those that proclaim God as an avenger against those who do evil.[16] One of the ways in which religion has attempted to harmonize these teachings is through "just-war" theory, or establishing the conditions under which war can be morally rationalized. One justification is through espousing the right of self-defense, whereby a state attacked by force can respond with force. The right to self-defense is not absolute, however, and conditions for its application have been codified, for example, by the United Nations.[17] However, religion still also espouses a moral authority that can be used to justify offensive war, to punish an evildoer outside a state's own borders.[18] Michael Walzer, one of the more positive analysts of just-war theory, refers to this as a war of law enforcement, in which a state fights not only for itself but also for the preservation of the entire society.[19] Jean Bethke Elshtain has described the dual nature of the just-war argument as: "On one end, the Catholic just-war tradition makes contact with pacifism; on the other, it elides into holy wars against infidels."[20] Sectors of religion thus contribute to what Elshtain calls the "heretical crusading offshoot," in which conflicts are seen as being between the righteous and the sinners.[21] Yet even the less emphatic interpretations of just-war theory provide a justification for war in terms of confronting evil. The underlying assumption is that war will remain as long as evil remains, and recently just-war theory has been utilized to validate the war against Iraq.[22] As Gen. Wesley Clark described it, the American *2002 National Security Strategy* espoused a new policy justifying preemptive action against the threat of global terrorism.[23]

A recent variation of the more crusading aspect of just-war theory has been provided by Samuel Huntington, who focused less upon religion per se but on the notion of culture or civilization as a whole, which includes religion. He predicted that the "clash of civilizations" will be the latest phase in the evolution of conflict and that such clashes will dominate global politics in the foreseeable future.[24] Civilizations are herein seen as the broadest group with which individuals identify, and they encompass and are to some extent identified by religious traditions. Though the number of civilizations varies, Huntington identified the current Western, Confucian, Japanese, Islamic, Hindu, Slavic-Orthodox, Latin American, and African civilizations.[25] These civilizations are marked by the growing power of fundamentalist religious movements, and it is the recent revival of religion that unites contemporary civilizations.[26] As people define themselves in terms of religion, they see conflicts in terms of the "us" versus "them" light, which encourages animosities to come to the fore. In particular, Huntington predicted that the former ideological conflict of the Cold War would be replaced by the increasing clash of civilizations.[27] Though the interactions between civilizations will vary in terms of the levels of violence they experience, Huntington saw a primary confrontation arising between Islam and the West.[28] This will lead to both inter-state wars and intra-state wars as countries that contain peoples of different civilizations are torn apart.[29]

War and Psychology

A contrasting source of understandings or myths about war is psychology, and theories that have linked war and a general propensity to violence to human nature have been fairly common. Probably the most well-known work in this area is that of Sigmund Freud, who noted that "conflicts of interest between men are settled by the use of violence" and that "killing an enemy satisfied an instinctual inclination."[30] Chris Hedges, who covered a series of wars in his career as a correspondent, summarized the perspective of Sigmund Freud as concluding that all human history reflects the struggle within human nature between the impulse to protect and the instinct to destruction. Hedges, who admitted his own attraction to war, concluded that Freud was consequently pessimistic about ever being able to eradicate war.[31] Yet Freud's overall view of war was also more complicated in that he saw some wars as bringing nothing but evil, while other wars led to the creation of larger societies in which the use of force became impossible.[32] Consequently, he also maintained some hope that the process of civilization would serve to reduce the tendency to war.[33]

Yet Hedges's observations about war highlight a slightly different link between human psychology and war. The title of his book, *War Is a Force That Gives Us Meaning*, summarizes his contention that "the enduring attraction of war is this: Even with its destruction and carnage it can give us what we long for in life. It can give us purpose, meaning, a reason for living."[34] In this vein, war is characterized as an addiction, a drug that is linked both to the universal human capacity for evil and conversely to a cause that allows us to be noble.[35] Yet, he also sees war as a myth, "peddled by mythmakers—historians, war correspondents, filmmakers, novelists, and the state—all of whom endow it with qualities it often does not possess: excitement, exoticism, power, chances to rise above our small stations in life, and a bizarre and fantastic universe that has a grotesque and dark beauty."[36] In terms of understanding contemporary wars, Hedges argues that it is the mythmakers who help us fold war into the black-and-white views of our belief system that depicts war as necessary for a higher good and makes us callous to those we battle.[37]

In discussing the psychological foundations of war, James Schellenberg has traced the theme of ingrained aggression back to the work of Charles Darwin, which contributed to the general view that "conflict over the means of subsistence is the underlying fact which shapes the nature of human society."[38] According to Schellenberg, the field of sociology extended the idea of innate aggression into a conclusion that war is a "constant feature of humanity," driven by the desire for domination.[39] However, sociology was also instrumental in developing the emphasis on social determinism in which human behavior is the product of societal requirements that in essence trump biological traits.[40] From this perspective, conflict is still seen as endemic in the nature of human society, yet societies are seen as evolving, which raises the possibility of creating avenues toward peace.[41]

Joshua S. Goldstein, in his exhaustive examination of the links between war and gender, also discussed the biological and cultural determinants of war. Similarly, he found war to be part of human nature.[42] However, his research specifically indicated that there is only a limited link between testosterone and aggression.[43] More importantly, he tied war to the development of masculinity as a social construct. Masculinity has become defined as man's ability to function as a combatant.[44] War is thus a means of demonstrating and testing one's manhood. He argued that all elements of society work together to create a culture that highlights the centrality of war to masculinity and provides rewards to warriors.[45] The consistency of the gendered roles in war is related to the "pervasiveness of war across cultures."[46] This emphasis on the gendered construction of war has similarly been raised by a number of feminist scholars, and it will be discussed below in the section on philosophy.

The psychological conventional wisdom that "war was an eradicable part of human nature"[47] was also problematic for John G. Stoessinger, prompting him to conduct case studies of seven wars to better understand the origin of war. He concluded that although "aggression may be inherent, war is learned behavior and as such can be unlearned and ultimately selected out entirely. Humans have overcome other habits that previously had seemed unconquerable. . . . It does appear, however, that people abandon their bad habits only when catastrophe is close at hand. The intellect alone is not enough."[48] His ultimate conclusion was that to understand the origins of war, one had to examine the personalities of leaders in greater detail, and that the most important single precipitating factor in the outbreak of war is misperception on behalf of the leaders.[49] Though Seyom Brown also saw the role of misperception by leaders as being important in the causes of war, he reached an opposite conclusion: "that the insights we gain from the fields of biology and psychology are an insufficient basis for understanding the highly organized and usually premeditated international violence we call war . . . and that we must grapple as well with a wider array of factors, encompassing the material conditions, social structures, and cultural and moral norms that influence the behavior of nations."[50]

The assumption of the premeditation of war is also seen as significant by Kenneth J. Campbell, who became disillusioned about war through his experiences in the U.S. Marine Corps in Vietnam. Campbell also sees leaders' misperceptions as fundamental in the origins of war, but even more critically he argues that deception by leaders is the basis of many wars. Though he does not criticize all wars, he focuses upon quagmires, including the current war in Iraq:

> Quagmires are built upon the quicksand of deception, deception about purpose, progress, methods, and exit. When the nation's leaders conceive of a war for questionable purpose, they deceptively portray it as a "just cause," because they know that the people of the nation will not long support an unnecessary war and that the nation's troops will not long risk their lives for an unnecessary war.[51]

Though Campbell's critique is addressed at the hubris of the United States and its leaders, which created two specific wars (against Vietnam and Iraq), his major thesis is more broadly applicable. Leaders used systematic deception to launch and conduct wars for ideological motives and personal gain.[52] Thus Campbell's work highlights the linkages between myths about war that arise from psychology and those that are developed by philosophy and ideology.

War and Philosophy

Political philosophers have been in similar disagreement about the relationship between humankind and war. As Michael W. Doyle described in *Ways of War and Peace*, the ideologies of realism, liberalism, and socialism each posit different explanations of the role of war in human history. Though the classification of "realism" includes a spectrum of perspectives (classified as complex, fundamentalist, structuralist, and constitutionalist), the underlying claim is that the use of force and thus war are the fundamental bases of international politics.[53] Consequently "realists" tend to expect the endurance of the phenomenon of war. "Liberalism" is seen as encompassing a similar range in its perspectives (including foci on rights and interests, commercial pacifism, and internationalism), each of which espouses a slightly different explanation for war. However, the underlying assumption of liberalism is the possibility of peace among independent states.[54] Wars are caused by authoritarian leaders and totalitarian ruling parties that violate the rights of others, and when citizens "elect their governments, wars become impossible."[55] Though Doyle identifies fewer variants of socialism, he notes that some socialists are closer to liberals in seeing the possibility of peace, while others focus upon the enduring feature of war.[56] The underlying premise of socialism is the importance of economic relations between countries and classes, and war is the result of capitalist exploitation.[57]

Each of these general philosophical perspectives—realism, liberalism, and socialism has had numerous proponents within international relations theoretical scholarship as well, and they each propose contrasting expectations about the pervasiveness and trends in war. Though the plethora of variations within these perspectives are too detailed to comprehensively address here, they will be briefly discussed in terms of their understandings (or myths) about war.

REALISM

Realism has been considered the dominant paradigm in the study of international relations since the 1950s. Scholars who espoused its tenets included Hans Morgenthau, E. H. Carr, Raymond Aron, Kenneth Waltz, and John Mearsheimer. The central themes of realism include a focus upon the anarchy within the international system and the consequent need for states to pursue power.[58] The standard justification for a state's going to war is to promote or advance its power, or in other words to secure or advance important national interests.[59] The ultimate determinant of international behavior is the distribution of power within the system, and realists contend that "international politics, like all politics, is a struggle for power."[60] Though this struggle means that there is always a possibility of war, the probability of war can be mediated by the balance of power and diplomacy.[61] However, there is disagreement about which type of system structure or balance of power is better able to reduce conflict. Karl Deutsch and J. David Singer argued that a multipolar system in which power is distributed among a number of states is more stable and thus reduces the intensity and frequency of war.[62] In contrast, Kenneth Waltz argued that a bipolar system, in which international power is concentrated in two states (such as the USSR and the United States after World War II), was relatively stable and this stability served to limit violence.[63] Similarly, John Mearsheimer noted that the relative stability of the bipolar balance of power during the Cold War dampened the number of wars, and he predicted that the amount of war would return to normal (higher) levels once this balance had ended.[64] In *The Causes and Prevention of War*, Seyom Brown also discussed the extent to which the distribution of power provokes wars. He differentiated among three types of polarity (unipolarity, bipolarity, and multipolarity—each in both tight and loose configurations). War is unlikely in tight bipolar systems (like the Cold War) and is much more likely in loose multipolar systems.[65] He concluded that a polyarchic structure, or a radically depolarized structure, was emerging in the wake of the Cold War in which wars would no longer be deterred. He ominously predicted that "we can look forward to a 'state of nature'—more brutal than ever imagined by Thomas Hobbes—in which the lives of many of the world's peoples, even the survival of the species itself, are in perpetual jeopardy."[66]

There have been numerous studies that have utilized empirical methodologies to test the central propositions of realism, and the findings have been mixed. According to Paul Diehl and Frank

Wayman, their survey of tests of realism provides "strong evidence for both the utility and the limitations of the realist framework. The framework does offer insights into why states decide to become involved in conflict and when they might use or threaten military force."[67] John Vasquez similarly found support for the realist assertion that the struggle for power can lead to war, and in particular he concluded that disputes over territory are the main source of conflict and war.[68] In addition to general support for realism, Vasquez furthermore noted that the use of "realpolitik," or power politics behavior, to try to resolve territorial disputes increases the probability of war. "This is because the main practices of power politics—alliances, military buildups, and the use of realpolitik tactics—increase insecurity and hostility motivating each side to take harder lines."[69] However, in contrast to realist assertions, Vasquez found that not all states are engaged in the struggle for power.[70] Consequently, states have found ways to maintain peace and to resolve conflicts without going to war.[71]

The same distinction between realism as a theory and realpolitik as political practice that is designed to promote the security of the state was discussed by Manus Midlarsky in the context of examining instances of genocide.[72] He found that both loss (frequently involving territory) and the adoption of realpolitik policies are implicated in cases of genocide and that genocide generally occurred in the context of war.[73] Interventions by powerful states have the potential to deter or stop attempted genocides; however, "[i]f power disparities between potential interveners and victimizers are substantial ... and no intervention occurs, then validation of massacre, if not genocide itself, can be even more pronounced."[74]

Richard Stoll explicitly examined the role of polarity and discussed the competing claims about whether the bipolar system of 1946–1976 was fundamentally different (either more or less peaceful) from the preceding multipolar era (1816–1945). His findings, though modest, indicated that there were fewer wars involving the major powers than would be expected in the post–World War II era,[75] while the number of militarized disputes did increase in the post–World War II era, particularly in terms of disputes involving the United States.[76]

LIBERALISM

In contrast to the realists' focus upon the anarchy of the international system with the expectations of the persistence or increase in wars, the liberals, sometimes referred to as the idealists, tend to perceive the international system as "a society of states bound by common rules, customs, and shared norms."[77] Though there is conflict within the system, it can be mediated by international law, limiting the arms race, open diplomacy, promoting democratic control, and intergovernmental organizations (such as the League of Nations or United Nations).[78] Among the various strands of liberalism, the common assumption is one of progress, that human society can be perfected. War does not stem from human nature but from "imperfect political institutions that an advancing civilization could eliminate."[79] Thus war could be reduced or eliminated by the creation of alternative political institutions. Some scholars emphasized the role of functional systems, or networks of transnational scientific, cultural, or economic linkages, as potentially replacing nation-states.[80] The work of Robert Keohane and Joseph Nye focused upon the development of "complex interdependence" and the extent to which states could be eclipsed by nonterritorial actors, including intergovernmental organizations.[81]

More recently, the focus within liberalism has been upon progress through the promotion of democratic governments. As briefly described in the Introduction, both policymakers and liberal international relations scholars have espoused the position that the contemporary world is characterized by the increase in democratic governments, and it is argued that the spread of democracy is rendering war obsolete or at least less common.[82] For example, Francis Fukuyama foresaw an ensuing liberal peace lasting indefinitely.[83] Since the 1990s, the topic of the "democratic peace" has become one of the most popular within international relations scholarship. Doyle traced this perspective to the work of Immanuel Kant, whose article "Perpetual Peace" explained that liberal or democratic states would be peaceful between/among themselves but not necessarily peaceful in their relations with nonliberal states.[84] The liberal republics would band together in a pacific federation in order to protect their rights, and peace would spread as additional states are included within the federation, leading to perpetual peace.

A virtual cottage industry of empirical studies has developed examining the evidence for, and attributes of, the Kantian "democratic peace." Melvin Small and J. David Singer conducted one of the early studies of the war-proneness of democratic states, and for the period between 1816 and 1965, they found that in general democracies were just as likely as autocratic regimes to be involved in and initiate international wars.[85] They did find, however, that democracies did not seem to fight one another, though they partially attributed this finding to the fact that democracies rarely bordered one another during this period, thus lessening opportunities for conflict.[86] Their overall conclusion was that democracies are not particularly peace-prone, and that citizens in democracies are not always a restraint upon the government's involvement in wars, since the citizens can be persuaded to support their government's involvement. Therefore, they noted that they "cannot agree with optimistic conclusions about either the relationship between bourgeois democracies and war or the continuing democratization of the world."[87]

Despite Small and Singer's cautioning conclusion, a plethora of scholars have adopted the more optimistic assumptions of the democratic peace and produced numerous studies in support of its propositions. As Zeev Maoz noted, "The evidence is seemingly overwhelming, making this the most replicated research program in the modern study of international politics."[88] These findings have led Jack Levy to argue that the democratic peace is "the closest thing we have to an empirical law in the study of international relations," and John Owen has similarly concluded that "the proposition that democracies seldom if ever go to war against one another has nearly become a truism."[89] One of the major proponents of the democratic peace, Bruce Russett, has contended that all the elements alluded to by Immanuel Kant, namely, joint democracy, shared trade, and membership in the same international organizations, independently contribute to peace between pairs of states.[90] Similarly, a study by John Oneal and Russett focused upon the finding that democracies are less likely to fight each other than one would expect.[91]

The primary corollary of the democratic peace argument is that the number of wars will decline as the number of democracies spreads, though empirical scholarship has been replete with competing understandings of this historical trend. Scholars have differed concerning the time frame of this decline and the states to which it applies. Most researchers generally focus upon inter-state war (excluding extra-state, intra-state, and non-state wars), and in arguing that warfare is declining, they have posited the distinctiveness of the long postwar (since 1945) peace.[92] Jack Levy describes the downward trend in terms of wars that involved the great powers.[93] Others, such as Peter Wallensteen and Margareta Sollenberg, see the decline in wars as taking place after the end of the Cold War and, after analyzing armed conflict from 1989 to 1995, posed the question of whether we were seeing "the end of international war."[94] Since then, Hilde Ravlo, Nils Petter Gleditsch, and Han Dorussen have claimed to find support for the democratic peace even among extra-state wars.[95] Bethany Lacina, Gleditsch, and Russett found a significant decline in battle-deaths since World War II and even since the end of the Cold War.[96] *The Human Security Report 2005* found a large drop in several indicators of armed violence over the recent decades and argued that the intervention by peacekeepers from the

UN and other agencies had helped create a more peaceful world since the end of the Cold War.[97] The overall perspective of these scholars is reflected by Ted Robert Gurr, Monty G. Marshall, and Deepa Khosla, who concluded in 2001 that we have "a world more peaceful than at any time in the past century."[98]

The optimism of the democratic peace proponents has been challenged on both theoretical and empirical grounds. Doyle suggested three areas in which the democratic peace argument is vulnerable or needs more careful elaboration: the dependent variables (or outcomes), the causal model, and the policy implications.[99] In terms of the dependent variable, he notes that the absence of war is not the same as peace, and he suggests expanding the analyses to include other types of conflict, such as conflict below war level, such as militarized interstate disputes (MIDs); internal violence, such as intra-state wars; peaceful territorial change; the effect of electoral cycles; and great power cooperation.[100] The propensity of democratic peace scholars to focus only upon inter-state wars has also been a significant topic of dissent. A number of scholars have noted that the post–World War II era has witnessed a great deal of warfare of different types. Furthermore, millions have died in conflicts classified as democide (murder of people by a government) that can include genocide (the planned annihilation of a racial or cultural group) and politicide (the annihilation of a political group), which often accompany war.[101]

In particular, a number of empirical studies documented the increase in conflict that accompanied the end of the Cold War (1989–1991). Ted Gurr found that the number of ongoing ethnopolitical conflicts in the world doubled from the 1950s to the 1990s.[102] *The State of War and Peace Atlas* of the International Peace Research Institute of Oslo indicated that the period 1990–1995 had seen seventy states involved in ninety-three wars (primarily civil).[103] Military historian Michael Clodfelter claimed that both international and civil wars (conventional and guerrilla) seem to have made a comeback,[104] while others decried the proliferation of what are called "ethnic wars."[105] Similarly, Wolf Dieter Eberwein and Sven Chojnacki noted that the transition to democracy may be accompanied by a high incidence of both domestic conflict and international violence.[106] Likewise, Michael Brecher and Jonathan Wilkenfeld argued that interstate turmoil had not abated in the post–Cold War years, since there were twenty-one full-scale international crises from 1990 to 1994, and they concluded that, "the post–World War II international system has been characterized by persistent violence in many regions."[107]

Charles Kegley admitted that speaking of a long postwar peace does run the risk of misrepresenting the reality that a "long war" is indeed ongoing if one examines the entire system and includes all three types of war that occurred (inter-state, extra-state, and intra-state).[108] In the same vein, Monty Marshall noted that the other side of the "long peace" is the "third world war" in which the pattern of violence has shifted to the international periphery and is characterized by civil warfare and ethnic conflict.[109] A number of scholars have argued that the current international system has seen the emergence of new types of war, frequently referred to as "ethnic wars," "wars of the third kind," "peoples' wars," or "wars on terror." These arguments will be addressed below in a separate section entitled "New Wars?"

Doyle's second area of concern for the democratic peace argument involves the causal model, or lack thereof.[110] Here, there are two general issues: what are democracies, and why should we expect democracies to be peaceful? The first issue is primarily definitional and raises concerns about the ways in which democratic peace scholars code states as being democratic. As Doyle notes, "[I]t is not at all clear that most lists of participating polities, including my own, are all Liberal republics."[111] Doyle goes on to discuss several specific historical "hard cases," some of which expose the complexity of making a simple "Liberal versus non-Liberal categorization," including imperial Germany before World War I.[112] A similar case could be Germany prior to World War II, which raises the question as to whether the way in which *democracy* is defined automatically eliminates many states as they prepare for war from remaining in the democratic category. The problem thus becomes one of trying to "weed out the false negatives, where the Liberal model may be getting undue credit to peace."[113]

The causal connection between democracies and peace concerns the question as to why we should expect democracies to be peaceful. This question was initially raised by Small and Singer[114] and is recurrently brought to the fore by empirical findings such as those by Henry Farber and Joanne Gowa, who note that though democracies are less likely to go to war with one another, they are in general just as likely as any other regime to go to war.[115] Though many empirical studies focus merely upon the statistical findings correlating democracies and peace without discussing the causal mechanisms at play, others have developed arguments that rely upon either a monadic or a dyadic analysis. The monadic view, which emphasizes the attributes of a single country, argues that democracies are always more peaceful than nondemocracies owing to their nonviolent norms or the restraint of the citizenry. The more constrained dyadic view, which looks at the relationships between a pair of countries, argues that democracies are less likely to go to war only against other democracies.[116] John Owen similarly noted that the democratic peace lacked a convincing theoretical foundation. "No one is sure why democracies do not fight one another and yet do fight non-democracies. That we do not really know the causal mechanism behind the democratic peace means we cannot be certain the peace is genuine. It may be an epiphenomenon, a by-product of other causal variables such as those suggested by realist theories of international politics."[117] Owen then attempts to defend the democratic peace by developing a causal model that generally argues that it is "liberal ideas that cause liberal democracies to tend away from war with one another, and the same ideas prod these states into war with illiberal states."[118] He examines the monadic or structural view that democracies are peaceful because democratic structures restrain leaders from waging war, and he rejects it because his case studies indicated that "democratic structures were nearly as likely to drive states to war as to restrain them from it. Cabinets, legislatures, and publics were often more belligerent than the government heads they were supposed to constrain."[119] He similarly rejects the dyadic or normative view that it would be unjust for democracies to fight one another, partially because of the impact of the misperceptions of leaders. Consequently he argues that both of these emphases combine into an overarching variable of liberal ideas that gives rise to the distinctive foreign policies of liberal democracies through the intervening variables of liberal ideology and democratic institutions.[120] The concept of liberal ideas takes into account the role of perceptions, and Owen concludes that "liberals trust those states they consider fellow liberal democracies and see no reason to fight them. They view those states they consider illiberal with suspicion, and sometimes believe that the national interest requires war with them."[121]

A similar test of the causal arguments for the democratic peace was conducted by Christopher Layne, who came to the opposing conclusion: that the "democratic peace theory's causal logic has only minimal explanatory power."[122] Like Owen, Layne notes that democratic institutional constraints do not explain the democratic peace, because "if democratic public opinion really had the effect ascribed to it, democracies would be peaceful in their relations with all states, whether democratic or not."[123] Layne argues that it was realism, and not democratic peace theory, that provided the better explanations of why war was avoided.[124] He concludes by rejecting the democratic peace argument with the caution that "in the end, as its most articulate proponents admit, liberal international relations theory is based on hope, not on fact."[125] Despite Layne's assertive conclusion, the debate over the democratic peace continued. In 1997 Zeev Maoz undertook an examination of the critiques of the democratic peace from both the realist and cultural perspectives and concluded that "none of these critiques damages the democratic peace result in any significant way."[126] However, despite the continued spate of articles about the democratic peace, several researchers were still troubled by the "lack of consistency with regard to the putative theoretical explanations of this 'empirical law.'"[127] As Steve Smith noted, though some see the liberal peace theory as a progressive research paradigm, he does not see it as progressive but merely as a political view of international relations that defines a set of parameters as given and then examines behavior within those parameters, never looking at what aspects of world politics are excluded from the analysis. Smith specifically objects to the fact that "the liberal peace theory defines both peace and democracy in a very U.S. way."[128]

Consequently, Errol A. Henderson reexamined both of the theoretical explanations of the democratic peace, the monadic and the dyadic. Finding both of these to be unimpressive, he undertook a reexamination of the empirical evidence that had been produced in favor of the democratic peace; in particular, he replicated one of the major democratic peace studies, that done by Oneal and Russett.[129] Overall, Henderson found no significant relationship between joint democracy and a lowered likelihood of international conflict. Instead he charges that Oneal and Russett's findings were the result of several questionable research design choices, which thus "call into question the dyadic version of the democratic peace thesis, thereby undermining the empirical support for democratic enlargement strategies."[130] Overall, Henderson concluded that his finding should disabuse scholars of the notion that democracies are more peaceful.[131] He found that democracies are in fact *more war-prone* than nondemocracies, and *more* likely to initiate inter-state wars than are nondemocracies.[132] When Henderson extended his analysis to extra-state wars, he did find that democracies in general were less likely to engage in that class of wars; however, Western democracies were more likely to be involved.[133] Overall, in rejecting the democratic peace argument, Henderson proposes that during the Cold War era, the likelihood of war was decreased by, among other things, bipolarity, nuclear deterrence, enduring alliances, and increased trade.[134] He then concludes with the observation that "the democratic peace is hardly an empirical law; in fact, it appears to be a 'great illusion.'"[135]

SOCIALISM/CRITICAL THEORY

The third of Doyle's ideological perspectives that provide understandings about the origins of war is socialism. Though Doyle specifically refers to this perspective as socialism, the discussion below will also include discussions of elements of critical theory that might not particularly identify themselves as socialist but that also provide insights into the relationship between humankind and war. This combination follows the work of Andrew Linklater, who describes critical theory as consisting of both Marxian-inspired critical social theory and postmodern critical theory.[136]

Socialism

For Doyle, the key element of socialist theory is that it "focuses on the material conditions of life and on the classes—workers and capitalists, and financiers, landowners, merchants, small farmers, peasants—that have defined their interests in relation to jobs and wealth."[137] Derived from the work of Karl Marx and Friedrich Engels, socialism argues that history is driven by the conflict between the classes within society. For example, the stage of capitalist production will be supplanted by socialism (the dictatorship of the proletariat) when the workers overthrow the bourgeoisie. Since the capitalists (bourgeoisie) were so entrenched, a violent revolution will be necessary for history to progress.[138] It was Lenin who particularly extended the discussion of socialism's understanding of the role of war. Capitalism depended upon expanding its overseas linkages, for investment opportunities, for gaining the raw materials for production, and for creating new markets. This drive led to imperialism and war.[139] Capitalism is thus tied to war in two distinct ways: as leading to revolution within the capitalists countries, and as a means of colonial expansion (imperialism) and conversely to wars of national liberation to throw off colonial domination.[140] Capitalism thus particularly fuels both extra-state and intra-state wars. Imperialism reflected capitalism's final stage, and imperialism would also lead to inter-state wars, specifically from the attempts of a state to establish hegemonic power. "In fact, in every case, the final stage of the struggle for hegemony involved a major military encounter, which we may call generically a 'thirty years' war.' ... In each case the power committed to maintaining the basic structure of a capitalist world-economy won out ... and the war itself increased enormously the military strength of the putative hegemonic power."[141] Conversely, peace, or the end of war, would result only from the global triumph of socialism, reflecting the global unity of the working classes.

Historical events also shaped the development of socialist theory. In contrast to some theorists, "Marx set out to change the world, as well as to interpret it."[142] For example, the spread of revolutions throughout Europe in 1848 prompted a shift in socialist ideology in a couple of ways. On the one hand, it led Marx into a more detailed study of capitalism.[143] Additionally, it persuaded the socialists that "political explosiveness was no guarantee of political success ... and that they needed to organize their own movements ... in order to create the pressure necessary to bring about the social transformation they advocated."[144] The emphasis on creating revolutionary groups was heightened by the events of the Russian Revolution, which provided the impetus for shifts in socialist theories of war. Though Marx and Engels had emphasized the urban working class (proletariat) as the revolutionary class in advanced capitalist societies, capitalism was still developing in Russia. Russia was an autocracy, and in *What Is to Be Done?* Lenin developed a conception of a revolutionary organization instead led by a small group of workers and intellectuals.[145] This group, guided by revolutionary theory, would be the vanguard of the proletariat.[146] The ability of the vanguard to lead revolutions that in essence skipped the economic stage of bourgeois democracy became a central element of Leon Trotsky's theory of the "permanent revolution," in which the development of socialism in one country would be assisted by revolutions elsewhere.[147]

In taking up the call for the spread of socialist revolutions, Mao Tse-tung shifted socialist understandings of revolutionary wars by arguing that the peasantry can serve as the revolutionary class.[148] In confronting two militarily powerful opponents, Japan and the Chinese Nationalist government, Mao developed the strategies of guerrilla warfare that would be adopted by a number of subsequent revolutionary movements.[149] The post–World War II era experienced a spread of anti-imperialist movements, prompting extra-state wars for independence in Asia and Africa, in particular. In Vietnam, Generals Vo Nguyen Giap and Van Tien Dung developed a military strategy that combined military combat with a political struggle.[150] Their military strategy included both guerrilla and conventional warfare. Politically the North Vietnamese utilized class grievances to mobilize support, and their platform included promoting the emancipation of women—consequently women played a number of roles in the revolutionary movement.[151] The doctrine of the necessity of revolutionary warfare spread in Africa as well. In arguing for independence for Algeria, Frantz Fanon claimed that violence and guerrilla warfare were necessary parts of decolonization.[152] Fanon also saw the peasants as the revolutionary class, and in the context of colonization he described the workers in colonized nations as being the bourgeoisie faction, or part of the colonizing power.[153] Similarly, Kwame Nkrumah argued that the anticolonial movement in Africa was part of the world socialist revolution that could be understood only in the context of the class struggle.[154] He specifically warned that two types of organizations could emerge from independence struggles: the genuine people's party that was committed to both national liberation and socialism and the other reactionary national liberation movement that was supported by imperialism as a result of its preservation of capitalist structures.[155]

Continuing the socialist analysis, Michael Harrington has argued that the post–World War II era was also the period of the emergence of American economic hegemony.[156] The New International Economic Order (NIEO), fashioned after World War II at Bretton Woods, New Hampshire (which included among other things the creation of the International Monetary Fund), benefited the rich countries, while "many of the poor countries were to suffer grievously."[157] Within this new system, referred to as neo-imperialism by Michael Parenti, the United States could continue its exploitation of third world countries without the burden of the direct rule that was the mark of traditional imperial or colonial empires.[158] American hegemony and the growing power of transnational corporations fueled wars worldwide, though especially in Latin America, as the United States sought to confront moves toward socialism that might threaten its economic interests, such as by the Allende regime in Chile.[159] The economic or socialist argument also helps to explain U.S. support of right-wing dictatorships and opposition to peasant movements for democracy.[160] Similarly, it provides a framework within which to understand revolutions against governments run by conservative elites, such as the Batista regime in Cuba.[161]

From the socialist perspective, the end of the Cold War created a new era of economic globalization, or imperial globalization, in which market forces took increasing priority over traditional security concerns.[162] However, according to Carl Boggs, both American hegemony and militarism became even more potent in the aftermath of the end of the Cold War and especially in the "wake of September 11, 2001, with the specter of an endless war on terrorism, mobilization for invasion of Iraq, and the promise of future 'resource wars.'"[163] As Frances Fox Piven has maintained, these conditions contributed to the heightened role of the United States as an imperial power, which entailed significant costs for the United States both at home and abroad.[164] American policies will face continuing "blowback," or continued resistance by those harmed by America's imperial projects.[165] As Noam Chomsky claimed after September 2001, "The people in the advanced countries now face a choice: we can express justified horror, or we can seek to understand what may have led to the crimes. If we refuse to do the latter, we will be contributing to the likelihood that much worse lies ahead."[166] Similarly, Richard Falk argued, "[T]he American response to the al Qaeda has accentuated its earlier failures of global leadership, plunging the world into a struggle between two extremist visions of how to achieve world peace and global justice."[167] From this general perspective, according to George Katsiaficas, wars should remain a feature of contemporary global politics: "In such a world, of course, there can be no lasting peace. As long as the wretched of the earth, those at the margins of the world system, are dehumanized, branded as terrorists, and kept out of decision-making, they have no alternative but to carry out insurrection and wage war in order to find justice."[168]

Critical Theory

The late 1980s and early 1990s saw the emergence of another overarching theoretical perspective referred to as postmodernism, or critical theory. Critical theory emerged from both the Marxian and Kantian liberal traditions, and these approaches have in common a rejection of positivism.[169] In describing positivism, which includes realism, liberalism, and globalism/structuralism, Steve Smith notes: "Positivism has involved a commitment to a unified view of science, and the adoption of methodologies of the natural sciences to explain the social world."[170] Critical theory, also called post-positivism, encompasses a broad range of views, including the Marxist (discussed above), postmodernists, feminist theorists, and post-structuralist, and these various approaches represent a massive attack on traditional, or mainstream, international theory, which has been dominated by positivist assumptions.[171] Andrew Linklater describes four main achievements of critical theory: (1) critical theory invites observers to reflect upon the social construction of knowledge, which in international relations has led to the critique of realism and a reworking of idealism; (2) critical theory objects to empirical claims that assume that existing social structures, which support inequalities of power and wealth, are immutable, and thus seeks greater freedom in social relations; (3) critical theory includes the project of restructuring the Marxian focus on historical materialism; (4) critical theory envisions new forms of political community, rejecting the realist assumption that relations between/among communities must be based on military power.[172]

In terms of Linklater's first point, critical theory emphasizes the observation that knowledge is always for the benefit of someone and some purpose. Existing political orders work to the advantage of privileged groups and marginalize others. Consequently critical theory rejects claims of objectivity of knowledge, such as those made by realism.[173] Realism's focus upon the state and primary institutions of government downplays the importance of other actors. For example, Cynthia Enloe suggests that to gain a more complete understanding of international relations, we need to hear the voices of the people and groups who are generally seen to be at the margins, such as the people of Chiapas, Mexico. This effort is likely to reveal that there is much more power and many more forms of power in operation in international relations than is conventionally assumed.[174] Similarly, government policies are not seen as the result of rational considerations of all the options, but as choices determined by the legitimization of certain perspectives and the delegitimization of others. Thus critical theory urges us to look at who benefits from discussions about war—which voices are included and which are marginalized or excluded. In this vein, Kenneth Campbell concluded that any change in U.S. policy in Iraq was unlikely because the Iraq Study Group carefully excluded "all of the authoritative voices calling for a rapid withdrawal of U.S. troops from Iraq."[175] Likewise, Kathy Kelly argues that American policy in Iraq would have been quite different had the United States listened to the voices of the Iraqi people.[176]

In terms of Linklater's second point, critical theorists reject the conception of the immutability of social systems, since they see humans beings as being capable of making their own history. Consequently critical theory objects to the claims of immutability evidenced in realism's emphasis on power, capitalism's focus on private property, the division of societies into rigid hierarchies (such as caste systems), and the exclusion of women from the political realm.[177] In terms of the critique of realism, critical theory explains that the incidence of war and the prospects for peace do not depend upon the immutable anarchic international system but upon the ambitions of the great powers themselves.[178] Furthermore, it is here that socialism and critical theory provide an understanding of the linkages between and among capitalism, racism, and sexism. As Wallerstein explained:

> Racism was not a mechanism of exclusion, but rather a mechanism of justifying inclusion in the workforce and the political system at a level of reward and status sharply inferior to that of some large group. Sexism had the same objective, but reached it via a different path. By restricting women to certain modes of producing income, and by defining such modes as non-work (the concept of the "housewife"), sexism promoted the semi-proletarian household and hence, as we have already discussed, worked to reduce wage levels in very large sectors of the world-economy.[179]

Feminism challenges sexism and its claim of the immutability of the division of labor that claims the public sphere exclusively for men and reserves the private sphere for women. In terms of international relations, a number of feminist theorists, including Ann Tickner, have argued that the entire field is dominated by gendered (male) conceptions.[180] Just as the basic conceptions of international relations are male, the majority of foreign policy decision makers are male, and international relations (and specifically war) have been seen as proving grounds for "real men."[181] Here, the goal of feminists such as Marysia Zalewski is to emphasize or "problematize masculinities, the hegemony of men, and the subject of man within the theories and practices of international relations."[182] As Christine Sylvester explains, "[F]eminist International Relations reveal the pervasiveness of gender power in a field that denies it has anything whatsoever to do with gender."[183]

> Very centrally, IR learns from everyday feminist theorising "how the conduct of international politics has *depended* on men's control of women" (Enloe 1989, 4), on gender mechanisms of power, and on women as unheralded resources for men and their institutions.[184]

Thus, feminists argue that international relations must be changed so that the field takes seriously the conception of gender as an organizing framework about world politics. Within this framework, "Everyday forms of feminist theorising privilege a logic of gender identity that highlights women's experiences as sources of knowledge."[185] Such a framework challenges the traditional understanding of the naturalization of male predominance in matters of international politics, finance, and war."[186] As Cynthia Enloe maintains, it is the development of a "feminist curiosity" that encourages the questioning of things that other people take for granted.[187] The focus upon women and their experiences expands the scope of traditional ideas about key elements in international relations. For example, V. Spike Peterson makes the case that gender relations are a key feature of group identities and thus form the basis of an understanding of nationalism.[188] Yet, as Peterson and Jacqui True note, summarizing the contributions of the feminist perspective is complicated by the diversity among women and within feminist theory.[189] Thus, realizing that it is impossible to do justice to the breadth of feminist scholarship here, only a few major elements will be discussed in terms of their specific links to the topic of war.

Enloe argues that a major contribution of the feminist perspective is that it allows one to make sense "of the links between two of the world's most potent trends: globalization and militarization."[190] Militarization is the process by which one adopts militaristic values, such as a belief in hierarchy, obedience, and support for the use of force.[191] Militarization affects individuals and elements of domestic politics, but it can also be globalized, for example, through wars and in the activities of large defense contractors.[192] As mentioned earlier, militarization is also linked to the development of masculine identity,[193] whereby femininity is generally manipulated.[194]

The understanding of militarization and war as gendered presents a more comprehensive view of war because it highlights the ways in which war affects women in profoundly different ways than it does men.[195] In their book *The Women and War Reader,* Lois Ann Lorentzen and Jennifer Turpin bring together thirty-seven articles, each of which describes different aspects of women's experience with war, as well as discusses the intersections of feminist concerns with those of class, race, and ethnicity.[196] Such stories, in addition to those collected by Mary Ann Tétreault and Krishna Kumar in terms of revolutions and civil wars, reveal the ways in which women have participated in war and have been affected by war, topics that are frequently ignored in traditional accounts.[197] Furthermore, utilizing a feminist perspective expands the analysis of the goals of revolutions to include discussion of the extent to which revolutions attempt to address and/or resolve women's problems in postrevolutionary societies.[198] Conversely, one consequence of the traditional denial or ignoring of women's contributions to wars and revolutions is that it erodes women's claims to equality.[199]

Reference to the gendered nature of war is becoming more widespread (though frequently from an affirming perspective), particularly as the participation of women in the military and war is growing.[200] As Judith Stiehm has noted, women's participation in the military is threatening men's very gender identity, that of warrior/protector.[201] The media, reflecting gendered stereotypes, frequently poses such questions as: "Does 'being a good soldier' [depend] on being an aggressive male?" "Can the warrior survive the feminization of the military, or are we sacrificing military effectiveness on the altar of political correctness?"[202] Feminists frequently seek to confront the supposed immutability of gender hierarchies by proposing alternative visions of society, where women are not subjugated and relegated to the margins. For instance R. Claire Snyder proposes trying to sever the connection between manhood and the roles of "citizen-soldiers and manly warriors."[203] Others have proposed an entire redefinition of security along the lines of a concept of human security that includes the provision of basic human needs and notions of justice and emancipation.[204] However, many feminists are less than optimistic about the possibility of such radical challenge to hegemonic masculinity, one that would confront not only the legitimization of war but also the process of militarization more generally. Consequently, as Ann Tickner explains, "Feminists have claimed that the likelihood of conflict will not diminish until unequal gender hierarchies are reduced or eliminated."[205]

Since the last two of Linklater's proclaimed contributions of critical theory relate to revisions of Marxism, they were partially addressed in the section on socialism, above, and thus will be only briefly mentioned here. In terms of the project of reconstructing historical materialism, Linklater argued that traditional Marxism focused too much of its analysis on the specific modes of production. Critical theorists have retained the economic basis of Marxism but have updated it to place a greater emphasis on war and state building.[206] In this context, Robert Cox has described critical theory as entering international studies through the study of international political economy (IPE). Though markets remain the key institutions, they function within a broader context that includes an analysis of the growing opposition to the alliance of state and corporate powers on both the national and transnational levels.[207] The core of much of the work in this area is a discussion of globalization and its impact upon the distribution of the world's wealth between the core and the periphery. As Michael Cox has noted, "unfettered capitalism (which is what we've now got) ... makes fertile ground for radical analysis."[208] This perspective highlights a wide array of negative attributes of neoclassical economics. Spike Peterson describes this perspective as:

> These wide-ranging critiques argue that globalization increases class inequalities, enhances the wealth and power of the elites, fails to lift the poorest out of poverty, erodes the gains and prospects of organized labor, worsens un- and under-employment, displaces subsistence agriculture and local craft production, increases the unpaid work of women, fuels licit and illicit informalization, lowers standards in advanced economies, increases surveillance and discipline of workers, weakens worker demands through the threat of job losses and capital flight, reduced the state's capacity or commitment to prioritize domestic welfare, promotes environmental damage and toxic dumping on poor countries, fuels speculative and volatile financial markets, and poses systemic risks due to the integration of financial markets.[209]

This critical perspective challenges the neoliberal belief that everyone benefits from the globalization of the market economy. As briefly mentioned in the section on liberalism, above, one of the elements of the Kantian peace is the argument that the spread of capitalism and growing economic ties contribute to the democratic peace. The critical perspective instead focuses upon the growing tendency toward instability in the financial markets and the extent to which the repercussions are unequally shared, with the costs falling more heavily on women and the poor.[210] There is a growing gap between the have and have-not states, and the unfettered power of finance capital is creating instability.[211] This increases the potential for internal conflict as workers begin to resist global capital.[212] The growing power of transnational corporations can also promote conflict over resources, especially within developing states, abetted by the growing utilization of private armed forces. The increased potential for conflict affects developed states as well, where the link between globalization and the "new militarism" was evident in the drive to protect the global economic system in the 1999 bombing of Yugoslavia and the 1991 Persian Gulf War.[213]

The final contribution of critical theory is that it highlights the changes in the social bonds that unite and divide states.[214] In particular, critical theory addresses the developments that are weakening the bonds between citizens and the state, or sovereignty. R. J. B. Walker maintains that critical theory sees the principle and practice of sovereignty as enormously complicated, and it thereby addresses a principle that is claimed to be at the core of international studies, but which is simply taken for granted there.[215] Walker argues that international relations traditionally saw sovereignty as an already attained condition of a plurality of communities and did not really examine the ways in which sovereignty is produced or reproduced.[216] In contrast, critical theory examined both the development of and challenges to sovereignty. As Noam Chomsky explained, sovereignty, or the modern nation-state system, was a European invention, that has no particular relation to the way people live or their associations, and thus had to be established by force.[217] Europe thus had a history of bloody wars as part of the effort to establish the nation-state system. Since the borders, particularly those established for colonial empires, were frequently arbitrary, wars also resulted from the challenges to national assimilation that were raised by subnational groups and indigenous peoples. Critical theorists have consequently proposed that new forms of community and sovereignty should be developed.[218]

New Wars?

A final source of knowledge (or myth, according to Hillman) about wars derives from the literature positing that the contemporary world is experiencing new types of wars, though there is a fair amount of disagreement concerning the exact nature of these new wars. The diversity within this scholarship is reflected in the competing terminologies of *peoples' wars, postmodern wars, wars of a third kind,* and most commonly *ethnic wars.* Similarly, the popularity of the term *ethnic conflict* belies the degree of disagreement over both the definition of the term and the degree of its importance or significance as a cause of conflict. Probably the most common representations follow that of David Lake and Donald Rothchild, who argued that the early 1990s can be characterized as a "new world disorder" characterized by a wave of ethnic conflict.[219] They further note:

> Since the end of the Cold War, a wave of ethnic conflict has swept across parts of Eastern Europe, the former Soviet Union, and Africa. Localities, states, and sometimes whole regions have been engulfed in convulsive fits of ethnic insecurity, violence, and genocide. Early optimism that the end of the Cold War might usher in a new world order has been quickly shattered. Before the threat of nuclear Armageddon could fully fade, new threats of state melt down and ethnic cleansing have rippled across the international community.[220]

Beyond the general agreement about the growing trend in ethnic wars, however, disagreement emerges about the exact nature of ethnic wars. In attempting to evaluate this literature, Lake and Rothchild differentiate three broad understandings of ethnicity and its relationship to conflict.[221] The *primordialist* approach takes ethnicity as a fixed characteristic of individuals, communities, and conflict.

In this view, ethnic divisions and tensions are "natural." Although recognizing that ethnic warfare is not a constant state of affairs, primordialists see conflict as flowing from ethnic differences and, therefore, not necessarily in need of explanation.... [C]onflict is understood to be ultimately rooted in ethnicity itself .... Analyses of conflict from within the primordialist approach stress the uniqueness and overriding importance of ethnic identity.... When viewed through this lens, ethnic conflict is sui generis; what one learns about ethnic conflict is typically not relevant to other social, political, or economic conflicts.[222]

In contrast, the second, or *instrumentalist,* approach understands ethnicity as a tool used by individuals, groups, or elites to obtain some end. In this view, "ethnicity is primarily a label or set of symbolic ties that is used for political advantage—much like interest-group membership or political-party affiliation.... If politicized ethnicity is not inherently different from other forms of political association, ethnic conflict should not necessarily be different from other conflicts based on interest or ideology."[223]

Finally, the *constructivist* approach represents, according to Lake and Rothchild, a bridge between the other two perspectives and reflects the emerging scholarly consensus that ethnicity is neither immutable nor completely open.[224] "Constructivists emphasize the social origin and nature of ethnicity.... Ethnicity is constructed from dense webs of social interactions.... Ethnicity is not an individual attribute but a social phenomenon.... As social interactions change, conceptions of ethnicity evolve as well."[225] For instrumentalists and constructivists, ethnicity is not inherently conflictual. "For instrumentalists, as noted, conflict is largely stimulated by elites who mobilize ethnicity in pursuit of their own narrow interests. For constructivists, on the other hand, conflict is caused by certain types of what might be called pathological social systems.... It is the social system that breeds violent conflict."[226]

Though Lake and Rothchild see the constructivist approach emerging as the dominant paradigm, much of the common understanding of ethnic conflict and significant portions of the research community utilize arguments more in line with the primordialist approach. For instance, both V. P Gagnon and Stuart Kaufman describe, but then reject, the "the myth of ethnic war," or the description of the wars in the Balkans as being caused by "ancient hatreds."[227] Lake and Rothchild similarly reject the primordialist position:

> We argue that ethnic conflict is not caused directly by intergroup differences, "ancient hatreds" and centuries-old feuds, or the stresses of modern life within a global economy. Nor were ethnic passions, long bottled up by repressive communist regimes, simply uncorked by the end of the Cold War. Instead, we maintain that ethnic conflict is most commonly caused by collective fears of the future.[228]

Overall, they conclude that "by itself, ethnicity is not a cause of violent conflict."[229] A similar position is adopted by Ted Robert Gurr and the Minorities at Risk project, which similarly rejects primordialism and instrumentalism and is based on the view that ethnic identities are enduring social constructions.[230] Gurr concludes that, "the politics of identity are based most fundamentally on persistent grievances about inequalities and past wrongs, conditions that are part of the heritage of most minorities in most countries."[231] Gurr's goal is to examine the "tsunami of ethnic and nationalist conflict that swept across large parts of Eurasia and Africa in the early 1990s" and the subsequent "short peace" that took place after the mid 1990s.[232] For the purposes of his study he is not interested in the construction of ethnic identity, but takes ethnic identities as a given in order to focus attention on their contemporary political consequences.[233] Additional research concerning the contemporary period has also examined the issues of diffusion and escalation of ethnic wars, and specifically on the link between ethnic and inter-state wars (or the internationalization of ethnic conflict), which points to the increasing propensity of outside states to intervene in intra-state wars.[234]

However, the petard upon which the constructivists have hoisted themselves is in reconciling the conceptions of identities as enduring social constructions with the argument of the distinctiveness of the 1990s. The emphasis only on the recent decades also seems to reflect a certain sense of superiority or triumphalism within Western scholarship (to the degree that it seems to imply that these are a new type of war that could only happen to "others" and are unlike anything in Western history).[235] The dangers, in both theoretical and political terms, of the hegemonic discourse around the terminology of ethnic conflict have been further addressed by Tamara Dragadze.[236] In this vein, John Stack links objections to the focus on ethnicity to the objections raised against Huntington's "clash of civilizations" article, described earlier in this chapter. Stack argues that some of the objections against Huntington arose from liberals who see ethnicity as an atavistic force that the progress of the recent centuries should have moved beyond, and that liberals are particularly "dismayed by the increase of intractable ethnic conflicts since World War II."[237] However, Stack also admits that some of the criticism arises from the perplexing issue of "why ethnicity is so potent now, at the end of the twentieth century, as opposed to ten, fifteen, or fifty years ago? If ethnicity is as important as it appears, why does it cast such a long shadow now, when it did not in the past?"[238] He does not resolve this dilemma and to a degree questions the distinctiveness of the contemporary period by referring to the primordial perspective to explain the enduring importance of ethnicity.[239] Michael Brecher and Jonathan Wilkenfeld address the issue of the distinctiveness ethnicity in the post–Cold War era by examining the incidence of ethnic crises among all crises in the period of 1918–1988. They divided the entire time period into eras of multipolarity (1918–1939), bipolarity (1945–1962), and polycentrism (1963–1988). They found that ethnopolitical crises existed in all three periods and were in fact "proportionately more prominent under multipolarity than in either of the two later systems."[240] Similar evidence against the distinctiveness of contemporary ethnic wars is presented by Joseph Rudolph, who sees ethnic conflict as occurring throughout the twentieth century, albeit with significant increases during the anticolonial period.[241]

Similar arguments about the distinctiveness of contemporary wars have been made by Kal Holsti and Mary Kaldor. Holsti contends that there is an emergence of a new kind of war, or "wars of the third kind":

> Wars of the "third kind" bear little relationship to the European wars of the eighteenth and nineteenth centuries or to the total wars of the first half of the twentieth century. The main criteria for distinguishing forms of war are: (1) the purposes of the war; (2) the role of civilians during wartime; and (3) the institutions of war.[242]

On the basis of this premise, Holsti sees war as falling into three categories: institutionalized war, total war, and wars of the third kind, also called "peoples' wars."[243] Such wars are deinstitutionalized in that they are not fought with classical military fronts but by guerrilla warfare. Citizens are involved as both combatants and victims. The goal is also different, involving the desire of people to create their own state.[244] The factor that highlights the prominence of "wars of the third kind" in the post–Cold War era is that groups seeking their own entity are spread through areas controlled by weak states.[245]

Similarly Mary Kaldor argues that the 1980s and 1990s saw the emergence of a new type of violence, or incidents of "new war." What differentiates these "new wars" is their political nature, the prevalence of low-intensity conflict, their economic role within the process of globalization, and the activities of private or paramilitary actors.[246] Kaldor describes the war in Bosnia-Hercegovina from 1992 to 1995 as an archetypal example of a new war.[247] The political goals included ethnic cleansing and nationalism. Yugoslavia was in the midst of an economic crisis fueled by globalization. It was a heavily militarized state, containing a wide array of military and paramilitary entities. Civilians were widely involved, both in paramilitary organizations and as targets of the violence.

These claims that there are new wars that are "quite unlike and appreciably different from all wars we have known and studied" were comprehensively evaluated by Errol Henderson and J. David Singer.[248] Overall they admit that there is some element of truth in the observations that war in the post–World War II era is different in terms of the locus of war and the increasing prevalence of intra-state over inter-state war.[249] However, they fundamentally disagree with the assertions that such wars are a distinctive category of "new wars" that is inexplicable using extant approaches in world politics.[250] In particular, Henderson and Singer contend that these wars are not really "new" at all. "We contend that the 'new wars' are actually an amalgam of different types of 'old wars.' ... Further, contrary to the assertion of 'new war' theorists, war has not changed 'fundamentally,' with respect to its 'purpose,' types of participants, and the manner of its prosecution."[251] In examining the claims of the "new wars" in detail, Henderson and Singer note that most of the "new wars" are wars within the existing category of civil wars between a state government and insurgents; that both "new wars" and wars of previous eras have involved civilian casualties; that the tactics of guerrilla warfare have been evident in a number of wars over the past 200 years; that many of the "new wars" involve both conventional as well as guerrilla strategies; that the supposed increasing trend in civil wars is largely a product of the increasing number of states in the system; that the supposed "lethality" of "new wars" never approaches that of many of the "old wars" such as the Taiping Rebellion, while other "new wars" are in fact just examples of low-intensity conflict; and that the purpose of the "new wars" is fundamentally the same. Consequently Henderson and Singer conclude that "the 'newness' of these wars largely derives from the fact that they are a hodgepodge of several types of war" including inter-state, extra-state, and intra-state wars, with different names.[252]

Though changes in military practices are not a critical aspect of their arguments, both Holsti and Kaldor do point to them as elements of their new types of war. Corresponding arguments have been made within specific studies of military history and technology. John Keegan does not particularly develop new categories of war; however, he has described a variety of elements in the changing nature of warfare throughout human history. One element is the increasing intensity of war, defined in terms of a significant change in the proportion of the population serving as soldiers. Prior to 1800, the percentage of the population in the military was small though it increased during the Napoleonic Wars, so that battle deaths did not have widespread repercussions.[253] Another element was the improvement in medical services, which reduced fatality levels in war. Keegan argues that the Boer War (1899–1902) was the last battle in which the British army suffered more fatalities from sickness than missiles and that by 1914 the scourge of disease had been lifted from battle.[254] However, World War I also exhibited several other changes in the practice of war. Prior to 1914, in none of the wars "had the combatants yielded to the delusion that the whole male population must be mobilized to prosecute a quarrel."[255] This element plus mechanical changes in weaponry led to a quantum leap in casualty rates.[256] During World War II, Adolf Hitler's utilization of the blitzkrieg and the Luftwaffe also displayed the evolving technology of war. In particular, Keegan argues that the practice of the war was changed by Hitler's abrogation of the tacit agreement to spare civilian targets in the bombing of Britain, which prompted the British to begin bombing German cities as well, a process that culminated in the U.S. bombing of Japan.[257] But Keegan also warns that the increasing frequency and intensity of war in the twentieth century should not lead us to idealize primitive warfare. Culture determines the nature of warfare, and slaughter and butchery have always been a part of war.[258]

Disparities in the levels of military technology between/among parties in war have continued to be significant. The U.S. conduct of the war in Vietnam was determined to a good extent by the technology of its weapons, and it was predicated upon faulty assumptions about their efficacy.[259] Israeli victories can be tied to superior weapons technology.[260] The 1991 Gulf War and the 2003 quick U.S. advance upon Baghdad demonstrated, according to Gen. Wesley Clark, the fact that the United States was "simply unchallengeable in their craft of warfare."[261] In many respects, these recent wars have marked a fundamental shift in warfare. Max Boot has described four major revolutions in military technology: the Gunpowder Revolution, the First Industrial Revolution, the Second Industrial Revolution, and the Information Revolution.[262] Boot admits that the 1991 Gulf War can be seen as either the last of the industrial wars (with the clash of tank armies in the desert) or the first of the wars of the information age (with its smart bombs), which is his position.[263] He argues that elements of the information age include advances in computers, advances in communications (the Internet), development of the globalized economy, and advances in the precision of weaponry. These advances contributed to a war in Iraq in which American deaths were relatively minimal.[264] However, as Boot admits, American technological superiority did not guarantee victory. The United States was not prepared to deal with unconventional challenges.[265] According to Boot, the United States is facing growing asymmetric threats from other states and from substate groups, and some of the advances of the information age are available to challengers as well.[266] Similarly, General Clark argues, the failure of U.S. policy resulted from a strategy that "focused the nation on a conventional attack on Iraq rather than a shadowy war against the perpetrators of the 9/11 attacks: Al Qaeda. I argue that not only did the Bush administration misunderstand the lessons of modern war, it made a policy blunder of significant proportions."[267] Both Clark and Boot see the real focus of the modern war as terrorism. Clark describes terrorism emerging in the late nineteenth century as a tactic against czarist Russia. Terrorism was subsequently a feature of twentieth century struggles for independence and wars of liberation, enabling weaker parties to fight back without risking defeat in conventional warfare.[268] However, the terrorist threat from al-Qaida was different, partially due to its supranational character.[269] The failure of American policy was due to both its inability to see al-Qaida as an independent transnational actor and consequently to its search instead for a state sponsor for terrorism.[270] Similarly Boot argues that even though the tactic of irregular attacks is as "old as warfare itself," it is the "technological advances that have made such attacks far more potent than in the past."[271]

Boot's and Clark's analyses point to an emerging feature of modern war, the growing number of nonstate entities that are capable of waging war; some of which function within states, while others operate across state borders. In this same vein, P. W. Singer describes the emergence of another type of nonstate entity, private or corporate military organizations.[272] Singer credits one such organization, Executive Outcomes, with saving the government of Sierra Leone, while another, Military Professional Resources Incorporated (MPRI), aided Croatia's military in 1995.[273] The importance of these firms is not only in their growing power and global reach but also in the degree to which the growing reliance of states, as well as individuals or corporations, upon their services demonstrates the fact that states are losing their former monopoly over the use of force.[274]

A Comprehensive View of Trends in Modern War

What do we thus know about wars? The discussions of war in the realms of theology, psychology, and philosophy have provided us with competing understandings (myths) about the nature of war. This book began with the questions of whether or in what ways war is evolving. In this regard, one of the most contentious issues has been the issue of trends in war, and the competing myths about war have provided differing expectations about wars' pattern. Is war becoming obsolete? Are we in the midst of an era of peace with a declining prospect of war (as the liberal democratic peace argument contends)? Is war ubiquitous, tied to human nature (as elements of theology, psychology, and feminist theory contend, unless gender relations are transformed)? Or is war on the increase, fueled by the end of the bipolar system, the global economy, or the emergence of new types of war, such as ethnic wars or "wars of the third kind" (as realism, socialism, critical theory, and new war theories propose)? A related series of questions concerns the practice of war: Are we seeing the emergence of new types of actors and tactics in wars? In what ways are advances in military technology changing wars? Answers to such questions are important, not only for international relations scholars but also for political leaders who are grappling with developing strategies to respond to contemporary conflicts.

Part of the difference in perceptions about the trends in war and/or the relative peacefulness of the system is due to the segmented nature of many of the existing conflict studies, in which only one type of war (inter-state or civil) or only wars between certain types of actors are examined. Obviously part of this dichotomy is linked to cleavages in the political science discipline, with international politics scholars concerned primarily with inter-state wars and comparative politics scholars focusing more often on internal developments, including revolutions and civil wars.[275] The general assumption of international relations scholars has been that inter-state wars, and frequently more specifically only major-power wars, are distinct from other types of violence, including minor-power wars, major–minor–power wars, extra-state wars, and intra-state wars. Thus inter-state wars have generally been studied separately. Consequently, though hundreds of books and articles have addressed the question of the trends in war, too few have examined the totality of war. This lack of scholarship treating multiple types of war has limited the accumulation of knowledge and has circumscribed our understanding of war by preventing an examination of the ways in which different types of war behavior might be interrelated.

In contrast to these segmented approaches, there are those who see similarities and linkages between intra-state, extra-state, and inter-state wars. One of the early proponents of this approach was Lewis Fry Richardson, who in *Statistics of Deadly Quarrels*, which was written before 1950 though not published until 1960, insisted that all wars be treated in one omnibus list in which the focus was on the magnitude of killing, regardless of whether the war took place between countries or within one country.[276] More recently, Eberwein and Chojnacki have claimed that the more narrow disciplinary focus on inter-state war is no longer justifiable.[277] Relatedly, Donald Snow proposed a more integrative approach, since he argued that contemporary internal wars are more like international wars than traditional civil wars, leading him to call them "uncivil wars."[278] Along the same lines, Marshall has argued that the bifurcations in war studies have become less tenable, particularly as the borders separating internal from external issues within states have become more permeable.[279] He thus contends that scholars must "acknowledge all forms of violence and warfare as being essentially related and similarly problematic."[280] Relatedly, Dennis Sandole argued that there are significant similarities among violent conflicts occurring at various levels of aggregation and thus asserted the need for a generic theory for "capturing the complexity of conflict."[281] Some work along these lines has been done by J. Joseph Hewitt, Wilkenfeld, and Gurr in *Peace and Conflict 2008*, which examined both inter-state and internal conflict.[282] Much more integrative work needs to be done, however. The development of an overarching view of war—combining the four types of war over a long time span—is one of the primary aims of this chapter.

What Do the New Data Tell Us?

In *Resort to Arms,* published in 1982, Melvin Small and J. David Singer analyzed three major types of war. They included a total of 224 wars: 67 inter-state wars, 51 extra-systemic wars, and 106 civil wars. Overall, they found no overarching trends indicating increasing or decreasing patterns of war, though they did find some evidence of war cycles or peaks of war activity every 20 to 30 years.[283] They were surprised by the similarities between their findings for international (inter-state and extra-systemic) wars and those for civil wars, though they conceded that the question of "why the civil wars should be related to the international wars is a question we leave for future analyses."[284] An updated analysis of Correlates of War (COW) wars covering the period of 1816–1997 was done by Sarkees, Wayman, and Singer in 2003. Our analysis in this work of the data on 401 wars from 1816 to 1997 (79 inter-state, 108 extra-state, and 214 intra-state) similarly found a general constancy in overall warfare.[285] There was a negative correlation between extra-state and intra-state war onsets, with intra-state wars increasing as extra-state wars declined. In the most recent version of the data, presented here, there are now 655 wars: 95 inter-state wars, 163 extra-state wars, 335 intra-state wars, and 62 non-state wars. In the preceding chapters we have discussed the patterns in each of these four categories. Some of the trends in warfare over time reflect changes within the international system (including the actors within it) and the impact of those changes on the specific definitions of the war types. For example, as more of the world's territory was incorporated into members of the interstate system, the number of nonstate territories declined, leading by definition to a decline in non-state wars toward the end of the nineteenth century. At that same time, the number of extra-state wars rose as the imperial powers sought colonial empires. However, the growth in the number of nonstate entities that are capable of waging war, coupled with the potential destructiveness of modern weaponry (which in some cases enables the battle threshold of 1,000 deaths per year to be reached more easily), has led to a recent resurgence of both extra-state and non-state wars.

Here, the focus upon the interplay in the incidence of war among the war types is addressed by combining the data on all four types of war together. A complete chronological list of all wars is included in the Appendix. With 655 wars over the 192 years from 1816 to 2007, if the wars were evenly distributed, there would be 3.4 war onsets per year. As Figure 7.1 shows, there were only 12 total years during this period with no war onsets.

The largest number of years experienced two or three war onsets, though there were two years, 1848 and 1991, that had the largest number (eleven) of war onsets. In examining the onsets of war per year over time, there is no specific pattern evident in terms of an overarching decline or increase in the onset of wars. As Figure 7.2 shows, there are peaks and valleys in the onsets of war but the pattern in the post–1945 era is not substantially different from patterns in the nineteenth century.

This general constancy in the incidence of war onsets can be more easily seen if the 192 years are combined into 19 decades (omitting the wars in the two end years, 1816 and 2007), which yields an average of 34 war onsets per decade. Figure 7.3 reveals a fairly consistent pattern of 30 war onsets per decade, which would be expected by those adopting a psychological, realist, or socialist perspective. There is some support for the realist argument concerning the stability of the bipolar post–World War II era, in which war onsets were slightly below average. However, the numbers of intra-state wars in particular began to rise by the mid-1960s and extra-state wars in the mid 1970s. Each of the last four decades (from 1967 to 2006) has experienced a greater-than-average number of war onsets, which again is in line with realist expectations about the collapse of bipolarity, socialist arguments about the impact of globalization, and arguments about emerging new wars.

FIGURE 7.1 **NUMBER OF WAR ONSETS BY INDIVIDUAL YEARS, 1816–2007 (NUMBER OF YEARS IN WHICH THE ONSET OF 0 THROUGH 11 WARS OCCURRED)**

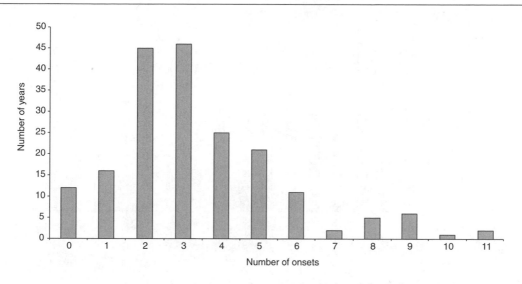

FIGURE 7.2 **WAR ONSETS BY YEAR, 1816–2007**

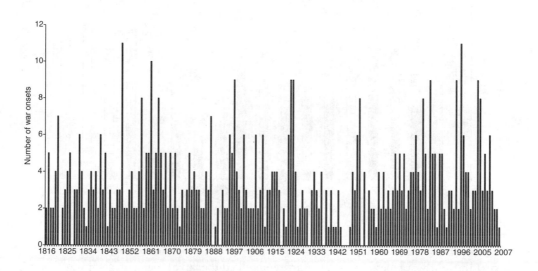

Figures 7.4 and 7.5 represent two ways of looking at the interactions among the four types of war. Figure 7.4 reports the number of war onsets per decade for each of the four types of war (inter-state, extra-state, intra-state, and non-state). Non-state and inter-state wars are the two smaller categories. As is clear, the number of non-state wars declined over time as more territory became incorporated as system members. The number of inter-state wars has fluctuated, but not greatly. However, there is a clear inverse relationship between extra-state wars, which declined as colonial empires were dissolved, and intra-state wars, which significantly increased since the end of World War II. The same

FIGURE 7.3 **WAR ONSETS BY DECADE, 1817–2006**

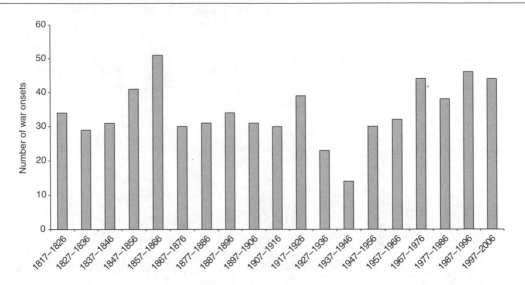

FIGURE 7.4 **WAR ONSETS BY TYPE PER DECADE, 1817–2006**

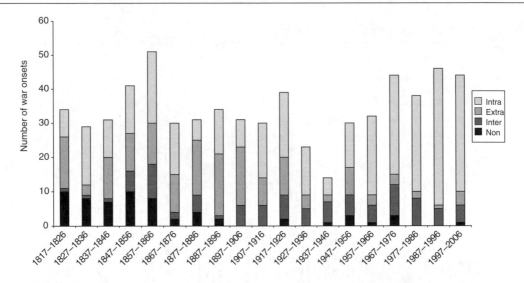

general patterns can be seen in Figure 7.5, which reports the percentage of all war onsets represented by each of the four war types. Inter-state wars represented the largest percentage of war onsets in the 1937–1946 decade, while intra-state wars constituted the largest percentage between 1987 and 1996. The growing percentage of intra-state wars is partially a reflection of changes in the post–World War II system in which a number of colonies gained independence and became system members. Thus wars that might have been extra-state in the past are now classified as intra-state. As mentioned in the discussion of military technology above, one of the facets of technological advance has been the development of weapons that can kill significant numbers of people from a relatively safe vantage point, enabling a plethora of groups to engage in hostilities at the war level. Weapons technology has also played a role in the reemergence of extra-state and non-state wars as groups that are not necessarily territorially identified (terrorist groups or private armed forces, for instance) have the wherewithal to

FIGURE 7.5 **PERCENTAGE OF WAR ONSETS BY TYPE PER DECADE, 1817–2006**

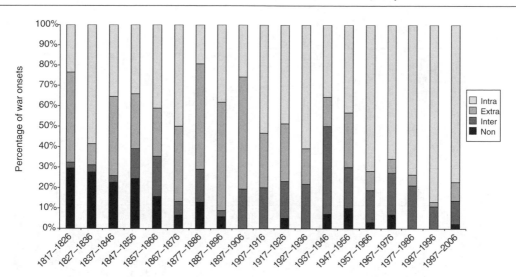

conduct war. The revival of extra-state wars can also be seen as reinforcing arguments about the expanding hegemony of the United States (in wars against al-Qaida, for instance). The data do not, however, point to the emergence of a new type of war. Nonstate actors have participated in wars throughout the entire period of this study. Terrorism is not inherently a new type of war but is a tactic that has been used in numerous wars throughout the 1816–2007 time period. Many of the so-called new wars are included within the COW existing war categories, and utilizing all of the COW datasets on war can provide an overarching view of war that is missing from the more segmented studies.

Another difference of opinion among international relations scholars concerns whether the international system is uniformly prone to war or whether zones of war and peace exist. The structural realists see a uniform international system characterized by anarchy and war. Peace can emerge in certain times and places, in this theory, only as a result of balances of power and structures such as bipolarity.[286] Other authors see the international system as characterized, for a variety of reasons, by zones of war and zones of peace. For instance, Max Singer and Aaron Wildavsky divided the world into a zone of "peace, wealth, and democracy" based in the rich democracies and a zone of "turmoil, war, and development" in the poorer portions of the globe.[287] Other scholars have proposed northern Europe or South America as zones of peace. An overall distribution of wars by the regions(s) in which they were fought over the entire period shows little appreciable pattern except for the higher number of wars in Asia and the relative absence of war in Oceania (see Figure 7.6). The bars that are described by multiple regions represent wars that occurred in more than one region, such as World Wars I and II and the Spanish-American War. Obviously, the number of wars in a region is influenced by the number of system members in that region, and the six regions utilized by the COW Project as the basis of the system membership list are not equal in terms of the number of system members each contains. As of 2007, Africa has fifty system members, Asia has thirty-two, Europe has sixty-five, the Middle East has twenty-two, Oceania has fourteen, and the Western Hemisphere has thirty-five, though the states have been system members for varying periods of time. Calculating a general measure of wars per system member by region where the wars occurred demonstrates Oceania as having

FIGURE 7.6 WAR ONSETS BY REGION, 1816–2007

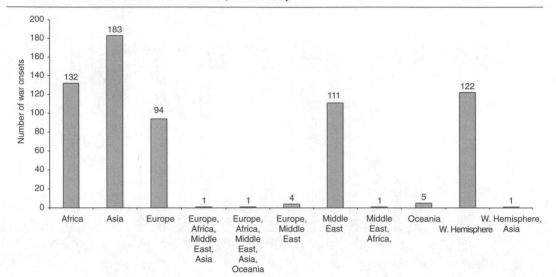

the least war-prone states (.4), followed by Europe (1.5), Africa (2.7), the Western Hemisphere (3.5), the Middle East (5.4), and Asia (5.8).

A related question refers to which specific states are the most war-prone. Some theorists see peace coming through military strength and expect the more powerful nations to be the most peaceful. Others expect that the states with the greatest capabilities will be the ones that are more likely to wage war. As Table 7.1 shows, for the entire 1816–2007 period, the majority of the most war-involved states are European. The singular most war-prone state is clearly the United Kingdom, followed by France, Russia, Turkey/Ottoman Empire, China, and the United States. There is some variation in terms of states' involvement in the different types of war. Participation in inter-state war is more evenly distributed; the United Kingdom and France (as major colonial powers) dominate extra-state war involvement; and large entities such as Russia, Turkey (Ottoman Empire), and China are the most likely to be involved in intra-state wars.

In terms of the theoretical debates about war, arguably the most significant finding here is the constancy of war. In this sense the results pose a challenge to the "democratic peace" literature and its projections of a declining trend in warfare. As mentioned in the Introduction, one of the more widely publicized set of findings from this perspective was that of the *Human Security Report 2005*. The report highlighted what it claimed was a steep decline in wars since 1990.[288] Moreover, it claimed that there had been "a dramatic and sustained decline in the number of armed conflicts" since the end of the Cold War.[289] The authors of the report seem puzzled by the fact that this "steep drop in the number of wars has passed largely unnoticed by policymakers, the media and the public alike."[290] However, the analysis in this chapter suggests several reasons why the *Human Security Report*'s findings may not be as significant as the report seems to believe they are.

The *Human Security Report* is based on data from Uppsala University's Conflict Data Program and the International Peace Research Institute, Oslo (PRIO). As noted by Sarkees and Singer, these projects utilize data-coding procedures that have a significant impact on the types of findings they generate.[291] The primary difficulty with these projects, and with much of the democratic peace literature, is their utilization of relatively short time frames. They tend to gather data only for the post–World War II era, which means that they are unable to consider war cycles, or the ways in which war onsets

TABLE 7.1 MOST FREQUENT STATE WAR PARTICIPANTS

	Inter-state	Extra-state	Intra-state	Total	Rank
Argentina	3	2	10	15	11
Austria-Hungary	6	2	5	13	14
China	14	5	23	42	5
France	19	35	13	67	2
Germany	9	3	2	14	12
Italy	13	5	2	20	8
Japan	9	2	5	16	9
Mexico	2	0	14	16	9
Netherlands	3	10	1	14	12
Russia/USSR	16	9	26	51	3
Spain	6	14	8	28	7
Turkey/Ottoman Empire	13	10	24	47	4
United Kingdom	13	59	9	81	1
United States	13	6	14	33	6
Total state participants	337	198	443	978	

regularly fluctuate over time. This also gives a misleading picture of war as necessarily declining from one of the historical peaks. More particular issues arise from their collection of data based upon calendar years, the disaggregation of some wars, the necessity of identifying the issue of the war for it to be included, the inclusion of civilian deaths as battle-deaths, and the practice of counting as one war a conflict that lasts for many years but has widely separated and limited periods of sustained combat. Though these issues may not sound particularly important, Eberwein and Chojnacki found that coding differences such as these contribute to the fact that one gets very different understandings of war, depending upon which of the major databases on war one utilizes.[292]

In particular, the selection of the time frame significantly shapes the arguments of the "democratic peace." Some of the earlier democratic peace studies had originally focused upon the supposedly peaceful era that occurred after the conclusion of World War II. However, as an increasing number of wars broke out in the late 1970s, this argument had to be modified. Democratic peace proponents now argue that it was the end of the Cold War that launched the new era of peace. Yet 1991 was one of two years that saw the largest number of war onsets since 1816. The *Human Security Report* is correct in indicating that there has been a decline in wars over the past decade, though it exaggerates its importance. It is relatively easy to find a decline once one is at a high point (especially if one makes one's time span short enough). However, the view from a longer historical period reveals that the number of war onsets rises and falls with great frequency. People may not see the decline in wars over the past few years as being significant, because wars have still been at a relatively high level, not because, as the *Human Security Report* contends, of the hypercoverage of wars by the media.

Trying to understand or critique the particular findings of the *Human Security Report* is complicated by a couple of major features of the report. A primary question arises from the distinction between war and armed conflict. Throughout the early pages of the report, numerous mentions are made of a steep drop in the number of *wars* being fought. A description of the decline in wars even

FIGURE 7.7 AREA ONSETS BY TYPE, 1946–2007

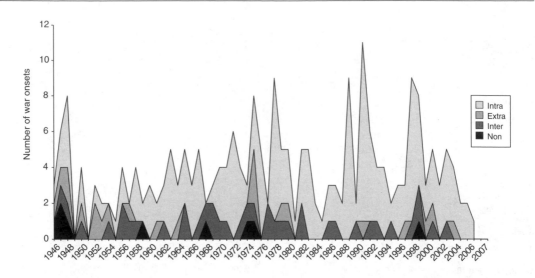

appears in the text surrounding Figure 1.1; however, the chart itself actually provides data on armed conflicts.[293] Armed conflicts are significantly different from wars in that they only must entail at least 25 battle-deaths per year (not the 1,000 death criterion for war). The judgment that conflicts with 25 deaths are a fundamentally different activity than the sustained combat necessary for a war was made by COW and led to the creation of the militarized interstate dispute (MID) dataset for armed conflicts with 0–999 battle-deaths per twelve-month period. It is hard to tell to what degree the patterns for this low-level conflict correspond to (or muddy the results) of their claims about war. Does the fact that weapons technology has made it easier to kill 25 people lead to a proliferation of low-intensity conflict? In order to decipher Figure 1.1, it would also be helpful to know exactly what the chart represents. Supposedly it represents the number of conflicts in each category, and presumably this means the number of conflicts ongoing rather than conflict onsets. Or could it be the "five-year moving averages" measure that appears in a number of other charts? Figure 7.7, above, is a chart that parallels Figure 1.1 of the *Human Security Report*. It likewise is a stacked area graph for the period starting in 1946, though it includes only wars, and specifically war onsets. Though some of the overall patterns are similar in the two charts, the *Human Security Report* does not pick up the increase in inter-state and extra-state wars in 2000.

The *Human Security Report* specifically provides data on wars in Part V of the report, where it analyzes a new dataset on wars from 1816 to 2002. In two charts, Figures 5.1 and 5.2, the report examines trends in international (inter-state and extra-state) and civil wars. Figure 7.8 (next page) is similar to the report's Figure 5.1 on international wars, though here what is being measured is specifically war onsets, while the report's Figure 5.1 uses a five-year moving average (of ongoing wars?), which apparently smoothes out the fluctuations.[294]

Even though the overall patterns of the two charts are similar, there is a variance in how the data are interpreted. Both analyses see no obvious trend in international war up through the 1970s; however, the *Human Security Report* optimistically highlights what it sees as the dramatic decline in war after the end of the Cold War. The *Human Security Report*'s analysis of civil wars (Figure 5.2) ends on a similarly optimistic note: it maintains that "civil wars soared after World War II, then declined even

FIGURE 7.8 INTERNATIONAL WAR ONSETS, 1816–2007

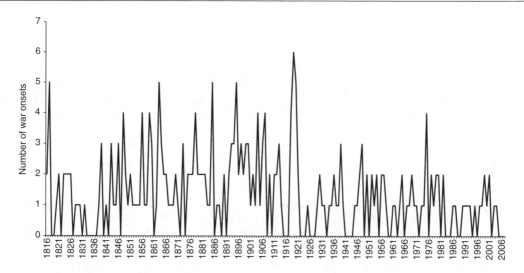

more rapidly after the end of the Cold War."[295] It fails to mention that the report data show that the number of civil wars in 2002 was still significantly above average. It would be nice to be so optimistic about the status of war in the world, but unfortunately such optimism does not seem to be supported by the evidence.

To a good extent, the findings of this COW study correspond to some of those of the *Peace and Conflict 2008* report, which noted that its newest data presented "a sobering reminder of the resiliency of human temptation to use force to resolve disputes."[296] David Singer once said, "One should not predict further into the future than one's data extend into the past." If the trends of the past 192 years provide insight into the future, the findings here portend a depressing endurance for war. As John G. Stoessinger observed:

> The nature of war in our time is so terrible that the first temptation is to recoil. Who of us has not concluded that the entire spectacle of war has been the manifestation of organized insanity? Who has not been tempted to dismiss the efforts of those working for peace as futile Sisyphean labor? Medusa-like, the face of war, with its relentless horror, threatens to destroy anyone who confronts it.
>
> Yet we must have the courage to brave the abyss. I deeply believe that war is a sickness, though it may be humanity's "sickness unto death." No murderous epidemic has ever been conquered without exposure, pain, and danger, or by ignoring the bacilli.[297]

Stoessinger encourages us to look Medusa in the face. We hope that scholars will continue to have such courage and will find fresh insights into the roots of warfare—and that citizens and leaders will seek ways to prevent it.

NOTES

1. James Hillman, *A Terrible Love of War* (New York: Penguin Press, 2004), front flap.
2. Women's International League for Peace and Freedom, "WILPF Women and Peace," www.wilpf.int.ch.
3. P. J. O'Rourke, *Give War a Chance* (New York: Atlantic Monthly Press, 1992), xix.

4. Chris Hedges, *War Is a Force That Gives Us Meaning* (New York: Public Affairs, 2002), 3.
5. Hillman, *A Terrible Love of War*, 9.
6. Ibid., 18.
7. Ibid., 22.
8. Ibid., 20.
9. Ibid., 205.
10. Beatrice Heuser and Cyril Buffet, "Introduction: Of Myths and Men," in *Haunted by History: Myths in International Relations*, ed. Cyril Buffet and Beatrice Heiser (Providence, R.I.: Berghahn Books, 1998), vii–viii.
11. Beatrice Heuser and Cyril Buffet, "Conclusions: Historical Myths and the Denials of Change," in *Haunted by History: Myths in International Relations*, ed. Cyril Buffet and Beatrice Heuser (Providence, R.I.: Berghahn Books,1998), 267.
12. Hillman, *A Terrible Love of War*, 215.
13. Ibid., 178–217.
14. Ibid., 182.
15. Ibid., 183.
16. Joseph C. McKenna, "Ethics and War: A Catholic View," in *International War: An Anthology*, 2nd ed., ed. Melvin Small and J. David Singer (Chicago: Dorsey Press, 1989), 112.
17. See McKenna, "Ethics and War: A Catholic View," 111–116; Michael W. Doyle, *Ways of War and Peace* (New York: W. W. Norton, 1997), 385–388.
18. McKenna, "Ethics and War: A Catholic View," 114.
19. Michael Walzer, "The Just War," in *International War: An Anthology*, 2nd ed., ed. Melvin Small and J. David Singer (Chicago: Dorsey Press, 1989), 141–145.
20. Jean Bethke Elshtain, *Women and War* (New York: Basic Books, 1987), 152.
21. Ibid., 157.
22. Jean Bethke Elshtain, *Just War against Terror* (New York: Basic Books, 2004).
23. General Wesley K. Clark, *Winning Modern Wars* (New York: Public Affairs, 2003), 144–145.
24. Samuel P. Huntington, "The Clash of Civilizations?" in *Classic Readings of International Relations*, ed. Phil Williams, Donald Goldstein, and Jay Shafritz (Fort Worth, Tex.: Harcourt Brace College, 1999), 633.
25. Ibid., 635.
26. Ibid., 636.
27. Ibid., 638.
28. Ibid., 640.
29. Ibid., 646.
30. Sigmund Freud, "Why War?" in *International War: An Anthology*, 2nd ed., ed. Melvin Small and J. David Singer (Chicago: Dorsey Press, 1989), 176–177.
31. Hedges, *War Is a Force That Gives Us Meaning*, 158.
32. Freud, "Why War," 178.
33. Ibid., 181.
34. Hedges, *War Is a Force That Gives Us Meaning*, 3.
35. Ibid.
36. Ibid.
37. Ibid., 10,17.
38. James A. Schellenberg, "The Biology of Human Aggression," in *International War: An Anthology*, 2nd ed., ed. Melvin Small and J. David Singer (Chicago: Dorsey Press, 1989), 166.
39. Ibid.
40. Ibid., 167.
41. Ibid., 175.
42. Joshua S. Goldstein, *War and Gender* (Cambridge: Cambridge University Press, 2001), 27.
43. Ibid., 179.
44. Ibid., 251.
45. Ibid., 252, 287.
46. Ibid., 22.
47. John G. Stoessinger, *Why Nations Go to War*, 7th ed. (New York: St. Martin's Press, 1998), xi.
48. Ibid., 208.
49. Ibid., 211.

50. Seyom Brown, *The Causes and Prevention of War* (New York: St. Martin's Press, 1994), 25–26.

51. Kenneth J. Campbell, *A Tale of Two Quagmires* (Boulder, Colo.: Paradigm, 2007), 9.

52. Ibid., 89.

53. Doyle, *Ways of War and Peace*, 43.

54. Ibid., 206.

55. Ibid.

56. Ibid., 321.

57. Ibid., 318–321.

58. Joseph M. Grieco, "Modern Realist Theory and the Study of International Politics in the Twenty-First Century," in *Millennial Reflections on International Studies,* ed. Michael Brecher and Frank P. Harvey (Ann Arbor: University of Michigan Press, 2002), 65–66.

59. Brown, *The Causes and Prevention of War,* 49.

60. Hans Morgenthau, *Politics among Nations,* 5th ed. (New York: Alfred A. Knopf, 1973), 27.

61. James E. Dougherty and Richard L. Pfaltzgraff Jr., "The Realist Approach to International Conflict," in *International War: An Anthology,* 2nd ed., ed. Melvin Small and J. David Singer (Chicago: Dorsey Press, 1989), 215.

62. Karl W. Deutsch and J. David Singer, "Multipolar Systems and International Stability," in *International War: An Anthology,* 2nd ed., ed. Melvin Small and J. David Singer (Chicago: Dorsey Press, 1989), 225.

63. Kenneth N. Waltz, "The Stability of a Bipolar World," in *Classic Readings of International Relations,* 2nd ed., ed. Phil Williams, Donald Goldstein, and Jay Shafritz (Fort Worth, Tex.: Harcourt Brace College, 1999), 78.

64. John Mearsheimer, "Back to the Future: Instability in Europe after the Cold War," *International Security* 15 (1990): 5–56.

65. Brown, *The Causes and Prevention of War,* 73.

66. Ibid., 235.

67. Paul F. Diehl and Frank W. Wayman, "Realpolitik: Dead End, Detour, or Road Map?" in *Reconstructing Realpolitik,* ed. Frank W. Wayman and Paul F. Diehl (Ann Arbor: University of Michigan Press, 1994), 249.

68. John A. Vasquez, *The War Puzzle* (Cambridge: Cambridge University Press, 1993), 7.

69. Ibid., 7.

70. Ibid., 158.

71. Ibid., 263.

72. Manus I. Midlarsky, *The Killing Trap* (New York: Cambridge University Press, 2005), 92.

73. Ibid., 374–375.

74. Ibid., 395.

75. Richard J. Stoll, "Major Power Interstate Conflict in the Post–World War II Era: An Increase, a Decrease, or No Change?" *The Western Political Quarterly* 35, no. 4 (December 1982): 597.

76. Ibid., 603.

77. Phil Williams, Donald Goldstein, and Jay Shafritz, eds., *Classic Readings of International Relations,* 2nd ed. (Fort Worth, Tex.: Harcourt Brace College, 1999), 8.

78. Ibid., 10.

79. Ibid.

80. Richard Mansbach, Yale H. Ferguson, and Donald E. Lampert, "Towards a New Conceptualization of Global Politics," in *Classic Readings of International Relations,* 2nd ed., ed. Phil Williams, Donald Goldstein, and Jay Shafritz (Fort Worth, Tex.: Harcourt Brace College, 1999), 192.

81. Robert O. Keohane and Joseph S. Nye Jr., *Power and Interdependence: World Politics in Transition,* 3rd ed. (New York: Addison Wesley Longman, 2000); Joseph S. Nye Jr., "Transnational Relations, Interdependence and Globalization," in *Millennial Reflections on International Studies,* ed. Michael Brecher and Frank P. Harvey (Ann Arbor: University of Michigan Press, 2002), 168.

82. John Oneal and Bruce Russett, "The Classic Liberals Were Right: Democracy, Interdependence, and International Conflict, 1950–1985," *International Studies Quarterly* 41 (1997): 267–293; Peter Wallensteen, "Universalism vs. Particularism: On the Limits of Major Power Order," *Journal of Peace Research* 21 (1984): 243–257.

83. Francis Fukuyama, "The End of History?" *The National Interest* 16 (Summer 1989): 3–5, 8–15, 18.

84. Doyle, *Ways of War and Peace,* 253.

85. Melvin Small and J. David Singer, "The War-Proneness of Democratic Regimes, 1816–1965," *The Jerusalem Journal of International Relations* 1, no. 4 (Summer 1976): 67.

86. Ibid., 67.

87. Ibid., 68.

88. Zeev Maoz, "The Controversy over the Democratic Peace: Rearguard Action or Cracks in the Wall?" *International Security* 22 (1997): 162.

89. Jack S. Levy, "Domestic Politics and War," in *The Origin and Prevention of Major Wars,* ed. Robert I. Rotberg and Theodore K. Rabb (New York: Cambridge University Press, 1989), 88; John M. Owen, "How Liberalism Produces Democratic Peace," in *Theories of War and Peace,* ed. Michael E. Brown, Owen R. Coté Jr., Sean M. Lynn-Jones, and Steven E. Miller (Cambridge, Mass.: MIT Press, 1999), 137.

90. Bruce Russett, "Evidence for the Kantian Peace: Democracy, Trade, and International Organizations, 1950–1992" (paper presented at the annual meeting of the International Studies Association, Toronto, March 19–22, 1997).

91. John Oneal and Bruce Russett, "Escaping the War Trap: Evaluating Liberal Prescriptions for Peace: Controlling for Expected Utility" (paper presented at the annual meeting of the International Studies Association, Toronto, March 19–22, 1997).

92. Charles W. Kegley, ed., *The Long Postwar Peace* (New York: HarperCollins, 1991); John Mueller, *Retreat from Doomsday: The Obsolescence of Major War* (New York: Basic Books, 1989).

93. Jack Levy, *War in the Modern Great Power System* (Lexington: University of Kentucky Press, 1983); updated in Jack Levy, Thomas Walker, and Martin Edwards, "Continuity and Change in the Evolution of Warfare," in *War in a Changing World,* ed. Zeev Maoz and Azar Gat (Ann Arbor: University of Michigan Press, 2001).

94. Peter Wallensteen and Margareta Sollenberg, "The End of International War? Armed Conflict 1989–1995," *Journal of Peace Research* 33, no. 3 (1996): 353–370.

95. Hilde Ravlo, Nils Petter Gleditsch, and Han Dorussen, "Colonial War and the Democratic Peace," *Journal of Conflict Resolution* 47, no. 4 (August 2003): 520–548.

96. Bethany Lacina, Nils Petter Gleditsch, and Bruce Russett, "The Declining Risk of Death in Battle," *International Studies Quarterly* 50 (2006): 673–680.

97. Human Security Centre, *Human Security Report 2005* (New York: Oxford University Press, 2005).

98. Ted Robert Gurr, Monty G. Marshall, and Deepa Khosla, *Peace and Violent Conflict 2001* (College Park, Md.: Center for International Development and Conflict Management, 2001), 1.

99. Doyle, *Ways of War and Peace,* 285.

100. Ibid., 286.

101. Barbara Harff and Ted Gurr, "Toward Empirical Theory of Genocides and Politicides: Identification and Measurement of Cases since 1945," *International Studies Quarterly* 3 (1988): 359–378; R. J. Rummel, *Death by Government* (New Brunswick, N.J.: Transaction, 1994); Frank Wayman and Atsushi Tago, "Explaining the Onset of Mass Political Killing, 1949–87," *Journal of Peace Research* 46, no. 6 (November 2009).

102. Ted Gurr, "Peoples against States: Ethnopolitical Conflict and the Changing World System," *International Security* 38 (1994): 347–378.

103. Dan Smith, *The State of War and Peace Atlas,* new rev. 3rd ed. (London: Penguin, 1997), 13.

104. Michael Clodfelter, *Warfare and Armed Conflicts: A Statistical Reference to Casualty and Other Figures, 1618–1991* (Jefferson, N.C.: McFarland, 1992), 971.

105. David A. Lake and Donald Rothchild, eds., *The International Spread of Ethnic Conflict* (Princeton, N.J.: Princeton University Press, 1998); David Carment and Patrick James, *Wars in the Midst of Peace: The International Politics of Ethnic Conflict* (Pittsburgh: University of Pittsburgh Press, 1997).

106. Wolf Dieter Eberwein and Sven Chojnacki, "Scientific Necessity and Political Utility: A Comparison of Data on Violent Conflicts," P01-304 (Berlin: Arbeitsgruppe: Internationale Politik, 2001), 3.

107. Michael Brecher and Jonathan Wilkenfeld, *A Study of Crisis* (Ann Arbor: University of Michigan Press, 1997), xviii, 1.

108. Kegley, *The Long Postwar Peace,* 8.

109. Monty Marshall, *Third World War* (Lanham, Md.: Rowman and Littlefield, 1999), 10.

110. Doyle, *Ways of War and Peace,* 286.

111. Ibid.

112. Ibid.

113. Ibid., 288.

114. Small and Singer, "The War-Proneness of Democratic Regimes."

115. Henry Farber and Joanne Gowa, "Politics and Peace," *International Security* 20, no. 2 (Fall 1995): 108–132.

116. For a complete discussion and testing of these two democratic peace propositions, see Errol A. Henderson, *Democracy and War: The End of an Illusion?* (Boulder, Colo.: Lynne Rienner, 2002).

117. Owen, "How Liberalism Produces Democratic Peace," 137.
118. Ibid., 138.
119. Ibid., 141.
120. Ibid., 143.
121. Ibid., 174.
122. Christopher Layne, "Kant or Cant: The Myth of the Democratic Peace," in *Theories of War and Peace*, ed. Michael E. Brown, Owen R. Coté Jr., Sean M. Lynn-Jones, and Steven E. Miller (Cambridge, Mass.: MIT Press, 1999), 137.
123. Ibid., 183.
124. Ibid., 209.
125. Ibid., 220.
126. Maoz, "The Controversy over the Democratic Peace."
127. Henderson, *Democracy and War*, 5.
128. Steve Smith, "Alternative and Critical Perspectives," in *Millennial Reflections on International Studies*, ed. Michael Brecher and Frank P. Harvey (Ann Arbor: University of Michigan Press, 2002), 205.
129. John R. Oneal and Bruce Russett, "The Classical Liberals Were Right: Democracy, Interdependence, and Conflict, 1950–1985," 267–293.
130. Henderson, *Democracy and War*, 16.
131. Ibid., 156.
132. Ibid., 146.
133. Ibid., 147.
134. Ibid., 148.
135. Ibid., 157.
136. Andrew Linklater, "The Achievements of Critical Theory," in *International Theory: Positivism and Beyond*, ed. Steve Smith, Ken Booth, and Marysia Zalewski (Cambridge: Cambridge University Press, 1996), 279.
137. Doyle, *Ways of War and Peace*, 316.
138. Ibid., 330.
139. Ibid., 342.
140. Ibid., 352.
141. Immanuel Wallerstein, "The Inter-state Structure of the Modern World System," in *International Theory: Positivism and Beyond*, ed. Steve Smith, Ken Booth, and Marysia Zalewski (Cambridge: Cambridge University Press, 1996), 99–100.
142. Tom Bottomore, ed. *Karl Marx* (Englewood Cliffs, N.J.: Prentice-Hall, 1973), 1.
143. Ibid., 11.
144. Wallerstein, "The Inter-state Structure of the Modern World System," 94.
145. Henry M. Christman, ed. *Essential Works of Lenin* (New York: Bantam Books, 1971), 53.
146. Vladimir Ilyich Lenin, "What Is to Be Done?" in *Essential Works of Lenin*, ed. Henry M. Christman (New York: Bantam Books, 1971), 70.
147. Adam Ulam, *The Bolsheviks* (Toronto: Collier Books, 1968), 248.
148. Mao Tse-tung, *Quotations from Chairman Mao Tse-tung* (New York: Bantam Books, 1967), 5–6.
149. Mao Tse-tung, "Preserving Oneself and Destroying the Enemy," in *Classic Readings of International Relations*, ed. Phil Williams, Donald Goldstein, and Jay Shafritz (Fort Worth, Tex.: Harcourt Brace College, 1999), 414–421.
150. Generals Vo Nguyen Giap and Van Tien Dung, *How We Won the War* (Philadelphia: Recon, 1976), 24.
151. Ibid., 56.
152. Frantz Fanon, *The Wretched of the Earth* (New York: Grove Press, 1963), 64.
153. Ibid., 109.
154. Kwame Nkrumah, *Class Struggle in Africa* (London: Panaf Books, 1980), 10.
155. Ibid., 57.
156. Michael Harrington, *Socialism Past and Future* (New York: Arcade, 1989), 157.
157. Ibid., 158.
158. Michael Parenti, *The Sword and the Dollar: Imperialism, Revolution, and the Arms Race* (New York: St. Martin's Press, 1989), 66.
159. Harrington, *Socialism Past and Future*, 171.
160. Parenti, *The Sword and the Dollar*, 106.

161. Ibid., 111.

162. Richard A. Falk, *The Declining World Order: America's Imperial Geopolitics* (New York: Routledge, 2004), 244.

163. Carl Boggs, ed. *Masters of War: Militarism and Blowback in the Era of the American Empire* (New York: Routledge, 2003), 2.

164. Frances Fox Piven, *The War at Home* (New York: New Press, 2004), 1.

165. Chalmers Johnson, "American Militarism and Blowback," in *Masters of War: Militarism and Blowback in the Era of the American Empire,* ed. Carl Boggs (New York: Routledge, 2003), 113.

166. Noam Chomsky, cited in *Understanding Power: The Indispensable Chomsky,* ed. Peter R. Mitchell and John Schoeffel (New York: New Press, 2002), xiii.

167. Falk, *The Declining World Order,* vii.

168. George Katsiaficas, "Conclusion: The Real Axis of Evil," in *Masters of War: Militarism and Blowback in the Era of the American Empire,* ed. Carl Boggs (New York: Routledge, 2003), 350.

169. J. Ann Tickner, *Gendering World Politics* (New York: Columbia University Press, 2001), 31.

170. Steve Smith, "Positivism and Beyond," in *International Theory: Positivism and Beyond,* ed. Steve Smith, Ken Booth, and Marysia Zalewski (Cambridge: Cambridge University Press, 1996), 11.

171. Ibid., 12.

172. Linklater, "The Achievements of Critical Theory," 279–280.

173. Ibid., 281.

174. Cynthia Enloe, "Margins, Silences and Bottom Rungs: How to Overcome the Underestimation of Power in the Study of International Relations," in *International Theory: Positivism and Beyond,* ed. Steve Smith, Ken Booth, and Marysia Zalewski (Cambridge: Cambridge University Press, 1996), 200.

175. Campbell, *A Tale of Two Quagmires,* 94.

176. Kathy Kelly, *Other Lands Have Dreams: From Baghdad to Pekin Prison* (Petrolia, Calif., 2005), 38.

177. Linklater, "The Achievements of Critical Theory," 282.

178. Ibid., 283.

179. Wallerstein, "The Inter-state Sstructure of the Modern World System," 97.

180. J. Ann Tickner, *Gender in International Relations: Feminist Perspectives on Achieving Global Security* (New York: Columbia University Press, 1992).

181. Among many others, see Nancy E. McGlen and Meredith Reid Sarkees, *Women in Foreign Policy: The Insiders* (New York: Routledge, 1993); Marysia Zalewski and Jane Parpart, eds., *The "Man" Question in International Relations* (Boulder, Colo.: Westview Press, 1998); Christine Sylvester, *Feminist International Relations: An Unfinished Journey* (New York: Cambridge University Press, 2002); and Goldstein, *War and Gender.*

182. Marysia Zalewski, "Íntroduction: From the 'Women' Question to the 'Man' Question in International Relations," in *The "Man" Question in International Relations,* ed. Marysia Zalewski and Jane Parpart (Boulder, Colo.: Westview Press, 1998), 1.

183. Christine Sylvester, "The Contributions of Feminist Theory to International Relations," in *International Theory: Positivism and Beyond,* ed. Steve Smith, Ken Booth, and Marysia Zalewski (Cambridge: Cambridge University Press, 1996), 260.

184. Ibid., 267.

185. Ibid.

186. Jane Parpart, "Conclusion: New Thoughts and New Directions for the 'Man' Question in International Relations," in *The "Man" Question in International Relations,* ed. Marysia Zalewski and Jane Parpart (Boulder, Colo.: Westview Press, 1998), 206.

187. Cynthia Enloe, *Globalization and Militarism* (Boulder, Colo.: Rowman and Littlefield, 2007), 1.

188. V. Spike Peterson, "Gendered Nationalism: Reproducing 'Us' versus 'Them,' " in *The Women and War Reader,* ed. Lois Ann Lorentzen and Jennifer Turpin (New York: New York University Press, 1998), 43.

189. V. Spike Peterson and Jacqui True, " 'New Times' and New Conversations," in *The "Man" Question in International Relations,* ed. Marysia Zalewski and Jane Parpart (Boulder, Colo.: Westview Press, 1998), 15.

190. Enloe, *Globalization and Militarism,* 2.

191. Ibid.

192. Ibid., 6.

193. Goldstein, *War and Gender,* 251.

194. Enloe, *Globalization and Militarism,* 147.

195. Lois Ann Lorentzen and Jennifer Turpin, eds., *The Women and War Reader* (New York: New York University Press, 1998), xi.

196. Ibid., xii.
197. Mary Ann Tétreault, ed. *Women and Revolution in Africa, Asia, and the New World* (Columbia: University of South Carolina Press, 1994); Krishna Kumar, *Women and Civil War: Impact, Organizations, and Action* (Boulder, Colo.: Lynne Rienner, 2001).
198. Tétreault, *Women and Revolution,* 18.
199. Ibid., 435.
200. Judith Hicks Stiehm, *Arms and the Enlisted Woman* (Philadelphia: Temple University Press, 1989), 7.
201. Ibid., 239.
202. *The New York Times Magazine,* cited in R. Claire Snyder, *Citizen-Soldiers and Manly Warriors: Military Service and Gender in the Civic Republican Tradition* (Boulder, Colo.: Rowman and Littlefield, 1999), 1.
203. Snyder, *Citizen-Soldiers and Manly Warriors,* 3.
204. Tickner, *Gendering World Politics,* 48.
205. Ibid., 6.
206. Linklater, "The Achievements of Critical Theory," 284.
207. Robert W. Cox, "Universality in International Studies: A Historicist Approach," in *Millennial Reflections on International Studies,* ed. Michael Brecher and Frank P. Harvey (Ann Arbor: University of Michigan Press, 2002), 214.
208. Michael Cox, "The Continuing Story of Another Death Foretold," in *Millennial Reflections on International Studies,* ed. Michael Brecher and Frank P. Harvey (Ann Arbor: University of Michigan Press, 2002), 219.
209. V. Spike Peterson, *A Critical Rewriting of Global Political Economy* (New York: Routledge, 2003), 6.
210. Ibid., 153.
211. Cox, "The Continuing Story of Another Death Foretold," 226.
212. Ibid., 230.
213. Boggs, *Masters of War,* 3, 5.
214. Linklater, "The Achievements of Critical Theory," 287.
215. R. B. J. Walker, "Alternative, Critical, Political," in *Millennial Reflections on International Studies,* ed. Michael Brecher and Frank P. Harvey (Ann Arbor: University of Michigan Press, 2002), 266.
216. Ibid., 266.
217. Noam Chomsky, "The Nation-State System," in *Understanding Power: The Indispensible Chomsky,* ed. Peter R. Mitchell and John Schoeffel (New York: New Press, 2002), 314.
218. Linklater, "The Achievements of Critical Theory," 288.
219. David A. Lake and Donald Rothchild, "Spreading Fear: The Genesis of Transnational Ethnic Conflict," in *The International Spread of Ethnic Conflict,* ed. David A. Lake and Donald Rothchild (Princeton, N.J.: Princeton University Press, 1998), 3.
220. Ibid.
221. Ibid., 5–6.
222. Ibid., 5.
223. Ibid., 6.
224. Ibid.
225. Ibid.
226. Ibid.
227. V. P. Gagnon Jr., *The Myth of Ethnic War* (Ithaca, N.Y.: Cornell University Press, 2004), xv; Stuart J. Kaufman, *Modern Hatreds: The Symbolic Politics of Ethnic War* (Ithaca, N.Y.: Cornell University Press, 2001), 3–5; also see the discussion in Raymond C. Taras and Rajat Ganguly, *Understanding Ethnic Conflict: The International Dimension,* 2nd. ed. (New York: Longman, 2002), 16–17, 25–27.
228. Lake and Rothchild, "Spreading Fear," 4.
229. Ibid., 7.
230. Ted Robert Gurr, *Peoples versus States: Minorities at Risk in the New Century* (Washington, D.C.: United States Institute of Peace, 2000), 4.
231. Ibid., xiv.
232. Ibid., xiii.
233. Ibid., 4.
234. See the essays in Steven E. Lobell and Philip Mauceri, eds., *Ethnic Conflict and International Politics: Explaining Diffusion and Escalation* (New York: Palgrave Macmillan, 2004).

235. Meredith Reid Sarkees, "Trends in Intra-state (Not Ethnic) Wars," (paper presented at the Joint Convention Globalization and Its Challenges in the 21st Century, sponsored by the International Studies Association, the University of Hong Kong, and eleven international studies associations, Hong Kong, July 26–28, 2001).

236. Tamara Dragadze, "Ethnic Conflict as Political Smokescreen: The Caucasus Region," in *Ethnicity and Intra-state Conflict*, ed. Håkan Wiberg and Christian P. Scherrer (Brookfield, Vt.: Ashgate, 1999), 262–279.

237. John F. Stack Jr., "The Ethnic Challenge to International Relations Theory," in *Wars in the Midst of Peace*, ed. David Carment and Patrick James (Pittsburgh: University of Pittsburgh Press, 1997), 13–14.

238. Ibid., 15.

239. Ibid., 16–18.

240. Michael Brecher and Jonathan Wilkenfeld, "The Ethnic Dimension of International Crises," in *Wars in the Midst of Peace*, ed. David Carment and Patrick James (Pittsburgh: University of Pittsburgh Press, 1997), 175.

241. Joseph R. Rudolph Jr., *Encyclopedia of Modern Ethnic Conflicts* (Westport, Conn.: Greenwood Press, 2003), xxiii.

242. Kal Holsti, *The State, War, and the State of War* (Cambridge: Cambridge University Press, 1996), 27.

243. Ibid., 28.

244. Ibid., 36–41.

245. Ibid., 124.

246. Mary Kaldor, *New and Old Wars: Organized Violence in a Global Era* (Stanford, Calif.: Stanford University Press, 1999), 2–5.

247. Ibid., 31–68.

248. Errol A. Henderson and J. David Singer, "'New Wars' and Rumors of 'New Wars,'" *International Interactions* 28 (2002): 165–166.

249. Ibid., 170.

250. Ibid., 170–171.

251. Ibid., 166.

252. Ibid., 174.

253. John Keegan, *A History of Warfare* (New York: Alfred A. Knopf, 1993), 360.

254. Ibid., 361.

255. Ibid., 364.

256. Ibid., 361.

257. Ibid., 374.

258. Ibid., 9, 387.

259. Clark, *Winning Modern Wars*, 165.

260. Ibid., 108.

261. Ibid., vii.

262. Max Boot, *War Made New: Weapons, Warriors, and the Making of the Modern World* (New York: Gotham Books, 2006).

263. Ibid., 14–15.

264. Ibid., 417.

265. Ibid., 416–417.

266. Ibid., 431.

267. Clark, *Winning Modern Wars*, xvi.

268. Ibid., 106–107.

269. Ibid., 110.

270. Ibid., 130.

271. Boot, *War Made New*, 433.

272. P. W. Singer, *Corporate Warriors* (Ithaca, N.Y.: Cornell University Press, 2003).

273. Ibid., 4–5.

274. Ibid., 18.

275. Ted Robert Gurr, *Why Men Rebel* (Princeton, N.J.: Princeton University Press, 1970); Manus Midlarsky, "Rulers and Ruled: Patterned Inequality and the Onset of Mass Political Violence," *American Political Science Review* 82 (1988): 491–509.

276. Lewis Fry Richardson, *Statistics of Deadly Quarrels* (Pittsburgh: Boxwood Press, 1960).

277. Eberwein and Chojnacki, "Scientific Necessity and Political Utility, 4.

278. Donald M. Snow, *Uncivil Wars* (Boulder, Colo.: Lynee Rienner, 1996), 1–2.

279. Marshall, *Third World War*, 19.

280. Ibid., 14.

281. Dennis Sandole, *Capturing the Complexity of Conflict: Dealing with Violent Ethnic Conflicts of the Post–Cold War Era* (London: Pinter, 1999), 1.

282. J. Joseph Hewitt, Jonathan Wilkenfeld, and Ted Robert Gurr, *Peace and Conflict 2008* (Boulder, Colo.: Paradigm, 2008).

283. Melvin Small and J. David Singer, *Resort to Arms* (Beverly Hills, Calif.: Sage, 1982), 293–294.

284. Ibid., 295.

285. Meredith Reid Sarkees, Frank Wayman, and J. David Singer, "Inter-State, Intra-State, and Extra-State Wars: A Comprehensive Look at Their Distribution over Time, 1816–1997," *International Studies Quarterly* 77 (2003): 49–70.

286. Kenneth Waltz, *Theory of International Politics* (Reading, Mass.: Addison-Wesley, 1979).

287. Max Singer and Aaron Wildavsky, *The Real World Order: Zones of Peace, Zones of Turmoil* (Chatham, N.J.: Chatham House, 1993).

288. Human Security Centre, *Human Security Report 2005*, 15, 17.

289. Ibid., 17.

290. Ibid., 15.

291. Meredith Reid Sarkees and J. David Singer, "Armed Conflict Past and Future: A Master Typology?" (paper presented at the European Union Conference on Armed Conflict Data Collection, Uppsala, Sweden, June 2001).

292. Eberwein and Chojnacki, "Scientific Necessity and Political Utility."

293. Human Security Centre, *Human Security Report 2005*, 23.

294. Ibid., 148.

295. Ibid., 151.

296. Hewitt, Wilkenfeld, and Gurr, *Peace and Conflict 2008*, 21.

297. Stoessinger, *Why Nations Go to War*, 207.

Chronological List of All Wars

Year	War name	War type & number
1816	Allied Bombardment of Algiers of 1816	Extra-state War #300
1816	Ottoman-Wahhabi Revolt of 1816–1818	Extra-state War #301
1817	Liberation of Chile of 1817–1818	Extra-state War #302
1817	First Bolívar Expedition of 1817–1819	Extra-state War #303
1817	War of Mexican Independence of 1817–1818	Extra-state War #304
1817	British-Kandyan War of 1817–1818	Extra-state War #305
1817	British-Maratha War of 1817–1818	Extra-state War #306
1818	First Maori Tribal War of 1818–1824	Non-state War #1500
1818	First Caucasus War of 1818–1822	Intra-state War #500
1819	Shaka Zulu-Bantu War of 1819–1828	Non-state War #1501
1819	Burma-Assam War of 1819–1822	Non-state War #1502
1820	Buenos Aires War of 1820	Non-state War #1503
1820	Sidon-Damascus War of 1820–1821	Intra-state War #501
1820	First Two Sicilies War of 1820–1821	Intra-state War #502
1820	Ottoman Conquest of Sudan of 1820–1821	Extra-state War #307
1821	Sardinian Revolt of 1821	Intra-state War #505
1821	Greek Independence War of 1821–1828	Intra-state War #506
1821	Second Bolívar Expedition of 1821–1822	Extra-state War #308
1821	Turco-Persian War of 1821–1823	Extra-state War #309
1821	Second Maori Tribal War of 1821–1823	Non-state War #1505
1821	Siam-Kedah War of 1821	Non-state War #1506
1821	Spanish Royalists War of 1821–1823	Intra-state War #503
1823	Franco-Spanish War of 1823	Inter-state War #1
1823	First British-Burmese War of 1823–1826	Extra-state War #310
1824	First British-Ashanti War of 1824–1826	Extra-state War #311
1824	Liberation of Peru of 1824 1825	Extra-state War #312
1824	Egypt-Mehdi War of 1824	Intra-state War #507
1825	China-Kashgaria War of 1825–1828	Non-state War #1508
1825	Dutch-Javanese War of 1825–1830	Extra-state War #313
1825	Mexico-Yaqui Indian War of 1825–1827	Non-state War #1509
1825	British-Bharatpuran War of 1825–1826	Extra-state War #314
1826	Brazil-Argentine War of 1826–1828	Extra-state War #315
1826	Central American Confederation War of 1826–1829	Non-state War #1510

(Continued)

Year	War name	War type & number
1826	Viang Chan-Siamese War of 1826–1827	Non-state War #1511
1826	Janissari Revolt of 1826	Intra-state War #508
1826	Russo-Persian War of 1826–1828	Extra-state War #316
1828	First Russo-Turkish War of 1828–1829	Inter-state War #4
1828	Peru-Gran Colombia War of 1828–1829	Non-state War #1512
1828	Miguelite War of 1828–1834	Intra-state War #510
1829	Argentine War for Unity of 1829–1831	Non-state War #1513
1829	Spanish Reconquest of Mexico of 1829	Extra-state War #317
1829	Sayyid Said War of 1829–1830	Non-state War #1514
1830	First Murid War of 1830–1832	Intra-state War #511
1830	First Albanian Revolt of 1830–1831	Intra-state War #512
1830	French Occupation of Algiers of 1830	Extra-state War #319
1830	First French Insurrection of 1830	Intra-state War #513
1830	Belgian Independence War of 1830	Intra-state War #515
1830	China-Kokand War of 1830–1831	Non-state War #1515
1831	Egyptian Taka Expedition of 1831–1832	Intra-state War #516
1831	First Polish War of 1831	Intra-state War #517
1831	Siam-Cambodia-Vietnam War of 1831–1834	Non-state War #1516
1831	First Syrian War of 1831–1832	Intra-state War #518
1832	First Mexican War of 1832	Intra-state War #520
1832	Ottoman-Bilmez-Asiri War of 1832–1837	Extra-state War #320
1833	Argentina-Ranqueles Indian War of 1833–1834	Non-state War #1518
1834	Egypt-Palestinian Anti-Conscription Revolt of 1834	Intra-state War #521
1834	First Carlist War of 1834–1840	Intra-state War #522
1834	Second Murid War of 1834	Intra-state War #523
1835	Cabanos Revolt of 1835–1837	Intra-state War #525
1835	Bolivia Conquest of Peru in 1835–1836	Non-state War #1520
1835	Farroupilha War of 1835–1845	Intra-state War #526
1835	Texan War of 1835–1836	Intra-state War #527
1836	First Bosnian War of 1836–1837	Intra-state War #528
1836	Third Murid War of 1836–1852	Intra-state War #530
1836	Boer-Matabele War of 1836–1837	Non-state War #1521
1837	Druze Rebellion of 1837–1838	Intra-state War #532
1837	Sabinada Rebellion of 1837–1838	Intra-state War #531
1837	Dissolution of the Bolivia-Peru Confederation of 1837–1839	Non-state War #1523
1837	Persian Siege of Herat of 1837–1838	Non-state War #1524
1838	Boer-Zulu War of 1838	Non-state War #1525
1838	First British-Zulu War of 1838	Extra-state War #321
1839	First British-Afghan War of 1839–1842	Extra-state War #322
1839	Anti-Rosas War of 1839–1840	Non-state War #1527
1839	Dissolution of the Central American Confederation of 1839–1840	Non-state War #1528
1839	Second Syrian War Phase 1 of 1839	Intra-state War #533

(Continued)

Year	War name	War type & number
1839	First Opium War of 1839–1842	Extra-state War #323
1839	First Franco-Algerian War 1839–1847	Extra-state War #324
1840	Lebanon Insurgency of 1840	Intra-state War #535
1840	First Colombian War of 1840–1842	Intra-state War #536
1840	Second Syrian War Phase 2 of 1840	Intra-state War #537
1841	First Argentina War Phase 2 of 1841–1842	Intra-state War #538
1841	Second Bosnian War of 1841	Intra-state War #540
1841	Dogra-Tibet War of 1841–1842	Non-state War #1530
1841	Triangular Revolt of 1841	Intra-state War #541
1841	Peru-Bolivian War of 1841	Extra-state War #325
1842	Karbala Revolt of 1842–1843	Intra-state War #542
1843	British-Sind War of 1843	Extra-state War #326
1843	Uruguay War of 1843–1851	Extra-state War #327
1843	Gwalior War of 1843	Extra-state War #329
1844	First Haiti-Santo Domingo War of 1844–1845	Non-state War #1531
1844	Franco-Moroccan War of 1844	Extra-state War #330
1845	First Maronite-Druze War of 1845	Intra-state War #543
1845	First British-Sikh War of 1845–1846	Extra-state War #331
1846	Cracow Revolt of 1846	Extra-state War #332
1846	First British-Xhosa War of 1846–1847	Extra-state War #333
1846	Mexican-American War of 1846–1848	Inter-state War #7
1847	Mayan Caste War Phase 1 of 1847–1848	Intra-state War #545
1847	Second Carlist War of 1847–1849	Intra-state War #546
1847	War of Seven Khojas of 1847–1848	Non-state War #1533
1848	Second Two Sicilies War of 1848–1849	Intra-state War #547
1848	First Venezuelan War of 1848–1849	Intra-state War #548
1848	Viennese Revolt of 1848	Intra-state War #550
1848	Milan Five-Day Revolt of 1848	Intra-state War #551
1848	Austro-Sardinian War of 1848–1849	Inter-state War #10
1848	First Schleswig-Holstein War of 1848–1849	Inter-state War #13
1848	First Dutch-Bali War of 1848–1849	Extra-state War #334
1848	Second British-Sikh War of 1848–1849	Extra-state War #335
1848	Second French Insurrection of 1848	Intra-state War #552
1848	Mayan Caste War Phase 2 of 1848–1855	Intra-state War #553
1848	Hungarian War of 1848–1849	Intra-state War #554
1849	War of the Roman Republic of 1849	Inter-state War #16
1849	Chinese Pirates War of 1849	Extra-state War #336
1850	Taiping Rebellion Phase 1 of 1850–1860	Non-state War #1534
1850	Second British-Xhosa War of 1850–1852	Extra-state War #337
1851	Ottoman-Yam Rebellion of 1851	Extra-state War #338
1851	La Plata War of 1851–1852	Inter-state War #19

(Continued)

Year	War name	War type & number
1851	First Chilean War of 1851	Intra-state War #555
1852	Second British-Burmese War of 1852	Extra-state War #339
1852	First Tukulor War of 1852–1854	Non-state War #1535
1852	Kashmir-Dards of Chilas War of 1852	Non-state War #1536
1852	First Turco-Montenegrin War of 1852–1853	Intra-state War #556
1853	Crimean War of 1853–1856	Inter-state War #22
1853	First Peru War of 1853–1855	Intra-state War #557
1854	Han-Miao War Phase 1 of 1854–1860	Non-state War #1537
1854	French-Tukulor War of 1854–1857	Extra-state War #340
1855	Second Haiti-Santo Domingo War of 1855–1856	Non-state War #1538
1855	Han-Nien War of 1855–1858	Non-state War #1539
1855	British-Santal War of 1855–1856	Extra-state War #341
1855	Puebla War of 1855–1856	Intra-state War #558
1856	Hodeida Siege of 1856	Extra-state War #342
1856	Filibuster War of 1856–1857	Non-state War #1540
1856	French Conquest of Kabylia of 1856–1857	Extra-state War #345
1856	Han-Panthay War Phase 1 of 1856–1860	Non-state War #1541
1856	Second Opium War of 1856–1860	Extra-state War #343
1856	Anglo-Persian War of 1856–1857	Inter-state War #25
1856	Second Peru War of 1856–1858	Intra-state War #560
1856	First Zulu Internecine War of 1856	Non-state War #1542
1857	Indian Mutiny of 1857–1859	Extra-state War #347
1857	Kucha and Khoja Uprising of 1857	Non-state War #1543
1858	Mexican Reform War of 1858–1861	Intra-state War #561
1858	Second Turco-Montenegrin War of 1858–1859	Intra-state War #562
1858	First Boer-Basuto War of 1858	Non-state War #1544
1858	First Ethiopian War of 1858–1861	Non-state War #1545
1858	First Franco-Vietnamese War of 1858–1862	Extra-state War #349
1859	Second Venezuelan/Federalist War of 1859–1863	Intra-state War #563
1859	Netherlands-Bone War of 1859–1860	Extra-state War #350
1859	War of Italian Unification of 1859	Inter-state War #28
1859	Argentine-Buenos Aires War of 1859	Extra-state War #351
1859	First Spanish-Moroccan War of 1859–1860	Inter-state War #31
1860	Garibaldi Expedition of 1860	Extra-state War #352
1860	Second Colombian War of 1860–1861	Intra-state War #565
1860	Second Maronite-Druze War of 1860	Intra-state War #566
1860	Second Tukulor War of 1860–1862	Non-state War #1546
1860	Italian-Roman War of 1860	Inter-state War #34
1860	Neapolitan War of 1860–1861	Inter-state War #37
1860	Taiping Rebellion Phase 2 of 1860–1866	Intra-state War #567
1860	Second Nien Revolt of 1860–1868	Intra-state War #568
1860	Miao Revolt Phase 2 of 1860–1872	Intra-state War #570

(Continued)

Year	War name	War type & number
1860	Panthay Rebellion Phase 2 of 1860–1872	Intra-state War #571
1861	U.S. Civil War of 1861–1865	Intra-state War #572
1861	Third Buenos Aires War of 1861	Intra-state War #573
1861	Third Turco-Montenegrin War of 1861–1862	Intra-state War #575
1862	Transvaal War of 1862–1864	Non-state War #1548
1862	Franco-Mexican War of 1862–1867	Inter-state War #40
1862	Tungan Rebellion of 1862–1873	Intra-state War #576
1862	Sioux-Minnesota War of 1862	Intra-state War #577
1862	Bolivian-Pérez Rebellion of 1862	Intra-state War #578
1863	Second Polish War of 1863–1864	Intra-state War #580
1863	Central American War of 1863	Non-state War #1550
1863	Second Argentina War of 1863	Intra-state War #581
1863	Spanish-Santo Dominican War of 1863–1865	Extra-state War #353
1863	British-Maori War of 1863–1866	Extra-state War #355
1863	Shimonoseki War of 1863–1864	Extra-state War #356
1863	British Umbeyla Campaign of 1863	Extra-state War #357
1863	Ecuadorian-Colombian War of 1863	Inter-state War #43
1864	Second Schleswig-Holstein War of 1864	Inter-state War #46
1864	Russian-Kokand War of 1864–1865	Extra-state War #359
1864	Xinjiang Muslim Revolt of 1864–1871	Intra-state War #582
1864	Lopez War of 1864–1870	Inter-state War #49
1864	First Australian Aboriginal War of 1864–1865	Non-state War #1551
1865	British-Bhutanese War of 1865	Extra-state War #360
1865	Second Boer-Basuto War of 1865–1866	Non-state War #1552
1865	Naval War of 1865–1866	Inter-state War #52
1866	Russian-Bukharan War of 1866	Extra-state War #361
1866	First Cretan War of 1866–1867	Intra-state War #583
1866	Seven Weeks War of 1866	Inter-state War #55
1866	Yellow Cliff Revolt of 1866	Intra-state War #585
1866	Third Argentina War of 1866–1867	Intra-state War #586
1867	Queretaro War of 1867	Intra-state War #587
1867	British-Ethiopian War of 1867–1868	Extra-state War #362
1868	Meiji Restoration of 1868	Intra-state War #588
1868	Third Venezuelan War of 1868–1871	Intra-state War #590
1868	Second Ethiopian War of 1868–1872	Non-state War #1553
1868	Spanish Liberals War of 1868	Intra-state War #591
1868	First Spanish-Cuban War of 1868–1878	Extra-state War #363
1869	Guerre des Cacos of 1869	Intra-state War #592
1869	Attack on Bahr el-Ghazal of 1869–1870	Extra-state War #364
1870	Uruguay Colorados-Blancos War of 1870–1872	Non-state War #1554
1870	Fourth Argentina War of 1870–1871	Intra-state War #593
1870	Franco-Prussian War of 1870–1871	Inter-state War #58

(Continued)

Year	War name	War type & number
1870	Bolivia-Criollos War of 1870–1871	Intra-state War #595
1870	Ottoman Conquest of Arabia of 1870–1872	Extra-state War #365
1871	Second Franco-Algerian War of 1871–1872	Extra-state War #366
1871	Paris Commune War of 1871	Intra-state War #596
1872	Third Carlist War of 1872–1876	Intra-state War #597
1873	Second British-Ashanti War of 1873–1874	Extra-state War #367
1873	First Dutch-Achinese War of 1873–1878	Extra-state War #370
1873	Second Franco-Vietnamese War of 1873–1874	Extra-state War #369
1874	Catonalist Uprising of 1874–1875	Intra-state War #598
1874	Fifth Argentina War of 1874	Intra-state War #600
1875	Bosnia and Bulgaria Revolt of 1875–1876	Intra-state War #601
1875	Kokand Rebellion of 1875–1876	Extra-state War #371
1875	Egypt-Ethiopian War of 1875–1876	Extra-state War #372
1876	Diaz Revolt of 1876	Intra-state War #602
1876	First Central American War of 1876	Inter-state War #60
1876	Defeat of Xinjiang Muslims of 1876–1877	Intra-state War #603
1876	Serbian-Turkish War of 1876–1877	Extra-state War #373
1876	Third Colombian War of 1876–1877	Intra-state War #605
1877	Satsuma Rebellion of 1877	Intra-state War #607
1877	Second Russo-Turkish War of 1877–1878	Inter-state War #61
1877	Third British-Xhosa War of 1877–1878	Extra-state War #374
1878	Egypt-Sudanese Slavers War of 1878–1879	Extra-state War #375
1878	Russo-Turkoman War of 1878–1881	Extra-state War #376
1878	Austrian-Bosnian War of 1878	Extra-state War #377
1878	Second British-Afghan War of 1878–1880	Extra-state War #379
1879	Second British-Zulu War of 1879	Extra-state War #380
1879	War of the Pacific of 1879–1883	Inter-state War #64
1879	Argentine Indians War of 1879–1880	Intra-state War #608
1880	Fourth Buenos Aires War of 1880	Intra-state War #610
1880	Gun War of 1880–1881	Extra-state War #381
1880	First Boer War of 1880–1881	Extra-state War #382
1881	Franco-Tunisian War of 1881–1882	Extra-state War #383
1881	First British-Mahdi War of 1881–1885	Extra-state War #384
1882	Third Franco-Vietnamese War of 1882–1884	Extra-state War #385
1882	Conquest of Egypt of 1882	Inter-state War #65
1883	Haitian Civil War of 1883–1884	Intra-state War #611
1883	Second Zulu Internecine War of 1883–1884	Non-state War #1556
1883	First Franco-Madagascan War of 1883–1885	Extra-state War #386
1883	Oman-Ibadi War of 1883–1884	Non-state War #1557
1884	Sino-French War of 1884–1885	Inter-state War #67
1884	Second Australian Aboriginal War of 1884–1894	Non-state War #1558
1884	Fourth Colombian War of 1884–1885	Intra-state War #612

(Continued)

Year	War name	War type & number
1885	Peru's National Problem of 1885	Intra-state War #613
1885	Second Central American War of 1885	Inter-state War #70
1885	Russo-Afghan War of 1885	Extra-state War #390
1885	Ethiopia-Mahdi War of 1885–1889	Non-state War #1559
1885	French-Mandinka War of 1885–1886	Extra-state War #389
1885	Serbian-Bulgarian War of 1885	Extra-state War #391
1885	Third British-Burmese War of 1885–1889	Extra-state War #387
1887	First Italian-Ethiopian War of 1887	Extra-state War #392
1888	Zambezi Conquest of 1888	Extra-state War #393
1888	German East Africa Company War of 1888–1889	Non-state War #1560
1890	First Franco-Dahomeyan War of 1890	Extra-state War #394
1890	First Yemeni Rebellion of 1890–1892	Intra-state War #616
1890	Franco-Jolof War of 1890–1891	Extra-state War #395
1891	Second Chilean War of 1891	Intra-state War #617
1891	Zaili-Jinden Revolt of 1891	Intra-state War #618
1892	Second Franco-Dahomeyan War of 1892–1893	Extra-state War #396
1892	Belgian-Tib War of 1892–1894	Extra-state War #397
1893	Brazil Federalists War of 1893–1894	Intra-state War #620
1893	Rabih Zubayr-Bornu War of 1893	Non-state War #1561
1893	Brazil Naval War of 1893–1894	Intra-state War #621
1893	Third British-Ashanti War of 1893–1894	Extra-state War #398
1893	Melilla War of 1893–1894	Extra-state War #399
1893	Mahdist-Italian War of 1893–1894	Extra-state War #400
1894	Tonghak Rebellion of 1894	Intra-state War #623
1894	Second Franco-Madagascan War of 1894–1895	Extra-state War #401
1894	Second Dutch-Bali War of 1894	Extra-state War #402
1894	First Sino-Japanese War of 1894–1895	Inter-state War #73
1894	Third Peru War of 1894–1895	Intra-state War #625
1895	Fifth Colombian War of 1895	Intra-state War #626
1895	Portuguese-Gaza Empire War of 1895	Extra-state War #403
1895	Ecuador Liberals War of 1895	Intra-state War #627
1895	Second Spanish-Cuban War of 1895–1898	Extra-state War #404
1895	First Gansu Muslim War of 1895–1896	Intra-state War #628
1895	Japan-Taiwanese War of 1895	Extra-state War #405
1895	Mazrui Rebellion of 1895–1896	Extra-state War #406
1895	Druze-Turkish War of 1895–1896	Intra-state War #630
1895	Second Italian-Ethiopian War of 1895–1896	Extra-state War #407
1896	Second Cretan War of 1896–1897	Intra-state War #631
1896	Second British-Mahdi War of 1896–1899	Extra-state War #409
1896	Spanish-Philippine War of 1896–1898	Extra-state War #410
1896	Third Brazil-Canudos War of 1896–1897	Intra-state War #632
1897	British-South Nigerian War of 1897	Extra-state War #411

(Continued)

Year	War name	War type & number
1897	Greco-Turkish War of 1897	Inter-state War #76
1897	British-Pathan War of 1897–1898	Extra-state War #412
1898	Hut Tax War of 1898	Extra-state War #413
1898	Spanish-American War of 1898	Inter-state War #79
1899	American-Philippine War of 1899–1902	Extra-state War #414
1899	Fourth Venezuelan War of 1899	Intra-state War #633
1899	French Conquest of Chad of 1899–1900	Extra-state War #415
1899	Second Yaqui War of 1899–1900	Intra-state War #635
1899	Second Boer War of 1899–1902	Extra-state War #416
1899	Sixth Colombian (War of the 1,000 Days) of 1899–1902	Intra-state War #636
1900	Last Ashanti War of 1900	Extra-state War #417
1900	Boxer Rebellion of 1900	Inter-state War #82
1900	Sino-Russian War of 1900	Inter-state War #83
1901	Somali Rebellion of 1901–1904	Extra-state War #419
1901	Fifth Venezuelan War of 1901–1903	Intra-state War #638
1902	Bailundu Revolt of 1902–1903	Extra-state War #420
1902	Kuanhama Rebellion of 1902–1904	Extra-state War #421
1903	British Conquest of Kano and Sokoto of 1903	Extra-state War #422
1903	Ilinden War of 1903	Intra-state War #640
1904	First Uruguay War of 1904	Intra-state War #641
1904	South West African Revolt of 1904–1906	Extra-state War #423
1904	Russo-Japanese War of 1904–1905	Inter-state War #85
1904	Second Dutch-Achinese War of 1904–1907	Extra-state War #424
1904	Younghusband Expedition of 1904	Extra-state War #425
1904	Second Yemeni Rebellion of 1904–1906	Intra-state War #642
1905	Bloody Sunday War of 1905–1906	Intra-state War #643
1905	Maji-Maji Revolt of 1905–1906	Extra-state War #426
1906	Sokoto Uprising of 1906	Extra-state War #427
1906	Third British-Zulu War of 1906	Extra-state War #429
1906	Third Central American War of 1906	Inter-state War #88
1907	Fourth Central American War of 1907	Inter-state War #91
1907	Romanian Peasant Revolt of 1907	Intra-state War #645
1907	Dembos War of 1907–1910	Extra-state War #430
1907	Anti-Foreign Revolt of 1907	Extra-state War #431
1907	Japan-Korean Guerrillas War of 1907–1910	Extra-state War #432
1907	Overthrow of Abd el-Aziz of 1907–1908	Intra-state War #646
1908	Iranian Constitution War of 1908–1909	Intra-state War #647
1909	Young Turks Counter-coup of 1909	Intra-state War #648
1909	French Conquest of Wadai of 1909–1911	Extra-state War #433
1909	Second Spanish-Moroccan War of 1909–1910	Inter-state War #94
1910	Second Albanian Revolt of 1910–1912	Intra-state War #650
1910	Asir-Yemen Revolt of 1910–1911	Intra-state War #651

(Continued)

Year	War name	War type & number
1910	Third Mexican War of 1910–1914	Intra-state War #652
1911	Paraguay War of 1911–1912	Intra-state War #656
1911	Italian-Turkish War of 1911–1912	Inter-state War #97
1911	First Nationalists War of 1911	Intra-state War #657
1912	French-Berber War of 1912	Extra-state War #434
1912	First Sino-Tibetan War of 1912–1913	Extra-state War #435
1912	Cuban Black Uprising of 1912	Intra-state War #658
1912	Ecuadorian Civil War of 1912–1914	Intra-state War #670
1912	First Balkan War of 1912–1913	Inter-state War #100
1913	Moroccan-Berber War of 1913–1915	Extra-state War #436
1913	Moro Rebellion of 1913	Extra-state War #437
1913	Second Balkan War of 1913	Inter-state War #103
1913	Second Nationalists War of 1913	Intra-state War #671
1914	China Pai-ling (White Wolf) War of 1914	Intra-state War #672
1914	World War I of 1914–1918	Inter-state War #106
1914	Fourth Mexican War of 1914–1920	Intra-state War #673
1916	Southern China Revolt of 1916–1918	Intra-state War #675
1916	Russia-Turkestan War of 1916–1917	Intra-state War #676
1917	Russian Civil War of 1917–1921	Intra-state War #677
1918	Second Sino-Tibetan War of 1918	Extra-state War #440
1918	Finnish Civil War of 1918	Intra-state War #680
1918	Caco Revolt of 1918–1920	Extra-state War #441
1918	Western Ukrainian War of 1918–1919	Intra-state War #681
1918	Estonian War of Liberation of 1918–1920	Inter-state War #107
1918	Latvian War of Liberation of 1918–1920	Inter-state War #108
1919	Sparticist Rising of 1919	Intra-state War #682
1919	Russo-Polish War of 1919–1920	Inter-state War #109
1919	Hungary's Red Terror War of 1919–1920	Intra-state War #683
1919	Hungarian Adversaries War of 1919	Inter-state War #112
1919	Third British-Afghan War of 1919	Extra-state War #442
1919	Second Greco-Turkish War of 1919–1922	Inter-state War #115
1919	First Nejd-Hejaz War of 1919	Non-state War #1567
1919	First British-Waziristan War of 1919–1920	Extra-state War #443
1919	Franco-Turkish War of 1919–1921	Inter-state War #116
1920	Franco-Syrian War of 1920	Extra-state War #444
1920	Iraqi-British War of 1920	Extra-state War #445
1920	First Chinese Warlord War of 1920	Intra-state War #685
1920	Lithuanian-Polish War of 1920	Inter-state War #117
1920	Green Rebellion of 1920–1921	Intra-state War #686
1920	Gilan Marxists War of 1920–1921	Intra-state War #687
1920	Conquest of Mongolia of 1920–1921	Extra-state War #446
1920	Italian Fascist War of 1920–1922	Intra-state War #688

(Continued)

Year	War name	War type & number
1921	Kronstadt Rebellion of 1921	Intra-state War #690
1921	Rif Rebellion of 1921–1926	Extra-state War #449
1921	Moplah Rebellion of 1921–1922	Extra-state War #450
1921	Bashmachi in Turkestan War of 1921–1923	Intra-state War #691
1922	Second Chinese Warlord War of 1922	Intra-state War #692
1923	Italian-Sanusi War of 1923–1931	Extra-state War #447
1923	Agrarian Rising of 1923	Intra-state War #693
1923	De La Huerta Rebellion of 1923–1924	Intra-state War #695
1924	Honduran Conservative War of 1924	Intra-state War #696
1924	First Afghan Anti-Reform War of 1924–1925	Intra-state War #697
1924	Second Nejd-Hejaz War of 1924–1925	Non-state War #1568
1925	Franco-Druze War of 1925–1927	Extra-state War #451
1925	Third Chinese Warlord War of 1925–1926	Intra-state War #698
1926	Chinese Northern Expedition War of 1926–1928	Intra-state War #700
1926	Cristeros Revolt of 1926–1929	Intra-state War #701
1928	Ethiopian Northern Resistance of 1928–1930	Intra-state War #702
1928	Second Gansu Muslim War of 1928–1930	Intra-state War #703
1928	Second Afghan Anti-Reform War of 1928–1929	Intra-state War #705
1929	Intra-Guomindang War of 1929–1930	Intra-state War #706
1929	Escoban Rebellion of 1929	Intra-state War #707
1929	Ikhwan Revolt of 1929–1930	Intra-state War #708
1929	Manchurian War of 1929	Inter-state War #118
1930	Yen Bai Uprising of 1930–1931	Extra-state War #452
1930	Chinese Civil War Phase 1 of 1930–1936	Intra-state War #710
1930	Saya San's Rebellion of 1930–1932	Extra-state War #453
1931	Xinjiang Muslim Revolt of 1931–1934	Intra-state War #711
1931	Second Sino-Japanese War of 1931–1933	Inter-state War #121
1932	Matanza War of 1932	Intra-state War #712
1932	Aprista Revolt of 1932	Intra-state War #713
1932	Paulista Rebellion of 1932	Intra-state War #715
1932	Chaco War of 1932–1935	Inter-state War #124
1934	Fukien Revolt of 1934	Intra-state War #716
1934	Saudi-Yemeni War of 1934	Inter-state War #125
1934	Spanish Miners War of 1934	Intra-state War #717
1935	Conquest of Ethiopia of 1935–1936	Inter-state War #127
1936	British-Palestinian War of 1936–1939	Extra-state War #454
1936	Spanish Civil War of 1936–1939	Intra-state War #718
1936	Second British-Waziristan War of 1936–1938	Extra-state War #455
1937	Third Sino-Japanese War of 1937–1941	Inter-state War #130
1938	Changkufeng War of 1938	Inter-state War #133
1939	Nomonhan War of 1939	Inter-state War #136
1939	World War II of 1939–1945	Inter-state War #139

(Continued)

Year	War name	War type & number
1939	Russo-Finnish War of 1939–1940	Inter-state War #142
1940	Franco-Thai War of 1940–1941	Inter-state War #145
1944	Greek Civil War of 1944–1949	Intra-state War #720
1945	Polish Ukrainians War of 1945–1947	Intra-state War #721
1945	Ukrainian Partisans War of 1945–1947	Intra-state War #722
1945	Forest Brethren War of 1945–1951	Intra-state War #723
1945	Indonesian War of 1945–1946	Extra-state War #456
1946	Chinese Civil War Phase 2 of 1946–1950	Intra-state War #725
1946	Partition Communal War of 1946–1947	Non-state War #1570
1946	French-Indochina War of 1946–1954	Extra-state War #457
1947	Taiwan Revolt of 1947	Intra-state War #726
1947	Paraguay War of 1947	Intra-state War #727
1947	Third Franco-Madagascan War of 1947–1948	Extra-state War #459
1947	Hyderabad War of 1947–1948	Non-state War #1571
1947	First Kashmir War of 1947–1949	Inter-state War #147
1947	Palestine War of 1947–1948	Non-state War #1572
1948	Yemeni Imamate War of 1948	Intra-state War #728
1948	Costa Rica War of 1948	Intra-state War #730
1948	Cheju Rebellion of 1948–1949	Non-state War #1573
1948	Seventh Colombian ("La Violencia") War of 1948–1958	Intra-state War #731
1948	Arab-Israeli War of 1948–1949	Inter-state War #148
1948	Malayan Rebellion of 1948–1957	Extra-state War #460
1948	First Burmese War of 1948–1951	Intra-state War #732
1948	Indo-Hyderabad War of 1948	Extra-state War #461
1950	Third Sino-Tibetan War of 1950	Extra-state War #462
1950	South Moluccas War of 1950	Intra-state War #733
1950	Korean War of 1950–1953	Inter-state War #151
1950	Hukbalahap Rebellion of 1950–1954	Intra-state War #735
1952	Franco-Tunisian War of 1952–1954	Extra-state War #463
1952	Bolivia War of 1952	Intra-state War #737
1952	British-Mau Mau War of 1952–1956	Extra-state War #464
1953	Moroccan Independence War of 1953–1956	Extra-state War #465
1953	Indonesia-Darul Islam War of 1953	Intra-state War #738
1954	Off-shore Islands War of 1954–1955	Inter-state War #153
1954	Third Franco-Algerian War of 1954–1962	Extra-state War #466
1955	Argentine Military War of 1955	Intra-state War #740
1956	Tibetan Khamba Rebellion of 1956–1959	Intra-state War #741
1956	Sinai War of 1956	Inter-state War #155
1956	Soviet Invasion of Hungary of 1956	Inter-state War #156
1956	Indonesian Leftists War of 1956–1962	Intra-state War #742
1957	French-Cameroon War of 1957–1958	Extra-state War #467
1957	Ifni War of 1957–1958	Inter-state War #158

(Continued)

Year	War name	War type & number
1958	First Lebanese War of 1958	Intra-state War #743
1958	Cuban Revolution of 1958–1959	Intra-state War #745
1958	Taiwan Straits War of 1958	Inter-state War #159
1958	Second Burmese War of 1958–1960	Intra-state War #746
1959	Iraq-Shammar War of 1959	Intra-state War #747
1959	Rwandan Social Revolution of 1959–1962	Non-state War #1574
1960	Vietnam War Phase 1 of 1960–1965	Intra-state War #748
1960	First DRC (Zaire) War of 1960–1963	Intra-state War #750
1960	First Laotian War of 1960–1962	Intra-state War #751
1961	Angolan-Portuguese War of 1961–1974	Extra-state War #469
1961	First Iraqi Kurds War of 1961–1963	Intra-state War #752
1962	Algerian Revolutionaries War of 1962–1963	Intra-state War #753
1962	War in Assam of 1962	Inter-state War #160
1962	North Yemen War of 1962–1969	Intra-state War #755
1963	Second Laotian War Phase 1 of 1963–1968	Intra-state War #756
1963	First Ogaden War of 1963–1964	Intra-state War #757
1963	First South Sudan War of 1963–1972	Intra-state War #758
1963	Second DRC (Jeunesse) War of 1963–1965	Intra-state War #760
1963	First Rwanda War of 1963–1964	Intra-state War #761
1964	Third DRC (Simba) Rebellion of 1964–1965	Intra-state War #762
1964	Zanzibar Arab-African War of 1964	Intra-state War #763
1964	Mozambique-Portuguese War of 1964–1975	Extra-state War #471
1965	Vietnam War Phase 2 of 1965–1975	Inter-state War #163
1965	Second Iraqi Kurds War of 1965–1966	Intra-state War #765
1965	Dominican Republic War of 1965	Intra-state War #766
1965	First West Papua War of 1965–1969	Intra-state War #767
1965	Second Kashmir War of 1965	Inter-state War #166
1966	First Uganda War of 1966	Intra-state War #768
1966	First Guatemala War of 1966–1968	Intra-state War #770
1966	First Chad (FROLINAT) Rebellion of 1966–1971	Intra-state War #771
1967	Cultural Revolution Phase 1 of 1967	Intra-state War #772
1967	Six-Day War of 1967	Inter-state War #169
1967	Third Burmese War of 1967–1980	Intra-state War #773
1967	Biafra War of 1967–1970	Intra-state War #775
1967	Cultural Revolution Phase 2 of 1967–1968	Intra-state War #776
1968	Second Laotian War Phase 2 of 1968–1973	Inter-state War #170
1968	Dhofar Rebellion Phase 1 of 1968–1971	Non-state War #1577
1969	Third Iraqi Kurds War of 1969–1970	Intra-state War #777
1969	War of Attrition of 1969–1970	Inter-state War #172
1969	Football War of 1969	Inter-state War #175
1970	Naxalite Rebellion of 1970–1971	Intra-state War #778
1970	War of the Communist Coalition of 1970–1971	Inter-state War #176

(Continued)

Year	War name	War type & number
1970	Black September War of 1970	Intra-state War #780
1970	Second Guatemala War of 1970–1971	Intra-state War #781
1971	Pakistan-Bengal War of 1971	Intra-state War #782
1971	First Sri Lanka-JVP War of 1971	Intra-state War #783
1971	Khmer Rouge War of 1971–1975	Intra-state War #785
1971	War for Bangladesh of 1971	Inter-state War #178
1972	First Philippine-Moro War of 1972–1981	Intra-state War #786
1972	Communist Insurgency of 1972–1973	Intra-state War #787
1972	Eritrean Split of 1972–1974	Intra-state War #788
1972	First Burundi War of 1972	Intra-state War #789
1972	Philippines-NPA War of 1972–1992	Intra-state War #790
1972	Rhodesia War of 1972–1979	Intra-state War #791
1973	Baluchi Separatists War of 1973–1977	Intra-state War #792
1973	Chilean Coup of 1973	Intra-state War #793
1973	Yom Kippur War of 1973	Inter-state War #181
1973	Dhofar Rebellion Phase 2 of 1973–1975	Intra-state War #795
1974	Fourth Iraqi Kurds War of 1974–1975	Intra-state War #797
1974	Turco-Cypriot War of 1974	Inter-state War #184
1974	Angola Guerrilla War of 1974–1975	Non-state War #1581
1975	Eritrean War of 1975–1978	Intra-state War #798
1975	Argentine Leftists War of 1975–1977	Intra-state War #800
1975	Second Lebanese War of 1975–1976	Intra-state War #801
1975	East Timorese War Phase 1 of 1975	Non-state War #1582
1975	East Timorese War Phase 2 of 1975–1976	Extra-state War #472
1975	Namibian War of 1975–1988	Extra-state War #473
1975	War over Angola of 1975–1976	Inter-state War #186
1975	Western Sahara War of 1975–1983	Extra-state War #474
1976	Second West Papua War of 1976–1978	Intra-state War #802
1976	Third Laotian War of 1976–1979	Intra-state War #803
1976	Angolan Control War of 1976–1991	Intra-state War #804
1976	Second Ogaden War Phase 1 of 1976–1977	Intra-state War #805
1976	East Timorese War Phase 3 of 1976–1979	Intra-state War #806
1977	Second Ogaden War Phase 2 of 1977–1978	Inter-state War #187
1977	Vietnamese-Cambodian Border War of 1977–1979	Inter-state War #189
1978	Third Lebanese War of 1978	Intra-state War #807
1978	Second Ogaden War Phase 3 of 1978–1980	Intra-state War #808
1978	Third Guatemala War of 1978–1984	Intra-state War #809
1978	Saur Revolution of 1978	Intra-state War #810
1978	Fourth DRC (Shaba) War of 1978	Intra-state War #811
1978	First Afghan Mujahideen Uprising of 1978–1980	Intra-state War #812
1978	Overthrow of the Shah of 1978–1979	Intra-state War #813
1978	Sandinista Rebellion of 1978–1979	Intra-state War #815

(Continued)

Year	War name	War type & number
1978	Ugandan-Tanzanian War of 1978–1979	Inter-state War #190
1979	Khmer Insurgency of 1979–1989	Extra-state War #475
1979	Anti-Khomeini Coalition War of 1979–1984	Intra-state War #816
1979	Sino-Vietnamese Punitive War of 1979	Inter-state War #193
1979	El Salvador War of 1979–1992	Intra-state War #817
1979	Mozambique War of 1979–1992	Intra-state War #818
1980	Soviet Quagmire of 1980–1989	Extra-state War #476
1980	Second Chad (Habre Revolt) War of 1980–1984	Intra-state War #820
1980	Iran-Iraq War of 1980–1988	Inter-state War #199
1980	Second Uganda War of 1980–1986	Intra-state War #822
1980	Nigeria-Muslim War of 1980–1981	Intra-state War #823
1981	Hama War of 1981–1982	Intra-state War #825
1982	Tigrean and Eritrean War of 1982–1991	Intra-state War #826
1982	Shining Path War of 1982–1992	Intra-state War #827
1982	Contra War of 1982–1990	Intra-state War #828
1982	Falklands War of 1982	Inter-state War #202
1982	War over Lebanon of 1982	Inter-state War #205
1983	Matabeleland War of 1983–1987	Intra-state War #831
1983	Fourth Burmese War of 1983–1988	Intra-state War #832
1983	Fourth Lebanese Civil War of 1983–1984	Intra-state War #833
1983	First Sri Lanka Tamil War of 1983–2002	Intra-state War #835
1983	Second South Sudan War of 1983–2005	Intra-state War #836
1984	Indian Golden Temple War of 1984	Intra-state War #837
1984	First Turkish Kurds War of 1984–1986	Intra-state War #838
1985	Fifth Iraqi Kurds War of 1985–1988	Intra-state War #840
1986	South Yemen War of 1986	Intra-state War #842
1986	Holy Spirit Movement War of 1986–1987	Intra-state War #843
1986	War over the Aouzou Strip of 1986–1987	Inter-state War #207
1987	Sino-Vietnamese Border War of 1987	Inter-state War #208
1987	Second Sri Lanka-JVP War of 1987–1989	Intra-state War #845
1987	Inkatha-ANC War of 1987–1994	Intra-state War #846
1988	Fifth Burmese War of 1988	Intra-state War #847
1988	First Somalia War of 1988–1991	Intra-state War #848
1989	Fifth Lebanese War of 1989–1990	Intra-state War #850
1989	Second Afghan Mujahideen Uprising of 1989–2001	Intra-state War #851
1989	Third Chad (Déby Coup) War of 1989–1990	Intra-state War #852
1989	First Aceh War of 1989–1991	Intra-state War #853
1989	Bougainville Secession War of 1989–1992	Intra-state War #854
1989	Eighth Colombian War of 1989–present	Intra-state War #856
1989	First Cambodian Civil War of 1989–1991	Intra-state War #857
1989	Romania War of 1989	Intra-state War #858
1989	First Liberia War of 1989–1990	Intra-state War #860

(Continued)

Year	War name	War type & number
1990	Gulf War of 1990–1991	Inter-state War #211
1990	Kashmir Insurgents War of 1990–2005	Intra-state War #861
1991	Shiite and Kurdish War of 1991	Intra-state War #862
1991	First Sierra Leone War of 1991–1996	Intra-state War #863
1991	Croatian Independence War of 1991–1992	Intra-state War #864
1991	Second Turkish Kurds War of 1991–1999	Intra-state War #865
1991	First PKK in Iraq of 1991–1992	Extra-state War #477
1991	SPLA Division (Dinka-Nuer) War of 1991–1992	Intra-state War #866
1991	Jukun-Tiv War of 1991–1992	Intra-state War #868
1991	Second Somalia War of 1991–1997	Intra-state War #870
1991	Georgia War of 1991–1992	Intra-state War #871
1991	Nagorno-Karabakh War of 1991–1993	Intra-state War #872
1991	Dniestrian Independence War of 1991–1992	Intra-state War #873
1992	Algerian Islamic Front War of 1992–1999	Intra-state War #875
1992	War of Bosnian Independence of 1992	Inter-state War #215
1992	Tajikistan War of 1992–1997	Intra-state War #876
1992	Bosnian-Serb Rebellion of 1992–1995	Intra-state War #877
1992	Second Liberia War of 1992–1995	Intra-state War #878
1992	Angolan War of the Cities of 1992–1994	Intra-state War #880
1993	Second Cambodian Civil War of 1993–1997	Intra-state War #881
1993	Azeri-Armenian War of 1993–1994	Inter-state War #216
1993	Abkhazia Revolt of 1993–1994	Intra-state War #882
1993	Second Burundi War of 1993–1998	Intra-state War #883
1994	South Yemeni Secessionist War of 1994	Intra-state War #885
1994	Second Rwanda War of 1994	Intra-state War #886
1994	First Chechnya War of 1994–1996	Intra-state War #888
1994	Iraqi Kurd Internecine War of 1994–1995	Intra-state War #890
1995	Cenepa Valley War of 1995	Inter-state War #217
1995	Croatia-Krajina War of 1995	Intra-state War #891
1996	Third Liberia War of 1996	Intra-state War #892
1996	Sixth Iraqi Kurds War of 1996	Intra-state War #893
1996	Fifth DRC War of 1996–1997	Intra-state War #895
1997	Third Rwanda War of 1997–1998	Intra-state War #896
1997	Second PKK in Iraq of 1997	Extra-state War #479
1997	First Congo (Brazzaville) War of 1997	Intra-state War #897
1998	Second Sierra Leone War of 1998–2000	Intra-state War #898
1998	Kosovo Independence War of 1998–1999	Intra-state War #900
1998	Badme Border War of 1998–2000	Inter-state War #219
1998	Guinea-Bissau Military War of 1998–1999	Intra-state War #902
1998	Africa's World War of 1998–2002	Intra-state War #905
1998	Fourth Chad (Togoimi Revolt) War of 1998–2000	Intra-state War #906

(Continued)

Year	War name	War type & number
1998	Third Angolan War of 1998–2002	Intra-state War #907
1998	Second Congo (Brazzaville) War of 1998–1999	Intra-state War #908
1999	Moluccas Sectarian War of 1999–2000	Intra-state War #910
1999	War for Kosovo of 1999	Inter-state War #221
1999	First Nigeria Christian-Muslim War of 1999–2000	Intra-state War #911
1999	Second Aceh War of 1999–2002	Intra-state War #912
1999	Kargil War of 1999	Inter-state War #223
1999	Oromo Liberation War of 1999	Intra-state War #913
1999	Hema-Lendu War of 1999–2005	Non-state War #1594
1999	Second Chechnya War of 1999–2003	Intra-state War #915
2000	Second Philippine-Moro War of 2000–2001	Intra-state War #916
2000	Guinean War of 2000–2001	Intra-state War #917
2000	Al Aqsa Intifada of 2000–2003	Extra-state War #480
2001	Third Burundi War of 2001–2003	Intra-state War #918
2001	Fourth Rwanda War of 2001	Intra-state War #920
2001	Invasion of Afghanistan of 2001	Inter-state War #225
2001	First Nepal Maoist Insurgency of 2001–2003	Intra-state War #921
2001	Afghan Resistance of 2001–present	Extra-state War #481
2002	Fourth Liberia War of 2002–2003	Intra-state War #922
2002	Ethiopian Anyuaa-Nuer War of 2002–2003	Intra-state War #923
2002	Côte d'Ivoire Military War of 2002–2004	Intra-state War #925
2003	Third Philippine-Moro War of 2003	Intra-state War #926
2003	Darfur War of 2003–2006	Intra-state War #927
2003	Invasion of Iraq of 2003	Inter-state War #227
2003	Iraqi Resistance of 2003–present	Extra-state War #482
2003	Third Aceh War of 2003–2004	Intra-state War #930
2003	Second Nepal Maoist War of 2003–2006	Intra-state War #931
2004	Waziristan War of 2004–2006	Intra-state War #932
2004	Second Nigeria Christian-Muslim War of 2004	Intra-state War #933
2004	First Yemeni Cleric War of 2004–2005	Intra-state War #935
2005	Philippine Joint Offensive of 2005–2006	Intra-state War #936
2005	Fifth Chad War of 2005–2006	Intra-state War #937
2006	Third Somalia War of 2006–2008	Intra-state War #938
2006	Second Sri Lanka Tamil War of 2006–present	Intra-state War #940
2007	Second Yemeni Cleric War of 2007	Intra-state War #941

Selected Bibliography

Abdel-Kader, A. Razak. *Le Conflit Judeo-Arabe*. Paris: Francois Maspero, 1962.

Abedin, Syed Z. *Russian Colonial Expansion to 1917*. New York: Mansell, 1988.

ABO/OLF. "OLF Mission." www.oromoliberationfront.org, 2005.

Abrahamian, Ervand. *Iran between Two Revolutions*. Princeton, N.J.: Princeton University Press, 1982.

Abun-Nasr, Jamil M. *A History of the Magreb*. Cambridge: Cambridge University Press, 1975.

Aburish, Said K. *The Rise, Corruption and Coming Fall of the House of Saud*. New York: St. Martin's Press, 1995.

Acevedo, Eduardo. *Anales Historicos del Uruguay*. Vols. 3–5. Montevideo: Barreiro y Ramos, 1934.

Adám, Magda. *The Little Entente and Europe (1920–1929)*. Budapest: Akadémiai Kiadó, 1993.

Adams, N.S., and A.W. McCoy, eds. *Laos: War and Revolution*. New York: Harper, 1970.

Adamson, David G. *The Kurdish War*. New York: Praeger, 1965.

"Afghanistan: 2001–2008 Timeline." *Guardian News and Media*, April 8, 2008. www.guardian.co.uk/afghanistan.

Agi, S. P. I. *The Political History of Religious Violence in Nigeria*. Calabar, Nigeria: Pigasiann and Grace, 1998.

Agoncilla, Teodoro A. *The Revolt of the Masses*. Quezon City: University of the Philippines, 1956.

Aguilar, Luis E. *Cuba 1933*. Ithaca, N.Y.: Cornell University Press, 1972.

Agung, Ide Anak Agung Gde. *Bali in the 19th Century*. Jakarta: Yayasan Obor Indonesia, 1991.

Agwani, M. S., ed. *The Lebanon Crisis, 1958: A Documentary Study*. London: Asia Publishing House, 1965.

Ahmed, Akbar. *Religion and Politics in Muslim Society, Order and Conflict in Pakistan*. Cambridge: Cambridge University Press, 1983.

——. *Resistance and Control in Pakistan*. London: Routledge, 1991.

Ahmida, Ali Abdullatiff. *The Making of Libya: State Formation Colonization and Resistance, 1830–1932*. Albany: State University of New York Press, 1994.

Ahort, Philip. *Pol Pot, Anatomy of a Nightmare*. New York: Henry Holt, 2004.

Ajayi, J. F. A., and Michael Crowder. *History of West Africa*. 2nd ed. 2 vols. London: Longman, 1976, 1987.

Akagi, Roy. *Japan's Foreign Relations: 1542–1936, A Short History*. Tokyo: Hokuseido, 1936.

Aker, Frank. *October 1973: The Arab-Israeli War*. Hamden, Conn.: Archon Books, 1985.

Akers, Charles E. *A History of South America*. London: John Murray, 1930.

Albertini, Luigi. *The Origins of the War of 1914*. 3 vols. Translated by Isabella Massey. London: Oxford University, 1952–1957.

Albrecht-Carrié, René. *A Diplomatic History of Europe since the Congress of Vienna*. New York: Harper and Row, 1958.

Alcock, Norman Z., and Keith Lowe. "The Vietnam War as a Richardson Process." *Journal of Peace Research* 7 (1970): 105–112.

Alessio Robles, Vito. *Coahuila y Texas*. 2 vols. Mexico City: Antigua Libreroa Robredo, 1945–1946.

Alexander, Robert J. *The Bolivian National Revolution*. New Brunswick, N.J.: Rutgers University Press, 1958.

Alford, Henry, and W. Denniston Sword. *The Egyptian Sudan: Its Loss and Recovery*. London: Macmillan, 1932.

AlJazeera. Multiple items concerning war in Yemen, January–April 2007. www.aljazeera.net.

Allen, W. E. D., and Paul Muratoff. *Caucasian Battlefields*. Cambridge: Cambridge University Press, 1953.

Allworth, Edward, ed. *Central Asia*. New York: Columbia University Press, 1967.

Almanach de Gotha. Gotha, Germany: Justus Perthes, 1764–1940.

Amaral, Ignacio M. Do. *Ensaio Sobre a Revolucao Brasileira*. Rio de Janeiro: Imprensa Naval, 1963.

American Heritage Dictionary. 2nd college edition. Boston: Houghton Mifflin, 1985.

Amnesty International. "Croatia: A Shadow on Croatia's Future: Continuing Impunity for War Crimes and Crimes against Humanity." EUR 64/005 (2004).

Amoo, Sam G. "Frustrations of Regional Peacekeeping: The OAU in Chad, 1977–1982." Carter Center Working Paper Series, 2003.

An, Tai Sung. *Mao Tse-Tung's Cultural Revolution.* Indianapolis: Bobbs-Merrill, 1972.

Anastasoff, Christ. *The Bulgarians.* Hicksville, N.Y.: Exposition Press, 1977.

_____. *The Tragic Peninsula: A History of the Macedonian Movement for Independence since 1878.* St. Louis: Blackwell Wiebendy, 1938.

Andaya, Barbara Watson, and Leonard Y. Andaya. *A History of Malaysia.* New York: Macmillan, 1982.

_____. *A History of Malaysia.* 2nd ed. Honolulu: University of Hawaii Press, 2001.

Anderson, Benedict. *Imagined Communities: Reflections on the Origin and Spread of Nationalism.* London: Verso, 1991.

Anderson, R. C. *Naval Wars in the Levant.* Princeton, N.J.: Princeton University, 1952.

Anderson, Thomas P. *Matanza.* Lincoln: University of Nebraska Press, 1971.

_____. *The War of the Dispossessed: Honduras and El Salvador.* Lincoln: University of Nebraska Press, 1981.

Andrews, George Frederick. "Spanish Intersts in Morocco." *The American Political Science Review* 5, no. 4 (November 1911): 553–565.

Angel, Barbara A. "Choosing Sides in War and Peace: The Travels of Herculano Balam among the Pacificos del Sur." *The Americas* 53, no. 4 (April 1997): 525–549.

_____. "The Reconstruction of Rural Society in the Aftermath of the Mayan Rebellion of 1847." *Journal of the Canadian Historical Association* 4 (1993): 33–53.

Anna, Timothy E. *The Fall of the Royal Government in Peru.* Lincoln: University of Nebraska Press, 1979.

_____. *Forging Mexico, 1821–1835.* Lincoln: University of Nebraska Press, 1998.

Annual of Power and Conflict. London: Institute for the Study of Conflict, 1971–.

Annual Register of World Events. London: Longmans, 1758–.

Anthouard, Albert F. *Les Boxeurs.* Paris: Plon-Nourrit, 1902.

Antonius, George. *The Arab Awakening.* London: Ham Ish Hamilton, 1938.

Aram, M. *Peace in Nagaland: The Eight Year Story, 1964–1972.* New Delhi: Arnold-Heinemann, 1974.

Arguedas, Alcides. *Historie Generale de la Bolivie.* Paris: Alcan, 1923.

Armstrong, David. "The Next Yugoslavia? The Fragmentation of Indonesia." *Diplomacy and Statecraft* 15, no. 4 (2004): 783–808.

Arnold, Anthony. *Afghanistan's Two-Party-Communism: Parcham and Khalq.* Stanford, Calif.: Hoover Institution Press, 1983.

Arnold-Forster, Mark. *The World at War.* New York: Stein and Day, 1973.

Aron, Robert. *The Vichy Regime 1940–1944.* London: Putnam, 1958.

Artz, Frederick B. *Reaction and Revolution, 1815–1832.* New York: Harper 1934.

Ashford, Douglas E. "The Irredentisi Appeal in Morocco and Mauritanis." *The Western Political Quarterly* 15, no. 4 (December 1962): 641–651.

Ashmead-Bartlett, Ellis. *The Passing of the Shereefian Empire.* Edinburgh: William Blackwood, 1910.

Askew, William C. *Europe and Italy's Acquisition of Libya 1911–1912.* Durham, N.C.: Duke University Press, 1942.

Assunção, Matthias Röhrig. "Elite Politics and Popular Rebellion in the Construction of Post-colonial Order, The Case of Maranhão, Brazil (1820–41)." *Journal of Latin American Studies* 31 (1999): 1–38.

Atamian, S. *The Armenian Community.* New York: Philosophical Library, 1955.

Atkin, Muriel. *Russia and Iran, 1780–1828.* Minneapolis: University of Minnesota Press, 1980.

"Atlantic Report: Rwanda." *The Atlantic Monthly,* June 1964. www.theatlantic.com.

Atwill, David G. "Blinkered Visions: Islamic Identity, Hui Ethnicity, and the Panthay Rebellion in Southwest China, 1856–1873." *The Journal of Asian Studies* 62, no. 4 (November 2003): 1079–1108.

Australian War Memorial. "United Nations Operation in Somalia (UNOSOM) 1992." www.awm.gov.au.

Averoff-Tossizza, Evangelos. *By Fire and Axe: The Communist Party and the Civil War in Greece, 1944–1949.* New York: Caratzas, 1978.

Avirgan, Tony, and Martha Honey. *War in Uganda.* Westport, Conn.: Lawrence Hill, 1982.

Axelrod, Alan. *Political History of America's Wars.* Washington, D.C.: CQ Press, 2007.

Axworthy, Michael. *A History of Iran: Empire of the Mind.* New York: Basic Books, 2008.

Ayers, R. William. "Cechnya and Russia: A War of Succession." In *History behind the Headlines: The*

Origins of Conflicts Worldwide, vol. 1, edited by Sonia G. Benson, Nancy Matuszak, and Meghan Appel O'Meara. Detroit: Gale Group, 2001.

Ayoob, Mohammed, ed. *Conflict and Intervention in the Third World.* New York: St. Martin's Press, 1980.

Ayoob, Mohammed, and K. Subrahmanyam. *The Liberation War.* New Delhi: S. Chand, 1972.

Azevedo, M. J. *Historical Dictionary of Mozambique.* London: Scarecrow Press, 1991.

Baabar [Bat-Erdene Batbayar]. *Twentieth-Century Mongolia.* Translated by D. Sühjargalmaa, S. Burenbayar, H. Hulan, and N. Tuya. Cambridge: White Horse Press, 1999.

Baddeley, John F. *The Russian Conquest of the Caucausus.* New York: Longmans, Green, 1908.

Baddour, Abd El-Fattah Ibrahim El-Sayed. *Sudanese-Egyptian Relations: A Chronological and Analytic Study.* The Hague: Martinus Nijhoff, 1960.

Baden-Powell, Robert. *Downfall of the Prempeh: A Diary of Life with the Native Levy in Ashanti, 1895–96.* New York: Ayer, 1972.

Badoglio, Pietro. *The War in Abyssinia.* London: Methuen, 1937.

Baégas, Richard, and Ruth Marshall-Fratani. "Côte d'Ivoire: Negotiating Identity and Citizenship." In *African Guerrillas: Raging against the Machine,* edited by Morten Bøås and Kevin C. Dunn. Boulder, Colo.: Lynne Rienner, 2007.

Baerlein, Henry. *The March of the Seventy Thousand.* London: Leonard Parsons, 1971.

———. *Southern Albania.* Chicago: Argonaut, 1968.

Bahru Zewde. *A History of Modern Ethiopia 1855–1974.* Athens, Ohio: Ohio University Press, 1991.

Bailey, David C. *!Viva Cristo Rey!* Austin: University of Texas Press, 1974.

Bailey, Thomas A. *A Diplomatic History of the American People.* 7th ed. New York: Appleton-Century-Crofts, 1964.

Baldry, John. "Al-Yaman and the Turkish Occupation 1849–1914." *Arabica* 23, no. 2 (June 1976): 156–196.

Baldwin, Frank. "Patrolling the Empire: Reflections on the USS *Pueblo.*" *Bulletin of Concerned Asian Scholars* 4, no. 2 (Summer 1972): 54–74.

Bamzai, P. N. K. *Culture and Political History, Kashmir.* Vol. 3. New Delhi: M D Publications, 1994.

Bancroft, Hubert Howe. *History of Mexico.* San Francisco: A. L. Bancroft, 1885.

Bannon, John F., and Peter Dunne. *Latin America.* Milwaukee, Wisc.: Bruce, 1963.

Barber, Robin. *Blue Guide Greece.* 6th ed. New York: W. W. Norton, 1995.

Barclay, C. N. *The First Commonwealth Division.* Aldershot, UK: Gale and Polden, 1954.

Barker, Kim. "Taliban Chief Vows to Drive Out Troops." *Chicago Tribune,* December 30, 2006, 1, 15.

Barman, Roderick J. *Brazil, the Forging of a Nation, 1798–1852.* Stanford, Calif.: Stanford University Press, 1988.

Barrios y Carrion, Leopoldo. *Sobre La Historia De La Guerra De Cuba.* Barcelona: Revista Cientifico-Military Biblioteca Militar, 1888–1890.

Bar-Siman-Tov, Yaacov. *The Israeli-Egyptian War of Attrition, 1969–1970: A Case Study of Limited War.* New York: Columbia University Press, 1980.

Basadre, Jorge. *Historia de la Republica del Peru.* Lima: Editorial Cultura Anartica S.A., 1940.

Bashore, Maj. Boyd T. "Dual Strategy for Limited War." In *Modern Guerrilla Warfare,* edited by F. Osanka. Glencoe, Ill.: Free Press, 1962.

Bassiouni, M. Cherif. *Final Report of the UN Commission of Experts, Annex III and Annex III.A.* New York: United Nations Commission of Experts, 1992.

Battaglia, Roberto. *La Prima Guerra d'Africa.* Rome: Einaudi, 1958.

Bauden, C. R. *The Modern History of Mongolia.* London: Kegan Paul, 1989.

Baynard, Sally Ann, Laraine Newhouse Carter, Beryl Lieff Benderly, and Laurie Krieger. "Historical Setting." In *The Yemens, Country Studies,* edited by Richard F. Nyrop. Washington, D.C.: American University, 1986.

BBC News. "Britain's Role in Sierra Leone." *UK,* September 10, 2000. http://news.bbc.co.uk.

———. "Counting Kosovo's Dead." (November 12, 1999). http://.bbc.co.uk/1/hi/world/europe/517168.stm.

———. "Country Profile: Chad." (January 5, 2006). http://news.bbc.co.uk.

———. "Country Profile: Guatemala." *BBC News,* July 20, 2002. http://news.bbc.co.uk.

———. "Deaths Mount in Liberian Capital." (July 22, 2003). http://newsvote.bbc.co.uk.

———. "Guide to the Philippines Conflict." (February 10, 2005). http://newsvote.bbc.co.uk.

———. "Horrors of Kosovo Revealed." (December 6, 1999). http://news.bbc.co.uk/1/hi/world/europe/551875.stm.

———. Multiple news items. 1999–2008.

——— "Q&A: Ivory Coast's Crisis." (January 17, 2006). http://newsvote.bbc.co.uk.

———. "Sierra Leone's Hostages." *Special Report 1999,* August 10, 1999. http://news.bbc.co.uk.

———. "Timeline: Guinea." (December 12, 2005). http://newsvote.bbc.co.uk.

_____. "UK to Boost Afghan Force by 1,400." (February 26, 2007). http://news.bbc.co.uk.

_____. "UN Gives Figure for Kosovo Dead." (November 10, 1999). http://news.bbc.co.uk/1/hi/world/europe/514828.stm

_____. "US Beefs up Forces in Afghanistan." (March 26, 2004). http://news.bbc.co.uk.

_____. "World: Africa." Multiple stories concerning Chad. (1998–2002). http://news/bbc/co/uk.

Beach, David. *War and Politics in Zimbabwe, 1840–1900.* Gweru, Zimbabwe: Mambo Press, 1986.

Beach, Vincent W. *Charles X of France.* Boulder, Colo.: Pruett, 1971.

Beachey, R. W. *A History of East Africa, 1592–1902.* New York: I. B. Tauris, 1996.

Beals, Carleton. *The Crime of Cuba.* Philadelphia: Lippincott, 1933.

Beasley, W. G. *Select Documents on Japanese Foreign Policy, 1853–1868.* New York: Oxford University Press, 1955.

Beattie, Hugh. *Imperial Frontier: Tribe State in Waziristan.* London: Taylor and Francis, 2001.

Becker, Seymour. *Russia's Protectorates in Central Asia: Bukhara and Khiva, 1865–1924.* Cambridge, Mass.: Harvard University Press, 1968.

Beckett, Ian F. W. *Modern Insurgencies and Counter-Insurgencies: Guerrillas and Their Opponents since 1750.* New York: Routledge, 2001.

Beebe, Gilbert, and Michael De Bakey. *Battle Casualties: Incidence, Mortality and Logistic Considerations.* Springfield, Ill.: C. C. Thomas, 1952.

Beehler, William H. *The History of the Italian-Turkish War.* Annapolis, Md.: Advertiser-Republican, 1913.

Beer, Francis A. *How Much War in History: Definitions, Estimates, Extrapolations, and Trends.* Sage Professional Papers in International Studies, vol. 3, series 02-030. Beverly Hills, Calif.: Sage, 1974.

_____. *Peace against War: The Ecology of International Violence.* San Francisco: W. H. Freeman, 1981.

Belden, Jack. *China Shakes the World.* New York: Monthly Review, 1949.

Belfield, Eversley. *The Boer War.* Hamden, Conn.: Archon Books, 1975.

Belich, James. *The New Zealand Wars.* Auckland: Auckland University Press, 1986.

Bell, John Patrick. *Crisis in Costa Rica: The 1948 Revolution.* Austin: University of Texas, 1971.

Bellew, W. H. "History of Kashghar." In *Report of a Mission to Yarkand in 1873,* edited by Thomas D. Forsyth. Calcutta: Foreign Department Press, 1875.

Bello, Jose Maria. *A History of Modern Brazil, 1889–1964.* Stanford, Calif.: Stanford University Press, 1966.

Bemis, Samuel Flagg. *A Diplomatic History of the United States.* New York: Henry Holt, 1936.

_____. *The Latin American Policy of the United States.* New York: Harcourt, 1943.

Bender, Gerald J. *Angola under the Portuguese: The Myth and the Reality.* London: Heinemann Educational Books, 1978.

Benes, Vaclav L. *Poland.* New York: Praeger, 1971.

Bennoune, Mahfoud. "Mauretania: Formation of a Neocolonial Society." *MERIP Reports,* no. 54 (February 1977): 3–13, 26.

Benoit, Emile, and Harold Lubell. "World Defense Expenditures." *Journal of Peace Research* 3 (1966): 97–113.

Benson, Sonia G., Nancy Matuszak, and Meghan Appel O'Meara, eds. *History behind the Headlines: The Origins of Conflicts Worldwide.* Vol. 1. Detroit: Gale Group, 2001.

Bentley, Kristina A., and Roger Southall. *An African Peace-Process.* Cape Town: Nelson Mandela Foundation, 2005.

Bercovitch, Jacob, and Judith Fretter. *Regional Guide to International Conflict and Management from 1945 to 2003.* Washington, D.C.: CQ Press, 2004.

Bercovitch, Jacob, and Richard Jackson. *International Conflict: A Chronological Encyclopedia of Conflicts and Their Management, 1945–1995.* Washington, D.C.: Congressional Quarterly, 1997.

Bergquist, Charles. *Coffee and Conflict in Columbia, 1886–1910.* Durham, N.C.: Duke University Press, 1978.

Berkeley, Bill. *The Graves Are Not Yet Full.* New York: Basic Books, 2001.

Berkeley, George F. H. *The Campaign of Adowa and the Rise of Menelik.* London: Constable, 1935.

_____. *Italy in the Making: 1815–1846.* Vol. 1. Cambridge: Cambridge University Press, 1932.

_____. *Italy in the Making: January 1st 1848 to November 19th 1848.* Cambridge: Cambridge University Press, 1940.

Bernard, Stephane. *The Franco-Moroccan Conflict, 1943–1956.* New Haven, Conn.: Yale University Press, 1968.

Berndt, Otto. *Die Zahl im Kriege.* Vienna: Freytag U. Berndt, 1897.

Bernstein, Harry. *Modern and Contemporary Latin America.* New York: Russell and Russell, 1965.

Berthe, Augustine. *Garcia Moreno.* Vol. 1. Paris: Librairie de la "Sainte Famille," 1903.

Bertier de Sauvigny, Guillaume de. *La Restauration.* Paris: Flammarion, 1955.

Best, Felix. *Historia de las Guerras Argentinas.* 2 vols. Buenos Aires: Peuser, 1960.

Bethell, Leslie, ed. *Brazil: Empire and Republic, 1822–1930.* New York: Cambridge University Press, 1989.

_____. *Cuba: A Short History.* Cambridge: Cambridge University Press, 1993.

Betts, Robert Benton. *The Druze.* New Haven, Conn.: Yale University Press, 1988.

Bhacker, M. Reda. *Trade and Empire in Muscat and Zanzibar: Roots of British Domination.* New York: Routledge, 1992.

Biangyi. "Tibetans' Fight against British Invasion." *China Tibet Magazine,* March 9, 2005.

Bilmanis, Alfred. *A History of Latvia.* Princeton, N.J.: Princeton University, 1951.

Bimberg, Edward L. *The Moroccan Goums: Tribal Warriors in a Modern War.* Westport, Conn.: Greenwood Press, 1999.

Bing, Li Ung. *Outlines of Chinese History.* Shanghai: Commercial Press, 1914.

Bird, M. B. *The Black Man; or, Haytian Independence.* Freeport, N.Y.: Books for Libraries Press, 1971.

Birmingham, David. *Portugal and Africa.* Rochester, N.Y.: University of Rochester Press, 2000.

Birwood, Christopher. *India and Pakistan.* New York: Praeger, 1954.

Bisher, Jamie. *White Terror: Cossack Warlords of the Trans-Siberian.* London: Routledge, 2005.

Blackey, Robert. *Modern Revolutions and Revolutionists: A Bibliography.* Santa Barbara, Calif.: Clio, 1976.

Blainey, Geoffrey. *The Causes of War.* New York: Macmillan, 1973.

_____. *The Causes of War.* 3rd ed. New York: Free Press, 1988.

Blakemore, Harold. "The Chilean Revolution of 1891 and Its Historiography." *Hispanic American Historical Review* 45 (August 1965): 393–421.

Blank, Stephen J., and Earl H. Tilford Jr. "Russia's Invasion of Chechnya: A Preliminary Assessment." *Strategic Studies Institute,* January 13, 1995.

Blaxland, Gregory. *Objective: Egypt.* London: Frederick Muller, 1966.

Bley, Helmut. *Namibia under German Rule.* Hamburg and Windhoek: Namibia Scientific Society, 1996.

Blick, Jeffrey P. "Genocidal Warfare in Tribal Societies as a Result of European-Induced Culture Conflict." *Man, New Series* 23, no. 4 (December 1988): 654–670.

Blok, Petrus. *A History of the People of the Netherlands.* New York: Putnam, 1912.

Bloom, Mia M. "Ethnic Conflict, State Terror and Suicide Bombing in Sri Lanka." *Civil Wars* 6, no. 1 (Spring 2003): 54–84.

Blum, Jerome. *Noble Landlords and Agriculture in Austria, 1815–1848: A Case Study in the Origins of the Peasant Emancipation of 1848.* Baltimore, Md.: Johns Hopkins University Press, 1948.

Blumenfeld, Ralph D. "A Hundred Years War of Today." *Harper's Monthly* 103 (August 1901): 367–374.

Blunt, Wilfrid Scawen. *Secret History of the English Occupation of Egypt: Being a Personal Narrative of Events.* New York: Howard Fertig, 1967.

Boahen, A. A., ed. *UNESCO General History of Africa.* Vol. 3. Berkeley: University of California Press, 1985.

BøÅs, Morten, and Kevin C. Dunn, eds. *African Guerrillas: Raging against the Machine.* Boulder, Colo.: Lynne Rienner, 2007.

Bobb, F. Scott. *Historical Dictionary of Democratic Republic of the Congo.* London: Scarecrow Press, 1999.

Bock, Carl H. *Prelude to Tragedy.* Philadelphia: University of Pennsylvania Press, 1966.

Bodart, Gaston. *Losses of Life in Modern Wars.* Oxford: Clarendon Press, 1916.

_____. *Militar-Historisches Kriegs-Lexikon (1618–1905).* Vienna: C. W. Stern, 1908.

Bogart, Ernest L. *Direct and Indirect Costs of the Great World War.* New York: Oxford University Press, 1919.

Boggs, Carl, ed. *Masters of War: Militarism and Blowback in the Era of the American Empire.* New York: Routledge, 2003.

Bollaert, William. *The Wars of Succession of Portugal and Spain From 1826 to 1840.* 2 vols. London: Edward Stanford, 1870.

Bond, Brian, ed. *Victorian Military Campaigns.* New York: Praeger, 1967.

Bonilla, Adrian. "National Interests and Political Processes of the 1995 Armed Conflict." Paper presented at the 19th International Congress of the Latin American Studies Association, Washington, D.C., September 28–30, 1995.

_____. "National Interests and Political Processes of the 1995 Armed Conflict." *Nueva Sociedad* (Caracas) 146 (May–June 1996).

_____. "Political Process and National Interests in the Ecuador-Peru Conflict." Manuscript of translation of key parts by Maria Inclan. Pennsylvania State University, 2000.

Boot, Max. *War Made New: Weapons, Warriors, and the Making of the Modern World.* New York: Gotham Books, 2006.

Bottomore, Tom, ed. *Karl Marx.* Englewood Cliffs, N.J.: Prentice-Hall, 1973.

Bourne, Peter G. *Men, Stress, and Vietnam*. Boston: Little Brown, 1970.

Bouthoul, Gaston, and René Carrere. "Deux Ans D'aggressivite Mondiale, 1967–1969." *Etudes Polemologiques* 2, Vol. 10 (1978): 83–108, and Vol. 11 (1979): 183–186.

_____. "List of Major Armed Conflict." *Peace Research* 10, no. 3 (July 1978): 83–108.

Box, Pelham Horton. *Origins of the Paraguayan War*. Urbana: University of Illinois Press, 1927.

Brackenbury, Henry. *The Ashanti War, A Narrative*. Edinburgh, London: Blackwood, 1968. Facsimile reprint of the first edition (1874).

Brackman, Arnold C. *Indonesian Communism*. New York: Praeger, 1963.

Bradley, J. F. N. *Czechoslovakia*. Edinburgh: Edinburgh University, 1971.

Bradley, John. *Allied Intervention in Russia*. New York: Basic Books, 1963.

Brantley, Cynthia. *The Giriama and Colonial Resistance in Kenya, 1800–1920*. Berkeley: University of California Press, 1981.

Bravo Ugarte, Jose. *Historia de Mexico*. Vol. 3. Mexico City: Editorial *Jus*, 1962.

_____. *Mexico Independiente*. Vol. 22 in *Historia de America*, edited by A. Ballesteros y Beretta. Barcelona: Salvat, 1949.

Brecher, Michael. *The Struggle for Kashmir*. Toronto: Ryerson Press, 1953.

Brecher, Michael, and Jonathan Wilkenfeld. *Crises in the Twentieth Century*. New York: Pergamon Press, 1988.

_____. "The Ethnic Dimension of International Crises." In *Wars in the Midst of Peace*, edited by David Carment and Patrick James. Pittsburgh: University of Pittsburgh Press, 1997, 164–193.

_____. *A Study of Crisis*. Ann Arbor: University of Michigan Press, 1997.

Brecke, Peter. "The Characteristics of Violent Conflict since 1400 A.D." Paper presented at the annual meeting of the International Studies Association, Washington, D.C., February 17–20, 1999.

Bremer, Ian, and Ray Taras, eds. *Nations and Politics in the Soviet Successor States*. Cambridge: Cambridge University Press, 1993.

Bridge, F. R. *The Hapsburg Monarchy among the Great Powers, 1815–1928*. New York: Berg, 1990.

Bridgman, Jon. *The Revolt of the Hereros*. Berkeley: University of California Press, 1981.

Brinkley, George A. *The Volunteer Army and Allied Intervention in Southern Russia, 1917–1921*. South Bend, Ind.: University of Notre Dame Press, 1966.

Brinton, Crane. *The Anatomy of Revolution*. New York: Prentice-Hall, 1938.

Britannica Book of the Year. Chicago: Encyclopaedia Britannica, 1963.

Britton, Peter, and Richard Nixon. "Indonesia's Neo-Colonial Armed Forces." *Bulletin of Concerned Asian Scholars* 7, no. 3 (1975): 14.

Broadhead, Susan H. *Historical Dictionary of Angola*. 2nd ed. London: Scarecrow Press, 1992.

Brody, Alter, Theodore M. Bayer, Isidor Schneider, and Jessica Smith. *War and Peace in Finland*. New York: Soviet Russia Today, 1940.

Brogan, Patrick. *World Conflicts*. Lanham, Md.: Scarecrow Press, 1998.

Bromberger, Merry, and Serge Bromberger. *Secrets of Suez*. London: Pan, 1957.

Broome, Richard. *Aboriginal Australians: Black Responses to White Dominance 1788–2001*. Crows Nest, NSW: Allen and Unwin, 2002.

_____. "The Statistics of Frontier Conflict." Voices from Black Australia: The Koori History Website Project. www.kooriweb.org, 2005.

Broussard, Ray F. "The Puebla Revolt: First Challenge to the Reform." *Journal of the West* 18, no. 1 (1979): 52–57.

Brown, Macalister, and Joseph J. Zasloff. "Laos 1973: Wary Steps toward Peace." *Asian Survey* 14, no. 2, A Survey of Asia in 1973: Part II (February 1974): 166–174.

_____. "Laos in 1975: People's Democratic Revolution–Lao Style." *Asian Survey* 16, no. 2, A Survey of Asia in 1975: Part II (February 1976): 193–199.

_____. "Laos 1979: Caught in Vietnam's Wake." *Asian Survey* 20, no. 2 (February 1980): 103–111.

Brown, Mervyn. *A History of Madagascar*. Princeton, N.J.: Markus Wiener Publisher, 2001a.

_____. *Madagascar Rediscovered*. London: Damien Tunnacliffe, 1978.

_____. *Madagascar Rediscovered*. Hamden, Conn.: Archon Books, 1979.

_____. *War in Shangri-La, A Memoir of Civil War in Laos*. New York: Radcliffe Press, 2001b.

Brown, Michael E., Owen R. Coté Jr., Sean M. Lynn-Jones, and Steven E. Miller, eds. *Nationalism and Ethnic Conflict*. Cambridge, Mass.: MIT Press, 1997.

Brown, Seyom. *The Causes and Prevention of War*. New York: St. Martin's Press, 1994.

Browne, Edward G. *The Persian Revolution of 1905–1909*. London: Frank Cass, 1966.

Brownstone, David, and Irene Franck. *Timelines of War: A Chronology of Warfare from 100,000 B.C. to the Present*. New York: Little, Brown, 1994.

Bruce, George. *Burma Wars, 1824–1886.* London: Hart-Davis MacGibbon, 1973.

_____. *Harbottle's Dictionary of Battles.* 3rd ed. New York: Van Nostrand Reinhold, 1981.

Brzozowski, Marie. *La Guerre de Pologne en 1831.* Leipzig: Brockhaus, 1833.

Buck, James H. "The Satsuma Rebellion of 1877: From Kagoshima through the Siege of Kumamoto Castle." *Monumenta Nipponica* 28, no. 4 (Winter 1973): 427–446.

Buell, Raymond Leslie. *The Native Problem in Africa.* Vol. 1. New York: Macmillan, 1908.

Bunkley, Allison W. "Sarmiento and Urquiza." *Hispanic American Historical Review* 30, no. 2 (May 1950): 176–194.

Burgess, Paul. *Justo Ruffino Barrios.* Philadelphia: Dorrance, 1926.

Burke, Edmund. "Pan-Islam and Moroccan Resistance to French Colonial Penetration, 1900–1912." *The Journal of African History* 13, no. 1 (1972): 97–118.

_____. *Prelude to Protectorate in Morocco.* Chicago: University of Chicago, 1976.

Burns, E. Bradford. *A History of Brazil.* New York: Columbia University Press, 1980.

Burr, Robert N. "The Balance of Power in Nineteenth Century South America: An Exploratory Essay." *Hispanic American Historical Review* 25 (February 1955): 37–60.

Burrowes, Robert D. *The Yemen Arab Republic: The Politics of Development.* Boulder, Colo.: Westview Press, 1987.

Burrows, Mantagu. "The Conquest of Ceylon." In *The Cambridge History of the British Empire,* Vol. IV: *British India 1497–1858,* edited by H. H. Dodwell. New York: Macmillan, 1929.

Burt, Alfred L. *The Evolution of the British Empire and Commonwealth.* Boston: Heath, 1956.

Bush, Kenneth. *The Intra-Group Dimensions of Ethnic Conflict in Sri Lanka.* New York: Palgrave Macmillan, 2003.

Buttinger, Joseph. *The Smaller Dragon.* New York: Praeger, 1958.

_____. *Vietnam: A Dragon Embattled.* Vol. 2. London: Pall Mall Press, 1967.

Byler, Charles. "Pacifying the Moros: American Military Government in the Southern Philippines, 1899–1913." *Military Review* (May–June 2005): 41–45.

Cady, John F. *Foreign Intervention in the Rio Del Plata 1838–1850.* Philadelphia: University of Pennsylvania Press, 1929, 1950.

_____. *A History of Modern Burma.* Ithaca, N.Y.: Cornell University Press, 1958.

_____. *The Roots of French Imperialism in Eastern Asia.* Ithaca, N.Y.: Cornell University Press, 1954.

_____. "The Situation in Burma." *Far Eastern Survey* 22, no. 5 (April 22, 1953): 49–54.

Cady, Richard H., and William Prince. *Political Conflicts, 1944–1966.* Ann Arbor, Mich.: Bendix Social Sciences Division, 1966. Data available from ICPSR at the University of Michigan.

Calahan, H. A. *What Makes a War End?* New York: Vanguard, 1944.

Caldwell, Malcolm, and Lek Hor Tan. *Cambodia in the Southeast Asian War.* New York: Monthly Review, 1973.

Callahan, Mary. *Making Enemies: War and State Building in Burma.* Ithaca, N.Y.: Cornell University Press, 2003.

Callcott, Wilfred H. *The Caribbean Policy of the United States.* Baltimore, Md.: Johns Hopkins University Press, 1942.

_____. *Santa Anna.* Norman: University of Oklahoma Press, 1936.

Calogeras, Joao P. *A History of Brazil.* Translated and edited by Percy A. Martin. New York: Russell and Russell, 1963.

Cammaerts, Emile. *A History of Belgium.* New York: D. Appleton, 1921.

Campbell, Kenneth J. *A Tale of Two Quagmires: Iraq, Vietnam, and the Hard Lessons of War.* Boulder, Colo.: Paradigm, 2007.

Campos y Serrano, Martinez de. *Espana Belica: El Siglo XIX.* Madrid: Aguilar, 1961.

Cardoza, Efraim. *Paraguay Independiente.* Vol. 21 in *Historia de America,* edited by A Ballesteros y Beretta. Barcelona: Salvat, 1949.

Carey, James C. "The Latin American Legacy: The Background for Civil War." In *Civil Wars in the Twentieth Century,* edited by Robin Higham. Lexington: University Press of Kentucky, 1972.

Carment, David, and Patrick James. *Wars in the Midst of Peace: The International Politics of Ethnic Conflict.* Pittsburgh: University of Pittsburgh Press, 1997.

Carmichael, Joel. *The Shaping of the Arabs.* New York: Macmillan, 1967.

Caroe, Olaf. *The Pathans 550 B.C.– A.D. 1957.* Oxford: Oxford University Press, 1958.

Carr, Raymond. *Spain: 1808–1975.* Oxford: Oxford University Press, 1982.

Carrère, Rene. "1870–1871, Guerre Ancienne ou Guerre Moderne?" *Etudes Polemologiques* 5 (July 1972): 23–24.

Carrère, Rene, and Pierre Valat-Morio. "La Violence Mondiale, 1970–1971." *Etudes Polemologiques* 6 (October 1972): 16–70.

Carroll, Berenice A. "Germany Disarmed and Rearming, 1925–1935." *Journal of Peace Research* 3 (1966): 114–124.

Case, Lynn M. *Franco-Italian Relations, 1860–1865.* New York: AMS Press, 1970.

Cashman, Greg. *What Causes War?* New York: Lexington Books, 1993.

Cashman, Greg, and Leonard C. Robinson. *An Introduction to the Causes of War: Patterns of Interstate Conflict from World War I to Iraq.* Lanham, Md.: Rowman and Littlefield, 2007.

Cassels, Alan. *Fascist Italy.* London: Routledge, 1969.

Castellanos, Pedro Zamora. *Vida Militar de Centro América.* Guatemala City: Editorial del Ejército, 1925.

Catchpole, Brian, and I. A. Akinjogbin. *A History of West Africa in Maps and Diagrams.* London: Collins Educational, 1983.

Cattaui, Rene, and Georges Cattaui. *Mohamed Aly et L'europe.* Paris: Librarie Orientaliste, 1950.

Cayley, Edward. *The European Revolutions of 1848.* 2 vols. London: Smith, Elder, 1856.

Cbe, Najib Alamuddin. *Turmoil: The Druzes, Lebanon and the Arab-Israeli Conflict.* London: Quarter Books, 1993.

Center for Balkan Development. "History of the War in Bosnia." 1996. www.friendsofbosnia.org.

Center for Defense Information. "Afghanistan: Re-Emergence of a State." December 21, 2001a. www.cdi.org.

_____. "Afghanistan: United Kingdom Deploys Commando Battlegroup." April 2, 2002b. www.cdi.org.

_____. "Forces in Play." October 26, 2001b. www.cdi.org.

_____. "International Security Assistance Force (ISAF)." May 1, 2002c. www.cdi.org.

_____. "Peacekeeping in Afghanistan: Local Requests vs. International Response." March 5, 2002a. www.cdi.org.

Central Intelligence Agency (CIA). *Balkan Battlegrounds: A Military History of the Yugoslav Conflict, 1990–1995.* Vol. 1. Washington, D.C.: Central Intelligence Agency, 2002.

CERAC. *Colombia Conflict Database.* Release 8 (January 11, 2008). www.cerac.org.co.

Chadwick, H. Munro. *The Nationalities of Europe and the Growth of National Ideologies.* Cambridge: Cambridge University Press, 1945.

Chaliand, Gerard. *Revolution in the Third World: Myths and Prospects.* New York: Viking Press, 1977.

Chambers, Frank, Christina Harris, and Charles Bayley. *This Age of Conflict.* New York: Harcourt, 1950.

Chan, Steve. "Mirror on the Wall . . . Are the Freer Countries More Pacific?" *The Journal of Conflict Resolution* 28, no. 4 (December 1984): 617–648.

Chanda, Nayan. *Brother Enemy: The War after the War.* New York: Free Press, 1988.

Chandler, James A. "Spain and Her Moroccan Protectorate 1898–1927." *Journal of Contemporary History* 10, no. 2 (April 1975): 301–322.

Chapman, Charles E. *A History of the Cuban Republic.* New York: Macmillan, 1927.

Chaqueri, Cosroe. *The Soviet Socialist Republic of Iran, 1920–1921, Birth of the Trauma.* Pittsburgh: University of Pittsburgh Press, 1995.

Charles, Eunice A. "Shaikh Amadu Ba and Jihad in Jolof." *The International Journal of African Historical Studies* 8, no. 3 (1975): 367–382.

Chasteen, John Charles. "Cabanos and Farrapos: Brazilian Nativism in Regional Perspective, 1822–1850." *Locus* 7, no. 1 (1994): 31–46.

Cheeseboro, Anthony Q. "Sudan: Slavery and Civil War." In *History behind the Headlines: The Origins of Conflicts Worldwide,* vol. 1, edited by Sonia G. Benson, Nancy Matuszak, and Meghan Appel O'Meara. Detroit: Gale Group, 2001.

Cheminon, J., and G. Fauvel-Gallais. *Les Evenements Militaires en Chine.* Paris: Chapelot, 1902.

Chen, King C. *China's War with Vietnam, 1979.* Stanford, Calif.: Hoover Institution Press, 1987.

Cheng, Peter. *A Chronology of the People's Republic of China.* Totowa, N.J.: Rowman and Littlefield, 1972.

Ch'en, Jerome. "Defining Chinese Warlords and Their Factions." *Bulletin of the School of Oriental and African Studies, University of London* 31, no. 3 (1968): 563–600.

Chesneaux, Jean. *Peasant Revolts in China, 1840–1949.* London: W. W. Porter, 1973.

Chew, Allan. *The White Death.* East Lansing: Michigan State University Press, 1971.

Chi, Hsi-Hseng. *The Chinese Warlord System, 1916–1928.* Washington, D.C.: American University, 1969.

Chiang Siang-Tseh. *The Nien Rebellion.* Seattle: University of Washington Press, 1954.

Chien-Nung, Li. *The Political History of China, 1840–1928.* Princeton, N.J.: D. Van Nostrand, 1956.

Chien Yu-Wen. *The Taiping Revolutionary Movement.* New Haven, Conn.: Yale University Press, 1973.

Chilcote, Ronald H. *Portuguese Africa.* Englewood Cliffs, N.J.: Prentice-Hall, 1967.

Ching, Erik, and Virginia Tilley. "Indians, the Military and the Rebellion of 1932 in El Salvador." *Journal of Latin American Studies* 30 (1998): 121–156.

Chomsky, Noam. *At War with Asia*. London: Fontana, 1971.

_____. "Destroying Laos." *New York Review of Books* 15, no. 2 (July 23, 1970): 21–33.

_____. "East Timor: The Press Coverup." *Inquiry* (February 14, 1979): 16–20.

_____. "The Nation-State System." In *Understanding Power: The Indispensible Chomsky*, edited by Peter R. Mitchell and John Schoeffel. New York: New Press, 2002.

Chorbajian, Levon, Patrick Donabedian, and Claude Mutafian. *The Caucasian Knot: The History and Geopolitics of Nagorno-Karabagh*. London: Zed Books, 1994.

Chow Ro-Bin. "The Chinese-Japanese Truce of Tangku." *Literary Digest* 115, no. 23 (June 10, 1933): 11.

_____. *Chung-eh Kuan-hih Shih*. Taipei: 1960.

Christie, Clive. "Great Britain, China, and the Status of Tibet, 1914–21." *Modern Asian Studies* 10, no. 4 (1976): 481–508.

Christman, Henry M., ed. *Essential Works of Lenin*. New York: Bantam Books, 1971.

Chronicle of the 20th Century. Mount Kisco, N.Y.: Chronicle Publications, 1987.

"Chronology of the Peasant War." *Korea Journal* (Winter 1994): 125–126.

Chu Wen-Djang. "The Moslem Rebellion in Northwest China, 1862–1878." *Central Asiatic Studies* 5 (1966).

Churchill, Charles Henry. *The Druzes and the Maronites under the Turkish Rule from 1840 to 1860*. London: Berbard Quaritch, 1862.

_____. *The Life of Abdel Kader, Ex-Sultan of the Arabs of Algeria*. London: Chapman and Hall, 1867.

Churchill, Winston S. *The River War*. 2 vols. London: Longmans, 1900.

Ciment, James, ed. *Encyclopedia of Conflicts since World War II*. 2nd ed. Volumes 1–4. Armonk, N.Y.: Sharpe Reference, 2007.

Cioffi-Revilla, C. *Handbook of Datasets on Crises and Wars 1495–1988*. Boulder, Colo.: Lynne Rienner, 1990.

Clark, Andrew F., and Lucie Colvin Phillips. *Historical Dictionary of Senegal*. 2nd ed. London: Scarecrow Press, 1994.

Clark, Chester Wells. *Franz Joseph and Bismarck: The Diplomacy of Austria before the War of 1866*. Cambridge, Mass.: Harvard University Press, 1934.

Clark, Peter. "The Maitatsine Movement in Northern Nigeria in Historical and Current Perpsective." In *New Religious Movements in Nigeria*, edited by Rosalind I. J. Hackett. Lewiston, N.Y.: Edwin Mellen Press, 1987.

Clark, Wesley K. *Winning Modern Wars: Iraq, Terrorism, and the American Empire*. New York: Public Affairs, 2003.

Clarke, Henry Butler. *Modern Spain, 1815–1898*. Cambridge: Cambridge University Press, 1906.

Cleage, Pearl. "Basic Training: The Beginnings of Wisdom." In *Deals with the Devil, and Other Reasons to Riot*. Westminster, Md.: Ballantine Books, 1993.

Clemens, Walter, Jr. *Baltic Independence and Russian Empire*. New York: St. Martin's Press, 1991.

Clements, Paul H. *The Boxer Rebellion*. New York: AMS Press, 1967.

Clendenen, Clarence C. "Tribalism and Humanitarianism: The Nigerian-Biafran Civil War." In *Civil Wars in the Twentieth Century*, edited by Robin Higham. Lexington: University Press of Kentucky, 1972.

Clessold, Stephen, ed. *A Short History of Yugoslavia*. Cambridge: Cambridge University Press, 1966.

Cleveland, William L. *A History of the Modern Middle East*. Boulder, Colo.: Westview Press, 1994.

Cline, Howard. *The United States and Mexico*. New York: Atheneum, 1963.

Cline, Lawrence E. "Spirits and the Cross: Religiously Based Violent Movements in Uganda." *Small Wars and Insurgencies* 14, no. 2 (Summer 2003): 113–130.

Clodfelter, Michael. *Vietnam in Military Statistics: History of the Indochina Wars, 1772–1991*. Jefferson, N.C.: McFarland, 1995.

_____. *Warfare and Armed Conflicts: A Statistical Reference to Casualty and Other Figures, 1500–2000*. 2nd ed. Jefferson, N.C.: McFarland, 2002.

_____. *Warfare and Armed Conflicts: A Statistical Reference to Casualty and Other Figures, 1618–1991*. Jefferson, N.C.: McFarland, 1992.

Cloud, David S. "U.S. Airstrike Aims at Qaeda Cell in Somalia." *New York Times*, January 9, 2007. www.nytimes.com.

Clough, Michael. "A Losing Bet in Ethiopia." www.oromoliberationfront.org, 2005.

Clubb, Edmund O. *Twentieth Century China*. New York: Columbia University Press, 1964.

CNN. "In-Depth Specials–Focus on Kosovo–A Timeline of Tensions." (1998). www.cnn.com/SPECIALS/1998/10/kosovo/timeline.

_____. "KLA Goes from Splinter Group to Potential Giant-Killer." (1999). www.cnn.com/WORLD/europe/9903/24/kla.history.

"Coalition Forces in Iraq." ProCon.Org. http://usiraq.procon.org.

"Coalition of the Willing." *Perspectives on World History and Current Events* (February 18, 2006). http://pwhce.org.

Coalition Public Awareness Working Group. *The Coalition Bulletin* 1, no. 1 (October 22, 2002).

Coates, Tim, ed. *The British Invasion of Tibet: Colonel Younghusband, 1904.* London: Stationery Office Books, 2001.

Coates, William P., and Zelda K. Coates. *The Soviet Finnish Campaign.* London: Eldon, 1941.

_____. *Soviets in Central Asia.* London: Lawrence and Wishars, 1951.

Cockcroft, James. *Neighbors in Turmoil: Latin America.* New York: Harper and Row, 1971, 1989.

Coffey, Rosemary K. "The Heart of Deterrence." *Bulletin of the Atomic Scientists* 21, no. 4 (April 1965): 27–29.

Coghlan, Benjamin, Valeria Nkamgang Bemo, Pascal Ngoy, Tony Stewart, Flavien Mulumba, Jennifer Lewis, Colleen Hardy, and Richard Brennan. *Mortality in the Democratic Republic of Congo, An Ongoing Crisis.* New York: International Rescue Committee, 2004.

Cohen, Ariel. *Russian Imperialism.* Westport, Conn.: Greenwood Press, 1996.

Cole, Juan I. R., and Moojah Momen. "Mafia, Mob, and Shiism in Iraq: The Rebellion of Ottoman Karbala 1824–1843." *Past and Present* 112 (August 1986): 112–143.

Collier, Richard. *The Sound of Fury.* London: Collins, 1963.

Collier, Simon, and William F. Slater. *The History of Chile, 1808–2002.* 2nd ed. Cambridge: Cambridge University Press, 2004.

Collier's Encyclopedia Yearbook Covering the Events of 1947. New York: P. F. Collier and Sons, 1948.

Collins, Robert O. "Africans, Arabs, and Islamists: From the Conference Tables to the Battlefields in the Sudan." *African Studies Review* 42, no. 2 (September 1999): 105–123.

Collins, Robert, and Robert Tignor. *Egypt and the Sudan.* Englewood Cliffs, N.J.: Prentice-Hall, 1967.

Collister, Peter. *Bhutan and the British.* London: Serindia Publications with Belitha Press, 1987.

The Columbia Encyclopedia. 5th ed. New York: Columbia University Press, 1993.

Columbia University, Faculty of, eds. *Studies in History Economics and Public Law.* Vol. 66. New York: Columbia University, 1915.

Commins, D. D. *Historical Dictionary of Syria.* London: Scarecrow Press, 2004.

Communist China, 1962. Hong Kong: Union Research, 1963.

Conetta, Carl. "Disappearing the Dead: Iraq, Afghanistan, and the Idea of a 'New Warfare.'" Project on Defense Alternatives (2004). www.comw.org/pda.

_____. "Operation Enduring Freedom: Why a Higher Rate of Civilian Bombing Casualties. January 18." Project on Defense Alternatives (2002). www.comw.org.

_____. "Strange Victory: A Critical Appraisal of Operation Enduring Freedom and the Afghanistan War." Project on Defense Alternatives Research Monograph #6 (2002). www.comw.org.

Confer, Vincent. *France and Algeria: The Problem of Civil and Political Reform, 1870–1920.* Syracuse, N.Y.: Syracuse University Press, 1966.

Congressional Quarterly. *The Middle East.* 8th ed. Washington, D.C.: Congressional Quarterly, 1994.

Congressional Research Service. "Kosovo Conflict Chronology: January–August 1998." Washington, D.C.: Library of Congress, 1998.

_____. "Kosovo: U.S. and Allied Military Operations." Washington, D.C.: Library of Congress, 2000.

Cook, Chris, and John Paxton. *European Political Facts 1900–1996.* New York: St. Martin's Press, 1998.

Cook, Earnshaw. *Percentage Baseball.* Cambridge, Mass.: MIT Press, 1964.

Cooke, James J. "Lyautey and Etienne: The Soldier and the Politician in the Penetration of Morocco, 1904–1906." *Military Affairs* 36, no. 1 (February 1972): 14–18.

Cooper, Chester. *The Lost Crusade.* New York: Dodd, Mead, 1970.

Coox, Alvin. *The Anals of a Small War.* Westport, Conn.: Greenwood Press, 1977.

_____. "The Forgotten War of 1939." *Conflict* 5 (June 20, 1973), 4–20.

_____. *Nomonhan: Japan against Russia, 1939.* Palo Alto, Calif.: Stanford University Press, 1985.

Coplan, David B., and Tim Quinlan. "A Chief by the People: Nation versus State in Lesotho." *Africa* 67 (1997).

Coplin, Ian. *The Princes of India and the Endgame of Empire.* Cambridge: Cambridge University Press, 1997.

Copper, John. *Taiwan: Nation-State or Province?* Boulder, Colo.: Westview Press, 1996.

Copson, Raymond W. *Africa's Wars and Prospects for Peace.* Armonk, N.Y.: M. E. Sharpe, 1994.

Cordesman, Anthony H. *After the Storm: The Changing Military Balance in the Middle East.* Boulder, Colo.: Westview Press, 1993.

_____. *Bahrain, Oman, Qatar, and the UAE: Challenges of Security.* Boulder, Colo.: Westview Press, 1997.

_____. *The Military Balance in Yemen and the Red Sea States: 1986–1992.* Washington, D.C.: Center for Strategic and International Studies, 1993.

_____. *A Tragedy of Arms: Military and Security Developments in the Maghreb.* Westport, Conn.: Praeger, 2004.

Cordesman, Anthony H., and Abraham R. Wagner. *The Gulf War,* vol. 4 in *The Lessons of Modern War.* Boulder, Colo.: Westview Press, 1996.

Cordier, Henri. *Histoire des Relations de la Chine avec les Puissances Occidentales.* Vol. 3. Paris: F. Alcan, 1902.

_____. *Histoire Generale de la Chine et de ses Relations avec les Pays Etrangers Depuis les Temps les Plus Anciens Jusqu'a la Chute de la Dynastie Mandchou.* Vol. 4. Paris: Geuthner, 1920.

Corfield, Frank. *Historical Survey of the Origins and Growth of Mau Mau,* Cmnd. 1030 (London: HMSO, 1960). Battle-death estimates at p. 316.

Cornell, Svante E. "The Nagorno-Karabakh Conflict." Report No. 46, Department of East European Studies, Uppsala University, Uppsala, Sweden, 1999.

Costello, Patrick. "Guatemala: Historical Background." *Accord* (2002).

Costeloe, Michael P. "The Triangular Revolt in Mexico and the Fall of Anastasio Bustamante, August–October 1841." *Journal of Latin American Studies* 20, no. 2 (November 1988): 337–360.

Costin, W. C. *Great Britain and China,* 1833–1860. London: Oxford University Press, 1937.

Coulthard-Clark, Chris. *The Encyclopedia of Australia's Battles.* Crows Nest, NSW: Allen and Unwin, 2001.

Cousin, Tracey L. "Eritrean and Ethiopian Civil War." ICE Case Studies. Washington, D.C.: American University, November 1997.

Covarrubias, Miguel. *Island of Bali.* New York: Knopf, 1937.

Coverdale, John F. *Italian Intervention in the Spanish Civil War.* Princeton, N.J.: Princeton University Press, 1975.

Cox, Michael. "The Continuing Story of Another Death Foretold." In *Millennial Reflections on International Studies,* edited by Michael Brecher and Frank P. Harvey. Ann Arbor: University of Michigan Press, 2002, 217–233.

Cox, Robert W. "Universality in International Studies, A Historicist Approach." In *Millennial Reflections on International Studies,* edited by Michael Brecher and Frank P. Harvey. Ann Arbor: University of Michigan Press, 2002, 209–216.

Craig, Albert M. *Chōshū in the Meiji Restoration.* Cambridge, Mass.: Harvard University Press, 1961.

Crais, Clifton. *White Supremacy and Black Resistance in Industrial South Africa: The Making of the Colonial Order in the Eastern Cape, 1770–1865.* New York: Cambridge University Press, 1992.

Crampton, R. J. *A Short History of Modern Bulgaria.* Cambridge: Cambridge University Press, 1987.

Crawford, Ann Fears, ed. *The Eagle: The Autobiography of Santa Anna.* Austin, Texas: Pemberton Press, 1967.

Crawley, Charles William. *The Question of Greek Independence.* Cambridge: Cambridge University Press, 1930.

_____. *The Question of Greek Independence.* New York: Howard Fertig, 1973.

Cribb, Robert. "Nation: Making Indonesia." In *Indonesia beyond Suharto: Polity, Economy, Society, Transition,* edited by Donald K. Emmerson. Armonk, N.Y.: M. E. Sharpe, 1999.

Crocker, Chester. *High Noon in Southern Africa: Making Peace in a Rough Neighborhood.* New York: W. W. Norton, 1992.

Croissant, Michael P. *The Armenia-Azerbaijan Conflict: Causes and Implications.* Westport, Conn.: Praeger, 1998.

Cross, Colin. *The Fall of the British Empire.* London: Hodder and Stoughton, 1968.

Crossette, Barbara. "War Adds 1.7 Million Deaths in Eastern Congo, Study Finds." *New York Times,* June 9, 2000. www.nytimes.com.

Crow, John A. *The Epic of Latin America.* Garden City, N.Y.: Doubleday, 1971.

Cumberland, Charles C. *The Mexican Revolution: The Constitutionalist Years.* Austin: University of Texas Press, 1972.

_____. *Mexico: The Struggle for Modernity.* New York: Oxford University Press, 1968.

Cunha, Euclides Da. *Rebellion in the Backlands (Os Sertoes).* Chicago: University of Chicago Press, 1944.

Curtis, Glenn E. *Kazakstan, Krygyzstan, Tajikistan, Turkmenistan, and Uzbekistan: Country Studies.* Washington, D.C.: Library of Congress, 1997.

Curtiss, John Shelton. *The Russian Army under Nicholas I.* Durham, N.C.: Duke University Press, 1965.

Cutter, Charles H. *Africa.* 42nd ed. Harpers Ferry, W. Va.: Stryker-Post Publications, 2007.

Daalder, Ivo H., and Michael E. O'Hanlon. *Winning Ugly; NATO's War to Save Kosovo*. Washington, D.C.: Brookings Institution Press, 2000.

Dakin, Douglas. *The Greek Struggle in Macedonia, 1897–1913*. Thessaloniki: 1966.

_____. *The Struggle for Greek Independence, 1821–1833*. London: B. T. Batsford, 1973.

_____. *The Unification of Greece, 1770–1923*. New York: St. Martin's Press, 1972.

Dallin, David J. *Soviet Russia and the Far East*. New Haven, Conn.: Yale University Press, 1948.

Dalzel, Archibald. *History of Dahomey: Inland Kingdom in Africa*. London: Frank Cass, 1967.

Darkwah, R. H. Kofi. *Shewa, Menilek and the Ethiopian Empire 1813–1889*. New York: Holmes and Meier, 1975.

Dau, Butros. *History of the Maronites: Religious, Cultural, and Political*. Lebanon: Butros Dau, 1984.

Davenport, Rodney, and Christopher Saunders. *South Africa: A Modern History*. 5th ed. New York: St. Martin's Press, 2000.

Davidson, Basil. *Africa: History of a Continent*. New York: Macmillan, 1972.

Davidson, James W. *The Island of Formosa Past and Present*. Oxford: Oxford University Press, 1988.

Davies, Charles E. *The Blood-Red Arab Flag: An Investigation into Qasimi Piracy, 1797–1820*. Exeter: University of Exeter Press, 1997.

Davies, Norman. *Europe: A History*. Oxford: Oxford University Press, 1996.

_____. *God's Playground: A History of Poland*. Vol. 2. New York: Columbia University Press, 1984.

_____. *White Eagle, Red Star: The Polish-Soviet War, 1919–1920*. New York: St. Martin's Press, 1972.

Davis, H. P. *Black Democracy*. New York: Biblo and Tannen, 1967.

Davis, Harold F. *History of Latin America*. New York: Ronald Press, 1968.

Davis, Paul K. *Encyclopedia of Invasions and Conquests from Ancient Times to the Present*. Millerton, N.Y.: Grey House, 2006.

Davis, William Columbus. *The Last Conquistadores*. Athens: University of Georgia Press, 1950.

Dawisha, Karen. *Conflict, Cleavage and Change in Central Asia and the Caucasus*. Cambridge: Cambridge University Press, 1997.

Dawson, Daniel. *The Mexican Adventure*. London: G. Bell and Sons, 1935.

De Klerk, E. S. *History of the Netherlands East Indies*. Vol. 2. Rotterdam: W. L. and J. Brusse, 1938.

De Silva, K. M. *Reaping the Whirlwind*. New Delhi: Penguin Books, 1998.

De Tarde, Alfred. "The Work of France in Morocco." *Geographical Review* 8, no. 1 (July 1919): 1–30.

De Waal, Thomas. *Black Garden*. New York: New York University Press, 2003.

De Watteville, H. *Waziristan, 1919–20*. London: Constable, 1925.

Deadline Data on World Affairs. New York: Deadline Data (weekly since 1955).

Deans, William. *History of the Ottoman Empire*. London: A. Fullerton, 1854.

"Deaths from the War in Iraq." ProCon.Org. www.procon.org, 2008.

Decalo, Samuel. *Historical Dictionary of Chad*. 2nd ed. Metuchen, N.J.: Scarecrow Press, 1987.

_____. *Historical Dictionary of Chad*. 3rd ed. Lanham, Md.: Scarecrow Press, 1997.

Decalo, Samuel, Virginia Thompson, and Richard Adloff, eds. *Historical Dictionary of Congo*. London: Scarecrow Press, 1997.

Decoux, Jean. *A la Barre de l'Indochine*. Paris: Hachette, 1949.

The Defense of Quemoy and the Free World. Taipei: Asian People's Anti-Communist League, 1959.

D'Encausse, Hélène Carrère. "Systematic Conquest, 1865 to 1884." In *Central Asia, 130 Years of Russian Dominance, A Historical Overview*, 3rd ed., edited by Edward Allworth. Durham, N.C.: Duke University Press, 1994.

Deflem, Mathieu. "Warfare, Political Leadership, and State Formation: The Case of the Zulu Kingdom, 1808–1879." *Ethnology* 38 (1999).

DeFronzo, James. *Revolutions and Revolutionary Movements*. Boulder, Colo.: Westview Press, 1996.

DeGeorge, Barbara. "Liberia in Civil War: Haven for Freed Slaves Reduced to Anarchy." In *History behind the Headlines: The Origins of Conflicts Worldwide*, vol. 1, edited by Sonia G. Benson, Nancy Matuszak, and Meghan Appel O'Meara. Detroit: Gale Group, 2001.

Del Val, Don Alfonso Merry. "The Spanish Zones in Morocco (Continued)." *The Geographic Journal* 55, no. 6 (June 1920): 409–419.

DeLancey, M. W. *Historical Dictionary of the Republic of Cameroon*. 3rd ed. Lanham, Md.: Scarecrow Press, 2000.

Dellepiane, Carlos. *Historia Militar del Peru*. Vol. 1. Lima: Imprenta del Ministero de Guerra, 1943.

Demarest, Geoffrey. "War of the Thousand Days." *Small Wars and Insurgencies* 12, no. 1 (Spring 2001): 1–30.

Demetriou, Spyros. "Rising from the Ashes? The Difficult (Re)Birth of the Georgian State." *Development and Change* 33, no. 5 (2002): 859–883.

Dennis, Lawrence. *The Dynamics of War and Revolution.* New York: Weekly Foreign Letter, 1940.

Denton, Frank H. "Some Regularities in International Conflict, 1820–1949." *Background* 9, no. 4 (February, 1966): 283–296.

Denton, Frank H., and Warren Phillips. "Some Patterns in the History of Violence." *Journal of Conflict Resolution* 12, no. 2 (June 1968): 182–195.

Deployment Health Clinical Center. "Operation Allied Force." www.pdhealth,mil/508/deployments/allied_force/background.asp.

Desch, M. "War and Strong States, Peace and Weak States?" *International Organization* 50 (1996): 237–268.

Deschamps, Hubert. *Histoire de Madagascar.* Paris: Berger-Levrault, 1960.

Deutsch, Karl W. "External Involvement in Internal Wars." In *Internal War,* edited by H. Eckstein. Glencoe, Ill.: Free Press, 1964.

Deutsch, Karl W., and J. David Singer, "Multipolar Systems and International Stability." In *International War: An Anthology,* 2nd ed., edited by Melvin Small and J. David Singer. Chicago: Dorsey Press, 1989, 225–237.

Deutschland in China, 1900–1901. Dusseldorf: A Bagel, 1902.

Devillers, P., P. Fistie, and Le Thilnh. *L'Asie du Sud-Est.* Paris: Sirey, 1971.

Dewey, Edward R. *The 177-Year Cycle in War, 600 B.C.–A.D. 1957.* Pittsburgh: Foundation for the Study of Cycles, 1964.

Di Pisani, Andre. *SWA/Namibia: The Politics of Continuity and Change.* Johannesburg: J. Ball, 1986.

Diehl, Paul F., and Frank W. Wayman, "Realpolitik: Dead End, Detour, or Road Map?" In *Reconstructing Realpolitik,* edited by Frank W. Wayman and Paul F. Diehl. Ann Arbor: University of Michigan Press, 1994, 247–265.

Dimbleby, Jonathan. *The Palestinians.* New York: Quartet Books, 1980.

Dixon, Jeffrey. "Coding Rules Memo." Personal communication with Meredith Reid Sarkees, May 6, 2006:1.

―――. "Suggested Changes to the COW Civil War Dataset 3.0." Paper presented at the annual meeting of the International Studies Association, Portland, Ore., February 25–March 1, 2003.

Dixon, Jeffrey, and Meredith Reid Sarkees. "Intervention, Recognition, and War Transformation: A Consistent Standard for Distinguishing Inter-State, Extra-State, and Intra-State Wars." Paper presented at the annual meeting of the International Studies Association, Honolulu, Hawaii, March 1–5, 2005.

Djilas, Milovan. *Wartime.* New York: Harcourt, 1977.

Dobby, E. H. G. *Southeast Asia.* 11th ed. London: University of London Press, 1973.

Dobyns, Henry H., and Paul L. Doughty. *Peru: A Cultural History.* New York: Oxford University Press, 1976.

Dodwell, H. H., ed. *The Cambridge History of India.* Vol. 5. New York: Macmillan, 1929.

Dodwell, Henry. *The Founder of Modern Egypt: A Study of Muhammad Ali.* Cambridge: Cambridge University, 1931.

Dominguez, Jorge I., with David Mares, Manuel Orozco, David Scott Palmer, Francisco Rojas Aravena, and Andrés Serbin. *Boundary Disputes in Latin America.* Washington, D.C.: United States Institute of Peace, 2003.

Donia, Robert J. *Sarajevo.* Ann Arbor: University of Michigan Press, 2006.

Donia, Robert, and John Fine. *Bosnia and Hercegovina.* New York: Columbia University Press, 1994.

Donnison, Frank S. V. *Burma.* New York: Praeger, 1970.

Dontas, D. N. *Greece and the Great Powers.* Thessaloniki: Institute for Balkan Studies, 1966.

Dorji, C. T. *A Political and Religious History of Bhutan, 1651–1906.* Delhi: Sangay Xam, Prominent Publishers, 1995.

Doroshenko, I. Mitro. *History of the Ukraine.* Translated by Hanna Chikalenko-Keller. Edmonton, Alberta: Institute Press, 1939.

Dorronsoro, Gilles. *Revolution Unending, Afghanistan: 1979 to the Present.* New York: Columbia University Press, 2005.

Dougherty, Carter. "Burundi Inching Closer to Ending Long Civil War." *World and I* 19, no. 11 (November 2004).

Dougherty, James E., and Richard L. Pfaltzgraff Jr. "The Realist Approach to International Conflict." In *International War: An Anthology,* 2nd ed., edited by Melvin Small and J. David Singer. Chicago: Dorsey Press, 1989, 212–216.

Doyle, Michael W. *Ways of War and Peace.* New York: W. W. Norton, 1997.

Dragadze, Tamara. "Ethnic Conflict as Political Smokescreen: The Caucasus Region." In *Ethnicity and Intrastate Conflict,* edited by Håkan Wiberg and Christian P. Scherrer. Brookfield, Vt.: Ashgate, 1999, 262–279.

Dresch, Paul. *A History of Modern Yemen.* Cambridge: Cambridge University Press, 2000.

Drew, Frederic. *The Northern Barrier of India*. London: Edward Stanford, 1877.

Droz, Jacques. *Les Revolutions Allmandes de 1848*. Paris: Presses Universitaires de France, 1957.

Du Quenoy, Paul. "Warlordism à *la Russe*: Baron Von Ungern-Sternberg's Anti-Bolshevik Crusade, 1917–21." *Revolutionary Russia* 16, no. 2 (2003): 1–27.

Duffy, James. *Portugal in Africa*. Cambridge, Mass.: Harvard University Press, 1962.

_____. *Portuguese Africa*. Cambridge, Mass.: Harvard University Press, 1959.

Duiker, William. *The Rise of Nationalism in Vietnam, 1900–1941*. Ithaca, N.Y.: Cornell University Press, 1976.

Duke, Simon, Hans-Georg Ehrhart, and Matthias Karadi. "The Major European Allies: France, Germany and the United Kingdom." In *Kosovo and the Challenges of Humanitarian Intervention*, edited by Albrecht Schnabel and Ramesh Thakur. New York: United Nations University Press, 2000.

Dumas, Samuel, and Knud Otto Vedel-Peterson. *Losses of Life Caused by War*. London: Oxford University Press, 1923.

Dumont, Jean, ed. *Les Coups d'État*. Paris: Hachette, 1963.

Duner, Bertil. "Military Involvement: The Escalation of Internal Conflicts." Swedish Institute of International Affairs, 1980.

Dunn, Kevin C. "Uganda: The Lord's Resistance Army." In *African Guerrillas: Raging against the Machine*, edited by Morten BøÅs and Kevin C. Dunn. Boulder, Colo.: Lynne Rienner, 2007.

Dunn, Ross E. "The Bu Himara Rebellion in Northeast Morocco: Phase I." *Middle Eastern Studies* 17, no. 1 (1981): 31–48.

_____. *Resistance in the Desert: Moroccan Responses to French Imperialism, 1881–1912*. Madison: University of Wisconsin Press, 1977.

Dupree, Louis. *Afghanistan*. London: Oxford University Press, 1973.

_____. *Afghanistan*. Princeton, N.J.: Princeton University Press, 1980.

Dupuy, Alex. *Haiti in the World Economy: Class, Race, and Underdevelopment since 1700*. Boulder, Colo.: Westview Press, 1997.

Dupuy, R. Ernest, and William H. Baumer. *The Little Wars of the United States*. New York: Hawthorn, 1968.

Dupuy, R. Ernest, and Trevor N. Dupuy. *The Harper Encyclopedia of Military History from 3500 B.C. to the Present*. 4th ed. New York: HarperCollins, 1993.

_____. *The Encyclopedia of Military History from 3500 B.C. to the Present*. New York: Harper and Row, 1970.

Dupuy, Trevor N. *Attrition: Forecasting Battle Casualties and Equipment Losses in Modern War*. Fairfax, Va.: Hero Books, 1990.

_____. *Elusive Victory: The Arab-Israeli Wars, 1947–1974*. New York: Harper and Row, 1978.

Dupuy, Trevor N., and Paul Martell. *Flawed Victory: The Arab-Israeli Conflict and the 1982 War in Lebanon*. Fairfax, Va.: Hero Books, 1986.

Eagleton, William, Jr. *The Kurdish Republic of 1946*. London: Oxford University Press, 1963.

Earle, Peter. *The Pirate Wars*. New York: St. Martin's Press, 2003.

Eastman, Lloyd E. *Throne and Mandarins*. Cambridge, Mass.: Harvard University Press, 1967.

Eberwein, Wolf Dieter, and Sven Chojnacki. "Scientific Necessity and Political Utility: A Comparison of Data on Violent Conflicts." P01-304. Berlin: Arbeitsgruppe: Internationale Politik, 2001.

Echard, William E. *Historical Dictionary of the French Second Empire, 1832–1870*. Westport, Conn.: Greenwood Press, 1985.

Eckstein, Harry, ed. *Internal War*. Glencoe, Ill.: Free Press, 1964.

Edgerton, Robert B. *Africa's Armies, From Honor to Infamy*. Boulder, Colo.: Westview Press, 2002.

_____. *The Fall of the Asante Empire: The Hundred-Year War for Africa's Gold Coast*. New York: Free Press, 1995.

Edmonds, Martin. "Civil War, Internal War, and Intrasocietal Conflict: A Taxonomy and Typology." In *Civil Wars in the Twentieth Century*, edited by Robin Higham. Lexington: University Press of Kentucky, 1972.

Edwardes, Michael. *Battles of the India Mutiny*. London: B. T. Batsford, 1963.

Edwards, H. Sutherland. *The Private History of a Polish Insurrection*. London: Saunders, 1865.

Eggenberger, David. *A Dictionary of Battles*. New York: Crowell, 1967.

Eggers, Ellen K. *Historical Dictionary of Burundi*. Lanham, Md.: Scarecrow Press, 1997.

Ekinci, Mehmet Ugur. "The Origins of the 1897 Ottoman-Greek War: A Diplomatic History." Master's thesis, Bilkent University, Ankara, 2006.

Eliade, M. N. *Crete, Past and Present*. London: Heath, Cranton, 1933.

Elleman, Bruce A. *Modern Chinese Warfare, 1795–1989*. London: Routledge, 2001.

Ellis, C, II. *The British "Intervention" in Transcaspia, 1918–1919*. Berkeley: University of California Press, 1963.

Elmslie, Jim. *Irian Jaya under the Gun: Indonesian Economic Development versus West Papuan Nationalism.* Honolulu: University of Hawaii Press, 2003.

Elshtain, Jean Bethke. *Just War against Terror.* New York: Basic Books, 2004.

_____. *Women and War.* New York: Basic Books, 1987.

Emmerson, Donald K. *Indonesia beyond Suharto: Polity, Economy, Society, Transition.* Armonk, N.Y.: M. E. Sharpe, 1999.

Encina, Francisco Antonio. *Historia de Chile.* Vol. 14. Santiago: Editorial Nascimento, 1950.

Enloe, Cynthia. *Globalization and Militarism.* Boulder, Colo.: Rowman and Littlefield, 2007.

_____. "Margins, Silences and Bottom Rungs: How to Overcome the Underestimation of Power in the Study of International Relations." In *International Theory: Positivism and Beyond,* edited by Steve Smith, Ken Booth, and Marysia Zalewski. Cambridge: Cambridge University Press, 1996, 186–202.

Entelis, John P. *Algeria: The Revolution Institutionalized.* Boulder, Colo.: Westview Press, 1986.

_____. *Comparative Politics of North Africa.* Syracuse, N.Y.: Syracuse University Press, 1980.

Eprik, Cecil. *War and Peace in the Sudan: 1955–1972.* London: David Charles, 1972.

Erickson, John. *The Soviet High Command.* London: Macmillan, 1962.

Ero, Comfort. "ECOMOG: A Model for Africa?" In *Building Stability in Africa: Challenges for the New Millennium,* Monograph 46 (February 2000).

Esposito, Mark A. T. "Nagorno-Karabakh: Self-Determination and Ethnic Identification." In *History behind the Headlines: The Origins of Conflicts Worldwide,* vol. 1, edited by Sonia G. Benson, Nancy Matuszak, and Meghan Appel O'Meara. Detroit: Gale Group, 2001.

Esposito, Vincent J., ed. *A Concise History of World War I.* New York: Praeger, 1964a.

_____. *A Concise History of World War II.* New York: Praeger, 1964b.

Essen, Leon Vander. *A Short History of Belgium.* Chicago: University of Chicago Press, 1916.

Etcheparaborda, Roberto. *La Revolucion Argentina del 90.* Buenos Aires: Editorial Universitario de Buenos Aires, 1966.

_____. *Tres Revoluciones, 1890–1893–1905.* Buenos Aires: Pleamar, 1968.

Etherton, Thomas P. *In the Heart of Asia.* London: Constable, 1925.

Europa Yearbook, 2005. "Afghanistan." New York: Freedom House, 2005.

Europa Yearbook, 2007. New York: Freedom House, 2007.

Evans, Alexander. "The Kashmir Insurgency: As Bad as It Gets." *Small Wars and Insurgencies* 11, no. 1 (Spring 2000): 69–81.

Evans, Grant. *A Short History of Laos: The Land in Between.* Chiang Mai, Thailand: Silkworm Books, 2002.

Evans, Grant, and Kelvin Rowley. *Red Brotherhood at War: Vietnam, Cambodia and Laos since 1975.* New York: Verso Books, 1990.

Evans, Martin. *Afghanistan: A Short History of Its People and Politics.* New York: HarperCollins, 2002.

_____. *Encyclopedia of the Boer War, 1899–1902.* Santa Barbara, Calif.: ABC-CLIO, 2000.

Evans, Martin, and John Phillips. *Algeria: Anger of the Dispossessed.* New Haven, Conn.: Yale University Press, 2007.

Evans, Stanley G. *A Short History of Bulgaria.* London: Lawrence and Wishart, 1960.

Eversley, Lord George J. S. *The Turkish Empire from 1288 to 1914.* London: T. Fisher Unwin, 1917.

Evron, Y. *War and Intervention in Lebanon.* Baltimore, Md.: Johns Hopkins University Press, 1987.

Fabunmi, L. A. *The Sudan in Anglo-Egyptian Relations.* London: Longmans, 1960.

Facts on File World News Digest. New York: Facts on File (weekly since 1940, multiple years).

Fage, J. D. *A History of West Africa.* Cambridge: Cambridge University Press, 1969.

Fage, J. D., and Roland Oliver, eds. *The Cambridge History of Africa.* Vol. 5. Cambridge: Cambridge University Press, 1976.

_____. *The Cambridge History of West Africa.* 8 vols. New York: Cambridge University Press, 1975–1980.

Fahmy, Khaled. "Mutiny in Mechmed Ali's New Nizami Army, April–May 1824." *International Journal of Turkish Studies* 8, no. 1–2 (2002): 129–138.

Fairbank, John K. *Cambridge History of China.* Vol. 10, *Late Ch'ing 1800–1911, Part 1.* Cambridge: Cambridge University Press, 1978.

_____. *China, a New History.* Cambridge, Mass.: Belknap Press, 1992.

Fairbank, John K., and Kwang-Ching Liu. *Cambridge History of China.* Vol. 11, *Late Ch'ing 1800–1911, Part 2.* Cambridge: Cambridge University Press, 1980.

Fairbank, John K., Edwin O. Reischauer, and A. M. Craig. *East Asia: Tradition and Transformation.* New York: Houghton Mifflin, 1958, 1960, 1989.

Fairbank, John K., and Denis Twitchett. *Cambridge History of China*, Vol. 12: *Republican China, 1912–1949, Part 1*. Cambridge: Cambridge University Press, 1983.

Falk, Richard A. *The Declining World Order: America's Imperial Geopolitics*. New York: Routledge, 2004.

Fall, Bernard. *Hell in a Very Small Place: The Siege of Dienbienphu*. New York: Da Capo, 2002.

———. *Street without Joy*. Harrisburg, Pa.: Stackpole Books, 1963.

———. *The Two Viet-Nams*. New York: Praeger, 1967.

Falls, Cyril. *The Great War*. New York: Putnam, 1959.

Falola, Toyin. *Violence in Nigeria: The Crisis of Religious Politics and Secular Ideologies*. Rochester: University of Rochester Press, 1998.

Falola, Toyin, and Matthew Heaton. *A History of Nigeria*. New York: Cambridge University Press, 2008.

Fanon, Frantz. *The Wretched of the Earth*, New York: Grove Press, 1963.

Far Eastern Economic Review. *Asia Yearbook*. Hong Kong: Far Eastern Economic Review, 1970–1972, 1974.

Farah, Caesar E. "The Anglo-Ottoman Confrontation in Yemen, 1840–1849." *International Journal of Turkish Studies* 3, no. 2 (Winter 1985/86): 69–93.

———. "The Lebanese Insurgence of 1840 and the Powers." *Journal of Asian History* 1, no. 2 (1967): 105–132.

———. *The Politics of Interventionism in Ottoman Lebanon, 1830–1861*. London: I. B. Tauris, 2000.

———. "Reaffirming Ottoman Sovereignty in Yemen, 1825–1840." *International Journal of Turkish Studies* 3, no. 1 (Winter 1984/85): 101–116.

———. *The Sultan's Yemen: Nineteenth-Century Challenges to Ottoman Rule*. London: I. B. Tauris, 2002.

Farber, Henry, and Joanne Gowa. "Politics and Peace." *International Security* 20, no. 2 (Fall 1995): 108–132.

Farer, Tom J. *War Clouds on the Horn of Africa: The Widening Storm*. New York: Carnegie Endowment, 1978.

Farmanfarmaian, Roxanne, ed. *War and Peace in Qajar Persia*. New York: Routledge, 2007.

Farsoun, Karen, and Jim Paul. "War in the Sahara: 1963." *MERIP Reports* no. 45 (March 1976): 13–16.

Farwell, Byron. *Prisoners of the Mahdi; The Story of the Mahdist Revolt from the Fall of Khartoum to the Reconquest of the Sudan by Kitchener Fourteen Years Later, and of the Daily Lives and Sufferings in Captivity of Three European Prisoners, a Soldier, a Merchant and a Priest*. London: Longmans, 1967.

———. *Queen Victoria's Little Wars*. New York: Harper and Row, 1972.

FAS Intelligence Resource Program. "Kosovo Liberation Army (KLA)." www.fas.org/irp/world/para/kla.htm.

Fay, Sidney B. *The Origins of the World War*. 2 vols. New York: Macmillan, 1928.

Fearon, James D., and David D. Laitin. "Burma." Ethnicity, Insurgency and Civil War Research Project. (July, 7, 2006). www.stanford.edu/group/ethnic/random narratives.

Featherstone, Donald. *Colonial Small Wars: 1837–1901*. Newton Abbot, UK: David and Charles, 1973.

———. *Victorian Colonial Warfare: Africa*. London: Blanford, 1992a.

———. *Victorian Colonial Warfare: India*. London: Cassell, 1992b.

Feierabend, Ivo K., and Rosalind L. Feierabend. "Aggressive Behaviors within Polities, 1948–1962: A Cross-National Study." *Journal of Conflict Resolution* 10, no. 3 (September 1966): 249–271.

Feith, Herbert. "Indonesia." In *Government and Politics in Southeast Asia*, edited by G. Kahin. Ithaca, N.Y.: Cornell University Press, 1964.

Feng, Cheng, and Larry M. Wortzel. "PLA Operational Principles and Limited War: The Sino-Indian War of 1962." In *Chinese Warfighting: The PLA Experience since 1949*, edited by Mark Ryan, David Finkelstein, and Michael McDevitt. Armonk, N.Y.: M. E. Sharpe, 2003.

Feraoun, Mouloud. *Journal, 1955–1962: Reflections on the Algerian War*. Lincoln: University of Nebraska Press, 2000.

Field, G. Lowell. *Comparative Political Development: The Precedent of the West*. Ithaca, N.Y.: Cornell University Press, 1967.

Figes, Orlando. *A People's Tragedy, The Russian Revolution: 1891–1924*. New York: Penguin Books, 1996.

Finkel, Caroline. *Osman's Dream: The Story of the Ottoman Empire*, 1300–1923. New York: Basic Books, 2005.

Finnegan, William. *A Complicated War: The Harrowing of Mozambique*. Berkeley: University of California Press, 1993.

Firkins, Peter. *The Australians in Nine Wars*. London: Robert Hale, 1972.

Firro, Kais M. *A History of the Druzes*. New York: E. J. Brill, 1992.

First, Ruth. *South West Africa*. London: Penguin, 1963.

Fisher, John R., Allan J. Kuethe, and Anthony Mcfarlane. *Reform and Insurrection in Bourbon New Granada and Peru*. Baton Rouge: Louisiana State University Press, 1990.

Fisher, Sydney N. *The Middle East: A History*. New York: Knopf, 1968.

Fitzgerald, C. P. *China, A Short Cultural History*. New York: Praeger, 1967.

Fitzgibbon, Louis. *The Betrayal of the Somalis*. London: Rex Collings, 1982.

Fitzgibbon, Russell H. *Cuba and the United States*. Menasha, Wisc.: George Banta, 1935.

Fleming, Peter. *The Siege at Peking*. London: Hart-Davis, 1959.

Flemion, Philip F. *Historical Dictionary of El Salvador*. Metuchen, N.J.: Scarecrow Press, 1972.

Fletcher, Arnold. *Afghanistan: Highway of Conquest*. Ithaca, N.Y.: Cornell University Press, 1965.

Florinsky, Michael T. *Russia: A History and an Interpretation*. Vol. 2. New York: Macmillan, 1953.

Fontaine, Pierre. *Abd-El-Krim*. Paris: Le Sept Couleurs, 1950.

Foreign Languages Press. *Documents on the Sino-Indian Boundary Question*. Peking: Foreign Languages Press, 1960.

Fortescue, Sir John W. *History of the British Army*. Vols. 11, 12, and 13. London: Macmillan, 1923, 1927, 1930.

Fortna, Page. "Where Have All the Victors Gone? War Outcomes in Historical Perspective." Paper presented at the annual meeting of the American Political Science Association, Chicago, September 3, 2004.

Foster, Charles. "Indonesia and West Papua." *Contemporary Review* 282, Issue 1645 (February 2003): 73–76.

Foster, Henry. *The Making of Modern Iraq*. Norman: University of Oklahoma Press, 1935.

Fowler, Will. *Tornel and Santa Anna: The Writer and the Caudillo, Mexico 1795–1853*. Westport, Conn.: Greenwood Press, 2000.

Fox, Grace. *Britain and Japan, 1858–1883*. Oxford: Clarendon Press, 1969.

Fraley, G., and Jovan Wlahovitj. *Le Montenegro Contemporain*. Paris: E. Plon, 1876.

France, Ministry of Foreign Affairs. *Les Origines Diplomatiques de la Guerre de 1870–1871*. Paris: G. Ficker, 1915.

Franke, Wolfgang. *A Century of Chinese Revolution, 1851–1949*. Oxford: Blackwell, 1970.

Fraser-Tyler, William K. *Afghanistan*. London: Oxford University Press, 1967.

Frazer, R. W. *British India*. New York: Putnam, 1897.

Frédéric, Louis. *The Japan Encylopedia*. Cambridge, Mass.: Harvard University Press, 2002.

Frederick, William H. *Visions and Heat: The Making of the Indonesian Revolution*. Athens, Ohio: Ohio University Press, 1989.

Freedom House. *Freedom in the World*. Lanham, Md.: Rowman and Littlefield, 2004.

_____. *Freedom in the World 2007: The Annual Survey of Political Rights and Civil Liberties*. New York: Freedom House, 2007.

Freeman-Grenville, F. S. P. *A Chronology of African History*. London: Oxford University Press, 1973.

Frère, Marie-Soleil. *The Media and Conflicts in Central Africa*. Boulder, Colo.: Lynne Rienner, 2007.

Freud, Sigmund. "Why War?" In *International War: An Anthology*, 2nd ed., edited by Melvin Small and J. David Singer. Chicago: Dorsey Press, 1989, 176–181.

Frey, H. *Francais et Allies au Petchlihi: Campagne de Chine de 1900*. Paris: Hachette, 1904.

Fried, Alfred H. "A Few Lessons Taught by the Balkan War." *International Conciliation* 74 (January 1914).

Friedjung, Heinrich. *Österreich von 1848 bis 1860*. Stuttgart: J. G. Cotta, 1912.

_____. *The Struggle for Supremacy in Germany 1859–1866*. Translated by A. J. P. Taylor and W. L. McIlvee. London: Macmillan, 1935.

Frilley, G., and Jovan Wlahovitj. *Le Montenegro Contemporain*. Paris: E. Plan, 1876.

Friters, Gerard M. *Outer Mongolia and Its International Position*. Baltimore, Md.: Johns Hopkins University Press, 1949.

Fukuyama, Francis. "The End of History?" *The National Interest* 16 (Summer 1989): 3–5, 8–15, 18.

Fuller, Francis. *A Vanished Dynasty: Ashanti*. London: John Murray, 1921.

Fuller, J. F. C. *The Conduct of War, 1789–1961*. London: Eyre and Spottiswoode, 1961.

Furneaux, Rupert. *Abdel Krim: Emir of the Rif*. London: Secker and Waburg, 1967.

Gabriel, Richard A. *Operation Peace for Galilee: The Israeli-PLO War in Lebanon*. New York: Hill and Wang, 1984.

Gabrielle, Leon. *Abd-El-Krim et les Evenement du Rif*. Casablanca: Edition Atlantides, 1953.

Gaddis, J. L. *The Long Peace: Inquiries into the History of the Cold War*. New York: Oxford University Press, 1987.

Gade, Kirsten, and W. Glyn Jones. *Blue Guide Denmark*. 2nd ed. New York: W. W. Norton, 1997.

Gagnon, V. P., Jr. *The Myth of Ethnic War: Serbia and Croatia in the 1990s*. Ithaca, N.Y.: Cornell University Press, 2004.

Galbraith, John S. *Mackinnon and East Africa 1878–1895: A Study in the "New Imperialism."* Cambridge: Cambridge University Press, 1972.

Galbraith, W. O. *Columbia*. London: Royal Institute of International Affairs, 1953.

Galdames, Luis. *A History of Chile*. Chapel Hill: University of North Carolina Press, 1941.

Galdmes, Luis. *A History of Chile*. New York: Russell & Russell, Inc., 1964.

Galey, John H. "Bridegrooms of Death: A Profile of the Spanish Foreign Legion." *Journal of Contemporary History* 4, no. 2 (April 1969): 47–64.

Galvez, Juan Ignacio. *El Peru Contra Colombia, Ecuador y Chile*. Santiago: Sociedad Imprentalitografia Universo, 1919.

Gambra, Rafael. *La Primera Guerra Civil de Espana (1821–1823)*. Madrid: Esceliecer, 1972.

Ganguly, Sumit. "Explaining the Kashmir Insurgency." In *Nationalism and Ethnic Conflict*, edited by Michael E. Brown, Owen R. Coté Jr., Sean M. Lynn-Jones, and Steven E. Miller. Cambridge, Mass.: MIT Press, 1996.

Garner, William R. *The Chaco Dispute*. Washington, D.C.: Public Affairs Press, 1966.

Gat, Azar. "The Pattern of Fighting in Simple, Small-Scale, Prestate Societies." *Journal of Anthropological Research* 55, no. 4 (Winter 1999): 563–583.

Gavin, R. J. *Aden under British Rule 1839–1967*. New York: Barnes and Noble Books, 1975.

Gebrandy, P. S. *Indonesia*. London: Hutchinson, 1950.

Gehl, Jurgen. *Austria, Germany, and the Anschluss, 1931–1938*. London: Oxford University Press, 1963.

Gelber, Yoav. *Palestine 1948*. Brighton: Sussex Academic Press, 2006.

Geller, Daniel, and J. David Singer. *Nations at War: A Scientific Study of International Conflict*. Cambridge: Cambridge University Press, 1998.

General Staff, Army Headquarters in India. *Operations in Waziristan, 1919–20*. Delhi: Government Central Press, 1923.

Geoffrey de Grandmaison, Charles Alexander. *L'expedition Francaise d'Espagne en 1823*. Paris: Plon, 1928.

Georgieva, Valentina, and Sasha Konechni. *Historical Dictionary of the Republic of Macedonia*. Lanham, Md.: Scarecrow Press, 1998.

Germany, Armee Grosser General Stab. *Die Kampfe der Deutschen Truppen in Sudwest Africa*. 2 vols. Berlin: Kriegsgeschicht Abteilung, 1906–1907.

Gerner, Deborah J. *One Land, Two Peoples: The Conflict over Palestine*. Boulder, Colo.: Westview Press, 1991.

Gernet, Jacques. *A History of Chinese Civilization*. Cambridge: Cambridge University Press, 1982.

Gerolymatos, André. *The Balkan Wars: Conquest, Revolution, and Retribution from the Ottoman Era to the Twentieth Century and Beyond*. New York: Basic Books, 2002.

Gerome, Frank A. "Race and Politics in Cuba and the U.S. Intervention of 1912." *SECOLAS Annals: Journal of the Southeastern Council on Latin American Studies* 28 (1997): 5–26.

Gerrard, Craig. "The Foreign Office and British Intervention in the Finnish Civil War." *Civil Wars* 3, no. 3 (Autumn 2000): 87–100.

Geschichte des Zweiten Weltkrieges 1939–1945. Wurzburg: A. G. Ploetz, 1960.

Gettleman, Jeffrey. "Somalia Forces Retake Capital from Islamists." *New York Times,* December 29, 2006. www.nytimes.com.

Gettleman, Marvin, ed. *Vietnam*. New York: Fawcett, 1970.

Gettleman, Marvin, S. Gettleman, L. Kaplan, and C. Kaplan, eds. *Conflict in Indochina*. New York: Vintage, 1970.

Gewald, San-Bart. *Herero Heroes: A Socio-Political History of the Herero of Namibia, 1890–1923*. Athens: Ohio University Press, 1999.

Ghosn, Faten, Glenn Palmer, and Stuart Bremer. "The MID3 Data Set, 1993–2001: Procedures, Coding Rules, and Description." *Conflict Management and Peace Science* 21 (2004): 133–154.

Giap, Vo Nguyen, and Van Tien Dung. *How We Won the War*. Philadelphia: Recon, 1976.

Gibbs, Brian, and J. David Singer. *Empirical Knowledge on World Politics: A Summary of Quantitative Research, 1970–1991*. Westport, Conn.: Greenwood Press, 1993.

Gilbert, Martin. *Recent History Atlas*. London: Macmillan, 1966.

Gillespie, Carol Ann. *Ethiopia*. New York: Chelsea House, 2002.

Gilmore, Robert L. *Caudillism and Militarism in Venezuela, 1810–1910*. Athens: Ohio University Press, 1964.

Ginor, Isabella, and Gideon Remez. *Foxbats Over Dimona: The Soviets' Nuclear Gamble in the Six-Day War*. New Haven: Yale University Press, 2007.

Girling, J. L. S. "Laos: Falling Domino?" *Pacific Affairs* 43, no. 3 (Autumn 1970): 370–383.

_____. "The Resistance in Cambodia." *Asian Survey* 12, no. 7 (July 1972): 549–563.

Gleijeses, Piero. *The Dominican Crisis*. Baltimore, Md.: Johns Hopkins University Press, 1978.

Glenny, Misha. *The Balkans: Nationalism, War and the Great Powers, 1804–1999*. New York: Viking Press, 1999.

Global Security.org. "Al-Aqsa Intifada." www.globalsecurity.org, 6/4/2005.

_____. "Congo Civil War." www.globalsecurity.org.

_____. "Free Aceh (Aceh Merdeka) Free Aceh Movement [Gerakin Aceh Merdeka (GAM)] Aceh Security

Disturbance Movement (GPK)." www.globalsecurity
.org.

_____. "Insurgency in Nepal." www.globalsecurity.org.

_____. "Iraq Coalition Troops." www.globalsecurity
.org, 8/18/2005.

_____. "Ivory Coast Conflict." www.globalsecurity.org.

_____. "1999 Kargil Conflict." www.globalsecurity
.org/military/world/war/kargil-99.htm.

_____. "Liberia–First Civil War–1989–1996." www
.globalsecurity.org.

_____. "Liberia–Second Civil War–1997–2003." www
.globalsecurity.org, 2005.

_____. "Maluku." www.globalsecurity.org.

_____. "Operation Allied Force." www.globalsecurity
.org.

_____. "Operation Enduring Freedom–Afghanistan."
www.globalsecurity.org, 2007.

_____. "Operation Enduring Freedom–Deploy-
ments." www.globalsecurity.org.

Glubb, John B. *A Soldier with the Arabs.* London: Hodder and Stoughton, 1957.

_____. *Syria, Lebanon, and Jordan.* London: Thames
and Hudson, 1967.

_____. *War in the Desert.* London: Hodder and
Stoughton, 1960.

Gnorowski, S. B. *Insurrection of Poland.* London: James
Ridgeway, 1839.

Godechot, Jacques. *Les Revolutions de 1848.* Paris:
Albin Michel, 1971.

Goertz, Gary, and Paul Diehl. "International Norms
and Power Politics." In *Reconstructing Realpolitik,*
edited by Frank Wayman and Paul Diehl. Ann Arbor:
University of Michigan Press, 1994.

Goldschmidt, Arthur J. *A Concise History of the Middle
East.* Boulder, Colo.: Westview Press, 1991.

_____. *Modern Egypt, the Formation of a Nation-
State.* Boulder, Colo.: Westview Press, 1988.

Goldstein, Erik. *Wars and Peace Treaties 1816–1991.*
New York: Routledge, 1992.

Goldstein, Joshua S. *War and Gender.* Cambridge:
Cambridge University Press, 2001.

Goldstone, Jack A. *The Encyclopedia of Political
Revolutions.* Washington, D.C.: Congressional Quarterly, 1998.

Gonzales, Michael J. "Neo-colonialism and Indian
Unrest in Southern Peru, 1867–1898." *Latin American
Research* 6, no. 1 (1987): 1–26.

Goodwin, Jason. *Lords of the Horizon: A History of the
Ottoman Empire.* London: Chatto and Windus, 1998.

Gopcevic, Spiridion. *Le Montenegro et les Montenegrins.* Paris: Plon, 1877.

Gordon, Charles Alexander. *Recollections of Thirty-
Nine Years in the Army.* London: Swan Sonnenschein,
1898.

Gordon, Stewart. *The Marathas, 1600–1818.* New York:
Cambridge University Press, 1993.

Gordon, Thomas. *History of the Greek Revolution.*
London: Blackwood, 1844.

Gough, Charles, and Arthur Innes. *The Sikhs and the
Sikh Wars.* London: A. D. Innes, 1897.

Gouvea, Rodger M., and Gerald T. West. "Riot Conta-
gion in Latin America, 1949–1963." *Journal of Conflict
Resolution* 25 (June 1981): 349–360.

Grant, Jonathan, Jonathan Unger, and Laurane A. G.
Moss, eds. *Cambodia: The Widening War in Indochina.*
New York: Simon and Schuster, 1970.

Graves, W. S. *America's Siberian Adventure, 1918–1920.*
New York: P. Smith, 1941.

Gray, Jack. *Rebellions and Revolutions: China from the
1800s to the 1980s.* Oxford: Oxford University Press,
1990.

Graz, Liesl. *The Turbulent Gulf.* London: I. B. Tauris,
1990.

Great Britain, Central Office of Information. *PAI-
FORCE.* London: H.M.S.O., 1948.

Great Britain, Colonial Office. *Historical Survey of the
Origins and Growth of Mau Mau.* London: H.M.S.O.,
1960.

Great Britain, Foreign Office. *Correspondence Relating
to the Asiatic Provinces of Turkey, 1896, 7.* London:
1896.

_____. *Documents Regarding the Situation in Greece:
January, 1945.* London: H.M.S.O., 1945.

Great Britain, Naval Intelligence Division. *Geographical Handbook Series, Algeria.* Vol. I. Oxford: Naval
Intelligence Division of the Admiralty (Oxford Sub-
centre), 1942.

_____. *Jugoslavia.* London: H.M.S.O., 1944.

Great Britain, Royal Institute of International Affairs.
The Middle East: A Political and Economic Survey. London: Royal Institute of International Affairs, 1950.

Gregorian, Vartan. *The Emergence of Modern Afghanistan.* Stanford, Calif.: Stanford University Press, 1969.

Gregory, J. W. *The Foundation of British East Africa.*
New York: Negro Universities Press, 1901.

Gregory, John S. "British Intervention against the
Taiping Rebellion." *Journal of Asian Studies* 19 (November 1959): 11–24.

_____. *Great Britain and the Taipings.* London: Rout-
ledge and Kegan Paul, 1969.

Grieco, Joseph M. "Modern Realist Theory and the
Study of International Politics in the Twenty-First
Century." In *Millennial Reflections on International*

Studies, edited by Michael Brecher and Frank P. Harvey. Ann Arbor: University of Michigan Press, 2002, 65–78.

Gross, Feliks. *World Politics and Tension Areas.* New York: New York University Press, 1966.

Grunder, Garel, and William Livezey. *The Philippines and the United States.* Norman: University of Oklahoma Press, 1951.

Grunfeld, A. Tom. *The Making of Modern Tibet.* Armonk, N.Y.: M. E. Sharpe, 1996.

Grunwald, Constantin de. *Tsar Nicholas I.* Translated by Brigit Patmore. New York: Macmillan, 1955.

Guérard, Albert. *France: A Modern History.* Ann Arbor: University of Michigan Press, 1959.

Guerra y Sanchez, Ramiro. *Guerra de los Diez Anos.* 2 vols. Havana: Cultural, 1950.

Guha, Ramachandra. *India after Gandhi: The History of the World's Largest Democracy.* New York: Ecco Press, 2007.

Guimaraes, Fernando Andresen. *The Origins of the Angolan Civil War: Foreign Intervention and Domestic Political Conflict.* Basingstoke, UK: Macmillan, 1998.

Gukiina, Peter M. *Uganda: A Case Study in African Political Development.* Notre Dame, Ind.: University of Notre Dame Press, 1972.

Gunaratna, Rohan. *Sri Lanka, a Lost Revolution? The Inside Story of the JVP.* Kandy, Sri Lanka: Institute of Fundamental Studies, 2001.

_____. *Sri Lanka's Ethnic Crisis and National Security.* Colombo: South Asian Network on Conflict Research, 1998.

Gunn, Geoffrey C. *East Timor and the U.N.: The Case for Intervention.* Trenton, N.J.: Red Sea Press, 1977.

Gunter, Michael M. "The KDP-PUK Conflict in Northern Iraq." *Middle East Journal* 50, no. 2 (Spring 1996): 225–241.

_____. "The Kurds Struggle for 'Kurdistan.'" In *Encyclopedia of Modern Ethnic Conflicts,* edited by Joseph R. Rudolph. Westport, Conn.: Greenwood Press, 2003.

Gupta, Shanteswarup. *British Relations with Bhutan.* Jaipur: Panchsheel Prabashan, 1974.

Gurr, Ted Robert. "Peoples against States: Ethnopolitical Conflict and the Changing World System." *International Security* 38 (1994): 347–378.

_____. *Peoples versus States, Minorities at Risk in the New Century.* Washington, D.C.: United States Institute of Peace Press, 2000.

_____. *Why Men Rebel.* Princeton, N.J.: Princeton University Press, 1970.

Gurr, Ted Robert, and Barbara Harff. *Ethnic Conflict in World Politics.* Boulder, Colo.: Westview Press, 1994.

Gurr, Ted Robert, Monty G. Marshall, and Deepa Khosla. *Peace and Violent Conflict 2001.* College Park, Md.: Center for International Development and Conflict Management, 2001.

Gurr, Ted Robert, and Phil Schrodt. "Updating and Expanding the Singer and Small Codes." Internal COW Memo. (September 30, 1988): 1–2.

Gurr, Ted Robert, with Charles Ruttenberg. *The Conditions of Civil Violence: First Test of a Causal Model.* Princeton, N.J.: Center for International Studies, 1967.

Guy, Jeff. *Destruction of the Zulu Kingdom: The Civil War in Zululand, 1879–1884.* London: Longman, 1979.

_____. *Remembering the Rebellion: The Zulu Uprising of 1906.* Scottsvile, South Africa: University of KwaZulu-Natal Press, 2006.

Gvosdev, Nikolas K. *Imperial Policies and Perspectives towards Georgia, 1760–1819.* Oxford: St. Antony's College, 2000.

Haas, Ernst B. *The Uniting of Europe.* Stanford, Calif.: Stanford University Press, 1958.

"Habib Bourguiba." *The Economist* (April 15, 2000).

Haglund, David G., and Allen Sens. "Kosovo and the Case of the (Not So) Free Riders: Portugal, Belgium, Canada, and Spain." In *Kosovo and the Challenges of Humanitarian Intervention,* edited by Albrecht Schnabel and Ramesh Thakur. New York: United Nations University Press, 2000.

Hagopian, Mark N. *The Phenomenon of Revolution.* New York: Dodd, Mead, 1974.

Haley, Edward P., and Lewis W. Snider, eds. *Lebanon Crisis.* Syracuse, N.Y.: Syracuse University Press, 1979.

Haliburton, Gordon. *Historical Dictionary of Lesotho.* African Historical Dictionaries, no. 10. Metuchen, N.J.: Scarecrow Press, 1977.

Hall, D. G. E. *A History of South East Asia.* New York: St. Martin's Press, 1968.

_____. *A History of South-East Asia.* 4th ed. New York: St. Martin's Press, 1981.

Hall, John Whitney. *Japan: From Prehistory to Modern Times.* Ann Arbor: University of Michigan Press, 1968.

Hall, Richard Andrew. "Theories of Collective Action and Revolution: Evidence from the Romanian Transition of December 1989." *Europe-Asia Studies* 52, no. 6 (September 2000): 1069–1093.

Hallett, Robin. *Africa to 1875.* Ann Arbor: University of Michigan Press, 1970.

Halm, Heinz. *The Empire of the Mahdi: The Rise of the Fatimids.* Translated from the German by Michael Bonner. New York: E. J. Brill, 1996.

Halpern, Jack. *South African Hostages*. Baltimore, Md.: Penguin, 1965.

Halstead, John P. "A Comparative Historical Study of Colonial Nationalism in Egypt and Morocco." *African Historical Studies* 2, no. 1 (1969): 85–100.

Hammer, Ellen. *The Struggle for Indochina*. Stanford, Calif.: Stanford University Press, 1954.

Hammer, Kenneth M. "Huks in the Philippines." In *Modern Guerrilla Warfare*, edited by F. Osanka. Glencoe, Ill.: Free Press, 1962.

Hammond, R. J. *Portugal and Africa 1815–1910*. Stanford, Calif.: Stanford University Press, 1966.

Hamnett, Brian. *A Concise History of Mexico*. Cambridge: Cambridge University Press, 1999.

_____. "Mexican Conservatives, Clericals, and Soldiers: the 'Traitor' Tomás Mejía through Reform and Empire, 1855–1867." *Bulletin of Latin American Research* 20, no. 2 (2001): 187–209.

Hane, Mikiso. *Japan: A Short History*. Oxford: Oneworld Publications, 2000.

Hanlon, Joseph. *Mozambique*. London: Zed Books, 1984.

Hanna, A. J., and K. A. Hanna. *Napoleon III and Mexico*. Chapel Hill: University of North Carolina Press, 1971.

Hanna, Henry B. *The Second Afghan War*. Vol. 3. London: Constable, 1910.

Harbottle, Thomas Benfield. *Dictionary of Battles from the Earliest Date to the Present Time*. London: S. Sonnenschein, 1904.

Harbottle, Thomas Benfield, and George Bruce. *Dictionary of Battles*. New York: Stein and Day, 1971.

Harcave, Sidney. *The Russian Revolution of 1905*. London: Collier-Macmillan, 1964.

Harden, Blaine. "Africa's Diamond Wars." *New York Times*. (Outlook 2001). www.nytimes.com/library/world/africa.

Harff, Barbara, and Ted Gurr. "Toward Empirical Theory of Genocides and Politicides: Identification and Measurement of Cases since 1945." *International Studies Quarterly* 3 (1988): 359–378.

Harrington, Michael. *Socialism Past and Future*. New York: Arcade Publishing, 1989.

Harris, Norman Dwight. "The New Moroccan Protectorate." *The American Journal of International Law* 7, no. 2 (April 1913): 245–267.

Harris, Walter. *France, Spain, and the Rif*. London: Arnold, 1927.

Harsgor, Michael. *Portugal in Revolution*. Beverly Hills, Calif.: Sage, 1976.

Hart, B. H. Liddell. *The Real War, 1914–1918*. Boston: Little, Brown, 1930.

Harvey, George E. *The Cambridge History of India*. Cambridge: Cambridge University Press, 1929.

Harvey, Robert. *Portugal: Birth of Democracy*. New York: St. Martin's Press, 1978.

Hasbrouck, Alfred. "The Argentine Revolution of 1930." *Hispanic American Historical Review* 18 (August 1938): 285–321.

_____. "The Conquest of the Desert." *Hispanic Historical Review* 15, no. 2 (May 1935): 195–228.

Haslip, Joan. *The Crown of Mexico*. New York: Holt, Rinehart and Winston, 1971.

Hasluck, E. L. *Foreign Affairs, 1919–1937*. New York: Macmillan, 1938.

Haumant, Emile. *La Formation de la Yugoslavie*. Paris: Bossard, 1930.

Headley, P. C. *The Life of Louis Kossuth*. Auburn, N.Y.: Derby and Miller, 1852.

Healy, David F. *Gunboat Diplomacy in the Wilson Era*. Madison: Wisconsin University Press, 1976.

Hearder, Harry, and Daniel P. Waley. *A Short History of Italy*. Cambridge: Cambridge University Press, 1977.

Hedges, Chris. *War Is a Force That Gives Us Meaning*. New York: Public Affairs, 2002.

Heflin, Jean. Unpublished notes about major power conflicts, memo to R. C. North, January 19, 1970.

Heidenrich, John G. "The Gulf War: How Many Iraqis Died?" *Foreign Policy*, no. 90 (Spring 1993): 108–125.

Heikal, Mohammed. *The Road to Ramadan*. London: Collins, 1975.

Heinl, Michael. *Written in Blood: The Story of the Haitian People 1492–1995*. Lanham, Md.: University Press of America, 1996.

Heinl, Robert. *Soldiers of the Sea*. Annapolis, Md.: U.S. Naval Institute, 1962.

Heitman, Francis B. *Historical Register and Dictionary of the United States Army*. Vol. 2. Washington, D.C.: GPO, 1903.

Helg, Aline. *Our Rightful Share: The Afro-Cuban Struggle for Equality, 1886–1912*. Chapel Hill: University of North Carolina Press, 1995.

Hellenic Resources Network. "Summary Data." www.hri.org/docs/nato, 2006.

Helmert, Heinz, and Hansjurgen Usczeck. *Bewaffnete Volkskampfe in Europa 1848/49*. Berlin: Militarverlag der Deutsche Demokratische Republik, 1973.

Helmreich, Ernst Christian. *The Diplomacy of the Balkan Wars, 1912–1913*. Cambridge, Mass.: Harvard University Press, 1938.

Henao, J. M,. and G. Arrubla. *History of Colombia*. Chapel Hill: University of North Carolina Press, 1938.

Henderson, Errol A. *Democracy and War: The End of an Illusion.* Boulder, Colo.: Lynne Rienner, 2002.

Henderson, Errol A., and J. David Singer. "'New Wars' and Rumors of 'New Wars.'" *International Interactions* 28 (2002): 165–190.

Hennessy, C. A. M. *The Federal Republic in Spain, 1868–1874.* Oxford: Clarendon Press, 1962.

Henriksen, Thomas H. *Revolution and Counterrevolution: Mozambique's War of Independence, 1964–1974.* Westport, Conn.: Greenwood Press, 1983.

Henriques, Robert. *100 Hours to Suez.* New York: Viking Press, 1957.

Hentea, Călin. *Brief Romanian History.* Lanham, Md.: Scarecrow Press, 2007.

Heppell, Muriel, and Frank Singleton. *Yugoslavia.* New York: Praeger, 1961.

Hernon, Ian. *Britain's Forgotten Wars.* Phoenix Mill, UK: Sutton, 2002.

Herold, Marc. W. "A Dossier on Civilian Victims of United States Aerial Bombing of Afghanistan: A Comprehensive Accounting (Revised)." 2002. www.cursor.org/stories/civilian_deaths.htm.

Herr, Michael. *Dispatches.* New York: Knopf, 1977.

Herring, George. *America's Longest War.* New York: Wiley, 1979.

Herring, Hubert. *A History of Latin America from the Beginnings to the Present.* New York: Knopf, 1966.

Herz, Monica, and João Pontes Nogueira. *Ecuador vs. Peru: Peacemaking Amid Rivalry.* Boulder, Colo.: Lynne Rienner, 2002.

Heuser, Beatrice, and Cyril Buffet. "Conclusions: Historical Myths and the Denials of Change." In *Haunted by History: Myths in International Relations,* edited by Cyril Buffet and Beatrice Heuser. Providence, R.I.: Berghahn Books, 1998, 259–274.

_____. "Introduction: Of Myths and Men." In *Haunted by History: Myths in International Relations,* edited by Cyril Buffet and Beatrice Heuser. Providence, R.I.: Berghahn Books, 1998, vii–x.

Hewitt, J. Joseph, Jonathan Wilkenfeld, and Ted Robert Gurr. *Peace and Conflict 2008.* Boulder, Colo.: Paradigm, 2008.

Hibbs, Douglas A. *Mass Political Violence: A Cross-National Causal Analysis.* New York: Wiley, 1973.

Higham, Robin, ed. *Civil Wars in the Twentieth Century.* Lexington: University Press of Kentucky, 1972.

Hill, Richard Leslie. *Egypt in the Sudan, 1820–1881.* Oxford: Oxford University Press, 1959.

_____. *On the Frontiers of Islam: Two Manuscripts Concerning the Sudan under Turco-Egyptian Rule, 1822–1841.* Oxford: Clarendon Press, 1970.

Hillman, James. *A Terrible Love of War.* New York: Penguin Press, 2004.

Hintrager, Oskar. *Sudwest Afrika in der Deutschen Zeit.* Munich: R. Oldenbourg, 1955.

Hiro, Dilip. *The Essential Middle East: A Comprehensive Guide.* New York: Basic Books, 2003.

_____. *The Middle East.* Phoenix: Oryx Press, 1996.

Hitti, Philip Khuri. *A History of the Arabs.* New York: St. Martin's Press, 1970.

_____. *Lebanon in History from the Earliest Times to the Present.* London: Macmillan, 1962.

Ho Han-Wen. *Chung-Eh Wai-Chiao Shih.* Shanghai: Chung Hua, 1935.

Ho Ping-Ti. *Studies on the Population of China, 1368–1952.* Cambridge, Mass.: Harvard University Press, 1959.

Hobbes, Thomas. *Leviathan.* Parts 1 and 2. New York: Liberal Arts Press, 1651; 1958.

Hochschild, Adam. *King Leopold's Ghost: A Story of Greed, Terror, and Heroism in Colonial Africa.* Boston: Houghton Mifflin, 1998.

Hodges, Tony. *Angola from Afro-Stalinism to Petro-Diamond Capitalism.* Bloomington: Indiana University Press, 2001.

_____. "How the MPLA Won in Angola." In *After Angola: The War over Southern Africa,* edited by Colin Legum and Tony Hodges. New York: Africana, 1978.

_____. *Western Sahara: Roots of a Desert War.* Chicago: Chicago Review, 1984.

Hoffman, Valerie J. "*Irbadi* Islam: An Introduction." Downloaded from http://www.uga.edu/islam/ibadis.html, 9/28/2008.

Hoisington, William A., Jr. *Lyautey and the French Conquest of Morocco.* New York: St. Martin's Press, 1995.

Holbrooke, Richard. *To End a War.* New York: Modern Library, 1999.

Holsti, Kal J. "International Theory and Domestic War in the Third World: The Limits of Relevance." Paper presented at the annual meeting of the International Studies Association, Toronto, March 18–22, 1997.

_____. *The State, War, and the State of War.* Cambridge: Cambridge University Press, 1996.

Holt, Edgar. *The Carlist Wars in Spain.* Chester Springs, Pa.: Dufour Editions, 1967.

Holt, P. M. *The Mahdist State in the Sudan, 1881–1898.* Oxford: Clarendon Press, 1958.

_____. *A Modern History of the Sudan, from the Funj Sultanate to the Present Day.* New York: Grove Press, 1961.

Holt, P.M., and M.W.Daly. *The History of the Sudan from the Coming of Islam to the Present Day.* 3rd ed. London: Weidenfeld and Nicolson, 1979.

_____. *The History of the Sudan from the Coming of Islam to the Present Day.* 5th ed. Harlow, Essex: Pearson Education, 2000.

Home Office. "Burundi Country Report." Country Information and Policy Unit (April 2004).

Hopkirk, Peter. *The Great Game: The Struggle for Empire in Central Asia.* New York: Kodansha, 1992.

Hordynski, Joseph. *History of the Late Polish Revolution.* Boston: Carter and Hendle, 1832.

Horne, Alastair. *A Savage War of Peace.* New York: Viking Press, 1977.

Horvath, William. "A Statistical Model for the Duration of Wars and Strikes." *Behavioral Science* 13, no. 1 (January 1968): 18–28.

Horvath, William, and Caxton C. Foster. "Stochastic Models of War Alliances." *Journal of Conflict Resolution* 7, no. 2 (June 1963): 110–116.

Hourani, Albert. *A History of the Arab Peoples.* Cambridge, Mass.: Belknap Press, 1991.

Howard, Michael. *The Franco-Prussian War.* London: Rupert Hart-Davis, 1962.

Howe, George Frederick. "Garcia Moreno's Efforts to Unite Ecuador and France." *Hispanic American Historical Review* 16, no. 2 (May 1936): 257–262.

Howe, Herbert. "Lessons of Liberia: ECOMOG and Regional Peacekeeping." In *Nationalism and Ethnic Conflict,* edited by Michael E. Brown, Owen R. Coté Jr., Sean M. Lynn-Jones, and Steven E. Miller. Cambridge, Mass.: MIT Press, 1997.

Hoyt, Edwin P. *Army without a Country.* New York: Macmillan, 1967.

Hozier, Henry Montague. *The Russo-Turkish War.* 2 vols. London: W. Mackenzie, 1878.

_____. *The Seven Weeks' War.* 2 vols. Philadelphia: Lippincott, 1867.

Hrushevsky, Michael. *A History of the Ukraine.* New Haven, Conn.: Yale University Press, 1941.

Hu-DeHart, Evelyn. *Yaqui Resistance and Survival: The Struggle for Land and Autonomy, 1821–1920.* Madison: University of Wisconsin Press, 1984.

Hughes, H. Stuart. *Contemporary Europe: A History.* Englewood Cliffs, N.J.: Prentice-Hall, 1961.

Hughes, John. *The End of Sukarno.* London: Angus and Robertson, 1967.

Human Rights Watch. "Afghanistan: Crisis of Impunity." *Human Rights Watch* 13, no. 3 (July 2001).

_____. *Angola: Arms Trade and Violations of the Laws of War since the 1992 Elections.* New York: Human Rights Watch, 1994.

_____. *Angola: Violations of the Laws of War by Both Sides.* New York: Human Rights Watch, April 1989.

_____. "Civilian Deaths in the NATO Air Campaign." (2000). www.hrw.org/reports/2000/nato/natbm200-01.htm.

_____. "Ituri: Blodiest Corner of Congo." (2003). www.hrw.org/campaigns/congo/ituri/ituri.htm.

_____. "Pentagon Report Whitewashes Civilian Deaths in Yugoslavia." In *HRW World Report.* (2000). www.hrw.org/press/2000.

_____. "Rwanda, Observing the Rules of War?" *Human Rights Watch* 13, no. 8 (December 2001).

_____. "Somalia, Human Developments." (1994). www.hrw.org/reports/1994.

_____. "Under Orders: War Crimes in Kosovo–2. Background." (2001). www.hrw.org/reports/2001/kosovo/underword-01.htm.

Human Security Centre, *Human Security Report 2005: War and Peace in the 21st Century.* Oxford: Oxford University Press, 2005.

Hume, Martin A. S. *Modern Spain, 1788–1898.* London: Putnam, 1900.

Hunefeldt, Christine. *A Brief History of Peru.* New York: Facts on File, 2004.

Hunt, M. H. *Ideology and U.S. Foreign Policy.* New Haven, Conn.: Yale University Press, 1987.

Hunt, Steve. "Rethinking a Model for Peace in Guatemala." *Reports, Science from the Developing World* (September 20, 2002).

Huntington, Samuel. "The Clash of Civilizations." *Foreign Affairs* 72 (1993): 56–73.

_____. "The Clash of Civilizations?" In *Classic Readings of International Relations,* edited by Phil Williams, Donald Goldstein, and Jay Shafritz. Fort Worth, Texas: Harcourt Brace College, 1999, 633–652.

_____. "Patterns of Violence in World Politics." In *Changing Patterns of Military Politics,* edited by Samuel Huntington. New York: Free Press, 1962.

Hupchick, Dennis P. *The Balkans: From Constantinople to Communism.* New York: Palgrave, 2002.

Hupchick, Dennis, and Harold Cox. *The Palgrave Concise Historical Atlas of Eastern Europe.* Rev. and updated ed. New York: Palgrave, 2001.

Hurd, Douglas. *The Arrow War.* London: Collins, 1967.

Hutchinson, Sharon E. "A Curse from God? Religious and Political Dimensions of the Post-1991 Rise of Ethnic Violence in South Sudan." *The Journal of Modern African Studies* 39, no. 4 (2001): 307–331.

Huth, Paul. *Extended Deterrence and the Prevention of War.* New Haven, Conn.: Yale University Press, 1988.

Huttenback, Robert A. *British Relations with Sind, 1799–1843.* Berkeley: University of California Press, 1962.

Hyamson, Albert M. *Palestine under the Mandate.* London: Methuen, 1950.

Ignotus, Paul. *Hungary.* London: Ernest Benn, 1972.

Ikuhiko, Hata. "The Japanese-Soviet Confrontation." In *Deterrent Diplomacy,* edited by James W. Morely. New York: Columbia University Press, 1976.

Iliffe, John. "The Organization of the Maji Maji Rebellion." *The Journal of African History* 8, no. 3 (1967): 495–512.

Independent International Commission on Kosovo. *The Kosovo Report.* Oxford: Oxford University Press, 2000.

India Ministry of Information and Broadcasting. *Defending Kashmir.* Dehli: Ministry of Information and Broadcasting, 1949.

Information Please Almanac. New York: McGraw-Hill, 1972.

Ingrams, Doreen, and Leila Ingrams, eds. *Records of Yemen, 1798–1960.* Vol 3. Slough: Archive Editions, 1993.

Ingrams, Harold. *The Yemen.* London: John Murray, 1963.

Institut Francais de Polemologie. "Periodicite et Intensite des Actions de Guerre de 1200 á 1945." *Guerre et Paix* 2 (1968): 20–32.

International Crisis Group. "Aceh: A Slim Chance for Peace." *Indonesia Briefing* (March 27, 2002): 1–15.

_____. "Liberia Unravelling." (August 2002). www.crisisweb.org/projects.

_____. "Rwanda/Uganda: A Dangerous War of Nerves." *Africa Briefing* (December 21, 2001): 1–15.

International Institute for Strategic Studies. "International Terrorism." Armed Conflict Database. (2003). http://acd.iiss.org/armedconflict.

_____. "Sri Lanka (LTTE)." Armed Conflict Database. (2006). http://acd.iiss.org/armedconflict.

International Rescue Committee. "The IRC in Democratic Republic of Congo." (December 2004). www.theirc.org/drc.

"Iraq Body Count." (2005). www.iraqbodycount.net.

Iraq Coalition Casualty Count. "Afghan Casualty Count." www.icasualties.org.

_____. "Iraq Coalition Casualty Count." www.icasualties.org, 2008.

Ireland, Gordon. *Boundaries, Possessions and Conflicts in South America.* Cambridge, Mass.: Harvard University, 1938.

IRIN (Integrated Regional Information Networks). "Burundi: IRIN Focus on Rebel Movements." UN Office for the Coordination of Humanitarian Affairs (November 2001).

_____. "DRC: IRIN Focus on the Hemda-Lendu Conflict." www.irinnews.org, 11/15/1999.

_____. "DRC: Ituri Conflict Linked to Illegal Exploitation of Natural Resources." UN Office for the Coordination of Humanitarian Affairs (September 3, 2004).

_____. "DRC: Who's Who in Ituri–Militia Organizations, Leaders." UN Office for the Coordination of Humanitarian Affairs (April 29, 2005).

_____. "West Africa Update 224." UN Office for the Coordination of Humanitarian Affairs (June 6–8, 1998).

Ironside, Edmond. *Archangel, 1918–1919.* London: Constable, 1953.

Isaacman, Allen. *Mozambique.* Boulder, Colo.: Westview Press, 1983.

Isaacs, Arnold R., Gordon Handy, Macalister Brown, and the Editors of Boston Publishing Company. *Pawns of War: Cambodia and Laos.* Boston: Boston Publishing Company, 1987.

Isaacs, Harold R. *The Tragedy of the Chinese Revolution.* Stanford, Calif.: Stanford University Press, 1961.

Isby, David C. *War in a Distant Country, Afghanistan: Invasion and Resistance.* London: Arms and Armour, 1989.

Ismael, Tareq Y., and Jacqueline S. Ismael. *PRD Yemen, Politics, Economic, and Society.* London: Frances Pinter, 1986.

Isono, Fujiko. "Soviet Russia and the Mongolian Revolution of 1921." *Past and Present,* no. 83 (May 1979): 116–140.

Israel Office of Information. *Israel's Struggle for Peace.* New York: Israel Office of Information, 1960.

Italy, Comitato per la Documentazione Dell'Opera Dell'Italia in Africa. *Italia in Africa.* Rome: Istituto Poligrafico Dello Stato, 1952.

Iyob, Ruth, and Gilbert M. Khadiagala. *Sudan, the Elusive Quest for Peace.* Boulder, Colo.: Lynne Rienner, 2006.

Jackson, Paul. "Legacy of Bitterness: Insurgency in North West Rwanda." *Small Wars and Insurgencies* 15, no. 1 (Spring 2004): 19–37.

_____. "The March of the Lord's Resistance Army: Greed or Grievance in Northern Uganda?" *Small Wars and Insurgencies* 13, no. 3 (Autumn 2002): 29–52.

Jacques, Hubert. *L'aventure Riffaine et Ses Dessous Politiques.* Paris: Bossard, 1927.

Jae-gon, Cho. "The Connection of the Sino-Japanese War and the Peasant War of 1984." *Korea Journal* (Winter 1994): 45–58.

James, Lawrence. *The Savage Wars: British Campaigns in Africa, 1870–1920.* New York: St. Martin's Press, 1985.

Jane's Defense. "Kosovo: Background to Crisis. (March 1999)." 1999. www.janes.com/defence/news/kosovo/misc990301_03_n.shtml.

Jaques, Tony. *Battles and Sieges: A Guide to 8,500 Battles from Antiquity through the Twenty-First Century.* Vols. 1–3. Westport, Conn.: Greenwood Press, 2007.

Jardine, Douglas. *The Mad Mullah of Somaliland.* London: Herbert Jenkins, 1923.

_____. *Mad Mullah of Somaliland.* Westport, Conn.: Greenwood Publishing Group, 1986.

Jardine, Matthew. *East Timor: Genocide in Paradise.* Tucson, Ariz.: Odonian Press, 1999.

Jasci, Oscar. *Revolution and Counter-Revolution in Hungary.* New York: Howard Fertig, 1969.

Jen Yu-Wen. *The Taiping Revolutionary Movement.* New Haven, Conn.: Yale University Press, 1973.

Jenkins, Gwilym M., and J. G. Watts. *Spectral Analysis and its Applications.* San Francisco: Holden Day, 1968.

Jenks, Robert D. *Insurgency and Social Disorder in Guizhou: The "Miao" Rebellion, 1854–1873.* Honolulu: University of Hawaii Press, 1994.

Jennings, Lawrence C. "French Diplomacy and the First Schleswig-Holstein Crisis." *French Historical Studies* 7, no. 2 (Autumn 1971): 204–225.

Jensen, Amy Elizabeth. *Guatemala.* New York: Exposition, 1955.

_____. *The Makers of Mexico.* Philadelphia: Dorrance, 1953.

Jochmus, Augustus. *The Syrian War and the Decline of the Ottoman Empire.* 2 vols. Berlin: Albert Cohn, 1883.

Joestin, Joachim. *The New Algeria.* Chicago: Follett, 1964.

Johnson, Chalmers. "American Militarism and Blowback." In *Masters of War: Militarism and Blowback in the Era of the American Empire,* edited by Carl Boggs. New York: Routledge, 2003, 113.

Johnson, Chalmers. *Revolution and the Social System.* Stanford, Calif.: Hoover Institution Press, 1964.

Johnson, Donald. *The Northern Expedition.* Honolulu: Hawaii University Press, 1976.

Johnson, Douglas H. *The Root Causes of Sudan's Civil Wars.* Bloomington: Indiana University Press, 2003.

Johnson, Richard A. *The Mexican Revolution of Ayutla, 1854–1855.* Rock Island, Ill.: Augustana College Library, 1939.

Johnston, Harry H. *A History of the Colonization of Africa by Alien Races.* Cambridge: Cambridge University Press, 1913.

Johnston, Robert. *The Roman Theocracy and the Republic.* London: Macmillan, 1901.

Joireman, Sandra Fullerton. "Ethiopia and Eritrea: Border War." In *History behind the Headlines,* vol. 1, edited by Sonia G. Benson, Nancy Matuszak, and Meghan Appel O'Meara. Detroit: Gale Group, 2001.

Jolliffe, Jill. *East Timor: Nationalism and Colonialism.* St. Lucia, Quebec: University of Queensland Press, 1978.

Jones, Adam. "Kosovo: Orders of Magnitude." *IDEA–A Journal of Social Issues* 5, no. 1 (2000). www.ideajournal.com/articles.php?Id=24.

Jones, Daniel, Stuart A. Bremer, and J. David Singer. "Militarized Interstate Disputes, 1816–1992: Rationale, Coding Rules, and Empirical Patterns." *Conflict Management and Peace Science* 15, no. 2 (1996): 163–213.

Jones, F. C. *Japan's New Order in East Asia.* London: Oxford University Press, 1954.

Jones, Ronald D. "Construct Mapping." Kansas City: University of Missouri, June 1966. Mimeo.

Jordan, Karl G. *Der Aegyptisch-Turkische Krieg, 1839.* Zurich: Borsig, 1923.

Jorga, N. *Geschichte des Osmanischen Reiches.* 5 vols. Gotha: Justus Perthes, 1913.

Judah, Tim. *Kosovo: War and Revenge.* New Haven, Conn.: Yale University Press, 2000.

Jutikkala, Eino. *A History of Finland.* New York: Praeger, 1962.

Kaas, Albert. *Bolshevism in Hungary.* London: Grant Richards, 1931.

Kadian, Rajesh. *The Kashmir Tangle: Issues and Options.* Boulder, Colo.: Westview Press, 1993.

Kahin, George. *Nationalism and Revolution in Indonesia.* Ithaca, N.Y.: Cornell University Press, 1952.

Kahin, George, and John Lewis. *The United States in Vietnam.* New York: Dial, 1969.

Kahin, George McTurnan. *Nationalism and Revolution in Indonesia.* Ithaca, N.Y.: Southeast Asia Programs Publications, Cornell University, 2003.

Kajima, Morinosuka. *The Diplomacy of Japan, 1894–1922.* Vol. 1. Tokyo: Kajima Institute of International Peace, 1978.

Kalaw, Teodoro M. *The Philippine Revolution.* Manila: Manila Book, 1925.

Kaldor, Mary. *New and Old Wars: Organized Violence in a Global Era.* Stanford, Calif.: Stanford University Press, 1999.

Kalyvas, Stathis N. *The Logic of Violence in Civil War.* New York: Cambridge University Press, 2006.

Kann, Robert A. *The Multinational Empire: Nationalism and Reform in the Hapsburg Monarchy, 1848–1918.* 2 vols. New York: Octagon Books, 1970.

Kaplan, Sam. "Documenting History, Historicizing Documentation: French Military Officials' Ethnological Reports on Cilicia." *Comparative Studies in Society and History* 44, no. 2 (April 2002): 344–369.

Karatnycky, A., ed. *Freedom in the World, 2000–2001: The Annual Survey of Political Rights and Civil Liberties.* Boston: Freedom House, 2001.

Karatnycky, A., F. House, A. Piano, and Freedom House Survey Team, eds. *Freedom in the World: The Annual Survey of Political Rights and Civil Liberties, 2001–2002.* Piscataway, N.J.: Transaction, 2002.

Karnes, Thomas L. *The Failure of Union: Central America 1824–1960.* Chapel Hill: University of North Carolina Press, 1961.

Karnow, Stanley. *Vietnam: A History.* New York: Viking Press, 1983.

Karpat, Kemal. "The Transformation of the Ottoman State, 1789–1908." *International Journal of Middle East Studies* 3, no. 3 (July 1972): 243–281.

Kaszeta, Daniel J. "Lithuanian Resistance to Foreign Occupation, 1940–1952." *Lituanus* 34, no. 3 (1988): 5–32.

Katjavivi, Peter H. *A History of the Resistance in Namibia.* London: James Currey; Addis Ababa: OAU; Paris: UNESCO Press, 1988.

Katsiaficas, George. "Conclusion: The Real Axis of Evil." In *Masters of War: Militarism and Blowback in the Era of the American Empire,* edited by Carl Boggs. New York: Routledge, 2003, 343–356.

Katumba-Wamala, Edward. "The National Resistance Army (NRA) as a Guerrilla Force." *Small Wars and Insurgencies* 11, no. 3 (Winter 2000): 160–171.

Kaufman, Stuart J. *Modern Hatreds: The Symbolic Politics of Ethnic War.* Ithaca, N.Y.: Cornell University Press, 2001.

_____. "Spiraling to Ethnic War: Elites, Masses and Moscow in Moldova's Civil War." In *Nationalism and Ethnic Conflict,* edited by Michael E. Brown, Owen R. Coté Jr., Sean M. Lynn-Jones, and Steven E. Miller. Cambridge, Mass.: MIT Press, 1997.

Kaul, B. M. *The Untold Story.* Bombay: Allied, 1967.

Kecskemeti, Paul. *Strategic Surrender.* Stanford, Calif.: Stanford University Press, 1958.

Keegan, John. *A History of Warfare.* New York: Knopf, 1993.

Keegan, John A., ed. *Atlas of the Second World War.* London: HarperCollins, 1997.

Keep Military Museum. "The Malabar Campaign (Moplah Rebellion)." Dorchester, UK: Keep Military Museum, 2000.

Keesing's Contemporary Archives. London. Multiple years.

Keesing's Record of World Events (formerly *Keesing's Contemporary Archive: Weekly Diary of World Events,* and published from 1931 to the present with continuously running page numbers): 42936, 42997, 43357, 43576, and 43628.

Keesing's Record of World Events. "Afghanistan." (October 2001). 44503–44504.

_____. "Afghanistan: Military Developments." (1981). www.keesings.com.

_____. "Developments in Bosnia-Hercegovina." (March 1992). 38832.

Kegley, Charles W., ed. *The Long Postwar Peace.* New York: HarperCollins, 1991.

Kegley, Charles, and Eugene Wittkopf. *World Politics: Trend and Transformation.* New York: St. Martin's Press, 1981.

Keller, Helen Rex. *A Dictionary of Dates.* 2 vols. New York: Macmillan, 1934.

Kelly, J. B. *Britain and the Persian Gulf: 1795–1880.* Oxford: Oxford University Press, 1968.

Kelly, Kathy. *Other Lands Have Dreams: From Baghdad to Pekin Prison.* Petrolia, Calif.: CounterPunch, 2005.

Kende, Istvan. "Twenty-Five Years of Local Wars." *Journal of Peace Research* 8 (1971): 5–22.

_____. "Wars of Ten Years (1967–1976)." *Journal of Peace Research* 15 (1978): 227–241.

Kennan, George F. *The Decision to Intervene.* Princeton, N.J.: Princeton University Press, 1958.

_____. *Russia and the West under Lenin and Stalin.* Boston: Little, Brown, 1960.

Kennedy, J. *A History of Malaya, A.D. 1400–1959.* London: Macmillan, 1962.

Kennedy, Paul. *The Rise and Fall of the Great Powers: Economic Change and Military Conflict from 1500 to 2000.* Jefferson, N.Y.: Random House, 1987.

Kenney, George. "The Bosnia Calculation: How Many Have Died? Not Nearly as Many as Some Would Have You Think." *The New York Times Magazine,* April 23, 1995. From the Balkan Repository Project.

Kent, Raymond. *From Madagascar to the Malagasy Republic.* Westport, Conn.: Greenwood Press, 1976.

Keohane, Robert O., and Joseph S. Nye Jr. *Power and Interdependence: World Politics in Transition.* 3rd ed. New York: Addison Wesley Longman, 2000.

Kerkvliet, Bernard J. *The Huk Rebellion.* Berkeley: University of California Press, 1977.

Kerr, George H. *Formosa Betrayed.* Boston: Houghton Mifflin, 1965.

_____. *Formosa: Licensed Revolution and the Home Rule Movement, 1895–1945.* Honolulu: University Press of Hawaii, 1974.

Kessel, William B., and Robert Wooster, eds. *Encyclopedia of Native American Wars and Warfare.* New York: Facts on File, 2005.

Kessler, Glenn. "Sudanese Rebels Sign Peace Plan for Darfur." *Washington Post,* May 6, 2006, A01.

Keurs, Pieter ter, ed. *Colonial Collections Revisted.* Leiden: CNWSPublications, 2007.

Keyte, J. C. *The Passing of the Dragon.* London: Carey Press, 1925.

Khadduri, Majid. *Independent Iraq, 1932–1958.* London: Oxford University Press, 1960.

Khalfin, N. A. *Russia's Policy in Central Asia: 1857–1868.* London: Central Asian Research Centre, 1964.

Khan, Mohammed Anwar. *England, Russia and Central Asia, 1857–1878.* Penshawar, Pakistan: University Book Agency, 1963.

Khobe, Mitikishe Maxwell. "The Evolution and Conduct of ECOMOG Operations in West Africa." *Boundaries of Peace Support Operations,* monograph no. 44 (February 2000).

Khoi, Le Thanh. *Le Viet-nam.* Paris: Editions de Minuit, 1955.

Kielstra, E. B. *Beschrijving Van Den Atjeh-Oorlog.* 3 vols. Gravenhage, Netherlands: Van Cleef, 1883.

Kiernan, E. V. *British Diplomacy in China, 1880–1885.* Cambridge: Cambridge University Press, 1939.

Kiernan, V. G. *The Revolution of 1854 in Spanish History.* Oxford: Clarendon Press, 1966.

Kikuoka, Michael. *The Changkufeng Incident.* New York: University Press of America, 1988.

Kim, C. I. Eugene, and Han-Kyo Kim. *Korea and the Politics of Imperialism 1876–1910.* Berkeley: University of California Press, 1967.

Kimche, Jon, and David Kimche. *A Clash of Destinies.* New York: Praeger, 1960.

King, Bolton. *A History of Italian Unity.* Vol. 1. London: James Nisbet, 1899.

King, Charles. *The Ghost of Freedom: A History of the Caucasus.* Oxford: Oxford University Press, 2008.

_____. *The Moldovans: Romania, Russia, and the Politics of Culture.* Studies of Nationalities. Stanford, Calif.: Hoover Institution Press, 2000.

Kingsbury, Damien. "The Free Aceh Movement: Islam and Democratisation." *Journal of Contemporary Asia* 37, no. 2 (2007): 166–189.

Kiritzesco, Constantin. *La Roumanie dans la Guerre Mondiale, 1916–1919.* Paris: Payot, 1934.

Kirk, Donald. "Cambodia 1973: Year of the 'Bomb Halt.'" *Asian Survey* 14, no. 1, A Survey of Asia in 1973: Part I (January 1974): 89–100.

Kirkby, Dianne. "Colonial Policy and Native Depopulation in California and New South Wales 1770–1840." *Ethnohistory* 31, no. 1 (Winter 1984): 1–16.

Kirkpatrick, Frederick A. *A History of the Argentine Republic.* Cambridge: Cambridge University Press, 1931.

_____. *Latin America.* New York: Macmillan, 1939.

Kisirwani, Maroun. "Foreign Interference and Religious Animosity in Lebanon." *Journal of Contemporary History* 15, no. 4 (October 1980): 685–700.

Kissinger, Henry. *A World Restored.* Boston: Houghton Mifflin, 1957.

Klarén, Peter Flindell. *Peru: Society and Nationhood in the Andes.* New York: Oxford University Press, 2000.

Klingberg, Frank L. *Historical Study of War Casualties.* Washington, D.C.: United States, Secretary of War Office, 1945.

_____. "Predicting the Termination of War: Battle Casualties and Population Losses." *Journal of Conflict Resolution* 10, no. 2 (June 1966): 129–171.

Knatchbull-Hugessen, C. M. *The Political Evolution of the Hungarian Nation.* London: National Review Office, 1908.

Kneisler, Pat. "Operation Enduring Freedom Fatalities." (2005). Icasualties. http://icasualties.org/oif.

Knight, Ian. *The Anatomy of the Zulu Army.* Mechanicsburg, Pa.: Stackpole Books, 1995.

_____. *Great Zulu Battles 1838–1906.* London: Arms and Armour Press, 1998.

_____. *Great Zulu Battles 1838–1906.* Edison, N.J.: Book Sales, 2003.

_____. *Zulu War 1879: Twilight of a Warrior Nation.* London: Osprey, 1992.

Knightly, Phillip. *The First Casualty.* New York: Harcourt, 1975.

Koebel, William Henry. *Uruguay.* New York: Scribner's, 1915.

Kohn, George Childs. *Dictionary of Wars.* New York: Checkmark Books, 1986, 1999.

_____. *Dictionary of Wars.* 3rd ed. New York: Checkmark Books, 2007.

Kolinski, Charles J. *Independence or Death.* Gainesville: University of Florida Press, 1965.

Korbel, Josef. *Danger in Kashmir.* Princeton, N.J.: Princeton University Press, 1959.

Korea Past and Present. Seoul: Kwangmyong, 1972.

Korean Institute of Military History. *The Korean War: Volume 1.* Lincoln: University of Nebraska Press, 2000.

Korean National Comission for UNESCO. *Korea Journal* 34, no. 4 (1994).

Korean Overseas Information Service. *A Handbook of Korea.* Seoul: Seoul International Publishing House, 1987.

Kostakos, Georgios. "The Southern Flank: Italy, Greece, Turkey." In *Kosovo and the Challenges of Humanitarian*

Intervention, edited by Albrecht Schnabel and Ramesh Thakur. New York: United Nations University Press, 2000.

Kostiner, Joseph. *The Making of Saudi-Arabia 1916–1936*. New York: Oxford University Press, 1993.

Kostiner, Joseph, ed. *Middle East Monarchies: The Challenge of Modernity*. Boulder, Colo.: Lynne Rienner, 2000.

Kosut, Hal, ed. *Indonesia: The Sukarno Years*. New York: Facts on File, 1967.

Kour, Z. H. *The History of Aden 1839–72*. Totowa, N.J.: Frank Cass, 1981.

Kraay, Hendrik. "'As Terrifying as Unexpected': The Bahian Sabinda, 1837–1838." *Hispanic American Historical Review* 72, no. 4 (November 1992): 501–527.

Kriel, Lizé. "Same War, Different Story: A Century's Writing on the Boer-Hananwa War of 1893." *Journal of Southern African Studies* 30, no. 4 (December 2004): 789–810.

Kruger, Paul. *The Memoirs of Paul Kruger: Four Times President of the South African Republic*. New York: Century, 1902.

Kubijovyč, Volodymyr E. *Ukraine: A Concise Encyclopedia*. Vol. 1. Toronto: University of Toronto Press, 1963.

Kumar, Krishna. *Women and Civil War: Impact, Organizations, and Action*. Boulder, Colo.: Lynne Rienner, 2001.

Kuneralp, Sinan. "Military Operations during the 1904–1905 Uprising in the Yemen." *Studies on Turkish-Arab Relations* 2 (1987): 63–70.

Kuo, P. C. *A Critical Study of the First Anglo-Chinese War*. Shanghai: Commercial Press, 1935.

Kuodytė, Dalia, and Roskas Tracevskis. *The Unknown War: Anti-Soviet Resistence in Lithuania in 1944–1953*. Vilnius: Genocide and Resistance Research Centre of Lithuania, 2006.

Kup, A. P. *Sierra Leone: A Concise History*. London: David and Charles, 1975.

Kurlantzick, Joshua. "Tilting at Dominoes: America and Al Qaeda in Southeast Asia." *Current History* 101, no. 659 (December 2002): 421–427.

Kutschera, Chris. "Mad Dreams of Independence: The Kurds of Turkey and the PKK." *Middle East Report*, no. 189 (July–August 1994): 12–15.

La Foy, Margaret. *The Chaco Dispute and the League of Nations*. Bryn Mawr, Pa.: Bryn Mawr Press, 1946.

La Porte, Pablo. "Civil-Military Relations in the Spanish Protectorate in Morocco: The Road to the Spanish Civil War, 1912–1936." *Armed Forces & Society* 30, no. 2 (Winter 2004): 203–226.

Lacey, Robert. *The Kingdom of Arabia and the House of Saud*. New York: Avon, 1981.

Lacina, Bethany, and Nils Petter Gleditsch. "Monitoring Trends in Global Combat: A New Dataset of Battle Deaths." *European Journal of Population* 21, nos. 2–3 (2005): 135–166.

Lacina, Bethany, Nils Petter Gleditsch, and Bruce Russett. "The Declining Risk of Death in Battle." *International Studies Quarterly* 50 (2006): 673–680.

LaFeber, Walter. *The American Age: United States Foreign Policy at Home and Abroad since 1750*. New York: W. W. Norton, 1989.

_____. *The American Age: United States Foreign Policy at Home and Abroad Volume 1 to 1920*. 2nd ed. New York: W. W. Norton, 1994.

_____. *Inevitable Revolutions: The United States in Central America*. New York: W. W. Norton, 1983, 1993.

Laffin, John. *The War of Desperation: Lebanon 1982–1985*. London: Osprey, 1985.

L'Afrique Francaise 36, no. 6 (June 1926): 327–337.

Laitman, Leon. *Tunisia Today, Crisis in North Africa*. New York: Citadael Press, 1954.

Laizer, Sheri. *Martyrs, Traitors and Patriots: Kurdistan After the Gulf War*. London: Zed Books, 1996.

Lake, David A., and Donald Rothchild, eds. *The International Spread of Ethnic Conflict*. Princeton, N.J.: Princeton University Press, 1998.

_____. "Spreading Fear: The Genesis of Transnational Ethnic Conflict." In *The International Spread of Ethnic Conflict*, edited by David A. Lake and Donald Rothchild. Princeton, N.J.: Princeton University Press, 1998, 3–32.

Lamb, Alastair. *Britain and Chinese Central Asia: The Road to Lhasa, 1767 to 1905*. London: Routledge and Kegan Paul, 1960.

_____. *The Kashmir Problem*. New York: Praeger, 1967.

_____. "Sinkiang in the Twentieth Century." In *Central Asia*, edited by G. Hambly. New York: Delacorte, 1969.

Lampe, John R. *Yugoslavia as History: Twice There Was a Country*. 2nd ed. Cambridge: Cambridge University Press, 2000.

Lancaster, Donald. *The Emancipation of French Indochina*. London: Oxford University Press, 1961.

Landau, Rom. *Moroccan Drama*. San Francisco: American Academy of Asian Studies, 1956.

Landen, Robert G. *Oman since 1856*. Princeton, N.J.: Princeton University Press, 1967.

Langer, Paul F. "Laos: Search for Peace in the Midst of War." *Asian Survey* 8, no. 1, A Survey of Asia in 1967: Part I (January 1968): 80–86.

Langer, Paul F., and Joseph J. Zasloff. *North Vietnam and Laos*. Cambridge, Mass.: Harvard University Press, 1970.

Langer, William L. *European Alliances and Alignments.* New York: Knopf, 1931.

_____. *Political and Social Upheaval, 1832–1852.* New York: Harper, 1969.

Langer, William L., ed. *An Encyclopedia of World History.* Boston: Houghton Mifflin, 1948, 1952.

Laserson, Max M. "The Recognition of Latvia." *American Journal of International Law* 37, no. 2 (April 1943): 233–247

Lasswell, Harold, and Abraham Kaplan. *Power and Society.* New Haven, Conn.: Yale University Press, 1950.

Latimer, Elizabeth Wormeley. *Russia and Turkey in the Nineteenth Century.* Chicago: A. C. McClurg, 1903.

Latvian Library. "The Story of Latvia: The First World War, Struggle for Independence." www.latvians.com/en/readings, 2008.

Latvian War Museum. "Research about Latvian War of Independence." Personal communication, March 12, 2008.

Layne, Christopher. "Kant or Cant: The Myth of the Democratic Peace." In *Theories of War and Peace,* edited by Michael E. Brown, Owen R. Coté Jr., Sean M. Lynn-Jones, and Steven E. Miller. Cambridge, Mass.: MIT Press, 1999, 176–220.

Laytano, Dante De. *Historie da Republica Rio Grandense.* Porto Alegre, Brazil: Livraria do Globo, 1936.

Le Gouhir y Rodas, Jose. *Historia de la Republic del Ecuador.* Quito: Prensa Catolica, 1925.

Le Thiinh. *Le Viet-Nam.* Paris: Editions de Minuit, 1955.

Le Vine, Victor T. *The Cameroons from Mandate to Independence.* Berkeley: University of California Press, 1964.

Lea, David. *A Political Chronology of Africa.* London: European Publications, 2001.

Leary, William M. "The CIA and the 'Secret War' in Laos: The Battle for Skyline Ridge, 1971–1972." *The Journal of Military History* 59, no. 3 (July 1995): 505–517.

Lebow, Richard Ned. *Between Peace and War: The Nature of International Crisis.* Baltimore, Md.: Johns Hopkins University Press, 1984.

_____. "Miscalculation in the South Atlantic: The Origins of the Falklands War." In *Psychology and Deterrence,* edited by Robert Jervis, Richard Ned Lebow, Janice Gross Stein, Patrick M. Morgan, and Jack L. Snyder. Baltimore, Md.: Johns Hopkins University Press, 1985.

Leckie, Robert. *Conflict.* New York: Putnam, 1962.

Lee, J. S. "The Periodic Recurrence of Internecine Wars in China." *China Journal* 14, no. 3 (March 1931): 111–115, 159–162.

Lee, Ki-Baik. *A New History of Korea.* Cambridge, Mass.: Harvard University Press, 1984.

_____. *A New History of Korea.* Translated by E. J. Schultz. Cambridge, Mass.: Harvard University Press, 2007.

Lee, Ta-Ling. *Foundations of the Chinese Revolution.* New York: St. John's University Press, 1970.

Leezenberg, Michiel. "Chapter 12: The Anfal Operations in Iraqi Kurdistan." In *A Century of Genocide: Critical Essays and Eyewitness Accounts,* edited by Samuel Totten, William S. Parsons, and Israel W. Charny. New York: Routledge, 2004.

Lefebvre, Jeffrey A. "Middle East Conflicts and Middle Level Power Intervention in the Horn of Africa." *Middle East Journal* 50, no. 3 (Summer 1996): 387–404.

Lefever, Ernest W. "Peacekeeping by Outsiders: The U.N. Congo Expeditionary Force." In *Civil Wars in the Twentieth Century,* edited by Robin Higham. Lexington: University Press of Kentucky, 1972.

Legum, Colin. "Angola and the Horn of Africa." In *Diplomacy of Power,* edited by Stephen S. Kaplan. Washington, D.C.: Brookings Institution Press, 1981.

_____. "The Role of the Big Powers." In *After Angola: The War over Southern Africa,* edited by Colin Legum and Tony Hodges. New York: Africana, 1978.

Lei, K. N., ed. *Information and Opinion Concerning the Japanese Invasion of Manchuria and Shanghai from Sources Other Than Chinese.* Shanghai: Shanghai Bar Association, 1932.

Leifer, Michael. "The International Dimensions of the Cambodian Conflict." *International Affairs (Royal Institute of International Affairs 1944–)* 51, no. 4 (October 1975): 531–543.

Leighton, Marian Kirsch. "Perspectives on the Vietnam-Cambodia Border Conflict." *Asian Survey,* Vol. 19, no. 5 (May 1978): 448–457.

Leiner, Frederick C. *The End of Barbary Terror.* Oxford: Oxford University Press, 2006.

Leitenberg, Milton, and Richard Dean Burns, comps. *The Vietnam Conflict.* Santa Barbara, Calif: ABC-CLIO, 1973.

Lemarchand, Rene. *Burundi, Ethnocide as Discourse and Practice.* Cambridge: Cambridge University Press, 1994.

_____. "Chapter 10: The Burundi Genocide." *In A Century of Genocide: Critical Essays and Eyewitness Accounts,* edited by Samuel Totten, William S. Parsons, and Israel W. Charny. New York: Routledge, 2004.

_____. "Ethnic Genocide." *Society* 12, no. 1 (January-February 1975): 50–60.

_____. *Rwanda and Burundi.* New York: Praeger, 1970.

LeMay, G. H. L. *The Afrikaners: An Historical Interpretation.* Oxford: Blackwell, 1995.

Lemke, Douglas. "The Twenty Territorial Entities in the Rio de la Plata Region, and Ten Wars, 1810–1862." Paper presented at the short course Improving Data on International System Membership at the annual meeting of the American Political Science Association, Philadelphia, 2006.

Lenczowski, George. *The Middle East in World Affairs*. 4th ed. Ithaca, N.Y.: Cornell University Press, 1980.

_____. *Russia and the West in Iran*. Ithaca, N.Y.: Cornell University Press, 1949.

Lenin, Vladimir Ilyich. "What Is to Be Done?" In *Essential Works of Lenin*, edited by Henry M. Christman. New York: Bantam Books, 1971, 70.

Lensen, George A. *The Russo-Chinese War*. Tallahassee, Fla.: Diplomatic Press, 1967.

Leslie, R. F. *Polish Politics and the Revolution of November, 1930*. London: London University, 1956.

_____. *Reform and Insurrection in Russian Poland*. London: London University, 1963.

Lettrich, Joseph. *History of Modern Slovakia*. New York: Praeger, 1955.

Levene, Ricardo. *A History of Argentina*. Chapel Hill: University of North Carolina Press, 1937.

_____. *A History of Argentina*. New York: Russell and Russell, 1963.

Levine, Robert M. "'Mud-Hut Jerusalem': Canudos Revisited." *Hispanic American Historical Review* 68, no. 3 (August 1988): 525–572.

Levy, Jack. *War in the Modern Great Power System, 1495–1975*. Lexington: University Press of Kentucky, 1983.

Levy, Jack S. "Domestic Politics and War." In *The Origin and Prevention of Major Wars*, edited by Robert I. Rotberg and Theodore K. Rabb. New York: Cambridge University Press, 1989.

Levy, Jack, Thomas Walker, and Martin Edwards. "Continuity and Change in the Evolution of Warfare." In *War in a Changing World*, edited by Zeev Maoz and Azar Gat. Ann Arbor: University of Michigan Press, 2001.

Lewis, Bernard. "Some Reflections on the Decline of the Ottoman Empire." *Studia Islamica*, no. 9 (1958): 111–127.

Lewis, David Levering. *The Race to Fashoda: Colonialism and African Resistance*. New York: Weidenfeld and Nicolson, 1987.

Lewis, G. L. *Turkey*. New York: Praeger, 1955.

Lewis, William H. "Morocco and the Western Sahara." *Current History* 84 (May 1985): 213–216.

Leys, M. D. R. *Between Two Empires*. London: Longmans, Green, 1955.

Li, Chien-Nung. *The Political History of China, 1840–1928*. Princeton, N.J.: Van Nostrand, 1956.

Li, Ung Bing. *Outlines of Chinese History*. Shanghai: Commercial Press, 1914.

Li, Xiaobing. "PLA Attacks and Amphibious Operations during the Taiwan Strait Crises of 1954 and 1958." In *Chinese Warfighting: The PLA Experience since 1949*, edited by Mark A. Ryan, David M. Finkelstein, and Michael A. McDevitt. London: M. E. Sharpe, 2003.

Lichbach, M. "Social Theory, Comparative Politics, and Conflict." Paper presented at the annual meeting of the American Political Science Association, San Francisco, August 29–September 1, 1996.

Liebman, Marcel. *The Russian Revolution*. New York: Vintage, 1970.

Lieven, Anatol. *The Baltic Revolution: Estonia, Latvia, Lithuania and the Path to Independence*. New Haven, Conn.: Yale University Press, 1994.

Linden, Herman Vander. *Belgium: The Making of a Nation*. Oxford: Clarendon Press, 1920.

Linebarger, Paul M. A. *The China of Chiang K'ai-Shek*. Boston: World Peace Foundation, 1941.

Ling, Dwight L. *Morocco and Tunisia: A Comparative History*. Washington, D.C.: University Press of America, 1979.

Linklater, Andrew. "The Achievements of Critical Theory." In *International Theory: Positivism and Beyond*, edited by Steve Smith, Ken Booth, and Marysia Zalewski. Cambridge: Cambridge University Press, 1996, 279–298.

Lin-Le. *Ti Ping Tien-Kwoh: The History of the Ti-Ping Revolution*. London: Day and Son, 1866.

Linn, Brian. *The Philippine War, 1899–1902*. Lawrence: University Press of Kansas, 2000.

Lipman, Jonathan N. "Ethnicity and Politics in Republican China: The Ma Family Warlords of Gansu." *Modern China* 10, Issue 3 (July 1984): 285–316.

Lisbon Correspondent. "East Timor." *The Economist* (May 26, 1979).

Listowel, Judith. *The Making of Tanganyika*. London: Chatto and Windus, 1965.

Littauer, Raphael, and Norman Uphoff, eds. *The Air War in Indochina*. Boston: Beacon, 1972.

Litten, Frederick S. "The CCP and the Fujian Rebellion." *Republican China* 14, no. 1 (1988): 57–74.

Little, Richard. *Intervention: External Involvement in Civil Wars*. Totawa, N.J.: Rowman and Littlefield, 1975.

Livermore, Thomas L. *Numbers and Losses in the Civil War in America: 1861–65*. Bloomington: Indiana University Press, 1957 (1900).

Lobanov-Rostovsky, Andrei. *Russia and Asia*. Ann Arbor, Mich.: Wahr, 1951.

Lobell, Steven E., and Philip Mauceri, eds. *Ethnic Conflict and International Politics: Explaining Diffusion and Escalation*. New York: Palgrave Macmillan, 2004.

Loeb, Vernon. "Yugoslav Military Is Formidable Foe." *Washington Post,* Saturday April 3, 1999, A9. www.washingtonpost.com/wp-srv/inatl/daily/april99/forces040399.htm.

London Times. Issues from July 1, 1875 to June 30, 1876.

Longrigg, Stephen Hemsley. *Iraq, 1900 to 1950.* London: Oxford University, 1953.

——. *Syria and Lebanon under French Mandate.* London: Oxford University Press, 1958.

Lopes, Carlos. *Guinea-Bissau: From Liberation Struggle to Independent Statehood.* Boulder, Colo.: Westview Press, 1987.

Lorch, Netanel. *The Edge of the Sword.* New York: Putnam, 1961.

Lorcin, Patricia M. E. *Imperial Identities: Stereotyping, Prejudice and Race in Colonial Algeria.* London: I. B. Tauris, 1995.

Lord, Robert. *The Origins of the War of 1870.* New York: Russell and Russell, 1966.

Lorentzen, Lois Ann, and Jennifer Turpin, eds. *The Women and War Reader.* New York: New York University Press, 1998.

Love, Joseph. *Rio Grande do Sul and Brazilian Regionalism, 1882–1930.* Stanford, Calif.: Stanford University Press, 1971.

Loveman, Brian. *Chile: The Legacy of Hispanic Capitalism.* New York: Oxford University Press, 1979.

Lowenheim, Oded. "'Do Ourselves Credit and Render a Lasting Service to Mankind': British Moral Prestige, Humanitarian Intervention, and the Barbary Pirates." *International Studies Quarterly* 47 (2003): 23–48.

Lowry, Robert. *The Armed Forces of Indonesia.* St. Leonards, NSW: Allen and Unwin, 1996.

Luard, C. E. "The Indian States, 1818–57." In *The Cambridge History of the British Empire,* vol. IV: *British India, 1497–1858,* edited by H. H. Dodwell. New York: Macmillan, 1929.

Luard, Evan, ed. *The International Regulation of Civil Wars.* New York: New York University Press, 1972.

Luckett, Richard. *The White Generals: An Account of the White Movement and the Russian Civil War.* New York: Viking Press, 1971.

Lukowski, Jerzy, and Hubert Zawadzki. *A Concise History of Poland.* 2nd ed. Cambridge: Cambridge University Press, 2006.

Luther, Narendra. "The Story of Kasim Razvi." *Legend and Anecdotes of Hyderabad,* no. 58 (June 1, 2000). http://narendralutherarchives.blogspot.com.

Lye, William F. "The Ndebele Kingdom South of the Limpopo River." *The Journal of African History* 10, no. 1 (1969): 87–104.

Lynch, John. *The Spanish-American Revolutions, 1808–1826.* New York: W. W. Norton, 1973.

Lyons, Eugene. *Assignment in Utopia.* New York: Harcourt, Brace, 1937.

Møsler, Bjørn. "The Nordic Countries: Whither the West's Conscience?" In *Kosovo and the Challenges of Humanitarian Intervention,* edited by Albrecht Schnabel and Ramesh Thakur. New York: United Nations University Press, 2000.

Maass, Walter B. *Assassination in Vienna.* New York: Scribner's, 1972.

Macartney, C. A. *The Hapsburg Empire, 1790–1918.* London: Weidenfeld and Nicolson, 1968.

Macauley, Neill. *The Sandino Affair.* Chicago: Quadrangle, 1967.

MacCallum, Elizabeth. *The Nationalist Crusade in Syria.* New York: Foreign Policy Association, 1928.

MacDermott, Marcia. *A History of Bulgaria.* London: Allen and Unwin, 1962.

MacKenzie, David. *The Serbs and Russian Pan-Slavism, 1875–1878.* Ithaca, N.Y.: Cornell University Press, 1967.

——. "Turkestan's Significance to Russia (1850–1917)." *Russian Review* 33, no. 2 (April 1974): 167–188.

Mackerras, Colin. *Modern China: A Chronology from 1842 to the Present.* London: Thames and Hudson, 1982.

Mackintosh, J. M. *Strategy and Tactics of Soviet Foreign Policy.* New York: Oxford University Press, 1963.

Maclean, Frank. *Germany's Colonial Failure.* Boston: Houghton Mifflin, 1918.

MacLeod, James Mcivey. "The Achievements of France in Morocco." *Geographical Journal* 52, no. 2 (August 1918): 84–101.

MacNair, Harley F. *China in Revolution.* Chicago: University of Chicago, 1931.

Macrory, Patrick. *Signal Catastrophe.* London: Hodder and Staughton, 1966.

Madden, Lori. "The Canudos War in History." *Luso-Brazilian Review* 30, no. 2 (1993): 5–22.

Magnus, Philip. *Kitchener.* London: John Murray, 1958.

Magocsi, Paul R. *A History of Ukraine.* Seattle: University of Washington Press, 1996.

Maier, Karl. *This House Has Fallen: Midnight in Nigeria.* New York: PublicAffairs, 2000.

Majumdar, R. C., H. C. Raychaudhuri, and Kalikinkar Datta. *An Advanced History of India.* London: Macmillan, 1948.

Makdisi, Ussama. "Corrupting the Sublime Sultanate: The Revolt of Tanyus Shahin in Nineteenth-Century Ottoman Lebanon." *Comparative Studies in Society and History* 42, no. 1 (January 2000): 180–208.

Malaquias, Assis. "Angola: How to Lose a Guerrilla War." In *African Guerrillas; Raging against the Machine*, edited by Morten Bøås and Kevin C. Dunn. Boulder, Colo.: Lynne Rienner, 2007.

Malcolm, Noel. *Bosnia: A Short History*. Washington Square: New York University Press, 1996.

Malet, Sir Alexander. *The Overthrow of the Germanic Confederation by Prussia in 1866*. London: Longmans, Green, 1870.

Malian Ministry of Foreign Affairs and International Cooperation. "Mapping of Non-State Armed Groups in the ECOWAS Region." Paper presented at the 6th Ministerial Meeting of the Human Security Network, Bamako, Mali, May 27–29, 2004.

Maliti, Tom. "Rebels, Troops Clash in Chad Capital." *Chicago Tribune*, February 3, 2008, 1, 15.

Mallat, Joseph. *La Serbie Contemporaine*. Vol. 1. Paris: Librarie Orientale et Americaine, 1902.

Mallay, Michael. "Regions: Centralization and Resistance." In *Indonesia beyond Suharto: Polity, Economy, Society, Transition,* edited by Donald K. Emmerson. Armonk, N.Y.: M. E. Sharpe, 1999.

Malleson, G. B. *An Historical Sketch of the Native States of India in Subsidiary Alliance with the British Government.* London: Longmans, Green, 1875.

Malloy, James M. *Bolivia: The Uncompleted Revolution.* Pittsburgh: University of Pittsburgh Press, 1970.

Maloba, Wunyabari. *Mau Mau and Kenya: An Analysis of a Peasant Revolt.* Bloomington, Ind.: Indiana University Press, 1998.

Mamdani, Mahmood. *When Victims Become Killers: Colonialism, Nativism, and the Genocide in Rwanda.* Princeton, N.J.: Princeton University Press, 2002.

Mangulis, Visvaldis. *Latvia in the Wars of the 20th Century.* Princeton Junction, N.J.: Cognition Books, 1983.

Manich Jumsai, M. L. *History of Laos Including the History of Lannathai, Chiengmai.* Bangkok: Chalermnit, 1967.

Mann, Erick. *Mikono Ya Damu: African Mercenaries and the Politics of Conflict in German East Africa, 1888–1904.* New York: P. Lang, 2002.

Mansbach, Richard, Yale H. Ferguson, and Donald E. Lampert. "Towards a New Conceptualization of Global Politics." In *Classic Readings of International Relations,* 2nd ed., edited by Phil Williams, Donald Goldstein, and Jay Shafritz. Fort Worth, Texas: Harcourt Brace College, 1999, 191–202.

Mansfield, Edward D. "The Distribution of Wars over Time." *World Politics* 41, no. 1 (October 1988): 21–51.

Mansfield, Peter. *The British in Egypt.* New York: Holt, Rinehart and Winston, 1971.

Mansford, Oliver. *The Battle of Majuba Hill.* New York: Crowell, 1967.

Mansingh, S. *Historical Dictionary of India.* 2nd ed. London: Scarecrow Press, 2006.

Manwaring, Max G. "Nonstate Actors in Colombia: Threat and Response." *Strategic Studies Institute* (May 2002).

Mao Tse-tung, "Preserving Oneself and Destroying the Enemy." In *Classic Readings of International Relations,* edited by Phil Williams, Donald Goldstein, and Jay Shafritz. Fort Worth, Tex: Harcourt Brace College, 1999, 414–421.

Maoz, Zeev. "The Controversy over the Democratic Peace: Rearguard Action or Cracks in the Wall?" *International Security* 22 (1997): 162–198.

_____. "Memo to the Correlates of War Community." (2007).

Marchak, M. Patricia. *Reigns of Terror.* Montreal: McGill-Queen's University Press, 2003.

Marcus, Harold G. *A History of Ethiopia.* Berkeley: University of California Press, 2001.

_____. *The Life and Times of Menelik II: Ethiopia 1844–1913.* Oxford: Clarendon Press, 1975.

_____. *The Life and Times of Menelik II, Ethiopia, 1844–1913.* Lawrenceville, N.J.: Red Sea Press, 1995.

Mares, David. "Deterrence Bargaining in Ecuador and Peru's Enduring Rivalry: Designing Strategies around Military Weakness." *Security Studies* 6, no. 2 (Winter 1996–1997): 91–123.

_____. Personal communications with Meredith Reid Sarkees, 2007–2008.

_____. *Violent Peace: Militarized Interstate Bargaining in Latin America.* New York: Columbia University Press, 2001.

Marett, Robert. *Peru.* New York: Praeger, 1969.

Margolis, Eric S. *War at the Top of the World.* New York: Routledge, 2002.

Markham, Clements R. *A History of Peru.* Chicago: Charles H. Sergel, 1892.

_____. *A History of Peru.* New York: Greenwood Press, 1968.

Markides, Kyriacos C. *The Rise and Fall of the Cyprus Republic.* New Haven, Conn.: Yale University Press, 1977.

Marks, Thomas A. "Insurgency in Nepal." *Strategic Studies Institute* (December 2003).

_____. "Making Revolution: the Insurgency of the Communist Party of Thailand (CPT) in Structural Perspective." PhD diss., University of Hawaii, 1991.

_____. "Spanish Sahara–Background to Conflict." *African Affairs* 75, no. 298 (January 1976): 3–13.

Marlin, Michael R., and Gabriel H. Lovett, eds. *Encyclopedia of Latin American History*. Indianapolis: Bobbs-Merrill, 1968.

Marlowe, John. *A History of Modern Egypt and Anglo-Egyptian Relations, 1800–1956*. Hamden, Conn.: Archon Books, 1965.

_____. *Spoiling the Egyptians*. New York: St. Martin's Press, 1975.

Marr, David. *Vietnamese Tradition on Trial, 1920–1945*. Berkeley: University of California Press, 1981.

Marr, Phebe. *The Modern History of Iraq*. Boulder, Colo.: Westview Press, 1985.

Marshall, Monty. *Third World War*. Lanham, Md.: Rowman and Littlefield, 1999.

Marshall, S. L. A. *Sinai Victory*. New York: William Morrow, 1958.

Marsot, Afaf Lutfi Al-Sayyid. *Egypt in the Reign of Muhammad Ali*. Cambridge: Cambridge University Press, 1984.

Martelli, George. *Leopold to Lumumba*. London: Chapman and Hall, 1962.

Martin, Christopher. *The Russo-Japanese War*. New York: Abelard Schulman, 1967.

Martin, Claude. *Histoire de L'algerie Francaise, 1830–1962*. Paris: Editions des 4 Fils Aymon, 1963.

Martin, Michael R., and Gabriel H. Lovett, eds. *Encyclopedia of Latin American History*. Indianapolis: Bobbs-Merrill, 1968.

Marure, Alejandro. *Bosquejo Historico de las Revoluciones de Centro America*. Guatemala City: El Progreso, 1837.

Mathieu, Henri. *La Turquie*. Paris: E. Dentu, 1856.

Maullin, Richard L. *Soldiers, Guerrillas and Politics in Colombia*. Lexington, Mass.: D. C. Heath, 1973.

Maurice, C. Edmund. *The Revolutionary Movement of 1848–49 in Italy, Austria-Hungary, and Germany*. New York: Putnam, 1887.

Maurice, F., and George Arthur. *The Life of Lord Wolseley*. Garden City, N.Y.: Doubleday, 1924.

Maurice, John Frederick. *Hostilities without Declaration of War*. London: H.M.S.O., 1883.

Maxwell, Gavin. *The Lords of the Atlas*. London: Longmans, Green, 1966.

Maxwell, Neville. *India's China War*. London: Jonathan Cape, 1970.

Mays, Terry M. *Africa's First Peacekeeping Operation: The OAU in Chad, 1981–1982*. Westport, Conn.: Praeger, 2003.

Mazade, Charles de. *Les Revolutions de L'espagne Contemporaine*. Paris: Didier, 1869.

Mazower, Mark. *Salonica City of Ghosts: Christians, Muslims, and Jews, 1430–1950*. New York: Knopf, 2005.

Mbaria, John. "Exit of the Islamists Will See a Revival of Clan Conflicts." *Analysis* (January 9, 2007). http://allafrica.com.

McAdam, D., S. Tarrow, and C. Tilly. "A Comparative Analysis of Social Movements and Revolution: Towards an Integrated Perspective." Paper presented at the annual meeting of the American Political Science Association, San Francisco: August 29–September 1, 1996.

McAleavy, Henry. *Black Flags in Vietnam*. New York: Macmillan, 1968.

_____. *The Modern History of China*. London: Weidenfeld and Nicholson, 1968.

McCaa, Robert. "Missing Millions: The Demographic Costs of the Mexican Revolution." *Mexican Studies/ Estudios Mexicanos* 19, no. 2 (Summer 2003): 367–400.

McCann, James. "The Political Economy of Rural Rebellion in Ethiopia: Northern Resistance to Imperial Expansion, 1928–1935." *The International Journal of African Historical Studies* 18, no. 4 (1985): 601–623.

McClure, William Kidston. *Italy in North Africa*. London: Constable, 1913.

McCoy, Alfred W., and Nina S. Adams, eds. *Laos: War and Revolution*. New York: Harper and Row, 1970

McCrum, Robert. "Timor's 'Mass' Resistance." *World Press Review*. Vol. 40, no. 6, June 1994: 18–19.

McGann, Thomas Francis. *Argentina, the United States, and the Inter-American System, 1880–1914*. Cambridge, Mass.: Harvard University, 1957.

McGlen, Nancy E., and Meredith Reid Sarkees. *Women in Foreign Policy: The Insiders*. New York: Routledge, 1993.

McGregor, Andrew James. *A Military History of Modern Egypt*. Westport, Conn.: Praeger Security International, 2006.

McHenry, J. Patrick. *A Short History of Mexico*. Garden City, N.Y.: Doubleday, 1962.

McKenna, Joseph C. "Ethics and War: A Catholic View." In *International War: An Anthology*, 2nd ed., edited by Melvin Small and J. David Singer. Chicago: Dorsey Press, 1989, 110–124.

McKiernan, Kevin. "Turkey's War on the Kurds." *Bulletin of the Atomic Scientists* (March–April 1999): 26–37.

McLintock, A. H., ed. *1966 Encyclopaedia of New Zealand*. Ministry of Culture and Heritage: Crown Copyright, 2005–2008. www.teara.govt.nz.

McLynn, F. J. "The Montonero Risings in Argentina during the Eighteen-Sixties." *Canadian Journal of History* 15, no. 1 (1980): 49–66.

Mearsheimer, J. "Back to the Future: Instability in Europe after the Cold War." *International Security* 15 (1990): 5–56.

Medlicott, W. N. *The Congress of Berlin and After: A Diplomatic History of the Near Eastern Settlement.* Hamden, Conn.: Archon Books, 1963.

Melady, Thomas Patrick. *Burundi: The Tragic Years.* Maryknoll, N.Y.: Orbis, 1974.

Mellor, Andrew. *India since Partition.* New York: Praeger, 1951.

Mende, Tibor. *The Chinese Revolution.* London: Thames and Hudson, 1961.

Menendez Pidal, Ramon. *Historia de Espana.* Vol. 26. Madrid: Espasa-Calpe, 1968.

Mennecke, Martin. "Genocide in Kosovo?" In *Century of Genocide,* 2nd ed., edited by Samuel Totten, William S. Parsons, and Israel W. Charny. New York: Routledge, 2004.

Menon, Parvathi. "Falsifying History." *Frontline* 15, no. 21 (October 10–23, 1998).

Menon, V. P. *The Story of the Integration of the Indian States.* Calcutta: Orient-Longmans, 1956.

Mentre, Francois. *Les Generation Sociales.* Paris: Bossard, 1920.

Meo, Leila. "The War in Lebanon." In *Ethnic Conflict in International Relations,* edited by Astri Suhrke and Lela Garner Nobel. New York: Praeger, 1977.

Meray, Tiboy. *Thirteen Days That Shook the Kremlin.* New York: Praeger, 1959.

Mercer, John. "The Cycle of Invasion and Unification in the Western Sahara." *African Affairs* 75 no. 301 (October 1976): 498–510.

Meredith, Martin. *The Fate of Africa: From the Hopes of Freedom to the Heart of Despair.* New York: Public Affairs, 2005.

Metcalf, Barbara, and Thomas Metcalf. *A Concise History of Modern India.* 2nd ed. Cambridge: Cambridge University Press, 2006.

Metz, Helen Chapin. *Persian Gulf States: Country Studies.* 3rd ed. Washington, D.C.: Library of Congress, 1994.

Meyer, Joan A. *The Cristero Rebellion.* New York: Cambridge University Press, 1976.

Meyer, Michael C., and William H. Beezley. *The Oxford History of Mexico.* New York: Oxford University Press, 2000.

Meyer, Michael C., and William L. Sherman. *The Course of Mexican History.* New York: Oxford University Press, 1983.

Meyer, Michael C., William L. Sherman, and Susan M. Deeds. *The Course of Mexican History.* 7th ed. New York: Oxford University Press, 2003.

Meza, Rafael. *Centro America: Campana National de 1885.* Guatemala City: Tipografia Nacional, 1935.

Michael, Franz. "T'ai Ping T'ien-Kuo." *Journal of Asian Studies* 17, no. 1 (November 1957): 67–76.

Michael, Franz, and Chung-Li Chang, eds. *The Taiping Rebellion: Documents and Comments.* Bellingham: University of Washington Press, 1966–1971.

Michael, Franz, and George Taylor. *The Far East in the Modern World.* Rev. ed. New York: Holt, Rinehart and Winston, 1964.

Michell, Robert. *Eastern Turkestan and Dzungaria and the Rebellion of the Tugans and Taranchis, 1862 to 1866.* Calcutta: Office of Superintendent of Government Printing, 1870.

Midlarsky, Manus. *Handbook of War Studies.* London: Unwin Hyman, 1989.

———. *The Killing Trap.* New York: Cambridge University Press, 2005.

———. "Rulers and Ruled: Patterned Inequality and the Onset of Mass Political Violence." *American Political Science Review* 82 (1988): 491–509.

Miege, Jean-Louis. *Le Maroc et l'Europe.* Vol. II. Paris: Presses Universaires de France, 1961.

Mijatovich, Chedomille. *The Memoirs of a Balkan Diplomat.* London: Cassell, 1917.

Mikus, Joseph. *Slovakia.* Milwaukee, Wisc.: Marquette University Press, 1963.

Miller, Benjamin. *States, Nations, and the Great Powers.* Cambridge: Cambridge University Press, 2007.

Miller, M. E. *Bulgaria during the Second World War.* Stanford, Calif.: Stanford University Press, 1975.

Miller, Robert Ryal. *Mexico: A History.* Norman: University of Oklahoma Press, 1985.

Miller, William. *The Ottoman Empire, 1801–1913.* Cambridge: Cambridge University Press, 1913.

Millett, Allan R. *The War for Korea, 1945–1950: A House Burning.* Lawrence: University Press of Kansas, 2005.

Milstein, Jeffery S., and William C. Mitchell, "Dynamics of the Vietnam Conflict: A Quantitative Analysis and Predictive Computer Simulation." *Peace Research Society Papers* 10 (1968): 163–213.

Milstein, Uri. *History of Israel's War of Independence.* Vol. 2. New York: University Press of America, 1997.

Minahan, James. *Encyclopedia of the Stateless Nations: Ethnic and National Groups around the World.* 4 vols. Westport, Conn.: Greenwood Press, 2002.

———. *Nations without States: A Historical Dictionary of Contemporary National Movements.* Westport, Conn.: Greenwood Press, 1996.

Mirbagheri, Farid. *Cyprus and International Peace-making.* London: Hurst, 1998.

Mitchell, Peter R., and John Schoeffel, ed. *Understanding Power: The Indispensible Chomsky.* New York: New Press, 2002.

Mitrany, D. *A Working Peace System.* London: Royal Institute of International Affairs, 1943.

"Mohammedanism and Slave-Trade in Africa." *Science* 12, no. 308 (December 28, 1888): 325–326

Molesworth, G. N. *Afghanistan 1919.* New York: Asia Publishing House, 1962.

Møller, Bjørn. "The Nordic Countries: Whither the West's Conscience?" In *Kosovo and the Challenges of Humanitarian Intervention,* edited by Albrecht Schnabel and Ramesh Thakur. New York: United Nations University Press, 2000.

Mooradian, Moorad, and Daniel Druckman. "Hurting Stalemate or Mediation? The Conflict over Nagorno–Karabakh, 1990–95." *Journal of Peace Research,* Vol. 36, no. 6 (Nov. 1999): 709–727.

Moore, Clement Henry. "The Neo-Destour Party of Tunisia: A Structure for Democracy?" *World Politics.* Vol. 14, no. 3 (April 1962): 461–482.

Moore, Harriet L. *Soviet Far Eastern Policy, 1931–1945.* Princeton, N.J.: Princeton University Press, 1945.

Moore, Joel R., Harry H. Mead, and Lewis E. Jahns, eds. *The History of the American Expedition Fighting the Bolsheviki.* Detroit: Polar Bear, 1921.

Moorehead, Alan. *The Russian Revolution.* New York: Harper, 1958.

Moosa, Matti. *The Maronites in History.* Syracuse, N.Y.: Syracuse University Press, 1986.

Morell, David. "Thailand: Military Checkmate." *Asian Survey* 12, no. 2 (February 1972): 156–167.

Morgenthau, Hans. *Politics among Nations.* 5th ed. New York: Knopf, 1973.

Moriarity, Robin. *Aims, Wars and Settlements Dataset.* 2005. Provided by author.

Moron, Guillermo. *A History of Venzuela.* New York: Roy, 1963.

Morris, Benny. *Righteous Victims.* New York: Knopf, 2001.

Morris, Donald. *The Washing of the Spears: A History of the Rise of the Zulu Nation Under Shaka and Its Fall in the Zulu War of 1879.* New York: Simon and Schuster, 1965.

———. *The Washing of the Spears: A History of the Rise of the Zulu Nation Under Shaka and Its Fall in the Zulu War of 1879.* New York: Da Capo, 1998.

Morris, Richard B., ed. *Encyclopedia of American History.* New York: Harper, 1970.

Morrow, John H. "Unrest In North Africa." *Phylon (1940-1956)* 16, no. 4 (4th Quarter 1955): 410–426.

Morse, Hosea Ballou. *The International Relations of the Chinese Empire.* Shanghai: Kelly and Walsh, 1910. Reprinted. Taibei: Wen Xing Shu Dian, 1966.

———. *The International Relations of the Chinese Empire.* Vol. 3. London: Longmans, Green, 1918.

Mortimer, Robert. "Islamists, Soldiers, and Democrats: The Second Algerian War." *Middle East Journal* 50, no. 1 (Winter 1996): 18–39.

Mosley, Melinda M. "Operation Deliberate Force." *Air Force Library* (March 2000). www.au.af.mil.

Mosse, W. E. "Queen Victoria and Her Ministers in the Schleswig-Holstein Crisis 1863–1864." *The English Historical Review* 78, no. 307 (April 1962–1963): 263–283.

Mostert, Noel. *Frontiers: The Epic of South Africa's Creation and the Tragedy of the Xhosa People.* New York: Knopf, 1992, 1993.

Mounsey, Augustus H. *The Satsuma Rebellion.* London: John Murray, 1879.

Mowafi, Reda. *Slavery, the Slave Trade, and Abolition Attempts in Egypt and the Sudan 1820–1882.* Stockholm: Esselte Studium, 1981.

Mowat, Robert Balmain. *A History of European Diplomacy 1914–1925.* London: E. Arnold, 1927.

Moya Pons, Frank. *The Dominican Republic, A National History.* New Rochelle, N.Y.: Hispaniola Books, 1995.

Moyal, J. E. "The Distribution of Wars in Time." *Journal of the Royal Statistical Society* (Series A), 112, no. 4 (1949): 446–449.

Mueller, John. "The Essential Irrelevance of Nuclear Weapons: Stability in the Postwar World." *International Security* 13 (1988): 55–79.

———. *Retreat from Doomsday: The Obsolescence of Major War.* New York: Basic Books, 1989.

Munro, Dana Gardner. *The Five Republics of Central America.* New York: Oxford University Press, 1918.

———. *Intervention and Dollar Diplomacy in the Caribbean.* Princeton, N.J.: Princeton University Press, 1964.

———. *The Latin American Republics.* New York: Appleton-Century-Crofts, 1942.

Muslim, Macapado A., and Rufa Cagoco-Guiam. "Mindanao: land of Promise." *Accord* (2002). www.c-r.org/accord.

Mydans, Carl, and Shelly Mydans. *The Violent Peace.* New York: Atheneum, 1968.

Mylonis, George E. *The Balkan States.* St. Louis, Mo.: Eden, 1946.

Nagaland Is Born. Kohmia: Government of Nagaland, 1964.

Nahaylo, Bohdan, and Victor Swoboda. *Soviet Disunion: A History of the Nationalities Problem in the USSR.* New York: Free Press, 1990.

Nahm, Andrew C., and James E. Hoare. *Historical Dictionary of the Republic of Korea.* Lanham, Md.: Scarecrow Press, 2004.

Nalivkine, Vladimir P. *Histoire du Khanat de Khokand.* Paris: Leroux, 1889.

Nantet, Jacques. *Histoire du Liban.* Paris: Editions de Minuit, 1963.

National Democratic Institute for International Affairs. *Nation Building: The U.N. and Namibia.* Washington, D.C.: National Democratic Institute for International Affairs, 1988.

NATO. "NATO's Role in Relation to the Conflict in Kosovo." (1999). www.nato.int/kosovo/history.htm.

————. "Operation Deliberate Force." *NATO-OTAN AF SOUTH Fact Sheets* (December 16, 2002). www.afsouth.nato.int/factsheets.

Natrajan, L. "The Santhal Insurrection." In *Peasant Struggles in India,* edited by A. R. Desai. Bombay: Oxford University Press, 1979.

Naval Intelligence Division. *Geographical Handbook Series, Algeria.* Vol. 1. Naval Intelligence Division, 1942.

Naylor, Phillip C. *Historical Dictionary of Algeria.* 3rd ed. Lanham, Md.: Scarecrow Press, 2006.

Nazzal, Nafez Y., and Laila A. Nazzal. *Historical Dictionary of Palestine.* Lanham, Md.: Scarecrow Press, 1997.

Ndarubagiye, Léonce. *Burundi: The Origins of the Hutu-Tutsi Conflict.* Nairobi: Léonce Ndarubagiye, 1996.

Neeson, Eoin. *The Civil War in Ireland.* Cork: Mercier, 1966.

Nelson, Harold D., ed. *Algeria, A Country Study.* Washington, D.C.: American University, 1979.

————. *Tunisia: A Country Study.* Washington, D.C.: American University, 1986.

Nelson, Harold D., and Irving Kaplan, eds. *Ethiopia, A Country Study.* Washington, D.C.: American University, 1981.

New York Times. *The Pentagon Papers.* New York: Bantam, 1971.

New York Times Index, 1909, 1947 (in addition to references listed in "Sources" throughout the book).

Ngoh, Victor Julius. *History of Cameroon since 1800.* Buea: Presbook, Limbe, 1996.

Nicholls, David. *From Dessalines to Duvalier: Race, Color, and National Independence in Haiti.* Rev. ed. New Brunswick, N.J.: Rutgers University Press, 1995.

Nicolini, Beatrice. *Makran, Oman, and Zanzibar: Three-Terminal Cultural Corridor in the Western Indian Ocean, 1799–1856.* Boston: Brill, 2004.

Nilsen, Av Kjell Arild. "Death Toll In Bosnian War Was 102,000." Norwegian News Agency, November 11, 2004). www.freerepublic.com/focus.

Niox, Gustave. *Expedition du Mexique 1861–1867.* Paris: J. Dumaine, 1874.

Nish, Ian. *The Origins of the Russo-Japanese War.* London: Longman, 1985.

Nkrumah, Kwame. *Class Struggle in Africa.* London: Panaf Books, 1980.

Nodal, Roberto. "The Black Man in Cuban Society: From Colonial Times to the Revolution." *Journal of Black Studies* 16, no. 3 (March 1986): 251–267.

Nolan, Edward H. *The Liberators of Italy.* London: J. S. Virtue, 1865.

Nolutshungu, Sam C. *Limits of Anarchy: Intervention and State Formation in Chad.* Charlottesville: University Press of Virginia, 1996.

Norbu, Dawn. "The 1959 Tibetan Rebellion: An Interpretation." *The China Quarterly* 77 (1979): 74–93.

Norris, J. A. *The First Afghan War 1838–1842.* Cambridge: Cambridge University Press, 1967.

Nutting, Anthony. *The Arabs.* New York: New American Library, 1964.

Nye, Joseph S., Jr. "Transnational Relations, Interdependence and Globalization." In *Millennial Reflections on International Studies,* edited by Michael Brecher and Frank P. Harvey. Ann Arbor: University of Michigan Press, 2002, 165–175.

Nyrop, Richard F., Lyle E. Brenneman, Roy V. Hibbs, Charlene A. James, Susan MacKnight, and Gordon C. McDonald. *Area Handbook for Rwanda.* Washington, D.C.: GPO, 1969.

Nzongola-Ntalaja, G. *The Congo: From Leopold to Kabila: A People's History.* London: Zed Books, 2002.

O'Ballance, Edgar. *Afghan Wars, 1839–1992.* New York: Brassey's, 1993.

————. *The Arab-Israeli War.* London: Faber and Faber, 1956.

————. *The Communist-Insurgent War in Malaysia 1948–1960.* London: Faber and Faber, 1966b.

————. *The Greek Civil War, 1944–1949.* New York: Praeger, 1966a.

————. *The Indo-China War 1945–1954.* London: Faber and Faber, 1964.

————. *The Kurdish Revolt: 1961–1970.* London: Faber and Faber, 1973.

_____. *The Kurdish Struggle 1920–1994*. New York: St. Martin's Press, 1996.

_____. *No Victor, No Vanquished: The Yom Kippur War*. San Rafael, Calif.: Presidio, 1978.

_____. *The War in the Yemen*. London: Faber and Faber, 1970.

Oberling, Pierre. *The Road to Bellapais: The Turkish Cypriot Exodus to Northern Cyprus*. New York: Columbia University Press, 1982.

O'Brien, Patrick K., ed. *Oxford Atlas of World History from the Origins of Humanity to the Year 2000*. New York: Oxford University Press, 1999.

Odhiambo, E. S. Atieno, and John Lonsdale, eds. *Mau Mau and Nationhood*. Columbus: Ohio State University Press, 2003.

Ogawa, Gotaro. *Expenditures of the Russo-Japanese War*. New York: Oxford University Press, 1923.

Ogot, Bethwell A. *Zamani*. New York: Longman, 1974.

Oh, John Kie-Chiang. *Korean Politics: The Quest for Democratization and Economic Development*. Ithaca, N.Y.: Cornell University Press, 1999.

Olcott, Martha B. "The Basmachi or Freemen's Revolt in Turkestan, 1918–24." *Soviet Studies* 33, no. 3 (July 1981): 352–368.

Oliver, Robert T. *A History of the Korean People in Modern Times, 1800 to the Present*. Newark: University of Delaware Press, 1993.

Oliver, Roland, and Anthony Atmore. *Africa since 1800*. Cambridge: Cambridge University Press, 1972, 1981, 1994, 2004.

Oliviera, A. Ramos. *Politics, Economics and the Men of Modern Spain*. London: Victor Gollancz, 1946.

Oneal, John, and Bruce Russett. "The Classic Liberals Were Right: Democracy, Interdependence, and International Conflict, 1950–1985." *International Studies Quarterly* 41 (1997): 267–293.

_____. "Escaping the War Trap: Evaluating Liberal Prescriptions for Peace: Controlling for Expected Utility." Paper presented at the annual meeting of the International Studies Association, Toronto, March 19–22, 1997.

O'Neill, Bard E. "Revolutionary War in Oman." In *Insurgency in the Modern World*, edited by Bard E. O'Neill, William R. Heaton, and Donald J. Alberts. Boulder, Colo.: Westview Press, 1980.

O'Neill, Robert. "Doctrine and Training in the German Army." In *The Theory and Practice of War*, edited by Michael Howard. New York: Praeger, 1966.

Onesto, Li. *Dispatches from the People's War in Nepal*. London: Pluto Press, 2005.

Onishi, Norimitsu. "Guinea in Crisis as Area's Refugees Pour In." *New York Times*, February 24, 2001.

Ono, Giichi. *Expenditures of the Sino-Japanese War*. New York: Oxford University Press, 1922.

"Operation Enduring Freedom: Coalition Fatalities." (5/25/2007). http://icasualties.org.

Organski, A. F. K., and Jacek Kugler. *The War Ledger*. Chicago: University of Chicago Press, 1980.

Orlansky, Jesse. "The State of Research on Internal War." Research paper, Institute for Defense Analysis, 1970.

O'Rourke, P. J. *Give War a Chance*. New York: Atlantic Monthly Press, 1992.

Orr, William J., Jr. "British Diplomacy and the German Problem, 1848–1850." *Albion: A Quarterly Journal Concerned with British Studies* 10, no. 3 (Autumn 1978): 209–236.

Orsi, Pietro. *Cavour and the Making of Modern Italy*. New York: Putnam, 1914.

Osborne, Milton E. *The French Presence in Cochin China and Cambodia: Rule and Response, 1859–1905*. Ithaca, N.Y.: Cornell University Press, 1969.

Osborne, R. *Indonesia's Secret War: The Guerilla Struggle in Irian Jaya*. Crows Nest, NSW: Allen and Unwin, 1985.

Ottaway, David, and Marina Ottaway. *Algeria: The Politics of a Socialist Revolution*. Berkeley: University of California Press, 1970.

Ottaway, Marina. *South Africa: The Struggle for a New Order*. Washington, D.C.: Brookings Institution Press, 1993.

Outram, Francis. *A Modern History of Oman*. London: I. B. Taurus, 2004.

Ovendale, Ritchie. *The Origins of the Arab-Israeli Wars*. 2nd ed. New York: Longman, 1992.

Owen, John M. "How Liberalism Produces Democratic Peace." In *Theories of War and Peace* edited by Michael E. Brown, Owen R. Coté Jr., Sean M. Lynn-Jones, and Steven E. Miller. Cambridge, Mass.: MIT Press, 1999, 137–175.

Oyewole, A., and J. Lucas. *Historical Dictionary of Nigeria*. Lanham, Md.: Rowman and Littlefield, 2000.

Page, Stanley W. *The Formation of the Baltic States*. Cambridge, Mass.: Harvard University Press, 1959.

_____. "Lenin, the National Question and the Baltic States, 1917–1919." *American Slavic and East European Review* 7, no. 1 (February 1948): 15–31.

Pakenham, Thomas. *The Boer War*. New York: Random House, 1994.

_____. *The Scramble for Africa, 1876–1912*. New York: Random House, 1991.

Palace, Wendy. *The British Empire and Tibet 1900–1922*. New York: Routledge, 2004.

Palmer, Alan. *The Baltic: A New History of the Region and Its People*. New York: Overlook Press, 2005.

_____. *The Decline and Fall of the Ottoman Empire*. New York: Barnes and Noble Books, 1992.

Palmer, David Scott. "Overcoming the Weight of History: Getting to Yes in the Peru-Ecuador Border Dispute." Manuscript, first draft, February 21, 2000. http://abayayala.nativeweb.org/ecuador/border.

_____. "Overcoming the Weight of History: Getting to 'Yes' in the Peru-Ecuador Border Dispute." *Diplomacy and Statecraft* 12, no. 2 (June 2001): 29–46.

_____. Personal communications with Meredith Reid Sarkees, 2007–2008.

_____. "Peru-Ecuador Border Conflict: Missed Opportunities, Misplaced Nationalism, and Multilateral Peacekeeping." *Journal of Interamerican Studies and World Affairs* 39, no. 3 (Fall 1997): 109–148, especially note 17, 141.

Palmer, R. R. *Atlas of World History*. Chicago: Rand McNally, 1957.

Palmer, R. R., and Joel Colton. *A History of the Modern World*. 2nd ed. New York: Knopf, 1964.

Paloczi-Horvath, George. "Thailand's War with Vichy France." *History Today* 45 (March 1995).

Papageorgiou, Stephanos P. "The Army as an Instrument for Territorial Expansion and for Repression by the State: The Capodistrian Case." *Journal of the Hellenic Diaspora* 12, no. 4 (1985): 21–34.

Parenti, Michael. *The Sword and the Dollar: Imperialism, Revolution, and the Arms Race*. New York: St. Martin's Press, 1989.

Paris, Timothy J. *Britain, the Hashemites, and Arab Rule, 1920–1925*. London: Frank Cass, 2003.

Parkes, Henry Bamford. *A History of Mexico*. Boston: Houghton Mifflin, 1960.

Parpart, Jane. "Conclusion: New Thoughts and New Directions for the 'Man' Question in International Relations." In *The "Man" Question in International Relations*, edited by Marysia Zalewski and Jane Parpart. Boulder, Colo.: Westview Press, 1998, 199–208.

Pasdermadjain, P. *Histoire de l'Armenie*. Paris: Libraire Orientale H. Samuelian, 1964.

Pattee, Richard. *Gabriel Garcia Moreno y el Ecuador de Su Tiempo*. Quito: Editorial Ecuatoriana, 1941.

Patterson, George N. "China and Tibet: Background to the Revolt." *The China Quarterly*, no. 1 (January-March 1960b): 87–102.

_____. *Tibet in Revolt*. London: Faber and Faber, 1960a.

Paul, T. V., ed. *The India-Pakistan Conflict: An Enduring Rivalry*. New York: Cambridge University Press, 2005.

Paxton, Robert. *Vichy France*. New York: Knopf, 1972.

Payne, Robert. *The Civil War in Spain, 1936–1939*. New York: Capricorn, 1970.

_____. *Massacre*. New York: Macmillan, 1973.

Payne, Stanley. *Politics and the Military in Modern Spain*. Stanford, Calif.: Stanford University Press, 1967.

Pazzanita, Anthony G., and Tony Hodges. *Historical Dictionary of Western Sahara*. New York: Rowman and Littlefield, 1994.

Peace Pledge Union Online. "Eritrea." www.ppu.org.uk//wars.

_____. "Kashmir." www.ppu.org.uk//wars.

Pearson, Frederic S. "Foreign Military Intervention and Domestic Disputes." *International Studies Quarterly* 18 (September 1974): 259–290.

Peckham, Howard, ed. *The Toll of Independence: Engagements and Battle Casualties of the American Revolution*. Chicago: University of Chicago Press, 1974.

Peires, J. B. *House of Phalo: A History of the Xhosa People in the Days of Their Independence*. Berkeley: University of California Press, 1982.

Pelissier, Roger. *The Awakening of China, 1793–1949*. London: Secker and Warburg, 1963.

Pemberton, W. Baring. *Battles of the Boer War*. London: B. T. Batsford, 1964.

Pendergast, John. *U.S. Leadership in Resolving African Conflict: The Case of Ethiopia-Eritrea*. Washington, D.C.: United States Institute of Peace, 2001.

Pennell, C. R. "Ideology and Practical Politics: A Case Study of the Rif War in Morocco, 1921–1926." *International Journal of Middle East Studies* 14, no. 1 (February 1982): 19–33.

_____. *Morocco since 1830: A History*. New York: New York University Press, 2001.

Perce, Elbert. *The Battle Roll*. New York: Mason Brothers, 1858.

Perkins, Dexter. *The American Approach to Foreign Policy*. Cambridge, Mass.: Harvard University Press, 1952.

_____. *Hands Off*. Boston: Little, Brown, 1941.

Perovic, Jeronim. "The North Caucasus on the Brink." *International Relations and Security Network* (August 29, 2006). www.isn.ethz.ch.

Perry, Elizabeth J., and Tom Chang. "The Mystery of Yellow Cliff: A Controversial 'Rebellion' in the Late Qing." *Modern China* 6, no. 2 (April 1980): 123–160.

Perry, Glenn E. *The History of Egypt*. Westport, Conn.: Greenwood Press, 2004.

Perry, James M. *Arrogant Armies: Great Military Disasters and the Generals behind Them*. New York: Wiley, 1996.

Perry Richard O. "Warfare on the Pampas in the 1870s." *Military Affairs* 36, no. 2 (April 1972): 52–58.

Pert, Jean Paul. *Les Mutations de la Guerre Moderne.* Paris: Payot, 1962.

Peterson, Clarence Stewart. *Known Military Dead during Mexican War, 1846–1848.* Baltimore, Md.: by author, 1957.

Peterson, V. Spike. *A Critical Rewriting of Global Political Economy.* New York: Routledge, 2003.

———. "Gendered Nationalism: Reproducing 'Us' versus 'Them.'" In *The Women and War Reader,* edited by Lois Ann Lorentzen and Jennifer Turpin. New York: New York University Press, 1998, 41–49.

Peterson, V. Spike, and Jacqui True. "'New Times' and New Conversations." In *The "Man" Question in International Relations,* edited by Marysia Zalewski and Jane Parpart. Boulder, Colo.: Westview Press, 1998, 14–27.

Petras, James. "Revolution and Guerrilla Movements in Latin America: Venezuela, Guatemala, Colombia, and Peru." In *Latin America: Reform or Revolution?,* edited by J. Petras and M. Zeitlin. Greenwich, Conn.: Fawcett, 1968.

Phayre, Arthur. *History of Burma.* Bangkok: White Orchid, 2002.

Philippines Information Bulletin 2, no. 2 (April 1974).

Phillips, Charles, and Alan Axelrod. *Encyclopedia of Wars.* Vols. 1–3. New York: Facts on File, 2005.

Phillips, G. D. R. *Russia, Japan and Mongolia.* London: Frederick Muller, 1942.

Phillips, Walter Alison. *The Confederation of Europe: A Study of the European Alliance, 1813–1823.* London: Longmans, 1914.

———. *The War of Greek Independence.* London: Smith, Elder, 1897.

Phillipson, Coleman. *Termination of War and Treaties of Peace.* London: T. Fisher Unwin, 1916.

Pierce, Richard. *Russian Central Asia, 1867–1917, a Study in Colonial Rule.* Berkeley: University of California Press, 1960.

Pieri, Piero. *Storm Militare del Risorgimento.* Turin: Giulio Elnaudi, 1962.

Pike, Douglas. *Viet Cong.* Cambridge, Mass.: MIT Press, 1966.

Pike, Frederick. *The Modern History of Peru.* New York: Praeger, 1967.

Pinson, Koppel S. *Modern Germany, Its History and Civilization.* New York: Macmillan, 1954.

———. *Modern Germany, Its History and Civilization.* 2nd ed. New York: Macmillan, 1966.

Pirenne, Henri. *Histoire de Belgique.* Vol. 6. Brussels: Lamertin, 1926.

Pitsch, Anne. "The Democratic Republic of Congo (Congo-Kinshasa): The African World War." In *History behind the Headlines: The Origins of Conflicts Worldwide,* vol. 1, edited by Sonia G. Benson, Nancy Matuszak, and Meghan Appel O'Meara. Detroit: Gale Group, 2001.

Piven, Frances Fox. *The War at Home.* New York: New Press, 2004.

Plakans, Andrejs. *The Latvians: A Short History,* Stanford, Calif.: Hoover Institution Press, 1995.

Playfair, R. L. *A History of Arabia Felix or Yemen.* Salisbury, N.C.: Documentary Publications, 1978 (1859).

Pohler, Johann. *Bibliotheca Historico-Militaris. Systematische Obersicht D. Erscheinungen Aller Sprachen auf dem Gebiete D. Geschichte D. Kriege und Kriegswissenschaft Seit Erfindung D. Buchdruckerkunst B. Z. Schluss des Jahres 1880.* 4 vols. New York: Burt Franklin, 1961.

Polites, Athanase G. *Le Conflit Turko-Egyptien.* Cairo: Institut Francaise d'Archeologie Oriental du Caire, 1931.

Polk, William R. *The Opening of South Lebanon, 1788–1840: A Study of the Impact of the West on the Middle East.* Cambridge, Mass.: Harvard University Press, 1963.

Ponte Dominguez. Francisco J. *Historia de la Guerra de los Diez Anos.* 2 vols. Havana: A. Muniz, 1958.

Pontecorvo, Gillo, and Franco Solinas. *The Battle of Algiers* ("La Battaglia di Algeri"). Producers, Antonio Musu and Yacef Saadi. Rizzoli, 1965. Film.

Pool, D. I. "Estimates of New Zealand Maori Vital Rates from the Mid-Nineteenth Century to World War I." *Population Studies* 27 (March 1, 1973): 117–125.

Poole, Peter A. "The Vietnamese in Cambodia and Thailand: Their Role in Interstate Relations." *Asian Survey* 14, no. 4 (April 1974): 325–337.

Poplai, S. L. *India, 1947–1950.* Vol. 2. London: Oxford University, 1959.

Portell Vila, Herminio. *Historia de la Guerra de Cuba y los Etados Unidos Contra Espana.* Havana: Jésus Montero, 1949.

Posada-Carbo, Eduardo. "Elections and Civil Wars in Nineteenth-Century Colombia: The 1875 Presidential Campaign." *Journal of Latin American Studies* 26, no. 3 (October 1994): 621–649.

Post, John D. "A Study in Meteorological and Trade Cycle History: The Economic Crisis following the Napoleonic Wars." *Journal of Economic History* 24 (June 1974): 315–349.

Powell, Eve. *A Different Shade of Colonialism: Egypt, Great Britain, and the Mastery of the Sudan.* Berkeley: University of California Press, 2003.

Powell, Geoffrey. *The Kandyan Wars 1803–1813*. London: Leo Cooper, 1973.

Power, Samantha. *"A Problem from Hell": America and the Age of Genocide*. New York: Basic Books, 2002.

Pratt, Keith, and Richard Rutt. *Korea: A Historical and Cultural Dictionary*. Richmond, Surrey, UK: Curzon Press, 1999.

Prazmowska, Anita. *A History of Poland*. New York: Palgrave Macmillan, 2004.

Preston, Matthew. "Stalemate and the Termination of Civil War: Rhodesia Reassessed." *Journal of Peace Research* 41, no. 1 (2004): 65–83.

Prinzing, Friedrich. *Epidemics Resulting from Wars*. Oxford: Clarendon Press, 1916.

Pritchard, Earl H. "Political Ferment in China, 1911–1947." *Annals* 277 (September 1951).

Project Ploughshares. "Armed Conflict Report." (2000). www.ploughshares.ca/content.

_____. "Armed Conflict Report." (2002). www.ploughshares.ca/content.

_____. "Armed Conflict Report." (2003). www.ploughshares.ca/content.

_____. "Armed Conflict Report." (2004). www.ploughshares.ca/content.

_____. "Armed Conflict Report." (2005). www.ploughshares.ca/libraries.

_____. "Armed Conflict Report." (2006). www.ploughshares.ca/libraries.

_____. "Armed Conflict Report." (2007). www.ploughshares.ca/libraries.

_____. "Armed Conflict Report." (2008). www.ploughshares.ca/libraries.

Prunier, Gérard. *Darfur: The Ambiguous Genocide*. Ithaca, N.Y.: Cornell University Press, 2005.

_____. "Rebel Movements and Proxy Warfare: Uganda, Sudan and the Congo (1986–99)." *African Affairs* 103, no. 412 (2004): 359–383.

Puddington, A., Eiess, C., and Piano, A., eds. *Freedom in the World 2007: The Annual Survey of Political Rights and Civil Liberties*. Lanham, Md.: Rowman and Littlefield, 2007.

Purcell, Victor. *The Boxer Uprising*. Cambridge: Cambridge University Press, 1963.

Puzyrewsky, Alexander. *Der Polnisch-Russische Krieg, 1831*. 3 vols. Vienna: Kreisel and Groger, 1893.

Pye, Lucien. *Guerrilla Communism in Malaya*. Princeton, N.J.: Princeton University Press, 1956.

Rabinavisius, Henrikas. "The Fate of the Baltic Nations." *Russian Review* 3, no. 1 (Autumn 1943): 34–44.

Rabinovich, Itamar. *The War for Lebanon*. Ithaca, N.Y.: Cornell University Press, 1985.

Rabinowitch, Alexander. *The Bolsheviks Come to Power*. New York: W. W. Norton, 1976.

Race Jeffrey. "Thailand: 1973: 'We Certainly Have Been Ravaged by Something…'" *Asian Survey* 14, no. 2 (February 1974).

_____. "Thailand in 1974: A New Constitution." *Asian Survey* 15, no. 2 (February 1975): 157–165.

Raffles, Y. Stamford. *The History of Java*. New York: Oxford University Press, 1985.

Raine, Philip. *Paraguay*. New Brunswick, N.J.: Scarecrow Press, 1956.

Ramet, Sabrina P. *Thinking about Yugoslavia, Scholarly Debates about the Yugoslav Breakup and the Wars in Bosnia and Kosovo*. Cambridge: Cambridge University Press, 2005.

Ranke, Leopold. *The History of Serbia*. London: Bohn, 1853.

Rapoport, Anatol. "Lewis F. Richardson's Mathematical Theory of War." *Journal of Conflict Resolution* 1, no. 3 (September 1957): 249–307.

Rasler, Karen, and William Thompson. "War Making and State Making: Government Expenditures, Tax Revenues, and Global Wars." *American Political Science Review* 79 (1985): 491–507.

Raun, Toivo U. *Estonia and the Estonians*. Stanford, Calif.: Hoover Institution Press, 1987.

Ravlo, Hilde, Nils Petter Gleditsch, and Han Dorussen. "Colonial War and the Democratic Peace." *Journal of Conflict Resolution* 47, no. 4 (August 2003): 520–548.

"Recent Disturbances in Morocco." *The American Journal of International Law* 1, no. 4 (October 1907): 975–978.

Reddaway, W. F., et al., eds. *The Cambridge History of Poland*. Cambridge: Cambridge University Press, 1941.

Reed, Nelson A. *The Caste War of Yucatán*. Rev. ed. Stanford, Calif.: Stanford University Press, 2001.

Reed, W. Cyrus. "Patronage, Reform, and Public Policy: The Role of Zaire in the Great Lakes Crisis." Unpublished manuscript, March 8, 1999.

Rees, David. *Korea: The Limited War*. New York: St. Martin's Press, 1964.

Refugees International. "Sri Lanka: Renewed Conflict Displacing Thousands." *Bulletin* (July 10, 2006). www.refugeesinternational.org.

Reid, Anthony. *The Indonesian Revolution, 1945–1950*. Westport, Conn.: Greenwood Press, 1986.

Rennie, Isabel F. *The Argentine Republic*. New York: Macmillan, 1945.

Reno, William S. "Liberia: The LURDs of the New Church." In *African Guerrillas; Raging against the Machine,* edited by Morten Bøås and Kevin C. Dunn. Boulder, Colo.: Lynne Rienner, 2007.

Report of the International Commission to Inquire into the Causes and Conduct of the Balkan Wars. Geneva: Carnegie Endowment for International Peace, 1914.

Report of the Kargil Review Committee. New Delhi: Government of India, March 2000.

Research and Documentation Center Sarajevo. "The Status of Database by the Centers." (2006). www.idc .org.ba/aboutus.

Reshetar, John S. *The Ukrainian Revolution, 1917–1920.* Princeton, N.J.: Princeton University Press, 1952.

Restrepo, Jorge, Michael Spagat, and Juan F. Vargas. "The Dynamics of the Colombian Civil Conflict: A New Data Set." Paper presented at the conference "Revolutions, Old and New," Villa Gualino, Italy, June 2003.

——. "The Severity of the Columbian Conflict: Cross-Country Datasets versus New Micro Data." Unpublished manuscript, 2004.

Rettig, Tobias. "French Military Policies in the Aftermath of the Yên Bay Mutiny, 1930: Old Security Dilemmas Return to the Surface." *South East Asia Research* 10 (November 2002): 309–331.

Reyntjens, Filip. *Small States in an Unstable Region—Rwanda and Burundi, 1999–2000.* Uppsala: Nordic African Institute, 2000.

Richani, Nazih. "Third Parties, War Systems' Inertia, and Conflict Termination: The Doomed Peace Process in Colombia, 1918–2002." *The Journal of Conflict Studies* 25, no. 2 (Winter 2005).

Richards, D. S. *The Savage Frontier: A History of the Anglo-Afghan Wars.* London: Pan Books, 1990.

Richardson, Hugh E. *A Short History of Tibet.* New York: E. P. Dutton, 1962.

——. *Tibet and Its History.* London: Oxford University Press, 1962.

——. *Tibet and Its History.* Boulder, Colo.: Shambhala, 1984.

Richardson, Lewis F. *Arms and Insecurity.* Pittsburgh: Boxwood, 1960b.

——. "The Distribution of Wars in Time." *Journal of the Royal Statistical Society* 107 (1945): 242–250.

——. "Frequency of Occurrence of Wars and Other Fatal Quarrels." *Nature* 148, no. 3759 (November 15, 1941): 598.

——. "Generalized Foreign Politics." *British Journal of Psychology.* Suppl. monograph 23 (June 1939): 1–91.

——. *Statistics of Deadly Quarrels.* Pittsburgh: Boxwood, 1960a.

——. "Variation of the Frequency of Fatal Quarrels with Magnitude." *Journal of the American Statistical Society* 43 (1948): 523–546.

Ricklefs, M. C. *A History of Modern Indonesia since c. 1300.* Palo Alto, Calif.: Stanford University Press, 1993.

——. *A History of Modern Indonesia since c. 1200.* 3rd ed. Palo Alto, Calif.: Stanford University Press, 2001.

Ricks, T. E. *Fiasco: The American Military Adventure in Iraq.* New York: Penguin, 2006.

Ridley, J. *Maximilian and Juarez.* New York: Ticknor and Fields, 1992.

Rieber, Alfred J. "Civil Wars in the Soviet Union." *Kritika: Explorations in Russian and Eurasian History* 4, no. 1 (2003): 129–162.

Riedinger, Edward A. "1907–1910: Dembos-Portuguese War." *Great Events from History: The Twentieth Century, 1901–1940,* edited by Robert F. Gorman. Pasadena, Calif.: Salem Press, 2007.

Riker, T. W. *The Making of Rumania.* London: Oxford University Press, 1931.

Rio Branco, M. *Efemerides Brazileiras.* Rio de Janeiro: Ministerio das Relacoes Exteriores, 1946.

Ripenburg, Carl J. *Oman.* London: Praeger, 1998.

Ritter, E. A. *Shaka Zulu.* London: Longmans, Green, 1955.

Ritter, William S. "The Final Phase in the Liquidation of Anti-Soviet Resistance in Tadzhikistan: Ibrahim Bek and the Basmachi, 1924–1931." *Soviet Studies* 37, no. 4 (October 1985): 484–493.

Roberts, Elizabeth. *Realm of the Black Mountain: A History of Montenegro.* Ithaca, N.Y.: Cornell University Press, 2007.

Roberts, Hugh. *The Battlefield: Algeria 1988–2002, Studies in a Broken Polity.* New York: Verso Books, 2003.

Roberts, Stephen H. *The History of French Colonial Policy.* Hamden, Conn.: Archon Books, 1963.

Robertson, Priscilla. *Revolutions of 1848: A Social History.* Princeton, N.J.: Princeton University Press, 1952.

Robertson, W. S. "Foreign Accounts of Rosas." *Hispanic American Historical Review* 10, no. 2 (May 1930): 124–137.

Robinson, Arthur E. "The Conquest of the Sudan by the Wali of Egypt, Mohammad Ali Pasha, 1820–1824." *African Affairs* 25, no. 97 (1925): 47–58.

Robinson, David. "French 'Islamic' Policy and Practice in Late Nineteenth-Century Senegal." *The Journal of African History* 29, no. 3 (1988): 415–435.

Robinson, Geoffrey. *The Dark Side of Paradise; Political Violence in Bali.* Ithaca, N.Y.: Cornell University Press, 1995.

Rodman, Selden. *Haiti: The Black Republic, The Complete Story and Guide.* New York: Devin-Adair, 1954.

_____. *Quiqueya: A History of the Dominican Republic.* Seattle: University of Washington Press, 1964.

Rodriguez Herrero, Enrique. *Campana Militar de 1904.* Montevideo: n.p., 1934.

Rogel, Carole. *The Breakup of Yugoslavia and the War in Bosnia.* Westport, Conn.: Praeger, 1998.

Roggio, Bill. "The Fall of Northwestern Pakistan: An Online History." *The Long War Journal* (September 13, 2006). www.longwarjournal.org.

Romani, George. *The Neapolitan Revolution of 1820–1821.* Evanston: Northwestern University Press, 1950.

Romanovski, Dmitrii Il'ich. *Notes on the Central Asian Question.* Calcutta: Office of Superintendent of Government Printing, 1870.

Rondon Marquez, R. A. *Guzman Blanco.* Caracas: Garrido, 1944.

Rood, Judith Mendelsohn. "Mehmed Ali as Mutinous Khedive: The Roots of Rebellion." *International Journal of Turkish Studies* 8, nos. 1, 2 (Spring 2002): 115–128.

Roque, Ricardo. "The Razor's Edge: Portuguese Imperial Vulnerability in Colonial Moxico, Angola." *The International Journal of African Historical Studies* 36, no. 1 (Special Issue: Colonial Encounters between Africa and Portugal, 2003): 105–124.

Rosberg, Carl G., Jr., and John Nottingham. *The Myth of "Mau Mau": Nationalism in Kenya.* Palo Alto, Calif.: Hoover Institution; New York: Praeger, 1966.

Rose, J. Holland. *The Development of European Nations 1870–1919.* Cambridge: Cambridge University Press, 1915.

Rosenau, James N., ed. *International Aspects of Civil Strife.* Princeton, N.J.: Princeton University Press, 1964.

Ross, David. "Dahomey." In *West African Resistance,* edited by Michael Crowder. London: Hutchinson Library for Africa, 1971.

Ross, Frank E. "The American Naval Attack on Shimonoseki in 1863." *Chinese Social and Political Science Review* 18, no. 1 (April 1934): 146–155.

Rouland, John. *A History of Sino-Indian Relations.* Princeton, N.J.: Van Nostrand, 1967.

Roy, Denny. *Taiwan: A Political History.* Ithaca, N.Y.: Cornell University Press, 2003.

Rubin, Neville. *Cameroun: An African Federation.* New York: Praeger, 1971.

Rubinstein, Alvin Z. *Soviet Foreign Policy since World War II.* Glenview, Ill.: Scott, Foresman, 1989.

Rubinstein, Murray. *Taiwan: A New History.* Armonk, N.Y.: M. E. Sharpe, 1999.

Rudolph, Joseph R., ed. *Encyclopedia of Modern Ethnic Conflicts.* Westport, Conn.: Greenwood Press, 2003.

Ruedy, John. *Modern Algeria, The Origins and Development of a Nation.* Bloomington: Indiana University Press, 1992.

Rummel, Rudolph J. *Death by Government.* New Brunswick, N.J.: Transaction, 1994.

_____. *The Dimensionality of Nations.* Beverly Hills, Calif.: Sage, 1972.

_____. "Dimensions of Conflict Behavior within and between Nations." *General Systems Yearbook* 8 (1963): 1–50.

_____. "A Field Theory of Social Action with Application to Conflict within Nations." *Yearbook of the Society for General Systems* 10 (1965): 183–211.

_____. *Statistics of Democide: Genocide and Mass Murder since 1900.* Münster: Lit Verlag, 1997.

Rupen, Robert A. *Mongols of the Twentieth Century.* Vol. I. Bloomington: Indiana University Press, 1964.

Russell, D. E. H. *Rebellion, Revolution, and Armed Force.* New York: Academic Press, 1974.

Russell, Frank S. *Russian Wars with Turkey.* London: Henry S. King, 1877.

Russett, Bruce M. "Delineating International Regions." In *Quantitative International Politics: Insights and Evidence,* edited by J. David Singer. New York: Free Press, 1968.

_____. "Evidence for the Kantian Peace: Democracy, Trade, and International Organizations, 1950–1992." Paper presented at the annual meeting of the International Studies Association, Toronto, March 19–22, 1997.

_____. *International Regions and the International System: A Study in Political Ecology.* Chicago: Rand McNally, 1967.

_____. *Trends in World Politics.* New York: Macmillan, 1965.

Russett, Bruce M., J. David Singer, and Melvin Small. "National Political Units in the Twentieth Century: A Standardized List." *American Political Science Review* 62, no. 3 (September 1968): 932–951.

Rwantabagu, Hermeneglide. "Explaining Intra-state Conflicts in Africa: The Case of Burundi." *International Journal on World Peace* 18, no. 2 (2001): 41–46.

Sabry, M. *L'Empire Egyptien Sous Mohamed-Ali et la Question d'Orient.* Paris: Librairie Orientaliste, 1930.

Safran, Nadev. *From War to War.* New York: Pegasus, 1969.

Sagar, D. J. *Major Political Events in Indo-China 1945–1990.* Oxford: Facts on File, 1991.

Salert, Barbara. *Revolution and Revolutionaries.* New York: Elsevier, 1976.

Salibi, Kamal S. *Crossroads to Civil War.* Delmar, N.Y.: Caravan, 1976.

Sandford, Christine. *Ethiopia under Haile Selassie.* London: J. M. Dent, 1946.

Salopek, Paul. "Headed for a Real Bad Showdown." *Chicago Tribune,* May 23, 2000, 1, 3.

Sanders, Peter. *Moshoeshoe, Chief of the Sotho.* London: Heinemann, 1975.

Sandole, Dennis. *Capturing the Complexity of Conflict: Dealing with Violent Ethnic Conflicts of the Post–Cold War Era.* London: Pinter, 1999.

Sanz, Timothy L. "The Yugoslav Conflict: A Chronology of Events, 1990–1993." *Military Review* (December 1992). From Foreign Studies Service Publications. http://calldp.leavenworth.army.mil.

Saray, Mehmet. *The Russian, British, Chinese and Ottoman Rivalry in Turkestan.* Ankara, Turkey: Turkish Society Printing House, 2003.

SarDesai, D. R. *Vietnam Past and Present.* Boulder, Colo.: Westview Press, 1998.

Sarkees, Meredith Reid. "The Correlates of War Data on War: An Update to 1997." *Conflict Management and Peace Science* 18, no. 1 (Fall 2000): 123–144.

_____. "Trends in Intra-State (Not Ethnic) Wars." Paper presented at the joint convention Globalization and Its Challenges in the 21st Century, sponsored by the International Studies Association, the University of Hong Kong, and Eleven International Studies Associations, Hong Kong, July 26–28, 2001.

_____. "A Typology of International Political Actors and War Participants." Draft manuscript, 2006.

Sarkees, Meredith Reid, and J. David Singer. "Armed Conflict Past and Future: A Master Typology?" Paper presented at the European Union Conference on Armed Conflict Data Collection, Uppsala, Sweden, June 2001.

_____. "Old Wars, New Wars, and an Expanded War Typology." Paper presented at the joint meeting of the International Studies Association and the Japan Association of International Relations, Tokyo, September 20–23, 1996.

Sarkees, Meredith Reid, Frank Wayman, and J. David Singer. "Inter-State, Intra-State, and Extra-State Wars: A Comprehensive Look at Their Distribution over Time, 1816–1997." *International Studies Quarterly* 77 (2003): 49–70.

Sarmiento, Domingo. *Life in the Argentine Republic in the Days of the Tyrants; or, Civilization and Barbarism.* New York: Hafner, 1971 (original in Spanish, 1868).

Sater, William. *Chile and the War of the Pacific.* Lincoln: University of Nebraska Press, 1986.

Saunders, Christopher, and Nicholas Soothey. *Historical Dictionary of South Africa.* London: Scarecrow Press, 2000.

Scarone, Arturo. *Efemerides Uruguayas.* Montevideo: Instituto Historico y Geografico del Uruguay, 1956.

Schafer, Phil. Report to the Correlates of War Seminar, University of Michigan, April 8, 1994.

_____. "States, Nations, and Entities from 1492 to 1992." Ann Arbor: University of Michigan Terminal System, for the Correlates of War Project, 1995.

Scheina, Robert L. *Latin America's Wars.* Vol. 1: *The Age of the Caudillo, 1791–1899.* Washington, D.C.: Brassey's, 2003a.

_____. *Latin America's Wars.* Vol. 2: *The Age of the Professional Soldier, 1900–2001.* Washington, D.C.: Brassey's, 2003b.

Schellenberg, James A. "The Biology of Human Aggression." In *International War: An Anthology,* 2nd ed., edited by Melvin Small and J. David Singer. Chicago: Dorsey Press, 1989, 162–175.

Scherer, John L. *Blocking the Sun: The Cyprus Conflict.* Minneapolis: University of Minnesota Press, 1997.

Scherrer, Christian P. "Dynamics, Characteristics and Trends." In *Ethnicity and Intra-State Conflict,* edited by H. Wiberg and C. P. Scherrer. Aldershot, UK: Ashgate, 1999.

_____. *Genocide and Crisis in Central Africa.* Westport, Conn.: Praeger, 2002.

Schiemann, Theodor. *Geschichte Russlands Unter Kaiser Nikolaus I.* Vol. 3. Berlin: George Reimer, 1913.

Schiff, Z., and E. Ya'ari. *Israel's Lebanon War.* New York: Simon and Schuster, 1984.

Schirokauer, Conrad, and Donald N. Clark. *Modern East Asia, A Brief History.* Belmont, Calif.: Thomson/Wadsworth, 2004.

Schlarman, Joseph. *Mexico: A Land of Volcanoes.* Milwaukee, Wisc.: Bruce, 1950.

Schlesinger, Max. *The War in Hungary, 1848–1849.* London: Richard Bentley, 1850.

Schmidt, Carl. *The Plough and the Sword.* New York: Columbia University Press, 1938.

Schmitt, Bernadotte. *Coming of the War, 1914.* New York: Scribner's, 1930.

Schneider, Ronald M. *"Order and Progress": A Political History of Brazil.* Boulder, Colo.: Westview Press, 1991.

Schofield, Ricahrs. "Negotiating the Saudi-Yemeni International Boundary." Paper presented to the British-Yemeni Society, March 31, 1999.

Schrecker, John E. *The Chinese Revolution in Historical Perspective.* New York: Praeger, 1991.

Schurmann, Franz, and Orville Schell. *The China Reader*. Vol. 2: *Republican China*. New York: Vintage Books, 1967.

Schuschnigg, Kurt Von. *The Brutal Takeover*. New York: Atheneum, 1971.

Schuyler, Eugene. *Turkistan: Notes of a Journey in Russian Turkistan, Khokand, Bukhara, and Kuldja*. New York: Scribner, Armstrong and Co., 1876.

Scobie, James R. "The Aftermath of Pavon." *Hispanic American Historical Review* 35, no. 2 (May 1955): 153–174.

Scott, J. G. *Burma: From the Earliest Times to the Present Day*. New York: Knopf, 1924.

Selbin, Eric. *Modern Latin American Revolutions*. Boulder, Colo.: Westview Press, 1993.

Selassie, Bereket Habte. *Conflict and Intervention in the Horn of Africa*. New York: Monthly Review Press, 1980.

Senn, Alfred E. *The Emergence of Modern Lithuania*. New York: Columbia University Press, 1959.

Sethi, Manpreet. "Novel Ways of Settling Border Disputes: The Peru-Ecuador Case." *Strategic Analysis* 33, no. 10 (January 2002).

Seton-Watson, Hugh. *The Decline of Imperial Russia, 1855–1914*. London: Methuen, 1952.

_____. *A History of the Czechs and Slovaks*. Hamden, Conn.: Archon Books, 1965.

_____. *The Russian Empire 1801–1917*. Oxford: Oxford University Press, 1967.

Seton-Watson, Robert William. *Britain in Europe 1789–1914*. Cambridge: Cambridge University Press, 1938.

Shah, Surdan Ikbal Ali. *The Tragedy of Amanullah*. London: Alexanderouseley, 1933.

Shak, Shakeeb. "The British Druze Connection and the Druze Rising in the Hawran." *Middle Eastern Studies* 13 (1977): 251–257.

Shakabpa, Tsepan W. D. *Tibet: A Political History*. New Haven, Conn.: Yale University Press, 1967.

Shaplen, Robert. "Our Involvement in Laos." *Foreign Affairs* 48, no. 3 (April 1970): 478–493.

Shaw, George A. *Madagascar and France*. New York: Negro Universities Press, 1969. Reprint of the first edition (1885).

Shek, Richard. "The Revolt of the Zaili, Jindan Sects in Rehe (Jehol), 1891." *Modern China* 6, no. 2 (April 1980): 161–196.

Sheridan, James E. *China in Disintegration*. New York: Free Press, 1975.

_____. *Chinese Warlord: The Career of Feng Yu-Hsiang*. Stanford, Calif.: Stanford University Press, 1966.

Shibeika, Mekki. *British Policy in the Sudan 1882–1902*. London: Oxford, 1952.

Shinn, Rinn S. *Italy, A Country Study*. Washington, D.C.: American University, 1985.

Shomo, D. J. "Oil Companies Buy an Army to Tame Colombia's Rebels." *New York Times,* August 22, 1996, A1, A8.

Short, Anthony. "Communism and the Emergency." In *Malaysia*, edited by Gung Wu Wang. London: Pall Mall, 1958.

Short, Philip. *Pol Pot, Anatomy of a Nightmare*. New York: Henry Holt and Company, 2004.

Siaroff, Alan. "Democratic Breakdown and Democratic Stability: A Comparison of Interwar Estonia and Finland." *Canadian Journal of Political Science/ Review Canadienne de Science Politique* 32, no. 1 (March 1999): 103–124.

Sicker, Martin. *Reshaping Palestine: From Muhammad Ali to the British Mandate, 1831–1922*. Westport, Conn.: Praeger, 1999.

Sillery, A. *The Bechuanaland Protectorate*. London: Oxford University Press, 1952.

Silverlight, John. *The Victor's Dilemma*. New York: Weybright and Talley, 1970.

Simmonds, Stuart. "Laos and Cambodia: The Search for Unity and Independence." *International Affairs (Royal Institute of International Affairs 1944–)* 49, no. 4 (October 1973): 574–583.

Simmons, Beth A. Personal communication with Meredith Reid Sarkees, 2007.

_____. *Territorial Disputes and Their Resolution: The Case of Ecuador and Peru*. Washington, D.C.: United States Institute of Peace, 1999.

Simpson, Bertram L. *The Fight for the Republic of China*. New York: Dodd, Mead, 1917.

Sinclair, Keith. *A History of New Zealand*. Harmondsworth, UK: Penguin, 1980.

Singer, J. David. "Accounting for International War: The State of the Discipline." *Journal of Peace Research* 18, no. 1 (1981): 1–18.

_____. "Armed Conflict in the Former Colonial Regions: From Classification to Explanation." In *Conflict and Development*, edited by Jan-Geert Siccama and Luc van de Goor. Hague: Clinqendael Institute, 1996.

_____. "The Correlates of War Project: Interim Report." *World Politics* 24, no. 2 (1972): 243–270.

_____. "The Global System and Its Sub-Systems: A Developmental View." In *Linkage Politics*, edited by James Rosenau. New York: Free Press, 1969.

_____. "Peace in the Global System: Displacement, Interregnum, or Transformation?" In *The Long Postwar Peace*, edited by Charles Kegley. New York: Harper Collins, 1991.

Singer, J. David, and Thomas Cusack. "Periodicity, Inexorability, and Steersmanship in Major Power War." In *From National Development to Global Community*, edited by Richard Merritt and Bruce Russett. Herts, UK: Allen and Unwin, 1981.

Singer, J. David, and Melvin Small. "The Composition and Status Ordering of the International System 1815–1940." *World Politics* 18, no. 2 (January 1966): 236–282.

_____. *The Wages of War, 1816–1965: A Statistical Handbook.* New York: Wiley, 1972.

Singer, Max, and Aaron Wildavsky. *The Real World Order: Zones of Peace, Zones of Turmoil.* Chatham, N.J.: Chatham House, 1993.

Singer, P.W. *Corporate Warriors.* Ithaca, N.Y.: Cornell University Press, 2003.

Singh, Kelvin. "Big Power Pressure on Venezuela during the Presidency of Cipriano Castro." *Revista/Review Interamericana* 29, nos. 1–4 (1999): 125–143.

Singh, Khushwant. *A History of the Sikhs.* 2 vols. Princeton, N.J.: Princeton University Press, 1966.

Singletary, Otis A. *The Mexican War.* Chicago: University of Chicago Press, 1960.

Singleton, Fred. *A Short History of Finland.* Cambridge: Cambridge University Press, 1989.

SIPRI. *Yearbook of World Armaments and Disarmament, 1968–69.* London: Duckworth, 1970.

Sivard, Ruth. *World Military and Social Expenditures.* 14th ed. Washington, D.C.: World Priorities, 1991.

Skocpol, Theda. *States and Social Revolutions: A Comparative Analysis of France, Russia, and China.* Cambridge: Cambridge University Press, 1979.

Slater, W. *Chili and the War of the Pacific.* Lincoln: University of Nebraska Press, 1986.

Sloan, Stephen. *A Study in Political Violence.* Chicago: Rand McNally, 1971.

Small, Melvin. "The Diplomatic Importance of States, 1816–1970: An Extension and Refinement of the Indicator." *World Politics* 25 (July 1973): 577–599.

Small, Melvin, and J. David Singer, eds. *International War: An Anthology.* 2nd ed. Chicago: Dorsey Press, 1989.

_____. "Patterns in International Warfare, 1816–1965." *Annals* 391 (September 1970): 145–155.

_____. "Patterns in International Warfare, 1816–1980." In *International War: An Anthology,* 2nd ed., edited by Melvin Small and J. David Singer. Chicago: Dorsey Press, 1989.

_____. *Resort to Arms: International and Civil War, 1816–1980.* Beverly Hills, Calif.: Sage, 1982.

_____. "The War-Proneness of Democratic Regimes, 1816–1965." *The Jerusalem Journal of International Relations* 1, no. 4 (Summer 1976): 50–69.

Smith, C. Jay, Jr. *Finland and the Russian Revolution.* Athens: University of Georgia Press, 1958.

Smith, Charles D. *Palestine and the Arab-Israeli Conflict.* 2nd ed. New York: St. Martin's Press, 1992.

Smith, Dan. *The State of War and Peace Atlas.* New rev. 3rd ed. London: Penguin, 1997.

Smith, Denis Mack. *A History of Sicily, Modern Sicily after 1713.* New York: Viking Press, 1968.

_____. *Victor Emanuel, Cavour, and the Risorgimento.* London: Oxford University Press, 1971.

Smith, Iain R. *The Origins of the South African War, 1899–1902.* New York: Longman, 1996.

Smith, Joseph. "Britain and the Brazilian Naval Revolt of 1893–4." *Journal of Latin American Studies* 2, no. 2 (November 1970): 175–198.

Smith, Justin H. *The War with Mexico.* 2 vols. New York: Macmillan, 1919.

Smith, Michael G. *Peacekeeping in East Timor: The Path to Independence.* Boulder, Colo.: Lynne Rienner, 2003.

Smith, Michael Llewellyn. *The Great Island: A Study of Crete.* London: Longmans, 1965.

Smith, Rhea Marsh. *Spain: A Modern History.* Ann Arbor: University of Michigan Press, 1965.

Smith, Ronald Bishop. *Siam; or, the History of the Thais from 1569 A.D. to 1824 A.D.* Bethesda, Md.: Decatur Press, 1967.

Smith, Steve. "Alternative and Critical Perspectives." In *Millennial Reflections on International Studies,* edited by Michael Brecher and Frank P. Harvey. Ann Arbor: University of Michigan Press, 2002, 195–208.

_____. "Positivism and Beyond." In *International Theory: Positivism and Beyond,* edited by Steve Smith, Ken Booth, and Marysia Zalewski. Cambridge: Cambridge University Press, 1996, 11–44.

Smith, Tony. "Comparative Study of French and British Decolonization." *Comparative Studies in Society and History* 20, no. 1 (January 1978): 70–102.

Smyth, Howard McGraw. "Piedmont and Prussia: The Influence of the Campaigns of 1848–1849 on the Constitutional Development of Italy." *American Historical Review* 55, no. 3 (April 1950): 479–502.

Smythe, Donald. *Guerrilla Warrior: The Early Life of John J. Pershing.* New York: Scribner's, 1973.

Snow, Donald M. *Uncivil Wars.* Boulder, Colo.: Lynne Rienner, 1996.

Snow, Edgar. *Far Eastern Front.* New York: H. Smith and R. Haas, 1933.

_____. *Red Star over China.* New York: Grove Press, 1961.

Snow, Peter J. *Hussein.* Washington, D.C.: Luce, 1972.

Snyder, R. Claire. *Citizen-Soldiers and Manly Warriors: Military Service and Gender in the Civic Republican Tradition.* Boulder, Colo.: Rowman and Littlefield, 1999.

Soggot, David. *Namibia.* New York: St. Martin's Press, 1986.

Solomon, Robert L. *Saya San and the Burmese Rebellion.* Santa Monica, Calif.: RAND Corporation, 1969.

Sonyel, Salahi R. "How the Turks of the Peloponnese Were Exterminated during the Greek Rebellion." *Belleten* 62, no. 233 (1998): 121–135.

Sorokin, Pitirim A. *Social and Cultural Dynamics.* Vol. 3: *Fluctuation of Social Relationships, War and Revolution.* New York: American Book, 1937.

Soucek, Svat. *A History of Inner Asia.* Cambridge: Cambridge University Press, 2000.

Southall, Aidan. "Social Disorganization in Uganda: Before, during and after Amin." *Journal of Modern African Studies* 18, no. 4 (December 1980): 627–656.

Spain, James W. *The Pathan Borderland.* The Hague: Mouton, 1963.

Spain, Servicio Historico Militar. *Historia de las Cami'anas de Mar-Rueces.* Vol. 1. Madrid: Impr. del Servicio Geografico del Ejercito, 1947.

Spence, Jonathan. *God's Chinese Son: The Taiping Heavenly Kingdom of Hong Xiuquan.* New York: W. W. Norton, 1996.

Sperling, Elliot. "Don't Know Much about Tibetan History." *New York Times,* April 13, 2008, Op-ed.

Spicer, Edward H. *The Yaquis: A Cultural History.* Tucson: University of Arizona Press, 1980.

Spielmann, Christian. *Die Taiping-Revolution (1850–1864).* Halle, A.S.: Hermann Gesenius, 1900.

Spindler, Frank. *Nineteenth Century Ecuador.* Fairfax, Va.: George Mason University Press, 1987.

Sremac, Danielle S. "War of Words: Washington Tackles the Yugoslav Conflict." Praeger Security International (1992). www.psi.praeger.com.

Stack, John F., Jr. "The Ethnic Challenge to International Relations Theory." In *Wars in the Midst of Peace,* edited by David Carment and Patrick James. Pittsburgh: University of Pittsburgh Press, 1997, 2–25.

Starr, S. Frederick. *Xinjiang: China's Muslim Borderland.* Armonk, N.Y.: M. E. Sharpe, 2004.

Stašaitis, Arûnas. "Lithuania's Struggle against Soviet Occupation 1944–1953." *Baltic Defence Review,* no. 3 (2000): 115–122.

Statesman's Yearbook. Multiple years.

Stavrianos, Leften. *The Balkans since 1453.* New York: Holt, Rinehart and Winston, 1958.

Stearns, Peter N. *1848: The Revolutionary Tide in Europe.* New York: W. W. Norton, 1974.

Stearns, Peter N., ed. *Encyclopedia of World History: Ancient, Medieval, and Modern, Chronologically Arranged.* Wilmington, Mass.: Houghton Mifflin, 2001.

Steefel, Lawrence C. *The Schleswig-Holstein Question.* Cambridge, Mass.: Harvard University Press, 1932.

Steel, Rodney. *History of West Africa.* New York: Facts on File, 2003.

Steinberg, David I. "International Rivalries in Burma: The Rise of Economic Competition." *Asian Survey* 30, no. 6 (June 1990): 587–601.

Stephenson, Nathaniel W. *Texas and the Mexican War.* New Haven, Conn.: Yale University Press, 1921.

Stevenson, Francis Seymour. *A History of Montenegro.* New York, Conn.: Arno Press/New York Times, 1971.

Stewart, George. *The White Armies of Russia.* London: Macmillan, 1933.

Stickney, E. P. *Southern Albania and Northern Epirus in International Affairs, 1912–1923.* Stanford, Calif.: Stanford University Press, 1926.

Stiehm, Judith Hicks. *Arms and the Enlisted Woman.* Philadelphia: Temple University Press, 1989.

Stoessinger, John G. *Why Nations Go to War.* 7th ed. New York: St. Martin's Press, 1998.

Stojanovic, M. D. *The Great Powers and the Balkans, 1875–1878.* Cambridge: Cambridge University Press, 1939.

Stoll, Richard J. "Major Power Interstate Conflict in the Post–World War II Era: An Increase, a Decrease, or No Change?" *The Western Political Quarterly* 35, no. 4 (December 1982): 587–605.

Stone, David R. *A Military History of Russia from Ivan the Terrible to the War in Chechnya.* Westport, Conn.: Praeger Security International, 2006.

Stone, Lawrence. "Theories of Revolution." *World Politics* 18 (January 1966): 159–176.

Stone, Martin. *The Agony of Algeria.* New York: Columbia University Press, 1997.

Stora, Benjamin. *Algeria, 1830–2000: A Short History.* Ithaca, N.Y.: Cornell University Press, 2001.

Storey, Moorfield, and Marcial P. Lichauco. *The Conquest of the Philippines by the United States.* New York: Putnam, 1926.

Stracey, P. D. *Nagaland Nightmare*. Bombay: Allied, 1968.

Strakhovsky, Leonid I. *Intervention at Archangel*. Princeton, N.J.: Princeton University Press, 1944.

Straziuso, Jason. "U.S. General Takes Command of NATO Force in Afghanistan." *Washington Post*, February 5, 2007, A11.

Strobel, Edward H. *The Spanish Revolution, 1868–1875*. Boston: Small Maynard, 1898.

Stuart, J. *A History of the Zulu Rebellion of 1906 and of Dinizulu's Arrest, Trial, and Expatriation*. New York: Macmillan, 1913.

Stuart-Fox, Martin. *A History of Laos*. Cambridge: Cambridge University Press, 1997.

Suhrke, Astri. "Smaller-Nation Diplomacy: Thailand's Current Dilemmas." *Asian Survey* 11, no. 5 (May 1971): 429–444.

Suhrke Astri, and Lela Garner Noble, eds. *Ethnic Conflicts in International Relations*. New York: Praeger, 1977a.

_____. "Muslims in the Philippines and Thailand." In *Ethnic Conflicts in International Relations*, edited by Astri Suhrke and Lela Garner Nobel. New York: Praeger, 1977b.

Sula, Abdul B. *Albania's Struggle for Independence*. New York: Family Press, 1967.

Sulé, Jorge Oscar. *Rosas y Sus Relaciones con Los Indios*. Buenos Aires: Instituto Nacional de Investigaciones Históricas Juan Manuel de Rosas, 2003.

Sullivan, Stacy. "Federal and Bosnian Serb Armies 'Were As One.'" Institute for War and Peace Reporting. (July 24, 2003).

Sullivant, Robert S. *Soviet Politics and the Ukraine, 1917–1957*. New York: Columbia University Press, 1962.

Sumner, Benedict H. *Russia and the Balkans 1870–1880*. Oxford: Oxford University Press, 1937.

Swami, Praveen. "Quickstep or Kadam Taal? The Elusive Search for Peace in Jammu and Kashmir." United States Institute of Peace, Special Report #133. (March 2005): 1–12.

Swarns, Rachel L. "Zimbabwe Says It Stands by Congo in Conflict." *New York Times*, January 20, 2001. www.nytimes.com.

Swire, Joseph. *Albania: The Rise of a Kingdom*. New York: Smith, 1950.

Sykes, Percy Molesworth. *A History of Afghanistan*. London: Macmillan, 1940.

_____. *A History of Persia*. 2 vols. London: Macmillan, 1951.

Sylvester, Christine. "The Contributions of Feminist Theory to International Relations." In *International Theory: Positivism and Beyond*, edited by Steve Smith, Ken Booth, and Marysia Zalewski. Cambridge: Cambridge University Press, 1996, 254–278.

_____. *Feminist International Relations: An Unfinished Journey*. New York: Cambridge University Press, 2002.

Tabeau, Ewa, and Jakub Bijak. "War-related Deaths in the 1992–1995 Armed Conflicts in Bosnia and Herzegovina: A Critique of Previous Estimates and Recent Results." *European Journal of Population* 21 (2005): 187–215.

Taboulet, Georges, ed. *La Geste Française en Indochine*. Paris: Adrien-Maisonneuve, 1955.

Takeuchi, Tutsuni. *War and Diplomacy in the Japanese Empire*. Garden City, N.Y.: Doubleday, 1935.

Tan, Andrew. "Armed Muslim Separatist Rebellion in Southeast Asia: Persistence, Prospects, and Implications." *Studies in Conflict and Terrorism* 23 (2000): 267–288.

Tan, Chester C. *The Boxer Catastrophe*. New York: Columbia University Press, 1955.

T'ang Leang-Li, ed. *Suppressing Communist Banditry in China*. Shanghai: China United Press, 1934.

Tang, Peter S. H. *Russia and Soviet Policy in Manchuria and Outer Mongolia, 1911–1931*. Durham, N.C.: Duke University Press, 1959.

Tanner, Stephan. *Afghanistan: A Military History from Alexander the Great to the Fall of the Taliban*. New York: Da Capo, 2002.

Tanter, Raymond. "Dimensions of Conflict Behavior within and between Nations, 1958–1960." *Journal of Conflict Resolution* 10 (March 1966): 41–64.

Tanter, Raymond, and Manus Midlarsky. "A Theory of Revolutions." *Journal of Conflict Resolution* 11 (September 1967): 264–280.

Taras, Raymond C., and Rajat Ganguly. *Understanding Ethnic Conflict: The International Dimension*. 2nd ed. New York: Longman, 2002.

Tareke, Gebru. "From Lash to Red Star: The Pitfalls of Counter-insurgency in Ethiopia, 1980–82." *Journal of Modern African Studies* 30, no. 3 (2002): 465–498.

Tatu, Michel. "Intervention in Eastern Europe." In *Diplomacy of Power: Soviet Armed Forces as a Political Instrument*, edited by Stephen S. Kaplan. Washington, D.C.: Brookings Institution, 1981, 205–264.

Tauber, Eliezer. *The Formation of Modern Syria and Iraq*. Ilford, UK: Frank Cass, 1995.

Taylor, A. J. P. *The Struggle for Mastery in Europe, 1848–1918*. Oxford: Clarendon Press, 1954.

Taylor, Charles Lewis, and Michael C. Hudson. *World Handbook of Political and Social Indicators*. New Haven, Conn.: Yale University Press, 1972.

Temperly, Harold. *England and the Near East*. Hamden, Conn.: Archon Books, 1964.

Teng Ssu-Yti. *Historiography of the Taiping Rebellion*. Cambridge, Mass.: East Asia Research Center, Harvard University, 1963.

_____. *The Nien Army and Their Guerrilla Warfare, 1851–1868*. The Hague: Mouton, 1961.

_____. *The Taiping Rebellion and the Western Powers*. Oxford: Clarendon Press, 1971.

Tessler, Mark. *A History of the Israeli-Palestinian Conflict*. Bloomington: Indiana University Press, 1994.

Tétreault, Mary Ann, ed. *Women and Revolution in Africa, Asia, and the New World*. Columbia: University of South Carolina Press, 1994.

Thant, Myint U. *The Making of Modern Burma*. Cambridge: Cambridge University Press, 2001.

Thayer, William Roscoe. *The Life and Times of Cavour*. Vol. 2. Boston: Houghton Mifflin, 1911.

Theobald, Alan Buchan. *The Mahdiya: A History of the Anglo-Egyptian Sudan, 1881–1899*. London: Longmans, 1951.

Thomas, Alfred Barnaby. *Latin America: A History*. New York: Macmillan, 1956.

Thomas, Hugh. *Cuba: The Pursuit of Freedom*. New York: Harper, 1971.

_____. *The Spanish Civil War*. New York: Harper, 1961.

_____. *Suez*. New York: Harper, 1967.

Thomas, Jeffrey. "President Puntin's North Caucasus Challenge." Center for Strategic and International Studies. (March 8, 2001).

Thomas, Lowell. *With Lawrence in Arabia*. New York: Century, 1924.

Thomas, Lowell, Jr. *The Silent War in Tibet*. Garden City, N.Y.: Doubleday, 1959.

Thompson, Edward John, and G. T. Garrett. *The Rise and Fulfillment of British Rule in India*. London: Macmillan, 1934.

Thompson, Leonard. *A History of South Africa*. New Haven, Conn.: Yale University Press, 1995, 2001.

_____. *Survival in Two Worlds: Moshoeshoe of Lesotho 1786–1879*. Oxford: Oxford University Press, 1975.

Thompson, Virginia. *French Indochina*. New York: Octagon Books, 1968.

Thompson, Virginia, and B. Richard Adloff. *The Malagasy Republic*. Stanford, Calif.: Stanford University Press, 1965.

Thornton, Richard C. *China, A Political History, 1917–1980*. Boulder, Colo.: Westview Press, 1982.

Thurner, Mark. "Atusparia and Caceres: Rereading Representations of Peru's Late Nineteenth-Century 'National Problem.'" *Hispanic American Historical Review* 77, no. 3 (August 1997): 409–441.

Tibawi, Abd-Al Latif Al. *A Modern History of Syria*. London: Macmillan, 1969.

Tickner, J. Ann. *Gender in International Relations: Feminist Perspectives on Achieving Global Security*. New York: Columbia University Press, 1992.

_____. *Gendering World Politics*. New York: Columbia University Press, 2001.

Tilly, Charles. "Reflections on the History of European State Making." In *The Formation of National States in Western Europe*, edited by Charles Tilly. Princeton, N.J.: Princeton University Press, 1975.

_____. *The Vendee*. Cambridge, Mass.: Harvard University Press, 1964.

Tilly, Charles, and James Rule. *Measuring Political Upheaval*. Princeton, N.J.: Center of International Studies, 1965. Mimeo.

Tilman, Robert O. "Burma in 1986: The Process of Involution Continues." *Asian Survey* 27, no. 2 (February 1987): 254–263.

Timasheff, Nicholas S. *War and Revolution*. New York: Sheed and Ward, 1965.

Timberg, Craig. "Sudan's Offensive Comes at Key Time." *Washington Post*, September 5, 2006, A01.

Tinker, Hugh. *The Union of Burma*. London: Oxford University Press, 1957.

Tirona, Tomas C. "The Philippine Anti-Communist Campaign." In *Modern Guerrilla Warfare*, edited by F. Osanka. Glencoe, Ill.: Free Press, 1962.

Todorov, N., L. Diney, and L. Melnishki. *Bulgaria: Historical and Geographical Outline*. Sofia: Sofia Press, 1968.

Toft, Monica Duffy. *The Geography of Ethnic Violence*. Princeton, N.J.: Princeton University Press, 2003.

Tomasek, Robert D. "Caribbean Exile Invasions." *Orbis* 17 (Winter 1974): 1354–1382.

Townsend, John. *Oman: The Making of the Modern State*. London: Crown Helm, 1977.

Toye, Hugh. *Laos: Buffer State or Battleground*. London: Oxford University Press, 1968.

Totten, Samuel, William S. Parsons, and Israel W. Charny, eds. *A Century of Genocide: Critical Essays and Eyewitness Accounts*. New York: Routledge, 2004.

Traboulsi, Fawwaz. *History of Modern Lebanon*. London: Pluto Press, 2007.

Tregar, Edward. "The Maoris of New Zealand." *The Journal of the Anthropological Institute of Great Britain and Ireland* 19 (1890): 96–123.

Tripp, Aili Mari. "Women, Violence, and Peacebuilding in the Great Lakes Region." Unpublished manuscript, 2005.

Tripp, Charles. *A History of Iraq*. Cambridge: Cambridge University Press, 2000.

Tse-tung, Mao. *Quotations from Chairman Mao Tsetung*. New York: Bantam Books, 1967.

Tuchman, Barbara. *The Guns of August*. New York: Ballantine Books, 1994.

Tull, Denis M. "The Democratic Republic of Congo: Militarized Politics in a 'Failed State.'" In *African Guerrillas, Raging against the Machine*, edited by Morten Bøås and Kevin C. Dunn. Boulder, Colo.: Lynne Rienner, 2007.

Turbull, Michael. *The Changing Land: A Short History of New Zealand*. Aucksland: Longman Paul, 1975.

Turner, Robert T. *Vietnamese Communism: Its Orgins and Development*. Stanford, Calif.: Hoover Institution Press, 1975.

Twagilimana, Aimable. *The Debris of Ham: Ethnicity, Regionalism, and the 1994 Rwandan Genocide*. Lanham, Md.: University Press of America, 2003.

Twitchett, Denis, and John K. Fairbank. *Cambridge History of China*, vol. 10: *Late Ch'ing*. New York: Cambridge University Press, 1978.

Tyler, Christian. *Wild West China: The Taming of Xinjiang*. Piscataway, N.J.: Rutgers University Press, 2004.

Udoidem, Sylvanus I. "Religion in the Political Life of Nigeria." In *New Strategies for Curbing Ethnic and Religious Conflicts in Nigeria*, edited by F. U. Okafor. Enugu, Nigeria: Fourth Dimension, 1997.

Ulam, Adam. *The Bolsheviks: The Intellectual and Political History of the Triumph of Communism in Russia*. Toronto: Collier Books, 1968.

Ullman, Richard. *Intervention and the War*. Princeton, N.J.: Princeton University Press, 1961.

United Asia 14, no. 12 (December 1962): 691–708.

United Nations. "Somalia–Unosom I." Department of Public Information. (March 21, 1997): 1–4.

United Nations Command. "Report to United Nations Secretary General." (October 23, 1953).

United Nations Committee on Rights of the Child. "Initial Reports of States Parties Due in 1994: Azerbaijan. 29/05/96." Office of the United Nations High Commissioner for Human Rights. (1996).

United States Central Command. "France: Support to Global War on Terror (Operation Enduring Freedom)." www.centcom.mil/sites/uscentcom2.

United States Institute of Peace. "Civil Society under Siege in Colombia." Special Report 114. (February 2004): 1–16.

_____. "Rwanda: Accountability for War Crimes and Genocide." Report on a United States Institute of Peace Conference. (2002).

U.S. Congress. Senate. Committee on Foreign Relations. *Hearings before a Subcommittee on U.S. Security Agreements Abroad*. 91st Cong., 1st sess., part 2, October, 20, 21, 22, 28, 1969.

U.S. Congress, Senate Committee on the Judiciary, Subcommittee to Investigate Problems Connected with Refugees and Escapees. *Crisis on Cyprus*. Washington, D.C.: American Hellenic Institute, 1975.

U.S. Department of the Army. Historical Section. *Order of Battle of the United States Army Forces in the World War*. Washington, D.C.: GPO, 1937.

U.S. Department of State. "The Question of the Pacific. America's Alsace and Lorraine. The Conquest by Chile in 1879." Report, date unknown [early 1900s].

"U.S. Invasion of Afghanistan." *Aljazeera Magazine*, January 1, 2003. www.aljazeera.com.

U.S. Library of Congress. "The Finnish Civil War." http://countrystudies.us/finland, 2008.

Unterberger, Betty. *America's Siberian Expedition 1918–1920*. Durham, N.C.: Duke University Press, 1956.

Uppsala Universitet Conflict Data Project. "Afghanistan–Detailed Information–Whole Conflict." (2004). www.pcr.uu.se.

_____. "Angola." (2002). www.pcr.uu.se/database.

_____. "Azerbaijan." (1997). www.pcr.uu.se/database.

_____. "Bosnia-Hercegovina." (1995a). www.pcr.uu.se/database.

_____. "Congo, Democratic Republic of (Zaire)." (2003). www.pcr.uu.se.

_____. "Congo–Detailed Information–Whole Conflict." (2006). www.pcr.uu.se.

_____. "Croatia." (1995b). www.pcr.uu.se/database.

_____. "Eritrea vs. Ethiopia." (2005a). www.pcr.uu.se/database.

_____. "Liberia." (2005b). www.pcr.uu.se/database.

_____. "Mozambique." (1995c). www.pcr.uu.se/database.

Urlanis, Boris T. *Voini I Narodo-Nacelenie Evropi (Wars and the Population of Europe)*. Moscow: Government Publishing House, 1960.

_____. *Wars and Population*. Moscow: Progress Publishers, 1971.

Usborne, C. V. *The Conquest of Morocco*. London: Stanley Paul, 1936.

Utting, Francis. *The Story of Sierra Leone*. Reprint. Manchester, N.H.: Ayer, 1931.

Valdes, Nelson P. "Revolutionary Solidarity in Angola." In *Cuba in the World*, edited by Cole Blasier and Carmelo Mesa-Lago. Pittsburgh: University of Pittsburgh Press, 1979.

Vali, Ferenc A. *Rift and Revolt in Hungary*. Cambridge, Mass.: Harvard University Press, 1961.

Van der Kraan, Alfons. *Bali at War: A History of the Dutch-Balinese Conflict of 1846–49*. Clayton, Australia: Monash University, 1995.

Van Nederveen, Gilles K. "USAF Airlift into the Heart of Darkness, the Congo 1960–1978, Implications for Modern Air Mobility Planners." Airpower Research Institute Paper #2001–04. (September 2001): 1–31.

Vandervort, Bruce. *Wars of Imperial Conquest in Africa*. Bloomington: Indiana University Press, 1998.

Vanly, Ismet Cheriff. *The Revolution of Iraki Kurdistan*. Lausanne: Committee for the Defense of the Kurdish People's Rights, April 1965.

Vasquez, John A. *The War Puzzle*. New York: Cambridge University Press, 1993.

Vasquez, John A., ed. *What Do We Know about War?* Lanham, Md.: Rowman and Littlefield, 2000.

Vasquez-Machicado, Humberto, Jose De Mesa, and Teresa Gisbert. *Manual de Historia de Bolivia*. La Paz: Libreroas Editores, 1963.

Vassiliev, Alexi. *The History of Saudi Arabia*. New York: New York University Press, 2000.

Vatikiotis, P. J. *History of Modern Egypt*. Baltimore: The Johns Hopkins University Press, 1980.

Vaughn, Bruce. "Nepal: Background and U.S. Relations." Congressional Research Service. (June 8, 2005).

Vayda, Andrew P. "Maoris and Muskets in New Zealand: Disruption of a War System." *Political Science Quarterly* 85, no. 4 (December 1970): 560–584.

Vial, Jean. *Le Maroc Héroique*. Paris: Hachette, 1938.

Vickers, Miranda. *The Albanians: A Modern History*. London: I. B. Taurus, 1995.

Villacorta Calderon, Jose Antonio. *Historica de la Republica de Guatemala, 1821–1921*. Guatemala City: Tipografica Nacional, 1960.

Vinacke, Harold M. *Far Eastern Politics in the Post War Period*. New York: Appleton-Century-Crofts, 1956.

Vines, Alex. *RENAMO: Terrorism in Mozambique*. Bloomington: Indiana University Press, 1991.

Vlekke, Bernard. *Nusantara*. Chicago: Quadrangle, 1960.

Voevodsky, John. "Quantitative Behavior of Warring Nations." *Journal of Psychology* 72 (July 1969): 269–292.

Volgyes, Ivan, ed. *Hungary in Revolution, 1918–19: Nine Essays*. Lincoln: University of Nebraska Press, 1971.

Von Moltke, Helmuth. *Darstellung des Turkisch-Aegyptischen Feldzugs in Sommer 1839*. Berlin: Junker and Dunnhaupt, 1935.

_____. *The Franco-German War of 1870–91*. Translated by Michael Howard. London: Greenhill Books, 1992.

Von Rauch, George. *A History of Soviet Russia*. New York: Praeger, 1957.

Von Sax, Carl Ritter. *Geschichte des Machtverfalls der Torkel*. Vienna: Manziche K. U. K. Hof Verlags and Universitdts Buchhandlung, 1913.

Von Schlechta-Wssehrd, Ottokar. "Der Letzte Persiseh-Russische Krieg." *Zeitschrift der Deutschen Morgenländischen Gesellschaft* 2 (1866): 288–305.

Von Sternegg, J. K. *Schlachten-Atlas des XIX. Jahrhunderts: Der Deutsch-Dänische Krieg, 1848–1850*. Leipzig: P. Bäuerle, 1892–1898.

_____. *Schlachten-Atlas des XIX. Jahrhunderts: Der Russisch-Türkische Krieg, 1828–1829*. Leipzig: P. Bäuerle, 1891–1895.

_____. *Schlachten-Atlas des XIX. Jahrhunderts: Der Russisch-Türkische Krieg, 1877–1878*. Leipzig: P. Bäuerle, 1866–1899.

Wack, Henry Wellington. *The Story of the Congo Free State*. New York: Putnam, 1905.

Wakeman, Frederic. *Strangers at the Gate*. Berkeley: University of California Press, 1966.

Walder, Andrew G., and Yang Su. "The Cultural Revolution in the Countryside: Scope, Timing and Human Impact." *The China Quarterly* (2003): 74–99.

Waldman, Eric. *The Spartacist Uprising of 1919 and the Crisis of the German Socialist Movement: A Study of the Relation of Political Theory and Party Practice*. Milwaukee, Wisc.: Marquette University Press, 1958.

Walker, R. B. J. "Alternative, Critical, Political." In *Millennial Reflections on International Studies*, edited by Michael Brecher and Frank P. Harvey. Ann Arbor: University of Michigan Press, 2002, 258–270.

Walker, Robert. "Rwanda remembers the Holocaust." BBC News, http://news.bloc.co.uk, 1/27/2005.

Wallensteen, Peter. "Universalism vs. Particularism: On the Limits of Major Power Order." *Journal of Peace Research* 21 (1984): 243–257.

Wallensteen, Peter, and Karin Axell. "Conflict Resolution and the End of the Cold War, 1989–93." *Journal of Peace Research* 31 (1994): 333–349.

Wallensteen, Peter, and Margareta Sollenberg. "The End of International War? Armed Conflict 1989–1995." *Journal of Peace Research* 33, no. 3 (1996): 353–370.

Waller, Michael, Kyril Drezov, and Bülent Gökay. "Introduction." In *Kosovo: The Politics of Delusion*, edited by Michael Waller, Kyril Drezov, and Bülent Gökay. Portland, Ore.: Frank Cass, 2001.

Wallerstein, Immanuel. "The Inter-state Structure of the Modern World System." In *International Theory: Positivism and Beyond,* edited by Steve Smith, Ken Booth, and Marysia Zalewski. Cambridge: Cambridge University Press, 1996, 87–107.

Waltz, Kenneth N. "The Stability of a Bipolar World." In *Classic Readings of International Relations,* 2nd ed., edited by Phil Williams, Donald Goldstein, and Jay Shafritz. Fort Worth, Texas: Harcourt Brace College, 1999, 77–81.

_____. *Theory of International Politics.* Reading, Mass.: Addison-Wesley, 1979.

Walzer, Michael. "The Just War." In *International War: An Anthology,* 2nd ed., edited by Melvin Small and J. David Singer Chicago: Dorsey Press, 1989, 141–145.

Wan Lo. "Communal Strife in Mid-Nineteenth Century Kwangtung: The Establishment of Ch'ih Ch'i." In *Papers on China.* Vol. 19. Cambridge, Mass.: East Asian Research Center, Harvard University, 1965.

Wandycz, Piotr S. *Soviet-Polish Relations, 1917–1921.* Cambridge, Mass.: Harvard University Press 1969.

Warburg, Gabriel R. "The Turco-Egyptian Sudan: A Recent Histographical Controversy." *Die Welt Des Islams,* New Series BD. 31, no. 2 (1991): 193–215.

Ward, W. E. F. *A History of Ghana.* London: Allen and Unwin, 1959.

Warming, Louis. "The North Schleswig Question: A Forty Years' War." *American Journal of Sociology* 8, no. 3 (November 1902): 289–335.

Warren, Harris Gaylord. *Paraguay.* Norman: University of Oklahoma Press, 1949.

_____. "The Paraguayan Revolution of 1904." *The Americas* 36 (January 1980): 365–384.

Warwick, Peter, ed. *The South Africa War: The Anglo-Boer War, 1899–1902.* Harlow, UK: Longman, 1980.

Washburn, George. *Fifty Years in Constantinople.* Boston: Houghton Mifflin, 1909.

Wawro, Geoffrey. *The Austro-Prussian War: Austria's War with Prussia and Italy in 1866.* Cambridge: Cambridge University Press, 1996.

Wayman, Frank, and Paul Diehl. "Realism Reconsidered: The Realpolitik Framework and Its Basic Propositions." In *Reconstructing Realpolitik,* edited by Frank Wayman and Paul Diehl. Ann Arbor: University of Michigan Press, 1994.

Wayman, Frank Whelon, J. David Singer, and Meredith Reid Sarkees. "Inter-State, Intra-State, and Extra-Systemic Wars, 1816–1995." Paper presented at the annual meeting of the International Studies Association, San Diego, April 16–21, 1996.

Wayman, Frank, and Atsushi Tago. "Explaining the Onset of Mass Political Killing: The Effect of War, Regime Type, and Economic Deprivation on Democide and Politicide, 1947–1987." Paper presented at the annual meeting of the International Studies Association, Honolulu, March 2, 2005.

_____. "Explaining the Onset of Mass Political Killing, 1949–87." *Journal of Peace Research* 46, no. 6 (November 2009).

Wehl, David. *The Birth of Indonesia.* London: Allen and Unwin, 1948.

Wei, Henry. *China and Soviet Russia.* Princeton, N.J.: Van Nostrand, 1956.

Weidner, Glenn R. "Operation Safe Border: The Ecuador-Peru Crisis." *Joint Force Quarterly* (Spring 1996): 52–58.

Weiss, Herbert K. "Stochastic Models for the Duration and Magnitude of a Deadly Quarrel." *Operations Research* 11, no. 1 (1963a): 101–121.

_____. "Trends in World Involvement in War." Los Angeles: Aerospace Corporation, 1963b. Mimeo.

Welch, Claude Emerson. *Anatomy of Rebellion.* Albany: State University Press of New York, 1980.

Wenner, Manfred W. *Modern Yemen, 1918–1966.* Baltimore, Md.: Johns Hopkins University Press, 1967.

_____. *The Yemen Arab Republic.* Boulder, Colo.: Westview Press, 1991.

Werlich, David. *Peru: A Short History.* Carbondale, Ill.: Southern Illinois University Press, 1978.

Werth, Alexander. *Russia at War.* New York: E. P. Dutton, 1964.

Wheeler, Douglas. *Republican Portugal: A Political History, 1910–1926.* Madison: University of Wisconsin Press, 1978.

Wheeler, Douglas, and Réne Pélissier. *Angola.* New York: Praeger, 1971.

Wheeler, Raymond H. *War, 599 B.C.–1950 A.D.: Indexes of International and Civil War Battles of the World.* Pittsburgh: Foundation for the Study of Cycles, 1951.

Whetten, Lawrence L. *The Canal War: Four Power Confrontation in the Middle East.* Cambridge, Mass.: MIT Press, 1974.

White, Alistair. *El Salvador.* New York: Praeger, 1973.

White, George F. *A History of Spain and Portugal.* London: Methuen, 1909.

White, James D. "National Communism and World Revolution: The Political Consequences of German Military Withdrawal from the Baltic Area in 1918–1919."

Europe-Asia Studies 46, no. 8, Soviet and East European History (1994): 1439–1369.

White, John A. *The Siberian Intervention.* Princeton, N.J.: Princeton University Press, 1950.

Wickens, G. E. "J. D. C. Pfund, a Botanist in the Sudan with the Egyptian Military Expeditions, 1875–6." *Kew Bulletin* 24, no. 1 (1970): 191–216+iii.

Wieczynski, Joseph. *The Modern Encyclopedia of Russian and Soviet History.* Vol. 5. Gulf Breeze, Fla.: Academic International Press, 1977.

Wiencek, David G. "Mindanao and Its Impact on Security in the Philippines." In *The Unraveling of Island Asia? Governmental, Communal, and Regional Instability,* edited by Bruce Caughn. Westport, Conn.: Praeger, 2002.

Wilbur, Donald N. *Contemporary Iran.* New York: Praeger, 1963.

Wilcox, Cadmus M. *History of the Mexican War.* Washington, D.C.: Church News, 1892.

Wilkenfeld, Jonathan. "Domestic and Foreign Conflict of Nations." *Journal of Peace Research* 1 (1968): 56–69.

———. "Some Further Findings Regarding the Domestic and Foreign Conflict Behavior of Nations." *Journal of Peace Research* 2 (1969): 147–156.

Wilkinson, David. *Deadly Quarrels: Lewis F. Richardson and the Statistical Study of War.* Berkeley: University of California Press, 1980.

Wilks, Ivor. *Asante in the Nineteenth Century.* New York: Cambridge University Press, 1975.

Williams, C. F. Rushbrook. *The State of Pakistan.* London: Faber and Faber, 1962.

Williams, Henry Smith. *The Historian's History of the World.* Vols. 21–22. New York: Encyclopaedia Britannica Company, 1907.

Williams, Kristen P. *Despite Nationalist Conflicts: Theory and Practice of Maintaining World Peace.* Westport, Conn.: Praeger, 2001.

Williams, Mary W., Ruhl J. Bartlett, and Russell E. Miller. *The People and Politics of Latin America.* Boston: Ginn, 1955.

Williams, Matthew. *The British Colonial Experience in Waziristan and Its Applicability to Current Operations.* Fort Leavenworth, Kan.: School of Advanced Military Studies, United States Army Command and General Staff College, 2005.

Williams, Phil, Donald Goldstein, and Jay Shafritz, eds. *Classic Readings of International Relations.* 2nd ed. Fort Worth, Texas: Harcourt Brace College, 1999.

Williamsen, Marvin. "The Military Dimension, 1937–1941." In *China's Bitter Victory: The War with Japan,* 1937–1945, edited by James C. Hsiung and Steven I. Levine. Armonk, N.Y.: M. E. Sharpe, 1997.

Wilson, A. Seyalatnam. *Politics in Sri Lanka, 1947–1973.* London: Macmillan, 1974.

Wilson, Andrew. *The "Ever Victorious Army."* Edinburgh: Blackwood, 1868.

Wilson, Andrew. *Ukrainians: Unexpected Nation.* New Haven, Conn.: Yale University Press, 2000.

Wilson, Derek A. *A History of South and Central Africa.* London: Cambridge University Press, 1975.

Wilson, Dick. *The Long March: The Epic of Chinese Communism's Survival, 1935.* New York: Viking, 1971.

Wilson, John. "Drought Bedevils Brazil's Sertao." *National Geographic* 142, no. 5 (November 1972): 704–723.

Wilson, Monica, and Leonard Thompson. *The Oxford History of South Africa.* Vol. 2. Oxford: Oxford University Press, 1971.

Wilson, Woodrow. *Declaration of War.* 5th Congress. Senate Document no. 5. (April 2, 1917).

Windrich, Elaine. *The Cold War Guerrilla: Jonas Savimbi, the U.S. Media, and the Angolan War.* Westport, Conn.: Greenwood Press, 1992.

Windrow, Martin. *The Algerian War, 1954–1962.* London: Osprey, 1998.

Wise, George S. *Caudillo: A Portrait of Antonio Guzmán Blanco.* New York: Columbia University Press, 1951.

Wiseman, Paul. "Revived Taliban Waging 'Full-Blown Insurgency.'" *USA Today,* June 20, 2006. www.usatoday.com.

———. "Taliban on the Run in Afghanistan, but Group Is Far From Vanquished." *Army Times,* July 26, 2005. www.armytimes.com.

Wolf, Charles, Jr. *The Indonesian Story.* New York: John Day, 1948.

Wolff, Robert Lee. *The Balkans in Our Time.* Rev. ed. New York: W. W. Norton, 1978, c.1974.

Women's International League for Peace and Freedom. "WILPF Women and Peace." www.wilpf.int.ch.

Wood, Conrad. *The Moplah Rebellion and Its Genesis.* New Delhi: People's Publishing House (distributed by South Asia Books), 1987.

Wood, David. "Conflict in the Twentieth Century." *Adelphi Papers* 48. London: Institute of Strategic Studies, June 1968.

Woodhead, H. G. W., ed. *China Year Book 1931.* Shanghai: North China Daily News and Herald, 1931.

Woodhouse, C. M. *The Greek War of Independence.* New York: Hutchinson, 1952.

Woodman, Dorothy. *The Making of Burma.* London: Cresset, 1962.

_____. *The Republic of Indonesia.* New York: Philosophical Library, 1955.

Woods, Frederick Adams, and Alexander Baltzly. *Is War Diminishing?* Boston: Houghton Mifflin, 1915.

Woodward, Bob. *Bush at War.* New York: Simon and Schuster, 2002.

Woodward, Ralph. *Central America: A Nation Divided.* New York: Oxford University Press, 1985.

Woodward, Ralph Lee, Jr. *Rafael Carrera and the Emergence of the Republic of Guatemala, 1821–1871.* Athens: University of Georgia Press, 1993.

Woolman, David. *Rebels in the Rif.* Stanford, Calif.: Stanford University Press, 1968.

Worcester, Donald E. *Brazil from Colony to World Power.* New York: Scribner's, 1973.

World Alliance for Peace in Sri Lanka. *Peace in Sri Lanka, Obstacles and Opportunities.* London: World Alliance for Peace in Sri Lanka, 2005.

The World Almanac and Book of Facts. New York: World Almanac Books. Multiple years.

Wortzel, Larry M. *Dictionary of Contemporary Chinese Military History.* Westport, Conn.: Greenwood Press, 1999.

Wright, Ione S., and Lisa M. Nekhom. *Historical Dictionary of Argentina.* Metuchen, N.J.: Scarecrow Press, 1978.

Wright, John. *Libya.* New York: Praeger, 1969.

Wright, Quincy. *A Study of War.* Rev. ed. 2 vols. Chicago: University of Chicago Press, 1965.

_____. "When Does War Exist?" *American Journal of International Law* 26, no. 2 (April 1932): 362–368.

Wrobel, Piótr, with A. Wróbel. *Historical Dictionary of Poland, 1945–1996.* Westport, Conn: Greenwood Press, 1998.

Wuorinen, John H. *A History of Finland.* New York: Columbia University Press, 1965.

Wyatt, David K. *Thailand, A Short History.* New Haven, Conn.: Yale University Press, 1984.

_____. *Thailand, A Short History.* New Haven, Conn.: Yale University Press, 2003.

Wyckoff, Theodore. "Standardized List of National Political Units in the Twentieth Century: The Russett-Singer-Small List of 1968 Updated." *International Social Science Journal* 32 (1980): 834–846.

WYSIWYG. "Indonesia." *WYSIWYG* 24 (1978) and vol. 29 (1983).

Xinhua General Overseas News Service. "East Timor." (March–December 1977).

Yanaga, Chitoshi. *Japan since Perry.* New York: McGraw-Hill, 1949.

Yaroslavsky, E., and I. P. Tovstukha. *The Great Proletarian Revolution.* Vol. 2 of *The History of the Civil War in the U.S.S.R.,* edited by M. Gorky and S. Kirov. Moscow: Foreign Language Publishing House, 1946.

Yavuz, M. Hakan. "Five Stages of the Construction of Kurdish Nationalism in Turkey." *Nationalism and Ethnic Politics* 7, no. 3 (Autumn 2001): 1–24.

Yildiz, Kerim. *The Kurds in Iraq, The Past, Present and Future.* London: Pluto Press, 2007.

Young, George. *Nationalism and War in the Near East.* Oxford: Clarendon Press, 1915.

Young, Jordan M. *The Brazilian Revolution of 1930 and the Aftermath.* New Brunswick, N.J.: Rutgers University Press, 1967.

Young, M. Crawford. "The Obote Revolution." *African Report* 11 (June 1966): 8–14.

Young-hee, Suh. "Tracing the Course of the Peasant War of 1894." *Korea Journal* (Winter 1994): 17–30.

Youngs, Tim, Mark Oakes, and Paul Bowers. "Kosovo: Operation 'Allied Force.'" Research Paper series 99, no. 48. London: House of Commons Library, 1999.

Yu, Maochun. "The Taiping Rebellion: A Military Assessment of Revolution and Counterrevolution." In *A Military History of China,* edited by David Graff and Robin Higham. Boulder, Colo.: Westview Press, 2002.

Zaide, Gregorio F. *The Philippine Revolution.* Manila: Modern Book, 1954.

Zainu'ddin, Ailsa. *A Short History of Indonesia.* North Melbourne: Cassell Australia, 1968.

Zalewski, Marysia. "Introduction: From the 'Women' Question to the 'Man' Question in International Relations." In *The "Man" Question in International Relations,* edited by Marysia Zalewski and Jane Parpart. Boulder, Colo.: Westview Press, 1998, 1–14.

Zalewski, Marysia, and Jane Parpart, eds. *The "Man" Question in International Relations.* Boulder, Colo.: Westview Press, 1998.

Zartman, I. William, ed. *The Political Economy of Morocco.* New York: Praeger, 1987.

Zasloff, Joseph J. "Laos: The Forgotten War Widens." *Asian Survey* 10, no. 1, A Survey of Asia in 1969: Part 1 (January 1970): 65–72.

_____. "Laos 1972: The War, Politics and Peace Negotiations." *Asian Survey* 13, no. 1 (January 1973): 60–75.

Zhang, Xiaoming. "China's Involvement in Laos during the Vietnam War, 1963–1975." *The Journal of Military History* 66, no. 4 (October 2002): 1141–1166.

Ziegler, David. *War, Peace, and International Politics.* 7th ed. New York: Longman, 1997.

Zinner, Paul E. *Revolution in Hungary.* New York: Columbia University Press, 1962.

Zook, David H. *The Conduct of the Chaco War.* New York: Bookman, 1960.

Zoubir, Yahia H. "Western Sahara Conflict Impeded Maghrib Unity." *Middle East Report,* no. 163, North Africa Faces the 1990's (March–April 1990a): 28–29.

_____. "The Western Sahara Conflict: Regional and International Dimensions." *The Journal of Modern African Studies* 28, no. 2 (June 1990b): 225–243.

Zuljan, Ralph. *Armed Conflict Events Data.* (2003). www.onwar.com.

Index